* To Play a Giant's Part *

The role of the British Army at Passchendaele.

Robert Alan Perry

The Naval & Military Press Ltd

For my Grandfather

Leonard William Perry D.C.M. C.de.G

And the countless thousands of others whose stories were never told.

Published by
The Naval & Military Press Ltd
Unit 10 Ridgewood Industrial Park,
Uckfield, East Sussex,
TN22 5QE England

Tel: +44 (0) 1825 749494
Fax: +44 (0) 1825 765701

www.naval-military-press.com • www.nm.archive.com

© Robert Alan Perry 2014

In reprinting in facsimile from the original, any imperfections are inevitably reproduced and the quality may fall short of modern type and cartographic standards.

YPRES – The Ramparts and the Lille Gate

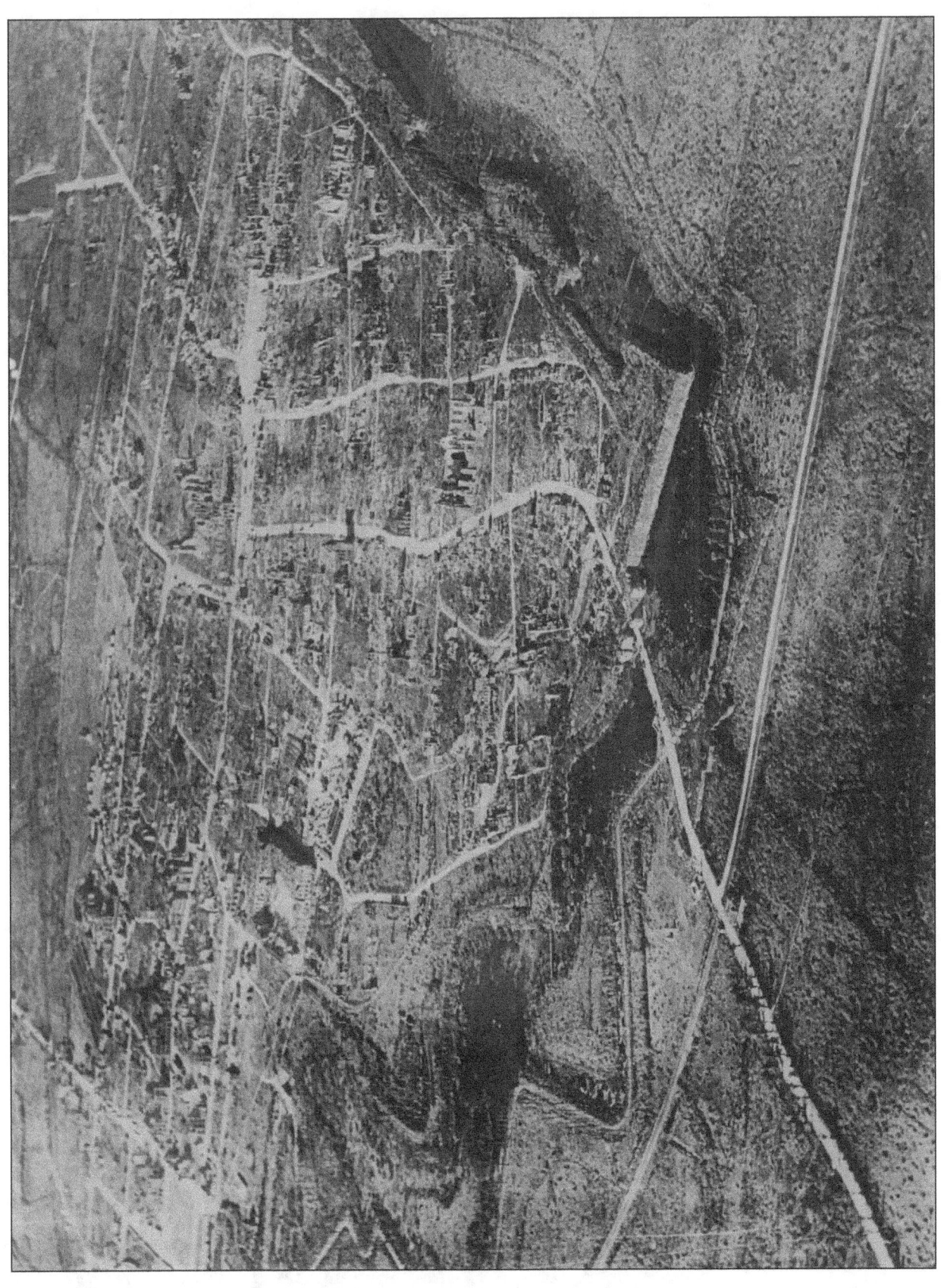

YPRES – The Grande Place. Ruins of Cloth Hall & Cathedral

To Play a Giant's Part – Contents

Title page

Dedication page

Author's note 6

Map Ypres Salient 9

Introduction 10

Chapter 1 - The Northern Operation
Part 1 The complexities of coalition warfare 13
Part 2 "A mere gamble would be both a folly and a crime" 45
Part 3 "A largely strategic objective" 77

Chapter 2 - "We are not on the Black Line" The Battle of Pilckem Ridge
Part 1 A stream too far 118
Part 2 "We were thus under fire from the North South and East" 181

Chapter 3 - "Too great a hurry" The Battle of Langemarck 195

Chapter 4 - "Magnificent in accuracy and volume" The Battle of the Menin Road Ridge 241

Chapter 5 - "In the face of confusion and great danger" The Battle of Polygon Wood 313

Chapter 6 - "We could have captured Passchendaele" The Battle of Broodseinde 348

Chapter 7 - "Almost unimaginable difficulties" The Battle of Poelcappelle 398

Chapter 8 - "Every man steeled his heart" The First Battle of Passchendaele 432

Chapter 9 - "All that was humanly possible" The Second Battle of Passchendaele
Part 1 "I urge unhesitatingly the continuance of the offensive" 465
Part 2 "Men set their teeth and wondered, who's next?" 512

Chapter 10 - The Ragged Sword 545

Postscript 584

Appendix 592

To Play a Giant's Part

The Rôle of the British Army at Passchendaele

Author's note

From a very early age I knew that my grandfather had been a soldier. How I first came by this information I cannot now recall. It certainly did not come from him, as I do not remember that he ever mentioned either the Great War through which he had fought in the infantry, or the Army, in which he had remained after the War to serve for a total of twenty seven years. He died in 1961 at the age of 69 when I was 12. Thirty five years later, it was to investigate what he had done in the Great War that first brought us to Ypres.

For anyone with a passionate interest in the Great War, the Ypres Salient is a dangerous place to visit. The atmosphere can soon take you under its spell. After many visits, the Salient held me firmly in its tenacious grip and it quickly became obvious that by hook or by crook, I would somehow have to live there. After operating a bed and breakfast business at Langemark for a short time I found that many of our guests required tours of the battlefields. This proved far less simple than I at first thought it would be. Over a number of years we had some wonderful guests, from Australia, Britain, Canada, New Zealand and the United States, who were keen to learn something of where their forefathers had fought and what they had endured at Ypres. But with the best will in the world it was clear that the time available to spend with our guests was completely insufficient to explain what had happened over four years of war in the Salient. The more information I acquired the greater was the difficulty of conducting tours, as it became a problem not of knowing what to show, but in knowing what to leave out.

So many accounts of the War emphasize the futility of the whole business, and the inadequacies of those in command. This commonly held belief was often the opinion of our guests. These emotions were understandable, but I found it increasingly difficult to relate the four years of endurance and courage shown by the British and Dominion troops in the Salient, to actions which were now considered utterly futile. To me it seemed an unintended insult to the memory of those who had served. I have often stood with our guests on the Butte in Polygon Wood close to the 5th Australian Division Memorial, overlooking the beautiful Buttes New British Cemetery, or at the Cross of Remembrance above the blockhouse at Tyne Cot Cemetery with its views back across the 'Immortal Salient' to the Cloth Hall and the Cathedral at Ypres. With tears in their eyes they have looked down upon the immaculately kept lawns and the headstones above the graves of their countrymen so far from home, and reflected on the futility. Sometimes I offered them what I believed to be another perspective. I had asked myself on many occasions, if those soldiers lying in the now peaceful Polygon Wood, or on the slopes above the Hanebeek had been given the option prior to the battles which made up Passchendaele, whether they should go on, or go home, how they would have replied? I believe that overwhelmingly the answer would have been, that with the job unfinished, they would have marched up, towards the front, for better or for worse. On expressing my belief to our guests I have sometimes detected a change in their faces from one of sadness to one of pride.

My own difficulties in attempting to show visitors the Salient in a meaningful way led to the decision that I should try to write about some aspect of what had happened here. The Third Battle of Ypres seemed to me the period of greatest interest to many. Certainly the Battle was the most controversial. Most historians writing about what is commonly referred to as 'Passchendaele', have generally depicted it as a disaster of great magnitude, and have emphasized in detail the ineptitude of the high command responsible for its evil memory. A few have taken a more pragmatic approach and have viewed the outcome differently. With such polarized academic opinions it seemed that the only way to get to the truth of the matter was to closely examine the available information myself; to run a 'personal check' on what has been written. The exercise has been most enlightening, influencing my perception of the Battle, and providing an insight into the way the same story can be told, only to reach totally differing conclusions. My hope for this work is threefold: First, that by treating Passchendaele as one phase of an enormous ongoing conflict, and not as a means to an end in itself, will prompt readers to at least reconsider the question of futility, and the competence or otherwise of the Generals. Second, by setting the Battle against the backdrop of the sensitivities of coalition warfare and the complexities of political entanglements will encourage alternate avenues of evaluation. Third, that by bringing together in one volume detailed accounts of the actions of Australian, British, Canadian, Irish, New Zealand, and South African formations will add to the full picture of the battles which eventually became Passchendaele.

I make no claim to be an historian. I would offer this in defence of any professional inadequacies in the book; any mistakes are entirely my own and I make no claim to its accuracy or the completeness of its detail. I have attempted to gather information from many sources which I hope will add to the balance of the book. I have made every effort to describe exactly where the actions took place, and hope that for those interested in visiting the old Salient this book may be a useful guide. As most of the tracks, roads, streams and woods are now to be found exactly where they were in 1917 they are not difficult to locate, and there is no better way to find out about a battle than by visiting the battlefield, especially in its less well visited areas. If an infantry unit fought in the Ypres Salient during the Passchendaele offensive I have made every effort to mention them down to battalion level, as I feel they all deserve no less. Undoubtedly there may be some I have inadvertently missed. If this is the case and causes disappointment I can do no more than apologize, and if I am made aware will try to correct the omission at some future date.

There have been occasions when the records of certain actions required interpretation. It is sometimes interesting to compare the account of one division, to the account of the next division in line. On the divisional boundary the pieces of the jigsaw do not always fit, the account from one division, brigade, or battalion being at variance with the next. The more severe the fighting the more common is this problem, and it has then been necessary to make a judgment, to try and work out what actually happened. The facts are not always simple to establish, but living close to where these actions took place and being able to quickly view the ground has, I believe, been a great advantage. Living in Langemark, two minutes on a bicycle gets me to the Steenbeek, five minutes to the Lekkerboterbeek, and twenty minutes to Passchendaele. Where there are two accounts of the same action which differ in a major way I have given both sides of the story. On the other hand there have been numerous occasions when the descriptions of actions from several different sources all agree, and for me this has been like striking the mother load, 90 years on.

After giving the matter much thought, to maintain a consistent approach and hopefully to help in following the extraordinary complexity of the battles, I have always described the actions from south to north. For example the description of the Battle of Pilckem Ridge commences on the southern or right end of the British Line, with the attack of Second Army near the River Lys, and gradually works north, ending with the Fifth Army on the Yser Canal on the far left. I hope this helps with the understanding of the battles. If it has been necessary to change from this practice in description of a local event I have mentioned the fact in the text. There is a further detail that I think deserves mentioning. On occasions, battles although fought over one day were really in two phases, the first, fighting in the early morning to the point reached by a British advance, which was then often followed in the afternoon by a German counter-attack. Where this is the case I have divided the day battle into two sections, and described them separately, rather than describing the activities of one division for the whole day in one passage. Also, where the attacks such as those of General Plumer's Second Army in September against the Gheluvelt plateau, where controlled by advances to three definite and precise objectives, I have described the whole Army advance by divisions, brigades and battalions to the first objective *along the whole Army line*, and then repeated the process to the subsequent objectives. In the interest of clearer understanding, this takes the advance forward in gradual waves, rather than following one division to its final objective as an independent operation.

All place names in the book are in their old French spellings, as this is the way they appear on the 1917 trench maps. I have used sections of 1:10,000 trench maps to illustrate some actions. Each action covers a specific area on the ground, some smaller, some larger. This means the trench maps cannot all be reproduced in the book to the same scale. As a guide to measuring distance on the maps however, each heavily printed square is 1,000 yards by 1,000 yards, these divided by dotted lines into four smaller 500 yard by 500 yard squares. Distances in the text are given in yards and miles, and heights in metres, again in line with the old maps.

To write the story of the Third Battle of Ypres has been an enormous but incredibly rewarding undertaking. My never ending thanks go to my wife Alison for her enduring faith in the validity of my project. She has had to cope with more of my personal explanations and beliefs regarding the fighting at Ypres than is good for anyone's health.

In conclusion this book is dedicated to my grandfather Leonard William Perry D.C.M. and to all those of his generation who went away to war. Their endeavors were far from futile.

Robert A. Perry
Essex Villa
Langemark
1-1-2007

The Battles of Ypres 1917

To Play a Giant's Part

The Rôle of the British Army at Passchendaele

Introduction

Passchendaele – avoidable futility or cornerstone of victory?

This book is intended to give a full and accurate account of The Battles of Ypres 1917, which have become known collectively as the Third Battle of Ypres, or more commonly the Battle of Passchendaele. To use the name Passchendaele to identify the series of battles fought to the east of Ypres, during the Flanders offensive from the 31st July to the 10th November 1917 is strictly incorrect. There were six major battles between the 31st July and the 9th October, and each battle was to be given an independent title. It was the penultimate battle on the 12th October that was to become officially called the First Battle of Passchendaele, and the final series of attacks between the 26thOctober and the 10th November, that were to be called the Second Battle of Passchendaele. The conditions of mud and shell-shattered ground experienced during this final period were amongst the worst throughout the whole campaign. There were however periods in August, between the Battle of Pilckem Ridge and the Battle of Langemarck, when conditions were in places as bad, and optimism in the ranks dropped to an all time low. But the name by which the offensive was to be remembered around the world, and the name that was to arouse such emotion, and later controversy, was Passchendaele. Nearly 90 years later, mention of the word Passchendaele still evokes an atmosphere of grim foreboding, despair, and tragedy. The word has become synonymous with images of mud, mutilation and death, and the despair borne of hopelessness and futility. This account will attempt to show that the battles, and the efforts of the men who fought them under collectively the worst conditions the British Army has ever experienced, were far from futile.

Throughout these pages will be considered whether or not the military conduct of the Flanders offensive, and the repercussions of its results, benefited or were detrimental to the British War effort. Also discussed will be the rôle of the War Cabinet, and its influence or otherwise on military strategy. The impact on British War policy of many often trivialised issues, including the mutinies in the French Army, and the activities of the German navy from their bases on the Flemish coast will be examined in detail. The story told in this book encompasses all the intricate twists and turns, intentional and fateful, political, military, and of nature, that created Passchendaele. The Battle which would destroy countless lives and impose its enormous influence on the future course of the conflict was to become a national phenomenon destined to ruin reputations, and ignite endless bitter controversy.

It has become widely accepted that the blame for the hardships and misery suffered by the soldiers at the front may be laid at the feet of the high command, whose alleged crass incompetence and mindless bungling resulted in a disaster of catastrophic proportions to the Nation and the Empire. Residing in comfort, well behind the fighting fronts, the Generals sent thousands of men to a pointless and futile death. Their lack of humanity was wicked, their ineptitude scandalous. The Commander-in-Chief of the British Expeditionary Force, Field-Marshal Sir Douglas Haig, became the arch-villain, held chiefly responsible for what were seen as the tragedies of both the Somme and Passchendaele. There has never been a leading military figure so roundly condemned by his own country as Sir Douglas Haig. If Britain had lost the Great War the long term vilification could not have been worse. The high levels of casualties sustained during the Somme and Passchendaele fighting provide the dagger to thrust at Haig's reputation, the simplistic and naïve rationale being that anybody presiding over such shocking 'slaughter' must have been totally incompetent and callous. But it was the collective memory of Passchendaele that caused most damage. To explain in some meaningful way how those casualties occurred during the Flanders campaign, and what if anything was the benefit of the sacrifice, and whether in a military sense the casualties could or could not have been substantially avoided, is not possible without taking time to study the complexity and the enormity of the battle. Many will argue that nothing is worth that level of sacrifice, but that is a totally different argument, implying that no cause can justify so many casualties. But the British Generals did not define the cause, nor did they lead the Country into war. Their responsibility was to fight the war that the politicians ordered them to fight, in the best place and in the best way they knew how.

Criticism of the military (and political) conduct of the Battle comes from diverse sources. An increasingly ill-informed media will on occasions pounce on the reputation of Haig, inevitably and inextricably linked with Passchendaele, drag it further through the gutter, and then as boredom with the subject sets in quickly drop it and move on. If the editors involved had to write one meaningful and factual side of A4 explaining the background behind the 'scandal' they were highlighting they would most likely be hard pressed to do so. On the other hand, years of academic research can bring historians to extremely well informed conclusions, which are often at variance with other historians who are equally well informed, but have reached completely different conclusions. In analysing the Passchendaele battle, some will claim that there were better places to fight than Flanders, or that different tactics should have been used, and that little had been learnt from earlier battles. They will claim that there should have been a greater consideration of the possibility of adverse weather conditions, or difficult ground conditions, and that there should have been a clearer understanding of the strengths and weaknesses of both friend and foe. In fact they will claim that virtually every aspect of the battle, military, technical, political, and moral should have been considered more deeply, been handled differently; or even that the battle should not have been fought at all. But the bewilderment and confusion of the time imposed upon those responsible for making decisions in circumstances and conditions never experienced and rarely envisaged before the War, the crushing and ceaseless pressure of national responsibility, and the frustration of dealing with numerous Allied self interests, is not weighing upon modern, enlightened, and often self opinionated shoulders. To criticise is perfectly justifiable, but that criticism must be measured, and must endeavour to recognise the enormous difference in perspective created by the passing of ninety years.

However unpalatable it may be, the Armies, which in reality meant tens of thousands of men, were weapons to be wielded by the Generals. The cost of wielding the weapons was reflected in the huge casualty lists. The question which remained unanswered at the time, and for that matter is still unanswered, was how great these lists could become before enough was considered enough. Once the whole monstrous thing was set in motion, only outright victory, an acceptable negotiated peace which was only likely to be achieved from a position of strength, or a defeat which might include any armistice that the enemy may wish to impose, could bring it to a conclusion. If for one side the casualty list became unacceptably long it would mean defeat, as the only alternative to continuing the fight would be an armistice upon terms dictated by the enemy, or capitulation. The question of tactics, of how to use the Army, either in attack or in defence, which may or may not put a brake on the growing casualty list, was an ongoing dilemma, and a continual cause of controversy between the Cabinet on one hand, and the War Office and G.H.Q. on the other. Fresh strategies were earnestly considered, to move the fighting away from the Western Front and shift the chief responsibility for the fighting, with its associated devastating casualty lists away from the British Army. What should the priority be, lower casualties or final victory? The War Cabinet's position, for which it cannot be criticized, was that ideally the High Command should strive for both, always searching for a grand success, with the minimum of casualties. Unfortunately, however many alternate schemes the Cabinet may promote, they were devoid of workable ideas of how to achieve this Utopia, while the Generals struggled to operate in a real, but far from ideal world.

The myth and the controversy of the Great War prevails, both amongst those who know but little, and wish to know no more, and amongst many of the better informed who now claim the wisdom to explain how things should have been done. The traditional view of the Battle of Passchendaele endures; that it was utter futility and a total failure. Some are of the opinion that however it had been fought, this was the inevitable outcome. Others believe that a change of tactic here, or a firmer hand there, would have had a positive influence upon, what in their opinion, was to become a costly failure. What a sad epitaph to the proud memory of the officers and men who fought this epic battle, and to their heroic deeds described in this book, which at the time not all considered futile. A quote from a War Diary, written by a Canadian Major, 10 days after his unit had been involved in the operation to seize Passchendaele illustrates this point: 'But the measure of our success in Flanders, is not only to be estimated by the value of important positions taken. It is to be found also in the declining strength of the enemy's defences and diminished vigour of his counter attacks.' There is no sign here of despair or hopelessness. Many historians would argue that their academic assessment remains correct, and the Canadian Major was wrong. The historians could be right, as for every positive statement made by a veteran of the Passchendaele fighting there are probably 100 which are negative. But in reality that proves little, for even if the battle had achieved all its original objectives, it is unlikely that those who fought would have subsequently spoken fondly of it. Success in war can as often be partnered by misery, as misery can be the partner of failure. The conclusion of this book is that the Canadian Major was in the long term closer to the truth than he could have possibly known.

To question the old firmly-held beliefs that the whole offensive was futile and its management inept, in no way undermines the magnitude of the sacrifice, or the horror that the soldiers of the Great War had to endure. It is rather an attempt to truly understand a hugely complex period of history by re-examining it in way unclouded by dogma, sentiment, pathos, or an overdose of deep philosophical dissection. The Great War was not conjured up by demons in a dark netherworld: it was caused, started, maintained and fought by men, imbued with both great strengths and inevitable weaknesses. It must therefore be possible to examine the conflict in a rational way. So many critics have condemned the Battle of Passchendaele in speech or writing, when in all honesty it is clear from the factual mistakes and lack of detail or omissions within their content, that they really know insufficient about it to entrench their position so firmly. Attempts to present a convincing argument are often based on scant or unduly partisan evidence offered in a spiteful, deliberately distorted, and personally damaging way, intent on further ruining the reputations of great men no longer in a position to speak in their own defence. This is not the valid presentation of sound historical research. It does not help understanding of the complex issues involved. It is pointless, unsubtle, character assassination, unworthy of its perpetrators whose motive remains a mystery. Recognised and well respected historians, in roundly condemning Haig's folly, at doing this, or not doing that, have in their accounts of the offensive often omitted to discuss in any depth extraneous issues of vital importance to the Passchendaele story. Before anything can be understood, all facts pertaining to it must be available. Hopefully a more rational judgement can then be made. This book is devoted to presenting those facts, and to the memory of the men who fought the great battles. If it can begin to dispel the myth of futility, and show that the efforts of the High Command, the officers, and the men of the British Army at Ypres in the second half of 1917 were of enormous value in the final outcome of the conflict, then it will have served its purpose.

Robert A. Perry
Essex Villa
Langemark   1-1-2007

Chapter One

The Northern Operation

Part One

The complexities of coalition warfare

By the early summer of 1917 the Ypres sector of the Western Front had become a relatively quiet backwater. It had not always been so quiet, for in the autumn of 1914 it had seemed most likely that the city would fall to the relentless enemy advance. But what had begun as an offensive manoeuvre by a few regular British divisions under the command of Field-Marshal Sir John French had quickly and of necessity transformed into a desperate, stubborn defence that had stopped the German westward advance in its tracks. The enemy had pressed the British and French defenders hard but they had held on 'by their eye lids'. The vital defence line on the Yser, covering the Channel ports, was firmly anchored at its southern end at Ypres. By late November the fighting of the First Battle of Ypres had died down, but so severe had it been that the ranks of the hardcore of professional soldiers which had made up the old British Expeditionary Force were decimated. The enemy had failed to seize Ypres, but to the north and south of the city they had pressed so far forward that it was threatened with encirclement. The crucial defence had resulted in large bulge, or salient, which jutted eastward into the enemy line.

By early 1915, to the east of the city, around the arc of what was to become known to the British as the Ypres Salient, the gradually increasing trench systems and rudimentary barbed wire entanglements identified the high water mark of the German advance of 1914; they also signified for the moment the end of mobile warfare. The Western Front had reached stalemate. But the positions to the east of Ypres upon which the British and French had finally held the German advance gave the enemy an enormous strategic advantage. Their front line had settled on the western edge of a low ridge which curved around the city from the south, then forming a plateau 5,000 yards to the east near Gheluvelt. From the plateau, the ridge ran towards the north for about nine miles gradually loosing height. Along its crest from south to north were the hamlet of Broodseinde, and the villages of Passchendaele and Westroosebeke. From Westroosebeke the ridge arced to the west, to eventually become almost imperceptible at the town of Dixmude, which lay on the eastern bank of the River Yser, raised a few metres above the surrounding polders. By the end of the First Battle of Ypres, the German line to the north of the city had pushed west of this low ridge and curved forward as far as the bank of the Ypres - Yser canal, near the village of Bixschoote.

In October 1914 the Belgian Army, in a desperate and eventually successful attempt to thwart further German advance westward along the coast, had opened the sea locks at Nieuport, and at high tides had allowed the sea to gradually inundate a huge low lying area approximately 19 miles long and up to 2 miles wide, across the polder-like country to the north of Ypres through which flowed the partially canalized River Yser. The Belgian Army had dug-in in relative safety behind the impassable protection of the inundations, which stretched inland to within 12,000 yards of Ypres. At Diksmude, approximately mid way between Ypres and the coast, a narrow causeway split the inundations virtually in half, the crossing closely guarded by the Belgians on the west bank of the river. The defensive position thus created on the Yser, between Nieuport on the English Channel, and the Ypres Salient, anchored the northern end of the Western Front.

In the spring of 1915 the battle in Flanders had resumed. To indicate how strategically important the Germans considered the Ypres position to be, they again attempted to drive out the British and French from the city. If their attack succeeded they would outflank the Yser inundations to the south and resume their march on the Channel ports, and to the west of Ypres there was little by way of defences to stop them. But this attack was to be different. This time the world was to be introduced to a new weapon, provided by the ingenuity of German science, which its Army felt morally justified to use. The wonder weapon, unleashed upon an enemy totally lacking in any protection against it, very nearly sealed the fate of the Salient. The dogged resistance of a few brave Canadians allowed time for a more substantial defence to organise. For the enemy the first use of chlorine gas between Steenstraat on the Ypres-Yser canal, and the village of Langemarck, had nearly been decisive; but only nearly. By the end of May with British casualties approaching 60,000, the Second Battle of Ypres, the first and greatest chance of success for the new poison gas had ended in failure for the enemy; but the genie was out of the bottle. There would be new and more terrible gases, but the vital moment had passed and never again would gas come so close to being a war winning weapon. The city, sitting in its vital position at the southern end of the Ypres-Yser canal which flowed via the Yser inundations to the Channel coast, had for the second time been saved. But the Salient had been reduced, and the arc to the north had been driven in by 5,000 yards.

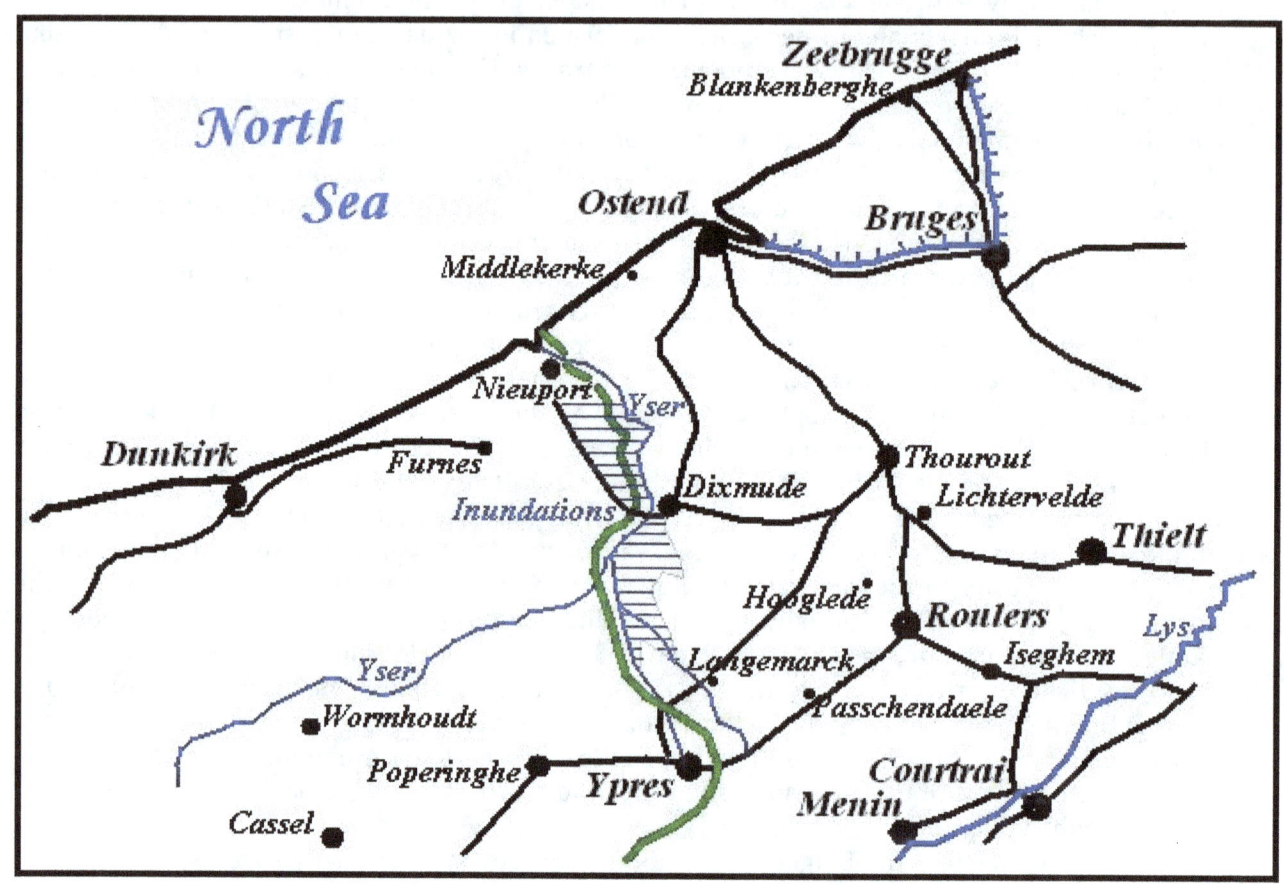

The Flemish coast and the Yser inundations
Showing principle railways and Front Line January 1917

Since the end of the Second Battle, the British Second Army under General Sir Herbert Plumer had held the uncomfortable, exposed, and continuously overlooked breastworks, along the foot of the Messines ridge south of Ypres, and around the arc of the Salient. From the end of the Second Battle in 1915, to the spring of 1917, there had been no major offensive action by either side, but Plumer's Army had been considering and developing various new ways to assault the enemy position.[1] Although a quiet sector compared with the major battlefields to the south, in the mind of the British soldier the Salient had become arguably the most hated place along the

---

[1] In the summer of 1916 a local but significant German attack between Hill 60 and Hooge had driven the British off three small, but nonetheless important hillocks, Mount Sorrel, Hill 61, and Hill 62, on the western edge of the Gheluvelt plateau to the east of the City, but the positions had soon been retaken by the Canadian Corps.

whole front line held by the B.E.F. Enemy shelling which had begun to seriously damage the fine old buildings of Ypres in 1914, had increased drastically in 1915, and by 1917 the city lay in ruins, few structures being left unscathed. The gaunt, broken central tower of the Cloth Hall, appearing as the abandoned keep of a medieval stronghold, stood out as a precise landmark to German observers, pinpointing what remained of the city centre. The Salient, now measured about 10,000 yards across its base and thrust eastwards up to a depth of 5,000 yards, to the western fringe of the main ridge. In their rapid advance southwards behind their gas cloud, from Bixschoote towards Ypres in April 1915, the Germans had taken possession of another low ridge, which protruded from the Gheluvelt plateau towards the northwest, and was separated from the main Passchendaele ridge by the shallow valley of the Steenbeek, a gentle stream meandering through a wide, flat depression. This low secondary ridge, known to the British as Pilckem ridge, formed the north-eastern rim of a shallow saucer with Ypres at its centre, and upon this curve of slightly higher ground sat the enemy, like the audience in an amphitheatre, with excellent observation across the whole low plain which was the British position. That the enemy could see every movement the British made, but the British could not easily see the enemy, was the reason for the evil reputation the sector had gained. The British positions in the nose of the Salient were continually exposed to observed enemy fire, both small arms and artillery, from front, from both flanks, and in places from the rear.

In the autumn of 1914, as the Germans advanced westwards along the Belgian coast, they had occupied in tact the ports of Zeebrugge, Blankenberghe and Ostend. From the time of their occupation, German submarines and torpedo boats could operate with mine and torpedo against the vital British cross Channel routes of supply and communications. In time, operating under the command of the *MarineKorps Flandern,* the U-Boats would also patrol into the North Sea, the Thames Estuary, the South Irish Sea, and the Bay of Biscay, returning to safe ports at Ostend and Zeebrugge with canal links to Bruges 10 miles inland, where there were soon to be extensive repair and docking facilities, eventually protected within great reinforced concrete pens. The Flemish coast had always been of prime strategic importance to the British and now it was largely in enemy hands. From late 1914 plans had been under consideration for an attack, both along the coastal strip and by a sea borne landing to remove the threat. This operation in Flanders was preferable to Sir Douglas Haig, who had replaced Sir John French as Commander-in-Chief of the British Expeditionary Force in December 1915, to the proposed combined Franco-British offensive on the Somme.

The available frontage on which to launch an attack along the coast was however, due to the inundations, limited to a narrow coastal strip of sand dunes. The inundations were in fact a double edged sword. They had prevented German advance westward in October 1914 but would also unless drained, except for the narrow causeway at Dixmude, restrict Allied movement eastward. To drain the inundations south of Dixmude after the closing of the locks, to allow the passage of troops, would take around three weeks, but would undoubtedly awaken the Germans to British intentions. Before 1914 was out, minds had already focused upon unlikely schemes to recover the Belgian coast. One such plan involved a combined operation, mounted from the mouth of the Yser at Nieuport along the coastal strip, supported by a landing at Ostend. This, another of Winston Churchill's amphibious plans, was opposed by General Joffre and was not attempted. Within a year the Admiralty's concern had deepened, stating that the use of the Belgian ports by the German navy constituted: 'a growing danger to the transport of troops and supplies to France', and on the 28th October began discussing a combined naval military operation once more. A memorandum on the subject was written by the General Staff at the War Office, in consultation with the Admiralty War Staff and Vice Admiral Roger Bacon Commanding the Dover Patrol. Issued on the 12th November 1915 the memorandum examined in detail the possibilities of a French attack from Nieuport along the coast (as they already held the coastal strip), supported by the guns of the British Fleet. When the French reached Westende Plage, it was envisaged that a British landing could be made in support at Middlekerke Bains, which would so threaten Ostend that the enemy would most likely flood the surrounding country, making the port unusable to them. Even if an advance to this depth was not achieved, the movement and deployment of heavy guns along the coast as far as Westende Plage would threaten enemy operations at Ostend. But Haig was already certain that the coastal attack would require a much greater military commitment than that suggested in the War Office memorandum, and requested that plans be drawn up for a more extensive operation. The instruction he issued on the 7th January 1916 read: '1/ Plan for landing and capture of Ostend to be worked out in detail. 2/ The success of the operation will depend on surprise of the enemy. With this in view, plan for engaging enemy in order to cause him to withdraw his reserves from the Ostend area will also be worked out - e.g., attack on Houthulst: advance on Middlekerke. 3/ The date on which these operations will take place must depend on the plans of the G.O.C.-in-C. French Army.'[2]

The first possible place south of the Yser inundations where a British force of suitable size would have sufficient length of front on which to assemble for an attack towards the Flemish coast ports was the salient at Ypres. Haig planned not just to take Ostend but to clear the whole Belgian coast, and if matters progressed well, the whole of northern Belgium up to the Dutch border. Once he was clear of the main ridge east of Ypres, but not before, a joint naval-military operation would be carried out from Nieuport along the coast, with simultaneous amphibious landings behind the German lines towards Ostend. The January 1916 plan proposed that General Sir Henry Rawlinson's Fourth Army should take over the northern sector of the Salient down to the line of the Ypres – Roulers railway, and that Rawlinson should prepare a plan for an initial breakout to the north-east towards Houthulst Forest, an extensive area of strategically important and heavily defended woodland held by the enemy 14,000 yards north of Ypres, with the support of General Sir Herbert Plumer's Second Army on his right. Lieutenant-General Hunter Weston, with experience of combined operations during the Gallipoli campaign, would meanwhile in conjunction with Vice-Admiral Sir Roger Bacon, compile a plan for a joint operation with the Navy, to launch an attack along the coastal strip from the Nieuport bridgehead, and a surprise seaborne landing against Ostend. It was understood from the beginning that a breakout from the Ypres Salient was not going to be easy. All the benefits of a strong defensive position and excellent observation lay with the enemy. Any breakout towards the north-east would entail first having to capture Pilckem ridge and cross the Steenbeek, and then advance another 2 to 3 miles to gain the main ridge around Passchendaele and Westroosebeke. Five-thousand yards to the east of Ypres, where the Ypres to Menin road crosses the Messines – Wytschaete – Passchendaele ridge lay the main German defensive strength, on and behind the Gheluvelt plateau, where at its highest points the ground reaches around 60 meters.

Haig met with his Army commanders on the 13th January to discuss the Northern Operation, as the breakout from the Salient was to be known, and the importance of capturing the Gheluvelt plateau before Fourth Army attempted to cross the Steenbeek was emphasised. From the plateau German artillery observers with direct sight of any British movement on the lower ground to the north-west across the Steenbeek depression could bring down fire from the many batteries sited on and behind the plateau and behind the main ridge between Gheluvelt and Passchendaele. There was however a further complication. General Plumer, who had been in the Salient since 1915 and knew the ground well, made it clear that as a preliminary to the capture of the Gheluvelt plateau, the occupation of the Messines – Wytschaete ridge to the south of Ypres would be essential.[3] Plumer announced that the preparations for this separate operation were already well advanced, including the tunnelling of a number of great mines beneath the German front line positions, at Hill 60, along the western face of the Messines ridge, and in the valley of the Douve stream just to the south of Messines. Haig agreed with Plumer's strategy to

---

[2] Brigadier-General Sir James Edmonds (1948), *Official History of the Great War: Military Operations in France and Belgium 1917 Vol.II 7th June-10th November, Messines and Third Ypres (Passchendaele)* (hereafter BOH) London: HMSO p399

[3] This ridge to the south of the City, reaching a height of around 80 metres at Wytschaete can best be imagined as the handle of a scythe, Gheluvelt plateau and Pilckem ridge forming the blade.

extend the scope of the Northern Operation to first include the capture of the Messines – Wytschaete ridge as a precursor to the main breakout battle towards the Belgian coast. The Northern Operation was intended to be the major British effort in 1916. But before the launch of the Flanders attack, the British were to co-operate with the French in a series of limited attacks on the Somme, to coincide with a Russian offensive on the Eastern Front.

On the 21st February 1916 the Germans totally upset Allied strategic planning, with a major attack on the French at Verdun. From the start the operation had been envisaged by the enemy as a battle of attrition to wear down the French Army, attacking them at a place where they could not refuse to fight. Continuing into the summer the battle drew in more and more French reserves, which had been earmarked for the Allied summer offensive operations. The arrangements for the planned battle on the Somme had to be drastically altered, the British now taking the leading role, as French manpower was increasingly thrown into the desperate fighting at Verdun.

The Battle of the Somme put on hold the plan to carry out the Northern Operation in 1916. Rawlinson's Fourth Army was totally committed, and would not in the foreseeable future be involved in the operation in Flanders. Plumer's Second Army meanwhile would have to operate alone in Flanders with strictly limited resources. On the 22nd May 1916 a Reserve Army (soon to become the British Fifth Army) had been raised under Lieutenant-General Sir Hubert Gough, with the intension of breaking through and exploiting any breach in the German line on the Somme created by Fourth Army. Any hope there had been that Gough's Army might be available to move north in support of the Second Army were also soon dashed by the severity of the Somme fighting. Consequently the limited Messines operation to seize the ridge south of Ypres was proposed as a subsidiary to the Somme offensive and given a provisional date for the 15th July 1916. But demands on manpower and equipment for the Fourth and Reserve Armies soon made it clear that sufficient resources were not available to Second Army, and even the preliminary Messines operation was for the moment cancelled.

From the German perspective however, matters were not all going their way. The battle of attrition which they had unleashed at Verdun, and the costly defence of their positions on the Somme were believed to have greatly weakened their fighting capacity. The true extent to which their morale had been affected was however unknown. On the other hand the French Army, although not 'bled white' at Verdun as the Germans had intended, was reaching the limits of its reserves of endurance and manpower. On the 13th November the last major attack of 1916 by the Fifth Army, began on the Somme. Two days later a conference to decide the future course of the War assembled at Chantilly.

The Inter-Allied Conference Chantilly the 15th and 16th November 1916[4]

The most important conclusions to come out of the Chantilly Conference were first, that the strategic forward planning for 1917 was to change little from the pattern of 1916, and second, that a major effort should be made in the Balkans. It was considered desirable that twenty-three divisions should be concentrated at Salonica, this being the largest number that could be supported due to the limited communications available in the area and constraints due to available British shipping. Pressure was brought upon the Italians to provide engineers and labour to construct roads and railways capable of supporting up to 30 divisions which according to General Milne, the British Commander-in Chief in the theatre, were required to carry out a decisive offensive against Bulgaria. So read the report of the Conference compiled by Cabinet Secretary Sir Maurice Hankey. Haig's Chief-of-Staff Lieutenant-General Kiggell later added a little more substance to the record of the proceedings of the Military Conference.[5] General Joffre

---

[4] National Archives, note by the Secretary of the War Committee on the results of the Paris Conference, November 15th and 16th 1916. CAB42/25/8
[5] Liddell Hart Centre for Military Archives, Kiggell papers 5/2 and 5/3

the French Commander-in-Chief had made it clear that the French had been badly shaken by their experience at Verdun, and his Army was suffering from dangerously dwindling levels of manpower. The French certainly desired a strong offensive, but looked unlikely to take a lead rôle on the Western Front; rather relying on the British to carry out the main attack, whilst avoiding severe casualties which they could themselves ill afford. In order to keep the German Army occupied in all theatres, a series of offensives were planned on the Western, Italian and Eastern Fronts, the timings to be arranged to prevent the movement of enemy forces from one threatened front to another. The general consensus was that the offensive of 1917 against the Central Powers should be mounted *simultaneously* on all fronts, but no agreement could be reached on an approximate date to begin.

Joffre pointed out that France had carried the main burden of the War for two years, and in order to forestall another German attack against his Army, pressed for an offensive to begin as early as February. Neither the Italians nor the Russians, partly due to concerns over possible winter conditions, could agree to such an early start, the February date also (according to Kiggell) rejected by Haig. Joffre however, rather than wait and adhere to the agreed principle and likely success of a simultaneous operation, appeared more concerned about an early German attack upon him and stuck to his demand for an early opening. The majority conclusion was that if simultaneous action was to be ensured, the offensive must not begin before the end of May, and Kiggell noted that, 'Sir D. Haig according to my recollection comforted Joffre with the assurance that he would act at once to draw pressure off the French if they were attacked before the general Allied offensive was ready to start'. But all present were agreed that the utmost pressure possible should be maintained on the enemy, and no opportunity should be offered to allow a recovery from the damage inflicted at Verdun and on the Somme. In the spring the Italians were to resume their offensive against the Austrians on the Isonzo, and the Russians would also launch an offensive in the east. Joffre was reluctant to allow the enemy a respite and gained the agreement of the Conference that offensive action should be maintained, weather allowing, throughout the winter months.[6] The French communiqué recording the agreements reached still spoke of the Allies making preparations, 'avec tous lès moyens dont elles disposent' to be ready during the first fortnight in February. Haig's initial plans for an offensive on the Western Front in 1917 in which the British were to take the lead were soon to be formulated in accordance with this general plan, but with a view to commence operations simultaneously with the Italians and the Russians, probably during May.[7]

British Prime Minister Asquith was accompanied at the Conference of Allied Governments by the Secretary of State for War, David Lloyd George. In pursuance of his great hope of attacking the enemy anywhere but on the Western Front, Lloyd Georeg raised with Joffre the question of Allied strength in the Balkans, and asked exactly how many divisions comprised the present Salonica force. Joffre replied that there were 7 British and 6 French, with the promise of 3 Italian, but Lloyd George doubted the General's assurance of the inclusion of 6 Serbian divisions, claiming that in reality only 3 were present. In his diary entry that day Haig claimed that Lloyd George was all for sending more divisions to Salonica to make good the numbers, and to support Romania in its fight with Bulgaria. He also noted that the suggestion was rejected by the French, and by General Sir William Robertson, the Chief of the Imperial

---

[6] This was also Haig's view. After talking with Joffre on the 23rd October Haig had noted: 'He gave me his views on the general situation and agreed with me that we must continue to press the enemy here on the Somme battle front throughout the winter'. Gary Sheffield and John Bourne Eds. (2005) *Douglas Haig, War Diaries and Letters 1914-1918*. London: Weidenfeld & Nicholson, (hereafter Douglas Haig. Diaries and Letters) p246

[7] The preference for waiting until May so firmly stressed by Kiggell implies that Haig had apparently changed his mind on a start date, for after a talk with Robertson on the 22nd October Haig had rather confusingly noted in his diary: 'November Conference at Chantilly. General Joffre had suggested postponing a general offensive till next May because Russians and Italians could not advance until then. We both agreed that such a late date was quite unsound.' Douglas Haig. Diaries and Letters, p245

General Staff, who stressed the great difficulty in supporting greater numbers given the shortage of shipping and the difficulty with communications in the Balkans.[8] It was agreed however, undoubtedly to the dissatisfaction of Lloyd George, that the decisive operations in 1917 would be concentrated on the Western Front, and there should be no dissipation of forces to other theatres. The French Army, hopefully revitalised come the spring, would attack on the Aisne, with a Franco-British supporting operation on the Somme, to be followed in the summer by the major British effort, in Flanders. But dramatic events were soon to turn this whole scenario on its head.

The decision for the main British effort to be made in Flanders corresponded with the wishes of the War Committee of the British Cabinet, who on the 23rd November instructed the military that there was, 'no measure to which the Committee attached greater importance than the expulsion of the enemy from the Belgian coast'.[9] The importance that the British Government placed upon the maintenance of the vital Channel passage was expressed to Joffre in a letter from General Robertson, in which he stated that the occupation of Ostend and Zeebrugge should be an objective of the campaigns in 1917. On the 8th December Joffre replied indicating complete agreement, although his perception of the plan was a little different to the British. He considered the breakout from Ypres should commence several weeks after the attacks in the south, as a means of holding German reserves, and whether successful or not should be followed ten days later by a French attack along the coast from Nieuport with the amphibious landing of five divisions some two or three days after that. The British G.H.Q. plan differed in two major ways, in that the whole coastal operation depended on, and should not be attempted before, a successful breakout from the Ypres Salient and beyond the Passchendaele ridge, and that the maximum number of divisions the Admiralty thought could be landed from the sea was two not five.

Haig now began to seriously consider the arrangements for the Northern Operation, and on the 17th November requested Plumer to submit plans based on the assumption that 30 to 35 divisions would be available for the operation. Plumer was told that he must be prepared to launch an attack at Messines at a months notice (a tall order) in the spring or summer of 1917. His initial proposals were similar to those he had made in January, in that the first attack should include in its objectives the Messines ridge, Hill 60 (just south of the Gheluvelt plateau), and Pilckem ridge, to deprive the Germans of their key observations positions over Ypres before any attempt be made to cross the Steenbeek and approach the Passchendaele ridge. In a personal letter to Lieutenant-General Kiggell on the 15th December, Plumer's chief G.S.O. Major-General Charles (Tim) Harington pointed out that as the whole operation might prove too big for one Army to control, the attacking force should be split into two Armies, the Second Army to carry out the Messines operation with the Ypres – Comines canal as its northern boundary,[10] with another Army responsible for the main breakout towards the north-east from the Salient. The basic foundations for the Northern Operation had therefore been laid.

On the 20th November, following a visit to G.H.Q. by Admiral Bacon, Haig made an interesting note in his diary, based on comments which Bacon had made: 'He considers that the situation in the Channel is much less satisfactory than it was. The German sailors have learnt much and their recent raid has shown them that they can interfere with our communications without much danger or difficulty. He [Bacon] cannot prevent these raids. I gather from this that out command of the Channel is precarious, and that our ports may be closed oftener in the future than in the past.'[11] The activities of the *MarineKorps Flandern* from their bases on the Flemish coast were clearly of concern to the British Commander-in-Chief, and the dangers to

---

[8] Douglas Haig. Diaries and Letters, p256
[9] BOH p8
[10] A small canal which branched off the larger Ypres – Yser canal just north of Ypres, passed around the western side of the city to then run south-east, passing through a cutting in the main ridge at 'The Bluff' then past Hollebeke to reach the River Lys at Comines
[11] Douglas Haig. Diaries and Letters p258

vital British communication and supply across the narrow sea lane were obvious to all. Worryingly it was not just U-boats giving Bacon and Haig major cause for concern but also destroyers.[12]

The arrival of Nivelle

At the Chantilly Conference, although Joffre had stressed the need for a period of respite for the French Army, he had not grasped how precarious was his personal situation. The government of French Premier Aristide Briand, already under pressure for the perceived national disaster at Verdun, was more than pleased to deflect the growing resentment towards the ageing General, who now rather than a symbol of dogged French resistance became identified as the architect of failure. Joffre had been Chief of the French General Staff since 1911, and although undoubtedly responsible for the development and implementation of flawed strategy, had been a rock upon which all of the disasters that had befallen France since 1914 had beaten, but failed to disturb. But at the end of 1916, this was a crisis of confidence which not even Joffre could withstand. The Conference had proposed a series of wearing-down battles proceeding over a period of at least a year, before the possibility might arise to finally break through the enemy defences and deliver a final crushing defeat. But politically and socially France was being worn-down more quickly than the prospect of this depressingly predictable pattern of long drawn out war would allow. In some influential political groups there was call for a change of tempo, to be initiated by a change of military leadership.

The choice of successor to Joffre was not obvious. Pétain, Foch and Castelnau were all clear contenders, but one name had recently become prominent, and had risen to fame not for competence alone, but for delivering an element of success from the tragedy that had been Verdun. General Robert Nivelle the tough, talented, imaginative and highly personable victor of Fort Douaumont was the military man of the moment. His hard hitting, lightening-strike tactics, with novel use of massed artillery to blast a passage through the whole depth of the enemy position had worked very well on a limited scale at Verdun, and Nivelle saw no reason why they should not work on a much larger scale. On such a large scale in fact that if he were given the opportunity to develop them on a broad section of the Western Front, he foresaw a rapid breaching of the enemy line, and within 24 to 48 hours comprehensive exploitation to the extent that victory would be swift and sure. Nivelle also claimed that if the offensive failed to deliver what he promised of it within 48 hours he would immediately call it off. His bold, belligerent statements and guarantees of swift victory left some dubious of their worth, but certainly gave others reassurance and offered hope to an Army and a country which for long had been short on both.

By the 11th of December political pressure in France, due partly to general discontent with the conduct of the War so far, and partly to weaknesses in the Government of Premier Briand, had brought about a new French war cabinet, the 'Comité de Guerre', which demanded the removal of General Joffre, and the appointment of General Nivelle as Commander-in-Chief. On the 13th December Joffre was removed from his post, to be appointed technical advisor to the Government. By the 21st December Joffre, soon to be bestowed with the nominal title of Marshal of France as poor consolation, became aware that without consultation with the Government's 'technical advisor' Nivelle had entirely changed the plan of operations of the French Armies on the Western Front.

David Lloyd George becomes Prime Minister

At the same time political upheaval in Britain had brought about the fall of the Government of Herbert Asquith, and on the 6th December David Lloyd George had become Prime Minister of a coalition Government of Liberals and Conservatives. One of Lloyd George's first actions to better

---

[12] See Chapter 10 *MarineKorps Flandern*

conceive and control War policy was to create a small executive War Cabinet. Two days later, reacting before Lloyd George was even settled into Downing Street, Robertson presented him with a memorandum outlining his views on the present situation, and immediately emphasised the necessity to gain more control over the conduct of the war and prepare for a lengthy struggle based mainly on the Western Front.[13] He also stressed the importance of improving the French Nord Railway system, a real and acute problem to the British Army, soon to be at the centre of much political shenanigans. From the moment Lloyd George took up the premiership, the relationship between Haig, Robertson, and their political master was to become increasingly difficult, and both greeted the coming of Lloyd George's administration with grave misgivings. Haig recognised the new Prime Minister's enormous organisational abilities on the home front, but foresaw that there would now be far greater interference from London in matters of strategy and military planning than there had been under Asquith. Robertson had already crossed swords back in October with the then War Minister over his disregard for military advice, Lloyd George making it clear that he would not be bound by the views of the military. On the 15th December, one year to the day since Haig's appointment as Commander-in Chief, he and Robertson, met with Lloyd George for the first time as Prime Minister. The gulf between Haig's strictly Western Front approach to the War and Lloyd George's alternative front schemes were obvious from this first meeting. Haig noted in his diary: 'He pointed out the need for an early success, and was anxious to make an attack from Egypt on El Arish and so towards Jerusalem. For this he wanted two divisions from France. He was also anxious to help Italy with 200 heavy guns and take Pola. I was to provide these guns during the winter and get them back in the spring.'[14] Throughout the next year Haig was, for better or worse, to be consistent in his strategic outlook, whilst Lloyd George would wander and waver from one unlikely policy to another as the winds of change, and vision of spectacular or inexpensive results carried him. On one matter however the Prime Minister was resolute; he loathed the idea of another major British offensive in France or Flanders. He totally mistrusted Haig's abilities and concepts of fighting 'wearing-out battles' on the Western Front which in his view would inevitably result in high British casualties, as had been witnessed on the Somme. He much preferred a policy committed to fighting on alternative fronts, attacking Germany's weaker neighbours, where he would be prepared to give support by way of equipment and guns. By confronting the Turks in Palestine or Mesopotamia, the relatively low levels of manpower engaged would prevent the huge casualty lists of the Somme, whilst in Italy, hopefully others would do most of the fighting. By turning away from the main body of the enemy on the Western Front, and engaging Turkey, Bulgaria, or Austria, he could thus achieve his two purposes; to minimise British casualties, and curb what he saw as Haig's excesses. Lloyd George saw Italy as an obvious prospect to develop an alternative front, believing privately that the Italians had not shouldered sufficient burden of effort towards the War so far, whilst stating publicly that with the support of a British and French contingent of undisclosed size, and with a considerable supply of weaponry, great things could be achieved. The Italian Front strategy was seen by the 'Westerners' however as being defined more by what it may prevent happening (heavy British casualties on the Western Front), rather than by what it might achieve (knocking Austria out of the War through a separate peace), and was in any event considered by Haig and Robertson as being dangerously flawed. In their opinion, for the British and French to move forces to Italy in sufficient numbers of either men or guns to make a material difference would have the effect of handing the initiative to the Germans, who, by means of superior internal lines of communication, could support their Austrian Ally quickly; an action which would seriously threaten to overwhelm the Italians before the French and British could build up their forces on the Italian Front. Alternatively the enemy could sit safely on the Western Front in the knowledge that they were not at risk from an Allied offensive. The most dangerous scenario was that they might launch their own offensive on the weakened Western Front, and strike across the Aisne towards Paris,

---

[13] Robertson Papers 7/7/9 8th December 1916. Liddell Hart Centre for Military Archives, King's College London
[14] Douglas Haig. Diaries and Letters, p260

or of greatest worry to Haig, attack in Flanders and threaten to cut the British supply artery across the Channel by seizing the Channel ports. In opposition to this view, the Prime Minister was to pursue his argument against a British offensive on the Western Front, and his preference of an alternate front strategy throughout 1917; except that is for the brief period about to unfold under the influence of General Nivelle.[15]

Nivelle introduced himself to Haig by letter on the 19th December, congratulating him on his 'succès sur la Somme', upon the power and resolution shown by les troupes Britanniques, and of his confidence of achieving victory through a plan to combine the operations of both armies.[16] The two Commanders-in-Chief met for the first time on the 20th December. Haig initially liked what he saw of Nivelle: 'He was, I thought a most straightforward and soldierly man…He is confident of breaking through the Enemy's front now that the Enemy's morale is weakened, but the blow must be struck by surprise and go through in 24 hours….Altogether I was pleased with my first meeting with Nivelle.'[17] Within 3 days Haig was in receipt of Nivelle's detailed plans for his proposed offensive.[18] To achieve his aims of break through, exploitation, and destruction of the enemy, Nivelle explained that it would be necessary to assemble a large reserve of 27 divisions forming three French Armies. The offensive would be launched against the great German salient between Soissons and Arras, to entrap and defeat the enemy within in a pincer movement, with the overall intention of destroying the principal mass of the German forces on the Western Front. The execution of the plan would see the French Army taking the main rôle, attacking the southern end of the German defences north of the Aisne towards the high ridge of the Chemin des Dames, while the British played a subsidiary part by attacking *a few days earlier* on the northern flank of the German salient at Arras. The French were to assemble an overwhelming weight of artillery to pound the German defensive belts in depth, smashing the wire and fortifications, and enabling the infantry to pour through the gaps created toward Laon. In order to concentrate a sufficiently large French reserve capable of exploitation following the break through, it would be necessary for the British to take over a section of the French front between the Somme and the Oise, a task requiring by Nivelle's calculations the deployment of 7 or 8 British divisions. The redeployment of forces should be completed by the 15th January at the latest.[19] Nivelle recognised that this movement of British divisions would release them from the obligation of winter operations agreed at Chantilly in November, and of greater importance claimed that his plan did not exclude the possibility, if the need arose, of a future operation for the capture of Ostend and Zeebrugge. If his offensive succeeded Nivelle considered the Flanders operation would be unnecessary as the Germans would have already been compelled to withdraw from the Belgian coast, whilst if it were unsuccessful there would remain the opportunity for the British to attack in Flanders in good summer weather.[20]

---

[15] For another even briefer period after the failure of Nivelle, Lloyd George was to appear to support Haig's plan for a Flanders offensive, whilst in reality only bolstering French resolution to continue fighting.
[16] National Archives, Nivelle to Haig, letter No.15654 19th December 1916, WO158/37
[17] Douglas Haig. Diaries and Letters, p261
[18] National Archives, Nivelle to Haig, letter No.17856 21st December 1916, WO158/37
[19] The extension of the British Front Line was discussed at an Anglo-French conference on the 26th December, and again by the Cabinet on the 27th. Robertson informed the Cabinet that Haig had already agreed to take over nearly half the line required by Nivelle, but was reluctant to do more until he was informed from London of what drafts he would receive over the next few months. The C.I.G.S. reported that 2 divisions would proceed to France in January and a further 2 in February. The Cabinet decided to reply that they were in general sympathy with the French proposal, but would not commit themselves until they had gone into the matter in detail with Haig. National Archives, minutes of Cabinet meeting 27th December 1916 CAB23-1.
[20] Nivelle's letter concluded: 'Enfin, le plan d'operations que je vous si exposé n'exclue pas la possibilité d'effectuer, le cas échéant, l'operation visant la conquête d'Ostende et de Zeebrugge puisque celle-ci ne peut pas avoir lieu avant l'été….Si notre grande offensive réussit, il est certain que

Not only was this a complete departure from the agreements of Chantilly, but, as a matter of considerable surprise to Haig, Nivelle's planning went far beyond anything discussed at their cordial meeting on the 20th. There was for the moment no mention of timing in Nivelle's letter and therefore no mention of the matter considered so important in earlier planning of a simultaneous offensive by all the Allies. Gone was the requirement to maintain pressure on the enemy during the winter months, but more alarmingly also gone was the agreement to make the Flanders offensive and the clearing of the Belgian coast the main British priority for 1917, the operation previously considered of prime importance by the British Government, now relegated to secondary importance, or if Nivelle was to be believed probably altogether unnecessary. In addition the British were being asked to provide another 7 divisions to take over more line. Here was a major dilemma for Haig. It was becoming clear that to cooperate fully in Nivelle's plan would embroil his Army in a major offensive of indeterminate length, likely to jeopardise his planned concentration in Flanders. Should he continue to mould his policy around the requirements of the French, as to date in accord with Joffre he had always done, or consider his national interests first? Obviously without considerable reinforcement he could not do both. Haig responded to Nivelle by letter explaining that although he agreed in principle with the plan and wanted to help, the degree of help would depend on the level of reinforcements he received in the next two or three months from other theatres, specifically mentioning Salonica.[21] Haig's hopes of reinforcement for the Western Front from alternate theatres were to prove completely out of phase with Lloyd George's strategic policy, which was generally more inclined towards a reversal of this movement. But there was soon to be a crucial change in the Prime Ministers thinking before he once more returned to his 'alternative front' course.

Inter-Allied Conference Rome
5th 6th and 7th January 1917

On the 2nd January Lloyd George accompanied amongst others by General Robertson set out for an Inter-Allied Conference in Rome, stopping in Paris en-route, where he was met off the train by Premier Briand. The journey to Italy continued on the 4th, the Prime Minister taking the opportunity whilst on the train to lobby the French Minister of War General Lyautey with an explanation of his proposal for a large Anglo-French artillery concentration on the River Isonzo in support of an Italian offensive against the Austrians. Upon arrival in Rome Lloyd George sent Cabinet Secretary Hankey on a mission to see Italian Commander-in-Chief General Cadorna, to sound him out on the proposed artillery concentration. Robertson had however beaten him to it. Hankey's arrival at Cadorna's house immediately followed the C.I.G.S. departure, and placed the Cabinet secretary in a difficult position, as he was aware of Robertson's disapproval of the plan to send the guns. Cadorna appeared at best luke-warm to the proposal, sighting a number of technical difficulties, which Hankey believed had possibly been suggested to the Italian by Robertson. Hankey subsequently passed on his appreciation of the meeting with Cadorna to Robertson, and also to Lloyd George, who was less than pleased with the account. The Prime Minister was not to be thwarted however and arranged a somewhat clandestine meeting that evening at the British embassy with Bissolati, a socialist member of the Italian Cabinet, considered an outcast by the Italian inner political circle. The perceptive and intelligent Bissolati seemed more receptive towards Lloyd George's proposal, and left promising to try to convince Cadorna.

The Conference was held at the Consulta on the evening of the 6th, and Lloyd George, with little or no reference to his military advisors, with usual eloquent persuasiveness,

---

la côte belge tombera entre nos mains du fait de la retaite des Armées allemandes, et sans attaque directs. Si au contraire nos attaques échouent, il sera toujours possible d'exécuter à la belle saison les operations projetées en Flandre.' National Archives, Nivelle to Haig, letter No.17856 21st December 1916, WO158/37

[21] National Archives, OAD255, 25th December 1916, Haig to Nivelle WO158/37

introduced his plan for a heavy concentration of supporting artillery on the Isonzo, details of which he had circulated to attendants of the Conference that morning. Whereas a shortage of shipping precluded the despatch of 2 divisions to Salonica he explained, trucks and guns could be sent to the Italian Front without any demand upon shipping. He urged that his proposed plan should be carefully considered by the General Staffs; but this he considered was not enough, because 'it would never be carried out unless ministers themselves took the matter in hand and insisted on it being considered favourably'.[22] Intent on gaining general approval of his plan Lloyd George read out the following resolution. 'The Conference are impressed with the advantages afforded by the Italian Front for a combined offensive by the three Western Allies, which are as follows:

1) It would relieve the pressure on Russia, Rumania, and the Balkans. 2) It would attack the enemy on a front where his forces are weaker in numbers, quality and equipment, than at any other point accessible to the Allied Armies of the West. 3) It might enable the Allies to capture Trieste, which would bring important political advantages. 4) It might enable the Allies to capture Pola, the principle Austrian naval base, thereby reducing the submarine menace in the Mediterranean. 5) No additional demand on shipping transport is involved. 6) The Allies would be fighting on enemy territory.

The Conference refer this question for immediate examination, by the ministers, in conjunction with the Military representatives, more particularly, from the point of view of the form the French and British cooperation should take.' Lloyd George then explained that the last sentence enquired in effect whether General Cadorna required guns only, or infantry divisions as well. Premier Briand cast doubt on the plan in view of the advanced stage of preparations for the Nivelle offensive and the associated requirement for guns, the Prime Minister countering that his proposal should receive full consideration and the undoubted reluctance of Nivelle or Haig to relinquish guns should not be considered the final word. Briand, and French Armaments Minister Albert Thomas, maintained a unified front in opposition to the plan, and General Cadorna was called in to hear and comment on Lloyd George's proposals. Cadorna was under the impression that any guns he received would need to be returned to the Western Front by May, and taking into account the delays in transportation and for technical familiarity with the new weapons, he felt that insufficient time was available to make the deployment viable. Lloyd George, struggling against the flow to press his case, and showing a clear disregard for the demands of the Western Front, claimed that although this may be the case with French guns, he had not excluded the possibility of allowing British guns to remain longer with the Italians. This was obviously too much for the French, Albert Thomas pointing out that Lloyd George spoke as if he had unlimited resources, talking of sending guns at the same time to both Italy and Russia. The Prime Minister retorted that he new more than most about the availability of British guns, and further did not wish to hear that General Cadorna simply *wanted* the weapons, as that could be taken for granted; but rather could he *guarantee success* if he received them.

However eloquently and sincerely he had presented his case, Lloyd George's plan had received scant support. The Italians were reluctant to accept a greater weight of the War upon their shoulders, especially on the eve of a major Franco-British initiative, which if it lived up to expectations would in any case negate the necessity for an Italian offensive. Neither was it liked by the French who baulked both at the thought of placing elements of their Army under Italian command, and at withdrawing more forces from the Western Front with the Nivelle offensive at the forefront of their minds. The proposal was formally rejected, with the proviso that it would be remitted for further examination by the military staffs.[23]

---

[22] National Archives, Cabinet Secretaries account of Rome Conference CAB/21/40

---

[23] Cadorna's reply implied that he required more than just a few hundred guns: 'In conclusion the Italian Commando Supremo is convinced that the co-operation of the Allies on the Isonzo front would have the most important results in the joint interests of the Allies and appeals for the support of the Government to convince the Allied Governments that no other part of the front, in all the Western

This however was to prove far from the last word from Lloyd George on the proposal to send guns to Italy. The Military Conference meanwhile had fared little better in endeavouring to reach an accord. Its conclusions had been entirely negative, one account of the proceedings being edited by the British and Italian representatives, and another by the French and Russians, and both presenting diametrically opposite points of view.

The Prime Minister's first initiative to shift the main war making effort to the Italian Front had failed, and he had little alternative but to re-examine the possibilities the proposed Nivelle offensive offered him towards curbing Haig's Western Front adventures. It was not to be long before he recognised opportunities, this time as a direct result of the Nivelle plan. With the French taking the lead rôle, and Nivelle in command of the operation, it dawned on Lloyd George that he would in effect gain both objectives of his still-borne Italian project; first in hopefully limiting British manpower involvement and therefore casualties, and second in subjugating Haig (and his Army) to Nivelle's command.

Nivelle's plans jeopardise Haig's Northern Offensive

Nivelle meanwhile had again written to Haig on the 2nd January in optimistic but imprecise tones, loosely describing his perception of the phases of his proposed offensive. In grand fashion he explained that the break through phase was to include the capture of the whole of the enemy's artillery on the front attacked, but most worryingly to Haig disclosed that he considered the exploitation battle would be a long one. This was inconsistent with the original conception of a lightening-strike attack, and a battle that would be as good as won within 24 to 48 hours after the opening of the French offensive. Haig was now deeply concerned over the vague aspects of Nivelle's plan to which he would soon be expected to conform, especially the unknown and possibly open ended duration of the exploitation period. To gain a deeper clarification before reaching an agreement he wrote a precise and unambiguous letter to Nivelle on the 6th January, the wording of which is of the utmost importance in understanding his reaction to the extraordinary events of the spring of 1917, and his conduct of the Northern Offensive throughout the summer and autumn.

'I will deal first with the plan of operations, on which the solution of all minor problems depends. It is essential that there should be no room for misunderstanding between us on this question.
In your letter of January 2nd, you divide the operations into three phases. In the first phase, you propose that strong attacks shall be made by our respective armies with the object, not only of drawing in and using up the enemy's reserves, but of gaining such tactical success as will open the way for decisive action on the fronts of attack, either immediately or – later on – as a result of success obtained by you in the second phase. During this first phase adequate reserves are to be held ready either to exploit success immediately, or to continue to use up the enemy's reserves, according to the development of the situation.

---

theatre of war is so vulnerable to the adversary as that of the Isonzo, and that a vigorous and powerful offensive would result in an enemy concentration on that front which would check any other enemy offensive and at the same time greatly assist a Franco-British attack on the Western Front'. That may have been true but Robertson recognized that the Entente were insufficiently strong to spread their forces so wide. He gave his formal reply in a memorandum of the 29th January, subsequent to the Cabinet receiving General Cadorna's plan. He came down firmly against the Prime Ministers plan, due to the British commitment to the Nivelle Offensive, and advised that Cadorna should immediately be made aware of the British inability to be part of his planning, summarizing: 'In these circumstances it is not possible at present to prepare a definite plan for combined operations on the Italian front, or to make any offer of support to Italy as regards either time or amount, but as such operations may become desirable we should, pending the execution of the Franco-British plan, closely watch the general situation on all fronts, keep in mind the possibility of undertaking these operations and be prepared with a plan when the situation shows them to be feasible and desirable'. National Archives WO106-1511.

I have already agreed to launch such an attack as you describe, but not to an indefinite continuation of the battle to use up the enemy's reserves. Such continuation might result in a prolonged struggle like that on the Somme this [last] year, and contrary to our agreement that we must seek a definite and rapid decision.

In the second phase you propose that my offensive shall be continued while you seek a decision on another front. This I have also agreed to on the definite understanding that your decisive attack will be launched within a short period – about eight to fourteen days – after the commencement of the first phase; and, further, that the second phase also will be of very short duration. You will remember that you estimated a period of 24 to 48 hours as sufficient to enable you to decide whether your decisive attack had succeeded or should be abandoned.

The third phase as described in your letter of January 2nd, will consist in the exploitation by the French and British Armies of the success previously gained. This is, of course, on the assumption that the previous successes have been of such magnitude as will make it reasonably certain that by following them up at once we can gain a complete victory and, at least, force the enemy to abandon the Belgian coast. On this assumption, I agree to the third phase on the general lines described in your letter.

But I must make it quite clear that my concurrence in your plan is absolutely limited by the considerations I have explained above, on which we have already agreed in our conversations on the subject. It is essential that the Belgian coast should be cleared this summer. I hope and believe that we shall be able to effect much more than that, and within limitations of time, I will cooperate to the utmost of my power in the larger plans which you have proposed.

But it must be distinctly understood between us that if I am not satisfied that this larger plan, as events develop, promises the degree of success necessary to clear the Belgian coast then I not only cannot continue the battle but I will look to you to fulfil the undertaking you have given me verbally to relieve on the defensive front the troops I require for my northern offensive.

Thus, there is, in fact, a fourth phase of the battle to be provided for in our plans. The need to carry it out may not, and, I hope, will not arise. But the clearance of the Belgian coast is of such importance to the British Government that it must be fully provided for before I can agree to your proposals.

In regard to the date of the Allied offensive, it was agreed at the last Conference of Commanders-in-Chief that the Allies should be prepared to attack by the date mentioned in your letter of the 27th December if circumstances should render it necessary to do so. At the same time, however, I pointed out that my Armies could not be ready to attack in full force before the 1st May, and both the Russian and Italian representatives were also in favour of this later date.

It was recognised that it is of great importance that all the Allies should attack practically simultaneously and in the greatest force possible, and personally I hold that view very strongly. Circumstances may compel us to take offensive action, with such forces as can be made available, before we are all fully ready; but we must regard it as a grave disadvantage if this should occur and we must strive to avoid it. We have evidence that the enemy fears the results of combined simultaneous action by the Allies in force. We must expect him to take steps intended to prevent such combination, and we must beware of being deceived into complying with his intentions by launching attacks prematurely on any one front, or even on all.' [24]

This letter allowed for no possibility of further ambiguity and demanded an equally precise response. As had already been agreed, Haig's support was dependant upon Nivelle's

---

[24] National Archives, OAD262 6th January 1917 Haig to Nivelle. WO158/37. Given the plain talking in this letter and the absolute transparency with which it was written, making it totally clear that the Northern Operation was key to British planning for 1917, it is strange that Denis Winter claims that the policy of the British Government 'made Haig responsible for hiding Passchendaele up his sleeve and appearing to offer Nivelle stronger assistance than he ever intended to deliver'. Denis Winter (2001) *Haig's Command-A Reassessment* London: Penguin, (hereafter Haig's Command) p78

rapid success, and there was no promise of continued support if the battle became prolonged. Exploitation would only be undertaken if there appeared a strong probability that it would result in the abandonment by the enemy of the Belgian coast. Operational developments which gravitated towards the clearance of the coast were the requirement which punctuated every step of the agreed cooperation, and this was clearly stated in every paragraph of Haig's letter. If the plan did not develop in this way then Haig gave notice that he would abandon it and would require Nivelle to relieve his forces holding the defensive front between the Somme and the Oise, to enable him to proceed with the fourth phase; the Northern Operation to clear the coast. The letter tethered Nivelle by the cords of his own claims and promises. If they proved founded Haig was bound to support him. If they proved false, and to most seasoned critics this seemed most likely, then Haig had given due notice of his intended actions; to disengage and concentrate in Flanders. For the first time Nivelle knew that Haig was looking through the smoke and behind the mirrors, and it was now necessary for the flamboyant General to add detail to his tempting generalities.

Nivelle's reply was hardly reassuring, as drawing him into the open succeeded in little more than exposing the fact that the 24 to 48 hour timetable was the sham that many already believed it to be. He claimed that to be precise regarding the timing of the phases of his operation was not possible, and implied that once both armies were engaged he could not believe that Haig, solely on his own appreciation of the situation, would disengage the British Army and leave the French fighting alone. He agreed that in the *unlikely event* of the Flanders offensive becoming necessary he would relieve the British divisions south of the Somme, and repeated his plea that the quicker the joint offensive was launched the better were its chances.
A gulf was quickly developing between the positions of the two commanders, the decision as to whether the 1st and 2nd phases had been sufficiently successful to launch the 3rd phase, and who would make that decision and when, being the chief erosive element. With Haig's mind preoccupied by his responsibility to clear the Belgian coast, it appeared that the final decisions on the degree of British commitment to Nivelle must rest with the Cabinet, once they were fully informed of the situation.

Anglo – French Conference
London the 15th January

In London on the morning of the 15th January, Haig and Robertson again met with Lloyd George at Downing Street. Haig noted: 'After I had explained the general plan for the offensive, and General Nivelle's proposals and wishes made to me, the PM proceeded to compare the success obtained by the French Army during the last summer with that the British had achieved. His general conclusion was that the French Army was better all round, and were able to gain success at less cost in life'.[25] It was not a promising start, and no broad front of agreement was reached between the military and the politicians before they met with the French. In the afternoon Nivelle, accompanied by the French Ambassador, was invited to attend a meeting of the War Cabinet to formally come to an understanding on the commitment of the British to his plans. He wished to obtain the British Government's agreement on two issues sensitive to Haig. First, as we have seen, to release more of their own forces the French required the British to take over an extended length of front, which in Haig's opinion would threaten his supporting operation at Arras. Second, Nivelle also wished to bring forward the date of the Arras attack to better suit his own plans, which again Haig and Robertson considered inadvisable and a threat to the operation. The meeting broke up having failed to reach agreement, the French proposals to be further discussed by the politicians without the military being present. After only brief consideration of matters of such huge importance, the Cabinet announced their findings to Haig and Robertson the next morning. 'The PM then said that the War Cabinet had considered by themselves the 2 questions now before us', noted Haig. 'They felt that we must agree to take

---

[25] Douglas Haig. Diaries and Letters, p266

over the Roye road for the following reasons: 1. We had refused to send divisions to Salonika though strongly pressed by the French Government. We must if possible oblige them now. 2. We were fighting in France and the C.-in-C. of the French Army had elaborated a plan which we must do our utmost to make successful. 3. The French Army was the largest force.
We must also agree to the date which the French wished. Their country was invaded and they wished to clear the Enemy out as soon as possible. Lastly by attacking early, we would be able, if the attack by the French failed, to launch another attack later in the year.'[26]

The French requirements were therefore accepted by the British Cabinet, and the *commitment was signed by Nivelle, Robertson, and contrary to his better judgement, by Haig*. That any agreement had in fact been signed was soon to be denied by the Prime Minister, leading to an unfortunate episode which was to further discolour the relationship between the politicians and the military. The only concessions granted to Haig meanwhile were that he would get his reinforcements, and that the agreed date to take over the French line would be the 1st March, not the 15th February as requested by Nivelle. The date of the attack, in line with Nivelle's proposal, was to be not later than the 1st April. The Prime Minister's transformation was complete, and for once and once only he was supportive of a major offensive on the Western Front, committing the British Army to full cooperation in an offensive conceived and commanded by Nivelle. What repercussions this policy may have upon any future British operation in Flanders, which had until this point been intended as the principle theatre for 1917 remained to be seen. On the following day when Haig was not present, to ensure his total compliance with the French plan, Robertson was charged by the War Cabinet to give him special written instructions emphasising the importance they placed upon his cooperation with Nivelle. The relevant minute of War Cabinet 36 was very clear in its meaning: 'The War Cabinet decided that the Chief of the Imperial General Staff should record, in the form of a special instruction to Field-Marshal Sir Douglas Haig, the importance to which they attach to the utmost dispatch in carrying out both in the letter and in the spirit, the agreement made with General Nivelle on the 16th January 1917, in order that the British Expeditionary Force may be able to carry out its share of the operations at the date laid down in the aforesaid agreement, or even before that date, with the forces available at the moment, if the weather and other conditions make the operations possible and advisable. It should be noted that on no account must the French have to wait for us owing to our arrangements not being complete. Further, it was to be borne in mind that, as the Germans might attack before we do, we, by making every effort to advance our arrangements, should be assisting to stultify any effort of theirs.'[27] The question of the starting date for the offensive was soon to be joined by controversy over the command structure of the Franco-British operation, and both issues were within weeks to erupt into a bitter, major, and on-going clash between the military and Downing Street.

Both French and British Cabinets had agreed that with the Western Front offensive requiring all the strength they could muster, for the moment no forces were available to send to Italy. With attentions fully engaged upon the protracted negotiations surrounding the Nivelle offensive, little notice was given to the fact that by the end of January the Italians had further considered the offer made to them at the Rome Conference, and now requested the assistance of heavy guns *and infantry divisions*, which Lloyd George had implied could be made available. But the request had arrived at the wrong time and fell on largely deaf ears.

The turn of the year had certainly witnessed sweeping changes in many quarters. With Nivelle had come a new, vigorous, and bold approach to the future conduct of the War which was supported fully by the previously doubtful British Prime Minister; but amongst the senior ranks of the French and British Armies there remained grave concerns. Lloyd George however was clearly delighted with Nivelle's plan, whilst oblivious to the hazards, seeing in it his longed for knock-out blow on the enemy to be landed mainly by the French, with the added benefit of a

---

[26] Douglas Haig. Diaries and Letters, p269
[27] National Archives, minutes of War Cabinet 36, 17th January 1917, CAB23-1 and CIGS to War Cabinet WO106/1511 0.1/77/233

limitation on Haig's control over events. Whether or not Nivelle's claims were realistic, his reassuring and plausible nonchalance had convinced the Prime Minister, and also, for the moment at least, influenced the way future plans for the War were regarded. But neither Haig nor Robertson were fully convinced, recognising the impossibility of many of Nivelle's claims, and doubting the ability of stopping a major offensive after 48 hours should it be unsuccessful. Robertson revealed his position to the King via Lieutenant-Colonel Clive Wigram, the King's Assistant Private Secretary in a letter on the 16th, apparently unimpressed with Nivelle's success at Verdun, and feeling that little had been achieved during the Conference other than Haig having to take over more front than he had hoped. The opening date of the offensive was already contentious, as Robertson pointed out to Wigram: 'Strange to say the Prime Minister has always been a great opponent to making an attack before all the Allies are ready. He has constantly laid great stress upon this and has in fact thrown a good deal of cold water upon any attack being made on the West Front. But Nivelle, like Sarrail [French Commander-in-Chief at Salonica], seems to have impressed him and he was all for attacking on the 15th February until we more or less convinced him that that would not do. As it now stands the attack will be made when Haig and Nivelle are ready and that will not be before April.'[28]

Haig was still in England on the 18th and wrote to Kiggell in a positive vein informing him of the outcome of the Conference. 'In my opinion there were three satisfactory points established: 1st All efforts are to be devoted to making the Western Attacks decisive. 2nd The French are determined to put in as big a blow as they possibly can. 3rd If they fail, then we are to be supported to their utmost ability.'[29] But he was unhappy with Robertson's note written at the instigation of the Cabinet, instructing his full compliance with the agreements made in London, and replied to it on the 22nd making a case for not attacking until all the Allies were prepared, and preferably not until after Italy and Russia had launched their offensives; which meant waiting until May.[30] Robertson was in accord with Haig's thinking and compiled a lengthy memorandum for the War Cabinet detailing the case for waiting until all were fully prepared. He concluded: 'The whole question is, as is usual in War, one of balancing advantages and disadvantages, and in my opinion the disadvantages of voluntarily initiating offensive operations at an unduly early date are so great, and may be so far reaching in their consequences, that the risk of incurring them would be justified only by very pressing and special circumstances.' [31] But it was Nivelle in the driving seat, not Haig or Robertson, and however much the French Commander-in-Chief wished to press on with the preparations for his offensive the limiting factor dictating how rapidly the British build up would be completed, according to Haig, was the creaking and over burdened railway system of the Chemin de Fer du Nord. The railway problems were about to emerge as a key factor in the relationships between Haig, Nivelle and Lloyd George.

As the preparations for the spring offensive slowly progressed, Haig continued to devote time and thought to the British operation he still believed would be necessary to clear the Belgian coast. It seems however that he was not immune to the revitalised, optimistic atmosphere, as he

---

[28] Robertson Papers 7/1/31 16th January 1917, Robertson to Sir Clive Wigram. Liddell Hart Centre for Military Archives, King's College London

[29] Kiggell papers 1/47, 18th January 1917, Haig to Kiggell. Liddell Hart Centre for Military Archives, King's College London

[30] Robertson Papers 7/7/2, 22nd January 1917, Haig to Robertson. Liddell Hart Centre for Military Archives, King's College London. Haig's note was based on a memorandum prepared by Kiggell on the 12th January in response to Nivelle's letter No.7162 of the 11th. Both can be found in National Archives, WO158/37 The contents of the memorandum were again used as a basis for Robertson's answer to the War Cabinet on the 24th.

[31] Robertson Papers 7/5/49 24th January 1917, Robertson to War Cabinet, Mr Balfour and First Sea Lord, Liddell Hart Centre for Military Archives, King's College London. Robertson's conclusions were basically those reached by Kiggell which had subsequently been sent in a letter from Haig to Robertson.

now scrapped Plumer's plans for the Northern Offensive agreed in January 1916, which had proposed a systematic and measured approach in Flanders. What was now required was rapid action creating a break through of the enemy's defences on a wide front, and the infliction of a decisive defeat, to replace the slow tactics of attrition the battle the Somme had become. But far too much was being taken for granted both by Nivelle and those under his influence. The enemy's morale had not been seriously weakened even after the costly battles of 1916, but rather it was the French Army that had not fully recovered; and worse, the forthcoming attack was to be anything but a surprise. A whole new world of optimism had meanwhile spread through both the French and British camps, carried by the exuberant oratory of Nivelle, and the message had been happily accepted by many as a tonic for war-weariness and depression. But questions were being asked by others, albeit mostly in private. Would the results match the promises, and if they did not how hard would be the fall?

The genesis of Passchendaele

The new desire for optimistic determined action ensured that the plan for the Flanders offensive was to awake from hibernation as a very different creature to that previously envisaged by Plumer. As we have seen Plumer had concluded that after the capture of the the Messines ridge in a preliminary operation, the capture of the Gheluvelt plateau and Pilckem ridge should be the limit of the first attack of the main offensive from Ypres before attempting to cross the Steenbeek. In a letter from Kiggell on the 6th January,[32] Plumer was required to submit new plans by the 31st, which were to propose rapid action and entail the breaking through of the enemy's defences on a wide front without delay. Plumer's November plan was now considered obsolete, as it had proposed a sustained and deliberate offensive such as had been carried out on the Somme. Two days later, on the 8th, a special sub-section of the Operations Branch, G.H.Q., was appointed under Lieutenant-Colonel C. N. Macmullen, to work out details for a campaign in Flanders in line with Haig's new thinking. There were now two planning groups for the Northern Offensive, Second Army and G.H.Q.

But Plumer was not to be the man chosen to command the Northern Operation. His careful approach was now viewed by Haig as out of step with the bold new policy; a policy which offered Haig the chance of a major strike at the enemy in Flanders if Nivelle's promises did not come to fruition. A new man would be chosen, but for the moment that choice had yet to be made. As requested by Kiggell, Plumer had represented his fresh proposals on the 30th January but even in their reworked form they were not what Haig required. Plumer proposed that the first part of the operation, at Messines, should be carried out in three phases. His latest plan had however adopted Harington's idea of a two army attack, both armies to assault simultaneously, Second Army at Messines, and the other (northern) army from the Ypres Salient.[33] But Plumer persisted in his belief that the northern army should confine its attack to the capture of the eastern slope of Pilckem ridge before crossing the Steenbeek, an average advance limited to 2,000 yards. This he argued would allow for the forward movement of the field artillery and observers to the intermediate ridge to enable the next move across the Steenbeek to be covered under observed fire. He also explained that as it was *not possible* to assemble a sufficient strength of artillery and infantry in the confined space west of the Gheluvelt plateau, a 2,000 yard gap from Mount Sorrel to Bellewaarde Lake (on the western face of the plateau) would be necessary between the flanks of the southern and northern assaults.

---

[32] BOH p406 Appendix V

[33] This was in accord with Kiggell's letter to Plumer on the 6th January 1917 which had stated: 'The operations naturally divide themselves into two sectors and will be organized under two separate Army commands: a) The attack on the Wytschaete Messines Ridge and Zandvoorde, with the objective of forming the defensive flank for the decisive attack, will be carried out by the southern Army. b) The decisive attack, from the approximate front Hooge – Steenstraat with the objectives Roulers and Thourout, will be executed by the northern Army. It is essential that this attack should be carried out *with the least possible delay*. (Authors italics) BOH p406 Appendix V

The priority, after the initial attacks, would be the closing of the inner flanks of the two armies to gain a firm foothold on the Gheluvelt plateau. This he claimed must be accomplished to cover the right flank of the northern army, before that army continued its advance across the Steenbeek two days after its initial attack, to a line Broodseinde – Gravenstafel – Langemarck – Bixschoote. The coastal operation was to commence once the main advance had arrived level with Cortemarck, 8 miles north of Passchendaele, or earlier if the enemy showed signs of demoralization. Two coastal divisions would then advance from the Nieuport bridgehead, simultaneously with the landing of a division from the sea at Middlekerke. The line gained by the landing force would then be reinforced and extended towards Ostend by two reserve divisions moving up from Nieuport.

Plumer and Macmullen were now to be joined in their deliberations by General Rawlinson. This was understandable as at this stage, the proposal was, as it had been prior to the Somme, for Rawlinson's Fourth Army to carry out the northern attack from the Ypres Salient, and on the 9th February he made a number of observations regarding Plumer's plan. The first was that the Messines operation could be carried out in one day. Secondly Rawlinson was as concerned as Plumer about Gheluvelt, and emphasised that the progress of the northern army was absolutely dependant on the success of the inner flanks of both armies closing on and securing the plateau to cover his right flank. He agreed that to carry out an assault on the plateau simultaneously with the southern attack was impracticable due to inevitable crowding of infantry and guns on the ground south and south-west of Ypres, but suggested as an alternative that the southern attack should be made first, followed *in 48 to 72 hours* by a combined central and northern attack in one operation between Mount Sorrel (on the south-west edge of the Gheluvelt plateau), and Steenstraat (on the Ypres – Yser canal). Haig countered, that according to Colonel Macmullen the three assaults could be made simultaneously if tanks were to make a surprise attack in the centre to capture the high ground between Observatory Ridge and Broodseinde. Although this dispenses with the argument that Haig was dismissive of technical innovation it does expose a degree of naivety in the abilities of the tanks. Thankfully the proposal was soon to be condemned as completely unworkable by the tank experts. But Rawlinson's plan for a 'two stage' offensive *was* ultimately to be adopted, although as initially presented was clearly flawed. It seems strange even at this early planning stage, that no serious consideration was given to how the guns and materials necessary for the huge northern attack could be moved from the Messines front into the Ypres Salient in 48 to 72 hours, as it was fully realised that insufficient equipment was available to carry out preparations for both southern and northern attacks simultaneously. The plan also assumed that the enormous engineering preparations to develop the infrastructure necessary before launching the northern attack could be undertaken in the Salient, simultaneously with those at Messines. This proved not to be the case, as in reality insufficient men and materials were available to prepare both fronts at the same time. But as the 'two stage' attack was not to be the plan *initially* adopted no further consideration was given to the feasibility or otherwise of the 48 to 72 hour delay until the abandonment of the 'single stage attack' plan some weeks later.

After consultation with Plumer and Rawlinson, Colonel Macmullen had meanwhile submitted a memorandum on the 14th February which summarised Plumer's plan, but with the addition of the proposal for the use of tanks. In this plan the southern, central, and northern attacks would be made *simultaneously*, and the first day's objective was to be limited to the German Second Line on the eastern slope of Pilckem ridge. The most significant points in the memorandum were: 'On Zero Day a simultaneous attack by the Second and Fourth Armies on a front from St. Yves [2,500 yards south of Messines] to Lizerne [3,000 yards north of Boesinghe] with the object of penetration to a depth of approximately 1,500 to 2,000 yards.

On Zero+2 Day, or ealier, if found possible, an attack by the Fourth Army on the enemy's third line north of the Ypres – Roulers railway, combined with an attack supported by a strong force of tanks on to the Becelaere – Broodseinde line. Second Army to push forward simultaneously to a line running from the Ypres – Comines railway by Gheluvelt to Becelare.

The attack on Zero+2 Day to be followed immediately by a rapid continuation of the advance by the Fourth Army towards the line Roulers – Thourout, Second Army taking over the defensive flank up to Broodseinde.

An attack at Nieuport as soon as the main advance has reached the neighbourhood of Cortemarck [7 miles north of Westroosebeke], or earlier if the enemy shows signs of great demoralization.'[34] The memorandum recognised the capture of the Gheluvelt plateau as a matter of first importance to subsequent operations. But it also endorsed a *simultaneous* attack by both Second and Fourth Armies, emphasising the *'value of dispersal of hostile artillery fire resulting from an attack on the broadest front possible, a factor which becomes of increased importance when attacking from a salient. Moreover an attack by the Second Army as a first phase is opposed to the idea underlying the whole scheme, which is a heavy surprise attack followed by a rapid break through...'*[35] (Authors italics) Here then was another plan for the Flanders offensive, which was tentatively - almost reluctantly, but in the end only temporarily accepted by Haig. The minor alteration to be made in the next few weeks was subsequent to a proposal by Plumer on the 18th March, in line with Rawlinson's previous suggestion, that the Messines operation should be carried out in two rather than three phases. The jutting enemy strongpoint at Spanbroekmolen Knoll was to be included on the first day, and not as part of a preliminary operation prior to the general Messines attack. On the 3rd April Haig was to carry this plan a stage further, proposing that both phases of the Messines attack should be incorporated into one. The capture of the near ridge crest and the back ridge crest should be achieved during the morning and a deeper advance to capture the German Third, or Oosttaverne Line, should continue in the afternoon. This was to be the Messines plan in its final form, but the plan for the Northern Operation was yet to see enormous changes which were not be made known until the 7th May.

The preparations for Nivelle's spring offensive were meanwhile being seriously hampered, from the British perspective, by a serious lack of carrying capacity on the French Nord railway system. The problem was one of great complexity, but in some accounts has been dangerously over simplified in an effort to throw the blame for future difficulties associated with the Nivelle offensive, squarely onto Haig's shoulders. In simple terms it has been suggested that Haig attempted to use the railway crisis as an excuse to delay the date of the opening of the British attack until May, as opposed to February or at worst early April as required by Nivelle. This argument, however plausibly it may be presented, is simply not true.

The French railway crisis

The operating system of the Chemin de Fer du Nord, responsible for the region north of an approximate line between Paris, Soissons and Laon, that is a small section of the French Army front and the whole of the British Army front in France, was experiencing shortages in every commodity necessary for the transport of men and material; personnel, track, locomotives, and trucks. That the system was groaning under the strain of carrying the essential war materials for the British build-up for the campaign of 1917 had not come as a surprise, as the problem had been recognised by Haig as far back as October and November 1916[36], long before the inception of the Nivelle plans. Complaints and warnings regarding the railways reflected perfectly legitimate concerns. By January 1917 Robertson was explaining the difficulties to the War

---

[34] BOH p410 Appendix VII
[35] BOH p414 Appendix VII Timing of Attacks.
[36] Douglas Haig. Diaries and Letters, p256-257 6th November: (Haig to Allenby, with reference to proposed attack at Arras) 'It was particularly important to improve the railway communications, making new lines and perhaps doubling the main line to Arras.' 18th November: 'Railways must be seen to at once. Geddes (Director General of Transportation) explained a few of our difficulties. Shortage of steel, wagons, etc.etc.'

Cabinet. 'The Chief of the Imperial General Staff reported that the departure of additional divisions from home was being delayed owing to congestion on the French railways. The French authorities had stated that they could not convey the troops for a period of three days.'[37] Although not critical in itself the delay was symptomatic of a growing problem. Haig and Nivelle had exchanged correspondence around the same time, the former describing a major hold-up at the Channel ports due to lack of wagons, the latter pointing out, 'the situation of the Nord Railway line, which conveys the greater part of the supplies to the British Armies, is extremely strained and the traffic has reached its maximum; the slightest hitch causes delays which reflect immediately on the supply of empty rolling stock at the bases'.[38] Nivelle was telling Haig what he already knew, but insisted that the situation could only be improved by: '1) The increase of the import of [British] rolling stock to the fullest possible extent, at the same time supplying a suitable proportion of powerful [British] engines and brake-wagons. 2) The acceleration of the execution of the work in connecting with traffic, notably the doubling of the lines now in progress, for which I shall have to ask you to take an increased share. [It had been previously agreed at Conferences in November and December 1916 that these works would be undertaken by the French] 3) Instructions given to all the depts. of the British Army to reduce to a minimum the holding up of rolling stock'. But Nivelle could not see a major problem. 'In any case it does not seem to me that the delays resulting from the present crisis in transportation should cause any serious modification in the plan of operations already made.' It is interesting to note that since the beginning of the War, the French railways had been controlled and managed by the French, who had discountenanced any association of the British Armies in their management.

Haig met with Nivelle on the 29th January at Beauvais to discuss the problem. Haig advised that 250,000 tons of imported stores and supplies and 100,000 tons of local traffic, (roadstone and timber etc.) required moving to his Armies weekly. Nivelle suggested that the railways, with special effort, might move 200,000 tons plus the local traffic. But matters failed to improve, and on the 8th February in Downing Street, 'it was brought to the notice of the War Cabinet that, owing to delays on French railways, our military preparations for the campaign of 1917 were being interfered with, and the general situation was, in consequence, becoming very unsatisfactory'.[39] Robertson was instructed to obtain a statement from Haig at an early date, with a view to the Foreign Office forwarding its contents to the French Government. Haig replied as follows: 'I have no means of knowing to what extent the railway situation has delayed preparations for the French offensive, nor do I know what proportion of the railway facilities has been retained by the French for their own use. In the absence of full and reliable information as to future railway prospects it is not in my power to give a date by which it will be possible to carry out my attack on the scale I had intended. At my meeting with General Nivelle on the 29th January, 1917, it was agreed that my Transportation Department should be brought into closer touch with the French railway experts, and I hope that this will lead to a fuller knowledge of what facilities I can rely on, and when they will be available. Meanwhile, if the French commence their operations on the 1st April – and still more if they commence earlier than that – I can only comply with the War Cabinet's instructions, as to combination with them, to the extent of a very modified attack. This course, so far as the British Armies in France are concerned, could have no more than a very local and temporary effect on the enemy, and would use up resources which would prejudice the success of subsequent operations.'[40] On the 9th Haig's Director General of Transport, Major-General Sir Eric Geddes, spelt out the problem for the War Cabinet, also providing a full memorandum. Geddes pointed out that 'on the 11th November General Joffre asked Sir Douglas Haig for general assistance on the railways, [which had already exceeded the limits of their carrying capacity even during the Somme battles] and this was the first indication given by the French that they were not completely masters of the railway situation. But there was no admission of inability to deal with the required tonnages

---

[37] National Archives, minutes of War Cabinet 47, 29th January 1917, CAB23/1
[38] Nivelle to Haig, letter No.21,631 26th January 1917, National Archives, WO158/37
[39] National Archives, minutes of War Cabinet 57, 8th February 1917, CAB23/1
[40] National Archives, Appendix I War Cabinet 64, 13th February 1917, CAB23/1

which were before the French in full at the time'. Since the meeting at Beauvais on the 29th January word had been received that the French were able, as Nivelle had promised, by special efforts to raise the movement capacity to 200,000 tons of imported stores plus 100,000 tons of local traffic.[41] Up till the end of January however only 150,000 tons of imports and 60,000 tons of local traffic were being handled. Geddes claimed that although British Army traffic was seriously restricted there was still a considerable amount of civilian traffic being carried by the Nord. The War Cabinet concluded that: 'The Foreign Office should make a strong representation to the French Government on the subject, pointing out that unless the French carried out their undertakings we could not guarantee to carry out the undertakings on which General Nivelle had laid so much stress at the London Conference on the 15th – 16th January. These representations should be supported by a reasoned memorandum by the Chief of the Imperial General Staff, which might be based partly on the statement from the Commander-in-Chief of the British Expeditionary Force called for at the previous Meeting (War Cabinet 57, Minute 3), and partly on information provided by Sir Eric Geddes.' The vital issue was raised again by Robertson at the War Cabinet on the 13th February. He pointed out that as Haig had been instructed to conform to the orders of Nivelle, even if this meant attacking early much against his better judgement, the responsibility of possible failure should *not* rest with Haig. He wished to know whether the breakdown of the French railway system had encouraged the War Cabinet to change their views. It had not, but in order to defend their position, made more precarious as it flew in the face of official Military advice, the Cabinet proposed to write to the French telling them of the circumstances of great responsibility under which they had complied with Nivelle's wishes, and declaring that: 'The War Cabinet consider that they are fairly entitled to say how disappointed they are at the breakdown in the French railway system, because the feasibility of carrying out the plan of operations agreed upon must obviously be greatly affected by the railway facilities afforded, and they wish this point of view to be fully apprehended by the French authorities.'

    The dialogue continued in similar vein on the 14th. Robertson read to the War Cabinet the contents of a signal from Haig, which stated that there seemed little likelihood of an early improvement. Unaware that the War Cabinet had already decided to write to the French, and also unaware of the drama which would unfold as a result of his action, Haig recommended an inter-allied conference to discuss the crisis. He concluded: 'In the present circumstances, if the operations are carried out on dates proposed, they will probably lead to very heavy losses with inadequate results'. Robertson was not at all impressed with the suggestion for another conference and made this clear in a letter to Haig that day: 'So long as Ministers take part in the discussions of plans of operations we shall always have trouble of the worst kind I am sure.' [42] He suggested to the War Cabinet that Haig should have a further meeting with Nivelle in a few

---

[41] These are presumably the figures referred to by Denis Winter in his claim of 'A rail crisis which had been brought to a head by Haig's demand that the Nord railway carry 200,000 tons weekly for the British in addition to its usual 100,000 for the French. Nivelle took inevitable umbrage. Haig's statistics meant that an army half the size of the French was claiming the use of three and a half times the number of railway wagons per day.' See *Haig's Command A Reassessment* p79. This is clearly an incorrect understanding of the figures leading to an inaccurate and misleading conclusion of their meaning. The 100,000 tons was stated by Geddes as being 'local traffic' and not specifically traffic destined for the French Army but rather materials such as roadstone and timber required by the British for the operation, but coming from local supply and not through the ports. In any event as the Nord railway only operated down roughly to the line of the Oise, it was not responsible for the bulk of the French Army which held the Western Front south of that line, making a nonsense of Winter's claims. See National Archives, CAB23/1 8th February 1917 and WO158/41. Winter's point is that '200,000 tons only made sense if Haig was preparing for two battles [i.e. Arras and the Northern Operation]'. This was not the case, as during this period Second Army in Flanders was continually short of labour and materials.

[42] Robertson Papers 7/7/7 14th February 1917, Robertson to Haig. Liddell Hart Centre for Military Archives, King's College London

days and report back on any progress, the Cabinet minutes recording: 'The War Cabinet fully sympathised with him [Haig] with regard to the difficulties with which he is faced in this matter, and are *quite prepared to have a Conference* as proposed *if he cannot come to an agreement with General Nivelle*'.(Authors italics) By the next day the War Cabinet had shifted its position slightly, and rather than being 'quite prepared' to hold a conference, now decided that, 'whatever might be the result of the Conference between Sir Douglas Haig and General Nivelle, it was *desirable to hold a Conference* with the French Government on the subject, and they authorised the Chief of the Imperial General Staff to inform Sir Douglas Haig in this sense'.(Authors italics)[43] By the 20th the shift was even more discernable. Robertson announced to the Cabinet that from the positive account of the discussions between Haig and Nivelle at Chateau Beaurepaire on the 16th an improvement in the position of the French railways in the north looked hopeful.[44] In brief Haig's conclusions of his meeting with Nivelle were quite satisfactory and stated: '1) We agree that attack is not to be made until preparations for attack are completed on British front. 2) This depends on state of the Compagnie du Chemin de fer du Nord. 3) General Nivelle sent wire to French Government urging vital importance of putting Ch de fer du Nord in efficient state without delay. Date of attack depends on it. 4) General Nivelle has information that certain steps have already been taken with this object, and hopes that by 10th April we may be ready. I shall do my best to be ready by that date, but again it is a question of when the Ch. De fer du Nord can give us 200 trains per diem'.[45] Haig's previous desire for a Conference now seemed premature as most difficulties seemed virtually settled. But the 'War Cabinet nevertheless, adhered to their previous decision, that a Government Conference should take place, so that a definite understanding might be reached and an agreement drawn up and signed by the Heads of the two Governments respectively, not only so far as railways are concerned, but also in regard to the operations of 1917. The Secretary of State for Foreign Affairs undertook to see the French Ambassador in London immediately, in order to make the necessary preliminary arrangements with him for the holding of the Conference'.[46] Robertson's nightmare of 'trouble of the worst kind', prompted by the unwitting hand of Haig, had unfortunately come to fruition. The real reasons behind Lloyd George's insistence to hold another Conference were about to become painfully clear, and the outcome of the proceedings was to present a very different result to that initially envisaged by Haig.

The Calais Conference
26th February 1917

At the heart of the manoeuvrings and intrigues that were to taint the negotiations over who commanded the British Forces engaging in the Nivelle Offensive, lay the overwhelming desire of Lloyd George to subordinate Haig to French Command; but to do so would require another Anglo-French conference to be convened. The Prime Minister's opinion of the Commander-in-Chief had hardly been improved by a storm which had erupted around an interview Haig had given on the 1st February at G.H.Q. to reporters of the French press, the contents of which, whilst being of a general nature and not divulging military secrets were seen as inopportune. The various reports appearing in the French newspapers, claiming to carry the facts of Haig's interview but much reworked in the personal style of their authors, were picked up by the British press, which in turn asked permission of the G.H.Q. censor to carry the piece in the British papers. Neither Haig nor Brigadier-General Charteris, whose intelligence gathering department at G.H.Q. also handled Public Relations and Censorship, saw the request for

---

[43] National Archives, minutes of War Cabinet 67, 15th February 1917, CAB23/1
[44] See Notes on discussion with General Nivelle on the 16th February 1917. National Archives WO158/37
[45] National Archives, Meeting between Haig and Nivelle 16th February 1917 at Chateau Beaurepaire WO158/37
[46] National Archives, minutes of War Cabinet 75, 20th February 1917, CAB23/1

permission to publish. The result was a disaster, as the British newspapers carried forward the French reports with further embellishments, proclaiming Haig's confidence in victory, that the year would see the Germans beaten, and that 1917 would be the year of peace. Whilst the reports were well received in war-weary Paris, by the middle of February they had caused uproar in political circles in London, with questions being put to the Prime Minister in the House of Commons. Minister of War Derby wrote to Haig warning of the dangers to morale if such optimistic predictions as those reported were dashed by failure, but mainly condemned Charteris for not submitting the requests for permission to publish to Haig. An exchange of letters began, with Haig, obviously much angered by the whole affair, questioning who was most likely to gain from the misrepresentations of the French press reports, and adding that if Lloyd George had someone else in mind to command the Army he would bow out gracefully. Lord Derby responded by declaring the matter closed and reaffirmed his confidence, and that of the country and the Army in Haig.

But from the moment Lloyd George heard of the matter it had rankled with him, deepening his resentment of Haig, and focusing his determination to take steps to remedy the situation. On the 1st February, at an impromptu meeting with Hankey and Commandant Bertier de Sauvigny the French Liason Officer at the War Office, the Prime Minister indicated that whilst he had complete confidence in Nivelle, the success of his offensive depended ultimately upon his ability to make use of all Allied forces involved, both British and French. According to Bertier, Lloyd George stated that it was imperative that the War Cabinet should be in full accord with this policy, but their agreement could not be assured unless Nivelle and the French Cabinet firmly insisted on the point. Lloyd George recognised that the strength of feeling in the country and in the Army would make it difficult for him to simply subordinate Haig to French command, but once the Cabinet understood how essential it was to adopt this arrangement, they would not hesitate to give Haig secret instructions to this effect, and if necessary, if he did not comply with their wishes, to replace him.

Since the Downing Street Conference on the 15th January, two important issues, one logistical, one administrative, had arisen, each of which could be presented as requiring the attention of the British and French Governments, providing Lloyd George with a plausible excuse to call another Inter-Allied Conference. The first matter, which we have examined at length, was the inadequate state of the French railways, and whilst Haig's unfortunately premature request aided in legitimising the Conference, it also helped Lloyd George cover his real reason for calling it. The second matter was less legitimate, but nevertheless also helped cover the true reason for another Conference with the French. At the Cabinet meeting on the 24th February, according to the testament of Secretary of State Lord Derby, Lloyd George announced that although agreement had been reached on the 16th January upon cooperation with Nivelle, the French had signed nothing and were therefore not bound to the agreement. To obtain the necessary signatures another conference was required. This was blatantly not so, as Haig, Robertson and Nivelle had all signed on the 16th, but as Lloyd George had taken steps through the offices of the Cabinet Secretary to ensure that Robertson would not be present at the Cabinet meeting on the 24th this fact would not become apparent to the other members.[47] It

---

[47] Denis Winter claims that both Robertson and Haig were aware of 'exactly what was on the minds of the politicians before the conference, despite their claims to the contrary over the next ten years', *Haig's Command* p82. The claim is based on Winter's contention that Robertson was present at the War Cabinets on the 20th and 22nd February at which the Cabinet discussed their tactics for the Conference. We have already seen that on the 20th (War Cabinet 75) it had been recorded in the minutes that the two Governments would draw up an agreement 'in regard to the operations of 1917'. This was a very vague statement and indicated no precise intent or objective. On the 22nd (War Cabinet 78) the minutes indicate the only discussion at Cabinet regarded who was to be present at the Conference, and did not consider what was to be discussed. War Cabinet 79 on the 24th February, *at which Robertson was not present* was the first occasion, according to the minutes of the Cabinet Secretary when the question of detailed content of the Conference was discussed. Winter's statement

was therefore decided that: 'Having regard to the great importance of avoiding any misunderstanding in regard to the forthcoming operations in the Western theatre, and of preventing any recrimination after the operations, the War Cabinet authorised the Prime Minister to ask General Nivelle and Field-Marshal Sir Douglas Haig to give him a full explanation of their plans for the campaign of 1917; to use his best endeavours to ascertain any points on which there might be a difference of opinion between the two Commanders-in-Chief; in concert with M. Briand to decide any such differences of opinion on their merits; and to aim more especially at the adoption of such measures as might appear best calculated, as a result of the discussion at the Conference, to ensure unity of command both in the preparatory stages of and during the operation.'[48] The deceptions necessary to gain Cabinet acquiescence to call another Conference were now in place; the railway crisis in France and lack of formal documentation allegedly to be top of the agenda. Unity of command had also been mentioned, but not until the 24th, and most conveniently Robertson had been advised by Hankey that his presence was not required this day. But behind the façade the Prime Minister and the French had other, more ambitious plans afoot.

On the 26th February the political and military leaders of France and Britain met in conference at Calais. As the discussion regarding the railways became somewhat technical it was suggested that those officers responsible should withdraw to continue their talk independently. Lloyd George, seemingly anxious to expose and develop any rift which would undermine Haig's position, required of Nivelle not just an explanation of his plan, but more especially to expand upon any differences between himself and Haig regarding the British compliance with the plan. A tactical disagreement had arisen with Nivelle, over Haig's decision to include Vimy Ridge within his area of attack at Arras. Haig made it clear to the conference that in his opinion the terms of the agreement were that British forces would attack north of the Somme, break the enemy's front, and advance on Cambrai, but the tactical decision as to where and how this was to be achieved was his alone. With suitable modesty Lloyd George claimed he had no understanding of strategy or tactics, but on obviously more confident ground asked the French to draw up their proposals for a system of command for the period of the Nivelle offensive, to be discussed by himself, Robertson and Haig before the next meeting, which was to be held on the following day. That evening, an angry Robertson informed Haig that he had been handed by the Prime Minister, for consideration, a draft French proposal to establish a British Chief-of-Staff, with Quartermaster-General and full staff under him, at French General Headquarters, the Chief-of-Staff to report directly to the War Cabinet in London, leaving Haig responsible for no more than administration, discipline and reinforcements of his own Army. The British Army would under these circumstances be placed under the French Commander-in-Chief's orders. Confronted in his room by Robertson and Haig, the Prime Minister in Haig's words 'told us that the War Cabinet had decided last week that since this was likely to be the last effort of the French, and they had the larger numbers engaged, "in fact, it was their battle", the British Army would be placed under the French C.-in-C's orders'.[49] With an astounding lack of sincerity, whilst agreeing that the French demands were 'absurd',[50] Lloyd George asked Haig and Robertson to go away and give consideration to a scheme for giving effect to the *War Cabinet's decision*. Haig's diary takes up the story. 'I went with Robertson to his room. He seemed thoroughly upset with the attitude of our Prime Minister. Colonel Hankey (Secretary War Committee) further added to our dissatisfaction by saying that LG had not received full authority from the War Cabinet for acting as he was doing. General Kiggell took part in our discussion and we agreed we would rather be tried by Court Martial than betray the Army by agreeing to its being placed under the French. Robertson agreed that we must resign rather

---

that Robertson's memory was at fault or that he was lying is a wholly wrong and most unfortunate claim.
[48] National Archives, minutes of War Cabinet 79, 24th February 1917, CAB23/1
[49] Douglas Haig. Diaries and Letters, p271
[50] Later tempered by Haig in the transcript diaries to 'excessive'

than be partners in this transaction. And so we went to bed, thoroughly disgusted with our Government and Politicians.'[51] By next morning Haig had considered the matter further and had prepared the following note for Robertson: 'I have in the short time available considered the decision of the War Cabinet (of which Mr. Lloyd George informed us last night) to place the British Army in France under the orders of the French Commander-in-Chief, and the proposal of the French to give effect to that decision. In my opinion there are only two alternatives, viz:- 1) To leave matters as they now are, or 2) To place the British Army in France entirely under the French Commander-in-Chief. The decision to adopt the second of these proposals must involve the disappearance of the British Commander-in-Chief and G.H.Q. What further changes would be necessary must depend on the French Commander-in-Chief and the French Government under whom he acts. So drastic a change in our system at a moment when active operations on a large scale have already commenced seems to me to be fraught with the gravest danger.'[52]

The next morning the French Minister of War General Lyautey, and Nivelle, requested an urgent meeting with Haig, and expressed their disgust at the French proposal, falsely claiming that they were only recently made aware of its contents, and that it had been drawn up in Paris with the approval of Lloyd George and the French Premier Briand. Robertson meanwhile had received a paper from Lloyd George, suggested and drawn up by Cabinet Secretary Hankey, offering a compromise solution to the problem, which divided the question of command into two periods, one before the beginning of Nivelle's offensive, the second after it had commenced. In the first period Haig would be expected to conform to Nivelle's instructions regarding preparation, but could depart from them by appeal to the War Cabinet if he thought the Army was endangered or that success was prejudiced. Once the battle began the Army was to act entirely as Nivelle ordered. Haig objected strongly to the latter proposal and insisted on having added to the agreement, 'that I have a free hand to choose the means and methods of utilising the British troops in that sector of operations allotted by the French C-in-C in the original plan'.[53] Nivelle agreed with Haig's amendment. The working arrangement had in fact changed little from that to which Haig and Joffre had always adhered, with the exception that Haig was relieved of responsibility of the plan of the battle being prepared by Nivelle, and for the details of the execution of the plan. For the moment therefore the Conference had recovered from the brink of a potential constitutional disaster. To a point all was settled, albeit uneasily, but the bad feeling and mistrust resulting from knowledge of the subterfuge would, for a time, inevitably have an adverse knock-on effect on the relationship between Nivelle and Haig. Neither Robertson nor Haig would ever trust Lloyd George again, and his animosity towards them would fester and lead to greater upheavals and inconsistency of policy, to the inevitable detriment of the Allied cause. But had the Conference, at least for the moment, established an agreement within which all concerned could work? The answer was quickly to be no; as the unacceptability of what had been signed crowded in on Robertson, and a degree of dissatisfaction with the Calais agreements became apparent within the War Cabinet giving rise to the necessity for yet another Conference before the complexities of 'who commanded what' in the Nivelle offensive were finally settled.

When on the 28th, Haig returned to G.H.Q. at Beaurepaire, his B.G.G.S. Brigadier-General Davidson was there, having recently returned from visiting the French Armies preparing for the offensive. Davidson reported that General Micheler, the G.O.C. French Reserve Army Group had stated gloomily, 'it does not matter what the politicians may decide, the French soldier is not going to fight after the autumn!'.[54] Here was a worrying portent of future trouble, coming in the midst of an existing maelstrom of administrative difficulties, and as yet simply at the preparation stage of the major offensive.

---

[51] Douglas Haig. Diaries and Letters, p272
[52] National Archives, part of Robertson's memorandum to War Cabinet, 2nd March 1917, CAB104/145
[53] Douglas Haig. Diaries and Letters, p273
[54] Douglas Haig. Diaries and Letters, p273

That evening a letter arrived from Nivelle, which an obviously ruffled Haig considered was 'couched in very commanding tones….a type of letter which no gentleman could have drafted, and it also is one which certainly no C-in-C of this great British Army should receive without protest'.[55] The letter requested a copy of the orders issued to the British Army for the forthcoming offensive: 'Je vous serais reconnaissant en conséquence de me communiquer le plus tôt possible les instructions que vous avez données à vos commandents d'Armée ainsi que les dispositions qui ont été prises par eux en exécution de vos ordres.'[56] But of greatest difficulty for Haig, it also asked that Sir Henry Wilson (with whom Haig was not always on the best of terms, feeling that rather than concentrating on substance, he was inclined to revel in intrigue) should be appointed Chief of the British Mission at G.Q.G., a post Wilson had previously held in 1915. 'Je vous demande donc de mettre à la tête de cette Mission le Général Wilson dès qu'il sera de retour de Russie', wrote Nivelle. Haig decided, 'to send a copy of the letter with my reply to the War Committee, with a request to be told whether it is their wishes that the C-in-C in command of this British Army should be subjected to such a treatment by a junior *foreign* officer'.

Robertson, already full of misgivings about the Calais agreement, the signing of which he now considered to have been totally unwise, wrote to Haig on the 28th, hoping that no great harm had been done whilst expecting the worst. 'I know that certain harm has been done all the same, but we must forget it and try and avoid conferences in future. They always lead to evil.'[57] He wrote again on 2nd March, and did his best to reassure Haig regarding Wilson's appointment to head the British Mission at G.Q.G. for which Nivelle was pushing. On the same day he wrote a detailed memorandum for the War Cabinet stating very clearly that he did not agree with the principles of unity of command established at the Calais Conference. It began: 'As my signature is appended to the Calais Agreement of the 27th ultimo regarding the future relations between Field-Marshal Sir Douglas Haig and General Nivelle, I ask the permission of the War Cabinet to explain that the signature does not mean that I approve of the principles under-lying the Agreement. The Prime Minister informed me and Sir Douglas Haig at Calais that the principle is, as decided by the War Cabinet on the 24th ultimo, that General Nivelle should be in command of the French and British Armies during the battle in question, and that Sir Douglas Haig should carry out the orders of General Nivelle in the same way as they would be carried out by a Commander of a Group of French Armies. It is obvious that I am not in a position either to approve or disapprove of the principle the War Cabinet decided to adopt, because I am not a member of the War Cabinet; my advice was not asked when the question was discussed by the War Cabinet, nor had I any opportunity of giving it as I was not present at the Meeting, having previously been told by the Secretariat of the War Cabinet not to attend unless I had anything special to bring forward. The first intimation I had that any such change in principle was contemplated either by the British or the French Government was when I received General Nivelle's proposal at 9 p.m. on the first day of the Conference. (As the Cabinet know, these proposals were not accepted by the Prime Minister. Other proposals were drafted under his direction by Sir M. Hankey, and these, with certain additions made by myself and General Nivelle, eventually formed the agreement signed).'[58] The opening of Robertson's memorandum settles the assertion that both he and Haig knew of the Cabinet's intentions before the Conference, as it makes it quite clear that they did not. He went on to make the point that not only did he consider it fundamentally wrong to place the British Army under French control, but that the Governments of the Dominions, who had not been consulted, may strongly object, 'and that entirely to entrust the fortunes of this great battle to a foreign Commander, who as yet has had no opportunity of proving his fitness for the position, was a serious step viewed from the standpoint of the Empire'. The Prime Minister had been unable to accord with his views,

---

[55] Douglas Haig. Diaries and Letters, p275
[56] National Archives, Nivelle to Haig, letter No.24250, WO158/37
[57] Robertson Papers, 7/7/8 28th February 1917, Robertson to Haig. Liddell Hart Centre for Military Archives, King's College London
[58] National Archives, Memorandum 2nd March 1917, Robertson to War Cabinet CAB104/145

continued Robertson, and he now further distanced himself from the agreement, placing the responsibility for the decision firmly where it belonged: 'I trust that I have now made it clear that I did not, and in fact could not agree with the principles of placing the British Armies under General Nivelle, and therefore that my signature merely means that the procedure laid down in the Agreement appears to me to be the one best suited to give effect to the principle which the War Cabinet had already decided to adopt.'

By the 3rd the possible repercussions of the Calais arrangements were troubling him still more deeply. He informed Haig that he meant to raise the matter at Cabinet and requested any representations he may wish to make, whilst casting further doubts over the sincerity of Nivelle: 'I think you may have great difficulties in carrying out the hybrid arrangement. I trusted Nivelle to play the game. It all depends upon him and I hardly dare trust him.'[59]

Nivelle meanwhile was convinced that Haig was not adhering to terms of the Calais agreements, resulting in a complaint on the 7th March from Premier Briand to the British Government,[60] requesting that Hiag be ordered to conform to the decisions of the Conference, and to the instructions issued to him by Nivelle.[61] The French were in high dudgeon and roundly criticised Haig for: '1) An inclination not to accept the decisions of the Calais Conference; 2) A tendency continually repeated to reconsider the plan of operations accepted by the Conference which was attended by the Chiefs of the British and French Governments provided with full powers by the two Governments and by their War Cabinets, a tendency all the more dangerous in that the period of the offensive is approaching; 3) A tendency calculated to lose the initiative in the operations shown by praise of everything which the Germans can do or plan without dreaming for one instant that we can benefit by the same advantages.'[62] The War Cabinet, with the exception of the Prime Minister, after taking time to digest the full implications of command of British forces being subordinated to the French, were less inclined to sympathise with Briand's view, and steps were to be taken to address their concerns. On the same day Robertson informed Haig, who had meanwhile received yet another strident communication by way of a 'directive' from Nivelle, that another conference (to be the third) was to be held in London on the 12th. Robertson was adamant that he and Haig must grasp the opportunity the *second London Conference* was to offer, to regain control over the British Armies.

---

[59] Robertson Papers, 7/7/9 and 7/7/10, 2nd and 3rd March 1917, Robertson to Haig. Liddell Hart Centre for Military Archives, King's College London

[60] French Ambassador to War Cabinet, Spears papers 2/1/14, Liddell Hart Centre for Military Archives, King's College London

[61] An interesting document exists amongst Lloyd George's papers, which is a typed copy of a letter apparently from Nivelle, recipient unknown (possibly the French Minister of War), dated the 7th March 1917. 'I consider that the situation cannot improve as long as Sir Douglas Haig remains in command; if the British Government decides to replace him, there are two possible alternatives: A. The British Expeditionary Force might be divided into two Army Groups, of which the Northern Army Group, consisting of the First and Second Armies, would have a defensive rôle, whereas the southern Army Group, consisting of the Third, Fourth and Fifth Armies, would take part in the combined France-British offensive, these two Army Groups being actioned by a British General acting in conformity with my plans and keeping in close touch with the War Committee: B. Another Commander in Chief could be chosen, in which case I should prefer General Gough to any other General….Though I fully realise the difficulties which the British Government may encounter in the application of the first solution, I nevertheless consider that it would meet the general interests of the Allies in a more satisfactory way. Meanwhile, the French Government have asked the War Committee to require Sir Douglas Haig that he should comply with the decision reached at the Calais Conference. Please keep me informed of Mr. Lloyd George opinion on the subject.' Parliamentary Archives. Lloyd George Papers. LG/F/162/1(6)

[62] Spears papers 2/1/14, Liddell Hart Centre for Military Archives, King's College London

The London Conference the 12th March 1917

In contrast to the divisions in the ranks witnessed at Calais, broad agreement on a united policy had been reached by the British participants before the London Conference, which resulted inevitability in the Prime Minister somewhat moderating his position. Two significant changes were quickly settled; the first that Nivelle should not communicate direct with London but only through Haig, the second placing beyond any doubt that British forces remained at all times under the command of their own officers, and of the British Commander-in-Chief. It was agreed however that in line with Nivelle's request Wilson should be appointed Head of the British Mission at G.Q.G., and that all instructions or communications transmitted from him to Haig must bear Nivelle's signature. At last, a compromise had been reached within which everyone could work, but still with significant reservations. On the morning of the 14th Haig received from Robertson a copy of the agreement for signature, which was urgently required by Nivelle who was leaving for France at 11:00 a.m. Still unhappy with the final draft Haig went to see Robertson at the War Office to add a final note of clarification to the document: 'I agree with the above on the understanding that, while I am fully determined to carry out the Calais Agreement in spirit and letter, the British Army and its Commander-in-Chief will be regarded by General Nivelle as Allies and not as subordinates, except during the particular operations which he explained at the Calais Conference. Further, while I also accept the Agreement respecting the functions of the British Mission at French Headquarters, it should be understood that these functions may be subject to modification as experience shows to be necessary.'[63] The War Cabinet, meeting at 12:30, approved the amendment and Haig duly signed.[64] For the benefit of the Cabinet he once more outlined the general plan for the offensive which he summarised as: '1. Continue pressing Enemy back with advanced guards wherever he is giving way. 2. To launch our main attack as soon as possible. But in view of the possibility of these attacks falling in the air, at once prepare for attacks elsewhere.' The plan for the British Army within these general arrangements was: '1. To continue to make all preparations (as arranged) for attacks by First and Third Armies, keeping adequate reserves available either to support Second Army (Ypres) or to exploit success of attacks near Arras. These reserves are obtained from Fifth Army. 2. If successful, at Arras, exploit with all reserves and the cavalry. 3. If not successful, prepare to launch attacks near Ypres to clear the Belgian coast. All cavalry will be required probably if this attack is successful.....The attack on Messines Ridge might be made in May if desirable.'

The whole affair had underlined the complexity of coalition warfare, laying bare the damaging conflicts which were the result of national and personal self-interests, exacerbated by a severe level of distrust between the British High Command and a Prime Minister bent on curbing their powers. But this time Lloyd George had failed in his first major attempt since becoming Prime Minister to meddle in military matters; his main design not in this instance being a laudable campaign to create a unity of purpose between two Commanders-in-Chief, but rather, due to little more than personal animosity, to subordinate the whole British Army and its Commander-in-Chief to French command.

---

[63] Douglas Haig. Diaries and Letters, pp276-277
[64] Spears papers 2/1/23, whole document in English and French, Liddell Hart Centre for Military Archives, King's College London

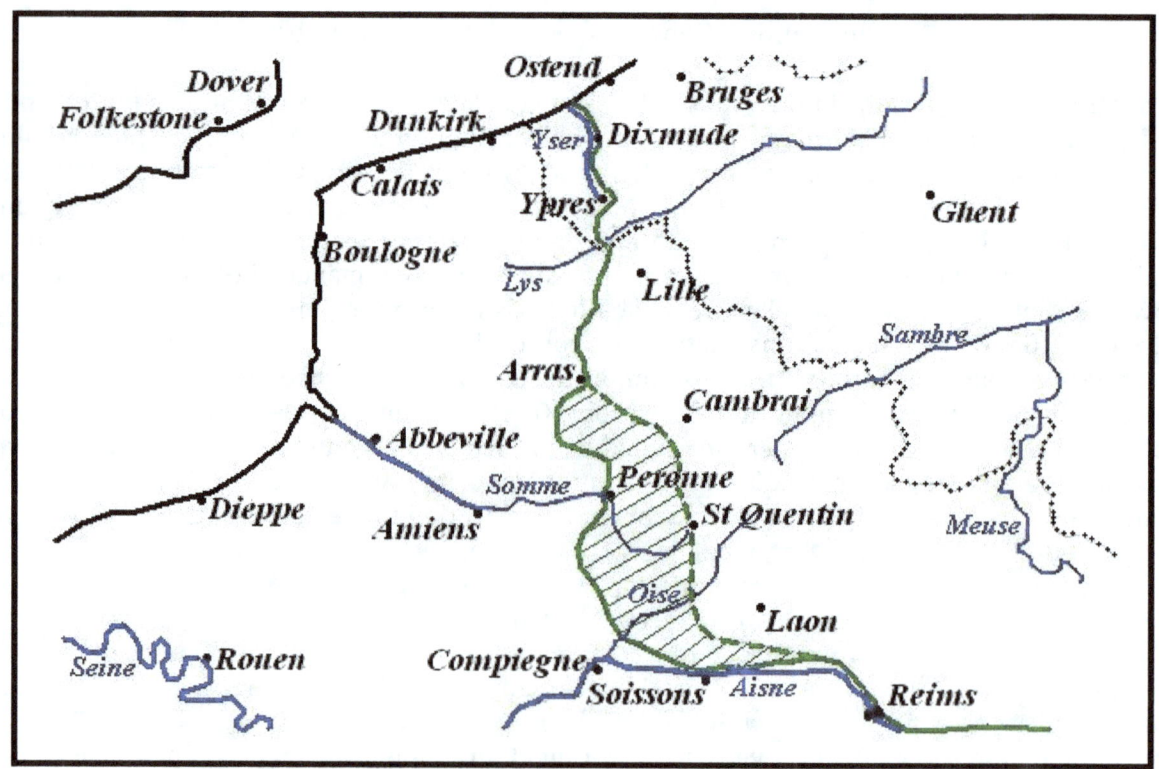

German withdrawal to the *Siegfried Stellung* – the Hindenburg Line

The German withdrawal

Whilst the intriguing and manoeuvring went on amongst the Allied politicians and military staffs, and the promises and hopes of the new offensive clouded many judgements, the enemy were hatching their own plot which was destined to scupper Nivelle's plans before they even got under way. Beginning on the 9th February the Germans had stolen a march by withdrawing from the great westward bulge in their line to a pre-prepared position, the *Siegfried Stellung*, known to the British as the Hindenburg Line, between Soissons and Arras, shortening their front by 27 miles and adding in effect 8 divisions to their defensive strength. Upon confirmation of the German intension General Franchet d'Espèray proposed that his Northern Army Group should immediately launch a general attack. To acknowledge that the enemy was withdrawing from the salient, which was the trap in which their main body was intended to be caught, was impossible for Nivelle without accepting that the plan for the offensive was already obsolete, or at best compromised. For three weeks Franchet d'Espèray's request was denied. By the time it was authorized the belated French action was ineffective. Bad weather and ground conditions, the total wanton destruction of the infrastructure by the enemy, and effective mining and booby-trapping, helped slow the Allied pursuit. The absence of mobile warfare over the past two years had introduced a partial paralysis which even the cavalry found it hard to overcome. The German withdrawal was completed by the 5th April. Strategically Nivelle's whole offensive plan had lost its purpose. To make matters worse the Germans were now stronger and defending a tactically sounder position. Brushing these awkward facts aside Nivelle had merely commented that the greater the enemy numbers the greater would be his victory. But before his offensive had begun, things were already going badly wrong.

Haig, initially optimistic that the withdrawal was a manifestation of German weakness and a sure indication of the damage they had sustained in the Somme fighting, soon changed his opinion. He became more convinced, although incorrectly, that the withdrawal was a prelude to a massive enemy offensive, but was unsure of where the blow might fall, and was most concerned about the safety of his Army if he were to over-extend his commitment at Arras. On the 4th March he explained his concerns to Nivelle indicating that he wished to keep sufficient reserves in hand to cover the most vulnerable sector of his front, that of Second Army at Ypres, covering his supply line through the Channel ports.[65] Nivelle was neither moved by the concerns of his principle ally, by the doubts of his own commanders, or by the actions of the enemy.

Far away on the other side of the Alps however, different concerns were focusing Italian minds.

The Italians reconsider

Towards the middle of March intelligence reports indicated to the Italians that large quantities of warlike stores were being accumulated on both the Isonzo and Trentino fronts, and it appeared that an Austrian attack was being prepared in both sectors. Weather conditions in the Trentino made it unlikely that an attack would take place before end of April, but on the Isonzo severe fighting was anticipated by the end of March. At a meeting between Rennell Rodd, the British Ambassador in Rome and Italian Foreign Minister Sonnino, it became clear that the Italians were having a change of heart over the proposals Lloyd George had made at the Rome Conference back in January. In fact General Cadorna had prepared a plan which had been forwarded to Lloyd George by the Italian Government during the last week of January, which envisaged that 300 heavy guns and 8 infantry divisions should be sent to Italy commencing the 15th February.

By March they were becoming alarmed that the Germans may have come to regard the Italian front as a point where they could achieve a positive result, both to raise flagging spirits and morale at home, and to enable them to secure new territory for use as a bargaining tool. The Italians were now of the opinion that they had insufficient numbers of heavy guns to thwart an attack on two fronts, and even if attacked on one front they did not have the capability of moving guns quickly from one sector to the other. The Austrians had held the Asiago plateau throughout the winter and a concentration of heavy guns in that area would threaten Vicenza. If they broke through to Vicenza they would cut the lateral railway communications, inevitably resulting in the Italians having once more to fall-back behind the Isonzo. Sonnino pressed his case further, expressing doubt that the Franco-British offensive in France would be sufficient to prevent an Austro-German offensive against Italy, and explaining that if the suggestion made by Lloyd George in January had been carried out the whole position in Italy would be more secure. In a letter to Lloyd George on the 18th March Rennell Rodd made these points, and suggested that any military setback would dangerously threaten Italian morale.

The concerns of the Ambassador sat well with the Prime Minister's high regard to increase British aid to the Italians, and in his reply he pointed out that he had for months presented the case to both the General Staff and the Cabinet, to consider the best way to come to the assistance of Italy should she become hard pressed. He was unable to resist pointing out however that at the Rome Conference in January he had felt himself, 'in the position of appearing to thrust an undesirable gift upon a reluctant recipient'.[66] On the 17th March Robertson had produced a memorandum on the subject for the Cabinet, which whilst recognising that Italy may at some point justifiably require Allied assistance, considered for sound strategic reasons that any assistance should primarily come from the French.[67] By the time Lloyd George's letter had reached Rome, Rennell Rodd had spoken at length with General Cadorna who as we have seen had been non-receptive (as had the French) to the suggestion of the guns back in January. Cadorna was now singing a very different song, claiming with some justification that his coolness over the guns had been due to the requirement of quickly returning them, and the fact that he had not received political agreement to accept the offer. His reserves were now tied up covering Vicenza against a possible Austrian attack from the Asiago, and he had not the strength therefore to press on beyond the Isonzo towards his main goal, Trieste. With the assistance of

---

[65] National Archives, Haig to Nivelle OAD326 4th March 1917 WO158/37
[66] Parliamentary Archives, Lloyd George Papers. Rennell Rodd-L.G. LG/F/56/1/25 L.G.-Rennell Rodd
[67] Memorandum CIGS to Cabinet 'Despatch of Reinforcements from the Western Front to the Italian Front', 17th March 1917, National Archives, WO106/1512

Allied forces however, he could use them to either push on towards Trieste, or to stiffen his defences in front of Vicenza. Following Sonnino's lead he also warned of the grave danger to Italian morale, and the possible upsurge of pacifist elements in the country, which were already rife, if there should be a military setback. Cadorna was sure that an Austro-German mobile reserve could easily outnumber his own forces, and if Italy was attacked in the Trentino by overwhelming numbers he would require the direct intervention of an Allied force, and not just the indirect intervention of an Allied offensive in France. The bottom line of the Italian argument was that the situation had changed for the worse and Cadorna not only wanted the guns he had rejected in January, but also required 20 infantry divisions. As far as the guns were concerned, it was to become a mission of the Prime Minister to agitate until he got them.

Part Two

"A mere gamble would be both a folly and a crime"
David Lloyd George

The Nivelle Offensive – British sector north of the Somme

The Battle of Arras the 9th April

On the 9th April, in rain, sleet, and flurries of snow, the British attacked at Arras, in line with the strategic plans of General Nivelle. By the end of the day all the enemy front positions had been seized and in places the third line had been breached to a depth of 4,500 yards. The Canadians had secured most of the vital Vimy ridge to the north of the city, and 10,000 prisoners and 38 guns had been captured. The weather soon proved a major handicap, hampering the forward movement of the supporting artillery. After three days' fighting the German defences were broken along a front of 12 miles, and the spoils had increased to 12,000 prisoners and 150 guns. Under heavy fire from the British guns which had now been dragged forward, the enemy, having lost all hope of recovering Vimy ridge, began falling-back upon their new defensive position behind the Hindenburg Line, the Drocourt – Queant Switch. But German resistance stiffened as more guns and three fresh divisions arrived, and all hopes of a British strategic break through vanished.

Three days before the British attacked at Arras, the United States had declared war on Germany. Like the acorn destined to become the mighty oak, the Great Democracy was awakening, and although the situation for the moment changed little, the Germans were acutely aware that the clock timing the ultimate race for supremacy on the battlefield had begun to tick. Time was now of critical importance to the enemy, and would be even more so if the hoped for success of the unrestricted U-boat campaign, which had been reopened on the 1st February, did not quickly come to fruition.

The Nivelle Offensive
French sector south of the Oise 17th to 27th April

For his offensive Nivelle had amassed 1,200,000 men and around 5,000 guns. After an 11 day bombardment, which was greatly hampered by rain and snow, at 6:00 a.m. on the 16th April Nivelle's Armies attacked. The plan was to break through 3 German positions, to a depth of 5 to 6 miles on the first day. Throughout a day of bitter snow storms, 4 corps of the French Sixth Army and 5 corps of the Fifth Army threw themselves at the strong German positions. On the right of the Sixth Army line the II Colonial Corps gained the crest of the Chemin des Dames but as they descended into the valley of the Ailette beyond, they were decimated by hidden enemy machine guns which had not been destroyed as planned by Nivelle's mighty barrage. As night fell amid sleet and pouring rain the day's achievements were assessed. Most of the German front position had been secured but only small sections of the second position. In many places the French had been driven back to their start line, and although 11,000 prisoners had been taken nowhere did the penetration exceed 2,500 yards. It was soon to become clear, made starkly apparent by the rash promises of immediate success, that Nivelle's great strategic adventure was unlikely to succeed.

On the 17th April Haig found it impossible to get any news from the French regarding the offensive on the Aisne, which indicated to him things were not going well. The next day he received a letter from Henry Wilson, with the French G.Q.G. at Compiegne, which confirmed his fears, stating that the attack of the French Sixth Army had been a failure, but that the Fifth Army and subsidiary attack of the Fourth Army may have done better. Throughout the 17th, 18th, and 19th the battle continued, to be joined on the night of the 19th/20th by the Tenth Army, which was according to the plan to have passed through to exploit the rupture in the enemy line. Nivelle was now forced to recognise the total failure of the breakthrough, and the objectives were limited to freeing Reims from danger and completing the capture of the Chemin des Dames plateau.

Lloyd George was at this time on his way to Italy with French Premier Ribot, (who had succeeded Briand in March) to attempt, with the help of the Italian Premier, to address the threat of Russia making an independent peace with Austria. Major-General Maurice, Director of Military Operations at the War Office, accompanying the Prime Minister on his mission, was sent to see Haig and to gain his views regarding a meeting which Lloyd George had had in London with Albert Thomas, the French Minister of Armaments. Thomas had claimed, with great vision if not inside information, that if the battle on the Aisne did not develop successfully and very quickly, the French would call off the offensive and stand on the defensive until 1918, awaiting the arrival of the Americans (who as we have seen had only declared war with Germany on the 6th April). Haig told Maurice that he would reply in writing directly to Robertson, but that in general he considered the idea of the French giving up the offensive a grave mistake, as it would give the Germans chance to recover from the blows they had suffered in 1916 on the Somme and at Verdun. The seeds of doubt concerning the ability and intention of the French to fight in 1917 were sown in Haig's mind. In Lloyd George's mind they were already well established.

To help settle these doubts, on the 24th April Haig went to Amiens to meet with Nivelle. Before seeing him he spoke with Sir Henry Wilson who indicated that Nivelle, who had only recently been acclaimed the great military hope for France, was after only a few months under political pressure, and already his position was extremely vulnerable. The French President, Poincaré, and some members of the French Government lacked confidence, and there was jealousy of his position within the Army. This summary was supported by a telegram from Lord Esher, the British Ambassador in Paris, which arrived with Haig at the same time, informing that there was 'strong determination on the part of Minister of War [Paul Painlevé] here to make radical changes in High Command'.[68] Meeting with Nivelle privately, Haig raised the matter that the French Government, through Thomas, had already informed Lloyd George of their intention to stop the offensive on the Aisne in the first few days of the attack unless a distinct success was obtained. Indirectly the Flanders operation was also discussed, with Haig emphasising the importance of clearing the Belgian coast, due to the destructive level of the U-boat campaign. This he felt could be accomplished by an attack either directly from Ypres, or indirectly in the direction Charleroi – Liege, which in fact was the operation already under way at Arras in his attacks against the Hindenburg Line towards Cambrai. The success of his present operation depended on the continued action of the French Army. Haig explained his concern that his Army at Arras may exhaust itself in supporting the French attack on the Aisne, only for the French Government to stop offensive action at a later date, at which point the British would have insufficient strength to attack in Flanders to capture the Channel ports. Nivelle gave his assurance that neither he nor his Government had any intention of calling off the offensive, at least until Reims was safe, and further that an Army Reserve would be assembled on the left rear of General Franchet d'Espérey's Army Group North, which if necessary could support the British at Arras. There was nothing in Nivelle's words that came anywhere near revealing the true situation of his offensive. Unknown to Haig, on the 20th April, four days before this meeting, the first phase of the offensive on the Aisne had already been suspended, to be resumed at a scaled down level between the 5th and 9th May. Haig already knew of the weakness of Nivelle's position before the meeting, but was apparently satisfied with assurances given by him, both personally and on behalf of the French Government. But he still harboured reservations, and wisely decided that he would go to Paris on the 26th to better gauge the situation with the politicians.

In Paris knowledge of both the failure of the offensive and the threat to Nivelle's position had been made known to Lord Esher by Painlevé. The Minister of War had indicated that Nivelle

---

[68] Parliamentary Archives, Lloyd George Papers, Lord Esher to L.G., LG/F/16/1/6

would likely be removed, to be replaced by Pétain, but also gave further assurances that the attack between Soissons and Reims would continue so as to prevent the whole weight of the German Army being thrown upon Haig. The tactics would be amended to 'change an expensive method for a more economical one'.[69] Esher passed this information to Lloyd George in a letter on the 25th adding, 'there is a general 'malaise' or ferment of weariness here among the people, the shopkeepers, and in the factories. They are so intelligent and well informed that they realise perfectly the failure of their offensive – the French offensive – and they are aware of the differences of opinion among their generals'.[70]

On 26th April Haig arrived in Paris stepping into a web of intrigue, and began by trying to measure the level of political resolution in maintaining the offensive. He met first with Minister of War Painlevé, whose main intention was not to discuss the cohesion of Anglo – French military strategy, but more to gain Haig's support in replacing Nivelle with Pétain, then Commander of Army Group Centre east of Reims. Painlevé appeared to Haig both agitated and anxious, and appeared already to feel that the offensive on the Aisne had failed. He gave assurances however that the French would still support the British in all that had been agreed, including the clearing of the Belgian coast, and that the Aisne offensive would go on. In the afternoon Haig met with Premier Ribot who informed him that no decision had been made regarding Nivelle and that he was disinclined to make a change in High Command in the middle of an offensive, but went on to ask Haig's opinion of Pétain. He claimed that there was no intention to stop the offensive or to change the plans already made and requested that Haig pass his sentiments on to the British Government. Another private meeting took place between Haig and Painlevé on the 27th. The Minister of War seemed quieter and steadier than at the previous meeting, and Haig asked him directly, 'can I rely on the French Army to go on with the preparations for an attack on my right as agreed between Nivelle and myself?'[71] Once again Haig received assurance that there would be no change in plan, and left feeling more confident than he had on the previous day. But the vagueness of the French position both with regard to the future of Nivelle and the future of the French offensive placed Haig in a major dilemma. If, as appeared likely, the Nivelle Offensive had failed, then it was imperative to check further major British action at Arras to conserve manpower and resources, and as quickly as possible shift the main focus of attack to Flanders. But if the Northern Operation was to stand a chance of success it was imperative for the French to continue fighting and drawing off German reserves, which they likely would not do if Haig stopped his 'supporting operations' at Arras. There seemed little alternative but to proceed by way of a balancing act; maintain the offensive at Arras to the point that the French stayed in the fight, risking the effect that action may have on future operations, whilst gradually disengaging and shifting assets to the north. The part of the dilemma regarding Nivelle's position however, was about to solve itself.

For the French, the Nivelle offensive was a tragedy from the start, not solely through military failure, but more because the hopes raised by the many promises of quick, easy victory had been so rapidly dashed. The Germans in a strong position and with prior warning of the attack gained from captured documents, withdrew their artillery out of range of the French guns, and in a foretaste of their deployment in Flanders arrayed their counter-attack formations in great depth to absorb the French thrust. After some initial success, in a few days the offensive had been brought to a standstill, and the assurances given to Haig by Nivelle, and more importantly by senior members of the Government in Paris, once more came into question. It was clear to Haig that the consequences of Nivelle's failure would have a knock-on effect on his forthcoming Flanders campaign.

Haid discussed the situation with Kiggell. It was now known to them that Pétain had been appointed Chief of the Staff on the 28th April, but information from Paris suggested that it was likely he would soon be promoted Commander-in-Chief. There was little doubt that the

---

[69] Parliamentary Archives, Lloyd George Papers, Lord Esher to L.G., LG/F/16/1/6
[70] Parliamentary Archives, Lloyd George Papers, Lord Esher to L.G., LG/F/16/1/6
[71] Douglas Haig. Diaries and Letters, p288

French position would shift drastically under the command of Pétain, and that the French Armies would be limited to 'aggressive defence' at best. This possibility must have an immediate influence on the future of the operation at Arras, as to continue to press the attack towards Cambrai would produce a salient in the British line which would attract a greater weight of the enemy reserves, resulting in greater British casualties as the French effort slackened. The aim therefore should be limited to; first reaching a good defensive line, second to prepare several attacks to go in by surprise so as to hold the enemy and wear him out, and third to launch the Ypres attack, for which purpose troops should now be economized. It general terms it was considered imperative to press the enemy in France in order to help the Italians and Russians, by retaining enemy reserves, and to induce the Italians and Russians to start attacking as soon as possible.

On the 1st May Haig wrote a memorandum to the War Cabinet laying out the present situation and future plans. He advised that the fighting at Arras had not yet broken the enemy's fighting strength, but that it was essential to realize that the only way it could be broken was by hard and continued fighting. He warned that to persevere with the Arras offensive without strong and active French co-operation would be unwise, the very point he had made to Nivelle on the 24th April. Haig took the opportunity to remind the Cabinet that his divisions were 60,000 men below establishment, and that he was ever mindful of the urgent need, and the expressed desire of the Cabinet, to clear the Belgian coast. To ensure the Northern Operation of a reasonable chance of success he laid down four conditions. 1. That the French should take back at least as much front as the British had taken from them since Nivelle had taken command. 2. The French must undertake a simultaneous offensive. 3. His infantry divisions and artillery must be brought up to establishment. 4. That the Belgians should hand over a small frontage required for the British attack, (north of Boesinghe on the Ypres – Yser canal). Under the circumstances all these requests were perfectly reasonable, bearing in mind with regard to point 2, that at this time Haig was unaware of the serious problems erupting within the French Army. In Haig's mind the moment had now arrived to begin to shift the priority of operational planning to Flanders, and to firm-up arrangements with the French to take back the section of line between the Oise and the Somme, whilst at the northern extremity of the Western Front the British, in preparation for the coastal advance, should take over the French positions at Nieuport. If these arrangements could not be settled between Haig and Nivelle, or with whomever the French chose to replace him, then they would have to be settled at the forthcoming conference in Paris.

Paris Franco British Military Conference
Inter Allied Conference 4th/5th May

Held in Paris on the morning of the 4th May the Franco-British Military Conference must have been difficult for Nivelle, coming as it did two weeks after the failure of the first phase of his offensive. As a direct consequence of the failure, and only five days before the Conference, mutinous misconduct had broken out in the ranks of the French Sixth Army. France was represented by Nivelle, still nominally Commander-in-Chief, Pétain in his new position of Chief of the Staff with extended powers, and Admiral Lacaze French Minister of Marine, with Haig, Admiral Jellicoe and General Robertson representing Britain. The reality of events had quickly dampened the optimism of December. Pétains long held views had been vindicated and it was now accepted that to attempt to *quickly* punch a hole through the German defences was not possible and the tactic of relentless attacks with limited objectives, over a broad front beneath the protective umbrella of the artillery should be employed; in many ways this was back to Joffre's plans of the Chantilly conference of November 1916. Much of the dilemma as to whether or not the French would maintain the offensive was now answered with the gradual eclipse of Nivelle, and the obvious ascendance of the cautious Pétain. Clearly the task of wearing down the enemy's strength and resistance would now inevitably fall mainly upon the British. The French were to take a subsidiary rôle but would attempt to make a number of vigorous attacks. They would also relieve the British along 16 miles of front as far north as Havrincourt, 8 miles southwest of Cambrai, releasing 6 British divisions for operations elsewhere. The great French hopes of February and March had come to nothing, but the full repercussions were yet to be felt.

In the late morning the military representatives joined their political masters at the Quai d'Orsay in an Inter-Allied conference, which continued on the following day, at which Greece and Salonica were the prime subjects discussed, uncomfortably from the British viewpoint as there was no previously agreed policy on the subject. With regard to the Western Front, Pétain had the painful task to report that within the French Army the confidence in its Generals and in the Government was undermined. There was however no mention of the dangerous instability in the French Sixth Army. For their part the British representatives were equally concerned about the loss of merchant shipping tonnage, which, due to the unrestricted U-boat campaign, had reached the record level of 800,000 tons during April. Lloyd George obviously in bullish mood stated that 'the enemy must not be left in peace for one moment, we must go on hitting and hitting with all our strength until the German end, as they always do, by cracking'.[72] He claimed that their losses on the Aisne and at Arras must have had a material and psychological effect and that he and the British Government were ready to put the whole weight of the British Army into the attack, but emphasised, 'it will be no good doing so unless the French do the same, otherwise the Germans would bring their best men and guns and all their ammunition against the British Army, and then later against the French'.[73] The change in the Prime Ministers attitude since the low point at the Calais Conference nearly ten weeks ago was marked. Haig could not have improved upon his script; but the words were easy to say. Whether the transformation would be long-lived remained to be seen, but for certain he appeared a different man, fulsome in his praise of Haig and the recent British achievements. Did this sudden fluctuation of his mercurial character indicate a softening towards Haig and Robertson, or should it be considered a major play towards keeping up French morale and keeping them in the fight?[74] Unfortunately for Haig events were to prove the latter to be the case; but meanwhile Premier Ribot praised Lloyd George for his resolute language and bound France to the agreements of the Military Conference, on the understanding that French reserves, which now amounted to no more than 35,000 in depots would not be squandered. He also laid emphasis on the appalling casualties the French Army had sustained since the beginning of the War. Painlevé also spoke, indicating that previously his views had been misinterpreted, and that although he was in favour of an offensive, he remained concerned about the methods of execution, which was understandable in light of the recent Nivelle fiasco and its possible repercussions. Pétain repeated the warnings he had given before the Nivelle offensive. He advised that as German counter-attacks in superior force would soon have to be faced, objectives should be limited within a zone that could be covered by an overwhelming artillery barrage, and losses out of all proportion to gains occurred when attacking infantry passed beyond that zone. He added, 'it is important to grasp clearly the distinction between action in depth and action in breadth; to contain and destroy the enemy's forces, action in breadth will give the best results'.[75] The military questions had been settled by the military and endorsed by the politicians, so complete agreement had been achieved upon the War making policy to be pursued on the Western Front. A series of attritional attacks with 'limited objectives' within the range of the guns, to wear down the German divisions and prevent them launching an offensive in 1917, while awaiting the arrival of the Americans; what was to become generally referred to as 'Pétain Tactics'. The difficulty, soon to emerge in Flanders, was an apparent inability to accept an agreed definition of the vague term *'limited objectives'*.

---

[72] BOH p23
[73] BOH p23
[74] Hankey had no doubt as to what Lloyd George was about. 'The main object of this visit was to ginger up the French to renew their efforts on the Western Front, and to give the enemy no respite.' Hankey Diaries, Churchill Archives, Churchill College Cambridge HNKY 1/2
[75] BOH p23

Pétain's cautious words however had left huge question marks in British minds regarding the capacity of the French to maintain an offensive capability. It was not so much what Pétain had said, but rather what he had omitted to say. According to the recollections of the Prime Minister, aware of British puzzlement, Pétain approached Lloyd George after the Conference and said 'I suppose you think I can't fight?' Lloyd George turned to the Frenchman, 'no General, with your record I could not make that mistake, but I am certain that for some reason or other you won't fight'. Pétain made no reply.[76] Cabinet Secretary Hankey, who had been present at the Conference, had little confidence in the solidarity of the key Ally. 'The general atmosphere of Paris struck me as very bad – a weak Government, a tiresome chamber, intrigue everywhere, and a troubled and rather dejected people.'[77]

On the 5th May Haig struck while the iron was still hot, writing to Nivelle, (or as a note from Kiggell to Wilson attached to the letter instructed, whoever was now in the position of Commander-in-Chief) requesting immediate relief of his divisions up to the Omignon River, to be followed between the 7th and 20th June, commencing immediately after the operation at Messines, with relief of the line up to Havrincourt.[78] On the 10th May Nivelle replied, notably now addressing himself as le General Commandent en Chef, and not le General Commandment en Chef les Armées du Nord et du Nord-Est, advising that he had issued orders for the relief of the British divisions holding the front up to the line of the River Omignon by the French Northern Army Group. Nivelle's tenure as Commander-in Chief was rapidly approaching its end.

The choice of Gough

The planning for the Northern Offensive was now Haig's major priority, but those plans did not necessarily sit easily with the agreements just settled in Paris. As we have seen, Haig had initially accepted the Plumer-Rawlinson-Macmullen plan for the Northern Offensive, but he was obviously not happy with it. It is possible that he was still overly-influence by the general change of tempo and optimism which had been Nivelle's trademark; but more likely the eclipse of Lloyd George's unqualified support for the now fallen Frenchman and temporary swing towards outward acceptance of the Flanders operation, presented him with the ideal opportunity to exploit the situation and follow his preferred path with a bold and decisive offensive from Ypres, a position from which the Germans did not have the option to simply withdraw. Haig was looking beyond the inevitable set piece infantry battles envisaged before clearing the Messines – Gheluvelt – Broodseinde – Passchendaele higher ground, towards break through and exploitation, and Plumer's steady approach was for the present out of phase with his current thinking. Energy, thrust, and drive were the desired qualities of the moment; the ability to press-on at all costs, irrespective of the council of others, and the possible stress and strain upon subordinates at all levels. The time was fast approaching for quick decision and bold action. The task was enormous, but so was the possible prize that success would bring; the breaking of the northern end of the Western Front and the clearing of the coast. Equally possible was the deep bewilderment and dejection of failure but now was the time to be positive, and for better or worse, General Sir Hubert Gough, the 42 year old cavalryman commanding the British Fifth Army was to be Haig's choice, to smartly drive the offensive beyond the low ridge. Gough was a man of great wit and enthusiasm, in whose company the Commander-in-Chief felt at ease. Haig also had a high regard for Gough's high sense of professionalism, optimism, and aggression. But he was arguably also impetuous, inclined to push forward too far too fast, and was distrusted by some elements within his Army. What was at first regarded as an attribute was soon to emerged as a flaw, and left unchecked by Haig, was to result in serious consequences in the planning and handling of the Northern Operation.

In 1916 before the Battle of The Somme, Gough had been entrusted by Haig with command of the Reserve Army, to await the expected break through of Rawlinson's Fourth

---

[76] David Lloyd George (1938). *War Memoirs of David Lloyd George Vol IV* London: Odhams p2129
[77] Hankey Diaries, Churchill Archives, Churchill College Cambridge HNKY 1/2
[78] National Archives, Haig to Nivelle the 5th May 1917, OAD433, WO158/48

Army, at which point he would thrust through the breach in the German position with the cavalry and two infantry divisions. It had been wishful thinking, but he was now to get another chance to pierce the enemy line. Gough was first told of his appointment by Haig on the 30th April. On the 13th May, the order was issued that Gough, with little local knowledge of the Flanders battlefield, would command the main Northern Operation at Ypres, the greatest campaign yet undertaken by a British Army in the War. Years after the event Gough would question the wisdom of offering him the command, especially as Haig was aware of his lack of experience of Flanders. But on the 10th March 1917 he had written to Haig, 'we can now beat the Germans when and where we like if we have time for a fairly good artillery preparation; five of my divisions can hold the front line east of Bapaume, and all the rest of the Fifth Army is at your disposal for any offensive you may decide on'.[79] Bold words indeed. It is interesting to reflect, that by the time of Gough's appointment, the Nivelle offensive, which in some ways had so influenced Haig's choice of commander and tactics, had already collapsed in dismal failure and with dire results. On the 14th May, Colonel Macmullen handed to General Gough the Northern Operations file with the G.H.Q. 1917 plan and all the correspondence leading up to it, as a working basis for his scheme for the main attack out of the Ypres Salient.

Haig's appointment of Gough served to reinforce the point that a rapid break through was his chosen strategy. But how was this break through to be achieved? Perhaps by a number of advances of *limited depth*, in accord with the Paris agreements, but nevertheless planned to quickly pierce the enemy Flanders position which would be necessary to reach the Belgian ports? The conundrum which immediately presented itself was, what was to be the accepted definition of *limited*. In his memorandum to the War Cabinet on the 1st May Haig had concluded, 'even if a full measure of success is not gained, we shall be attacking the enemy on a front where he cannot refuse to fight, and where, therefore, our purpose of wearing him down can be given effect to' for the first step he wrote, 'must always be to wear him down ("soften" as is said nowadays) the enemy's power of resistance until he is so weakened that he will be unable to withstand a decisive blow'.[80] Haig's choice of words is important for it reveals his belief that even if the break through battle did not succeed, the enemy would be compelled to fight an attritional, wearing-down battle in Flanders. This fact was eventually to become of ultimate importance to the Allied cause, even if the wearing-down battle was not Haig's initial prime intention. But for the moment the situation existed, that whilst theoretically operating under the constraints of the Paris agreement, the British Army was about to attempt to clear the Channel coast, and if all went well northern Belgium up to the Dutch border.

Between the 12th and 23rd May a flurry of correspondence passed between Ribot and Lloyd George, mostly concerning possible peace negotiations between Italy and Austria. Lloyd George considered the matter important enough to arrange a meeting with Ribot, but also indicated in a letter of the 14th May, that information he had received subsequent to the agreements made in Paris, indicated a good deal of uncertainty as to the military policy the French Government intended to pursue on the Western Front during the year. The Prime Minister again emphasised that a 'British only' offensive was impossible, as it would enable the Germans to defeat the one army making the attack, with a subsequent dire effect on Allied morale, especially in Russia. But Lloyd George, through no fault of his own, was making plans based on incorrect appreciations of the condition of his Allies. He totally underestimated the depth of the fermenting French military malady, and he misunderstood the gravity of the problems in Russia, failing to foresee that the situation in that county was already irretrievable.

---

[79] BOH p20
[80] National Archives, Haig to CIGS OAD 248 CAB27-7

Army Commander's Conference Doullens the 7th May

At the Army Commander's conference at Doullens on 7th May, Haig reported that the Nivelle offensive had achieved only a limited advance. The French attack would not move on Laon as had been planned, and the agreement for British co-operation in the offensive was now at an end. Although no longer on the offensive, the French were to continue with a series of methodical attacks to wear-down the enemy reserves. The Sixth and Tenth Armies were in a simultaneous but limited action to seize the heights north of the Aisne, and were if possible to establish a defence line along the Ailette. The Fourth and Fifth Armies were to continue with their mission to disengage Reims. The Third Army was to continue to prepare its front, and be ready to come into action immediately to provide artillery support when required. Under the new conditions Nivelle had ordered the operations north of the Aisne in the direction of the north-east suspended. The great offensive was over.[81]

The Italians and Russians however had also planned for offensives which were hoped to at least hold the enemy forces deployed on their fronts. Haig went on to give an account of the decisions reached at the Paris Conference, explaining that the French were to stand on the defensive, and that the Arras battle would be continued in an attempt to further wear-down the enemy and to obscure the real intention of attacking in Flanders. As he did not possess the strength to maintain the offensive at two points on the British front at once, there would be a steady running-down of the fighting at Arras, as men and material were gradually moved north.[82] The orders issued to the Army Commanders concerning the continuation of operations on other fronts were understandable in the circumstances stating, 'the ruling principles in the conduct of these operations are the careful selection of important objectives of a limited nature, the deliberate preparation of the attack, the concentration of artillery, and the economy of infantry, combined in each case with feint attacks, smoke, and gas elsewhere on the remainder of the front'.[83] Whether this deception plan worked or not, there was little alternative but to try. Preparations for major offensives on the Western Front were notoriously difficult to conceal, and it was more a case of disguise them as well as possible, whilst not expecting miracles from the deception. The French, it was hoped, would take over the southern end of the British line as far north as Havrincourt by the middle of June. The intention was to convey the impression to the enemy that the IV Corps of Fifth Army, relieved by the French south of Havrincourt, were concentrating as a continuation of the Arras battle for an attack towards Havrincourt, whilst the incoming French threatened St. Quentin.[84] But unknown to Haig at the time, this part of the

---

[81] National Archives, Nivelle to French Army Group Commanders copied to Haig, GQG 6th May 1917, WO158/48

[82] The deception plan to continue with local attacks at Arras has come in for some unfounded criticism, see Prior and Wilson *Passchendaele the Untold Story* pp51-52 'Haig had already pointed out that he did not have the guns and men to launch offensives both at Arras and Ypres, yet he was expecting the Germans not to notice that he was acting offensively at Arras only with token weaponary and forces hastily assembled…..Haig's deception plan, in sum, seemed to have the capacity only to deceive Sir Douglas himself.' This attack on Haig does not stand up to even brief examination, for other than to stand down the forces remaining at Arras and have them do nothing, he had little option but to keep up local attacks with those forces available. On the 5th May, the day after the Paris Conference, he had written to Nivelle: 'My operations in the immediate future will consist of continuing to engage and wear out the enemy on my present front (Arras – Vimy) by attacking definite local objectives from time to time with such forces as I can make available for this purpose'. National Archives, Haig to Nivelle the 5th May 1917, OAD433, WO158/48. It is quite obvious that Haig recognised the limitations of the deception plan, rather than 'expecting the Germans not to notice' as suggested by Prior and Wilson, but had no other course open to him.

[83] National Archives, Record of verbal instructions, Haig to Army Commanders, Doulens 7th May, WO158/311

[84] National Archives, Haig to Nivelle the 5th May 1917, OAD433, WO158/48: 'As I have already stated, I am continuing to engage the enemy on the Arras – Vimy front and shall continue to do so

complex planning was to soon be dashed by the inability of the French to take over the section of the British line between the Omignon valley and Havrincourt.

In reality neither the attack on the Aisne or at Arras had worn-down the enemy reserves in line with the hopes of February.[85] Nevertheless the date for the opening of the Flanders offensive at Messines was to be about the 7th June, with 'the Northern Operation (some weeks later) with a view to securing the Belgian coast'.[86] This was a departure from the proposals of the 3rd April, which had foreseen the Messines and Ypres operations occurring *simultaneously*. As Messines was now to be a stand alone operation the problem of lack of room to assemble south and south-west of the Gheluvlet plateau was alleviated. The tank operation, which had in any event been considered inappropriate given the unsuitable conditions on the western face of the plateau was cancelled. The *'some weeks'* delay between the two operations now being proposed introduced a very different and more realistic timetable compared to the 48 to 72 hours initially suggested by Rawlinson. The April plan to attack both the Messines ridge and Pilckem ridge simultaneously, and Rawlinson's plan to attack from the Salient 48 to 72 hours after Messines, would have required the deployment of around 4,500 guns between St Yves and Steenstraat, plus all the necessary engineering preparations required before launching in effect two great offensives, at both Messines and Ypres. Obviously between the 3rd April and the 7th May much more thought had been given to the logistical difficulties of attacking both at Messines and out of the Salient, either simultaneously or within three days, and both plans had clearly appeared impossible to achieve. There were simply insufficient guns available to attack in both places at the same time. Once the Messines attack was over, then the majority of guns from that front, and other guns from further south, would be moved up to Ypres. It was not just guns which had to be moved. The enormous amount of work necessary to prepare the infrastructure of the Salient for the forthcoming battle would require both time and a huge labour force. The time delay between the operations was critical, but on the 1st June there were to be only (nominally) 6,157 guns in the whole B.E.F. along 163,500 yards (93 miles) of front,[87] and as approximately 2,250 guns were required at Messines and another 2,250 at Ypres, there was little alternative but to introduce a delay. The reasons for the delay between the end of the Messines battle on the 14th June and the opening of the Passchendaele battle on the 31st July has itself become a battleground of much debate; a subject which we shall soon examine in more detail.

---

until after the attack on the Messines – Wytschaete Ridge has been delivered. The impression I wish to convey to the enemy by the latter attack is that it is a diversion in the north to draw off his reserves from my main battle front, which continues to be east of Arras, and I hope to produce an impression that the troops relieved south of Havrincourt are intended to renew the original offensive.' These plans had therefore been made prior to Haig being informed by Pétain on the 18th May that the French could not take over the whole 16 miles of British front line up to Havrincourt.

[85] Denis Winter claims the opposite, stating that the Germans sent 105 of their 157 Western Front divisions against the French by the end of July, and that 'the wearing out process had therefore gone according to GHQ's most favourable calculations'. *Haig's Command* p86. But GHQ's calculations up to the end of April were undoubtedly based on the hope that the Nivelle offensive would be successful and the enemy routed from a large area of the Western Front including, if Nivelle was to be believed, the Belgian coast, rather than the failure it turned out to be. It is inconceivable that GHQ felt the Germans were worn out according to their most favourable calculations.

[86] National Archives, Record of verbal instructions, Haig to Army Commanders, Doulens 7th May, OAD 434 page 3 WO158/311

[87] National Archives, GHQ statistics WO95/14

Amiens the 18th May
Haig confers with Pétain

Major unrest was developing meanwhile within the ranks of the French Army. Undertaking Nivelle's offensive in a weakened state after the months of fighting at Verdun the Poilus had been promised that this one last effort would bring them victory. There was no victory, only mounting casualties, inadequate medical support, poor food, and depressing and degrading conditions behind the lines. On the 29th April there occurred in one division an outbreak of 'collective disobedience'; mutiny in all but name. The malady quickly spread through other French units which had now lost all faith in their leaders and all hope of victory. But it was not until the 15th May that G.Q.G. was sufficiently alarmed to send a formal communiqué to War Minister Painlevé explaining how bad matters were. Also on the 15th May in Paris, demonstration marches, mostly by women workers, moved along the boulevards, ostensibly striking for a wage rise to meet the ever rising cost of living. The unrest was willingly fermented by communist and anarchist agitators through publications some of which were surreptitiously financed through the German intelligence services. Most worryingly, soldiers on leave were joining the demonstrations, which now occurred on a daily basis. A hint of revolution was in the air, fed by war-weariness and political subversion. The French War Cabinet was under no illusions regarding the potential dangers.

On the 12th May Robertson had written to Haig expressing his unease regarding the affect the unstable situation in France, and any possible separate peace which Russia may make, would have on promised French co-operation in the forthcoming Northern Offensive. Haig replied on the 16th, stating that his opinion remained, 'that the action of a wearing-down character must be continued; that pressure on the present offensive front must be gradually relaxed; and that my efforts must be concentrated on completing preparations for clearing the coast this summer'.[88] He proposed maintaining 'just sufficient pressure on the Arras front to prevent the enemy from weakening his forces there', whilst optimistically believing that 'the enemy's frequent counter-attacks have assisted appreciably in wearing down his strength'. At this time, unaware of the full situation in the French Army, he remained convinced that 'similar counter-attacks with similar results also continue to be directed against the positions recently captured by the French and they serve the purpose I have in view almost as well as offensive activity by the French. It is not unlikely that the enemy's efforts to recapture these positions – especially the Chemin des Dames – will be continued for some time, and perhaps increase in strength; but even if this should not be so I feel sure that, when the question of command has been finally settled, the French Armies will not fail to maintain the degree of offensive activity promised by the French Government at the recent Paris Conference'.[89] Haig also explained that the Northern Operation was to be split into two phases and that although he thought it unlikely that the Russian situation would develop that quickly, if it did, the Messines operation could be abandoned, and the second phase would not be carried out unless the situation at that time was favourable to success. Haig's reply crossed with another letter from Robertson, informing that a printed version, in French, of the resolutions of the May 5th Paris Conference had been received in London. The document, he told Haig, made no mention of the promise given at the Conference by the French Government to continue offensive action, which may mean that on reflection they had decided not to bind themselves to the resolution. Of almost equal concern to future French cooperation, on the 15th May Pétain succeeded Nivelle in command of the French Armies of the

---

[88] National Archives Haig to CIGS OAD 449 CAB27-7

[89] This memorandum throws into doubt Denis Winter's claim that Haig believed the French would remain on the defensive come what may, rather than coming to this conclusion in June upon hearing of the mutinies. See endnote 93 below. Denis Winter (2001) *Haig's Command* London: Penguin p86-87. It also shows that Haig accepted that French defence against strong German attacks could seriously weaken the enemy. The question soon to arise was how much pressure could the French Army withstand?

North and North-East. The high spirits displayed by Lloyd George at the Paris Conference had now seriously declined, to be replaced by great doubts, fuelled by the apparent lack of French commitment, and the appointment of Pétain which further threatened the same. Robertson's letter was followed the same day by a telegram to Haig stating that the British War Cabinet would only support the plans for the Northern Offensive if the French played their full agreed part, and that Haig was to be insistent on this point in any discussions with Nivelle, Pétain, Foch, or whoever it might be who was now responsible for deciding operations. The danger as the Cabinet saw it was that any suggested intention to embark on costly operations, whether the French co-operated or not, may result in Britain fighting practically alone, and to this or to a plan which contains the danger of it the they could not agree.

To clarify in his own mind the true state of the French Army, Haig arranged a meeting with General Pétain on the 18th May at Amiens,[90] first establishing that Pétain was commander of the field army, and the correct man with which to negotiate. With Henry Wilson present he handed Pétain the telegram from Robertson which stated: 'Prime Minister desires me to remind you of War Cabinet intentions to support your policy as was in fact done by him at the recent Paris Conference but on express condition that French also play their full part as agreed upon at our Conference with Nivelle and Pétain. He is anxious that you should clearly realize this in your discussion with Nivelle [now Pétain] because Cabinet could never agree to our incurring heavy losses with comparatively small gains which would obviously be the result unless French cooperate whole-heartedly.'[91] Pétain confirmed his intention to comply, 'in accordance with the assurances given at the Paris Conference'. He claimed that the French had planned four attacks. The first was an operation by the Sixth Army using 6 divisions to secure the crest of the Chemin-des-Dames (Malmaison) on a front of 7 to 8 kilometres, followed a few days later by an attack of the Tenth Army on a front of 4 kilometres, the start planned for the 10th June to coordinate approximately with the British attack at Messines. The second was to be an attack on a large scale using two Armies from Sapigneul and from Moronvillers, on a front of 25 kilometres, with the intention of disengaging Reims, and timed to coincide with the British attack at Ypres at the end of July. The third attack, the date of which had not yet been settled would be at Verdun on a front of 10 kilometres. The fourth was to be in Alsace, at a time and of a scale as yet undecided. Pétain could not however hold to the agreement made on the 4th May in Paris, to take over the 16 miles of British front line up to Havrincourt but would take over 8,000 yards releasing 3 British divisions, and the cooperation of the French Third Army in an attack towards St. Quentin and Cambrai agreed previously with Nivelle was no longer possible. He agreed to the temporary handing over of the Nieuport bridgehead to the British and suggested that the 2 French divisions of the XXXVI Corps holding that sector, plus 4 more, should take up the line on the British left between Boesinghe and the inundations, (assuming the Belgians were willing to relinquish it), and should co-operate with 6 Belgian divisions d'armée (each equivalent in strength to 2 British divisions), all under the command of the King of the Belgians, with General Anthoine as Chief of Staff.

Haig handed a detailed copy of his plans for the Northern Operation and two maps to Pétain, emphasising the importance of French support about the 1st July, pointing out that by this time British activity at Arras would have subsided. Pétain promised to comment on their content as soon as possible, acknowledging the Flanders offensive as the main operation and ensuring his utmost efforts to attract as many hostile divisions as possible. Haig telegraphed the same evening to the War Cabinet that he believed the French would carry out their part, and their co-operation would be wholehearted. In repeating what Pétain had said he appeared to harbour no serious doubts, claiming that he found him, 'businesslike, knowledgeable, and brief of speech. The latter a rare quality in Frenchmen!'[92]

---

[90] National Archives, record of Conference held at Amiens at 5:00 p.m. on Friday, the 17th May 1917, OAD454, WO158/48
[91] National Archives, telegram cipher 34467, 14th May 1917, CIGS to Haig WO158/48
[92] Douglas Haig. Diaries and Letters, p294

Sir Henry Wilson was however less convinced; in fact he did not trust Pétain's assurances, and also doubted the steadfastness of Painlevé. A week before the Amiens meeting Pétain had already told Wilson that he was opposed to Haig's plan of attack, and Wilson determined to make Haig aware of that fact. But first, in an endeavour to pin Pétain down more firmly to his commitments, Wilson met with him on the 20th May. Wilson intimated that although French support for the Messines attack was settled there was no written agreement, and that the extent to which the French would support the main operation from Ypres also remained vague. Further, Wilson claimed that if the British got it into their heads that French cooperation for the Ostend – Zeebrugge offensive was not to be forthcoming it would have grave consequences on the future course of the War. Pétain asked Wilson if he had a solution. Wilson's reply was that the French should either agree to attack practically the whole time the British were engaged, even if this meant with a reduced number of divisions, or to explain there and then precisely the reasons for only proceeding with smaller operations divided into much shorter periods of fighting. Wilson's worse fears were justified as he was introduced to what would soon become commonly referred to as 'Pétain Tactics'. To adhere to the first proposal, said Pétain, was out of the question and was not in line with new policy. Rather, the French attacks would be towards limited objectives, and once these were gained the movement would cease. The French held too much line, and although Pétain had nothing like the number of divisions that Haig had at his disposal he would try to employ 25 divisions throughout the summer. But of overwhelming significance, Pétain claimed that he was opposed to any operation with such distant objectives as those proposed in Flanders, and that with the amount of assistance he felt able to give, Haig faced an impossible task, *but that it was no business of his*. He promised to write to Haig indicating exactly what he was willing and able to do, and to show Wilson the letter before it was sent. The alarming content of the meeting was conveyed by Wilson in a letter to Hiag. On the 23rd Haig received a reply from Pétain in response to the plan and maps Haig had presented at Amiens.[93] The contents of the two letters contained very different stories. In Pétain's reply (which he had failed to show to Wilson as promised), there was no cautionary note regarding distant objectives in Flanders, simply a repeat of the agreements to support the Messines attack with an attack on the 10th June and another during July to correspond with the attack at Ypres. He also drew Haig's attention to the inadvisability of relieving the Belgians on the Yser with French troops too soon, as this movement simultaneous with the British taking over the bridgehead at Nieuport would be noticed by the enemy. He also remarked that a Britsh attack at Lens would have a considerable impact if the Lens – Bethune coalfield could be disengaged; but there was no word of caution regarding the distant objectives of the Northern Offensive. Haig was baffled. Wilson was angry, not just because Pétain had failed to show him the letter first, but because it addressed not one of the vital points he had raised on the 20th. Who was Haig to believe? Did Pétain have no faith in the Northern Operation, and did he really believe that a massive offensive to be conducted by his principle ally was *not his business* to comment upon? Although the full impact of the mutinies in his Army were not yet upon him, there had been absolutely nothing stopping Pétain informing Haig of his doubts regarding the operation to clear the Belgian coast. Neither had his doubts prevented him handing the French First Army to Haig's command on the 27th May in support of the attack at Ypres. Perhaps he considered it preferable, in the interests of France, not to questions Haig's plan but better to let him go on. Whatever the reason, Sir Henry Wilson had rumbled Pétain, but he had still failed to get the Frenchman to come clean.

It is claimed anecdotally, that to those on his staff with the temerity to question Pétain's judgment, and advise active co-operation with the British, he simply replied 'I am waiting for the Americans and the tanks'. Whether he actually made this statement or not is immaterial, as this was in any case the stance which the French took. In time Pétain was to launch two offensives with strictly limited objectives, the first on the 26th August at Verdun, and the second on the 23rd October at Malmaison (originally planned for the 10th June), against an enemy enormously weakened by the Flanders fighting and unable to counter-attack, as they possessed

---

[93] Letter No. 21444, Pétain to Haig 23rd May 1917, National Archives WO158/48

hardly enough troops to hold even the passive defence line.[94] Pétain had so far made no mention to Haig of mutiny within his Army, but it was becoming increasingly questionable whether some of the promises given to Haig on the 18th May would be fulfilled. Wilson's information had given Haig prior warning of what Pétain was about, even if it had not been entirely accepted by the Commander-in-Chief. But there were undoubtedly grave concerns in London in view of the War Cabinets insistence that the French must play their full part, for if the growing reports of their predicament were correct it was now probable that they could not.

At the end of May disquieting information was reaching the ears of the Prime Minister from Lord Esher in Paris regarding what the Ambassador described as 'this socialist difficulty' confronting the French Government. Esher regarded international socialists, a powerful force in French politics at the time and determined on a path of making peace on their terms, as a great danger to the cause of the Allies. Esher's language was alarmist in the extreme. 'The governing forces of this country are losing all control. Without firm control the French have always drifted and then plunged into excess. We are on the high road to a peace such as no one ever dreamed of, arranged over the heads of statesmen, parliaments, and armies.'[95] His observations, however overstated from a political viewpoint, had an underlying ring of truth. From all quarters, on the eve of the British offensive, the news from France was giving due cause for anxiety. The news however was about to get much worse.

Pétain's message to Haig   2nd June

On the 2nd June the serious escalation of the mutinies was at last made clear to Haig, as Pétain sent him a letter, carried by his Chief of Staff, General Debeney, which signified its extreme secrecy. It explained that the planned French attack at Malmaison in the Champagne in support of Haig's attack at Messines could not, due to conditions within the Army, take place on the 10th June, but that the artillery battle on the Aisne and in Champagne would continue. Debeney believed the earliest the French could launch an offensive would be at the end of July at Verdun. A disappointed but undoubtedly unsurprised Haig expressed his hope that Pétain would do all he could by offensive measures, to at least hold the German divisions on his front. The true situation within the French Army was now known by the British Commander-in-Chief, or at least enough of it to raise considerable alarm. In reality things were worse than Pétain had admitted. The Chemin des Dames front was under counter-attack, and as exhausted French divisions gave way under pressure, those held in reserve to relieve them were already rife with sedition. Divisions in a doubtful state of discipline were being sent into the line, but the very fact that the mutinies were happening placed France in great danger. As Painlevé the French Minister of War pointed out, that with the Germans lying only 100 kilometres from Paris, the single fact of not being certain that an order given by a regiment would be executed automatically was a grave peril.

On the day Pétain's letter arrived, Haig had received a report from Major Lytton, the Press Liaison Officer at G.H.Q., informing that there were accounts of strikes, widespread war-weariness, and despondency in the French press. It was an extremely low period in the fortunes of France, and the obvious dangerous implications had a major and entirely understandable effect upon Haig. Later, away from the stress and emotion of the moment Painlevé was to write, (repeating a statement that he had made to a meeting of the French War Cabinet in early June) that at this period there were between Soissons and Paris only two divisions upon which he could confidently rely. It is not surprising that Haig was only partially informed regarding the depth of the trouble, as G.Q.G. kept the tightest possible security net over the Zone of the Armies, and the French Cabinet, who the Army Staff did not trust with matters of great secrecy, were also kept only partially informed.[96]

---

[94] See Chapter 10
[95] Parliamentary Archives, Lloyd George Papers, LG/F/16/1/13
[96] There are other very different viewpoints. Denis Winter claims that Haig and Lloyd George each knew the real situation, which was that the plan of both Pétain and more especially the French

The Messines offensive was to be launched in five days time on the 7th June. Haig had visited the three Corps of Plumer's Second Army during the previous week, was satisfied with what he had seen, and had the utmost confidence in the result. Without further reference to the War Cabinet, Haig made his decision. Messines would go ahead. It was inevitable, given the scale of preparations involved that the enemy had warning of the forthcoming offensive. Given the perfect observation the Germans enjoyed from the ridges, to construct roads, railways, camps, ammunition dumps, and dig-in artillery, in the build up to an offensive without revealing the intension was impossible. Any attack to be made from the low Flanders plain towards the ridges had to take this enemy advantage into account, and to partially alleviate this problem was in any event the main reason for the preliminary attack at Messines. Crown Prince Rupprecht, Commander of the German northern Army Group had asked for 15 divisions to make his preparations to resist the attack. He was sent 10 divisions and much heavy artillery, much of it moved north from the Aisne front. The inevitable consequence of the forthcoming offensive, in influencing the movements of the German reserves to Flanders and away from the French, a critical issue looming increasingly large in Haig's mind, was already in progress. Many more enemy divisions would travel north before the Northern Operation was over, and the French would have their badly needed respite.

On the eve of battle a review of the international situation, from Haig's perspective, provided not a shred of comfort; not from France, not from Russia, not from Italy, not from the high seas, and even not yet from the United States. He now placed his faith in the only hands he could always trust; those of his ever reliable British Army.

Messines, Plumer's battle the 7th June

The final plan of attack at Messines was to be an assault on a broad front of nearly 10 miles from St.Yves just south of the Douve stream on the flat plain of the River Lys in the south, to Mount Sorrel in the north, on the south-western edge of the Gheluvelt plateau. The objective was to be strictly limited to a maximum depth of 3,000 yards and an average of around 2,000 yards into the enemy's position. The high ground of the Messines - Wytschaete ridge was to be captured during the morning of the day of assault, and in line with Haig's requirements, in the afternoon a short advance down the eastern slope was to be made to better secure possession.

As we have seen, at the planning stage for Messines (on the 18th March), Haig had intervened, suggesting that Plumer's objective for the first day of the battle, an advance of around 2,000 yards to an observation line beyond the German Second Line but still quite close to the ridge top, was insufficiently bold. It should he ordered, be extended down the eastern slopes of the ridge to a maximum distance of around 3,500 yards to include the German Third or 'Oosttarverne' Line. In so doing it was hoped that around 120 German guns within this area would be taken, although later in practice this was not to be the case as the enemy had already moved his undamaged guns.

The operational orders for the battle were issued by Second Army headquarters on the 10th and 19th of May, and three corps of the Second Army were to be employed. On the right (south) the II Anzac Corps (Lieutenant-General Sir A. J. Godley), comprising the 3rd Australian, New Zealand and 25th British Divisions, was to assault north-eastwards and capture the southern shoulder of the ridge, including Messines village. In the centre the IX Corps (Lieutenant-General Sir Arthur Gordon), with the 36th, 16th and 19th Divisions, advancing due east astride the Spanbroekmolen saddle was to capture the central sector of the ridge including the village of Wytschaete. On the left the X Corps (Lieutenant-General Sir T. N. L. Moorland), with the 41st, 47th and 23rd Divisions, was to assault south-eastwards and gain the northern part

---

Government, was to cease major offensive operations and wait for the Americans, not as a result of mutinies but as a matter of policy. The 'mutinies' it is claimed were made a convenient excuse for 'doing nothing in the latter half of 1917'. Denis Winter (2001) *Haig's Command* London: Penguin p86-87 This topic is discussed more fully in Chapter 10-'The threat of disaster, the French mutinies'.

of the ridge between the St.Eloi - Oosttaverne road and Mount Sorrel. XIV Corps (Lieutenant-General Lord Cavan), would be in GHQ reserve. From Mount Sorrel northwards to the Belgian front, the left wing of the Second Army was held by the II Corps, with the 30th Division, from Mount Sorrel to Bellewaarde Lake, and by the VIII Corps from there to Boesinghe on the Belgian right.

Each of the three attacking corps would deploy 3 divisions in the line, the 9 divisions being equally spaced along the 17,000 yard frontage of the battle sector. In addition 3 divisions, the 4th Australian, 11th, and 24th were attached one two each corps as a reserve making a total of 12 divisions available for the operation. Elements of the 4th Australian Division and the 11th Division were to carry forward the advance in the afternoon. The attack was to be supported by a strong concentration of artillery and also by the exploding of 19 great mines which had been specially prepared over a long period for the purpose.[97] Also 72 of the new Mk IV tanks were to make their first appearance in action.

South of the Ypres – Comines canal the German Front Line formed a marked salient thrusting to the west into the British position, similar in size and shape to the British salient in front of Ypres, the whole position forming a reversed S. Consequently the two flank corps, II Anzac to the south and X Corps to the north, had only to cover 1,200 and 1,800 yards respectively to reach their objectives whereas the central corps, IX had over 3,000 yards to cover to the final objective. As compensation the front of the central corps was gradually narrowed from over 5,000 yards to around 2,000 yards at the objective on the ridge. The very shape of the battlefield, the length of the front reducing as the advance proceeded into the salient, was to complicate the movement and deployment of the infantry, and this tactical problem was to lead to some difficulties. Preparations for the battle were arranged meticulously by Plumer and Harington. Great attention was paid to the training of all involved, including the construction of large scale models of the areas to be assaulted. Progressive arrangements in artillery methods were introduced, including greater attention to counter-battery work and a careful creeping barrage timetable. There was also to be an integrated machine gun barrage.

In one respect the Messines operation was unique. The fixed German positions on the ridge, which as we have seen had been established since 1914, made them a prime target for major mining operations. These operations had not received official sanction until 6th January 1916. But the engineers had not waited for this approval, and several deep shafts were in existence and half a dozen deep tunnels had already been started, including one at Hill 60, by August 1915 and four others in December. The establishment of the German Front Line and its strong outposts along the western face of the ridge favoured the British mining plan. Near horizontal tunnels, some short, others over 700 yards long, driven beneath the German positions from behind the British lines would place the mine galleries 80 to 120 feet beneath the German strong-points, and at such depth they would prove difficult for German counter-mining efforts to discover. The geology also favoured the British. From the lower ground which they held at the foot of the ridge, shafts could be sunk that would more readily cut into the important beds of blue clay, which on the lower ground were closer to the surface than on top of the ridge. As long as the galleries kept within these clay beds, and did not cut above them into the saturated alluvial deposits and sand beds at higher levels, they would remain *relatively* dry. German counter-mining shafts sunk from the higher ground on the ridge inevitably cut straight down into the wet sandy clay and saturated Kemmel Sands, (*Schwimmsande*), which lay just beneath the surface, causing the shafts to be much wetter than those of the British. The mining was however more difficult where the British positions were on the sandy clay beds at Hill 60, the

---

[97] There were at least 4 more charged mines, which were deliberately not fired on the 7th June, and others were under construction. All mines intended to detonate on the 7th fired correctly. For an excellent account see Peter Barton, Peter Doyle and John Vandewalle, *Beneath Flanders Fields*, Spellmount, Staplehurst 2004. At Le Pelerin, (Trench 121), 4 mines were deliberately left unfired as they were off the southern edge of battlefield, around 1,000 yards south of the most southerly mine blown at Factory Farm. One of these four exploded in a thunderstorm in 1955. The three remaining mines (plus some others further north) still lie beneath the old battlefield.

Bluff, and St. Eloi, and on the wet alluvial deposits at Ontario Farm, where operations were also hampered by dreadfully wet conditions. This wetness led German miners to believe that British deep mining operations were most unlikely, whilst under ground in the deepest systems, 95,600 lbs. of ammonal were being placed at a depth of 125 feet at St. Eloi, and 60,000 lbs.103 feet deep at Ontario Farm. Great care had to be taken in the disposal of the blue-grey clay from the deep galleries. Being of a different colour to any surface soil, it would quickly disclose the existence of the deep British systems if spotted by German reconnaissance aircraft. It was removed from the vicinity of the shafts in sandbags via light gauge railway, and disposed of usually at night in old trench systems, shell craters or woodland. Enemy counter-mining operations were of continual concern to the British Tunnelling Companies. Generally at the depths they were mining they were relatively safe from enemy tunnellers, but at times the Germans had come very close to discovering the British galleries, and the firing of camouflets, small-charge mines fired to destroy the British tunnels, came close to causing disaster in some systems. The possibility of discovery of the mines was a perpetual worry especially at Hill 60 and Spanbroekmolen.

In addition to the mining work of the Tunnelling Companies, the Royal Engineers were engaged in preparations to move tons of ammunition, stores and equipment towards the battle front on a scale not previously attempted. 115 miles of broad gauge and 58 miles of narrow gauge railway track were laid for the purpose. Water pipe lines were earmarked for forward extension to supply each corps with 150,000 to 200,000 gallons of water per day in advance of the old front lines. Artillery from other fronts was gradually assembled throughout the last three weeks of May, and eventually 2,266 guns and howitzers were available 756 being of heavy or medium calibre. Ammunition was dumped throughout March and April, and in May 166 trains delivered 65,000 tons. A total of 144,000 tons was dumped for the whole operation.

In Flanders the German defence system was very different from that which the British had faced on the Somme in the summer of 1916. From experience, the enemy tactics had evolved, as the wet sand and clay beds of Flanders were very different to the chalk of Picardy. Gone were the deep chalk dugouts incorporated into the massive trench systems, as was the heavily manned front line. They had been replaced by a series of strong-point localities established like hornworks where ever the German front line jutted into the British position, these linked by relatively shallow trenches protected by thrown-up breastworks. From south to north, the strong-points at Trench 122, Trench 127, Ontario Farm, Kruistraat, Spanbroekmolen, Peckham Farm, Maedelstede Farm, Petit Bois, Hollandscheschuur Farm, and St. Eloi projected like powerful bastions into the British line, enabling enfilade fire to smite the flanks of any attack. Each of these strong-points and two more near the northern end of the battlefield at the Caterpillar and Hill 60, were earmarked for destruction at the very start of the battle by the series of great mines.

The enemy front line system, of front, support, and reserve trench, ran roughly along the western face of the ridge. The second line had been established nearer the top of the ridge and incorporated the ruined but fortified ridge-top villages of Messines and Wytschaete. Along the front line, in the forward zone between the front and second lines, and in the battle zone between the second and third lines, a position between 1,500 and 3,500 yards deep, had been constructed a great number of concrete blockhouses and small machine gun bunkers. The defensive plan called for 30 machine gun nests and 8 strong-points to each regimental sector of 1,500 yards of front and 3,000 yards depth. The forward zone, between the first and second lines along the ridge was expected to be devastated by the preliminary bombardment and was only lightly manned. Local counter attack formations were held behind the forward zone, and behind these again, two counter attack (*Eingreif*) divisions, two to each front division, would move up if the second line were breached. A third (Oosttaverne) line ran east of the ridge, between La Basse-Ville and the Ypres-Comines canal east of The Bluff, and 1,500 to 2.000 yards behind this ran a fourth (Warneton) line. Although the British held much higher ground at Mount Kemmel (159 metres), around 6,000 yards due west of the Messines ridge, this gave them only partial observation of the enemy held ground to the east. The folds in the eastern slope formed by the valleys of the Blauwepoortbeek, Wambeek, and Roosebeek, across which ran the German Third Line, were all below the British line of sight. Only where the line crossed the Messines spur, the Wambeek spur and the Oosttaverne spur could it be seen, at a range of 8,000 yards from Kemmel. The British also held a small area of high ground at Hill 63, 3,000 yards south-west of Messines, but only the section of the Oosttaverne Line south of Owl Trench, near Huns Walk 1,000 yards east of Messines could be seen from the hill, most of the ground east of the ridge being hidden behind the Messines spur. The artillery bombardment was arranged to take all these factors into account. On the 21st May systematic shelling and counter battery fire began, becoming intense on 31st May. Over the following eight days up to the day of the assault, the artillery fired concentrically into the German salient, unleashing a total of 3,258,000 rounds.

Owing to the generally high water table in Flanders, and as a result of the saturated sand beds being so close to the surface of the Messines ridge, the Germans had opted to build their bomb proof shelters above rather than below the ground. These shelters, known to the Germans as *Mannschafts-Eisenbeton-Unterstande,* varied in size and construction, but were all fabricated from concrete with steel reinforcements. The structures being constructed in considerable numbers not just at Messines but also along the length of the enemy Flanders Position around the Ypres Salient, were referred to by the British alternatively as Mebus, blockhouses, bunkers, pillboxes or shelters, some having one or more machine gun embrasures, while others which were purely shelters did not. For all the structures three main methods of construction were used, one of concrete poured into timber formwork amongst steel reinforcing rods, the second using pre-cast concrete blocks with steel bars passing through the blocks to secure the structure, and the third of larger blocks without the steel rods. The blocks were cast at special units well behind the lines, and transported to the front via light gauge railway. Some blockhouses had hinged closable steel rear doors, while others remained open. Size and shape of the constructions varied from large blockhouse shelters to accommodate about forty men, to the average shelter accommodating around 10 to 15, to small pillboxes to house a single machine gun and its crew. Front faces and roofs of the medium and large blockhouses were of reinforced concrete 4 feet or more thick. The structures were of an excellent quality construction, the pebbles mixed with the cement being of fine water washed gravel. Heavy steel girders and sections of old railway line strengthened the roofs and faces, whilst hooped round steel bars were used to produce a birdcage-like reinforcement for the concrete.

Artillery preparations planned for the smashing of these structures, the larger of which required a direct hit from a howitzer shell of at least 8 inches to cause its destruction. Hits or near misses from lighter calibre guns could however be catastrophic for the occupants due to concussion. A special bombardment directed at the village of Wytschaete on the 3rd June, and Messines on the 4th June, reduced anything still standing above ground in these two fortress villages to rubble, with the exception of the Mebus. The field artillery concentrated on smashing the maze of wire entanglements in the forward zone. In an attempt to make the Germans disclose the positions of their batteries and thus allow their destruction by counter battery fire, a full dress rehearsal of the creeping barrage to simulate an attack was carried out on the 3rd and 5th of June. Subsequent location of German batteries by the II Brigade Royal Flying Corps, lead to a great concentration of counter-battery fire with outstanding success. On the 4th June a continuation of fine weather was forecast and Corps Staff were informed that Zero Day would be 7th June. At midday on the 6th watches were synchronized for the simultaneous explosion of the mines at 3:50 a.m. next morning when it was believed visibility would be about 100 yards. In fact it was to be about 50 yards. By 3:00 a.m. the assault divisions, except for the 3rd Australian Division on the far right, which had been hampered by German gas shelling while moving up through Ploegsteert Wood, had gathered in their assembly trenches, and bayonets were silently fixed.

British artillery fire which had been active throughout the night calmed towards dawn and the battlefield fell silent, to the extent that nightingales could be heard singing in distant woods. The eye witness accounts of the moment the great mines erupted vary greatly depending upon the vantage point and which mine was being watched. Some were spectacular, throwing huge mushrooms of earth and debris many hundreds of feet into the air, to burst with a brilliant flash of white or orange flame, while others were less so, leaving little evidence of their power even on the surface. The 19 mines, some of which had been in the ground for over a year, had exploded without a single failure creating an earthquake-like effect which was felt for miles around. The shock wave terrified the German garrison in Lille 15 miles distant, and is reported to have been felt in London. Unintentionally the mines had not all been fired entirely simultaneously, there being a time spread of about 22 seconds between the first explosions at Factory Farm in the south, which fired 7 seconds early, to the last at Spanbroekmolen in the centre, which fired 15 seconds late. Subsequent descriptions of the heart of the ridge being blow out by the mines were totally exaggerated, as even these great explosions were not capable of such a movement of earth; but the result of their firing certainly shattered the morale of the enemy. The effect on the German garrisons in the front line positions was either fatal or sufficient to stun, to the extent that in the area of the eruptions little or no resistance was offered, the time delay between the detonations serving to increase the panic effect right along the enemy line. Immediately after the explosions, the whole might of the Second Army artillery opened at its planned rate of fire. The three barrage belts descended on the first 700 yards of the German lines and the counter battery groups deluged all known German battery positions with gas. Plumer had given his infantry the best possible start. It was now their turn. Officer's whistles blew, they climbed from the assembly trenches, and the forward assault companies of 9 divisions advanced towards the enemy.

The bastion strong-points within the German Front Line had ceased to exist, large craters marking the positions where they had once menaced the British line.[98] Within 35 minutes the lightly manned forward zone had been easily overrun, and by 5:00 a.m. the front trench of the German Second Line along the forward face of the ridge had been taken. After a two hour halt on this line the protective barrage thickened and the advance continued across the flat ridge top towards the first main objective, the rear trench of the German Second Line on the back crest of the ridge. The New Zealand Division had a tough fight clearing strong-points in the rubble remains of Messines, while 3,000 yards to the north the Irish had cleared most of Wytschaete and by 8:00 a.m. the 36th and 16th Divisions were on their objectives, east of the ridge-top road. At around 8:40 a.m. another short advance was made to secure an observation line, from which the battalions to continue the advance towards the Oosttaverne Line in the afternoon would jump-off. At this point it was expected the enemy counter-attack divisions would attempt to throw the British back off the ridge. But not until around 11:00 a.m. were German columns, around two battalions in strength, first seen crossing the Ypres – Comines canal. At 11:45 others were seen approaching up the Wambeek valley, and then another group at 12:45 up the Blauwepoortbeek valley. The counter-attack finally crossed the Oosttaverne Line at around 1:45 but was broken by artillery fire, and machine gun fire from the observation line, the enemy falling back into shell-holes and onto the Oosttaverne position by 2:10 p.m. The second phase of the attack was initially planned to begin at 1:10 p.m., but at 10:00 a.m. due to difficulties experienced in getting forward over bad ground, Plumer postponed the advance to the Oosttaverne Line until 3:10 p.m. So far everything had gone remarkably well but now there was to be a reverse. At 3:10 in the afternoon two brigades of the 4th Australian Division advanced towards the Oosttaverne Line, the right brigade, the 12th, supported by the 37th Battalion of the 3rd Australian Division. After some very tough fighting this brigade group secured most of the southern end of the Oosttaverne Line. To the left, the northern brigade, the 13th, quickly ran into trouble. The 33rd Brigade of the British 11th Division, in support of IX Corps, was to have moved across the ridge between Messines and Wytschaete and advanced to the left of the Australian 13th Brigade. They were late arriving on the battlefield and the Australian left flank was left totally exposed. Instead of attacking eastwards down the Wambeek spur towards the Oosttaverne Line, the 52nd battalion on the left of the 13th Australian Brigade veered far too the left in an endeavour to gain touch with the 33rd British Brigade. The 52nd reached the Oosttaverne Line with little trouble, but a dangerous gap had developed on their right, and for 1,000 yards to the south no attack had been made on the German Third Line.

---

[98] At Ontario Farm, due to the geology and the depth of the mine there was no crater, just a steaming and foul smelling swamp where the German strong-point had once stood.

The 12th Brigade, 3,000 yards to the south, had meanwhile inadvertently advanced about 300 yards beyond their objective. An S.O.S. signal to the artillery to assist in stopping a German counter-attack at around 5:30 p.m. caused a number of casualties from friendly fire, and a premature order to retire to get clear of the barrage resulted in some of the 12th Brigade falling-back through the observation line towards the ridge. Most of the 37th Battalion however stayed put. Forward artillery observers of the New Zealand Division, from their positions on the ridge saw, in poor light, at between 8:00 and 9:00 p.m. what they believed was a German-counter attack approaching the observation line, and asked for a barrage to search between that line and the Oosttaverne Line. The resulting fire caught the remainder of the 12th Brigade and the 37th Battalion who were still holding their forward positions. Suffering considerable casualties beneath their own barrage the last of the Australian garrison holding the southern end of the Oosttaverne Line also fell back towards the British line. The whole southern section of the German Third Line, plus the 1,000 yard gap between the Blauwepoortbeek and Wambeek brooks was now left open to the enemy. A similar situation arose in the central and northern sectors of the battlefield at around 8:30 p.m. when a suspected counter-attack prompted a barrage to be fired too short, resulting in a withdrawal from the Oosttaverne Line. Wrongly informed that the withdrawal was due to an enemy counter-attack, the artillery shortened its range even more, to stand just forward of the observation line, inflicting further friendly casualties. When the protective barrage ceased fire at around 10:00 p.m. the infantry again moved forward and reoccupied the German Third Line. An order from Lieut.-General Godley commanding II Anzac Corps for the artillery to only fire east of the German Third Line solved most of the friendly fire problems, and the southern section of the line was reoccupied by the Australians the following morning. After a number of partially successful but costly attacks, the enemy finally abandoned the last sections of the Oosttaverne line in the early hours of the 11th June. The observation over the enemy old third line position was considered inadequate, and Plumer ordered a further short advance which was carried out successfully between the 12th and 14th June with little enemy intervention.

    The battle had been a complete success, but there were inevitably some lessons to be learnt. Casualties on the morning of the first day had not been as high as expected, but were nevertheless higher than necessary, due to some unfortunate tactical errors. Crowding on the ridge-top through the premature deployment of reserves, and the funnelling effect of the shape of the battlefield had resulted in numerous casualties from hostile shelling. After the initial success the friendly fire casualties had been a bitter disappointment. Some have blamed the level of casualties on Haig's desire to push on over the ridge to the Oosttaverne Line on the first day. But the capture of the German Third Line was certainly important to future operations, and was well within the capacity of Second Army to attempt on the first day. The setbacks had largely not been due to enemy action, but to misunderstandings in command and control of the battle, and the hazy June weather and smoke had hindered good observation. Most of the problems encountered would not have occurred if there had not been two independent defensive operations, one responsible for the divisions which attacked and held the first objective, and the other for the reserve forces which attacked the German Third Line, each group with its own artillery support. That the 33rd Brigade had not arrived on the battlefield at the allotted time had also caused a serious problem. These were tactical errors in the timing of infantry movement and in artillery support planning and control. They were not an inevitable result of Haig's requirement to capture the enemy Third Line on the first day. The belief by observers on the ridge that enemy counter-attacks had thrust west of the Oosttaverne Line, (which later they had not), and the fact that some infantry had pushed too far forward, had resulted in much of the friendly fire. Explaining the mistakes at the southern end of the battlefield the Australian Official Historian says, 'Thus, owing to the action of its own artillery – for which defects in the maps, over eagerness of the infantry, over anxiety of some of the staff and commanders, and a dangerous degree of inaccuracy in the barrage, were responsible, the whole of the final objective between the Blauwepoortbeek valley and the Douve had by 9:00

p.m. been left open to the enemy'.⁹⁹ The Oosttaverne Line was well protected by many Mebus and if it had not been at least partly secured on the first day, it is likely that it would have been reinforced more heavily by the enemy before any renewed attack. The difficulty the Australians experienced later in evicting the enemy from the blockhouses in the Blauwepoortbeek depression proved the wisdom of attempting its capture on the first day.

The lessons of better control of reserves and artillery were both well learnt by Second Army, and changes were made to prevent the same mistakes happening again. It became clear that to be successfully overcome the concrete blockhouses required a special attack technique by infantry, and this experience was of vital importance in training for the forthcoming main attack to the north. By the 14th June the battle was over with virtually all objectives taken. The careful and painstaking planning and preparation had paid off. Messines was heralded as a thorough success, albeit of a local nature which was completely in accordance with its concept. Total casualties between the 1st and 12th June had been over 24,500, and around half of these had been in II Anzac Corps. There had been 7,350 prisoners taken, and 48 guns, 218 machine guns, and 60 trench mortars had been captured. German casualties, although difficult to establish were also believed to have been around 25,000.¹⁰⁰ It had been a preliminary and essential part of the master plan to free the Belgian coast of the enemy, but now the work must begin in earnest and with all speed to prepare the next step.

Political machinations
Cassel, Pétain meets Haig the 7th June

On the day of the Messines battle, Pétain had taken his train to Cassel where he again met with Haig. He was at pains to make it clear that although the situation had improved, he was still concerned about the doubtful state of discipline within the French Army. Two divisions had refused to relieve two others in the line due to lack of leave. Men had been tried and some had been shot, with the support of the Government. In the Army morale was improving, as the

---

⁹⁹ Charles E. W. Bean. *Official History of Australia in the War of 1914-1918 Vol IV. The Australian Imperial Force in France 1917* (hereafter AOA) Sydney: Angus and Robertson p641. 2007 Australian War Memorial, Canberra.

¹⁰⁰ John Mosier claims that the Germans had already evacuated the ridge four days before the attack and it was therefore an empty section of terrain. He also claims British casualties of 'perhaps 50,000'. John Mosier. *The Myth of the Great War* p282. Denis Winter concurs stating 'the much-trumpeted victory of Messines was little more than the capture of a few scattered pillboxes'. *Haig's Command* p96. Neither author explains exactly where they believe the Germans had withdrawn to prior to the attack. But they had certainly not withdrawn from the Bluff, from White Chateau, or from the Damm Strasse where around 400 prisoners were taken, as bitter fighting was experienced in all three locations. Nor do they explain the high levels of fighting by the Irish Divisions in the ruins of Wytschaete, or for the bunkers along the ridge top at Pick House and Swayne's Farm, or the fighting and high casualties in the New Zealand Division for the ruins of Messines, and the resistance faced around the Douve by the 3rd Australian Division. In fact all they tell us is that the area was evacuated by the enemy. It is a pity that the British and Dominion Divisions which fought on the 7th June did not find it so abandoned. Prior to the attack Colonel von Lossberg and Lieutenant-Colonel Wetzell had warned that it was essential to withdraw from at least the positions threatened by mines. Rupprecht and Chief of Staff Kuhl went further considering it wise to evacuate the Messines – Wytschaete salient. This proposal was put to a *Fourth Army* conference on the 30th April but was rejected by local commanders who felt the recently improved positions *on the forward face* of the ridge were favourable for mobile defence and the launching of counter-attacks. By the 3rd May Rupprecht considered that withdrawal to the third line (Oosttaverne – Warneton) was no longer practical. After the event Kuhl lamented that Rupprecht had not 'simply ordered the withdrawal despite the objections made to his proposal at the *Fourth Army* conference on the 30th April; the German Army would thereby have been spared one of the worst tragedies of the War'. Kuhl ii p144 quoted in BOH p94

spreading of the mutiny appeared to have been checked, but in Paris the domestic situation was still volatile, with French Socialists wishing to make a trip to Stockholm to parley with German Socialists, but being prevented in doing so by the Government.[101] Whether Haig's fears for both the French Army and Government were in reality unduly excessive, or are now considered to be unfounded, is of no consequence. The important point is that all Haig knew for certain was the little that Pétain was telling him, and none of it was good news. He would have been guilty of gross dereliction of duty and professional incompetence had he risked ignoring the possibilities of the immense dangers posed by the fragile state of the French. Some word of the troubles in the French Army had *certainly got back to the War Cabinet* in London. In the minutes of War Cabinet 156 held at Downing Street on the 6th June is noted the following. 'Trouble in French Army. The Director of Military Operations reported that there was serious trouble, amounting to mutiny in a number of French regiments, partly as a result of Socialist propaganda, partly on the ground that native troops had been allowed to fire on strikers in the neighbourhood of Paris. It was hoped that this disaffection would be set right in five or six days.'[102] At the meeting of the War Cabinet on the 8th June, Lieutenant-General Wilson, (as senior British liaison officer at G.Q.G., with his subordinate Lieutenant-Colonel Spears probably the closest British officers to the heart of the trouble) warned that the French 'would not stick it much longer',[103] and that Pétain could not support Haig's Messines attack with his promised action at Malmaison on the 10th. The report had been practically confirmed from Paris by Lord Esher, and according to Cabinet Secretary Hankey, made all present very anxious.

The Cabinet Committee on War Policy

On the 8th June, in an effort to streamline policy-making, the whole question of the future conduct of the War had been handed over to a Cabinet Committee on War Policy. Its members were the Prime Minister, Lord Curzon, Lord Milner, Mr Bonar Law and General Smuts, with Sir Maurice Hankey as secretary to the Committee. Although in a position and with the power to make decisions on policy and planning, little advice, few suggestions, and no rational alternatives were to emerge from this Committee, to either challenge or modify Haig's plans for the Northern Offensive. The lack of precise leadership or helpful support from Lloyd George or any other member of the Committee raises the question of its relevance to military policy. Between the 11th of June and its final meeting on the 11th October, the substance and value of the Committee's considerations was not to improve.

At its first meeting on the 11th June, the Committee were again given *a full account of the problems within the French Army* by Colonel Spears, the very experienced British liaison officer at G.Q.G. who had been with the French since the early days of 1914. Spears confirmed that a state of mutiny existed in some regiments. He went on to claim that the British attack at Messines had come as a great tonic to the French, that British actions were the mainstay of their morale, and that in his opinion there would be most serious results if the Germans launched a major offensive against them. He advised that the situation should be watched very carefully, since he felt that a small incident may lead to very serious trouble or even to revolution, which if it occurred would take the form of anarchy, as there was no commanding individual or group responsible for the subversion.[104] The War Cabinet had therefore been warned from several different but reliable sources of the grave state of the French Army.[105]

---

[101] Extensive leave facilities were granted to the French soldiers (ten days in every four months), resulting in the permanent weakening of the effective strength of the French Army by some 340,000 men This compared to an average figure of 80,000 men on leave in the British Army. Charteris *Field Marshal Haig* p266 and Davidson *Haig:Master of the Field* p19
[102] National Archives, minutes of War Cabinet June 6th 1917 CAB23/1
[103] Hankey Diaries, Churchill Archives, Churchill College Cambridge HNKY 1/2
[104] National Archives, WO106/404 Spears (Spears) report 11th June 1917
[105] National Archives Cabinet Committee on War Policy, 1st meeting 11th June CAB27-6. For an alternative view see Denis Winter *Haig's Command* pp86-87

Haig's memorandum to the Cabinet and the Chateris intelligence appraisal. 12th June

At G.H.Q. the problems within the French camp were also exercising the mind of the Commander-in-Chief. On the 2nd June, five days before the Messines battle Pétain had made it clear to Haig that the French Army, for reasons already mentioned, would not be able to entirely fulfil its commitments. Now that this had been made apparent, in theory Haig's future actions were limited, as without French support, in line with the wishes of the Cabinet the Northern Offensive should be postponed. At around the same time however intelligence information provided by Brigadier-General Charteris, the head of the Intelligence Section at G.H.Q., led Haig to believe that the German Army, due to losses suffered in the Champagne, on the Aisne, and at Arras in the spring and early summer, was in fact in a parlous state, both in manpower and morale. A summary of the so called 'facts' put in writing on the 12th June stated that it was a fair deduction that, given a continuance of the existing circumstances and of the effort of the Allies, Germany may well be forced to conclude a peace on Britain's terms before the end of the year.

This information, however critically it may now be viewed, was in Haig's opinion, sufficiently positive to present to the Cabinet in support of his argument to proceed with the Northern Offensive, even without unqualified French support. On the 12th June he wrote a memorandum to the War Cabinet, attaching the intelligence summary as an appendix, and also driving home the fact that his forces were not, due to inadequate drafts, up to War strength and had not yet been provided with their full compliment of guns. This memorandum was written in a considerably more bullish tone than the memorandum sent on the 1st May. He gave his perception of the state of the German Army, based on the information from Charteris, and stated that he was adverse to any delay which allowed the Germans opportunity to recover. 'With the drafts and guns already promised, however, I consider, on present indications, that it will be possible to carry through *at least a portion* of the operations intended, and my plans and preparations are being made to *advance by stages* so arranged that, while each stage will give a definite and useful result, it will be possible for me to discontinue the advance if and when it appears that the means at my disposal are insufficient to justify a further effort....

According to reports, the endurance of the German nation is being tested so severely that discontent there has already assumed considerable proportions. The German Government, helped by the long disciplinary training of the people, is still able to control this discontent; but every realization of the failure of the submarine campaign increases the difficulty of doing so, and further defeats in the field may have unexpectedly great results, which may come with unexpected suddenness.

The German Army, too, shows unmistakable signs of deterioration in many ways and the cumulative effect of further defeats may at any time yield greater results in the field than we can absolutely rely on gaining.

From a careful study of the conditions, I feel justified in stating that continued pressure with as little delay as possible certainly promises *at least very valuable results*; whereas relaxation of pressure now would strengthen belief that the Allies are becoming totally exhausted, and that Germany can outlast them. Waning hope in Germany would be revived, and time would be gained to replenish food, ammunition and other requirements. In fact many of the advantages already gained by us would be lost, and this would be certainly be realized by, and would have a depressing effect on, our Armies in the field, who have made such great efforts to gain them.

The depressing effect in France would be especially great and especially dangerous. At the present crisis in the war French hope must have something to feed on. The hope of American assistance is not sufficient for the purpose. It is still too distant and the French at the moment are living a good deal on the hope of further British success. They can and will assist in these by keeping the enemy on their front fully employed, wearing him down, and preventing him from withdrawing divisions to oppose us. But they feel unable to do more at present than

this, and *it is useless to expect it of them* – although any considerable British success and signs of a breakdown in German power of resistance would probably have an electrifying effect.....
On the other hand I am equally convinced that to fail in concentrating our forces in the Western theatre, or to divert them from it, would be most dangerous. It might lead to the collapse of France. It would certainly encourage Germany. And it would discourage our own officers and men very considerably. The desired military results, possible in France, are not possible elsewhere. I am aware that my motives in stating this may be misunderstood, but I trust that in the interests of the Empire at what is undoubtedly a critical period in the war, whatever value the War Cabinet may attach to my opinion may not be discounted by any doubt of such a kind.....
Given sufficient force and provided no greater transfer of German troops is made in time from East to West, *it is probable* that the Belgian coast could be cleared this summer and the defeats of the German troops entailed in doing so might quite probably lead to their collapse....
Without sufficient force I shall not attempt to clear the coast, and my efforts will be restricted to gaining such victories as are within my reach, thereby improving my position for the winter and opening up possibilities for further operations hereafter if and when the necessary means are provided.'[106] (Authors italics) It is interesting to compare Haig's measured predictions for his offensive with the rash promises that Nivelle had made back in January, which Lloyd George had accepted with confidence when it was the French who would be doing much of the fighting. Haig was putting the likelihood of a break through at no better than *probable*, whilst claiming the advance would be in line with the agreements reached in Paris, by stages.

There is no question however, that backed by the optimistic G.H.Q. intelligence assessments, Haig was painting too rosy a picture of the decline in enemy strength, both in Germany and at the front. But whilst he was clearly attempting to sell the offensive which he believed so necessary to a sceptical War Cabinet, he was also quite forthright in declaring that there was every possibility he may not clear the Belgian coast, but felt the operation was essential for other equally valid reasons. Haig had not mentioned his personal knowledge of the dangerous mutinies in the French Army. By the 12th June he had been aware of Pétain's situation for ten days, but made no mention of this very secret information to the War Cabinet. He had however gone as far as he could to hint at it, and made the point that to expect too much of the French, as Lloyd George already knew from other sources, was pointless.
Others were however of very different opinion regarding the G.H.Q. intelligence assessments. Brigadier-General G.M.W. Macdonogh, Director of Military Intelligence, General Staff, at the War Office, was in disagreement with Charteris regarding the state of the German Army and was of the opinion that a probable Russian collapse would greatly increase German rifle and gun strength on the Western Front, to slightly greater than that of the Allies. A memorandum from Robertson, to the War Cabinet summarising the D.M.I's findings stated that without French support, 'it is obvious that offensive operations on our front would offer no chance of success; and our best course would be to remain on the defensive, strengthen our positions, economise our reserves in man-power and material, and hope that the balance would be *eventually* redressed by American assistance'.[107] This was a position from which Haig was becoming somewhat isolated. The Commander-in Chief was, at least on paper, certainly at variance with the D.M.I. if not the C.I.G.S. The difference in interpretation of the intelligence was smoothed out by Robertson's telegram to Haig on the 13th suggesting that the G.H.Q. intelligence summary appendix should not be circulated to the War Cabinet, and mention of it should be removed from the memorandum, making the point that different estimates of German strength coming from two military sources would be regrettable. He advised Haig, 'you will have opportunity during discussions here to give such information regarding enemy's reserves as you deem necessary'.[108] Haig agreed to the omission, and the War Committee judged his conclusions in conjunction with the intelligence interpretation of the General Staff at the War Office, not that of G.H.Q. The War Committee, given their doubts regarding the situation in the French Army, and

---

[106] National Archives, Haig to CIGS for War Cabinet (OAD 478) CAB27/7
[107] National Archives, Robertson to War Cabinet CAB27/6
[108] National Archives telegram C.I.G.S. to Haig, WO158/24

the General Staff's interpretation of the possible consequences of the Russian situation, considered Haig's outlook overly optimistic, and for the moment *hesitated* to give its approval to the second phase of the Northern Operation.

Two days after writing his important memorandum for the War Policy Committee, the conclusions of which had been for the moment rejected, Haig held an Army Commanders Conference at Lillers. He stated that there were no changes to the general plans made on the 7th May. 'Underlying the general intention of wearing out the Enemy is the idea of securing the Belgian coast and connecting with the Dutch frontier. The nature and size of the several steps which we take towards that objective must depend on our *effectives* and the replacement of our *guns*. Roughly these [steps] are.... 1/ Capture bridgehead formed of the Passchendaele – Staden – Clerken ridge. 2/ Push on towards Roulers – Thourout so as to take coast defences in rear. 3/ Land by surprise in conjunction with attack from Nieuport.....If effectives or guns inadequate it may be necessary to call a halt after No.1 is gained.'[109] (Haig's italics) On the 5th July he produced a memorandum to summarise the main issues covered at the conference. Second Army's task was confirmed as cooperating with the right flank of Fifth Army, and to be prepared to gradually take over the defence of the main ridge as far north as Passchendaele, or possibly even further. The point regarding an advance to the Courtrai – Roulers line, taken out of context and much ridiculed in some accounts, was made at this juncture. Haig's memorandum, written for the advice of the Army Commanders actually read, 'the Commander of the Second Army will also be prepared with plans to develop an advance towards the line Warneton – Menin, or push forward on the right of the Fifth Army to the line Courtrai – Roulers (throwing out a flank guard along the line of the Lys), if circumstances should render such movements desirable as the situation develops'.[110] The suggestion does not sound so ridiculous or fanciful when presented in its entirety.[111] An outline of Fifth Army operations, and the diversionary actions expected of those Armies operating south of the Lys was included in the memorandum. Haig also made the point, 'the above outline of possibilities is issued to enable Army Commanders to foresee and prepare for what may be required of them. The progress of events may demand modifications or alterations of plan from time to time and, - especially in view of the comparatively short period of fine weather we can count on, - our progress before winter sets in may fall short of what would otherwise have been within our power for this year'.[112] The latter statement, although of great importance, is less often mentioned, as it does not suit the conventional 'anti-Haig' argument. Once more Haig had repeated that there was no guarantee that the offensive would reach the coast.

On the 17th June Haig backed up his memo of the 12th with a further paper to the War Policy Committee outlining in greater detail his strategic objectives, introducing the argument that a short advance would bring Ostend within range of his guns and place Dunkirk beyond the range of German guns. He pointed out that the enemy communications ran through a narrow corridor between the front lines and the Dutch border, and a limited advance sufficient to bring the Roulers – Thourout railway within range would severely restrict railway communication with the coast through Ghent and Bruges. A further short advance would bring Bruges within gun range which would probably induce the evacuation of Zeebrugge. Haig expanded the argument still farther and explored the enormous possibilities should the Dutch frontier be reached, with the possibility of the Dutch joining the Allies, and the freeing of Antwerp, placing

---

[109] Douglas Haig. Diaries and Letters, pp299/300
[110] National Archives, Haig to Army Commanders 5th July, WO158/311
[111] Haig's objectives were certainly less optimistic than those expressed by Nivelle for Hiag's Armies issued on the 4th April.: 'Dans tout les Armées, les opérations d'exploitation doivent être conçues dans l'espirit le plus large et le plus audacieux. Dans cet ordre d'idéas: - Les Armés Britanniques, après s'être emparées de Cambrai et de Douai, devront se porter sue Valienciennes, puis sur Mons, Tournai et Courtrai, en élargissant sans cesse leur action vers le Nord, au fur et à mesure de leur progression à l'intérieur du territoire reconçuis.' Nivelle to Haig 4th April 1917, National Archives, WO158/37.
[112] National Archives, Haig to Army Commanders 5th July, WO158/311

the enemy right flank in an impossible position, the Germans then either accepting terms or undertaking a disastrous retreat. He then reiterated a number of points on which his strategic argument was based, and which directly countered any argument supporting an offensive on any other front. The Flanders offensive would directly and seriously threaten the main enemy on which the opposing Coalition depended. The main front was in easy reach of the supply bases, covered these bases from attack, and was infinitely more easily developed and maintained than any other theatre. A short advance would assist the navy and prevent further air attacks on England, and on no other front would such a limited advance promise such far reaching results on Germany. As a direct counter to Lloyd George's Italian plan Haig claimed that, 'in other theatres we can only employ detachments, seeking to attain results by indirect methods, and under most difficult conditions of maintenance. Time and space considerations would be so unfavourable to us that if any indirect threat appeared dangerous to Germany it would be well within her power to take timely steps to counteract it either by direct attack on us at a more vital point or by moving troops to meet our indirect thrust. Lastly, while an increase in our force in the Western theatre would have an encouraging effect on France, where encouragement is of very high importance now, any reduction of our force here at this juncture might have most severe consequences'.[113]

The Prime Minister had meanwhile compiled his thoughts into a memorandum of his own, entitled 'Arguments for the plan of a Great Offensive in France'. It began with three short paragraphs outlining Haig's arguments *for* the Northern offensive. The next section, over six times as long as the first, stated his arguments *against* the plan. He began by pointing out the possible hazards to morale should the offensive fail, and explained the lack of Allied numerical superiority to launch such an attack. He intimated that to some degree he was aware of the French disarray, and that he felt it unwise to assume that the French soldier could match the Germans man for man. 'In the face of repeated warnings we have received from well informed and competent observers, it would be madness on our part to proceed on such an assumption. Our two military representatives with the French Army [Spears and Wilson] have deemed it to be their painful duty to intimate in the most explicit terms that we cannot this year rely upon the French Army to take its full part in such an enterprise as we contemplate. For the moment its fighting spirit is impaired – it is full of distrust, suspicion and discouragement.'[114] He continued, emphasising the dangers of the British attacking alone without full French support. 'It is therefore proposed that we should rush into the greatest battle of the War, against an enemy almost equal in number, quite equal in equipment, still the greatest army in Europe in everything that constitutes an efficient fighting force, with larger reserves than our own, to make up the deficiency during this year, holding formidable defensive positions which he has taken three years to strengthen and perfect; and we are to launch this attack with doubtful support from our most powerful and important ally....I ask whether the C.I.G.S. anticipates anything better than Vimy and Messines can ensue as the result of this attack. Brilliant preliminary success followed by weeks of desperate and sanguine struggles, leading to nothing except perhaps the driving of the enemy back a few barren miles – beyond that nothing to show except a ghastly casualty list.' Ironically, mindful of very much the same concerns, Lloyd George and Haig had come to diametrically opposed ideas. The Prime Minister's greatest reason for *not* mounting the offensive, the weakness of the French, had become one of Haig's principle reasons for doing so. Lloyd George summed up his 'anti-offensive' argument. 'Since our last review of the situation, when the Commander-in-Chief was present, we have had a good deal of authoritative fresh evidence as to the condition of the French Army. We should be guilty of a serious dereliction of duty if we did not give full weight to the very grave reports presented by General Wilson, Colonel Spears, and the Naval Attaché and to the important information we have received as to the report made to the French Ambassador by M. Abel Ferny. Their reports have more than confirmed the apprehensions we had formed, and we should not be justified in

---

[113] National Archives, Haig to War Policy Committee 17th June, WO158/24
[114] Parliamentary Archives, Lloyd George Papers, June 1917 LG/F/161/1/2

risking scores of thousands of British lives on the assumption that we could disregard the solemn admonitions involved in these documents.'

The Prime Minister then launched into his main theme, the alternative strategy to Haig's offensive. The main errors of the War so far, as he saw it, were first the refusal to recognise the European battlefield as one indivisible whole, and second concentrating the strongest armies to attack on the strongest fronts. Austria and Turkey were the weakest fronts, and the overthrow of either would begin the disintegration of the Central Powers. The defeat of Austria might lead to a separate peace. To defeat Austria it would be necessary for the Italians to capture Trieste, for the Austrians had vowed not to relinquish it by agreement. But the Italians were only 8 miles from Trieste. French and British guns could be provided to support this venture, and the Italians with plenty of reserves of manpower could do the fighting. Austria had no reserves of manpower and Trieste might be captured before the Germans came up in support of their ally. Turkey and Bulgaria would be left isolated without supplies or support from Germany and could be easily defeated. The Russian Armies could then concentrate against Germany, and the Italians could release men either for an attack on Turkey, or to support France. Lloyd George clearly felt that Italy was by far the best place to confront the main enemy. 'What does it matter whether we fight Germans in the north of France or in Italy? The only difference would be that if we fought them in France we should be doing it at the expense of our own troops, whereas in Italy we can use the enormous reserves of the Italians.' He recognised that the French were tired, so why not 'give the Italians a turn' while the French were resting. If the Germans did come to the aid of the Austrians, then at least the fighting would not be on the Western Front and the 'wastage would be Italian not British and French.' The Prime Minister thought it unlikely in any event that the Germans would detach great numbers from the Western Front, but if they did the 'French might make a push there'. He considered that Italy would be so reliant upon the Allies after the defeat of Austria that she could be 'forced to carry out her bargain' in an attack on the Turks or in supporting the French. The Germans, subsequent to the defeat of the Austrians, would not dare to leave the border un-garrisoned and the Allies could then concentrate the whole of their strength in breaking German power. The Prime Minister was certain in his own mind that the defeat of Austria was possible and that she would make a separate peace. The actions proposed would all help the Russian offensive planned for September, which might then become decisive.

How the Prime Ministers plan was to be put into practice, relying as it did on the political and military agreement and co-operation of *all* the Allies, and founded on the belief that the armies of those Allies were of equal fighting worth man-for-man to his own Army and could be relied upon to carry out his great scheme, remained unclear. Lloyd George was moving forces on his war map whichhe did not have the power to move. According to the French, and the advice of British liaison officers, the French Army could not be relied upon, and there was turmoil within France. There was civil unrest in Italy, and the C.I.G.S. did not have a high regard of Italian military capabilities. In the case of the Russians they could already be regarded as virtually out of the game. In Petrograd the Winter Palace had been stormed, in Kronstadt the fleet had mutinied, and on the 15th March the Tsar had abdicated. Power in the country was now split, nominally in the hands of the provisional government drawn from the ranks of the wealthy and middle classes, but with communications and banks controlled by the executive committee of the Soviet. It was not only Lloyd George who misunderstood the Russian situation. The provincial government held to the belief that the revolution had been an uprising against autocracy. But to the Russian people and the soldiers it was a revolt against tyranny, poverty, but above all *against the War*. On March the 14th the passing of 'Order No.1' legalised soldier's soviets, and placed the Army under the orders of the Soviet in all political matters. The Russian Army was continuing its slow disintegration. Minister of War Kerensky, under great pressure from the Allies, including the threat of withdrawal of financial support, had embarked on a tour of the Army to attempt to win back the allegiance of at least some of the soldiers, with a view to launching an offensive in Galicia. The doomed Kerensky offensive was to be opened by Russian artillery on the 29th June. It was to be the last hold the Allies were to have over Russia. The Allied opponents of the Central Powers, which Lloyd George had lined up so carefully on his war map, appeared to be dropping out of line one-by-one. But the Prime Minister had put forward no alternative strategy, other than the fanciful and unworkable proposal directed against Austria. If the War Cabinet wished to endorse a major offensive, they had no realistic alternative plan to Haig's offensive in Flanders, and in all honesty they must have known it.

The 7th, 8th and 9th Meetings of the Cabinet Committee on War Policy – 19th 20th and 21st June[115]

At the 7th meeting of the Committee at 11:00 a.m. on the 19th June, Haig, who had crossed to England for the purpose, was to present for the first time the details of his Flanders project with its distant objectives including the clearing of the Belgian coast. Lloyd George opened by commending Haig on the powerful statement made by his recent paper arguing his case.
From the outset it was clear that the possible scope of Haig's offensive went far beyond anything agreed at the Paris Conference. But the issue was undoubtedly clouded by the fact that Haig had always promised a step by step advance which should take him through the enemy Flanders position *first*, before considering a breakout beyond the ridge, once beyond the heaviest of the German defences. Then holding the present Committee hostage to the concerns expressed by Asquith's administration, he reminded the members that his choice of Flanders for the offensive was in line with the much quoted War Cabinet resolution of the 23rd November 1916, in that there was 'no measure in which it attached greater importance than the expulsion of enemy forces from the Belgian coast'. The strength of the opposing armies on the Western Front was discussed, the Allied figure being 2,455,000 and the enemy 2,149,000. Haig pointed out that he had superiority in field guns, but not in the more important heavy guns, in which there was approximate parity. Information indicated that the enemy were short of ammunition and were restricting its use. The Prime Minister stated his concern that Haig did not posses sufficient superiority in either men or guns, and went on to query projected estimated casualties. Haig hoped that the loss rate of 100,000 men per month, which had been the case since the opening of the Arras battle, should not be so great in the forthcoming offensive, pointing out that he had persisted with operations at Arras to show that he had fully supported the Nivelle offensive, and that the tactics to be used in Flanders would be different. Lord Curzon returned to the question of numbers, asking Haig if he had enough men and guns to succeed, and Lord Milner also expressed concern that Haig had the necessary strength to carry the operation through. Haig said he was happy to start with the forces at his disposal to at least secure the first objective, the 'Clercken (Passchendaele) Ridge'. Lloyd George persisted with the lack of resources theme, indicating that German reserves were greater than those of the Allies. Curzon astutely requested exact figures of the size of the force Haig intended to employ, whether Robertson could maintain that force in men and guns, and whether further forces were available to develop Haig's offensive in the manner planned. Haig replied that 42 British and 6 French divisions were being concentrated in Flanders, and Robertson added that ammunition supplies were adequate, and as long as no guns were moved to other theatres their numbers were also adequate. With regards to manpower Robertson claimed that the Army in France was presently 20,000 -30,000 men below strength, but that the War Office hoped to send another 150,000 men by the middle of August, and considered the position sufficiently favourable to proceed in accordance with Haig's plan. The politicians were doubtful that the French would be able to support the initiative, and Lloyd George was sure that the main strength of the enemy would be deployed against Haig. The argument flowed backwards and forwards, the Committee generally negative, whilst Haig and Robertson attempted to counter the suggested pitfalls as positively as they could. With a degree of frustration Haig claimed that his plan was 'the best he knew of', that it was necessary to go on engaging the enemy, and he was confident that he could reach the first

---

[115] National Archives, 7th, 8th and 9th meetings of the Cabinet Committee on War Policy – 19th 20th and 21st June, CAB27/6

objective, *but nothing was certain in war and he could give no guarantees*. Attempting to balance the possible advantages of success against the inevitable distress of failure, Bonar Law wrestled with whether enough would be gained from the attack to justify the gamble, whilst Lord Milner declared that to clear the Belgian coast of the enemy was 'worth half a million men'. Lord Curzon referred to two memoranda from the Admiralty which had so far not been discussed, but which in his opinion carried weight. Lloyd George questioned whether it would be possible to attempt the first phase of the operation in the event of insufficient forces being available for the whole, to which Haig replied that it would be possible to initially capture at least the ridge. The Prime Minister wound up the conference by making clear the political difficulties involved in endeavouring to raise manpower for the Army, adding that the Russian revolution had had an unsettling effect in all countries, and that there was a good deal of talk of revolution everywhere. He questioning whether it would not be preferable to wait until 1918 to mount an offensive, to a time when the French Army had been resuscitated by the intervention of America. He reminded Haig and Robertson that Britain was carrying the full burden of the War at that time. Lloyd George had closed the proceedings with no inspirational or uplifting message, and had for the moment in no way endorsed the plans of his military commanders to resume the offensive at Ypres.

The 8th meeting of the Committee was held at 11:00 a.m. on the 20th June and was mainly concerned with how to counter recent German air raids on London. Haig had placed two scout squadrons from the Western Front at the disposal of Field-Marshal French, Commander-in-Chief Home Forces, one based at Calais and one in Kent, to attempt to intercept the enemy raids. At that time home defence consisted of three squadrons of obsolete aircraft, incapable of confronting the Gotha bombers, which had recently commenced raids on London from airfields on the Flemish coast. Lloyd George was as ever asking the military for precise answers to completely unanswerable questions, requesting Major-General Trenchard to confirm that if a raid was seen leaving the Belgian coast how many enemy machines could he count on being shot down by the scouts based in Kent.

At noon on the same day the 9th meeting of the Committee was convened, the proceedings being opened by a long statement by Robertson. He began by making clear his opposition to the Prime Ministers preferred offensive against Austria, which he considered was not in a position to make a separate peace in any event. He pointed out the considerable advantage the enemy possessed in operating on internal lines of communication, reiterating the points Haig made in his paper of the 17th. He added that the Allies relied on two inadequate railways into Italy, whereas the enemy enjoyed the use of five, one into the Trentino and four to the Isonzo, and any concentration they may wish to make could be accomplished more quickly than the Allies. He saw the surest way of preventing the Germans moving against Italy in mass, and of keeping Russia in the War, was to maintain pressure upon them on the Western Front. Robertson summed up his argument. 'The conclusions I have arrived at, taking the broadest possible view of the general situation, is that our chances of obtaining good results are certainly no grater in Italy than they are in the north, while the risks involved are much greater in the former case than in the latter.'[116] Whilst not advocating the case as positively as Haig it was clear that both men were now in broad agreement with the declared military policy. They remained however at variance with the Prime Minister, but Robertson did accept supplying Italy with ammunition for the heavy weapons she had already got.

Haig proceeded with his case, stating that he had no intention of entering into a great offensive incurring heavy losses, but favoured a step by step approach which was aggressive without too great a committal. He then read another four page statement repeating all his previously outlined reasons for launching his offensive. With the conference reaching a point of stalemate, and with the arguments of either side having been repeatedly aired to the point of exhaustion, it was decided that the First Sea Lord, Admiral Jellicoe, should join the proceedings. Jellicoe had recently issued two papers, the most recent dated the 18th June, which had already been circulated to the Committee outlining his views on the naval policy with regard to Ostend

---

[116] National Archives, Robertson statement to War Policy Committee 20th June, CAB27/6

and Zeebrugge. The conclusions of the findings expressed in his paper were, 'the absolute necessity of turning the Germans out of Northern Belgium at the earliest possible moment. It must be done during the present summer: every day that we wait the difficulties will increase, and every day that we wait the threat from the sea and the air become greater. The operation cannot be carried out by the Navy alone, but can be carried out as a joint business'.[117] The verbal statements he was about to make did not therefore come as a shock, as his views had been read by the Committee members previously. Jellicoe was asked to develop his case by Curzon, and responded by stating that he had two points in his mind. The first was that 'immense difficulty would be caused to the Navy if by the winter the Germans were not excluded from the Belgian coast',[118] but generally the Admiral felt that he could do no better than refer the Committee to his previously submitted papers. In these he had claimed that the position would become impossible if the Germans realised the full use they could make of the Belgian ports. 'These two ports [Ostend and Zeebrugge] provide harbours which, together with Bruges, can accommodate a very large number of destroyers, and, if the Germans were to concentrate destroyers at the ports up to the full limit of their capacity, there is no doubt whatever that if they realised the strength of their own position they could with great ease raid the Straits of Dover so effectively as to make almost a clean sweep of our forces.'[119] Jellicoe outlined the forces he thought the enemy had based at the ports making special mention of the destroyer flotillas which he recognised as such a danger to cross-channel communications, adding that if they were deployed in force they could 'wipe the ships on patrol out of existence'. He believed that only twelve small submarines were based on the Belgian coast, (in fact there were about thirty-two, which in March had sunk 195 Allied ships of around 234,871 tons, nearly half the whole German fleet total) and they were so close to the east coast war channel that they could operate there every night, with regular mine laying exercises. His second point was that if Zeebrugge could not be cleared in the winter of 1917 it probably could not be cleared at all, as it was improbable that the country could go on with the War into 1918 due to shortage of shipping. Jellicoe also pointed out the strength of the German position on the coast for operating aircraft against shipping, and the lack of suitable Royal Naval aircraft to combat them. Lloyd George picked up on the most significant issue regarding lack of shipping to support the War effort. He felt that Jellicoe's statement must be carefully checked, for if it was found to be accurate, 'then we should have far more important decisions to consider than our plans for operations for this year, namely the best method of making tracks for peace'.[120]

The story has gained acceptance that Jellicoe's statement came as a surprise to all present, but as his papers had already been circulated to the Committee this cannot be so. However it may have come as a surprise to Haig, and the story may have subsequently grown from his diary entry for that day. As with all well known moments in the story of Passchendaele, there are differing interpretations on the way Jellicoe's remarks were received, and what level of credence was placed upon them.[121] It has been claimed that there is no evidence that Jellicoe's warnings carried conviction either with the Committee or with the military. But Haig, in his diary entry on the 20th June, writing as usual for his wife's attention, titled the passage 'Secret. (Not to be copied.)' and went on to disclose, '[A most serious and startling situation was disclosed today.] At today's Conference Admiral Jellicoe as First Sea Lord stated that owing to [the great shortage of shipping due to German submarines], it would be impossible for Britain to continue the war in 1918. This was a bombshell for the Cabinet, [and all present] and a full enquiry is to be made as to the real facts on which this opinion [of the Naval Authorities] is

---

[117] National Archives, Jellicoe memorandum to War Policy Committee 18th June, CAB27/6
[118] National Archives, Jellicoe memorandum to War Policy Committee 18th June, CAB27/6
[119] National Archives. Jellicoe memorandum to War Policy Committee 18th June CAB27/7
[120] National Archives, minutes of 9th meeting of War Policy Committee 20th June, CAB27/6
[121] In the British Official History Edmonds claims: 'Admiral Jellicoe's statements bore great weight in the discussions which followed.' BOH p102. See also Prior and Wilson *Passchendaele the Untold Story* Notes 1/The Conundrum (7) for a different view.

based'.[122] The use of 'secret', 'not to be copied', 'most serious and startling situation', and 'bombshell', indicate that Haig was indeed quite concerned.[123] It must however be made clear that the square bracket entries are Haig's later typescript additions to his manuscript diaries, and could have been added for greater effect. This does not detract from the fact that he had made it clear to his wife that the information was highly confidential, more so than most of his diary entries, and that Jellicoe's statement came, at least to him, as a 'bombshell'.

There is no doubt that Jellicoe had strengthened Haig's hand, but how drastically the loss of Ostend and Zeebrugge would affect U-boat operations in any event was not discussed. The U-boats and destroyers operating from the Belgian ports with the support of repair facilities and shelter from attack at Bruges, and operations by seaplanes, landplanes, and torpedo boats, certainly posed a huge and unique threat to allied shipping. The shorter distance to the prime target areas of the South Irish Sea and Bay of Biscay, enabled the Flanders U-boats to remain on station for an extra four days, compared to U-boats operating from Germany. Mine laying in the Channel by enemy submarines and minelayers, and attacks on British transports, escorts, and boom protection vessels by destroyers and torpedo boats also operating from the Belgian coast were, as Jellicoe had outlined, further problems to the Admiralty. From Jellicoe's perspective he had not intentionally overstated the case. In fact not knowing the true strength of the Flanders bases, he had if anything understated the threat. He was adamant that his opinion was justified and that it could be supported by the Shipping Controller, and pointed out that he had made a similar statement to the Cabinet earlier in the year. The discussion then settled around why it was not possible to bombard Zeebrugge from the sea, but the First Sea Lord made clear the strength of the German batteries on the coast and the ability of the enemy to move their warships up the canal to Bruges.[124]

The Cabinet Committee reconvened on the 21st at 11:00 a.m. Lloyd George began by stating that it would be too great a responsibility for the Committee to take the strategy of the War out of the hands of the military advisors. Haig and Robertson, he explained, should therefore take time to carefully consider the misgivings and doubts that had been raised, but if after giving them full consideration they adhered to their original viewpoint, 'then the responsibility for their advice must rest with them'.[125] They must make a momentous decision, and a wrong step could bring disaster to the cause of the Allies. The Prime Minister then retraced the whole scope of the argument once again from his point of view, in one last desperate effort to tempt Haig and Robertson to falter. What reasons were there he asked to lead him to believe that the enemy could be driven back 15 miles, and that a place 10 miles away could then be captured? To achieve a success of this magnitude one of the following conditions would be necessary; an overwhelming force of men and guns; that the enemy should be attacked so strongly elsewhere that his reserves should be drawn off; or that the enemy's morale should be so broken that he could no longer put up a fight. In his view none of these conditions obtained at that time. He made the point that during three years of War no offensive had begun without sure predictions of success from the military, and that that experience had left him a little sceptical. But in this case due to the lack of numerical superiority he was 'especially sceptical'. The chances of success were very low and the cost in human life would be very high. The first part of the Prime Minister's statement ran to six pages, every word intended to dissuade Haig and Robertson. He concluded the first part by saying that it was his belief that none of his colleagues, whether they were in favour of, or opposed to, the adoption of Sir Douglas Haig's plan were convinced of success. The second part of Lloyd George's statement ran to another six pages. He wanted to make it clear that although he did not want to attack in Flanders this did not mean that he did not wish to attack anywhere. Everything from 'Pétain tactics', attacking the enemy at a weak point, or attacking Austria in Italy was raked over

---

[122] Douglas Haig. Diaries and Letters, p301
[123] In their introduction to 'Douglas Haig, Diaries and Letters', John Bourne and Gary Sheffield believe that: 'a shocked Haig' recorded the entry, and there seems little reason to doubt this.
[124] For an account of the German coastal strength see Chapter 10 – *MarineKorps Flandern*
[125] National Archives, minutes of 9th meeting of War Policy Committee 20th June, CAB27/6

thoroughly again. By the end of the presentation the rhetoric had been plenty but the conclusions were few. Lloyd George made it clear that even if his colleagues were in complete agreement with his views, he did not feel inclined to impose his preferred policy on his military advisors, but that he would not be doing his duty if he concealed the fact that he had grave misgivings over the advice they had given. The proceedings now reached a pitch of climax and high drama. The Prime Minister claimed that if after full reflection they advised against the suggestions *he* had proposed, he would nevertheless support them. He felt however that they were at the 'parting of the ways', believing that one course (his) would lead to victory, and the other course (theirs) to a hopeless and costly struggle, bringing victory no nearer. Putting up a game fight to the last Lloyd George instructed Cabinet Secretary Hankey to speak with Haig and Robertson when the meeting had broken up with a view to encouraging them to liaise personally with General Cadorna regarding his Italian plan.

So after three days of talking, and countless repetitions of the same arguments, what had been concluded? Very little beyond the fact that the positions of the Prime Minister and his military advisors were irreconcilable and that the whole matter must be considered further by the Chief of the Imperial General Staff. The Prime Minister had held the opportunity within his grasp to abort the offensive before it began. He failed to take it, even though it would have been impossible for anyone to have made a stronger and lengthier case against Haig's plan. Whatever the reason may have been, the Committee had declined to overrule the naval and military authorities on a question of strategy. The most likely reason is that there was no realistic alternative, and privately the Committee knew it. It was safer neither to say yes nor to say no, to what potentially could become a military and therefore political shambles. It was preferable to leave the final decision, and therefore the ultimate responsibility to the military.

The meeting of the Committee on War Policy which should have made the final decision on the future of Haig's offensive was held four days later at 11:00 a.m. on the 25th. Haig and Robertson had, as requested, produced further papers commenting on the misgivings expressed by Lloyd George. This time the Prime Minister found Haig's submission, which (over) emphasised the declining morale in the German Army, both positive and encouraging, especially in its statement that, 'if our resources are concentrated in France to the fullest possible extent, the British Armies are capable and can be relied on to effect great results this summer, results which will make final victory more assured, and which may even bring it within reach this year'.[126] He was however less impressed with Robertson's submission which had in part rather pointlessly criticised the Governments pre-war military manpower policy. As usual he wanted to know what Robertson thought were the chances of success of the operation, as only there lay the answer to the question which challenged him, upon which so far he had successfully avoided making a decision. Robertson, claimed the Prime Minister, was the constitutional military advisor and on his evidence he should make his decision, even though he had already stated that whatever evidence was placed before him *he* would *not* make the decision, but would in any event leave it to the military. The whole situation must have seemed rather pointless. Robertson's answer that the chances of securing good results were certainly no greater in Italy than they were on the Western Front, had at least been honest, even if it was not as positive and hopeful as was required. The C.I.G.S. pleaded that the whole problem depended on factors such as the actions of France and Russia which were beyond his control, and that whilst Haig was commenting in full knowledge of the morale of his own troops, and to a point those of the enemy, he was considering things on a broader canvas. Robertson's reply did however contain the following interesting passage. 'It seems to me we must give the French the opportunity to fight. If they do not fight we must act accordingly, and the plan will permit of this. In any case the French defection is not a good reason for sending British troops to another theatre, for Germany may counter us by heavily attacking the French, and under the assumption that they will not fight this attack might be disastrous to the Entente.'[127] Lord Curzon observed astutely

---

[126] National Archives, Haig to War Policy Committee 25th June, WO158/24
[127] National Archives, Robertson to War Policy Committee, CAB 27/7

that however differently the two soldiers had expressed their case, they had come broadly to the same conclusion. Bonar Law wanted to know if Ostend could be taken. Robertson cagily answered that Hiag's plan was the best plan possible. Bonar Law demanded a more direct answer and Robertson directed him to Haig's passage regarding concentration of forces, which had so encouraged Lloyd George. The proceedings then took a turn for the worse, as the Prime Minister, desperate to avoid the main issue, introduced the somewhat irrelevant point that General Foch thought it desirable to send guns to Italy. Robertson wished he would do so. The situation would have been laughable had it not been so serious. Lloyd George, perhaps mildly annoyed at Robertson's brusqueness, returned to the point that he thought Robertson's attitude had changed since May, when he had advised in Paris how essential it had been for the French to attack at the same time. Robertson pointed out that the visit to Paris had been largely to persuade the French to fight, and for that reason he may have over stated the case. Lloyd George then asked Robinson what he would do if the French refused to fight now, and was there a half-way-house between a complete offensive and a defensive? Robertson, probably by now boiling beneath his red tabbed khaki, declared that he had not changed his opinion. The Committee then made the decision not to make a decision, but to let matters rest for a period of two weeks when another meeting would be arranged, this time with the French, to attempt to better secure their assistance. Lord Curzon then asked very reasonably, who would settle the question for France, Painlevé, Foch or Pétain? Bonar Law expressed the opinion that it would not be unnatural if the French, who had sustained such tremendous losses, took the line that it was the turn of the British to do the fighting. Robertson pointed out that without fighting the War would never be won. In the meanwhile it was agreed that Haig could continue with his preparations.

Lloyd George's opposition to Haig's plan was founded on admirable motives, reinforced by a deep vein of mistrust in the military, as his June memorandum had made clear. 'The Cabinet must regard themselves as trustees for the fine fellows that constitute our army. They are willing to face any dangers, and they do so without complaint, but they trust to the leaders of the nation to see that their lives are not needlessly thrown away, and that they are not sacrificed on mere gambles which are resorted to merely because those who are directing the War can think of nothing better to do with the men under their command….It is therefore imperative that before we embark upon a gigantic attack which must necessarily entail the loss of scores of thousands of valuable lives, and produce that sense of discouragement which might well rush nations into premature peace, that we should feel a fair confidence that such an attack has a reasonable chance of succeeding. A mere gamble would be both a folly and a crime.'[128] But in the fashion of the shrewd political operator, and ever mindful of lurking military pitfalls, he refused to grasp the inevitable fact that the War was one great gamble, and repeatedly explored every possible alternative rather than make a firm policy decision. But the greatest gamble of taking the country to War had already been made, and further gambles would inevitably continue at every step, until the War ended, for better or for worse, as however much he may have dislike it, risks were the nature of war. We are left to ponder whether the Prime Minister gave an equal degree of thought to the possible 'folly and crime' of backing the Nivelle offensive, or a future offensive by the Italians. Presumably the risk of the gamble was more acceptable when it was scores of thousands of French or Italian lives at stake. Lloyd George huffed-and-puffed but allowed the military to proceed with a plan he detested, whilst attempting to ensure that any repercussions for failure would fall on them and not on him. Despite the Cabinet's lack of firm leadership, its refusal to accept the responsibility for what should have been a political decision based on military advice, or to accept head-on the risks imposed by the War, for the moment at least, Haig had got his battle.

---

[128] Parliamentary Archives, Lloyd George Papers, June 1917 LG/F/161/1/2

Part Three

"A largely strategic objective"
Charles Bean

July – The countdown

During July the situation in Russia continued to alarm. The Kerenski offensive, after a strong beginning against the Austrians, was routed by the counter-attacks of six German divisions of the general reserve. Political power had never really been in the hands of Kerenski's provisional government, although they had been returned with overwhelming majorities in the elections of the local dumas in April and May. The election success was more due to lack of alternative candidates than for support of the moderate Socialists and Mensheviks. It was to the local Soviets that the people turned for the deep social changes they yearned, and within the Soviets small groups of Bolsheviks were rapidly becoming more influential.

Threats of Allied financial pressure had driven Kerenski to raise what loyal forces he could, and launch his offensive into Galicia. On the 2nd July, the day after the offensive began, demonstrations on the streets led by the Bolsheviks had shown overwhelmingly that there was no support amongst the people for continuing with the war. Even within the government there was no faith in the offensive, rather a desire that it should fail, the resulting disaster hopefully stimulating an upsurge of national resolve which may go some way to restoring the situation. The offensive, disrupted by dissents and desertion, was checked by the disciplined and motivated German divisions. Soon 300,000 Russians were fleeing before 50,000 Germans. By the 3rd August Galicia was to be cleared of the Russians, only lack of communications and reserves stopping a deeper German thrust into Russia.

The British failure against the Turks at the Second Battle of Gaza was a distinct blow to Lloyd George who had placed great hopes in the abilities of General Murray. Murray had now been sacked to be replaced on the 27th June by General Sir Edmund Allenby, but for the moment the Prime Minister's hopes of seizing the morale boosting prize of Jerusalem had also gone.

Any chance of French support through a proposed wide front attack at Verdun, to correspond with the Flanders offensive was dashed due to a minor German attack, further French action being postponed until the 20th August. In the Allies favour, and there is little that was, political discontent was growing in Germany, expressed on the streets in a lack of confidence in the Army, doubts regarding the effectiveness of the submarine blockade, and the apparent lack of commitment on the part of the Government to state its peace terms.

Irrespective of what was happening elsewhere, Haig proceeded with the arrangements for his Northern Operation. The artillery had begun to concentrate at Ypres and the preparatory bombardment had commenced on the 16th July. The War Cabinet however still hesitated. On the 18th July Robertson wrote to Haig, 'up to the present no official approval of your plan has been given by the War Cabinet'.[129] The War Policy Committee had expressed concern that the infantry attacks would be pressed too far forward beyond the range of the protective artillery support with resulting heavy loss. Robertson stated that he had impressed on the Committee that their fears were unfounded and a step by step advance within the range of the guns was planned until such time as a break through occurred. His letter to Haig concluded simply, 'the Committee seem to favour the Flanders plan so long as a step by step advance is adhered to'.[130] Understandably, due to the lateness of the hour, this message stung Haig. In a reply on the 21st July, ten days before the planned opening of the great offensive he wrote to Robertson that he found it, 'somewhat startling at this advanced stage of the preparations to learn that the War

---

[129] National Archives, Robertson to Haig 15th July, WO158/24
[130] National Archives, Robertson to Haig 15th July, WO158/24

Cabinet have not yet determined whether the attack is to be permitted to proceed'.[131] He asked Robertson to explain to the Cabinet the lengthy and involved nature of the preparations and to reiterate much of what he had said at the meetings in London in June.

Lloyd George had meanwhile been agonizing over making the final decision on Haig's offensive. On the 15th July he had summoned Hankey to Sunday lunch, to enable him to further churn over the pros and cons with the Cabinet Secretary, as if more words could solve his dilemma. Hankey commented in his diary, 'he is still hankering after a great attack on Austria on the Italian Front. I agree with him in principle but am convinced that he must first allow Haig to have his attack. I urged him to get Cadorna to make preparations to receive a great accession of heavy guns and to pile up ammunition and make all plans. If Haig is successful then the combined attack on Austria will not come off and Cadorna will have to do the best he can without our assistance. But if Haig fails to get on we can switch all the artillery we can spare, after providing for the defensive, to Italy'.[132] The Prime Minister was making the best of social occasions to wrestle with his great question, in the company and with the support of others. To dinner at Downing Street on the 16th were invited Curzon, Milner, Smuts, Balfour (Foreign Minister), Carson (First Lord of the Admiralty), and Hankey. The ground which had been covered so many times before was covered again, and at last a decision of sorts was reached. Haig was to be allowed to open his offensive but it was not to draw out into a long indecisive battle of the 'Somme type'. If this happened it would be stopped, and the plan for the attack on the Italian front would be tried. Lloyd George's process of decision making appears somewhat illogical. He had required assurances of success from his military advisors, had not accepted or agreed with the advice they had given, and had then asked them to fully consider his alternative plan. But he had already stated that whatever they decided to do he would back them, as he felt the War Cabinet could not take the responsibility of overruling their decisions. Then, although having declared that the military had the final word, he had continued to seek further political opinion, which in any event due to his reluctance to overrule the military could be of no relevance to his decision making whatsoever. The whole process was nothing short of a charade, giving the appearance of War Cabinet control of policy, which in effect did not exist.

On the 20th July the War Cabinet met to consider a report drawn up by Hankey, entitled 'Recommendations in regard to Military Policy', which spelt out the terms under which Haig was to be authorised to operate. It read as follows:

a) The Field-Marshal commanding the British Expeditionary Force in France should be authorised to carry out the plans for which he has prepared, as explained by him to the Cabinet Committee on War Policy on June the 19th.

b) If it appears probable in the execution of these plans that the results are not commensurate with the effort made and the losses incurred, the whole question should be re-examined by the War Cabinet with a view to the cessation of this offensive and the adoption of an alternative plan.

c) The only alternative plan which at present commends itself to the Cabinet Committee is General Cadorna's proposal for a great offensive against Austria supported by British, and if the French are willing to co-operate French heavy artillery.

d) In order that this alternative plan may be feasible in the event of a decision being taken to desist from Field-Marshal Sir Douglas Haig's plan of operations, arrangements should be made forthwith for giving effect to it; for a gradual accumulation of reserves of ammunition for an eventual force of British heavy guns on the Italian front; and for all other measure that can be taken in advance to facilitate the execution of the plan.

e) The Chief of the Imperial General Staff should take immediate steps to make effect to these decisions.

---

[131] National Archives, Haig to Robertson 21st July, WO158/24
[132] Hankey Diaries, Churchill Archives, Churchill Colleague, Cambridge HNKY 1/2

f) Pressure should be put on the French Government to co-operate with all their forces in the forthcoming British offensive in Flanders; and to send heavy guns to Italy if the proposal in (d) is adopted.[133]

This document could scarcely be regarded as an unqualified endorsement for the greatest operation the British Army had yet undertaken. The first paragraph was clearly relevant to the Flanders offensive. The next four discussed stopping it, or the arrangements for alternatives; this around ten days before it was about to commence. The extraordinary state of indecision continued, with Haig's letter to Robertson of the 21st crossing with a letter from the War Cabinet to Haig, containing the above conclusions of the meeting of the Cabinet on the 20th, forwarded on the 21st. The Cabinet were carefully covering their own backs, offering commitment with qualifications. Haig had finally received official authorisation to proceed with his offensive in line with the plan he had outlined to the War Committee, but if, during its execution, it appeared not to be progressing to the satisfaction of the War Cabinet the alternative plan to support an Italian effort against Austria with heavy guns would be tried. To emphasise the qualifications, Haig had been instructed to make arrangements to switch to the Italian plan in case of its adoption, this in the middle of preparations to commit the British Army to the greatest attack in its history. In a covering letter Robertson said that the War Cabinet wished to know the first objective of the Flanders offensive so that they might judge whether the operation had, up to that stage succeeded or not. It is odd that such a fundamental question which had already been answered at the many Cabinet conferences which Haig had attended should be asked again at such a late hour. The War Cabinet's lack of commitment, subsequent to their agreement that the offensive should proceed, now appears staggering.

Haig's reply to the War Cabinet of the 22nd, sent via Robertson was polite, but he made his feelings very clear. He again explained the length of time necessary to prepare for great offensives and warned the War Cabinet of the dangerous effect to morale of cancellation. Haig could not understand why the Cabinet had taken so long in reaching its conclusions, and earnestly hoped that, 'the War Cabinet may never again find it necessary to postpone such a decision to the last moment'.[134] He was obviously put out by the timbre of the proposal to review the progress of the offensive, and possibly stop it, commenting, 'no doubt, before such an order is issued, the effort and losses of the enemy as well as our side will be duly considered, as also the possible effect on the enemy and our own Army of stopping the action, as foreshadowed in this conclusion'. Probably of greatest importance, he stated his impression that the War Cabinet was not giving him their full support, and lacked confidence in his ability to conduct the operation and to make the necessary strategic decisions on the spot. He requested that if his impressions were unjustified that the Cabinet should assure him to that effect. Being concerned about a possible shortage of artillery and ammunition for the offensive he added, 'I desire to allude particularly to the shortage of 6-inch howitzer ammunition in France, of which ammunition I notice that 'ample supplies' are being sent to Italy; and also to the probable shortage of artillery personnel and of guns in the Armies under my Command'. His illumination of the gun shortage was to forewarn of a critical problem soon to affect the whole operation. Once again he repeated that his views on diverting resources from the Western Front were so well known that it was pointless repeating them. In response to the Cabinet's enquiry he gave the first objective of the offensive as, 'the ridge extending from Stirling Castle (Gheluvelt plateau), by Passchendaele, Staden and Clerken to near Dixmude'.

A memorandum compiled at G.H.Q. and passed as a note to Robertson gives a clear insight into Haig's views at the time. 'The British troops are the only troops in the field at the moment on whose capacity to carry through successful attacks against the German we can rely....The weariness and disappointment of the French is a factor of greatest importance at the moment. Germany knows it, is trying to take advantage of it, and will continue to do so. She is in a position to do so and we are not in regard to Austria. If we have a really good success in our forthcoming operation the value of the French troops will be much increased and while their

---

[133] National Archives, Hankey memorandum to War Cabinet 20th July, CAB27/7
[134] National Archives, Haig to Robertson 22nd July, WO158/24

reawakened enthusiasm lasts we should concentrate our endeavours on developing this success. If we do not have a really good success our most urgent and serious care will be to nurse France through the winter without impairing our offensive power for next years campaign, which is practically certain to be the last campaign we shall induce France or Russia to face (even if we can get them to face that which is doubtful). To nurse France through the winter and to give ourselves the best chance of success next year will tax all our power. We cannot afford to dissipate any of it. We could see Italy and even Russia drop out, and still continue the War with France and America. But if France drops out we not only cannot continue the War on land but our Armies in France will be in a very difficult position....Every man and gun that we send to Italy reduces our power in one respect or another. I consider it dangerous and so unsound to adopt such a course that, in my opinion any responsible soldier who consents to issue an order for it must expect to be judged by history to have failed in his duty to his country.'[135]

On the 24th July Robertson forwarded Haig's request for acknowledged Cabinet support to Hankey (who was in Paris with the Prime Minister for a conference with the French), for the attention of the War Cabinet, and requested early instructions on two points. '1) I presume I may inform the Field-Marshal that, the War Cabinet having approved of his plans being executed, he may depend on their wholehearted support. 2) I also presume I may tell him that if and when the War Cabinet decide again to reconsider the situation they will obtain his views before coming to any decision as to cessation of the operation.'[136] Hankey added a reply in his own hand to the bottom of Robertson's note saying, 'The Prime Minister has instructed me to inform you that on behalf of the War Cabinet he authorises you to give the assurances as you propose in 1) and 2) above. M.P.A. Hankey, Hotel Crillon, Paris July 25th 1917'.

On the 25th July, six days before the planned opening of the offensive, Haig at last received a telegram of assurance from Robertson which stated that, 'War Cabinet authorises me to inform you that having approved your plans being executed, you may depend upon their whole hearted support; and that if and when they decide to reconsider the situation, they will obtain your views before arriving at any decision as to the cessation of operations'.[137] The wording is interesting, in as much as it may have been assumed that the words and sentiments expressed in Robertson's fateful telegram, authorising the opening of the greatest offensive ever mounted by the British Army to that date, were those of the Prime Minister. It is clear however that they were not, but were Robertson's words which he had been authorised to use by Hankey. There had therefore been no remarkable change in attitude on the part of Lloyd George, which the telegram seemed to imply. There had been no change of heart, just a reluctant acceptance of Robertson's written proposals. Having no other realistic policy, the Prime Minister, against his better judgement, had bowed to the inevitable taking the Cabinet with him.

Haig's reply to Robertson's telegram is important as it provides a clear view of the principles he would apply throughout the course of the coming campaign, 'even if my attacks do not gain ground, as I hope and expect, we ought still to persevere in attacking the Germans in France. Only by this means can we win; and we must encourage the French to continue fighting'.[138] It is clear from the outset that Haig's single priority was to engage the German Army in Flanders, to soften up, grind down, or by any other means at his disposal reduce their capacity to fight, and restrict their ability to deploy elsewhere, especially against the French. His reference to encouraging the French to keep fighting is indicative of his concern over their situation at that time, whether or not those fears are now considered by some to be unfounded. One way or the other – break through or attrition, Haig was committed to continue with the offensive until the weather, lack of resources, or an order from the War Cabinet caused him to stop.

---

[135] National Archives, GHQ memorandum OAD565 22nd July, WO158/24
[136] National Archives, Robertson to Cabinet 24th July, WO106/407
[137] National Archives, telegram Robertson to Haig, 25th July, WO158-24
[138] National Archives, Haig to Robertson, 26th July WO158-24

Preparations for battle

The Battle of Messines had officially ended on the 14th June. The first attack of the Third Battle of Ypres, to be called the Battle of Pilckem Ridge, was not to open until the 31st July. After Messines the enemy had undoubtedly been off-balance, and had not had time to complete their defensive preparations around Ypres. Delay was the last thing Haig needed. So why was the pause so long? Numerous theories abound and are worth considering in some detail. One theory suggests that Messines was commenced prematurely, either due to concerns of the Tunnellers over their mines being discovered, or concerns regarding the difficulties of the French. It is true that there was a good deal of tension within the Tunnelling Companies regarding their mines; enemy trench raids had come precariously close to discovering at least one tunnel entrance, whilst underground counter-mining activities had given grave cause for concern. But there is no evidence or likelihood that the Messines attack was brought forward for this reason. As Haig knew nothing formally about the French mutinies until the 2nd June, it is not possible that he brought forward the attack to support them, as the Messines date had been already announced at the Army Commanders Conference at Doullens on the 7th May. Messines was therefore not brought forward, but Pilckem Ridge, for whatever reason, was delayed, or more correctly took a long time to prepare. Some claim that Haig had already decided that there would be a 'seven week' period between the end of Messines and the opening of the fighting in the Salient. This is not correct and the point is an important one. Haig had in fact said 'some weeks' not seven weeks and there is a world of difference between the two. There are also claims that the selection of Gough as Army Commander in charge of the Northern Operation brought with it an inbuilt delay, due to the time it would take for him to establish headquarters, familiarize himself with the ground, and produce a plan. But Gough established his headquarters at Lovie Chateau on the 31st May, assumed command of his battle front between Observatory ridge and Boesinghe at 12 noon on the 10th June, and as we shall see had thrashed out the Fifth Army plan with his Corps Commanders on the 6th and 16th June, the latter date only two days after the end of the Messines battle. The theory that the delay was due to the choice of Gough, which was the direct responsibility of Haig, seems mainly devised to support the argument that he was a bad choice, and the delay was part of the baggage which came with that bad choice. He may well have been a bad choice but that had nothing to do with the delay. The argument appears to ignore the complexities of concentrating the Fifth Army and most especially its artillery in the Salient, in an effort to present a case against Haig's selection of commander. The delay was clearly nothing to do with the choice of Gough and had certainly not been planned at 'seven weeks' by Haig on the 7th May. We shall soon examine the real reasons for the delay.

Messines had been a great success, within the bounds of its limited intensions. The German counter salient to the south of Ypres, which had frowned over the British position since November 1914 had been removed. No longer could the German artillery observers, situated all along the gentle ridge at the excellent vantage points of Spanbroekmolen and St. Eloi, direct their searching gunfire onto the vital British supply arteries. The road from Poperinghe through Vlamertinge and into Ypres was safer, but far from safe. German batteries, previously just behind the Messines – Wytschaete ridge were now much further back behind the Warneton line, but of greater menace to the coming offensive, batteries were being concentrated behind the Zandvoorde hill and the Gheluvelt plateau.

Back on the 24th May Haig had written to Plumer, emphasising the importance of quickly exploiting any success made by Second Army. As the capture of the Messines ridge was the opening phase of the battle to capture the Passchendaele ridge, reserves were to be placed at the disposal of Gough's Fifth Army, in order to enable him to co-operate in the securing of that ridge. On the 3rd June, four days before Messines, Plumer had stated that it was essential that the opportunity for exploiting a success should be taken advantage of at the earliest possible moment. In order to gain this advantage he had arranged for II Corps and VIII Corps to attack respectively, to the north side and south side of Bellewaarde Lake (on the western face of the plateau, just north of the Menin Road) to a depth of 1,200 yards, the line Stirling Castle –

Westhoek ridge being the objective. As artillery support for this proposed attack upon the conclusion of the Messines battle, Plumer required 60 heavy and medium guns and howitzers moved north from the Messines front, and to accomplish this movement he required three days. On the 6th June Haig explained the proposed attack to Gough, who was less than enthusiastic, preferring to carry out the attack on the Gheluvelt plateau himself as part of the main offensive. Patrols sent forward by II and VIII Corps early on the 8th June reported stiff enemy resistance and at midday Haig asked Plumer if the attack could be carried out at once. Plumer true to character, was disinclined to commit his infantry with insufficient artillery support, and repeated his request for the three day delay to move the guns. At that point with uncharacteristic impetuosity Haig transferred II and VIII Corps to Gough, with orders that the attack should be carried out by the Fifth Army, details of the plan being sent by Plumer to Gough on the 9th June. However, at the Army Commander's Conference at Lillers on the 14th June, Gough after discussion with his divisional commanders expressed his unhappiness with the plan, believing that if the II and VIII Corps moved forward to the proposed position they would be in a dangerously exposed salient, and it would be wiser to include the attack within the main Northern Operation.[139] The postponement was approved. Gough's rejection of the plan to attempt to push forwards on to the Gheluvelt plateau on a limited front was undoubtedly correct, with the proviso that due to the activities of the enemy, the longer the attack was delayed the more difficult it was to become. The insufficient concentration of forces, especially in artillery, to deal with the Gheluvelt position was to have major repercussions later.

    The Germans expected the British plan to develop much as Plumer had proposed, Crown Prince Rupprecht recognising the capture of the Messines Ridge to be the first phase of an operation to clear the Belgian coast, most likely assisted by a landing from the sea. Rupprecht saw the second phase as the establishment of a firm British right flank stretching from the Lys about Comines, through Zandvoorde to the Gheluvelt plateau, and an attack in the area Zandvoorde – Gheluvelt was expected daily after the Messines success. If this attack developed, Rupprecht contemplated a withdrawal initially on a line Hooge - Zandvoorde - Wervicq, and subsequently, due to perceived British artillery superiority, to the Flanders I position along the Passchendaele ridge, and behind the Lys in the south. He then foresaw the third phase as a general British breakout to the north-eastwards from Ypres, commencing with attacks on a narrow front supported by an overwhelming weight of artillery to drive deep wedges into the German position, followed by a break through on a broad front. But the German high command firmly believed in the strength of their two great bastions, Houthulst Forest to the north of Langemarck, and Gheluvelt plateau to the east of Ypres, and considered whilst they held at least one of these positions a breakout was unlikely. As the British assault on the Gheluvelt position had not taken place immediately following Messines as feared, at the critical point of relative German weakness, they had not had to withdraw as envisaged by Rupprecht, and there was a breathing space to reorganise and strengthen their positions. They were to use it well. Shortage of labour, due to the construction of the Hindenberg and Wotan positions further south had limited the amount of work completed on the Flanders position until early June. Although for very different reasons, lack of labour had also placed the British in the same predicament, but now the build-up race in and around the Salient was on.

The British concentration in Flanders.

Final instructions for the concentration in Flanders were issued by G.H.Q. on 22nd May. All available resources were to be employed, estimated at fifty Allied divisions, thirty-eight of which would be British. A major regrouping of divisions and of Army and corps artillery was entailed, the artillery mostly coming up from the Messines front after the 14th June. The main attack by the Fifth Army under Gough was to be made on a 11,500 yard front from Mount Sorrel in the

---

[139] National Archives, Advanced GHQ OAD291/27 p4 15th June WO158/311

south, to Boesinghe on the Ypres-Yser canal in the north, held at this time by the II and VIII Corps, which as we have seen were to be transferred from Second to Fifth Army. The Second Army was to cover the right flank of the main operation, with the II Anzac, IX and X Corps, fielding five divisions.

On the 31st May Gough moved with his chief General Staff officer Major-General Neil Malcolm, to his new headquarters at Lovie Chateau,[140] 8 miles W.N.W. of Ypres, taking over his new frontage with the II and VIII Corps, (30th, 55th, 39th and 38th Divisions) in the line on the 10th June.[141] Towards the end of June and into July further divisions arrived to bring Fifth Army strength up to eighteen divisions, with one in G.H.Q. Reserve. The front was allotted between four corps, the II, XIX, XVIII, and XIV, in sectors mainly corresponding to the positions held by the divisions of II and VIII Corps, who stayed in line to avoid premature reliefs arousing enemy suspicion.

At the end of June the French First Army, which was to protect Gough's left flank requested that its length of front be reduced. In accordance with these wishes, Fifth Army took over the line for 1,000 yards north of the Boesinghe railway bridge on the Ypres – Yser canal.

The final allotment of forces to Fifth Army was:

II Corps	8th, 18th, 25th and 30th Divisions, (Plus 24th Div. from Sec. Army on 4th July).
XIX Corps	15th, 16th, 36th and 55th Divisions
XVIII Corps	11th, 39, 48th and 51st Divisions
XIV Corps	Guards, 20th, 29th and 38th Divisions
VIII Corps	(reserve) 61st Division
V Corps	(GHQ reserve) 56th Division

Each attacking corps was to use two divisions for the initial assault to the first day's objectives, and keep two in support for future operations. The exception, as we shall see, was to be II Corps which was to use the 24th, 30th, 8th Divisions and elements of 18th Division against the strong Gheluvelt plateau position. The Second Army was reduced to twelve divisions of II Anzac, IX and X Corps, to cover the right flank, but importantly received the I Anzac Corps (1st, 2nd and 5th Australian Divisions) into reserve in the latter part of July. More than half of Second Army's artillery was transferred to Fifth Army and of the 243 heavy howitzers and 546 field guns remaining, 112 howitzers and 210 field guns were concentrated on the left in X Corps sector, to support the Fifth Army attack against the Gheluvelt plateau. By 31st July Fifth Army's artillery strength had risen to 752 heavy howitzers and 1,422 field guns, and three tank brigades each of 72 tanks were at its disposal. Combined air strength at the disposal of Second and Fifth Armies totalled 406 aircraft and 18 kite balloon sections.

The left, (northern) flank of the main offensive was to be covered by the French First Army under General Anthoine, which had been in reserve at the time of the Nivelle offensive. It is probable that it had not therefore been overly influenced by the disaster or the subsequent mutinies, and comprised of the I Corps, (1st, 2nd, 51st and 162nd Divisions), joined later by the XXXVI Corps moving south from Nieuport, (29th and 133rd Divisions) which replaced the Belgian

---

[140] National Archives, Advanced GHQ OAD455 19th May WO158/311
[141] National Archives, War Diary Headquarters Fifth Army, WO95/519

4th and 5th Divisions on the front Boesinghe – Nordschoote between the 5th and 10th July. The Army group that Pétain had suggested would include the Belgians had not been formed. French First Army were to attack in conjunction with the British on a 6,500 yard front, from 1,200 yards north of the Boesinghe railway bridge on the Ypres-Yser canal, to Nordschoote, the main concentration being in the southern sector between Boesinghe and Steenstraat. The attack towards Bixschoote was to be supported by 300 heavy and medium guns and 240 75mm field guns. The left flank of the advance was to rest upon the Yser inundations. Six Belgian divisions held the thirteen mile line from Nordschoote behind the Yser inundations towards the coast at St Georges, and were possibly to attack through a gap in the inundations near Dixmude if the opportunity offered.

The offensive along the coast, and the German attack of the 10th July

A coastal operation, to be launched both from the Lombartzyde bridgehead, east of the Yser near Nieuport, and also by an amphibious assault, to include the landing of tanks from special craft (the HUSH Operation) had long been under consideration, and was to be launched at a suitable state of the tides to cooperate with the main Northern Offensive. This was the only place on the Western Front that there remained a possibility of outflanking the German line. On the Swiss border there was no such possibility. The proposal was to make four simultaneous attacks, one from the bridgehead at Lombartzyde, and three seaborne landings, to be made by three brigade columns of 1st Division, totalling 5,000 men, onto open beaches. A western landing was to be made at Westende Bains, a mile behind the German Second Line, a central landing 1,200 yards to the east on the flank of the German Third Line and an eastern landing 3,000 yards east of the German Third Line just beyond Middelkirke Bains. The lightly equipped columns, each supported by three tanks, and with artillery and machine gun detachments, were to seize pre-arranged tactical targets. On the afternoon before the landings two divisions were to attack from the Lombartzyde bridgehead and capture the forward zone up to the German Second Line. On the day of the landing two support divisions were to pass through those on the Second Line, and carry the attack towards Ostend, and link up on their right with a Belgian attack advancing from Dixmude.

The plans for the amphibious landing were most innovative given the technical ability of the equipment available at the time. Shallow draught monitors were to tow three huge armoured lighters inshore from which the infantry, field artillery and nine tanks would disembark onto the beaches. For the tank operation special and very secret training was undertaken at Merlimont just south of le Touquet where a special section of sea wall was constructed. To enable the tanks to mount the sea wall they would be equipped with ramps specially made for the purpose, carried forward on the front of the machine to the wall, where it would be detached in a position to allow the tank to climb over. The tracks would also be fitted with special spikes to better grip the concrete wall. The climbing tanks were also fitted with power winches at the rear, to tow up other tanks, guns and stores once the wall was mounted. Given the problems experienced with amphibious landings with more sophisticated equipment in a later war, it is probably for the best that this early initiative was finally not attempted.

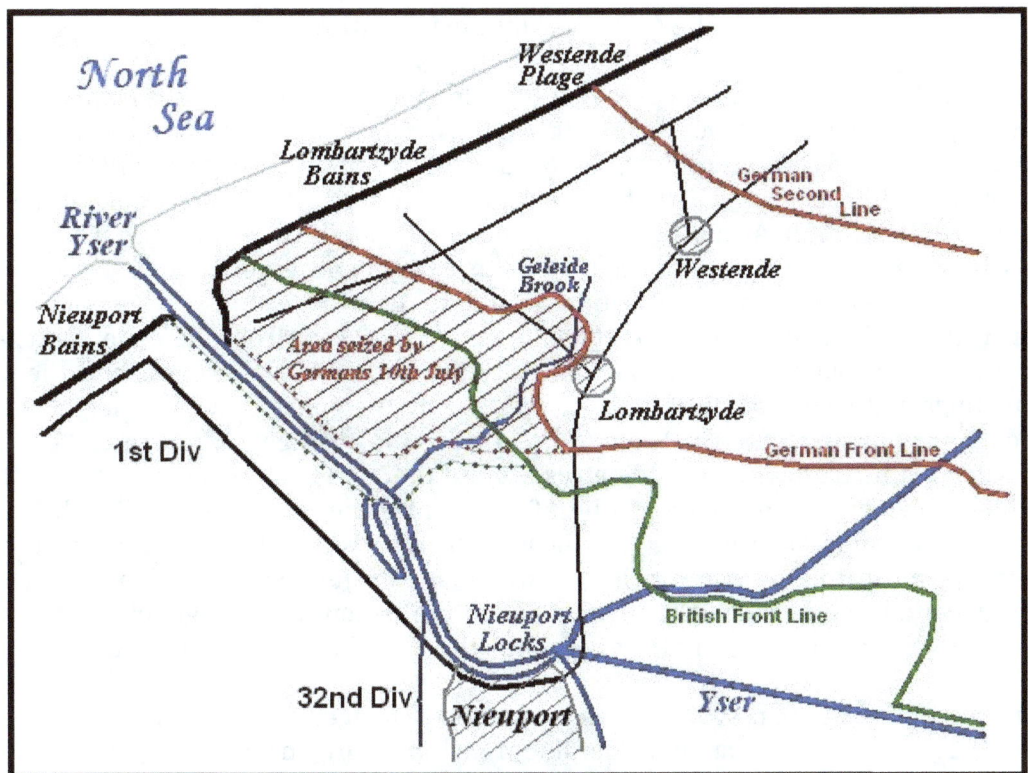

The Lombartzyde bridgehead seized by the Germans 10th July

Upon the cancellation by Pétain on the 18th May of the combined Anglo-French attack towards St. Quentin and Cambrai, General Rawlinson's Fourth Army headquarters had been given command of the northern coastal sector of operations with headquarters at Malo les Bains. On the 20th June under command of the XV Corps, the British 32nd Division, (coming from Second Army, and soon to be joined by the 1st Division), took over from the French XXXVI Corps, which moved south to join French First Army on the Yser canal. In an attempt to forestall what was seen as a Britsh build-up towards an attack along the coast, the Germans launched a pre-emptive attack on the 10th July against the Nieuport bridgehead. From the 6th July onwards the enemy gradually increased artillery pressure on the British positions. At 5:30 a.m. on the 10th there was severe shelling of the whole area, which was most intense between the Geliede Brook and the beach. At 8:00 p.m. an infantry assault began which evicted the 2nd Brigade of the newly arrived British 1st Division holding the poorly prepared defences of the Lombartzyde position north of the Yser and west of the Geleide Brook. The artillery available to Fourth Army, which as it took over from the French had only begun to take up its positions at the same time as the British infantry in late June, was totally inadequate to resist the attack, being outnumbered three to one, many guns not having had time to register. A counter-attack using the 32nd Division to regain the lost bridgehead ordered by Rawlinson for the 11th, was subsequently considered unwise, as the artillery situation had not improved, and the position remained the same with the Germans in possession of part of the bridgehead north-east of the Yser. A revised plan was drawn up by Rawlinson to attack from the narrow section of bridgehead still held by the British, and then with a flanking attack drive the enemy from between the Geliede Brook and the beach. The coastal attack was then to proceed as previously arranged. Rawlinson was aware of the overwhelming necessity to dominate the enemy artillery prior to any further operations, and it was agreed with Haig to work for the 8th August as the date for the Fourth Army attack, as a time when the main offensive should have made sufficient progress, and which corresponded with a satisfactory state of the tides. The pre-emptive enemy strike, although a severe embarrassment, had not affected the plans for the Northern Offensive.

The German Flanders Position

The German defensive position at Ypres had been long in the making and it incorporated over two years experience in defensive warfare. It had the overwhelming advantage of being, (except for a few hundred yards around Hill 62, Hill 61, and Hill 59-Mount Sorrel) on the higher ground with fine observation across the British forward and rear areas. Along the whole of the front to be assaulted by the Fifth Army, the German defences other than the forward observation positions, lay on a reverse slope out of sight of British ground observers.

Although having total observation over the British positions, this view was not necessarily gained from any great advantage in elevation, except from the main Passchendaele ridge and Gheluvelt plateau. Due to the generally flat nature of the ground, and the fact that many buildings and trees had already been reduced by the guns, a minimal height advantage provided a great viewing platform. From Pilckem ridge the average advantage in elevation was no more than ten metres, rising to 15 metres around the Ypres – Roulers railway. On the main ridge the Germans had been driven off Hill 60 in the Messines battle, and Hills 62, 61, and 59 were in British hands, overlooking the German front position in Shrewsbury Forest. The Gheluvelt plateau in the areas of Stirling Castle, Clapham Junction and Glencorse Wood did however give a full 45 metre height advantage and the Bellewaarde ridge 35 metres, over the low ground towards Ypres and northwards into the Steenbeek valley towards St. Julien and Langemarck.

The principle of the German system of defensive had changed significantly since the Somme battles of 1916. The strongly manned front line trench network, incorporating deep dugouts for the protection of the garrison holding the line had gone. It had been replaced with a defence in great depth, consisting of a front, second (*Albrecht Stellung*) and third (*Wilhelm Stellung*) line, constructed in front of a fourth position, *Flandern I* known to the British as the Staden – Zonnebeke Line, or simply Flanders I. The building of Flanders I, which ran northwards from the Lille defences, to reach the sea between Ostend and Middlekerke was commenced in February 1917, and two positions in rear, Flanders II and Flanders III were partially prepared, or under construction during the campaign. The zones between these lines varied in depth. Across the Gheluvelt plateau between the front line, the second line, and the third line, known to the British as the Langemarck – Gheluvelt Line, the zone depth was a fairly equal 1,000 to 1,500 yards. To the north in the upper Steenbeek valley, north of Frezenberg and south of St Julien the zone between the front line and the *Albrecht Stellung* or second line opened to 2,500 yards where the latter line conformed to a natural defensive position east of the Steenbeek. Further north across Pilckem ridge and the Steenbeek valley towards Langemarck, the distance between the *Albrecht Stellung* and the *Wilhelm Stellung* extended to a full 4,000 yards, although between the front line on the Ypres-Yser canal and the *Albrecht Stellung* in front of Pilckem it was only 1,000 yards. The front, second and third lines were oriented approximately southeast to northwest forming the northern arc of the Salient. The Flanders I Line, the forth defence position, was oriented approximately south to north, the zone between it and the third (*Wilhelm*) line widening towards the north. For example the distance between the *Wilhelm Stellung* at Kansas Cross on the Langemarck to Zonnebeke road, across Gravenstafel Ridge to the Flanders I line at the base of Wallemolen Spur was approximately 3,000 yards.

The forward zone between the front and second lines was to be very lightly manned to avoid heavy casualties from any initial barrage. Concern about possible British mining after the Messines experience also encouraged a limited forward garrison. The second line was to form the first main defence line, providing a number of strong-points and fortified localities to break up any attack, which would then be thrown back by the supports and reserves of the front line battalions which garrisoned the forward zone. Along the second line, and behind it in the battle zone between the second and third lines, numerous fortified strong points of reinforced concrete construction had been built. Where suitable the remains of old farm buildings had been used, often incorporating parts of the original red brick structure to camouflage concrete and steel bunker construction beneath, housing many machine guns, and in some cases in the battle zone field artillery. The concrete Mebus, bunkers, blockhouses and shelters, many presenting a very low profile, were well camouflaged beneath banks of earth, and arranged in such a pattern as to give covering fire one to another. In this battle zone, between the second and third lines with its numerous echeloned bunkers and pillboxes, providing lethal fields of machine gun crossfire, most of the serious fighting would take place. These structures were linked by communication trenches, and protection of strong-points was increased with fighting trenches and strong wire entanglements. The second line also formed the artillery defensive line covering the mass of field batteries, although many of these were largely to be withdrawn east of the Steenbeek to around the third line before the 31st July.[142]

As usual the Germans had made best use of the topography, natural features being incorporated into their defence system. Of greatest importance to the enemy, the salient from which the British were about to attempt to break out fell between two great bastions of German strength, the natural strong position of the Gheluvelt plateau, and the position within Houthulst Forest north of Langemarck, which was itself endowed with even greater protection from frontal attack, being positioned just behind the southern extremity of the inundated areas, along the valley of the St Jansbeek north of Bixschoote. There was however a significant strategic weakness in the whole German position in north-west Belgium. The main supply arteries from Germany across Belgium to the coast and to the Ypres – Yser front, relied primarily on two railways. The line of greatest importance ran from the German border at Aachen, to Liege, then through Brussels and Ghent to Bruges, with further branches to Zeebrugge and Ostend. This line was 25 miles from Ypres. The second line, of only slightly less significance, ran from Brussels to Courtrai, then to Roulers, Thourout and to Ostend, with an important branch from Courtrai to Menin. This line was about 11 miles from Ypres, and little more than 4 miles from the Passchendaele ridge. The first railway was the lifeline to the enemy operation at Bruges, Zeebrugge and Ostend. Without it the Germans would be left with a far less significant supply line by road and canal, as communication by sea was highly precarious. The second railway kept the Army at Ypres and along the Yser supplied. The capture of Roulers and Lichtervelde and the cutting of the railway would almost certainly seal the fate of the German position on the Yser. Without this line their ability to reinforce and re-supply their Flanders Position would be so reduced as to make the section of the Western Front north of Ypres untenable. German recognition of this weakness had dictated the construction of the great defensive positions around Ypres and along the Yser. The other possible route of Allied attack was from the Channel itself, and a great line of fortifications had been built along the coast amounting to no fewer than 41 batteries which mounted around 164 guns of calibres up to 380 mm.[143] The enemy were therefore as acutely aware of the vulnerability of their position as were the British, the loss of railway communication inevitably leading to a loss of the U-boat bases, and to a possible catastrophe by a fatal outflanking of the Western Front.

Disposition of German forces in defence of the Flanders Position

The Flanders front from the Lille – Armentieres road to the Belgian coast was held by the German *Fourth Army* under General Sixt von Armin, and on the 13th June Colonel von Lossberg the recognised defensive battle expert, arrived to take over as Chief of Staff. Upon the framework of the already prepared defence lines, von Lossberg was to arrange the dispositions of the German infantry and artillery. On the 27th June *Fourth Army* issued the order for the

---

[142] The Mebus had not totally replaced deep underground shelter systems. Whereas those on the Somme had been cut into the supportive chalk, at Ypres the German deep dugout systems were sunk to around 16 metres into the clay and were totally timber lined, and continuously pumped, exactly the same as their British counterparts. See Barton, Doyle, Vandewalle, *Beneath Flanders Fields* pp224-263
[143] See Johan Ryheul *MarineKorps Flandern 1914-1918*

defensive battle it knew it was about to fight, which was to encompass the whole range of new German defence tactics.

Just as the construction of the physical defence lines were in depth, so were the dispositions of the defending forces. Resistance to attack was to come from two distinct groups. Initial resistance was to come from the divisions holding the line, but if this proved inadequate, a separate force of super counter-attack divisions, (*Eingreif-Division*) would be available to recover any lost ground. It was accepted that the front line would soon be crossed, the attacking infantry then entering the forward zone. Reserves of the forward battalions held back near the second line would then carry out local counter-attacks. From the strong-points in rear of the forward zone the defending garrison would further attempt to break up the cohesion of the attack. The deeper the attack advanced beyond this forward zone the more strong points and fortified locations it would encounter. Behind the second line, the reserves of the front division would be ready to counter attack at the point when the already disorganised assault would be exhausted after fighting its way past the strong-point line or *Stutzpunktlinie*. The main clash of the encounter battle would be fought in the battle zone between the second and third lines. If the front line divisional reserves failed to retake the lost ground, the *Eingreif* divisions, one regiment of which with its attached divisional artillery, would be held back in an assembly area in the rearward zone behind the third line, could be rapidly called on by the front line divisional commander to counter-attack once the British intensions were known. The remaining two regiments of this super counter-attack division would be in assembly areas 2,000 to 4,000 yards further back (well behind the Gheluvelt plateau, and behind the Passchendaele ridge), less at risk from barrage fire. Behind the *Eingreif* divisions Army Group reserves would be available to take the place of any of the first line reserve ordered forward. Fifth Army estimated German strength opposing them at 42 battalions comprising 21,000 rifles in the line (approximately 5 divisions); between 27 to 36 battalions of 13,500 to 18,000 rifles in close reserve west of the Thourout – Menin railway (3 to 4 divisions); and a further 27 battalions (3 divisions) in the rear around Ghent – Antwerp – Oudenarde, a total of between 48,000 to 52,500 rifles, or approximately 11 divisions.[144]

A great strength in artillery had been concentrated behind the Gheluvelt plateau and Passchendaele ridge, which could support counter-attacks to the north or the south with fire controlled from the excellent observation points provided by the higher ground. On the 31st July German artillery strength facing Fifth Army between Hollebeke and Steenstraat on the Yser canal amounted to 345 heavy / medium guns and 392 field guns. Facing Second Army between Warneton and Hollebeke were 127 heavy / medium guns and 176 field guns. This was the very tough and able opposition, established in well prepared positions in great depth, which was now to be assaulted by the British Fifth Army. The actual enemy gun strength opposing Fifth Army was in fact neary 42% greater than Gough's intelligence gatherers believed, as an optomistic report on the 30th July claimed the figures to be approximately 200 field guns and 230 heavies.[145]

---

[144] National Archives, Estimate of Enemy strength opposite Fifth Army front 30th July 1917, War Diary Headquarters Fifth Army, WO95/519
[145] National Archives, Estimate of Enemy strength opposite Fifth Army front 30th July 1917, War Diary Headquarters Fifth Army, WO95/519

The German *Fourth Army* on the day of the British offensive was deployed as follows, from south to north.

Line divisions

Group Lille:
Lille-Armentieres road to Warneton on the Lys. Not engaged.

Group Wytschaete:
Warneton on the Lys to Bellewaarde Lake (exclusive) north of the Menin road.
Five front divisions. *16th, 18th Reserve, 10th Bavarian, 22nd Reserve, 6th Bavarian.*

Group Ypres:
Bellewaarde Lake to Ypres-Staden railway.
Three front divisions. *38th, 235th, 3rd Guards.*

Group Dixmude:
Ypres-Staden railway to Noordschoote, (much of which behind the inundations). One front division, *111th Division* plus the *104th* (left) *Regiment* of the *40th Division.*

Group Nord:
Noordschoote to the coast. Mostly behind the inundations.

MarineKorps Flandern:
Coastal sector *1st, 2nd* and *3rd Marine Divisions*

As *Groups Lille* and *Nord* were not expected to be heavily engaged no Army reserves were provided.

Counter-attack divisions

Behind *Groups Wytschaete, Ypres and Dixmude*, six *Eingreif* division were assembled close to the Flanders I position and disposed as follows:

Group Wytschaete:
207th, 12th and *119th* covering the important Gheluvelt plateau.

Group Ypres
: *221st* and *50th Reserve.*

Group Dixmude:
2nd Guard Reserve.

Reserve divisions

Behind the six *Eingreif*-divisions of *Fourth Army* reserve was a second line of two divisions, *3rd Reserve* east of Roulers, and *79th Reserve* at Thourout, these in *Group of Northern Armies* reserve. Behind these about Ghent and Bruges was *Group Ghent* of two divisions, *23rd* and *9th Reserve* and the *5th Bavarian Division* was in Antwerp, all in position to oppose any possible British landing on the Dutch coast.

Gough's plan

As we have seen, on the 14th May the Northern Operations files containing the G.H.Q. plan for the forthcoming offensive were handed to General Gough by Colonel Macmullen. This plan envisaged a limited advance of about one mile on the first day, to capture as second objective, the German Second Line, to enable observation posts to be established both on the higher ground of Pilckem ridge and upon the Gheluvelt plateau. A two day pause was then planned for the forward movement of the field artillery to allow observed fire to cover the next advance, and to complete the capture and consolidation of the Gheluvelt plateau, prior to a further advance across the Steenbeek.

To Gough, this plan did not allow him to achieve the swift progress that the Commander-in-Chief had required. It contained no evidence of a rapid and vigorous drive towards the Passchendaele ridge, but rather a limited advance to the *Albrecht Stellung*. After all the thorough preparations to assemble his mighty Army, this plan fell woefully short of achieving Gough's requirements, not even threatening the German gun line. It did not meet with his approval and he set about revising it. At conference with his Corps Commanders on the 6th June the general plans for the first attack of the Northern Operation were discussed. Initially the direction of attack was to be north-northeast, pivoting on the left flank just north of Steenstraat and pasing south of Houthulst Forest, while the right flank advanced along the Passchendaele ridge. It is significant to note that Gough's initial proposal was for the final objective for the first day to be the line of the Steenbeek, an advance of between 2,500 and 3,000 yards. It was to prove a pity that this embryo plan was not adhered to. On the second day of attack the objective would be a line approximately Broodseinde – Gravenstafel – Schreiboom – Wijdendrift, an advance of between 2,000 and 3,000 yards. It was envisaged that if the enemy was particularly demoralised it may be possible to gain at least part of this line during the first attack, but the conference notes cautioned: 'As regards the proposed extension of objective for the first day's attack, the A.C. said that the question of the artillery support was the principle difficulty.'[146] It cannot be argued that Gough had not considered his artillery problems. Neither were the enemy's tactics of counter-attack unknown to Gough: 'The A.C. said that recently the enemy had delivered heavy counter-attacks after our initial attack. He wished to ensure prompt dealing with such attacks by improving the co-operation between artillery and aircraft after the initial attack had taken place.' The issues that were to be the principle problems on the 31st July had therefore been carefully, but subsequently ineffectively considered.

The next conference at Lovie on the 16th June considered the start date for the offensive. The French had reported that they would be ready by the 21st July; Fifth Army believed they would be ready by the 25th but this depended mainly on the supply and dumping of sufficient ammunition for the guns. The conservative objectives of the previous conference had now however been abandoned and a new scheme had been evolved, in which the second (and final) objective for the first day which had been proposed on the 6th June and conformed to the G.H.Q. plan, (the German Second Line, or approximately the line of the Steenbeek), should be pushed forward a further mile to a third objective to include the capture of the German Third Line. If things went well and the Third Line was taken, at the discretion of divisional commanders and without appreciable pause, the Army was to push on another mile to a fourth objective, to include the German Fourth Line, (Flanders I) on the Passchendaele ridge at Broodseinde. To address the already recognised problem of maintaining field artillery protection for the further advance, the report of the conference rather vaguely stated: 'As regards the provision of mobile artillery for the latter stages, it is *hoped* that the Divisional Artilleries of the two Army Reserve Divisions will be available to go forward and will not be in action previous to Zero. They will *probably* be allotted to the XVIII and XIX Corps.'(Authors italics)[147] This would be progress

---

[146] National Archives, report of Army Commanders conference Lovie Chateau 6th June 1916, War Diary Headquarters Fifth Army, WO95/519

[147] National Archives, report of Army Commanders conference Lovie Chateau 16th June 1916, War Diary Headquarters Fifth Army, WO95/519

indeed and just what Gough thought Haig required. The left flank would rest on the hamlet of Gravenstafel, and thence north-west along the London (Gravenstafel) ridge to Langemarck. The third objective (the German Third Line), once reported taken, was to be occupied by the battalions which had rested on the first objective after the initial assault. In places this plan envisaged, if the attack continued to the Flanders I Line, an advance of over 6,000 yards by heavily laden and by then undoubtedly exhausted troops, through two distinct defence zones infested with concrete machine gun bunkers. To compound the dangers, an advance to the fourth objective on the Flanders I Line would be beyond the effective support range of the covering field artillery batteries. By way of compensation for the lack of protection from the field artillery, all available heavy artillery would be standing by to fire a protective barrage in front of the advanced posts along Flanders I in the event of an S.O.S. call. Further, if the opportunity arose and enemy resistance was light, the advance was to be continued the same afternoon, the II Corps on Passchendaele, the XIX Corps on Goudberg, and the XVIII Corps on Poelcappelle. As stouter resistance from German reserves was considered likely along the fourth objective, a two or three day halt was planned in which to bring up artillery support in preparation for a further attack on the fourth day. On the fourth day of the offensive, it was hoped to reach the Passchendaele-Staden area of the main ridge. Optimism was obviously running riot, and the agreement reached in Paris for *limited* advances guaranteed not to pass beyond the range of supporting filed artillery appeared to have been totally brushed aside.

This was the bold Fifth Army plan for the rapid and vigorous thrust which Gough believed was required by Haig. The position and length of his front was settled and not in doubt. His right would rest on Observatory ridge on the south-west of the Gheluvelt plateau, while his left 13,000 yards to the north-west would be on the Ypres – Yser canal, 1,000 yards north of Boesinghe. The Second Army would protect his right flank between the Lys and the plateau, and the French First Army his left, up to the edge of the Yser inundations. To deal with the strength and depth of the German defences a prolonged preliminary bombardment of around nine days duration would be required. But there was little in the plan that reflected the agreed step by step approach, and careful sheltering of the infantry beneath the barrage of the field artillery. With the benefit of hindsight and with the knowledge of the future course of events, the whole scheme appears reckless in the extreme, given the strength and depth of the enemy's defensive position. An assault to this depth, where the attacking infantry would outstrip the support range of their field artillery, and would advance such a distance, guaranteeing exhaustion, even at the third of the four objectives, was surely to court disaster. From their point of view the Germans could not have wished for a better plan from the British. It was the type of attack von Lossberg had planned for, and it played nicely into the hands of his defence tactics. This was the attack the deep defence lines and multitude of concrete bunkers had been designed to disorganise and stop, and the battle the *Eingreif* divisions, should the British get that far forward, had been trained to fight. A seam of naivety appears to run through narrative of the conference report of the 16th June. Amongst the twelve key points recorded outlining the plan, including issues of immense importance such as objectives and barrages, numbers ten and eleven are worthy of note: '10) With reference to Artillery preparations, the Army Commander did not wish the H.A. to fire on roads more than was absolutely necessary in order to preserve them as much as possible for the future. 11) The necessity for every possible means to be taken to camouflage locations was impressed on Corps Commanders. There was no need for tents to be arranged in rigid lines, which only rendered their positions all the more conspicuous. Tents should be scattered, thereby taking advantage of cover available.' A sense of detached nonchalance appears to leaps from Neil Malcolm's words.

However filled with danger the plan may have appeared, Haig decided not to overrule his Army Commander, and to allow Fifth Army to continue in its own way and try for the further objectives. Even so Haig was uneasy in his own mind about the Fifth Army plan, undoubtedly influenced by his assurances given at the War Cabinet conference in June, (and subsequently by Robertson), when he had claimed that he had no intention of launching a tremendous offensive involving heavy losses, but rather to proceed using the step by step 'Pétain tactics' that had worked so well, but with limited results at Vimy and Messines. But in any event the objectives of the Northern Offensive, complying approximately to the nature of the enemy defence lines were in every respect different from Vimy and Messines, as was the geography of the Salient to which those lines clung. Could the tactics of the two previous successes be applied to Ypres? And could the Fifth Army plan possibly be passed off as a step by step approach, or was Gough offering an attempted break through? Where was the clear line to be drawn which defined one from the other, both in theory and on the ground? North of St. Julien the German Third Line lay well beyond the Steenbeek, and it had all along been considered unwise to cross the stream before the Gheluvelt plateau was secure. At the stream the field gun barrage was reaching its extreme range. So was the Steenbeek the defining line for a safe advance, as had been proposed on the 6th June? On the other hand the plan did not include a definite proposal to 'break through' the Flanders 1 Line, nor did it propose an immediate subsequent exploitation, for the German Flanders Position was just too deep to allow this, and Gough envisaged a number of large battles before this could be acheived. The next attack of a similar weight was to come in between three and ten days. Gough had not been in Paris so was not about to be influenced by 'Pétain tactics' and Haig had not gone out of his way to spread the Pétain gospel. In Gough's interpretation, which may now appear to lack imagination and common sense, he had planned for a limited step by step advance and at the time his plan did not lack support, even amongst the most outspoken of his Corps Commanders. To other observers however it smacked of an attempted break through. Again the confusion was in the interpretation of the word *limited*.

The Davidson memorandum

On Haig's return from London on the 25th June he was handed a memorandum written by Brigadier-General J.H. Davidson, head of Operations Branch at G.H.Q., roundly criticising in detail Gough's plan. Davidson made all the logical points again. Only proceed with a series of limited attacks. Do not attempt to seize objectives beyond an advance of about one mile on the first day. Confine the attack to a task within the capability of the infantry and the protection of the field artillery. The artillery softening up bombardment within a relatively shallow zone would be far more concentrated and therefore more effective. It was foreseen that there would be immediate German counter-attacks and it would be far preferable, 'to accept battle with those reserves when we are in an organised state, our guns in position, our troops not tired and our communications in good state, than to engage them in some forward position where we have none of these advantages. We shall not be in a position to obtain a victory or exploit success until we have thoroughly demoralised the enemy and defeated at all events the first series of divisions which he will bring up as reinforcements to the battle'.[148] He made several important points regarding the arrangements for the artillery. He argued that the enemy must be kept under remorseless fire, and that it would be unwise to plan for any forward movement of guns whilst the battle was in progress, for the simple reason that while guns were being moved they could not be in action. He observed that with an advance of limited depth the destructive barrage zone would be more concentrated. With a greater concentration of firepower in a smaller area this would go some way to negate the shortage of guns. Both these points were to come into prophetic focus on the 31st July.

It could be surmised that General Plumer would have endorsed these sentiments. But at a meeting convened by Haig at Cassel on the 28th June, at which Gough, Plumer and Davidson were present a different side to Plumer's tactical thinking became apparent, which seems in contrast to his more methodical image. In a private conversation with Davidson, Plumer, at odds with the memorandum said, 'Do you think that after making the vast preparations for attack on this position over a long period of months, if not years, and after sitting in the salient all this time, I am going to agree to limiting the progress and advance of my troops at the outset of the first day? I say definitely no, I would certainly not agree to any such limitation'.[149] This

---

[148] BOH p129
[149] Davidson *Haig:Master of the Field*. p31

statement adds another twist of complexity to understanding what Gough and to a point Plumer believed their objectives to be. Plumer seems to contradict his original plans, and his usual support of the shallow penetration, step by step approach. Had he been in the Salient too long, or was he trying, through Davidson, to show Haig his true offensive spirit?[150] In any event it was not Plumer's Army, that was to attempt a deep penetration of the enemy position, as Second Army south of the Ypres – Comines canal was only to establish a line of strong posts just short of the Warneton Line, an average advance of 500 yards. Whatever the reason for the change of heart, it must have encouraged Haig in making his final decision to have both his Army Commanders concur with the Fifth Army plan. Later, General Sir Charles Harington, Plumer's G.S.O. wrote, 'I can say without any hesitation that my Chief, General Sir H. Plumer, welcomed and endorsed the plan. He had known what it was to have his troops sitting day after day and winter after winter under the Messines – Wytschaete ridge and in front of Ypres, with the enemy holding all the commanding ground'.[151]

General Gough replied to the Davidson memorandum saying he agreed in its broad principles, 'in so far as it advocates a continuous succession of organised attacks'.[152] He then proceeded by weight of written argument to make it plain that he far from agreed with its broad principles. Some of his reasoning made sound sense and was shared with other senior officers of the Fifth Army. Lieutenant-General Sir Ivor Maxse, who, like Gough had gained his experience the hard way through practical lessons, concurred with his Army Commander. Gough was adamant that in previous campaigns opportunities had been missed by failing to strike deeply enough and subsequently failing to follow up the first attack immediately with another, and then another. He believed that the forces at his disposal were adequately organised to conduct an operation in this manner. Not to penetrate the enemies defences to a sufficient depth, risked failing to capture significant numbers of guns and prisoners. His argument implied that to advance to only the "Black Line", (the German Second Line), would not threaten the German field batteries, which could then be moved back to resist further assaults. To advance only to the "Black Line" on the first day with subsequent attacks to the "Green Line", (German Third Line), and then to the "Red Line", (German Fourth Line), would mean the moving of the artillery twice, instead of only once as would be the case with an advance to the Red Line on day one. This was a logical argument, but the execution of its logic depended upon the physical ability of the British infantry to carry it through, the powerful enemy artillery to remain passive, and the co-operation of the *Eingreif* divisions in not counter-attacking the overstretched and exhausted British who would by then be beyond the effective range of their field artillery. One of the most telling paragraphs in Gough's memorandum stated: 'The operations for the capture of the Passchendaele - Staden Ridge envisaged by me, and put I trust clearly before my corps commanders, do in truth constitute a succession of organised attacks at short intervals'.[153] Obviously there was not in Gough's mind a major difference between the Fifth Army plan and the G.H.Q. proposals, but simply a minor difference in interpretation and degree. The Australian Official Historian précis the situation perfectly. 'The fact stands out that not only was the whole Flanders offensive planned with a largely strategic objective, but the first stroke in it was delivered, not as a closely limited battle of attrition on the lines favoured by Pétain and Robertson, but with mixed aims – to penetrate as well as to wear out….Here again it by no means follows that Haig was wrong, but in this mixture of motives lay grave disadvantages.'[154]
Haig's optimistic hopes of a break through resulted in his ordering of the Cavalry Corps to move in July from behind the front at Arras and to concentrate at Merville and St Pol, 25 and 40 miles west of Ypres. The theory was that if the blows about to be struck upon the German line

---

[150] On the 22nd May after a meeting with Plumer, Haig had claimed in his diary: "I felt that the leaders have been on the defensive about Ypres so long that the real offensive spirit has to be developed". Douglas Haig Diaries and Letters p295
[151] Harington, *Plumer of Messines*. p111
[152] Harington, *Plumer of Messines*. p111
[153] BOH Appendix XV
[154] AOA p697

produced the hoped for results the Cavalry were still the only arm capable of exploitation. This was true, but the infantry would need to advance through, in some places, six lines of German defence before the cavalry could be in open country. Their premature use was soon to prove disastrous, but only on a mercifully small scale.

The importance of the Gheluvelt plateau

At Cassel on the 28th June Haig had discussed the Davidson memorandum with both Gough and Plumer. It was agreed that the Fifth Army plan should stand, but again Gough was warned by Haig, undoubtedly with Plumer's full support, to pay particular attention to the strong enemy defences on the Gheluvelt plateau. Once his right flank was firmly established upon it, and only then, should he proceed with the attack along the ridge to Broodseinde. This exposed another major difference between Fifth Army plan and G.H.Q. plan. On one hand Haig had agree to Gough's plan, but on the other he had introduced a major caveat possibly dislocating it entirely. Gough's plan for day one envisaged to push on if at all possible, and at the discretion of divisional commanders, to Flanders I, the Red Line on Broodseinde - Passchendaele ridge. It seemed however that on the instructions of the Commander-In-Chief, this action was dependant on, and subject to, the securing of the Gheluvelt plateau. But what if the centre successfully advanced across the Steenbeek, while the right made little progress on the plateau? The answer was soon to become all too apparent.

Fifth Army intelligence summaries during July had pointed to a great deal of German preparation on the Gheluvelt plateau. The report of the 7th July indicated that work to strengthen the position was being carried out more intensely than on any other part of the front and that a great concentration of artillery was being gathered to the east of the high ground. It was recognised that this would be the pivotal point of the German line in the event of that line being pushed back to the Steenbeek. The obvious danger had been pointed out many times that German artillery east of the plateau, through observed enfilade fire could seriously disrupt British progress in the Steenbeek and Hanebeek valleys, towards the main Passchendaele ridge to the north. Gough had planned to spread his divisions and guns evenly along the length of his front and no change in planning was made to allow for the greater German defensive strength at Gheluvelt, either by way of extra infantry or concentration of artillery fire. For some unknown reason the matter was not subsequently pursued by Haig to the point where any decisive action was taken. The consequences were to be severe.

The dispositions of Gough's four attacking corps were now to be, south to north:
Boundary with Second Army to:

II Corps	Klein Zillebeke road to Ypres – Roulers railway
XIX Corps	Ypres – Roulers railway to 500 yards north of Ypres – St Julian road at Wieltje
XVIII Corps	500 yards north of Wieltje to 400 yards north of Lancashire Farm
XIV Corps	400 yards north of Lancashire Farm to bend in canal 1,250 yards northwest of Ypres – Staden railway bridge over Yser canal at boundary with French First Army.

The positions of attacking divisions by Corps were now to be, south to north:

II Corps:	24th, 30th, 8th
XIX Corps	15th, 55th
XVIII Corps	39th, 51st
XIV Corps	38th, Guards, to boundary with French First Army

On the 27th June, while visiting Lieutenant-General Sir Claud Jacob at II Corps (which was to attack the plateau), Haig was advised that the Corps flank should be moved further south, to include within the area of its attack the German positions on Tower Hamlets spur. Jacob had recognised the danger of a counter attack from this position against his right flank as he advanced towards Zonnebeke. Haig continued to be concerned about the Gheluvelt plateau, of which Tower Hamlets spur was a southern extension, and agreed to the plan. It was arranged that 24th Division, the left division of the Second Army, should be transferred to Fifth Army at once with a quantity of field and heavy artillery. Fifth Army's front was subsequently moved south on the 4th July to the Klein Zillebeke - Zandvoorde road.

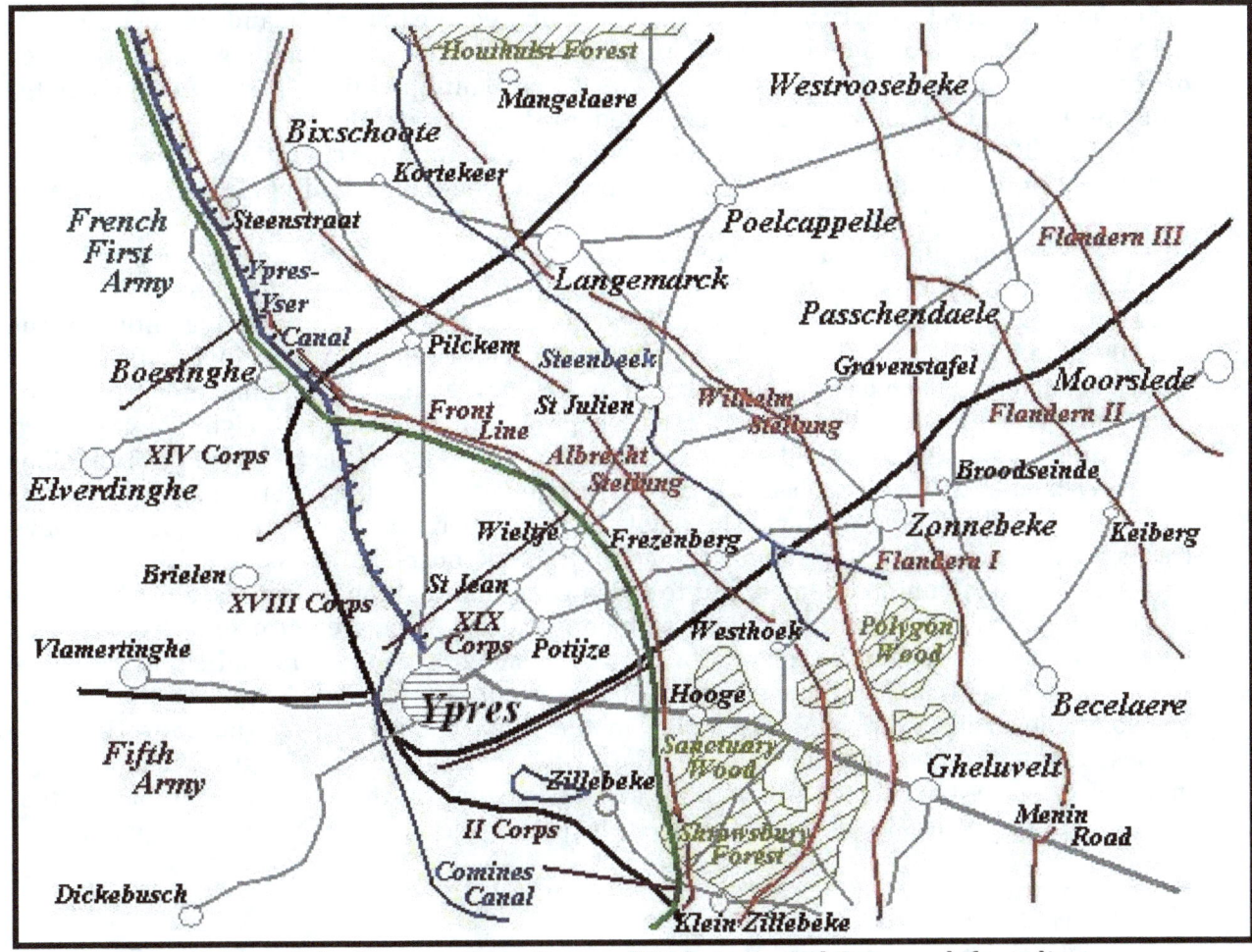

Dispositions of the four attacking Corps of Fifth Army and German defence lines

The attack of First Army at Lens the 28th June

Thirty miles south of Ypres, on the 28th June, Sir Henry Horne's First Army was to carry out a feint attack towards Lens in accordance with instructions issued at Doullens on the 7th May, for those Armies not involved in the Northern Operation to tie down and wear out the enemy wherever possible. Horne was to attack with three corps, the XIII, to attack on a 2,300 yard front between Gavrelle and Oppy, and the inner divisions of the Canadian Corps and the I Corps, to attack on a front of 4,800 yards astride the River Souchez, and capture Hill 65. The plan had been to attack in the middle of July, but as Horne had been told on the 15th June that most of his siege and heavy artillery would be on the way to Flanders, he brought forward the attack to the 28th. The attacks succeeded in capturing most of the objectives, although heavy rain hampered the operation. It had also been hoped to use the left division of I Corps to attack Hill 70, north of Lens, but due to lack of resources this was postponed until August.

An unfortunate postponement in Zero Day

The preparations for the Battle of Messines had taken many weeks, but when the battle ended on the 14th June the work necessary on the infrastructure to allow for Gough's attack from the Salient had not seriously begun. Unfortunately there was no chance of immediately taking up where Plumer had left off, and continuing the attack on the shaken enemy. It was to take six weeks from the 14th June to carry out the engineering works, and assemble the massive forces required by the Fifth Army to launch the main offensive. The digging of the Messines mines had been under way since the end of 1915, but as we have seen the operation orders for that battle had not been issued by the Second Army until the 10th May 1917.[155] Manpower resources throughout January, February and March had been limited due to the demands of operations on the Somme and at Arras, but engineering preparations for Messines, including the construction of roads and railways had begun slowly in April, and built-up with greater urgency after the date for the opening of the battle had been made clear on the 7th May.[156] Dumping of ammunition had commenced in March. Taking into consideration preparations already in hand, and accepting the middle of April as a start point for the main build-up, it had taken seven weeks to prepare for Messines.

It was not until the Battle of Messines was over that the labour required to prepare for the main offensive was available. Sixty-four labour companies were moved to the Ypres front, in addition to six Chinese labour companies. The area which was handed over to the Fifth Army on the 10th June was well provided with shelters, water, and communications, but sufficient only for the small force which had held it to that point. On the 6th June, Corps commanders had been asked how long they required to complete their preparations. II Corps thought about 40 days were required, and XIX Corps had asked for the same dependant on the arrival of the Tunnelling Company labour. XVIII Corps had required two months. XIV Corps, which had to cross the Ypres-Yser canal required 65 days. The whole massive operation to construct roads, railways, tracks, bridges, camps, water supplies, communications, hospitals, dressing stations, battery emplacements, ammunition dumps, and to move guns, ammunition, materials, and supplies of all kinds had now to begin in the Salient, all hampered to a much greater extent than they had been at Messines by enemy artillery. Corps and divisional headquarters and staffs had to be established in the limited confines of the Salient around and behind Ypres, and the infantry divisions and artillery brigades assembled in the same cramped area. The pause between battles was unfortunate but inevitable, as the British did not posses the guns, manpower or material to make major preparations both at Messines and in the Ypres Salient. Many other reasons for the pause have been suggested, including the claim that Gough's appointment

---

[155] BOH p416 appendix VIII
[156] National Archives, Record of verbal instructions, Haig to Army Commanders, Doulens 7th May, WO158/311

brought with it an inevitable delay, due to the time required for him to settle in and make his plans. But as we have seen Gough was in his headquarters by the 31st May, and had drawn up the Fifth Army plan by the 16th June, two days after the end of the Messines battle and over six weeks before the beginning of the main offensive. Clearly there was another reason. Irrespective of other engineering considerations, the moving of the artillery alone was an enormous task. Distribution of artillery figures show that in the four weeks from the 8th June to the 6th July 1,083 guns were moved into the Salient, 349 of which were heavy. A further 1,227 arrived in the two weeks from the 6th to the 20th July, 406 of which were heavy.[157] Whilst ignoring the enormous task of preparing for a great offensive, some minds have striven gamely to identify other causes for the pause. It was not the appointment of Gough that held up the opening of the next phase, but simply the enormous logistical tasks of engineering, construction and movement to complete the required preparations.[158]

At the Lillers conference on the 14th June the date of the opening of the Northern Offensive had been discussed: 'As regards the date of the main offensive the Commander-in-Chief stated that the sooner our attack is launched, the less will be the opposition encountered. Therefore we must aim at attacking as early as possible. The French have stated that they hope to be ready by the 21st July. The Commander-in-Chief repeated that we should try to be ready by the 25th July.'[159] General Anthoine commander of the French First Army which was to operate on the British left, reported on the 1st July that he would not be ready by the 25th due to lack of labour to construct gun emplacements and ammunition dumps for his artillery. To help with the problem Haig sent 7,200 men to assist with the work but was most unhappy with the further postponement.

The further delay can in no way be placed solely upon French shoulders, for on the 7th July at a G.H.Q. conference at Watou, it was Gough's turn to request a postponement of five days, until the 30th July, to allow for the replacement of damaged guns, (an indication of the efficiency of the German counter-battery fire) and the late arrival of much of his artillery. With the benefit of the extra time, Gough suggested that the artillery could get into a more forward position to enable it to better support the infantry advance from the second to the third objectives, and the prolonged bombardment period, with resultant destruction of enemy positions would enable the next advance to be carried out by the same divisions, thus in the long run saving time. This argument convinced Haig sufficiently to agree to a three day postponement until the 28th.

On the 21st July General Anthoine, upon whose shoulders Pétain had placed the added responsibility of *guaranteeing* the success of the French First Army, reported that due to recent dull and cloudy weather the French artillery had been unable to complete necessary counter battery fire and demanded three more days until the 31st for completion of the task. There were

---

[157] National Archives, distribution of artillery statistics for June and July WO95/14

[158] See Prior and Wilson *Passchendaele the Untold Story* p51.'But of course the choice of a new man meant that time would be needed for him to establish a headquarters, familiarize himself with the ground, and produce a plan. So the introduction of Gough also inexorably meant the introduction of a significant gap between operations at Messines and the commencement of the main campaign.' It is also claimed by John Mosier in *The Myth of the Great War*, that the German use of mustard gas was the primary cause of the delay, and the British, in an effort to minimise the impact of the new gas threw the blame for the delay on the French. 'The gas shelling forced the offensive to be delayed (the British attempted to minimize the impact of the gas shelling by blaming the French for the delay)'…See John Mosier, *The Myth of the Great War* p283. In *A Short History of the Great War* Albert Frederick Pollard rather tenuously claims Belgian reluctance to accept collateral damage as another possibility for reasons for the delay. 'Probably they were political. Belgium, notwithstanding her passion for liberation, cannot have desired the rest of her soil to be restored in the condition of the Wytschaete ridge--a horror of desolation unfit for man or even for nature's growths; and there seemed little prospect of driving the Germans out except by a succession of ruinous tactical victories.' *A Short History of the Great War* Chapter XVI. The real reason is more prosaic, and as has been shown it is unlikely that any of the above assertions are correct.

[159] National Archives, Advanced GHQ OAD 291/27 p4 15th June WO158/311

no calls from Fifth Army for extra time for the artillery to complete its work, but this did not necessarily indicate that all had gone to plan. Haig was now becoming extremely anxious for two reasons. The flank attack along the coastal strip required the right period of the tides between the 7th and 8th of August to launch the operation. It was now becoming doubtful whether sufficient progress would be made out of the position in the Salient to coordinate with the coastal operation. The greater chances of the weather turning wet towards late August and September were also a concern. Gough reported that he would be ready by the 28th, but rather than alter his plans he would prefer to wait until the 31st when the French would be ready. Bearing in mind the precarious state of the French Army further south, and with a will to allow Anthoine the best chance of success in accordance with Pétain's wishes,[160] Haig reluctantly agreed to the further delay. General Rawlinson was informed that the coastal operation would also be postponed until the next high tides. The 31st July it would be, at 3:50 am. The consequences of delay and of the lost dry days between the 25th and the beginning of the heavy rain on the 29th July would prove to be most severe.[161]

The training and assembly of the infantry

Throughout late June and early July the battalions that would comprise the striking force of Fifth Army began to move to Flanders. Camps west of St.Omer began to fill as the battalions gradually regrouped into their brigades and the brigades into full divisions. The attacks in which they were soon to be engaged were going to be complex operations requiring advances to deep objectives, involving infantry movements closely coordinated with the protective artillery barrages. Precise objective lines were to be allocated to specific units, and pauses on each objective were to be precisely timed to enable consolidation of the position won, under the protection of a standing barrage. During the pause the supporting wave of infantry would have time to assemble before passing-through or 'leap-frogging' the front wave, and continuing the advance, in concert with a creeping barrage.

The lessons of Messines had been well learned and training in new tactics to deal with the German concrete blockhouses proceeded relentlessly on a daily basis. Divine services were the only exception to days otherwise filled with physical exercises, musketry practice and bayonet training. Contrary to some accounts, the Lee Enfield .303 rifle was still considered the infantryman's best friend, and as will soon be accounted, huge numbers of wounds were inflicted on the enemy with the bayonet, (or 'sword' in Rifle Regiments), which was of little use without the rifle.[162] The Hales and Mills rifle grenades, fired from the Lee Enfield rifle, were also

---

[160] Petain had written to Haig on the 30th June, 'l'offensive des Flandres doit etre assure d'un success absolu, 'imperieusement exige par les facteurs moraux du moment'
[161] Interestingly, Sixt von Arnim, in a *Fourth Army* report dated the 12th August 1917 claims the Germans believed the date for the opening of the offensive to be the 19th July. The delay was put down to: 1) The effective results of the German H.E. and gas bombardments. 2) The German attack at Nieuport on the 10th. 3) The delay incurred by bringing up the French reserves. National Archives, information collected from German archives CAB45/172. von Arnim was certainly correct as far as points 1 & 3 were concerned.
[162] See Prior and Wilson *Passchendaele the Untold Story* p81 'Of least value was the Lee Enfield rifle. It retained a role in repelling counter-attacks once an enemy position had been overrun, but it was difficult to employ during the actual advance on a defended position and anyway was presented with few targets.' Possibly not a statement with which, at the time, most RSM's would have concurred. As in 1917 the British Army did not posses an automatic assault rifle, or light machine gun (other than the Lewis which was rather too heavy for use as an assault weapon, although at times it was used in that rôle), it is difficult to imagine an infantry attack striking fear and dread in the heart of the enemy without the threat of the 1907 pattern bayonet atop the Mk III* SMLE. As the Lee Enfield rifle with bayonet fixed was at the core of the infantry assault, it could hardly be considered as 'of least value', and it is difficult to imagine what could have readily replaced it. There was a major difference between advancing to the assault, and trench raiding, where the rifle was certainly of less

to become important assets. Special attention was given in training to platoon fire and movement attacks, with Lewis gunners and rifle grenadiers bringing mock blockhouses under fire, while bombing parties worked around the flanks, and crept in close enough to bomb out the garrison, a task soon to become frighteningly commonplace resulting in numerous acts of gallantry. Full scale representations of the ground to be attacked were created, complete with routes of approach, headquarters dugouts, front lines, and enemy trenches and strong-points. Trench maps of the enemy positions were provided, and if the practice field could not precisely replicate the orientation of the map grid, correction bearings were to be applied accordingly, to enable a correct line of attack. To allow proper forming up, jump-off positions and company boundaries were marked out. Objectives were identified at an equivalent position and distance as they appeared on the ground. Mock attacks were practised, with forward companies advancing in artillery formation, then stopping at their objective, and allowing support companies to leap-frog through to continue towards their further target. Advances were practiced keeping a strict distance of 100 yards between the front and second waves, and 200 yards between the second and third.

The training was not limited to battalion operations, but included full divisional exercises. On the 14th July, the 30th Division carried out a practice attack on the Tournehem training ground, near Nordausques, mid-way between Calais and St. Omer.[163] Battalions marched out to the training area at 9:45 p.m. on the 13th and Zero hour was to be 3:40 a.m. on the morning of the 14th, the battalion cookers accompanying the exercise to provide the men with hot tea an hour before Zero. The 30th Division was to attack the vital Gheluvelt plateau, with three objectives, the Blue, Black and Green Lines and these were identified as such on the training field. Two brigades were to advance to the Black Line where the barrage would pause, and from where at a precise time and with the support of two tanks a third brigade was to advance towards the Green Line. A contact aircraft was also to be part of the exercise to identify the position of flares fired by the forward infantry. The exercise was as realistic as could be devised, the only participants not included being the enemy. All went extremely well and by around 6:30 a.m. the battalions were back at their billets enjoying breakfast, some looking forward to an annual inter-battalion sports meeting in the afternoon. If the battle went as smoothly it would be a walk over.

Less than a week later the attacking divisions began moving up in buses, by train, or by march towards Ypres, mostly into hutted or bivouac camps about Poperinghe. Nights in these camps were inevitably disturbed by aerial bombing, which caused many casualties. For some, safer accommodation was available closer to the front in a system of deep tunnels and dug-outs, in places excavated 15 to 20 yards deep into the clay and capable of housing many hundreds of infantry. All available time was spent on intensive training of every skill required to carry out an effective attack. Over the next few days the concentration of forces continued, moving by the 27th to camps about Dickebusch, Vlamertinghe and Elverdinghe, battalions then being within an hour's march of the front line. On the 28th / 29th the march up across allotted tracks into support positions 1,000 yards behind the lines was completed, the final march up to the assembly trenches and jumping off positions to be made on the 30th.

The Artillery

From the viewpoint of the Royal Artillery, the attack from the Salient presented many more problems than had faced them at Messines. The very shape of the German Flanders position now to be bombarded was unfavourable, and was totally different from either Messines or Vimy. At Messines, the outline of the German salient pushing west into the British lines had allowed the British gunfire to be concentrated, shooting concentrically towards the centre of the

---

use, more compact weapons being more appropriate. See Anthony Saunders, 2000, *Dominating the Enemy* Stroud, Sutton Publishing pp128-145
[163] National Archives, War Diary of 30th Division, WO95/2329

arc. In the Ypres Salient the situation was reversed. The British guns would be firing out of the arc and the effective weight of fire on any given area would therefore be lessened. The batteries were packed into the restricted space of the Salient, in positions obvious to observers on the higher ground, providing an excellent target to enemy gunners.

In the Salient the depth of the German position was also much greater, many targets being east of the Gheluvelt plateau – Broodseinde ridge. From Brielen, an area of concentration of Fifth Army heavy artillery 1,500 yards west of the Ypres-Yser canal, the distance to the Flanders I Line near Broodseinde, which Gough hoped his infantry may reach on the first day, was 11,000 yards, (six and a quarter miles), and into the German assembly and communication areas on the eastern side of the Passchendaele ridge around the Flanders II position was over 14,000 yards, towards the extreme range of the biggest guns. From the northern concentration of guns in the Elverdinge – Woesten group, the distance to Flanders I was around 15,500 yards. The length of the enemy position around the Salient was in turn also much greater, tactical targets such as German batteries having to be engaged from Zandvoorde in the south, to Houthulst Forest in the north, an arc length of around 21,000 yards, (approaching 12 miles).

At Messines there had been 2,266 guns and howitzers, 756 of which were medium or heavy, firing on a front of 15,000 yards. At Ypres on the Fifth Army front, there were to be 2,174 guns and howitzers deployed, 1,098 of which were 18-pounders, 324 4.5-inch howitzers, and 752 of which were medium or heavy, firing on a front of 11,500 yards.[164] But of greater importance is to compare the number of guns on each front, with the target length of the German Third Line on that front. At Messines the Oosttaverne Line (German Third Line) was about 11,000 yards long, whereas in the Salient the *Wilhelm Stellung* (German Third Line) was about 16,000 yards long. This gives a startling figure of around one gun per 5 yards targeting the German Third Line at Messines, reduced to one gun per 7.5 yards targeting the German Third Line in the Salient. To have achieved an equivalent weight of fire on the German Third Line in the Salient as had been the case at Messines, Gough would have required at least 3,200 guns, 1,000 more than he actually had. The further the infantry advanced out of the Salient the worse the situation would become. The greater the distance from the British gun line the less damage would be inflicted on German defences. The opposite had been the case at Messines.

An even more revealing figure can be obtained by comparing the total area between the German Front and Third lines at Messines, and in the Salient. At Messines there was approximately 26,000,000 square yards between the front and Oosttaverne lines, giving a concentration of one gun per 12,000 square yards. In the Salient between the German Front Line and the *Wilhelm Stellung* there were approximately 54,000,000 square yards, giving a concentration of one gun per 24,500 square yards. The figures, although somewhat academic, do give an illustration of the problem, as real targets could be located anywhere within these areas. Simply put there was twice the gun concentration per square yard at Messines up to the German Third Line. Given Gough's plan to advance to the *Wilhelm Stellung* and possibly even beyond, the gunners faced a daunting and near impossible task in attempting to reduce the German defences in preparation for the attack of the Fifth Army. The lack of density of firepower could be solved in two ways. Increase the time available to bombard the target, or reduce the depth of the attack. Neither was an option to Gough, even if the problem had been identified in the first place.

The total number of shells of all calibres fired also points to the weakness of the artillery preparation for the battle on the 31st July. At Messines there had been 3,258,000 shells fired along the 9 mile front. The number of shells fired in preparation for the 31st July was 4,283,550, but this was along a 15 mile front, as it included the 6 ½ miles between la Basse Ville and the Kleine Zillebeke road to be attacked by the Second Army. A total of 789 guns and howitzers remained on the front of the Second Army, of which 112 heavy and 210 field guns were concentrated near the right flank of the Fifth Army to support the main offensive. The French

---

[164] BOH p135 The figures from the GHQ distribution of artillery statistics are slightly different showing 1,176 18-pounders, 370 4.5-inch howitzers, but concurring in the number of medium and heavy guns, National Archives WO95/14

First Army on the left would add another 300 heavy guns and 240 75's, but again in simple terms given the length and depth of the target, there were just not enough guns. That there were not enough guns did not however alter the fact that those that were firing against wire belts, trenches, strong-points, enemy batteries and blockhouses, were doing enormous damage to the ground, which was gradually becoming a cratered waste of churned earth, and smashed and blocked ditches and streams. The ground was to become very difficult to cross for both men and machines. Another disturbing problem was soon to become evident. Irrespective of how many times the guns fired at them, the concrete blockhouses were proving virtually impossible to destroy with artillery. There were glaring weaknesses in the plan for the long preparatory bombardment, and although there was sufficient firepower to reduce the enemy's first and second lines of defence, there was insufficient strength to guarantee in doing more than this.

The protective barrage

The protective barrage was to be provided by approximately two-thirds of the field guns in each corps sector. Its purpose was to provide the infantry with protection from immediate retaliation by enemy infantry, and to allow assembly and organization at each objective, before advancing to the next objective. The numerous objective lines to be reached by the infantry, at varying ranges, along different sections of the front, with different timings for stands, lifts and creep rates, inevitably led to an extraordinarily complex fire-plan for the field artillery. Variations such as ground conditions, serious obstacles or stronger enemy defences would inevitably require a slower barrage creep. As the advance was planned to continue for up to 8 hours (which did not include any subsequent S.O.S. calls), it was to going to be a long and tiring day for the gunners. The barrage plan for each division was different, due to the varying shape and size of the sector to be attacked.[165] The overall plan provided for a barrage to be put down on the enemy's front line at Zero Hour, and remain stationary for 5 minutes. For the first ten minutes after Zero each gun would fire at a rate of 4 rounds per minute, subsequently slackening to 2 rounds per minute. After the 5 minute concentration on the enemy front line, the barrage would lift, and creep forward at a set rate, until at about 1 hour after Zero it stood around 300 yards beyond the first objective for around ½ an hour. During this period the barrage would thin to 1 round per two minutes. After the pause the barrage would again thicken to 4 rounds per minute to indicate its intention to move, and then lift towards the second objective, until at around 2 hours after Zero it stood 300 yards beyond. After a 4½ hour pause 300 yards beyond the second objective the barrage would lift towards the third objective where it would finally stand 300 yards beyond until 7 hours 48 minutes after Zero.

    The rate at which the barrage moved was critical, as if it crept too quickly it would move away from the advancing infantry and they would loose the benefit of its protection in suppressing enemy retaliatory machine gun and rifle fire. If the ground conditions were bad due to wire, the obstruction of smashed timber, mud, shellfire damage, or if the enemy resistance was extra stubborn, the movement of the infantry would be drastically slowed. All these factors were to be taken into account when planning the barrage. A rate of 25 yards per minute was chosen after the first 250 yards (which would be at a faster rate), but in many places especially on the very difficult ground of the Gheluvelt plateau this was found to be too fast, as it had been suspected it would be. The fact that the advance to the deeper objectives would be getting dangerously close to the maximum effective range of the field guns was to be addressed.

During the pause on the second objective a number of the field batteries were to move forward to positions sufficiently advanced to support the attack to the third objective. The G.H.Q. and Operations Branch plans had allowed two days to carry out this redeployment of the field batteries. Gough's plan allowed for 4 ½ hours, but as Davidson had rather obviously pointed

---

[165] See Chapter Two, endnote 13 for a detailed description for the plan of 30th Division and for a comparison with 8th Division.

out, whilst they were moving they could not be firing. The guns were to be in position and ready to open fire by 10:00 a.m. It was certainly aggressive; it was also near impossible.

The Artillery Plan

The main artillery Plan was issued on the 30th June, and was modelled on that which had worked so well at Messines. Preparation to reduce the German defences began formally on the 16th of July. The medium and heavy guns were organised into counter battery and bombardment groups, each with a distinct task. Four main concentrations of batteries were dispersed to the west of Ypres, each approximately 3,500 to 5,000 yards behind the British Front Line. The artillery of three Australian divisions 1st, 2nd and 5th of I Anzac Corps, whose infantry were not yet in the Salient were added to this strength, being deployed from about the 19th July.

The II Corps, whose heavy batteries were concentrated around Dickebusch, had with the addition on the 4th July of the 24th Division, a three division frontage, and therefore had been allocated extra artillery, which consisted of three counter battery and three bombardment double groups of heavy artillery, each single group consisting of four to six siege, heavy, or medium batteries. The heavy and medium artillery of XIX Corps was situated on the western side of Ypres, XVIII Corps about Brielen, and XIV Corps about Elverdinge – Woesten, each of these three corps deploying two counter battery double groups and three bombardment single groups, one of which was a reinforcing group. X Corps on the left flank of Second Army were to assist II Corps with a concentration of guns around Vierstraat to give fire support on the corps boundary, 4th Australian Divisional artillery being moved up from Messines as part of this concentration.

The field batteries were gradually deployed closer up to the front lines. In II Corps, guns were concentrated into the areas east of Zillebeke Lake, with forward batteries up towards the woods on the western slope of the ridge. These included a field artillery group of 2nd Australian Division with batteries just south of the Comines canal supporting 24th Division, and a group from 1st Australian Division near Zillebeke Lake supporting 18th Division. The II Corps was also stronger in field artillery, each of its divisions supported by around nine field artillery brigades, while the divisions of other corps had six. But the front it was to assault was approximately a third as long again as the other three corps, and the shattered remains of the wooded areas along the western face of the Gheluvelt plateau were expected to make the going very hard for the infantry, all demanding the extra weight of barrage from the protective field artillery fire. Field batteries of XIX Corps were brought up about Potijze and St Jean, with others on the western bank of the Yser canal, which included the artillery of 5th Australian Division in support of 15th British Division. The guns of XVIII Corps were mainly west of the canal, with some in forward positions north and northwest of La Brique, whilst all those of XIV Corps were west of the canal, and mostly within 1,200 yards of it. The enormous preparations of constructing battery positions, moving and mounting guns and stockpiling ammunition were proceeding in full view of the German observation posts on the elevated ground across Pilckem ridge and on the Gheluvelt plateau, with the inevitable intervention and disruption by German artillery.

The German Artillery

The British estimate of German artillery strength at around 1,500 guns was very near correct. German artillery arrangements had been most thorough, up to three alternative emplacements being built for each battery, enabling them to be moved from one position to another, one gun sometimes remaining in position and firing to give the impression of a full battery in action. Under these circumstances, observation from the air of shoots on gun pits and accurate calculation of batteries destroyed was going to be difficult for the British gunners. It was soon clear that counter-battery fire and bombardment of German strong-points was not going to be as thorough or successful as it had been at Messines. In fact German counter-battery fire was itself proving most disruptive and destructive to British artillery, especially in the II Corps area. This was due mainly to the concentration of German guns to the east of the Gheluvelt plateau, about Becelare, Gheluvelt and Zandvoorde, which although outnumbered by British guns were very well co-ordinated under one commander and could bring down an overwhelming fire-concentration at short notice on any target within range. This organisation was employed on several occasions during the preliminary duels to knock out or drive back the British batteries which had crossed the Ypres - Comines canal and ventured forward towards the ridge in the neighbourhood of Zillebeke.

Group Wytschaete's artillery was achieving local superiority. The Germans were enjoying the advantage that they always held at Ypres, and the British had experienced at Messines; firing concentrically into a salient, and with the great advantage of the German forward positions on the ridges giving them the benefit of observed fire day and night. The German gunners also had a new and terrible weapon in their armoury, Mustard Gas. The work of the Royal Engineers and the Royal Artillery was made more arduous by the failure to dominate the German batteries, bearing in mind the British guns were only coming into action gradually as they arrived, and as soon as they could be established. The tasks of the Engineers throughout the Salient and rear areas back to a range of over seven miles, on roads, battery positions and supply dumps was under continuous H.E. and often gas shelling. The German use of their new weapon, Mustard Gas (dichlorethyl sulphide), added to the discomfort. During its first use in the Salient on the nights of the 12th / 13th of July, Ypres was deluged with the new gas causing 2,014 casualties, most of whom thankfully overcame the worst of the effects.[166] The new gas was delivered by shells

---

[166] Much has been made of the dire consequences inflicted upon Fifth Army due to the enemy use of Mustard gas during July. Denis Winter claims that, 'The impact of mustard was so great that British records were all but wiped clean to conceal the degree of embarrassment it caused'. *Haig's Command* p95. This is not so, as many references exist in official documents describing its use and affects. A report on the gas bombardment of the 12th / 13th by Surgeon-General Bruce Skinner written on the 15th July stated: 'It was clear that a lethal gas [phosgene] had been put over at the same time as the lachrymatory mustard oil. The mustard oil seemed to dull the sense of smell, so that those who had put on respirators removed them too soon as they could not smell gas. Consequently, they not only got the eyes affected but also were poisoned by the lethal gas. It is necessary therefore, during a gas shell bombardment of any nature, to keep respirators on until orders are issued for them to be discontinued. This applies especially to men in dug-outs or any place where air does not circulate freely, as in a town or wood. As far as I can gauge at present the majority of those affected with this mustard oil lachrymatory only, should be fit to return to duty in from 7 to 14 days. No permanent damage to the eyes has been noted to date. But the affection when severe is extremely painful, and for this reason men should be advised to wear their respirators as ordered.' A report by Captain Monier-Williams, Chemical Advisor to Fifth Army gives a full account of a visit to Ypres on the 13th July: 'Practically the whole of the town of Ypres was affected, and also some of the battery positions outside the town....Two blind shells have been collected and sent to Central Laboratory for examination. They were painted blue with yellow head and were marked on the base with a green cross and on the side near the shoulder, with a similar cross in yellow. Fuze:- EKZ 17....In all cases the symptoms appear to have been very much the same. First, a tendency to sneeze, with gradually increasing nose and throat irritation. Later on, in some instances as much as six or eight hours after exposure to the gas, intense and very painful irritation and inflammation of the eyes, accompanied by free discharge of mucus from the nostrils and occasional fits of vomiting. Many men complained also of pains in the forehead and stomach. The majority of cases passing through No. 47 Field Ambulance did not appear to be severely ill. And no deaths have been reported as yet....The cases which I saw today were almost all marked by intense and painful irritation of the eyes, making it impossible to open the eyes at all. The skin was also blistered in places, on the face and also on the buttocks, where men must have sat down on earth where a shell had burst previously. In all cases where Small Box Respirators were put on in time and worn until the bombardment had ceased and the gas had cleared away no ill-effects whatever were experienced.' National Archives, War Diary Fifth Army headquarters, 27th July 1917, WO95/520. It is evident that although Mustard Gas was a great hazard and caused terrible

which at first appeared to be duds, not bursting in the usual way but making an unusual plop sound upon landing. The gas had little smell, initial indication of its presence more usually being felt either by stinging in the eyes or respiratory tract, or on other parts of the body, especially moist areas. An extra filter fitted to the British small box respirator overcame most of the inhalation dangers, but the dangers of skin contact were more problematic.[167]

The preparatory and retaliatory barrages

It was evident that the results of the British bombardment, and especially the counter-battery fire were not as successful as the senior gunners were reporting them to be. The reports of Fifth Army intelligence, which told of continuous heavy fire from enemy guns on communications and battery areas was in direct contradiction to information given to Haig on the 25th July by Lieutenant-General Sir Noel Birch, Artillery Advisor at G.H.Q. who claimed that he was confident that the upper hand had been gained over the German artillery. In and around the Salient and on the gun lines this clearly was not the situation, especially in the case of the continual destructive fire from the *Group Wytschaete* guns east of Gheluvelt. Haig was naturally impressed with Birch's reports, but unfortunately was also misled. Birch claimed to have discussed the situation with Major-General Uniacke the C.R.A. of Fifth Army, who had apparently expressed himself 'very satisfied'. He was obviously not reading his own Army's intelligence reports. Haig noted in his diary on the 28th July, 'in fact my artillery advisor is of opinion that "we have already cowed the Enemy's artillery"...'.[168] A more realistic picture was portrayed in the Fifth Army War Diary: '26th July; Considerable shelling of our front line and communication trenches except in XVIII Corps area. Fewer gas shells used and Ypres intermittently shelled. Our bombardment continues, many destructive shoots being carried out. Hostile artillery very active during the night on II Corps front, and intermittent shelling of communication trenches and support line in XIV Corps sector. 27th July: During the day the front trenches of the II Corps were heavily shelled, also the area east of Zillebeke. A heavy 5 minute barrage was put down west of Cambridge Trench in the XIX Corps area at 11.30 a.m. The XIX Corps area was shelled considerably. A very heavy barrage was put along the front of the XIV Corps at 9.30 p.m. and the Canal in the XVIII Corps area was also heavily shelled till 11.30 p.m. After dark the XIV Corps old front line [the Guards had crossed the Canal this day] was heavily shelled, also Ypres and the area to the south with gas shells.' Over the next three days the hostile shelling decreased but

---

injuries, its immediate affect on the build up for the offensive has been over stated in some accounts. Denis Winter also claims that there is a reference in Fifth Army War Diary to 'one man in six becoming a mustard casualty in a single division after the barrage of the 26th July' citing WO95/519 as his reference, *Haig's Command* p95. WO95/519 is in fact the Diary for June and not July, and Mustard gas was not used at Ypres until mid July. The author has not been able to find any reference in the July Diary (WO95/520) for any such casualty figures.

[167] Yperite, or Yellow Cross as the gas was also known, left the shell as an oily liquid, which evaporated very slowly, and would penetrate clothing easily. As a liquid, it would lay for some time in trenches before evaporating, where inevitably it would be sat in, and in other ways come into contact with clothing and eventually the skin, when it would cause severe blistering. The longer the exposure, the worse the blistering, and serious cases would become gangrenous. The effect on the eyes could be horrific, causing the eye lids to swell and forcing the eyes to close. In serious cases the cornea would become ulcerated and would decay, causing permanent blindness. The effect on the respiratory tract could be even worse, causing swelling of the throat, difficulty in swallowing and shortness of breath. Serious exposure with large quantities inhaled would lead to failure of lung tissue. Bronchitis and pneumonia would follow, causing internal bleeding and collection of dead tissue. The secretion of mucous would add to the congestion causing blocking of the airways, suffocation and death. The devastating effect of this weapon could become evident long after initial exposure, many developing cancers and dying painful deaths years later.

[168] Douglas Haig. Diaries and Letters, p306

was still considerable. The Fifth Army casualty figures for the July period indicate the true capabilities of the German batteries: 6th to 13th July 2,275...13th to 20th July 5,930... 20th to 27th July 7,354. Many of these casualties were however caused by mustard gas, the majority of whom recovered to a greater or lesser extent within 7 days.

But as more of the British guns came into action the Germans also felt the pressure. Prince Rupprecht's figures gave *Group Wytschaete* equipment losses by the 25th July as 50% of the heavy guns, 30% of the heavy howitzers, 17% of the mortars, and 10% of the 10 cm guns.[169] There are reports that as the British bombardment intensified most of the German field batteries withdrew behind the Steenbeek. But when Captain J. Herbertson later examined the German archives and was asked if there was evidence of any guns being withdrawn he answered, 'I can find no trace of any such order. On the contrary everything pointed to the artillery being strongly reinforced. The Archivists here who were in the artillery do not think that the idea of artillery in depth had got past the stage of theory on the 31st July 1917, so that no guns would have been moved back even with this idea in mind'.[170] The claim also made, that the enemy withdrew their infantry, 'to leave a zone of marshland between their new forward positions and the British front line' is quite untrue.[171] On the 27th July Fifth Army War Diary recorded: 'After dark patrols were sent out along the whole Army front. Reports from these patrols showed that the enemy was holding his front system if anything in greater strength than usual', and again on the 28th, 'The situation remained unchanged this day. The enemy showed no signs of evacuating his front trenches'.[172] The claim that the enemy had mostly withdrawn from his front line positions is as wrong for the Salient in July as it was for Messines in June. Casualties from the British bombardments in the *6th Bavarian Division* holding the key front line position on the Gheluvelt plateau between the Klein Zillebeke road and the Menin Road were 1,228, of which 682 had been gassed.[173] A report issued by German *Fourth Army* on the 25th 'complained of the not inconsiderable casualties incurred by heavy enemy gas attacks', caused mainly by the late or incorrect donning of respirators, and the fact that troops were often deceived when fired on by gas and H.E. mixed, the near identical mistakes duplicated by their British counterparts. The last three days from the 28th July saw the culmination of the preparatory barrages, the big guns and howitzers concentrating on the known German battery positions, while the field guns covered the forward enemy field batteries with shrapnel and gas shell. This bombardment enabled some but not all of the assaulting divisions to reach their assembly trenches largely unhindered by the enemy, the main exception being west of the Gheluvelt plateau. The destructive result of this weight of fire upon the very ground across which the infantry, and more especially the tanks were to advance, was soon to become depressingly clear.

The Air

The same problems that had always faced the British gunners in the Salient were still evident. They could not see their targets, but their adversary could clearly see them. To attempt to hide the intent of their current preparations was impossible. The building of roads, and gun emplacements and the movement of huge quantities of ammunition could not go on unnoticed. The careful sighting of the German positions on rearward slopes added to the British difficulties. The only way to see the target being fired at, and to see the results of the shooting, was from above the battlefield.[174] It was therefore essential to acquire air supremacy over the battlefield

---

[169] Rupprecht. *In Treue fest. Mein Kriegstagebuch ii* Munich: Deutscher National Verlag p230
[170] National Archives, information collected from German archives CAB45/172
[171] See Denis Winter *Haig's Command* p96
[172] National Archives, War Diary Fifth Army headquarters, 27th July 1917, WO95/520
[173] National Archives, information collected from German archives CAB45/172
[174] Whilst describing the Messines – Passchendaele ridge Denis Winter tells us that 'it was in fact of little significance in 1917, since artillerymen had detailed maps and used aeroplanes to observe their shooting'. *Haig's Command* p93. This statement would undoubtedly have drawn a wry smile from

both to allow for effective artillery spotting from balloons and from Corps Squadron aircraft, and to deny the same to the enemy. The British observation balloon line ran (south to north) from around 6,000 yards west of Armentières, over Neuve Eglise, Kemmel hill, la Clytte, west of Dickebusch, just west of Vlamertinghe, to Elverdinghe.[175] The balloons worked with the heavy artillery of the corps to which they were attached. The Corps Squadron aircraft were responsible for artillery observation, photography, reconnaissance, and infantry contact patrols in the corps area to which they were assigned, and were protected in their work both by their own defences and by the scouts of the Army Squadrons.

In early July the air fighting in the Ypres sector was already at a high pitch, fifteen British airmen being killed in action on the 7th July alone. This was a portent of what was to come in the struggle for air supremacy over Flanders. The air offensive, subject to a programme issued by Major-General Trenchard on the 7th July and intended to commence on the 8th, was delayed by bad weather until the 11th, and was finally launched amongst existing concerns regarding the high level of air – artillery co-operation being demonstrated by the enemy. The intention was to gain air supremacy over the whole battle area from the Lys to the coast and back to the German observation balloon line five miles behind their front. Throughout June and July the German air strength had been steadily increased in Flanders, aircraft available to the *Fourth Army* being roughly doubled, until it stood in the Ypres sector, excluding the coastal sector of *MarineKorps Flandern*, at a strength of around 200 scouts (fighters), and 400 other types. The beginning of July saw local German air superiority helping with accurate counter-battery fire which seriously delayed and disrupted the deployment of Gough's artillery.

Jagdgeschwader I

The German Air Force, the *Luftstreitkräfte,* rose to the challenge presented by the Royal Flying Corps. Of great importance was the presence of *Jagdgeschwader I*, an elite fighter wing of four squadrons, *Jagdstaffeln* - 4, 6, 10 and 11. Formed on the 24th June and commanded by Manfred von Richthofen it operated from airfields around Courtrai, *Jasta 11* at Marcke, *Jasta 4* at Ceune, *Jasta 6* at Bisseghem, and *Jasta 10* at Heule. Von Richthofen was however in St Nicholas hospital in Courtrai at the beginning of the R.F.C. offensive, recovering from a near fatal head wound.[176] He was to return to command of *JG I* on the 25th July. *JG I* was a serious menace to the growing strength of the R.F.C., bringing together the very best of the German pilots in the very best of their aircraft. As a tactical weapon, and used as a concentrated force, it could command local air superiority in the face of British numerical superiority in a reflection of what *Group Wytschaete's* guns were achieving on the ground.

Things were improving however for the R.F.C. The introduction of new aircraft types like the S.E.5a, the Bristol Fighter, and the Sopwith Camel were beginning to address the German technical superiority, and gradually the improved quality and increasing quantity began to tell. The allotted strength in aircraft amounted to 508 British, including 230 single-seater scouts, plus 200 French, including 100 single-seater scouts, and 40 Belgian; 748 aircraft in total. As the British fought to master the situation in the air over the battle area, so the artillery performance improved. The last two weeks in July witnessed some of the most bitter and certainly largest air battles so far experienced in the war, an indication of how vital command of

---

both the gunners and airmen of July 1917, bearing in mind the complexity involved in coordinating operations between the guns and the air for target spotting and correction of shooting, plus the grave danger to the aircrew flying over the enemy lines. Low cloud, of which there was plenty, also led to a breakdown in these fragile arrangements. German battery control on the other hand was possible from ground observation on the ridges via telephone line, a somewhat simpler and safer operation. Both British difficulty and German facility were due solely to the enemy occupation of the Messines – Passchendaele ridge. The very reason for fighting the Messines battle was to throw the enemy off this high ground south of Ypres.

[175] National Archives, Maps showing co-operation and tactical work of RFC in WO153/493
[176] The shot fired by the observer of an F.E.2d on the 6th July.

the air was to both sides. On the 26th July above Polygon Wood an air-battle which lasted nearly an hour took place at four levels from 5,000 to 17,000 feet, when around 100 aircraft were involved in the general melee. Probably due to the confused nature of the fighting most combats appeared inconclusive, but it is believed six German and two British aircraft were shot down.

Towards the end of the month the Royal Flying Corps believed it had largely succeeded in its aim, a summary of air activity claiming that the enemy had shown less individual activity and had not crossed the British lines as often as he used to. The Germans were reported to be concentrating in large formations which had been successfully encountered on many occasions, and nearly all encounters had taken place on the enemy side of the lines. With regard to enemy air activity remaining over the German lines, the report should perhaps have added, 'except in night skies'.

The Tanks

Three tank brigades of the Heavy Branch Machine Gun Corps, (to become officially known as the Tank Corps from the 28th July), each of 72 tanks were to be available to Fifth Army. The II Brigade was to support II Corps, III Brigade XIX Corps, and I Brigade was in Fifth Army Reserve at Oesthoek Wood, near Lovie Chateau, with 24 of its tanks forward to support XVIII Corps. No tank support was planned for XIV Corps, as its position on the bank of the Ypres – Yser canal made tank deployment there impossible.[177]

As we have seen, in February, a plan had been proposed by Macmullen, to reduce the German positions on the Gheluvelt plateau and even advance towards Broodseinde by use of tanks alone. The idea had been rapidly rejected by those who understood the capability of the machines, although on other matters their opinions were largely over-ruled. To attack the plateau, the tanks would have to pass through the clearings between the shattered remains of the woods, as it was impossible for them to operate through the areas of smashed timber. The gaps between the woods formed natural defiles up the western slopes of the ridge, and for the tanks to attack through these would leave them easy pray to the German batteries and anti-tank guns, many of which were situated around Clapham Junction on the Menin Road. These anti-tank batteries were to cause II Tank Brigade many casualties in its attempts to support II Corps. The Mark IV tank was capable of a wide range of battlefield tasks, within the limits of its very recent design.[178] It had already performed well at Messines, and great things were hoped of it

---

[177] Headquarters of the new arm was at Bermicourt, near St.Pol where there were workshop which tested all new vehicles from the factories and had facilities for repairing battlefield recoveries. The corps was gradually being built up to a strength of three brigades, each brigade consisting of three battalions, each of three companies with 12 tanks per company.

[178] It was more capable than its predecessors the Mark I, which had first gone into action the previous September on the Somme, and the Mark II, which without the special heating and rapid cooling treatment to its plating was without armour and intended only for training. The experimental Mark III was visibly almost identical to the Mark II but with the addition of 12 mm armour, which was an improvement over the 8 mm in the Mark I, and proof to small calibre armour piercing rounds. The Hotchkiss machine guns of the earlier male models were replaced with Lewis guns in the Mark III, the Lewis also replacing the heavier Vickers guns in the females. All the modifications of the Mark III were carried over to the Mark IV which had a crew of eight, weighed 28 tons and had a theoretical maximum speed of 3.7 mph over good ground. A new fuel tank had been re-positioned outside the tank at the rear, where the wheeled tail had once been in the Mark I. The fuel tank was encased in armour and with a capacity of 70 gallons gave the tank a theoretical range of 35 miles with a consumption of a half mile to the gallon. With the repositioning of the fuel tank gravity was no longer helpful, and a new "Autovac" vacuum fuel feed system was introduced.

The tracks were modified to allow the fitting of extra plates known as spuds to help traction on heavy ground. A timber un-ditching beam was carried on top of the tank, which required attaching to the tank tracks by means of shackles and chains, at least two crew members having to get out of the tank

again. The limitations in its capabilities were however already clear to those who knew and understood the tank. Those limitations could be summarised as follows: It was highly liable to "belly out", over soft wet ground and this was almost a certainty over ground heavily cratered by artillery. Its speed was low, especially over bad ground, to the point that in some instances it would be left behind by advancing infantry. It quickly exhausted its crews, who worked in an atmosphere of great heat, noise, and toxic exhaust fumes, even when not under fire. It was vulnerable to anti-tank and general artillery fire. It had limited range, especially under battlefield conditions. On the other hand given reasonably good going, and without too much rain and 'cratering', it could be of great assistance to the infantry. Enemy trenches did not create a great obstacle. It could break down wire entanglements with ease. The male tank could attack enemy concrete bunkers and dugouts effectively with its 6-pounders, and all tanks could drive off infantry with their machine guns. If close cooperation with the infantry was possible great things could be achieved. When going well it gave a great boost to infantry morale, and had an equally disastrous effect on the morale of the enemy.

It rained heavily on the 29th July a little on the 30th, and it was to rain heavily again on the 31st July. The area across which the tanks were to advance had been under heavy shell-fire from the 7th July and the most concentrated of artillery barrages since the 16th July. The intricate network of ditches and streams which drained the Flanders sandy-clay had been broken by the guns. The rainwater had nowhere to go but to spread from the blocked, broken streams, and lie on the surface and fill the shell craters. On the slightly higher ground of Pilckem ridge and up the gentle slopes toward the Gheluvelt plateau the picture was little different. Around the Steenbeek and at Frezenberg it was to be even worse. This was the shattered muddy ground across which the tanks were now about to attack.

The Guards make an early advance on the 27th July

At the northern end of the British Front Line in the sector of XIV Corps, the opposing front lines faced each other across the Yser canal. During the first desperate battle of 1914 the canal had presented an obstacle which the Germans had been unable to cross, although they had done so briefly during the Second Battle of Ypres in April 1915, assisted by the first use of poisonous gas. The canal was in fact the southern limit of the great defensive position provided by the inundations which stretched to the Channel coast at Nieuport, and to the west of which the Belgian Army had since 1914 held its sector of the Western Front. Whilst the Germans were on the offensive, the inundations, and to some extent the canal, had been a secure defence line for the Allies, but now with the British and French about to launch an offensive, the waterway provided a strong defensive line for the enemy.

The German position had further strengths, in that it offered excellent observation across the British forward and rear areas for many thousands of yards. About 800 yards east of the canal the ground rose gently to a small hill no more than 20 metres above sea level, across which ran the German Second Line, the *Albrecht Stellung*. Although little more than a slight rise, 20 Metre Hill gave the Germans a height advantage of 10 metres over the British lines which in this very flat country allowed a considerable advantage in observation. The hill was a north-western extension of Pilckem ridge, which, rising to 22 metres near Pilckem village also gave an

---

to carry out this operation, often under fire. A steel framework of parallel rails across the top of the tank allowed the beam to pass over the top, upon becoming (hopefully) un-ditched.
Although similar in appearance to the Mark III, there were other structural changes in the Mark IV. Modified gun sponsons could now fold into the hull to facilitate rail transportation, and were also modified in shape being shaved off at the front lower corners to help prevent digging in over bad ground. A modified gun in the male tank, the Quick-Firing Hotchkiss 6-pounder, 6cwt, had a shorter barrel at 47 inches, which was now capable of being run back on the mounting, making it possible, with a great deal of hard work to retract it with the sponson. See David Fletcher (2001), *The British Tanks 1915-1918*, Marlborough: Crowood

excellent observation position both of the canal, and directly into Ypres to the south. As a result of the constant shelling of the canal and the streams and ditches which fed it, the once navigable waterway was reduced to a muddy morass an average of 25 yards wide, through the centre of which ran a filthy stream which in many places formed stagnant pools, which could increase substantially in depth during periods of heavy rain.

This was the line along which on the 15th June the 2nd Guards Brigade relieved the 38th Welsh Division, whose front had been reduced, but remained in position to the right of the Guards.[179] The 1st Guards Brigade moved up into bivouacs near Woesten 5,000 yards to the west. The Guards quickly started to improve the access to their 1,200 yards of front line along the canal, which ran northwards from the ruined Boesinghe railway bridge. Communication trenches were improved and four distinct lines of approach were constructed in preparation for the great movement of materials towards the lines which would soon become necessary. The primary concern of the divisional staff was the fording of the canal under fire. To accommodate the stores required for this operation, 19 chambers were dug into the western face of the canal bank, with the provision of opening them on the eastern face to enable bridging material to be carried directly forward to the canal side when the assault began. All of these operations attracted a great deal of enemy shelling, as did the major repairs of the Ypres – Staden railway track to the south of the railway bridge.

The problems of passing the division over the wide muddy obstacle, under the observed fire of the German batteries taxed the ingenuity of those involved. A solution to bridging muddy shallows was provided by Belgian engineers, well used to operating under these conditions along the Yser inundations. A length of canvas matting, longer than the widest part of the canal and one yard wide was reinforced with wire mesh and wooden slates fixed close together. The whole assembly would roll up and still be light enough to manhandle to the canal side. When laid across the canal bed a rope would also be passed across to indicate the position of the mat in any deeper water, and to provide a hand line. Under simulated conditions the mats proved to be extremely effective, but obviously relied on the water level remaining low. In case of a rise in water level in the canal, portable single file wooden bridges were also constructed, with wooden piers to be supported on petrol cans. All of the bridging material was stored in the 19 chambers, and the 4th Coldstream Guards, pioneers to the division, were given special training in their use. The whole operation took on huge proportions and in each chamber in the canal bank was stored, one petrol tin bridge, five duckboard bridges, and behind each tunnel nine of the canvas mats. The work involved in carrying this vast amount of stores forward, mostly in the dark and under conditions of constant shelling, took the carrying parties and their Royal Engineer guides over a week, some having covered about 160 miles of arduous toil over a two week period.

As soon as 2nd Brigade took up its place in the line nightly patrols were commenced to test the strength of the forward German garrison, and on most occasions found the front line unoccupied. On the 25th June a large party of the 1st Scots Guards carried out a raid to test the efficiency of the mats, and after about two hours in the enemy lines returned without seeing any Germans, but reported the wire and trenches badly damaged by shelling. Before the end of June, 1st Brigade relieved 2nd Brigade, and the 3rd Brigade moved up to Woesten. The 1st Brigade continued with the raids, and on the 2nd July the 2nd Grenadier Guards crossed the canal near the ruined Boesinghe railway bridge and found the German trenches empty. The enemy in the support line were however alert, and moving forward up a communication trench attacked with bomb and rifle fire, causing the raiders to withdraw. Two days later it was the turn of two parties of the 2nd Coldstream which returned from the German trenches with one wounded prisoner. Information provided by the prisoner and from captured documents indicated that the Guards were facing the *228th Regiment* of the *49th Reserve Division* in the line, with the *23rd Reserve Division* on its left. German retaliation to the raids came at 1:50 a.m. on the 14th July in the form of a German box barrage which hemmed in the two right platoons of the 1st Irish Guards. Forty-five minutes later around 50 Germans attacked the Irish Guards but were driven

---

[179] Cuthbert Headlam, *History of the Guards Division in the Great War 1915-1918*, London: John Murray

off by vigorous rifle and machine gun fire. The artillery preparations which started on the 16th July were supported on the Guards front by 16 2-inch mortars, soon to be joined by three 9.45-inch and one super 9.45-inch mortars and two 6-inch mortars, firing into the enemy front, support and reserve lines. The building of emplacements and bringing up of ammunition for the mortars proved a difficult task.[180]

As Zero Day had now been postponed to the 31st July, Major-General Fielding decided on the relief of the 2nd and 3rd Brigades, which were to carry out the main offensive, by the 1st Brigade in order to give them two days rest. Before this relief was carried out, on the night of the 19th / 20th July a raid, with no artillery support, along much of the enemy line was made by the 2nd Irish Guards on the right, and the 2nd Grenadier on the left. Mats laid by the 4th Coldstream were of little help as due to recent rains the water level in the canal had risen appreciably. One party of the Irish successfully crossed in water up to their armpits, made their way into the German trenches, and found them to be unoccupied and much damaged by the bombardment. Another party struggled across and into an occupied trench where a bombing fight ensued. The remaining Irish found the crossing impossible. Four parties of the Grenadier managed with difficulty to cross just north of the railway bridge to find an alerted enemy ready to fight. Danger of envelopment by considerable numbers of Germans caused one party to retire, covered by the rifle fire of the 4th Coldstream on the opposite bank. Between the 22nd and 24th further raids reported deepening water and some enemy resistance.

The 1st Brigade relieved the 2nd and 3rd, holding the line with the 3rd Coldstream. Great anxiety was now felt by all concerned as deep water and an alert enemy could put the whole operation in jeopardy, and increased shelling of the forward British positions indicated what a costly business crossing the canal under fire might become. The anxieties were however proved unfounded as in the early hours of the 27th July two wounded men of the 38th Division were seen on the eastern bank of the canal, and were brought back to the British side with no sign of enemy intervention. A Royal Flying Corps patrol had also reported at 9:00 a.m. that the German front and support lines appeared empty and their seemed to be few if any enemy west of the Steenbeek. This was good news indeed, and Fielding decided to act without delay. The canal would be crossed by the 3rd Coldstream, then holding the line, in daylight and with no preparatory barrage to warn the enemy. The reason the air patrol had seen no Germans was probably that, on hearing the sound of the approaching aircraft they had dived for their bunkers and out of sight, to avoid the inevitable barrage which would be called in. It is thought also that the sounds of tunnelling caused by the digging in the west bank of the canal had understandably alarmed the forward German infantry after their experience at Messines, and further that shelling of the forward positions had become intolerable, resulting in an unauthorised withdrawal from the line by the *228th Regiment*. Whatever the reason, the line was certainly empty.

---

[180] Initially the Divisional Ammunition Column brought up ammunition to Bluet Farm 2,000 yards behind the front line from where it was transported to the front by trench tramway to Boesinghe Chateau 500 yards behind the line from where carrying parties distributed it to the batteries. On the 17th July a shell blew-up an ammunition dump which so damaged the tramway all ammunition had subsequently to be carried up from the X line which was 1,000 yards short of the batteries, to provide the 5,200 rounds fired by the divisional mortars during the bombardment period.

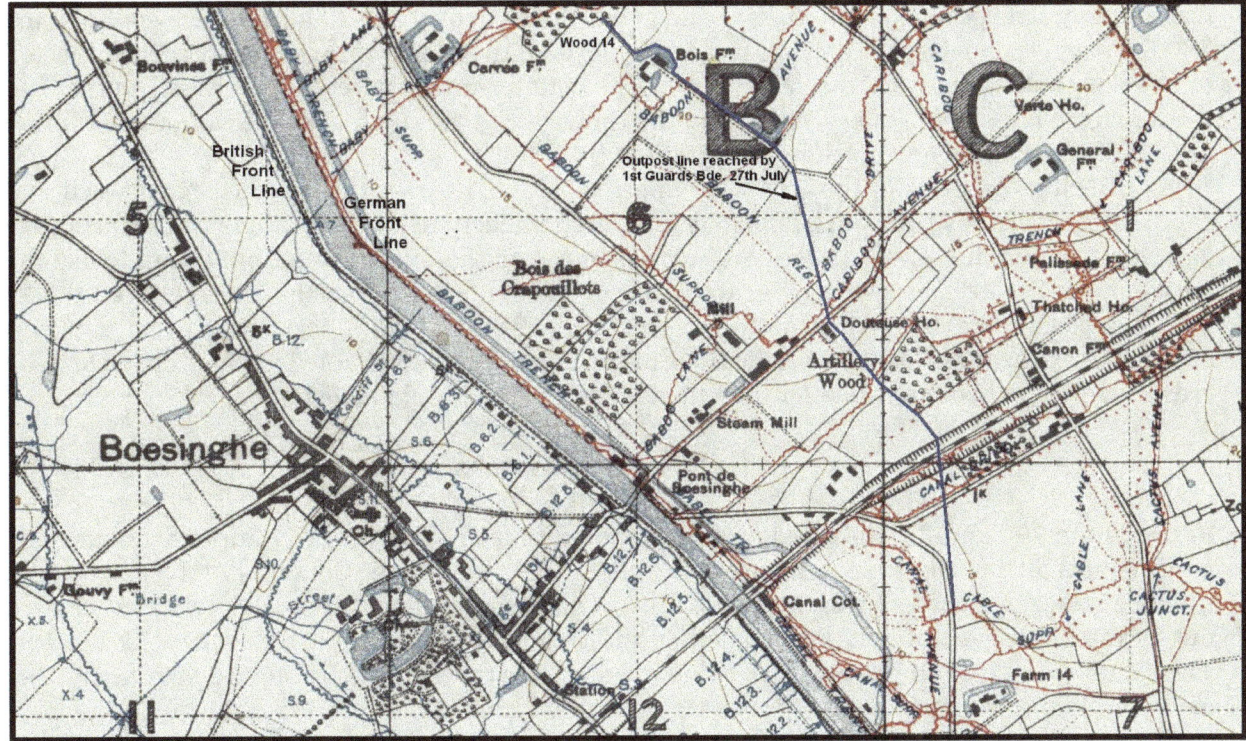

Outpost line on east side of canal reached by 1st Guards Brigade 27th July

At 5:30 p.m. four patrols of the 3rd Coldstream crossed the canal on their canvas mats, and finding the enemy trench completely deserted cautiously made their way forward along the communication trenches, finding a few Germans who they either killed or captured. The four patrols were quickly supported by another four which mopped-up more of the enemy in dug-outs along the southern side of the railway. The patrols eventually reached a position 500 yards beyond the canal, along a line from Wood 14, through Baboon Reserve trench to the south-western side of Artillery Wood. South of the railway bridge the 38th Division had crossed the canal and gained touch with the Guards right, at the junction of the railway track and Canal Avenue, while on the left the French had also crossed and were in touch. By this time the Germans had grasped the situation and had moved forward in sufficient force to threaten the Guards position which came under rifle and machine gun fire. To better defend their new line the Guards commenced to dig a support trench behind Baboon Reserve. Two companies stayed in the forward position, one held the support position, and the remaining company moved back to the canal bank.

After dark the French retired from east of the canal, being happier to stay on their breastworks on the west bank. The 38th Division, threatened by the same pressure as the Guards, found their position in Canal Avenue untenable and also withdrew west of the canal. In consequence, with both flanks in the air it was necessary for the Guards to throw back defensive posts to the right and left. Overnight and into the morning of the 28th the Guards continued to consolidate their position, in constant contact with the enemy, one German officer and 20 other ranks being captured and a number killed or wounded. No counter-attack was attempted but the hostile artillery subjected the canal bank to a vigorous shelling. The new front line was firmly consolidated by morning, and also by 5:00 a.m. the 4th Coldstream had thrown fourteen wooden bridges across the canal notwithstanding the heavy shelling. During the morning the French returned to their position east of the canal relieving the pressure on the left, but on the right the defensive flank along the railway and Canal Avenue was maintained. On the 28th July, which was fairly quiet in the new front line, the 1st Irish Guards were able to relieve the Coldstream between Douteuse House and Wood 14. An intercepted German wireless message indicated that a counter-attack to drive the Guards back across the canal was to concentrate on the junction of Canal Avenue and Cable Support, (on the front of the 38th Division), and the line was suitably strengthened with Vickers and Lewis guns to cover this flank. By the evening of the 28th German reconnaissance aircraft had finally located the new front which was then subjected to heavier shelling, as were the canal banks. The counter-attack, already expected, approached the line from between Artillery Wood and the railway, and although in significant numbers was driven-off by artillery and machine gun fire.

During the night of the 28th / 29th patrols of the 1st Irish Guards pushed forward and captured a blockhouse in front of Bois Farm, seizing a machine gun and killing or capturing the garrison. The 29th July saw a persistent bombardment on the Guards front, but around dusk the battalions of the 2nd and 3rd Brigades to carry out the main assault on the 31st, relieved the 1st Irish Guards in the line. The continual pressure of the infantry patrols and the artillery, supported by the ingenuity and hard labour of the engineers, had enabled a major obstacle to be crossed with a casualty toll smaller than the most optimistic could have hoped.

The Final Preparations

Between the 19th and 23rd July, Haig embarked on a tour of all Fifth Army Corps headquarters, and of most of the divisions who were to undertake the attack. On the 17th he attended a practice attack against a representation of Shrewsbury Forest and Tower Hamlets spur carried out by the 73 Brigade of the 24th Division, in the area of II Corps. He was pleased with what he saw. 'The troops looked extremely fit and well after nearly a month out of the line. It gave me great confidence as to the result of the attack, to talk to the officers and men. Jacob is also most confident as to the result.'[181]

The preparations had been most thorough. In corps training areas 1:50 scale models of the ground over which the battalions would assault had been made, and various attack scenarios considered by the commanders involved. The full scale assault courses had been utilised to the full by all divisions to simulate trenches and strong points to be attacked, and there had been much practice in the assault of blockhouses and pillboxes by bombing parties, with the support of Lewis guns, rifle grenades, and Stokes mortars in the fashion that had worked so well at Messines.

The complex operation of moving the assaulting brigades to their final assembly areas commenced after dark on the 28th July. On the following night the brigades holding each divisional front were relieved by the assault brigades who now moved into the line, this operation being carried out successfully, apparently unnoticed and unheard by the enemy outposts.[182] The men were heavily laden with their personal equipment which weighed not far short of 100 pounds. Equipment and ammunition carried varied by unit, but the following can be considered typical. Weighed down with Lee Enfield rifle and bayonet, two full front pouches and an extra bandolier of .303 ammunition totalling up to 220 rounds, two grenades, steel helmet, small box respirator and gas helmet, water bottle, three days rations, folded ground sheet and entrenching tool, fighting their way forward to the distant objectives was not going to be easy. Bombers and leaders of bombing parties were to carry 10 Mills bombs and 50 rounds of rifle ammunition, and bomb carriers 20 bombs, with 50 rounds. Rifle grenadiers were to carry 10 Hales grenades, 5 Mills grenades, 50 blanks to fire the grenades, and 50 rounds of .303 ammunition. For signalling each platoon would carry forward 8 1-inch and 24 1.5-inch Very pistol flares and 2 signal rifle grenades all with S.O.S. colours, and to deal with any uncut entanglements a quantity of wire breakers and wire-cutters.

During the same period and under cover of darkness the tanks were also moving towards the front, from their concentration areas at Ouderdom and Oosthoek. They crossed the canal in two echelons during the nights of 28th / 29th and 29th / 30th. Four specially constructed causeways had been built to carry them across the shallow muddy bed of the canal. The

---
[181] Douglas Haig. War Diaries and Letters, p303
[182] The assault brigades were to attack with an initial strength of 16 officers and 660 other ranks, 18 officers and 265 other ranks being held back as casualty replacements.

movement was completely successful, 133 tanks including supply and signal tanks, out of 136 completing the journey. The only reported incidents were of one company being heavily gas shelled, causing seven officer casualties, and one tank in collision with a train at a level crossing, the tank subsequently going into action after minor repairs. They rumbled to their assembly points around Zillebeke, Potijze, St. Jean, and at Frascati (just northeast of La Brique), and helped by the dull overcast weather nowhere were they discovered. Movement had not been easy in the dark without lights, and the showers of the last few days had made the roads and tracks muddy and slippery. It was difficult to avoid the crowded artillery positions, and to try not to churn through the endless network of telephone cables which criss-crossed the rear areas. Their positions were camouflaged as well as possible with tarpaulins and nets, but the Germans certainly already knew of the arrival of large numbers of tanks from information gained from prisoners, and had ordered the overhaul of their anti- tank measures. Cooperation between the tank unit commanders and infantry formation commanders was close, the infantry headquarters being shared, and touch was gained where possible down to battalion and company level before the operation. Two cavalry divisions had also been moved forward to positions about Dickebusch and Elverdinghe to be available to exploit any opportunity for a breakout, beyond the entrenched enemy positions.

At last, during the night of the 30th / 31st many tens of thousands of men, of the nine front line divisions of the Fifth Army, plus those of the Second Army to their right and the French First Army to their left moved into the final assembly positions from which in a few short hours they would attack. The battle front extended from the River Lys in the south to Nordschoote near the Ypres – Yser canal in the north, a distance of around 27,000 yards. Some were to start from forward trenches, short scaling ladders at hand to help them over the top. Some had already moved out into No Mans Land, following tracks previously marked out with small boards or discs on posts, or by tapes; moving silently up to wait pensively in shallow, poorly dug trenches, which had been prepared closer up towards the German lines. Others already out in No Mans Land, lay down in depressions and shell-holes between the wire belts for anything up to three hours, praying they would not be observed. The Germans seemed nervous and restless, sending up many flares, followed by some sporadic shelling from their artillery including the usual gas, which, given the number of men assembling inevitably caused some casualties. The ground was wet and slippery from the rain of the last few days, and the night was dark and oppressive with heavy cloud cover. At around 2:00 a.m. it began to drizzle. In places the drizzle soon set in to a fine wetting rain.

The British guns were not silent but their fire was relatively light, mostly being of longer range from the bigger guns, the shells rumbling far over the heads of the awaiting infantry. The gunners of the field batteries had little time left to make the final preparations to their incredibly complex barrage tables, some involving up to 45 'lifts' with different angles and ranges for each gun. Their protection from the weather was primitive and their careful calculations were often taking place in wet muddy gun-pits under shielded torch-light.

On the 29th July, Haig had moved to his Advanced G.H.Q. closer to the front, situated in railway coaches in a siding under a row of trees on the Bergues to Proven line near Westcappel, 19 miles W.N.W. of Ypres. All was now as ready as it could be. The 'subtle' differences between the Fifth Army plan and the G.H.Q. plan now counted for nothing. What the War Cabinet did or did not think of Haig's strategy for the moment was irrelevant. For better or for worse it was now the turn of the infantryman with his rifle and bayonet, the gunner ramming the charge into the breach of a field gun or howitzer, and the driver struggling at the controls of his slow cumbersome tank, who held the stage. The nation had supplied them with the best tools it could provide for the task, and the Army had trained them to the best of its ability. They and their junior officers were now the key actors in the drama which would decide how the future of world affaires would proceed. At 3:50 a.m. on the 31st July 1917, the greatest artillery barrage the world had ever witnessed engulfed the whole Salient with mind shattering sound and flame, beyond any reasonable level of human tolerance.

15" Howitzer – probably at Dickebusch

12" Howitzer on railway mountings

8" Howitzer near Lock 8 on Ypres-Comines canal 15th Sept 1917

Australian 2nd Division field artillery – 18 pounder

Ground unsuitable for tanks

About the Menin road

Remains of Hill 60. Zillebeke Lake in background.

18 Pounder ammunition crossing Yser Canal probably 31st July

Chapter Two

"We are not on the Black Line"
Major-General W. de L. Williams 30th Division

The Battle of Pilckem Ridge 31st July

Part One

A stream too far

The protective right flank.

Between la Basse Ville on the River Lys and Boesinghe on the Ypres – Yser canal, over a distance of around 27,000 yards, 12 divisions of two British Armies were about to hurl themselves at the enemy. General Plumer's Second Army, the victor of Messines now in a subsidiary rôle, was to support the Fifth Army by providing a protective flank to the south of the Gheluvelt plateau. It was also hoped the Germans would be deceived into believing that the attack was targeted against Lille, causing them to make the necessary deployment of forces, both infantry and artillery to resist such an attempt. The Second Army was to push forward using elements of 5 divisions on a front of approximately 9,100 yards, between la Basse-Ville and the Klein Zillebeke road, to improve on the positions reached by the end of the Messines battle. By the end of that battle the Germans had withdrawn to their fourth defence line, east of the Messines ridge, known to the British as the Warneton Line. Isolated raids made towards this line from the middle of July had been unsuccessful and had been stopped on Plumer's order, but now the three Corps of Second Army, II Anzac, IX and X, were to attack to establish a series of posts in front of the German position. The advance was to be made in three steps, with the distance to the first, second and final objective varying depending upon local conditions. These objectives were indicated on the operation maps with a colour code, the first being the Red Line, the second the Blue Line, and the third the Green Line.

Facing Second Army, the Divisions of *Group Wytschaete (IX Reserve Corps)* holding the line were from south to north; *16th Division, 18th Reserve Division, 10th Bavarian Division, 22nd Reserve Division,* and *6th Bavarian Reserve Division* (in poor fighting condition and soon to be replaced by *52nd Reserve Division*), with the *38th (*soon to be replaced by the *119th), 12th, and 207th* all as *Eingreif Divisions* in reserve.

The rain on the 29th had turned the ground to wet heavy mud, a mass of shell-holes half-filled with water, and a quagmire in the communication and forward trenches. To the south of the Gheluvelt plateau, by the early hours of the 31st July a light drizzle had already set in. At 3:50 a.m. as night reluctantly gave way to a heavily overcast dawn, the Second Army barrage erupted with a roar, but with nothing like the power it had displayed on the 7th June, as many of its batteries had been moved north into the Salient. As the mighty Fifth Army barrage thundered to the north, Second Army barrage was noticeably thinner than it had been on the day of Messines, although remaining accurate and damaging to the enemy.

Weather conditions, rainfall Vlamertinghe, temperature Ypres[183]

	26th July	**27th July**	**28th July**	**29th July**	**30th July**	**31st July**
Rainfall	Nil	Nil	Nil	11.5mm	0.5mm	21.7mm
Temp	75F	75F	78F	69F	65F	69F

The Attack of Second Army 3:50 a.m. 31st July

II Anzac Corps
Lieutenant -General Sir Alexander Godley

At the very southern end of the battlefront, on the right of the Second Army line, and within 700 yards of the River Lys, the II Anzac Corps was to attack with the New Zealand Division and the 3rd Australian Division along a front of around 3,600 yards. Since the Battle of Messines and the capture of the ridge, the higher ground lay behind the British line. From the forward trenches near la Basse-Ville the rise of Hill 63 could be seen 3,000 yards to the west, while 2,000 yards to the north-west the low rubble mound that had been the village of Messines, captured by the New Zealand Division on the 7th June, perched at the end of the low ridge which ran away to the north towards Ypres. Looking forward from the trenches, towards the east and the enemy, the battlefield appeared as a flat featureless plain dipping gently towards the Lys. Across No-Mans-Land the long scrubby undergrowth that had reclaimed the once neatly cultivated fields, concealed many machine gun outposts established in fortified shell-holes, beyond which could be seen the wire entanglements and breastworks of the Warneton Line. A number of dense hedges and ditches criss-crossed this forward area, also concealing more deadly machine guns and well hidden rifle pits.

New Zealand Division
Major -General Sir Arthur Russell

At the far right of the British line the New Zealand Division was to make a feint thrust towards the River Lys. The objective was to establish a line of strong outposts about 500 yards forward of the present front line, which had moved little since the end of the Messines battle nearly seven weeks before. The front along which the division was to attack was approximately 1,800 yards in length, from the hamlet of la Basse-Ville on the north bank of the Lys at the southern end, to the Douve stream in the north. In front of the division's line the river and the stream converged, with the small town of Warneton situated within the confluence. Across the western outskirts, the Germans had established the wired and entrenched Warneton Line, defending the town and the road bridge over the river. To the south of the town, the Warneton Line was on the south bank of the Lys, with a number of vulnerable outposts thrown across to the northern bank, and connected to the main line north of the river only by a small bridge near la Basse-Ville.
A railway track ran along the north bank, about 500 yards from the river, between la Basse-Ville and Warneton.
    In support of the Division the field artillery had been separated into two groups, the southern group supporting the attack on la Basse-Ville village with one gun to cover every 47

---
[183] National Archives, GHQ statistics WO95/14

yards of front, and the northern group, firing onto the open ground south of the Douve with one gun every 23 yards. The machine guns which were to provide a barrage were also split into two groups with the same targets as the field artillery. To allow the infantry the best chance of success, the enemy strong-points and machine gun emplacements south of the Douve and in the Warneton Line had been subjected to a softening-up bombardment by field and medium howitzers.

1st New Zealand Brigade[184]
The 1st New Zealand Brigade was to attack with the 2nd Wellington Regiment towards la Basse-Ville and the south-western outskirts of Warneton,[185] while the 1st Auckland Regiment supported by the 2nd Auckland attacked along the Douve and towards the northern outskirts of the town. 1st Otago Regiment, of 2nd New Zealand Brigade, were to establish a post safeguarding the right flank.

At 3:50 a.m. two and a half companies of the Wellington attacked behind the creeping barrage towards the western edge of la Basse-Ville, and immediately walked into machine gun fire from a series of heavily fortified shell-holes. Quickly overwhelming these positions the leading platoon seized the wrecked Sugar Refinery near the bank of the Lys. Two further platoons worked their way into the hamlet, one on each side of the road, whilst a fourth headed towards the remains of a factory at the northern end. Working along the road the Wellington attacked the bunkers in ruined houses bombing and bayoneting their garrisons, clearing the southern end and seizing the factory. Enemy snipers in ditches and hedges beside the Lys put up little fight and fled along the river bank towards Warneton, many being shot down as they ran. By 4:50 a.m. la Basse-Ville was clear of the enemy and consolidation had begun.

Two sections under Lance-Corporal Leslie Wilton Andrew were detailed to work further along the road towards Warneton, to seize a bunker in a wrecked estaminet which had caused serious problems on an earlier raid. As the party moved forward behind the protective barrage, they threatened to outflank a German machine gun post on the railway track 200 yards to their left, which was holding up another company of the Wellington. Diverting from their original task they worked behind the machine gun post, and then rushed it killing the gun crew. Quickly returning to the road, the two sections caught up with the barrage and moved on towards the estaminet, from where they could see a machine gun firing continuously. Working around the bunker concealed by undergrowth, they moved in close enough to throw a shower of bombs at the garrison, most of which fled along the river, the remainder being shot, and the machine gun being captured. Lance-Corporal Andrew and Private Ritchie continued their patrol towards Warneton for another 300 yards, as far as the standing British barrage would allow, and soon spotted another machine gun firing from an open trench beside the wrecked In den Rooster Cabaret, which had been turned into a fortified bunker. Many of the enemy fleeing from the fighting in la Basse-Ville had taken shelter in the bunker and the cellar of the estaminet. Andrew and Ritchie rushed the post, bombed out the cellar and bunker, and then gradually worked their way back towards the New Zealand lines. Andrew was to be awarded the V.C. for his leadership and gallantry.

Advancing behind the barrage, the centre company of the Wellington led by Lieutenant Biss, had experienced bitter fighting. The right of the two assaulting platoons was to establish a post on the railway line. As they neared the track they came under heavy machine gun fire from two nests on the embankment. These were the guns which Andrew and his party had seen from the road. The centre platoon were pinned down by the fire, but slowly worked their way forward from water filled shell-hole to shell-hole all the time suffering casualties, and finally were held up under the muzzles of the guns, but still gamely exchanging fire with the gun crews. At this moment Andrew was working behind the guns on the other side of the railway, and the Germans, realising their position was now precarious began to look around for a way of escape. Biss decided this was the moment for action and shouted to his men to attack. They struggled

---

[184] National Archives, War Diary 1st New Zealand Brigade WO95/3687
[185] National Archives, War Diary 2nd Wellington WO95/3690

from their muddy shell-holes under fire, and rushed one gun killing the crew, as Andrew and his party did the same with the other.

After a five minute bombardment of the enemy positions, and under cover of Lewis and machine gun fire from the flanks, the left platoon split into three parties and advanced behind the barrage, but immediately came under severe rifle and machine gun fire from hedges and ditches to the west of the railway. Two of the parties were practically annihilated, while the third reached its objective on the railway bank, but being fired at from the railway and both flanks was forced to fall back. The enemy garrison on the railway seeing the demise of the two machine gun teams just south of them began to make off along the embankment, 8 being shot and 24 soon surrendering. The hedges and banks were then quickly cleared, another machine gun being captured, and posts were consolidated along the embankment.

About 800 yards to the north, a company of the 1st Auckland attacked behind the barrage in four parties towards Warneton. A platoon of the 2nd Auckland following up was to construct the outpost line on the objective west of the embankment upon its capture. The 1st Auckland was confronted by numerous fortified shell-holes constructed with timbered and matted roofs, covered with 6 inches of soil, well camouflaged, shrapnel-proof and with a looped front for a machine gun. The three platoons on the right quickly overran these positions most of the occupants fleeing, those who fought being killed. The fourth platoon, on the left, was hit by severe machine gun fire and a trench mortar bombardment and could not get forward. The two centre platoons with their left flank exposed were not able to reach the railway, although this was not serious as in any event the outpost line was to be established west of the embankment. In this attack 1st Auckland had killed 80 Germans, taken 12 prisoners and captured two machine guns.

Near the Lys in la Basse-Ville a strong-point was established near the Sugar Refinery to cover the foot bridge over the river. From here a line of outposts was established by the 2nd Wellington for about 500 yards along the railway embankment towards Warneton, from which point the outpost line consolidated by the 2nd Auckland, ran northwards towards the Douve. At 5:30 a.m. a contact aircraft reported flares fired in the line of posts along the whole objective.

The German reaction to the attack was typically robust, the new positions in la Basse-Ville and along the outpost line coming under intense shelling. Machine gun fire from the German positions south of the Lys to the front of the New Zealand, and from In den Rooster Cabaret in enfilade, swept the outpost line and the approaches from the old front line. The first enemy counter-attack was launched from Warneton shortly after dawn, but as it attempted to concentrate near In den Rooster Cabaret it was dispersed by a machine gun and artillery barrage fired in response to S.O.S. signals. In the afternoon 50 Germans attempted to outflank the far right post near la Basse-Ville by working their way along the river bank in dead ground, and trying to edge round behind the New Zealand line. A Wellington party of an officer and around 15 men from the post, cheering loudly and hurling bombs charged the Germans, 20 of whom were shot, and 13 bayoneted, while the remainder fled. In the evening and in heavy drizzle, sentries in the outpost line spotted a large number of Germans once more concentrating near the Cabaret. The S.O.S. was again fired and as the enemy advanced towards the outposts they were struck by the British shellfire which had responded promptly. Some however came on to within 100 yards of the New Zealand positions only to be decimated by Lewis gun and rifle fire, the attack dwindling away.

By the late evening when the 1st Wellington relieved the 2nd in la Basse-Ville and the outpost line, the rain was even heavier and the trenches and outposts had become muddy water-filled ditches and pools.

In the operation 2nd Wellington had captured an officer and 41 other ranks, plus 5 machine guns and 2 trench mortars, while their own casualties had been 27 killed and 104 wounded. The Germans opposing the New Zealand Division were from the *29th Regiment* of the *16th Division*.

The New Zealand Division had been entirely successful in establishing an outpost line close up to, and threatening the Warneton Line, at the most southerly point of the battlefield.[186]

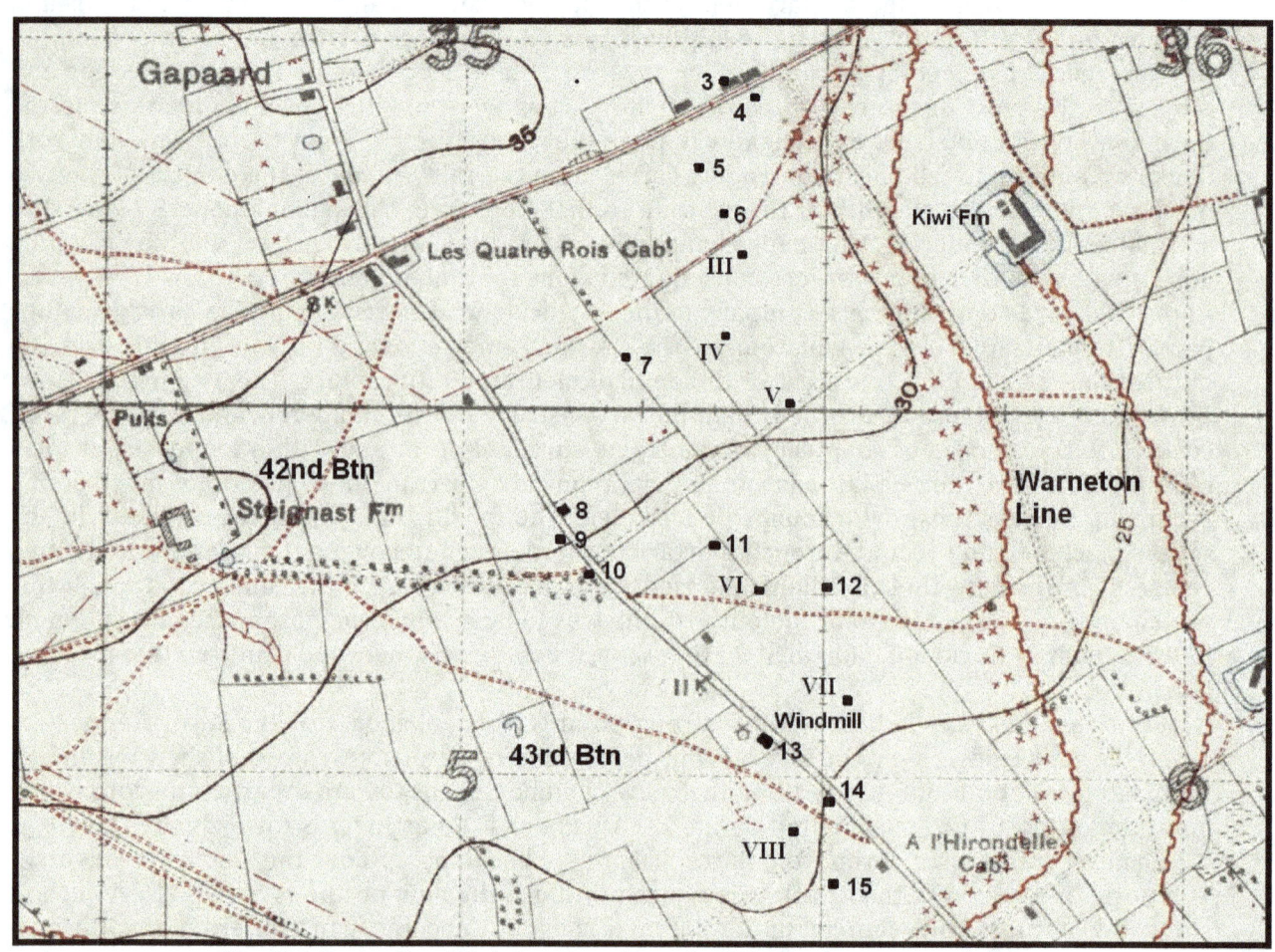

The 3rd Australian Division attack on the Warneton outpost line

3rd Australian Division
Major-General Sir John Monash

11th Australian Brigade[187]
The 11th Australian Brigade, with its 43rd and 42nd Battalions was to attack north of the Douve stream on a 1,800 yard front, with its left just south of the Blauwepoortbeek.[188] Astride the Warneton road, which ran obliquely across the front, the Germans had dug upwards of 20 outposts about 300 yards in front of the wire entanglements of the Warneton Line, and the task of the Australian battalions was to capture the line of enemy posts identified from left to right as 3 to 14, and set up a line of outposts of their own to be numbered III to VIII. The Warneton Line was held by the *28th*, *68th* and *29th Regiments* of the *16th Division*.

The troops moved up through communication trenches deep in mud, and worked forward to their jumping-off tapes only 100 yards short of the German outposts. The 43rd Battalion on the right attacked behind the barrage which contained a proportion of smoke shell to cover their movement. A number of the German machine gun posts lined the ditch along the Warneton road, and the 43rd, obscured by the smoke was quickly amongst them. From the start the defenders put up a stout resistance hurling stick bombs at the Australians at close quarters,

---

[186] Colonel H. Stewart (1921), *The New Zealand Division 1916-1919*, Auckland: Whitcombe and Tombs
[187] National Archives, War Diary 11th Australian Brigade WO95/3425
[188] National Archives, War Diary 43rd Battalion WO95/3436, 42nd Battalion WO95/3434

causing many casualties. The fighting along the ditch was fierce but the posts were gradually bombed and taken. The garrison at post 13 on the road, near the ruins of a windmill did not give up without a resolute fight, in which all the Australian officers and all N.C.O's. except one were wounded.

On the left, machine gun fire from enemy posts 8 and 9, on the Warneton road a little way north of the mill, held up the 42nd Battalion, but were outflanked, bombed and captured. Within 15 minutes the first wave of Australians had reached the wire of the Warneton Line, and here as planned lay down in shell-holes, while the protective barrage held just forward of the entanglements. The second wave began to dug-in on the planned III to VII outpost line, 250 yards short of the wire. Soon the third wave was digging a fire trench in support of the outpost line, with saps running forward to join with the outposts, while the supporting artillery and Stokes mortars cloaked the operation with smoke.

On the far right, the Germans in post 15 had not been affected by the initial Australian bombardment and still held out, raking the consolidating troops with enfilade machine gun fire. The Australians attacking post 14, although badly shot up and with many casualties finally worked to their right and silenced post 15, capturing a machine gun. As a party of the 43rd Battalion attempted to establish post VIII on the right, they were continually under heavy fire, but held on to their position. At post VII near the windmill, nearly all the officers had become casualties, command passing to N.C.O's., but the post was successfully established. At the planned time and behind the smokescreen, the forward wave retired from the wire to the fire trench, and by 9:00 a.m. the outpost line was completed including post VIII. The smokescreen was probably mistaken by the Germans as another attack against the *29th Regiment*, the enemy also noting a further attack (not recorded by the Australians) against the *28th Regiment* at 10:30 a.m. which was reported as broken by an artillery barrage and machine gun fire.

Spotted in their new positions by a German reconnaissance aircraft the Australian outposts came under heavy shelling from 2:00 p.m. to 6:00 p.m., an enemy counter-attack driving the hard pressed garrison from post VII. The other outposts held out although the drizzle which had set in during the afternoon caused the ground conditions to become steadily worse towards the evening.

Just after 9:00 p.m. and in steady rain, a counter-attack developed from the direction of Warneton, but was scattered by a mass machine gun barrage soon backed up by the artillery. Germans records claim they counter-attacked at 9:00 p.m. but were driven back, a further counter-attack taking place at 10:10 p.m. by the *84th Regiment (18th Reserve Division), 28th* and *68th Regiments* succeeding on the left, probably when post VII was captured.

Post VII was recaptured at 12:30 a.m. on the 1st August, when according to the German account, by 2:00 a.m. their garrison at the Windmill was killed to a man.[189] The II Anzac Corps had succeeded in its task, and a new outpost line sat close up to the entanglements of the Warneton Line. By the evening of the 31st the weather was awful and the drab battlefield near the Lys was quickly turning into a quagmire, adding to the misery of all involved. The fighting along the Warneton road had been severe, 11th Brigade sustaining 550 casualties in the attack. Total casualties in II Anzac Corps had amounted to 1,352. Casualties for the *16th Division* are not known, but those of the *18th Reserve Division* alone were 268 killed 1,070 wounded and 265 missing.

IX Corps
Lieutenant -General Sir Alexander Gordon

In the centre of Second Army line the IX Corps, attacked with elements of the 37th and 19th Divisions, which were to make their main assault down the spur between the Wambeke and the Roosebeek streams, to a depth of around 500 yards. The Corps right flank was on the Blauwepoortbeek, with the left flank 500 yards south of the village of Hollebeke, a front of about

---

[189] National Archives, record of German accounts CAB45/172

3,500 yards. The attack was to be made towards a patchwork of German machine gun bunkers constructed of reinforced concrete some hidden within the remains of ruined farmhouses, which formed strong a defensive outpost line around 750 yards west of the Warneton Line. The operational order was complex, and the attack was to be executed in two phases. Part 1 was to be an attack by the 56th Brigade of 19th Division plus two battalions of 63rd Brigade under command of the 19th Division up to Zero plus 3 hours (6:50 a.m.). Part 2, at Zero plus 4 hours (7:50 a.m.), was to be an attack by 37th Division with 63rd Brigade, with one battalion of 112th Brigade (attached to 63rd Brigade), back under command of 37th Division.

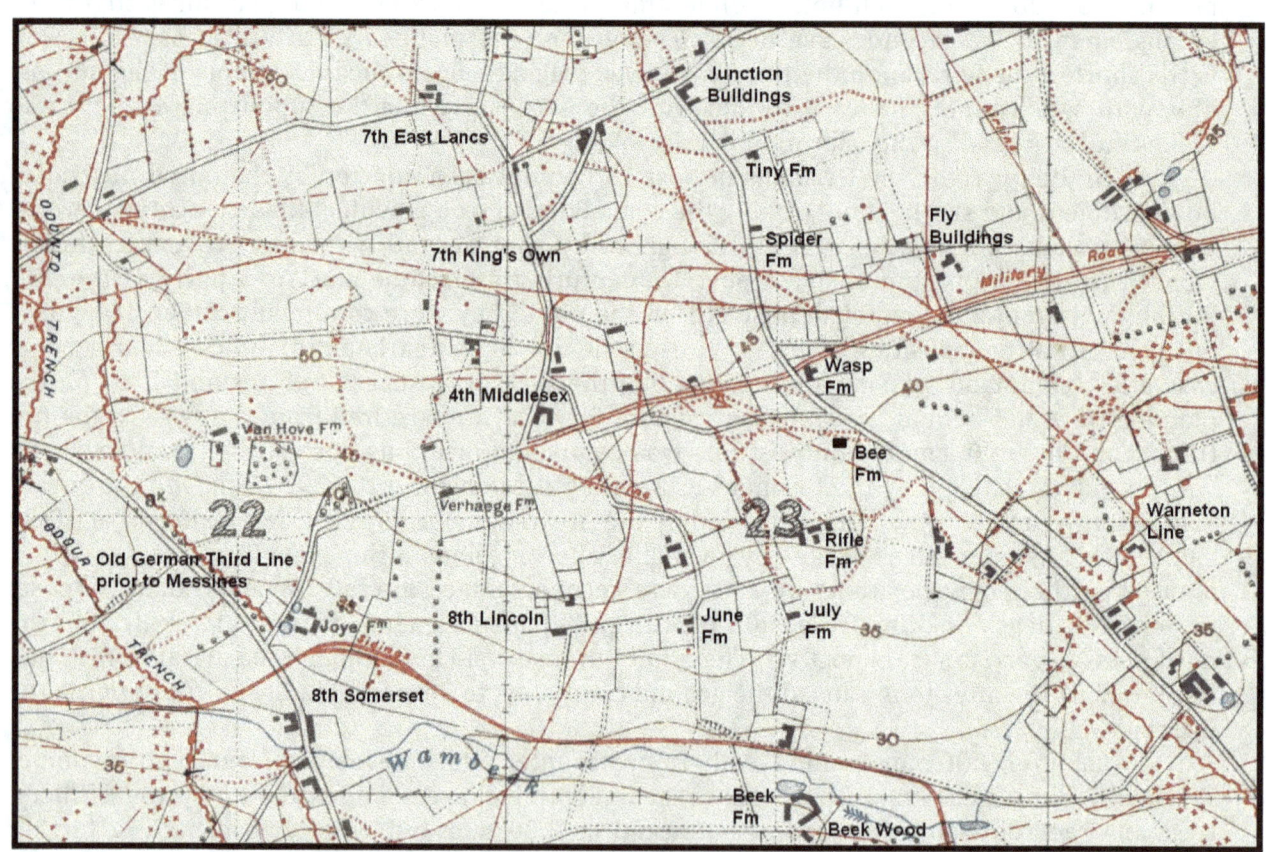

German fortified farm outposts attacked by 63rd and 56th Brigades

37th Division
Major-General H. Bruce

19th Division
Major-General G. T. M. Bridges

63rd and 56th Brigades[190]
Under orders of 19th Division, the 8th Lincolnshire Regiment and 4th Middlesex Regiment (63rd Brigade, 37th Division), formed up on the right of the line with the 7th King's Own Royal Lancaster, 7th East Lancashire and 7th Loyal North Lancashire Regiments (56th Brigade, 19th Division), on their left.[191] The Lincoln advanced behind the barrage between the Wambeek and Rifle Farm, with the Middlesex continuing the line north towards Wasp Farm. In the poor light the attacking waves struggled forward across the heavy ground, and quickly came under severe machine gun fire from the numerous German bunkers. In the dreadful conditions touch was

---

[190] National Archives, War Diary 56th Brigade WO95/2075/76
[191] National Archives, War Diary 7th East Lancs WO95/2081, 7th Loyal North Lancs WO95/2080

soon lost between the Middlesex and the King's Own, (to be regained east of Bee Farm at about 4:10 a.m.). On the right of the Middlesex, "C" Company, with the Lincoln, took Rifle Farm by 4:30 a.m., the Lincoln then establishing a flank to protect their exposed right between June Farm and July Farm. At this time "A" Company, the support company of the Middlesex, sent a patrol forward to Bar Farm, and immediately came under counter-attack by the Germans in which both Middlesex "C" Company and the Lincoln became embroiled. Severe hand-to-hand fighting took place in front of Bar Farm with mounting casualties on both sides. The remainder of the Middlesex and Lincoln on the flanks, and not involved in the fighting near Bar Farm, came under heavy machine gun fire from the front, and in enfilade from right and left, which caused further severe casualties. Another enemy counter-attack was launched against the left flank of Middlesex "C" Company, who fought it out amongst the muddy shell-holes until they were all either killed or wounded.

On the left of the Middlesex the King's Own and East Lancs experienced tough and confusing fighting in attacks against enemy bunkers at Spider Farm, Tiny Farm and Junction Buildings, but succeeded in reaching the Blue Line by about 5:00 a.m., as did the right companies of the North Lancs to their left. Patrols then began to work east from Spider Farm towards Fly Buildings. A little to the north, to the west of Hollebeke in X Corps sector, 122nd Brigade were held up and involved in severe fighting to clear the ruins of the village. With their left dangerously exposed, the left company of the North Lancs threw back a defensive flank to the north-west towards Forret Farm, which lay 500 yards south-west of the village.[192]

At about 6:45 a.m. a German counter attack covered by a smoke barrage struck at the junction of the Lincoln and the Middlesex at Rifle Farm, which the enemy succeeded in retaking. The Middlesex and King's Own fell back a few hundred yards, and the left of the Lincoln also fell-back to conform to the Middlesex. An hour later another counter-attack from the direction of Fly Buildings thrust at the line between the King's Own and the East Lancs, pushing the flanks of both battalions back to Tiny Farm.

At around 7:50 a.m. with the results of the first phase inconclusive, the second phase of the attack began. On the far right, the 8th Somerset Light Infantry of 63rd Brigade advanced along the Wambeek, the right flank of the Lincoln moving forward from June Farm with them. One company of the Somerset dug-in west of Beek Farm while two platoons attempted unsuccessfully to work forwards towards Beek Wood. Later the 8th East Lancashire Regiment (112th Brigade attached) relieved the exhausted Middlesex.

The fighting on IX Corps front had been confused and costly, 4th Middlesex alone suffering casualties of 8 officers and 203 other ranks. Most of the German outpost line at the eastern foot of the Wambeek spur, 750 yards west of the main Warneton Line, and consisting of the deadly fortified farm ruins had been taken, but at great loss to the battalions engaged. The final line consolidated ran from near Delporte Farm on the Blauwepoortbeek in the south, across the Wambeek west of Beek Farm, through June Farm, Junction Buildings, to Forret Farm in the north, and the line between the Australians south of the Blauwepoortbeek and X Corps at Hollebeke was secure. Total casualties in XI Corps had amounted to 2,003.

X Corps
Lieutenant-General Sir T. L. N. Morland

On the Second Army left flank, the X Corps was to use one division, the 41st along a front of about 2,000 yards to provide the southern support buttress for Fifth Army's main attack on the Gheluvelt plateau. The Corps front was complicated by the channel of the Ypres – Comines canal and the embankment of the Ypres – Comines railway. The recent rains had resulted in the cratered ground becoming a mass of water-filled shell-holes and very heavy to cross. The ruins of Hollebeke village lay on the right of the Corps front, about 500 yards west of the canal. As

---

[192] Forret Farm was later to be secured by the 12th East Surrey of 122nd Brigade, at which point touch was gained with the Loyal North Lancs.

planned, most of X Corps artillery was engaged in counter battery fire with the German guns behind the Zandvoorde hill, to protect the right flank of II Corps (Fifth Army), the bombardments on X Corps front being proportionately lighter.

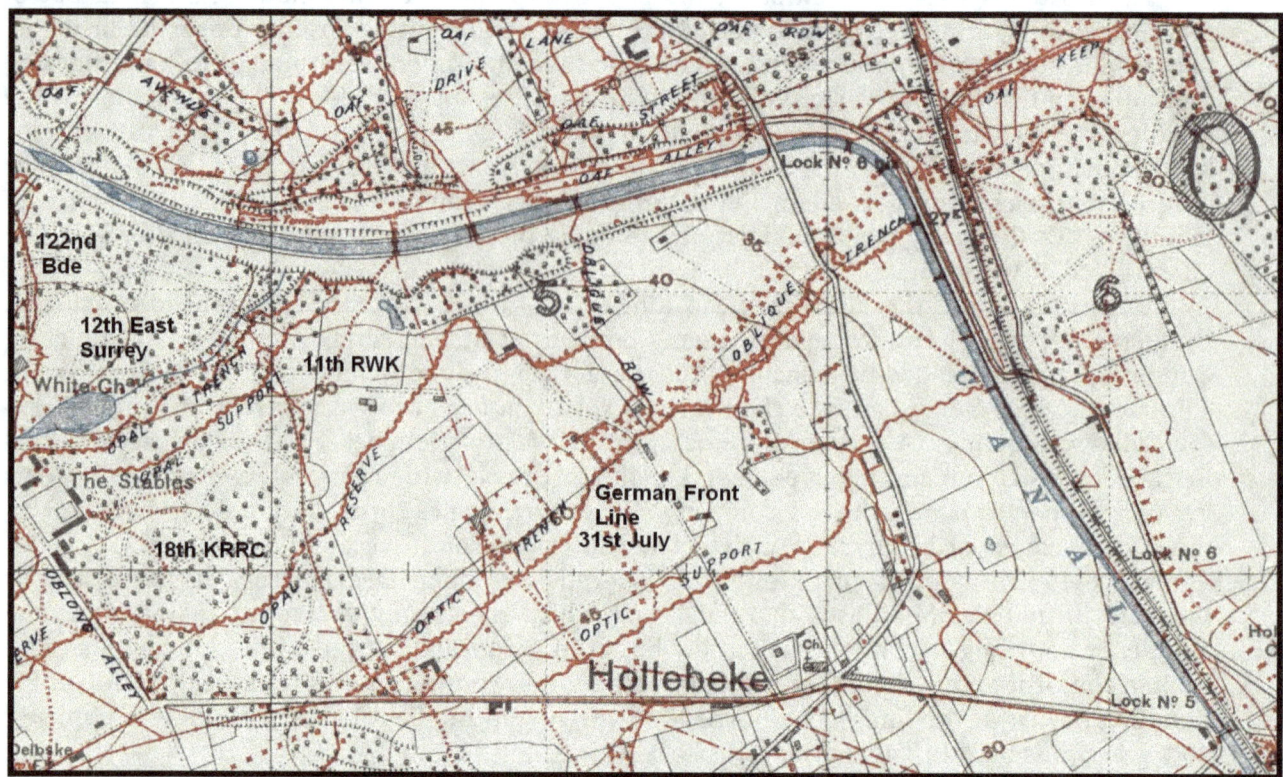

122nd Brigade attack at Hollebeke (showing German trenches prior to Messines)

41st Division
Major-General S. T. B. Lawford

The 41st Division was to attack with the 122nd Brigade to the south of the Ypres – Comines canal and the 123rd Brigade to the north. The paths of the canal and the railway, from the point at which they converged just south of Battle Wood bisected the divisional front, in some places hampering the advance. The division had three objectives. The first, the Red Line, a distance forward of about 300 to 400 yards, ran from just north of the village of Hollebeke along Optic Support and Oblique Trench, across the canal through Oaf Keep and along Imperial Trench to the Klein Zillebeeke road. The second objective, the Blue Line, was about 300 to 400 yards beyond the Red Line, and the final objective, the Green Line being about 300 yards beyond the Blue.

The approach march of the attacking battalions was made more difficult by extensive German shelling especially about the Bluff, along the line of the canal forward of Iron Bridge, and about White Chateau Woods.

122nd Brigade[193]
From their jumping off points, just south-east of White Chateau, which had been gained by the end of the Battle of Messines, the brigade attacked in semi darkness and in a slight drizzle, with the 18th King's Royal Rifle Corps on the right and 11th Royal West Kent Regiment to the left, in

---

[193] National Archives, War Diary 122nd Brigade, 18th KRRC, 12th East Surrey, 15th Hants, all in WO95/4243

the initial assault wave, and the 12th East Surrey Regiment in support. The brigade left flank was to be along the south-east side of the Comines canal.

The forward "A" and "D" Companies of the West Kent, attacked across very bad ground only just keeping up with the barrage, and into fierce enemy machine gun fire, arcing across the canal from the railway embankment on the left, and from the ruins of Hollebeke on the right. Some wire entanglements had not been cut, and there was stout opposition from the enemy before Oblique Trench (the Red Line) was taken, where the West Kent soon established outposts in shell-holes 150 yards forward of the first objective. On the right of the West Kent, the K.R.R.C. in the advance towards Optic Trench was silhouetted against the dim skyline, and seen by the enemy. Severe machine gun fire from bunkers in ruined houses along the Hollebeke road, in rear of the trench, and from the ruins of Hollebeke church to their left scythed into the attacking waves causing severe casualties, the survivors dropping into the shelter of shell-holes near Optic Trench, 300 yards short of the village which was their objective. As the barrage lifted towards the second objective "B" and "C" Companies of the West Kent, took up the advance, and were struck by the same withering machine gun fire, some getting forward to the Blue Line, but here under the hail of rifle and machine gun bullets they too were checked and forced to take cover. One platoon on the right worked forward through the mud from shell-hole to shell-hole, eventually reaching the final objective 200 yards south of Hollebeke and setting up a post, but with the risk of being outflanked soon fell back to the company line. Meanwhile touch had been lost between the West Kent and the K.R.R.C. on their right. The advance was totally stalled in front of Hollebeke and at 5:15 a.m. a party of "A" Company of the West Kent which was consolidating on the Red Line, was sent forward to support "C" Company in their more forward posts. The Germans, machine gunners who had unleashed the hail of fire at the K.R.R.C. from the houses along the Hollebeke road, had now withdrawn into the village with their guns where they helped stiffen the defences.

    At around 5:30 a.m. at brigade H.Q. the situation appeared confused but it was clear that all was not going well, as reports had come in stating that Hollebeke had been taken which was plainly not the case. The brigade major was sent to the H.Q. of the East Surrey in brigade support, with an order for the battalion to go forward and take the village. Prior to his arrival the C.O. of the K.R.R.C. had arrived in the sap trench where the East Surrey H.Q. was situated and reported the decimated state of his battalion. By 6:15 a composite company, mostly "D" Company of the East Surrey, began its move forward towards Hollebeke, and at around 7:00 a.m., passing behind the right rear of the West Kent, through the remnants of the K.R.R.C. attacked from the flank and took some houses on the road south-west of the village. The company then assisted the West Kent to clear this section of the ruins, and then later extended the line a further 250 yards to the south-west to Forret Farm, where touch was made with the 7th North Lancs of 56th Brigade.

    The Brigade Major sent up a report to Lieutenant -Colonel Corfe of the West Kent, indicating the orders given to the East Surrey. Corfe felt that in attacking the ruins from the north-west and not the north-east, the East Surrey may well suffer the same fate from the enemy machine guns as the K.R.R.C. By 7:40 a.m. the situation in front of Hollebeke appeared not to have changed and Corfe took responsibility upon himself to send a further 25 men up from the Red Line, with as many remnants of "C" Company as could be spared, to attempt to force their way into the wrecked village. Just before 8:00 the West Kent assault party attacked the ruins, from which the enemy put up a stout defence. Working from bunker to bunker they systematically bombed out the concrete dug-outs hidden within the rubble, and gradually knocked out the lethal machine guns. The German garrison had held out for a long time, the courageous defence of the rubble being sustained by no more than an officer and about 20 men. At around 11:00 a.m. a report was sent back that the village was at last clear of the enemy, and the West Kent was then able to move up to within 100 yards of its final objective and begin to consolidate the line.

    The fighting for the heavily defended ruins of Hollebeke had been tough and confusing and casualties in the 18th K.R.R.C. had been high. The brigade had advanced across atrocious waterlogged and gas soaked ground towards a determined and brave enemy. The ruins once taken had been consolidated, and the outpost line had been pushed out, down the slope south-east of the village only 100 yards short of the final objective, and in touch with the 7th North Lancs of 56th Brigade.

123rd Brigade[194]

The 123rd Brigade attacked with three battalions in the line, its right being in the south-east corner of Battle Wood, its left on the Klein Zillebeke road. The 23rd Middlesex Regiment, the right battalion, started from a difficult position between the converging angle of the canal and the railway. To their left were the 11th Queens, and the 10th Royal West Kent with the 20th Durham Light Infantry in support.

 The Middlesex attacked with its "A" Company forward and "D" Company forming the second wave with "B" and "C" Companies in support. The line of advance was immediately into the bottleneck created by the canal and railway, narrowing towards the first objective. The left flank had the difficult job of crossing the railway embankment at the point it met the German front line at Oaf Keep. Here the embankment was 25 feet high, honeycombed with dugouts, and had a number of pillboxes with machine guns trained into the bottleneck. As the Middlesex advanced behind the barrage it became clear to those in "A" and "D" Companies that the ground between the canal and the railway was an impassable bog, causing the forward wave to move to the left, and attempt to advance along the railway embankment. By 3:54 a.m. four minutes after Zero and on time, the first objective was seized. As the barrage lifted toward the Blue Line the advance continued across the dreadful quagmire, but the forward wave of the Middlesex was unable to keep up with the line of bursting shells. An officer and twenty men attempted to consolidate a position in shell-holes on the Red Line north-east of the embankment, in touch with the 11th Queens on their left. Heavy machine gun fire from two dugouts along the railway embankment, and from higher ground 500 yards to the left struck the first, third and fourth waves, many casualties being sustained. At around 4:35 a.m. a party of two officer and about 40 men with three Lewis guns dug-in on the Blue Line about 100 yards north-east of the embankment also in touch with the Queens. The fire from the dugouts on the embankment was causing severe casualties, and proved very difficult for the Middlesex to silence. Some uncut wire, an expanse of waterlogged ground and water filled shell-holes prevented them from being outflanked, although the Middlesex worked up close enough to sustain casualties through stick bombs thrown from them. The dugouts were eventually bombed out by a team who worked down the embankment, 40 prisoners being taken, and by 5:30 a.m. battalion headquarters had been set up in one of the captured dugouts. By 6:00 a.m. the Blue Line was clear of the enemy, but machine gun fire from two pillboxes on the Green Line 400 yards to the north-east, swept the Middlesex as they consolidated on the Red and Blue Lines and along the embankment. No further forward movement was possible and after being seen by German reconnaissance aircraft the muddy and water-filled forward outposts also began to be shelled. It was a similar story with the Queens and the Royal West Kent along the whole brigade line, the Blue Line secured and consolidated up to the track of the Klein Zillebeke road on the left, but machine gun fire from the Green Line holding up any further advance.

 Having attacked across awful waterlogged ground and under harassing machine gun fire, 41st Division had been checked a few hundred yards short of their final objective, but had secured the left flank of the main attack of II Corps along the Klein Zillebeke road. Second Army had been successful in its task of providing a firm flank upon which the main advance to the north could now pivot, but any further advancement of X Corps would depend on the progress made by II Corps onto the Gheluvelt plateau, north of the Klein Zillebeke road. Total casualties in X Corps had been 1,494.[195]

---

[194] National Archives, War Diary 123rd Brigade WO95/4243

[195] In their book *Passchendaele the Untold Story*, Prior and Wilson claim: 'Little aid was accorded Jacob's men [II Corps on the Gheluvelt Plateau] by the endeavours of Plumer's Second Army on their right. X Corps did manage to capture a small section of the plateau to the east of Battle Wood. But, more importantly, along the remainder of the 13,000 yards front Plumer's other corps advanced only

The Main Attack

The Attack of Fifth Army 3:50 a.m. 31st July

Throughout the arc of the British Front Line which defined the dreaded Ypres Salient, in places no more than 3,500 yards from the ruined Cloth Hall in the centre of the city, tens of thousands of young men leaned against trench walls or lay in wet, muddy shell-holes as the time for action drew agonisingly close. As thousands of watches ticked away the final minutes to Zero, the waiting and the tension for both officers and men became unbearable. The time for other thoughts and considerations had now passed as the order to fix bayonets was quietly passed along the trenches or whispered across No Mans Land, and at the last moment the protection covers fitted in an effort to keep them clear of the pervading mud had been removed from the muzzles and breaches of their rifles. The fleeting hopes in the minds of some, of a minor injury keeping them out of the line, or the attack being called off were now forgotten, and many more whispered a silent prayer. There may even have been those who could not wait to get to grips with the enemy, but they were surely few in number. The rum ration had helped a little to settle ragged nerves, and provide a degree of fire which had perhaps previously been absent. Soon they would all pass into a different dimension where the future was beyond their control, and survival was in the hands of luck, or their creator. Those who had been into battle before knew what faced them, those who had not were the lucky ones. In a short while there was to be no more sheltering, but rather the insanity of exposure to careless, tearing, white-hot shards, and zipping, whining bullets and shrapnel balls. The capacity for self control, the ability to think clearly under conditions of utter confusion, and the very will to survive, were now to be put to the ultimate test. Each man's own strength of character, the quality of his training, and the conduct and example of those around him, would all go into the melting pot, as the ability to endure was closely examined. To be found wanting would be laid bare for all to see. This was the greatest demon lurking in the dark corners of many young minds. Some would conquer these demons and transcend their fears to carry out such acts of valour, courage and bravery, which, away from the battlefield defied the logical reasoning of non military men. The fear of fear was the worst.

    Over No-Mans-Land, across the cratered ground where a few scrubby weeds and tufts of rank grass grew amongst the shell-holes, the screw-pickets and the rusty barbed wire, all seemed dark and quiet. A few random flares were evidence of the tension also felt by the ever jumpy enemy. Any friendly shelling was sporadic, mainly from the bigger guns, the shells rumbling over head, no different to any other night. The enemy guns which had been more active earlier were now reduced to sporadic firing. If the Germans had any inkling that they were on the brink of Armageddon they did not show it. They were about to receive a rude awakening.

There was little visibility through the gloom of the early dawn. A heavy low cloud base at around 500 to 800 feet was driven on a moderate westerly breeze. On some parts of the battlefront it was already drizzling, but mainly to the south of the Menin Road. Under these conditions the air co-operation which had been so carefully planned was not going to be possible.

    The final fateful seconds were counted down, willed on by those whose nerves could wait no longer, until at the moment of 3:50 a.m. the artillery massed along the whole front opened fire in one great, shattering crescendo. Like a colossal electrical storm thousands of brilliant rippling gun flashes darted amongst the low fleeting clouds, closely followed by the

---

500 yards. No important German positions were captured, no great number of casualties inflicted, and no German troops diverted from the north'. As we have seen, this is a misleading, simplistic, and unnecessarily unfair criticism of the operations of the Second Army on this day, which had succeeded in reaching virtually all its objectives, *within the plan*. The author hopes he has gone some way towards putting the record straight. See *Passchendaele the Untold Story* p93

thunder of their report. Within seconds the screaming and whining of countless field artillery shells, were joined by the rumble of the huge projectiles from the bigger guns which filled the upper air. In an instant the atmosphere pulsed with noise, heat and light, as the lethal deluge erupted amongst and above the forward enemy outposts, which quickly disappeared beneath a veil of hurled earth, smoke and flame. The shrill of officer's whistles was drowned out by the general cacophony. The great battle had started and whatever the outcome was to be, the Tommies were on their way.

The protective barrage fired by the 18-pounders and 4.5-inch howitzers of the field artillery, positioned a few thousand yards behind the lines, cracked above and blasted into the German front positions, where it rampaged in accordance with the intricate fire plan for five minutes. The infantry, released at last from the agony of anticipation climbed heavily from their shallow jump-off trenches or shell-holes, shook out into artillery formation, and, led forward by their officers, moved further out into No-Man's-Land to within fifty yards of the wall of bursting shells.[196] As the guns at last lifted off the enemy front line the forward waves of skirmishers followed up closely, nosing for the enemy, the menacing bayonets of their Lee Enfield rifles glinting in the vicious flashes. To assist them in keeping direction in the poor visibility, trench mortars had fired many illuminating rounds of bright burning Thermit bombs. Batteries of Livens projectors, a crude but effective large bore mortar tube, firing a lozenge shaped projectile and hated by the enemy, had launched oil filled canisters into the German positions, the glare of the yellow-orange oil flames creating an unearthly light which danced amongst the thick black oily smoke. From 500 hundred yards behind the British front line, and unheard amongst the uproar, a massed machine gun barrage was fired by 64 Vickers guns on each corps sector, the streams of fire drifting over the heads of the advancing infantry to rake the ground ahead of the creeping field artillery barrage.[197]
    Along much of the front from the Klein Zillebeke road to the Yser canal at Boesinghe, the initial assault went well. As the infantry attack advanced, the German Front Line and supports were quickly overrun while the barrage thundered forward. The wire that one year before on the Somme had caused such agony was less in evidence, and what there was had been well cut, an indication of the successful work of the artillery. Those of the German garrison who had remained in the front line were quickly overwhelmed, dazed and stunned by the tumultuous barrage, and either surrendered promptly, or were immediately thrust with the bayonet or shot down, their dugouts methodically bombed-out in turn. The response of the German artillery was not immediate. It was not until about ten minutes after Zero that their retaliatory barrage began to be noticed, and along much of the battlefront it appeared rather weak and erratic. But that was not the case on the western slopes of the Gheluvelt plateau, were it fell with disconcerting power along the old British Front Line and assembly trenches, and amongst the shattered remains of the woods. *Group Wytschaete's* artillery concentration behind the higher ground had

---

[196] The barrage was provided by about two thirds of the field guns in each corps sector.
[197] National Archives, War Diary of 30th Division, WO95/2329. 30th Division was to have a heavier barrage provided by the 48 machine guns of 18th Division, to give support up to and including the capture of the Blue Line. In the Fifth Army on the 31st July, the various objectives designated in the divisional orders were given a colour code for ease of definition. The first objective, which was generally between the German Front and Second Lines was coded the Blue Line. The second objective, was on or about the German Second Line, (*Albrecht Stellung*), and was coded the Black Line. The third objective, was on or about the German Third Line, (*Wilhelm Stellung*), except for north of St. Julien where it was just west of the Steenbeek, and was coded the Green Line. The fourth objective, was on or about the German Fourth Line, (*Flandern I*), and was coded the Red Line. Intermediate objectives were described as Dotted Lines, e.g. Black Dotted Line. It will be noted that confusingly these colour codes did not follow the same order as those in Second Army.

immediately made itself felt, an early indication that the plateau was going to be defended at all costs.[198]

By 4:40 a.m. and in marginally better light, it was evident that across Pilckem ridge, the first objective, the Blue Line, had been taken in a model advance of an average 800 yards. The ground had been heavy but the opposition so far had been remarkably light. Along the slight ridge, the principle German observation positions were, after over two years of occupation by the enemy, at last in the hands of the British. Only on the right, in the area of II Corps, attempting to gain the enemy bastion of the Gheluvelt plateau was there an ominous check.

At 5:05 a.m., the protective barrage, which had calmed and stood just forward of the first objective, suddenly roared and thickened, as the gunners quickened the feeding of their guns to four rounds per minute, indicating their intension to commence the steady creep toward the second objective. The assault companies took up the advance, close up to the dubious protection of the curtain of exploding projectiles, and moved forward on their way to the Black Line, the *Albrecht Stellung* 1,000 yards beyond. They were now entering the main "Battle Zone" where all had been warned the worst of the fighting would begin. The whole area was a battered crater-field in which the soft targets, the enemy trenches with their wicker revetments and open gun-pits, had been tumbled and smashed. But the carefully positioned concrete blockhouses and pillboxes had mostly survived the preparatory bombardment with their machine guns intact and would have to be overcome the hard way, by infantry attack. The platoon training to outflank the bunkers under the covering support fire of Stokes mortar, rifle grenade and Lewis gun was now to be put into shocking, trembling, practice.

Over Pilckem ridge the realities of the assault bit home, as towards the shallow valley of the Steenbeek the advance continued, the stubborn blockhouses being systematically outflanked and seized, the garrisons either fleeing or being killed or captured. It was quite evident however that the further the advance penetrated the stiffer the resistance became. This was to be no walkover. The German artillery fire, much of which was coming from the right in enfilade, from behind the Gheluvelt plateau, became more intense and destructive, as did the machine gun fire from the numerous, carefully positioned bunkers. Casualties increased as the air thickened with scything, hissing, projectiles. But the heavily laden infantry struggled forward, picking their way between the craters, across the clinging muddy ground; and they were still making good progress.

The situation in the II Corps sector on the right was not so encouraging, especially on the front of the 24th and 30th Divisions given the main task of assaulting the Gheluvelt plateau. Even at this early stage, the warnings repeated so many times by Plumer, Rawlinson, Haig and other Staff Officers at G.H.Q. regarding Gheluvelt were proving correct. In places *Group Wytschaete's* artillery had battered the assembling battalions even before they deployed to their jump off positions, causing casualties, disruption and delay. With the shells falling amongst them, the infantry had pressed forward beyond the edge of what had once been Sanctuary Wood; across the featureless and desolate wasteland of muddy, water filled shell-holes and smashed trenches, and advanced into an increasing hail of machine gun fire from the numerous well hidden pill boxes. Battalions became hopelessly mixed up, drastically weakened by casualties, with many companies without officers. Those who survived the first advance took what cover they could in the old smashed German positions, as the impetus and cohesion of the attack was lost. The protective barrage moved relentlessly forward, leaving them stranded and at the mercy of the efficient German machine gunners, well protected in their pillboxes. Men huddled and trembled in filthy shell-holes and old trenches, pressing their faces to the ground as bullets ripped and spattered into the muddy parapets, all their training of little material use, self preservation now the main objective. To make matters worse, if that were possible, the drizzle had now increased to a light rain, the ground quickly becoming a quagmire, the shell-holes filling more deeply.

---

[198] Up to the 25th July *Group Wytschaete* artillery losses had been considerable at the hands of Fifth Army counter battery fire, amounting to 50% of the heavy guns and 30% of the heavy howitzers, but such were the German powers of replacement at this time, most of these losses had been made good by the 31st.

II Corps
Lieutenant-General Sir Claud Jacob

The attack on the Gheluvelt plateau

On the right of the Fifth Army front the II Corps was to attack with three divisions in the line, the 24th, 30th and 8th, with elements of the 18th Division supporting the 30th Division. The II Corps had by far the most important and difficult task on this first day, in forming a firm defensive flank on the Gheluvelt plateau to secure the right wing of the main thrust towards the Broodseinde – Passchendaele ridge. The Corps front was around 5,000 yards long, between the Klein Zillebeke – Zandvoorde road in the south, and the track of the Ypres – Roulers railway to the north. The advance was to be over most difficult ground, much of it consisting of the shattered remains of woods which provided excellent defensive positions to the enemy, concealing strong-points and well hidden pillboxes. Seizing this area was going to be a tough proposition for the British infantry, as they faced the most numerous and formidable enemy preparations along the whole front. Incorporated within a depth of 3,000 yards were three German systems, their Front Line, Second Line (*Albrecht Stellung*), and Third Line *(Wilhelm Stellung)*, all protected by the strongest concentration of artillery, and between which were arranged numerous concrete bunkers and shelters. The German Second Line, wound across the narrow neck of the plateau, which was here about half a mile wide, between the natural obstacles of the heads of the valleys of the Hanebeek draining to the north, and the Bassevillebeek draining to the south. The enemy recognised the plateau as the keystone to their Flanders position and they were intent on holding it at all costs.

    The tanks of A and B Battalions of the 2nd Tank Brigade (21 tanks in all engaged in action), were to co-operate with the 30th and 8th Divisions, but the ground was particularly unsuitable for tank operations. The smashed wooded areas limited the lines of advance to the narrow defiles between them, which had been rendered virtually impassable by shell craters, and were well covered by enemy anti-tank artillery. Understanding of the tank's capabilities was, like the machines themselves, in its infancy. This did not detract from the courageous efforts the tank crews were to make in assisting the hard-pressed infantry.[199] It was to become obvious to the infantry from the outset, that to keep proper direction and to identify correct position on this devastated battlefield, whilst lashed by machine gun fire and pounded by the enemy artillery was near impossible, and in the general mêlée many companies were to veer way off course and become hopelessly mixed with other battalions.

24th Division
Major-General L. J. Bols

The right division of the II Corps, the 24th was to form a protective flank to the main advance, across the south western edge of the plateau, their right in contact with the 123 Brigade of the 41st Division, (Second Army). The right and centre brigades had only 2 objectives to reach, the Blue and Black Lines, while the left brigade, protecting the right flank of 30th Division would have an extra 400 yards to advance in order to reach the third objective on the Green Line.
The division was to advance on a front of around 1,600 yards. The 72nd Brigade on the right with its right flank on the Klein Zillebeke to Zandvoorde road, was to attack towards Groenenburg (Greenbug) Farm and Bulgar Wood, the 73rd Brigade in the centre through Shrewsbury Forest towards the Bassevillebeek valley, while on the left the 17th Brigade was to attack between Shrewsbury Forest and Bodmin Copse, cross the Bassevillebeek valley and at the final objective, gain Tower Hamlets spur and the Menin Road west of Gheluvelt. This advance of 2,700 yards to

---

[199] 20 of the 21 tanks engaged became casualties.

the third objective would thus secure the right flank of 30th Division. In common with the whole of the Gheluvelt plateau, the ground over which the division was about to advance had been turned into a muddy quagmire by the recent wet weather. The network of German fire, support, reserve and communication trenches had been continuously blasted by the preparatory barrage, which had laid waste the desolate surface leaving only the shattered remains of woods, which were now reduced to a few stubborn, limbless trunks. Scarred by a plethora of water-filled shell-holes, one sector of the desolation looked the same as the next, and without carefully following a compass bearing, maintaining correct direction was going to be most difficult. If officer casualties mounted it was going to be impossible. Numerous enemy machine guns waited in bunkers within thick concrete protection, to make those officer casualties a certainty.

During the 29th and 30th the attacking battalions had made their way towards the forward assembly areas, a task made more difficult by the wet and slippery ground. The series of communication trenches and tunnels behind the British Front Line, leading to the grim western slopes of the Gheluvelt plateau and the dubious heights of Mount Sorrel, Hill 61 and Hill 62 became heavily congested, as thousands of wet and muddy men and their equipment competed for what little space existed. Officers desperately tried to establish temporary battalion headquarters in muddy trench or filthy overcrowded tunnel, and on the 30th made strenuous last minute efforts to reconnoitre the front line and check the jump-off positions already posted and taped for their battalions. Quartermasters strove valiantly to get the basic requirements of food and drink as far up the line as they could, assuming their battalion could be located. In the dank unhealthy tunnels even basic sanitary arrangements became near impossible. As vigilant and powerful as ever, the enemy artillery joined in the party with high explosive and its new mustard oil, adding to the difficulties and quickly establishing the first names on the inevitable casualty lists.[200]

72nd Brigade[201]
On the right of the 24th Division, the 72nd Brigade was to attack on a two battalion front, with the 8th Queens on the right and the 1st North Staffordshire Regiment on the left.[202] The 8th Royal West Kent Regiment was in support and the 9th East Surrey Regiment in reserve. Typical of the brigade arrangements were those of the 1st North Staffs, which was to attack on a two company front, "C" and "D" leading, with "B" Company in support and "A" Company in reserve. Assembly positions for "C", "D" and "B" Companies were in the protective confines of the Mount Sorrel Tunnel system, while "A" Company assembled in Image Crescent trench. In order to miss the worst of the enemy barrage which usually fell upon the British support areas around 2:00 p.m. the attacking companies of the brigade began to move out of the tunnels and trenches and up to their tape lines around midnight, to lay out in wet muddy shell-holes and await Zero Hour.

---

[200] The positions of Hill 59, (or Mount Sorrel), Hill 61 and Hill 62 were somewhat unique in the Salient as being the only place where the British Front Line was on higher ground than the opposing German section of front. The Canadians had fought hard to regain the position in the summer of 1916.
[201] National Archives, War Diary 72nd Brigade WO95/2211, War Diary 8th Queens WO95/2214
[202] National Archives, War Diary 1st North Staffs and 8th Queens WO95/2114

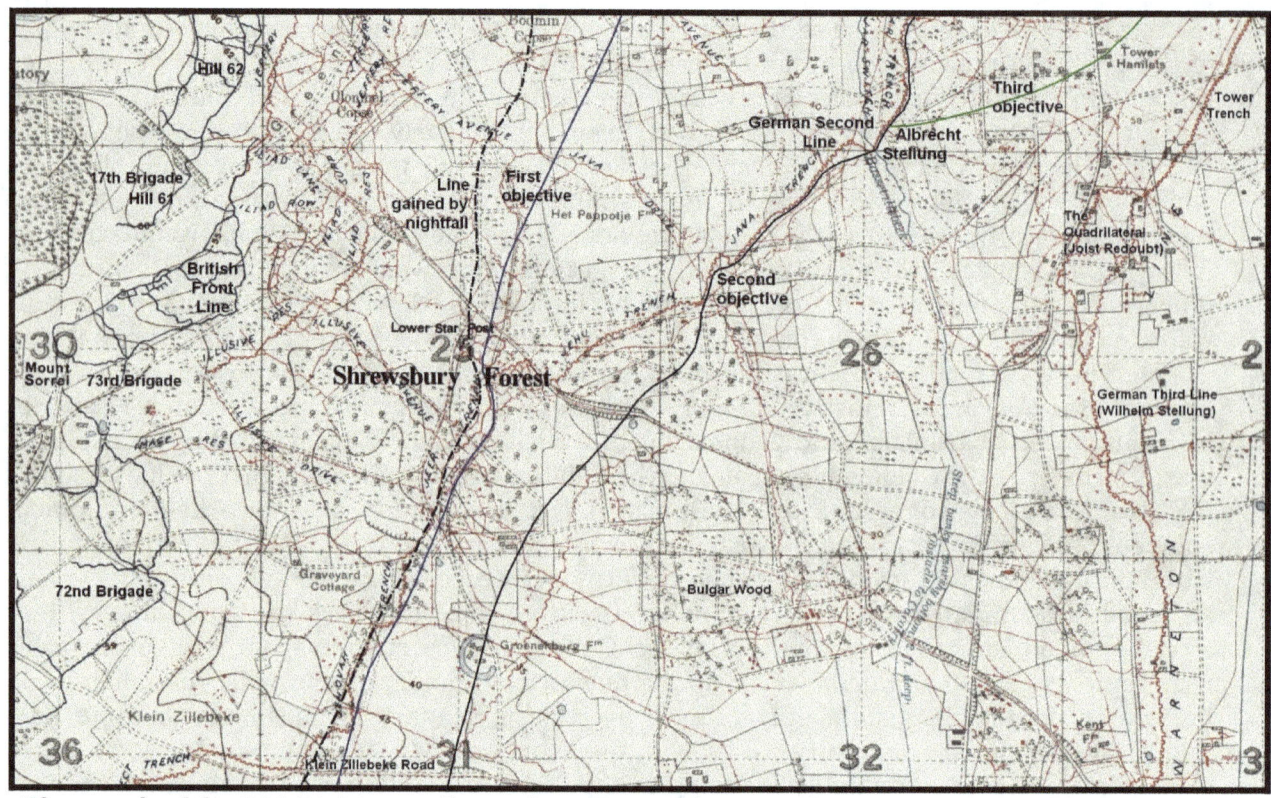

The attack of the 24th Division at Shrewsbury Forest showing objectives and actual line gained by nightfall

From midnight onwards the German artillery kept up a fairly active but erratic bombardment on the British support and communication trenches with guns of all calibres which caused a few casualties. At 3:50 prompt the British barrage came down with tremendous force, the gun flashes and shell-bursts lighting an otherwise dark scene. The front skirmish lines of the Queens and North Staffs climbed from their shell-hole protection, or over the parapets of the shallow assembly trenches, formed up, and moved forward behind the dense maelstrom of protective blasts. Within minutes the enemy guns were in action, a hail of 77's falling on the British Front Line while 4.2's and 5.9's searched the support and reserve positions. The attacking line got quickly clear of the enemy shells and pushed on across the wet, heavy ground. The enemy were soon encountered occupying shell-holes just beyond No-Mans-Land, but most surrendered quickly; those that did not were bayoneted or shot down. There were few casualties in the first 600 yards, but as the barrage lifted off Jehovah Trench the enemy rapidly emerged from a bunker and succeeded in bringing a machine gun into action, which began to rip into the Queens and North Staffs. While Lewis guns and rifle grenades were concentrated on the hostile machine gun, parties worked forward and entered the trench. The gun crew abandoned the gun and ran into the concrete shelter from where they began to throw stick bombs at their assailants. A Sergeant of the North Staffs, firing a Lewis gun from the hip opened up on the entrance to the shelter, while a bombing party worked in close enough to threaten the garrison, at which point 14 men emerged and surrendered. Jehovah Trench was occupied, but it was clear that all was not well to the left of the North Staffs in 73rd Brigade sector. Parties of the 7th Northants were veering right to avoid enfilade machine gun fire emanating from a strong-point on some higher ground amid the stumps and gaunt trunks of Shrewsbury Forest. Because of the heavy ground and confusion of blasted timber and craters, the Northants were having great difficulty getting forward, and having lost the barrage were being cut down by machine guns from the high point in the wood. A gap had opened between the left of the North Staffs and the right of the Northants and now the North Staffs were also being hit by the same machine gun fire from the wood to the north. The difficulties in attacking the featureless wastes in virtual darkness soon became apparent, as in Jehovah Trench there now gather parties from the 7th Northants, the

North Staffs, the Queens and even men of the 20th Durham Light Infantry of 41st Division, who should have been south of the Klein Zillebeke road. Enemy machine gunners in Bulgar Wood 700 yards in front of Jehovah Trench also opened fire, and by 5:30 casualties had risen alarmingly. All except two company officers of the North Staffs had been hit. Some men of "C" Company led by Lieutenant Allen and others led by their N.C.O's made further progress east of Jehovah Trench towards Groenenburg Farm, and there checked by fire from front and flanks took cover in shell-holes in the marshy ground just west of the farm moat. To cover the gap with the Northants, Allen formed a defensive left flank of riflemen and Lewis gunners in shell-holes, who then engaged the enemy machine guns in Shrewsbury Forest as best they could. Some of the leading platoon of "C" Company under 2nd Lieutenant Pierson reached as far as Jordan Trench. But at 6:00 a.m. with 41st Division checked short of their objective on the right, and the 7th Northants held up on the left, the Brigade Commander gave orders that the attack would not continue, and that the ground gained was to be consolidated. The front post at Jordan Trench held by Pierson and his party, being totally isolated and exposed to fire from Bulgar Wood and Shrewsbury Forest was withdrawn. Consolidation west of Groenenburg Farm was hampered by intermittent enemy shell-fire, which although by 6-inch guns caused little damage, while machine gun fire from the woods remained lethal.

This was to be the pattern for the attacks against Gheluvelt plateau by II Corps, with darkness, shell-fire, machine guns, and atrocious ground all conspiring to create confusion, disorganisation and high casualties. But this was only on the southern fringe of the plateau. To the north things were to be much worse.

73rd Brigade[203]

In the centre of 24th Division the 73rd Brigade was to attack through Shrewsbury Forest with the 7th Northamptonshire Regiment and the 2nd Leinster Regiment.[204] The 13th Middlesex Regiment was in support.[205] The brigade had two objectives, the first the Blue Line near the centre of Shrewsbury Forest close to Jeer Trench, the second, the Black Line east of the wood towards the Bassevillebeek. On the night of the 29th / 30th, both attacking battalions had begun to move up to their assembly positions in Canada Street and Larch Wood Tunnels, or in nearby dug-outs. The ground conditions were already so bad that "A" Company of the Northants was ordered to remain at its forward camp as the trench it was to occupy was flooded. The Northants established battalion headquarters in the miserable cramped conditions of Canada Street Tunnel, where at least it was relatively safe from the enemy shell-fire, which had sporadically searched between the support trenches and the eastern slope of Mount Sorrel throughout the night. The 2nd Leinster, also in Canada Street Tunnel had taken the precaution on the night of the 30th / 31st to lay a tape running forward from the tunnel exit to its forward jumping-off tapes to avoid any mix up in the final assembly. At 9:30 p.m. on the 30th Lieutenant -Colonel Hobbs D.S.O. of the Northants, and Lieutenant -Colonel Murphy D.S.O., M.C. of the Leinster accompanied by Lieutenant Berridge M.C. the Brigade Intelligence Officer went forward to reconnoitre the front line, checking the stakes indicating the flank positions of the assaulting companies, and the jump-off tapes, which had already been fixed by the 9th Royal Sussex Regiment. At around midnight the attacking companies began the slow movement out of the claustrophobic tunnels and by 3:30 a.m. all were in position, taking what shell-hole shelter they could find along the jumping-off tapes. Shelter was essential, for a little before Zero Hour the enemy artillery dropped a few shells amongst the anxiously waiting troops causing some casualties. The waiting was at last over as the British barrage crashed down, and the Northants and Leinster gathered themselves and began to advance. Within three minutes the enemy retaliated with a barrage of 77's which burst along the jump-off line, causing many casualties including some officers, whilst the heavier 4.2's and 5.9's thumped into the support trenches to the west of Mount Sorrel.

---

[203] National Archives, War Diary 73rd Brigade WO95/2217
[204] National Archives, War Diary 7th Northants and 2nd Leinster WO95/2118
[205] National Archives, War Diary 13th Middlesex WO95/2119

The darkness and officer casualties created immediate difficulties for the Northants. Previously identified landmarks, a shattered tree or mound of an earthwork, were impossible to see in the darkness, and many officers with their invaluable compasses had already gone down. Before the worst of the fighting started the Northants were already veering off course. The ground was proving very hard going, mud and fallen timber hindering the advance, which gradually lost the barrage. It appeared that the enemy had dragged machine guns forward of Jeer Trench into shell-holes, for as the British barrage pilled onto the trench these guns opened fire causing a further check and disorganisation. As riflemen and Lewis gunners, taking cover in shell-holes engaged the enemy machine guns, bombing parties worked forward from crater to crater. The German guns were gradually put out of action, but now a greater menace emerged as enfilade machine fire from a strong-point on higher ground to the left smashed into the left flank and rear of the already scattered Northants.

To the left of the Northants the Leinster had quickly overcome defended shell-holes just east of no-mans-land, but then came under rifle fire from Iliad and Illusive Reserve trenches, 250 yards from their jump-off line. The momentum of their advance soon overcame the resistance, some Germans being shot while about 20 were taken prisoner. Within 5 minutes the trenches were taken and the Leinster continued towards their first objective, but were soon confronted with muddy broken ground and, under considerable machine gun fire, also lost the barrage. This fire was soon identified as coming from the main German defensive position 400 yards ahead on higher ground. This strong-point had a commanding view allowing for an excellent all-round field of fire. It was this fire which was so affecting the Northants and also 72nd Brigade 800 yards to the right, and now cut into the advance of the Leinster. The group of enemy pillboxes at the strong-point of Lower Star Post, and Jeer Trench running north and south of it were heavily garrisoned, well concealed and protected by wire, and armed with many machine guns. Approaches from the north and west were covered, and a clear field of fire was available along the shallow valley to the south down to Groenenburg Farm and the approach to Bulgar Wood. It was clear that the barrage had done little to soften the defences as the Leinster had been under fire from the position virtually throughout its advance. All the officers of the Leinster right company became casualties, only one Sergeant remaining to take command. The shallow valley which reached into the centre of Shrewsbury Forest and then ran to the southwards was swept by machine fire, and to avoid the worst of this fire the right company veered to their left, northwards towards the higher ground were the left company were already suffering severely from enfilade and frontal machine gun and rifle fire.

In an attempt to avoid the shallow valley, the left company of the 7th Northants had veered far to the right, in an almost southerly direction, accompanied by an officer and some men of the right Leinster company, all these movements being carried out under heavy fire over awful ground and in virtual darkness. The Northants assault companies were now highly disorganised, but were holding a small section of the Blue Line in Jeer Trench, around 500 yards south of Lower Star Post. Walking wounded also reported that the Black Line was secure, but the situation was so confused and obscure that Lieut.-Colonel Hobbs personally went forward to ascertain the position. With all the company officers casualties, 2nd Lieutenant Berridge with two N.C.O's reorganised at least part of the line and sent a message back to battalion headquarters for reinforcements. A company of the 13th Middlesex were sent forward to reinforce the Northants line at Jeer Trench, but were themselves badly shot-up by the Lower Star Post guns on the way up. At first moving beyond a section of Jeer Trench, upon seeing none of the Northants in front of them the remnants fell-back and dug-in between Illusive Drive and Illusive Reserve, within a few hundred yards of the jump-off line.

A little to the north of Lower Star Post small parties of the Leinster left company had reached the eastern edge of Shrewsbury Forest. Casualties had been most severe and only isolated groups of men were left to push the advance beyond the Blue Line. The left of the battalion was in touch with the 1st Royal Fusiliers in 17th Brigade sector as they had veered to their left to avoid the worst of the fire, and the remnants of all 3 Leinster assaulting companies were gathered together as best possible, to join with the Fusiliers in an further attempt to advance. By this stage the barrage was out of sight, and the edge of the wood near the Blue Line was found to be thickly wired with low trellis wire. The Germans were still resisting strongly from a group of loop-holed concrete dug-outs on the Blue Line. Isolated groups desperately attempted to capture the dug-outs head on, enemy machine gun fire stopping many attempts and causing dreadful casualties. Eventually a double flanking manoeuvre was organised and after much delay the dug-outs were bombed out, and the northern end of Jeer Trench near Jeffery Avenue was occupied. Another section of the Blue Line was now secure, but a large gap existed in the line either side of Lower Star Post, and without the necessary reinforcements of men and re-supply of ammunition and bombs no further forward movement was possible. Consolidation of the position gained was started, under heavy fire from the front and right flank, and a patrol was sent out to the right in an attempt to gain touch with the Northants. The patrol was not seen again.

With orders to follow up behind the advance as far as the Blue Line, the reserve company of the Leinster had meanwhile left Larch Wood Tunnel and shaken out into artillery formation. A little before 6:00 a.m. it had reached a point 200 yards beyond the old British front line, when it came under heavy machine gun fire from the high ground in the wood at Lower Star Post. A Vickers gun and a Stokes mortar had been brought forward, and at a range of 550 yards, with the support of the company riflemen engaged the enemy machine guns. Movement forward was impossible and the company consolidated as best possible about Illiad Reserve to await information regarding the position and situation of the forward companies, and where the left flank of the Northants rested. During the morning an enemy aircraft flew low over Shrewsbury Forest and apparently observed the position of the Leinster reserve company, for soon a severe hostile bombardment shook Illiad Reserve. As quickly as possible the company moved slightly forward and to the flanks to avoid the worst of the shelling, but so devastating was the fire that by noon half of the company were casualties.

Throughout the morning and afternoon the enemy kept up a continuous heavy bombardment along the old British front line and an area up to 300 yards either side, dislocating communication with the new front line, and rendering the evacuation of the many wounded virtually impossible. By about 1:00 p.m. the situation in the new front line had become clearer, and it was now known that a gap of about 400 yards existed between the left on the Northants and the right of the Leinster, in the centre if which sat Lower Star Post. At 3:15 the support company of the 13th Middlesex was sent forward in a forlorn hope to fill the gap. Already weakened as it had supplied one platoon to gain contact between the Leinster reserve company at Illiad Reserve trench and the 17th Brigade, the Middlesex support company eventually reached the front line at 6:30 p.m. via the 17th Brigade sector, and then extended the right flank of the front line by about 100 yards and established a defensive flank facing south.

It had been clear by early in the morning that 73rd Brigade in a disorganised state was held up, at best on the Blue Line, and was not going to achieve its final objective. Lower Star Post had been expertly positioned and garrisoned, and had not been effected by the British barrage or closely approached by infantry. Most ominously the enemy artillery fire had been severe, had obviously not been dominated, and throughout the day had not been quietened by counter-battery fire. But this was still only the flank of the attack on the plateau, and an even worse situation had developed to the north.

17th Brigade [206]

On the left of 24th Division the 17th Brigade was to use the 1st Royal Fusiliers to attack the first objective, from where the 12th Royal Fusiliers were to pass through towards the further objective,[207] while the 3rd Rifle Brigade were to follow up in support. The battalions began to move up into the Canada Street and Hedge Street Tunnels on the night of the 29th / 30th. Some patrolling of the line was attempted, and although the enemy were not encountered the operation was hampered towards the 30th Division front line by enemy gas shelling. The atmosphere in Hedge Street Tunnel was foul and the conditions cramped, with many units

---

[206] National Archives. War Diary 17th Brigade WO95/2204
[207] National Archives, War Diary 1st Royal Fusiliers WO95/2207

jostling for space. At one point the battalion headquarters of the 1st Royal Fusiliers was threatened when a 5.9-inch shell knocked in part of the tunnel. No casualties were caused, and all ranks were successfully provided with hot tea before forming up. At about 10:30 the 1st Royal Fusiliers began moving out of the tunnel towards the tape lines, and formed up "A" Company on the right, "C" Company on the left, with "B" and "D" Companies in support, and all were in position soon after 2:00 a.m.

At Zero Hour as the barrage came down the support companies moved up close behind the assault companies to avoid the enemy barrage, which as expected soon fell on the British front line. From the start the machine guns at Lower Star Post raked the forward waves of Royal Fusiliers as they worked forward across the muddy cratered ground. As the left Leinster company veered to its left to avoid the fire, it crowded the Fusiliers right company forcing them also to the left, the advance moving northeast instead of east. Illiad Reserve and Jeffery Reserve were taken with little enemy resistance, but casualties were mounting from the fire from Lower Star Post. About 200 yards east of Illiad Reserve the Germans had established machine guns in shell-holes which opened fire directly in front of the Fusiliers, causing more casualties and forcing some to take cover. Before these guns could be attacked the enemy had dragged them back towards the northern end of Jeer Trench. No effort was made by the Germans to make a stand until the Fusiliers approached a strong-point just south of Jeffrey Avenue. Here "B" Company were checked and forced to take cover by a machine gun, which they quickly engaged with Lewis guns and rifle grenades. Lieutenant Flack M.C. the Company Commander personally knocked out the gun with a rifle grenade, but sniper fire continued to take a heavy toll on the Fusiliers. "B" Company then commenced to consolidate between Jeer Trench and Jeffery Avenue. The left Fusilier "C" Company, although also veering slightly left, had generally maintained better direction, and under severe and accurate sniper fire, with some men of "A" Company had taken a section of Java Drive in Bodmin Copse, and had commenced to consolidate. Here the Company Commander Captain Leeming was shot and killed by a sniper. The left support company "D" had succeeded after stiff fighting in entering Jeffery Avenue, and began to consolidate the position in touch with "B" Company.

At around 5:30 the 12th Royal Fusiliers passed through the 1st, and advanced down the exposed slope towards the Bassevellebeek, but soon came under machine gun fire from Dumbarton Woods to their left, and from Tower Hamlets spur across the Bassevillebeek valley. Advancing out of the remains of the wood, and down into the marshy ground within 200 yards of the stream, the hail of fire from the pillboxes on the spur was too heavy, and those who could were forced to fall-back up the slope, to a position near Java Avenue, 500 yards short of the stream. The 3rd Rifle Brigade had moved up in support of the 1st Royal Fusiliers, and with men from the Leinster helped in consolidation of the position.

The 24th Division had advanced a maximum of 1,000 yards, but in some places was pinned down by the guns at Lower Star Post and had advanced less than 500 yards. At best they were still 1,000 yards short of their objective. The fighting had been severe as the casualty figures of nearly 2,250 showed. Most seriously the enemy had confined the fighting within the forward zone, between their Front Line and Second Line. Their Third Line, the *Wilhelm Stellung* sat inviolate; solidly on top of Tower Hamlets spur, at the crest of the muddy slope 800 yards on from the Bassevellebeek, protected by its wire entanglements and line of concrete blockhouses which the British artillery had not harmed. The men of 24th Division must have wondered how they were ever to conquer the heights and breach the German Third Line. It was to be many weeks of toil and heartache before anyone did.

30th Division
Major -General W. de L. Williams

Having been heavily engaged in the Somme and Arras battles, the mainly Liverpool and Manchester Pals battalions of 30th Division had not fully recovered from their losses, and were now being asked to attempt the most difficult job of the day, the storming of the central part of the Gheluvelt plateau. To replace them with a fresher division had been considered, but rejected through lack of time. To compensate, the 53rd Brigade of the 18th Division was allotted to assist in gaining the further objectives. The addition of the 18th Division was not just to bolster any perceived weaknesses in the 30th Division, but was an indication of how difficult the capture of the central plateau was recognised to be, and the weight of infantry which was considered necessary to be pushed through the narrow front to achieve success. The division was to attack on a frontage of about 1,600 yards, (through which 12 infantry battalions would have to pass), to an average depth of about 2,700 yards to the third objective, or the Green Line. But the divisional frontage widened from 1,600 yards at the jump off point, to nearer 2,700 yards closer to the distant objectives. This meant driving a great number of infantry through the Blue and Black Lines once captured, if there was to be any hope of capturing the Green Line, let alone the Red Line another 800 yards further forward. It also meant that the further the infantry advanced the thinner their protective barrage would become.

The division was to attack in an east north-easterly direction, using 3 brigades, the 21st, 90th, 89th between just south of Bodmin Copse, and the northern end of Sanctuary Wood. They were to assault towards the higher ground at Stirling Castle and Dumbarton Lakes, then across the moonscape of the flat, blasted plateau top, cross the Menin Road 1,500 yards west of Gheluvelt, and advance towards Inverness Copse, Glencorse Wood, and Nonne Boschen. Ultimately if all went to plan they would reach the western edge of Polygon Wood, an advance of 3,000 yards, and throughout this advance would be a prime target for the concentration of *Group Wytschaete* guns east of the plateau. The skeletal remains of Inverness Copse and Glencorse Wood were protected by, and incorporated within the defence system of the *Albrecht Stellung*, and across the western face of Polygon Wood ran the *Wilhelm Stellung*. Both on and between the second and third German lines many concrete pillboxes and blockhouses had been built, giving the deep, integrated system great strength. The blockhouses had been positioned with great skill, with excellent fields of fire commanding the approaches from the west, and most importantly the eastern slope of Westhoek ridge and the valley of the Hanebeek, stretching away from the plateau to the north. In the central section of the divisional front, the British trench lines bisected the shattered Sanctuary Wood. Here the initial advance would be uphill, through the fallen splintered trunks, the blasted stumps and rusted wire entanglements which lay within the smashed shambles of what had been the wood.

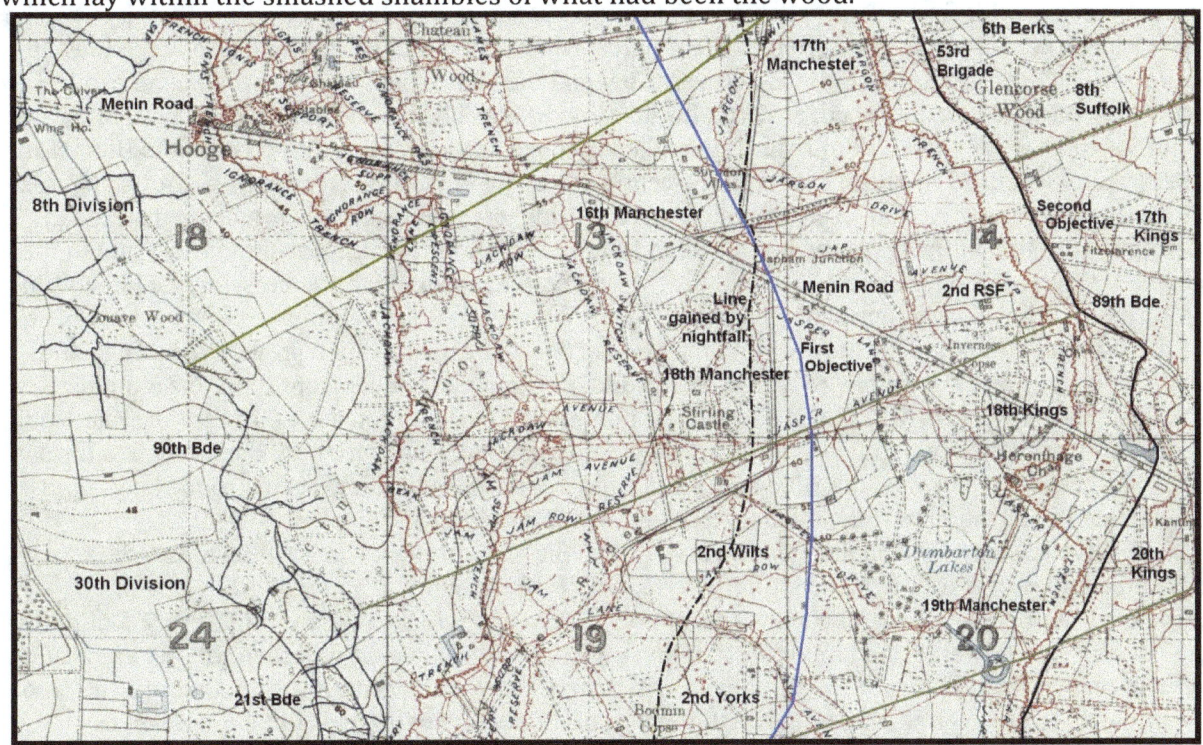

Attack of 30th Division showing objectives and intended positions of battalions on Blue and Black Lines and actual line gained by nightfall

The shape of the area to be captured was not simple, and neither were the planned dispositions of the forces to attack it. The initial assault to the Blue and Black Lines was the task of the 21st and 90th Brigades. On the Black Line the 89th Brigade was to pass through both the 21st Brigade, and the right sector of the 90th Brigade (18th Manchester and 2nd Royal Scots Fusiliers), and advance to the Green Line. Through the left section of the 90th Brigade (16th and 17th Manchester), the 53rd Brigade of the 18th Division was to pass through on the Black Line and advance towards the Green Line, which in its sector ran through the centre of Polygon Wood, at the western end of the "Racecourse".[208] The attack by the forward assault battalions of 21st and 90th Brigades was to be carried out in three waves, the first wave to advance to the Jeffery Support-Jam Support-Jackdaw Support line, the second wave to Jeffery Reserve-Jam Reserve-Jackdaw Reserve line, and the third wave at double the strength of the 1st and 2nd waves to the Blue Line 400 yards beyond. The second phase of the attack by the support battalions of 21st and 90th Brigades to the Black Line would be in two stages, by a fourth and fifth wave, with locally defined objectives.

The whole operation was one of great complexity which would have undoubtedly been difficult to perform in daylight with identifiable landmarks, and with little resistance from the enemy. On Salisbury Plain maybe, but in darkness and against determined and well established opposition it was asking too much.[209]

21st Brigade[210]

---

[208] The remains of a pre-war exercise track for ponies and horses of the Belgian Army.

[209] The barrage plan for the 30th Division attack on the Gheluvelt plateau was extremely complex due to the shape of the area to be assaulted and was as follows. The barrage was to be put down on the enemy's front line at Zero hour and remain there until Zero plus 5 minutes. It would then advance over the first 100 yards in 3 minutes, the next 75 yards in 2 minutes, and the next 75 yards in 4 minutes, and at this point would advance at a uniform rate of 100 yards in 4 minutes. Because of the irregular shape of the objective lines, the barrage would reach the objective at a different time along different parts of the front. At the northern and southern ends of the 30th Division's first objective, the Blue Line, it would reach it at Zero plus 30 minutes, while in the middle it would be at Zero plus 38 minutes. The barrage would continue 300 yards beyond the Blue Line, where it would stand and a protective barrage be established, at Zero plus 46 minutes at each end and at Zero plus 54 in the centre. At Zero plus 1 hour 23 minutes it would commence to advance, until it crossed the Black Line at Zero plus 1 hour 39 minutes, except in the centre where just east of Inverness Copse it would cross at 1 hour 47 minutes. At 300 yards beyond the Black Line it would stand as a protective barrage at Zero plus 1 hour 55 minutes at the north end and Zero plus 1 hour 51 minutes at the south and in the centre. At Zero plus 6 hours and 28 minutes, it would commence to advance, crossing the Green Line at Zero plus 6 hours 48 minutes at the north end and Zero plus 6 hours 32 minutes at the southern end of the front, continuing 300 yards beyond the Green Line and establishing a protective barrage until 7 hours and 48 minutes. Rate of fire would be 4 rounds per gun per minute from Zero to Zero plus 10 minutes, and subsequently 2 rounds per gun per minute. During the protective barrages the rate would reduce to 1 round per two minutes, then die down to occasional rounds to mark the protective lines. During the last 8 minutes on the Blue and Black lines the rate would increase to 4 rounds per minute to indicate the intention to lift. National Archives, War Diary of 30th Division, WO95/2329
The 8th Division barrage plan differed in detail due to the less complex shape of the area to be assaulted and was as follows. The artillery barrage will lift normally at a rate of 100 yards in 4 minutes. It will be put down on enemy's front line at Zero and will remain on it till Zero + 5 minutes. It will then lift 100 yards and remain on that line till Zero + 8 minutes. It will then lift 100 yards and remain on that line till Zero + ten minutes. It will then lift 100 yards and remain on that line till Zero + 14 minutes, after which lifts and times will be normal. Protective barrages will be put down as follows: i) 300 yards east of Blue and Black Lines respectively. ii) 500 yards east of Green Line. iii) 500 yards east of Nordemdhoek – Broodseinde road from Red Line. BOH Appendix XIV section 12.

[210] National Archives, War Diary 21st Brigade WO95/2329

On the division right flank, the 21st Brigade was to attack with their right on Hill 62 and their left in Sanctuary Wood. On the brigade right the 2nd Green Howards were supported by the 19th Manchester Regiment, and on the left the 2nd Wiltshire Regiment were supported by the 18th King's Liverpool Regiment.[211]

On the night of the 29th / 30th all battalions had moved up into trenches and dug-outs about Maple Copse. The move had been arduous, deep mud in the tracks and trenches leading up hampering the heavily laden men. Most had marched the 8,000 yards from camps about Dickebusch, via Café Belge, Chateau Segard, across the Comines canal at Iron Bridge, past Bedford House and through the remains of Zillebeke village. Here they entered the maze of communication trenches about Valley Cottages and Dormy House, many moving towards the front by Zillebeke Street, and Vince Street trenches, to rear assembly positions in Maple Copse, Ritz Street and Vigo Street. Some of the assault battalions, and the first wave companies of the support battalions moved up into the protective shelter of the tunnel systems, but not before the enemy had shelled the more exposed sections of the route with high explosive and gas, causing a few casualties. The British batteries east of Zillebeke and immediately in rear of Ritz Street had been the main enemy target, but Crab Crawl and Maple Copse had taken their share of the pounding. Battalion headquarters were established in the thick, squalid, smoke-filled atmosphere of Crab Crawl tunnel, now crammed tight with sweaty, mud-caked men and their equipment.

At around 9: p.m. on the evening of the 30th the final move up to the battle assembly positions had begun, the Green Howards and Wiltshire taking position in the Cross Trench, Vancouver Avenue and Grab Street assembly trenches between midnight and 1:30 a.m. At around 1 hour before Zero "A" and "C" Companies of the 2nd Green Howards moved out into No-Mans-Land accompanied by 21st Machine Gun Company and 21st Trench Mortar Battery carrying forward 2 Vickers guns and 2 Stokes mortars, while to their left 3 platoons of "B" Company of the 2nd Wiltshire likewise supported by 2 Vickers guns and 2 Stokes Mortars, all to go over in the first wave, also took up position in shell-holes, the movements completed by 10 minutes before Zero.

At Zero Hour the British barrage crashed down around 100 yards forward of the jump-off lines, and the awaiting infantry quickly formed up within 40 to 50 yards of it. The enemy response was immediate, putting down a barrage on the British Front Line, and in an attempt to hinder reinforcement on Crab Crawl. The Green Howards set off and quickly came under machine gun and rifle fire from their right, from the direction of Shrewsbury Forest, but made good progress with little opposition. As the barrage lifted off Jeffery Reserve it was swiftly occupied, a few of the enemy being killed and 6 captured. "B" and "D" Companies, following up closely arrived at the trench, where "A" and "C" had already begun to consolidate, and passed trough towards Jeffery Support. On the right "B" Company converged with groups of the 1st Royal Fusiliers, which were veering left to avoid the fire from Lower Star Post, causing the Green Howards to do the same. The fighting in the near darkness, amongst the tumble of part blown-in, muddy and water-logged enemy trenches was very confused. "B" Company, which had lost direction and moved towards the north-east, finally took up a position around the junction of Jeffery Reserve and Jam Lane, near Green Jacket Ride, and believing they were on or about the Blue Line, (which they were not), commenced to consolidate. "D" Company had meanwhile passed through "C" Company at Jeffery Support and after attacking and capturing a concrete shelter, had worked its way to just east of Bodmin Copse. It was here checked by a German strong-point and being in too few numbers to make an attack, stopped and consolidated in an old German trench, probably a section of Java Avenue about 1,000 yards forward of the old British front line and close on the Blue Line. The situation now saw the right company about 400 yards to the north-west, or to the left of, the left company. Such was the confusion of the morning. Enemy machine gun and sniper fire were heavy, and "D" Company, sustaining casualties in its forward exposed position beyond Bodmin Copse, requested support from "A"

---

[211] National Archives, War Diary 2nd Yorkshire, 2nd Wiltshire, 19th Manchester, 18th King's, all in WO95/2329

Company. "A" Company did the same as so many others were to do on this dark bewildering morning, and in attempting to move east, veered too far north, finally coming upon "B" Company near Jam Lane, where they remained.

To the left of the Green Howards, "B" Company in the first wave of the Wiltshire had done well and had captured their section of Jeffery Trench, Jeffery Support and Jam Support and had taken 40 prisoners. Company headquarters had been established at the head of Jam Row near Green Jacket Ride. The second wave was formed by 3 platoons of "C" Company, which were soon in action with the enemy in Jam Row and Jam Lane, where a number of Germans were killed but none taken prisoner. Company headquarters was established in a muddy enemy trench-mortar dug-out near the junction of Jam Lane and Jar Row, with two platoons in a defensive position in shell-holes astride Jam Lane, and a third near the junction of Jeffery Reserve and Jam Row. The third wave consisting of "A" Company and 2 platoons of 'D" Company came against strong enemy resistance in the form of heavy machine gun and rifle fire from woods west of Dumbarton Lakes, and from the direction of Inverness Copse, across the Menin Road. The fighting was heavy in Jam Lane and Jar Row, around 12 of the enemy taken prisoner, with a further 12 killed as the Wiltshire advanced towards an enemy strong-point near Jasper Drive. A strong-point was established by 2nd Lieutenants Lewis and Bowen with about 20 men, close to the junction of Jasper Drive and Green Jacket Ride, where with the support of Lewis guns taken from a disabled tank they could cover the lower ground towards Dumbarton Lakes, and the junctions of Jar Row and Jasper Drive. They were soon to be joined there by filthy and exhausted men of other units. By around 6:15 a.m. most of the Wiltshire objective had been captured, a little in rear of the Blue Line on the right and slightly forward on the left, and the enemy trenches and bunkers cleared. Battalion headquarters moved up into the line at around 9:30 and by 10:15 the Commanding Officer Lieutenant -Colonel Gillson D.S.O. and the Adjutant were established in the poor and vulnerable accommodation of Jam Lane trench, with the 2 remaining platoons of "D" Company in reserve in Jam Reserve. Although casualties had been high most of the Blue Line had been captured by 21st Brigade. But the initial success was to be short lived, and long before Gillson had moved forward disaster had overtaken the 19th Manchester.

At Zero Hour "A" and "B" Companies of the 19th Manchester Regiment had begun to file out of the Crab Crawl tunnel, "A" by the Crab Crawl entrance and "B" by Peter Street. No sooner had the barrage commenced and the Green Howards moved off, than wounded men began staggering back into the entrances, which rapidly became choked, enabling the Manchester men to only exit in ones and twos. So slow was the evacuation that attempting to form up in the dark in good order to advance, and beneath the enemy retaliatory barrage which now burst amongst the men, was near impossible. In an effort to get clear of the hostile barrage many isolated groups of men in an uncoordinated movement began to push forward into No-Mans-Land, preventing the organised assembly of the two companies. At least half of the company officers became casualties before even crossing the British Front Line. The support companies "C" and "D" were to leave Maple Copse, 700 yards behind the line, at Zero Hour and previous reconnaissance had shown that the only practicable way forward given the time constraints was over the Observatory Ridge road and Hill 62. With "D" Company leading, the march over the dangerously exposed ridge was in progress when a heavy enemy barrage fell amongst the Manchester causing many casualties, including 2 officers of "D" Company, which then became badly disorganised. Although continuing to march up, and reaching the firing-line, "D" Company was incapable of maintaining any further advance. "C" Company had sustained serious casualties but remained under the control of its Company Commander. Subsequently passing through the hostile barrage, and correctly shaking out into lines of platoons it succeeded by around 5:00 a.m. in advancing as far as the line to the east of Bodmin Copse held by the Green Howards at Java Trench. The 2 leading platoons had veered left and were north of the battalion boundary, but were still not in touch with the 18th King's Liverpool which should have been there, (although contact was made later). On four occasions the remnants of "C" Company of the Manchester attempted to push the advance forward towards the Black Line. But by this stage the barrage was long gone, the Germans had re-mounted their machine guns, and a devastating hail of fire from the edge of Dumbarton Wood 200 yards distant swept the ground in front of Java Trench. They could do no more than attempt, under intense machine gun fire, to consolidate the line they had reached around the eastern edge of Bodmin Copse using the remains of the German earthworks and shell-holes. With the Manchester, in their weak and exposed position were men of all four battalions of 21st Brigade, and they were soon to be joined by the 20th King's Liverpool of 89th Brigade. A small party of the 19th Manchester had also worked further north and were with the Wiltshire in the strong-point at Jasper Drive.

All four companies of the 18th King's Liverpool Regiment were assembled just east of Maple Copse by midnight, and had commenced their move towards the front shortly before Zero Hour, "1" and "3" Companies leading and "2" and "4" Companies following up. The battalion was to come into the line on the left of the 19th Manchester and in support of the 2nd Wiltshire. Movement across the muddy and difficult ground through the atrocious tangle of Sanctuary Wood was made by platoon columns in single file, stumbling in the darkness around the blasted stumps and water-filled shell-craters. The plan for each company when in position was to attack with two platoons in the line and with one in support. As the King's passed the old British Front Line and advanced beyond No-Mans-Land, in a correct direction slightly north of east, they soon became embroiled with groups from many other units including the 2nd Wiltshire, the 18th and 19th Manchester and the 2nd Royal Scots Fusiliers, most of which appeared to be lost in the dark and were moving north-east, diagonal to the line of the King's advance. The general drift to the left so prevalent along the whole line now also affected the King's. The two front companies succeeded in passing through and maintaining direction, and entered the line in their correct position, where the 2nd Wiltshire was near the Blue Line. The support companies however lost formation and cohesion, and inevitably were dragged in the general melee to the left.

Captain Heywood M.C. had guided "1" and "3" Companies through the Wiltshire positions and had successfully deployed his force along the allotted frontage between Jar Row and a tramway just south of Stirling Castle, and close to Jasper Drive, taking cover as best they could in shell-holes and old trench sections to avoid the heavy machine gun fire from Dumbarton Wood and Inverness Copse. They were in fact forward of the Wiltshire line on the right, in the belief that the position of the Blue Line had been mistakenly established too far in the rear. Under extremely difficult conditions, although by now the light was improving, the King's had deployed in good order and Heywood quickly led them forward again towards the Black Line, but was soon wounded by machine gun fire. Against the severe enemy fire from Dumbarton Wood, and with the loss of officers, the cohesion of the King's attack broke down, parties of "1" Company joining the 19th Manchester in an attack on a strong-point in Jar Row, which was driven back by a shower of German stick grenades and machine gun fire. Some of "3" Company meanwhile, under 2nd Lieutenant Graham attacked and captured a strong-point just south of Stirling Castle, which they held until relieved. Graham was to be tragically killed a little later by gunfire from a tank, which mistakenly fired on the King's position. It is possible that some men of the King's got into Dumbarton Wood, and even Inverness Copse, although this cannot be confirmed. About 60 men of "1" and "3" Companies under 2nd Lieutenant Futvoye held a 50 yard section of trench near Jam Reserve, in touch with the 19th Manchester on their right, and a patrol had made touch with the King's party at Stirling Castle. The whereabouts of "1" and "3" Companies was not known at battalion headquarters until 1:30 p.m. when a message informing that it was in front of Stirling Castle was finally delivered by a runner who had left at 8:10 a.m. The advance of "2" and "4" Companies of the King's had been totally disrupted at the start by the chaos in Sanctuary Wood, and isolated groups of men did the best they could to continue the advance. Some became engaged in the heavy fighting around Clapham Junction and Surbiton Villas, north of the Menin Road, while others fought near the German Menin Road tunnel.

The attack of 21st Brigade was at a standstill, stalled with little hope of movement, close to but in places not on the Blue Line.

90th Brigade[212]

The 90th Brigade was to attack with the 18th and 16th Manchester Regiment, supported by the 2nd Royal Scots Fusiliers and the 17th Manchester Regiment, with the brigade right flank opposite "The Beak" in Sanctuary Wood, and the left on the southern face of Zouave Wood.[213]

The 18th Manchester had relieved the 19th King's Liverpool in the line on the night of the 28th / 29th July the operation being complete by 3:00 a.m. The companies remained in the front line and support trenches throughout the 29th and 30th, and at 10:00 p.m. on the 30th moved out into wet and muddy shell-holes along their taped line in No-Mans-Land to await Zero Hour. At 3:50 the battalion followed closely under the barrage, moving forward through the stumps and craters of Sanctuary Wood, and meeting little opposition from Jackdaw Trench, Jackdaw Support, or Jackdaw Reserve, was on the Blue Line, just east of Stirling Castle by 5:30 a.m.

The 16th Manchester was clear of its assembly positions in Stanley Street by 1:15 a.m. It then had the unenviable task of deploying along its jump-off line within the devastation of Sanctuary Wood, a task found exceedingly difficult for a large body of men in the dark. The movement was however completed well before Zero, in touch with the 18th Manchester on the right but not with the 1st Worcestershire Regiment of 24th Brigade to its left. At Zero Hour the battalion closed up under the barrage; so close that it sustained about 6 casualties in the first wave from the shell-fire. By 4:15 "A" Company had succeeded in taking Jackdaw Support, having encountered little opposition. "B" Company then passed through behind the barrage and by 4:30 had reached Jackdaw Reserve, again with little resistance from the enemy, a few of which had been seen to run away. In the confusion of the dark and the maze of featureless blown-in trenches, instead of moving on and entering Jackdaw Switch, about a dozen men of "B" Company strayed right and into the devastated stables area of Stirling Castle, where the Company Commander was shot and killed. From the Jackdaw Reserve / Jackdaw Switch line, "C" and "D" Companies were to continue the attack across the Menin Road at Clapham Junction towards Surbiton Villas. On the right "C" Company worked forward close behind the barrage to the Menin Road at Clapham Junction, to find the area wrecked by British shell-fire, reduced to a mass of craters and blown-in enemy dug-outs. A few Germans were encountered at the tunnel under the road but were swiftly dealt with. The right platoon pushed on across the road and reached the Blue Line between the end of Green Jacket Ride and the Westhoek road. Enemy resistance began to stiffen as "C" Company came under machine gun fire from Inverness Copse and other positions north of the Menin Road, and here the Company Commander succeeded in knocking out one gun with rifle fire. Touch was gained on the right with the 18th Manchester near Green Jacket Ride, and on the left with the right platoon of "D" Company just south of Surbiton Villas. The left platoon of "D" Company, accompanied by an officer and 15 men of "C" Company had meet with a more determined enemy and had lost touch with the barrage, subsequently coming under heavy machine gun fire and having difficulty crossing over to the north of the Menin Road at the bend 300 yards west of Clapham Junction. Once across the road the fighting continued, and about 40 to 50 prisoners, a machine gun and a trench mortar were taken from dug-outs and trenches as they were cleared north of the bend.

The 2nd Royal Scots Fusiliers were to pass through the 18th Manchester and advance to the Black Line. The intended manoeuvre did not happen. In the confusion and semi-darkness, instead of moving through Sanctuary Wood and following a direction of east-north-east, the battalion moved virtually north almost parallel to the enemy front line, along the line of Jackdaw Trench and Ignorance Lane, crossing the Menin Road somewhere between Hooge and the bend and entering Chateau Wood from the south. Here they were 1,000 yards west of their objective which was on the southern edge of Glencorse Wood. In support of the 16th Manchester, "A" Company of the 17th Manchester was to pass through on the Blue Line, and after the 30 minute pause and under the covering fire of 2 Stokes mortars was to advance to Jargon Drive, and bomb along the trench to the known strong-point in the sunken road. "B" Company was then to advance and capture Jargon Trench, and bomb up Jargon Switch on the left flank. "C" and "D"

---

[212] National Archives, War Diary 90th Brigade WO95/2337
[213] National Archives, War Diary 16th 17th and 18th Manchester WO95/2339

Companies were then to pass through "A" and "B" and advance to the Black Line in Glencorse Wood. It was a great pity that the attack on the strong-point at the sunken road on Jargon Drive did not take place for its machine guns were soon to decimate the attack of 53rd Brigade. The severe machine gun fire sweeping the Menin Road from Inverness Copse and Glencorse Wood which had stopped the 16th Manchester now stopped the 17th which took cover with men from many other battalions about Clapham Junction and west of Surbiton Villas.

Between 5:15 and 6:00, the confusion amongst units south of the Menin Road was so great that men of 8 different battalions had crossed the road west of Clapham Junction, and were sheltering in shell-holes or old trenches in isolated groups, all exposed to and pinned down by heavy machine gun fire. The advance of the 16th Manchester, which up to the Menin Road had, at least on the right been little opposed, was now checked by severe and damaging machine gun fire from numerous positions east and north of Clapham Junction; as was the advance of the 17th. A strong-point was established just east of the bend in the Menin Road from which Lewis guns covered the area towards Surbiton Villas and the higher ground at Clapham Junction, but they had little hope of suppressing the fire from the well concealed and protected enemy pillboxes and dug-outs.

89th Brigade[214]

The 20th and 17th King's Liverpool Regiment were to pass through 21st Brigade and the right sector of 90th Brigade on the Black Line, and at 10:10 a.m. continue the advance to the Green Line, where it all went to plan its right would be beyond Kantinje Cabaret on the Menin Road, its centre on Veldhoek, and its left on Black Watch Corner at the south west corner of Polygon Wood.[215]

Between 5:00 and 5:20 p.m. on the 30th both battalions marched up to forward positions between Maple Copse and Sanctuary Wood. The enemy shell-fire, by this time heavy and directed at the British support positions caught the assembly, causing a number of casualties. At 7:50 the final movement towards the front line began, under continual hostile shell-fire which now increased to the level of a barrage. As the 20th approached Jam Reserve it became apparent that all was not going well in the front line, as mixed groups of men from battalions that had attacked earlier were, amongst a high level of confusion, pinned down by heavy enemy machine gun fire near the Blue Line. A message sent back by the 20th informed Brigade headquarters that the Black Line had not been taken, and that they were establishing a defensive line running from south of Stirling Castle, in touch with the 17th on their left. By this time the 10:10 barrage had passed on towards the Green Line, and a message received from Brigade headquarters advised the 20th that the barrage was being brought back at 10:20 on to Jargon Trench, Jap Trench and Inverness Copse, a full 800 yards forward of the King's present position, and that they were to co-operate in pushing forward a further attack. As the message was not received until 11:06, 46 minutes too late for compliance, the placing of the barrage was purely academic. A message from the Commanding Officer of the 20th King's to Brigade headquarters stated: 'Front line now roughly along road south of Clapham Junction (Green Jacket Ride). Enemy machine guns very active and any movement in forward positions is at once stopped by machine gun fire. Without careful artillery preparation further attacks will be useless. I am therefore holding on to present line.'[216]

The 17th King's had also suffered under the hostile barrage in Sanctuary Wood. Approaching Stirling Castle at around 8:40 a.m. reports were received that the attack was stalled on the Blue Line, and the Commanding Officer ordered his men forward with the intention of reinforcing the Blue Line and carrying forward the attack to the Black Line. On

---

[214] National Archives, War Diary 89th Brigade WO95/2332, War Diary 2nd Bedford WO95/2333, War Diary 20th King's WO95/2335

[215] Everard Wyrall (1928-30) *The History of the King's Liverpool Regiment Vol III* London: Arnold p495.

[216] Everard Wyrall (1928-30) *The History of the King's Liverpool Regiment Vol III* London: Arnold p495.

crossing the high ground at Sterling Castle the true situation was evident as no British troops could be seen to the east of the position, but the battalion pushed on under heavy machine gun fire from north of the Menin Road until the left flank rested on Clapham Junction. Under the severe fire from Inverness Copse and Glencorse Wood, and increasing hostile shell-fire the 17th could make no further movement and took shelter in craters and old trenches.[217] No further movement was possible by either battalion of the King's, and the remnants of a total of 12 battalions of 30th and 18th Divisions, in a state of great confusion and exhaustion were now all stopped on or near the Blue Line.

The difficulties in attacking in poor light across the desolate waste, the ground churned by the guns, through a confusing network of blown-in enemy trenches with few landmarks remaining are well illustrated, as one patch of smashed, cratered woodland looked very much the same as the next. In many cases it had been impossible to keep up with the barrage. The Divisional Commander Major-General Williams, had complained to both Army and Corps, that he considered the lifts of 25 yards per minute too quick, given the state of the ground the heavily laden infantry had to cover, and thought 20 yards per minute more appropriate. He was told that it was too late to alter the fire plan.

The German artillery had demonstrated how hard the fight for the plateau was going to be, for around 5:00 a.m. it began an intense and persistent bombardment of Sanctuary and Chateau Woods, to the extent that British communications were virtually paralysed. All types of electrical connection to rearward positions were cut with only pigeons left to be used and a few runners eventually getting through to battalion or brigade headquarters. No news of the situation at the front was received at divisional or II Corps headquarters until 10:00 a.m. At 9:50 a.m. a message from a contact aircraft had reported that it had been fired on by machine gun and rifle fire from Inverness Copse just west of the German Second Line. No British troops were to be seen on the ground in the area, nor had answers been given to signals directed to that area. Carrier pigeon messages sent from the front line near Stirling Castle at 8:30 a.m. to divisional headquarters stating the position, and again at 9:00 a.m. to division and divisional artillery headquarters asking that the barrage be re-opened between the Blue and Black lines were not received.

At 10:10 a.m. on time, the barrage had commenced its forward creep towards the third objective to the east of the Bassevillebeek, to Tower Hamlets spur and north of the Menin Road towards Veldhoek and Polygon Wood, but there were no infantry that far forward to follow it. Finally at 10:40 a.m. Major-General Williams, got a message back to II Corps headquarters at Hoogeraaf south of Poperinghe, underlining the uncertainty of the situation by stating that apparently he was not on the Black (Second) Line anywhere, but that he held the Blue (First) Line in tact. This message proved later to be incorrect for not only had the Black Line not been penetrated anywhere, but in fact neither had the first objective the Blue Line, been secured entirely. On realising the situation at the front, Williams passed on the information to Major-General Lee, commanding 18th Division, whose 54th Brigade was about to continue the advance in the left of 30th Division sector, from the third to the fourth objective, which implied to beyond Polygon Wood. Fortunately this brigade was stopped in time, but as we have already seen the two battalions of the 89th Brigade had already gone forward. Unfortunately, just after 7:00 a.m. so had two battalions of the 53rd Brigade.

---

[217] The support battalions of the 89th Brigade in Divisional Reserve, the 19th King's and 2nd Bedford, had moved up to south of Zillebeke Lake by 10:00 a.m. and were informed that they were to attack at 4:00 p.m. The King's moved up to Maple Copse, but shortly were informed that the attack had been cancelled. Under heavy shell-fire the battalion took shelter in shell-holes to await orders. At 10:00 p.m. the battalion received orders to relieve the hard pressed Suffolk and Berkshire of 53rd Brigade, and moved up past Zouave Wood and the Menin Road under continual hostile shelling, the Commanding Officer and the Medical Officer being wounded. The relief was completed by 3:30 a.m. on the 1st August.

53rd Brigade[218] (18th Division attached)

The 8th Suffolk Regiment and 6th Royal Berkshire Regiment were to pass through the left flank of 30th Division once that division had secured its second objective on the Black Line,[219] which included the capture of the German Second Line along the western edge of Glencorse Wood. Here 53rd Brigade was to move on to take the third objective beyond Nonne Bosschen, and half way through Polygon Wood.

Both battalions had marched up from Dickebusch on the night of the 30th / 31st to take up rear assembly positions between Valley Cottages and Yeomanry Post east of Zillebeke. The poor ground conditions had made the march tiring, and although enemy shelling had not been heavy the Berkshire had sustained casualties of 2 officers and 17 other ranks. "C" Company of the Suffolk had also lost 5 men killed, 3 wounded and a Lewis gun destroyed as they passed through Zillebeke.

At 3:50 the sky was illuminated with the flashes of the guns and as the sounds of battle thundered on the ridge 1,000 yards to the east, the men of 53rd Brigade anxiously waited their turn to enter the fray. It was obvious that the enemy were putting down a heavy barrage on No-Mans-Land and the British Front Line, but little shelling affected their rear assembly area. The success or otherwise of the brigade would depend on 30th Division seizing the Black Line, and at 5:00 a.m. the news arrived that the Blue Line was secure. By 6:50 a.m. further unofficial news had been received by telephone at brigade headquarters, that an aircraft had reported the Black Line also secure. Between 7:15 and 7:45 the Suffolk and Berkshire commenced the short march up towards Sanctuary Wood, after which they would cross the Menin Road to reach the Black Line part way through Glencorse Wood, from where at 10:10 a.m. they were to continue the attack behind the barrage.

Moving in artillery formation up to Sanctuary Wood there was little problem, but on reaching the north-eastern section of the wood the brigade came under a heavy indirect machine gun barrage and a severe barrage by 77 mm field guns. The hostile shelling continued to the eastern face of the wood, and was obviously intended to prevent reinforcement of the front line. The two battalions struggled forward towards the Menin Road, remaining well organised under the circumstances. Between Sanctuary Wood and the Menin Road, past Jackdaw Reserve and Jackdaw Switch at about 8:10 a.m., they had not met with any of 90th Brigade, the only information of the situation in front coming from their own observations and a patrol guide.

On reaching the road at about 8:45, "C" Company on the right of the Suffolk extended its right flank in an effort to gain touch with the 17th King's of 89th Brigade, and ominously came under direct machine gun fire from positions east and north of Clapham Junction, an area which they believed to have been already secured. To their left "A" Company also came under fire as they approached the road, but met an officer of the Manchester who advised that Glencorse Wood was taken. This information was quickly contradicted by Lieutenant Bollingbroke, an 8th Suffolk scout who had been forward to Surbiton Villas and had ascertained that the enemy were still in control of ground west of Glencorse Wood. Near the road the machine gun fire was so severe that movement was only possible by rushes between shell-holes, and then only by sections moving one at a time. "B" Company worked across the road near Clapham Junction by a series of rushes. On working gradually forward to the area about Surbiton Villas, fire from Glencorse Wood caused numerous casualties and cover was quickly taken in nearby shell-holes. The Suffolk "D" Company had followed up in support, sustaining serious casualties from the shelling through Sanctuary Wood, and had seen no sign of 90th Brigade. Approaching the Menin Road it was clear that a gap existed between "C" Company on the right and "A" Company in the centre and "D" Company moved up to fill it. Machine gun fire also raked "D" Company, which could only make further movement across the Menin Road by short rushes by section, covered as best possible by rifle and Lewis gun fire. The worst of the enemy fire appeared to come from a strong-point in Jargon Drive, (the one the 17th Manchester had hoped to tackle), 300 yards

---

[218] National Archives, War Diary 53rd Infantry Brigade WO95/2037
[219] National Archives, War diary 8th Suffolk WO95/2039

north-east of Clapham Junction, and from the south-west corner of Glencorse Wood. "D" Company, after striving to work slowly forward under sustained fire were also driven to ground about 150 yards north of the Menin Road.

The 6th Berkshire had exactly the same experience of hostile shelling moving up through Sanctuary Wood, and neither had it seen any evidence of 90th Brigade, but on reaching Jackdaw Reserve had come upon a machine gun detachment of 30th Division, which claimed that the Germans were still in control of Inverness Copse, and that their machine guns were active north of the Menin Road. On approaching the bend in the road just north of Jackdaw Reserve, the Berkshire was caught by the machine gun fire which mercilessly swept the cratered track which had once been the road, defying the British to cross. It was obvious that the Black Line was not secure, but at about 8:50 the Berkshire determined to fight its way forward to Jargon Trench, from where it was to attack at 10:10. Shaking out into extended order the advance resumed and was immediately caught in a cross-fire as the German machine gunners opened up. In a desperate attempt to regain the initiative, a Lewis gun, rifle fire, and a Stokes mortar battery attached to the Suffolk gave what covering fire they could, and the advance continued. Under hostile fire from the same guns at Jargon Drive and Glencorse Wood that were assailing the Suffolk, the Berkshire advanced an average of 300 yards, finally establishing a line in shell-holes facing east about 150 yards west of the Westhoek road, facing Glencorse Wood. Although there was no sign of 30th Division, the Berkshire could see British troops in Jabber Drive 500 yards north at Westhoek, and two platoons of "D" Company were sent north in an attempt to gain contact. This was done successfully the troops being of the 2nd Berkshire of 25th Brigade, in support of the 8th Division, but a 500 yard gap still existed between the two Berkshire battalions with no forces to fill it. The 6th Berkshire extended over as long a line as possible, and with very thin ranks advanced towards Glencorse Wood, succeeded in taking Jargon Switch and advanced to the line of the Westhoek road, all the while under severe machine gun fire. Surbiton Villas was also taken as was the crossroads on the Westhoek road 400 yards to the north. It was now 9:50 a.m. and the battalion, having sustained severe casualties from machine gun fire, with dangerously thinned ranks, and exhausted from it exertions, recognised that it was not going to be possible to reach Jargon Trench in time to continue the advance at 10:10. The decision was taken however to advance from the position they now held, in concert with the barrage at 10:10. The gunners were precise with their timing and at 10:10 the shells again crashed down. But the gunners were also accurate and the barrage landed right on target, just forward of the Black Line which ran through the centre of Glencorse Wood 200 yards behind Jargon Trench. Nevertheless the remnants of the 6th Berkshire, as ordered, lifted themselves heavily from their shell-holes and advanced towards the enemy. They were met by a hail of machine gun cross-fire from Jargon Trench, and from the strong-point in Jargon Drive, and those who did not immediately take cover were shot down. Further attempts were then stopped. A message had got through to the 2nd Lincoln of 25th Brigade to request assistance to cover the left flank, but the Lincoln themselves had been hard hit by the machine guns in Glencorse Wood and could do little to help, except for the digging of a strong-point which was subsequently reinforced by a party of the Manchester of 30th Division. The 6th Berkshire finally consolidated on a line just west of the Westhoek road with a second defensive line of shell-hole posts just in rear.

About an hour and a half earlier, as we have seen, "C" Company of the 8th Sussex, to the right of the Berkshire had reached the Menin Road near Clapham Junction and had extended its right to gain touch with the 17th King's, but in fact was still not in contact with any other units. The Menin Road, swept by German machine gun fire could only be crossed by small parties rushing between shell-holes, but so intense was the fire that once over the road "C" Company was forced to take what cover they could in craters to await the next move. It was the fire from the strong-point in Jargon Drive that was mainly responsible for the hold up, and a Stokes mortar and a Vickers machine gun, which had been carried forward by the gun teams with great difficulty, were set up and came into action against the enemy strong-point, with the added fire of the rifles of the company. The covering fire was sufficient to allow parties to work forward and enter Jap Avenue 50 yards beyond the road, where the company gradually assembled and organised to renew the assault. From here the Jargon Drive strong-point 150 yards to the north was engaged with Lewis guns, rifles and rifle grenades, and the enemy fire suppressed sufficiently for parties to work forward to within 100 yards of the position. The German gunners could not be suppressed for long and the Suffolk parties were driven to ground in shell-holes, also under hostile rifle and machine gun fire from Inverness Copse to the south-east and Glencorse Wood to the north. "C" Company had already sustained severe casualties, and now pinned down under fire from front and in enfilade. The remnants of the Suffolk vainly attempted to consolidate their hopelessly exposed position, but it was clear that it could not be held for long and another desperate effort was made to capture the enemy strong-point. Under 2nd Lieutenant Argles a party rushed towards the enemy guns and succeeded in gaining a foothold, bombing their way into a section of the German defences, putting 1 machine gun out of action, taking 20 enemy prisoners, and killing a considerable number more. "C" Company was now even more dispersed and isolated, and the enemy added a trench mortar to the machine gun fire directed at them. The situation became more critical as British heavy artillery, possibly attempting to knock out the enemy strong-point, began landing amongst the shell-holes they held, and hostile artillery, seemingly guided by an enemy observation aircraft also found their range. To their left "D" Company had also been pinned down by the same machine guns and could not get forward, and was consolidating in craters 100 yards short of Jargon Drive, and "A" Company after sustaining serious casualties had been checked on a line about 200 yards east of Surbiton Villas just to the east of the Westhoek Track. By about 2:00 p.m. "C" Company's position had become untenable and it gradually began to fall-back towards the Menin Road to the line of Jap Avenue, where touch was eventually gained with the 17th King's. "A" Company also fell-back about the same time, under fire from both friendly and hostile artillery to the line of the Westhoek road, in touch with the 6th Berkshire on its left.

The results of the mornings fighting on the Gheluvelt plateau were disappointing, but in many ways predictable. Nowhere had the first objective been secured, and the attack was now at a largely disorganised, bloody and exhausted standstill. There had been a dreadful mix up of battalions, largely due to the darkness at the beginning of the attack, and the effective German artillery and vicious machine gun fire. Many battalions had lost cohesion and were way out of their intended positions. Eight different battalions were represented in dugouts at Clapham Junction, and the well planned and exercised arrangements to leap-frog units forward to continue the advance had collapsed under the reality of events. The well sited and strongly constructed German strong-points at Lower Star Post and in Inverness Copse, Jargon Drive and Glencorse Wood, had done their job admirably and true to form, having been unaffected by the days of British bombardment. Unfortunately the Germans had retained possession of vital high points near Clapham Junction and the area east of the Westhoek road near Surbiton Villas, which was to have serious repercussions on the 8th Division attacking to the left.

All the warnings regarding the strength of the German positions on the plateau repeated so many times had been proved correct. The plan had been over-complicated, with impossibly over-ambitious objectives. It also relied on close co-ordination between infantry and artillery, which, due to the inadequacies of rudimentary communications, once the operation got out of synchronisation, could not be quickly corrected. It had asked too much of even the best trained battalions. An insufficient concentration of gun strength had not enabled counter-battery fire to dominate the German artillery east of the plateau, and insufficient howitzer concentration on the bunkers and strong points about the first and second objectives had left the infantry with an impossible task. Enemy aircraft had been in evidence far more than the Royal Flying Corps, and had accurately directed German gun-fire onto the precarious British positions. The room to concentrate sufficient infantry forces within the boundaries allocated to a division within the devastated area of the Salient was inevitably inadequate, and the rearward assembly areas were too congested to hold more reserves. Brigadier-General G.D. Goodman of 21st Brigade made clear in a report how problematic the assembly of forces had been. 'This presented a most difficult problem. I have never seen an area that had been more shelled by the enemy.' He also commented on the assembly of the 19th Manchester. 'On the right there was no area behind the trenches that was not frequently shelled and I therefore decided to put 2 Companies of the 19th

Bn. Manchester Regiment in the Tunnel and 2 Companies in Maple Copse. The two latter passed through a heavy barrage in coming up (but for the state of the ground they could have missed the barrage by moving north), but the two leading Companies were caught coming out of the Tunnel and there was much congestion. Assembly in the Tunnel had been practised by this Battalion, who had got out of the Tunnel in 12 minutes. But I am now satisfied that the risk of confusion is too great and it would have been better to put the Battalion anywhere (even in a shelled area) than where they were, or else they should have left the Tunnel before Zero. There are at least 10 exists.'[220]

Given the depth of the objectives, it was not possible to make sufficient allowance for what might go wrong. But before the event few seemed to have wanted to say so, being carried along by the positive thrusting approach and not wishing to seem negative. A more cautious Army Commander may have tried to organise things differently. On the positive side, (and on the plateau there was not a lot that was), the German observation positions on the western edge had been overrun, except for one small area on the Menin Road near Clapham Junction from where Ypres was still just visible. Less positive was the fact that although 24th and 30th Divisions had been fought to a standstill, no significant German counter attacks had taken place, and the *Eingreif* divisions had not been engaged. The inability of 30th Division to capture the German Second Line, the strong-point line, was to have a serious knock-on effect on 8th Division which was to be severely hit in enfilade by the formidable German machine gun positions in Glencorse Wood and in Nonne Bosschen.

2nd Tank Brigade's actions with 30th Division

It has been said that the tanks were unable to substantially improve the situation on the plateau. In the reports of some infantry battalions the tanks appeared to be of little use. Lieut.-Colonel Gillson of the 2nd Wiltshire reported, 'the tanks did not give our men confidence, and the men did not follow the tanks. The tanks drew hostile fire and caused a few casualties to our men in a post at J.19.b.95.60 [Jasper Drive], and we could have got on as well if there had been no tanks'.[221] This may be true but does little justice to the tremendous efforts made by the tank crews to assist the infantry. A more thorough examination of the action of the tanks is therefore justified.[222] 30th Division was supported by "B" Battalion, II Tank Brigade which was to be employed in two waves, 8 tanks to "mop-up" about the Black Line while the second wave had 12 tanks to attack the Green Line and 4 tanks to operate beyond the Green Line.[223] Due to the difficulties of the ground the tanks had been held back until daylight before moving forward.

Four tanks of No.5 Company were to be in the first wave supporting 21st Brigade in their attack on the Black Line. One tank was hit by shellfire at the start, the remaining three tanks reaching the Blue Line, where they found the infantry held up by machine gun fire. The section commander, on ascertaining the situation from the infantry sent the three tanks forward to engage the enemy machine guns between the Blue and Black Line in Shrewsbury Forest. They successfully attacked machine gun emplacements causing casualties to the enemy, but the infantry were still unable to advance. Eventually the "Bogey" was hit by a shell, the "Bohemian" and "Bushranger" becoming ditched in front of the forward line of the infantry.

Four tanks of No.6 Company were to be in the first wave supporting 90th Brigade in their attack on the Black Line. Two tanks were knocked out on the approach march and the remaining two became ditched in the neighbourhood of the Blue Line. No assistance to the infantry was therefore possible.

---

[220] National Archives, War diary 21st Brigade WO95/2329
[221] National Archives, War diary 2nd Wiltshire, Operation Report WO95/2329
[222] When considering tank operations reference should be made to the notes regarding their use in Chapter
[223] National Archives, War Diary II Brigade Tank Corps WO95/101

Four more tanks of No.5 Company were to operate with 89th Brigade in its attack on the Green Line. One tank had engine trouble, two became ditched, while the fourth "Barbarian" reached a point just south of Stirling Castle, in touch with the infantry. The tank moved against enemy machine guns on the west side of Dumbarton Woods where it engaged them inflicting casualties. It continued to patrol in this area until crew exhaustion caused its withdrawal to its starting point.

The remaining four tanks of No.5 Company were to have attacked the southern portion of the Green Line (German Third Line) at the point it crossed the Menin Road. All four came up to just north of Bodmin Copse, where they got in touch with the infantry, who indicated that they were held up by machine guns southeast of Stirling Castle. The tanks informed that they would move against Inverness Copse and the west side of Dumbarton Woods and would attempt to draw the machine gun fire from Stirling Castle. The infantry however, due to disorganisation were unable to co-operate. "Bloodstone" engaged machine gun emplacements in front of Inverness Copse with Lewis gun fire killing some of the enemy, until it was put out of action by a direct hit. "Black-Arrow" engaged enemy machine guns west of Dumbarton Woods killing some gun crews, and was proceeding to run down some uncut wire in front of Java Avenue when it was hit on the petrol tank and burnt out. "Ballyhacle" engaged enemy machine guns and infantry, but again British infantry were not able to co-operate, the tank eventually being hit on a track when returning to its starting point.

Four more tanks of No.6 Company were to operate with 53rd Brigade in their attack on the Green Line. Three of the tanks arrived on time at Clapham Junction where they found the infantry held up by machine gun fire from Glencorse Wood and Inverness Copse, which the section commander then ordered them to attack. Two tanks "Boomerang" and "Backslider" went forward but became ditched near Inverness Copse. They did however continue in action engaging a local enemy counter attack and a machine gun. The third tank "Battle-Axe" crossed the Menin Road towards Glencorse Wood, engaging several machine guns on the edge of the wood and also in the north-west corner of Inverness Copse, killing some gun crew. "Battle-Axe" finally became ditched just southwest of Glencorse Wood, in front of the infantry line. The tank commander then moved his men out of the tank while under direct fire, into an adjacent shell-hole where they continued to engage the enemy machine guns in Glencorse Wood and an enemy aeroplane with Lewis gun fire, until their position came under such intense fire the crew withdrew back to the infantry line. The fourth tank of the company the "Behemoth" arrived at Clapham Junction almost half and hour after the others, and proceeded towards Glencorse Wood where it engaged enemy machine guns until knocked out by a direct hit from an anti-tank gun 100 yards north of Inverness Copse. Again the tank commander moved his men into a nearby trench, (possibly the eastern end of Jap Avenue), 200 yards in front of the infantry which they continued to hold for two hours. The remaining four tanks of No.6 Company were to work with 53rd Brigade beyond the Green Line, and all reached Clapham Junction where they found the infantry held up. They moved forward against the machine guns in Glencorse Wood. "Britannia" and "Bridget", moving down the Menin Road were both knocked out by anti-tank guns, the other two tanks becoming ditched south of the Menin Road.

This was the story of the day from the perspective of the tank crews. It is not surprising that it differs in detail with the reports of the infantry. The warnings given concerning the limitations of the tanks had been shown to be largely correct, especially regarding their unsuitability to operate in areas of direct artillery fire, and across heavily cratered and deeply muddy ground. Such were the conditions under which they had fought. The tank crews had done all that could be expected of them, and more. Undoubtedly the inability of the infantry to co-operate, due to no fault of their own did not help. In an ideal situation the infantry needed to immediately consolidate the positions overrun by the tanks; but the Gheluvelt plateau was not an ideal situation.

8th Division
Major-General W. C. G. Heneker

The success or otherwise of the attack of the 8th Division, was to a large part dependant on the results of the attack of the 30th Division and the attached battalions of 18th Division to its right. Major-General Heneker commanding the division had warned on the 10th July that the whole success of his attack depended on the 30th Division on his right, and should they be held up at any point, the remainder of his advance (beyond the second objective), would be seriously exposed to commanding enfilade fire from the Stirling Castle – Polygon Wood ridge. The 30th Division was in trouble, stalled in front of the first objective, and although Stirling Castle was secure, some high ground near Clapham Junction, and the whole of Glencorse Wood and Nonne Bosschen were not. Polygon Wood had not even been approached. As feared by its commander, 8th Division's right flank was to be exposed to enfilade fire, and this combined with the fact that the division's second objective was on a forward slope and exposed to direct fire was to prove very difficult.[224]

The 24th 23rd and 25th Brigades 8th Division advance to Westhoek Ridge and line gained by nightfall

The area the division was to attack, on a frontage of about 1,800 yards, with an average distance of about 3,000 yards to the third objective, while having fewer concrete pillboxes than the central plateau still presented a major challenge. Here the German Front Line ran across two spurs, and between the spurs lay the swamp which had been Bellewaarde Lake. On the southern bank of the lake the blasted remains of Chateau Wood would prove an obstacle. To the east, beyond the lake and towards the higher ground were two low parallel ridges. The first and smallest, the Bellewaarde ridge (upon which lay the first objective), at a height of 50 metres was 800 yards behind the German Front Line. The second and larger Westhoek ridge, again at a height of 50 metres, was 1,700 yards behind the line, and along it ran the second objective, the German Second Line. Westhoek ridge formed a finger of higher ground attached to the fist of

---

[224] Lt.-Colonel J.H. Boraston (1926) *The Eighth Division in War, 1914-1918* London: The Medici Society

Gheluvelt plateau pointing roughly northwest towards Frezenberg and thence to Pilckem ridge. East of Westhoek ridge, the ground dipped into the shallow valley of the Hanebeek and at the crest of the eastern slope of this valley, along Anzac spur, were the concrete shelters and pillboxes of the third objective the German Third Line, the *Wilhelm Stellung*, a full 3,000 yards beyond the front lines.

The 8th Division was to attack with two brigades in the line, the 24th and 23rd to secure the first two objectives, with one brigade, the 25th in support to attack the third objective. The tanks of "A" Battalion, II Tank Brigade operated with the division, 4 tanks with each leading brigade, and 12 tanks with the 25th to attack the final objective. The 23rd Brigade was also to support 25th Brigade in the attack on the third line, after handing over its sector of the second objective to 24th Brigade.

24th Brigade[225]

The 24th Brigade attacked with two battalions the, 1st Worcestershire Regiment and the 2nd Northamptonshire Regiment, which were to take the Blue Line. The 2nd East Lancashire Regiment and 1st Sherwood Foresters were then to pass through them to the Black Line on Westhoek ridge.

On the right the 1st Worcester set of well into the gloom, surmounting the bare Hooge spur and taking their first objective with little opposition. One platoon per company acted as moppers-up behind the leading waves, quickly bombing out a number of dug-outs. The German tunnel beneath the Menin Road proved no serious obstacle and yielded 41 prisoners. After "C" and "D" Companies secured Ignorance Support, "A" and "B" Companies passed through, into the rusty wire entanglements and shell-shattered debris of Chateau Wood, and attacked the strongly held James Trench on the eastern edge of the wood, quickly capturing the position. Moving forward and bombing along the communication trenches running east of James Trench the battalion reached its second objective on the east side of Bellewaarde ridge overlooking Westhoek ridge and began to dug-in.

The 2nd Northants, jumping-off from Kingsway Trench and Kingsway Support was immediately confronted with the obstacle of Bellewaarde Lake. A trench mortar bombardment of Thermit shells was concentrated on the banks of the lake which were soon cleared. Half the battalion moved to the left of the lake and struggled in the semi-darkness to keep up with the barrage across the muddy cratered rise, but succeeded in doing so and occupied the first objective, Jacob Trench on Bellewaarde Ridge. The smartness of the advance here was in no small part due to an officer of the 2nd Northants whose actions were to gain him the V.C. 2nd Lieutenant, (acting Captain) Thomas Riverdale Colyer-Ferguson, Commanding "B" Company, with ten men succeeded in keeping up close to the barrage and was first to reach the objective on Bellewaarde ridge. But the enemy garrison which had at first run back over a wide front, were soon rallied and attempted a counter attack. At a range of 100 yards Colyer-Ferguson and his party knocked out around 30 of the enemy with rifle fire at which point the remainder either surrendered or dived for shell-holes. On seeing an enemy machine gun in action nearby, Colyer-Ferguson accompanied only by his orderly attacked and captured the gun and turned it on another group of the enemy, killing a large number and driving the rest into the hands of an adjoining British unit. He was killed by a stray machine gun bullet shortly after the action.

To the right of the lake "C" Company struggled across the swampy ravine in Chateau Wood, keeping touch with the Worcester advancing on their right. From a strong-point around 50 Germans were seen to be directing fire at the Worcester. The enemy garrison was attacked by 2nd Lieutenant Frost who killed an officer and 14 men. Two bunkers were bombed out, and one, apparently a bomb store, blew up killing around nine of the enemy. By 5:30 a.m. Jacob Trench, the first objective, had been entered by both "B" and "C" Companies of the Northants and an outpost line was dug 150 yards forward, near the crest of Bellewaarde ridge.

---

[225] National Archives, War Diary 24th Brigade WO95/1717, War Diary 2nd East Lancs WO95/1720, War Diary 1st Sherwood Foresters WO95/1721, War Diary 2nd Northants WO95/1722

To the brigade right the 2nd East Lancs passed through the Worcester and were swept by machine gun fire from the higher ground to their right front, in the direction of Inverness Copse and Glencorse Wood. Under this damaging fire the East Lancs moved forward, throwing out Lewis gun sections in posts to protect their right and reached the final objective on Westhoek ridge at about 6:00 a.m., and the 1st Worcester worked forward along the communication trench at Jabber Drive to maintain touch. To the left of the East Lancs, the 1st Sherwood Foresters moved up behind Bellewaarde ridge and as the barrage lifted towards the Black Line passed through the Northants. The battalion came under heavy machine gun fire from Westhoek ridge to their front, and also most worryingly in enfilade from Surbiton Villas and Clapham Junction to their right, which made it difficult to keep up with the barrage. They continued forward under harassing machine gun fire and, overcoming strong-points at The Snout and Westhoek crossroads, reached their final objective on the forward (eastern) slope of Westhoek ridge, taking shelter and establishing a defence line in shell-holes. The failure of 30th Division to secure the area about Clapham Junction was causing the 8th Division major problems, as its Commanding Officer had warned it would.

At around this time the 8th Suffolk and 6th Berkshire made their gallant but unsuccessful attempt to advance towards Glencorse Wood, which left the ground around Clapham Junction and east of the Westhoek track still in the hands of the enemy. The right flank of 8th Division was now totally exposed to enfilade fire which swept their line of approach across Bellewaarde ridge and as far back as Chateau Wood, and which lashed into the right rear of the forward positions on Westhoek ridge. As 24th Brigade Headquarters moved up under this vicious fire to Jacob Trench, the Brigade Major Captain Holmes Scott, R.E. was shot dead, as was Leiutenant -Colonel Sunderland of the 2nd Devonshire who had gone forward to the Kit and Kat blockhouses on Westhoek ridge to reconnoitre.

23rd Brigade[226]

The 23rd Brigade attacked to the left of the 24th, with its left on Railway Wood and the Ypres – Roulers railway, with two battalions, the 2nd West Yorkshire Regiment, with the 2nd Devonshire Regiment to their left. The 2nd Scottish Rifles with the 2nd Middlesex Regiment were in support to carry the advance to the Black Line. The West Yorks, successfully attacked the Ziel House bunker on Bellewaarde ridge, and soon secured the Blue Line. The Devonshire with well practiced tactics using rifle grenades and Lewis guns overcame two strong-points and also reached its objective on time. Both battalions then began to consolidate a shell-hole line on the exposed Bellewaarde ridge, the urgency increased as they soon came under searching artillery fire from German 4.2 field batteries and heavier 5.9's.

Crossing the difficult crater-field in No-Mans-Land at 4:20 a.m., the Scottish Rifles quickly passed the old German front line, leaving behind the enemy barrage which was firing long. Machine gun fire from nests on the right and sniper fire from shell-holes was overcome with Lewis guns and rifle grenades, many of the enemy being killed or taken prisoner. As the barrage lifted from the Blue Line the battalion passed through the West Yorks. The 2nd Middlesex had followed closely behind the Devonshire to avoid the German retaliatory barrage and at 5:00 a.m. was assembled on the Blue Line awaiting the British barrage to lift. At 5:29 they moved off alongside the Scottish Rifles, and with little opposition the left of the second objective at Jaffa Trench was taken by "A" and "D" Companies of the Middlesex, but machine gun and rifle fire from the fortified ruins of houses along the ridge north of Westhoek, and from the Kit and Kat blockhouses caused a check to the Scottish Rifles. Hostile machine gun fire from pillboxes on the left along the railway and at Sans Souci hampered the advance of Middlesex "C" and "B" Companies east of the ridge.

Enemy snipers were seen to be infiltrating forward amongst the shell-holes east of the Hanebeek, and observers were pushed out in front by the Scottish Rifles to direct the fire of Lewis guns and rifle grenades at the blockhouses north of the Westhoek hamlet, which soon

---

[226] National Archives, War Diary 23rd Brigade WO95/1710, War Diary 2nd Devon WO95/1712, War Diary 2nd West Yorks WO95/1714

enabled the enemy bunkers to be surrounded, bombed-out and captured. By 9:00 a.m. the enemy snipers had also been driven back and a ragged outpost line had been established with Lewis guns in shell-holes just east of the ridge top.

25th Brigade[227]

The support brigade of the 8th Division, the 25th Brigade left their dugouts at Halfway House around 8:00 a.m. and moved forward across the fire-swept 3,000 yards to Westhoek Ridge, their objective being the *Wilhelm Stellung*, (the Green Line) across the Hanebeek valley. The fact that 30th Division had been unable to secure the right flank was not known until the brigade was crossing Westhoek ridge, by which time they were virtually committed. On hearing of the capture of the Black Line Brigadier -General Coffin had gone forward to establish the position of Brigade Headquarters and to carry out preliminary reconnaissance with his four battalion commanders, but found the situation very different from that which he expected. To attack seemed suicidal with the right flank totally exposed to machine gun fire from Glencorse Wood and Nonne Bosschen, but to change the plan at the last moment involved dangers of its own. To gain further information regarding the position he returned to 23rd Brigade headquarters at Ziel House, and there received the more reassuring news that the Scottish Rifles had cleared the Kit and Kat blockhouses and the ruined houses on the Westhoek track. He therefore decided to press ahead with the original plan and issued orders to that effect at 9:20 a.m. The brigade was to attack with three battalions, the 2nd Lincolnshire Regiment, 1st Royal Irish Rifles and 2nd Rifle Brigade, and was in position on Westhoek ridge around 10:10 a.m. ready for the next advance. The support battalion 2nd Royal Berkshire Regiment was to use one company to cover the exposed right of the Lincoln with Lewis gun posts and if necessary send up the remainder of the battalion to form a defensive flank.

On the right, at 10:10 a.m. as the barrage began its forward creep the Lincoln moved off under the command of a 2nd Leiutenant, both the Colonel and the Adjutant having been wounded before the order to advance was given. The full weight of the German machine gun fire from the plateau swept the Lincoln, the British barrage in front of 30th Division having moved forward and now falling well beyond the enemy machine guns and thus not disrupting their action.

In the centre the Irish Rifles were also suffering under the machine gun fire from Glencorse Wood and Nonne Bosschen. The right company made gallant efforts to keep going with the barrage but were finally checked and desperately attempted to consolidate in shell-holes where they were, still under heavy enfilade fire. The centre company fought its way forward to the muddy Hanebeek stream, some even crossing the mire and advancing up the slope of Anzac ridge towards the *Wilhelm Stellung*. Being completely unsupported and with the enemy attempting to get around their right, they eventually fell back until in contact with the battalions on either flank.

The 2nd Rifle Brigade on the left and farthest away from the scything enfilade fire from the higher ground and the woods got well forward. The right company established an outpost in Hanebeek Wood, near the edge of the stream, about 800 yards east of the crest of the ridge, but in so doing lost all its company officers. A gap developed between the Rifle Brigade and the Irish Rifles, dangerously exposing the formers right flank. In consequence the battalion was forced to withdraw from the wood to a position just forward of the Black Line on their left, and with their right drawn back to the Kit and Kat blockhouses on the ridge.

Under the withering enfilade fire no further progress could be made and the decision was taken to withdraw the brigade line into shelter to the west of Westhoek ridge leaving a line of Lewis gun posts along the ridge top. The whole brigade gradually fell-back and line was established just forward of Jabber Trench, slightly west of the original Black Line. The tanks had been largely bogged down in the crater-field or disabled before coming into action, but tank A.30, "Argyll", had assisted in silencing machine guns firing from a bunker just east of Jabber

---

[227] National Archives, War Diary 25th Brigade WO95/1727

Trench with 6-pounder and Lewis gun fire. The tank had also attacked German infantry in Jabber Trench who then scattered.

The position held by the 25th Brigade was precarious indeed, and the German reaction was growing in strength, to the point that there was concern as to whether even the present line could be held. The situation was extremely serious, as further withdrawal would dangerously expose the right flank of 15th Division north of the Roulers railway, so threatening the success of the whole advance to the north. Brigadier-General Coffin's example now proved a salvation to his men. He moved around the battlefield from post to post, organizing, encouraging and reassuring and becoming engaged in all tasks including the carrying of ammunition. Continually under fire, he appeared to live a charmed life and by his magnificent courage and calm behaviour he inspired all ranks. For these actions he was to be awarded the V.C.

The work of consolidation proceeded and a German counter-attack launched before midday was driven off. Two more determined counter-attacks just after 2:00 p.m. were supported by a German barrage which carpeted 8th Division's area, falling upon Bellewaarde ridge, the depression behind Westhoek ridge, and on the British forward outposts. On the right in their very exposed positions the Lincolns gave some ground, and in the centre the enemy entered the trench held by the Irish Rifles. Vigorous counter-attacks were immediately launched and the line was soon restored, no ground subsequently being lost and many Germans being killed. For the rest of the afternoon the Lincoln and Irish Rifles were left unmolested to continue with consolidation.[228] The situation on the left was for some hours less reassuring as a gap still existed between the Irish Rifles and the Rifle Brigade. The Middlesex supports were brought up from Bellewaarde ridge to fill the gap and the Rifle Brigade drew back its right slightly to conform to this line.[229] The whole of the II Corps attack upon the Gheluvelt plateau had therefore by 1:30 p.m. come to a complete standstill and Lieutenant-General Jacob had informed Fifth Army headquarters accordingly.

German forces facing II Corps

The three divisions of II Corps were faced by approximately four German regiments, each roughly equivalent to a British brigade. The *6th Bavarian Reserve Division* with two regiments in the line the *20th and 17th Bavarian Reserve Regiments,* with the *16th Bavarian Reserve* in support, had held from Lower Star Post to Westhoek since the 15th July. On the 31st they were in course of relief by the *52nd Reserve Division, 240th and 238th R.I.R's* with the *239th R.I.R.* in close support when the assault was launched. After the shock of Messines and with the fear of further mines, the outpost system was garrisoned at only half strength and this to be withdrawn to the Second Line in the event of an assault. To the south between Lower Star Post and the Klein Zillebeke – Zandvoorde road the line was held by the right flank of the *82nd* and later *94th Reserve Infantry Regiments* of the *22nd Reserve Division*, and to the north between Westhoek and the Ypres – Roulers railway was held by the left flank of the *95th Regiment, 38th Division*.[230]

---

[228] Another counter attack which began to form up around 5:00 p.m. in the Hanebeek valley still threatened the position. The remaining companies of the Berkshire were sent up to support the Rifle Brigade and the artillery was asked to draw back the defensive barrage by 300 yards. The counter-attack was subsequently broken up by artillery, Lewis gun, machine gun and rifle fire.
[229] The situation as darkness fell remained the same.
[230] National Archives, maps showing distribution of enemy forces on 29th and 31st July in WO153/601

XIX Corps
Lieutenant-General H. E. Watts

A very different prospect faced the attacking battalions of XIX Corps. They were to advance up the gentle slope of Pilckem ridge between the Ypres – Roulers railway, and a line running southwest to northeast 500 yards north of Wieltje, a total frontage of around 2,800 yards, but were not faced with the problems of the smashed woods on II Corps front. They were however faced with crossing a barren crater field of shell-holes and overcoming some formidable German strong points, in the forward zone, on and around the *Albrecht Stellung*, and in the battle zone beyond. The average distance to the third objective at the *Wilhelm Stellung* was about 3,400 yards.

The XIX Corps attacked with the 15th (Scottish) Division and the 55th (1st West Lancashire) Division. The III Brigade tanks of "C" Battalion (24 tanks) worked with the 15th Division, and "F" Battalion (24 tanks) with the 55th Division.[231] The ground conditions in the area around Frezenberg were generally poor being heavy and thoroughly cratered, but there were no woods to cause obstacles allowing the tanks a greater chance than those operating with the II Corps. The tanks were to deploy into sections in line, either in No-Mans-Land or on crossing the enemy line, were to work as close up to the barrage as possible and ideally take the lead in front of the infantry from the Blue Line. Upon reaching the Black Line the tanks were to patrol behind the line until consolidation had begun at which time they should return to a rallying point near Rupprecht Farm, 200 yards north-east of Verlorenhoek. Signalling between tanks and infantry was rudimentary. Tank signals were to be shown by a sectioned coloured disc; red and green disc to indicate "have reached objective", red, red and red disc to indicate "I have broken down", and red white and white disc to indicate "no enemy in sight". To call for tank assistance the infantry were to wave their helmets hoisted on their bayonets!

In the early hours there was a drizzle falling, causing the already bad ground conditions to become gradually worse.

15th (Scottish) Division
Major-General H. F. Thuillier

To the north of the Ypres – Staden railway the 15th Division was to attack with the 44th and 46th Brigades in the line to capture the Blue and the Black Line, with the 45th Brigade in support to continue the advance to the Green Line. The attack was on a frontage of around 1,200 yards between the railway, and the line of the western tributary of the Hanebeek, opening to 1,500 yards on the third objective, the Green Line. The division was to attack across the low hump of Frezenberg ridge, (rising to no more than 35 metres but from which the Germans had an excellent view into Ypres), then down into the shallow valley of the Hanebeek. The line of the third objective ran from where the Ypres – Zonnebeke road crossed the Roulers railway track on the right, then northwards through Bostin Farm to Dochy Farm, and then north-west parallel with the Zonnebeke – Langemarck road. To reach the Green Line the 45th Brigade would have to cross the Hanebeek, fight its way through the *Wilhelm Stellung*, and would have to advance 3,000 yards forward of the British Front Line. The ground conditions were bad with heavy mud and many shell-holes half filled with water, making the march up by No.2 Track to the assembly positions at Cambridge Trench extremely arduous.

44th Brigade[232]
The 44th Brigade attacked with two battalions in the line, the 8/10th Gordon Highlanders and the 9th Black Watch with the 8th Seaforth Highlanders in support.[233] The leading battalions advanced

---
[231] National Archives, War Diary III Brigade tank Corps WO95/104
[232] National Archives, War Diary 44th Brigade WO95/1935, War Diary 8th Seaforth WO95/1940
[233] National Archives, War Diary 8/10th Gordon Highlanders WO95/1938, National Archives, War Diary 8th Seaforth Highlanders WO95/1940

with two companies in the forward wave, each with two platoons forming a line of skirmishers in front with the remaining two companies in close support. The third company moved up in rear in similar formation, while the fourth company, some distance back moved up in artillery formation. The darkness caused difficulty in forming-up, but there was little mixing of companies and by the time the hostile retaliatory barrage crashed down at 3:54 a.m. the forward waves were well clear of the British Front Line.

    The Gordons went of in good order behind the barrage but found it difficult in the poor light and across the badly shell-pocked, muddy ground to trace the battalion boundaries. The German front, support and reserve trenches were cleared with little delay, but within 700 yards it was plain that the enemy was going to put up stiff resistance. Machine gun fire increased and a viscous hand-to-hand bayonet fight ensued between the Gordons and the enemy garrison holding Wilde Wood. The Black Watch was also involved in the fighting with local strong-points, and the two leading companies of the 8th Seaforth, "A" and "D", following up closely became engaged in the same melee the as the Gordons, assisting in the capture of a bunker in the north-west corner of the wood. Fire from the bunker was suppressed with Lewis guns and rifle grenades, and the garrison surrendered when approached, 2 enemy machine guns being put out of action. Seaforth "A" Company meanwhile overwhelmed and captured a machine gun at the junction of Ibex Avenue and Ibex Reserve, and then advancing with the Black Watch, assisted in the capture of Bill Cottage the garrison of which surrendered as the Highlanders closed in, and the bunker being burnt out with Phosphorus bombs. The Gordons and the Black Watch, under increasing hostile machine gun and shell fire, kept well up to their own barrage and reached the Blue Line on time at 4:25 a.m., maintaining touch with the 2nd Devonshire of 23rd Brigade on the other side of the Roulers railway embankment. After a short pause on the Blue Line, at 5:05 the Gordons and the Black Watch continued the advance towards the Black Line, those of the Seaforth which were not already there moving on to the Blue Line and beginning to consolidate. Hostile shell-fire became so heavy on this line that it was impossible to dig-in and the position had to be moved, "A", "C" and "D" Companies consolidating between Douglas Villa and the railway, with "B" Company 50 yards in rear.

    The wire around North Station Buildings adjacent to the railway and around the village of Frezenberg had been well cut, but the Gordons and Black Watch were held up by machine gun fire from a number of bunkers at a redoubt in Frezenberg hamlet. The fighting was fierce, the fire from the enemy garrison pinning down the Highlanders, who returned fire from the cover of shell-holes with Lewis guns and rifle grenades. The infantry waved their helmets, signalling for assistance and two tanks of "C" Battalion, "Challenger" and "Conqueror", worked their way around the flanks of the redoubt and opened fire on the bunkers, subduing the machine guns sufficiently for the bombers to work up close. The strong-point fell by about 9:00 a.m. The Gordons and Black Watch, by this time having sustained many casualties continued the advance to the Black Line, 500 yards east of Frezenberg and by 5:55 a.m. proceeded to consolidate the position. Two counter-attacks, one at 8:30 a.m. and one at 10:00 a.m. were fought off, assisted by 6-pounder and Lewis gun fire from two tanks "Coquette" and "Crusader", which had become bogged just east of the Black Line but continued to give valuable gunfire support.

46th Brigade[234]

The 46th Brigade attacked to the left of the 44th with the 7/8th King's Own Scottish Borderers and the 10/11th Highland Light Infantry, with the 10th Scottish Rifles in support.[235] The brigade had assembled with the front wave of its forward companies about 30 yards beyond the British wire, with the second wave in the British Front Line. Between these two waves were companies of the 10th Scottish Rifles, which were to mop-up the enemy front system. The support companies of the King's Own Scottish Borderers and Highland Light Infantry had their forward wave between the front line and Crump Trench, and their second wave in Crump Trench.

---

[234] National Archives, War Diary 46th Brigade WO95/1950
[235] National Archives, War Diary 10th/11th Highland Light Infantry WO95/1952

Following closely behind the barrage, which reassuringly appeared to annihilate the enemy trenches, the brigade made good progress across very bad ground which had been previously devastated by shell-fire. Around 2 minutes after Zero the enemy put down a barrage on Crump Trench, which quickly shortened to the communication trenches especially Haymarket at its junction with the Front Line, while heavy shells dropped occasionally on Cambridge Road 300 yards to the rear. The K.O.S.B. and the H.L.I. successfully reached the Blue Line having encountered little resistance from enemy infantry. A few machine gunners had remained by their guns, but most had either surrendered, or quickly made off towards their Second Line. Battalion headquarters of the H.L.I. moved up 600 yards beyond the British Front Line into the old German trench at Cameroon Avenue, while advanced headquarters was established at Grey Ruin, another 500 yards forward. No sooner had the H.L.I. headquarters moved into Cameroon Avenue, than the enemy dropped a heavy barrage around nearby Rupprecht Farm and their old reserve area, which killed the Battalion Lewis gun Officer and the Medical Officer.

At 5:05 a.m. the advance continued towards the Black Line. The K.O.S.B. became engaged with 44th Brigade in the fight for the redoubt in Frezenberg, and was also involved in its capture. As the leading waves of the H.L.I. came over the crest of Frezenberg ridge just beyond Grey Ruin they came under intense machine gun fire, and began to experience the full effect of the numerous German blockhouses and bunkers. Direct fire from Hill 35 at the western end of Zonnebeke spur 1,000 yards to the northwest, and in enfilade from Frost House, near Frezenberg hamlet cut into the advancing ranks causing considerable casualties. The garrison of Square Farm, a considerable fortress, 300 yards from the crest of the ridge and right in the path of the H.L.I. put up little resistance and was moped up by "C" Company, 130 prisoners being taken.[236] The two forward companies "A" and "D" of the H.L.I. pushed on under intense fire, especially from Frost House, and by 5:50 were 100 yards east of Square Farm, still supported by "C" Company which had lost three of its Company Officers. "C" Company inclined slightly to the right to face this fire, and in a flanking manoeuvre attacked with Lewis guns and rifle grenades the bunker at Low Farm, bombing out a machine gun which had been causing casualties.

By about 9:00 a.m. the K.O.S.B. had taken its section of the Black Line, but the H.L.I. was held up. To their left, 55th Division was checked in front of Pommern Castle at the foot of Hill 35.[237] Machine gun fire from the hill directed on the H.L.I. was still acute making movement even by short rushes costly, although a number of the enemy could be seen falling-back across the hilltop road. Led by its one remaining officer, "A" Company of the H.L.I. finally reported the Black Line taken and consolidation had commenced at around 10:35 a.m. To this point the battalion had sustained casualties of 10 officers and around 150 other ranks. The position of the Black Line was not however considered advantageous, and the battalion moved forward and dug-in between a position 150 yards forward of Beck House on the right and the Iberian strongpoint on the left. At around the same time a hostile barrage landed about the Blue Line, Square Farm and in the Hanebeek valley, but by this stage the 45th Brigade in support had already passed through towards the Green Line.

By 9.25 a.m. thirteen field batteries had been moved up close to the position of the old British Front Line, to give barrage support for the next advance. Great difficulty had been experienced moving the guns due to the awful condition of the ground and German shelling, and as the infantry were beginning to notice, whilst they were being moved they were out of action. Around 10:00 a.m. the drizzle had stopped, the sun made a brief appearance, and it became hot and sultry, causing mist to rise from the soaking ground which reduced the visibility again. At 10:10 a.m. the barrage began its forward creep towards the third objective, but as some of the

---

[236] This is different to the account of 165th Brigade which claims that Square Farm fell to the 1/7th King's Liverpool Regiment. It may be that the King's had already taken the farm when the H.L.I. moped-up, but as the H.L.I. claim they were 100 yards east of the farm at 5:50 a.m. this seems unlikely. The discrepancy must be put down to the confusion of battle.
[237] A fortified position within the *Albrecht Stellung* at the western foot of the Zonnebeke spur, 800 yards to the north.

batteries struggled forward, it was obvious to the infantry that the protective curtain of shells was much thinner than before.

45th Brigade[238]

The 45th Brigade was to continue the advance towards the Green Line, about 1,200 to 1,500 yards forward. The brigade attacked with the 6/7th Royal Scots Fusiliers and the 6th Cameron Highlanders, on the divisional front, with the 11th Argyll and Southerland Highlanders, and the 13th Royal Scots in support.[239] The objective of the brigade was around 300 yards beyond the German Third Line, which ran north from the Roulers railway to the Bremen Redoubt, then crossed the Zonnebeke brook at Zevencote and then northwards again across the Zonnebeke spur at Hill 37.

As the 45th Brigade worked forward towards the Green Line, to their right south of the railway the 8th Division was still held up on the Black Line with little chance of getting forward. This left the right of 45th Brigade dangerously exposed and two platoons of the Argylls were ordered to move south of the railway to form a defensive flank between the 8th and 15th Divisions. At the request of the Argylls, tank C.1 moved towards some machine gun shelters along the railway, from where at the approach of the tank the enemy quickly retired. C.1 soon became ditched in a shell-hole but continued to fire on the enemy whilst un-ditching. At 11:30 the Argylls, again pinned down, asked for further assistance from the tank which succeeded in knocking out machine guns dug-in to the railway embankment, and then proceeded to patrol the front while the Argylls established their Lewis guns in shell-hole posts along the flank.

Even with the efforts of the Argylls and C.1, the 45th Brigade's right flank was very much in the air. As a result of heavy machine gun fire from south of the railway, the right companies of the 6/7th Royal Scots Fusiliers, after sustaining heavy casualties, had to stop and take what cover they could in German trenches and gun-pits about Potsdam House, just north of the railway and 500 yards short of the Hanebeek. By 11:30 a.m. however the left companies of the battalion had succeeded in fighting their way forward to the Bremen Redoubt, a large bunker system within the *Wilhelm Stellung*, on the third objective. To the left of the Fusiliers, the Camerons pressed on relentlessly out of effective range of the enfilade fire from south of the railway, and tanks C.11 and C.13 assisted them in silencing machine guns and snipers at the Beck House blockhouse. At 11:45 a.m. after a sharp fight for the defences, the Camerons captured the section of the *Wilhelm Stellung* on Hill 37, the most dominant point on this part of the battlefield, gaining their objective on the Green Line and taking 150 prisoners. They then proceeded to push forward patrols, down the eastern slope of the hill towards the northern side of the Langemark – Zonnebeke road, where they occupied the strong-points at the Dochy Farm and Otto Farm blockhouses. Here, incredibly, they were only 1,700 yards short of the fourth objective, the *Flandern I* line.

The failure of the 30th Division to seize Glencorse Wood and Nonne Bosschen on the Gheluvelt plateau was having the foreseen repercussions. The subsequent inability of 8th Division to get forward south of the railway had produced an inevitable knock on effect on 15th Division. Vicious enfilade fire from the area south of the railway which should have been secured by the 8th Division had cut into the right companies of the Royal Scots Fusiliers which were stopped 500 yards short of their objective. But the left companies had got forward to the third objective, and to their left the Camerons were 700 yards beyond the *Wilhelm Stellung* at Hill 37, but in insufficient numbers to withstand any concerted counter-attack. Although the division had broken the resistance of many blockhouses, it was plain that the structures had been little damaged by the preparatory bombardments, and had been extremely active and quite capable of maintaining their fire whilst subjected to the creeping barrage. The reinforced concrete fortresses were to see a great deal more action over the coming weeks.

---

[238] National Archives, War Diary 45th Brigade WO95/1943, War Diary 6th Camerons WO95/1945, War Diary 13th Royal Scots WO95/1946
[239] National Archives, War Diary 11th Argylls WO95/1944

55th (West Lancashire) Division
Major-General H. S. Jeudwine

The 55th Division held the 1,600 yard sector between the Ypres – Zonnebeke road and a point 300 yards north of the Ypres – St.Julian road, which widened to 1,800 yards at the third objective on the Green Line, and was to attack with the 165th and 166th Brigades in the line and the 164th in support.[240] The direction of attack led over the shell-pocked rise of Pilckem Ridge, and down into the shallow depression of the Steenbeek valley, the stream being 1,900 yards beyond the British Front Line. The second objective near the German Second Line lay just beyond the Steenbeek, which at this part of the battlefield was beginning to widen from a brook into a stream. The banks had been so damaged by shellfire, and the watercourse so choked with blasted earth, that the flow had been totally disrupted and instead of draining lazily to the north, it now spread across the flat meadows, spilling into the multitude of surrounding shell-holes. The German Third Line was 3,700 yards from the British Front Line, and was the division's third objective. This line of wire entanglements and trenches, supported by numerous pillboxes ran along the southern-western tip of the London, or Gravenstafel Ridge, then turned south to cross the northern Hanebeek and the Langemark – Zonnebeke road at Kansas Cross,[241] then crossed the Zonnebeke spur at Hill 37. Numerous blockhouses and fortified positions of great defensive strength had been constructed in the forward zone, along the Black Line, in the battle zone, and along the Green Line, and all were to severely test the British infantry. Twenty four tanks of "F" Battalion operated with the division, 12 to attack the Blue and Black Lines with 165th and 166th Brigades, and 12 to support the attack on the Green Line with 164th Brigade.

165th Brigade[242]
The 165th Brigade was to attack with the 1/5th and 1/6th King's Liverpool Regiment in the line, and the 1/7th and 1/9th King's Liverpool in support. In the early hours of the 30th / 31st the 1/5th and 1/6th King's assembled in the assembly trenches opposite Camel Trench (Kaiser Bill).[243] At Zero Hour in the gloomy half-light the troops attacking in four waves, experienced great difficulty in keeping proper distance across the broken muddy ground, but following close up to the barrage quickly overran the German forward trench systems and advanced with little resistance to the Blue Line on the eastern face of Pilckem ridge. Both battalions began to consolidate the position under constant sniper and machine gun fire, the 1/6th establishing a strong-point on the left flank between Jasper Farm and the Blue Line. Hostile machine gun fire was heavy from Plum Farm, beyond the Blue Line, greatly hampering consolidation. Although beyond the first objective the strong-point was attacked and taken whilst the barrage still fell upon it, 3 machine guns being captured. To this point the 1/5th had taken 80 prisoners and the 1/6th around 100.

The 1/7th had moved off from the assembly trenches and crossed No-Mans-Land at 4:20, encountering many Germans who had remained in dug-outs and broken sections of trench in their front system, and had been passed over by the 1/5th. These were swiftly mopped-up and just after 5:00 the 1/7th reached the Blue Line. The 1/9th had been caught by the hostile retaliatory barrage just after Zero, and had already lost several men. Moving forward out of the barrage area at 4:30, they were on the Blue Line up to time.

At 5:05 the 1/7th and 1/9th passed through, but from this point the advance became more difficult the resistance stiffening considerably, with heavy machine gun fire being

---

[240] The Rev. J.O. Coop (1919), *The Story of the 55th (West Lancashire) Division*, Liverpool: 'Daily Post' Printers
[241] There are three separate tributaries of the upper Steenbeek all named Hanebeek, one (the western), rising near Verlorenhoek, the second (the southern), near Westhoek, and the third (the northern), near Zonnebeke.
[242] National Archives, War Diary 165th Brigade WO95/2925
[243] Everard Wyrall (1928-30) *The History of the King's Liverpool Regiment* London: Arnold pp499-501

encountered from the numerous strong-points and blockhouses towards the German Second Line. The support battalions continued the advance towards the Black Line, "A" Company of the 1/7th soon being held up by machine gun fire from the blockhouse at Square Farm in the 15th Divisional area on the extreme right. Parties of the 1/7th moved over the divisional boundary and attacked Square Farm, a machine gun and a small number of Germans being overwhelmed. (See footnote 19 and H.L.I. account). On the left "C" Company seized Plum Farm. "B" Company under Captain Heaton, after advancing through both shell and machine gun fire, and over bad ground, crossed the spreading Steenbeek by bridges and scrambling through the shattered wire entanglements of Pommern Castle at 6:05, attacked the redoubt from both flanks.[244] Pommern Castle was just in rear of the Black Line. This had been a considerable advance of over 2,000 yards from the British front line, and "B" Company had inevitably sustained many casualties. Whilst some of "B" Company mopped-up Pommern Castle, a small party worked forward 500 yards under heavy machine gun fire, and succeeded in setting up a post on the north-west side of the Hill 35, 200 yards south of Gallipoli, having captured a field gun and shot down a number of the enemy on the way. Tanks "Foggy", "Furious" and "Formosa" all answered calls for assistance from the infantry. One such call was made by "A" Company of the 1/7th, held up by machine gun fire near the Steenbeek. To get the message to the tank which was operating 600 yards to the left, Private Shaw volunteered to work across the exposed fire-swept craters, the tank then returning to successfully knock out the offending machine gun. Soon "A" and "D" Companies also arrived at Pommern around 9:30, but were in small numbers and had lost all but one company officer. Captain Heaton took command of all 3 companies, and organised for defensive posts to be pushed out 150 yards forward of the redoubt.

The 1/9th was checked by the blockhouse at Bank Farm on the *Albrecht Stellung*, just east of the Steenbeek, here a spreading mire of mud which the battalion had crossed with difficulty. The 1/9th signalled for tank assistance and the blockhouse was captured with the help of tank F.23, which also cleared the enemy from a communication trench running east. The tank "Five Nights" of "F" Battalion, trundled forward and cleared a strong-point at Apple Villa which had held up the 1/9th, where eight Germans and a machine gun were captured and two more machine gun crews were forced to retire. This tank then proceeded to the redoubt at Pommern Castle where it assisted in clearing the enemy from a length of trench. Second-Lieutenant G. Elderd with 6 men of "A" Company of the 1/9th had worked forward with his small party, forded the Steenbeek, and attacked the Pommern Redoubt, taking 40 prisoners. At around 9:30 he was supported by Second-Lieutenant Ellam with 50 men of "B" Company and the tally of prisoners soon rose to about 90. Small groups of "C", "D" and "A" Companies of the 1/9th after crossing the Steenbeek were arriving on the Black Line from 7:30 onwards in small numbers of 6 to 7 men, having sustained many casualties and been held up by heavy machine gun fire. The line was far from secure, but with the arrival of the 50 men of "B" Company the situation improved. But by this time in an effort to stem the flow of supports to the front the enemy dropped a heavy barrage by guns of all calibre up to 8-inch on No-Mans-Land, and right back as far as Potijze on the outskirts of Ypres. At 11:45 165th Brigade headquarters had ordered all available men up to reinforce the Black Line, and that the 1/6th was to send up 2 companies to support the 1/9th.

166th Brigade[245]

The 166th Brigade was to attack with the 1/5th King's Own Royal Lancaster Regiment and the 1/5th North Lancashire Regiment leading and the 1/10th King's Liverpool Regiment (Liverpool Scottish) and the 1/5th South Lancashire Regiment in support. The King's Own and South Lancs fought their way past enemy machine gun nests, the gun teams stunned by the weight of the barrage, and kept up with the curtain of fire to reach the Blue Line with little opposition. Following up closely from the assembly trenches to the Blue Line the Liverpool Scottish and the

---

[244] The account of the attack on Pommern Castle or Pommern Reboubt is confusing as the capture of the position is credited to both the 1/7th and the 1/9th. It is likely therefore that both battalions had a hand in its capture.

[245] National Archives, War Diary 166th Brigade WO95/2829

South Lancs reorganised before continuing the advance behind the barrage towards the Black Line. From the start the Liverpool Scottish came under fierce machine gun fire from Spree Farm (450 yards beyond the Steenbeek and just forward of the Black Line), towards which they were advancing, and from its protective earthwork Capricorn Trench. Machine gun fire at longer range also swept the Liverpool from another blockhouse at Pond Farm 500 yards beyond the Black Line. The great strength of the German blockhouse system now became all too clear. Each blockhouse was so arranged as to give its neighbours covering fire, and to attack one meant exposure to deadly fire from the others. It appeared that the preparatory bombardments over many days had devastated the ground into a wilderness of water-filled craters, but had made no impression on the reinforced concrete structures, which kept up a steady stream of fire upon the advancing British even as the creeping barrage had passed over them. The hail of machine gun fire from front and flanks struck the South Lancs and the Liverpool Scottish causing many casualties. Soon confronted by a belt of uncut wire the advance faltered in front of Capricorn Trench, and those remaining in the much thinned ranks were forced to take cover. With the advance obviously in trouble the North Lancs moved up from the Blue Line in support of the two weakened battalions. Helmets were waived urgently to attract help, the call soon answered by tank F.39 which, though hit by anti-tank fire succeeded in breaking down the uncut wire. The way was now clear for the infantry to rush Capricorn Trench which quickly fell, and by 7:00 a.m. was held by the Liverpool Scottish, in touch with the South Lancs on the right. Tank F.39 also temporarily suppressed the machine guns at Spree Farm just beyond the trench, but although the brigade was on most of the Black line by 9:00 a.m., the enemy garrison in Spree Farm still held out. The brigade attempted to construct supporting strong-points in shell-holes, but enemy shelling and continual sniping from Spree Farm and Pond Farm greatly hampered consolidation, causing many casualties.[246]

164th Brigade[247]

Moving up in support from the Blue Line to continue the advance, 164th Brigade immediately came under fire from the machine guns in Spree and Pond Farms which had so hampered 166th Brigade. Passing through the shell-hole posts of the 165th and 166th, 164th Brigade attacked at 10:10 a.m. behind the renewed, but noticeably thinner barrage, and continued the advance towards the Green Line. The 1/4th Loyal North Lancashire Regiment was to the right and the 2/5th Lancashire Fusiliers to the left, supported by the 1/4th King's Own Royal Lancaster and the1/8th King's Liverpool Regiment (Liverpool Irish).[248] Before setting off the Liverpool Irish,

---

[246] Captain Noel Godfrey Chavasse V.C. of the 1/10th Liverpool Scottish, had moved his first aid post forward to a German dug-out at Setques Farm. Although the area was under heavy enemy fire Captain Chavasse had stood up and waved to indicate the position of the aid post. He was hit in the head by a shell splinter, possibly suffering a fractured skull. After having his wound dressed at the large Weiltje dugout, he returned to his work at the forward first aid post, continuing to help the wounded until sundown. After dark he proceeded to search for survivors across the bleak and desolate battlefield. The following morning with the aid of a German medical orderly prisoner he continued to work on the wounded in the filthy and appalling conditions of the dug-out. The danger of using enemy bunkers with the entrances facing east soon became clear, as a shell entered the dug-out and exploded, killing some of those inside, and again wounding Captain Chavasse. He refused to go to the rear and continued with his work. At around 3:00 a.m. on the morning of the 2nd August, another shell exploded in the dug-out killing nearly all inside and wounding him in many places, including a serious wound to the abdomen. Managing to crawl out of the dug-out and across the foul ground outside he eventually found assistance, and was taken back to No.32 Casualty Clearing Station at Brandhoek, where he was immediately operated upon. Although regaining consciousness, he died at 1 p.m. on the morning of the 4th August. For his acts of selfless gallantry he was to be awarded a bar to his V.C., the only soldier to be awarded two such decorations, both won in the Great War.

[247] National Archives, War Diary 164th Brigade WO95/2920/21, War Diary 1/4th King's Own WO95/2922

[248] Everard Wyrall (1928-30) *The History of the King's Liverpool Regiment* London: Arnold p502

waiting to follow up behind the Lancashire Fusiliers had sustained officer casualties from snipers, even though they wore Private's uniforms. The fighting now became most severe as the brigade encountered the numerous strong points and blockhouses in the battle zone beyond the Black Line. The preparatory artillery barrages had not been successful in destroying the blockhouses and although the Germans had withdrawn much of their field artillery behind the Green Line during the pause on the second objective, many of the bunkers and emplacements contained fixed field guns which continued to fire into the advancing infantry over open sights. Numerous machine guns in the many mutually supporting blockhouses filled the air with the zip and whine of machine gun bullets, the severe fire causing numerous casualties.

Most fire seemed to come from the Somme and Hindu Cot blockhouses on the higher ground to the left and centre, and from Schuler Farm to the left in the valley of the northern Hanebeek. On the right the North Lancs, fighting hard along the northern edge of the Zonnebeke spur put their training into practice, and captured the garrisons at Somme Farm and Gallipoli by platoon outflanking attacks, both positions containing machine guns and a German battery. To the right of Gallipoli and on top of the Zonnebeke spur, Hill 35 was taken. Six hundred yards forward at Kansas Cross on the third objective, a battery firing over open sights at 100 yards, was rushed by parties of the North Lancs and King's Own, a number of prisoners being taken. During this attack Corporal Tom Fletcher Mayson of the King's Own, single-handedly destroyed two machine guns and killed their crews. For his remarkable valour and initiative he was to be awarded the V.C. The advance, in which five 77 mm field guns had been captured, had been successfully carried to the Green Line and both battalions commenced to consolidate, with a line of shell-hole outposts thrown forward. Touch was gained with the 45th Brigade on the right, but on the left although there was no touch with either the Lancs Fusiliers or the Liverpool Irish, parties of British infantry could be seen up Gravenstafel ridge about Wurst Farm.

But on the left of the brigade attack the fighting was much tougher. The Lancashire Fusiliers were soon held up by a battery and the machine guns at Pond Farm 500 yards beyond the second objective, and subsequently lost the barrage. Without the protection of the barrage the advance was all the more difficult, but after fierce fighting, both Pond Farm, and Hindu Cottage 200 yards beyond were taken. The ranks of the Lancashire Fusiliers were thinning drastically and the Liverpool Scottish moved up to fill the gaps, and support the attack on the Green Line. Moppers-up of the Liverpool clear the bunkers and trenches at Pond Farm, Hindu Cot and Border House, and "D" Company attacked a line of dug-outs taking 150 prisoners.

By this time the British barrage was noticeably thin and ragged, and had little if any effect on suppressing the hostile fire. The depth of the defences was very clear as no sooner had Hindu Cot been cleared than heavy machine gun fire struck the Fusiliers and Liverpool from Schuler Farm, another blockhouse down the gentle slope towards the Hanebeek. The farm was 500 yards forward and still 500 yards short of the Green Line. A battery supporting the strong-point a few yards west of the Langemark – Zonnebeke road, fired at close range causing total disorganisation to the advance, until the Battalion Commander of the Lancashire Fusiliers Lieut.-Colonel Bertram Best Dunkley rallied the foremost companies, and mounted an attack which succeeded in outflanking and seizing the blockhouse and battery. For this act of conspicuous bravery he was to be awarded the V.C. posthumously, as he later died of wounds received in the action. Severe machine gun fire from a long row of concrete dug-outs, Schuler Galleries, again swept the advance, protected behind a wire entanglement which had not been broken by the British bombardment. There were exceedingly few men left in the leading waves of the attack, and these remnants were driven to ground by the savage fire. The tired survivors mounted yet another determined attack against the Galleries this time with success, killing a number of the enemy and capturing others. But Schuler Farm just west of the Zonnebeke – Langemarck road resisted all attempts at capture and held out, although the bunker at Winipeg to the east of the road was seized.

By now all battalions had suffered most severe casualties in their long advance towards the third objective. The wired German trench system at the Galleries covering a number of empty battery positions, was mistaken for the German Third Line and here most of the surviving Fusiliers and Liverpool Irish in a state of total exhaustion remained and dug-in, about

600 yards short of their objective. Incredibly a platoon of the Lancashire Fusiliers detailed to occupy outposts on Gravenstafel ridge continued the advance across the shallow Hanebeek valley and up the bare slope onto the ridge at Wurst Farm. An officer's patrol reached Aviatik Farm 400 yards beyond the *Wilhelm Stellung*, where a German officer and 50 other ranks were taken prisoner. Once aware of the situation, the Commanding Officer of the Liverpool Irish ordered the survivors of his "B" Company to push forward to join the Lancs Fusiliers at Wurst Farm, and "D" Company to dig-in on the Green Line near Fokker Farm. Small parties of the 2/5th Lancashire Fusiliers were dug-in along the Green Line between the two positions.[249]

The 12 tanks of "C" Battalion and the 12 tanks of "F" Battalion of the III Tank Brigade had been successful, given the bad state of the ground especially around Frezenberg. Where they could come into action they gave great assistance to the infantry. Of the 24 tanks available 8 had mechanical problems, 4 were knocked out, and 8 became ditched.
Except for the section between Kansas Cross and Schuler Farm the 55th Division was on the Green Line, but in greatly reduced numbers and in a state of exhaustion and shock, with a small forward outpost hopelessly exposed up on Gravenstafel ridge at Wurst Farm. The fighting for the blockhouses had been tough and costly. The infantry had learnt the hard way, that although the lengthy bombardment prior to the attack had mostly cut the wire and blown in the enemy earthworks, it had also succeeded in creating a multitude of water-filled craters across the muddy wastes, but had done little to knock out the numerous concrete emplacements. It was also very clear that the further they had penetrated the stronger the resistance of the enemy had become and the weaker had become their own barrage. The two forward battalions of the brigade had now lost more than half their strength and the two support battalions were merged into them. Typical was the Liverpool Irish with total casualties of 18 officers and 307 other ranks. Exhausted, shocked, filthy, thirsty and short of ammunition, they could now do little but await the enemy onslaught.

German forces facing XIX Corps

The inner flank regiments, the *94th I.R.* (with the *96th I.R.* in close support) of the *38th Division*, and *456th I.R.* of the *235th Division* (which had all three regiments in the line) opposed the XIX Corps. Each regiment was of slightly less strength than a British brigade. The *38th* and *235th* had been in the line for only 3 and 4 days respectively.[250]

XVIII Corps
Lieutenant-General Sir Ivor Maxse

The British Front Line from which the XVIII Corps was to attack extended from north of the Ypres - St Julien road at Wieltje, to north-west of the Ypres - Pilckem road (1,000 yards west of the Yser canal near Lancashire Farm), a total frontage of around 2,800 yards. The Corps was to form the right sector of a northern defensive flank. If all went to plan, the advance would carry the 39th and 51st Divisions through the German Front Line, across the low rise of Pilckem Ridge, through the Second Line, or *Albrecht Stellung* (the Black Line), on the eastern slope of the ridge, towards the shallow valley of the Steenbeek. Straddling the stream in the right of the sector lay the shattered ruins of the village of St Julien. The left flank, had the greatest distance to advance, it being nearly 4,000 yards from the British Front Line to the Steenbeek, with the third objective on the Green Line laying another 1,300 yards beyond the stream. Pilckem ridge and the Steenbeek valley presented another host of German defensive positions, being infested with strong points, many on the sites of the old farms, beneath the ruins of which lay the concrete and steel bunkers with their arsenal of field batteries and machine guns. There were many of

---
[249] After the subsequent withdrawal from this position later in the day, it was not destined to be re-taken until the 4th October.
[250] National Archives, maps showing distribution of enemy forces on 29th and 31st July in WO153/601

the smaller lower Mebus, constructed in lines of mutual protection, and also larger formidable independent bunkers in the ruined farmhouses to break up the cohesion of the advance. The tanks of "G" Battalion I Tank Brigade operated with the Corps, 16 tanks with the 39th Division and 8 with the 51st Division.[251]

39th Division
Major-General G. J. Cuthbert

Along a 1,200 yard section of the British Front Line between a point 500 yards north of the Ypres – St Julien road, and a point opposite Canadian Farm (in the German Front Line), the 39th Division was to attack with the 116th and 117th Brigades with the 118th Brigade in support. The objective widened to 1,600 yards beyond the Steenbeek. Facing the division across 500 yards of battered No-Mans-Land the German strong-point of Mouse Trap Farm, behind Caliban Reserve Trench 250 yards beyond the German Front Line, dominated the slight rise of the bare fire-swept Pilckem ridge.

116th Brigade[252]
The 116th Brigade was to attack with the 11th and 12th Royal Sussex Regiment forward and the 13th Royal Sussex and 14th Royal Hampshire Regiment in support.[253] The Blue Line was captured with little difficulty, and the advance continued, the 13th Royal Sussex and the Hampshire facing heavy machine gun fire from blockhouses and fortified trenches as they neared the German Second Line. Help arrived in the form of tanks G.3 and G.4 which attacked a series of concrete shelters in a redoubt at Juliet Farm and the earthworks to the rear at Canopus Trench, knocking out two machine guns and assisting in the capture of up to 60 of the garrison. The 13th Royal Sussex moved on and occupied the ruins of St Julien, taking prisoner the garrison of 17 officers and 205 other ranks, tanks G.2, G.3, G.4 and G.5 assisting in this operation. Another tank G.7, although broken down just east of the Steenbeek about 250 yards south of St. Julien, formed a strong-point with the infantry, quickly exhausting all its Lewis gun ammunition, then fighting on with rifles. The Hampshire encountered stubborn resistance on their left, coming under heavy machine gun fire from the fortified locality at Alberta 700 yards northwest of St. Julien. The defences were overcome by two tanks G.9 and G.47, while the Sherwood Foresters of 117th Brigade worked forward and captured the position, assisted by men of the Hampshire. During the pause on the Black Line, 2nd Lieutenant Denis George Wyldbore Hewitt of the 14th Hampshire was severely wounded by a shell which set fire to signal rockets in his pack. Although in great pain he led his company forward in the advance to the Black Dotted Line. Here while organising consolidation he was shot and killed by a sniper. He was to be awarded the V.C. for his courage and leadership.

By 8:00 a.m. the brigade had successfully forded the muddy Steenbeek with little trouble, and was consolidating on the Green Dotted Line just east of both the stream and St. Julien.

---

[251] National Archives, War Diary I Tank Brigade WO95/98
[252] National Archives, War Diary 116th Brigade WO95/2921
[253] C.T. Atkinson (1952) *The Royal Hampshire Regiment Vol II 1914-1918* Glasgow: Robert Maclehose

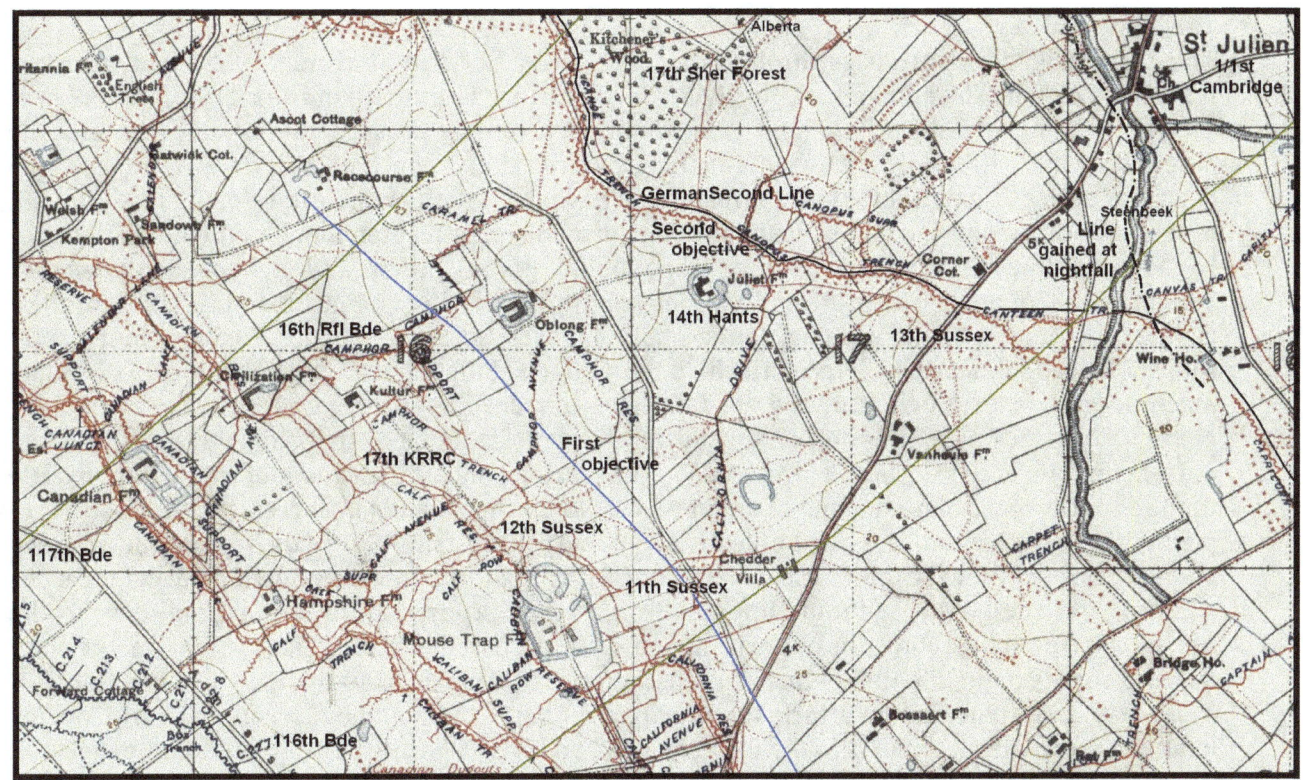

The advance of the 116th Brigade and 117th Brigade 39th Division over Pilckem ridge to the Steenbeek and line gained by nightfall

117th Brigade[254]

The 16th Sherwood Foresters and the 17th King's Royal Rifle Corps successfully captured the Blue Line, where the brigade's support battalions the 16th Rifle Brigade and 17th Sherwood Foresters passed through. The advance across Canoe Trench and through Kitcheners Wood was assisted by tank G.47, which silenced one machine gun and caused the crew of another to surrender to the Sherwood Foresters. On the left of the advance machine gun fire from three strong blockhouses at Regina Cross 600 yards west of the Steenbeek held up the 17th Sherwood Foresters. Using the assault weapons which they had brought forward, a barrage of Stokes mortar rounds and rifle grenades subdued the garrison sufficiently for it to be outflanked and the entrances rushed, the garrison of 30 being either bayoneted or captured. As the advance progressed past Kitcheners Wood strong-points, not always easy to see amongst the debris were overlooked, and tank G.46 helped mop-up a party of Germans still in the wood who were firing into the backs of the advancing Sherwood Foresters.

Further to the right, the large Mebus and defensive earthworks of the Alberta strong-point, 500 yards west of the Steenbeek, threatened another hold up. The tanks, G.9 and G.47 attacked the strong-point, G.9 running down the uncut wire in front of the breastwork, upon which the defenders surrendered to the infantry. Both tanks then opened fire upon the blockhouses and effectively subdued the defences, enabling the Sherwood Foresters to capture the position, with the assistance of the 14th Hampshire. The muddy morass of the broken Steenbeek was then crossed, and by 8:00 a.m. the brigade was consolidating a line in very heavy ground just east of the stream.

---

[254] National Archives, War Diary 117th Brigade WO95/2585

118th Brigade[255]

The 118th Brigade was to pass through the 116th and 117th and at around 10:10 a.m. attacked with the 1/6th Cheshire Regiment, the 1/1st Hertfordshire Regiment and the 4/5th Black Watch. The 1/1st Cambridgeshire Regiment was in support. Having crossed the muddy but fordable Steenbeek, the battalions began the advance towards the Green Line behind a barrage which was now noticeably thinner. Their important task was to link the main attack along the left flank of the XIX Corps, with the defensive flank to be formed along the Steenbeek to the north.

The Cheshire passed through the rubble of St. Julien and advanced across the Langemark –Zonnebeke road near Winnipeg, coming under heavy machine gun fire from their right rear, their right flank being dangerously exposed as the 2nd Lancs Fusiliers and 1/10th King's (Liverpool Scottish), were still held up about Schuler Farm and Kansas Cross. Enemy machine guns shot down many of the Cheshire, but despite the heavy losses the remainder continued the advance, pressing on up the gentle cratered slope to their objective at the wired entrenchments of the German Third Line, on the western end of Gravenstafel ridge. Here a large number of Germans behind a line of uncut wire held up their hands in surrender. Outposts were pushed forward beyond the third objective to von Tirpitz Farm 250 yards beyond the *Wilhelm Stellung*, but very few of the Cheshire had got forward, and they were now in a very dangerous position and completely without support. From these outposts there was a good view to the north-east, for those with the opportunity to look, across the Stroombeek valley to the wire entanglements of the Flanders I line at Wallemolen, 2,800 yards from the Cheshire position. But of greater importance to the attack, the fourth and final objective, the discretional Red Line, lay near the Stroombeek about 1,500 yards beyond von Tirpitz Farm. The depleted and exhausted Cheshire was already virtually out of the effective range of their field batteries, and the German counter-attack divisions were not yet engaged. To reach the Red Line appeared a forlorn hope. The 1/1st Herts meanwhile, on passing to the left of St. Julien came under a hail of machine gun fire lashing into their left flank from the direction of the blockhouses at Triangle Farm and Maison du Hibou, and suffered severe casualties before working forward to their objective east of the St.Julien – Poelcappelle road. To their left the 4/5th Black Watch advanced to a position just short of Triangle Farm, west of the St. Julien – Poelcapelle road, where they drew their left flank back to the Steenbeek to conform to the 51st Division to their left.[256]

The 1/1st Cambridgeshire Regiment in brigade reserve had moved forward and crossed the Hanebeek 400 yards east of St. Julian at 10:25 a.m. and had dug-in across the St.Julien to Winnipeg road, already under rifle fire from Fortuin 500 yards to the south, which should have been secured by 55th Division. Battalion headquarters was established in an old gun pit on the east bank of the Steenbeek, 300 yards south of St. Julian. The battalion War Diary of the 1/1st Cambridge takes up the story. '11:00a.m. From Battalion headquarters the whole area of the objective East of the St.Julien – Keerselare road could be seen. West of this road the country is covered with trees and hedge rows which obscure the view except for some 200 yards West and N.W. of the most Northerly houses in St. Julien. Patches of the fields were, however, visible. Crossing these patches of grass and East of the St. Julien – Keerselare road, the 1/6th Cheshire and 1/1st Herts and a few men of the 4/5th Black Watch could be seen. The 1/1st Herts appeared to be experiencing some difficulty in clearing "nests" of the enemy and be too far from the barrage. The 1/6th Cheshire were progressing but were not near enough to the barrage…11:20 a.m. The 1/1st Herts and the 1/6th Cheshires were seen to be retiring in disorder under heavy fire pursued by the enemy. The original orders for the 1/1st Cambridge were to move in support of the 4/5th Black Watch when the latter had reached their objective. With this move in view, "B" Company was held in readiness…11:35 a.m. The hostile counter-attack was now west of the Winnipeg – Springfield road. The time for a counter-attack by the 1/1st Cambs had come. O.C. "B" Company was ordered to move West of the Wieltje – St. Julien raod, to cross the river Steenbeek West of St. Julien and to counter attack the enemy's right flank. By this action it was

---

[255] National Archives, War Diary 118th Brigade WO95/2588/89
[256] Of the tanks operating with 118th Brigade the "Gladiator", "Gravedigger" and "Gloster" advanced as far forward as Springfield on the Langemarck – Zonnebeke road in support of the infantry.

hoped (1) to relieve the pressure on the 1/1st Herts and 1/6th Cheshire. (2) to protect the right rear of the Black Watch. (3) to save St. Julien. (4) to allow the retiring Herts to reform…12:12 p.m. The enemy (strength about one battalion) attacked "D" Company and the right of "A" Company from the direction of Springfield and Winnipeg. This attack was beaten off by rifle and machine gun fire, but a number of the enemy reached the Winnipeg – St. Julien road where they obtained good cover about 50 yards in advance of our trenches…12:40 p.m. The enemy attempted to assault our position but were driven back with heavy losses by rifle, L.G. and M.G. fire. ..During this period enemy reinforcements were seen coming from Springfield to the Northern end of St.Julien…1:15 p.m. A strong enemy attack developed from Wurst Farm to Vancouver. "B" Company and two platoons of "C" Company were driven back from the Northern houses of St. Julien to the left bank of the Steenbeek where they consolidated with the survivors of the 1/1st Herts…Ammunition was now running short.'[257] The actions of the Cambridge had for the moment checked the enemy counter-attacks, intent on throwing the British back across the Steenbeek. But so far these had been made only by local reserve regiments, initially held behind the Passchendaele ridge, the supports of the divisions holding the front line. The *Eingreif* divisions had not yet come into action.

 The 39th Division had succeeded in linking the main attack in Fifth Army centre with the defensive northern flank. The ruins of St. Julien had initially been cleared with little opposition and the muddy shell-broken Steenbeek had been readily forded. Small parties of British infantry had, as ordered, reached the third objective. A few had advanced beyond the Zonnebeke – Langemarck road, a platoon of the 2nd Lancs Fusiliers and a small party of the Liverpool Scottish having reached Gravenstafel ridge, and the party of the 1/6th Cheshire at von Tirpitz Farm. They had complied with the plan which had expected them to pass 1,500 yards beyond the Steenbeek. But they were in pathetically small numbers, and except for those few 18-pounders which had already been brought forward to the old British front line, were beyond the effective range of their field artillery batteries. At St. Julien, they had already fought-off a serious counter-attack, but the main German effort was still to come. The dangers inherent in the Fifth Army plan were soon to become all too obvious.

51st (Highland) Division[258]
Major-General G. M. Harper

The 51st Highland Division was to attack along a front of approximately 1,600 yards between Canadian Farm, (within the German Front Line) to just north of Lancashire Farm (behind the British line), which reduced to around 1,200 yards at the Steenbeek, and was to use the 152nd and 153rd Brigades in the attack. Each brigade was to attack on a two battalion front, the two front battalions to capture the Blue Line, with the two support battalions to pass through and

---

[257] National Archives, War Diary 1/1st Cambridge WO/95/2590
[258] The area just behind the 51st Division front had for many days been under severe enemy bombardment. The support lines between Turco Farm and Lancashire Farm were regularly pounded by German artillery as were forward headquarters in the dug-out positions along the canal bank. The division's centres of command and communication were shelled to the extent that movement was very dangerous, and casualties even in the dug-outs were inevitable. Shells of all calibres were fired, some of 11-inch smashing into the canal banks and reducing the positions along them to a shambles. The front line also received its share of shelling, on one occasion 200 trench-mortar bombs being fired into the trenches on one battalion front alone.
In an attempt to disrupt and confuse the enemy a Chinese attack was carried out at 5:00.a.m. on the 28th July, in which a feint attack from the British lines, opened by a creeping bombardment by the field artillery and the hoisting of dummies above the parapet, resulted in the Germans deploying in their forward positions only to be smitten by the 18-pounders as the barrage quickly returned. Major F.W. Bewsher (1921) *The History of the 51st (Highland) Division* Edinburgh: William Blackwood

capture the Green Line. The 154th Brigade was to be held in divisional reserve and not initially to be engaged.

In the centre of the divisional front the British lines bulged eastwards around the ruins of Turco Farm. The advance was to be across a featureless waste of cratered earth, initially up a slight slope, the German forward positions on Pilckem ridge being no higher than five metres above the British lines, the term ridge here being somewhat of a misnomer. The German Second Line ran along the eastern side of the ridge, midway between the Front Line and the Steenbeek, the stream being between 3,000 and 3,500 yards from the British Front Line. The division would have to overcome numerous strong points and bunkers, and fortified farm ruins in both the forward zone and the battle zone before it reached its objective. On the left flank, towards Langemarck, the German Third Line ran away to the north-west 1,750 yards beyond the Steenbeek and around 5,000 yards from the British lines. To moderate the distance of the advance the division's third objective, the Green Line, was therefore drawn back on the left flank. The objective on the right was on the Steenbeek, and on the left some 800 hundreds yards short of the stream near Varna Farm.

The division had a larger than average allocation of Vickers machine guns, 112 guns available for the attack, a fourth machine gun company having recently increased the strength, as had 48 guns from 11th Division.[259] The 8 tanks of "G" Battalion were to operate with the division in two waves, 4 tanks against the Black Line and 4 against the Green Line. As an aid to direction and to suppress the German forward area, at the moment of the attack 206 drums of burning oil were to be launched from Livens projectors towards the German support and reserve lines, and three minutes after zero 150 Thermit shells were to be fired into Fort Caledonia in the enemy support line on Pilckem ridge.[260]

152nd Brigade[261]
The 1/5th Seaforth Highlanders and the 1/8th Argyll and Sutherland Highlanders attacked in the first wave to the Blue Line, with the 1/6th Gordon Highlanders and the 1/6th Seaforth in support to attack the Black and Green Lines. The German artillery was slow in retaliating, and not until ten minutes after Zero did it crash down, doing but little harm mainly on or behind the British Front Line. The ground was very heavy and the going difficult, made more so by the mass of water filled shell-holes. The German Front Line was found to be virtually obliterated by the

---

[259] The guns were arranged with 64 firing three successive barrages covering the ground in front of the Blue, Black and Green Lines, 16 under orders of the Brigadiers to support consolidation, and 32 kept in reserve.

[260] The Livens projector, created by the British army officer Captain William H. Livens, Royal Engineers, was a large-bore steel mortar tube around three feet long. Usually arranged in batteries of 20 or more, the tubes were buried in the ground and inclined at an angle of approximately 45 degrees towards the enemy trenches. The closed end of the cylinder was spherical and located into a spherical depression in a separate circular steel plate which, buried beneath the tube, absorbed the recoil on firing so preventing the tube pushing deeper into the ground. A charge in the base of the cylinder was fired electrically enabling the whole battery to be released simultaneously, each tube launching a large drum, containing usually 30-lbs of liquid phosgene, or oil, through a high arc trajectory for a range of up to one mile. A bursting charge blast the drum open soon after impact, either releasing and igniting the oil, or emitting liquid phosgene which then vaporized into gas. The weapon was detested by the enemy. See: Albert Palazzo (2002), *Seeking Victory on the Western Front: The British Army and Chemical Warfare in World War I.* University of Nebraska Press p103. United States Department of War. (1942) *Livens Projector M1* TM 3-325. Unexploded drums and rusty base-plates are not an uncommon find on the battlefield today. The launch tubes are also a common sight, filled with concrete and still used as rollers, or set in the ground as bollards and posts.

[261] National Archives, War Diary 152nd Brigade WO95/2862, National Archives, War Diary 1/5th Seaforth WO95/2866, National Archives, War Diary 1/6th Seaforth WO95/2867

British shell-fire.[262] As the attack waves worked towards the Blue Line they met with some opposition, engaging strong-points with Lewis gun and rifle grenade and skilfully overwhelming the resistance. Mopping-up parties accounted for many Germans sheltering in shell holes and dug-outs.

At the Blue Line the 1/5th Seaforth and the Argyll began digging-in and improving shell-holes, and after the pause in the barrage the Gordons and 1/6th Seaforth took up the advance across the increasingly heavy ground. The nature of the fighting now changed as the attacking infantry were soon confronted by the machine guns of the concrete bunker defences, which it became clear, the artillery had failed to reduced. The Gordons were held up by machine gun fire from Ascot Cottage 600 short of the Black Line. Signals for tank assistance were answered by tank G.43 which trundled forward, silenced one machine gun and encouraged the crews of two others to surrender, 12 Germans being either killed or captured. The heavy going and maze of shell-holes resulted in the tanks of the first echelon reaching the Black line mostly behind the infantry. By 5:15 a.m. with the advance proceeding to plan, orders were passed to the field artillery for two batteries to move forward to positions close to the old Front Line, a most arduous task for the gunners, across the muddy and cratered fields while under fire. Near the Black Line at Hurst Park, between Canon and Canister Trenches, machine gun fire from two concrete bunkers checked the advance, the highlanders taking cover from the searching fire in shell-holes. The infantry signal for tank assistance was answered by tank G.44 which slowly manoeuvred across the muddy ground, crushing wire and earthworks in it path and attacked the bunkers. The garrison quickly surrendered, and two other machine gun crews were forced to retire. Just beyond the large Gournier Farm bunker a section of Canister Trench was entered from each end by half a platoon of the Seaforth, which bombed down the trench killing or capturing the whole garrison.

By 7:45 a.m. a general forward movement by all arms was underway, some of the field artillery already established and firing from about the old British Front Line. Stokes mortar teams had laboured to carry 108 pounds of gun tube, base-plate and bipod, and ammunition forward, ready to support the next advance.[263] The Vickers machine gun crews man-handled their cumbersome 110-pound weapons, gun, tripod, water container and ammunition boxes, across the muddy ground up the slope of Pilckem ridge, in order to advance the machine gun barrage.[264]

Fighting was still in progress to mop-up the Black and Black Outpost Line as the 1/6th Seaforth and 1/6th Gordons continued the advance towards the Green Line, the troops detailed to carry forward the attack inevitably getting involved in the close-quarter fighting. A platoon of the Gordons was detailed to assist two platoons of the Seaforth who were pinned down by vicious machine gun fire from strong-points at Macdonald's Farm and Macdonald's Wood 200 yards behind the farm. The Gordons engaged the enemy in the wood in enfilade with rifle and Lewis gun fire. Tank G.50 had already accounted for the surrender of three strong points in its advance. It now proceeded to attack Macdonald's Farm and after firing 6 six-pounder rounds, accompanied by a shower of rifle grenades from the two infantry platoons, the stunned garrison

---

[262] At the time of the assault, the *392nd Regiment* holding the forward zone were in process of relief by the *Lehr Regiment* of the *3rd Guard Division*.

[263] The 3-inch Stokes mortar was a simple but ingenious light support mortar, consisting of a 51-inch long, 3-inch bore barrel tube (43-pounds), base-plate (28 pounds), and bipod (37 pounds). The mortar fired a 'rolling-pin' shaped high explosive shell weighing 11 pounds over a maximum range of 800 yards. The shell, containing around 2 ¼ pounds of explosive, was fired by dropping it into the tube, when a shotgun-like blank cartridge was detonated as it struck a firing pin on the base-plate, then igniting propellant rings fitted to the round.

[264] The Vickers machine gun weighed around 30 pounds, the tripod 50 pound, 250 round ammunition box 22 pounds, plus 7½ pints of water in the cooling jacket and the condenser water container. With an effective range of 800 to 1,000 yards, the gun could fire indirect barrages up to 4,500 yards at a rate of 450-600 .303-inch rounds per minute. See Ian Hogg and John Batchelor (1976) *Weapons & War Machines*. London: Phoebus, p 62.

of 70 evacuated the bunker, and stumbled into captivity. A 4.2-inch (105mm) howitzer and two machine guns were also taken, and many German dead lay around the farm as evidence of the bitter fighting. Enemy machine gunners at Ferdinand Farm held up the advance once more, 500 yards west of the Steenbeek, until tank G.43 ground forward, crushed the outer defences, silenced the machine guns and scattered enemy infantry from surrounding shell-holes. Sergeant A. Edwards of the 1/6th Seaforth, lead his men against a machine gun position, killing the crew and capturing the gun. Although twice wounded he continued to fight forward with the advance, encouraging the men with him and assisting in the consolidation, for which action he was to be awarded the V.C.

The brigade pressed on towards the Steenbeek, and as they approached the stream machine gun fire from Maison Bulgare on the eastern bank became severe, cutting down many of the Gordons. It was clear that all the foot-bridge crossings over the stream were swept by well aimed machine gun fire. The proposed fording of the Steenbeek by a company of the 1/6th Seaforth to establish a bridgehead outpost around Maison du Rasta was postponed, the company digging-in 100 yards southwest of the stream. Private G. Mc Intosh of the 1/6th Gordons crossed the muddy Steenbeek without orders and armed with only a revolver and a Mills grenade, worked round behind a machine gun pit, killed the crew with the grenade, and returned across the stream with two light machine guns, an act for which he was to be awarded the V.C.

As the companies detailed to consolidate the Green Line west of the stream approached the Steenbeek, heavy fire from the other bank raked their lines. By short rushes between shell-holes, Lewis guns were worked forward and set up to sweep the far bank, and a tank was called up to give covering fire.[265] This support subdued the hostile machine gun fire sufficiently to enable the Gordons and Seaforth to dig-in and occupy shell-holes 250 yards short of the stream at around 7:30. The line dug amongst the craters by the Gordons was observed by low flying German aircraft, prompting the company commander to move his front line 100 yards forward and his support line 100 yards back. Shortly after the completion of this movement an enemy barrage descended on his original position.

153rd Brigade[266]

The 1/7th Gordons and 1/7th Black Watch attacked in the first wave of 153rd Brigade, the Gordons having a stiff fight in taking the blockhouse at Hindenburg Farm before reaching the Blue Line. The highlanders attacked in the well practiced way with Lewis gun and rifle grenade and the position was soon taken, ten of the enemy being killed or wounded and an uninjured officer and 22 men being taken prisoner. The Blue line was reached up to time and the 1/7th Gordons and 1/7th Black Watch had begun to consolidate before the supporting wave reached the line.

As the barrage thickened and lifted towards the Black Line the advance was continued by the 1/5th Gordons and the 1/6th Black Watch, which walked forward slowly into stiffening opposition. The 1/6th Black Watch had already suffered casualties, when at 30 minutes before zero they had been caught in a German barrage as they lay out in their assembly positions behind the British Front Line. Again while waiting for the barrage to advance from the Blue Line they had been swept by machine gun fire from the Gournier Farm blockhouse. As the barrage lifted No.1 platoon worked towards the farm, and working from shell-hole to shell-hole under punishing machine gun fire, engaged the enemy gun teams with Lewis gun and rifle grenade. Others meanwhile worked around the flanks and crept up and overwhelmed the garrison with bombs, taking 20 prisoners and capturing two machine guns and a field gun. The 1/5th Gordons

---

[265] At 28 pounds the air-cooled Lewis gun was just light enough to be carried by one man and on occasions was fired from the hip. More usually supported by a small bipod the gun could fire 550 .303-inch rounds per minute from a cam driven 47 round shallow drum magazine fitted on top of the action.

[266] National Archives, War Diary 153rd Brigade WO95/2872/73, War Diary 7th Black Watch WO95/2879, War Diary 5th Gordon WO95/2881

were confronted by machine guns in a row of pillboxes in front of the Black Line, but these were rushed, the crews bombed, and the guns speedily silenced. On the right flank of the Gordons attack, a pocket of Germans resisted stubbornly, but parties of both Gordons and Black Watch, supported by a Stokes mortar team and covered by Lewis guns overwhelmed the position, where the trench the enemy had held was found to be choked with dead, most of whom had been shot. About 100 prisoners were taken in the same action.

On the Black Line, near Cane Trench just northeast of Gournier Farm, tank "Gog" responded to a call for help from the infantry held up by a strong point, which the tank proceeded to attack, 60 of the enemy being taken prisoner. By 6:40 a.m. an outpost line in front of the Black Line had been established along the brigade front. In the advance towards the Green Line machine gun fire from pillboxes in Crane Wood and from Rudolphe Farm caused heavy casualties, until outflanked and silenced by platoons of the 1/6th Black Watch, (the latter in conjunction with a platoon of the 15th Welsh), 70 prisoners being taken. Searching machine gun fire from another bunker at Francois Farm 500 yards further east and from a blockhouse in a cemetery just behind the farm caused more casualties and delay, before being overrun by the Black Watch assisted by the 1/5th Gordons, three machine guns, 4 officers and 140 other ranks being captured. Varna Farm on the far left of the brigade front was taken in cooperation with the 38th Division.

By 7:30 a.m. the platoons detailed to take the Green Line, their numbers much depleted, consolidated a line amongst the shell-holes just west of the Steenbeek, in touch with 39th Division on the right and 38th Division on the left. At 10:30 a.m. a reconnaissance of the Green Line by Lieut.-Colonel Booth of the 1/6th Black Watch, indicated that a crossing of the Steenbeek was now possible and 30 to 40 men of "D" Company rushed the stream and crossed by a bridge just north of the Military Road. Four outposts were set up in shell-holes east of the stream and just north of the road. After hard and costly fighting against numerous bunkers and fortified positions, 51st Division had on the right reached its third objective, whilst on the left having advanced around 3,500 yards, to within a short distance of the Steenbeek, was well forward of its third objective, with a company over the stream north of Maison du Rasta. With the Steenbeek providing a reasonable defensive position the division was well placed to fight off any counter-attack, although some way beyond reliable field artillery protection.

The actions of the 24 tanks of "G" Battalion of the I Tank Brigade operating with the XVIII Corps had been most successful assisting the infantry at many points and losing only 2 tanks knocked out and one tank ditched.

German forces facing XVIII and XIV Corps
The 39th, 51st, 38th and Guards Divisions of the XVIII and XIV Corps were faced by approximately 4 German regiments in the line: *455th Regiment* of the *235th Division*, the *392nd* and *100th Regiments* of the *23rd Reserve Division* (in process of being relieved by the *Lehr., 9th Grenadier,* and *Guard Fusilier Regiments* of the *3rd Guards Division*), and the *73rd Fusilier Regiment* of the *111th Division*. These divisions had two regiments in the line and one regiment in reserve behind the *Flandern I* Line. Each regiment in the line had one battalion in the forward zone, one in support about the Second (*Albrecht*) Line and the third in reserve behind the Third (*Wilhelm*) Line.[267]

XIV Corps
Lieutenant -General Earl of Cavan

The task of XIV Corps was, with the French First Army to their left, to form a northern defensive flank to the main attack, using the 38th (Welsh) Division, and the Guards Division. The Corps was to attack on a frontage of around 3,000 yards from just north of Lancashire Farm, to the bend in the Ypres – Yser canal 1,200 yards north of the bridge of the Ypres – Staden railway. From the

---

[267] National Archives, maps showing distribution of enemy forces on 29th and 31st July in WO153/601

far left of the Corps front, to a point nearly 500 yards south of the railway bridge over the canal, the opposing front lines were dug along either bank, the breastworks being no more than 60 yards apart. From this point the lines parted from the canal banks and ran in a south-easterly direction beginning the long arc around the Salient.

The distance between the front lines and the German Third Line increased towards the north, giving XIV Corps the greatest distance to cover to reach the third objective. The track bed of the Ypres – Staden railway formed the centreline of the Corps frontage, and heading directly towards Langemarck, provided a perfect aid to direction. The attack was to pass through the hamlet of Pilckem (from which the slight and unimpressive ridge gained its name), the ruins of which were incorporated within the *Albrecht Stellung,* 1,700 yards east of the canal. Although the elevation on this northern part of the ridge reached no more than 22 metres above sea level, by standing on the Langemarck road in Pilckem hamlet and looking due south, it was possible to see directly into Ypres. Such was the German advantage of observation. Beyond Pilckem to the east the ground dipped slightly into the shallow lowlands across which meandered the Steenbeek, 3,750 yards from the front lines and 700 yards beyond the third objective. The shattered remains of the large village of Langemarck lay 1,000 yards beyond the Steenbeek, the *Wilhelm Stellung* or German Third Line being a further 1,000 yards beyond the village to the north-east. The ground beyond the ridge, especially that north of the railway presented a generally flat and featureless but shell-pocked landscape, between 10 and 15 metres above sea level, declining imperceptibly downstream along the Steenbeek, until at a point 4,000 yards to the northeast of Langemark the stream flowed into the southern extremity of the inundations near St. Janshoek.

The usual pattern of German defences had been constructed, including bunkers built into the low railway embankments, but the corps began with an advantage; the Guards Division as we have seen having already occupied the German forward positions east of the canal.

38th (Welsh) Division[268]
Major-General G. C. Blackadder

The division's 1,700 yard front, which narrowed to 1,400 yards towards the Steenbeek, was clearly defined by the track of the Ypres – Staden railway to the left, and was to be attacked by the 114th Brigade and 113th Brigade, with the 115th Brigade to pass through and establish a bridgehead across the Steenbeek. The division had been unfairly criticised by Haig after its bloody actions at Mametz Wood on the Somme, just over a year before. It had taken a long time to recover from its losses which had amounted to 190 officers and 3,803 other ranks, and was about to prove its capabilities and lay low its doubters.

114th Brigade[269]
Moving off with the barrage the 10th and 13th Battalions of the Welsh Regiment secured the Blue Line with little problem, although some Germans put up a fight from dugouts in Caesar's Support trench. The 10th and 13th Welsh began to dug-in on the first objective, and as the barrage thickened and lifted towards the Black Line, two companies of the 15th and 14th Welsh Regiment passed through behind the covering smoke screen to continue the advance, but soon came under intense fire from blockhouses which had not been affected by the barrage. The right flank were swept by machine gun fire from a blockhouse at Rudolphe Farm, which was attacked in the well practiced fashion and overrun by a platoon of the 15th Welsh in conjunction with 1/6th Black Watch of 153rd Brigade. As the advance progressed the two companies of the 14th Welsh met with stiffening resistance. The enemy put up a stout fight from the defences in the rubble of Pilckem and along the Langemarck road, where the ruins of many buildings had been fortified and from which came bursts of machine gun fire. Beyond Pilckem near the Iron Cross crossroads heavy losses were incurred by the 14th Welsh. There was heavy fighting before the

---

[268] Lieut.-Colonel J.E. Munby Ed. (1920) *A History of the 38th (Welsh) Division* London: Hugh Rees
[269] National Archives, War Diary 114th Brigade WO95/2558

strongly defended position and pillboxes were overcome, 20 of the garrison being killed, 40 taken prisoners, and three machine guns captured. The Black Line was taken by 6:00 a.m. and consolidation had begun on the outpost line when at 7:15 the two remaining companies of the 14th and 15th Welsh Regiment continued the advance behind the barrage to attack the Green Line, across ground which became progressively heavier towards the Steenbeek.

113th Brigade[270]

The Blue Line was to be taken by the two forward companies of the 13th and 16th Royal Welsh Fusiliers, at which point the remaining two companies were to pass through to attack the Black Line. Machine guns in concrete emplacements in Pilckem were successfully attacked by the 13th Royal Welsh Fusiliers. Corporal James Llewellyn Davies advancing through the barrage single-handedly attacked a machine gun post, killing one of the team and bringing in another with the captured gun. Then although wounded he led a bombing party in an attack against a defended house, gallant acts for which he was to be awarded the V.C.[271] As the advance continued beyond Pilckem, heavy machine gun fire from the railway embankment raked the lines of the 16th advancing on the left flank, causing severe casualties especially in officers. At 7:15 a.m., as the barrage lifted towards the Green Line, the 15th Royal Welsh Fusiliers passed through the forward companies of the 13th and 16th and immediately came under heavy machine gun fire from Battery Copse near the railway, where again many officers became casualties. Through a combination of this machine gun fire, hostile artillery fire and heavy ground, the barrage crept far ahead of the Welshmen, but the advance was maintained and the objective was gained by a series of short rushes by the 15th Royal Welsh Fusiliers. The Fusiliers then joined with the 14th and 15th Welsh Regiment of 114th Brigade in digging-in on the Green Line.

115th Brigade[272]

As the 114th and 113th Brigades advanced east of Iron Cross towards the Green Line, the 11th South Wales Borderers and 17th Royal Welsh Fusiliers of 115th Brigade moved up from the Blue Line where they had assembled, to the east side of Pilckem ridge. Here they were to organise behind the Green Line and at 8:00 a.m. advance towards the Steenbeek to establish a bridgehead.

The 11th S.W.B. on the right flank reached the stream in good time at 9:53 a.m. and proceeded to ford the muddy bed, successfully attacking three strong points, including a bunker in an old inn, Au Bon Gite, 200 yards from the stream beside the Langemarck road. In this action Sergeant Ivor Rees, 11th South Wales Borderers, rushed a machine gun from 20 yards and killed the crew. He then attacked a large concrete shelter and bombed out the garrison killing 5, capturing 30, and an undamaged machine gun. For his gallantry and initiative he was to be awarded the V.C.

On the left the 17th R.W. Fusiliers had a more arduous advance being raked by machine gun fire from the dug-outs along the railway embankment, and pinned down as the barrage crept relentlessly forward. Working forward slowly without artillery support and after a costly struggle with defended positions in ruined houses along the Langemarck road, the battalion reached the Steenbeek around 12:30 p.m. with its strength reduced to 4 officers and 200 other ranks. The losses sustained by 115th Brigade in the advance to the Steenbeek were severe, to the extent that one company of the 10th South Wales Borderers moved up to reinforce the 11th on the eastern bank of the stream, and one company of the 16th Welsh to reinforce the 17th Royal Welsh Fusiliers.

The 38th Division had accomplished a successful but costly advance of nearly 4,000 yards, while being badly held up on the left by the bunkers undamaged by the British bombardment along the Staden railway, and the fortified ruins along the Pilckem - Langemarck

---

[270] National Archives, War Diary 113th Brigade WO95/2553
[271] He later died of wounds received in the action.
[272] National Archives, War Diary 115th Brigade WO95/2560

road. By mid-day it was on all of its objectives, with the South Wales Borderers pushed across the Steenbeek in front of Langemarck.

Guards Division[273]

On the far left of the British line, the Guards Division were to attack on a 1,400 yard front with the track of the Ypres – Staden defining their right flank. The Ypres – Yser canal had been successfully crossed on the 27th July, and the German front and support lines, up to depth of 850 yards had been occupied. The leading battalions of the 2nd and 3rd Guards Brigades would wait until Zero+ 34 minutes for the forward creep of the 38th Division barrage to advance the 850 yards on the right, before their own barrage descended on the German line, at which point they would begin their advance to the Black Line. The 1st Guards Brigade in support was to move through the 2nd and 3rd Brigades and continue the advance to the Steenbeek.

As the British barrage thundered forward south of their assembly positions the Guardsmen could do no more than anxiously count down the 34 minutes before their turn came to move. Although the enemy knew their positions, the German artillery when it struck at the Guards line did so with little ferocity.

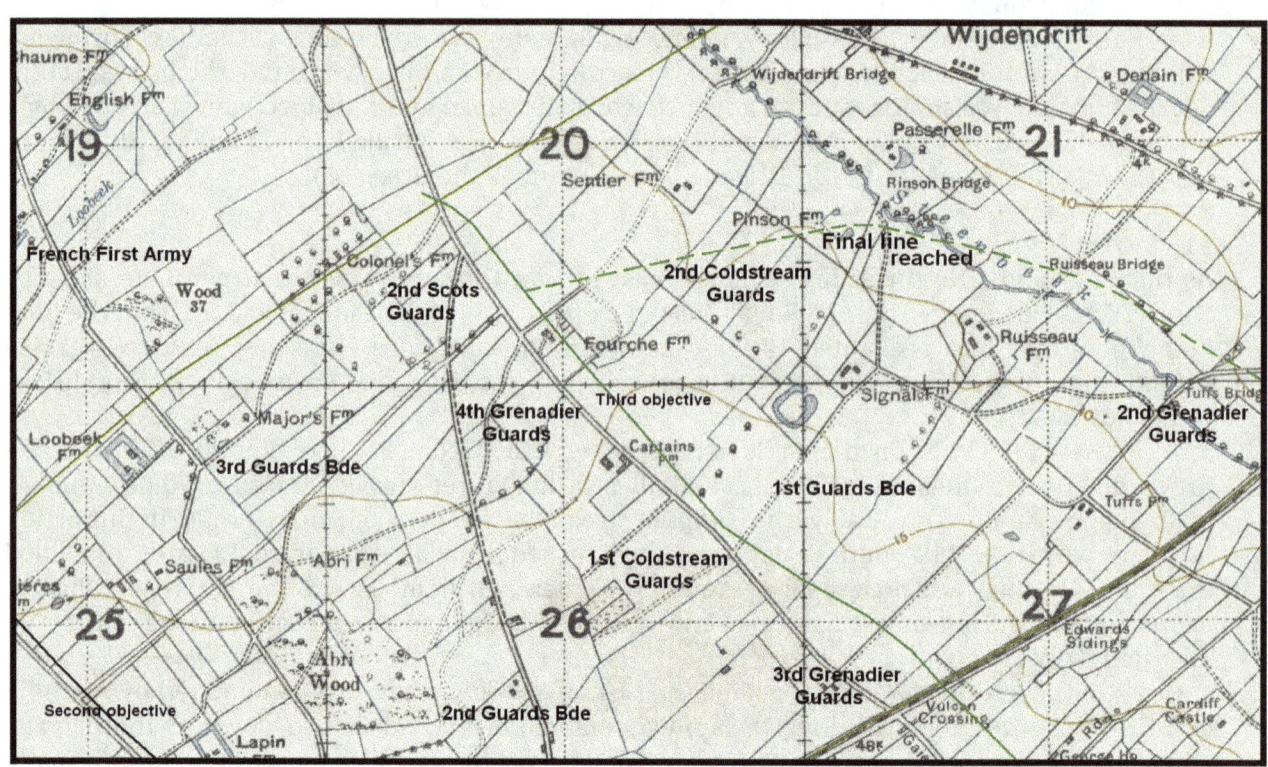

2nd and 3rd Guards Brigades to Green Line - 1st Guards Brigade to Green Dotted Line

2nd Guards Brigade[274]

At 4:24 a.m. with the 38th Division coming up on their right, the 1st Scots Guards and 2nd Irish Guards attacked towards the dim, low rise of Pilckem Ridge. Within fifteen minutes, after facing little opposition they were beginning to consolidate in front of Caribou Trench in the old German Second Line which was here the first objective, in touch with the 16th Royal Welsh Fusiliers on their right. As they commenced to dig-in, the Scots Guards, alarmingly, came under heavy machine gun fire from the rear, which caused many casualties. Well concealed enemy shelters in the scrub of Artillery Wood had been overlooked and not mopped-up in the advance,

---

[273] Cuthbert Headlam (1924) *The History of the Guards Division in the Great War 1915-1918* London: John Murray National Archives, War Diary Guards Division WO95/1193
[274] National Archives, War Diary 2nd Guards Brigade WO95/1218

and on being passed over had come into action. Once the enemy machine gun team had opened fire the position was exposed and was quickly knocked enabling consolidation of the first objective to proceed.

Soon after 5:00 a.m. as the barrage commenced its forward lift, the supporting companies of the Scots and Irish Guards continued the short 500 yard advance towards the Black Line. The Scots had little trouble, overcoming some resistance from German machine gunners in shell-holes. The Irish however came under heavy enfilade machine gun fire from their right in Hey Wood, the enemy taking advantage of a gap in the British barrage to bring their guns into action. A determined defence by the *73rd (Hanoverian) Fusilier Regiment* was gradually overwhelmed by the Irish Guards which captured the colonel and adjutant of the regiment, 4 machine guns, 2 trench mortars. In their advance to the Black Line they had killed or captured many Germans, the objective being reached by 6:00 a.m. Tragically the battalion commander of 2nd Irish Guards, Lieutenant -Colonel E. B. Greer had been killed during the advance.

The support battalions of the brigade, 3rd Grenadier Guards and 1st Coldstream Guards left their assembly trenches west of the canal around 5:00 a.m. by which time German shelling of the canal area had become severe. Crossing the canal was a lengthy process, made worse by the destruction of some of the wooden bridges. The crossing was accomplished without major incident, the two battalions moving up towards Pilckem ridge and then on to the Black Line in artillery formation, their casualties surprisingly few. At 7:15 as the barrage thickened and crept forward once more the support companies of both battalions began the advance to the Green Line. The 3rd Grenadiers which had already supported the Scots Guards in the capture of the second objective were struck in enfilade by concentrated bursts of machine gun fire from a blockhouse in the north side of the low railway embankment. The right company were pinned down and required reinforcement in their attack on the strong-point, which was supported by Lewis gun fire from the left. After causing the Guards many casualties the blockhouse was eventually overcome, three officers, 52 other ranks, and four machine guns being captured in the process. Fire from the blockhouse had also held up the advance of the 38th Division on the other side of the embankment south of the railway. The enemy were gradually driven out of their strong-points and fell-back on both sides of the embankment, and by 8:00 a.m. the Guards and the Welsh joined up near Vulcan Crossing, on the Guards third objective, 850 yards short of the Steenbeek. The left support battalion, 1st Coldstream Guards, a company of which had assisted the Irish Guards in their attack on the Black Line, extended their left to support the 4th Grenadiers of 3rd Guards Brigade, held up in front of Abri Wood. Private Thomas Whitham 1st Coldstream Guards, on his own initiative worked around a machine gun enfilading the 4th Grenadiers on the left, and working from shell-hole to shell-hole whilst under heavy fire he captured the gun, an officer, and two other ranks, an act for which he was later awarded the V.C. During their advance the 1st Coldstream had captured many prisoners, several machine guns and had seized a field gun in a concrete emplacement on the third objective.

By 8:00 a.m. and on time, the 2nd Guards Brigade was on the whole of its objective, the Green Line on the Kortekeer Cabaret road, and as the Welsh fought their way forward, was soon to be in touch with the 15th Royal Welsh Fusiliers on the right.

3rd Guards Brigade[275]

At 4:24 a.m. 3rd Guards Brigade advanced to the left of 2nd Guards Brigade towards the slight hump of 20 metre hill. Before the advance began, 1st Grenadier Guards on the brigade right had suffered some casualties from shelling, including a company commander. On moving forward on the left, 1st Welsh Guards were hit by machine gun fire from blockhouses in Wood 15. Sergeant Robert James Bye, on his own initiative rushed one of the blockhouses and bombed out the occupants. The thorough training in attacking bunkers was put into practice as the Guards manoeuvred to outflank the hostile machine guns, which the Lewis gunners and rifle grenadiers held under fire as the bombing parties crept in. Subsequently after the attack had moved on

---

[275] National Archives, War Diary 3rd Guards Brigade WO95/1222

Sergeant Bye volunteered to take charge of a party to clear out other blockhouses, which he did, showing remarkable initiative and taking many prisoners. For his actions he was to be awarded the V.C. By 5:00 a.m. the 3rd Guards Brigade had reached the first objective, in close touch with the French to their left, having killed wounded or captured around 150 of the enemy.

The distance to the second objective was less for the 3rd Guards Brigade than it was for the 2nd, and the advance to the Black Line was achieved by the support companies of both battalions with little hindrance from the enemy, a troublesome machine gun post on the right of the Grenadiers being silenced by a few Stokes mortar rounds.

The 4th Grenadier Guards and 2nd Scots Guards, to continue the advance to the third objective, had crossed the canal successfully with the support battalions of 2nd Guards Brigade, and had advanced in artillery formation beneath a severe hostile barrage east of the canal, through which they had passed practically unscathed. Upon reaching the Black Line, which the 1st Grenadier Guards and 1st Welsh Guards were consolidating, they deployed into shell-holes waiting for the moment the barrage lifted towards the Green Line. Whilst deploying the 4th Grenadier Guards came under heavy enemy machine gun fire from Abri Wood 300 yards forward. Under cover of a smoke barrage, support from Stokes mortars, and with the assistance of parties of the 1st Coldstream to their right, the Grenadiers outflanked and closed in upon the machine gun positions, most of the gun teams surrendering before the bombing parties reached them. The blockhouse at Abri Farm just behind the wood was also taken, where 3 trench mortars were captured. The 2nd Scots Guards on the left advancing in close touch with the 201st French Regiment overwhelmed the blockhouse at Major's Farm capturing 2 field guns and about 50 prisoners. Both battalions pressed on towards the Green Line, the Grenadiers taking the blockhouses at Fourche Farm and Captain's Farm on the Kortekeer Cabaret road, and then began digging-in and consolidating the objective at around 8:00 a.m. A company of 1st Grenadiers assisted in the consolidation, which by 2:00 p.m. was complete and effectively wired. Although initially touch had been kept with the French on the left, the 201st Regiment had been held up by a blockhouse at Colonel's Farm 400 yards short of the Green Line, and the 2nd Scots Guards threw back a defensive left flank to cover this part of the line.[276]

1st Guards Brigade[277]

To push forward from the Green Line to the Steenbeek was the task given to the 1st Guards Brigade. Upon reaching the stream they were to seize the crossings and the 2nd Grenadier Guards on the right were cross over and establish an outpost line 200 yards north-east of the bank. On the left 2nd Coldstream Guards were to reach the Steenbeek and then wheel left to face north and throw back a flank to conform to the French line. The two battalions had marched from their rear assembly areas at 4:00 a.m. and by 6:00 had successfully crossed the canal, reaching the Green Line just after it had been secured. The German barrage was continually shortening its range and forward movement of the Grenadiers was performed more safely by carefully timing the lifts, shelter being taken in shell holes between moves. At 8:50 a.m. the British barrage lifted towards the Steenbeek, but as some of the guns were already on their way forward towards the old British front line, it was noticeably thinner. To further hamper the advance the German resistance from the numerous fortified farms and blockhouses west of the Steenbeek now became intense, machine gun and rifle fire increasing drastically. On the right the Grenadier Guards were swept by a hail of machine gun fire from blockhouses south of the railway. These positions would have been taken but for the hold up of the 17th Royal Welsh Fusiliers about the Green Line, where they were still fighting for the stubbornly held ruined houses along the Langemarck road. This fire checked the Grenadier right company which of necessity took shelter in shell-holes and lost the protection of the barrage. Parties worked forward on the right by rushes, using the cover of shell-holes, supported by Lewis gun and rifle fire, and established a defensive flank facing the railway and the hostile fire. Having finally

---

[276] 3rd Brigade had captured 102 prisoners during the advance including men from *76th Regiment* and from the *73rd Fusilier Regiment*.
[277] National Archives, War Diary 1st Guards Brigade WO95/1214

knocked out the bunkers along the Langemarck road the Welsh Fusiliers came up around 12:30 p.m. driving the Germans from their positions south of the railway, and securing the Grenadiers right flank.

The Grenadiers continued the advance towards the Steenbeek coming under intense shelling and machine gun fire from the bunkers in the ruins of Langemarck and from blockhouses just east of the Langemarck- Wijdendrift road 400 yards beyond the stream. The fire, from many different directions, proved so intense and caused such severe casualties that the right company of the Grenadiers were forced to dig-in 80 yards short of the stream, which was their final objective. This position however gave them a reasonable field of fire for the Lewis guns, covering the enemy positions across the Steenbeek. The left leading company with the assistance of their support company, having taken the blockhouses at Signal and Ruisseau Farms, where thirty prisoners including a battalion commander were captured, forced a crossing of the Steenbeek and by 9:30 a.m. were digging outposts 80 yards beyond the eastern bank. The 2nd Grenadier Guards were by this time, except for the slight check just north of the railway, in possession of the greater part of their objective. On the left the 2nd Coldstream Guards had reached their objective with little opposition, in touch with the Grenadiers on their right, and had succeeded in making the difficult wheel to face north. On their left, they were not in touch with the French until after 2:30 p.m. by which time the 201st Regiment had moved up after clearing Colonel's Farm.

The Grenadier outposts east of the Steenbeek came under heavy sniping and machine gun fire from pillboxes along the line of the Langemarck – Weidendreft road which remained strongly held by the enemy.[278] The British artillery barrage was by this time noticeably thin and ragged, and the intention to push out patrols towards the road was abandoned. The new position was consolidated as quickly as possible and the machine guns which had been brought forward were set up in pre-planned positions, on the Green Line, on the railway at Vulcan Crossing, and near the Steenbeek to cover the new line. The 55th and 76th Field Companies Royal Engineers, each sent forward two sections with a carrying party of 100 Guardsmen to wire the Green Line, and a further two sections with a carrying part of 80 to wire the final objective on the Steenbeek.[279]

French First Army on the left defensive flank

The French, attacked with two divisions of its I Corps on a 3,000 yards frontage which reached as far north as Steenstraat on the canal, and supported admirably by its excellent artillery made good progress. Initially checked on the right at the wood about Colonel's Farm, it was by 2:30 p.m., in touch on the Guards left and had secured the defensive northern flank up to the outskirts of Bixschoote. An attempt at 9:00 p.m. in pouring rain, to push forward the centre to the cross-roads at Kortekeer Cabaret was unsuccessful.

Forward movement of the artillery and cavalry

The artillery plan had allowed for the forward movement of a number of field batteries, once the Black Line was secure, to better support any advance from the Green Line. On XVII Corps front, six field batteries had advanced to positions on or about the old British Front line and by 9:00 a.m. were in action alongside eleven "silent" batteries which had previously withheld fire to avoid detection. On XIV Corps front three brigades of field artillery were also in position around the same time to give support to the consolidation of the northern defensive flank along the

---

[278] The *73rd Regiment* holding the position had in fact been reinforced by two sections of the machine gun brigade of the *111th Division*, and other reinforcements had come up to the road and also into Langemarck.
[279] During the night of 31st July / 1st August, the 2nd Coldstream under appalling conditions in heavy rain, pushed forward their north facing flank and captured Sentier and Pinson Farms.

Steenbeek, or to any further advance beyond the stream. Behind the Guards Division the field batteries were moved up to the X-line about Gouvy Farm, 1,000 yards short of the canal, under the continuous and harassing fire of enemy guns. Movement of the guns was already found to be most difficult due to the ground conditions which were becoming steadily worse and increasingly damaged by enemy shelling. Hastily laid tracks were collapsing under the weight causing major problems for the Royal Engineers, some guns being stranded until new tracks could be made for them across the mire. As the batteries were established in new positions it became obvious the saturated ground would not support the weight and much timber was required to prevent them from sinking after a few rounds. Ammunition hastily dumped in the mud required cleaning before use, and ponies were already employed in bringing up the 18-pounder shells. All this added to the reduction in both weight and accuracy of the barrage, which had become noticeably thinner the further the infantry advanced. During the night 31st July / 1st August the Royal Horse Artillery Brigade attached to the Guards Division crossed the canal and moved forward about 500 yards into positions in rear of Artillery Wood and Wood 15. The 4th Guards Brigade Machine Gun Company which had commenced its move forward as soon as the Blue Line had been taken, took up position 500 yards beyond the Black Line on the eastern side of Abri Wood in range to give covering barrage fire on S.O.S. call.

The lessons learnt on the Somme when the cavalry were not brought forward soon enough to exploit any success were not to be repeated, and in each divisional sector a squadron of cavalry was to be moved up once the Black Line was secure, to 'reconnoitre ahead of the foremost infantry and exploit any local success'. This now seems an extraordinary decision. The situation on the Steenbeek was precarious even for the forward infantry battalions, who still faced heavy machine gun fire from firmly entrenched and wired German positions east of the stream, and artillery fire was still heavy. How much more precarious for the cavalry? Any thoughts of sending cavalry across the Steenbeek against these defences would surely mean sending them to certain destruction. The arrangements in the 15th Division may be used as a good example. One troop of the North Irish Horse was to be allotted to the division on Z-Day, to act under the orders of the Brigadier Commanding 45th Brigade. The troop was to rendezvous in the field immediately east of Goldfish Chateau, 3,000 yards west of Ypres at Zero plus 6 hours, and was to push forward patrols to the high ground north-east of Keerselaarhoek on the Passchendaele ridge, moving through the Green Line after the protective barrage lifted, or in other words 1 hour after the Green Line had been occupied. Another patrol was to be sent by 55th Division across the Stroombeek and up to reconnoitre the Flanders I Line about Wolf Farm, near Wallemolen, nearly 7,000 yards from the British Front Line. The patrols were to signal by visual signals on reaching each of the enemy defensive lines and their final objectives. They were to carry white flares for the purpose to signal to aircraft, and also to take forward carrier pigeons.

The crossing of the Steenbeek by the forward elements of 51st Division was the signal for their allotted cavalry to move towards the Steenbeek. The results were totally predictable, most of the horses being killed before ever reaching the stream. The squadron in the sector of the 51st Division, 1st King Edward's Horse, got forward as far as Ferdinand's Farm just 150 yards west of the Steenbeek and in sight of the defences of Langemarck, before the few survivors dismounted to fight as infantry, where they remained until the following morning. The squadron commander, Major Swan was shot down in a forward position. Sergeant Alexander Edwards of the 1/6th Seaforth went out and dressed the officer's wounds in a shell-hole and succeeded in helping him back to the British lines. For this act and other acts of bravery on this and the following day, during which he was twice wounded, he was to be awarded the V.C. To sacrifice the cavalry squadrons for no valid reason now seems a tragedy and indicates a total lack of understanding of the conditions and nature of the battlefield west of the Passchendaele ridge. It would have been more sensible to have left the horses west of Ypres.

Part Two

"We were thus under fire from the North, South and East"
War Diary 1st Battalion the Cambridgeshire Regiment

The British "high water mark" 31st July

The results of the mornings fighting were from the British viewpoint mixed. For many of the infantry it had been a bloody slog across terribly heavy ground, amongst a multitude of water filled shell craters, and through stoutly held defences. In some places the casualties had been very heavy, the battlefield littered with the dead and wounded of both sides. But the advance to the Black Line, mostly accomplished between 8:00 and 9:00 a.m. had gone exceptionally well, occupying the German observation positions along most of the front. The exception was in the vital area of the Gheluvelt plateau south of the Menin Road, where 24th and 30th Divisions were checked in Shrewsbury Forest, and in front of Dumbarton Lakes, Inverness Copse and Glencorse Wood, and 8th Division's position was precarious on Westhoek ridge with a totally exposed right flank. In the G.H.Q. plan, and the G.H.Q. Operations Branch memorandum written by Brigadier - General Davidson, and in the decisions agreed upon at the Paris conference of the 4th / 5th May, the operation should have now stopped on the Black Line for at least two days, as to immediately go further ran all the risks so strongly felt and frequently expressed. This was not however the plan to be followed on this day, and in accordance with decisions of Fifth Army, at 10:10 a.m., Zero+ 6hours and 20 minutes, the barrage had again started its forward creep. But the advance to the Green Line had also been largely successful. Perhaps Gough's less cautious approach was right after all? However it was certainly the case that the farther the advance had progressed the stiffer the resistance from the unscathed blockhouses had become. The deeper the penetration the more the casualties had increased, and it was plain to all how much weaker the protective barrage had become.

By 1:30 p.m. II Corps front was at deadlock. On Westhoek ridge 8th Division, as had been predicted by its commander, could not move forward largely due to enfilade fire from Glencorse Wood which had not been taken by 30th Division. On the XIX Corps sector 15th Division, with a weak right flank along the Ypres – Roulers railway, exposed due to the check of 8th Division at Westhoek, had been held up about Potsdam redoubt. On the left however the Camerons were on Hill 37 and 45th Brigade had established outposts beyond the Langemarck – Zonnebeke road at Dochy and Otto Farms, but all weak in numbers and dangerously exposed. After severe fighting, 164th Brigade had stopped just 600 yards short of its objective, and the surviving Lancashire Fusiliers and Liverpool Irish had dug in between Schuler Farm and Kansas Cross. A few had however crossed the Hanebeek and were in a dreadfully exposed position up on Gravenstafel ridge near Aviatic Farm.

The XVIII Corps engaged in forming the defensive flank to the north, had crossed the Steenbeek along the whole front. 39th Division had taken St. Julien and their 118th Brigade was across the St.Julien - Poelcappelle road with the left flank thrown back to the Steenbeek to conform to the 51st Division. 1/6th Cheshire had gone on beyond their third objective and had crossed the German Third Line, with outpost in positions of extreme danger about von Tirpitz Farm on Gravenstafel ridge. In the sector of the 51st Division the 152nd and 153rd Brigades had been stopped by intense machine gun fire just west of the Steenbeek, but the 1/6th Black Watch on the left had outpost positions just east of the stream. On the northern defensive flank XIV Corps had reached all its objectives, with the 38th Division on or slightly across the Steenbeek, with the Guards Division on the stream to their left.

The broad 8,500 yard offensive front of the II and XIX Corps was, due to the deadlock on the Gheluvelt plateau, reduced to the 3,500 yards held by the XIX Corps. The decision as to whether to press on to the fourth objective, Flanders I, was discretional and in the hands of the divisional commanders. But because of the almost total failure of communications it took a great deal of time for information regarding the situation at the front to get back to divisional headquarters six miles behind the lines. Bad visibility had caused problems with signalling and had also made it difficult for contact aircraft to observe the ground, (although there had been considerable enemy air activity directing their barrages). Telephone cables had been continually cut. Forward brigades were reduced to sending messages by multiple runners who could take up to two hours to reach the telephone cable heads on the old British Front Line.[280] When at 1:13 p.m. the information was finally received at 15th Division headquarters that the 45th Brigade was held up at Potsdam, the advance to the fourth objective was immediately postponed. In 55th Division, it was not until 2:30 p.m. that information was received that 164th Brigade was on the third objective, (they were in fact mostly 600 yards short), and orders were issued immediately for the two battalions holding the first objective to move forward to the second objective in readiness to push forward to the fourth objective. This order seems to have been considered a little reckless even by Gough's standards as he cancelled it at 3:10 p.m. and ordered all available XIX Corps troops to reinforce the third objective. As with the sea upon reaching high tide, there was now, except for continual hostile shelling, a pause and almost a calm. The British advance had for the moment reached its high water mark.

The forward brigades on the XIX and XVIII Corps fronts were well spread out, some in precarious positions and in small numbers due to heavy casualties. Because of the communication difficulties they had received no support or reinforcements since they reached their objective around 11:00 a.m. They were running short of ammunition, bombs and water, they were exhausted, and undoubtedly many were in shock. Those battalions holding the Black Line had however been far from idle, and substantial consolidation of the position was well under way, many Vickers guns being brought up to stiffen the defence. But the artillery as per plan had ceased its protective barrage around midday and those tanks still in action had, as ordered, returned to their rearward rallying points. The tide was now surely set to turn.

The German response

By 11:00 a.m. information regarding the extent of the British break-in was becoming known at German *Fourth Army* headquarters and was, correctly, believed to be at its most serious between Zonnebeke and Langemarck. The two *Eingreif* division of *Group Ypres* were therefore ordered to counter attack the flanks of the break-in along the line of the Zonnebeke – Langemarck road, on the left between Hill 40 and Hill 37, and on the right between Winnipeg and Keerselare. Information regarding the movement of German reinforcements had been slow in reaching Fifth Army or Corps headquarters. The programme of air spotting had been abandoned because of poor visibility in the morning and had not been fully replaced since, although the enemy had flown over the British positions with impunity. Aircraft of Corps squadrons had limited their reconnaissance activities to spotting the forward positions of the infantry, while Army squadrons had been busy attacking German rear areas. No aircraft it appeared had been searching for the enemy, and the concentration of the *Eingreif* divisions behind the ridge between Broodseinde and Passchendaele, and about Poelcappelle had gone ahead unseen. The first report of counter-attack forces moving forward came from a forward artillery observer with 45th Brigade, who upon approaching Bremen Redoubt around 11:30 a.m. saw 2,000 yards ahead, 'a vast amount of German infantry going along Passchendaele Ridge'. This message was received at 15th Division headquarters at 12:53 p.m. and from 1:00 p.m. onwards more messages were received from ground observers that a counter-attack was massing all along the battle front, but soon after a drizzling rain had set in once again reducing visibility. The outpost positions of the infantry were not known to the artillery, forward artillery observers were not in contact with the guns, and from observation points on the second

---

[280] On occasions up to 4 runners were sent with the same message in the hope that at least one would get through.

objective it was not possible to see what was happening further forward.[281] At about 2:00 p.m. an intense German barrage began to fall about the *Wilhelm Stellung* between the Ypres – Roulers railway and St. Julien. The inevitable counter-attack was about to descend upon the 45th, 164th and 118th Brigades, which were by now in no fit state, with insufficient strength, insufficient ammunition, and insufficient gunfire support to face it.

At about 4:00 p.m. three German aircraft flew along the British positions about St. Julien and dropped white flare balls to mark the target for their gunners. No British aircraft were in sight. The German right wing then struck the first blow, falling upon the forward battalions on the left of the 118th Brigade, the 1/1st Herts, east of the St.Julien – Poelcappelle road, the 4/5th Black Watch which was just short of Triangle Farm and west of the St. Julien – Poelcapelle road, and the 1/1st Cambridge in support at St,Julien. The *50th Reserve Division*, the northern *Eingreif* division of *Group Ypres* counter-attacked with the *230th* and *231st Reserve Regiments* which having marched from Westroosebeke (on the ridge north of Passchendaele), deployed south west of Poelcappelle, their first objective being to attack either side of St. Julien, and to the west of Schuler Farm and to retake the original German Second Line.

The Hertfordshire and Black Watch, unable to withstand the onslaught, and lacking artillery support, rapidly fell-back towards the Steenbeek and St. Julien. On the right the remnants of the 1/6th Cheshire in an already dangerously vulnerable position on Gravenstafel ridge, swung back their now exposed left to cover the withdrawal. The enemy who had previously held up their hands in surrender behind their wire took advantage of the situation to collect their weapons, but immediately had to take shelter to avoid their own barrage which fell on and around the *Wilhelm Stellung*. The Cheshire, suffering casualties from the barrage fell-back to the south-east of St. Julien, towards Border House. The War Diary of the 1/1st Cambridge again offers a graphic account. '4:10 p.m. The enemy (strength about two battalions) advanced along a line 500 yards East of Wurst Farm – Springfield covered by a barrage of H.E. Our position came under an intense bombardment of H.E. and shrapnel. The enemy could be seen advancing from the crest of the hill 1,000 yards to our right front [Gravenstafel ridge] in waves at about 150 yards to 200 yards distance. They were visible the whole way. They began to envelope our position, our casualties were heavy. There were no officers in "C" and "D" Companies which were now commanded by C.S.M. Burbridge…4:30 p.m. The enemy had crossed the Hanebeek South of Winnipeg [towards Fortuin]. Orders were sent to "A" and "D" Companies to withdraw to a trench line between Border House and St. Julien. "C" Company were to hold Border House. Two platoons of the 13th Royal Sussex Regt which had withdrawn from St. Julien were directed to entrench themselves 100 yards South of our new line. "B" Company and two platoons of "C" Company were holding both banks of the Steenbeek N.W. of St. Julien with their left in touch with the right of the Black Watch…5:45 p.m. By this time the enemy had reached the line of the Hanebeek between Border House and St. Julien and had advanced as far as Fortuin on the right rear. We still held Border House with the survivors of "C" Company, with about 40 Liverpool Scots guarding the right flank, and "B" Company and the two platoons of 'C" Company holding the ground N.W. of St. Julien…6:15 p.m. We had lost all officers East of St. Julien except the Commanding Officer (Lt. Col. E. P. A. Riddell D.S.O.) the Adjutant (Lt. H. W. Baynes Smith) 2nd Lt. F. W. Ford and 2nd Lt. G. B. Jarvis. Our casualties were now 16 officers and 250 other ranks. The hostile bombardment was very heavy. Our own guns opened on our positions. We were thus under fire from the North, South and East. The Commanding Officer went to the Brigade forward station to stop our guns and ordered the withdrawal to the Black Dotted Line in front of Canteen Trench [on the west bank of the Steenbeek, 400 yards south of St. Julien]…7:00 p.m. Our guns stopped firing on us.'[282] **The newly won possessions east of the**

---

[281] There was in fact in places some contact with the guns. At about 1:30 p.m. the C.O. of the 1/1st Cambridge had apparently made contact with the batteries from the Forward Brigade Station at Vanheule Farm, 1,000 yards south-west of St. Julien on the Wieltje road, and had successfully requested gunfire support, which had effectively opened up on the line Winnipeg – northern houses of St. Julien at around 2:30 and had prompted a retirement of the local German counter-attack.
[282] National Archives, War Diary the 1/1st Cambridge WO/95/2590

Steenbeek were thus lost to the enemy. As the British battalions withdrew, their casualties had been extremely severe, the 1/1st Herts having suffered 136 killed and 400 wounded out of an initial strength of 650.

The southern (*221st Eingreif*) division of *Group Ypres* was to attack across the Zonnebeke – Langemarck road, to the east of Schuler Farm with the *60th Reserve* and *1st Ersatz Reserve Regiments*. The withdrawal of 118th Brigade had exposed the left of 164th Brigade, which already in a weekend state, received orders at 2:15 p.m. to form a defensive left flank towards St. Julien along the Hanebeek, between Schuler Farm and Border House. As this movement began, six waves of German infantry of *60th Reserve* appeared over Zonnebeke spur, preceded by a protective barrage most of which was fired in enfilade and came from the direction of Zonnebeke and from behind the Gheluvelt plateau. Of the Lancashire Fusiliers and the Liverpool Irish in the advanced outposts on Gravenstafel ridge, about Aviatik Farm north of the road nothing more was heard. The hard won positions between Kansas Cross and Schuler Farm were abandoned as the brigade fell-back through the ghastly battle zone, where, through lack of artillery support, shortage of ammunition, and sheer exhaustion, all attempts to from a new line failed. Orders issued by 55th Division at 4:35 p.m. for the brigade to hold the line Hill 35 – Somme Farm – Border House, and to be supported where possible by 165th and 166th Brigades were obsolete even before they were issued, as the Hill 35 – Border House line had already fallen. Most of the Lancashire Fusiliers and Liverpool Irish attempting to hold the line were surrounded, only about 30 men returning to the second objective. On the right the North Lancs and King's Own, narrowly escaping envelopment on Hill 35, also retired to the second objective. On the left, 118th Brigade withdrew west of the Steenbeek for 500 yards either side of St. Julien abandoning the ruins.

To the left of *60th Reserve Division*, the *1st Ersatz*, which was to counter-attack between Hill 40 and Hill 37, roughly the positions of 45th Brigade, had lost direction and did not become engaged. The left of the *60th Reserve* however began to work their way between Hill 35 and the left flank of the Camerons on Hill 37. At about 2:30 p.m. the Camerons began to fall back to avoid envelopment, but of the outpost parties forward about Otto and Dochy Farms nothing more was heard. At around 4:00 p.m. to add to the misery and discomfort, if that were possible, the persistent drizzle developed into a downpour. By 4:15 p.m. the survivors on the left of 45th Brigade were back on the second objective. On the right those of the Royal Scots Fusiliers who in the morning had been held up and had dug-in about Potsdam Redoubt, had fallen-back to a defence line which had already been consolidated by supports, 400 yards in front of the second objective on the Iberian Beck House line, where the 10/11th Highland Light Infantry had dug-in earlier. Touch was gained with the 8th Division south of the railway.

The six hours which had elapsed since gaining the second objective had been well used, and the British artillery and machine guns positioned to defend the Black Line were well organised and ready. In front of Square Farm the H.L.I. had positioned 11 Vickers machine guns to stiffen an otherwise weak second defence line held mainly by headquarters staff. The heavy rain was making the conditions around the Steenbeek terrible, and the advancing Germans were up to their knees in mud and water, as were the British in their hastily dug defences, which quickly crumbled and fell-in under the downpour. From the British rear the steadily strengthening artillery fire and indirect and direct machine gun fire was now slowing up the counter-attack and it was not until around 6:00 p.m. that the forward German infantry, many with rifles and light machine guns choked with mud, approached within 300 yards of the Black Line. At this point the pre-arranged British S.O.S. signals brought down a withering protective barrage from both the artillery and machine guns. The German attack faltered, stopped, and then those that could turned and fell-back painfully up the gentle muddy slope east of the Steenbeek. They had however retaken the ruins of St. Julien, and from these they did not withdraw.

The German counter-attacks in the XIX and XVIII Corps sectors had been partially successful, the British being pushed back from the German Third Line along the whole front, west of the Steenbeek at St Julien, (but maintaining a small foothold east of the stream 500 yards south of the village), and to a line 300 yards forward of the Black Line beside the Ypres –

Roulers railway, 600 yards west of the Hanebeek. All three brigades, 118th, 164th and 45th, which had carried the attack so far forward and had then borne the brunt of the counter-attacks, were withdrawn at 10:00 p.m. having lost approximately 70% of their strength,. They dragged themselves across the shell-pitted and waterlogged morass, back to the old British Front Line to reorganise, the Black Line still being held in miserable wet and filthy conditions by the brigades who had captured it many hours earlier.

The relative success of their counter-attack in the centre encouraged the Germans to now press the flanks. But the situation on the northern defensive flank formed by the 51st, 38th and Guards Divisions was more secure than the fronts of the 39th, 55th and 15th Divisions in the centre where the Germans had succeeded. The position along the Steenbeek which had now been consolidated by 51st Division and XIV Corps presented a clearly defined and defendable line, beyond which a defensive barrage could safely fall. The infantry were not too far forward in exposed positions, and the field artillery was gradually getting forward in support.

Towards this hastily prepared line along northern defensive flank, and in appalling conditions, the *Eingreif* divisions now launched their counter-attacks. To the south of Langemarck between 2:30 and 3:00 p.m. the right companies of the *231st Regiment* advanced towards the Steenbeek, and the 51st Division positions on the west bank. The attack was met with an intense artillery barrage and a fusillade of machine gun, Lewis gun and rifle fire from the Seaforth, Gordons, and Black Watch, which turned the advance into a disorderly flight, in the wake of which a company of the 1/6th Seaforth, accompanied by two platoons of the Argyll and Sutherland dashed across the stream, seized a bridgehead opposite Ferdinand Farm, and established the outposts in Maison du Rasta and Maison Bulgare which had not been possible earlier.[283]

From the village of Langemarck at around the same time, the *229th Reserve Regiment* of the *50th Reserve Division* attacked towards the forward positions of the 38th Division which in some places were just east of the Steenbeek. The Germans suffered many casualties from British artillery and machine gun fire as they moved through the rubble to the west of the village. The Au Bon Gite blockhouse, garrisoned since its capture by the 11th South Wales Borderers, held up the advance of both leading battalions of the *229th* with machine gun fire, and German heavy artillery was finally required to evict the Welshmen, who withdrew across the swollen Steenbeek at around 5:00 p.m. to the water-logged line already consolidated west of the stream.[284]

To the north of the Welsh, the Guards held firmly to their gains of the morning along the Steenbeek. The *77th Reserve Regiment* of the *2nd Guard Reserve Division* attacked in the early afternoon with its right against the French at St. Janshoek and its left towards the Guards around Weidendreft. At around 4:30 p.m. the two support regiments of the division attacked, the *91st Reserve* against the Guards and the *15th Reserve* against the French about Bixschoote. The French not only withstood the counter-attacks but moved forward beyond their objective and by 6:00 p.m. had gained a foothold in the ruins of the village of Bixschoote.[285]

On the Gheluvelt plateau to the south, in the sector of II Corps, the Germans attempted with the *95th Regiment* and a battalion of the *41st Regiment (221st Division)*, at 2:00 p.m. and again at 7:00 p.m., to retake the positions held by 8th Division on Westhoek ridge. After initial local enemy success the position was regained by the 25th Brigade which was subsequently withdrawn into reserve behind Bellewaarde Ridge, the front then being held by 23rd and 24th Brigades. About the Menin Road and in the Bassevillebeek valley 30th Division had withstood local counter-attacks by the German front line divisions, the *Eingreif* divisions here not having been engaged as the British advance had not reached the German Second Line. A renewal of the attack against the Second Objective was ordered by 30th Division to commence at 6:30 p.m. but

---

[283] These outposts were withdrawn later in the evening.
[284] The *229th Reserve* suffered casualties of 19 officers and 614 other ranks in this attack.
[285] In *The First World War* John Keegan says the Germans remained in command of the vital ground. They did not; just a small area around Clapham Junction. He also says they had committed none of their counter-attack divisions. As we have seen, they had. John Keegan (1998) *The First World War* London: Hutchinson p388

at 5:30 p.m. II Corps headquarters ordered consolidation of the ground gained, and wisely the attack order was cancelled. Away to the south, on the front of Second Army, the Germans made a serious attempt to retake La Basse Ville at about 3:30 p.m. but were repulsed, the New Zealand Division holding their ground.

Any further attempts at major operations were stopped by heavy rain which had set in by the evening, turning the whole battlefield into a quagmire, especially along the swollen and spilling Steenbeek. Misery and discomfort there was in plenty, and only local efforts to improve the positions gained were possible. The tired battalions did their best to dig themselves in to the waterlogged mud, and the deeper they dug the deeper became the water they stood in. The more they threw up defensive breastworks the more the rain washed them back into the trench. The average monthly rainfall for August in Flanders is about 70mm. There were 21.7mm of rain on the 31st July 1917. At around 6:05 p.m. a heavy German barrage including a lavish use of gas shells fell on the line of the Steenbeek held by 51st Division. Owing to casualties and the risk of being outflanked, the forward outposts of 1/6th Black Watch east of the stream were withdrawn as were those of the 1/6th Seaforth and 1/8th Argyll, the withdrawal taking place none too soon as the rain was quickly turning the Steenbeek into a muddy torrent in the midst of a spreading quagmire. In the early hours of the 1st August the German garrison at Lower Star Post in Shrewsbury Forest, which had so effectively held up 24th Division was withdrawn, the movement being detected and the position occupied by 73rd Brigade.

Over the next two days, although the ground conditions were appalling the Germans maintained the pressure to regain their Second Line, along the Steenbeek south of St. Julien in the sector of XIX Corps. To strengthen their right defensive flank here, would better secure the vital position on Gheluvelt plateau. An enemy attack on the 1st August on the front of 15th Division, about Beck House gained initial local success, until a counter-attack by 45th Brigade retook the lost ground. On the 2nd August another attempt against 55th Division was broken up by artillery fire about Pommern Redoubt. Also on the 2nd August in XVIII Corps sector Germans were seen massing in front of 39th Division, but were dispersed by heavy shelling, 116th Brigade then crossing the Steenbeek and reoccupying St. Julien. A line of outposts was established north of the village and to the east of the stream, the ground conditions there being utterly dreadful with mud and water in places waist deep.

Evaluation of the results

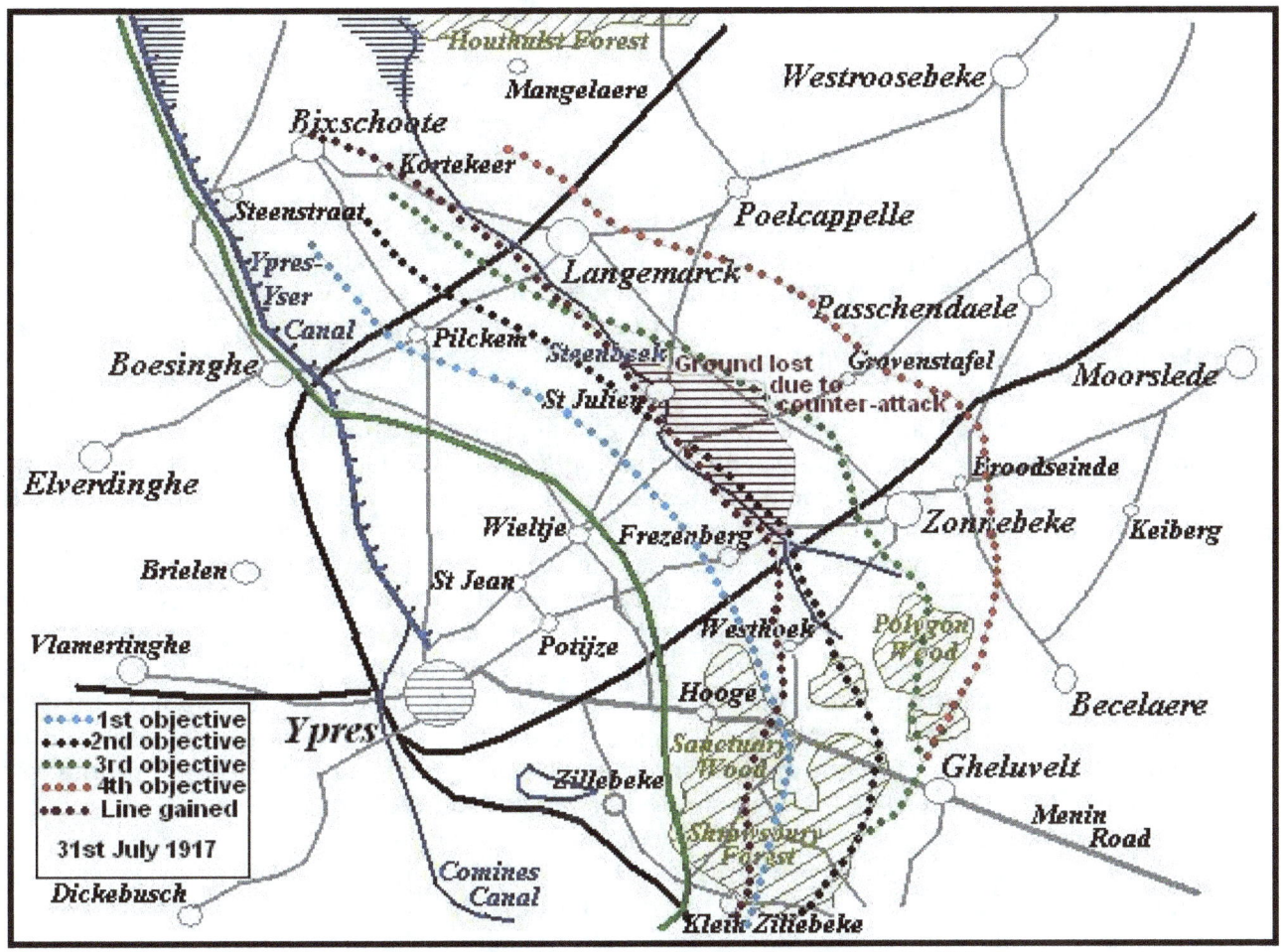

Objectives and line gained by nightfall - Battle of Pilckem Ridge

Haig visited Gough on the afternoon of the 31st and, even before the results of the days fighting were clear, instructed him to proceed with the operation as soon as possible, 'but only after adequate bombardment and after dominating the hostile artillery',[286] a situation not likely to be achieved in the immediate future. These words were to be repeated many times over the next fourteen weeks. When at 5:43 p.m. it was known at Fifth Army headquarters that II Corps had not, except north of Westhoek hamlet, advanced to the Black Line, and XIX Corps were driven back about this line, Order No.11 was issued for the offensive to be renewed by the two corps on the morning of the 2nd August. A few hours later at 8:45 p.m. this order was changed, the order to attack in the centre and to push on beyond the Steenbeek (XIX Corps) being withheld, dependent on II Corps securing the Black Line on the Gheluvelt plateau, and this to be achieved on the 2nd August. Two days later it was envisaged that II, XIX, and the right of XVIII Corps would resume their attacks towards the *Wilhelm Stellung,* the original Green Line, and the same day the left of XVIII Corps, with XIV Corps and French First Army would advance the northern defensive flank to the line of the Winnepeg - Langemarck - Weidendreft roads at its junction with the Green Line.[287]

On the morning of 1st August G.H.Q. issued an order confirming the Fifth Army decision. On the same day Brigadier-General Davidson, Operations Branch G.H.Q., produced a memorandum, as he had previously, warning of the dangers of continuing the operation across the Steenbeek before the main German positions on Gheluvelt plateau had been gained and

---

[286] Douglas Haig. Diaries and Letters, p307
[287] National Archives, Fifth Army Order No.11 31st July 1917 8:45 p.m. WO95/520

consolidated. The previous warnings were being repeated but with the benefit of the proof of recent experience. Davidson appreciated that to attack again at Gheluvelt as soon as possible to secure the Black Line was necessary, to prevent German reorganisation, and because the whole Fifth Army operation was checked until the position was secure, but to attack too soon and without thorough preparation was folly. To use the same divisions that carried out the original attack, which were tired and depleted by their efforts and through casualties that amounted to up to 60% of their fighting strength was inadvisable, and they should be withdrawn and replaced with three fresh divisions. The strength and location of the German machine gun positions about Inverness Copse was now known and they could be engaged by artillery with observed fire. The corps artillery could concentrate on the one objective and not be spread across three. Careful control and accurate shooting aided by two or more day's good flying weather were necessary to complete the artillery preparations. To secure the Black Line across the plateau was the most vital task on the whole Fifth Army agenda and the position at Westhoek was precarious until this was achieved. The message came over with great clarity; attack as soon as possible, but only after careful and thorough measures had been taken to achieve success. Davidson also recognised that the *Eingreif* divisions had not yet been engaged on the plateau and a German counter-attack on a large scale was likely soon along the whole II Corps front.

The German perception of the situation was very much the same, Crown Prince Rupprecht considering the results of the days fighting all the more satisfactory as the counter attack divisions of *Group Wytschaete* behind Gheluvelt plateau had scarcely been used. *Group Wytschaete* also believed that the British could not continue their intended break through north eastwards towards Roulers until they had secured their right flank, by pressing back the *52nd Reserve Division* on Gheluvelt plateau. It was expected therefore that the next blow would be delivered with all the strength the British could muster against the *52nd Reserve* and the *12th Divisions*, which held the line between Shrewsbury Forest and Westhoek.

By the evening of the 1st August it was clear that it was not going to be possible to carry out Order No.11 in its initial form, Order No 12 issued at midnight stating: 'As the operations mentioned in para 1 of O.O. No.11 may be delayed by bad weather the Army Commander wishes Corps Commanders to consider the possibility of carrying out the second operation [as detailed above] in modified form'. The revised plan was for the two separate attacks on the 2nd and 4th to be carried out simultaneously. But the whole Fifth Army plan was now postponed, not due to the Davidson memorandum, but because of the rain which persisted for three days and nights and turned the forward areas into a bog of water-filled shell holes, overflowing ditches and spilling streams approaching 4,000 yards wide, passable only by a few specially constructed tracks which received the regular attention of the German batteries. There were a few torrents of water in the steeper valleys of the Bassevillebeek and the Hanebeek, but along much of the Steenbeek, and across the flat meadows the Salient took on the appearance of a vast muddy lake.

The results of the first few days of the offensive were therefore mixed. The nine attack divisions which had been intended to reach the Passchendaele – Staden ridge before relief, had in fact reached less than half way and had lost from 30% to 60% of their fighting strength in doing so. It had been hoped that the tanks would play a major role in the later battles to break-out of the Salient, but out of the 177 which had gone into action on the 31st, 77 had been hit by enemy fire, or had become ditched or suffered mechanical breakdown, and 42 of these were a total loss. They were not to be quickly replaced. The southern and northern flanks were secure, but this was not the focal point of the attack. The wise prophases had proved to be tragically correct. The Gheluvelt position needed special attention, which it had not received in sufficient measure, and it stubbornly held out. To push too far forward beyond the capability of the field artillery to protect from counter-attack, and beyond the ability of the infantry to dig-in in sufficient strength to repel counter-attack was to risk failure, or more correctly without further disruption of the enemies artillery, to guarantee it. The weather had been as bad as it could be, but that was nobody's fault.

In his diary entry for the 1st August the Cabinet Secretary noted that the 200th meeting of the War Cabinet had been passed. There had in fact been two War Cabinet meetings that day but there was no mention of the great battle raging 130 miles away. On the 2nd August Robertson informed the War Cabinet of the fact that the attack was progressing successfully and the first objective had been achieved, but as they appeared to want to hear little more he did not elaborate.

Haig considered the fighting most satisfactory, and that casualties had been light for so great a battle, and so reported to the War Cabinet on the 4th August. To the modern reader the casualty figures for Fifth Army for the period 31st July to the night 2nd / 3rd August can hardly be considered slight, being in the region of 27,000 of which 3,700 were killed. Second Army casualties were just under 5,000. It is difficult to be precise regarding German losses, although for the period of most severe fighting they are believed to have been at least 30,000 and possibly as high as 40,000. 6,000 German prisoners had been taken, including 133 officers, and 25 guns had been captured.

Haig did not fail to point out in his report that, 'unfortunately however, the consistent bad weather which has persisted since the 31st July has rendered impossible the resumption of our advances and has imposed very great hardships on the troops...The delay will doubtless entail a renewal of the struggle for artillery and air supremacy before a fresh infantry assault can be launched. This supremacy can undoubtedly be gained, and there is no reason to doubt that, given a sufficient duration of suitable weather, the attainment of the objectives in view is within our power....I must point out, however, that the delay is throwing an increased strain on our guns and on the artillery personnel; while the wastage in both infantry and artillery will be increased by the hardships due to exposure to such bad weather and the enormous labour resulting from it in maintaining the troops and getting forward ammunition, etc., over ground which is reported to be as bad as that which we had to deal last winter on the Somme and Ancre'.[288] This was not the inaccurate and rosy picture which it has often been claimed Haig persistently painted for the consumption of the War Cabinet, but rather gave a fair assessment of the conditions and the outlook.

To advance east of the Steenbeek had been a mistake; an unnecessary gamble which had not paid off. But of great importance was the fact that nine German front line divisions had been so badly mauled that they required pulling out of the line within the next few days. To replace those divisions would ultimately mean bringing in other divisions from other areas, and this steady flow of resources into Flanders as the Third Battle of Ypres progressed denied the enemy the initiative, and inevitably helped reduced their capacity to attack the weakened French, or for that matter the Russians or the Italians, and that had been at least part of the plan.

---

[288] National Archives, Haig to CIGS 4th August WO158/24

British casualties for the period 31st July to 3rd August

Fifth Army	Killed	Wounded	Missing	Total
24th Division	386	1,502	354	2,242
30th Division	465	2,462	438	3,365
8th Division	415	2,293	368	3,076
18th Division	128	758	59	945
15th Division	388	2,368	687	3,443
55th Division	449	2,302	696	3,447
39th Division	439	2,644	788	3,871
51st Division	278	1,319	129	1,726
38th Division	394	2,126	402	2,922
Guards Division	355	1,432	177	1,964

R. A. Perry
Essex Villa
Langemark   27-03-2006

The difficulties in moving even the smaller guns – 18 pounder

The infamous Hell Fire Corner – Menin Road

The Menin Road towards the Culvert and Hooge

The road up to Ypres from Poperinghe

Shelter from the guns in a deep dugout

Near the Menin Road. Observatory Ridge in background

Moving up past knocked out tanks – Menin Road

Prisoners at Potijze Chateau

Chapter Three

"Too great a hurry"
Field-Marshal Sir Douglas Haig

The Fifth Army Offensive continues
Gheluvelt 10th August – The Battle of Langemarck 16th August

The rain on the 31st July had been awful, and the resulting bad ground had undoubtedly slowed the advance and caused great hardship to the attacking infantry. It had however also impeded the German counter-attacks of the afternoon, which had floundered in the mud and rain around the slough of the Steenbeek. The enemy may have been even more successful had it not been for the weather. Over the period of the 1st to the 4th August there was 41.6mm of rain, which meant no improvement in ground conditions, and movement of men and materials was arduous and fatiguing. The tanks were not to be able to assist in any planned operation until the ground had begun to dry out, and in fact were not to do so until the 19th August.

Weather conditions, rainfall Vlamertinghe, temperature Ypres[289]

	1st Aug	2nd Aug	3rd Aug	4th Aug	5th Aug	6th Aug	7th Aug
Rainfall	21.5mm	5.3mm	9.9mm	4.9mm	trace	0.1mm	Nil
Temp	59F	59F	59F	66F	73F	71F	69F

Bad weather or not, the enemy continued with their counter-attacks, and at 3:30 p.m. on the 1st August assaulted at divisional strength astride the Ypres – Roulers railway at the junction between the 8th and 15th Divisions. Preceded by an intense barrage and under cover of smoke the attack initially pushed back the 8th Division south of the railway. North of the railway the counter-attack was at first checked by the artillery, but the 8/10th Gordons on the right flank of the 45th Brigade, their right exposed, in turn fell-back until their left rested on North Station Buildings. The brigade right flank was soon supported by the 6/7th Royal Scots Fusiliers and the 11th Argyll and Sutherland Highlanders, and by 9:00 p.m. the enemy had been driven back and the Black Line reoccupied. Again on the 2nd August the enemy thrust at the precarious British line, this time at the junction between the 15th Division and the 55th Division at Pommern Castle, first at 1:30 p.m. and again at 5:00 p.m. Both attacks were driven-off by artillery and small arms fire. On the 4th and 5th the Germans shifted their point of attack to south of the Menin Road and made some efforts to retake Hollebeke. Both the 19th and 41st Divisions were involved in the fighting, which by the end of the day on the 5th saw the British back in possession of the ruins.

Haig was looking closely at his strength of reserves, and due to lack of drafts recognized that his divisions would be required to attack a second time below war strength, and that divisions holding the defensive front must be allowed to fall to as low as 8,000 to 9,000 infantry. His political masters meanwhile were meeting on the 7th and 8th August at an Anglo-Franco-Italian conference in London, at which Lloyd George, whilst not approving of nor condemning the situation in Flanders, again put forward his case for sending large quantities of men and guns to

---

[289] National Archives, GHQ statistics WO95/14

Italy. Hankey commented in his diary, 'P.M. once more compounded his theories for action on the Italian front, but got no support for this year. I agree with him that rain has spoiled Haig's Flanders plan and that we ought to do something else.'[290] The lack of political support for the offensive, and disinterest in the massive efforts of Haig's Armies, remains depressing even after the passage of time. Lloyd George's chairmanship of the meeting was criticized by Foch as being weak and weary, and according to Sir Henry Wilson, the Frenchman thought the conference an absolute fiasco and that Lloyd George was beaten. On the 11th August Hankey castigated the War Cabinet for wasting time in taking four hours for six people to compose a somewhat trivial letter. 'Yet the days are slipping by, it is time to consider whether Haig's offensive should be permitted to continue in the bad weather conditions, and whether the alternative for a great offensive on the Italian front should not be adopted.'[291]

In the harsher reality of the miserable Salient, the conditions had caused the cancellation of the order for the attack on the 2nd August, and on the 3rd, Fifth Army produced Order No.13 in a desperate effort to restore some momentum to the rain-stalled attack:
'1) Fifth Army Orders Nos. 11 and 12 and the tracing and map issued with them are cancelled and should be destroyed.
2) Operations will be carried out as follows :- a) August 6th. The II Corps will complete the capture of the Black Line. b) August 7th. The XIV, XVIII and left of XIX Corps will attack the Yellow Line [a modified position of the original Green Line]. The French First Army will cooperate, its task being, as before, to cover the left flank of Fifth Army. c) August 9th. The right of the XVIII, the XIX and II Corps will attack the Green Line. d) August 16th. The whole Army, in cooperation with the French, will attack the Red and Dotted Red Lines.
3) The date fixed for (a) is dependant upon weather conditions. If this attack takes place after August 8th it will be made simultaneously with (b). Subsequent dates are dependent upon the date on which (b) is carried out.'[292]

But the rain did not ease until the 5th, resulting in a continuation of the offensive being once more delayed, Fifth Army headquarters, finally ordering II Corps to recommence its attacks against the Gheluvelt plateau on the 9th August, with the main offensive to be resumed on the 13th. At an Army Commanders Conference at Lovie Chateau on the 7th Gough asked his Corps Commanders whether the dates selected were suitable. All agreed that, if no more rain fell, they would be in a position to attack on the 13th, so long as visibility allowed of counter-battery work being carried out, as 'none had been done for days'. Jacob of II Corps also agreed that unless more rain fell, he considered the ground would be alright for his attack on the 9th.[293] Although temperatures improved there was insufficient sun or drying wind to help improve the ground on the 5th, 6th and 7th, and on the 8th a violent thunderstorm with torrential rain again resulted in a quagmire sufficient to postpone the plans for both operations by 24 hours, meaning that II Corps would attack at Gheluvelt at 4:35 a.m. 10th August, and the next main offensive would commence on the 14th. Between the 8th and 12th August there would be another 18.4mm of miserable rain.

---

[290] Hankey Diaries. Churchill Archives, Churchill College, Cambridge. HNKY 1/2
[291] Hankey Diaries. Churchill Archives, Churchill College, Cambridge. HNKY 1/2
[292] National Archives, War Diary Fifth Army, Order No.13 3rd August 1917 WO95/520
[293] National Archives, War Diary Fifth Army, notes of Conference held at Lovie Chateau, S.G. 653/18 7th August 1917 WO95/520

Weather conditions, rainfall Vlamertinghe, temperature Ypres[294]

	8th Aug	9th Aug	10th Aug	11th Aug	12th Aug
Rainfall	10.2mm	0.2mm	1.5mm	4.8mm	1.7mm
Temp	71F	68F	69F	65F	72F

The situation regarding the strength of *Group Wytschaete* batteries east of the plateau had not changed and their undiminished fire ranged heavily over the 6,000 yards of British line from the plateau northwards into the valley of the Steenbeek, in the areas of II and XIX Corps. When Haig visited Gough on the 31st July he had ordered the offensive to proceed, but he had also indicated that domination of the enemy artillery was a pre-requisite, as had the Davidson memorandum. This had not been achieved. British batteries in the Verbranenmolen – Zillebeke area were continually shelled, prime targets for the hostile batteries east of the plateau. The German shelling was still fearsomely accurate, one battery, B/83 of 18th Division guns on the banks of Zillebeke Lake being hit four times before finally being relocated to Halfway House. It took from 4:30 a.m. to 11 p.m. to drag one 18-pounder 250 yards through the ooze and slime, so dreadful were the ground conditions. Subsequent to the advance, many of the British guns had been moved forward under appalling conditions and now needed time to re-register. The cooperation of the Corps Squadrons was essential for this work, but flying conditions had been dreadful, and the position of German batteries with their alternative sites had been near impossible to locate. The British artillery continued to disperse its fire at targets on a 12,000 yard frontage, and the *Group Wytschaete* batteries still maintained their local superiority.

The utter misery experienced by the infantry in the appalling weather was compounded, especially in the sectors of II and XIX Corps by continual German shell-fire upon the water filled trenches along the weak front line positions, and on the waterlogged lines of communication and supply. Those divisions which had suffered worst in the fighting of the 31st July and subsequent shelling had been gradually pulled out of the line. On the 1st August the 8th Division had been relieved by the 25th Division at Westhoek. On the 3rd / 4th August the 30th Division had relieved by the 18th Division on the plateau, the 15th Division by the 16th (Southern Irish) Division to the north of the Roulers railway, and the 55th Division by the 36th (Ulster) Division in front of Frezenberg. This was good news for the weary infantry coming out of the line but did not bode well for those going in, as they would be already exhausted from just holding the line before the attacks planned for the 10th and the 14th. On the far right, 24th Division was to stay in the line and hold its sodden, blood-soaked ground overlooking the Bassevillebeek.

Gheluvelt 10th August

The hammer of II Corps was again to fall upon the unyielding anvil of the plateau, this time as an independent operation using 18th and 25th Divisions to secure the right flank prior to the next main assault. This showed right thinking, as it identified the plateau as the key German defensive position, but went only part way as it did not provide the concentration of firepower or the time required to destroy the German batteries hidden to the east, and the lethal machine gun bunkers and blockhouses in front of the German Second Line, already painfully encountered on the 31st July. For the infantry it looked like a re-run, with the added danger that as the front to be attacked was limited, German artillery would be able to concentrate their firepower more

---

[294] National Archives, GHQ statistics WO95/14

closely upon it. On the 7th August, 24th Division extended its left from Bodmin Copse to just south of Stirling Castle, from where 18th Division was able to close up on its frontage of 1,200 yards to just north of Surbiton Villas. From this line it was to attack with two brigades to a depth of 800 yards and take the German Second Line across the narrow waist of the plateau, including the stubbornly defended strong-points in Inverness Copse and Glencorse Wood. To the left, the Hamlet of Westhoek and the German Second Line just east of the Westhoek ridge (where the 8th Division had experienced such a rough time on the 31st July), was also to be taken, this time by one brigade of the 25th Division, which was to push its front forward by a few hundred yards to conform to 18th Division on its right.

The bombardment in preparation for the attack commenced on the 8th August, in torrential rain, with heavy and medium howitzers firing around 3,000 rounds into Inverness Copse and Glencorse Wood, the shelling carrying on throughout the 9th. On the day of the attack a general bombardment along whole Fifth Army front was to be maintained throughout the period of the assault. The two brigades of the 18th Division were to proceed to their objective without a pause and behind a barrage allowing 46 minutes for the advance. The one attacking brigade of 25th Division would advance behind a 25 minute barrage to their objective. Ground conditions were still atrocious, the area being a mass of water-filled shell craters and especially so in and around the remains of the woods, which were nothing more than oozing mud and smashed skeletal trees, in front of which lay the remains of many of those fallen in the fighting of 10 days ago. Also in the filthy tangle lurked the numerous and well camouflaged machine gun bunkers, little affected by the British bombardment and waiting to decimate the struggling attackers. The Germans however had also been roughly handled. Many of those of the *240th, 239th* and *238th Reserve Regiments* of the *52nd Reserve Division* holding the position between Tower Hamlets and Nonne Bosschen had been in the line since the 31st July and were now thoroughly demoralized, largely due to the continual artillery bombardments. The *90th R.I.R.*, the left regiment of *54th Division* with the *27th R.I.R.* in close support, held the German Front Line north of Nonne Bosschen.

18th Division

During the night of the 3rd/4th August, in the pitch dark and pouring rain and under the continuous attention of the German field artillery, the 55th and 54th Brigades took up their positions in the 18th Division front in relief of 30th Division. The 7th Queens and 7th Royal West Kent moved up into support positions on the old British front line in Sanctuary Wood. The West Kent set up battalion headquarters in a shell-hole at the back of the Stirling Castle blockhouse, but an attempted relief by the Queens at 7:30 p.m. on 7th August became a shambles. The battalion became lost in a thick mist, not reaching the West Kent in the line until next morning, at which point they set up battalion headquarters in relative safety in the foul interior of the blockhouse. Three battalions were to carry the attack to the German Second Line. On the right the 55th Brigade was to use the 7th Queens on a frontage of 400 yards and 54th Brigade to their left was to use the 11th Royal Fusiliers and the 7th Bedfordshire Regiment to cover a front of 750 yards.

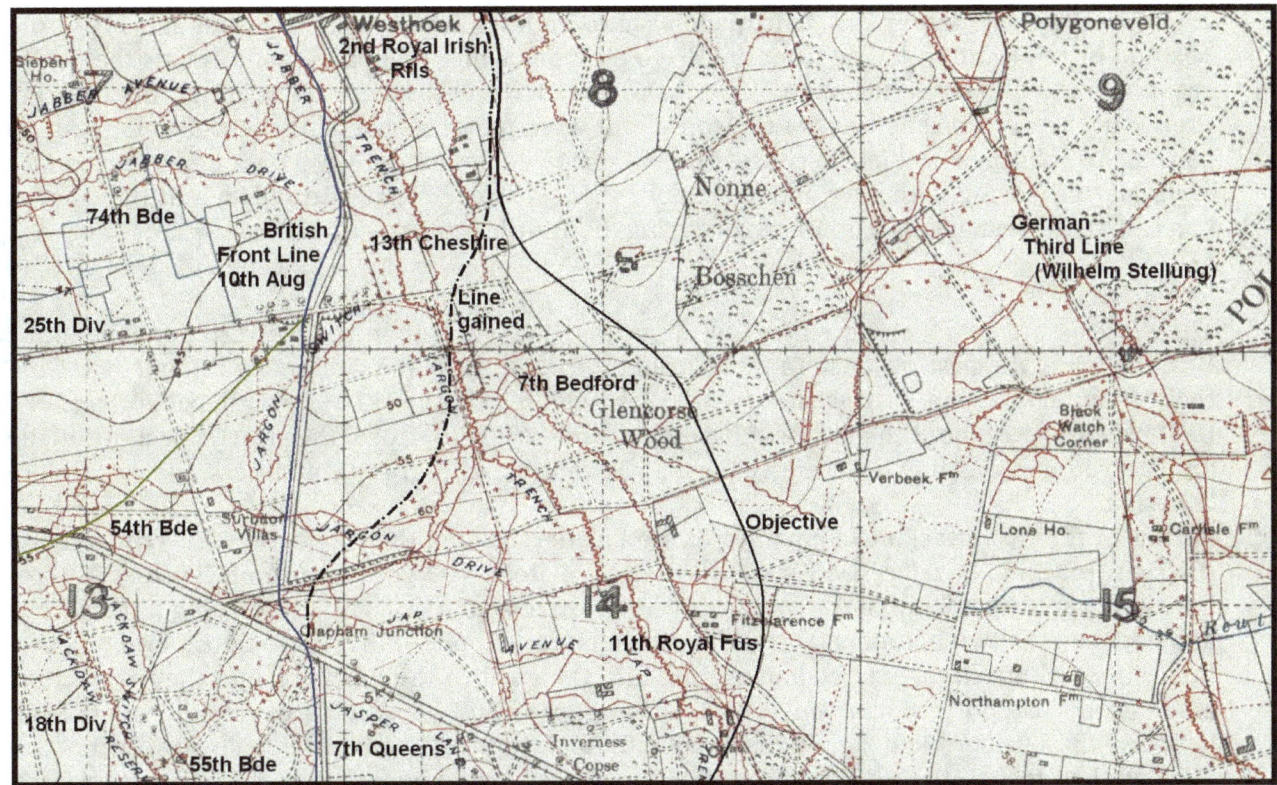

The capture of Westhoek 25th Division and failure at Inverness Copse and Glencorse Wood

55th Brigade [295]

For the moment the rain had stopped, as the attacking and support companies of the 7th Queens moved up towards their jumping-off line between Stirling Castle and Clapham Junction. They had an unfortunate start, for as they moved forward across the muddy cratered wastes along the higher ground, silhouetted against a moonlit sky, they stumbled into fresh barbed wire recently strung by the nervous Germans. The noise was overheard by enemy sentries. Rifle shots rang out and green flares went up along the enemy line. It was clear the attack was imminent, and soon the Queens were engulfed by artillery and machine gun fire, which smashed into the right company and three platoons of the left. At 4:35 a.m., Zero hour, another German barrage caught the battalion as they moved forward to the attack, but those who could continued the advance, to be met by withering machine gun and rifle fire in enfilade from Jasper Avenue and in front from organized shell-holes. Few of the front wave survived, those that did taking what cover they could in water filled craters or crawling back to the British line. The rear waves were held up amongst the uncut wire, shattered trees and shell-craters and few got forward. A small party got into Jasper Avenue and attempted to bomb their way forward along the trench but failed, as German reinforcements moved up through another communication trench to block the way to Inverness Copse. Some reached the south-west corner of the copse to find it defended by a machine gun post and a well guarded tunnel, all but one of this party becoming casualties. One hundred and fifty yards to the north two platoons had managed to keep up with the barrage and work along the northern edge of the copse to reach their objective. With no support and with the threat of being outflanked on the left they edged back to the north-west corner of the copse, bombing out a machine gun bunker which had been causing casualties on the way. The party then took shelter in Jasper Lane just south of the Menin Road and was assisted in holding the position by the arrival of two teams with Vickers guns. They remained there until relieved 18 hours later. As the Queens withdrew the Germans moved back into their original positions and re-occupied the bombed bunker. On the left flank, after getting

---

[295] National Archives, War Diary 55th Brigade WO95/2047

some way forward under constant machine gun and artillery fire, the Queens fell back to a position just in front of the old front line. Two platoons which had veered of towards the north-east while the others withdrew to Jasper Lane, may have become involved in fighting near Jap Trench at the north-east corner of the copse, but were never seen again. The right mopping-up platoon also disappeared in the copse. The ill-conceived assault on Inverness Copse in the face of an alerted enemy with very active artillery firing at close range had failed, and the Queens had lost 10 officers and 272 other ranks during their futile attack.

54th Brigade [296]

The *Albrecht Stellung,* behind which lay Glencorse Wood and then the western edge of Nonne Bosschen was the first obstacle to be cleared by the 54th Brigade. Following the barrage from their jumping-off line just west of the Westhoek track the 11th Royal Fusiliers and 7th Bedfordshire Regiment had more luck than the Queens from the start, being initially unobserved and pushing on into the German Second Line in greater numbers and with more cohesion.

Parties of the two attacking companies of the Fusiliers gained their objective, "D" Company on the right reaching Fitzclarence Farm on the open plateau 400 yards south of Glencorse Wood. But they were not able to make contact with the Queens on the right, there being a dangerous gap between the two battalions. The Germans had worked out of Inverness Copse into this gap, their rifle and machine gun fire hammering into the right of the Fusiliers, and they were soon amongst the support companies. A dangerous gap of 300 yards also developed on the left between the Fusiliers and the Bedford. By 6:00 a.m. the fighting had been so severe that the Fusiliers had lost all their officers, command of the surviving men now in the hands of N.C.O's. The remnants gradually fell back. All available men were sent forward from battalion headquarters in the Menin Road tunnel to reinforce the line, Lewis guns and later Vickers guns quickly covering the exposed right flank.

The Bedford, following the barrage across the torn ground through the wired remains of the *Albrecht Stellung* and into the tangled morass of Glencorse Wood, quickly overran the enemy bunkers, many Germans coming forward to surrender, and at 5:13 a.m. sent a message back to brigade H.Q. that the wood was taken. Due to the dreadful state of the ground consolidation proved extremely difficult, it only being possible to dig outposts, and these being in very exposed positions. To the right the 300 yard gap between the Bedford and the Fusiliers was placing that flank under great pressure from the enemy. In consequence the right company was drawn well back, and at 9:17 a.m. a message was sent explaining the situation. On the left, it appeared that the 13th Cheshire on 25th Division front was not so far forward, and this flank was also in the air. The Bedford was now very exposed, their forward outpost line in a vulnerable salient and receiving machine gun fire from pillboxes in front and on the right flank. By midday a main support line had been established in rear of the outposts, using the old German Jargon Trench on the *Albrecht Stellung,* along the west face of the wood, and three outposts in shell-holes protected the left and gained touch with the 13th Cheshire. The positions of both battalions was made more isolated due to a German box barrage which effectively prevented supports, ammunition, water and food being brought up during the day, the situation becoming increasingly critical.

Local German counter-attacks launched throughout the day against the Bedford from Nonne Bosschen were fought off. Soon after 5:00 p.m. the Germans were seen to be again massing in Nonne Bosschen and in Polygon Wood for a counter-attack, but were dispersed by artillery fire. Around 7:00 p.m. an intense German artillery barrage fell upon Glencorse Wood and its surrounds, followed by an attack under cover of smoke from the east of the wood against the Bedford outposts, and also from Inverness Copse on the right flank of the Fusiliers. An enemy bombing party moving south down Jargon Trench, got behind the Fusiliers who, now short of men and ammunition, were forced to retire to a position about 200 yards east of Clapham Junction, very nearly the point from where they had started. The Bedford also in an

---

[296] National Archives, War Diary 54th Brigade WO95/2041, War Diary 7th Bedford WO95/2043

exhausted state were forced back on their right through Glencorse Wood to Jargon Trench, but their left still held on in the north-west corner of the wood.

The two support battalions of the brigade, the 6th Northants and the 12th Middlesex had been considered too exhausted, due to holding the line over the last ten days and through casualties already sustained to go into action, but were now sent forward to support the weak line. The brigadier of the 54th had at 7:40 a.m. requested the 53rd Brigade be brought forward from divisional reserve to give further support, but the request was denied. The casualties of the 11th Royal Fusiliers were 17 officers and 335 other ranks, and the 7th Bedford 6 officers and 255 other ranks, and except for the north-western corner of Glencorse Wood they were virtually back to their start line.

German forces engaged [297]

The *239th* and *238th Reserve Infantry Regiments* of the *52nd Reserve Division* held the German front line south of Nonne Bosschen, and the *90th R.I.R.* and the *84th I.R.* of the *54th Division* between the wood and the Ypres – Roulers railway. The *238th R.I.R.* had been reinforced with one battalion of the leading regiment, *6th Reserve* of the *9th Reserve (Eingreif) Division*, for the counter attack against the Fusiliers and Bedford from Inverness Copse.

53rd Brigade

The brigade was brought forward from divisional reserve at Dickebusch at 3:20 p.m. the two leading battalions, the 8th Norfolk and 6th Royal Berkshire arriving at the assembly area at Sanctuary Wood at 7:00 p.m. and going into the line at 11:55 p.m. to relieve the three attacking brigades and to hold the divisional front.

25th Division
Major-General E. G. T. Bainbridge

74th Brigade [298]

To the left of 54th Brigade the 74th Brigade attacked across the length of Westhoek ridge, from Surbiton Villas, to the Roulers railway on their left flank, a total front of around 2,200 yards. Four battalions were engaged in the assault, the 13th Cheshire, 2nd Royal Irish Rifles, 9th Loyal North Lancs, and the 11th Lancashire Fusiliers.

The German outpost line was quickly overrun, and the hamlet of Westhoek was stormed by the Irish Rifles and two active blockhouses were taken. The new position, already reached on the 31st July but subsequently abandoned was now once again on the forward easterly slope of Westhoek ridge and exposed to artillery fire. The Germans shelled the ridge remorselessly throughout the day, causing severe casualties, the strengths of the battalions involved being reduced by half. The enfilade fire from the right which had so smitten the 8th Division on the 31st was now reduced by the actions of the Bedford in Glencorse Wood. The Hanebeek valley, 600 yards to the front was, due to the weather, a morass of mud and standing water 30 yards across. This presented a secure obstacle to deter counter-attack by the *90th R.I.R.* of the *54th Division* facing the 74th Brigade. But the *90th Reserve* were not easily deterred and made great efforts to concentrate a counter-attacking force in the terrible conditions of the Hanebeek valley, in an attempt to retake Westhoek ridge. The S.O.S. rockets of the British infantry were quickly answered and the enemy concentration was shattered by a succession of artillery barrages which left the dead and dying laying in huge numbers in the mud and squalor around the stream.

The second poorly planned but gallantly executed assault against the Gheluvelt plateau had therefore failed once again to seize the German Second Line across the narrow waist

---

[297] National Archives, maps showing distribution of enemy forces at 5 pm on the 10th August, in WO153/601
[298] National Archives, War Diary 74th Brigade WO95/2245

between the heads of the Bassevillebeek and Hanebeek valleys. But to the left a toehold had been gained in the southwestern corner of Glencorse Wood, and Westhoek hamlet and ridge were free of the enemy, although still dangerously exposed to their enfilade fire. This situation was obviously unsatisfactory and at 11:55 p.m. II Corps Commander Lieutenant-General Jacob ordered consolidation of the new positions, but added that the attack against the Second Line must be renewed as soon as practical. The commander of 53rd Brigade, who now held the line, pointed out the difficulties involved, especially as one of his battalions whilst moving up had lost direction in the dark. The attack was postponed for 24 hours and then, although artillery preparations were already underway, was cancelled. It was not just in the front lines that there had been casualties, as in carrying forward 80,000 rounds of ammunition during the day a company of the 12th Middlesex had lost 30 per-cent of their number.

It must have seemed to some that to make further recommendations regarding the conduct of operations was rather a waste of effort, all their previous warnings ignored, but subsequently proven correct by events. Gough had attempted to carry out Haig's orders by thrusting at the plateau, but had done so before the enemy artillery was dominated, which was one of the Commander-in-Chief's requirements. Time was pressing, and if Gough delayed the assault until after the domination of the enemy's artillery, what may be the consequences of this delay? It does however seem logical that the next step should have been a concentrated effort, allowing sufficient time for the necessary preparations, against the Gheluvelt plateau, before the resumption of a general offensive. Twice now it had been tried, the first time with insufficient concentration, and the second time with both insufficient concentration and insufficient preparation, and both efforts had failed. What chance the third time? On the other hand, what if the Army Commander accepted all the well meaning advice, and postponed and concentrated its forces? Did Fifth Army in any event have the necessary firepower to neutralize the local superiority of *Group Wytschaete's* guns behind Gheluvelt and Zandvoorde, or would this duel drag into an inconclusive artillery slogging match of indeterminate duration? The German ability to replace damaged guns had been clearly shown before the 31st July. The condition of the ground was dreadful, the movement of guns, howitzers, and ammunition backbreaking, and the casualties already suffered by the gun crews due to German counter battery fire alarming. Was to delay, also going to allow the Germans more time to concentrate and prepare? It was questionable whether Fifth Army had sufficient infantry reserves available for this concentration. The eight divisions which had been in reserve to the four attacking corps were all now in the line. Of the two divisions in Army reserve, the 56th went to II Corps on the 6th August, and the 61st to XIX Corps on the 14th August as partial replacement. Second Army had been asked to transfer three of its best divisions to Fifth Army, the 47th Division and 14th Division (less its artillery), going to II Corps on the 14th and 15th August, and 23rd Division going to XVIII Corps on the 15th. These three divisions were not scheduled to be used in the forthcoming operation, as they were now all that was left in Fifth Army reserve, and were thus earmarked for subsequent operations. This was however wishful thinking, as all were to be in the line before the end of the month. Evidently manpower was not available in sufficient numbers to replace the losses, and create an overwhelming concentration to attack the plateau. Lieutenant-General Jacob, unhappy with the situation at Gheluvelt requested a delay, to at least enable him to capture the German Second Line before the main offensive was launched. Major-General Heneker who's 8th Division had suffered so badly at Westhoek on the 31st July, and was to attack again in the next operation, asked that Glencorse Wood and Nonne Boschen should be taken in a preliminary attack, rather than expose his division to the same fate again.

The stark, cold realities of the War now placed Gough in a dilemma. Should he stop and attempt to concentrate forces which were not readily available, or press on with what he had without further delay? Should he allow II Corps more time to secure the German line along the waist of the plateau? What did the Commander-in-Chief really expect of him? Would it be best to pause and wear down the enemy at Gheluvelt first? Or should he attempt to thrust on where he could make some progress, towards the ridge and Passchendaele? And what of the operation on the coast, which had to catch the end of month high tides to act in coordination with the Fifth Army break out past Roulers, or be delayed for another four weeks? Did he really have the forces immediately at his disposal to do any of these things? Ideally he should wait until his artillery had dominated that of the enemy, but this surely is what he had been attempting to do since the middle of July with little result, and it was with reality and not ideals that he must contend.

Gough had to make the decision. He considered the situation and made up his mind. A postponement of 24 hours would be granted to allow for reliefs, and then the main offensive would recommence along the whole front on the 15th August. But the weather, in the fashion of that season had the final word, with 18.1mm of rain falling on the 14th August, and nearly 8mm on the 15th. Once more the battlefield took upon itself the qualities of a slough, and there was another postponement of a further 24 hours. What would become known as the Battle of Langemarck, and would herald probably the most depressing and discouraging period ever experienced by the British Army in war would begin at 4:45 a.m. on the 16th August.

Weather conditions, rainfall Vlamertinghe, temperature Ypres[299]

	13th Aug	14th Aug	15th Aug	16th Aug	17th Aug	18th Aug	19th Aug	20th Aug
Rainfall	Trace	18.1mm	7.8mm	Trace	Trace	Trace	Nil	Trace
Temp	67F	70F	65F	68F	72F	74F	69F	71F

Battle of Langemarck 4:45 a.m. the 16th August

On paper the objectives on the 16th August appeared less daunting for the eight divisions now in the line, than the distant targets which had challenged those on the 31st of July. The 8th Division, which had relieved the 25th Division on the 14th August, was back in the line on their old ground at Westhoek ridge and was the only division now present which had started on the 31st July. The Fifth Army was to attack along a front from Stirling Castle in the south to a line 1,500 yards north of the Ypres – Staden railway track near Langemarck in the north, beyond which it was again to be supported by the French First Army.

Once more the main task was to break through the German Third Line, referred to with familiarity and marked on the trench maps as the Gheluvelt – Langemarck Line. The objective was limited to an advance of around 1,500 yards, and lay beyond the German Third Line by a distance of between 100 and 600 yards. If the attack succeeded XIX Corps in the centre would be back on the positions it had reached at its high water mark on 31st July, about the Zonnebeke – Langemarck road, just beyond Hill 37, and would again be up on Gravenstafel ridge, as would XVIII Corps on its left. On II Corps front on the plateau, a defensive flank would be established through the awful Inverness Copse; the appalling Glencorse Wood would be cleared, as would the waterlogged squalor of Nonne Bosschen, and the western side of Polygon Wood would be penetrated. The quagmire in the Hanebeek valley would be crossed and the ridge beyond with the powerful German blockhouses and observation positions at Anzac Spur would be secured. On the northern flank the penetration would be slightly deeper carrying the attack about 1,500 yards beyond Langemarck and Wijdendrift, to the muddy banks of the Broenbeek, the French conforming on the left. Such were the Fifth Army plans.

In preparation for the assault great efforts had been made in the XIV Corps area to place bridges across the Steenbeek between Langemarck and Wijdendrift, to help ford the morass on

---

[299] National Archives, GHQ statistics WO95/14

the day of the battle, and many local operations took place in awful conditions to secure minor bridgeheads on the eastern bank of the stream. The 20th Division had been busy bridging the stream before the 7th August, for on this day at Chien Farm near the bridge on the Langemarck road the Germans succeeded in blowing up one of their constructions. On the 11th August, 29th Division, having relieved the Guards Division on the 7th had been active near Passerelle Farm. At 4:14 a.m. the 1st Lancashire Fusiliers and 16th Middlesex had forded the Steenbeek and attacked the farm which fell at the second attempt to the Middlesex. The position was consolidated with outposts established on the east bank, and twelve timber bridges were laid across the stream. At 4:00 a.m. on the 14th August again in 20th Division sector, on the Pilckem – Langemarck road, the 10th Rifle Brigade with the 11th in support had crossed the stream with the aid of bridges and attacked the blockhouse at Au Bon Gite, failing to take it but consolidating a shell-hole position 20 yards short by 6:00 a.m. On the 15th August at 5:00 a.m. the Germans attempted to drive the bridgehead back across the stream but were repulsed by the 11th Rifle Brigade.

At dawn on the 16th August, a ground mist limited visibility to 300 yards, but it had stopped raining. The assault brigades had moved up through a very dark night, which had made their journey up the wooden tracks, which had been laid where possible across the crater fields of water filled shell-holes, both treacherous and fatiguing. They were however all formed up in position and ready on the tapes, when at 4:45 a.m. as the barrage opened right along the front, they again advanced into the abyss. As the sun rose above the tortured landscape, the day became bright and sunny.

II Corps on the plateau

From the position established on the 10th August along a line from Clapham Junction through the north-west tip of Glencorse Wood and on across Westhoek ridge, the 56th and 8th Divisions of II Corps were to advance to an average depth of around 1,500 yards, into the western side of Polygon Wood and across the Hanebeek valley and onto Anzac spur. This was a much deeper penetration than had been attempted on the 10th, but to compensate the battalions were to attack on a much narrower frontage of 250 rather than 400 yards. The front battalions would advance behind a barrage that would lift 100 yards in five minutes, and they would then stop on an intermediate line where the support battalions would pass through them on to the objective. The creeping barrage would be provided by 180 18-pounder field guns, about one gun for every 12 yards of front, and standing barrages by 72 4.5-inch howitzers and 36 18-pounder guns would be fired at targets in and beyond the area to be occupied. A machine gun barrage provided by the 8 machine gun companies of each division would fire overhead up to a range 2,500 yards. A defensive right flank between Stirling Castle and Black Watch Corner, at the south-western tip of Polygon Wood, was to be formed along a line of eight selected strong-points which were to be captured and consolidated by the 56th (1st London) Division. The 8th Division was to attack from the ground it knew well on Westhoek ridge.

From the 14th August the attack battalions began moving into the line, and the ground conditions which were universally dreadful greatly hampered the reliefs. On the morning of the 16th enemy shelling of the British forward lines on the plateau, on support and rear areas on the western slopes and on Westhoek ridge continued to be heavy. Much of this fire, which was mainly high explosive, came in enfilade from the south-east, from the Zandvoorde group of guns.

German forces facing II Corps[300]
The *34th Division* held the line between Tower Hamlets and Nonne Bosschen with the *30th I.R.*(left), the *67th I.R.* (centre) and the *145th I.R.* (right) in the line. North of Nonne Bosschen and up to the Ypres – Roulers railway the front was still held by the *54th Division*, with the *27th R.I.R.* (left) the *90th R.I.R.* (support / centre) and the *84th I.R.* (right), in the line.

---

[300] National Archives, maps showing distribution of enemy forces at 5 pm on the 15th August, in WO153/601

56th (1st London) Division
Major-General F. A. Dudgeon

On the 13th August the 56th Division had relieved the 18th Division, in the line between Stirling Castle and Surbiton Villas. The 18th Division handed over the 53rd Brigade to the 56th Division which had held the line since the night of the 10th August. The brigade commander Br.-General Higginson had made it known on the 12th and again on the 14th of August that 53rd Brigade, after severe losses sustained in holding the line over the last five days, was not in a fit state to accomplish its task of securing the right flank of the attack. Subsequently on the 15th he was sent two battalions to assist, but only one, the 1/4th London, from 56th Division reserve, could be considered fresh, as the other, the 7th Bedford, had only rested for three days since its punishing ordeal in Glencorse Wood. These two battalions, one in a very weak condition, would now form the divisional defensive flank between Stirling Castle and Black Watch Corner. It was not a promising start. The 169th Brigade was to attack towards Glencorse Wood to the left of the 53rd and the southern end of Nonne Bosschen, while the 167th Brigade attacked to the left of 169th towards the northern end of Nonne Bosschen. Around 9:00 p.m. on the 15th amidst heavy enemy shell-fire, the assault companies began moving into their assembly positions in the front line. By 2:00 a.m. most were in position, but the hostile fire had already caused many casualties.

53rd Brigade (18th Division attached)
At 4:45 a.m. the 7th Bedford, prematurely back in the line, attacked behind the barrage towards the north-west corner of Inverness Copse, but immediately came under heavy shellfire from the south-east, seemingly from the German batteries around Zandvoorde, causing severe casualties and disruption.[301] Known German blockhouses in the north-west corner of Inverness Copse which housed at least three machine guns, and at Fitzclarence Farm on the open plateau just north of the copse, were to have been the targets of heavy artillery at 5:00 p.m. and 7:00 p.m. the previous evening, but the bombardments had not materialized, and preparatory shelling by 4.5-inch howitzers against the stubborn concrete structures had been ineffective. The remnants of the gallant Bedford were now cut down by machine gun fire from these blockhouses, which brought their attack to a standstill.

The 1/4th London was also hit by the shelling from south-east of the plateau and machine gun fire from the blockhouses, and eventually formed a weak protective flank along the southern edge of Glencorse Wood. Further attempts by support companies to get forward also failed. The attempt to form the southern defensive flank had rapidly stalled.[302]

169th Brigade [303]
With the 1/5th and 1/2nd London Regiment in the line and the 1/9th in support the 169th Brigade were to attack through Glencorse Wood and the central and southern section of Nonne Bosschen.[304] The leading waves of the 5th and 2nd moved up into their assembly positions in Jargon Trench by 2:00 a.m. Enemy shelling was heavy causing casualties and inevitable confusion, and the condition of the ground was appalling. At 4:45 the forward wave of the 1/2nd London, with a company of the 1/16th (Queen's Westminster Rifles) attached as moppers-up, advanced and encountered a shelled area of marsh 30 yards across, one foot deep in standing water. They attempted to edge round it by veering to the right, crowding into the 5th London and causing it to do the same. Both battalions were now much disorganized, but the advance worked forward slowly towards fortified enemy shell-holes and bunkers, well camouflaged

---

[301] National Archives, War Diary 7th Bedford WO95/2043
[302] The brigade was faced by the *67th Infantry Regiment* holding the centre of the of the *34th Division* sector of *Group Wytschaete* front, which had been in the line since the 12th August.
[303] National Archives, War Diary 169th Brigade WO95/2958
[304] National Archives, War Diary 1/2nd London WO95/2960, War Diary 1/5th London WO95/2961/62

amongst the debris of the wood. The enemy posts were gradually bombed and cleared. Hostile fire became heavier, and the barrage which had lifted too quickly for the infantry to keep pace was of little assistance. The leading wave now in reduced numbers pressed on through Glencorse Wood towards the German Third Line. The enemy resisted from a number of concrete shelters along a sunken track in the wood, but the posts were soon cleared by the moppers-up of the 1/16th. The front wave worked beyond Glencorse Wood, but came under increasing fire from the numerous pillboxes on the *Wilhelm Stellung.* Enfilade fire from both flanks became more intense, as the brigades to right and left were held up. A few men may have reached Polygon Wood, but most survivors of the forward wave, having reached their objective, were driven back to the shelters in the sunken track where the second wave and the 1/16th had taken cover. The 1/9th London moved up in support of the 1/5th and 1/2nd but could do little more under the intense machine gun fire than reinforce this line. The few forward outposts which the London had been able to establish gradually became untenable, and at around 7:00 a.m. the brigade fell back to the shelters along the sunken track in Glencorse Wood. Here some of the London assault waves remained, but most fell-back further through the wood to be finally rallied and re-organized on the line from which they started in Jargon Trench.

Casualties had been severe, and the number of missing illustrated the confused nature of the fighting. Typical were the casualties of the 1/2nd London which had sustained a total of 33 killed, 126 wounded and 167 missing.

167th Brigade [305]
The 1/8th Middlesex Regiment and 1/1st London Regiment,[306] whose left abutted the Westhoek – Zonnebeke road, were to advance through the northern end of Nonne Bosschen, towards Polygon Wood on the right, and across the upper Hanebeek valley towards the southern end of Anzac spur on the left. The battalions assembled with the first wave in Jabber Support, the second wave in Jabber Trench, and the following two waves echeloned in trenches and shell-holes just in rear. The 7th Middlesex was in support.

The enemy were already shelling Westhoek ridge heavily when the British barrage came down at 4:45 a.m. Advancing into the northern end of Nonne Bosschen the Middlesex found the conditions in the wood to be appalling with small lakes of muddy water up to four feet deep. The same quagmire which had caused the 2nd London to veer to the right, caused the leading Middlesex "B" Company to veer to the left to attempt to get around it, a gap opening between the two battalions. The barrage had now been lost and hostile machine gun and rifle fire from the pillboxes on the *Wilhelm Stellung* was increasing drastically. "B" Company now supported by "C" Company could get no farther forward and attempted to consolidate, but the ground conditions prevented even this, the only shelter available provided by the water-filled craters. An attempt to bring up Stokes mortars to break the deadlock also failed, the teams being shot down as they struggled to drag their weapons and ammunition forward. At 7:00 a.m. 169th Brigade were seen to be falling back on the right and by 10:00 a.m. the Middlesex shell-hole outpost line, now dangerously exposed, was withdrawn west of Nonne Bosschen, to within 300 yards of their jumping-off line at Jabber Trench.

The 1/1st London, advanced into the upper Hanebeek valley north of Nonne Bosschen, but was disorganized at the start by heavy enemy shell-fire. Anxious to get forward out of the hostile fire the front waves closed up together beneath the barrage, the moppers-up becoming engulfed with the third wave which also closed up to the barrage. The terrible ground added to the confusion, further breaking the cohesion of the attack, and parties of Germans passed-over in shelters and shell-holes caused disruption from behind as the battalion attempted to move forward. Very few got beyond the intermediate objective. As machine gun fire from Anzac spur increased, the forward companies desperately took shelter in water-filled shell-holes.

---

[305] National Archives, War Diary 167th Brigade WO95/2947
[306] Everard Wyrall *The Die Hards in the Great War Vol II 1916-1919* London: Harrison and Son pp108-110

By mid-morning the brigade was generally back at a position a few hundred yards forward of Jabber Trench, with a number of Lewis gun outposts thrown forward protecting the line. The enemy barrage remained severe all day on Westhoek ridge. Communications between the front outposts of 1/1st London, battalion headquarters, and 167th Brigade had been non existent. There were no telephone lines, the power buzzer sets had broken, visual signaling had failed, and even if it had been established the volume of shell-fire on the ridge had rendered it impossible to keep a signaler at the most exposed point. Most runners had been killed, as to get back from the forward outposts meant passing the enemy strong-points which had not been cleared. At battalion headquarters the pigeons, which would have been the only means of communication with the rear had been buried by an enemy shell.

The 56th Division had failed In its attempts to form a strong defensive southern flank, and to break the German Third Line along the eastern face of Polygon Wood and along Anzac spur, due partly to machine guns in bunkers still not reduced by the artillery, partly to *Group Wytschaete's* undefeated artillery, but mainly to the appalling state of the ground in the bogs of the watershed of the upper Hanebeek. The filthy tangled woods continued to be virtually impregnable. Undoubtedly the use of a tired and depleted battalion had not helped the situation, and nowhere were there sufficient supports available to secure any positions which had been reached. In places the barrage was considered weak and partly ineffective due to the use of burst on graze fuses which were useless on the soft muddy ground.[307] There were too many reasons for the failure and there had been too little chance of success. Parties of the *145th Regiment* were still behind the isolated detachments of the four forward British battalions, and in places more were infiltrating forward, and the serious German counter-attacks of the *Eingreif* divisions had not yet begun. A passage from the War Diary of the 1/7th Middlesex, which relieved the 1/8th Middlesex and 1/1st London on the 17th August is poignant and well illustrates the conditions. 'After passing a horrible day amidst the most ghastly conditions, with masses of badly wounded men on all sides, whom it was impossible to evacuate and for whom practically nothing could be done until after dark, the battalion was relieved by the 9th Rifle Brigade.'[308]

8th Division [309]

Directly across its line of advance the 8th Division was confronted by the muddy Hanebeek valley which had been considered an excellent barrier against German counter-attack on the 10th August. The state of the ground was now little better. Once across, the division would advance up the eastern slope towards the German Third Line, held by the *27th Reserve Regiment* of the *54th Division*, along the fortified line of blockhouses and shelters through Iron Cross Redoubt, Anzac, Jagged Trench, Zonnebeke Redoubt, and Dragon Trench as far north as the Roulers railway embankment. Since suffering 3,076 casualties in the Pilckem ridge battle and being pulled out of the line on the 1st August, the division had come back into the line on the 14th August after only two weeks rest, when it was usually accepted that at least four to six weeks were necessary to refit. The concerns already expressed by Major-General Heneker which had been shown on the 31st July to be well founded, regarding the dangers to his division of enfilade fire from an enemy still active in Nonne Bosschen 500 yards on his right flank, were once more to be proven correct. The failure to drive the enemy from the woods on the edge of the plateau in a preliminary operation, and the failure of 56th Division to do so now, would once more bring failure to 8th Division. By 4:15 a.m. all attacking battalions were in position on the eastern side of Westhoek ridge. As the British barrage descended the German artillery replied almost immediately landing on top of the ridge and on the eastern slope, but mainly west of the jumping-off tapes and so causing little damage.

---

[307] This situation was soon to be addressed with the introduction of the more sensitive French 106 fuse.
[308] Everard Wyrall *The Die Hards in the Great War Vol II 1916-1919* p115
[309] Lt.-Colonel J.H. Boraston (1926) *The Eighth Division in War, 1914-1918* London: The Medici Society

25th Brigade [310]

Things started well at 4:45 for the assaulting battalions, the 2nd Royal Berkshire Regiment advancing to the right of the Westhoek – Zonnebeke road, with the 1st Royal Irish Rifles on their left. The 2nd Lincolnshire Regiment was in support. Moving forward with the barrage, carrying small portable bridges to cross the dreadfully muddy Hanebeek, the Berkshire pressed on up the slope towards Iron Cross Redoubt. As the battalion struggled towards the ridge it came under damaging flank fire from the north-west corner of Nonne Bosschen and from Polygon Wood. It was clear that the 167th Brigade was held up to the right and a company of the Berkshire was detailed to form a defensive flank. The remainder continued up the slope, and on Anzac spur fought their way into the *Wilhelm Stellung* at Iron Cross Redoubt, which was soon largely secured.

The Irish Rifles also started well being less effected by the fire coming from the right flank, wading through the mire in Hanebeek Wood and struggling across the stream to continue up the slope to the battered defences of the *Wilhelm Stellung*, and secure Anzac and Iron Cross Redoubt, reaching their final objective 200 yards beyond the German Third Line by 7:00 a.m.

23rd Brigade [311]

On the right of the 23rd Brigade front the 2nd West Yorkshire Regiment started well and advanced with the Irish Rifles to their right.[312] Little opposition was met as the barrage had done its work well. In Hanebeek Wood two German machine guns were captured, lying on the muddy parapet without their sledge like mountings, the guns still hot from firing but the crews all dead or wounded. The attack moved forward up the slope beyond the Hanebeek and reached the final objective at Zonnebeke Redoubt on Anzac spur, where by 7:00 a.m. the West Yorks began consolidating, an outpost line being pushed forward down the eastern slope by 7:30. To the left of the West Yorks the 2nd Middlesex advanced with their left on the Roulers railway. The 2nd Devonshire Regiment was to act as moppers-up for the two forward battalions while the 2nd Scottish Rifles were in brigade support. Machine gun fire from the railway embankment, and from Potsdam Redoubt 150 yards beyond the railway and 500 yards in front of the German Third Line soon checked the progress of the Middlesex left. North of the railway 16th Division had been checked in front of Potsdam, allowing the left of the Middlesex to be exposed to machine gun fire. At 5:05 a.m. with the right company also being held up by the same fire, the battalion formed a flank facing the railway with the right on a small enclosure just north of Sans Souci.

The right and centre of 8th Division was now 1,000 yards forward of both the 56th and the 16th Division and was in a vulnerable and exposed position. By 6:00 a.m. the isolated forward detachments of the London battalions of 56th Division east of Nonne Bosschen found themselves surrounded, due to infiltration by the *145th Regiment*. At about this time a German counter-attack preceded by a creeping barrage forced the few survivors of the 5th and 2nd London back to the shelters along the sunken track in Glencorse Wood where at 7:00 a.m. they rallied behind a protective machine gun screen fired by Vickers guns of the 9th London, which checked the counter-attack. To the left the 8th Middlesex and 1st London were forced back beyond the western edge of Nonne Bosschen to within a few hundred yards of their jumping-off line at Jabber Trench, the Germans quickly re-establishing their machine guns in the intact blockhouses in the north-west corner of the wood. A number of low flying German aircraft attacked the precarious line of 167th Brigade positions machine gunning the shell-hole outposts. The infantry cowering in muddy shell-holes, brought what rifle and Lewis gun fire they could to bear on the enemy aircraft and had the unusual satisfaction of shooting one down. The 53rd Brigade had issued an order for a support battalion to once more try to form a defensive flank by an attack southward from the southern edge of Glencorse Wood, but on receipt of the

---

[310] National Archives, War Diary 25th Brigade WO95/1727
[311] National Archives, War Diary 23rd Brigade WO95/1710
[312] National Archives, War Diary 2nd West Yorks WO95/1714

information of the German counter-attack, the hopelessness of the situation was recognized and this order was cancelled.

The retaking by the Germans of the blockhouses in the north-west corner of Nonne Bosschen was now to have a serious effect on 25th Brigade consolidating 1,000 yards to the north-east along Anzac spur, who were soon fired upon by these machine guns from their right rear. Even more alarming, at around 9:00 a.m. was the arrival by motor lorry of further German reinforcements, who dismounting west of Zonnebeke began to advance behind a creeping barrage and under cover of smoke towards Anzac spur. The 1st Royal Irish Rifles were forced of the crest of the spur, and back to the road to the west of the Anzac position, exposing the flank of the Berkshire on their right, who also began to fall-back. The infantry sent up their S.O.S. Very-light flares, but due to the smoke in the barrage they were not seen by the artillery observers. Only one contact aircraft was employed on each divisional front (which was subsequently considered inadequate), and only one indefinite air-call was received by the artillery. Support from the guns did not arrive until 10:15 a.m. by which time it was too late to influence the outcome, as by then the infantry, after suffering heavy losses had retired back across the Hanebeek, and the enemy had established themselves in the bogs close up to the stream. The *27th Regiment* had been reinforced by the *34th Fusilier Regiment of the 3rd Reserve (Eingreif) Division* for this counter-attack, and now they pressed forward across the quagmire, threatening the flank of the 23rd Brigade. At 8:30 a.m. the West Yorks holding a weak line on Anzac spur and out of touch on both flanks had come under heavy machine gun fire, which compelled them to withdraw to the western side of the ridge. By 9:30 they also observed the hostile counter-attack in considerable numbers developing along the ridge. Again they fell-back toward the Hanebeek, establishing two posts east of Hanebeek Wood, the remainder of the battalion sheltering in the muddy tangled remains of the wood itself. On the right elements of both 25th and 23rd Brigades, in a disorganized and intermixed state were now back to within 200 yards of their start line just forward of Jabber Trench, where they were finally rallied. To the left, the 2nd West Yorks were a little farther forward near the stream, with the 2nd Middlesex still holding their defensive left flank where the Hanebeek passed under the railway. The situation along this line remained precarious throughout the afternoon, as the Germans fired a standing barrage at the position boxing-in the battalions in the Hanebeek valley who had carried out the morning assault, and preventing the forward movement of ammunition, and food. At around 3:30 p.m. another enemy counter-attack nearly reached Hanebeek Wood, and worked around the right rear of the two West Yorks posts in front of the wood, which were subsequently withdrawn west of the Hanebeek. Artillery support was called for to prevent the enemy crossing the Hanebeek, and the S.O.S. was again fired, but it was another 30 minutes before the barrage came down.

To the right the fragile line held by 56th Division was threatened about 4:00 p.m. as a German counter-attack, reinforced by all three support battalions of the *9th Reserve Regiment*, developed through and on both sides of Polygon Wood. On the line of the shelters along the sunken track in Glencorse Wood the 169th Brigade had expended virtually all their ammunition, and fell-back to their start line on the west side of the wood, exposing the flank of the 167th Brigade to enfilade machine gun fire, at which point they in turn also fell-back. A small party of the 1/1st London with stragglers of the 2nd Royal Berkshire of 25th Brigade, and of the 3rd London (which had been relieved by the 1/1st), had remained in shell-holes and gun-pits forward of Jabber Reserve most of the day. It had proved impossible to get ammunition forward to them from Jabber Trench, and on seeing the general enemy advance coming over Anzac spur at around 5:00 p.m. the party had fallen-back slowly on Jabber Support, under cover two of Lewis guns. Enemy infantry estimated at 1,000 strong began following up the general British withdrawal, but at 5:00 p.m. S.O.S. signals brought down artillery fire which checked the counter-attack with severe losses. The German reoccupation of their positions in Nonne Bosschen allowed enfilade machine gun fire once more to inflict damage on the forward positions of 8th Division along the Hanebeek, and later in the evening a full withdrawal was carried out nearly to the morning start line, back up on Westhoek ridge.

The II Corps assault on the vital Gheluvelt position had floundered in frustrating, bloody, failure. The woods and the upper Hanebeek valley had gathered another full harvest of the dead and dying of both sides. The casualties in the 56th Division amounted to 2,175, and in the 8th Division to 2,111 to be added to the 3,076 of the Pilckem battle. 56th Division was pulled out of the battle line on the night of the 17th/18th August to be replaced by the 14th Division, and the 8th Division suffered on until the night of the 18th/19th when it was relieved by the 47th Division, (both relieving divisions coming from Second Army). After a second major attempt, the right flank of the main attack was still not secure, the German Third Line and the bastion of the Gheluvelt plateau had still not been broken, and there seemed little hope, unless there was a drastic change of tactics, that it ever would.

XIX Corps

The attack of XIX Corps was to be very much an Irish operation, the 16th (Southern Irish) Division and the 36th (Ulster) Division being in line side by side as they had been at Messines where they had done so well. They were now however seriously under strength and not fully capable of carrying out the task required. The huge casualties sustained by the 15th and 55th Divisions on the 31st July had made it essential in the opinion of the Corps Commander to quickly relieve them both. On the 3rd August the 16th Division commenced the relief of the 15th Division in the front line, and the 36th Division relieved the 55th. Previously In Corps reserve, both the 16th and 36th had since the last week in July been employed in the arduous duties of digging and carrying under the most trying conditions, in and across the most dreadful ground, and had remained in the forward areas of the Hanebeek and Steenbeek valleys during the whole period of the offensive. Working in these exposed forward areas, the casualties caused through artillery and machine gun fire from the German positions on the higher ridges, had been approaching the levels of those divisions which had been engaged in the fighting, and sickness had also taken a toll. Now they were to take up their positions in the line 12 days before they were to go into battle. Between the 1st to the 15th August, the 16th Division had suffered over 2,000 casualties, and the 36th over 1,500 casualties, and in this state they were to take up the assault, the divisional battle strengths being down by around one third of full establishment. In some battalions the strength was down to one half. Between the 31st July and the 18th of August the 6th Connaught Rangers of the 47th Brigade, 16th Division, although not having been in the line during the period had sustained 250 casualties. Just to get up to the flooded forward trenches was a battle in itself, the indefinite outpost line being little more than muddy, water-filled shell-holes. The 7th Leinster of the 47th Brigade, went into the front line in relief of the 8/10th Gordon of the 15th Division on the 3rd August, with the battalion H.Q. in an old German bunker at Frezenberg Redoubt. Iron rations and water were the only sustenance available, as to get food into the line was simply impossible. Under constant hostile shelling and air attack, by the time the battalion was relieved on the 5th it was in a pitiable state, nearly every man suffering from trench foot.

The ground over which the Southern Irish and Ulster were to attack was totally exposed, and was in a deplorable state of muddy quagmire and water-filled craters, the very same shell-torn ground over which the attack of the 31st July had ebbed and flowed. On the right of the Corps front the 16th Division was to advance down a gentle slope, then across the Hanebeek, and up a slight rise towards Zonnebeke spur, with their right against the Roulers railway and their left across Zonnebeke spur between Hill 35 and Hill 37. Their final objective was about 500 yards beyond the German Third Line. To the left of the 16th, the 36th Division extended the front nearly to St. Julien, their attack starting from ground just to the east of the Steenbeek. The division was to advance up the gentle rise towards Zonnebeke spur, beyond which lay the Zonnebeke – Langemarck road, and the shallow valley of the northern Hanebeek. The final objective lay in this valley, an average of 500 yards beyond the German Third Line.

Across the whole front the German blockhouses and bunkers, which had caused such agony on the 31st, were fully ready for action. They had not been neutralized by the series of short concentrated bombardments fired by the heavy guns at ranges between 6,000 and 8,000 yards, which had been intended to smash them. These relatively small targets were difficult to both identify and to hit directly, and anything less did not destroy them. The German line was held by the *5th Bavarian Division* with the *19th* and *7th Bavarian Infantry Regiments* in the line, and the *21st Bavarian Infantry Regiment* in reserve, plus elements of the *12th Reserve Division* at Passchendaele.[313]

16th (Southern Irish) Division [314]
Major-General W. B. Hickie

The 16th Division had begun to come into the line on the 3rd August. Following the Leinster, the 8th Royal Dublin Fusiliers of the 48th Brigade entered the front line on the 5th August and the 7th Royal Inniskilling Fusiliers of 49th Brigade on the 6th. With battalions already reduced in numbers, holding the line under appalling conditions for up to 11 days prior to attack was a recipe for disaster. The division was to attack with the 48th Brigade and the 49th Brigade, and was faced by a formidable array of blockhouses, at Potsdam, Vampir Farm, Borry Farm, Beck House, Iberian, and Pommern Castle, that guarded the approach to the *Wilhelm Stellung*. It has been questioned whether the division was trained sufficiently in attack against the new German defence systems. The atrocious ground also gave the advantage to the defence, making rapid out-flanking movements impossible. The creeping barrage of fourteen 18-pounder batteries and standing barrage of twenty-four 4.5-inch howitzer batteries had negligible effect on lessening the fire from the blockhouses. This was even more true of the machine gun barrage fired overhead on three successive lines by 40 guns of the division from west of the Frezenberg – St. Julien road.

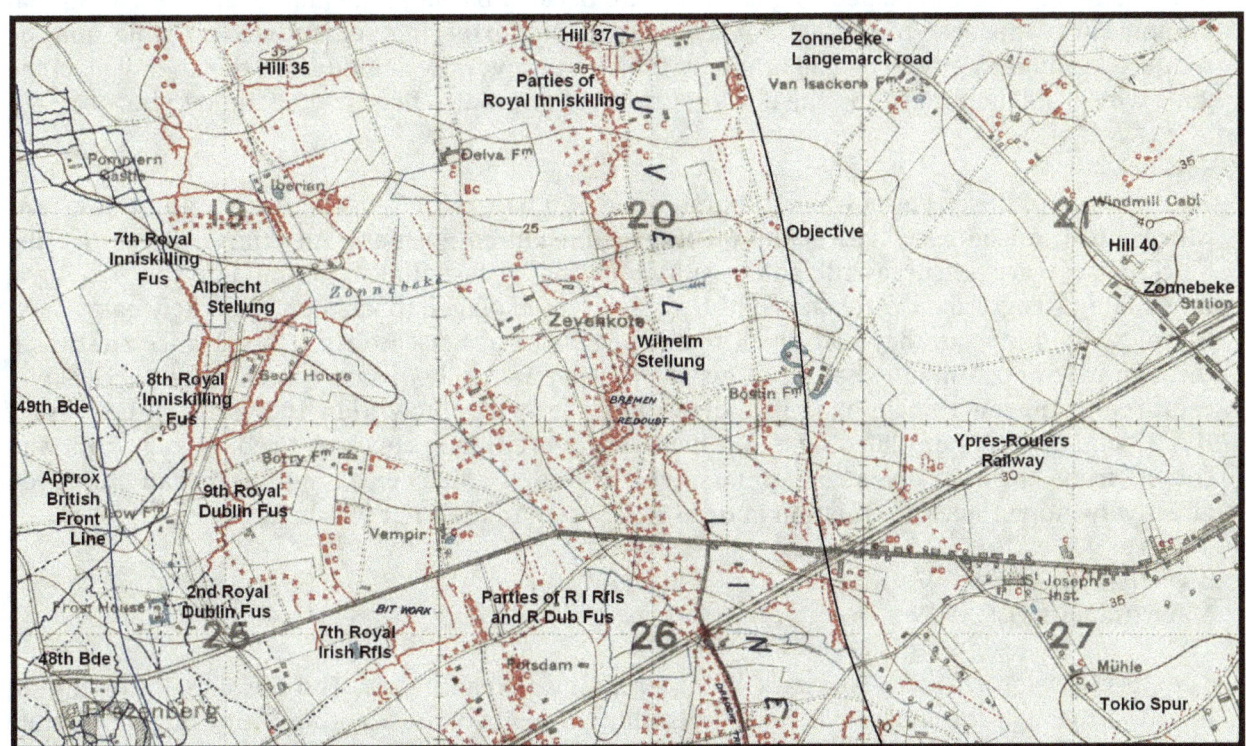

The attack of the 48th and 49th Brigades 16th (Southern Irish) Division

---

[313] National Archives, maps showing distribution of enemy forces at 5 pm on the 15th August, in WO153/601
[314] Terence Denman *Ireland's Unknown Soldiers The 16th (Irish) Division in the Great War 1914-1918* Irish Academic Press pp121-124

The 48th Brigade could initially muster no more than 27 officers and 700 other ranks. In the 2nd Royal Dublin Fusiliers "D" Company was broken up and the officers and men were attached to the other 3 companies. One company of the 8th Royal Dublin was attached to the 2nd in place of "D" Company, bringing the 2nd Royal Dublin strength up to no more than 400. In an effort to make up numbers the 1st Royal Munster Fusiliers from 47th Brigade were attached to 48th Brigade. In 49th Brigade the 7th Inniskilling could muster only 19 officers and 472 men for the attack.

48th Brigade [315]

The brigade was to attack with the 7th Royal Irish Rifles and the 9th Royal Dublin Fusiliers, with "A" and "B" Companies of the 2nd Royal Dublin Fusiliers in close support, "C" Company in support, and the attached company of the 8th Royal Dublin in reserve. Before Zero Hour the enemy opened a heavy barrage on the assembled battalions causing a number of casualties. Immediately the assault began machine guns from Potsdam, and Vampir Farm raked the thin ranks of the 7th Royal Irish Rifles, while to their left the 9th Royal Dublin Fusiliers were similarly struck from both Vampir and Borry Farms. The leading companies lost two thirds of their number to the intense fire, but isolated parties had past beyond the blockhouses and continued to struggle forward through the mire. The mopping-up sections of the 2nd Dublins came under the same hail of machine gun fire as they approached Potsdam and Vampir Farm, very few getting close enough to come to grips with the enemy garrisons. On the right, some of "A" Company of the 2nd succeeded in working forward and reaching the support company of the 7th Royal Irish Rifles which was held up under heavy machine gun fire short of the German Third Line having lost all its officers. On the left, in front of Vampir Farm the enemy machine guns had practically annihilated "B" Company of the 2nd Dublin which was reduced to 2 officers and 3 other ranks, but had managed to get a message back to battalion headquarters informing that Vampir Farm appeared to contain 5 machine guns. No further movement was possible, and the scattered groups in pitifully small numbers took what cover they could from the enemy machine guns which, still holding out in the blockhouses, were now also fired from behind them.

49th Brigade [316]

The garrison of Borry Farm, was estimated to be 100 men with 3 machine guns, and these guns raked into the leading waves of the 8th Royal Inniskilling Fusiliers. All efforts to capture the blockhouse were unsuccessful and resulted in many casualties. To the left the 7th Royal Inniskilling struggled on with a few of the 8th, and just managed to keep up with the weak
barrage. By 4:50 a.m. they had taken the strong-point at Beck House. The advance continued through machine gun and shell-fire towards Iberian and Delva Farm, which were successfully captured by the few remaining Inniskilling. Some got forward to within 400 yards of the crest of Hill 37 and the German Third Line. But here they were finally checked, fired at from front and sniped from the rear by strong-points which, due to their weak numbers had not been effectively moped-up. The situation in the 36th Division to their left was little better.

36th (Ulster) Division [317]
Major-General O. S. W. Nugent

The 36th Division was also to attack in an already weakened state. The divisional jumping-off line was through the morass of the over-spilling Steenbeek, presenting a thoroughly terrible section of the battlefield. The division was to use the 108th Brigade on the right, the 109th Brigade on the left with the 107th Brigade held in reserve. Each brigade was to attack with two battalions in the line, one in support 1,000 yards in rear, and the fourth in reserve in the old

---

[315] National Archives, War Diary 48th Brigade WO95/1973
[316] National Archives, War Diary 49th Brigade WO95/1976
[317] Cyril Falls (1922) *The History of the 36th (Ulster) Division* Belfast: McCaw, Stevenson & Orr pp114-118

British front and support lines. Each battalion was to attack on a 2 company front in 4 waves, but so weak were the battalions in numbers that the second and fourth waves were at half strength as each company had been reduced to 3 platoons. The objective of the leading companies, the Green Line, ran between Gallipoli and Schuler Farm, a distance of around 900 yards. Here the rear companies were to pass through to the final objective, the Red Line between 300 and 500 yards beyond the German Third Line. A company from each supporting battalion was allotted to the leading 2 battalions as moppers-up, and special platoons were given the responsibility to clear the dangerous bunkers at Somme, Pond Farm, Hindu Cot, Green House and Schuler Farm. On the night of the 15th as the attacking battalions waited in the assembly trenches they were hit by an enemy bombardment, causing casualties of about 50 men in each of the 4 leading battalions. No more than 2,000 men in total went 'over the top', the front wave being no stronger than 300, enemy machine gun fire probably reducing this figure by a third in the first half minute.

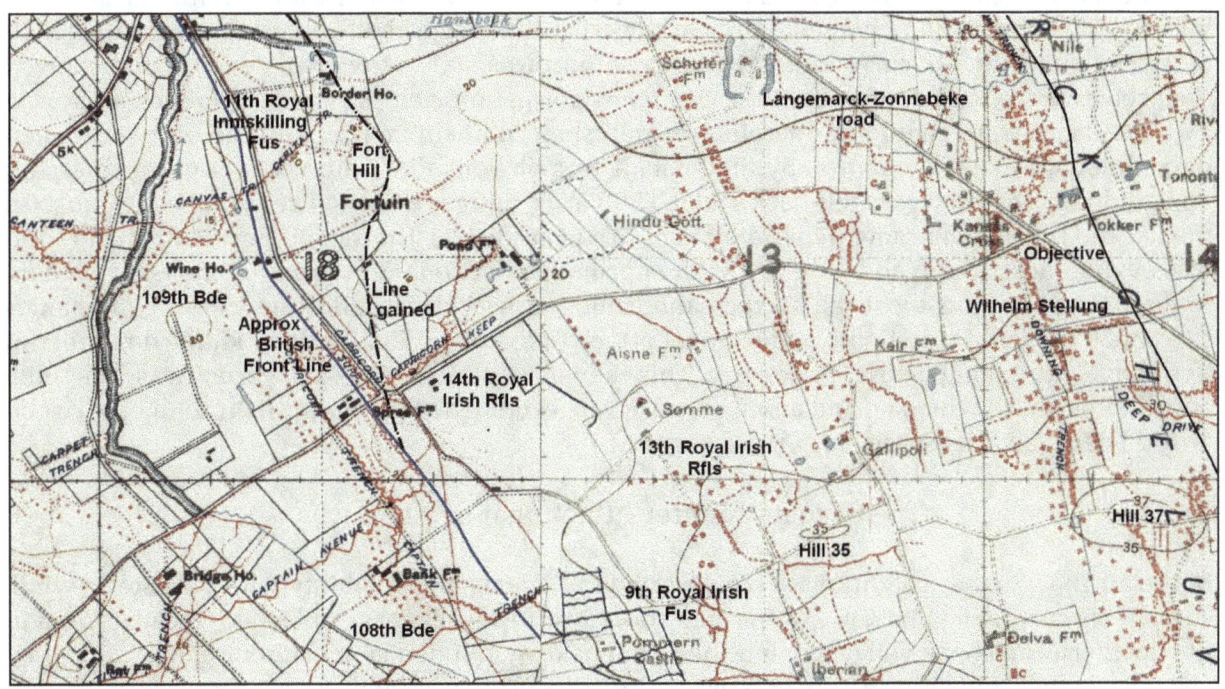

The attack of the 108th and 109th Brigades 36th (Ulster) Division

108th Brigade [318]

Advancing at 4:45 across atrocious ground and behind a weak barrage the 9th Royal Irish Fusiliers pressed forward from the broken entanglements and debris of Pommern Redoubt, and worked up across Hill 35, clearing the enemy from gun-pits on the western slope before them. The 13th Royal Irish Rifles on the left working between the shell-holes towards the Gallipoli and Somme blockhouses were immediately struck by severe machine gun fire. Hampered by the heavy mud they were easy targets for the enemy gunners. Moving forward painfully slowly they attempted to work around the blockhouses, but were held up by a recently strung diagonal line of wire entanglements which protected the approach. Breaks in the wire opened by the preparatory barrage were covered by German machine guns from the mutually supporting strong-points, and attempts by bombing parties to work round and bomb out the bunkers failed with ever mounting casualties.

    A few of the Irish Rifles, still under heavy fire, worked past the Somme blockhouse, hopeful that they could get forward and that it could be cleared by following waves. A subsequent attack to try and capture the blockhouse was unsuccessful, and with the 16th Division checked and driven back on the right by a counter-attack, at around 6:00 a.m. the 108th Brigade also began to fall-back. Upon seeing the withdrawal, and the damage being caused to his

---

[318] National Archives, War Diary 108th Brigade WO95/2504

battalion by the machine guns at Somme, Lieutenant -Colonel Maxwell of the Irish Rifles led forward his battalion headquarters in a desperate attack against the blockhouse. The attack was again unsuccessful and Maxwell was severely wounded in the attempt. Lieutenant -Colonel Somerville of the 9th Royal Irish Fusiliers had already been mortally wounded, but the battalion fought desperately to hold on to the top of Hill 35. The attack of 108th Brigade was at an end. The few survivors were driven back through the mud by the machine gun fire, almost to the start line. With the front in a disorganized state, the 12th Royal Irish Rifles were moved up from support to establish a defensive position on the Black Line, and made preparations to face any counter-attack.[319]

109th Brigade [320]
Struggling through the swamp east of the Steenbeek, across ground which was in places completely under water, the 14th Royal Irish Rifles and 11th Royal Inniskilling Fusiliers came under destructive fire from the blockhouses at Pond Farm and Border House. With machine gun bullets zipping all around a small party of the Irish Rifles worked forward amongst the shell-holes and succeeded in surrounding Pond Farm on three sides. Any of the enemy that showed themselves were shot down, but the Rifles were not in sufficient strength to mount an attack. Two messages were sent back for reinforcements, but no help arrived and the party remained pinned down by the enemy fire. By 8:00 a.m. it was obvious that help was not going to arrive, and gradually the survivors fell-back about 150 yards, under covering fire from Lewis guns. On the left the Inniskilling came under a blast of fire from Border House and Fort Hill. The ground was beyond description and although with enormous effort one officer and 7 men struggled on to the Green Line, most lost the barrage and could not get forward. But the support companies succeeded in mounting a bomb and bayonet attack upon Fort Hill at Fortuin, killing a number of Germans and taking some prisoners. This advance of around 400 yards was the only appreciable gain of the day, and a line of posts was established from the slight 20 metre rise of Fortuin back towards Spree Farm.[321]

The German counter-attack against XIX Corps

In the air the weather conditions were described as 'ideal, good visibility with a westerly wind' so it seems surprising that a major German counter-attack could assemble in the dead ground in the northern Hanebeek valley, behind the Zonnebeke – St. Julien spur without being noticed by air observation. But as in II Corps area so in XIX Corps area; only one contact aircraft was operating with each division and the German concentration went unnoticed with no information of it passed back to the guns. At around 9:00 a.m. German infantry, elements of the *12th Reserve (Eingreif) Division*, which had moved from Passchendaele and concentrated unseen behind the spur began to advance from the *Wilhelm Stellung* over the crest of Hill 37, towards the 16th and 36th Divisions. They reinforced the three battalions of the *21st Bavarian*, the support regiment of the *5th Bavarian Division*, and advanced behind a crushing artillery barrage, which contained an element of smoke sufficient to shield the advance from the British artillery ground observers. Those very few of the 7th Royal Irish Rifles and 9th Royal Dublin Fusiliers of 48th Brigade, and 8th Royal Inniskilling of 49th Brigade, which had fought through with such gallantry towards the German Third Line now fought again until they were killed or overrun. Others seeing the danger of being outflanked, fell-back around 1,000 yards through the blockhouse defence screen to the point from where they had started. Over the next hour a tragic re-enactment of the events of the 31st July was played out in exactly the same area, and the exhausted survivors of the two divisions, in filthy condition and with weapons choked with mud, struggled back towards their start line with the enemy in pursuit, only the tiny gain at Fortuin being held. At 9:30 a.m. "C" Company of the 2nd Dublin was sent up in support of the 9th

---

[319] The 11th Royal Irish Rifles were in brigade reserve.
[320] National Archives, War Diary 109th Brigade WO95/2508/09
[321] The 9th Royal Inniskilling was in brigade reserve.

Dublin. They succeeded in getting forward about 300 yards to within 100 yards of the German strong-point at Bit Work, just south of the Frezenberg – Zonnebeke road. Here, reduced to 2 officers and 10 men the survivors attempted to take cover in shell-holes. Two platoons of the composite company of the 2nd/8th Dublin moved up at 10:30, struggled forward a few hundred yards towards the blockhouses and into the remorseless machine gun fire. They lost all their officers and also took cover in shell-holes.

To defend the original position from the continuing counter-attack, the Corps Commander at 10:15 a.m. after discussion with the divisional commanders reluctantly decided to order a defensive barrage to stand in front of the start line, knowing that scattered survivors must be still holding out within the German position. Like a recurring nightmare, at 2:08 p.m. Fifth Army headquarters issued further orders which in reality were totally impossible to execute: 'II Corps will make every effort to clear up his right flank. Meanwhile XIX Corps will capture line Borry Farm – Hill 35 – Hindu Cot, and will get into touch with XVIII Corps at Winnepeg. With view to further advance at earliest possible moment, XVIII Corps and XIV Corps will reconnoiter line, von Tirpitz Farm – Quebec Farm – Rose House – U.24 central – U.18 central [2,000 yards north-east of Langemarck!] – Koekuit – U.10 central.[322] What forces were to be used to reach Hindu Cot 600 yards further forward than the small gain already made at Fortuin, and past the guns of Border House and Pond Farm was not immediately clear. Nor was it clear who was going to storm the menacing Borry Farm, or once again try to get up on to Hill 35. The shattered 7th Inniskilling was ordered to make another assault upon the Borry Farm blockhouse. The battalion had already reported that it had sustained losses approaching 400. The order was without meaning as there was no 7th Inniskilling to carry out the attack. The 7th / 8th Royal Irish Fusiliers were then sent up in an effort to support those of the 7th and 8th Inniskilling that still survived. The Fusiliers sustained 200 casualties in an unsuccessful attempt to get forward. The 2nd Royal Irish Regiment from 47th Brigade was also ordered forward in another futile and unsuccessful assault on the blockhouse at Borry Farm. By now the battlefield was strewn with the dead and wounded of many Irish battalions. Acting Lance-Corporal Fredrick George Room of the 2nd Royal Irish Regiment was to be awarded the V.C. for his courage and fearlessness as a stretcher bearer in recovering the wounded from the battlefield and saving the lives of many of his countrymen.

The remainder of the Fifth Army order required that II Corps should clear up the situation on its right flank. It must have seemed to Corps and Divisional Commanders that Army H.Q. was living in a different world, which to all intents and purposes it was. The stupidity of the order now seems inexcusable. It is a testament to the rigid discipline which dictated the actions of senior officers that the Corps Commander passed this order to his Divisional Commanders at 4:00 p.m. and questioned when they proposed to carry it out. The restraint natural to these senior officers now appears remarkable. Major-General Nugent commanding 36th Division suggested he could not comply until the following morning at the earliest.

At 4:10 p.m. the survivors of "A" Company of the 2nd Royal Dublin Fusiliers, fell-back from their hopelessly exposed position. One N.C.O. and 6 men reached the British Front Line. The remnants of the composite platoons of the 2nd/8th Dublin remained out on the battlefield until 10:00 p.m. the next day. Unsupported, raked by enemy fire and in a state of shock and total exhaustion they also finally withdrew to the British Front Line. In the 36th Division the casualties on the right had been severe, and after dark the survivors of the small party that had reached the Green Line crawled back to the British outposts. The 10th Inniskilling were brought forward from support to establish a defence line against counter-attack on the Black Line

What would have been the outcome of a renewed attack by the 16th and 36th Divisions the next morning is frightful to consider. However, both Nugent and Hickie, knowing from the reports of their brigadiers and battalion commanders that their divisions were now virtually broken, were against the idea to attack at all. No brigade could muster more than 500 men and the divisional reserve brigades were desperately trying to hold the original front line. At 8:00 p.m. Lieutenant-General Watts informed Fifth Army, undoubtedly to the great relief of all

---

[322] National Archives, War Diary Fifth Army, telegram in WO95/520

concerned, that XIX Corps could not carry out the attack ordered. The evacuation of the wounded from the battlefield was to prove an enormous task. The XIX Corps attack to capture the German Third Line, like that of II Corps, had ended in bloody, heart-braking failure. The 16th and 36th Division had fought courageously in the filthy conditions and through the murderous machine gun and shell fire. They could have done no more, and nothing more could have been asked of them. Losses in the two already weak divisions over the period of the battle from 16th to 18th August were: 16th Division 2,157, and 36th Division 2.076. Between the 1st August and the 20th August the 16th Division had lost 221 officers and 4,064 other ranks. Between the 2nd and the 18th August 36th Division had lost 144 officers and 3,441 other ranks.

XVIII Corps

The ground conditions either side of the Steenbeek from which Lieutenant -General Sir Ivor Maxse's XVIII Corps were about to attack with the 48th and 11th Divisions continued to be dreadful, there having been no sufficient period of drying to improve them. The area presented a muddy waste a mile wide and one of the worst parts of the battlefield. All movement in and around the line was difficult and keeping weapons working efficiently and clear of mud near impossible. Steel elephant shelters, heavy curved sheets of corrugated iron, were provided giving crude shelter for up to five men, and the numerous captured German bunkers were put to use as shelters, although inside often knee deep in water and putrid with decaying bodies. The bunkers could themselves be dangerous shell traps, as the exposed entrances were vulnerable to fire from the German lines. New entrances were gradually being blown in the four foot thick walls on the safe side, and when time and conditions permitted concrete shields were built by the engineers over the now exposed original entrance.

    The infrastructure behind the lines however had been greatly improved, work here being less molested by enemy artillery. The track of the Ypres – Staden railway had been carried across the canal at Boesinghe and repaired up towards the front lines of both XVIII and XIV Corps with spurs leading to newly laid 18 foot wide timber roads which in turn led on to narrow gauge railways and trench tramways and duck board tracks. All these works improved the movement of men and materials, especially those required by the artillery, the shell-dumps west of the canal now being more readily connected with the gun batteries. A web of plank roads, duckboard tracks and mule tracks wove their way towards the lines between the shell-craters, many emanating from the upwards of twenty four bridges and causeways thrown across the Ypres – Yser canal. Food and equipment and supplies of all types were reaching the troops in the front line more easily. The lighter cross-country routes were found to be less vulnerable to shell fire and more easily repaired than the heavier constructions. In many cases the mules picked their way across the ground rather than use the duck board walks which they easily blocked and damaged. The ground either side of the tracks however was still a slough. These organizational improvements had greatly assisted the build up to the new attack on the 16th. The field artillery to support the corps attack was impressive with 216 18-pounder field guns, amounting to one gun for every 13 yards of front, and 72 4.5-inch howitzers. On the 11th Division front alone for the 24 hour period of 16th August, 108 field guns fired 47,000 rounds, or three rounds every ten minutes, and 36 4.5-inch howitzers fired 13,409 rounds, or one round every four minutes. The heavy batteries would also add their support, concentrating on counter battery fire and communications targets deeper into the German position. On the other hand the German blockhouse and bunker system in front of the Langemarck – Gheluvelt Line was still strong and intact, having been little effected by the preliminary barrage which had however turned the battlefield into a waste of water-filled shell craters.

Opposite the right and centre of XVIII Corps the *183rd Division* held the enemy Front Line with the *418th I.R.* on the left and the *184th I.R.* on the right with the *440th I.R.* in support. The left of XVIII Corps was faced by the *121st Infantry Regiment,* on the left of the *26th Division*.[323]

48th (1st South Midland) Division
Major-General R. Fanshaw

To the right of the Corps sector, the 48th Division which had relieved the 39th Division on the 4th August was to attack with the 145th Brigade along a front approximately 1,300 yards, from just south of St. Julien to the point where the Regina Cross to Triangle Farm road crossed the Steenbeek. Its advance, a distance of about 1,250 yards, would be up the gentle slope east of the stream, across the Zonnebeke – Langemarck road and on to the objective just beyond the German Third Line which here ran along the western end of Gravenstafel Ridge.

145th Brigade [324]
The brigade attacked along the whole divisional front and was immediately raked by machine gun fire from the blockhouses which guarded the road to Poelcappelle at Border House, Hillock Farm, Triangle Farm, and Maison du Hibou. Advancing through the rubble of St. Julien, the 1/5th Gloucestershire Regiment were held up by fire from a German strong-point in a ruined house on the edge of the village, which they overcame with Lewis guns and rifle grenades, capturing forty of the enemy and a machine gun. The right company of the battalion, after advancing about 750 yards took by platoon attack, the moated strong-point at Border House, beside the northern Hanebeek. The centre companies secured strong-points at Jew Hill and Gun Pits, but were struck by machine gun fire from a bunker at Janet Farm 300 yards in front. On the left machine gun fire in enfilade, from Hillock Farm and Maison du Hibbou 1,000 yards distant the north, cut into the exposed flank. Unable to get further forward the Gloucester took cover in shell-holes, and attempted while still under long range fire to establish a defence line in the old German posts at Jew Hill and Gun Pits.

The 1/1st and 1/4th Oxfordshire and Buckinghamshire Light Infantry attacked to the left of St. Julien and came under intense machine gun crossfire as they topped the gentle rise 200 yards east of the Steenbeek. The 1/1st Ox and Bucks captured Hillock Farm, and some small parties of the battalion were seen to advance across the St. Julien – Poelcappelle road as far as Springfield on the Zonnebeke – Langemarck road, when all contact with them was lost. A blockhouse just west of Hillock Farm was used as a battalion headquarters and was established there at 7:00 a.m. The 1/4th Royal Berkshire Regiment in brigade reserve were brought up to strengthen the left flank and at 9:00 a.m.[325] German infantry were seen to be concentrating about Triangle Farm. A local counter-attack which developed around 10:00 a.m. was driven off with rifle and Lewis gun fire.

The brigade had made little progress on the right, and whilst the left had done better it was well short of its objective, due primarily to the dreadful state of the ground and to the vicious crossfire from the unsuppressed blockhouses.

11th Division
Major-General H. R. Davies

The 11th Division, which had relieved the 51st Division on the 7th August, held the line to the north-west of St. Julian for approximately 1,500 yards, with its right resting on a point about 250 yards short of the bridge where the Triangle Farm – Regina Cross road crossed the

---

[323] National Archives, maps showing distribution of enemy forces at 5 pm on the 15th August, in WO153/601
[324] National Archives, War Diary 145th Brigade WO95/2761
[325] National Archives, War Diary 1/4th Berks WO95/2762

Steenbeek. The 34th Brigade would be used to attack to the east of the stream and up a gentle rise towards the Zonnebeke – Langemarck road, a distance of about 1,600 yards to their objective, which would be reached after overcoming the strong breastworks of the German Third Line at Pheasant Trench.

34th Brigade

In front of the 34th Brigade, which was to carry out the attack along the whole 11th Division front, the blockhouses at Maison du Hibbou and Triangle Farm, covering the Steenbeek valley and the Poelcappelle road, commanded an extensive field of fire to their front and flanks due to the general flatness of the ground. Those which held up 145th Brigade at St. Julien, were now to hold up 34th Brigade.

On the brigade right flank the 8th Northumberland Fusiliers were struck by machine gun crossfire from strong-points to their front,[326] and due to 145th Brigade not being able to get forward, in enfilade from Maison du Hibbou and Triangle Farm to their right. Slowed by the heavy ground and severe enemy fire they lost the barrage, but got forward to within about 100 yards of the Langemarck road and there dug-in facing east, their right thrown back to conform to 145th Brigade. To the left the 5th Dorsetshire Regiment advanced steadily up with the barrage and in touch with the 61st Brigade to their left,[327] but was not in touch with the Northumberland to their right. On reaching the Langemarck road they commenced to dig-in a line of posts, throwing back a defensive flank to their right to the south of Hannixbeek Farm, to cover the gap with the Northumberland.

The 11th Manchester Regiment moving up in support of the Northumberland,[328] upon crossing the Steenbeek was also struck by the machine gun fire from Maison du Hibbou and Triangle Farm. They pressed on through the Northumberland to the Langemarck road, and past the blockhouse at the Cockcroft which they found abandoned. Here part of the battalion formed a defense line, still under enfilade fire from Maison du Hibbou, while others pushed on until machine gun fire from Bulow Farm 700 yards forward caused them to fall-back to a line of huts, just forward of the road and south of the Lekkerboterbeek.

In support of the Dorset the 9th Lancashire Fusiliers passed through and across the Langemarck road until they also came under fire from the blockhouse at Bulow Farm, at which point the right company fell-back towards the road and consolidated the position with the Manchester by the Lekkerboterbeek. The left company moved on to the left of the bunker at Rat House which held out, and then fought their way into Pheasant Trench in the German Third Line. The trying advance over heavy ground and under fire had caused them to becoming somewhat disorganized, but a section of Pheasant Trench was blocked and the position consolidated. A platoon was ordered forward to take White House on the lower Langemarck – Poelcappelle road, which it succeeded in doing forward of the barrage, soon coming under heavy shell-fire from their own guns. The survivors of the party were then withdrawn back towards Pheasant Trench 500 yards west of White House, which was later to be captured by 60th Brigade. The left of the brigade had done well, partly in touch with 60th Brigade of the 20th Division to their left which had taken Langemarck, and the Lancashire Fusiliers had reached and partially occupied Pheasant Trench in the German Third Line. Towards the right a defence line was gradually established, that ran back west of Rat House (which still resisted capture), to the Lekkerboterbeek at the position consolidated by the Manchester and Lancashire Fusiliers. It then crossed the Langemarck road at the Cockcroft, and swung gradually back towards the Steenbeek along the line held by the Northumberland.[329] The casualties had been heavy at 873 in 145th Brigade, and 749 in 34th Brigade, but not as disastrous as elsewhere.

The XVIII Corps fortunes had been mixed. Having just reached the Langemarck – Gheluvelt Line on the left, it had completely failed on the right, the disaster to Irish Divisions of

---

[326] National Archives, War Diary 8th Northumberland Fusiliers WO95/1821
[327] National Archives, War Diary 5th Dorset WO95/1820
[328] National Archives, War Diary 11th Manchester WO95/1821
[329] The 7th South Staffs and 9th Sherwood Foresters were in brigade reserve.

XIX Corps having a knock-on effect. No serious counter-attacks had developed, the Germans being more of the opinion that so long as the Gheluvelt bastion held, and Houthulst remained inviolate behind the inundations to the north, what gains the British made here mattered little. The new Front Line was formed by a ragged series of outposts, as attempting to dig any sort of continuous system was found to be nearly impossible in the waterlogged ground. The Germans subsequently infiltrated forward across the morass, and the blockhouses at Hillock Farm, Border House, and Cockcroft were reoccupied as were White House and Pheasant Trench, and all had to be fought for again on other days.

XIV Corps

The 20th Division, had relieved the 38th Division on the 5th August, and 29th Division, had relieved the Guards Division on the 7th August, The battlefield of the northern defensive flank across which they were about to attack, presented arguably the worst ground conditions of the whole offensive front, being in the muddy, shell-pitted swamp of the lower Steenbeek valley. But transport and communication facilities behind the lines had vastly improved since the Pilckem advance, in line with the improvements in XVIII Corps area, and numerous local raids had provided bridgeheads across the Steenbeek along much of the front, including at Au Bon Gite on the Langemark road, where however, the blockhouse 200 yards beyond the stream still held out. Great efforts had been made to ensure that weapons in a clean and mud-free state were available, armourer's workshops being set up near the front lines to pass rifles up during the advance.

To the right of the Ypres – Staden railway 20th Division was confronted with the desolation of the ruins of Langemarck, which they would have to pass through or round to reach their objective, the Langemarck – Gheluvelt Line being to the east of the village. Here the great breastworks of Eagle Trench would have to be overcome. Left of the railway 29th Division were to attack across the Langemarck – Wijdendrift road and over the slight rise, never above 10 metres, between the Steenbeek and the Broenbeek, their objective being virtually on the latter stream. The divisional artillery concentration would amount to around 108 field guns and 36 4.5-inch howitzers, plus about 24 heavy guns of the heavy artillery groups. Close support would be provided by the brigade trench mortar batteries and machine gun companies plus an overhead machine gun barrage from 48 machine guns.

The Corps was faced by the *79th Reserve Division* which had been in the line since the 4th August, was due for relief, and consisted of mainly young soldiers who were considered by their commanders inadequate to cope with prolonged shelling. The left of the division front was held by the *121st I.R.* and the right by the *119th I.R.* with the *125th I.R.* in support.

20th (Light) Division [330]
Major-General W. Douglas Smith

The ruins of Langemarck were to be attacked by the 60th Brigade to the right and the 61st Brigade to the left. Since entering the line the 20th Division, with the help of the Royal Engineers, had been working hard to establish bridgeheads east of the Steenbeek. The advance was to be made in stages to three designated objectives. Two specially trained companies of the 11th Rifle Brigade of 59th Brigade, who had been involved in holding the bridgehead established on the 14th August, were held ready to carry out an attack on the Au Bon Gite blockhouse, near the bridge on the Langemarck – Boesinghe road.

60th Brigade [331]

---

[330] Captain V.E. Inglefield *The History of the Twentieth (Light) Division* London: Nisbet pp155-166
[331] National Archives, War Diary 60th Brigade WO95/2118/19

From around 4:00 a.m. for some 30 minutes, German shelling on the assault waves formed up near the Steenbeek had been heavy. Then at 4:45 a.m. precisely the powerful British barrage crashed down on the German line east of the Steenbeek, and was here considered excellent. The advance towards Langemarck, east of the stream was made more arduous by the dreadful state of the ground, the water filled muddy craters and debris having to be negotiated in single file by the leading battalion, the 6th Ox and Bucks Light Infantry, supported by the 6th King's Shropshire Light Infantry, and the 12th King's Royal Rifle Corps. A carefully planed attack against Au Bon Gite by the 11th Rifle Brigade, was arranged in which a low flying aircraft was engaged to machine gun and distract the defenses. The two companies used smoke to cover their attack, which was completely successful, and an officer and fifty other ranks were taken prisoner.

The first objective, the Blue Line, was about Belleview Avenue (the Wijdendrift road), and was taken by the 6th Ox and Bucks who halted there for 25 minutes. They then advanced towards the second objective which lay beyond the rubble of the village along the Vancouver – Langemarck road. Here they were held up by machine gun fire from pillboxes to their front centre and separated towards the flanks. The 6th K.S.L.I., advancing from the first objective, where with the 12th K.R.R.C. they had rested for 20 minutes, moved forward and cleared the pillboxes and shelters towards the second line, where Alouette Farm was captured and used as battalion headquarters. The battalion then moved forward in two waves coming under fire from Rat House, White Mill and White House, but continued the advance to the Red Line, the final objective, capturing White House where nine Germans were killed and five taken prisoner, the position from where the 9th Lancashire Fusiliers had been forced to withdraw. From White House the line was then drawn back on the right to where Rat House still stubbornly held out. On the left 12th K.R.R.C. had moved up from the second objective and with the left of the 6th K.S.L.I. took the third objective including White Trench at around 7:45 a.m. and began to consolidate the position, digging an outpost line in improved shell-holes 150 yards forward. In front Germans were seen leaving Kangaroo Trench and heading towards a small wood east of White House. Sergeant (later Major) Edward Cooper of the 12th K.R.R.C. was to be awarded the V.C. for gallant conduct in the attack in rushing a blockhouse armed only with a revolver, silencing the garrison and capturing 45 Germans and seven machine guns.

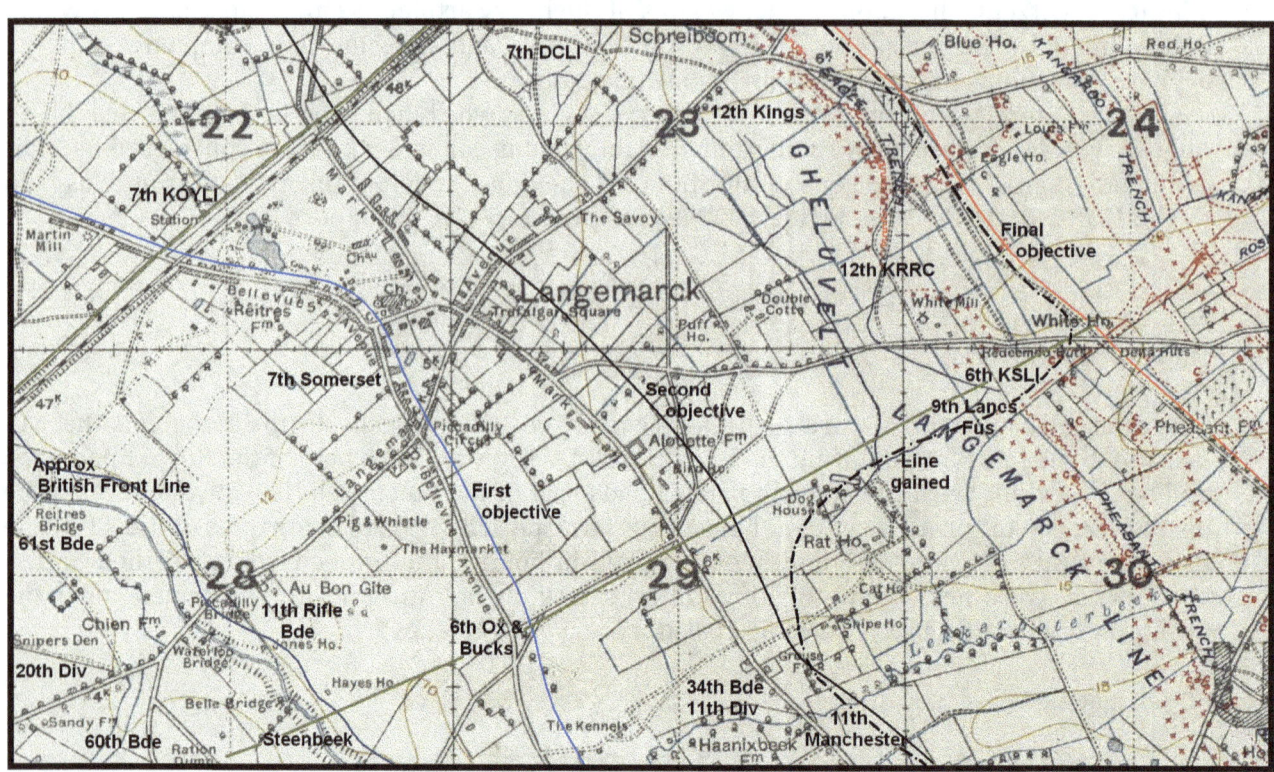

The capture of Langemarck by the 60th and 61st Brigades 20th Division

61st Brigade [332]

The capture of the ruins of Langemarck was the task of 61st Brigade. In the first wave over at 4:45, a half battalion of the 7th Somerset Light Infantry and half battalion of the 7th King's Own Yorkshire Light Infantry attacking on a two battalion front, were to secure the first and second objectives, at which point the 12th King's Liverpool Regiment and the 7th Duke of Cornwall's Light Infantry were to pass through to the final objective. The Somerset and K.O.Y.L.I. immediately came under enfilade fire from Au Bon Gite until it fell to the 11th Rifle Brigade, and moving on came under further machine gun fire from a blockhouse and concealed positions around the sidings and railway wagons near Langemarck station. The enemy were vigorously attacked with Lewis guns and rifle grenades and swiftly overcome. Private Wilfred Edwards of the 7th K.O.Y.L.I. was to be awarded the V.C. for conspicuous bravery in attacking a German blockhouse and bombing the garrison into surrender, taking 36 prisoners.

By 7:20 a.m. the brigade was on the third objective, although still under fire from concealed enemy positions, and was in touch with the 60th Brigade on their right. The final objective was under consolidation by 7:45 a.m. and the 20th Division had been successful in reaching the Langemarck – Gheluvelt Line. Germans began infiltrating forward at around 9:00 a.m. and attacked the 12th K.R.R.C. holding Eagle Trench. The fighting spread to involve the left company of the K.S.L.I. who although hard pressed, sent assistance to the K.R.R.C. by way of two Vickers guns, a Stokes mortar and a supply of ammunition. A small counter-attack was then launched, once more driving the enemy from Eagle Trench.

No fewer than five enemy counter-attacks against the position at White House occurred during the day, but all were driven off by artillery fire. A more serious counter-attack developed at around 4:00 p.m. preceded by a heavy German barrage along the divisional front. Enemy infantry infiltrated forward along hedges and ditches striking at the junction between the 60th and 61st Brigades. On the left the 12th King's Liverpool were driven back about 200 yards, exposing the left flank company of the 12th K.R.R.C. who fought until annihilated. The left of the K.R.R.C. then drew back to form a defensive flank to conform with the King's, a company of the 6th Ox and Bucks being sent up in support. The left company of the K.S.L.I. was ordered to hold on at all costs and the battalion again sent two rifle sections, two bombing sections, and two Lewis guns to the aid of the K.R.R.C. Two companies of the 12th Rifle Brigade from brigade reserve were sent up to the Green Line in support, and the 10th and 15th Welsh Regiment were placed at divisional disposal. With rapid action a dangerous enemy incursion had thus being staunched.[333]

29th Division
Major-General Sir B. de Lisle

The 29th Division was to use the 88th and 87th Brigades north of the railway to push its attack across the Langemarck - Wijdendrift road. In a similar fashion to the Guards on the 31st July great efforts had been made by the 86th Brigade to push bridgeheads across the Steenbeek. On the night of the 10th/11th August troops of 86th Brigade had forded the quagmire and set up a bridgehead of outposts on the east bank. The fortified ruins of Passerelle Farm which had held out on the night were taken by the 16th Middlesex the following night. During the night of the 12th/13th the Royal Engineers, assisted by carrying parties brought forward twelve double wooden bridges and erected them across the stream. On the night of the 15th/16th, the first wave of the two leading battalions crossed the stream and formed up on the pre-laid jumping-off tapes, but the support battalions still had the arduous task of negotiating the pontoons across the stream. The division had 3 objectives. The first, the Blue Line was on the Wijdendrift road where it crossed the Staden railway on the divisional right boundary, and around 500 yards

---

[332] National Archives, War Diary 61st Brigade WO95/2124
[333] The 6th K.S.L.I. had moved forward at 5:00 a.m., the 12th Rifle Brigade being held in brigade reserve west of the Steenbeek. National Archives, War Diary 12th Rifle Brigade WO95/2121

forward of the road on the left. The second objective, the Green Line was a uniform 500 yards beyond the first, and the third objective, the Red Line was about 100 yards beyond Leopard Trench, between the trench and the Broenbeek.

88th Brigade [334]

On the brigade right the forward companies of the 2nd Hampshire Regiment beside the railway, with the Newfoundland Regiment to their left,[335] were already across the Steenbeek awaiting the moment to attack when at 4:45 the British barrage opened. The German batteries were active but were mostly firing long, over the heads of the waiting infantry. Advancing behind the excellent barrage the Hampshire in touch with the Somerset south-east of the railway, were fired upon from dug-outs along the Wijdendrift road, the machine guns causing some casualties. Moving steadily on behind the barrage the Hampshire soon overran the enemy posts including the ruins of Martin Mill, and secured the Blue Line. On the right flank they assisted 61st Brigade with enfilade and reverse fire across the railway.

As the barrage lifted towards the second objective, the Newfoundland, advanced across very bad ground with mud in places knee deep, and struggling to keep up with the barrage, succeeded in capturing Denain Farm. Here they came under fire from the bunker at Cannes Farm, which after being outflanked was also taken. The advance continued to the Green Line where there was a one hour halt. The Newfoundland began to consolidated as best possible in the dreadful ground, mainly by improving shell-holes, whilst the protective barrage played along Leopard Trench the final objective on the Red Line, from which the enemy could be seen to be running towards the rear, across the Broenbeek.

At 7:45 a.m. the barrage lifted forward from Leopard Trench towards the Broenbeek and the advance from the Green Line was taken up by the 1st Essex Regiment on the right, and the 4th Worcestershire Regiment on the left.[336] The Essex right company advanced close up to the barrage and cleared four strong-points along the railway where 20 Germans were captured, while the left company opened rifle fire on enemy snipers holding up the Worcester to their left. The battalion then moved through Langemarck Cemetery and attacked Leopard trench where around 30 Germans raised their hands in surrender. The Red Line, on the southern side of the Broenbeek was then consolidated, the task being most difficult in the muddy ground, and on the right patrols attacked and occupied the strong-point at Japan House, where a further 23 prisoners were taken. Heavy shelling of the area continued, by both German and British guns until 9:00 a.m. and at times it was found necessary to take shelter in captured German bunkers. The Essex had captured 170 prisoners, 6 machine guns and a trench mortar, but had sustained 124 casualties in the fighting.

87th Brigade [337]

The Blue Line was reached quickly up with the barrage by the 2nd South Wales Borderers with the 1st King's Own Scottish Borderers on the left,[338] next to the French. The 1st Border Regiment was in support.[339] In the advance to the first objective by the K.O.S.B., Quarter Master Sergeant William Henry Grimbaldson, seeing that his company was held up by a blockhouse, in the face of heavy fire and although wounded, reached the entrance and threatening bombing with a hand grenade, caused the garrison of 36 Germans with 6 machine guns to surrender. He was to be awarded the V.C. for extraordinary courage and boldness. After waiting on the first objective for twenty minutes the support companies of the K.O.S.B. moved off behind the barrage towards the second objective, and were immediately held up by machine gun fire from three blockhouses. To the left, the French had not come up and the battalion flank was in the air. On his own initiative

---

[334] National Archives, War Diary 88th Brigade WO95/2307
[335] National Archives, War Diary 1st Newfoundland Regiment and 2nd Hants WO95/2308
[336] National Archives, War Diary 1st Essex WO95/2309
[337] National Archives, War Diary 87th Brigade WO95/2303
[338] National Archives, War Diary 2nd South Wales Borderers WO95/2304
[339] National Archives, War Diary 1st Border Regiment WO95/2305

and with an officer giving covering fire, Company Sergeant Major John Skinner, under heavy enemy fire worked his way behind the blockhouse on the left, and with Mills bombs thrown through the rear entrance bombed out the garrison. The next blockhouse was also silenced by Skinner, who managed to throw a bomb through the front machine gun embrasure, the occupants being either killed or captured. The third blockhouse was captured by the rest of the company but with heavy casualties. Sixty Germans, six machine guns and two trench mortars were captured in the action and C.S.M. Skinner was awarded the V.C. for his dash and gallantry.
In the advance to the second objective both battalions came under fire from Montmirail Farm and also came under enfilade machine gun fire from Champaubert Farm, 600 yards to their left within the French sector. Under cover of the barrage, Montmirail Farm was taken, the advance continuing to the final objective which was consolidated about 10:00 a.m. with patrols pushed forward in outposts towards the Broenbeek. A local German counter attack was broken up by artillery and small arms fire at around 4:00 p.m.

The XIV Corps had been successful in its endeavors to push forward the defensive northern flank, both 20th and 29th Divisions having reached and held the Langemarck – Gheluvelt Line around Langemarck, and also reached the line of the Broenbeek. The ground had been awful but the barrage had been excellent. It could be claimed that the German defences were not as numerous or as strong as in other parts of the front, but it is interesting to note that all four Victoria Crosses awarded this day, were awarded to soldiers of the XIV Corps. No serious German counter-attacks developed but with the benefit of observation from the higher ground east of Langemarck they were still able to direct artillery and machine gun fire onto the newly won positions, causing many casualties especially to 20th Division. But the cost of success had been very high, casualties from the time of entering the line being; 20th Division from 5th to 16th August 3,204, and 29th Division from 15th to 18th August 1,452.

French First Army
After heavy fighting about the numerous German strong-points in their sector the French had also been successful in reaching their objective, in touch with XIV Corps on the Broenbeek, and along the St. Jansbeek. The ground conditions were appalling, but they had also cleared the enemy from the area between the canal and the St. Jansbeek inundations, taking the ruins of Poesele and Drie Grachten.

The results of the second step

The second of Gough's great thrusts at the Flanders Position had ended, very much in line with the logical predictions, which had warned that without a change of tactics, and without new thinking and new ideas success was unlikely. The Langemarck – Gheluvelt Line had held except at Langemarck, where 20th Division had had a costly success in taking perhaps 1,500 yards of the line at Pheasant Trench and Eagle Trench, both of which were to be strongly contested and were at times destined to fall back into German hands. North-west of Langemarck, although 29th Division had successfully pushed on to the Broenbeek, the strength of the German line still held north of the stream. Along the rest of the front there had been total, demoralizing, failure. Now surely there must be a change in tactics? Was it not obvious to the Fifth Army Staff, that they did not possess the strength to break through the enemy Third Line, especially at Gheluvelt, which with its powerful concentration of artillery and seemingly unburstable blockhouses was still the key to the whole position? Could Fifth Army with the forces at its disposal redeploy them in such a way to make break through possible, at least on a limited front? Where did the hope of break through now stand, when balanced against attrition or wearing down, and who was being worn down the quickest? If extra resources were required the means to provide them lay in the hands of the Commander-in-Chief.

On the 17th August Haig met with Gough and his Corps Commanders. Both Gough and Lieutenant-General Watts of XIX Corps expressed dissatisfaction with the performance of 16th and 36th Divisions, Gough of the opinion they were not good under shellfire. Haig in his diary seemed somewhat more charitable recognizing that they had a tiring march to the lines and that most of the blockhouses had not been knocked out by the artillery, but made no comment regarding their losses prior to the battle and their subsequent weakness in numbers. Haig's attitude was at variance with the comments of his Army and Corps Commander's and makes them sound all the more unreasonable and unfair, as did the evidence of the casualty totals for the already weak divisions.

Lieutenant -General Jacob of II Corps reported that 8th and 56th Divisions had done splendidly, and but for bad luck would have done even better, if it had not been for the concentration of enemy artillery on his small front of attack. Jacob's expressed plan was to renew the attack locally using two battalions against Inverness Copse and two against Nonne Bosschen. What was to prevent the concentration of enemy artillery smashing this attack which was proposed on an even narrower front is not clear, for if this was to be a local attack the Germans could surely concentrate all their weight of fire upon it alone. As usual the plan required the reduction of the enemy artillery to stand a chance of success. It is quite clear that Haig recognized at least part of the problem, for in his diary entry for 17th August he stated, 'the cause of the failure to advance on the right centre of the attack of the Fifth Army is due, I think, to Commanders being in too great a hurry! 3 more days should have been allowed in which if fine the artillery would have *dominated* the Enemy's artillery, and destroyed the concrete defences! After Gough has got at the facts more fully I have arranged to talk the matter over with him.'[340] That Haig had some understanding of the problem is clear, but he failed to mention the question of manpower or extra guns to carry the job through, probably as he still underestimated the strength of the German position, and the capability of their artillery. Neither was there recognition that his artillery were having little effect on the blockhouses which, it was now realized by the men at the front, could only be reduced by gallant but costly infantry attacks. It is reasonable to argue that if Haig had retained a firmer personal control and not been so apparently confident in the performance of his Army Commander, he would have undoubtedly intervened at this point, assuming he fully understood the problems himself. Extra resources were in Haig's hands, and the man to wield them effectively was available, but it was to be eleven more dreadful days before he finally reached the decision to use them both. In the meantime the nightmare would go on and orders would continue to flow from Fifth Army Headquarters which did not have a hope of being carried out in the real world upon the deplorable battlefield.

Operations 17th to 21st August

At his post battle conference on the 17th August Gough told his corps commanders that the offensive would be resumed on the 25th by II, XVIII and XIX Corps, to reach the objectives not attained on the 16th, with the intention of launching another offensive to capture the Passchendaele ridge between Broodseinde and Westroosebeke as soon as possible afterwards. Before the operation on the 25th local attacks were to be made on the 22nd to establish satisfactory positions from which to launch the major offensive. It came as no surprise that II Corps' objective was Inverness Copse, and XVIII and XIX Corps were to advance to within a few hundred yards of the Langemarck – Gheluvelt Line. There was to be no change of tactics and to rational minds it must have seemed that Fifth Army Staff were both devoid of creative thinking, and were living in wonderland.

The tanks at St Julien on the 19th August

It had not rained on the 16th August and was not going to again until the 26th, and with a drying breeze the ground slowly began to improve, or at least got no worse. On the 19th August what was to become accepted as a model of co-operation between the tanks and infantry took place in XVIII Corps area north of St. Julien, to retake the strong-points which had held up the corps so

---

[340] Douglas Haig. Diaries and Letters, p318

badly on the 16th. The artillery had attempted to destroy the bunkers on numerable occasions without success, and it was considered feasible that if the tanks could keep to the roads, and given an element of surprise, they could with close infantry co-operation be successful. In co-operation with 48th Division, 11 tanks of G Battalion, I Tank Brigade,[341] were to attack the German positions at Gun Pits, Hillock Farm, Vancouver, Triangle Farm, Maison du Hibou and Cockcroft. The tanks were to advance just in front of the infantry, and on a signal from the tanks indicating success, the infantry would advance and secure the strong-point.

On the 19th, due to mechanical problems, or possibly ditching, the number of tanks to be engaged was reduced to 7, one male and six female, one allotted to each of the strong-points and one with a roving commission to assist where needed. The female tanks were not ideal for the purpose but were all that was available. The Royal Engineers had arranged crossing points by laying fascines across the bed of the Steenbeek, and the advance along the Poelcappelle road was to be covered by a smoke barrage laid upon all the rising ground beyond St. Julien from which the enemy could observe the deployment, and by aircraft flying low to disguise the noise. At 4:45 a.m. the tanks began their laborious advance at irregular intervals along the road out of St. Julien covered by a shrapnel and smoke barrage and closely followed by the 1/8th Warwickshire Regiment. To keep to the pave surface of the roads where possible was essential, as to attempt to negotiate the heavy muddy ground meant almost certain ditching. The first strong-point, at Hillock Farm, about 550 yards beyond St. Julien was reached at about 6:00 a.m. giving an idea of the speed at which the tanks were proceeding along the Poelcappelle road. The position was either unoccupied or the garrison had fled and it was quickly secured by the Warwick.

The only male tank G.29, commanded by Second Lieutenant A. G. Barker was to attack Maison du Hibou, machine fire from which had caused so many casualties to the advancing infantry on the 16th. At the junction by Triangle Farm it was found that the road to the west towards Maison du Hibou was obliterated by shell-fire, so Baker had to continue along the Poelcappelle road for about 125 yards beyond the junction, to a position now behind the blockhouse, from where he attempted to close the range by turning off the road to the left and approaching across country. At about 250 yards he engaged the blockhouse from the rear firing around 40 six-pounder shells from his left gun into the rear entrances at which point around 60 Germans emerged some 30 of whom were captured by the Warwickshire. The tank then inevitably became ditched, but continued to engaged targets about 600 yards to the east in the German Third Line with its right six-pounder, until the tank sank so deep into the mud the gun would not elevate onto the target. At about 11:15 a.m. the tank was abandoned, the crew taking the hammers from the six-pounders, and the Lewis guns and ammunition which they handed over to the infantry. Tank G.31 supported G.29 from the road, engaging Maison du Hibou with its Lewis guns, until experiencing engine problems which the crew managed to rectify, the tank then returning to its rallying point.

---

[341] National Archives, War Diary I Tank Brigade WO95/98

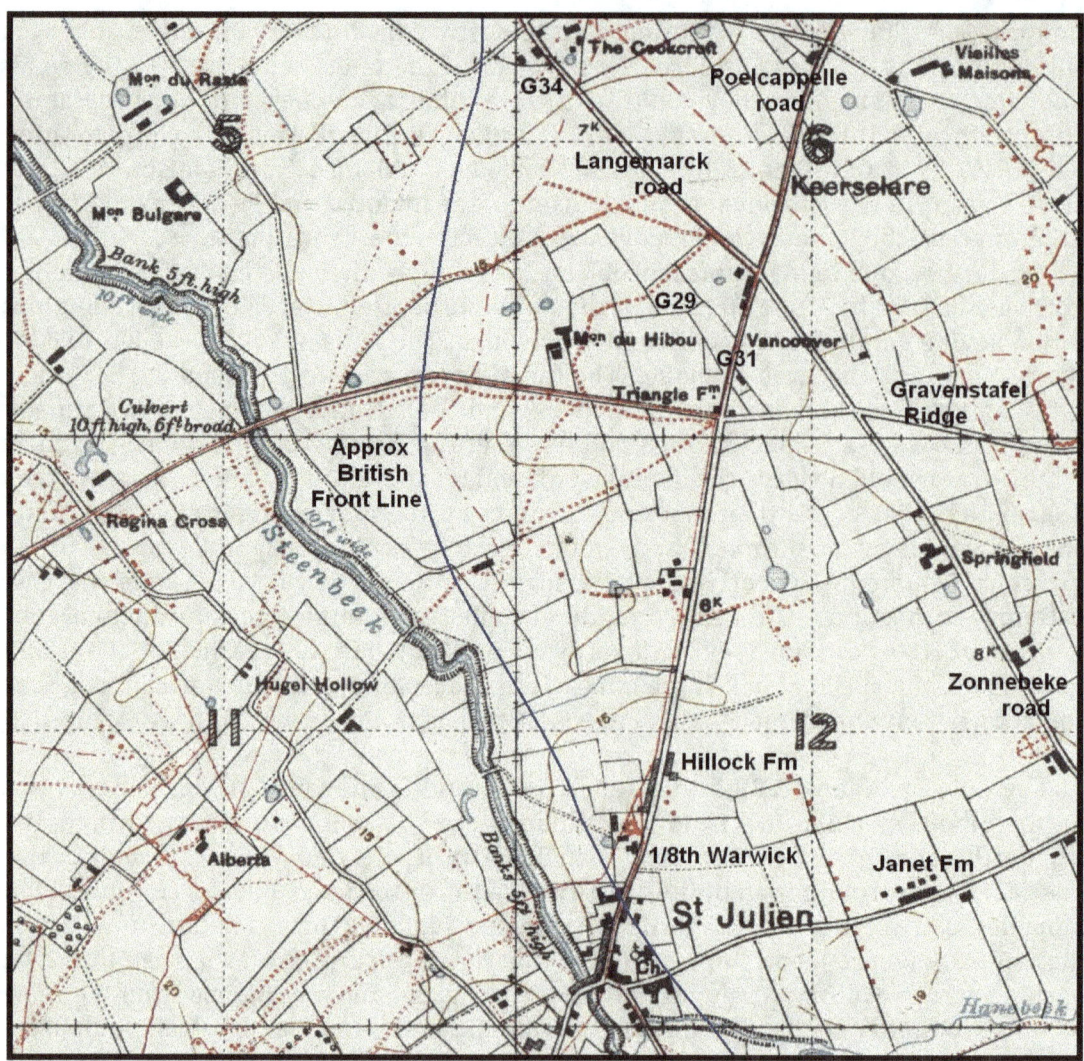

The Tank attack at St Julian on the 19th August

The garrison in the bunker within the ruins of Triangle Farm put up a stout resistance until, with the support of a tank, possibly G.31, the infantry entered the interior and cleared it at the point of the bayonet. Tank G.34 detailed to attack the Cockcroft blockhouse had the greatest distance to cover, around 2,400 yards from St. Julien to reach its objective, and did so around 6:45 a.m. Second Lieutenant Coutts approached the bunker along the Langemarck road and came under heavy machine gun fire to which the tank replied vigorously. After about 15 minutes around 50 Germans were seen to run out from the bunker and adjacent dugouts, the tank accounting for many of them with its Lewis guns. It then became ditched at the side of the road just south of the Cockcroft, the crew leaving the tank and setting up their Lewis guns in adjacent shell-holes. The Warwick were nowhere to be seen so Coutts sent a message by pigeon and also sent back two of the crew to bring up the infantry, which they failed to do as the infantry would not move. He then went back himself and found a senior officer who detailed 60 men to return to the tank and dig-in on the tank Lewis gun line. The tank crew remained with the infantry until 5:25 p.m. at which point after camouflaging the machine and posting a sentry of three rifle bombers inside, the crew at last retired.

    At the other strong-points the appearance of the tanks had put the enemy garrisons to flight. The operation had been spectacularly successful. The blockhouses had been eliminated and the outpost line had been pushed up close on the western side of the Poelcappelle road, and five of the seven tanks engaged had returned safely to the rallying point. Infantry casualties had been remarkably low at fifteen wounded, with tank crew losses two killed and eleven wounded. German casualties were estimated at 100 with 30 prisoners taken. To the Tank Corps the success was something of a double edged sword, as those who did not understand the capabilities of the machines now expected them to work wonders, even under less favorable conditions.

Attempts to approach the Langemarck – Gheluvelt Line 4:45 a.m. the 22nd August

At 4:45 a.m. on the 22nd August XIX Corps and XVIII Corps were to once again attempt to push forward with the objective of straightening the line, and gaining an improved attacking position for the assault to be made against the Langemarck – Gheluvelt Line on the 25th. Later in the morning at 7:00 a.m. and probably of greater strategic importance, II Corps were to attempt once more to capture the patch of mud and blasted, shattered stumps quaintly referred to as Inverness Copse.

XIX Corps 4:45 a.m.

In XIX Corps area the 15th Division had relieved the shattered 16th, and the 61st (Second South Midland) Division had relieved the equally battle weary 36th. The 15th Division using the 45th and 44th Brigades were to attack across the awful ground towards the lower Hanebeek, where so many lives and limbs had already been claimed by the now infamous forts before the German Third Line. The German machine gun crews at Potsdam, Vampir, Borry, Iberian, Pommern, in front of Bremen Redoubt, and Gallipoli and Somme in front of Hill 35 were ready and waiting to do their work again, before the Langemarck – Gheluvelt Line which they guarded so well was even approached. The night was very dark and for the heavily laden troops the march from Ypres up to the front along slippery duck boards and through trenches knee deep in mud was grueling. The rear assembly areas were as usual being shelled, and as gas was reported respirators had to be worn adding to the discomfort.

45th Brigade was to be supported by four tanks which all became ditched along the Frezenberg – Zonnebeke road before reaching the front.[342] Attacking with the 13th Royal Scots and the 11th Argyll and Sutherland Highlanders, both of which made slow progress forward, flares showed the advance had approached Potsdam, Borry and Vampir Farms at which point machine gun fire accounted for most of the forward waves. The survivors fell-back to join support companies of the 6th Cameron about the Railway Dump – Beck House track, near their starting point. The Royal Scots made repeated attempts to get forward during the day but without success. Of the Argylls all their officers and around 200 other ranks were casualties.

On the left, 6 tanks were to support 44th Brigade but 4 became ditched near their starting point west of Pommern Redoubt.[343] The 8th Seaforth Highlanders and 7th Cameron were scythed by machine gun fire from the start and made little progress, but some of the Cameron with the assistance of at least one tank made some headway up the slope towards Hill 35, until held up by machine gun fire from the Gallipoli blockhouse, which was engaged by the tank Fray Bentos with its six-pounders. The tank became ditched, and at around 7:00 a.m. the infantry began to retire some way leaving the tank isolated. The Germans worked forward towards the tank and were engaged by one gun which would still bear and the Lewis guns. The crew was in a desperate position as rifle and machine gun rounds smacked against the armour showering the interior with hot shards. Sniped at by both sides they remained with the tank until 9:00 p.m. by which time they were all wounded, and then after handing the Lewis guns and ammunition to the infantry, and arranging a covering party for the tank, they retired.

To the left, 61st (2nd South Midland) Division (Major-General C. J. Mackenzie), using the 184th Brigade had a little more success.[344] Attacking with the 2/1st and 2/4th Ox and Bucks Light

---

[342] National Archives, War Diary 45th Brigade WO95/1943
[343] National Archives, War Diary 44th Brigade WO95/1935
[344] National Archives, War Diary 184th Brigade WO95/3063

Infantry with 2/5th Gloucestershire Regiment in support there was hard fighting for Somme Farm and Pond Farm before they fell, the latter to the Gloucester who also took Hindu Cot. The line had been pushed forward about 600 yards. North and east of St. Julien there was some forward movement of the line although the success of the 19th August was not to be repeated, the attack turning into a confused affair with positions being taken and retaken. The casualties incurred in this fighting and in holding the slender gains on the next day were extremely high, being in 44th Brigade 1,052, 45th Brigade 1,019 and in 184th Brigade 914. Of the men of the three brigades 365 in total were killed.

XVIII Corps 4:45 a.m.

The XVIII Corps was to attack with the 48th Division which had been in the line under dreadful conditions since the 4th August, and the 11th Division which had been in the line since the 7th August. This time 48th Division was to use 143rd and 144th Brigade to push forward to the Zonnebeke – Langemarck road. The infantry were again to follow the tanks which were to spearhead the operation as they had on the 19th. At 4:45 a.m. and behind a protective barrage, ten tanks detailed to operate with 48th Division advanced out of St. Julien, six of them along the road to the east towards Winnipeg. Of these tanks operating with the 1/5th Warwickshire Regiment of 143rd Brigade,[345] all six either became ditched along the cratered road near Janet Farm or were knocked out before reaching the front line. The remaining four tanks, moving out of St. Julien along the Poelcappelle road had more success and assisted the Warwick in temporarily securing the Springfield blockhouse, which however was soon retaken by the enemy. The Warwick also attacked Winnipeg and the Gun Pits (between Winnipeg and Springfield) securing the latter, then losing the position to a counter attack, but re-taking it later in the day. Shelling and machine gun fire was heavy, making it impossible for support companies to get forward to assist in the confused fighting. On the left the 1/6th Gloucestershire Regiment of 144th Brigade got forward,[346] up near the Zonnebeke – Langemarck road in touch with the Warwick on their right. The tanks on the Poelcappelle road attacked the Vancouver blockhouse, which fell about 8:15 a.m. but was subsequently retaken. The Divisional line had been pushed forward about half way to the Zonnebeke road and that night outposts were established forward towards the road.

Towards Langemarck, 11th Division using the 33rd Brigade was to carry out the attack with the 6th Lincolnshire Regiment and the 6th Border Regiment, and attempt to bring the line up to conform with that established by the XIV Corps on the 16th August, when the Langemarck – Gheluvelt Line had been broken.[347] Two tanks were to co-operate with the infantry in an attack on Bulow Farm, one male commanded by Lieutenant Knight and one female, Delysia, commanded by Lieutenant Enoch. These tanks had the greatest distance to cover, their objective being 2,500 yards from St.Juien. Following the barrage the tanks left St. Julien by the Poelcappelle road with the Lincoln following close behind and proceeded to the crossroads at Vancouver. From this point onwards the road had been obstructed by the Germans, who had felled the shrapnel-torn bare trunks of the avenue of trees which had led towards Poelcappelle. The trunks presented a difficult obstacle for the tanks, as if they were not approached head on they would tend to pivot on the narrow pave roadway and could cause the tank to swing off the road and become ditched. The tanks, machine-gunning targets of opportunity on the way, successfully negotiated the obstacles and upon approaching Bulow Farm found it already under attack by the Lincoln which had got there before them, but were however by this time held up by machine gun fire from the blockhouse. At that point the leading tank of Lieutenant Knight was hit by a shell and slewed almost off the road, just allowing Lieutenant Enoch's tank, which had been 20 yards behind to pass. This tank although only armed with Lewis guns proceeded to attack Bulow Farm, which with the co-operation of the Lincoln was taken. Delysia on the return

---

[345] National Archives, War Diary 143rd Brigade WO95/2755
[346] National Archives, War Diary 144th Brigade WO95/2757
[347] National Archives, War Diary 33rd Brigade WO95/1811

journey to St. Julien picked up two badly injured crew members from the other tank, but Lieutenant Knight had been killed. The 144th Brigade had been held up on the right, and was still west of the Zonnebeke road. To cover the open flank the Lincoln threw back a defensive line along the Poelcappelle road through Keerselare. To the left of the Lincoln, the Border Regiment had advanced behind the barrage and got up well securing their objective, and in touch with the 38th Division of XIV Corps now holding the line near White House.

II Corps 7:00 a.m.

Further south at 7:00 a.m. it was to be the turn II Corps, with the 43rd Brigade of 14th (Light) Division,[348] (Major-General V. A. Couper), which coming from Second Army, had relieved 51st Division on the 17th /18th August, to make another attempt to secure Inverness Copse and the open plateau a few hundred yards to the north about Fitzclarence farm.

It was clear that before the main offensive could cross the Passchendaele ridge, the right flank on the plateau must be secured and Polygon Wood must be taken, but Polygon Wood lay beyond the Langemarck – Gheluvelt Line. Although the German Second Line had already been broken at Westhoek Ridge, it was not secure at Glencorse Wood, 1,000 yards in front of Polygon. From Glencorse Wood the Second Line ran south across the open plateau past Fitzclarence Farm to Inverness Copse. The dangers of attacking the Third Line from Westhoek Ridge, before the troublesome woods on the plateau to the right were secure had already been well illustrated. The order was clear; first Inverness Copse and Fitzclarence Farm, then Glencorse Wood and Nonne Bosschen and then Polygon Wood, and the position would be broken. The British new this and so did the Germans who were going to fight tooth and nail to hold Inverness Copse, "at all costs".

But Lieutenant -General Jacob commanding II Corps had already told Haig on the 17th August that his difficulties on the 16th had been caused because of his narrow frontage of attack, allowing the Germans to concentrate their artillery upon him. This time his attack frontage was even narrower and as there had been no additional concerted effort to dominate the German artillery the outcome of the attack was sadly all too predictable. The assault along the 800 yard front would be made by the 6th Somerset Light Infantry towards Inverness Copse and the 6th Duke of Cornwall's Light Infantry towards Fitzclarence Farm.[349] The Somerset got off well behind the barrage and crossed the shattered waste that had been a copse, taking 130 prisoners in the advance. The Cornwall to their left was soon held up by machine gun fire from the blockhouse at Fitzclarence Farm and also from another strong-point at an L-shaped Farm about 200 yards to the north. The Somerset left flank was therefore exposed and their now depleted ranks were counter-attacked from three sides, causing them to fall-back about 250 yards. Here with the assistance of two tanks firing from the Menin Road they were able to consolidate the line, in touch with the Cornwall on the left. This line was gradually strengthened by brigade supports during the morning, the 10th Durham Light Infantry supporting the Somerset and the 6th King's Own Yorkshire Light Infantry supporting the Cornwall, which drove off three counter-attacks in the afternoon. At 7:00 p.m. a message from the Somerset claimed that with two fresh battalions the eastern edge of the copse could be taken and held, but the message crossed at 9:00 p.m. with an order from II Corps H.Q. that the line now held should be consolidated, and added that at 4:00 a.m. next morning the Cornwall with the assistance of four tanks should capture Fitzclarence and the L-shaped Farms.

It rained heavily overnight and three of the four tanks ditched coming up, causing postponement of the attack. At 6:50 a.m. the Germans counter-attacked along the northern side of the copse and the one tank which had subsequently arrived gave valuable assistance in driving them off. The plan had allowed for the 41st Brigade to relieve the 43rd on the night of 23rd / 24th but II Corps was now running dangerously short of manpower. Jacob was mindful of the

---

[348] National Archives, War Diary 43rd Brigade WO95/1904
[349] National Archives, War Diary 6th Somerset L.I. WO95/1909

forthcoming major offensive planned for the 25th, and although he was fighting on the most crucial point of the whole front, he had no division in Corps reserve. He therefore held back the 41st Brigade and cancelled the planned relief of 43rd Brigade. He also protested to Fifth Army that he had insufficient infantry to carry out the proposed attack against Fitzclarence Farm and Nonne Bosschen on the 25th August, as the 23rd and 25th Divisions promised to II Corps were earmarked for later operations against Polygon Wood.

On the 21st Haig reported to the Cabinet on the fighting between the 4th and 20th August. He pointed out the continuing bad state of the battlefield, and that rather than having attacked on the 16th it would have been preferable to wait a longer period for the ground to dry, but for the exhaustion caused by holding men in the line for any longer in the dreadful weather. He presented an accurate description of the conditions, whilst overstating the achievements so far, and revealed to the Cabinet that 'in many places the men could only get forward by assisting each other out of breast-high mud and water in the shell holes...Reviewing the results of this operation up to and including this battle of the 16th August, I am well satisfied with them, although the gain of ground would have been much more considerable but for the adverse weather conditions....If we are favoured by a fine autumn, therefore, I regard the prospects of clearing the coast before winter sets in as very hopeful, not withstanding the loss of time caused by the bad weather during the first half of August. At the least I see no reason to doubt that we should be able to gain positions from which subsequent operations to clear the coast will present a far easier problem than we had to cope with at the outset of this offensive, and in which the losses and hardships suffered around Ypres in previous winters will be much reduced. In these circumstances the right course to pursue, in my opinion, is undoubtedly to continue to press the enemy in Flanders without intermission and to the full extent of our power; and, if complete success is not gained before winter sets in, to renew the attack at the earliest possible moment next year'.[350]

Weather conditions, rainfall Vlamertinghe, temperature Ypres [351]

	21st Aug	22nd Aug	23rd Aug	24th Aug	25th Aug	26th Aug
Rainfall	Trace	Nil	1.4mm	0.1mm	Trace	19.6mm
Temp	72F	78F	74F	68F	67F	70F

Inverness Copse and Glencorse Wood the 24th August

For certain the Germans would not let matters rest, with the British threatening their Second Line at the vital sector between Inverness Copse and Glencorse Wood, and on the morning of the 24th at about 4:00 a.m. an intense hostile barrage fell upon the copse and 600 yards to the north on the wood. The German shelling mainly seemed to fall short and it did little damage to 43rd Brigade, but half an hour later a major attack began spearheaded by the *4th Assault Sturmtrupp Battalion* and a battalion of the *177 Regiment, 32nd Eingreif Division* which both supported the *67th Regiment* of the *34th Division* which held the line. Across the plateau parties of enemy bombers and others with flame throwers broke through the position of the K.O.Y.L.I. and the Cornwall, which were driven back to their start line of the 22nd. The German barrage had fallen short upon its own advance, and the attack into the copse lacked cohesion, and although some Durham and Somerset fell back to the western edge, the line was quickly re-established. It was now the turn of the British to be shelled by their own artillery. The gunners, believing not only the K.O.Y.L.I. and Cornwall on the left, but also the Durham and Somerset on the right had

---

[350] National Archives WO158/24 Haig to Robertson 21st August
[351] National Archives WO95/14 GHQ statistics

retired to the old line, now began shelling the copse and their own infantry. Messages sent back to lengthen the range failed to stop the shelling until 2:00 p.m., by which time the exhausted Durham and Somerset, after being in action for three days and nights had retired once more out of the copse, and at the cessation of the shelling the Germans re-occupied the western edge, except for the north-west corner. The importance of the position to the Germans is illustrated by the fact that over the three days of fighting they made no fewer than eleven counter attacks to retake it.

The casualties of 43rd Brigade during this action to secure Inverness Copse and Fitzclarence Farm were 1,523 of whom 218 were killed. Since the opening of the second major assault on the 16th August, Fifth Army's attempt to move up close to the Langemarck – Gheluvelt Line had not been successful anywhere except on the far left near Langemarck. The failed attempt to pierce the Second Line at Inverness Copse proved to be the catalyst which was to bring about many changes of great magnitude, which would soon alter virtually every aspect of the campaign.

The moment of decision

The local but costly action at Inverness Copse on the 24th August was of great significance, as it appeared to define the point at which Haig realized he had to take personal control over events, and even change his philosophy regarding the overall strategy of the campaign. The hoped and planned for break through had plainly not happened. All the confident talk at the time of Nivelle's appointment about a change in the tempo of the War, which had so excited Haig, had now been brought down to earth by the reality of events. The battle, while still under Gough's command, had already become attritional, and if a denomination were to be used on a balance sheet, it would be measured in units of divisions engaged and exhausted, and not units of territory gained. So far the number of German divisions engaged against Fifth Army had been 30, two of them twice, and in the first three weeks of battle, 17 had been exhausted and withdrawn and 6 more would join them by the 28th August. But a German division numbered around 12,000 men,[352] not the over 20,000 men of a British division. On the other side of the balance sheet Fifth Army had deployed:

In II Corps, 24th, 30th, 8th (twice), 18th, 25th, 14th, 47th, and 56th Divisions.
In XIX Corps, 15th (twice), 55th, 16th, 36th, and 61st Divisions.
In XVIII Corps, 39th, 51st, 48th, 11th, 23rd Divisions.
In XIV Corps, 38th, Guards, 20th and 29th Divisions.

This was a total of 22 British divisions of which two had been engaged twice and 14 had been exhausted and withdrawn to refit. The two sides of the sheet, given the complexity of the accounting, were not far off balancing. If the four French divisions fighting to the north of Fifth Army were included in the figures, then 26 Allied divisions (nominally 520,000 men) had engaged 37 German divisions (nominally 440,000 men). As a plus, 9 of these 37 German divisions had been transferred into the Flanders battle from Champagne or Alsace-Lorraine, lessening the danger to the French. But conventional military wisdom dictated that to evict an enemy who was equal in courage, training, morale, and equipment, from a strong and well defended position, the attacking force would require a numerical superiority of 3 to 1. In the battles of August 1917 Gough had a numerical superiority in manpower of around 1.2 to 1. Even to have achieved an advantage of 1.5 to 1 Gough would have required another 7 divisions. To have achieved a superiority of 3 to 1 he would have required the absurd number of an extra 40 divisions.

---

[352] Fifth Army intelligence believed that: 'A German battalion has an average trench strength of 500 rifles. Thus the infantry strength in rifles of a German division is approximately 4,500, allowing for men employed on various duties'. National Archives, War Diary Fifth Army, WO95/520

On the 19th August Fifth Army Intelligence estimated German artillery strength opposing them at 558 guns. This gave the British superiority in guns of over 3 to 1, but there are other factors to consider. Generally the Germans had the advantage of observation even after they had been driven from the western edge of the Gheluvelt plateau, and had multiple prepared positions for their guns, which were still concealed behind the ridges, making finding and targeting them very difficult for the British batteries. Also the German gunners were firing into a salient and so concentrating their fire, the advantage the British had enjoyed at Messines. Air reconnaissance was always an essential element in British counter-battery work, and bad weather of which there had been plenty, had disrupted the programme totally. The ground conditions within the Salient, across which the British guns had on times to be moved, and upon which the gunners tried to stabilize their guns, were generally atrocious. The British were also firing out of a salient, at great depths and across a 15,500 yard frontage, so dissipating their weight of fire. The British numerical superiority was to a degree negated by these conditions, to the extent that the enemy batteries were never dominated as Haig had hoped, and in many instances continued to enjoy a local superiority,

It was little wonder there had been no break through, as the forces needed to have made that possible had not been made available to Gough. That Fifth Army had done as well as it had, in the cold calculations of the balance sheet was largely due to the fighting spirit and endurance of its junior officers and men, who by now were all totally exhausted. But so were the enemy exhausted and the flow of German divisions to Flanders continued, denying them the initiative, all to the benefit of French recovery. The fighting, although severe, inconclusive, and not having achieved a break through, had severely shaken the enemy. From a British viewpoint, as a battle of attrition it had not been a disaster. On the assumption that the Germans did not move divisions other than for a good reason, the enemy had also taken a severe mauling.[353]

A Fundamental Change

Haig learned of the failure at Inverness Copse during the afternoon of the 24th August and was understandably greatly disappointed with the news, but surely could not have been greatly surprised. He now made the decision which could not have been easy to make for a man who so reluctant to meddle with the day to day business of his Army Commander. On the morning of the 25th August he visited General Plumer at Second Army headquarters at Cassel, and after explaining the failure of Gough's endeavors informed that he wished him to assume overall control of the offensive. The importance of the Gheluvelt position was again emphasized by Haig, although this was unnecessary as Plumer knew Ypres better than anyone. Ever mindful of the German artillery concentration behind the plateau, and the associated dangers of a narrow front attack, Haig wished to broaden the front to the south as far as the Ypres – Comines canal and to include an attack towards Zandvoorde, in order to dissipate the German fire over this wider area. Second Army would assume control of the front between the Ypres – Comines canal and the Ypres – Roulers railway, and would throw the majority of its strength against the Gheluvelt plateau. The steady, conscientious Plumer must have mused ruefully upon his request back in June for a three day delay after Messines to move his 60 guns up to Ypres to support the attack of II and VIII Corps at Bellewaarde, at a time when the Germans were completely off balance; three days which were subsequently denied him by Haig, but which in the long term may have cost Haig his break through.

Most important of all was the Commander-in-Chief's decision that the strategy of the offensive would now change completely. As a break through seemed to be impossible, a step by

---

[353] The following German divisions had arrived in Flanders between the 31st July and the 16th August: *5th Bav. I.D., 12th R.D., 24th I.D., 26th R.D., 27th I.D., 32nd I.D., 34th I.D., 54th I.D., 121st I.D., 204th I.D., 214th I.D.* Since the 31st July and following the battle on the 16th August the following German divisions had been moved out of Flanders: *3rd G.I.D., 6th Bav. R.D., 10th Bav. I.D., 12th R.D., 16th Bav. I.D., 18th R.D., 22nd R.D., 26th R.D., 27th I.D., 34th I.D., 38th I.D., 40th I.D., 49th R.D., 52nd R.D., 54th I.D., 79th R.D., 111th I.D., 204th I.D., 214th I.D., 221st I.D., 235th I.D.*

step approach with limited objectives, achievable by the infantry within the support of the guns would now be adopted, at least until the position Zandvoorde – Polygon Wood – Broodseinde had been gained. This however was how Gough claimed he had been fighting the campaign so far, but Plumer's step by step, bite-and-hold tactics, were soon going to look very different to Gough's. It all came down to interpretation.

Gough met with his Corps Commanders at Lovie Chateau on the 25th and informed them of Haig's decision, but warned them that Fifth Army was expected to continue to push its left towards Poelcappelle. There appeared to be little enthusiasm and few fresh ideas were forthcoming. Watts considered XIX Corps could *draw back* its right from Bremen Redoubt and Potsdam to conform to II Corps, whilst Maxse understandably thought it virtually impossible to find sufficient battery positions for his XVIII Corps field artillery along the mire of the Steenbeek to support an attack on Poelcappelle. The Earl of Cavan felt that any advance by the XIV Corps towards Poelcappelle could only be made by a simultaneous advance of XVIII Corps. Incredibly the only discussion regarding II Corps, which held the key to unlock the other three Corps by securing the Gheluvelt plateau, was Jacob's claim that 23rd Division would not be ready until the 31st. Kiggell, reported Gough, considered it might not be necessary to secure the whole of Inverness Copse in order to secure the right flank of II Corps (and thus the whole offensive), a suggestion with which Jacobs did not agree, pointing out that possession of Herenthage Chateau and the concrete bunkers on the east side of the copse was essential. The thrusting eagerness of late July had disappeared, to be replaced by a confused impotence. The command and control of Fifth Army was obviously drifting; there was no firm grip on the situation, and little idea of how to proceed. The future of the whole operation appeared to be floundering on the inability of Maxse's field batteries to deploy along the Steenbeek and of Jacob to take Inverness Copse; and to all intents and purposes it was.[354] It would seem that nobody at Fifth Army could recognize, that with the strength presently at their disposal, and the ongoing appalling state of the battlefield, the goal was beyond their means; or in any event no one felt in a position to say as much. That responsibility rested with the Commander-in-Chief.

At G.H.Q. that afternoon with both Plumer and Gough present, it was established that Second Army would take over control of II Corps area in early September. Kiggell issued the order on the 26th confirming the arrangements.[355] But for the moment Fifth Army was to continue with the costly and fruitless local attacks on the Gheluvelt plateau, the order confirming, 'this transfer will be carried out as soon as the Fifth Army has secured a position on the high ground about Inverness Copse and including Glencorse and Nonne Bosschen Woods'. Haig was also clearly

---

[354] National Archives, War Diary Fifth Army S.G.653/23 notes on Conference held at Lovie Chateau 25th August 1917, WO95/520

[355] National Archives, GHQ order OAD 606 WO158/049. Gough's account of this period puts a different slant on matters. He later wrote: 'It was evident that if we were to clear the ridge and get possession of all the high ground, it was essential to extend considerably the front of the II Corps. It was too narrow to hope for a successful advance, taking into consideration the concentration of German guns against it. It was essential that Second Army on the right should push forward and so draw off a considerable proportion of the enemy's artillery fire. I put these conclusions to G.H.Q., and in consequence General Kiggell, the Chief of Staff, came over to Cassel, and there a small conference was held with myself and Plumer and our senior staff officers to discuss the proposition. Plumer at first did not like the suggestion and demurred, saying that he had been in the Salient for two years and "he had no intention of pushing himself into another." Kiggell, although a profound military student, did not possess the personality which was necessary to overcome the scruples and objections of Army Commanders, and the matter had to be referred to Sir Douglas Haig, who had been called away. The latter saw the cogency of the arguments I had put forward, and it was decided that the Second Army should now play a more active role.' **General Sir Hubert Gough** *The Fifth Army*. London: Hodder & Stoughton pp206/207 Davidson's recollection was as follows: 'The third effort to gain ground on the Gheluvelt Plateau having failed on the 24th August and being reported to G.H.Q. the same afternoon, Haig decided at once to suspend operations for the moment and change the plan, transferring the principle role from 5th to 2nd Army.' Davidson, *Haig:Master of the Field* p41

unaware that Fifth Army, given its present strength and tactics was incapable of the task, and this unfortunate state of affairs was to last until the 31st August. But he was aware of the strain which had been imposed upon the men of Fifth Army, recognizing that many were desperately tired. On the 28th Kiggell instructed Gough: *'In view of the unfavourable weather, of the inadvisability of pushing forward too far on your centre and left before the capture of the main ridge, and for the need that you should have in hand a thoroughly efficient force for the capture of the Staden ridge, the Commander-in-Chief considers it inadvisable that you should attempt any operation on a great scale before the Second Army is ready to cooperate...He therefore desires that in the present circumstances your operations may be limited to gaining a line including Inverness Copse and Glencorse and Nonne Bosschen woods, and to securing possession, by methodical and well combined attacks, of such farms and other tactical features in front of your line further north as will facilitate the delivery of a general attack later in combination with the Second Army. Proceeding on this principle he trusts that you will be able so to arrange for reliefs, and for the rest and training of your divisions, as to ensure having a fresh and thoroughly efficient force available for the severe and sustained fighting to be expected later,. He considers these questions of relief, rest, and training to be of great importance.'*[356]

Plumer asked for three weeks in which to make his preparations to resume the offensive, which on this occasion Haig granted. In the meantime Fifth Army would continue to attempt to improve its position with further attacks by II Corps against Inverness Copse, Glencorse Wood and Nonne Bosschen. In other words between the 27th and 31st August, *business as usual*.

Fifth Army operations 27th August to 10th September

In retrospect it would certainly have been better for Fifth Army to have consolidated the positions it already held, and to have built up and conserved its strength in preparation for the offensive which was to be begin as soon as Second Army was ready, in around three weeks time. Agreement had been reached however to resume the so far futile attacks at the now infamous points along the front, and that was how it was going to continue.

Weather conditions, rainfall Vlamertinghe, temperature Ypres [357]

Aug/Sept	27th	28th	29th	30th	31st	1st	2nd	3rd
Rainfall	15.3mm	0.9mm	2.6mm	0.7mm	0.7mm	0.2mm	1.1mm	Nil
Temp	57F	62F	61F	63F	64F	59F	63F	59F

Sept	4th	5th	6th	7th	8th	9th	10th	
Rainfall	Nil	6.1mm	24.6mm	0.1mm	Trace	Nil	Trace	
Temp	71F	74F	77F	72F	72F	71F	66F	

---

[356] National Archives, OAD 609 GHQ to Fifth Army 28th August 1917, WO95/520
[357] National Archives, WO95/14 GHQ statistics

Since the 16th August the rain had only been intermittent, there having been around 3mm in total, but there had been little warmth and the battlefield had not begun to dry out. The general offensive planned for the 25th August was cancelled but a further attempt by II Corps against Inverness Copse and Glencorse Wood was to take place on the 27th August at 4:45 a.m. But then nearly 20 mm of rain fell on the 26th. It rained all through the night and by the end of the day on the 27th there had been another 15 mm. The 23rd Division (Major-General J. M. Babington), which had relieved the 14th Division on the 25th August was to use the 41st Brigade (14th Division attached) to attack with the co-operation of four tanks, half a company of infantry being allotted to each. Due to the conditions all four tanks became ditched near Clapham Junction and the infantry attack ended in costly failure.

On the same day, in the centre and on the left flank XIX, XVIII, and XIV Corps were to attack later at 1:55 p.m. The conditions for the assaulting companies in the front line were atrocious. Having been marched up over night through torrential rain, they then had to stand around knee deep in water or lie in the filthy mud, for around ten hours awaiting the time to attack. Twenty minutes before the assault, the rain which had ceased during the morning again came on in torrents, with a driving wind adding to the mounting misery. Here amongst the filth and seeming futility, the British Army again proved its character and steadfastness beyond any doubt.

On XIX Corps front where 15th Division had already suffered so much, the ground around Hill 35 was once more a quagmire, where the 10/11th Highland Light Infantry of 46th Brigade, struggling through the mud and assailed by machine gun fire tried in vain to assault the Gallipoli blockhouse, the survivors dragging themselves back to the start line. To the left of Gallipoli and along the line towards Schuler Farm, 183rd Brigade of 61st Division attacked towards the Zonnebeke – Langemarck road with the 2/4th Gloucestershire Regiment and the 2/8th Warwick. The story was the same; the ground and machine gun fire were terrible and the remnants of the battalions fell-back to the start line, one third of the men and half of the officers becoming casualties.

In XVIII Corps sector north-east of St. Julien, the blockhouses at Springfield and Vancouver which had been captured during the confused fighting of the 22nd August had been re-occupied by the enemy and the heartbreaking job of clearing them began over again, in another attempt to establish a forward position along the Zonnebeke – Langemarck road. The 48th Division was to use the 144th Brigade with 145th Brigade in support. Germans sheltering in muddy water-filled shell-holes were cleared by the 1/8th and 1/7th Worcestershire Regiment as they advanced, the battalion also capturing a blockhouse. The advance across awful ground towards the road continued but came under increasing enfilade fire from the Springfield blockhouse on the right and the Vancouver blockhouse on the left. 1/4th Royal Berkshire Regiment and 1/4th Ox and Bucks Light Infantry moving up in support also came under fire from Springfield, but later in the day and with the assistance of two tanks which had moved up the St. Julien - Poelcappelle road, the blockhouse was outflanked and taken from the rear by the 1/8th Worcester. The Vancouver blockhouse also fell with the assistance of another tank.

To the left 11th Division using the 32nd Brigade was to make another attempt against Pheasant Trench. The 9th West Yorkshire regiment with the 8th Duke of Wellingtons to their left attacked with the 6th York and Lancaster Regiment and the 6th Yorkshire Regiment in support. The West Yorks started well but soon came under fire from Pheasant Trench and enfilade fire from the right from Vancouver, and from the Vieilles Maison blockhouse east of the Poelcappelle road. Seizing a bunker they began consolidating as best they could in the dreadful ground short of the objective, two platoons of the 6th York and Lancs coming up in support. The Duke of Wellingtons came under fire from a machine gun on top of the blockhouse at Pheasant Farm 300 yards behind the trench, and the right companies being worst hit took shelter in shell-holes and attempted to dig-in, only 60 yards forward of their start line. The left pushed on through the mud and occupied part of Pheasant Trench, the 6th Yorks coming up in support.

Trenches in the German Third Line north-east of Langemarck had in places been entered on the 16th August, but the occupation by the British of parts of the line had been far from secure, sections of Eagle and Pheasant trench being taken and then re-taken by the enemy. The XIV Corps were to assault the Third Line along 600 yards of trench either side of the Langemarck – Poelcappelle road at Schreiboom, where fighting had been severe on the 16th. The 38th Division attacked with the 16th Welsh Regiment of 115th Brigade at 1:55 p.m. The men had been lying out in shell-holes all morning but before midday it had started to rain, and when the moment came to move they found it difficult to even lift themselves out of the filthy water. The battalion failed in its struggle to keep up with the barrage and was soon hit by a hail of machine gun fire from Eagle Trench and in enfilade from White House, the survivors being back at their starting points by evening.

Along the whole front the effort had been costly, futile and mostly fruitless and fought under the worst possible conditions. XVIII Corps had pushed the line a little further forward and secured the blockhouses at Springfield and Vancouver, but the cost for such minor gains were ludicrous. The attacks need not and should not have happened.

The 28th August was another day of gales, but with less rain, and 15th Division were at last relieved by 42nd Division of XV Corps, having been in the line since 17th. The Germans, who were obviously also feeling the pressure, had withdrawn from the Vieilles Maison blockhouse during the night and it was occupied subsequently by the 6th York and Lancs.

Haig was now, at last, exercising more control over the situation, and was obviously unhappy about the results of the fighting on the 27th August, for on the 31st Kiggell issued the following order. 'In view of the continued wet weather and the consequent indefinite delay in delivery of the attack on Inverness Copse, Glencorse Wood and Nonne Bosschen Wood, the Field-Marshal Commanding-in-Chief has decided that this attack will not now take place under the orders of Fifth Army. The II Corps and Corps front will be transferred on the 3rd September from Fifth to Second Army under orders which are being issued separately. The G.O.C. Second Army will include the above mentioned local attack in the Second Army operations, either preliminary to or as part of the main operations as he may consider desirable after full consideration and when the weather conditions become more definite.'[358] Thankfully the attack planned for the 31st August against the woods was cancelled, and the next operation against them would be very different indeed.

But this was not quite the final swansong for Fifth Army's local attacks against tactical features. The 182nd Brigade of 61st Division had completed the relief of 15th Division on the 31st August about Gallipoli and Hill 35, and on the 1st September 2/5th Warwick attacked the enemy positions on the hill making a small gain. On the 4th September 2/8th Warwick of the same brigade attacked Aisne Farm 500 yards north of Hill 35 and got to within 30 yards of the blockhouse before being driven back. At 7:30 a.m. on the 6th September, 125th Brigade of 42nd Division using 1/5th and 1/6th Lancashire Fusiliers in the attack, and 1/7th and 1/8th in support attacked the infamous Borry Farm, Beck House and Iberian. Beck House fell to a company of the 1/6th but two companies attacking Iberian came under machine gun fire from Hill 35. A German bombing counter-attack at 10:45 a.m. re-took Beck House, where all but two of the Fusiliers were killed or captured. The survivors of the 1/6th Lancs Fusiliers were driven back to their start line by persistent machine gun fire from Hill 35. The left flank of the 1/5th in front of Borry Farm was now exposed and an enemy counter-attack at 7:30 p.m. drove back all but the right company which held a position about 150yards in front of their start line and attempted to consolidate. At night the 2/5th Warwick made another unsuccessful attack on Hill 35.

On the 7th September the ground that had been consolidated by the 1/5th Lancs Fusiliers on the 6th was given up. North-east of Langemarck, on the 13th September at 2:40 a.m. about 200 *Wurttembergers* many wearing body armour attacked the outposts of the 2nd Irish Guards, (the Guards Division having relieved the 29th Division on the 28th August) north of the Broenbeek, driving them back some way into shell-holes, the outpost positions being subsequently withdrawn south of the stream. On the 14th September at 3:00 a.m. the 2/1st London attacked Winnipeg on the Zonnebeke – Langemarck road from the blockhouse at Springfield, and at 7:30

---

[358] National Archives, GHQ order OAD612, WO158/311

p.m. 200 Germans attacked Springfield. On the 15th September the 7th London attacked a strongpoint in the ruins of a farm between Glencourse Wood and Inverness Copse, taking 36 prisoners and a machine gun. A counter attack the next day was resisted, but Lieutenant Cryer who had led the attack was killed, the position subsequently being known as Cryer Farm. On the 16th September, during a fierce artillery duel along the Guards front, a few Irish Guards who had been cut off north of the Broenbeek fought their way back across the stream to their own lines. Other local attacks planned by Fifth Army, to be carried out by V Corps on the 13th September, XVII Corps on the 11th and XIV Corps on the 15th, were stopped at last by Haig's order. The last few engagements in the attempt to draw up close to the Langemarck – Gheluvelt Line ended inconclusively, as most had done previously. Both sides had experienced the most traumatic, exhausting and harrowing time, under inconceivably atrocious conditions of rain and mud.

Conditions in the Salient August 1917

In the planning of the offensive it was known that it was never going to be possible to move tens of thousands of men, thousands of guns, and enormous quantities of stores and equipment into the restricted confines of the Ypres Salient without creating a vast area of badly cut-up and rutted, but hopefully not too soft ground. Given that the campaign had started in July, the hope of reasonable weather allowed for the above conditions, which it was realized would never be easy, but were to be expected and would be acceptable. Small amounts of rainfall were not unexpected in August, and would introduce muddy conditions that with luck would only be short-lived, as warm summer weather quickly baked the mud hard. But the hopes for a dry period had been dashed more firmly than could ever have been imagined. From late July and throughout August, between the downpours of rain, there had been insufficient sun to effect an improvement in ground conditions. Throughout the Salient the morass had become deeper and wider wherever the thousands men and animals trod, and wherever the wagons and guns rolled, or more often stuck. To work under such conditions was extremely difficult; to fight was near impossible.

To be anywhere near the Salient was dangerous. Ypres and all the villages around it were in total ruin, and many German shells had reached Poperinghe about ten miles behind the lines. The main route up to Ypres from Poperinghe through Vlamertinghe, either by bus, rail, or foot, and taken at some time by most who fought in the Salient, was continuously raked by German gunfire. Within the Salient itself, anywhere east of the Ypres – Yser canal to the north of the city, or east of the Ypres – Comines canal south of the city were areas in which movement in daylight was to be avoided, and even at night was highly risky. Within this area it was impossible to hide from the enemy guns, and the only way to ensure safety was to stay below ground. Any feature giving a degree of shelter was utilized to the full, the canal banks and the city ramparts being examples. Where no other shelter existed, deep underground tunnel systems were dug, many metres down into the clay, and this timber lined, putrid, wet, rat and fly infested world was the subterranean home to thousands. Pumps pushing air in and water out were operated constantly, the atmosphere always foul, but safe from the guns. An excellent description of one such dug-out appears in the history of the 36th (Ulster) Division. 'Wieltje dug-outs! Who that saw it will forget that abominable mine, with its "town major," its thirteen entrances, the water that flowed down its main passages and poured down its walls, its electric light gleaming dully through steam-coated lamps, its sickly atmosphere, its smells, its huge population of men – and of rats? From behind sack-curtained doorways the coughing and groaning of men in uneasy slumber mingled with the click of type-writers. In the corridor one would fall over a runner, slimy from head to foot with mud, resting while he waited for a return message to the front line. One advantage only it had: it was safe within. And that was in part counter-balanced by the danger of exit and entrance, constantly menaced by storms of fire.'[359]

---

[359] Cyril Falls *The History of the 36th (Ulster) Division* p113.

Several methods of transport were available to the troops. Up to Poperinghe most would be moved by train. From Poperinghe the standard gauge railway line ran to the Asylum sidings at Ypres. Later when the front moved east, the tracks were to be re-laid up the western side of the Ypres – Yser canal to Boesinghe and then across the canal towards Langemarck. A network of 60 centimetre railway tracks with steam locomotives was used to carry enormous numbers of men and materials, especially heavy ammunition, about the battlefield, with trench tramways relying on manpower to move the wagons pushing closer to the front lines. Buses, trucks and endless horse-drawn G.S. wagons loaded with troops and stores plied the inadequate tree lined road between Poperinghe, Vlamertinghe and Ypres, while many, less lucky, marched up or out on the pave. About the villages of Dickebusch, Vlamertinghe and Elverdinghe, an abundance of vast, tented or hutted camps gave very basic although less safe shelter, facing the continual risk of enemy shell-fire, and the nightly danger of air attack. They were at least better ventilated than the deep dugouts. But if it had rained, there was always endless, ankle deep mud. In the dugout systems and hutted camps boots could be removed to sleep, and there were chicken netted bunks to sleep on. There was hot food usually available and some basic facilities to wash both body and clothing, and compared with the trenches this was a luxury.

The battery positions of the medium and heavy guns were under the constant risk of hostile counter-battery fire. White hot case splinters lashing from high explosive shells were bad enough, but their killing zone was relatively local. Gas was another matter, as a heavy gas bombardment could saturate large areas and cause widespread fear and alarm, although good gas drill helped to keep casualties down. Since early July the German use of mustard gas had introduced a new hazard, for although the excellent small box respirator with its new filter could protect from the gas, it could not protect from the sticky oily paste which lay around and easily contaminated uniforms with disastrous results. The battery positions were always prime targets for gas shelling, and the gun crews suffered accordingly.

Enough has been said about the weather to know that throughout this period it was often very wet. For the troops, the gas cape gave some protection from the rain but the wool uniform was excellent at soaking up the water, adding to its natural discomfort. Opportunities to clean and dry clothing were few, especially in the line, and the problems with lice are well recorded. The puttees worn around the bottom of the trousers as gaiters were not the most convenient or comfortable of leg-ware. To the regulars of 1914 these discomforts had been a soldier's lot, but to the civilians in uniform of 1917 it seemed an endless nightmare. Under normal circumstances, opportunities to bathe and change clothing were made available at routine intervals, usually at local breweries, common in Belgium and France, or mobile bath units. But during an offensive there was little time for such routine. Clean dry socks were one item of clothing made available whenever possible even in the line, but it would not take long before they were wet and filthy again.

Preparations for the offensive meant for the attacking infantry endless training, and for the gunners, the engineers, and sappers endless labour. Before and during any major fighting, countless trips would be made night after night, across vulnerable duckboard tracks, or even across country, and then up communication trenches carrying forward the myriad of supplies required in the build up to, and maintenance of the offensive. The loads were heavy, and the ground was dreadful. The boarded tracks towards the lines were slippery and treacherous when wet, and often smashed by the guns. Just to find the way in the dark across the cratered wastes and up the network of trenches could be troublesome, especially to those new in the line. Work on paths, tracks, wire, ammunition dumps, gun emplacements, communication cables, and a host of other essential battlefield tasks was endless. Work would continue through the night and the firing of rockets and flares into the night sky by friend or foe would create a stark, silhouetted, bleak landscape, and would endanger revealing these nocturnal labourers.

Training for the infantry was usually directed towards one major aim; the most effective way to kill the enemy. This may not have always rested easily with the civilians in uniform, for killing, or even the thought of it, did not come to many as natural behavior. The hardships and privations were many in this place where the sight and smell of dead and mutilated men and animals, accompanied by the ever present danger of shellfire was considered the norm; and all this was behind the lines and before battle had even started.

After the opening of the offensive on the 31st July the situation in the forward positions which had been gained were simply awful. Use was made of the existing German defences where possible, enemy trenches and bunkers providing some shelter from sniping and shelling. The state of these trenches and shelters, often knee deep in filthy water and mud was appalling, the dead and parts of the dead of both sides lying around in abundance. Reliefs were very difficult. To move companies up to the line from the rear assembly areas west of Ypres took hours of treacherous struggle, along the communication trenches, or through the narrow, dank tunnels up to the Gheluvelt plateau, or for the last few thousand yards along the duckboard tracks up towards the Steenbeek. To get rations forward under such conditions was an on-going nightmare for quartermasters, who on occasions could not even find their battalions. The situation regarding latrine facilities is unimaginable.

For the dead the hardships no longer mattered, but for the wounded, numbered in thousands their plight was piteous. Those that could walk or stagger back to the overwhelmed Regimental Aid Posts were lucky. For those that could not their situation was dire. In agony and shock, and assuming they were in a position that was not still under fire, they could do no more than hope to be recovered by stretcher parties, which were themselves floundering in the mud, up to eight men often being required to evacuate one stretcher case. The journey back to the dressing stations could take many hours across the crater field and through the mud, continually harassed by shellfire, which on occasions would claim the whole party.

From the evidence of photographs taken of the battlefield it was an utter chaos of tangled wire, splintered timber, shattered concrete, rubble, discarded and broken equipment, blasted breastworks and bunkers, thousand upon thousand of water-filled shell-holes, and broken and bloated corpses of animals, and men. Such was the unholy awfulness of the Ypres battlefield in August 1917. With regard to the weather the British could consider themselves unlucky. But the tactics they had adopted throughout August were unlikely to have succeeded in achieving the aims of the Commander-in Chief even on a dry battlefield. On a battlefield of endless mud the results were now obvious. The conditions and apparent lack of success throughout the month had reduced the morale of the fighting troops in the Salient to an all time low. The British Official History sums it up thus. 'The memory of this August fighting, with its heavy showers, rain filled craters and slippery mud, was so deeply impressed on the combatants, who could not be told the reason for the Commander-in Chief's persistency, and such stories of it were spread at home by the wounded, that it has remained the image and symbol of the whole battle, overshadowing the subsequent successful actions of the campaign and preventing the true estimation of them, even in some cases stopping any knowledge of them from reaching the public ear.'[360] On the order of the Commander-in Chief there was now to be a change in tactics, and although not influenced by Haig's order, also a change in the weather.

British casualties from 31st July to 28th August 1917

	Killed	Wounded	Missing
Officers	684	2,563	177
Other ranks	9,582	47,589	7,406
Total	68,010		

---

[360] BOH p210

Their faces say it all. Battle of Langemarck

Taking the railway across the Yser Canal at Boesinghe

Chapter Four

"Magnificent in accuracy and volume"

Plumer's First Step

The Battle of The Menin Road Ridge, 20th September

The situation in Flanders at the end of August

The attempt by II Corps to capture Inverness Copse, which had ended in failure on the 24th August, had finally convinced the Commander-in-Chief to make fundamental changes to the conduct and control of the campaign. For Haig this had been a difficult decision. His direct involvement was now to increase, at least initially. Simply giving advice had proved insufficient to prevent the series of piecemeal attacks by Fifth Army which had totally lacked the initiative and innovation required to succeed, if indeed with the strength available that success had ever been achievable. The decision to intervene should have come sooner. If the initial advice had not been rejected by Gough, intervention may not have been required at all. The attempted break through, which had been so desperately hoped for, was for the moment put aside, to be augmented by a revised plan which would allow for the reduction of the German position on the Gheluvelt plateau by a serious of powerful attacks with strictly *limited objectives*, as opposed to the lip service paid to this tactic to date. To accomplish this, the principal command rôle had been transferred to General Plumer, and although the overall objectives would remain unaltered, the tactical arrangements would be drastically revised.

The weight of Second Army was now to fall upon a front, slightly shorter than that which had previously been the responsibility of II Corps. The tactical finesse with which Plumer and Major-General Charles (Tim) Harington his M.G.G.S. had planned and fought Messines would be applied to this new challenge, and the forces necessary to achieve success would be made available. The plan in simple terms was a series of four separate forward steps, each of around 1,500 yards, using four divisions of Second Army, each attacking on a frontage of about 1,000 yards. These limited steps would allow the infantry to consolidate the newly won position with fresh supports, while still under the protective umbrella of their field artillery barrage, and be able to not just resist, but moreover defeat any counter-attack. A six day interval between each step would enable the batteries, ammunition and other supplies to be brought forward ready to support the next step. In retrospect the new plan made Gough's previous failure all the more understandable. Haig had always warned him that he must concentrate on Gheluvelt, but must also attack along as broad a front as possible, to prevent concentration of gunfire by the German batteries. For Gough to have done both with the forces available to him, especially in artillery, had simply not been possible. To concentrate at Gheluvelt in sufficient strength in infantry and guns to break the German position would mean having insufficient forces elsewhere to attack along his broad front.

Gough had been short of guns, but had not made this known, and Haig had been sadly ill-informed of the true situation by his artillery chief.

The concentration of infantry and guns which Plumer now planned to engage to finally break the German Second Line on the Menin Road, and across the narrow saddle between the Bassevillebeek and Hanebeek valleys, would make it clear why Gough's attempts had continually failed. Whilst attempting deep penetrations of the Flanders position, Fifth Army had simply not possessed the strength to accomplish the task, however its forces had been deployed. It has been argued that whilst Fifth Army was failing to dominate the German artillery east of the plateau, British gun strength was dissipated unnecessarily along the Western Front, especially with the Second Army. It was now to be seen if with the additional strength Plumer was about to deploy, the German batteries would at last be dominated.

Distribution of Artillery in the British Expeditionary Force:[361]

	First Army		Second Army		Third Army		Fourth Army		Fifth Army		LOC*
	Field	Heavy	Field	Heavy	Field	Heavy	Field	Heavy	Field	Heavy	
July 27th	778	311	576	243	845	257	416	189	1568	758	461
August 17th	810	311	528	242	875	245	442	209	1620	757	521
Sept 21st	888	271	1268	629	725	245	272	131	1130	503	598

*Includes Anti Aircraft defences at Calais, Cavalry field artillery, G.H.Q. field and heavy battery reserves.

Approximate length of front in yards (prior to 20th September)				
First Army	Second Army	Third Army	Fourth Army	Fifth Army
61,000	16,500	37,500	6,000	11,500

Yards per gun (prior to 20th September approx)				
56	20	34	10	5

Approximate length of front in yards (on 20th September)				
61,000	20,500	37,500	6,000	7,500

Yards per gun (on 20th September approx)				
52	27* 3**	38	15	6

*South of Klein Zillebeke road. **Attack north of Klein Zillebeke road.

---

[361] National Archives, GHQ statistics, Distribution of Artillery in the British Expeditionary Force WO95/14

International situation at the end of August

The situation of the Allies made it clear that the British Army alone, for the time being, would have to continue to maintain the maximum pressure against the German Army on the Western Front. Although the United States was now gradually building an army to fight in Europe, it would not begin to arrive in any numbers sufficient to affect the balance of power before some point in 1918.

On the Eastern Front the situation of the Russian Army was fast disintegrating, and the ability of the faltering ally in the east to continue to resist was waning fast. If it ceased to resist, which now seemed likely, German fortunes would rise enormously with the establishment of a single major front on which to concentrate its forces. Since the end of the ultimately disastrous Kerensky offensive, the political pendulum had swung at first against and then in support of the Russian Premier. News of the disaster had been broadcast widely in the country by the provisional government, in the hope of a nationalistic upsurge, but the plan had backfired and the behaviour of the government had only provoked angry resentment. In consequence a premature uprising had begun, against the will of Lenin and Trotsky, who recognised that revolution at this time would prove abortive. The crowds marched on the Tauride Palace and demanded members of the Soviet executive committee to accept the power which was theirs to take. But the Bolshevik members declined to give a definite lead. The street protests generally lacked cohesion and direction, and with the opportune introduction of a rumour that Lenin and Trotsky were German agents, the provisional government soon had the situation back under control. For the moment Lenin and Zinovieff fled to Finland, while Trotsky and several others were imprisoned. Kerensky's popularity soared, except amongst the Bolsheviks. The pendulum swung back in favour of the Premier, with Kerensky now in a stronger position flirting with the idea of a dictatorship, and the pro-military right wing, led by the new Commander-in-Chief Korniloff, considering a counter-revolution. Kerensky also veered towards the right becoming more dictatorial in his dealings with the Soviet. With the Russian State in this fragile predicament and at a moment of impending internal crisis, Ludendorff, who was accurately informed of all that was happening in Petrograd, chose this moment to strike at the most sensitive point on the northern end of the Russian line, attacking on the 30th August near the coast at Riga. The result was not entirely a rout, but more an orderly retreat of Russian forces, and it had been those regiments most affiliated to Bolshevism which had fought hardest. Petrograd was now seriously threatened by German arms, and a tussle for political supremacy began between Premier Kerensky and Commander-in-Chief Korniloff. As forces loyal to Korniloff marched on Petrograd, Kerensky placed himself at the mercy of the Soviet's, who having foreseen Korniloff's actions had raised a Red Guard of 40,000 volunteers from the factories to defend the capitol. By the 13th September Korniloff's attempted coup had failed and after a bitter interview with Kerensky he committed suicide. Although there were to be other offers of military support from Kerensky in exchange for further monetary inducements, Russia had virtually ceased co-operation with the Allies in the future conduct of the War.

On the Italian Front matters looked a little more hopeful. The series of battles to be called the Tenth Battle of the Isonzo fought in May and June had ended in stalemate. But Cadorna was to reopen the fighting on the 17th August on the Bainsizza plateau, and the Eleventh Battle of the Isonzo was to see the Austrians pressed so hard they were soon to be calling for German help. The Italians in turn were warning that their offensive would soon stall for want of reserves, heavy artillery and other munitions, and were again calling upon the French and British for assistance.

The situation in the French Army, that Army being from Haig's perspective the keystone in the arch of Allied strategy, had improved, and the mutinies in the Second, Fourth, Fifth, Sixth and Tenth Armies subsequent to the Nivelle offensive were now under control. This did not imply in any way however, as Haig well knew, that it was back to full fighting strength. As had been promised by Pétain on the 2nd June, the French Second Army had on the 20th August, after a massive 8 day bombardment, successfully attacked on an 11 mile front astride the Meuse near Verdun. The heights of le Mort'Homme and Hill 304, taken by the Germans at such cost in February 1916 were regained and 10,000 prisoners taken. At le Mort'Homme 1,000 Germans had perished terribly when an underground tunnel was sealed by French gun fire. The Germans had found it impossible to launch a powerful counter-attack, for as we have seen many divisions had already been transferred to the Flanders front. This was all positive and in line with the Haig's strategy. But on the 19th September Haig noted in his diary, 'in fact the French Army has not only ceased to be able to take the offensive on a large scale but according to Pétain's opinion, its discipline is so bad it could not resist a determined German offensive'.[362] It has been claimed notoriously that on the 19th September Pétain made a special visit to Haig's Headquarters, and implored him to continue the British offensive in Flanders, and stated that between the British right and the Swiss border he had not a man upon whom he could rely, and that a determined German attack against them could not be resisted.[363] There appears to be no documentary evidence to indicate that Pétain ever made this statement. It is most likely that this meeting never took place, and it may just be a convenient later reconstruction of Haig's diary entry. It is also claimed that Pétain warned that there were fears France was nearing the limit of her man-power and the danger existed that the French Government would demand a separate peace rather than face a German offensive with another huge tariff of casualties. Whether or not this pessimistic summation was ever made is not of overwhelming importance. Of greatest importance is the fact that it undoubtedly sums up Haig's appreciation of the French situation at that time, both military and political, perpetuating his conviction that maintaining the pressure on the Germans in Flanders in order to allow the French a further breathing space in which to fully recover must be his top priority.

Painlevé, who had become premier after the fall of Ribot's Government on 12th September, later wrote that a memorandum written by G.Q.G. for the Minister of War on the condition of the French Army at the end of September 1917, stated that any reverse would provoke anew, and this time probably beyond remedy, the dangerous crisis through which the Army had passed in May and June. If G.Q.G. believed this to be the situation in September, why should it be considered unreasonable for Haig, whose scant information was coming from the French, to believe it also?

Further doubts within the War Cabinet

Lloyd George was taking a break and staying with newspaper proprietor Sir George Riddell at his home, Lindfield in Sussex, and was according to Hankey, 'in a ferment of excitement about Cadorna's victory on the Carso'.[364] On the 26th the Prime Minister wrote to Robertson urging him to go to Italy and establish the situation with a view to sending a large number of guns in an attempt to exploit the victory. He also wrote to Bonar Law pointing out the great opportunity offered in assisting the Italians, 'particularly in view of the failure of the Flanders offensive, consequent on the continuous rain'.[365] The War Cabinet met on the 27th August,[366] without Lloyd George who was still at Lindfield, and without its military advisor Robertson. Lloyd George sent a message in his absence, urging the dispatch of guns to Italy to assist with General Cadorna's offensive on the Isonzo, but made no comment regarding Flanders. In Robertson's absence, General Maurice gave the Cabinet an account of the fighting at Ypres. The news was not unduly inspiring and reflected the desperate fighting for Inverness Copse. From Italy the story was more encouraging, as the Italians had now taken most of the Bainsizza plateau, and had captured 28,000 prisoners and 100 guns, some up to 12-inch. It would undoubtedly not have

---

[362] Douglas Haig. Diaries and Letters, p329
[363] See BOH p235
[364] Hankey Diaries, 26th August
[365] Hankey Diaries, 26th August
[366] National Archives, minutes of War Cabinet 224 noon 27th August CAB23/2

crossed the minds of the Cabinet members that the Austrians were a very different enemy to the Germans. This fact was soon to become tragically clear to the Italians.

At Lindfield meanwhile the Prime Minister was anxiously awaiting a telegram, not of news from Flanders, but from Italy regarding stocks of heavy ammunition, his mood made no better by a bout of neuralgia and the fact that high winds had brought down the telephone lines, cutting off his communication with the outside world. Lord Milner arrived in the evening and was in substantial agreement with Lloyd George on the Italian question. It was decided that Robertson would be summoned to Lindfield, and he duly arrived, accompanied by Maurice on the morning of the 29th. The Prime Minister was well aware of Robertson's opinion that a Cabinet decision on strategic policy between support for the Western Front or the Italian campaign was essential. Using this as a convenient shield, Lloyd George and Milner had concocted a telegram to the British Ambassador in Rome which sank to new depths of skullduggery. Not content with surreptitiously subordinating their own responsibility for policy making to the British military, they now looked to the Italians for solace before formulating British strategy. In the telegram Lloyd George claimed that the British Cabinet was willing to abandon the Flanders operation. Although this would be hailed by the enemy as a victory, he was nevertheless prepared to suffer this embarrassment, and would assist in the Italian campaign, but only if he received assurances that British assistance would *guarantee* an Italian success. To add even greater conceit, the telegram, in a slight to the integrity of the Italian military, demanded a 'convincing appreciation' [367] from the Italian high command, as the Cabinet claimed it knew by experience the misguided optimism of Generals. To whom in Italy the British Ambassador was intended to hand the telegram was as unclear as the thinking behind it, and Hankey felt that Robertson only put his name to it in the belief that the Italian reply would not be sufficiently convincing. Lloyd George and his Cabinet had once more hedged the Flanders issue, and had abandoned any pretence of statesmanship by bringing the Italians into a decision making process, which was the responsibility of the British Government alone.

Not all news from Italy however was as encouraging as that from the Bainsizza which had so impressed Lloyd George. Colonel Spears, liaison officer at French General Headquarters had on the 28th written a note to General Maurice at the War Office informing of serious riots in Turin where there had been 30 deaths. Work in the factories was stopped, and there were cries of 'down with the War' on the streets. The anti-war activity of socialist pacifists was as rife in Italy as it was in France. But of more immediate danger, the first news of a possible check to Cadorna's highly regarded offensive had been picked up by the intelligence services at Italian General Headquarters, in that Austria, enabled by the deteriorating condition of the Russian Army was moving troops from the Russian front to the Italian, and of greatest importance had requested assistance from the Germans. There was already a good deal of talk of sending more guns to Italy, sixteen batteries of 6-inch howitzers and a liberal supply of ammunition having already been sent back in July. Robertson asked Spears to find out if the French were going to send either men or guns, and if so how many? Spears replied on the 2nd September. 'General Cadorna is asking for more artillery saying that the success of his operation depends directly upon the amount of heavy artillery with which he can be furnished. General Foch and French War Committee are disposed to send this artillery. The only reserve of heavy artillery at French disposal is the 350 heavy guns with the 1st Army; [supporting Haig's left] General Weygand will suggest that, say, 100 of these guns should be sent to Italy and then returned to Flanders to take part in operations there...French War Committee attaches sufficient importance to this proposal to make direct political request to British War Committee to endorse this view in the event of the C.I.G.S. refusing to take the French view.' [368] The French proposal to back the Italians was therefore to be at the cost of Haig's already slender resources of artillery at Ypres. From the French point of view it was immaterial whether the enemy was engaged on the Flanders front, in the Trentino, or on the Isonzo, so long as his reserves were kept off the French. But they were

---

[367] Hankey Diaries, 29th August
[368] National Archives, Spiers to CIGS, WO106/404

clearly intent, if necessary, on having British military advice overruled to achieve their aim of bolstering the Italians, the cost to be borne, again, by Haig.

In his reports to the War Cabinet during this period there is no doubt that Haig emphasized the positive achievements of the campaign so far. But as we have seen, he had not under-stated the difficulties. Haig's position was simple and his thinking understandable. That Russia and Italy should remain in the field and active was of immense importance to the Allied cause, tying up German and Austrian forces on the Eastern Front and in the north of Italy. The only way to give effective support to both Russia and Italy was to maintain pressure on Germany on the Western Front. But it was the questionable solidarity of the French, not of the Russians or the Italians that was the ultimate danger. If either Russia (which seemed most likely), or Italy were eliminated by German arms, or internal conflict, the repercussions would be very serious but not instantly catastrophic. But a concerted attack against France, which could not be withstood by her militarily, her politicians, or her people, would be catastrophic to Britain within weeks if not days. If Russia or Italy went out of the fight, the War could (and did) go on. But there was no contingency plan which envisaged continuing the fight without France. French collapse meant British collapse. The only way to support France which guaranteed denying the Germans the opportunity to move against her was to continue with the offensive in Flanders. To do nothing but sit on the defensive did not in the short term impose sufficient pressure on the enemy, and in the mind of the Commander-in-Chief was not an acceptable risk.

    To Haig his enormous responsibilities were crystal clear. Given the fact that a breakthrough now looked unlikely, the British Army, the only totally reliable and fully operational weapon in the Allied arsenal, should maintain its offensive in Flanders with all available resources until a satisfactory result was obtained, or until such time that for reasons of weather, man-power, or other factors outside his control it should cease. The greatest amount of damage possible should be done to the enemy, to prevent him gaining the initiative and moving his forces to another theatre. The operations now planned may well, given a period of clement weather, still prove decisive in driving the enemy from his position in Flanders, and from the Belgian coast. If the operations were not decisive, then at least the enemy was pinned in Flanders, and although he did not want to, he would have to fight.

    On the 2nd September Haig sent a brief résumé of offensive operations since the 21st August to the Cabinet via Robertson. His description of the fighting on the Gheluvelt plateau on the 27th was inaccurate as he claimed useful progress had been made, which it obviously had not. He explained however that greater force was being assembled to attack towards Polygon Wood, but again pointed out the limits of his manpower and artillery strength. 'Owing to the limited number of divisions and guns – especially the latter – at my disposal this extension of the main front of attack will entail curtailment of offensive energies on the front of my other armies. I have also been compelled to cut down ammunition expenditures in certain natures, especially in 6-inch howitzer, owing to insufficiency of supply.' [369] With the British Army fighting the greatest battle in its history, to which the Cabinet had in theory given its 'wholehearted support' it did nothing but continually talk of sending guns and ammunition, desperately needed in Flanders, to Italy, where in fighting the Austrians and not the Germans, the Italians were doing very well already. The shortage of ammunition was not just petty complaining on Haig's part, as the 6-inch howitzer comprised approaching 50% of his medium-heavy guns, 260 being with the Second Army and 208 being with the Fifth Army.

Not all members of the War Cabinet shared Haig's views, and at a meeting on the 4th September at which both Haig and Foch were present Lloyd George again cast doubts over the wisdom of continuing with the Flanders operation. The ability, or more especially determination of Russia to continue the War was now most unlikely. The probable defeat of Russia and present incapacity of the French led him to believe that to stand on the defensive for the remainder of

---

[369] National Archives, Haig to Robertson 2nd September WO158/24

1917 on the Western Front, whilst supporting the Italians with both men and materials was a far preferable policy.[370]

Foch had arrived in London, sent on his mission by Painlevé, to propose that French and British support for the Italian front should be backed by sending 100 heavy guns to Italy from Flanders. With the battle about to be rejoined at Ypres, Foch suggested, as Spears had predicted he would, removing the guns from the front of the French First Army on the Yser, presently supporting the left flank of Fifth Army. Haig was wholly and understandably opposed to removing any guns from Ypres and made it clear that they were still desperately needed. Foch claimed, undoubtedly under instruction from the French War Minister, (who had probably in turn been prompted by Minister of Munitions Albert Thomas), that it was politically expedient to send guns to Italy, which would otherwise be doing nothing at Ypres. But Haig refuted this, explaining how vital the French guns were in engaging the enemy batteries to the north of the Salient. The Cabinet, who were as usual split on the issue, finally agreed that the decision should be left with Haig. As the whole topic of sending the guns was of greater political than military significance, and was the brainchild of Painlevé and not Foch, it should undoubtedly have been the British politicians who made the final decision. Lloyd George 'spoke' to Haig privately and emphasized the political importance of the British being seen to be as supportive towards the Italians as were the French. The Prime Minister wrote to Painlevé the same day suggesting that, if Haig agreed, 50 guns might be found from the French First Army front, whilst the remaining 50 should be found by Pétain, at least partially relieving the burden on the main offensive front.[371] At least Lloyd George had gone out of his way to avoid a row with Robertson and Haig over the guns, undoubtedly supporting the 50 – 50 compromise. After the meeting he said to Hankey, 'I think this is the best we can do don't you? I do not think this is the moment for a row with the soldiers'.[372]

Painlevé's motives in sending the guns were as much if not more in the interest of France as they were in the interest of Italy. Ever mindful of the weakness of his own military and political situation, anything that could be done to inexpensively bolster the Italians was worth trying. France was already relying upon the British offensive to draw off the German reserves and allow time for recovery, so why not pay an added (but materially slight) insurance premium of 100 guns to stiffen Italian resolve, which would indirectly assist France. If the guns did not come from the French front so much the better, for the cost to France of the added insurance would then in fact be nothing. At a military conference at Amiens between Haig, Foch and Pétain, on the 7th September at which War Minister Lord Derby was present, full, but undoubtedly reluctant agreement was reached on the sourcing of the guns, which were destined soon to be on their way to Italy. Lord Derby wrote to the Prime Minister on the 8th September advising that the meeting had gone off amicably, and offered an astute appreciation of the French position, '...there is no doubt this is a political and not a military move as it was very evident neither of the French Generals liked sending the guns. Pétain was very insistent on the guns being returned from Italy as soon as ever the offensive was over and my own belief is that many of the guns will never go at all'.[373]

In a way Lord Derby was right, for although the guns so desperately needed at Ypres were on their way, they were never destined to reach the Italian front. As we shall see, on the 12th September, with the threat of German intervention looming large, General Cadorna was to call of his offensive east of the Isonzo. This information was not to come to the attention of the

---

[370] Lloyd George's perception of the incapacity of the French Army was partly due to his knowledge of the Nivelle disaster, but as we have seen he had also been informed by Spears, Wilson, General Maurice, and Lord Esher of the mutinies. Other members of the War Cabinet had been briefed in a similar way and all were aware that there had been problems. But the French were keeping a tight lid on information, and a matter of such extreme military sensitivity could not be made general knowledge, even in top political circles. See Chapter 10.
[371] Parliamentary Archives, Lloyd George Papers LG/F/50/1/17
[372] Hankey Diaries, 4th September
[373] Parliamentary Archives, Derby-L.G. Lloyd George Papers, LG/F/14/4/67

War Cabinet until the 21st September,[374] but when it did was to stimulate a far greater response than was ever achieved by any report from the great battle raging in Flanders.

Alternative Attack Sectors

Concerns regarding manpower troubled Haig in early September, as they had in early August. In August Robertson had written to G.H.Q. stating that during September probably less than 8,000 men would arrive in France as drafts, which would do little more than replace normal wastage. On the 21st August Haig had told his Army Commanders that the British Divisions in France would probably be 100,000 men below establishment by October. A decision had to be made regarding the best course of action should either bad weather or a lack of man-power draw the Flanders operation to an early conclusion. Operations Branch at G.H.Q. produced a memorandum with recommendations for making switches to certain selected fronts in case of need, initially considering Lens, where First Army had been planning the capture of the town, or Lombartzyde, to strengthen the hold of Fourth Army on Nieuport. On the 16th September, General Byng commanding Third Army, produced details of a proposed attack upon the Hindenburg Line at Cambrai using massed tanks. Haig had high regard for the Cambrai proposal and promised his support, if it was possible.

Lloyd George had altogether different ideas of alternative fronts. His eyes were again turning eastwards, and on the 16th September, on a break at Criccieth in North Wales, was noted by Hankey as saying that, 'He wants to abandon all activity on the Western Front and to concentrate our effort against Turkey'.[375] The next day Lord Milner arrived and again the talk returned to the mistake of the current military policy. Hankey noted, 'we all had a good talk as a result of which it was agreed that our proper course in the War was to concentrate on Turkey as there is little hope of achieving definite success on the Western Front'.[376] Away from the war gaming of the politicians the real War proceeded urgently towards the next major episode.

Plumer's requirements

The planned landings along the coastal strip had now been postponed until the first week in October and some realists may have begun to doubt whether they would now happen at all. Other strategic aspects of the campaign had not altered and the seizure of the high ground Gheluvelt - Broodseinde - Passchendaele - Staden - Clerken, followed by exploitation east towards Thourout and Roulers was still the aim. The way this aim was to be achieved had altered radically. Second Army was now responsible for capturing the German Third Line which ran along Tower Hamlets spur, across the Menin road near Gheluvelt, through Polderhoek and north to Polygon Wood. Once this right flank was secure the job of Fifth Army would be to continue its advance eastwards from the Steenbeek valley, through the German Third Line (Langemarck – Gheluvelt Line), then towards Zonnebeke – Gravenstafel – Poelcappelle, and then through the Fourth Line, Flanders I, and on to the high ground of the Passchendaele Ridge. General Plumer discussed his plan with his Corps Commanders on the 27th August and presented the scheme to G.H.Q. on the 29th. Five corps were available to Second Army to cover the 7.5 mile front from the River Lys in the south to where the left flank met with Fifth Army. From the south the VIII Corps, Lieutenant -General Hunter Weston, would cover from the Lys to just north of Messines with two divisions. From here the IX Corps, Lieutenant -General Gordon, would hold the line to the Ypres – Comines canal with one division, and would extend its left to 1,000 yards north of the canal, over which distance it would form a defensive southern flank with the 19th Division. The X Corps, Lieutenant -General Moorland, and the I Anzac Corps,

---

[374] National Archives, minutes of War Cabinet 237 21st September CAB23/2
[375] Hankey Diaries, 16th September
[376] Hankey Diaries, 17th September

Lieutenant-General Birdwood would carry out the main attack against the plateau, with the II Anzac Corps, Lieutenant-General Godley, in reserve for later fighting.

To better concentrate his infantry Plumer proposed that the length of front of his main attack be reduced from that first discussed with Haig of 6,800 yards, to 4,000 yards. An attack towards Zandvoorde to broaden the front had been one of Haig's requirements, but Plumer pointed out that the simultaneous attack by Fifth Army on the left would have the desired effect of dispersing the fire of the German batteries, and that as conditions in the lower Bassevillebeek valley would make attacking towards Zandvoorde a very difficult proposition, this attack should be postponed until a later date. Haig agreed to the suggestion which shortened Plumer's main front of attack by 2,000 yards, and on the 30th August also agreed that Fifth Army should take over 800 yards of Second Army front south of the Ypres – Roulers railway, north of Westhoek. Plumer now had his 4,000 yards front on which to concentrate the two attacking divisions of X Corps (41st and 23rd) and two of I Anzac Corps (1st and 2nd Australian), a frontage of 1,000 yards per division. The third division of X Corps, the 39th would, with 19th Division of IX Corps form the defensive southern flank.

This concentration of infantry was satisfactory to Plumer's requirements. He now needed the firepower, especially in heavy guns to smash the German batteries beyond the high ground, and burst their blockhouses on the plateau, to give the infantry the best chance of doing their job. He asked for 1,339 guns and howitzers for his attack front, and received 1,295 of which 575 were heavy and medium, and 720 were 18-pounders and 4.5-inch howitzers. Second Army received a total of 1,830 guns, the balance of 535 guns going to the defensive fronts of VIII and IX Corps. The huge concentration of guns on the fronts of X Corps and I Anzac Corps was more than double the number, (282 heavy and 576 field guns and howitzers), allotted to II Corps for the attack on the 31st July. With twice the number of guns and an objective depth of less than half that attempted by II Corps, the concentration of firepower would be more than four times that of the 31st July. But there was not a limitless supply of artillery, and to bring Second Army strength to this level Third and Fourth Armies guns were brought to Ypres to add to those which had already been taken over from II Corps. During the build-up period between the 28th August and 12th September, 626 guns and howitzers were transferred to Second Army, of which 14 were super heavy, 120 were heavy, 252 were medium, and 240 were field pieces. Total nominal gun strength of Second Army on the 14th September was, 990 18-pounders, 336 4.5-inch howitzers, 108 60-pounders, 4 9-inch howitzers (30 cwt), 292 6-inch howitzers (26cwt), 16 6-inch guns, 72 8-inch howitzers (Mk I-VI), 24 8-inch howitzers (Mk VII), 70 9.2-inch howitzers (Mk I), 12 9.2-inch howitzer (Mk II), 4 9.2-inch guns, 10 12-inch howitzers (Mk I & II), 11 12-inch howitzers (Mk III - V), 2 15-inch howitzers.[377]

At noon on the 3rd September II Corps and its frontage was taken over by Second Army from Fifth Army, the II Corps headquarters staff being relieved on the 5th. The divisions holding the line, 24th, 30th, and 8th would stay in position at the disposal of X and I Anzac Corps until a few days before the attack. The manpower and the guns, the two major component parts necessary to build Plumer's offensive machine were now available. They now required painstaking assembly and final detailed instructions to be issued on exactly how the whole complex mechanism was to be put into operation, for nothing was going to be left to chance. The one other element required was time, and Plumer had got three weeks.

Plumer's planning

The detailed instructions of the offensive were issued in two parts on the 1st and 10th September by way of Second Army Operation Order No 4, plus a subsequent addendum, with a probable date for the first step of the 20th September being given to corps commanders. The order of the 1st September defined the objectives of the first step. The final objective at an average depth of around 1,500 yards in accordance with the plan, formed a line from Groenenburg Farm in the

---

[377] National Archives, GHQ statistics, distribution of artillery, noon 14th September. WO95/15

south, northeast across the Bassevillebeek to just forward of the German Third Line on Tower Hamlets spur, then along the Third Line and across the Menin Road to a point on the Reutelbeek, this line to be captured by X Corps. From the Reutelbeek northward the line passed through Carlisle Farm and Black Watch Corner to a point on Anzac spur, 250 yards north of the Anzac blockhouse. The objective north of the Reutelbeek was upon or beyond the German Third Line and was to be captured by I Anzac Corps.

The addendum issued on the 10th September issued colour coding to the two intermediate objectives and the final objective, which were Red, Blue and Green respectively, (confusingly different from those used by Fifth Army on the 31st July). It also detailed the complexities of the barrage, including targets, lift rates, and sequences, arranged to protect the attacking infantry.

The artillery

Instructions had been issued to the artillery by Second Army on the 29th August with additions on the 14th September, the former explaining the requirements of the preliminary bombardment and the artillery role during the attack. The destruction of obstacles and strong-points, the isolation of the enemy forward batteries, disorientation of the enemy's forward infantry with a succession of dense creeping barrages to a depth of 2,000 yards beyond the final objective, and intensive counter-battery operations were the primary tasks of the preliminary bombardments. Prior to, and during the attack, (which would advance behind five separate barrage belts with a combined depth of about 1,000 yards), counter battery fire would be maintained on all known enemy battery positions. This point regarding the continuation of counter-battery fire during the attack was most important to the attacking infantry, and with the number of medium and heavy guns now available it could be maintained, without the risk of insufficient firepower being at hand to deal with potential counter-attack concentrations.

The additions issued on the 14th September went into exhaustive detail explaining further the tasks of the artillery. The complexity of the planning and its intention to continuously vary the target, timing, rate, and weight of fire, and the mixture in type of shell, fuse and use of gas is quite extraordinary. In its attempt to bring destruction, dislocation, disorientation and demoralization upon the enemy it was undoubtedly successful, but the work load it must have placed on the officers and men of the Royal Artillery can only be surmised. Destruction of the German batteries was paramount, and from the date of the order they were to be systematically attacked. On two nights before Zero day between 2:00 a.m. and 6:00 a.m., and again on Zero day for four hours before Zero hour, they were to be deluged with gas.

The preparatory barrage

The preparatory barrages would be carried out for five days preceding the attack, and communication trenches, observation points, wire entanglements, machine gun emplacements, strong-points and telephone exchanges would all be prime targets for the batteries. Isolating barrages, which would close the approaches to the front by two tiers of fire, would be carried out during this period, two thirds of the fire by night and one third by day. The tiers would be provided by machine guns at shorter range, field artillery up to 6,000 yards, with 60-pounder and 6-inch guns and howitzers beyond. Gas would be used where atmospheric conditions allowed against any position occupied by the enemy. The gas shelling was to be preceded by high explosive, the amount of gas shell fired then being gradually increased. The more sensitive No. 106 direct action fuse was to be saved where possible for barrage fire and not for counter-battery fire, and was to be used in a proportion of half 106 to half delay action for the 6-inch, 8-inch and 9.2-inch howitzers.

The protective barrage

The protective barrage would be put down 150 yards forward of the front line and would commence its advance after three minutes. It would cover the first 200 yards at a rate of 100 yards in four minutes, and then advance to the Red Line at a rate of 100 yards in six minutes, where it would halt for forty-five minutes. It would then advance from the Red to the Blue Line at a rate of 100 yards in eight minutes, where it would halt for two hours. It would then advance from the Blue to the Green Line at a rate of 100 yards in eight minutes, and upon arrival at the final objective the barrage would be put down 200 yards in front of the line gained and a searching barrage commenced. Such was the intricate fire programme to be followed by the field batteries. The rate of fire of the 18-pounder field guns was to increase to four rounds per minute for the first two minutes of the advance and reduce to one round per minute during pauses on the intermediate objectives, these barrages to be thickened with smoke shell if necessary. Liaison was to be maintained between appropriate departments, a field artillery officer was to live at the H.Q. of the infantry brigade his guns supported, and an officer, not under the rank of major should live at the H.Q. of the division whose front he covered, with direct telephone link to the bombardment and counter-battery groups. In the compilation of these orders issued to the artillery every conceivable detail was considered by Plumer and his chief G.S.O. Charles Harington, and a course of action directed to cover every foreseeable eventuality.

Five tiers of 1,000 yard depth would make up the protective barrage. Between the five tiers would be a gap of around 200 yards, which could be increased to 300 yards to increase the overall barrage depth if required. The first belt of fire, was a shrapnel barrage fired by half (336) of the available 18-pounder field guns. The second belt, consisted if high explosive shells fired by the remainder of the 18-pounders, with 70 per cent No.106 fuses and 30 per cent delay action, and by the 114 4.5-inch howitzers. The third belt, was fired by 240 machine guns, 128 in X Corps and 112 in I Anzac and was intended to keep the German forward counter-attack reserves in their shelters. The fourth belt comprised of 120 6-inch howitzers. The fifth belt was made up of 120 60-pounder guns, 28 8-inch and 14 9.2-inch howitzers, using the half No.106 and half delay fuse arrangement. The estimated artillery ammunition requirement for the seven day preliminary bombardment and for the day of the assault was 3.5 million rounds, about the same as had been fired at Messines, but here to be concentrated on a front under one quarter of that length.

The complexities of the artillery arrangements were extraordinary. To issue an order was simple, but that order had to then be transformed into action, involving thousands of men operating many hundreds of guns. Field artillery, medium and heavy batteries, all firing on different targets over different ranges had to be orchestrated into one programme. The variations and target changes involving each and every gun of the preparatory barrage were enormous, and the sequence of lifts and stands of the protective barrage required precise pre-planning and accurate compilation of and adherence to barrage tables and maps. Precision was vital as any inaccuracies would either result in insufficient destruction of enemy targets or even worse, disastrous casualties to friendly troops. The dumping of the correct caliber ammunition, of the correct shell type, with the correct fuses, at the correct battery, was an administrative and logistical nightmare all carried out in dreadful conditions under the fire of the enemy's guns. Of greatest importance was the ability to concentrate as soon as required, a great weight of fire upon selected fixed targets or targets of fleeting opportunity. This is what the German batteries behind the plateau had previously been able to achieve. To this end heavy and medium batteries were allocated defined target types and were formed into, bombardment, counter-battery, barrage, and fleeting-opportunity groups, allocated to corps or divisions.

Fifth Army artillery preparations involved a change to previous approach and were to attempt to surprise the Germans by dispensing with a long and systematic preliminary bombardment over a period of days, but rather to unleash an intense, "hurricane" bombardment over twenty four hours before the assault. Gough believed the element of surprise would give his infantry a better chance, and his planning in some ways pointed towards the future, for the days of the massive preparatory barrage were already numbered.

The infantry

The organization of the infantry would benefit in three principle ways from lessons learned at Messines. Firstly the German defence system was now well understood and a scheme of flexible attack would be developed to best overcome the strong-points. One or two lines of skirmishers at five-pace intervals would lead the attack, which during their advance would identify points of resistance, allowing time for the flexible assault groups following to deploy effectively against them. The assault groups, loosely distributed across the battlefield would then be responsible for outflanking and destroying the strong-points. This had become a recognized battlefield drill and much emphasis had been placed on it during training. Each group knew its task and much depended upon the resolution of junior commanders to carry them out. Following up the assault groups, mopping-up-parties would ensure thorough clearing of bunkers and dug-outs and would then consolidate on these positions.

Secondly it was recognized that the deeper the attack penetrated the stronger the resistance would become. To allow for this, the progressive objectives would be set at decreasing depths, and halts on each would gradually become longer. Within each brigade frontage, the number of infantry to attack each objective would be commensurate with their task. The first objective would be at about 800 yards and would be attacked by no more than one battalion, which would quickly overrun the enemy outpost zone. A forty-five minute halt would allow time for consolidation on the first objective and for the mopping-up parties to clear the area. After the halt a second battalion would pass through the first. This battalion would advance over a shorter distance towards the second objective 500 yards forward, but here the fighting around the strong-points encountered near the German Third Line would become more severe. A two hour halt would allow time for consolidation against counter-attacks by the German forward divisions. The final advance of no more than 300 yards would be carried out by two fresh battalions previously held back, which on reaching the final objective in strength, and not worn out by previous fighting would consolidate against an expected organized counter-attack. Depending on the local situation in some cases the final objective would be attacked by only one battalion, the other remaining in brigade reserve.

Thirdly the use of reserves was revised, becoming now more under control of local commanders and only to be used where necessary. At Messines the situation on the ridge later in the morning had resulted in unnecessary casualties from enemy shellfire due to overcrowding. It was believed that casualties in the initial attack would be higher than they in fact were, and reserves had been sent up as part of the pre-battle plan and not because they were required. This situation had now been addressed and reserves were only used when and where they were needed. The number of reserves per unit at company and battalion level was to be one quarter of the unit strength, (i.e. one platoon per company and one company per battalion), to be available in close support to overcome local opposition or local counter-attacks, and to be used at the unit commander's discretion. One brigade was to remain in reserve of each assaulting division, and available at the divisional commanders discretion and in a position to offer rapid support, with for example two battalions around one mile from the front, one battalion around two miles from the front and the fourth battalion around four miles behind the front. The reserves echeloned behind each assaulting divisional front would stretch back eight miles behind Gheluvelt plateau. A further full division would remain in reserve behind each assaulting division close enough to give support, or if necessary, relieve the division in the line that night or next morning. Either by chance or design this revised organization of reserves now mirrored the German system of counter-attack forces echeloned in depth behind their front line. In the three week period before the attack both Second and Fifth Army were given intensive training in this new attack organization, and counter-attack situations were simulated to ensure the competence of the reserve forces in dealing with them.

The infrastructure

The forces to carry out the offensive had now been gathered and were beginning to concentrate, and orders had been issued explaining the theory of how it was all going to work. But a concentration of such magnitude could not be placed in the position from which it was to operate quickly or easily. Plumer had asked for three weeks to make his preparations and the time had been put to good use.

To move the huge quantity of guns ammunition and other materials required by Second Army into position in the Salient would require the building of extra roads and light railways. It was now necessary for II Corp's heavy and medium batteries to move closer to the front, and with the addition of the extra guns arriving from Third and Fourth Armies, a vast number of new battery emplacements would have to be built, all additional work for the engineers. Hostile shelling had become less severe, the Germans having lost at least some of their commanding observation points, and throughout the middle of September with a period of dry weather the ground began to harden, both improvements helping in the burying of thousands of yards of new telephone cables, the building of the new battery positions and in improving the infrastructure. The light railways, from their junctions at the railheads with the standard gauge tracks ran forward to the shell dumps and battery emplacements, and towards the front lines. Although quick and easy to lay, and of tremendous help in moving heavy loads across the battlefields, they were not easy to repair if smashed by shellfire, and much movement of ammunition was still made by road. Throughout August, the roads due to the bad weather and enemy shelling had deteriorated, even with the ceaseless work of repair gangs. The main routes up to the fronts from where X and I Anzac Corps would attack were an obvious priority but were in an atrocious state. The Menin Road at Hooge was not recognizable as a road at all, with crater to crater shell-holes, smashed wagons, and knocked-out tanks in profusion.

New roads constructed of heavy timber planks measuring 9 feet by 1 foot by 2½ inches were laid across the crater fields and a one-way traffic system enforced to avoid congestion. The Menin and Verbrandenmolen roads out of Ypres were linked via Zillebeke to both Hellfire Corner and Hooge, and a loop road was built from Hooge forward through Chateau Wood then back around Bellewaarde lake and back to the Menin Road at Birr Cross Roads, (between Hooge and Hellfire Corner). One train load of 240 tons of planks arrived each day to supply I Anzac Corps alone with road building material. The timber was taken from the sidings at Ouderdom (5 miles south-west of Ypres) 3 tons at a time in 80 motor lorries, then through Ypres, to be dumped at Birr Cross Roads on the Menin Road, from where it was taken up mainly at night to the road working parties by 120 two-horse wagons.

Time was short and roads were built with single track only with passing places, and hostile shelling or accident could cause major congestion. The road circuits were finished just in time, on the 19th September. The working parties engaged on road building were always in the most exposed positions, many being under direct observation by the enemy forward positions, and therefore prime targets for German batteries, much of the work therefore having to be done at night. To assist the infantry to move across the ravaged fields, duckboard tracks led forward all the way from the city ramparts at Ypres and from the Yser canal bank right up to the front lines. For three weeks, night and day, the work on the infrastructure, dumping of ammunition, and carrying forward of a mass of stores and equipment had continued. The infantry and artillery had been concentrated, briefed and trained, and the engineering work necessary to give them improved access to and movement across the battlefield completed, just in time.

German observations

The three week lull in the offensive had somewhat confused the Germans. Some believed that the assault against their Flanders position had ceased, and misinformation gleaned from prisoners only added to this belief. It was assumed that the British would open an offensive elsewhere along their front.

On the 13th September Rupprecht's Chief of the Staff, stated that he was convinced the battle in Flanders was over.[378] At this time Second Army preparations were in full swing and it now seems incredible that German intelligence were unaware of the fact that the offensive was far from over. The loss of key observation points from which the whole Salient had previously been so open to scrutiny had obviously been significant, and German aircraft reconnaissance in daylight must have been drastically reduced by the work of the Royal flying Corps, (although at times this was not evident from the experiences of the men on the ground). Given these considerations it is still difficult to understand how the mass movement of guns, for which huge numbers of battery positions were under construction, and the laying of thousands of yards of new roads and light railways, plus the movement of tens of thousands of troops in rear areas was misinterpreted or went unnoticed.

It must be assumed that Rupprecht's officers changed their minds soon after the 13th September, for on this day and for the next week the preparatory barrages gradually increased in intensity. From the 15th September twice daily practice barrages were fired on either Army or Corps fronts of between 30 and 100 minutes duration which crept across the German defence system. Taking advantage of the barrages, the infantry carried out numerous raids taking prisoners where possible to identify the German units in the line. For the final two days the counter-battery groups concentrated on the German guns in their multiple emplacements behind the Gheluvelt plateau. Good flying weather allowed the Corps Squadrons to co-operate with accurate spotting, and wireless communications were established by the aircraft both with the batteries and Army Report Centre. Sometime during this period the Germans must have begun to realize the offensive was about to begin again, and by the 17th September *Fourth Army* headquarters were certain that a renewed attack was imminent.

The Air War continues

Officially it was claimed that the air superiority gained by July was largely maintained throughout August and into September by the Royal Flying Corps and Royal Naval Air Service, and those German aircraft that broke through the fighter patrols in daylight to photograph developments over the British lines were few in number. But there were to be times when the alleged British superiority was strongly challenged, the Germans making strenuous efforts to disrupt infantry and artillery with ground attacks, and in night skies German intruders had become a perpetual nuisance. In practice enemy aircraft remained very active both in a reconnaissance and ground attack role over the lines, and on many occasions were more in evidence that those of the Royal Flying Corps. The loss of ground observation was a great handicap to the German gunners who with lessening aircraft cooperation could do no more than carry out area shoots against the British battery positions, with decreasing accuracy, although observation balloons still floated precariously in the sky east of the ridge providing what information they could to their batteries .

In the battle areas of Second and Fifth Armies twenty six squadrons were now available, seven Corps Squadrons (Nos. 4, 6, 7, 9, 21, 42, and 53, all flying RE8's), two fighter reconnaissance squadrons (Nos. 20 and 22 flying Bristol Fighters), twelve single seat fighter squadrons (Nos. 1 flying Nieuports, 19 on SPADs, 45 on Sopwith Camels, 60 on SE5's, and 1 R.N.A.S. flying Sopwith Triplanes, all of II Brigade; Nos. 23 on SPAD's, 29 on Nieuports, 32 on DH5's, 70 on Sopwith Camels, and 10 R.N.A.S. flying Camels, all of V Brigade; and Nos. 56 on SE5's, and 66 on Sopwith

---

[378] BOH footnote p244

Pups, of 9th (Headquarters) Wing); three day bomber squadrons (Nos. 27 flying Martinsydes, and 55 and 57 DH4's), and two night bomber squadrons (Nos. 100 and 101 flying FE2b's). The heavy Handley Page V/1500's of the R.N.A.S. were also available for bombing of railway targets.[379]

To the west of Ypres the whole rear area back for many miles was packed with hutted and tented camps, hospitals, ammunition and supply dumps, fuel dumps, vehicle and tank parks, horse lines, railway sidings, communication centres and every other facility required by the Army. What the Germans could not hit so easily with artillery they now attempted to strike from the air. On most nights a steady stream of intruders, crossing the lines one at a time, flew towards the west with their small but lethal bomb loads heading sometimes beyond Poperinghe as far west as St. Omer. On dark nights their targets were not clearly defined, but so numerous were they that even if nothing was hit the disruption was intense. If the night was brighter the results could be most serious, on one such night a battalion in camp at Locre receiving 100 casualties from an air raid. Some accounts mention daylight raids and attacks on infantry columns, the Australian Official Account stating that at no time within the experience of Australian infantry were the German airmen so active behind the lines, although this is at variance with the British account which speaks of occasional reconnaissance aircraft which broke through by day. The raids began to have an effect more upon morale than material, and actions were taken to try to disrupt the disrupters. Standing night patrols were flown by the Flying Corps and although a system of co-operation between the pilots, the searchlights and the anti-aircraft guns was established, no enemy aircraft were brought down.

On the other side of the lines the two night bombing squadrons of the Royal Flying Corps were returning the favour. The same assortment and concentration of targets existed behind the German lines, the main enemy supply junction at Menin on the River Lys with its rail links to Courtrai, and the Courtrai to Roulers railway line with its associated branch lines and sidings were bombed, as were the R.F.C's most important target, the enemy airfields. The R.F.C. and R.N.A.S. were also very active in daylight skies over, and well east of the German lines. The interception of German two-seater reconnaissance aircraft at medium altitude and offensive sweeps against the enemy's fighters at higher altitudes was the responsibility of V Brigade, but return from patrols was to be at low level, machine-gunning troop concentrations and columns, or any other worthwhile targets. They would join II Brigade in this low level work, which was extremely dangerous due to ground-fire, and hated by the pilots. Anti-aircraft shellfire at medium and higher altitudes was disruptive but not too often lethal, whereas at low level, machine gun fire from the ground, against which the pilot had no defence, was the airman's worst nightmare, short of burning up. II Brigade was to maintain a permanent presence east of the barrage line and operating beneath 500 feet would report and attack any target of opportunity, including backing up the raids on airfields. The fighter aircraft would carry light bombs to add to their strafing and ground attack capability.

The day bombers were to fly deep into the enemy rear areas, the airfield groups about Courtrai being a prime target as again were the railway detraining centres at Menin, Courtrai, Roulers and Lille. Nearly all daylight operations during this period took place east of the German lines indicating the offensive spirit of the R.F.C. and R.N.A.S., and the undoubted air superiority they had gained with their excellent new Camels, SE5's and Bristol Fighters. This may well be the reason why enemy aircraft appeared more prevalent over the trenches to the British infantry than their own.

With the weather now much improved since the previous battles, the RE8's of the Corps Squadrons flying spotting and contact patrols would soon have their busiest period so far.

---

[379] Trevor Henshaw (1995) *The Sky Their Battlefield* London: Grub Street p226

The Offensive is resumed

The disposition of forces on 20th September
The disposition of British divisions, from south to north:
Second Army:
19th, 39th, 41st, 23rd, 1st Aus, 2nd Aus.

Fifth Army:
9th, 55th, 58th, 51st, 20th

The disposition of German divisions, from south to north:[380]
Line divisions:

Group Wytschaete:
9th Reserve, Bavarian Ersatz. Group Ypres: 121st, 2nd Guard Reserve, 36th, 208th, with the *26th Reserve Division* and *119th Division* of *Group Dixmude* north of Langemarck

Counter-attack divisions:
16th Bavarian, 234th, and *236th*

Second echelon counter-attack divisions:
3rd Reserve, 50th Reserve

Plumer's offensive machine, which had taken three weeks to prepare was gradually coming to life, and was soon to begin methodically grinding down the German resistance in preparation for evicting the enemy from the positions in which he was so firmly established. This was at least the theory and the intention, and the end result to which all the careful planning and training had been leading. It was recognized by all concerned however that this would be neither quick nor easy, and the infantry and the guns were in for a very tough fight. Those guns which were already emplaced began on the 31st August a desultory bombardment, which gradually increased in intensity as more guns came into line. The process was hindered by German shellfire which was still heavy and destructive, but as the number of guns increased the plan became reality as the specific target groups commenced their methodical build-up.

The RE8's of the Royal Flying Corps were the eyes of the gunners behind the ridge. Each aircraft would operate with its own battery which would indicate the target area by a coded signal from the ground, the signal made by way of a letter of the alphabet laid out in large sheets of white cloth. The aircraft would then fly behind the enemy lines towards the target which the code letter had designated, relying mainly on the protection of British scouts from enemy attack, but running the gauntlet of anti-aircraft fire and the flight of numerous British shells. The observer in the flimsy and exposed rear cockpit would place a celluloid disk known as a clock code over his trench map, pinning the centre of the disc on the target. On a morse signal from the aircraft the gun would open fire on the target. The disk was marked with twelve radial lines as with a clock face numbered one to twelve, and eight concentric circles lettered from the centre Y, Z, A, B, C, D, E, F each representing a measurable distance from the target. The fall of shot would be observed from the aircraft and identified on the map, giving it a position on the disk relative to the target, from which the radial lines gave a bearing and the concentric circles gave a distance. The aircraft would then fly back towards the battery and signal by Morse the necessary correction by way of a number and letter code, then fly back towards the target to observe the correction, and if necessary repeat the whole operation.

---

[380] National Archives, maps showing distribution of enemy forces at 5 pm on the 20th September, in WO153/601

The two tier slow barrage system, fired in the first tier by machine guns and field artillery upon the approaches to the enemy front line and forward field batteries, partially isolated these positions, its roving fire making it difficult to carry out reliefs and to bring forward supplies. Deeper into the German rear areas the 60-pounder and 6-inch gun and howitzer barrages of the second tier, fired one third by day and two thirds by night, further disrupted movement and communication. Initially from the 13th September, then more heavily from the 15th September, the depth and intensity of the barrages increased, and from the 15th the planned practice barrages for the main attack were fired each day, creeping forwards and then back across the depth of the German defences, and behind these barrages the infantry carried out their prisoner snatching raids. The bombardment by the medium and heavy guns on all the carefully identified targets, and the concentrated counter-battery fire, which was reported, directed, and corrected by the crews of the RE8's, now reached a crescendo.

German fire in response reduced pro-rata, but could still be destructive, lashing Westhoek and the western slopes of the plateau on the 15th September, a number of enemy batteries subsequently being withdrawn out of line to avoid retaliatory destruction. Some doubts still lingered in German minds as to the British intention, Rupprecht noting on this day that the British barrage was 'probably only for demonstration'. Others nearer the action in the German front line and some at *Fourth Army* headquarters were adamant that attack was imminent, and were alarmed that in spite of their warnings guns were being transferred from Ypres to other fronts.

Towards the end of the second week in September the divisions which were to take up their positions in the line for the attack, began the march up from their training areas towards the rear assembly camps east of Ypres, where they would be only a few hours march away from the front. Although the enemy now had a good idea they were coming, he did not know who he would face, or when he would have to face them. To relieve the divisions now holding the front line would not be a simple matter without warning the enemy of the imminence of impending attack, and the operation would have to be carried out quickly and quietly to avoid detection. It required careful planning, given the limited tracks available across the crater-field over which tens of thousands of men had to pass in both directions. Relief of the divisions holding the line began as early as the 16th September, by holding brigades of the attacking divisions. By the 18th September all divisions were in their allocated assembly areas west of Ypres, and at dusk on the 19th the brigades detailed for the attack began the march to the front.

	Weather conditions, rainfall Vlamertinghe, temperature Ypres[381]				
	11th Sept	**12th Sept**	**13th Sept**	**14th Sept**	**15th Sept**
Rainfall :	Trace	Trace	1.7mm	0.4mm	0.1mm
Temp :	71F	62F	61F	66F	67F
	16th Sept	**17th Sept**	**18th Sept**	**19th Sept**	**20th Sept**
Rainfall :	Nil	Nil	0.4mm	5.1mm	Nil
Temp	73F	67F	65F	72F	66F

---

[381] National Archives, GHQ statistics WO95/15

At around 11:00 p.m. when the move to the front was well underway and after a long period of good drying weather in which ground conditions had improved markedly, the rain began again, and the ground quickly became slippery and muddy slowing up movement. Gough telephoned Plumer enquiring whether or not the attack should proceed. After much consultation with his meteorologist and with corps and divisional commanders Plumer decided that the attack should proceed and Fifth Army was informed accordingly. Meanwhile the infantry had become thoroughly soaked, but soon after midnight the rain ceased leaving a clear starlit night. The routes up to the line, some by duck-board track, others across the bare ground which had now become difficult, were well marked by signposts, and closer to the front, after dusk, tapes had been laid marking the paths. Much care was taken in getting the brigades and then battalions up in the correct order in which they were to attack, those to attack the first objective logically being in front of those to attack the second and third. Not all divisions were to deploy their battalions in the same pattern, but in most brigades the battalion to attack the first objective moved silently out into no-mans-land onto their jumping-off tapes, about 150 yards short of the forward German sentry outposts, upon which the opening barrage was to fall. The second battalion to attack the second objective formed up about the British front line, and the two battalions to carry the attack later to the final objective formed up about 1,000 yards to the rear. This was not the case in 1st Australian Division whose commander, hoping to ensure his assault forces were quickly clear of any German retaliatory barrage, assembled all eight battalions of the 2nd and 3rd Australian Brigades up close by the front line.

Zero hour was to be at 5:40 a.m. but around 3:50 a.m. a moderate German barrage fell on the western slopes of the Gheluvelt plateau. At 4:30 a.m., before the complicated assembly was complete, and apparently in response to a coloured flare fired by a German post near Glencorse Wood, a heavy hostile barrage fell on the crowded assembly areas of 1st Australian Division, up close to the front line. In the 2nd Brigade, the 11th Battalion already forward, avoided most of the shellfire, but the 12th Machine Gun Company moving up to the line, and the 9th and 10th Battalions as they moved up through Chateau Wood, were caught fully by the barrage suffering many casualties, but with the help of the remaining officers proceeded up into line. Counter-battery fire stopped the German barrage at about 5:15 but at 5:20 it came down again and this time hit the brigade's fourth battalion, the 8th as they arrived at Clapham Junction. Two-thousand yards to the left, the barrage had also hit the line about Westhoek ridge, but here the Australian 2nd Division was held back in more sheltered positions behind the ridge. To the right of the Australians, machine gun fire had broken out in X Corps area where 69th Brigade of 23rd Division was assembling, but nothing more transpired. On the Australian far left at about 5:36, after German signal rockets had lit up the sky, their field artillery opened fire on the front of 2nd Australian Division, where 20th Battalion of 5th Brigade were in the line. Immediately the 20th Battalion advanced to get clear of the barrage, followed by the 18th Battalion which was also well forward, and all but the tail of the 18th missed the worst of the shelling.

It is possible that the shelling was due to information acquired earlier by the Germans of the imminence of the attack. An Australian officer of the 7th Machine Gun Company, 2nd Australian Division, having moved too far forward in the dark, had been taken prisoner in the early hours of the 20th by a patrol of the *56th Reserve Infantry Regiment,* in the line opposite Westhoek. He had unfortunately been carrying an operational order of the attack, from which by 3:00 a.m. the Germans had ascertained that two Australian Divisions would attack astride the Menin Road and about one kilometre south of the Roulers railway at an unclear time, but probably this day. This was very nearly correct but not exactly so, as the officer had attempted partly successfully to destroy his papers. The position that I Anzac was about to attack lay between the junction of two German corps. To the south opposite 1st Australian Division were the two northern regiments, *4th* and *15th Bavarian R.I.R.,* of the *3rd Bavarian Ersatz Division* of *Group Wytschaete (IX Reserve Corps),* and to the north at Westhoek in front of 2nd Australian Division were the two southern regiments, *56th* and *7th R.I.R.* of *121st Prussian Division* of *Group Ypres (Guard Corps).* As the Australian officer had been taken prisoner on *121st Division* front there was time for that division to order a barrage against the 2nd Australian Division on their divisional front, but not time for orders to be issued for other divisions to do the same. *Groups*

Wytschaete and *Ypres* had however been pre-warned of the attack, and had in tern warned the *Eingreif* divisions held back behind the ridge, of imminent action.

Across the fronts of *3rd Bavarian* and *121st Divisions* were deployed 160 field guns and howitzers, (84 and 76 respectively) and 106 medium and heavy guns, (46 and 60 respectively), plus an unknown number of corps controlled guns. Opposing about half this joint divisional front, I Anzac deployed 216 field and 208 medium and heavy guns, an advantage in firepower of 1.6 to 1.

At 5:40 a.m. precisely, and to the relief of everyone on the British side of the line, the British barrage opened with such force and power it exceeded even that of the 31st July.

The attack of the Second Army 5:40 a.m. 20th September

The attack against the Gheluvelt plateau

The same German positions that had so resolutely resisted so many attacks by Fifth Army were now to be attacked once more. But this time the Second Army were full of confidence in their General, in their training and in their ability to succeed, sentiments which were now heightened by the power and ferocity of the protective barrage which thundered mightily upon the German positions. Although confident, all involved suffered the inevitable tension and stress prior going into action. The 4,000 yard front of the main assault, upon which Plumer had so firmly insisted, was to be attacked by the 41st and 23rd Divisions of X Corps, and 1st and 2nd Australian Divisions of I Anzac Corps, the assault concentrated on 1,000 yards per division. It was now to be put to the ultimate test of battle to see if all the painstaking care in preparation, and theoretical step by step training tactics would withstand the cauldron, and succeed where previous efforts had failed. The 23rd Division and 1st and 2nd Australian Divisions were to carry out the main attack on the plateau, while the 41st and 39th Divisions of X Corps were to form the left, or northern sector of a southern defensive flank to protect the main attack, the right sector of this flank to be formed by one division, the 19th of IX Corps. The total front on which Second Army would attack stretched from the embankment of the Ypres – Comines railway alongside the canal in the south, to 800 yards south of the Ypres – Roulers railway in the north, a distance of around 6,350 yards.

It had been hoped that at 5:40 a.m. the visibility would be around 200 yards, but the rain of the previous evening had caused a mist to envelope the battlefield and as the dawn tinged the eastern horizon with red, the British battalions were shrouded from the view of the enemy as they deployed. The initial barrage was considered the best ever witnessed, and the lines of skirmishers followed by the leading assault companies, keeping up close to the dense line of exploding shells which moved forward at a pace of 50 yards every two minutes, quickly overran the German outpost line and forward shelter positions before many of the local counter-attack groups had time to emerge. The mopping-up parties dealt with the shelters and dugouts with grenade and phosphorous bombs resulting in rapid capitulation by the garrisons. After the first two hundred yards the barrage slowed to 100 yards every six minutes. Second Army rolled forward, behind its annihilating barrage as Plumer had predicted it would. What German retaliatory barrage there was soon died down, probably due to the overwhelming counter-battery fire, although the counter-battery gas barrage originally planned to be fired from Zero minus four hours had been cancelled for fear of betraying the imminence of the attack.

The advance continued across the plateau close behind the 1,000 yard deep maelstrom of exploding projectiles, the infantry carefully negotiating the mass of shell-holes and debris. As they penetrated deeper into the enemy position resistance was no more than patchy. In some places the enemy ran forward to surrender, but in others put up a dogged and violent resistance. Along the front of 1st Australian Division, the planned three wave attack had, due to the German shelling of the forming up positions near the British front line, led to all three waves bunching-up together and moving forward as one, but so intense was the protective barrage and so shaken and demoralized were the enemy that no great harm came to the over dense Australian wave.

The concentration of concrete bunkers further forward had not all been destroyed, even by the weight of fire which had been concentrated upon them, but in some places the garrison had been so numbed and shaken by the continual battering that their one thought was to surrender to the khaki clad enemy emerging from the mist and smoke. Some ran forward waving white handkerchiefs or bandages. As the bunkers became evident to the advancing infantry through the mist and thick dusty atmosphere, they were quickly surrounded. In some, dazed and despondent machine gunners who had been in the line for too long without relief were found sitting beside their undamaged and unfired guns waiting to be taken prisoner, so prolonged had been their exposure and so intense had been the barrage. Some stalwarts however, maintaining the tradition of their fine Army still resisted from pillboxes and bunkers, but the thorough training and use of local reserves enabled the assaulting waves to outflank and overwhelm them, greatly assisted by the shrouding mist and the firmer ground. The advance continued, but now at some cost to the attackers.

By about 7:45 a.m. this was generally the situation across most of the plateau with the first and second objectives taken. The position was not quite so successful however across the whole battlefront. It has been said of this day that the guns won the ground, the infantry merely occupied it, but this was not the way it was in the muddy Bassevillebeek valley just a few hundred yards to the south of the Menin Road.

Southern protective flank, right (southern) section

IX Corps

19th Division
Major-General G. T. M. Bridges

The southern flank from the Ypres – Comines canal north to Groenenburg Farm, a distance of 1,600 yards was the responsibility of 19th Division. Two brigades were to be used in an advance of about 600 yards to the first objective with another 400 yards in a second advance to the final objective, the 58th Brigade to the southern edge of Hessian Wood, and the 57th Brigade to the south-east edge of Belgian Wood. As the attack would be in full view of German observation points on Zandvoorde Hill a smoke screen was to be fired for four hours on to the hill. The protective barrage was to be less powerful than for the northern attacks, and was to be fired by 132 18-pounders providing a creeping barrage, while 300 yards ahead a searching barrage was fired by 32 4.5-inch howitzers. A standing barrage was to be distributed in depth beyond the searching barrage by 32 6-inch howitzers, 6 8-inch howitzers, 4 9.2-inch howitzers and 18 60-pounder guns, with a machine gun barrage fired 300 yards ahead of the searching barrage by 82 machine guns.

58th Brigade [382]
The protective barrage, although not as powerful as it was to be further north came down promptly at 5:40 a.m., and the assault waves of 58th Brigade began their advance. On the brigade right front, the 6th Wiltshire Regiment came under enfilade fire from German machine gun dug-outs in the railway embankment of the Ypres – Comines railway, (which formed the southern flank of the battlefront). In the centre the 9th Welsh Regiment with the 9th Cheshire Regiment to their left came under fire from machine guns in dug-outs in Hessian Wood which was sufficiently heavy to check the advance.[383] The forward wave of the Welsh and Cheshire were also caught in crossfire as machine gun fire from the ruins of Hollebeke Chateau 1,000 yards to the front right

---

[382] National Archives, War Diary 58th Brigade WO95/2088
[383] National Archives, War Diary 9th Cheshire WO95/2091

and from bunkers at Jarrocks Farm and Pioneer House 150 yards and 300 yards to the front centre zipped and whined amongst their ranks. The Wiltshire gradually edged forward along the railway and silenced the machine guns bunkers on the embankment, then continued the advance to the first objective. There was now a gap to their left there, and a defensive flank of posts was established in shell-holes to keep touch with the Welsh, who were still held up by the volume of crossfire in front of Hessian Wood. The Welsh, under heavy fire slowly crept towards the wood from shell-hole to shell-hole, whilst to their left a platoon of the Cheshire worked around the side and attacked the enemy dug-outs from the north. Assailed from two directions, the enemy either surrendered or died at their guns, as gradually the machine gun nests and dug-outs were silenced. In this action 2nd Lieutenant Hugh Colvin of the 9th Cheshire, cleared a number of dug-outs one after the other, entering them alone and forcing the enemy to surrender, finally taking about fifty prisoners, an act for which he was to be awarded the V.C. His gallant action enabled the advance to continue. The Welsh then moved up in touch with the Wiltshire on their right which had already reached the final objective. The 9th Royal Welsh Fusiliers were in brigade support and the moppers-up cleared and secured Moat Farm.

57th Brigade [384]
The 57th Brigade attacked with the 10th Worcestershire Regiment, 8th Gloucestershire Regiment and the 8th North Staffordshire Regiment. The battalions jumped-off from the line of Jehovah Trench and attacked across very heavy ground towards Belgian Wood. Heavy crossfire from machine guns at Wood Farm south of Belgian Wood, from the wood itself, and from dugouts near Top House north of the wood, held up the Gloucester and North Staffs, which were also hampered by the very muddy ground and lost the barrage. Pushing on through the mud they succeeded in reaching the first objective, the Red Line, which lay about 100 yards short of the wood, and began establishing a defence line in shell-holes. Whilst they consolidated, the protective barrage stood along the edge of the wood, 150 yards forward of the Red Line until Zero plus 1 hour and 20 minutes, when it lifted towards the wood and the final objective. The support wave of the Gloucester then advanced into Belgian Wood clearing snipers and strong-points with the bayonet, whilst the Worcester advanced to the right of the wood and the North Staffs to the left. The Germans were quickly driven out and the brigade secured the final objective just east of the wood by about 8:00 a.m.[385]

By 8:10 a.m. with the mist clearing, 19th Division was on its final objective along the whole divisional front, and the southern section of the defensive flank was secure, but at a high cost with casualties approaching 2,000. About midday the division suffered another serious loss as its commanding officer Major-General Bridges, who had gone forward to congratulate his brigade commanders, was severely wounded, loosing a leg.

Southern protective flank, (centre section)

X Corps

39th Division
Major-General E. Feetham

The 39th Division with the 41st Division to its left, was to form the right of the defensive flank of X Corps on the southern edge of the plateau, and was to capture the slopes down to the eastern side of Bulgar Wood and to the western side of the Bassevillebeek, a total advance of around 1,000 yards across very heavy and muddy ground.

---

[384] National Archives, War Diary 57th Brigade WO95/2084
[385] The 10th Royal Warwickshire Regiment was in brigade reserve about Klein Zillebeke 400 yards behind the jump-off line, but were not called on to support the attack battalions.

117th Brigade [386]

The 117th Brigade was to attack in an easterly direction, with the 17th Sherwood Foresters supported by the 16th Sherwood Foresters along an 800 yard front towards Bulgar Wood, and with the 16th Rifle Brigade supported by the 17th King's Royal Rifle Corps along a 600 yard front to the north of the wood. The brigade front broadened to nearer 2,000 yards at the final objective. The Germans were known to hold an outpost line between Groenenburg Farm and a strong-point at Lower Star Post where they had re-established their old position, which had caused such havoc on the 31st of July.[387] The first objective, the Red Line, ran through the western side of Bulgar Wood then northwards and past the eastern end of the sunken road in Shrewsbury Forest. The second objective, the Blue Line, was around 400 yards beyond the first objective, to the east of Bulgar Wood and 200 yards short of the Bassevillebeek. The third objective, the Green Line, was limited to the left sector of the attack and was to be reached by only one company of the left flank support battalion, the 17th K.R.R.C.

The 17th Sherwood Foresters and the 16th Rifle Brigade were to capture an intermediate objective, the Black Line, close to the enemy forward outpost line, and then move on and capture and consolidate the first objective. The 16th Sherwood Foresters and the 17th King's Royal Rifle Corps less one company would then pass through and capture and consolidate the second objective. The remaining company of the 17th K.R.R.C. would then pass through the left sector of the Blue Line and capture and consolidate the third objective, where its left flank would be thrown forward across the Bassevillebeek. Each company was to attack on a two company front, each company with three platoons in the first wave and one platoon in the second. On the night of the 18th / 19th September the 17th Sherwood Foresters and the 16th Rifle Brigade took over their sectors of the line, with a company each in the Larch Wood and Spoil Bank tunnelled dugouts.

At 5:40 punctually as the British barrage shook the ground 150 yards forward, the 17th Sherwood Foresters supported by the 16th advanced across heavy muddy ground towards the western edge of Bulgar Wood. They were immediately swept by machine gun fire from a number of dug-outs about the first objective causing a check to the advance. The German posts were gradually outflanked and overcome with the assistance of the 16th Sherwood Foresters. At around 7:00 a.m. as the advance to the final objective began it was realized that due to the mist and smoke some dug-outs had not been cleared and remained in enemy hands, as the Germans now began firing into the flanks and rear of the advancing Sherwood Foresters causing heavy losses. Corporal Ernest Albert Egerton of the 16th volunteered to clear the dug-outs, and rushing them under heavy fire at short range, had within 30 seconds shot three of the enemy, at which point 29 more surrendered. With the enemy positions cleared the advance continued to the final objective on the eastern side of Bulgar Wood. Corporal Edgerton was to be awarded the V.C. for his courageous actions.

To the left of the Sherwood Foresters the 16th Rifle Brigade moved off under the barrage but immediately came under machine gun crossfire from right and left flanks. Within 10 minutes "B" and "D" Companies had succeeded in capturing the Black Line but had faced stiff opposition at Lower Star Post and the sunken road. Whilst the enemy strong-points were cleared, "A" and "C" Companies passed through towards the Blue Line. Expecting strong resistance from Lower Star Post, rifle grenadiers had fired a barrage of No.23 and No.27 grenades at the area at Zero Hour. The anxieties were justified for as the platoon of "D" Company detailed to the task approached the position they met with fierce machine gun fire from two guns and a shower of stick grenades. Casualties increased rapidly, but an attack was mounted around either flank of the strong-point. The enemy soon gave way and Lower Star Post was cleared.. About 200 yards to the east, the Germans also resisted stoutly from a strong-point at the western end of the sunken road. The post was rushed at sword point by a platoon of "D" Company and many of the

---

[386] National Archives, War Diary 117th Brigade WO95/2585
[387] The line held by parts of the *395th Regiment* and the *6th Reserve Infantry Regiment*

enemy were thus dispatched.[388] In the fight to secure the Black line all the company officers had become casualties as had 95 other ranks. The enemy now began to fall-back in numbers from their forward defence line and came under a hail of Lewis gun fire sustaining many casualties.

"A" and "C" Companies pressed on towards the Red Line, but came under heavy machine gun fire from a strong-point in the sector of 124th Brigade to their left, and sent a party across the divisional boundary to capture the post, which after overcoming some resistance they succeeded in doing. The enemy still held out, machine guns in isolated dug-outs causing serious casualties. Sergeant William Francis Burman of the 16th Rifle Brigade whose company was held up by a machine gun, went forward into a hail of fire to what seemed like certain death, killed the gunner and then carried the machine gun forward to the objective where he used it to good effect against the enemy. By Zero plus 18 minutes the Rifle Brigade was on the Red Line on their right flank, but as the Queens were held up on the left, had on this flank thrown back a line of defensive posts, with Lewis guns positioned in shell-holes along the Red Line to stiffen the defence. On the right about 15 minutes after consolidation had begun, it became clear that the 16th Sherwood Foresters were held up in Bulgar Wood, under enfilade fire by a 40 strong party of the enemy lying along Forest Road 200 yards east of the sunken road. Sergeant Burman with two others again went forward and outflanked the position. The Germans at first wavered and then surrendered, Burman's party killing 6 and taking prisoner two officers and 29 other ranks. Sergeant Burman was to be awarded the V.C. for his gallant action.

The 17th King's Royal Rifle Corps had moved up in support of the Rifle Brigade, and passed through on the Red Line just after 7:00 a.m. On the left were "C" Company, with "B" Company in the centre and "A" Company on the right, and their task was to capture and consolidate the Blue Line. "D" Company was to pass through on the left and capture the Green Line across the Bassevillebeek. Enemy strong-points slowed the advance and caused many casualties but were eventually captured, the three leading companies seizing the Red Line. As the Queens were still held up on the left it was not possible for "D" Company to push across the Bassevillebeek, and the final line was consolidated on the Blue Line, west of the stream. In the advance the 17th K.R.R.C. had lost many officers, 2 companies finally being commanded by Corporals.

Partly due to acts of great personal bravery and partly to the dogged determination of the men even after the loss of so many of their officers, 117th Brigade had achieved its objective on the Bassevillebeek, in touch with 57th Brigade of 19th Division to the right and 124th Brigade of 41st Division to the left. Casualties were very high, approaching 1,000, out of whom nearly 50 were officers.

The German units opposite 19th and 39th Divisions had been in the line a considerable time without relief, and consisted of regiments of two divisions. The *19th* and *6th Reserve Regiments,* and the *395th Regiment* of the *9th Reserve Division* had been in the line since mid-August, and the *213th* and *209th Reserve Regiments* of the *207th Division* had been in the line since the 2nd August.

The southern protective flank, left (northern) section

(X Corps)

41st Division
Major-General S. T. B. Lawford

At the centre of X Corps, the 41st Division had topographically the most difficult ground to cross, as the three divisions making the main attack across the plateau to the north had at least flatter ground to cover. The division was to form part of the southern defensive flank for the main attack. The final objective, the German Third Line, held a commanding position atop Tower

---

[388] The Rifle Brigade referred to their bayonet as a sword

Hamlets spur. To reach Tower Hamlets the 41st Division had to cross the Bassevillebeek valley and climb the relatively steep eastern slope under the guns of the numerous German bunkers on the spur. Although there had been a period of drying weather, the ground around the stream remained a quagmire. Possession of the Tower Hamlets spur was of great importance to the British as it would anchor the right flank of the main attack on the plateau. It was therefore equally imperative to the Germans to retain it, as their presence there would be a continual threat to the British right. The defences the enemy had built to guard the spur were formidable. Hidden machine gun nests and fortified shell-holes were scattered across the valley of the Bassevillebeek, and were themselves covered by the fire of further machine guns around 600 yards to the east in numerous pillboxes and bunkers along the top of the spur, which had a commanding view over the valley from a height advantage of 22 metres. The British front line ran through the northern end of Shrewsbury Forest, then east of Bodmin Copse and Stirling Castle, and was on or about the position which had been reached on the 31st July, between 600 and 1,200 yards forward of the old front line. The advance would be at first downhill for about 600 yards, then across 200 yards of the flat and muddy valley floor, followed by a fairly steep climb of around 400 to 500 yards to the top of the spur, the whole assault front covered by numerous German machine guns. It would soon become clear whether or not the British barrages had destroyed the concrete machine gun bunkers.

The attack was to be made by the 124th and 122nd Brigades with the 123rd Brigade in support. By 1:00 a.m. the battalions to lead the assault were lying out in shell-holes along the tapes marking their jump-off positions, through Shrewsbury Forest and Bodmin Copse. Before starting 124th Brigade were shelled in their assembly areas, but at 5:40 a.m. as the British barrage shattered the dawn, the front waves moved forward. The support battalions closed up behind them to avoid the German barrage, which soon crashed down, but well behind the British line, doing little damage.

124th Brigade [389]

On the right the 124th Brigade attacked between the northern end of Shrewsbury Forest and Bodmin Copse. The 10th Queens and 21st King's Royal Rifle Corps (Yeoman Rifles) leading, were to take the first and second objectives,[390] two companies of each battalion forward to take the first objective the Red Line, just east of Java Trench and Java Drive. The two companies following were to take the Blue Line, in the bottom of the valley a few yards west of the stream on the right and a little east of the stream on the left. From here the 32nd and 26th Royal Fusiliers in support were to pass through to take the final objective,[391] the Green Line, the section of the *Wilhelm Stellung* formed by the fortified position of Joist Redoubt up on Tower Hamlets spur. The support battalions moved of directly behind the forward battalions to avoid any German retaliatory barrage, but after advancing 50 yards the leading companies 'came under heavy machine gun fire from concrete machine gun emplacements and dugouts'[392] at close range. There were numerous casualties including many officers, (including the C.O. of the Queens, Major Andrews M.C.) and the barrage was lost. A message received at 41st Division headquarters from 117th Brigade at 7:00 a.m. read: '10th Queens held up by strongpoint at J25b8.2 [300 yards east of Lower Star Post] and have lost barrage and are having heavy casualties'.[393] At 7:50 a.m. the 32nd Royal Fusiliers reported that they were completely held up by machine gun fire, but were holding the original front line. At 8:20 a.m. however the Queens had reached the Red Line and were advancing towards the Blue Line, whilst the 21st K.R.R.C. and 26th Royal Fusiliers reported that they were held up by machine gun fire at J26a00.85, Het Pappotje Farm. The resistance at the farm was mopped up and by 9:10 a.m. parties of the 21st K.R.R.C. and remnants of the 26th Royal Fusiliers had pushed forward to the Red Line and crossed the Bassevillebeek. The attack of

---

[389] National Archives, War Diary 124th Brigade WO95/2641
[390] National Archives, War Diary 10th Queens and 21st KRRC WO95/4243
[391] National Archives, War Diary 26th Royal Fusiliers WO95/4243
[392] National Archives, War Diary 124th Infantry Brigade WO95/2641
[393] National Archives, War Diary 41st Division WO95/2617

the Queens was now led by 2nd Lieutenants Hare and Toombs and Sergeant Busby. With the strong-point east of Lower Star Post and other gun-pits and fortified shell-hole now overcome, remnants of the battalion were believed to be on the Blue Line . Many men had fallen, but small parties had continued through the mire of the Bassevillebeek valley to secure the first two objectives. Here remnants of the Queen's and K.R.R.C. commenced to dig-in in shell-holes, under murderous machine gun fire from the Quadrilateral up on the spur, (a fortified position of wired entrenchments 400 yards east of the stream, where three ruined cottages had been reinforced into machine gun bunkers). From here the enemy machine guns could sweep the valley to the west, the south, and along the spur to the north, the preparatory British barrage having failed to destroy them. By 10:45 a.m. little more had been heard of the 26th Royal Fusiliers, although it was believed that remnants were still attacking the Green Line. By 11:20 a.m. a message received at 41st Division from 124th Brigade confirmed that the Blue Line was held but that the Brigade was too weak to advance against the Green Line. Only around 50 men however held the right of the Brigade line (at J20d2.2). Here they were about 100 yards east of the Bassevillebeek, 300 yards short of the Blue Line, and 700 yards short of the Green Line at Tower Trench. This remained roughly the situation for the rest of the day, with the left holding on part ways up the slope east of the Bassevillebeek, and the right only just east of the stream, where, well short of their final objective the leading companies of all battalions dug-in as best they could.

122nd Brigade [394]

On the left, the 122nd Brigade in the line between Bodmin Copse and just south east of Stirling Castle, was to attack with the 18th King's Royal Rifle Corps and the 15th Hampshire Regiment,[395] to take the first objective just west of the Bassevillebeek, and the second objective just east of the stream. The 12th East Surrey Regiment and the 11th Royal West Kent Regiment were in support to take the final objective the *Wilhelm Stellung* at Tower Trench up on the spur.[396] The infantry plan was not without its complexities. After the two leading battalions captured the Red and Blue Lines, the support battalions were to advance on a two company front, with two platoons in the leading wave advancing in columns of sections up to the Blue Line, where the two support companies were to extend into battle formation. The leading companies were to advance to within 300 yards of the Green Line where they would stop and consolidate, the support companies then following the barrage to the final objective at the Green Line. Each battalion was to designate reserve platoons to mop-up strong-points in shell-holes and bunkers, and map references were issued of known enemy positions to be dealt with. This was the plan of attack in detailed theory, but the intervention of German machine gunners was destined to somewhat upset the arrangements.

From the start the 18th K.R.R.C. ran into trouble, being held up for about an hour by machine gun fire from a pillbox around 150 yards east of Bodmin Copse, and just in front of Jar Trench. They were supported by the East Surrey moving up immediately behind them, and eventually overcame the position with rifle grenades, but had subsequently lost the barrage. Continuing down the slope they also came under a hail of fire from machine gun nests in fortified shell-holes in the valley, from the bunkers at Tower Hamlets, and from the Quadrilateral. The Hampshire started well but in a few hundred yards came up against heavy machine gun fire from a strong-point near Java Avenue, where all company commanders and many other officers and men became casualties. Parties rushed and captured the position. The advance doubled forward, caught up with the barrage, and continued to gradually mop-up further dug-outs and strong-points. At around 6:15 a.m. the forward companies of both leading battalions attempted to

---

[394] National Archives, War Diary 122nd Brigade WO95/2634
[395] *The King's Royal Rifle Corps Chronicle* 1917 (1920) London: John Murray p213 (18th Btn p213), and C.T. Atkins *The Royal Hampshire Regiment Vol II* Glasgow: Robert Maclehose pp238-241
[396] Colonel H.W. Prarse and Brig.-General H.S. Sloman (1924) *History of the East Surrey Regiment Vol III 1917-1919* London: The Medici Society p91, Captain R.O. Russell (1934) *The History of the 11th (Lewisham) Battalion The Queens Own Royal West Kent Regiment* London: Lewisham Newspaper Co Ltd pp162-164

consolidate on the first objective in the muddy ground west of the stream, whilst under considerable fire. At 7:08 as the barrage lifted forward, the Hampshire, rallied by Lieut.-Colonel Corfe of the West Kent, who was himself soon wounded, stumbled on through the muddy cratered valley, swept by continuous machine gun fire from the pillboxes on the spur. The Hampshire veered right and worked their way around the morass of lower Dumbarton Lake. The advance continued across the Bassevillebeek to the second objective 300 yards beyond, and at around 7:40 the Hampshire began to dig-in and consolidate as best possible in shell-holes. Soon parties of the K.R.R.C. and the East Surrey were up, also digging-in on the second objective, but were destined to get little further forward.

By 9:10 a.m. 122nd Brigade had reported that they were on the Blue Line, but thinly, having sustained heavy casualties, and parties were ready to advance to the Green Line, in touch with the 23rd Division on the left and with parties of the 124th Brigade on the right. Having already sustained many casualties, as the barrage lifted at 9:35 a.m. the West Kent made an attempt to continue the advance up the slope towards the final objective. They came under a hail of fire in enfilade from the Quadrilateral to their right, and from the bunkers and pillboxes of the Tower Hamlets position directly in front on top of the spur. Few in numbers, they continued up the slope and gained a foothold in Tower Trench. An enemy counter-attack and heavy enfilade machine gun fire soon drove the survivors back down the slope, where they attempted to dig-in under fire near the Blue Line just east of the stream, where the Hampshire were already consolidating. Here after throwing back a right flank, they were in touch with 124th Brigade, and posts were pushed forward with Lewis guns positioned in shell-holes. At 1:48 p.m. a pigeon message received at 41st Division headquarters from 18th K.R.R.C. reported that the Red and Blue Lines were secure, and in touch on the left, but that their right was in the air. The Red Line was held by 60 men with 4 Lewis guns and the Blue Line by 65 men and 3 Lewis guns.

At 5:30 p.m. the 15th Hampshire and 11th R.W.K. were again ordered to attack towards the Green Line on the spur. Due to the casualties already sustained by the West Kent, the attack was carried out by 130 men of the Hampshire alone, with the cover of a special barrage. 123rd Brigade, in support, was also to attack on the right in an effort to push forward the positions of 124th Brigade. The Green Line was taken, and over 40 men, a battalion commander and his adjutant, two machine guns and a field gun were captured. From their new position on the spur the Hampshire once more threw back a right flank, to where 124th Brigade was trying to maintain its precarious foothold on the side of the slope, whilst contact was also made with 23rd Division on their left. During the evening a number of counter-attacks were driven off by the exhausted 122nd Brigade.

123rd Brigade [397]

At about midday, due to the check to 122nd and 124th Brigades, the 123rd Brigade received orders to reinforce the brigade firing line, and to take the Green Line. At about 4:30 p.m. with the 23rd Middlesex on the right,[398] the 10th Royal West Kent in the centre and the 20th Durham Light Infantry on the left, the Brigade moved forward in artillery formation through Shrewsbury Forest via Lower Star Post to Java Trench. They immediately came under heavy machine gun fire from Tower Hamlets and the Quadrilateral across the Bassevillebeek valley. At about 6:30 p.m. under the cover of a special barrage which bombarded Tower Hamlets spur, the forward companies of the 23rd Middlesex advanced down the slope into the valley, and under very heavy fire reached the Bassevillebeek, but here got pinned down. At 8:25 they requested small arms ammunition and reinforcements, and by 8:50 p.m. small parties were reported consolidating on the Green Line with some of the 1/6th Cheshires of 118th Brigade, who had moved up on the right in support of 117th Brigade. At 9:20 the 20th Durham and 10th R.W.K. were ordered to push forward fighting patrols to gain touch with the Middlesex, but a later message reported the Middlesex digging-in back on the line of the Bassevillebeek. The severity of the fire from the spur

---

[397] National Archives, War Diary 123rd Brigade WO95/2637
[398] National Archives, War Diary 23rd Middlesex, 10th Royal West Kent, 20th Durham all in WO95/4243

had made it near impossible to advance up the slope and the majority of the Brigade had remained pinned down short of the Blue Line.

The 41st Division had failed, short of its final objectives.[399] The German Third Line had held even under the strain of the huge bombardment unleashed upon it, and despite the desperate and costly attempts of the infantry to climb the muddy slopes and come to grips with it. The strength of the bunkers at Tower Hamlets and the Quadrilateral had been sufficient to withstand the onslaught, as had the nerves and courage of the garrisons who manned them after undergoing many days of barrage fire. The Germans had paid a high price for their local victory at Tower Hamlets. The position was held by the *395th Regiment, 9th Reserve Division* and the *28th Ersatz Regiment, 3rd Bavarian Ersatz Division*. The front battalions of both regiments were virtually wiped out and only remnants of the support battalions survived, around 70 men of the *395th* holding Tower Hamlets when relieved on the night of 21st/22nd September. But the south-eastern edge of the plateau remained unconquered. The 41st Division may have failed to take Tower Hamlets, but it was not due to lack of effort as the total casualty figure of over 3,000 bears witness. The right flank of the main Second Army attack against the plateau was however secure, with the worrying exception of the important positions at Tower Hamlets, and the nearly 1,000 yard section of the *Wilhelm Stellung* to the south, which was still covered by the machine guns of the Quadrilateral. The cost of this 90 percent success was a casualty figure for all three divisions,

---

[399] A very different account of this action is given by Prior and Wilson in *Passchendaele-The Untold Story*, Newhaven and London: Yale University Press see p121 in which they claim: 'There was one division on the 20th September (41st Division, X Corps) which suffered a different experience and one unusual enough to warrant closer scrutiny. This experience, it should be noted, cannot be reconstructed from the usual array of reports and battle narratives in the war diaries. For this division on that day none survive.' This claim is strange and completely incorrect. In their account, Prior and Wilson say that the whole of the 124th Brigade 'fled' as 'a mob', the statement based on information from the private diary of Captain Harry Yoxall. It is not the case that War Diaries are not available for the 41st Division, or its Brigades and Battalions for the 20th September. As we have seen the War Diary of the 41st Division for 20th September is available at the National Archives Kew in WO95/2617 and covers the day's actions most fully in a twelve page, hour-by-hour account. The 124th Brigade War Diary is available at the National Archives Kew in WO95/2641, the 10th Queens is available under reference WO95/2643, and the 21st King's Royal Rifle Corps (Yeoman Rifles) also under WO95/2643. The Diaries for the 122nd and 123rd Brigades and the battalions in those brigades are also available. The 10th Queens War Diary states: 'Very disorganized, the Btn. pushed on and succeeded in reaching both its objectives in spite of heavy machine gun fire.' There is little doubt that due to the machine gun fire across the Bassevillebeek the attack became most disorganised, and the final positions reached by 124th Brigade were in right rear of 122nd Brigade which had got further forward across the stream. But the claim made that 'the remainder of the [124th] Brigade fled' as a mob (presumably meaning all those still capable of movement and not already casualties) seems difficult to substantiate based on one eye-witness account. As Prior and Wilson so rightly say on the first page of their introduction, 'Participant accounts are revealing, but by there nature they are partial.' It is interesting that Captain Yoxall did not make the claim that 124th Brigade had fled en-masse, but rather that around 150 men were collected about forward brigade headquarters where Yoxall was positioned. 124th Brigade headquarters was in fact around 2,000 yards east of the Bassevillebeek, back near the old British front line between Lower Star Post and Mount Sorrel. The disgraceful and ill researched claim that the *whole Brigade* left the field is made by Prior and Wilson. The casualties for 124th Brigade were: 10th Queens 192, 26th Royal Fusiliers 335, 32nd Royal Fusiliers 285, 21st King's Royal Rifle Corps 318; a total of 1,130 for the Brigade. Of the Battalion Commanders, The Commanding Officer of the 10th Queens Major Lesley Ernest Andrews MC was killed, the CO of the 26th Royal Fusiliers Lientenant-Colonel G. McNicoll died of wounds, and Lieutenant-Colonel Talbot McLeary Jarvis commanding 21st K.R.R.C. was wounded. If they fled as a mob as Prior and Wilson claim, it seems 124th Brigade got involved in some stiff fighting first. The reader must decide which version of events to accept.

19th, 39th and 41st of approaching 6,000, of which tragically around 1,000 had been killed. But at the head of the Bassevillebeek valley, up on the plateau, General Plumer's main assault was continuing apace, and to there we must now return.

The main assault on the plateau

Between the heads of valleys of the Bassevillebeek which flows south, and the Hanebeek which flows north, (neither watercourses being really more than brooks, or at best streams), is a distance of about 2,000 yards, creating a narrow waist across the Gheluvelt plateau. Across this narrow waist the *Albrecht Stellung*, or German Second Line ran, from behind the quagmire quaintly known as Dumbarton Lakes, past the wilderness of Inverness Copse across the flat, bleak, open plateau about Fitzclarence Farm, towards the shambles of Glencorse Wood, and although battered and penetrated on numerous occasions, the line had defied all previous gallant attempts to both seize and secure it. The whole area consisted of lip to lip shell-holes with hardly a skeletal tree left standing, but with the wreckage and awful flotsam of previous attacks still littering the ground. The only structures which remained were those reinforced against shellfire by the Germans, and these were mostly of low profile and well camouflaged with earth and debris. The entire plateau surface was an exposed, pocked, wasteland of churned earth with all usual points of reference and orientation long gone. Only the underlying shape of the landscape's surface remained, which now denuded of foliage and structures, more clearly defined the small rises and depressions in the ground, and those even the relentless guns could not eradicate.

Just north of Glencorse Wood, along Westhoek ridge, the *Albrecht Stellung* had fallen previously, but 400 yards to the east lay the bogs of the shattered Nonne Bosschen defending the approach to the *Wilhelm Stellung* and Polygon Wood, and most importantly the southern end of the Broodseinde ridge. For the next 1,000 yards north towards the Roulers railway the mire of the Hanebeek valley guarded the approach to the *Wilhelm Stellung*, which here ran towards the north across the western face of Anzac spur, and about 1,000 yards from the British Front Line. Farther to the east, beyond Anzac spur, were two more shallow depressions formed by small tributaries of the Hanebeek and separated by the small Tokio spur, which projected to the north-west from the main Broodseinde ridge like a hooked finger. Across the base of the finger where it joined Broodseinde ridge ran the German Fourth Line, *Flandern I*, around 2,000 yards to the east of the *Wilhelm Stellung*. Across this bloody, desolate and much disputed ground the Second Army was now to attack. The brief account of the main attack on the plateau given earlier, implied that General Plumer's tactical planning and thorough training had allowed the infantry to advance successfully into the German positions. This is certainly true, but as was expected from the outset, this battle was never going to be a walk-over, and there was to be much hard fighting before the day was through, and the enemy finally evicted from his stubbornly held defences. The artillery had prepared the way, it was now up to the infantry to bite into the enemy position, and hold what they had seized.

The advance to the Blue Line

X Corps

23rd Division[400]
Major-General J. M. Babington

The 23rd Division was to attack with the 68th Brigade on the right and 69th Brigade (strengthened by an extra 4 mortars of the 70th Light Trench Mortar Battery) on the left, on a 1,000 yard frontage. A half section of the 3rd Canadian Tunnelling Company was attached to each brigade. Four tanks were to be attached to 69th Brigade to assist in the clearing of enemy strong-points, two to move along the Menin Road and two north of Inverness Copse. The 70th Brigade was held in divisional reserve west of Zillebeke. The direction of attack was due east along the axis of the Menin Road which bisected the narrow waist of the plateau, towards the head of the Bassevillebeek valley at Dumbarton Lakes, and towards Inverness Copse just north of the road. There were to be three objectives, with the final objective (the Green Line), on the *Wilhelm Stellung* 1,500 yards east, at the point where it crossed the Menin Road. Each brigade would use one battalion for the capture of each of the three objectives, the fourth battalion held in brigade reserve or used to strengthen attacking battalions. The 23rd Division was faced by the left and centre regiments of the *Bavarian Ersatz Division*, the *28th Ersatz*, and *4th Bavarian R.I.R.*

The capture of Inverness Copse and advance to the Wilhelm Stellung 68th and 69th Brigades 23rd Division

68th Brigade [401]
The 68th Brigade was to attack with the 11th Northumberland Fusiliers to the first objective, the 10th Northumberland Fusiliers to the second objective and the 13th Durham Light Infantry to

---

[400] Lieut.-Colonel H.R. Sanilands (1925) *The 23rd Division 1914-1919* London: William Blackwood pp174-209
[401] National Archives, War Diary 68th Brigade WO95/2181

capture and consolidate the final objective.[402] The 12th Durham Light Infantry were held in brigade reserve, with one company at the disposal of the 11th and 10th Northumberland. Before the brigade could reach its third objective near the *Wilhelm Stellung,* at the northern end of the Tower Hamlets spur, it would have to negotiate the obstacle of the bogs in the upper Bassevillebeek valley and around Dumbarton Lakes. A direct assault across this area was considered impossible.

At 5:40 a.m. the British guns shattered the calm of the misty early dawn. South of the Menin Road the 11th Northumberland Fusiliers closed with the barrage which smothered the German lines, and 3 minutes later began their advance. The vagaries of the ground conditions were now to become apparent, for on the higher ground above the valleys the surface had dried to a hard crust. In places, the Northumberland were finding it difficult to keep direction amidst the dust and smoke of the barrage, whilst the 41st Division was floundering in the mud a few hundred yards to the south. Other parts of the brigade front around Dumbarton Lakes however were still a morass. The attack was made more difficult from the start, as the initial barrage was slightly too long and had landed beyond a German strong-point in Dumbarton Wood just west of the lakes. Machine gun fire from this strong-point swept the advance of the 11th Northumberland, and "D" Company of the 12th Durham which was moving forward in support. After a vicious fight the strong-point was taken, the battalion now being faced with the quagmire of a small stream which ran between the upper and lower Dumbarton Lakes. Delay in finding a crossing point resulted in the barrage being lost, and as the Northumberland struggled through the mire machine gun fire caused many casualties which included all the company commanders. Much of the fire which now swept the 11th Northumberland, came from a strong-point on a slight knoll on the battalion left flank, and from a bunker in the ruins of Herenthage Chateau 100 yards east of the knoll, within 69th Brigade's sector. Special arrangements had been made to deal with these strong-points and a platoon of the Northumberland had advanced with the 11th West Yorks (69th Brigade), to protect 68th Brigades left flank. With the support of 6-inch Newton mortars directed on the enemy positions they were both successfully captured. Meanwhile the remainder of the 11th Northumberland with "D" Company of the 12th Durham waded the stream, and although having lost all their officers had reached the Red Line.

During the pause, while the 11th Northumberland dug-in on the first objective, the 10th Northumberland supported by "A" and "B" Companies of the 12th Durham, assembled behind the standing barrage on the Red Line, and as the barrage lifted at 7:08 advanced towards the second objective. To avoid the morass of mud and water which was Dumbarton Lakes, two companies of the 10th Northumberland assembled behind the left rear of 122nd Brigade, and the other two companies behind the right rear of the 9th Green Howards of 69th Brigade between Herenthage Chateau and the Menin Road. This enabled the 10th Northumberland to advance either side of the mire. Moving forward around the lakes, the left company soon came under severe machine gun fire in which all it officers became casualties the company then loosing direction. "A" Company of the 10th Northumberland in support, moved forward and after severe fighting took the second objective, capturing 80 prisoners, 2 field guns and 2 howitzers. The two companies on the right after stiff fighting passed to the south of the quagmire, waded the stream, and joined "A" Company on the Blue Line on the east side of the Bassevillebeke depression.

The 11th Northumberland now held and began to dig-in along the whole brigade front on the second objective, with its left on Kantinje Cabaret on the Menin Road, and with the two support companies of the 12th Durham, which had inevitably become embroiled in the fighting, digging-in in close behind just in rear of the Blue Line.

69th Brigade [403]

The 69th Brigade was to attack with the 11th West Yorkshire Regiment to capture the first objective, the 9th Yorkshire Regiment (The Green Howards) to capture the second objective, and

---

[402] National Archives, War Diary 10th and 11th Northumberland Fusiliers WO95/2182
[403] National Archives, War Diary 69th Brigade WO95/2183

the 10th Duke of Wellington's Regiment to capture and consolidate the final objective. Two companies of the 8th Green Howards were to support the 10th Duke of Wellington.

The remains of Inverness Copse shrouded in the early morning mist were the first obstacle to the advance of the 69th Brigade. Leading off behind the barrage the 11th West Yorks entered the blasted and squalid remains of the copse, but were soon checked by machine gun fire from two dug-outs in a strong-point unaffected by the shell-fire. For the moment the advance was stopped as the leading wave took cover, the enemy fire causing a number of casualties. A sergeant of the 69th Trench Mortar battery fired 25 rounds at the strong-point with a Stokes mortar. The position was cleared in a smart action in which 35 Germans surrendered. Due to the smoke, dust and tangle of debris, a gap developed between the left and centre companies of the West Yorks, but the situation was quickly recognized and the reserve company was brought forward to fill it. By 6:10 a.m. the battalion was on the first objective.

Amongst the mist and smoke, small parties of Germans hidden in shell-holes had been missed by the moppers-up of the 11th West Yorks, and opened fire on flanks and rear the 9th Green Howards as they advanced in artillery formation. Vicious close quarter bayonet fighting ensued, with the Germans throwing bombs and opening fire at close range with rifles and light machine guns. Sixteen officers including two company commanders of the Green Howards had been killed or wounded before the fighting was over and the shell-holes and dug-outs finally cleared. Around 60 of the enemy had been killed. Those of "A" and "B" Companies of the Green Howards that had survived the advance through the copse moved up close behind the standing barrage, and at 7:08 moved off as it lifted towards the second objective. In front of the Blue Line in the centre of the brigade front, stood a concrete tower, and along a line running south between it and a small pond beside the Menin Road, were a number of pillboxes and dug-outs, which had been recognized as potential centres of resistance. The bombardment had done little to suppress these positions and the Green Howards came under heavy fire as they approached. Some Germans seeing they risked being outflanked abandoned their machine guns and ran forward to surrender, while others stayed put and engaged in viscous hand to hand fighting, before they were either shot or bayoneted, 40 dead being counted later around the tower. In the shelters along this short defence line the Green Howards had captured no less than 10 machine guns, 15 *flammenwerfer*, 5 trench howitzers and 4 trench mortars. While "A" and "B" Companies had been clearing the pillbox line, "C" and "D" Companies had passed through and captured the battalion objective on the Blue Line, and had begun to consolidate, the ground for once being found good for digging. Prisoners had indicated that the morale of their division, the *Bavarian Ersatz*, was low and many Germans could be seen streaming back towards the Reutelbeek to the left front, followed by a hail of rifle and Lewis gun fire. The job of consolidation was made more difficult by continual enemy machine gun and sniper fire, but before the next advance was to take place at 9:35 a.m. the forward companies were well dug-in with good cover.

At last the bunkers and dugouts about the *Albrecht Stellung* had been overcome and the line taken, with the first waves of infantry consolidating east of the broken German defence line, in touch with 41st Division to the right, and awaiting their support battalions to move up in readiness to advance to the final objective on the *Wilhelm Stellung*. The horrific Inverness Copse with its stubborn concrete shelters was at last behind them, but had once again claimed another bounty to add to its toll of dead and wounded.

I Anzac Corps

For the first time in the War two Australian divisions were to fight side-by-side, a situation which their senior commanders and men, and the Australian Government, believed would be of inestimable benefit to their fighting value. I Anzac Corps now comprised four Australian divisions 1st and 2nd, and 4th and 5th, the latter two being in Corps reserve to relieve the 1st and 2nd in subsequent fighting. There had been a period of rest for 1st, 2nd and 5th Divisions, but 4th Division, as part of II Anzac (Lieutenant-General Godley), had recently been heavily engaged in the fighting at Messines. At the instigation of Lieutenant-General Birdwood (commanding I

Anzac), 4th Division had been transferred to I Anzac Corps to create an all Australian Corps. Godley had been sorry to see them go but understood the reasoning, and whilst believing that I Anzac would gain in value, stated that he did not anticipate that the introduction of two good British divisions would lessen the value of his Corps. II Anzac was to become heavily involved in the later fighting, and now comprised 3rd Australian Division, New Zealand Division, plus the 49th (West Riding) and 66th Divisions. Australian artillery had been involved in the offensive since July, having moved up to their battery positions around the 19th and 20th and being heavily engaged on the 31st supporting British divisions. Now it was the turn of the Australian infantry, to attack across the Hanebeek towards Polygon Wood and Anzac spur, names which would become inextricably linked with Australian military history.

1st Australian Division to the Red Line
Major-General H. B. Walker

Glencorse Wood and Nonne Bosschen, both of evil reputation, would have to be taken before the leading battalions of the 2nd and 3rd Australian Brigades reached their first objectives on the Red Line.

As we have seen, on the order of the divisional commander all eight battalions to carry out the attack had been assembled well forward, in an attempt to avoid German shelling in the rear assembly areas. But the severe enemy barrage that had crashed down on the British Front Line around 4:30 a.m. had led the battalions in the rear waves to close right up towards the front to avoid the shelling. As a direct result at 5:40 as the British barrage lifted towards the first objective, the six support battalions had moved off too soon and caught up with the forward wave that were slowly advancing behind the creeping barrage.

2nd and 3rd Australian Brigades advance to the Red Line[404]
The carefully arranged and practiced plan of attack of the 2nd and 3rd Brigades had arranged for the 6th and 11th Battalions, which were to lead the attack to the first objective, to assemble on their jumping-off tapes 150 yards ahead of the front line trench, but behind the outpost line. The second objective was to be attacked by the 5th and 12th Battalions which would jump-off from the front line, while the 8th, 7th, 10th and 9th to attack the final objective, formed up just behind the front line. The plan now fell apart as all eight battalions, which should have shaken out into three distinct waves, moved forward as one mass, the 12th Battalion also veering to the left. In the words of the Australian infantry the British barrage was, 'Excellent, the best ever put up' and 'as near to perfect as possible' also 'magnificent in accuracy and volume'.[405] It was lucky for the dense wave of men moving forward that it was, as it undoubtedly saved them from what could have been a disaster under the muzzles of the German machine guns.

---

[404] National Archives, War Diary 2nd Aus Brigade WO95/3231, War Diary 5th Aus Battalion WO95/3233, War Diary 6th Aus Battalion WO95/3235, War Diary 7th Aus Battalion WO95/3237, War Diary 8th Aus Battalion WO95/3240, War Diary 3rd Aus Brigade WO95/3243, War Diary 9th Aus Battalion WO95/3247, War Diary 10th Aus Battalion WO95/3248, War Diary 11th Aus Battalion WO95/3251, War Diary 12th Aus Battalion WO95/3252
[405] AOA p761

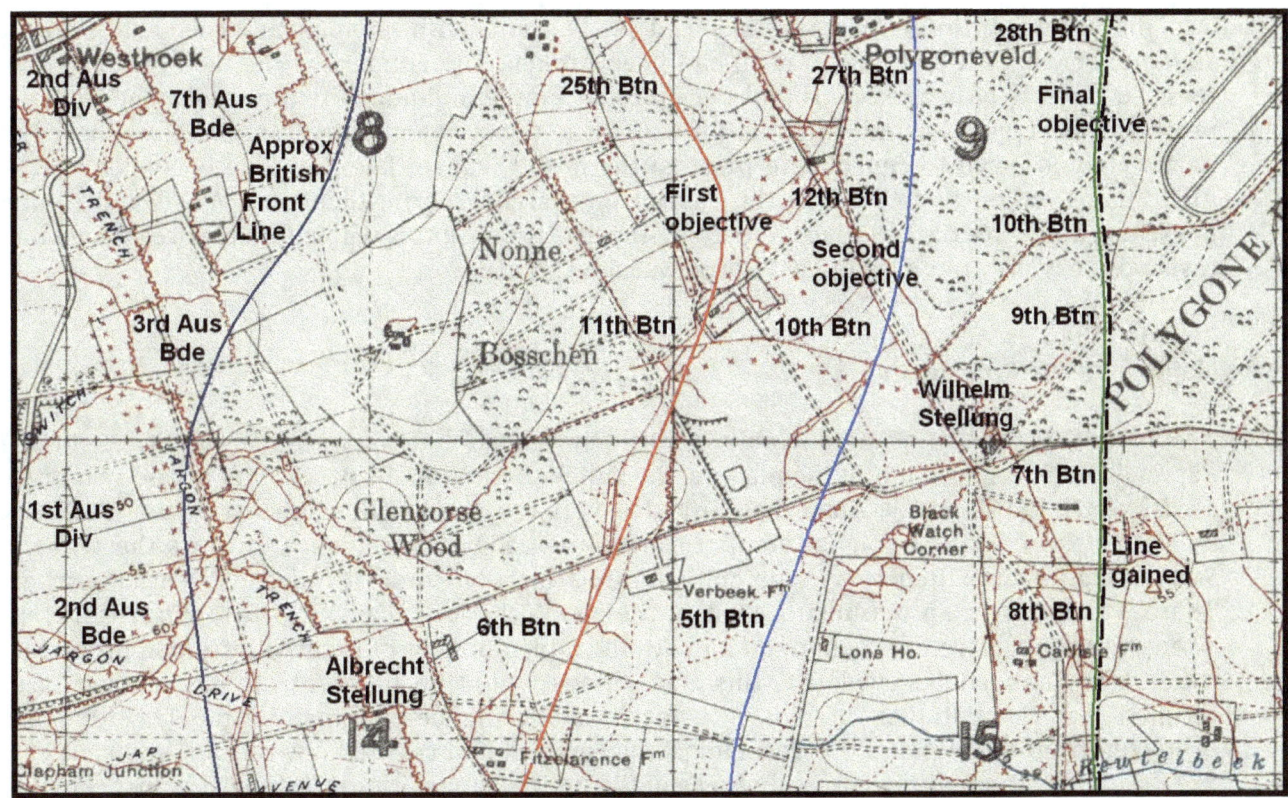

The capture of Glencorse Wood and Nonne Bosschen and advance to Polygon Wood
2nd and 3rd Australian Brigades - 1st Australian Division

There was little opposition from the line of pillboxes pounded by the barrage on the western edge of Glencorse Wood, only a few shots being fired and a few bombs thrown, and most were rushed or attacked from the rear and quickly over-run. The shambles of the devastated wood presented little obstacle, but machine gun fire from one bunker held up the 6th Battalion. 2nd Lieutenant Frederick Birks of the 6th, accompanied by a corporal rushed the bunker. The corporal was wounded but Birks continued alone and entered the bunker, killing the gun crew and capturing the gun. The advance continued. Later with a small party he again attacked a strong-point where fifteen Germans were captured and ten killed. 2nd Lieutenant Birks was to be awarded the V.C. for his gallantry.

The bunker at Fitzclarence Farm was suppressed by rifle grenades and Lewis guns of the 6th Battalion which fired at the loop-holes until it was outflanked, at which point the garrison of an officer and forty men surrendered. On the left of the 6th, the 11th Battalion, having negotiated most of the tangle of wire and debris through Glencorse Wood, came under machine gun fire from one of the pillboxes situated in the row of concrete shelters along the sunken road at its northern end. The Germans had mounted the gun on the roof of the pillbox and swept the line of the 11th causing a check. As the Western Australians closed in, a fierce close-quarters melee ensued with the use of bombs and pistols on both sides. Due to the initial bunching the 10th Battalion was also involved in the fight, and there was much slaughter of the German garrison before the remnant of an officer and 40 men were eventually taken prisoner. Another strong-point held up the advance and Private Reginald Roy Inwood of the 10th went forward through the barrage and single-handedly captured the strong-point and nine Germans, killing several others. He was to carry out a similar attack on the following day, gallant acts for which he was to be awarded the V.C. Mopping-up parties were left to clear the remaining bunkers as officers hurried the men forward to catch up with the advancing barrage.

On the left towards Nonne Bosschen, the bunching caused at the start resulted in a mixing of units, with parties of the 12th Battalion, and even men from the 2nd Division joining with the 11th Battalion. By careful negotiation around the edges of the water filled shell craters, the tangled quagmire where the wood had once been was crossed, but a machine gun in a blockhouse ripped into the crowded line until it was silenced. At last and with comparative ease the *Albrecht Stellung*, or what little remained of it, had been broken. The gunners of the field artillery now reduced the rate of fire to one round per gun per minute and added white smoke shells to the protective barrage as an indication that it would stand just beyond the first objective where the infantry could begin to consolidate prior to the next advance. The Red Line on which the 1st Australian Division halted ran to the east of Fitzclarence Farm, Glencorse Wood and Nonne Bosschen, and with the 23rd Division holding Inverness Copse this whole terrible area which had resisted every previous assault by II Corps was now secure.

2nd Australian Division to the Red Line
Major-General N. M. Smyth

The battlefield had dried appreciably during September, but as with the conditions in the Bassevillebeek valley south of the plateau, the valley of the Hanebeek was still a muddy morass across which the 7th and 5th Australian Brigades were to attack, from a line astride the Westhoek to Zonnebeke track. Previous attempts to cross the valley and advance towards the *Wilhelm Stellung* had been halted by vicious enfilade fire from Glencorse Wood and Nonne Bosschen. There was however an optimistic spirit in the air. With fresh plans, fresh troops with recent intensive training to carry them out, and with the added benefit of their countrymen protecting their right flank, all believed that this time things would be different. As has already been recalled the 25th Battalion of the 7th Brigade, sheltering behind the Westhoek ridge were protected from the worst of the German barrages which had crashed down from 4:30 a.m. This fire was aimed more at the assembly areas of the 1st Division, with the 2nd Division just catching the edge, but at 5:36 German field artillery opened fire across the valley and into the lines where 5th Brigade were formed up. The 20th Battalion immediately moved forward to avoid the shelling followed by the 18th, causing a degree of confusion right at the start.

7th and 5th Australian Brigades advance to the Red Line[406]
As the British barrage crashed down a few minutes later, the 20th Battalion to the left of the 25th, closely followed by the 18th Battalion, were already on their way, and were up very close to the bursting line of shells. Germans in shell-holes forward gave up the fight without firing a shot, and a party sheltering in shell-holes behind a hedge with fixed bayonets were so surprised by the advancing Australians that they were killed before they could us them. A few resisting bunkers opened up with machine gun fire and held up the right for a few minutes, but moving quickly to within bombing distance the 20th soon silenced them. The ground for 100 yards either side of the Hanebeek was a quagmire but the slow pace of the barrage allowed the 25th Battalion on the right of the 20th to choose their path through the mire carefully, and although some got stuck and had to be helped out, the majority advanced straight across. As the barrage fell about them, pillboxes east of the mire opened machine gun fire on the 25th and the right of the 20th, but with suppressing fire from Lewis guns, some fired from the hip, they were outflanked and bombed out, and the objective just east of the Hanebeek was reached. The left of the 20th Battalion had a more difficult time, being at first confronted by a line of old concrete shelters which were rushed as the garrison emerged, many being killed in a vicious fight. In the centre of the valley the Hanebeek Wood was an impassable quagmire, the 20th moving round rather than through it. This somewhat dislocated the advance, giving some German machine gunners in pillboxes beyond the wood time to open fire once the barrage had passed, and allowed some nests to be missed by the mopping-up parties which subsequently opened fire from behind. Those in front were rushed by the 20th while those in the rear were silenced by parties of the 20th and the 18th Battalion following up. The artillery timetable had allowed a maximum of 43 minutes for the

---

[406] National Archives, War Diary 7th Aus Brigade WO95/3243, War Diary 25th Aus Battalion WO95/3340, War Diary 27th Aus Battalion WO95/3342, War Diary 28th Aus Battalion WO95/3343, War Diary 5th Aus Brigade WO95/3308, War Diary 17th Aus Battalion WO95/3314, War Diary 18th Aus Battalion WO95/3316, War Diary 20th Aus Battalion WO95/3319

advance to the first objective. By around 6:00 a.m. the 20th Battalion was on their first objective east of the Hanebeek, and the Red Line was secured.

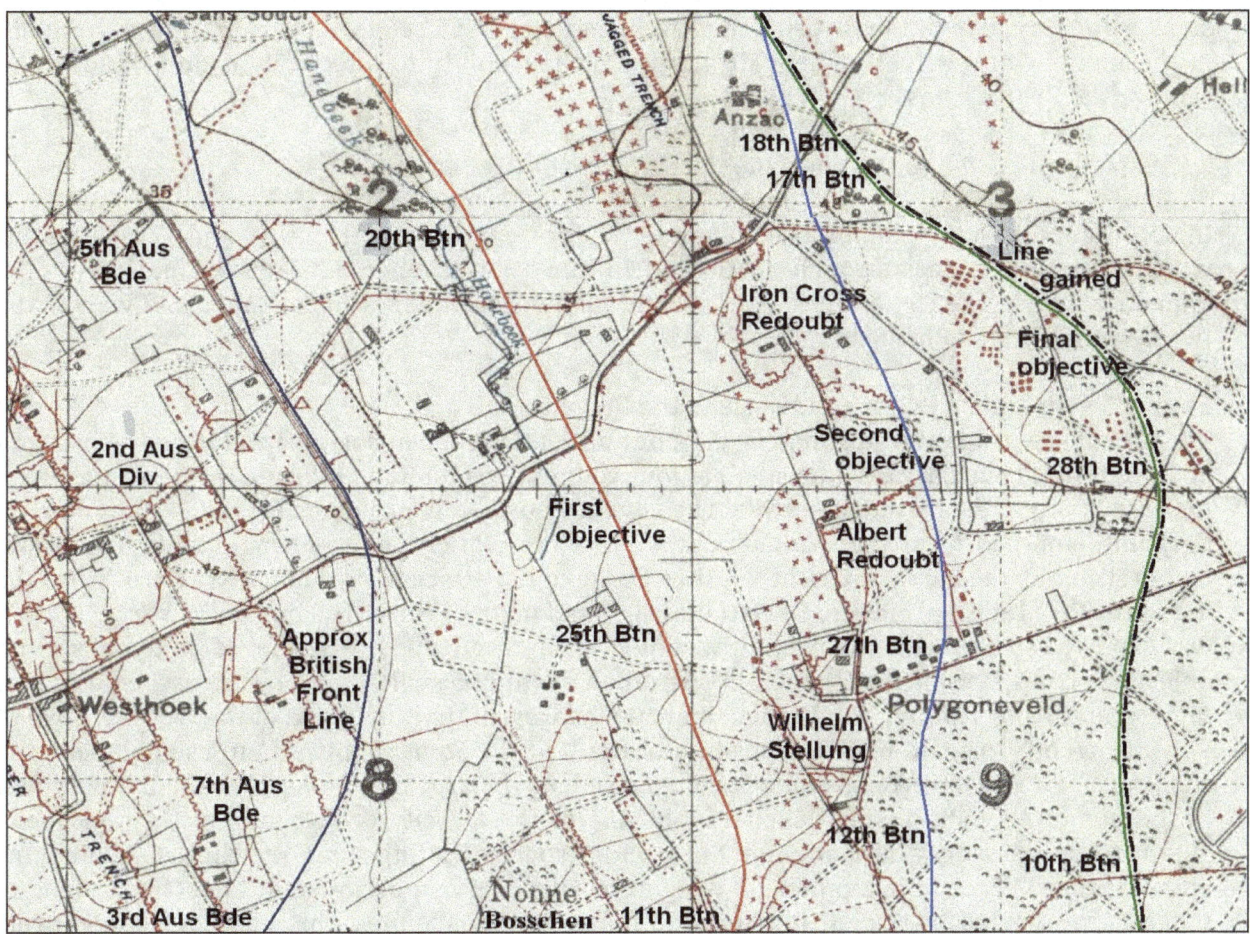

Breaking of the Wilhelm Stellung 7th and 5th Australian Brigades - 2nd Australian Division

The battalions on the first objective began to dig-in as the heavier guns searched the rear German positions, while the thinner protective barrage covered the consolidation. A few hundred yards beyond the Hanebeek two German bunkers opened machine gun fire on the right of the 20th where the New South Wales battalion was digging-in. Although beyond the first objective, it was obviously necessary to quickly silence these guns. An attack was made, through the barrage, by parties of the 18th and 20th and an officer and four men of the 20th reached the position and routed forty Germans and a machine gun.

The 45 minute halt on the first objective was now put to good use in sorting out the mixing of battalions that had occurred due to the bunching at the start. The German shelling had also caused some of the 1st Division to stray to the north, and a few were found so far left they were mixed with the left battalions of the 2nd Division. Even more were in the area of the right battalions, and officers gradually directed the men back to their correct positions.

The Germans had expected the attack but had been surprised when it started, as they believed it would be preceded by several hours of intense bombardment, which had not happened. So far only the three front companies of each regiment holding the forward area had been engaged, and the well organized defensive system still held large reserves and counter-attack forces echeloned to the rear. In front of 2nd Australian Division each regiment of *121st Division*, the *56th R.I.R.*, *7th R.I.R.*, and *60th R.I.R.*, had two companies held back in shelters about the *Wilhelm Stellung*, with three more close behind them, and a further four in reserve behind the Passchendaele ridge, with a similar arrangement for the *Bavarian Ersatz Division* in front of 1st Australian. Behind the two line divisions, *Group Wytschaete* and *Group Ypres* held back the main strength of the *Eingreif* divisions, *234th* and *236th* behind *121st Division*, and *16th Bavarian*, and if necessary *3rd Reserve* behind *Bavarian Ersatz*. *50th (Prussian) Reserve Division* was also moving down from about Westroosebeke. The *Eingreif* divisions, *234th, 236th* and *16th Bavarian* had three battalions at readiness with divisional artillery in support, and were to move off as soon as the direction of the British penetration was clear.[407] The enemy was therefore confident in the number of reserves at their disposal and their ability to affectively counter-attack and recover the British gains.

1st Australian Division to the Blue Line

In accordance with the plan of its commander Major-General Walker, the 5th and 12th battalions which were now to pass through the 6th and 11th, in their advance to the Blue Line, were to be joined by the 8th, 7th, 10th and 9th which would follow close behind the advance and wait at the two hour halt on the Blue Line.

2nd and 3rd Australian Brigades advance to the Blue Line
The mix up caused at the start had largely, but not entirely, been sorted out during the halt and at 7:08 the field gun barrage intensified to four rounds per minute to indicate the beginning of its forward creep to the second objective. The advance posed few problems for the 5th Battalion, as Germans emerged from their bunkers waving white cloths having been totally shaken and demoralized by the barrage. On the southern edge of the attack a blockhouse was firing into the left of the 23rd Division, and the 5th Battalion assisted in its capture. The bunker at Verbeek Farm was expected to cause a hold up, but it was quickly captured, and the 5th moved on to the second objective. To the left of the 5th the 12th Battalion advanced swiftly, and soon reached a line of undergrowth and saplings barely chest high, which was all that remained of the western edge of Polygon Wood. This had been the position of the *Wilhelm Stellung*, but so intense had been the shelling that it was unrecognizable as a line. The enemy in large numbers were still in occupation of the numerous pillboxes and shelters, but due to the ferocity of the barrage they had been stunned into passivity and many remained under cover awaiting captivity. Nine machine guns were captured, three in one pillbox. A dangerous situation had occurred at the start as some of the 12th had veered to the left to avoid the initial hostile shelling. This had not been entirely corrected at the halt on the first objective, and now a gap existed between the 5th and the 12th in which there remained active pillboxes. The right platoon of the 12th attacked and overwhelmed one pillbox. The 10th Battalion moving up close behind the 12th bridged the gap, and captured a machine gun and its crew which had caused a check. Between 7:30 and 7:45 a.m. the 1st Division had secured the Blue Line, and the 5th and 12th Battalions were digging-in. On the right, where the advance had to cover a greater distance, the *Wilhelm Stellung* with its pillboxes and formidable bunker at Black Watch Corner lay further forward and had still to be overcome. But on the left in front of Polygon Wood the enemy line had been easily breached.

7th and 5th Brigades to the Blue Line
The 27th Battalion met with only weak resistance as it advanced from the Hanebeek valley up the western slope of the Anzac spur towards the Albert Redoubt and the *Wilhelm Stellung*. The gun crews in the pillboxes scattered across the crater field put up little fight, those that did firing off a few rounds before being overwhelmed. Here too the *Wilhelm Stellung* having been obliterated by the shelling, had ceased to exist as a trench system. To the left the 18th Battalion advancing up the spur faced equally weak resistance, and as they approached Iron Cross Redoubt most of the garrison fired a few demonstrative shots and turned and ran, helped on their way by bursts of Lewis gun fire, while fifteen others emerged shaken and demoralized from a nearby pillbox and surrendered. The Anzac blockhouse was surrounded and the fifteen occupants were captured as they attempted to drag out two machine guns. The two storey blockhouse was found to have two lower rooms and a small upper room reached by a ladder. The upper room had excellent views

---

[407] National Archives, maps showing distribution of enemy forces at 5 pm on the 20th September, in WO153/601

from loops over the Steenbeek valley to the north, towards Ypres to the west, and with the gun battery group's targets at Westhoek and Bellewaarde marked on the loops. It was equipped with a field wireless set for communication with the batteries whose fire it controlled.

At around the time 1st and 2nd Australian Divisions, with the 23rd British Division to their right arrived on the second objective, a fresh breeze from the south-west began to clear the early mist and the extent of the morning's achievement became apparent. The neck of the plateau between the Bassevillebeek and the Hanebeek was clear of the enemy and the *Wilhelm Stellung* along the eastern side of the Hanebeek valley was broken. The Australians about the Anzac blockhouse had a clear view away to the north, of the brown pocked crater field of destruction stretching beyond Zonnebeke and along the ridge towards Passchendaele. Digging-in and wiring of the second objective began as the protective barrage thinned and stood just forward of the position, where it would remain for the next two hours. The battalions now dug-in with some urgency to prepare for the counter-attacks which they expected, and the heavy guns combed 2,000 yards back into the German rear for the anticipated concentration of reserves which were surely forming up behind the ridges. At the front, sniping from pillboxes and bunkers both within, and at longer range beyond the protective barrage began to cause casualties amongst the digging parties and also impeded the forward movement of the support battalions.

At the south-west corner of Polygon Wood where the 5th and 12th Battalions were digging-in, the Germans opened machine gun fire from bunkers just beyond the standing barrage. The blockhouse at Black Watch Corner in the *Wilhelm Stellung* defences was about 150 yards in front of the left company of the 5th Battalion, which was now suffering casualties from its sniping fire. A party of around 20 men of the 5th worked their way around the blockhouse, at which point the garrison then indicated their desire to surrender. The Captain commanding the raiding party ran forward to the bunker as the enemy began to emerge and was immediately shot by a German who had already surrendered. Only firm action by the officers of the 5th prevented annihilation of the whole garrison, and an officer, 15 men and two machine guns were captured. To prevent the enemy re-occupying the blockhouse the 5th moved their line forward and dug-in around it, not realizing that they were up within the protective barrage line. After the bunkers just beyond the Blue Line had been secured, sniping at longer range still continued, and with the breeze clearing the shell-smoke, the long mound of the Butte de Polygon which had a commanding view over the Anzac forward area could be clearly seen. From observation of enemy movement about the Butte it was obviously a position of importance. From dug-outs about the mound enemy machine gun fire over a range of 1,500 yards whined and smacked around the Blue Line, about which the Australians could do little but take cover. It was the same situation up on the spur at Anzac blockhouse, where the Germans opened fire on the 18th Battalion as they dug-in, from the Garter Point blockhouse 200 yards forward. The blockhouse, which was flying a red-cross flag, was about on the line of the final objective, but to prevent further casualties a party of the 18th moved forward and seized it. It was found to be a dressing station and two doctors with a number of wounded were in occupation, but as the bunker had been used offensively the red-cross flag was torn down.

The advance to the final objective, the Green Line

The British machine guns that had provided the third of the five barrage belts which had plunged over the heads of the infantry were now outranged, and had to be manhandled forward over 1,000 yards to take their place within the final protective barrage. The crews struggled forward with over 200 of the heavy weapons, up across the cratered ravaged ground. The field artillery stayed-put, as the limited advance enabled it to easily maintain the range, and provide continuous protective fire for the infantry. The advance to the third objective was to be the shortest at between 200 and 400 yards, but was to be undertaken by the greatest number of infantry, which for the last two hours had been assembling behind the second objective. Once the Green Line was secure the whole of the German Third Line across the plateau would be broken.

Rapid consolidation of the final objective was therefore essential, as it was expected that major German counter-attacks would soon threaten the newly won line, which now endangered the integrity of the whole German Flanders Position. This was a situation which for certain the enemy would not accept without violent reaction. After the two hour halt the protective barrage thickened once more, and at 9:53 a.m. began its slow forward creep of 100 yards in eight minutes, towards the final objective.

X Corps

23rd Division

The next step forward by the 68th and 69th Brigades from the Blue to the Green Line was critical, as once it was successfully taken General Plumer's main objective for this day would be achieved and the great German defensive position on the plateau would be broken, thus allowing the principal attack to the north to proceed with its right flank secure. The great strength of the German defences was still to be encountered by both brigades, with many more concrete bunkers to be overcome in the final 400 to 500 yard advance towards the *Wilhelm Stellung*.

68th Brigade

At Zero Hour the 13th Durham Light Infantry had moved up from Tor Top, to its preliminary assembly positions just south of Stirling Castle, vacated by the 10th Northumberland. After the capture of the Red Line it had moved forward to its jump-off positions on the Blue Line across the base of Tower Hamlets spur south of the Menin Road with its left on Kantijne Cabaret. To reach the Blue Line two companies of the 13th Durham, supported by "C" Company of the 12th Durham had passed to the south of Dumbarton Lakes, while the other two companies of the 13th proceeded to the north of the Lakes. At 9:35 the 13th Durham moved off behind the barrage towards the final objective the left companies crossing the flat northern end of Tower Hamlets spur. The axis of the road ran across the brigade front and the Durham were soon heavily engaged clearing bunkers in the ruins of houses along the roadside. As the left companies worked forward they were hit by machine gun fire from a bunker in 69th Brigade sector. A party of the 10th Duke of Wellington attacked the enemy bunker from the front and rear and knocked out the machine gun, enabling the Durham to continue their advance. With the left flank secure the Durham fought on along the road between the ruins. The remaining bunkers were slowly outflanked and captured, around 200 of the enemy being taken prisoner. The battalion moved forward and crossed what remained of the *Wilhelm Stellung*, and on to the final objective about 500 yards short of the ruins of the village of Gheluvelt. From this position they had a commanding view into the German rear areas to the south and south-east of the plateau.

69th Brigade

To north of the Menin Road the 10th Duke of Wellington's Regiment with two companies of the 8th Yorkshire Regiment advanced across flat open ground towards Veldhoek and Northampton Farm. The farm fell to "B" and "D" companies of the Duke's and a company of the Green Howards with little trouble, but beyond the farm the assault groups came under heavy machine gun fire from about 12 pillboxes about the *Wilhelm Stellung*, which caused considerable casualties. Touch was temporarily lost with the centre and right of the attack and a platoon with two Lewis guns was brought forward to protect the right flank. Advancing towards Velhoek, within a few hundred yards "A" and "C" Companies of the 10th Duke's came up against machine gun and rifle fire from a strongly defended hedgerow covering a row of concrete dug-outs. The hedgerow was outflanked and the defenders either surrendered or ran back, abandoning the dug-outs. Fighting to overcome twelve pillboxes on the *Wilhelm Stellung* defences was intense. Most of the final objective had been reached by 10:30 a.m. but the pillboxes were not finally cleared until around noon. The Duke of Wellington and the Green Howard began to dig-in and wire the Green Line, using much captured material as wire and shovels had been found abandoned about all the days objectives and put to good use. The Green Line became the forward observation line consisting largely of an unconnected line of defended shell-holes. Greater consolidation took place about the second objective which became the main line of resistance against counter-attack, machine guns being installed in many of the captured bunkers and pillboxes, these becoming strong-points with wire defences being erected where possible, and here the infantry would defend its gains. Best use was made of natural cover, reverse slopes and folds in the ground being selected for greatest protection against hostile artillery.

The 23rd Division having experienced some of the toughest fighting of the day, was on its final objective, and had advanced about 1,600 yards, the greatest penetration of the day. But due to the failure of 41st Division to reach its final objective, the right flank of the 13th Durham was left dangerously exposed and a company each of the 10th and 11th Northumberland were sent up to form a protective flank north-west of Tower Hamlets.

I Anzac Corps

During the two hour halt on the second objective, which some amongst the I Anzac Corps thought too long, the opportunity had been taken to re-organize those battalions of 1st Australian Division which had become most disorganized at the start, the 8th, 7th, 10th and 9th, which now sheltered in shell-holes behind the Blue Line. They were in the words of the Australian Official Account, eating sandwiches and smoking German cigars, and awaiting the barrage to lift towards the Green Line. German observers on the Butte in Polygon Wood and at Broodseinde had recognized the penetration of 2nd Australian Division, which had resulted in a weak enemy barrage falling along the Hanebeek. Timing the fall of the shallow curtain of shells, the 28th, 26th and 17th Battalions had been moved up from the shelter of Westhoek ridge to the Blue Line with hardly a casualty to await the advance to the final objective.

Consolidation on the Blue Line had been assisted by 2nd, 3rd, 7th and 5th Field Companies who with the infantry had begun to dig-in a line of trenches to better defend the position against counter attack. The divisional machine guns, (32 to each division) and Stokes mortars had been brought up and incorporated into the defence. The consolidation against counter-attack was urgent, as a German signal recovered from a messenger dog that had run happily into the Anzac blockhouse defences, had ordered the forward battalion commander of the *7th Reserve Infantry Regiment* (*121st Division*) to throw in his local reserves. Also at 8:30 a.m. an aircraft contact report indicated a large assembly of possibly 3rd (*Eingreif*) *Reserve Division* troops south of Zonnebeke. This was more likely a *121st Division* concentration of half a reserve battalion of the *60th Infantry Regiment* who were to attack along the Roulers railway at the junction between I Anzac and V Corps (Fifth Army). It is also probable that at this time *56th Reserve Infantry Regiment* was organizing a counter-attack along the northern edge of Polygon Wood.

1st Australian Division

The two battalions of 2nd Brigade and two of 3rd Brigade were now organized about the Blue Line and ready to continue the attack to the final objective. But at the designated time part of the barrage behind which they were to advance fell alarmingly short in front of Polygon Wood, a situation made worse by the fact that many had advanced beyond the Blue Line to silence the German bunkers that had threatened their consolidation. At Black Watch Corner parties digging-in about the blockhouse were caught beneath the British barrage and had to hastily withdraw back towards the Blue Line, as the assaulting battalions were just starting in the opposite direction. Generally however the barrage was of such weight and power the defenders were more than ready to give up the fight, but although the enemy caused few problems the barrage, to which the advancing Australians kept up very close, in places continued to fall short. At least one 18-pounder caused about 30 casualties, while some of the heavy guns whose shells should have been falling 300 yards beyond the final objective, were still falling on or even behind the second objective. At the southern edge of Polygon Wood a group of nine pillboxes, which by the artillery map should have been 250 yards behind the barrage, were attacked and seized by a party of the 8th Battalion, but came under heavy British shell-fire mortally wounding their officer Major Tubb. Slightly to the north parties of the 7th, 10th and 9th Battalions who had advanced into their own barrage had to withdraw to the Blue Line until efforts could be made to lengthen the range.

By 10:15 the advance to the final objective was accomplished except in the centre where the barrage still fell short. It was quickly arranged that the range be increased by 200 yards, and subsequently the whole objective was secured. The Germans appeared totally crushed and as consolidation began, with a number Lewis gunners in shell-holes 50 yards forward as protection, it was hardly interrupted by sniping. But once more a few pillboxes in front of the 8th Battalion on the right and just forward of the objective opened a harassing machine gun fire and had to be silenced. One such pillbox was stalked by the intelligence officer of the 8th, Lieutenant Errey, where a German battalion commander, his adjutant, 30 men and two machine guns were captured. Another troublesome pillbox in the same vicinity was seized by the 7th battalion with the aid of Stokes mortars.

2nd Australian Division

On the far left of 5th Brigade front the final objective at Garter Point had already been secured by the 18th Battalion, and the 17th Battalion could not believe they had no advance to make. The right company, within 50 yards of the barrage saw the white smoke shells indicating the end of the advance and stopped, but the three left companies continued to advance into their own barrage and suffered casualties. The 17th then began to consolidate with the 18th, and as they did so eight German aircraft that had broken through the R.F.C. screen attacked them with machine gun fire, but doing little damage.

On the right, 28th Battalion of 7th Brigade finding that their final objective lay on a rearward slope pushed their line a little further forward to the crest of Anzac Spur and started to dig-in. German artillery fire now became directed upon the positions of 17th, 18th and 28th Battalions, but was to some extent avoided by the battalions moving slightly further forward. The
barrage was heavier on the Hanebeek, but was mostly avoided by the 20th and 25th Battalions who also moved forward into shell-holes higher up the rearward slope of the spur.[408]

The confidence with which 1st Anzac Corps had entered the battle had not been unfounded, and it had been successful in taking all its objectives. The fighting had however been severe and it had been no walkover, 1st Australian Division having suffered a near disaster at the start from which it had rapidly recovered. Due to the usual lack of communication between the front line, brigade and divisional headquarters to the rear, it was not immediately clear that the third objective was secure, especially about Black Watch Corner. A message dropped at 11:20 a.m. by a contact RE8 of 4 Squadron at 1st Division headquarters put the matter beyond doubt, reporting that flares lighted by the infantry had been spotted along the third objective, and in some places in front of it.

The morning's achievement Second Army

There is little doubt that the morning's achievement greatly uplifted the spirits of the battalions now consolidating about the second and final objectives, as word of the general success spread along the line. Except at Tower Hamlets spur on the defensive right flank south of the Menin Road, where the enemy stubbornly held out, all the objectives had been taken and the *Wilhelm Stellung* was broken.

---

[408] This direct fire came at a range of around 1,750 yards from the *4th* and *5th Batteries* of the *241st Field Artillery Regiment (121st Division)* which was positioned at Molenaarelsthoek on the western side of the Broodseinde Ridge.

No German counter attacks of significance had occurred, although it was taken for granted that they would soon move to retake the vital position across the waist of the plateau, which had been so bitterly contested. But across the tortured ground in front of the forward infantry positions, now shimmering in the midday sun, there was little sign of enemy activity save for some sniping and machine gun fire from a few nests, some local shelling, and a few observers who were driven to ground by Lewis gun fire. It was unclear where the bulk of the enemy counter attack divisions were, but the major German effort to retake the plateau was still to come.

The attack of the Fifth Army 5:40 a.m. 20th September

General Gough's Fifth Army was to attack at 5:40 a.m. in conjunction with the Second Army with three corps which were to deploy five divisions along a front of approximately 8,400 yards, from 800 yards south of the Ypres - Roulers railway, to the line of the Ypres – Staden railway northeast of Langemarck, the distance to the final objectives being between 1,000 and 1,500 yards. The attack was to be carried out in two stages with only one intermediate objective, referred to as the Red Line, the final objective being the Green Line.

The objective of the V Corps, which was to attack on the right with the 9th and 55th Divisions, was the capture of the *Wilhelm Stellung*, from the Zonnebeke Redoubt, through the Bremen Redoubt, across Hill 37 to the Langemark – Zonnebeke road, and then northwest along the road to the point where the road crossed the Hanebeek at Schuler Farm. Each division in the corps had an attack frontage of around 1,800 yards, as opposed to the 1,000 yards front of 2nd and 1st Australian Divisions of Second Army to the right.

In the centre XVIII Corps was to attack with the 58th and 51st Divisions, the objective being to break the *Wilhelm Stellung* and reach a line from the Langemarck – Zonnebeke road crossing of the Hanebeek, north-east to Wurst Farm, then north across the Stroombeek 500 yards east of Hubner Farm, across the Lekkerboterbeek 750 yards east of Pheasant Trench, to a point 700 yards east of Eagle Trench. The corps frontage was around 3,200 yards.

On the left the XIV Corps using the 20th Division was to form a northern defensive flank along a front of around 1,200 yards, the objective being from the point 700 yards east of Eagle Trench, the line then following the Laudetbeek, finally swinging west to a point on the Ypres – Staden railway just north of Schreiboom.

The Artillery Fifth Army

As previously mentioned, Gough's plan for his artillery was to dispense with a long preparatory barrage, and instead fire a "hurricane" bombardment beginning twenty-four hours before the attack. In this way he hoped to improve the element of surprise. In contrast to the great build up of artillery in Second Army, the provision of guns for Fifth Army was to remain generally unchanged, having lost the guns of II Corps but now firing on a front 4,000 yards shorter. This situation did not allow for the five belt barrage of Second Army. The barrage was here limited to three or in some instances four belts, and as the guns had to spread their fire over a much longer front the overall gunfire support was therefore considerably weaker. Between them X Corps and 1st Anzac fielded a total of 1,295 guns of all calibers on a 4,000 yard front, whereas V Corps fielded 519 along a 3,600 yard front. The weight of artillery supporting 51st Division is typical of Fifth Army divisions. The division attacked with the 154th Brigade, which was supported by twenty-two 18-pounder batteries which fired 67,000 rounds on the 20th September and the same number on the 21st, six 4.5-inch howitzer batteries which fired 14,000 rounds on the 20th and the same number on the 21st, and twelve batteries of 6-inch howitzers which fired 5,551 rounds on the 20th. Also one battery of 6-inch and one of 9.2-inch guns, and one battery of 8-inch, three of 9.2-inch and one of 15-inch howitzers fired a total of 982 rounds in the first four and a half hours of the attack, all in support of 154th Brigade.

A typical barrage pattern was that fired by the artillery supporting 51st Highland Division of XVIII Corps. In the first belt the 18-pounder batteries of four brigades of Royal Field Artillery fired a creeping barrage initially falling 150 yards in front of the British positions, which advanced 100 yards in four minutes for the first 200 yards and then 100 yards every six minutes up to the first objective. At the first objective the barrage would stand for one hour and No. 3 gun of each battery would fire smoke to help conceal consolidation and the advance of supports. The barrage would then lift towards the final objective at the rate of 100 yards every eight minutes. Two hundred yards in front of the creeping barrage, a combing barrage was fired by the 18-pounders of one brigade of field artillery, while 300 yards beyond that all the 4.5-inch howitzers at the disposal of the division dwelt on pillboxes, strong-points and communication trenches. Beyond the combing barrage a neutralizing barrage of 6-inch howitzers and 60-pounder guns searched for further blockhouses and strong points, whilst beyond this a standing barrage of heavy howitzers and 60-pounder guns dwelt on the avenues of approach and probable assembly areas of the *Eingreif* divisions. The depressions behind the higher ground at Hill 37, Hill 40, and the Passchendaele and Gravenstafel ridges were all targeted by Fifth Army heavy guns searching for the assembly of the counter-attack divisions.

Although not on the same scale as Second Army, Fifth Army still arrayed an impressive number of heavy and medium guns, comprising in V Corps alone; 66 6-inch howitzers, 16 8-inch howitzers, 14 9.2-inch howitzers, 4 12-inch howitzers, 1 15-inch howitzer, 48 60-pounders, 8 6-inch guns, and 2 9.2-inch guns. V Corps field artillery comprised of 270 18-pounders and 90 4.5-inch howitzers. Total Fifth Army gun strength was, 798 18-pounders, 254 4.5-inch howitzers, 138 60-pounders, 4 6-inch howitzer (30cwt), 208 6-inch howitzer (26cwt), 20 6-inch (Mk VII) guns, 60 8-inch howitzers (Mk I-VI), 12 8-inch howitzers (Mk VII) 42 9.2-inch howitzers, 4 9.2-inch guns, 16 12-inch howitzers, 1 12-inch gun and 3 15-inch howitzers.[409]

The attack towards the Zonnebeke and Bremen Redoubts, Hill 37, and the Lower Hanebeek

V Corps
Lieutenant -General E. A. Fanshaw

Across the whole of Fifth Army front, it was V Corps which had by far the toughest task to accomplish. On the 16th, 22nd and 27th August XIX Corps had carried out despairing attacks across the same awful ground, only to be driven back virtually to their starting line in front of the fortresses of Potsdam, Vampir, Borry, Iberian, Pommern, Gallipoli and Somme, which guarded the approaches to Bremen Redoubt, Hill 35 and Hill 37 across which ran the *Wilhelm Stellung*. Despite the efforts of the heavy artillery to smash them, the blockhouses were still operational and presented a formidable task to overcome. V Corps was weaker than 1st Anzac (to its right) in heavy and medium guns, (159 against 208), but it was better provided with field guns, (369 against 216), these guns however firing across a wider front. The bitter lessons of the previous attacks had been learned and the necessity to comprehensively clear out the bunkers and blockhouses as the advance went forward was of paramount importance. To this end the usual practice of mopping-up parties had been dispensed with, in favour of special assault groups up to half a platoon strong, which had been trained especially to seize and most importantly occupy the blockhouses. Although the weather had sufficiently improved to allow the battlefield to partially dry out, in places such as the Hanebeek valley it still presented a quagmire with knee deep mud, and in many other areas the ground was very heavy and exhausting to advance across.

Holding the positions in front of V Corps were parts of four German regiments, the *60th (121st Division)*, and the *77th Reserve, 15th Reserve*, and *91st Reserve*, (of the *2nd Guard Reserve Division*). *121st Division* was worn out having been in the line since the 19th August, but *2nd Guard Reserve* was comparatively fresh having been in the line since the 13th September.

---

[409] National Archives, GHQ statistics, distribution of artillery, noon 14th September. WO95/15

9th (Scottish) Division[410]
Major-General H. T. Lukin

Moving from their camps near Ypres on the 12th September, by the 16th to 17th September 9th Division had relieved 42nd Division on Frezenberg ridge. The dangers of the Ypres Salient were again made brutally clear to the division for as the 11th Royal Scots detrained at the Asylum sidings a heavy shell landed causing around 50 casualties. On the night of the 19th the assaulting battalions moved up along the duckboard tracks made treacherous by the overnight rainfall, but thankfully enemy shelling was slight and few casualties occurred. By 5:00 a.m. on the 20th the division was assembled for the attack. The division was to attack with two brigades, the 27th astride the Ypres – Roulers railway, (with the 5th Australian Brigade to its right), across the lower Hanebeek valley towards the northern end of Anzac spur and the Zonnebeke Redoubt, and to the north of the railway towards Potsdam Redoubt. To the left of the 27th, the South African Brigade were to attack towards the Bremen Redoubt across one of the most bitterly contested and squalid parts of the whole battlefield.

A novelty of the divisional artillery arrangements was that on the insistence of the divisional commander Major-General Lukin, the 18-pounders of the protective creeping barrage would fire a mixture of high explosive and smoke shells in place of the usual shrapnel. It was believed this would help overcome the strongly held blockhouses and fortified positions, which proved to be the case. If stubborn local resistance was encountered the gunfire would stand upon that position, whilst most of the barrage crept forward. This gave the infantry the chance to surround the position and attack it from all sides once the guns lifted, a refinement not practicable when firing shrapnel. The divisional machine guns were to play an active part in the barrage, approximately 30 guns firing on to the final objective until the infantry reached the first objective at which point they would lift on to an S.O.S. line in front of the final objective. Around 20 guns would also be taken forward with the assaulting battalions to help strengthen consolidation against counter attacks. A similar procedure was applied throughout Fifth Army. The 2-inch trench mortar and Stokes mortar batteries also added their fire to the barrage. At 5:40 a.m. the attack began behind the creeping barrage which was described as first rate. The visibility was down to around 50 yards due to the mist, which helped the attackers who could identify the German strong points, but were themselves only vaguely visible to the enemy.

27th Brigade [411]
The brigade attacked with three battalions in the line, the 6th King's Own Scottish Borderers, the 9th Cameronians (Scottish Rifles), and the 12th Royal Scots, with the 11th Royal Scots in support. The K.O.S.B. was soon confronted by the remains of Hanebeek Wood in a quagmire along the stream, which held a number of German pillboxes. The field-guns firing on the wood stood on that target, high explosive shells ripping into the roots and stumps and throwing them high into the air, keeping the German machine guns suppressed and partly blinded by the additional smoke. To the left of the wood a company of the K.O.S.B. moving forward to outflank the pillboxes, intercepted and killed a party of Germans attempting to reinforce their positions in the wood. When the barrage lifted, the wood which was by then surrounded was attacked from the front and rear by both the K.O.S.B. and by parties of the 5th Australian Brigade, and the pillboxes overwhelmed before their machine guns could be brought into action. Four machine guns and about 50 prisoners were taken. The K.O.S.B. casualties were light, but were caused mainly by enemy rifle fire and friendly shrapnel, being fired by the neighboring division into the right flank of the wood. The K.O.S.B. then moved on to the first objective east of the Hanebeek.

To the left of the K.O.S.B. the 9th Scottish Rifles encountered little opposition reaching the first objective behind the barrage, but the left company north of the railway line was seriously held up by machine gun fire from a series of pillboxes, R1, R2, R3, R4 and R5, dug into the

---

[410] John Ewing (1921) *The History of the 9th (Scottish) Division 1914-1919* London: John Murray pp222-245
[411] National Archives, War Diary 27th Brigade WO95/1772

railway bank, which were also covered in enfilade by the Potsdam machine guns about 100 yards north of the railway. A support company of the 12th Royal Scots was detailed to seize the pillboxes in the railway bank up to the Red Line, but the attack was immediately held up by machine gun fire and bombs hurled from R1. Two platoons of the reserve company of the 12th Royal Scots were then ordered to attack the pillboxes from the southern side of the railway. This movement distracted the garrison sufficiently to allow it to be rushed by the platoons on the railway who captured 40 prisoners and three machine guns. The resistance on the railway soon gave way and the right company of 12th Royal Scots advanced to the Red Line. The left company of the battalion was to capture a strong-point called "A" and also the Potsdam position. Machine gun fire from "A" held up the advance, but Captain Reynolds supported by six men, moving from shell-hole to shell-hole under consistent fire, rushed the bunker and attempted to throw a Mills bomb through the loophole. The attempt was thwarted by the garrison who blocked the aperture with a pack while keeping up their fire. The machine gun was causing a major hold up and the attacking party persevered, Captain Reynolds finally forcing a phosphorous bomb through the loophole, the explosion setting the bunker on fire and smoking out the garrison, 7 prisoners and two machine guns being captured. Captain Reynolds was to be awarded the VC for his conspicuous bravery in this action.

At the Potsdam strong-point two machine guns were in action in the open, holding up the left of the 12th Royal Scots. Two platoons made a frontal assault whilst a third assisted by two parties of South Africans outflanked the position and attacked from the north, as another platoon attacked from the south. The garrison was quickly overpowered and 70 prisoners and the two machine guns were captured, the left company of the 12th Royal Scots then advancing to the Red Line.

All the assault battalions, except for the two left companies of the Scottish Rifles which had been held up by the pillboxes on the railway, were now on the Red Line and here the creeping barrage stood for one hour, whilst mopping-up and consolidation continued and the support companies which were to carry the attack forward to the Green Line assembled. On the right the support company of the K.O.S.B. had already suffered severely from the enemy's barrage, resulting in the whole battalion being required in the attack upon the Green Line. Two companies of the 11th Royal Scots in brigade reserve were then requested to support the K.O.S.B. on the Red Line. Due to the late arrival of the left companies of the Scottish Rifles, the right companies were swung towards the railway, one platoon keeping touch with the K.O.S.B. on the right. By the time the barrage began its forward creep towards the Green Line all attacking companies were up in line. The advance was virtually trouble free, a solitary German machine gun in a shell hole being outflanked by the K.O.S.B. and its crew bayoneted. The garrison at Zonnebeke Redoubt had no stomach for a fight and 40 prisoners were taken. The Scottish Rifles and Royal Scots were equally successful, two pillboxes in front of the Rifles putting up slight resistance.

The Green Line was reached up with the barrage and consolidation began, linking shell-holes by short sections of trench, while the operation was covered by Lewis guns in craters forward of the line. No enemy retaliatory action hampered this work, but a low flying aircraft gave rough indication of the position to the German artillery which sent over a few shells. The opportunity was taken by half the men to clean their rifles whilst the other half stood guard, and the divisional machine guns were brought forward to further strengthen the new position.

South African Brigade [412]
The 3rd South African Regiment attacked on the right and the 4th to the left of the brigade front. Machine gun fire from the fortified area at Potsdam House initially held up the 3rd. The commanding officer of the 1st Regiment moving up in support of the 3rd gathered a party of 50 men with two Lewis guns and a machine gun, and attacked the position from the rear, capturing 25 prisoners and 7 machine guns. This attack, with another led by Captain Sprenger of the 3rd Regiment, in cooperation with the 12th Royal Scots on their right, soon outflanked and secured

---

[412] National Archives, War Diary South African Brigade WO95/5345

the position. On the left, Borry Farm and Beck House which had caused so many problems previously, were treated to the same isolating barrage of high explosive and smoke which had been successful at Hanebeek Wood, and before they could bring their machine guns into action were outflanked and overrun by the 4th Regiment.

Both regiments arrived on the Red Line on time and during the one hour pause the 1st and 2nd Regiments moved up in support. At 7:08 a.m. they followed the lifting barrage towards the Green Line. On the right the 1st Regiment advanced to the Green Line without incident, but on the left, due to the 55th Division being seriously held up on their left flank, the 2nd Regiment had great difficulty getting forward, receiving enfilade machine gun fire from German positions at Waterend House, Tulip Cottages, and Hill 37, which tore into their flank. A large gap now developed between the 165th Brigade of the 55th Division and the South Africans. Fighting their way forward the 2nd Regiment eventually carried Zevencote and Bremen Redoubt, and threw back a defensive left flank protected by machine guns along the marshy Zonnebeke stream to cover the gap. During this attack Lance-Corporal William Henry Hewitt of the 2nd Regiment, though twice wounded attacked a pillbox single handedly which had been holding up the advance, and eventually throwing a bomb through the loophole dislodged the occupants. Lance-Corporal Hewitt was to be awarded the V.C. for his gallantry.

Consolidation of the Green Line commenced but losses to the 2nd Regiment, (half their strength) were so heavy they had to be reinforced by 5th Scottish Rifles of 26th Brigade from divisional reserve. Casualties for the whole South African Brigade from the night of the 19th / 20th September, until its relief on the night of the 21st / 22nd September were tragically high. Out of initial brigade strength of 91 officers and 2,488 other ranks, 51 officers and 1,204 other ranks became casualties, 16 officers and 237 other ranks being killed.

A German counter attack made by three companies of the *60th Regiment*, the line regiment of *121st Division*, attempted to move forward north of the railway against the South Africans. It was quickly seen and came under a "fearful drum-fire", which broke it up into small parties attempting to infiltrate forward. These parties came under heavy rifle fire when within 300 yards of the British line and were unable to approach further. Along the whole divisional front the *Wilhelm Stellung* had been broken, the new position consolidated on the Green Line, and the awful areas around Potsdam, Borry Farm and Beck House finally overrun. As with X Corps on the plateau, and I Anzac on Anzac spur, the main German counter-attack effort was yet to be faced by 9th Division.

55th Division (1st West Lancashire Division)[413]
Major-General H. S. Jeudwine

The ground over which the division was about to attack was the same ground over which it had fought on the 31st July, and almost from the same line which it had established on that day. Once again the key objective of 55th Division was Hill 37, at the right of the divisional front, across the top of which ran the *Wilhelm Stellung*. The line of pillboxes at Schuler galleries and the blockhouses at Schuler Farm presented a familiar major obstacle on the left flank of the division. In the action of the 31st July the division had suffered grievous casualties losing around 150 officers and 3,500 other ranks. Whilst in camp at St. Omer these losses had not been totally replaced in time for the attack on the 20th September. About 1,000 men arrived too late for training and had to be left behind when the division began its move to the front, which resulted in the division entering the line under-strength and deficient in training. However the divisional history claims that it returned to the line on the 12th September, 'thoroughly refreshed, rested, re-equipped, in splendid spirits, and thoroughly on its mettle'.[414] The division was destined to

---

[413] Rev. J. O. Coop (1919) *The Story of the 55th (West Lancs) Division* Liverpool: Daily Post Printers pp46-64

[414] Rev. J. O. Coop (1919) *The Story of the 55th (West Lancs) Division* Liverpool: Daily Post Printers p56

have the most costly fight of the day. German observers of the *91st Reserve Regiment* had noticed, at least three days before Zero, the tapes marking the jumping off points, and were therefore prepared for the imminent attack. The front battalion of the *91st Reserve* had been relieved by a fresh battalion during the night of the 18th / 19th and the machine gun companies had been relieved without loss during a lull in the British bombardment.

    The jumping-off points were to be mainly from shell-holes just forward of the British Front Line, the support companies being established in the old German front line a little to the rear. At the outset the forward companies of the 165th and 164th Brigades advancing to the assault as their protective barrage began its forward creep, were smitten by an accurate German barrage of 4.2 and 5.9 shells which targeted the jump-off line and the assembly trenches to the rear, causing considerable casualties and much confusion. A hail of machine gun and rifle fire from the pre-warned German lines also ripped in to the front companies as they began to deploy. Companies of the support battalions of the 166th Brigade in divisional reserve were soon to become involved in the confused and bitter fighting. Communication with the front line was poor, and at the headquarters of the three brigades and the two supporting artillery groups in the tunnelled dug-out at Wieltje information was scanty and slow in arriving. The mist and subsequent smoke made visual communication with the front virtually impossible and the heavy German barrage had severed most phone lines. Casualties amongst runners were heavy and under these conditions there was little chance of giving artillery support where it was needed, other than by the pre-arranged barrages.

                                           Map next page.

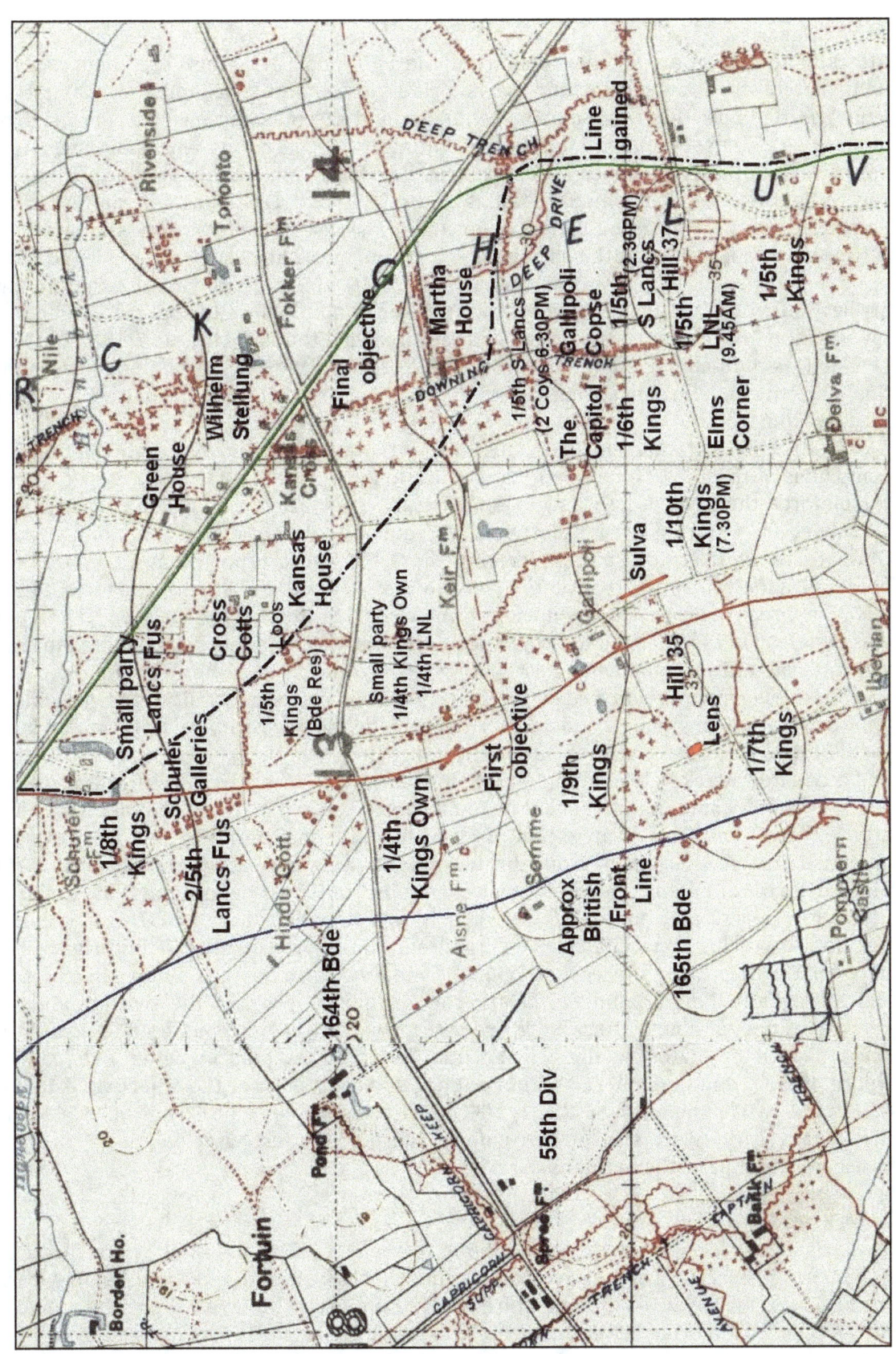

The attack on the *Wilhelm Stellung* 165th and 164th Brigades - 55th Division

165th Brigade [415]

Attacking to the right of the divisional front, the 1/7th and 1/9th King's Liverpool Regiment were immediately struck by the machine gun and rifle fire from the blockhouses at Kaynorth, Iberian, Lens and Gallipoli. Due to casualties, confusion and the morning mist the forward companies omitted to clear some enemy dugouts, resulting in the garrisons emerging and engaging the advancing support companies with machine gun fire. Both battalions were fully engaged in severe fighting in which some companies of the 1/5th and 1/6th King's in support also became embroiled. On hearing firing behind them the forward companies either stopped or began to retire, and to a large extent the barrage was lost, and as we have seen a gap opened between the brigade and the South Africans on the right. By 6:45 a.m. and after intense fighting, with little artillery support, Iberian and Kaynorth were taken, but at 7:08 as the barrage began to move on towards the final objective the brigade had not reached the Red Line. At 7:45 the blockhouse at Lens fell, as did Gallipoli soon after around 8:00. By this time the barrage had moved on to the final objective but German strong-points still held out about Hill 35, causing severe casualties to the attacking troops.

At 9:45 long after the South Africans on the right had secured their final objective, two companies of the 1/5th Loyal North Lancashire Regiment from divisional reserve were ordered to reinforce the 1/6th King's and to attack Hill 37. At around 11:20 the Loyal North Lancs. succeeded in capturing the hill but were subsequently driven off by a counter attack by local German reserves. To the south of the hill the 1/5th King's reported at 11:45 that they were holding Ditch Trench, but that no one was on their left and the enemy appeared to be holding Hill 37 in great strength. Meanwhile it became clear that the ground between Hill 35 and Hill 37 was not clear of the enemy and firing from occupied strong-points was making movement very difficult. The officer commanding 1/9th King's was ordered to gather as many men as possible and form two mopping-up waves to clear the Germans out as quickly as possible, prior to another attack being made against Hill 37 as soon as the necessary reinforcements had arrived. By 2:00 p.m. the eastern side of Hill 35 including the Sulva blockhouse was clear of the enemy, and a counter attack between 2:00 and 2:30 was driven off by artillery fire. Two companies of the 1/5th South Lancashire Regiment from divisional reserve arrived around 2:30 with orders to attack Hill 37 with the co-operation of all available men from 1/9th and 1/6th King's, and in conjunction with this attack from the west, 1/5th King's were ordered to attack from their position south of the hill. The attack was seen to be under way at around 3:35 p.m. but no firm news of progress arrived until 5:10 when it was reported that Hill 37 was secure and the position was being consolidated. Four-hundred yards north of Hill 37 the brigade held a line between Capitol, (250 yards east of Gallipoli) and Keir Farm dugouts. But a gap existed between Hill 37 and this line, around the position of Gallipoli Copse and the two remaining support companies of 1/5th South Lancs were ordered forward to capture and hold the copse. This they accomplished by 6:20 p.m. the brigade then being on its final objective between Waterend House, Hill 37, and Gallipoli Copse, but about 500 yards short of the objective at Keir Farm. At 7:30 p.m. two companies of the 1/10th King's (Liverpool Scottish) from 166th Brigade in divisional reserve were sent up to reinforce the position just west of Hill 37, in readiness to resist any attempt by the Germans to retake the hill.

164th Brigade [416]

The brigade attacked with three battalions in the line, the 1/4th King' Own Royal Lancaster Regiment,[417] the 2/5th Lancashire Fusiliers and the 1/8th King's Liverpool Regiment (Liverpool Irish). The 1/4th Loyal North Lancashire was in support of the 1/4th King's Own, and the 1/5th King's Own was in brigade reserve. From the outset the brigade were smitten by shell, rifle, and machine gun fire, as were the 165th to their right. The weight of the enemy barrage falling on the assembly positions of the support battalion, the 1/4th Loyals caused them to move forward to the

---

[415] National Archives, War Diary 165th Brigade WO95/2925
[416] National Archives, War Diary 164th Brigade WO95/2921
[417] National Archives, War Diary 4th King's Own WO95/2922

extent that they became intermixed with the 1/4th King's Own and became prematurely involved in the fighting. Having suffered significant casualties and subsequent disorganization, the 1/4th King's Own in their advance past Aisne Farm had failed to clear a number of German positions, with which the 1/4th Loyals now became engaged. Both battalions were hit by heavy enfilade machine gun fire from the direction of Gallipoli and Hill 35 on their right, making re-organization very difficult.

In the centre the 2/5th Lancs. Fusiliers advancing towards their first objective, a line of interconnected machine gun nests at Schuler Galleries, immediately came under a hail of machine gun fire from their left flank, and also from a post north of the Hanebeek 800 yards further forward. The fire was so heavy that the battalion lost half its number in the advance towards the right section of Schuler Galleries, which nonetheless they proceeded to capture. The left battalion, the Liverpool Irish, whose first objective was the left section of Schuler Galleries, came under the same withering fire, their advance being even more disorganized. The two support companies which were to carry forward the attack beyond the German position were, due to casualties in the leading waves, in action before the position was taken. Under heavy machine gun fire from the direction of Kansas Cross, after very heavy fighting, and only after the southern section of the Galleries was secured by the Lancs Fusiliers, did the Liverpool Irish take the northern section. The Galleries where then fully occupied. At 7:08 a.m. and in very small numbers the Fusiliers followed the creeping barrage forward from the Red Line towards the Green Line on the Langemarck – Zonnebeke road, some actually reaching their objective, but in such small numbers that holding the position was impossible and communication with these advanced posts was lost.

At around 10:00 a.m. some 500 Germans were seen to be massing behind the *Wilhelm Stellung* between Nile and Fokker Farm. Communication with the artillery was now thankfully established and this concentration was devastated by an artillery barrage and machine gun fire. A second attempt a few hours later by a similar number of the enemy from the same position suffered a similar fate. The enemy casualties were said to be appalling.

The 1/4th King's Own on the right meanwhile, had established a position on the Dotted Red Line but in no great strength. The support battalion, the 1/4th Loyals as we have seen had been hard hit by machine gun fire from Gallipoli on their right, and around 8:00 a.m. some had become involved in taking the Gallipoli blockhouse with the 165th Brigade. Those of the battalion who got forward to the position of the 1/4th King's Own on the Dotted Red Line were in insufficient numbers to continue the advance to the Green Line, and had in any case missed the barrage.

The 1/5th King's Own in brigade reserve had already been deployed and had also become hopelessly intermingled with the other assaulting battalions. Despite the best efforts of the brigade commander Brigadier -General C. I. Stockwell, due to the weight of hostile fire and the dreadful state of the ground, it had proved impossible to effectively control the brigade attack. In an attempt to establish some control those parties of the 1/5th King's Own who could be assembled were concentrated around the Loos blockhouse, about 600 yards west of Kansas Cross, where they were to establish a position in readiness to engage any counter-attack. Further confusion existed on the far left where at 11:10 a.m. a report from the 58th Division indicated that Schuler Farm, near the final objective of the Liverpool Irish had fallen to that battalion. At 2:30 p.m. 164th Brigade reported that the farm had not fallen, and by 4:25 it was confirmed that the farm was still in enemy hands and that hostile machine gun fire was causing problems. Schuler Farm did not fall to the 1/8th Liverpool Irish until 4:30 p. m. on the following day.

The fighting across the whole front of the division had been severe and confused, due mainly to the fact that the Germans were well prepared and ready, and from the start had broken up the cohesion of the initial advance of the attack, which was never fully regained. Nevertheless through dogged fighting, sometimes with little support from reserves or artillery, and across some atrocious ground, the division had largely won through and was on most of its objectives. The 165th Brigade, had fought its way up alongside the South Africans, and was on the Green Line except at Keir Farm, and most importantly the *Wilhelm Stellung* had been broken between Waterend House and across Hill 37. On the left 164th Brigade held the Dotted Red Line in strength with outposts pushed forward in shell-holes and old German defence positions up to the Green Line, although touch with these forward positions had largely been lost.

It is a worthwhile exercise to examine the results of this days fighting by the 55th Division with limited objectives, with the fighting of the 31st July, when some parties of 164th Brigade had got up onto Gravenstafel ridge at Aviatik Farm, only to be driven back to the Steenbeek. Casualties for the division on the 20th September were high at nearly 2,000 of whom around 170 were killed, but were not nearly as bad as those of nearly 3,500 on the 31st July.

XVIII Corps
Lieutenant -General Sir Ivor Maxse

Although better than it had been in August, the ground east of the Steenbeek between St. Julien and Langemarck, across which XVIII Corps were to attack was pitted with endless water filled shell-holes, and still very muddy and heavy going, the delicate network of drainage ditches having been destroyed by the guns. The primary objectives of the Corps were the western end of the Gravenstafel ridge, being little more than 30 metres above sea level, to be attacked by the 58th Division, and the western end of the Poelcappelle spur where the ground rose to barely 20 meters, to be attacked by the 51st Division. Both spurs presented low ridges running westward from the main Passchendaele ridge and along the western extremities of both, between 1,500 and 1,700 yards east of the Steenbeek ran the *Wilhelm Stellung*. Successful capture of the higher ground would allow for the safer deployment of the forward batteries along the Steenbeek valley, in preparation for the advance upon Poelcappelle. The tanks, which had been successful in previous operations in the area, were again to support the infantry in capturing German strong-points accessible from the St. Julien to Winnipeg and the St. Julien to Poelcappelle roads. Thirty tanks of I Tank Brigade were allotted, two companies of E Battalion to support 58th Division and one company of D Battalion to support 51st Division. As testimony to the state of the ground made infinitely worse by the shelling, only one tank succeeded in reaching its objective.

58th (2/1st London) Division
Major-General H. D. Fanshawe

On the 16th August the 48th Division had attacked towards the Gravenstafel ridge with precious little success. On the 19th and 22nd August the line had been pushed a little further forward. The 58th Division was now to attack across the same ground. The division was to use two brigades, but in a more subtle way than the usual method of direct frontal attack. Rather than make a direct attack up the face of the ridge, the right brigade, the 173rd, was to feint a frontal attack against the Winnipeg crossroads and along the Langemarck – Zonnebeke road towards the ridge, whilst the left brigade the 174th made the main attack moving initially east, and then in a generally south-easterly direction along the ridge, getting behind the *Wilhelm Stellung* defences and taking them in the rear. Divisional artillery was detailed to fire standing barrages of gas shell onto approach valleys and tracks in an attempt to further isolate the forward German positions. Defending the *Wilhelm Stellung* in front of 58th Division were the *175th Regiment* and part of the *128th Regiment* of the *36th Division*.

173rd Brigade [418]
One battalion, the 2/4th London was used in the holding attack, which as an additional task and with the assistance of two tanks was to assist 164th Brigade in taking Schuler Farm. The tank support failed to arrive, bogged down in the mud before reaching the farm, and heavy machine gun fire from the farm checked the London, the task then falling to the Liverpool Irish. As we

---

[418] National Archives, War Diary 173rd Brigade WO95/3000

have seen the farm was not secured until the following day. The holding attack however was successful. Advancing behind a creeping barrage which was described as excellent and contained a large proportion of smoke shell to obscure their movement the 2/4th moved forward 400 yards to capture the Winnipeg crossroads on the Langemarck – Zonnebeke road.

174th Brigade [419]
The main thrust of the divisional attack, to be delivered in a somewhat novel manoeuvre was to come from the Vancouver – Keerselare position on the left, and after passing through the German Third Line was to swing right, or south-east up the western end of Gravenstafel ridge. The thick early-morning mist, although concealing the movement from the enemy also hampered sense of both direction and distance.

The attack was led by the 2/8th London (Post Office Rifles) on a one battalion front, supported in turn by the 2/5th London (London Rifle Brigade), and the 2/6th London (Rifles). The brigade jumping-off line was only 500 yards from the *Wilhelm Stellung*, and the strong-points on that line were quickly overrun by the 2/8th London, whose movements were largely obscured from German observers by the mist and by the smoke shell in the barrage.[420]

Machine gun fire from fortified shell-holes and from Hubner and Dimple Trench caused casualties and machine gun fire from the blockhouses at Hubner Farm on the eastern side of the *Wilhelm Stellung* defences checked the 2/8th. The farm was surrounded with assistance from a party of 9th Royal Scots sent from 154th Brigade on the left, and the 2/5th London in support, and the garrison of over 70 men surrendered. Sergeant Alfred Joseph Knight of 2/8th London, (Post Office Rifles) was awarded the V.C. for his extraordinarily good work, exceptional bravery and initiative during this attack. Single-handed, he rushed twelve of the enemy in a shell-hole, bayoneted two and shot a third, the remainder scattering and abandoning a machine gun. Shortly afterwards he rushed a machine gun in action, bayoneted the gunner and captured the gun. The 2/8th was now on the Red Line from Marine View, through Genoa, to Hubner Farm. At this point the 2/5th and 2/6th London passed through and with great precision moved south-east along the top of the ridge taking the German strong-points from the rear. Much care had been taken in training for this enveloping manoeuvre, and each platoon had a definite objective, pillbox, or emplacement to clear and occupy. The German defenders, attacked seemingly from front and rear by an enemy who was difficult to see through the mist and smoke, soon gave way, and six officers and 285 men were taken prisoner, and 50 machine guns were captured. An outpost line was established in shell-holes between Stropp and Von Tirpitz Farms, and a large section of the *Wilhelm Stellung* on 58th Division front had fallen. Outpost groups then moved north and into the depression of the Stroombeek to the divisional boundary near Flora Cottages, where contact was established with the 9th Royal Scots of 51st Division, and consolidation of the new position began.

A competent plan and thorough training had produced excellent results. The attack had been a model of manoeuvre, somewhat unique in the fighting at Third Ypres, but its total success had come at the cost of nearly 1,250 casualties of whom sadly approaching 260 had been killed.

51st (Highland) Division[421]

In the line between Keerselare, and the Langemarck – White Huts road, the division was to attack with the 154th Brigade towards the shallow Lekkerboterbeek valley in the centre, and on the left, up a gentle gradient towards the low Poelcappelle spur, no feature in this area much influencing the general flatness of the ground. The primary objective of the attack was to secure

---

[419] National Archives, War Diary 174th Brigade WO95/3003
[420] The enemy barrage gradually increased, reaching its height around 6:45 a.m. and being maintained until 11:00 and falling mostly along the line Arbre – Marine View – Hubner Farm and forward to Von Tirpitz Farm and Stroppe Farm.
[421] Major F.W. Bewsher (1921) *The History of the 51st (Highland) Division* Edinburgh: William Blackwood pp192-232

an advantageous jump-off point for a subsequent assault upon Poelecappelle, the distance to this line being approximately 1,500 yards. The first objective was on a line from Flora Cottages and the confluence of the Stroombeek with the Lekkerboterbeek, to Delta Huts and White House. The final objective was along the line Quebec Farm, Beer Trench, Church Trench, Delta House, to Rose House 150 yards east of Kangaroo Trench.

In some ways the German defence system here was unique in the Salient, as it included major defended trench systems, as well as the usual blockhouses. The powerful breastworks of Pheasant Trench on the *Wilhelm Stellung* presented a major obstacle and lay about 150 yards beyond the brigade jumping-off line. About 150 yards beyond the trench and near the first objective was the strong-point of Pheasant Farm, at the foot of Poelcappelle spur, and 1,000 yards beyond the trench lay Kangaroo Trench another formidable earthwork. Artillery support for the attacking brigade was impressive, but did not drive the Germans entirely from their shelters in Pheasant Trench.

Once again the smashed drainage system and mass of water filled shell-holes presented conditions of a dreadful muddy quagmire, although improving to a degree towards the higher ground. The bold decision of the divisional commander to use only one brigade was made after careful consideration. It was believed that the number of defenders holding the forward positions would be limited by the number of concrete shelters, Mebus, or fortified farms available to shelter them, as in no other positions would they be protected from the British shelling. The garrisons of these blockhouses although small in number, would most likely survive the shelling and could cause heavy casualties to a dense wave of attackers, whereas the attackers were they to be successful, would only bag a limited number of German prisoners. In any case 152nd Brigade was in close support should the necessity arise.

Confronting the 51st Division along the *Wilhelm Stellung* defences were part of the *128th Regiment* and the *5th Grenadiers* of the German *36th Division,* each regiment holding around 800 – 900 yards of the front. Both regiments had been in the line since the 8th September, with one battalion in the outpost zone, one in support, and one in reserve behind the Flanders 1 Line. The *5th Grenadiers* opposite the 4th Seaforth and 4th Gordons, had an average company strength of 2 officers, 10 N.C.O.'s and 65 men. The regiment possessed 35 heavy and 32 light machine guns, and 12 *Minenwerfer,* but much of this equipment had been made unserviceable by the British bombardment.

154th Brigade [422]

The overnight rainfall caused the usual difficulties for the troops moving up with treacherous duckboards and water filled muddy shell-holes. The assembly was carried out successfully but with 27 casualties. The brigade was to attack with two battalions in the line, the 9th Royal Scots to the right, and the 4th Seaforth Highlanders to the left to take the first objective, with the 7th Argyll and Sutherland Highlanders and the 4th Gordon Highlanders in support to take the final objective.

As "A" and "B" Companies of the Royal Scots moved off behind the barrage, they were immediately engaged by machine gun and rifle fire from Pheasant Trench. "C" Company in support of "A" Company, and whose main task was the capture of the first objective, soon became involved in the attack on the trench. With great skill and determination, moving from shell-hole to shell-hole in twos and threes the assault parties infiltrated towards the trench, while supporting covering fire from rifles, Lewis guns and rifle grenades were poured into the German position. The defences were soon overwhelmed and "C" Company continued its advance towards the first objective. To the left "B" Company supported by "D" Company were similarly engaged, but the centre of "B" Company quickly entered Pheasant Trench. The two platoons on the left were however seriously held up by heavy machine gun fire from the trench, and a potentially dangerous situation arose as the assault parties retired to the British lines. Realizing the danger, the company commander with the battalion intelligence officer and the artillery liaison officer rapidly reorganized the men, and with parties of the 7th Argyll and Sutherland,

---

[422] National Archives, War Diary 154th Brigade WO95/2884

which were to go on to take the final objective, again advanced towards the trench. Meanwhile the right platoons already established in the trench had fought their way along it to the left, and with the fresh attack from the front the machine gun was knocked out and the position soon fell. The 4th Seaforth attacking to the left, mainly north of the Lekkerboterbeek, also encountered serious resistance from Pheasant Trench. The Germans had recently constructed new machine gun posts in shell-holes up to 40 yards in front of their line, and heavy fire was encountered from other machine guns sited on top of the numerous blockhouses, as well as from Pheasant Trench itself. The company attacking the trench were held up, and again had to gradually infiltrate forward from shell-hole to shell-hole, covered by Lewis guns and rifle grenades. The support company detailed to secure the first objective quickly assessed the situation and proceeded to move to attack the trench from a different position. Much hand-to-hand fighting ensued in which the Seaforth was entirely victorious, and the trench was taken. The fire of three machine guns from the trench and from a pillbox 30 yards beyond held up the left company until the guns were eventually knocked out, the enemy fighting most gallantly about the pillbox, where 30 were killed. At this point Pheasant Trench was entirely in British hands.

On the right meanwhile, "C" Company of the 9th Royal Scots continued their advance towards the first objective, having a stiff fight in front of Flora Cottages where around 15 Germans were killed. Enfilade machine gun fire from Hubner Farm 300 yards south of the divisional boundary, in 58th Division sector, was causing casualties, the company commander detaching two Lewis gun and two rifle sections to assist the 2/8th London. The party brought the farm under heavy fire for twenty minutes, inflicting such severe casualties upon the enemy that the 2/8th London was able to take it by frontal attack. The first objective was reached successfully by the Royal Scots "D" Company on the left of the battalion, although in weakened numbers due to the fighting for Pheasant Trench. The first objective had also been gained by 4th Seaforth on the brigade left. Pheasant Farm and Delta Huts had been taken and consolidation of the line was commenced.

The British artillery fire targeted against Pheasant Trench had been extremely heavy and the resolute German defence of the position had been all the more notable because of it. The ferocity of the fighting was now obvious. One 200 yard section of the trench contained 150 German dead, so overwhelming and ferocious had been the attack of the Royal Scots and Seaforth, and in the machine gun outposts the artillery had also taken a fearful toll. A huge quantity of rifle ammunition had been used to subdue the German positions and 12,000 rounds were sent up to the companies now holding the first objective.

The German retaliatory barrage had commenced about five minutes after the British attack had begun and fell predominantly between the original front line and the Langemarck road. But it also fell in front of that line where it caught "D" Company of the 7th Argyll and Sutherland, (who were detailed to attack the final objective), as they advanced. Further casualties had been suffered by both the Argyll and Sutherland and the 4th Gordon in the attack on Pheasant Trench, and they were in depleted numbers as they prepared to move off under the barrage as it lifted towards the final objective. The Argyll and Sutherland took Flora Cottages, crossed the Stroombeek and attacked and took Quebec Farm, supported mainly by the firing of rifle grenades. Bavaroise House was also taken with about 30 prisoners, and Church Trench was occupied. Of the four machine guns captured one was turned on the enemy with good results. The battalion was on the final objective at around 8:25 a.m. and within site of Poelcappelle village 750 yards to the north.

The 4th Gordon Highlanders which were to attack the final objective had already come under fire and lost five officers whilst forming up under the barrage. Following the curtain of shells, within one hundred yards the defence stiffened about Pheasant Farm Cemetery, where a Lance-Corporal was successful in capturing 28 prisoners and two machine guns. There was stiff fighting as the advance continued with bunkers at Malta House, Delta House and Rose House being taken up towards the final objective, on reaching which the Gordons were reduced to three officers and six platoons of about ten men each with which to hold the line. Two officers with the reserve company of the battalion were sent up to reinforce.

To the north of 51st Division, 20th Division had run into severe difficulties and was not up alongside. A defensive flank to a depth of 1,000 yards had therefore to be swung back by the 4th Seaforth and 4th Gordon to protect the left of the division. Under these circumstances the final objective on the far left could not be achieved, the line forward at Rose House being bent back towards the west to White House.

The 7th Argyll and Sutherland attempted to consolidate between Quebec Farm and Church Trench but in too few numbers, and requested the support of two platoons of the 9th Royal Scots. The latter battalion was unable to oblige and two platoons of the 8th Argyll and Sutherland of 152nd Brigade were sent up from divisional reserve. The severity of the German barrage is indicated by the fact that only 30 men out of the two platoons reached the 7th Argyll in the line. Soon after when consolidation was barely under way, the German barrage, which had been steadily pounding away at the Steenbeek valley, drew back its bombardment and began to shell heavily the western end of the Poelcappelle spur and the Stroombeek. The forward movement of reserves and machine gun teams was severely hampered by this shelling which caused many casualties, and was testimony to the inability of Fifth Army counter-battery fire to suppress the German artillery.

The exposed left flank was obvious to the Germans, and at 11:45 a.m. they demonstrated against the positions held by the 4th Gordon. Rifle and Lewis gun fire broke up this attack, which the enemy repeated at 12:30 p.m. in greater numbers but with similar results. To strengthen the position held by the 4th Gordon north of the Lekkerboterbeek, "A" Company of the 8th Argyll and Sutherland were sent up into the line north of the stream, two platoons deployed in Stroom Trench just south-east of the Poelcappelle road, and two platoons on a line from that road through Pheasant Farm Cemetery to just north of Delta Huts.

The sole tank of "B" Battalion of the I Tank Brigade to come into action reached Malta House about this time where it broke down, subsequently being used as a company headquarters, two of its Lewis guns being distributed between the positions at Delta House and Beer Trench, while 200 rounds of rifle ammunition were issued to each man in Beer Trench. One Lewis gun was retained in the tank for defence and a corporal was detailed to man one of the 6-pounders. During the morning the line of the final objective was further consolidated by machine guns set up in prearranged positions, two near Quebec Farm, two at Bavaroise House, four about Pheasant Farm Cemetery, two at Malta House and one on the left at Rose House. During the afternoon the enemy infantry became more active infiltrating forward in ones and twos. Taking shelter in shell-holes and gradually moving towards the British positions they began to concentrate in dead ground in preparation for a counter-attack, and around 2,000 yards further back larger groups could be seen massing.

XIV Corps
Lieutenant-General Earl of Cavan

To form a defensive flank between the Poelcappelle spur and the Ypres – Staden railway, at the northern end of the main battlefront was the task of XIV Corps. The flank to be made by the 20th Division, was to be formed by two brigades each with two battalions leading over a front of 1,400 yards, and to a depth of approximately 1,000 yards curving back to the original British front line on the Staden railway. The breastworks of another huge earthwork, Eagle Trench, traversed most of the divisional front. The trench ran between two great earth embankments about eight feet high and was to prove even more troublesome to the 20th Division than Pheasant Trench was to the 51st.

20th (Light) Division [423]
Major-General W. Douglas Smith

On the 11th September 20th Division relieved 38th Division in the line east of Langemarck, and by the 20th September, the 60th Brigade and the 59th Brigade held the front line with the 61st Brigade in divisional reserve, with divisional headquarters at Elverdinghe. The fighting strength of the division had not been made up since the costly fighting of the Battle of Langemarck on the 16th August, and battalion fighting strength averaged about 350. Signal communications had been much improved over the five weeks, the 38th Division having buried a telephone cable from Langemarck to Au Bon Gite, not a simple task across the shell-torn and devastated area. The Signal Company of the 20th Division continued the work, burying a cable across another 1,500 yards west of the Steenbeek back to the divisional forward communications bunker at Stray Farm, just south-west of Iron Cross. Signal communication was thus maintained throughout the days fighting, with continual telephone connection and an additional 1,010 telegrams were dealt with.

The preparatory bombardment was to be augmented by the firing from Livens projectors of 290 oil drums to be directed at Eagle Trench. As the trench was difficult to observe from the British lines it was not clear what its defences were, although it was believed to be strongly held, and the resulting oil fire was intended to weaken this defence.
The 20th Division was faced by the *185th Regiment* of the *208th Division* which had been in the line since the 5th September

60th Brigade [424]
On the right of the brigade front, the 12th Rifle Brigade made some headway but soon came under machine gun fire from blockhouses to their right at White House and Rose House,[425] and was soon checked. The oil drums which had been fired at Eagle Trench had overshot the mark and most had landed about 200 yards behind the trench, doing little harm to the enemy, but illuminating the attacking 6th Oxfordshire and Buckinghamshire Light Infantry as they approached the trench. The weight of machine gun fire from the trench stopped the Ox and Bucks, who could make no further progress and both they and the Rifle Brigade lost the barrage.

59th Brigade [426]
The 11th King's Royal Rifle Corps suffered the same fate as the Ox and Bucks in front of Eagle Trench.[427] To the left near the railway where there was no intermediate objective the 10th K.R.R.C. made good progress breaking into the network of enemy trenches about Beak Trench, and taking 't Goed ter Vasten Farm. Parties of the 11th Rifle Brigade were widely separated in support of the other battalions. By 8:00 a.m. the situation in front of Eagle Trench had reached stalemate and the protective barrage had long since moved on to the final objective. In the next hour the left of 59th Brigade reached its final objective and the right of 60th Brigade had made a little more progress, but in the centre in front of Eagle Trench no movement was possible.
At 1:30 the Divisional Commander ordered another attack to be made at 6:30 p.m. with a repetition of the artillery barrage, and with a concentration of smoke shells upon Eagle Trench. The smoke was ineffective in front of 11th Rifle Brigade, attempting to reform after their separation in the morning, and their observed concentration resulted in a heavy enemy barrage on Langemarck, whilst machine guns from Eagle Trench raked their ranks. By 9:15 p.m. 60th Brigade had secured the southern section of Eagle Trench, but the northern section immediately east of Schreiboom resisted all efforts to take it. The 11th Rifle Brigade succeeded in gaining a short section just north of the Schreiboom crossroads but suffered 60% casualties and lost 11

---

[423] Captain V.E. Inglefield *The History of the Twentieth (Light) Division* London: Nisbet pp143-177
[424] National Archives, War Diary 60th Brigade WO95/2119
[425] National Archives, War Diary 12th Rifle Brigade WO95/2121
[426] National Archives, War Diary 59th Brigade WO95/2113
[427] National Archives, War Diary 11th Rifle Brigade WO95/2116

out of 16 officers in doing so. The line now gained ran from about Eagle House, some 250 yards beyond the trench and near the southern divisional boundary, then swung back to the west to the enemy held section of Eagle Trench and then north of Schreiboom where it again swung eastward to 't Goed ter Vasten Farm and the railway.

The fighting for the stubbornly defended Eagle Trench had been costly, and the ground conditions had been awful. The trench did not finally fall to the 20th Division until the 23rd September. The division's casualties amounted to over 1,300 with over 225 killed.

Fifth Armies achievements

As expected the fighting had been hard, bloody, and costly. But there had been a major difference in this battle compared with the 31st July and the 16th August. What the Fifth Army had planned to take, the objectives being limited to at most 1,500 yards, it had taken, and more importantly held. The artillery had given the infantry the protection and support they required, and consolidation of the hard won positions had been in most instances sufficient to repel the counter-attacks.

As will soon be seen the Fifth Army divisions also stood firm in the face of concerted counter-attacks by the previously successful *Eingreif* divisions.

The German attempt to retake the Gheluvelt plateau

General Plumer had every confidence that his carefully planned attack against the plateau would be successful, and this had proved to be the case. He also firmly believed that the newly won positions would soon be subjected to powerful German counter-attacks in an effort to retake the high ground and the *Wilhelm Stellung* which was so vital to their whole Flanders position.

The Second Army Intelligence Summary of 16th September had foreseen that the main German effort would be made against the plateau, the most likely lines of attack being towards Tower Hamlets spur, up the Reutelbeek valley just south of Polygon Wood, and towards Polygon Wood itself. This assessment proved to be totally correct, but equally the Germans were quite clear as to British intentions. On the 21st September Crown Prince Rupprecht wrote in his diary that it was evident that the British intention to gain Gheluvelt plateau was the preliminary to a break-through northwards, combined with a landing on the Belgian coast. Rupprecht clearly believed that Haig was still attempting a breakthrough.

Plumer was well aware of the effort that his artillery had put into the attack, which by early afternoon had been in constant action for eight hours, and he was also mindful that their support would be required until nightfall. The morning mist had now given way to a clear sunny day which greatly improved the ability of the seven corps squadrons of the R.F.C. to spot for troop concentrations and other targets. In the course of the day a total of 394 wireless messages were received from aircraft, about one third of which resulted in immediate artillery fire. The communication between the aircraft and the batteries was now far more sophisticated than hitherto, with standardized coded messages being received directly at batteries equipped with the necessary equipment. Each corps had two radio equipped aircraft on reconnaissance, one patrolling over the lines spotting British and forward German positions, while the second operated farther over enemy lines watching for the concentration and movement of counter-attack forces. Shortly before midday German field artillery was seen moving guns and limbers in the Reutelbeek valley in front of 23rd Division, and infantry appeared to be gathering about Cameron Covert. More artillery activity was noticed on the Passchendaele ridge around 1,500 yards in front of 2nd Australian Division, and infantry were also noticed arriving at, and deploying from the Butte in Polygon Wood. The protective barrage which was still searching the German positions soon concentrated upon these operations, after which further movement ceased. The guns had already been instrumental in breaking up the local counter-attacks by the forward German battalions, but their greatest test was still to come as the major German counter-thrusts developed. But by 1:48 p.m. when the protective barrage ceased the *Eingreif* divisions had not appeared in any numbers at the front, although there was information from air reconnaissance that strong enemy formations were moving forwards from the Flanders III Line from the direction of Menin, Moorslede, and Westroosebeke.

Disposition of the German counter-attack divisions

The German Staff, relying on past experience, and believing the 1,500 yard advance to have only reached an intermediate objective, were expecting the British to make a further attack, and held back the *Eingreif* divisions accordingly until the situation was clearer. From 8:00 a.m. they had been at instant readiness to move and by late morning they could wait no longer. The deployment was divided into three major groups.

The southern group - *16th Bavarian Division* (The *50th Reserve Division* and if the whole Corps were attacked the *3rd Reserve Division* were also available to *Group Wytschaete*)
Moving up from Gheluwe, 6,000 yards east of Gheluvelt, and then up to Becelaere 2,500 yards east of Polygon Wood, the *16th Bavarian Division*, the northern division of *Group Wytschaete*, was to counter-attack with its three regiments . The *21st Bavarian Reserve Infantry Regiment,* (its movement seen and estimated by the British at about three battalions), arrived at around 5:15 p.m. It approached along the Reutelbeek valley, towards the line held by 23rd Division and 1st Australian Division. The *11th Bavarian Reserve* moved south of the Reutelbeek towards the 23rd Division, and the *14th Bavarian Reserve*, crossing to the south of the Menin Road moved against the 41st and 39th Divisions positions near Tower Hamlets spur and in the Bassevillebeek valley.
The central group - *236th Division* HQ at Roulers *(Group Ypres)*

From Moorslede, 7,000 yards northeast of Polygon Wood, the *458th Regiment* of the *236th Division*, the southern *Eingreif* division of *Group Ypres*, (a force again estimated by the British at about three battalions), advanced towards the wood and Anzac ridge, the positions of 1st and 2nd Australian Divisions, and 9th Division astride the Ypres – Roulers railway. The *459th Regiment* advanced towards Hill 37 and the front of 55th Division. The *457th Regiment* moving from Baythem, six miles east of Broodseinde was to join the *458th* in the attack north of Polygon Wood against Anzac spur.

The northern group - *234th Division* HQ at Roulers *(Group Ypres)*

As we have seen, a northern force, the *452nd Regiment* of the *234th Division*, the northern division of *Group Ypres*, having marched from Oostnieuwkerke 8,000 yards northeast of Poelcappelle, (correctly estimated at regimental strength), was seen approaching down the Poelcappelle spur from Westroosebeke towards 51st Division. It halted near Poelcappelle at 5:00 p.m. to await the arrival of *453rd* and *451st Regiment* to its left. With the three regiments in line the division was to attack on a 2,500 yard front.

The counter-attack of the *Eingreif* divisions

Soon after 2:30 p.m. the expected counter-attack forces, both infantry and field batteries, were reported moving towards the front. No sooner were the columns found than the British medium and heavy artillery commenced an intense barrage upon them, which was so effective that they rapidly had to deploy. So disruptive was this fire that confusion and delay was inevitable, some battalions not arriving within 2,000 yards of the front line until around 5:00 p.m.

At about 2:30 p.m. movement was detected as enemy parties were seen to slowly infiltrate from the Butte in Polygon Wood in a north-westerly direction towards the upper end of Albania valley, (between Anzac spur and Tokio spur). At about the same time, across the front of the 2nd Australian and 9th Division a column of infantry with attached field batteries marched from Zonnebeke in a southerly direction towards Molenaarelsthoek. This movement was reported at 2:40 p.m. by an observer for 2nd Australian Divisional Artillery from an observation post on Anzac spur. The report added that the enemy appeared likely to attack from near the cemetery in Albania valley and from Tokio spur. The observer had seen the deployment of the forward elements of the *458th Regiment* accompanied by the attached *7th Battery* of the *241st Field Artillery Regiment*, moving forward in support of the remnants of *121st Division*. At 3:15 p.m. the S.O.S. rockets went up along the front of 2nd Australian, but even before they were fired the divisional artillery had opened a crushing barrage upon Tokio spur and Albania valley. The organized German advance quickly disintegrated into a desperate attempt to push a few parties forward using shell-holes and whatever other cover it could find, and then finally stopped completely a few hundred yards in front of the British outpost line. At 4:00 p.m. at the request of the infantry of 2nd Australian the shelling was stopped and for the moment there was no further movement on that part of the battlefield.

This was to be the worst day in the Third Battle of Ypres for the *241st Field Artillery Regiment*. The commander of the counter-attack detachments, the *2nd* and *7th Batteries* was an early casualty. Positioned just behind the Butte in Polygon Wood, the *8th* and *9th Batteries* of the *241st F.A.R.* lost all its guns to British artillery fire before it could engage the advance of 1st Australian Division. The German forward batteries were no more than 800 to 1,500 yards forward of the British positions on the final objective and suffered considerable casualties from machine gun and shell fire.

Around 2,500 yards to the south, between 2:30 and 3:00 p.m., the leading assault groups of the *21st Bavarian Reserve Regiment* were seen moving up the Reutelbeek valley towards the front of the 23rd British and 1st Australian Divisions. Another crashing barrage from the British guns, assisted by trench mortar batteries in the front line broke this attack before it had really started. The initial efforts of the counter-attack divisions had been effectively broken, mainly by the British artillery. What German artillery fire there had been in support of their infantry had mostly passed over the heads of the British forward outposts, and had landed in a ragged barrage further to the rear, doing little damage. The loss of their excellent observation positions now placed the Germans at a severe disadvantage and it became obvious that their artillery were unclear as to where the new British positions were.

The misty morning had turned into a clear sunny day and now towards evening as the sun began to set behind the gaunt ruins of Ypres it lit up the gentle western slopes of the Broodseinde – Passchendaele ridge across which the Germans were now advancing. All movement was easily discernable and attracted the inevitable barrage. The approaches up the Reutelbeek valley were equally exposed, and even those movements hidden behind the ridge were reported from the air. From the outset the German counter-attacks were at a great disadvantage. But the main effort by the *Eingreif* divisions was still to come, and at around 6:00 p.m. grey clad infantry were again seen infiltrating forward from Molenaarelsthoek, across Tokio spur and into Albania valley towards 2nd Australian, and just to the north moving down the Broodseinde ridge across the Zonnebeke valley in front of 9th Division.

Once more the S.O.S. was fired by 2nd Australian on Anzac ridge. The response was virtually instantaneous and within a few seconds the supporting machine guns fired their overhead barrage, followed in half a minute by the artillery which kept up its bombardment for around forty minutes. This attack ordered by the *236th Division* was made by the *457th Reserve Regiment* together with the *458th* and the remnants of the *121st Division*.[428] The *458th* had already been disorganized due to the shelling in the earlier attack, and the *457th* caught by the barrage was unable to negotiate the crater-field and could not get forward. The German barrage in support of their infantry became severe, doing some damage in the British front line, but the counter-attack was broken by the guns and no infantry got near the British outpost line.

In the Reutelbeek valley to the south of Polygon Wood, the main German advance against the 23rd Division and 1st Australian Division began around the same time, and had been under close observation for over an hour. By consolidating on the old German outposts and bunkers the infantry had made thorough preparations to meet the counter-attacks with rifle and machine

---

[428] 121st Division casualties were to amount to approximately 2,600 on the 20th / 21st September, National Archives CAB45/172

gun fire. The German protective barrage thickened towards 6:30 as *21st* and *11th Bavarian Regiments* moved forward towards the positions of 69th Brigade south of the stream. The reply to the S.O.S. of 69th Brigade at 7:02 was instant and another devastating barrage broke the cohesion of the counter-attack.

At just after 7:00 p.m. a German artillery barrage concentrated on the Blue Line just behind 1st Australian front and *21st Bavarian* were seen to be advancing north of the Reutelbeek. Within twenty seconds of the S.O.S. a tremendous barrage ended any hope of the Germans getting to grips with the Australians. It is recorded that the British infantry were somewhat disappointed that the guns had broken the attack, as they were eager to destroy the enemy with their own fire. The *21st Bavarian*, attacking with three battalions had been ordered to reinforce the right and centre of the *Bavarian Ersatz Division* in the line. The *1 Battalion* on the right flank of *Group Wytschaete,* was to hold "at all costs" the *Wilhelm Stellung* across the west side of Polygon Wood, but arrived to find the line already lost. The two other battalions were ordered to retake the line north and south of the Reutelbeek, whilst the attached field artillery battery shelled Black Watch Corner. Both battalions had suffered heavily from the British searching barrage on their march up before even reaching the Flanders I Line, and now according to their regimental history 'overpowering artillery fire drove them quickly to earth'. Those that could struggle on did so, some of the *21st* and *11th Bavarian* to the south of the stream scrambling across the crater-field up to Polderhoek Chateau, while small parties of the *21st* north of the stream reached the Flanders I Line and infiltrated into Polygon Wood in an attempt to locate the Australian outpost line. It was discovered that to reach the other end of Polygon Wood was no longer possible, and touch was only gained with the Australian outposts after the greater part of the *1 Battalion* had worked forward into odd gaps in the crater-field.

South of the Menin Road the *14th Bavarian Regiment* had an equally tough time, creeping forward beneath the barrage in twos and threes from shell-hole to shell-hole in an effort to reinforce the remnants of the *395th Regiment* and *28th Ersatz Regiment* at Tower Hamlets, and to reach the Bassevillebeek valley across the southern end of the spur. Two attempts were made by *14th Bavarian* at 6:30 and 7:00 p.m. to threaten the positions of 39th Division in the valley, but upon the S.O.S. signal they were both broken by machine gun and artillery barrages.

German counter-attacks against Fifth Army

The counter-attack of the *236th (Eingreif) Division* against 55th Division

Shortly after 5:00 p.m. a more serious attempt was made by the *Eingreif* divisions to once again push the British advance back to the Steenbeek. Towards the right front of the 55th Division the enemy launched a counter attack from around Boetleer Farm on Gravenstafel ridge directed against Hill 37 and accompanied by a major effort by his artillery. This counter attack was made by the *459th Reserve Regiment*, on the right of the *236th Division*, and was to reinforce the *91st Reserve Regiment* in the front line. That regiments history states that every effort made to press the attack failed owing to the terrible artillery barrage and machine gun fire, which tore great gaps in the advancing companies and caused complete disorganization. Machine gun fire from the guns of 164th Brigade at Schuler Galleries and the nine guns of 165th Brigade at Keir Farm were instrumental in breaking this attack.

The Germans had found that launching counter-attacks, as they had to the north of Hill 37, between local salients in the British line which had been effectively consolidated with machine guns left them terribly vulnerable to enfilade fire, and they had paid a high price. The much vaunted system of defence in depth underwritten by the *Eingreif* divisions had failed.

The counter-attack of the *234th (Eingreif) Division* against the 58th Division

The counter attack at around 6:00 p.m. by the *451st, 452nd* and *453rd Regiment* of the *234th Eingreif Division* fell less heavily on the 58th Division than on the 55th and 51st on either flank, and was defeated by rifle, machine gun and artillery fire. As the *453rd* attacked, machine gun and Lewis gun fire was opened at 1,500 yards causing the numerous German columns to deploy into open formation. As the thinning ranks approached to within 150 yards of the outpost line the British barrage crashed down and according to an eye-witness was 'beyond description and the enemy stampeded'. The Germans did not attempt to move up again to occupy their most forward positions about Wurst Farm until sunset.

The counter attack of the *234th (Eingreif) Division* against 51st Division

An increasingly intense artillery barrage fired at around 5:00 p.m. was the precursor of the full scale counter attack by the *234th (Eingreif) Division*, in which the guns of the Houthulst, Poelcappelle and Passchendaele groups all co-operated in support of the German infantry in their attempt to force the British back across the Steenbeek. The leading regiment of the division, the *452nd* had halted near Poelcappelle awaiting the two other regiments of the division, the *451st* and *453rd* to come up on its left, and at around 5:00 p.m. continued its advance. On the right of the 51st Division, the *451st Regiment* advanced between York House and Tweed House, towards the positions of the 7th Argyll and Sutherland. This attack did not reach the British line, being broken by rifle, machine gun and most importantly protective artillery fire from the British batteries.

In the centre *452nd Regiment* pressed their attack with the *5th Grenadiers* to their right, against the positions of the 4th Gordon and the three support platoons of the 8th Argyll and Sutherland. For a while the assault was held but the huge expenditure of rifle and Lewis gun ammunition in the taking of Pheasant Trench now resulted in a serious problem, as pouches became empted and reserves exhausted. Gradually the line gave way at the point of greatest pressure between the Lekkerboterbeek and Rose House, although the latter position continued to hold out. The three platoons of the 8th Argyll and Sutherland broke up repeated attacks, causing many enemy casualties. German pressure against the V formed by the Lekkerboterbeek and the Poelcappelle road became acute. The 4th Gordon, after all their officers of the original attack had become casualties gave way, and Beer Trench was overrun, quickly followed by Malta House. The garrison in Stroom Trench including the party of the 8th Argyll and Sutherland were forced back, and at around 6:00 p.m. a general withdrawal began from the V between the Lekkerboterbeek and the Poelcappelle road.

The necessity to contain the dangerous incursion was obvious and immediate steps were taken by the local commanders to form two containing flanks. To the south of the Lekkerboterbeek a hasty deployment of "C" Company of the 7th, and two platoons of the 8th Argyll and Sutherland, accompanied by "D" Company of the 9th Royal Scots formed up facing north. To the north-west of the Poelcappelle road parties of the 8th Argyll and Sutherland and the 4th Seaforth faced south-east catching the *452nd Regiment* in enfilade from two sides and inflicting serious losses. Those of the Gordons and Argyll and Sutherland that had withdrawn from the V were rallied and having replenished ammunition from the dead and wounded were again led forward to Pheasant Trench, and with "A" Company of the 8th Argyll and Sutherland, who had previously been sent forward to reinforce the line, counter-attacked the Germans in the V. The attack was successful and drove the enemy out of the V and back towards Poelcappelle, a new line then being consolidated from a point a few hundred yards north of Delta Huts, through Pheasant Farm Cemetery, across the Poelcappelle road to the Lekkerboterbeek, then along the stream to the original final objective. At dusk the one remaining company of the 8th Argyll and Sutherland was brought up to reinforce the line.

During the night the *452nd Regiment* which had attacked the "V" was, due to the level of casualties, withdrawn and replaced with the *371st Regiment* of the *10th Ersatz Division*. The best efforts of the *Eingreif* divisions, strongly supported by their artillery, had not pushed the British back across the Steenbeek as planned, and had in fact been repulsed by 51st Division, although north of the Letterboterbeek the new line was consolidated about 600 yards in rear of the final objective. Compared with other British divisions in action this day the 51st Division casualties were less severe at nearly 1,200, but around 170 had been fatalities.

There were no further attempts, by the German counter-attack divisions to retake the *Wilhelm Stellung* on the 20th September. It had been a costly effort, many casualties being sustained before they got anywhere near the fighting zone. The fact that the Germans had been well prepared for, and in some sectors waiting for the attack, had been of overall advantage to the British. The more regiments that were thrust forward, the greater their destruction under the massive weight of fire of the guns. It is clear that the Germans did not yet appreciate that British tactics had changed. Their Official History states that the counter-attack divisions actually recaptured a line 1,500 metres east of the original British Front Line. In fact nothing of the sought had happened. Along most of the front the counter-attack divisions had not come to grips with the British infantry, being shattered by artillery before reaching the outpost line. Only in the sector of XVIII Corps, had the 51st Highland Division been driven back by *451st Division* but the ground lost had been largely retaken, and *451st Division* had sustained such casualties that it required immediate relief. Some battalions in *234th Division* had lost up to 60% of their officers and 50% of their men. It is now clear that to have held back the *Eingreif* divisions until after dark, and then reinforce the decimated front line regiments, would have been the best course of action for the German command. They would have achieved the same result but at far less cost.

As darkness fell over the battlefield it was clear to the British Staff that no further major effort by the German counter-attack divisions was imminent, their strength and momentum having for the moment been crushed beneath the British barrage. Plumer's insistence to attack only after concerted preparations, and with sufficient force had been correct, and maybe obviously so. The plan to hold an area of limited penetration which he believed his Army capable of defending under the weight of concerted counter attacks had also been proven sound. The change in tactics had not gone unnoticed by the troops. Not only the tactics, but also the results were different this time. This battle they had won, and the Germans for once had been worsted. The gains they had made and held were obvious for all to see. They had not been asked to achieve that which was beyond their capability. Those in the thick of the fighting were promptly relieved by fresh forces, the words of a young officer of 8th Australian Battalion probably summing up the general view. 'Had a good march out. If only every attack could be carried out so cleanly and followed by relief so quick, the men would be well content.'[429] In short things had finished on a high and positive note. Whether the change, (which to those not at the front and with little military understanding may have seemed rather subtle), was noticed by the politicians at home is a matter for debate. Lord Esher the British Ambassador in Paris noted in his diary, 'We have done a good offensive which is much appreciated. But will it lead to anything really important'.[430] That remained to be seen.

Subsequent actions

On the 21st September action was resumed at a few points along the front. During the night the movement of field artillery, which had begun on the afternoon of the 20th continued, many batteries being brought forward to Bellewaarde and Westhoek ridges. At 4:30 a.m. the whole weight of the barrage, including the machine guns descended once more on the German positions, sweeping forward some 2,000 yards. At 9:30 a.m. 41st Division again attacked the last stubbornly held section of the *Wilhelm Stellung* at Tower Hamlets using 123rd Brigade from divisional reserve. The 10th Royal West Kent Regiment with the 20th Durham Light Infantry, supported by the 23rd Middlesex made little headway in the dreadful conditions in the Bassevillebeek valley, the Quadrilateral still holding out even after a heavy bombardment. At 5:30 p.m. the enemy barrage in the Bassevillebeek valley became intense, being described as a seething furnace of bursting shells. Just before 7:00 the German barrage lifted and the enemy counter-attacked the West Kent and Durhams, but was driven off with heavy losses. A short time

---

[429] AOA p790
[430] AOA p790

later another counter-attack was made against the Middlesex which held it off with Lewis gun and rifle fire until in response to S.O.S. signals the British barrage totally annihilated it.

During the morning, movement 200 to 300 yards in front of the 1st Australian Division outposts in Polygon Wood indicated the Germans were attempting to consolidate a line. Stokes mortar fire of 2nd Brigade drove about a company of Germans out of their shell-holes, and the Australians pushed their outposts in the wood some 300 yards beyond the Green Line. The position of a machine gun was detected in the wood by Lance Corporal Inwood of the 10th Battalion. He and another soldier from 7th Battalion crept forward and got behind the gun, bombing it out. A survivor of the gun crew was made to carry the gun back to the Australian lines. For his courageous action Inwood was to be awarded the V.C.

German aircraft were active over the British lines during the day, making harassing machine gun and bombing attacks against both infantry and artillery. Little damage was done by the aircraft, but subsequent shelling became heavier and more accurate, indicating the German artillery now had a better idea of the British positions. Towards evening forty-five enemy aircraft were counted on one raid.

The positions of 2nd Australian Division about Anzac House and Garter Point came under heavy bombardment at 6:30 p.m., and expecting a counter-attack to follow, the S.O.S. went up about 7:00 to be followed almost immediately by 1st Australian Division. The artillery of both sides was soon competing, with barrages of tremendous force, but no counter-attack ensued and at 8:00 p.m. the shelling ceased.

In late afternoon a lightening German barrage crashed onto the positions of the 55th Division holding Hill 37 and Hill 35. It soon became clear that the Germans were making a serious effort to retake the important position, as dense waves of infantry followed by numerous columns advanced, whilst their artillery shelled all roads and approaches in an attempt to isolate the garrisons on the hills. The outpost line was penetrated in some places, but well positioned machine guns caught the enemy in enfilade and by 8:00 p.m. the attack collapsed and was driven back. By 9:15 the line had been restored by local supports. The line was also penetrated at Kier Farm dug-outs 500 yards to the north, but the enemy was swiftly ousted and the position restored.

Relief of the divisions in the line

The careful Staff planning had allowed for rapid relief on the 21st September, of those brigades which had been most heavily engaged on the 20th. Over the next few days, in preparation for the next major step the relief of the forward divisions took place.

In Second Army, on the 23rd September in X Corps, the battered 41st Division was relieved by the less heavily engaged 39th Division which side stepped northwards. Relief of the 23rd Division by the 33rd Division from corps reserve began on the night of the 24th, completing early morning of the 25th.

In I Anzac Corps 1st and 2nd Australian were relieved by 5th and 4th Australian Divisions overnight on the 22nd / 23rd.

In Fifth Army, 9th Division of V Corps was relieved by 3rd Division on the 22nd and during the night of 22nd / 23rd September, 55th Division was relieved by 59th Division. In XVIII Corps 58th Division maintained its place in the line, but relieved the 173rd and 174th Brigades with the 175th Brigade. On the 25th September 51st Division were relieved by 11th Division, (the latter not destined to be heavily engaged in the next phase).

Engagements near Langemarck 22nd – 23rd September
20th Division and 51st Division

On the night of 21st / 22nd September 152nd Brigade had relieved the 154th in the line held by 51st Division. A plan for a further attack to be made on the 22nd against the section of Eagle Trench still held by the Germans, by detachments of two battalions of the 20th Division supported by two tanks, was postponed as the tanks had become bogged in Langemarck. On the morning of the 23rd an initial plan to attack at 5:30 a.m. was again postponed as the tanks could still not move, an alternative plan to attack at 7:00 a.m. without them then being adopted.

At 6:30 on the morning of the 23rd the Germans advanced down Poelcappelle spur against the 5th Seaforth Highlanders on the left of the front held by 152nd Brigade of 51st Division, and against the right battalion of 20th Division, the 12th King's Royal Rifle Corps. One enemy platoon about forty strong was seen approaching the line of the 5th Seaforth, and were quickly wiped out. An assault group attempting to raid the line of the 12th K.R.R.C. on the left were caught in enfilade by fire of the Seaforth at which point 23 survivors, ran forward to the K.R.R.C. with their hands up and surrendered. A hurricane Stokes mortar bombardment against Eagle Trench in support of the detachments of 12th K.R.R.C. and 10th Rifle Brigade which were to make the attack was planned for 7:00 a.m. and the German attack did not alter these arrangements. After a very effective mortar bombardment, bombing parties of the 12th K.R.R.C. bombed up the trench from the south, whilst the 10th Rifle Brigade did the same from the north. One company of the 10th Rifle Brigade made a frontal assault, showering the enemy with rifle grenades from the west and the trench was soon taken, 94 prisoners and 10 machine guns being captured. By the evening, outposts of the 60th and 59th Brigades were established to the east of Eagle Trench, being relieved by the 61st Brigade at dusk.

During the afternoon of the 23rd an intense German barrage descended on the 152nd Brigade front as a precursor to a major attack along the Lekkerboterbeek valley which developed just after 7:00 p.m. The attack at first advanced in great columns, which then extended to the south and east of Malta House. The inevitable call for artillery support resulted in a devastating barrage. On the brigade right the 6th Seaforth Highlanders joined in with Lewis gun, Vickers machine gun and rifle fire. Five Lewis guns were in action, of which one fired twenty-eight drums into the enemy. The morning light of the 24th revealed great carnage in front of Malta House with the enemy dead strewn about in heaps.

The German spoiling attack on the 25th September

To the German Staff it was now obvious that the British were preparing to launch another great strike at the Gheluvelt plateau, which was in fact planned to take place on the 26th September. It was also clear to them that the counter-attack system of defence, so successful in the past, had failed on the 20th September. In order to gain the time necessary to assemble sufficient forces to resist the next British effort Crown Prince Rupprecht had ordered a counter-attack for the 24th September, later postponed to the 25th in order to delay the British preparations, and recapture the pillboxes and shelters of the *Wilhelm Stellung* along a 1,800 yard front from the Menin Road to the southern edge Polygon Wood. The *Wilhelm Stellung* was to be captured and crossed, and a position 100 to 150 yards forward of the line was to be consolidated and held at all costs.

On the 21st September the *50th Reserve Division* moved up from Menin to relieve the battered *3rd Bavarian Ersatz Division*, and the *231st Reserve Regiment* had gone into the line south of the Menin Road, the *230th Reserve Regiment* south of the Reutelbeek, with the *229th Reserve Regiment* to the north of the stream. Each regiment was to attack with one battalion leading, and the attack was to be reinforced by a special company of *Fourth Army* storm troops to act as a shock assault force, which was to hold the *Wilhelm Stellung* once it was taken. To support this effort the German artillery had been heavily reinforced with 27 batteries of field artillery and 17 field howitzer batteries. The artillery of the *25th* and *207th Divisions* (south of the *50th Reserve Division*), the *3rd Reserve Division* (which had relieved the *2nd Guard Reserve*), and the long range guns (*Fernkampfgruppe*) of the *Ypres Corps* all cooperated in the assault.[431] The heavy battery concentration of the Tenbrielen group amounted to 15 heavy howitzer batteries, and 5 batteries of H.V. guns, four times the normal divisional allotment and believed to be the greatest concentration of guns in any one divisional sector.[432]

For the British the attack was to come at the worst possible time. The relief of the 23rd Division by the 33rd Division was just completing, and preparations were finalizing for the next great attack on the morning of the 26th September. In order to reduce the I Anzac attack frontage for the next step to 2,100 yards, the left flank of X Corps had been shifted about 500 yards towards the north to encompass part of the *Wilhelm Stellung* captured by 2nd Australian Brigade on the 20th September. This would place the right flank of the incoming 5th Australian Division on the Black Watch Corner to Reutel village road, along the southern side of Polygon Wood. Although 33rd Division were not to take a major attacking role in the forthcoming battle, which was to be spearheaded by 5th and 4th Australian Divisions, its presence on the battlefield in the correct position was critical in protecting the Australian right flank.

Holding the left sector of 33rd Division front, 98th Brigade occupied an outpost line in the crater-field ahead of Carlisle Farm,[433] with supports about the ruins of the farm, and a reserve position 250 yards behind near Lone House on the old Green Line. At 6:50 p.m. on the 24th September the 1st Middlesex Regiment (19th Brigade attached) left Railway Dugouts at Zillebeke and moved up to relieve the 8th York and Lancaster in the line, battalion headquarters being in a concrete strong-point between Glencorse Wood and Fitzclarence Farm, which was taken over at 8:00 p.m. The battalion was to hold a front line of around 570 yards from Black Watch Corner southwards, which consisted of shell-holes with short sections of unconnected trench, with a support line to the rear, with "A" and "B" Companies to hold the front outposts, and "C" and "D" Companies in the support line. Although accompanied by guides, all companies had great difficulty finding their way forward, a situation made much worse by enemy shelling which increased in intensity throughout the evening. "D" Company arrived in relief of the York and Lancs by 11:30 p.m. the other three companies being located in position by officers patrols by 4:30 a.m. next morning. During the night a message was received from 98th Brigade to the effect that two practice barrages would be put down along Second Army front early in the morning.

German counter-attack between Menin Road and Polygon Wood 5.30 AM 25thSeptember.

Map next page.

---

[431] National Archives, p120 CAB45/172
[432] National Archives, War Diary 100th Brigade WO95/2429
[433] National Archives, War Diary 98th Brigade WO95/2425

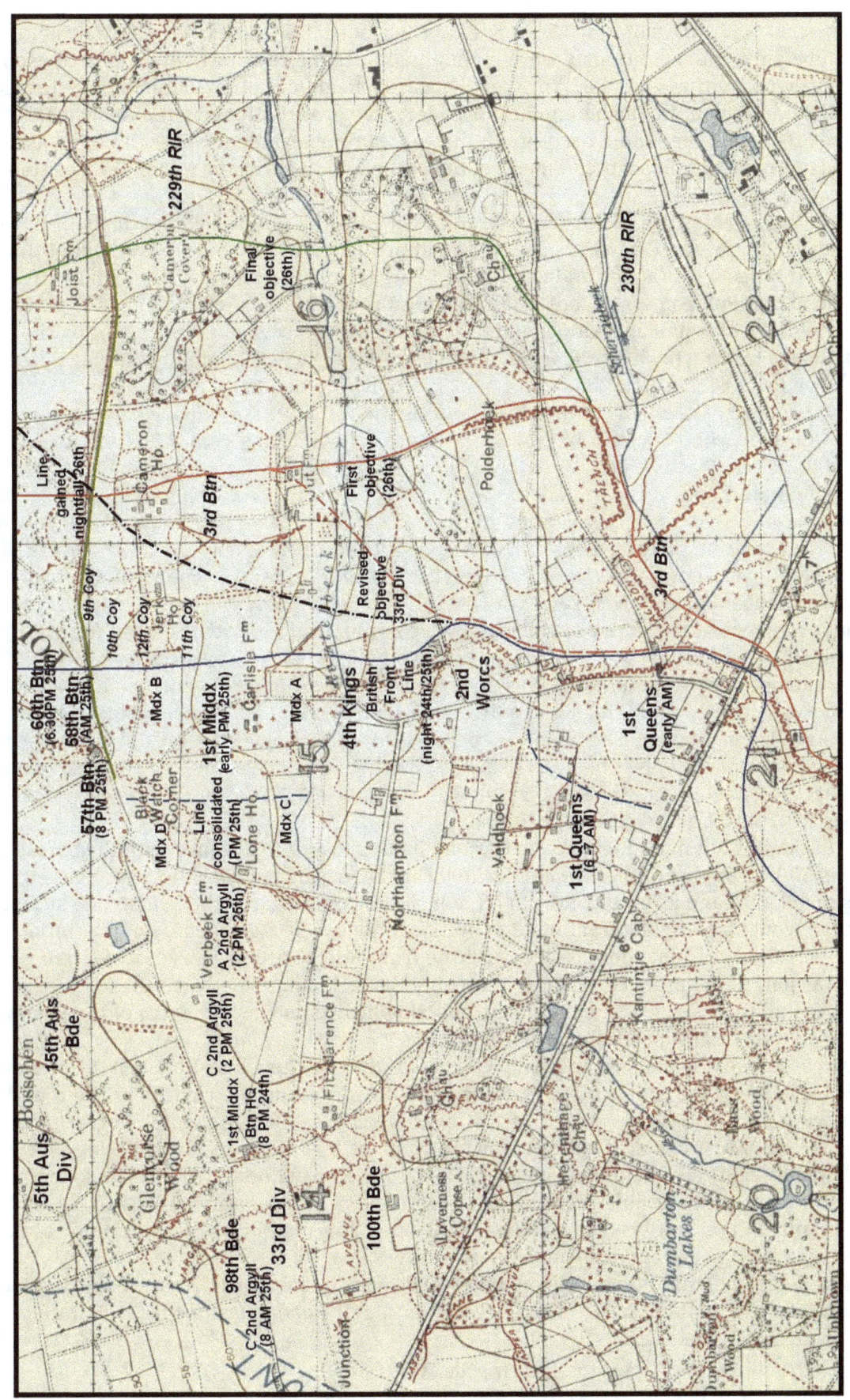

German counter-attack between Menin Road and Polygon Wood 5.30 AM 25th September.

To the alarm of 58th Battalion of 15th Australian Brigade,[434] 5th Australian Division holding the line in Polygon Wood, no outposts were maintained near the road to Reutel along the southern edge of the wood, either by the 8th York and Lancaster Regiment of the outgoing 70th Brigade, or by the 1st Middlesex of the incoming 98th Brigade. After protestations by the Australians, the 1st Middlesex were to later send a party to fill the gap, but meanwhile the 58th Battalion shifted its right and dug-in to obtain a fair command of the battlefield towards the Middlesex position.

At 5:15 in the morning of the 25th, only 45 minutes after the Middlesex had finally relieved the York and Lancaster, the German heavy and field artillery opened an intense bombardment of high explosive, heavy shrapnel, and gas shell, of barrage proportions upon the line between the Menin Road and Polygon Wood, but also targeting the road back towards Ypres. A party of the 8th Australian Field Ambulance attached to the Australian 5th Division was caught by the hostile shelling whilst moving towards the front. A member of the party William Ernest May noted in his diary, 'Reveille at 4:15 a.m. and moved off at 5.00 a.m. for the line at Menin Road, again as our division hops over at dawn in the morning. Leaving the A.D.S. we were just clear of a place called Hell Fire Corner, when a shell came over catching 5 of our chaps who dived into a shell-hole. Poor old Phil Murray was killed. McGoldrick, Raynor and Mole were all wounded. Going further along [the Menin Road] we were held up for two hours on account of his shelling the road. He caught and set on fire 6 motor lorries of ammunition and several dumps. I tell you it had everyone scared out of their lives. After doing 100 yards in even time, we arrived at our destination, Hooge Tunnel, where we started right away to carry the wounded. We had several lucky escapes again and arrived safely at the Culvert (relay post) where we leave our patient.' German aircraft were also active in closing down communications with the front for, 'on the way back we ran into 2 of Fritz's planes which played their machine guns along the road'. The German barrage on the Menin Road was now severe. 'Here another misfortune happened to us. Henry Merce's squad were bringing in a Stretcher Bearer who had been wounded when a shell landed straight on the stretcher, killing Lou Ballard, Matt Doyle, Henry and the patient and wounding Bill Happesley. Just then Peter Moore, Barlow and Les Townsend were also wounded. I tell you it is some Hot Shop, worse, I recon, than Bullecourt.'[435] The enemy was clearly doing his best to isolate the British front line positions.

In the fine but hazy morning the German infantry were to advance with the barrage from positions 500 yards east of the *Wilhelm Stellung*, but their barrage fell short causing the forward groups to fall back and await the guns to lift, which they did towards the British line at 5:30. The S.O.S. then went up along the front of 33rd Division, and also 5th Australian. But the initial British barrage was fired too long, possibly because the front line positions were not clear, or possibly as this was part of the practice barrage, but in any case fell mainly between the forward German companies and their supports further back, inflicting little damage. Just north of the Menin Road the German assault groups of the *3rd Battalion, 230th Reserve Regiment*, were seen between 300 and 500 yards away by the forward companies holding the British line. Between the Menin Road and the Reutelbeek the centre of 100th Brigade held firm but on the right near the road the 1st Queens were pushed back about 200 yards towards Veldhoek, while the 2nd Worcester on their left mostly held on to their positions. On the right of 98th Brigade, the 4th King's Liverpool, (astride the stream) also held their ground. The Germans used new storm troop tactics against the British line, their assault groups armed with *flamenwerfers* and 1908/15 pattern light machine guns in the first wave, and a heavy machine gun platoon with 1908 pattern machine guns accompanying each company in the next 3 waves.[436]

The main weight of the attack fell on three platoons in the centre and on the right of "B" Company of the 1st Middlesex.[437] The *11th, 12th* and *10th Companies* of the *3rd Battalion, 229th*

---

[434] National Archives, War Diary 15th Aus Brigade WO95/3638
[435] Private diary of William Ernest May 8th Australian Field Ambulance
[436] War diary 100 Machine Gun Company, 100th Brigade, 33rd Division. Part of captured enemy order. WO/95/2431.
[437] Everard Wyrall *The Die Hards in the Great War Vol II 1916-1919* London: Harrison pp124-130

Reserve Regiment, with their right guarded by the *9th Company* along Polygon Wood, advanced towards the Middlesex outposts, working between the gaps in the defensive line and taking the posts in the rear. To the right of "B" Company, towards the Reutelbeek, the initial attack against "A" Company was repulsed, but at about 6:30 the Germans again attacked in force, in five waves with supports closely following. They gradually closed in rushing from shell-hole to shell-hole, between and then behind the two companies of the Middlesex, eventually getting into the small trench sections where there was much bombing and hand to hand fighting, all the officers of "A" and "B" Companies being either killed or wounded. The remnant of "A" Company then fell back 250 yards towards the support line, where the German advance was temporarily checked by the support companies. Due to the shelling and misty conditions it was not clear to the support companies exactly what was the situation at the front, but as this became clear Lewis guns were pushed out to cover the gap in the centre, and rifle sections were sent forward into shell-holes. At battalion headquarters 1,000 yards back near Glencorse Wood the situation was even less clear, and urgent actions were taken to form a rearward defence line in case the enemy broke through. It was soon reported that the support companies had checked the advance but that the enemy were setting up machine guns in re-captured bunkers and were still attempting to infiltrate forward. At about 8:00 a.m. "C" Company of the 2nd Argyll and Sutherland Highlanders was placed at the disposal of the Commanding Officer 1st Middlesex and took up positions behind battalion headquarters. At this point the message was received from 58th Australian Battalion regarding the dangerous gap on the left and as the Australians threw back a right flank, one platoon of "C" Company of the Argyll were sent up to make contact and to help plug the gap.

At 12:35 p.m. while arrangements were being made at battalion headquarters to fill the gap between Middlesex "C" and "D" Companies, an order was received from brigade for the Middlesex to attack, with "A" and "C" companies of the Argyll and Sutherland, the objective being the original front line and the attack to commence with a covering barrage at 2:00 p.m. The attack was arranged with "A" Company of the Argylls to advance on a 180 yard front towards the gap between "C" Company on the left of the Middlesex line, and "D" Company on the right, with whom the remnants of "A" and "B" Companies were still fighting. As the Argyll company passed through, the Middlesex were to advance with them to recover the front line 200 yards forward. The three remaining platoons of Argyll "C" Company were to follow the attack in support. At 2:00 p.m. the arranged barrage fell, but well ahead of the Middlesex positions and the Argyll and Sutherland advanced without its cover. The movement was in full view of the Germans who dropped an accurate barrage on the advancing Argyll, who nonetheless succeeded in reaching the Middlesex position before being stopped by machine gun fire. A message from the front line was sent back to request a further barrage to allow for an attempt at another attack, but no message reached battalion headquarters. It appeared however to observers from the rear that the objective had been gained, this later proving not to be the case. The original Middlesex support line was then consolidated near Lone House, around 250 yards behind the original front line and 350 yards behind the Australian right flank, and in view of the Australians in the line, but unknown to both Australian and Middlesex headquarters. In this action on the 25th September 1st Middlesex sustained casualties of three officers killed, three wounded and three missing, with 34 other ranks killed, 69 wounded, 131 missing and 12 believed captured.

The dangers of the situation were not entirely obvious to the staffs of 33rd British and 5th Australian Divisions, as due to the intense shelling, communication with the front was near impossible. But to the local commanders of the battalions in the front line the situation was critical, as the ground which the Germans had captured included the jumping-off line for the great attack of the next day, and 15th Australian Brigade's right flank was dangerously exposed. As we have seen shelling of all approaches to the front was very heavy and even back at Hooge movement on the Menin Road was impossible. The barrage effectively boxed in the forward positions of 33rd Division making the re-supply of small arms ammunition, which was running extremely low, virtually impossible. During this period Lance-Corporal John Brown Hamilton of the 1/9th Highland Light Infantry, 100th Brigade, was to be awarded the V.C. for courageously distributing ammunition under direct enemy fire.

The danger to the Australian right flank was not realized by Brigadier-General Elliott at 15th Australian Brigade headquarters at Hooge crater until 8:46 a.m. when it became known that 1st Middlesex had retired and the Germans were setting up machine guns along the Reutel road. The Menin Road about Hooge was still an inferno of shelling, but word eventually came through from Major Freeman commanding 58th Battalion that he was throwing in one of his two support companies to strengthen his right and was in immediate need of reinforcement. All Elliott's battalions were in readiness for action in the great attack of the following morning, but quickly identifying the priority of holding the line, he sent forward a company of the 60th Battalion from Clapham Junction. The decision to use forces allocated for the attack next day was not instantly taken by Brigadier-General Heriot-Maitland commanding 98th Brigade, until he was so ordered by Major-General Wood commanding 33rd Division, (which had resulted in the two companies of the 2nd Argyll and Sutherland Highlanders being ordered up to Fitzclarence Farm to assist 1st Middlesex). When news of this proposal reached Elliott he immediately sent up another company of 60th Battalion to further reinforce Freeman. There followed a period of great confusion, caused largely by the persistent German barrage which continued to disrupt communications and box in the forward positions. At around 2:00 p.m. the Australians along the edge of Polygon Wood saw the two companies of the 2nd Argyll and Sutherland advance past Fitzclarence Farm down the Reutelbeek valley, but noticed that there was little or no protective barrage and that the Argyll had soon come under heavy shell and machine gun fire. They saw the advance continue in two waves, and as the first wave passed Lone House, it had stopped and dug-in (this on the position of the forward Middlesex companies), the second wave stopping 100 yards to the rear.

    Reports at 5:08 p.m. from 33rd Division headquarters implying that the front had been restored were not confirmed by the 58th Battalion in Polygon Wood, as their right flank was still not in contact with 98th Brigade. At 5:40 Major Freeman further reported to Elliott that large numbers of Germans were assembling near Cameron House, 500 yards east of Black Watch Corner near the Reutel road, which presented a major threat to his right flank. At 15th Brigade headquarters it became clear to Elliott that due to a misunderstanding the second company of 60th Battalion had not gone forward, but it was now ordered to do so under the battalion commander Lieutenant-Colonel Marshall, who then took control of the Australian right flank. Moving the company forward was almost impossible, the German barrage still being extremely heavy and accompanied by attacks from low flying aircraft. Marshall reported, 'Position appears bad. Idea of putting out tapes under present conditions is absolutely impossible. Consider you should insist on British brigade on our right [98th] retaking their front line at once.'[438] The time for marking out the jumping-off positions for the next mornings attack was getting perilously close.

By 6:30 p.m. the hard pressed 58th Battalion had been relieved by the two companies of the 60th. At around 7:00 p.m. Elliott received even more alarming news from 98th Brigade, that they were now pushed right back to Verbeek Farm, 500 yards west of Black Watch Corner. In fact the two companies of the 2nd Argyll and Sutherland, plus remnants of the Middlesex companies were still holding out on a line near Lone House but at the time this was not known to Elliott. The main crisis of the day had now arrived and at 7:05 on receipt of Marshall's message, Elliott sent forward Leiutenant-Colonel Stewart with the 57th Battalion, who upon arrival would assume command, with all the brigade's machine guns at his disposal. The remaining battalion of the brigade, the 59th was now brought forward to Clapham Junction. Three of Elliott's battalions intended for the morning's attack had now been thrown in, the 58th and 60th having suffered severe casualties, and the main 5th Australian Division ammunition dump and two forward dumps had been blown up in the shelling.

    The German spoiling attack to disorganize the preparations for the forthcoming major British effort had worked well. It was now almost certain that the Germans, who had taken prisoners from the front line companies, were well aware of the time and date of the next attack. Due to the dislocation of 33rd Division, X Corps had questioned whether the attack on the

---

[438] AOA p803

following morning should proceed, but had received orders from Plumer that the attack must be made. The objectives for 33rd Division were however modified with 98th Brigade alone covering the Australian right flank, whilst 100th Brigade was only to recover the lost ground.

At 7:00 p.m. Elliott telephoned Major-General Hobbs in command of 5th Australian Division and explained the seriousness of the situation. Already aware of the response X Corps had received from Army headquarters, Hobbs actions were limited to asking for greater effort from 33rd Division's counter-battery group, and to warn 8th Brigade from his divisional reserve that they may be required to carry out the next morning's attack, or at least to provide two battalions in support of the 15th. About 8:00 p.m. Elliott informed Hobbs that an attack by his 15th Brigade next morning was out of the question, and even assembly of any attacking force on his brigade front, given the proximity of the enemy machine guns on his right, would be exceedingly difficult. Hobbs promised to inform I Anzac headquarters but made it plain that the attack would be made, and this was quickly confirmed by Birdwood.

Although the whole situation still looked critical, the best possible plan was put into effect to overcome the problems. The counter-battery groups of 33rd Division would make every attempt to subdue the German artillery and two fresh battalions, the 1/4th Suffolk and 5/6th Cameronians (Scottish Rifles) were to restore the British front line south of Black Watch Corner at 5:15 a.m. 35 minutes before Zero Hour. If these battalions failed, a strike from the southern edge of Polygon Wood must be made to fill the gap and secure the Australian right. The main Australian attack would be carried out by the 59th Battalion to take the first objective, and the 31st and 29th Battalions of 8th Brigade to take the second, the whole operation being controlled by 15th Brigade. The movements from Dickebusch at about 8:00 p.m. of the two battalions of the 8th Brigade, and extra efforts by the Divisional Ammunition Column to bring up ammunition to replace that lost in the dumps were left in comparative peace, as at 8:15 p.m. the German artillery fell silent. Throughout the night the designated battalions were organized with difficulty into the positions from which they were to attack in the morning and guides from the 58th Battalion led them up to the hastily positioned tapes, in the glare of constant German flares but screened by the shattered stumps of Polygon Wood. Things were as well prepared as they could be for the next great step to begin at 5:50 a.m. on the 26th September.

Casualties 20th to 25th September

The victory of the 20th September had not been won without great sacrifice, and the mild euphoria was tempered with the knowledge that there were huge numbers who would never march off this battlefield. Casualty figures for the divisions engaged in the Battle of The Menin Road Ridge were as follows:

Second Army	**Total**	**Killed**
19th Division	1,933	340
39th Division	976	
41st Division	3,123	434
23rd Division	2,134	412
1st Australian Division	2,352	379
2nd Australian Division	1,773	325
Fifth Army		
9th Division	2,191	395
55th Division	1,994	170
58th Division	1,236	256
51st Division	1,184	195
20th Division	1,409	252
	20,305	

In comparison total casualties in the Battle of Pilckem Ridge from 31st July to 3rd August were 31,850 of which 27,000 were in Fifth Army. From 3rd August to 28th August including the Battle of Langemarck and subsequent actions total casualties were 36,160, the majority being in Fifth Army.

Robert Alan Perry
Essex Villa
Langemark
17th June 2006

Trench stores awaiting move to the line

Dug in on the Menin Road – knocked out tank in background

Austalian 5th Division on Westhoek Ridge 23rd Sept

Garter Point blockhouse

Chapter Five

"In the face of confusion and great danger"

The Second Step

The Battle of Polygon Wood 26th September

The Italian Offensive is suspended

The matter of the 100 guns (that were now on their way to Italy) which had been discussed at the meeting of the War Cabinet on the 4th September, was on the 21st September to be raised again. Back on the 4th, on account of Haig's reluctance (in contrast to Foch's anxiety) to send the guns, the matter had apparently caused Lloyd George a degree of embarrassment, and it was now about to do so once more. At a Cabinet meeting on the 21st, Robertson reported on the complete success of the attack at Ypres on the 20th September, which prompted little response from the members (Lloyd George still being at Criccieth), but he also reported that the Italian offensive on the Isonzo was, on the orders of General Cadorna, at a standstill and had been since the 12th September.[439] In contrast to the lack of enthusiasm aroused by the news from Ypres the news from Italy galvanized the War Cabinet into immediate and decisive action, and a note of disapproval was dispatched to Italy, stressing the *embarrassment* the Italian decision would cause on other fronts.

    The Italian G.H.Q. had cited worries over a collapse on the Russian front, the interior situation of Italy, and the possible effect of a setback on the country's morale, as the reasons for giving up the offensive. It was not only the British Cabinet who were shocked. Foch wrote to General Gondrecourt the French liaison officer at Italian G.H.Q.. 'My instructions to you are that you must insist with General Cadorna that the projected plan be maintained in its entirety. The difficulties in the interior of Italy, which are certainly the work of the enemy, testify to the enemy's anxiety under the repeated blows of the Italian Armies.'[440] Foch could instruct as much as he wished; Cadorna was to remain adamantly on the defensive.

    Three days later, on the morning of the 24th, the War Cabinet met again, with the Prime Minister back in the chair. A reply had arrived from Cadorna, stating that on the 19th the Italian government had decided that as the Austrian resistance was increasing and German intervention soon seemed likely, the offensive had been halted. He confirmed that if attacked the Italians would counter-attack, and was of the opinion that the Italian defensive stance would not affect the Allied situation on other fronts. This was at variance with the decisions made back in November 1916 when simultaneous offensives on all fronts had been considered advantageous. In an obvious state of excitement, which the news from Ypres had failed to rouse, but the disquieting although less significant news from Italy certainly had, the War Cabinet decided to reconvene a meeting of the War Policy Committee that very afternoon. This was to be the first meeting of the Committee since the 31st July, but the great battle that was raging in Flanders was not on the agenda.[441] As Lloyd George was plainly disappointed by the Italian reluctance to use the 100 guns in the way he had envisaged, plans were discussed to remove them and the accompanying troops from the supply line to the Italians, and ship them east through the Mediterranean to another theater, either to Salonica, or to Allenby in Palestine, or General Maude in Mesopotamia. Robertson however warned of the difficulties of using the guns in Palestine, pointing out that each battery required two trains for its transportation, and it was only possible to run seven or eight trains a day between Egypt and the Gaza front. Lloyd George

---

[439] National Archives, minutes of meeting of War Cabinet 237 21st September, statement by Robertson, and Appendix I telegram from Radcliffe in Rome.
[440] National Archives, Spiers to C.I.G.S. 22nd September WO106/404
[441] National Archives, minutes of the Cabinet Committee on War Policy 24th September CAB26/6

pressed the matter, and Robertson agreed to consult with Allenby. The question of the availability if shipping was discussed also with a view to moving men and guns from Marseilles and Italy, to either Salonica or Egypt. Consideration was given to reducing the country's grain reserve to make shipping available for the move through the Mediterranean. Whereas the Prime Minister had continually made it clear that he was no strategist as far as the Western Front was concerned, he was certainly becoming deeply involved in examining the strategic possibilities of cutting off the Turkish Army in Palestine, by a landing behind their front at Haifa, or further north at Ayas Bay (Alexandretta) to cut the main supply railway into Syria. Robertson pointed out that the Turks had recently completed the tunnels through the Taurus Mountains and could concentrate 70,000 to 80,000 men in a fortnight to oppose any landing. There were numerous objections raised to the Prime Minister's strategy, including the shortage of shipping, the difficulty of landing along the coast from an often rough eastern Mediterranean, rapid Turkish deployment, and, as pointed out by Lord Curzon, the long founded resistance of the French to a British landing in Syria or at Alexandretta. But Lloyd George was not to be put off, and suggested that the French should be encouraged to carry out the landing, partly carried in British transports and protected by British destroyers. Jellicoe and Wemyss explained that these could not be spared to carry out the operation. The Prime Minister then turned to his main passion and enquired of the possibility of shipping 150 heavy guns to Allenby. The Navy agreed it could be done, probably more quickly than Allenby could move them by train up to Gaza. Lloyd George's ever active and resourceful mind was one step ahead of the sailors, and suggested the guns could be carried in smaller ships then transferred to lighters and then to the shore. The charade continued back and forth between the politicians and the military, Wemyss pointing out to Smuts that there were no lighters available for the operation, having already described the near impossibility of landing guns from the often heavy seas. Wemyss suggested that Beirut may provide a safer landing point but Lord Curzon correctly pointed out that this was not far enough north to cut the Turkish communications with Mesopotamia. Wemyss then rather pointlessly suggested Haifa as a better landing point, 80 miles *further south.* Imaginations were truly being exercised to the extreme as Lord Curzon suggested that the British should reinforce Allenby in Palestine, the French should land at Alexandretta, and that the Japanese should send two divisions to support Maude in Mesopotamia. Lloyd George questioned what the effect would be on India of sending Japanese divisions to Mesopotamia. Curzon and Lloyd George felt that the Japanese would extract a high price for giving their assistance, which may well cost the British a possession in China. Their part in the meeting having concluded the representatives of the Navy then (undoubtedly thankfully) withdrew, and Lloyd George got down to the crux of his argument for the Palestinian enterprise. Should not Allenby be given overwhelming forces to ensure of his offensive being successful? 'He stated that the people in the country wanted some success to overcome war-weariness, *and the effect of an advance such as the recent one in Flanders did not last long.*'[442] (Authors italics) The conclusions of the meeting were that two divisions should be sent from France to act as a reserve in Egypt to Allenby's offensive in Palestine; Lloyd George should meet with Painlevé the next day and press for a French landing at Alexandretta; that to this end the French would have the use of Cyprus, the assistance of British transports, and the protection of 25 British destroyers, and that the French should begin to assemble lighters, horse boats, and barges and begin to tow them to the area of the eastern Mediterranean. The Japanese question would be put on hold until after talks with the Foreign Office.

    The minutes of the meeting illustrate how muddled and detached from reality the central political control of the British War effort had become. To explore every avenue of strategic possibility was only to be expected of the Committee, but to not make even one reference to the Flanders battle, at the moment it had begun to show positive results, shows a reluctance to face the subject of greatest importance. There was a willingness to discuss any and every issue, so long as that did not include facing up to the realities of the monumental struggle

---

[442] National Archives, minutes of the Cabinet Committee on War Policy 24th September CAB26/6

being enacted by the main body of their Army against the main body of the main enemy, *in Flanders*.

Three days later a letter was relayed to the War Cabinet from General Cadorna stressing that the decision for offensive or defensive action on the Italian front was his and his alone. This at least made it crystal clear to the Cabinet that it was not in a position to dictate military policy to Italy, even with a 100 gun stake in the game. The gaze of the Prime Minister now gradually shifted, not back to his most vital responsibility in Flanders, from where against the advice of Haig the desperately needed guns had been removed, but to hazy eastern horizons. While his soldiers suffered under the fire of *Group Wytschaete's* batteries, the downfall of Turkey was now to become the focus of Lloyd George's fertile but irresolute mind. More inclined to concern himself with a *morale boosting spectacle* rather than the reality of the Flanders battle, he now once more had his eyes fixed on Jerusalem. He could see little to celebrate in Plumer's 1,500 yard success of the 20th that would raise the spirits of a war-weary country. It was appearances not substance that concerned him, the quick buck, not the long-term investment. Better to reinforce Allenby in Palestine with two divisions and guns, and be certain of an historic but relatively pointless victory.

Future plans at Ypres

Weather conditions, rainfall Vlamertinghe, temperature Ypres[443]

	21st Sept	**22nd Sept**	**23rd Sept**	**24th Sept**	**25th Sept**	**26th Sept**
Rainfall	Trace	Trace	Trace	Nil	Trace	0.5mm
Temp	62F	64F	64F	69F	76F	69F

Between the 20th and 26th September no rain had fallen and the battlefield had continued to dry. Although cratered by hundreds of thousands of shell-holes which were still part water-filled, the surface of the ground began to form a hard dry crust, with the exception of the valleys of the shattered streams which were still quagmires to be avoided if possible. The improved ground helped the preparations necessary for the second of General Plumer's gradual steps towards the Passchendaele ridge, which had been sanctioned by Haig on the 21st September.

The Commander-In-Chief had been so encouraged by the results of the 20th September, that on the 22nd he sent an explanatory map to Plumer and Gough outlining his forecast for the next two phases of the campaign, to follow the hoped for success on the 26th. His intention for the third stage, to follow in about a week, required a further shift to the north by Second Army, with II Anzac Corps from that Army's reserve taking over the front now held by V Corps of Fifth Army. This would see I Anzac and II Anzac side by side attacking towards the Passchendaele ridge, with the right of I Anzac on Molenaarelshoek and the left of II Anzac virtually on the Stroombeek and thrusting towards the Wallenmolen – Bellevue spur. The objectives would be the main ridge around Broodseinde for I Anzac, and across Gravenstafel ridge into the Ravebeek – Stroombeek valley for II Anzac. On the right, X Corps would consolidate its position on Gheluvelt plateau to protect the Australian right flank, while on the left Fifth Army would strike towards Poelcappelle with the XVIII Corps. About a week later the fourth step would see Second Army on the ridge between Broodseinde and Passchendaele. Once this position was secure it would cover the right flank and rear of Fifth Army as it continued the main advance to the north-east towards Roulers and Staden. At Nieuport, Fourth Army would stand-by to co-operate with a strike across the Yser and with the long planned landings along the coast. The success of

---

[443] National Archives, GHQ statistics WO95/15

the 20th September following the previous disappointments had obviously raised Haig's spirits as they had those of his troops, enabling him to make these optimistic proposals.

Boulogne, 25th September

Haig's general optimism at this time may have been dampened somewhat, if had he been aware of a conference held in Boulogne on the 25th September, between the British and French to which, incredibly, the Commander-in-Chief had not been invited. A situation had arisen which had at its core the French mutinies. One element of Pétain's vital efforts to improve the morale of his Army had been an agreement to allow soldiers ten days leave in every four months. This had resulted in a permanent weakening of the effective strength of the French Army by some 340,000 men. The only immediate remedy open to the French was to reduce the length of front line held by them, and to request the British to extend their right flank southwards. Painlavé and Foch initially requested that the British take up the line as far south as Berry-Au-Bac. This was later moderated by Pétain, who requested the relief of six French divisions as far south as the Oise. This decision was to be presented to Haig in a letter from Robertson on the 3rd October, the day before the next great offensive at Ypres. It had previously been agreed, with the War Cabinet's approval that no discussion regarding operational matters would be held with the French without Haig being present, but that had not prevented Lloyd George from proceeding with the negotiations. He was also eager to introduce Foch to his plan for removing Turkey from the War, which would see the French land a force at Alexandretta 300 miles north of Jerusalem and cut the Turkish lines of supply to their forces in Palestine. Foch was not impressed with the idea, and Painlevé was found to be too preoccupied with his own political problems to be interested. Hankey was not impressed with the French, noting, 'One fact that emerged was that the French are not fighting at all. They put off their attack on Chemin des Dames until today or tomorrow and are postponing it again until October the 10th with the result that all the German strength is being concentrated against us in Flanders. Very fishy'.[444] Haig meanwhile, proceeded with the only operation which stood any real chance of damaging the main enemy, whilst in his absence the dispositions of his Army were discussed with the French.

Artillery preparations

Preparations for the attack on the 26th September had already begun on the afternoon of the 20th as the field artillery batteries had begun to move up 1,500 yards to their new support positions. An extension of the timber tracks and light railways had to be constructed into the recently won area, pushed further forward across the crater-field up to Westhoek ridge and Glencorse Wood. These tracks greatly assisted the movement of field guns and ammunition, the task of building and maintenance being the responsibility of the divisions in the line. Due to the hardening surface of the ground it was initially found possible to move the field artillery along earth tracks but without the properly prepared timber tracks the heavier pieces soon became stuck. Behind the old battle front the timber roads and light railways which had been constructed north and south of Zillebeke and connected with the main routes out of Ypres were used to move the medium and heavy artillery forward. The new battery positions were sited close to the tracks to ease the movement of the guns and ammunition, the work on roads and tracks behind the old front line being carried out by engineers from the resting divisions and Royal Engineer Tunnelling Companies.

The preparatory bombardment and counter-battery fire followed the pattern adopted for the first step, but this time there was more wire to cut leaving less ammunition available for practice barrages. These however took place twice a day at varying times on the 23rd, 24th, and 25th September. German counter-battery fire remained heavy and accurate, the British battery positions now moved to higher ground on the west of the plateau being under enemy ground

---

[444] Hankey Diaries 25th September

observation, and the concentration of German artillery in support of their attack on the 25th September gave them added fire power. In consequence artillery casualties began to rise. The protective barrage fired by Second Army was also to follow the routine of the 20th September, commencing at Zero Hour and creeping forward at the same rate. Fifth Army would fire a hurricane bombardment commencing two hours before Zero Hour, followed by a protective creeping barrage.

The Second Step

Carrying on from the successes of the 20th September, the second step was to again be limited to achievable objectives, within the capability of the infantry to secure and hold once they had been captured. The ability of the Germans to counter-attack any newly won positions was not underestimated, but as the enemy reaction was now predictable, measures could be taken to minimize its effect, and even turn it to British advantage. The defence in depth principle which up until 20th September the Germans had found so successful was being effectively used against them. The possession of the high ground east of Ypres which was so fundamental to their defensive grip on the city had been seriously compromised. Gheluvelt plateau had largely been lost, and gradually the German observation positions on the fingers of higher ground west of the main Passchendaele ridge were being wrested from them. Pilckem ridge had fallen, as had Anzac spur. The western end of Zonnebeke spur at Hill 35 and Hill 37 were, after dreadful fighting, in British hands and Hill 40 at the root of the spur was now threatened. The next attack which was known to be imminent may capture the whole of Polygon Wood and Tokio spur, and the British foothold on the western end of Gravenstafel ridge would undoubtedly be strengthened. There was little the Germans could do but to cling, at least for the time being, to their defensive principles however costly they may be. On the 25th September *Group Ypres* considered that many indications pointed to an immediate resumption of the offensive. Prisoner's statements and captured documents showed that the divisions which had attacked on the 20th had been relieved by fresh troops, and the presence of new lightly built forward battery positions had been confirmed. It was concluded that the British would attempt to seize at least the Passchendaele ridge (Zonnebeke crest) as the most favourable position for the winter. Every effort must be made to restrict their activity and delay their preparations until the weather again intervened. The British were not to be fought only with artillery, but the line divisions must maintain an offensive attitude continually harassing the enemy infantry and keeping them in a state of tension by frequent small attacks. Lost ground must be recaptured, to tempt the enemy into costly counter-attacks. The forces of the *Eingreif* divisions must not be called upon for this work; rather it was to be entrusted to the line divisions. So ran the simple doctrine of German defence tactics.

The main thrust of the attack to be made by three corps, one of Second Army and two of Fifth Army, at 5:50 a.m. on the 26th September was to be along a frontage of about 5,500 yards, from Black Watch Corner at the south-west corner of Polygon Wood on the right, to the track along Gravenstafel ridge near Wurst Farm on the left. The main assault with an advance of 1,000 to 1,500 yards should see I Anzac through Polygon Wood and into the Flanders I Line on their right, and across Tokio spur on their left. To the left of the Australian flank the western outskirts of Zonnebeke and Hill 40 just north of the station were the southern objectives of V Corps, with the 1,200 yard remnant of the *Wilhelm Stellung* about Kansas Cross still in German hands the corps objective to the north. As part of the general advance XVIII Corps would attempt to improve its position along Gravenstafel ridge.

Along a 2,500 yard line from the southern edge of Polygon Wood to about 1,000 yards south of the Menin Road in the Bassevillebeek valley, X Corps were to protect the right flank of the main attack. As we have seen, south of Black Watch Corner where 33rd Division had just relieved 23rd Division, the German spoiling attack on the 25th had punched two holes in the British line, one just north of the Menin Road which was not critical and had been contained, and another between the Reutelbeek and the southern face of Polygon Wood, which was serious exposing the Australian right flank and causing great disruption to preparations for the morning's attack.

The attack of the Second Army 5:50 a.m. 26th September

The German counter-attacks had caused huge problems to the battalions of 100th and 98th Brigades and 15th Australian Brigade, but by order of General Plumer were in no way to alter the planned timing of the assault. Special arrangements had been put in hand to overcome the difficulties, but the danger to the flank of 5th Australian Division was very real and might still jeopardize the whole offensive. As the attack by 33rd Division to recover the ground lost on the 25th September was to take place at 5:15 a.m. 35 minutes before Zero Hour on the 26th, an account of these operations will be given first.

X Corps north of the Menin Road

Operations to retake ground lost of the 25th

33rd Division
Major-General P. R. Wood

As we have seen, the task of 33rd Division to form a defensive flank had been made extremely difficult due to the German spoiling attack, and on being apprised of the situation General Plumer had redefined the divisional objectives. The 100th Brigade north of the Menin Road was to recover the ground lost on the 25th, while 98th Brigade alone was to cover the flank of 5th Australian Division along the southern edge of Polygon Wood. It was 98th Brigade that had been worst effected by the attack, and was now mostly back on a line just forward of Verbeek Farm, at least 700 yards behind where it should be. The task facing 98th Brigade appeared difficult in the extreme. The situation of 100th Brigade looked less precarious. Special arrangements had been made by 33rd Division to attempt to fill the dangerous gap in the Front Line on the exposed right flank of 5th Australian Division before the 5:50 a.m. Zero Hour.

98th Brigade 5:15 a.m.[445]
The fighting on the 25th September had been tough and confusing, made worse by the fact that the 98th Brigade had just taken up its position in the line and was on new territory. The German barrage throughout the day had hindered communication and it was unclear to brigade staff where the forward outposts of the 2nd Argyll and Sutherland were, although some, with the 1st Middlesex, were back as far as Verbeek Farm. Although German shelling had largely ceased over night, a thick ground mist had formed towards morning which conspired to deepen the confusion. At 4:00 a.m. Brigadier-General Elliott, 15th Australian Brigade, received a message from the 98th Brigade which stated, 'At the present time our left attacking battalion has three companies who have lost their way and are believed to be near Inverness Copse making there way forward. The left battalion hopes to have at least one company forward which will try to get as close to the original front line as possible'.
From prisoners taken on the 25th it was known to the Germans that a general attack would take place on the 26th. To protect the gains they had made south of Polygon Wood their artillery in the early hours of the 26th began to shell the area heavily, including the approaches in the vicinity of Inverness Copse, the shells coming in from the east and probably fired by the Terhand battery groups. The 33rd Division informed the 5th Australian Division several times that a line existed 200 yards forward of Verbeek Farm, but this line was not finally located until

---

[445] National Archives, War Diary 78th Brigade WO95/2426

after 6:00 a.m. when the two companies of the 2nd Argyll who had gone forward to support the Middlesex on the 25th were located there. The situation was obviously one of great confusion, the front positions of both the 98th Brigade and the enemy being completely unclear.

The 1/4th Suffolk Regiment,[446] with the 1/5th Cameronians (Scottish Rifles), (19th Brigade attached from divisional reserve), were ordered up to make a pre-emptive attack at 5:15 a.m. from the Verbeek Farm line towards the old *Wilhelm Stellung* position south of Black Watch Corner, a distance of around 500 yards. At the 5:50 a.m. Zero hour, the attack would then proceed with the barrage for another 1,000 yards towards the divisional objective just east of Cameron House. The Suffolk had received orders at 7:00 p.m. on the 25th to move up to the trench running from Fitzclarence Farm north towards Glencourse Wood and at 5:15 a.m. with the Scottish Rifles on their left, to advance to the line which it was believed was still held by the 1st Middlesex and the 2nd Argyll and Sutherland. The forward Suffolk companies were in position in the trench by 11:30 p.m. on the 25th with the two support companies in shell-holes to the rear. The line thought to be held by the Middlesex and the Argyll was at first believed to be around 150 yards east of Verbeek Farm, and later along the track behind Lone House 350 yards further forward.

The Scottish Rifles moved up to their support positions about Clapham Junction around 1:00 p.m. on the 26th. The assembly for the pre-emptive attack began badly with the Scottish Rifles, who were moving up from Clapham Junction with the assistance of guides across very difficult and unfamiliar ground, becoming lost in the vicinity of Inverness Copse. The darkness followed by the thick ground mist forming in the early hours and incessant enemy shelling totally confused direction and movement. By 3:30 a.m. the Commanding Officer of the Suffolk received permission to proceed independently, the Scottish Rifles having not arrived at their assembly point, but at this stage declined as to do so as it would necessitate the Suffolk attacking the whole brigade front previously held by the Argyll and the Middlesex. By 4:15, "A" and "B" Companies of the Scottish Rifles had arrived and a decision was taken to attack at 4:45 with the forces now available. At 4:30 however a heavy German barrage descended on the area further disrupting the situation, and the forward movement was postponed, first until 5:15 and subsequently until 5:30, when it was hoped matters would have improved sufficiently to proceed. By 5:30 it appeared the Scottish Rifles were still not organized and to make matters worse the German shelling became a concentrated barrage. The Suffolk, who were about to jump-off were therefore ordered to take what cover they could.

At 5:50, Zero hour and as the main attack commenced, parties of the Suffolk and Scottish Rifles advanced. Half of "C" Company of the Rifles also arrived at this time and were moved up in support of "A" and "B" Companies. Officer casualties were numerous causing much confusion in some companies, the attack advancing with little cohesion or unison. A ragged line was finally established by a few parties between Carlisle Farm and Black Watch Corner, in touch with the 4th King's Liverpool which was on the Reutelbeek to the right, but most were still 500 yards back in a line about Lone House. At around 9:00 a.m. the shelling became even heavier, now also coming from the south-east, the Tenbrielen group lending its weight to the Terhand group. When the other half of "C" Company and "D" Company of the Rifles arrived at 10:30 they were given orders to move up at 11:45 and attempt to push the line further forward, which they did but only by a few yards.[447]

Two hours after the attack had begun, the Australian right flank was still seriously exposed, now even more so as the 15th Australian Brigade had advanced through Polygon Wood with the 5:50 a.m. barrage. Provision had been made for this eventuality by Major-General Wood commanding 33rd Division and at 8:00 a.m. the 2nd Royal Welsh Fusiliers, (another battalion from 19th Brigade in divisional reserve) was ordered up. Its instructions were to pass round through the

---

[446] National Archives, War Diary 1/4th Suffolk WO95/2427, National Archives, War Diary 1/5th Scottish Rifles WO95/2422

[447] In this action 4th Suffolk sustained casualties of two officers killed and seven wounded, 43 other ranks killed, 150 wounded and 63 missing. The 1/5th Scottish Rifles sustained casualties of two officers killed, five wounded and one missing, 28 other ranks killed, 119 wounded and 52 missing.

Australian sector and enter Polygon Wood, from where it would attack at noon under a special barrage, in a south-easterly direction towards the first objective about Cameron House. After a wide detour through the back areas of 4th Australian Division the Fusiliers arrived at Black Watch Corner just before noon. As it was still believed that parties of the Argyll and Sutherland were still holding out east of the Black Watch Corner line, (when in fact they were mostly 500 yards west of this line), 98th Brigade ordered the special protective barrage to land beyond the days second objective near Cameron Covert, 900 yards forward of the jumping-off line of the Royal Welsh Fusiliers. To all intents and purposes there was no protective barrage for the attack of the Fusiliers, which were to be supported by elements of two Australian battalions. The full reason for this decision will soon be made clear.

Upon observing the three British battalions forming up, those parties of the *230th Reserve Infantry Regiment* who had been occupying Jerk House 400 yards east of Black Watch Corner began to retire around noon. The machine guns of the same regiment situated on Polderhoek spur 1,500 yards distant, south of the Reutelbeek, had the attack of the Fusiliers and Australians in full view and unleashed a devastating hail of machine gun fire at the advancing waves. The history of the *230th R.I.R.* states, 'When about 11 a.m. the wall of mist on the right flank of the regiment had disappeared, the men of the *230th* on Polderhoek spur saw the deploying enemy, behind his rolling barrage, advancing deep on its flank and manifestly in the act of pushing to the southeast. Enemy columns following after, were trying to reach Polygon Wood. On this incredibly favourable target there now fell at 1,000 to 1,800 metres the fire of all the heavy machine guns of the regiment that were still available, with annihilating effect, the British artillery being unable fully to suppress them. Seven heavy machine guns of the 1st Company sent streaming out in a short time 20,000 rounds.'[448]

This German account is substantially accurate except for the 'rolling barrage' which had been fired 900 yards in front of the attack. The Royal Welsh Fusiliers advanced around 350 yards through the machine gun fire and reached Jerk House, where they attempted to continue towards the first objective at Cameron House still 200 yards further forward. The attack was unsuccessful and Cameron House was to stay in German hands until finally captured by the Australians on the night of the 26th / 27th. (For map of the action see 5th Australian Division attack on Polygon Wood).

100th Brigade 5:15 a.m.[449]

The 100th Brigade had been originally tasked with pushing the front line forward from their position on the old *Wilhelm Stellung* by about 100yards along the Menin Road and to a depth of 600 yards across the Polderhoek spur on the northern flank. The German attack of the 25th had pushed the British line back from the *Wilhelm* position by around 200 yards towards Veldhoek. The objective had been redefined by Plumer and was now limited to the recovery of the shelters along the *Wilhelm Stellung*. The brigade attacked with the 1st Queens along the Menin Road with the 1/9th Highland Light Infantry on their left. The Highlanders reached their objective but the Queens were held up just short of the *Wilhelm Stellung* shelters. A company of 1st Scottish Rifles from 19th Brigade were sent up in support and by 9:00 a.m. most of the old line was retaken, and touch was made with the Sussex south of the Menin Road. On the Reutelbeek the 4th King's Liverpool had largely held firm on the 25th and by 1:30 p.m. were back in their original position. About 2:30 p.m. a local counter-attack against the left of the Queens was driven off by Lewis gun and rifle fire, with the fire support of 2 platoons of the Highland Light Infantry. The platoon commanded by 2nd Lieutenant Glen followed up the enemy retreat with a bayonet charge, the highlanders driving the Germans back from their original position. The line gained was then reinforced by the advance of the second platoon.

---

[448] AOA p821
[449] National Archives, War Diary 100th Brigade WO95/2429

X Corps
South of the Menin Road 5:50 a.m.

To further strengthen the southern protective flank another attempt was to be made at 5:50 a.m. to capture the section of the *Wilhelm Stellung* still held by the enemy between Tower Hamlets and the Quadrilateral position about Joist Redoubt.

39th Division   Major-General E. Feetham

The 39th Division had been less heavily engaged on the 20th September, and had retained the 118th and 116th Brigades in reserve. It had now side stepped to the left by around 1,500 yards and was confronted by a formidable task. A line which ran just beyond Tower Trench along the east of Tower Hamlets spur was the single objective for the two brigades. The jumping-off line was still in the muddy Bassevillebeek valley just east of the stream, and the advance was then faced with a climb up the valley side under the machine guns of Tower Hamlets and the Quadrilateral.

The divisional front ran for 1,500 yards from in the Bassevillebeek valley on the right, to the Menin Road on the left. In contrast to the very dry surface on the plateau, in the Bassevillebeek valley the mud was still heavy and glutinous. The Quadrilateral at Joist Redoubt had caused a serious hold up to the 41st Division on the 20th and had subsequently been subject to a systematic bombardment from the 23rd September to Zero Hour. Two tanks were to move along the Menin Road to Kantinge Cabaret and then along the Tower Hamlets track, to cooperate with the infantry in overcoming the Tower Hamlets pillboxes and the Quadrilateral position. Any movement across the plateau towards the front line, through Shrewsbury Forest and Bodmin Copse and down into the valley, was under constant observation from Tower Hamlets spur and was totally exposed to severe artillery, machine gun and rifle fire. The 14th Hampshire of 116th Brigade had already sustained casualties of 6 killed and 27 wounded in relieving the 15th Hampshire.

118th Brigade [450]

The 118th Brigade was to attack with the 1/1st Cambridgeshire Regiment with the 4/5th Black Watch in close support. The 300 yard line from which the battalions were to attack faced south east, aligned with the western face of Joist Redoubt. The right end of the line, being only 100 yards from the Bassevillebeek was mostly heavy mud, whilst at the left end of the line 350 yards from the stream and higher up the Tower Hamlets spur, the ground was much better. Two hours before the Cambridge assembled, platoon tapes had been laid on the jump-off positions, which were 300 yards short of the western face of Joist Redoubt, (the Quadrilateral), and white painted wooden pegs had been pushed into the ground 50 yards forward to give direction. The ground was so broken by shell-holes that companies were ordered to advance in section columns in single file.

The Cambridge moved of behind the barrage at 5:50, but immediately on the right and centre, "C" and "D" Companies in the bad ground near the stream become badly bogged-down. Many men became stuck in the knee deep in mud, and needing to be hauled out inevitably lost the barrage, the Black Watch in support experiencing the same problems. On the left "A" Company on the higher ground made good progress, kept up with the barrage and within 150 yards was amongst enemy dug-outs, the garrisons being cleared with the bayonet. As "C" and "D" Companies struggled out of the mud, "A" Company reached the western face of Joist Redoubt. Enemy resistance now increased at close quarters, as both sides desperately fought for possession of the redoubt. "A" Company cleared a dug-out in which 12 enemy machine gunners died by the bayonet in bloody and vicious combat. By the time "C" and "D" Companies cleared the south-western edge of the redoubt, "A" Company had reached the eastern face and the fighting became most severe. At the north-east corner of the redoubt, Tower Trench, the main

---

[450] National Archives, War Diary 118th Brigade WO95/2589

earthwork of the *Wilhelm Stellung* behind Tower Hamlets, entered the Quadrilateral perimeter from the north. The western face of Tower Trench was well wired and the trench and the northeastern corner of the redoubt were heavily defended by enemy machine gunners and riflemen, which opened a withering fire upon their attackers. To the left of the Cambridge and the Black Watch it appeared that the 116th Brigade was either held up or had veered left, for there was no sign of an attack against the southern end of Tower Trench. In fact there was a 400 yard gap between the Cambridgeshire and the 13th Sussex. By 6:30 a.m. the left flank of 118th Brigade was wide open and the determined and well positioned enemy fought stubbornly to evict the British from the redoubt. Casualties were now severe, and the Cambridge reserve "B" Company was ordered forward to support "A" Company and the left of the Black Watch, which had thrown back their left flank to face the gap, and to attempt to push forward to the final objective. Severe machine gun and rifle fire from the north-east corner of the redoubt and from the southern end of Tower Trench swept the Cambridge and Black Watch who had taken cover in shell-holes and were attempting to dig-in. "C" Company had reached the eastern edge of the redoubt but were pinned down by machine gun fire from the south, and "B" Company could get no further forward than the western face of the redoubt before being also forced to take cover.

It had been impossible for the tanks to negotiate the shell craters about the Menin Road and they had become bogged near Dumbarton Lakes. Their support would now have been very welcome, for as the Cambridge and Black Watch attempted to dig-in, they were swept by machine gun fire at close range from north and south. A determined counter attack by two companies of *115th Body Guard Infantry Regiment* of the crack *25th Division* emerging from shelters within the redoubt, drove the attacking companies of the Cambridge and Black Watch out of the Quadrilateral, and back to a line around 200 yards beyond the western perimeter, "A" Company having lost all its officers. This line on the eastern slope of the Bassevillebeek valley was then consolidated with support from the 1/6th Cheshire, and touch was eventually made with the Royal Sussex on the left.

116th Brigade [451]

The 116th Brigade attacked with the 13th Royal Sussex Regiment and the 14th Hampshire Regiment,[452] supported by the 11th and 12th Royal Sussex. The Sussex and Hampshire advanced through heavy ground across the flat top at the northern end of the spur towards the Tower Hamlets pillboxes and immediately met with heavy machine gun fire. Casualties soon mounted, the Hampshire loosing four officers, but the advance continued under the barrage and quickly outflanked and bombed the pillboxes and shelters at Tower Hamlets. The forward Hampshire companies had lost heavily and the support company commanded by 2nd Lieutenant Taberer was moved up to reinforce the attack. His leadership and initiative did much to ensure the success at this stage of the Hampshire advance and he was subsequently to be awarded the D.S.O. The advancing continued beyond the Tower Hamlet shelters, and a line of shell-holes just short of the northern end of Tower Trench was secured by about 150 men of the Hampshire by 7:30 a.m. A post was also established in the north-western corner of Gheluvelt Wood in touch with the Queens north of the Menin Road. As we have seen, in their attack on Tower Trench the Sussex appear to have veered to the left, as a reconnaissance carried out at 11:00 a.m. by Lieutenant -Colonel Riddell of the 1/1st Cambridge found the southern end of Tower Trench to be still in the hands of the *231st R.I.R.*, and the nearest Sussex troops in shell-holes 250 yards to his left, 150 yards short of Tower Trench. Companies of the 11th and 12th Royal Sussex were ordered forward to reinforce and help consolidate the new line.

A 600 yard section of the *Wilhelm Stellung* behind Tower Hamlets and to the south linking with Joist Redoubt at the Quadrilateral remained in the hands of the enemy. The tenacious resistance of the *25th Division* and elements of the *50th Reserve Division* which had

---

[451] National Archives, War Diary 116th Brigade WO95/2581
[452] C.T. Atkinson (1952) *The Royal Hampshire Regiment Vol II 1914-1918* Glasgow: Robert Maclehose p241-242

withstood all the British artillery and infantry could throw at them still denied the total possession of the Third Line south of the Menin Road.

I Anzac Corps
Lieutenant General Sir William Birdwood

Polygon Wood and Tokio Spur

From Black Watch Corner on the corps right flank to just north of the Anzac blockhouse on the left, a distance of about 2,200 yards, I Anzac was to attack at 5:50 a.m. with the 5th and 4th Australian Divisions, and advance to an average depth of 1,200 yards. There were to be two objective lines, the first at around 800 yards to include the Butte in Polygon Wood and Tokio on the spur, and the final objective 400 yards further forward to include the Flanders I Line behind Polygon Wood, and the whole of Tokio spur and southern outskirts of Zonnebeke. The mud which had been so synonymous with the offensive so far, had turned at least on the higher ground about Polygon Wood, to a dry crust upon which an exploding shell would raise dense clouds of dust. The attack began amongst great concern regarding the confused situation on the 5th Division right flank, which as we have seen, due to the difficulties of 33rd Division was dangerously exposed.

5th Australian Division
Major-General J. Talbot-Hobbs

The shattered remains of Polygon Wood was a wasteland of a few skeletal trees, blasted tree stumps, flattened and splintered trunks and countless water filled shell-holes. The inevitable low grey silhouettes of numerous blockhouses lurked amongst the shambles to confront the 15th and 14th Brigades as they advanced. The mound of the Butte, now exposed above the leveled trees at the north-eastern end of the wood, had been tunnelled by the Germans to give dug-out protection and also gave them excellent observation over the Australian position. On the night of the 25th / 26th September the situation of the 15th Australian Brigade on the right was dire, as 3 out of its 4 battalions had already been committed in the fighting to stem the German counter attack. In accordance with plans rapidly made, 2 battalions, the 31st and 29th of the reserve 8th Brigade, would now attack with the 59th Battalion, but under control of 15th Brigade. The battalions of 8th Brigade had the disadvantage of not being familiar with the ground. On the left, 14th Brigade had not been so affected by the German attack and its planning remained unchanged. The barrage at Zero Hour was considered the most perfect that ever protected Australian troops and was said to have broken out in a single monumental crash. The density of the shellfire was tremendous, great columns of dust from each explosion blending one with the other, and only the white puffs of shrapnel shell along the barrage face being seen as separate bursts.

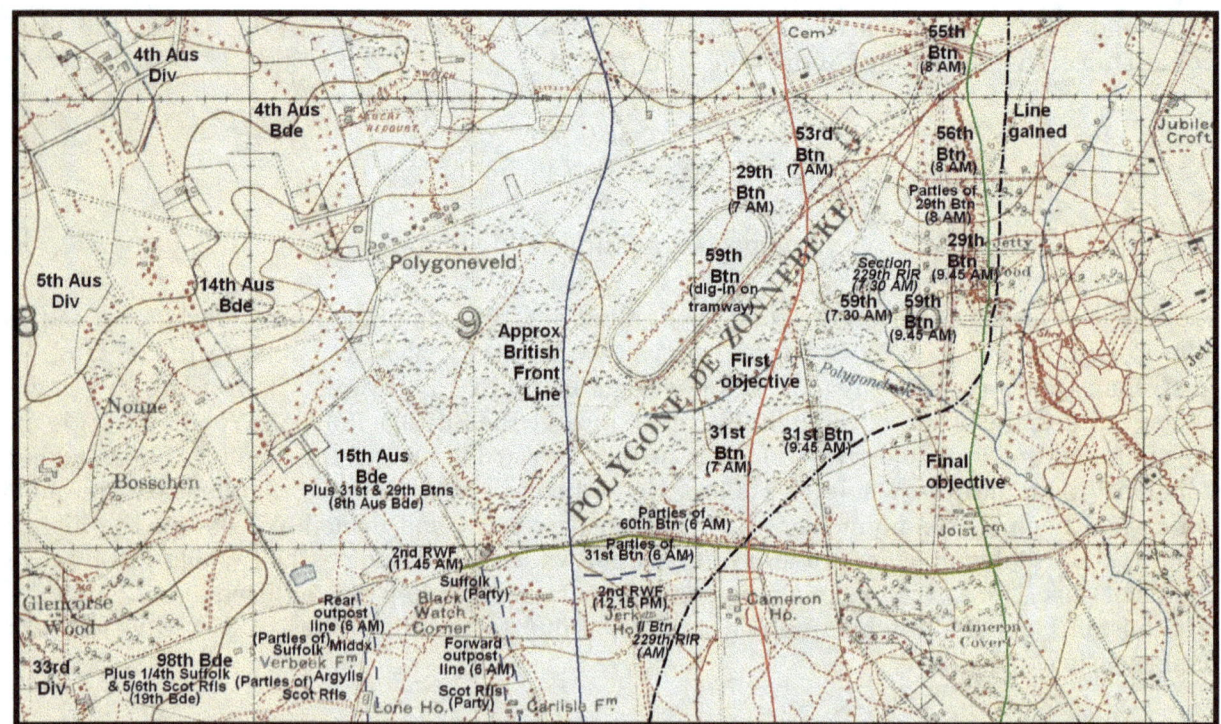

The capture of Polygon Wood 5th Australian Division – the danger to the right flank

15th Brigade / 8th Brigade [453]

The ferocity of the barrage and the great dust cloud it produced made it difficult to follow at a safe distance commensurate with keeping as close up as possible. Direction was also a problem and officers used their compass for guidance. Three minutes after the barrage descended 59th Battalion moved off as they had been trained, with a thin screen as close as possible to the shellfire, and with the successive waves following at a proper distance. They were to secure the first objective, where there would be a pause for about an hour, after which the 31st and 29th Battalions of 8th Brigade would take up the advance to the final objective. The two battalions of 8th Brigade had been trained rather differently, to keep up very close to the barrage, and soon they caught up and began to pass through the orderly pace of the 59th. Some of the 59th maintained their pace while others surged forward with the 31st and 29th.

The ground across which the three battalions were attacking had earlier been clear of the enemy, but since the German incursion on the 25th about 18 machine guns had been brought up into the wood. The fire of these guns added to those in blockhouses and others on the Butte, cut into the advancing waves. Enemy gun teams in shell-holes were quickly overwhelmed at bayonet point, but two pillboxes at the south-west corner of the wood and one near the old pony track or "racecourse" put up a fight, and many casualties occurred before the first objective was reached. On the 15th brigade left the attack was taken forward in touch with the 14th Brigade to the first objective, but nearer the centre, parties of the 59th mistaking the trench tramway to the right of the pony track to be its objective halted there, around 150 yards short of the first objective.

The exposed right flank now began to cause problems and confusion. As the 31st advanced towards its objective machine gun fire from a group of pillboxes on a low knoll west of Jerk House and beyond the southern side of the wood, caught them in enfilade and from the rear. Part of a support company following up turned half right towards this fire, and breaking beyond the wood attacked the pillboxes which due to their proximity close to the British line, had been missed by the barrage. This party of the 31st, after a serious of stubborn fights

---

[453] National Archives, War Diary 15th Aus Brigade WO95/3638, National Archives, War Diary 59th Battalion 3651, National Archives, War Diary 29th Battalion WO95/3638, National Archives, War Diary 31st Battalion WO95/3619

overcame the pillboxes, but was driven into shell-holes by heavy machine gun fire from the numerous guns at Jerk House. The ragged line stretched 200 yards south of the wood in front of Jerk House and was soon reinforced by a few Stokes mortars, while officers still tried to locate any trace of 33rd Division outposts. Inevitably more parties were drawn to the sound of fighting on what they knew was a dangerously exposed flank. The enemy was now concentrating at Jerk House and the *II Battalion* of the *229th Regiment* soon launched a counter-attack against the weak Australian line capturing an officer of the 29th and 20 men of the 31st of whom 14 were wounded.

Back in the wood meanwhile the main body of the 31st had captured its first objective but was in turn receiving heavy machine gun fire from Cameron House 100 yards south of the wood. The fire was so intense that a defensive flank was thrown back facing south towards Jerk and Cameron House.

Just after 6:00 a.m. messages from the front arrived at the joint battalion headquarters at Black Watch Corner, warning that as expected the right flank was wide open. A company of the 57th who had been involved in the previous day's fighting was intended to provide a defence line on this flank but had been caught squarely by the German retaliatory barrage and could not get forward. Parties of the 60th in the old front line had been forward of, and therefore missed by this barrage, and although in process of relief moved up in support of the exposed flank. A serious dilemma now faced the commander of the 31st. At 7:30 a.m. his battalion was to advance towards the final objective, but with the right flank totally open this would undoubtedly be extremely costly. The decision was made to remain on the first objective awaiting the advance of 33rd Division on the right.

Confusion now spread across the brigade front. On the left the 29th were also told to remain on the first objective although their flank was not immediately exposed. If the 29th stood fast this would produce a domino affect and expose the right of 14th Brigade as they advanced. To compound the confusion those of the 31st Battalion next to the 29th and on the first objective, did not receive the order to stand fast and as the barrage moved east the leading platoons moved off with it. Some, when 150 yards out were brought back to the first objective, back in line with the 29th while others moved on towards the final objective. Part of the rear company was deployed along the southern defensive flank where they were joined by those of the 60th to form a stronger line facing Jerk House.

On receipt of the news that 31st Battalion was standing on the first objective, Brigadier - General Elliott of 15th Brigade sent an unambiguous order for the 31st to go forward. Due to the total dislocation of the battalion, compliance with this order was not immediately possible and the situation remained the same. At this point the good news arrived with Elliott that 33rd Division were to attempt their attack with the Suffolk and Scottish Rifles. As we have seen this attack was unsuccessful resulting in the Royal Welsh Fusiliers being ordered up and moving through the sector of 4th Australian Division and into Polygon Wood to attack towards Cameron House at noon. To Elliott, upon receiving the news that the Royal Welsh Fusiliers were to attack, the situation looked more hopeful and at 11:00 a.m. he ordered that 31st and 29th would attack towards the final objective at noon in conjunction with the Welsh.

The situation at the front was very confused, as the battalions of 15th Brigade had become partially disorganized due mainly to the dangerous situation on the right flank. Most of 59th Battalion was mistakenly digging-in 200 yards short of their first objective. Part of 31st were out of the wood on the southern side pinned down in front of Jerk House, with part in the wood with orders to stand on the first objective, while others on the left, not having received the order to stand fast had moved off towards the final objective. Most of 29th Battalion was also standing fast on the first objective, but the left company had advanced alongside the 14th Brigade to protect that brigade's left flank.

At about 7:00 a.m. it was realized that the position near the pony track where 59th were digging-in was wrong. Some of the 31st were digging-in about 200 yards forward, on a slight rise beyond a depression through which ran the Polygonbeek, but to add further to the confusion some of them were drifting back towards the line of the 59th. At 7:30 the 59th were therefore organized to advance towards their correct position, the first objective on the Polygonbeek. As they did so Germans opened fire from an old battery position, but as the Australians moved forward quickly retired to a group of pillboxes beyond the stream. This advance coincided with that of 14th Brigade and the left company of the 29th Battalion. This company who against orders had decided to move forward with 14th Brigade in an attempt to protect that brigades flank, made their attack behind the barrage towards the final objective. With the 14th Brigade and the left company of the 29th Battalion now on the final objective a party of Germans emerged from the pillboxes beyond the Polygonbeek, which should have been secured by the right companies of the 29th which were still about the first objective. This local counter-attack made by a section of the *229th R.I.R.* and led by their battalion commander, attempted to work behind the front outposts of the 14th Brigade and attack the holding posts along the first objective. After a spirited attack against these posts, the battalion commander was wounded and the party fell back to their pillboxes from where they continued to fire. This action coincided with the arrival of the 59th on the Polygonbeek and the danger of the fire from the pillboxes was obvious. A party of the 59th was pushed forward to outflank the pillboxes from the south. The German positions were quickly subdued and the battalion commander, his staff and 60 men were made prisoners. The line through the German pillboxes east of the Polygonbeek, on which the 59th now began to consolidate, corresponded approximately with the final objective of the 29th, who had now moved forward to this position, and at about 9:45 a.m. touch was made on the right with the leading parties of the 31st. By the time the main barrage finished at 11:17 the line through the eastern edge of the wood was consolidated, with the right pulled back to conform to the defensive flank along the southern face. During the attacks by 31st Battalion, Private Patrick Joseph Budgen had on two occasions led small parties forward towards the final objective through heavy machine gun fire and attacked strongly held pillboxes. He proceeded to bomb the machine guns into silence and then capture the garrison at bayonet point. Later in the action whilst attempting to rescue wounded comrades, he was shot down and killed by machine gun fire, having already recovered five. For his most conspicuous bravery he was to be posthumously awarded the V. C.

Flares fired by the infantry in the forward positions were observed by the contact patrol RE8 of 4 Squadron and carefully marked on their map, and the news that the final objective was secure was dropped at 5th Division headquarters at 11:25 a.m. As a result of this information, and also because it was believed parties of the Argyll and Sutherland may still be beyond Jerk House, the special barrage by 33rd Division and 5th Australian Division guns to be fired at noon to support the attack of the Royal Welsh Fusiliers and part of the 31st Battalion, landed well forward at Cameron Covert, which on one hand did not help the Fusiliers but on the other did not land on the forward Australian positions, which were now in the southeast corner of the wood.

14th Brigade [454]

The 14th Brigade had not suffered the same degree of disruption on the 25th September that had so adversely affected the 15th Brigade. All three battalions detailed to attack, the 53rd to the first objective, and the 56th and 55th to the final, new the ground well. Two platoons of the 54th Battalion were to cover the assembly, but were not to take part in the attack. The 53rd Battalion in support positions in Nonne Bosschen had however caught the full fury of the German bombardment on the 25th and had lost 150 men, but still assembled on its jumping off tapes at midnight in good spirit. Brigadier -General Hopkirk assembled all three battalions close up to the front in twelve waves 60 yards deep, and a German precautionary barrage fired at 4:00 a.m. fell harmlessly behind the concentrated battalions.

Advancing at 5:50 a.m. close behind the barrage, the 53rd quickly outflanked the opposing pillboxes and after 500 yards the mound of the Butte could be seen silhouetted against the eastern sky through the smoke and dust. A few German machine gunners upon the mound

---

[454] National Archives, War Diary 14th Aus Brigade WO95/3625, National Archives, War Diary 53rd Battalion WO95/3628, National Archives, War Diary 55th Battalion WO95/3631, National Archives, War Diary 56th Battalion WO95/3633

ran off as the 53rd swarmed over the top, and bombed the entrances of the dugouts on the far side. Machine gun fire from a pillbox in the cemetery to the left of the Butte was soon suppressed and the position, which had been a regimental headquarters, was seized. Around 60 prisoners were taken in the dugout system beneath the Butte, most of them medical personnel.

At 7:30 a.m. the 56th and 55th continued the advance to the final objective beyond the wood on the Flanders I Line. The artillery had effectively pounded these defences, only shreds of the entanglements being evident, and the shelters and pillboxes along the line were quickly secured. Only on the right of 56th Battalion was there serious resistance, considerable machine gun fire coming from the pillboxes along the Polygonbeek which should have been secured by the 29th. Attempts by the 56th to take the pillboxes proved costly, the position finally falling as we have seen to parties of the 59th and finally consolidated by the 29th. Two blockhouses just beyond the Flanders I Line continued to fire on the forward Australian positions. Small parties of the 56th and 55th moved forward and captured them taking 45 prisoners, but then withdrew as the position was within the Anzac barrage line. The new outpost line along Flanders I was quickly consolidated to withstand the expected counter-attacks. The Butte 250 yards to the rear, so long used as an observation point by the enemy, was now put to the same use by the Australians, artillery observers and machine gunners acquiring an excellent view across the upper slopes of the ridge to the east and northeast.

The enemy line opposite the 14th Brigade was held on the right by the *229th R.I.R.* of the *50th Reserve Division* and on the left by the *49th R.I.R.* of the *3rd Reserve Division*.

After a very difficult start, 5th Australian Division had secured all its objectives except for the short section at the southeast corner of Polygon Wood, where the line was thrown back to conform to the 33rd Division position. The 14th Brigade had captured around 200 prisoners and 34 machine guns. Largely due to the tenacity and fighting spirit of the battalions of 15th and 8th Brigades success had been achieved in the face of confusion and great danger.[455]

4th Australian Division
Major-General E. G. Sinclair-Maclagan

The high drama on the right of I Anzac did not affect 4th Division. The 1,200 yards to be covered from the front line on Anzac spur to the final objective initially crossed the shallow Albania valley, then across the Tokio spur and into the depression the other side and the southern outskirts of the remains of Zonnebeke. Whereas Flanders I Line to the south had been taken by 5th Division, it was beyond 4th Division's final objective as here it ran away to the north, while the front of attack ran south-east to north-west. The advance, especially to the east of Tokio spur, would be exposed to enemy observation from the main ridge about Broodseinde, but equally any German counter-attack made in daylight would be clearly seen as it crested the bare ridge-top. The division was to attack with the 4th and 13th Brigades and both assembled well forward, avoiding the 4:00 a.m. German barrage which landed predominantly to the rear. The enemy line opposite 4th Australian Division was held by the centre and right regiments of the *3rd Reserve Division*, the *2nd R.I.R.* and the *34th Fusilier Regiment.*

---

[455] The author hopes that his description of the German counter-attack and the subsequent fighting of the 33rd Division and the 5th Australian Division is a more accurate and fare account than that given by Prior and Wilson in their book *Passchendaele the Untold Story*, and addresses the memory of the part played by the 98th Brigade: 'The 98 Brigade of this division [33rd] which was supposed to advance with the 15 Australian Brigade on its left, was nowhere to be seen at zero hour on account of its experience on the 25th. But the situation was retrieved by the Australians, who managed to capture their first objective and then use follow-up formations to side step to the right, thus capturing much of the territory assigned to 98 Brigade'. Prior and Wilson, *Passchendaele the Untold Story* p129

4th Brigade [456]

To secure the 4th Brigade's first objective was the task of 16th Battalion. The 15th and 14th Battalions were then to pass through to the final objective. At 5:50 a.m. as the assault began, the 13th Battalion in support began digging a communication trench across Anzac spur to enable safer access to the front line. Each battalion was to attack with four companies in line each on a one platoon front.

The inevitable pillboxes put up some resistance to the advance, but were soon subdued and the first objective was taken. The attack successfully reached the final objective on Tokio spur and consolidated just short of the Flanders I Line, the Germans then sniping from that line with machine guns upon the forward Australian outposts. At this time Sergeant James John Dwyer of 4th Company, Australian Machine Gun Corps rushed his gun forward to within 30 yards of a German machine gun which was enfilading troops on his flank. His fire at very close range killed the gun crew. Dwyer then captured the gun and returned with it to the Australian line. He continued to command his guns with great coolness on this day and on the 27th and was to be awarded the V.C. for his courage. The communication trench which had been started by 13th Battalion was completed as a track across Albania valley and in two hours was connected with the final objective, Stokes mortars being quickly brought forward to engage the troublesome machine gun sniping.

13th Brigade [457]

The 50th Battalion led the attack across Albania valley and the upper headwaters of the Steenbeek to the first objective across the nose of Tokio spur. Here the 49th and 51st passed through across the spur to the final objective, with the right and centre about 250 yards short of the outpost line of Flanders I, and the left of the 51st into the Brick Kiln Yard on the southern outskirts of Zonnebeke, with the British 3rd Division in touch on the left.

The I Anzac Corps was on its final objectives along the whole line and before the protective barrage ended consolidation was complete on the front of the 4th Division. Each brigade had taken forward eight machine guns to stiffen the new defense line against the expected counter-attacks.

The attack of the Fifth Army 5:50 a.m. 26th September

With I Anzac striking the main blow into the Flanders I Line, Fifth Army was to protect the Australian left flank, capture Hill 40, 750 yards northwest of Zonnebeke and at the same time push forward on the left towards the 32 metre ring contour near Aviatik Farm on Gravenstafel ridge. The capture of the latter position would provide a beneficial observation point across the Stroombeek and along the Ravebeek valley, and the northern section of the Flanders I Line where it crossed Wallemolen spur, another westward pointing sub-feature of the main ridge, 1,800 yards west of Passchendaele. Most importantly it would allow observation of part of the main ridge south of Passchendaele. The capture of Hill 40 was to prove elusive but fortunately not crucial, as observation east of the hill would be possible with the capture of Tokio spur by the Australians. Along a 3,500 yard front, V Corps was to provide the protective flank with the 3rd and 59th Divisions, while 58th Division of XVIII Corps would attempt the attack along Gravenstafel ridge.

---

[456] National Archives, War Diary 4th Aus Brigade WO95/3488, National Archives, War Diary 14th Battalion WO95/3495, National Archives, War Diary 15th Battalion WO95/3498, National Archives, War Diary 16th Battalion WO95/3499

[457] National Archives, War Diary 13th Aus Brigade WO95/3518, National Archives, War Diary 49th Battalion WO95/3521, National Archives, War Diary 50th Battalion WO95/3522, National Archives, War Diary 51st Battalion WO95/33523

V Corps Lieutenant
General E. A. Fanshaw

Hill 40 and Otto Farm

Three significant natural features confronted the V Corps. On the right where 3rd Division was to attack, the headwaters of the Steenbeek in Albania valley presented a quagmire which in places was impassable. Seven-hundred yards forward, the Zonnebeek stream, a small tributary of the Steenbeek, flowed diagonally across the assault area and in parts was also a morass. In the centre and on the left the final objective lay east of the Langemarck – Zonnebeke road and across Hill 40, an observation position near the base of the Zonnebeke spur which the Germans would not easily relinquish. To the left 59th Division were to capture the 1,200 yard section of the *Wilhelm Stellung* still held by the enemy, and the associated strong-points just to the east of that line. Four German regiments faced the two divisions of V Corps. Opposite the right of 3rd Division, the *34th Fusilier Regiment* held the right of the *3rd Reserve Division* line south of Zonnebeke, with the *102nd Reserve Regiment* of *23rd Reserve Division* in the line north of the town at Hill 40. The *392nd Regiment,* held the centre and the *100th Reserve Grenadiers* the right of the *23rd Reserve Division* sector opposite 59th Division. It was correctly believed by V Corps Intelligence that each division had all its regiments in the line, with one battalion holding the front line, one in support and one in immediate reserve, either west or just east of the Passchendaele ridge.

3rd Division
Major-General C. J. Deverell

The 3rd Division was to attack astride the Ypres – Roulers railway along a 1,500 yard front, its primary role to protect the left flank of 4th Australian Division. Careful planning was not the sole prerogative of Second Army, and much careful training had been done and many detailed arrangements had been made to assist the infantry of 3rd Division in their task. These arrangements are worth examining in detail being typical throughout Fifth Army. It was hoped that 10 tanks of No. 14 Company, "E" Battalion Tank Corps were to cooperate in the attack, ground conditions permitting. In an attempt to cover the assembly of the attacking battalions, and assuming the wind was favourable, it was planned to fire 200 gas projectors from Livens mortars at 9:00 p.m. on the 25th, from positions near Vampir Farm, over a distance of 1,400 yards to hit the area around the ruins of St. Josephs Institute on the Frezenberg road. This strongpoint, plus Bostin Farm, the blockhouses where the railway crossed the Frezenberg – Zonnebeke road, Draught House, and Muhle, were all identified to receive the special attention of "definite and complete units" of the infantry, who were to ensure their occupation and consolidation.

    The attack was to be supported by the Divisional Artilleries of the 3rd, 9th, and 42nd Divisions, the 64th and 65th Field Artillery Brigades, plus the heavy guns allotted by V Corps. A machine gun barrage was to be provided by the 8th, 9th, and 76th Machine Gun Companies, (less one section each to be placed at the disposal of their respective brigadiers), and the 253rd Machine Gun Company. Once the final objective was taken the machine guns would move forward to help secure and consolidate the position. Following a two hour hurricane bombardment the 18-pounders of the field artillery were to fire a protective barrage of high explosive and smoke 150 yards forward of the jumping-off line. In front of the protective barrage, the remaining 18-pounders, the 4.5-inch howitzers, and 60-pounders would fire a searching barrage, beyond which the remaining 60-pounders and 6-inch howitzers would fire a secondary barrage. The creeping barrage was to commence its forward lifts at Zero+3 minutes. Gradually lifting in 50 yard increments the barrage would advance 200 yards to the first objective, (the Green Line), at a rate of 100 yards in four minutes. At the first objective the infantry were to pause for 12 minutes, after which the artillery would signal the next lift by the firing of three rounds 'rapid smoke'. The barrage would then advance to the second objective, (the Red Line), at a rate of 100 yards in six minutes, at which point the infantry would halt for 41 minutes and consolidate the line. The support battalions would then leap-frog the leading battalions and on seeing the smoke signal from the artillery would continue the attack to the final objective, (the Blue Line). This was the planning behind the operation for which the division had been training so hard. As with so many previous attacks the plan relied on the infantry crossing the ground in good time and up with the barrage, but with the bogs of the Steenbeek and Zonnebeek to negotiate this was to prove difficult. The Royal Flying Corps was to provide two RE 8's of 21 Squadron; one 'Contact' aircraft flying over the objectives of the attacking infantry, and one 'Counter-attack Patrol' aircraft to be in the air from Zero+1 until dusk. The infantry were to indicate their position by red flares when requested by the contact aircraft by Klaxon horn or light signal. Any indication of enemy counter-attack would be signaled by the counter-attack patrol aircraft either by one long Klaxon blast or by dropping a smoke bomb.

The division was to attack with the 76th Brigade and the 8th Brigade in the line, each with one battalion of the 9th Brigade in immediate reserve with orders to assist upon their own initiative. The two remaining battalions of 9th Brigade would form a divisional reserve. The two support battalions of 9th Brigade would hold the line until relieved by the assault battalions of 76th and 8th Brigades prior to the attack at which point they would move into brigade reserve. The movement of divisions to their positions for battle were enormously complicated, and a perpetual headache to the administration and transport staff. From the outset it was realized that the 3rd Division move towards the front on Zero night would be difficult, due partly to the congestion of other units passing through Ypres and partly to the difficulty in navigating the maze of water-filled shell-holes up towards the line. Two battalions, one each of 76th and 8th Brigade were therefore moved up to the line on the night of 24th / 25th to relieve the two holding battalions of 9th Brigade which moved into support positions about Railway Wood. On the same night two further battalions, one of each brigade moved up just east of Ypres while one battalion of 76th Brigade moved into huts south of the city. The two remaining battalions of 8th Brigade and one of 76th moved up from the divisional concentration area at Brandhoek on the night of the 25th / 26th. All movements towards Ypres were made by bus or rail and all battalions were in position well up to time.

Great care was taken in preparation for the assembly along the jump-off line. Definite lines of approach were allotted and marked by coloured lamps, shaded on the enemy's side. These lines were marked with ropes, and discs for each platoon were placed in position. After dark on Zero night white tapes were laid along the rope lines and the lamps lighted. Each brigade was to advance on a two battalion frontage each of 400 yards, each battalion with two companies forward, and each company with two platoons forward and two following in a second wave. All platoons moved in section columns in file, and in diamond formation. The platoon H.Q. would be in the centre of the diamond with the corners formed by two rifle sections, one Lewis gun section and one rifle-grenade section. As with all complex plans things could go wrong and this night was to be no exception. The proposed gas bombardment had to be cancelled due to the direction of the wind, and the tank support was not to be forthcoming, the machines being bogged-down in the shell-torn ground on their way up to the front. It is recorded that the troops moved up to the attack in the most cheerful spirit and that all were full of confidence. Whether that was truly the case amongst the rank and file is a matter for conjecture. The night had been clear and reasonably quiet with only slight reaction from the German artillery in response to the opening of the hurricane barrage at 3:50. However at 5:50 a.m. as the attack advanced behind the barrage it was hampered by a thick mist which shrouded the ground.

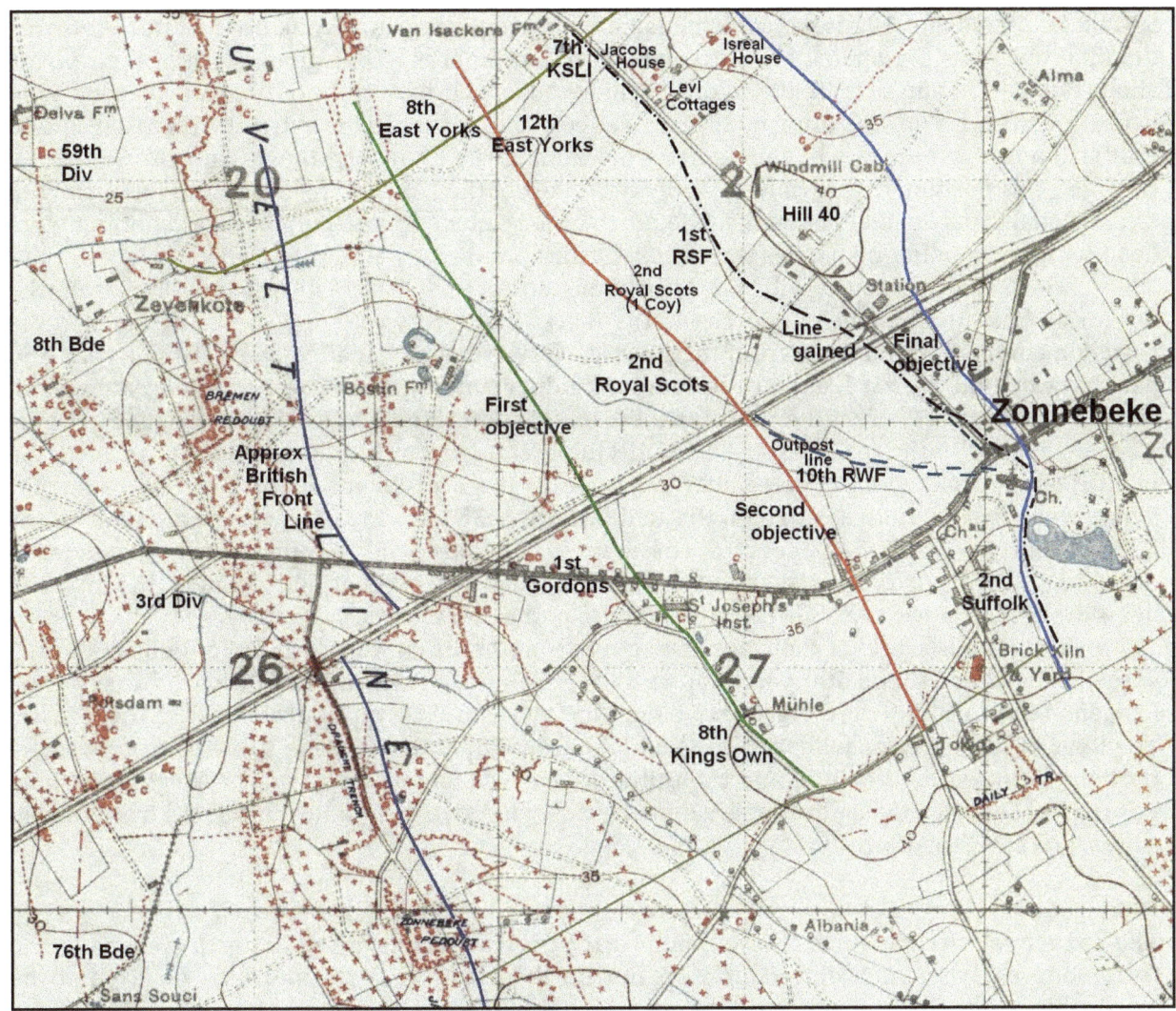
The attack of the 76th and 8th Brigades 3rd Division towards Zonnebeke and Hill 40

76th Brigade [458]
In front of the jumping-off positions just east of the old German Third Line, on the north-eastern slope of Anzac ridge, the brigade was immediately confronted with the quagmire of the upper Steenbeek. To the north of the brigade front the stream passed beneath the Ypres – Roulers railway, and here luckily the British Front Line was just east of the bad ground, which for 300 yards to the south was a morass 50 yards wide. The left company of the 1st Gordon Highlanders beside the railway was assembled to the east of the mire and to their right a 300 yard gap was left in the line across the virtually impassable ground.[459] The right company of the Gordons and both companies of the 8th King's Own Royal Lancaster Regiment would therefore cross the Steenbeek south of the bad ground where the going was somewhat better. This adjustment to the line, with the company of Gordons pushed slightly forward, required an equivalent adjustment to the barrage plan. To simplify matters the protective barrage along the whole divisional front was to come down on the 5 minute line and hold there for 5 minutes, the forming up lines of both brigades being fixed to suit this change. The companies detailed to cross the stream were to carry forward hurdle bridges to assist in the fording.

The preparations were well founded and following behind the excellent barrage both the King's Own and the Gordons captured their objectives up to time and began to consolidate. As the 2nd

---

[458] National Archives, War Diary 76th Brigade WO95/1433
[459] Cyril Falls *The Gordon Highlanders in the First World War 1914-1919* Aberdeen: University Press pp152-160. National Archives, War Diary 1st Gordons WO95/1435

Suffolk Regiment and 10th Royal Welsh Fusiliers passed through and took up the attack towards the final objective the opposition stiffened, especially from machine guns north of the railway about the station and on Hill 40. As the Fusiliers advanced just south of the railway they soon became embroiled in the mire of the Zonnebeek, but managed to extricate themselves and establish a line of outposts in shell-holes from Zonnebeke Church in touch with the Suffolk on the right, to a position on the railway 400 yards short of the Langemarck road, and in touch with the 1st Royal Scots Fusiliers of 8th Brigade north of the railway. Some pillboxes held out but were dealt with by mopping-up parties with phosphorous bombs.

The Suffolk, in touch with the Australians on their right established positions from the Brick Kiln Yard to Zonnebeke Church. As the Brick Kiln Yard was being constantly shelled the battalion commander moved part of the garrison forward across the Molenaarelshoek road and part back behind the yard, and at the same time distributed his left company in greater depth about the church. To strengthen the consolidation the machine gun section in brigade support was established with two guns just behind Muhle, one gun on the Frezenberg road near the Institution, and one gun at the railway crossing on the Frezenberg road. Two Stokes mortar teams were moved up to strengthen the Red Line. At 9:35 a.m. a message was sent back to the 529th Company Royal Engineers to come up to the area of the Institution to assist in consolidating the position. In the attack, the brigade had taken about 50 prisoners, the majority being *2nd Reserve* and *34th Fusilier Regiment*, both of the *3rd Reserve Division*.

The Suffolk were on their final objective from the Brick Kiln Yard to Zonnebeke Church with the Fusiliers about 500 yards short of their objective which lay 100 yards east of the Langemarck road, and were digging-in along that road for 150 yards northwest of the Church. The King's Own were consolidating the Red Line from Tokio to St. Joseph's Institute as were the Gordons between the Institute and the railway. The two companies of the 1st Northumberland Fusiliers of 9th Brigade just east of Frezenberg ridge and two companies in the old front line, in support of 76th Brigade, had not yet been engaged.

8th Brigade [460]

The Zonnebeek stream which crossed the brigade front from south-east to north-west had been reconnoitered where possible mainly to the north of Bostin Farm and was believed to be bridgeable with the use of trench boards or light hurdles. Upstream towards the railway however aerial photographs had identified a marshy area, and 60 bridges were to be taken forward to help with crossing.

The 2nd Royal Scots and 8th East Yorkshire Regiment advanced behind the barrage,[461] and although the line of the railway was an excellent guide to the Royal Scots, the morning mist considerably hampered the East Yorks, compasses being required to maintain direction. The 1st Royal Scots Fusiliers and 7th King's Shropshire Light Infantry moved forward immediately behind the leading battalions and all were clear of the jump-off positions just east of the old *Wilhelm Stellung* before the German retaliatory barrage came down at about 6:10 a.m. especially heavily 800 yards to the rear in the Hanebeek valley. Bostin Farm and its associated pillboxes was quickly overcome, a number of the enemy being killed or taken prisoner with some machine guns captured.

The problems caused by the mist were now compounded as the front waves approached the quagmire around the Zonnebeek. In places the broken stream and blocked culverts had spread into the adjacent shell-holes and produced an impassable bog 30 yards across. The worst ground was in the centre of the brigade front, causing the leading battalions to veer right and left. The ground to the left was however by far the worst and by 7:00 a.m. when the East Yorks had reached the Red Line they were well out of position being too far to the left and across the divisional boundary, a large gap having developed between them and the Royal Scots. As the K.S.L.I. passed through the East Yorks and moved forward towards the final objective the situation worsened as the forward companies veered even farther to the left, finally being

---

[460] National Archives, War Diary 8th Brigade WO95/1418
[461] National Archives, War Diary 2nd Royal Scots WO95/1423

checked by machine gun fire, with their left near Dochy Farm, and right some way south of the Langemarck road near Jacobs House. The battalion was here 500 yards left of its correct position.

Due mainly to the dreadful ground, the Royal Scots Fusiliers had arrived at the Red Line somewhat disorganized and as the battalion commander, Lieutenant -Colonel N. McD. Teacher D.S.O. attempted under heavy fire to improve the situation he was shot and killed. The Royal Scots Fusiliers continued the advance to attack Hill 40 without their commander and came under a hail of machine gun fire from the hill, which after inflicting many casualties brought them to a standstill in an arc around the foot of the slope. Their right was on the railway 150 yards west of the Langemarck road, their centre at the foot of Hill 40, 50 yards west of the Langemarck road, and their left on the Langemarck road 600 yards northwest of the hill. A company of the Royal Scots moved forward from the Red Line to reinforce the position and help in consolidation. An erroneous message implying the final objective had been taken resulted in a section of the 8th Machine Gun Company moving their guns forward, which however further strengthened the 6 Lewis guns and a captured German machine gun already defending the position. The 8th East Yorks and the 12th East Yorks from brigade reserve had meanwhile moved up on the left, and were in support 150 yards southwest of the K.S.L.I. and to an extent the gap between the battalions was closed.

59th (2nd North Midland) Division
Major-General C. F. Romer

The Langemarck – Zonnebeke road passed diagonally across the front to be attacked by the 59th Division. Where the German Third Line crossed the road at Kansas Cross, although it had been shelled to near oblivion, the bunkers shelters and pits still remaining were tenaciously held by the enemy. The division was to attack on a frontage of around 1,800 yards, from near Waterend House on the Zonnebeke in the south to near Schuler Farm in the north.
On the right, 177th Brigade would assemble along their jumping-off lines about the old *Wilhelm Stellung* which had fallen on the 20th September, while the left brigade, the 178th would form up mostly west of the 1,200 yard section of the old line still in enemy hands. The task of 178th Brigade was therefore somewhat greater, many bunkers still remaining active about Kansas Cross. This situation was addressed to a degree by the supporting attack to be made by 175th Brigade of 58th Division behind the German positions and along Gravenstafel spur. The boundary between the brigades ran in a straight line between Gallipoli and Otto Farm. The barrage was to include smoke shell to help cover the movement, and 40 machine guns per brigade were to put down a barrage on known hostile strong-points including Dochy Farm, Otto Farm, Toronto and Fokker Farm, and to lift from these points just before the artillery barrage came down on the Hanebeek valley. The machine guns would then lift and barrage the German support positions on a line between Bordeaux Farm, Boethoek and Gravenstafel. To help thicken the barrage a trench mortar battery was moved up to Schuler Galleries. A section of tanks was intended to support the infantry, but due to the dreadful state of the ground and the heavy hostile shelling most were knocked out before coming into action. At around 4:00 a.m. as the battalions assembled along their jumping-off tapes, the Germans put down a heavy barrage, causing considerable casualties. The thick early morning mist, made thicker still by shell-smoke, was to seriously hamper the attacking waves upsetting both cohesion and proper direction.[462]

177th Brigade [463]
With the 2/4th and 2/5th Leicestershire Regiment leading the attack and the 2/4th and 2/5th Lincolnshire Regiment in support the 177th Brigade was to jump-off from a line between

---
[462] National Archives, War Diary 175th Machine Gun Company 59th Division WO95/3025
[463] National Archives, War Diary 177th Brigade WO95/3023, National Archives, War Diary 2/4th and 2/5th Leicester WOP95/3022, War Diary 2/4th and 2/5th Lincoln WO95/3023

Waterend House and Downing Trench in the old German Third Line, with their final objective between Dochy Farm and Otto Farm. The Leicester battalions advanced behind an excellent barrage through the remains of the *Wilhelm Stellung* across the crest of Hill 37, and by about 7:20 a.m. had taken the second objective near the Zonnebeke – Langemarck road. As the barrage lifted towards the final objective the Lincoln passed through, and on the right captured the Dochy Farm blockhouse. Consolidation on the final objective was hampered on the left by machine gun fire from the Otto Farm blockhouses 200 yards further forward.

178th Brigade [464]

The 178th Brigade was to attack from a line from Downing Trench, on the *Wilhelm Stellung* near Keir Farm, to Schuler Farm, with the final objective on a line roughly between Otto Farm, Toronto and Nile. The 2/6th and 2/7th Sherwood Foresters were to lead the attack to the second objective where the 2/5th and 2/8th would pass through to the final.[465] The 2/6th and 2/7th captured the battered remains of the German Third Line 300 yards either side of Kansas Cross by about 7:00 a.m., digging-in on the second objective 150 yards beyond the Langemarck road.

The 2/5th and 2/8th formed up behind the second objective, and at 7:30 advanced behind the barrage. North-east of the Kansas Cross crossroad, the Wieltje – Gravenstafel road, which should have given a good indication of direction to the 2/5th, had been so smashed by the guns that it had virtually ceased to exist. The Commanding Officer of the 2/5th Lieutenant -Colonel H. R. Gadd, whose battalion was to capture the Otto Farm blockhouse, had disagreed with Brigadier -General T. G. Cope, regarding the size of force necessary to capture the blockhouse, Gadd wishing to use two companies, while the Brigadier considered two platoons sufficient. The Brigadier's wishes prevailed, and "B" Company of the 2/5th led the attack to the final objective line which was 200 yards short of Otto Farm. "C" Company was to come up level with "B" from which point, as the barrage lifted towards the blockhouse, the two platoons detailed were to go forward to seize it. At this point the two platoons were too weak in numbers to attack alone, and all those of "C" Company now available were assembled for the attack. As the barrage lifted off the blockhouse it was rushed by "C" Company and bombed out, many of the garrison running out, some being shot, and around 40 captured. Meanwhile what was left of 'B" Company had pushed out a line of posts to link up with Otto Farm, which, due to casualties was now being held by only 15 men of "C" Company. The remainders of the two companies were either casualties of severe enemy shelling, or lost in the mist. The remains of "D" Company in support, which had also sustained many casualties through the shelling, were moved up to Deep Trench, 200 yards behind the line held by "B" Company. Shortly after, it was noticed that the 2/5th Lincoln on the right were being heavily attacked and were falling-back about 500 yards, exposing the right flank of the 2/5th Sherwood Foresters, especially "C" Company at the Otto Farm bunker. A strong-point with a Lewis gun was subsequently established to cover the right flank.

XVIII Corps
Lieutenant General Sir Ivor Maxse

Gravenstafel Ridge

With the general assault in progress along the line to the south, an attempt was to be made to advance due east along the Gravenstafel ridge in an attempt to secure the excellent observation position where the road along the ridge top passed through the 32 metre ring contour. From this high point near Aviatik Farm, with a line of sight along the Ravebeek valley, German movements around Passchendaele would be exposed.

---

[464] National Archives, War Diary 178th Brigade WO95/3025
[465] National Archives, War Diary 2/5th Sherwood Foresters WO95/3025

58th (2/1st London) Division
Major-General H. D. Fanshaw

The attack in the mist
Using 175th Brigade the attack was to be made to try to repeat the excellent work on the 20th September by 173rd and 174th Brigades, which had pushed the line east along the Gravenstafel road to Wurst Farm. The assault of 175th Brigade, with its right along the (northern) Hanebeek valley would outflank the section of the *Wilhelm Stellung* to be attacked from the front by 178th Brigade. The attack was hampered from the outset by a thick mist and smoke, which made keeping direction and cohesion across the featureless ridge-top very difficult.

175th Brigade [466]
Along the northern bank of the Hanebeek the 2/12th London Regiment (The Rangers), attacked with the 2/9th London (Queen Victoria Rifles) to their left.[467] The 2/9th attempted to move off in a direction due east with, from right to left, "A", "C" and "D" Companies leading and "B" company in support behind "A". "D" Company's left was near Von Tirpitz Farm, 300 yards to the north of the track along the ridge top. The mist immediately caused major problems, and the platoons became badly mixed up, having little idea where they were in the crater-field, with Mebus and the enemy seemingly all around. Distances of advance were only established by laying out fifty yard tapes to give some idea of when the 250 to 300 yard objective had been reached. In attempting to keep direction compasses proved useless as it was impossible in the mist to take a bearing. The difficulties inevitably caused delay, and in places the barrage crept forward well ahead of the infantry. Many confusing minor engagements took place, in some places platoons getting well forward, while others were driven back by local resistance to take cover in shell-holes.

On the left of "D" Company, 13 Platoon closely followed by 15 Platoon were to attack towards the strong-point at Vale House 250 yards east of Von Tirpitz Farm, with 14 Platoon followed by 16 Platoon attacking to their right. Of the 22 men of 13 Platoon that moved off into the mist only three were subsequently accounted for. 15 Platoon did not locate Vale House and probably went well beyond it and took shelter in shell-holes waiting for the visibility to improve. Soon in front of them they saw members of 14 Platoon retiring, having previously attacked a wired strong-point, but then been driven out by a shower of enemy grenades. The officer leading 14 Platoon admitted to being lost, subsequently leading them away to the left, then appearing to fall-back and disappear from view. 14 Platoon had gone into action 23 strong. Of these 7 were killed, 5 wounded, 5 missing and only 5 returned. Their officer was amongst the missing. Later 15 Platoon also fell-back and came across 16 Platoon in the mist and helped consolidate a line.
16 Platoon had moved off behind 14 Platoon heading due east, and having advanced 200 yards, stopped and dug-in, being fired at by machine guns which they took to be north of the Stroombeek. Silhouettes of men seen to be falling-back through the mist on their position were soon identified as 14 Platoon, which had been ordered to retire in threes. 16 Platoon stayed in position for some time hoping for the visibility to improve, until their own barrage fell upon them. At that point they too fell-back by sections, their left finally being upon Stropp Farm about 50 yards in front of the jumping-off line. Out of two officers and 109 other ranks of "D" Company who went into action on this misty and frightening morning, one officer and 50 other ranks had become casualties to a mostly unseen enemy.

It was a similar tale all along 175 Brigade front. In places the Germans were seen retiring into the mist only to counter-attack a short time later. Lewis guns set up in shell-holes gave some covering fire at short range, firing at shadows to the limit of the visibility, and both sides nervously attempted to bomb out the others positions.

---

[466] National Archives, War Diary 175th Brigade WO95/3008
[467] National Archives, War Diary 2/12th and 2/9th London Regiment WO95/3009

On the far right of the 2/9th, 1 Platoon on the right front of "A" Company were to attack due east towards Aviatik Farm, followed by 3 Platoon, with 2 Platoon to their left followed by 4 Platoon. Moving forward quickly in an attempt to keep up with the barrage they gradually outpaced "C" Company to their left, but began to descend the slope of the ridge towards the Hanebeek, their direction of advance being too far to the right, and south-east rather than east. On their right flank parties of the 2/12th London soon loomed into view. Attempting to follow closely behind, 3 Platoon soon lost sight of 1 Platoon, but also drifted too far right, veering across the front of 2/12th which caused them to turn a little further to the east, but still well out of position.

Following in support of "A" Company, 7 Platoon on the right front of "B" Company were caught by their own barrage as they attempted to pass through "A" to their objective. They were then held up by machine gun fire from a Mebu at Cairo, where they also made contact with the Rangers. The Rangers were in as much trouble as the Q.V.R. having insufficient numbers to take their objective. 7 Platoon consolidated the position they held as best possible until counter-attacked in the afternoon, at which point on seeing others retiring, they also withdrew towards Dom Trench. After the counter-attack subsided 7 Platoon again moved forward, and at night returned to their forward position, there then being no sign of the enemy.

It seems the only platoons to get near their objective at Aviatik Farm were 6 Platoon of "B" Company who attacked to the left of 7 Platoon, and 5 Platoon which supported 6 Platoon. Both 6 and 5 got well forward into exposed shell-hole position where they were continually sniped, but managed to set up their Lewis guns and held on. The vital observation point on the 32 metre ring contour remained, albeit tenuously, in enemy hands. In the attack "B" Company sustained 41 casualties including an officer and 9 other ranks killed.

On the southern face of the ridge and in clearer conditions along the northern bank of the Hanebeek, the Rangers were a little more successful. The attack was led by "B" Company who reached their objective, where "C" Company passed through, moving on to secure the final objective at the Nile strong-point. The 2/12th had taken 74 prisoners in the advance.

The brigade had experienced a torrid time, the great problems of attacking in conditions of low visibility being obvious. It was also difficult to locate the new forward positions which were generally along a ragged line of fortified shell-holes strung between those enemy strong-points which had fallen and were still held by the London. The line ran approximately from Nile near the Hanebeek across the ridge between Wurst and Aviatik Farms, to near Vale House on the left. At Wurst Farm the 2/9th London were about 500 yards to the west of the farthest point reached by the 2/5th Lancashire Fusiliers of 164th Brigade eight weeks previously on the 31st July.

German counter-attacks

From the western face of the Quadrilateral south of the Menin Road where 118th Brigade clung to the edge of the Bassevillebeek valley, to Vale House 9,000 yards to the north on the slopes of Gravenstafel ridge above the Stroombeek valley where the shell-hole scrapes of the London had at last emerged from the mist, the attacking battalions of the Second and Fifth Armies dug-in and wired the ground they had won, in anticipation of the inevitable counter-attacks which would soon come. Powerful infantry reserves, held back in case of need, had not been required but were at hand should the front be pushed back by the enemy. At the spear-point of the battlefront, the two Australians divisions had each kept back a reserve brigade, held around Hooge, and each of the attacking brigades had kept back one battalion. Each of the two battalions attacking to the final objective on a brigade front had kept back one company in reserve and each company one platoon. In this way the British reserves were echeloned in depth.

The advantage of observation was now with the British, and it would not be easy for the Germans to move against them in any number without being seen by ground observers. But the German counter-attack divisions had also been held back, well east of the Gheluvelt – Passchendaele high ground, and until they entered the valleys to the east of the plateau or crested the Broodseinde – Passchendaele ridge they would not be seen from the ground. By noon the morning mists had cleared, the sun shone and the day became hot. It was ideal flying weather. It was not long before the wireless equipped RE8's patrolling east of the ridge, began to confirm to Army and Corps report centres large concentrations of German infantry moving towards the front. The assembly areas and likely approaches which the enemy divisions may take towards the battlefront had been foreseen on a Second Army Intelligence Summary counter-attack map issued before the battle, and the British heavy batteries were well prepared to fire on the frequently practiced targets. It appeared from the air that the roads from the east were crowded with grey clad infantry. There were three main groups; one to the south approaching from the direction of Menin along the Menin Road towards the Gheluvelt plateau; one in the centre approaching Polygon Wood from the direction of Becelare; and a northern group approaching the Keiberg and the Passchendaele ridge from the direction of Moorslede, which would probably cross the ridge between Broodseinde and Passchendaele. Between 1:00 and 2:00 p.m. the earlier air warnings were confirmed by artillery ground observers and the information of their position was passed to the guns. As the reports reached the batteries, working to the targets designated to their battery groups the British guns gradually brought the approaching columns under an ever increasing volume of fire, causing the Germans disorganization and delay.

At around 1:00 p.m. companies of the *89th Grenadier Regiment* of the *17th Division* moved forward from about Holle Bosch east of the Passchendaele ridge, and crossed the saddle north of Zwaanhoek on the Becelare spur. This was the central group reported by the RE8's, and was moving towards the positions held by the 5th Australian Division in Polygon Wood. The advance continued for about three hours under the constant observed fire of two 6-inch howitzers and a number of 18-pounders.

At around 1:20 p.m. first reports arrived from air observers that German infantry at battalion strength were moving up the eastern face of Broodseinde ridge and approaching towards the 4th Australian Division front. Prudently the artillery had fired a test barrage at 1:30 on the front of 4th Brigade and again at 2:30 on that of 13th Brigade to check its accuracy. At 3:00 p.m. 4th Brigade reported the enemy concentrating on its front, and a German barrage falling just behind its front line. The S.O.S. signal was fired at 3:25 p.m. The response from the British guns was immediate breaking the counter-attack before it came near the Australian outpost line. This counter-attack was mounted by the *236th Division*, the southern *Eingreif Division* of *Group Ypres*. The division had been aware that a major attack was imminent. The forward movement of British artillery and the preparatory bombardment along the Flanders I Line had made that plain. At 10:30 a.m. it had concentrated behind the Flanders II Position near Droogenbroodhoek, on the Keiburg spur south of Passchendaele. The division had been allotted, with the *234th Division,* to the *3rd Reserve Division* holding the front line between Polygon Wood and Zonnebeke. The counter-attack was ordered at 11:30, and at 1:20 the *457th, 459th* and *458th Regiments* of *236th Division,* identified by the Royal Flying Corps as the northern group, began moving across Keiburg spur towards the Australian front line and had at once been spotted from the air. A barrage of high explosive and gas from I Anzac guns caused them little problem and by 2:30 they deployed on the road along the ridge top at Broodseinde, 800 yards from the forward Australian outpost line. The attack was led by the *II Battalion, 457th Regiment* which advanced towards the northern end of Polygon Wood, while the *I and III Battalion* of the *459th Regiment* advanced through Molenaarelsthoek towards the base of Tokio spur, and the *I, 458th* to the south of Zonnebeke. As they crested the ridge the counter-attack waves came under heavy shrapnel and machine gun fire. The fire was heaviest from the direction of Polygon Wood causing the *II, 457th* to swerve north crowding into the front of the *459th*. Suffering losses from the Australian fire the counter-attack battalions continued their advance, but only as far as to reinforce the remnants of the front line battalions holding out in the shelters behind the still uncut wire of Flanders I. There they stopped, getting no nearer than 250 yards to the 4th Australian Division line.[468]

To the left of the 4th Australian Division line, the 3rd British Division position at the foot of Hill 40 was also to be threatened by counter-attack. At 8th Brigade headquarters at Square Farm 2,500 yards to the rear, and at divisional headquarters back at the Ramparts in Ypres, the situation at the front was unclear until 2:00 p.m. when it became known that the division was on the positions about the base of the hill which we have already noted. At about 2:30 p.m. Germans were seen to be assembling behind Zonnebeke station but the concentration was quickly broken by artillery, Lewis gun and rifle fire. At 3rd Division headquarters Major-General C. J. Deverell was of the opinion that a renewed attack to gain the station and Hill 40, combined with an advance by the 10th Royal Welsh Fusiliers to their final objective on the right stood every chance of success, and should be made before nightfall. The artillery was ordered to maintain a barrage on the approaches to the station and the hill and at 2:45 p.m. the brigade commanders were ordered to resume the attack behind a special barrage to commence at 6:30. All divisional reserves were placed at the disposal of 8th Brigade but only to be used as a last resort. In the line things looked a little different than they appeared 7,500 yards back at the Ramparts. There was a delay in the orders being received at the front, and organizing the forward troops, dispersed and scattered in shell-holes and under constant fire was not going to be easy. The attack when it began at 6:30 p.m. was therefore weak and disjointed, and was further disrupted by an enemy barrage which fell on the front positions, supports and reserves. This hostile barrage preceded a counter-attack from the hill by around 200 German infantry which brought the British attack to a standstill and then caused the few attacking parties to fall-back. This retirement, plus reports that the 176th Brigade on the left was also falling-back spread a degree of alarm along the centre of 8th Brigade, some troops withdrawing from their forward positions, and some in support positions joining them. The retirement was soon checked and most of the line was recovered, the loss of ground amounting to 100 yards on the right and 200 yards in the centre.

The German counter-attack extended to the right flank against the positions of the Suffolk, the battalion support companies rushing to the front to assist. The King's Own also came up to meet the counter-attack which by the time they arrived had already been broken by the Lewis gun and rifle fire of the Suffolk, the enemy having gone to ground near the lake 200 yards southeast of the Church. Some prisoners of the *452nd Regiment* were taken during this counter-attack which indicated that elements of the *234th Division* were by this time engaged. The *4th Bavarian Division* was also engaged using the *5th Bavarian Reserve Regiment* into Zonnebeke village, and the *9th Bavarian Reserve Regiment* against Hill 40. What had appeared from the front line to be a local counter-attack was in fact part of the concerted German effort, that had crossed the Passchendaele ridge and down the slopes from Broodseinde, and which was being enacted along the whole front from Tower Hamlets to north of Hill 40. At Zonnebeke the hill was still in German hands, but the counter-attack had totally failed, as it had all along the line.

Between 11:00 a.m. and noon, in the southern sector of the battlefield 3,000 yards south of Zonnebeke the right flank of the 5th Australian Division was still dangerously exposed. As we have seen, the 2nd Royal Welsh Fusiliers of 98th Brigade had passed through the rear area of the 5th Australian Division and had made a costly advance along the southern edge of Polygon Wood, towards Jerk House and Cameron House to cover the Australian right flank. The attack of the Fusiliers with parties of the 31st Australian Battalion supporting on their left, and with another group following up, had no barrage protection, (the barrage had been fired long), and was quickly struck by a storm of machine gun fire from Jerk House and Polderhoek spur far on the right. Jerk House was however taken by the Fusiliers and the 31st attempted to surround and take Cameron House 200 yards forward, but failed. The 59th and 60th Battalions holding the defensive flank along the side of the wood stayed in this position. By early afternoon the

---

[468] German reports claim their Eingreif divisions stopped the Australian advance. It in fact stopped where it was intended to stop. Only at Hill 40 was the British objective not achieved. National Archives, CAB45/172 p124

Fusiliers were running dangerously short of ammunition despite attempts to bring up more. About 4:00 p.m. a German counter-attack looked imminent as many columns were seen cresting the hill at Reutel 1,200 yards to the east and also advancing up the Reutelbeek valley, this the main body of the southern group observed by the Royal Flying Corps earlier in the morning. The counter-attack was to be carried out by the *89th Grenadier Regiment* of the *17th Division,* which was to pass through the *229th R.I.R.* (to the right of the *230th*) and recapture the old *Wilhelm Stellung* position. The ammunition promised to the Fusiliers had still not arrived and the battalion commander informed Captain McLennan of the 31st Australian Battalion that he was about to fall back. It was agreed that the 31st would cover the withdrawal of the Fusiliers back to Jerk House. The German thrust was not however to threaten the British line, as between 6:30 and 8:15 p.m. artillery fire broke the counter-attack of the *17th Division,* many of the *89th Grenadiers* failing even to reach the Flanders I Line.

Around the same time, south of the Reutelbeek, the *I* and *II Companies* of the *75th Infantry Regiment, 17th Division* advanced towards the 100th Brigade outposts. Those that got through the observed artillery barrage were smitten by the brigade's machine guns and rifle fire and got no further forward than the *230th R.I.R.* outpost line on Polderhoek spur.

The 98th Brigade outpost line was eventually established running through Jerk House, with the Australians taking Cameron House on the first objective during the night. The ground lost in the German spoiling attack on the 25th September had largely been retaken, but the line had not been pushed any further forward and the Australian right was still exposed, although reasonably covered by a defensive flank of their own forces. At dusk Brigadier-General Elliott received news that 33rd Division was again to attack to reach its final objective at the eastern end of Polderhoek spur and through Cameron Covert, and that he was to assist. He therefore moved forward two reserve companies of the 60th to reinforce the 31st. The 33rd Division made no sign of attack, but Elliott decided not to waste time and ordered the 60th to continue in the dark. A blockhouse close in front of the Australian line was surrounded and quickly captured. In the morning it was clear they had taken Cameron House, but it was not until the 27th that the Fusiliers advanced to their final objective.

Around 500 yards to the north on the eastern edge of Polygon Wood, parties of the *89th Grenadier Regiment*, that had crossed the Becelare spur at 1:00 p.m., although continually harassed by British artillery had by 5:00 p.m. infiltrated forward and now threatened the new line of 5th Australian Division. The Grenadiers had succeeded in assembling in a road, and gradually began to work through gaps in hedges, and by short rushes between shell-holes edged towards the Australian outpost line. At this point, within a few hundred yards of the line, they were engaged by the machine guns of 14th Australian Brigade on the Butte and by the 5th Division field-guns and howitzers. Some withdrew, some went to ground in shell-holes, but others came on. None however reached the Australian line.

On the front of 59th Division in the Hanebeek valley, in the early afternoon a local German counter attack against the survivors of 178th Brigade holding Otto Farm was driven-off by rifle fire. At about 5:00 p.m. a severe enemy barrage came down, especially on 177th Brigade front. A counter-attack developed towards Dochy Farm held by the 2/5th Lincoln, and it was seen from Otto Farm that a general withdrawal was proceeding, both to the right and the left. With the risk of being cut off and surrounded, the small party of "C" Company 2/5th Sherwood Foresters at Otto Farm withdrew to the line held by "B" Company, 200 yards behind the blockhouse, where a forward outpost line was finally established in fortified shell-holes.

The German counter-attack divisions moving forward in the early afternoon from east of the ridge had encountered the same problems as befell them on the 20th September, and had again been broken before endangering the British line. At about 6:00 p.m. the final German effort of the day was made by the *457th Regiment*. The S.O.S. was fired in front of 4th Australian Brigade and the resultant bombardment stopped the counter-attack which again only succeeded in reaching the position of the *49th Reserve Regiment* holding the outpost line. Once more no counter-attack had threatened the Australian positions and by 8:15 p.m. the guns fell silent and the front was quiet.

In places however there were still concerns, as a report at about 9:00 p.m. indicated that another withdrawal had occurred from the 3rd Division positions in front of Hill 40, and although Major-General Deverell was doubtful of its authenticity the possibility was too serious to ignore. Brigadier-General Holmes of 8th Brigade was ordered forward from Square Farm with the 4th Royal Fusiliers and 13th King's Liverpool Regiment from divisional reserve with instructions to restore the line. But the report was found to be exaggerated and the line at the foot of Hill 40 was still secure.[469] The Royal Fusiliers and King's Liverpool were held at the Red Line where they remained in support of 8th Brigade which at this time remained somewhat disorganized.

In the counter-attacks throughout the afternoon, two *Eingreif* divisions and elements of a third had been seriously engaged against Second Army and Fifth Army, the *17th and 236th Divisions* using in total six regiments, (*75th, 90th Fusilier, 89th Grenadier, 457th, 459th, and 458th*), supporting the two line divisions, the *50th Reserve* and *3rd Reserve*. Prisoners of *452nd Regiment* of *234th Division* had also been identified at Zonnebeke. It is significant that both *234th Division* and *236th* had been in action on the 20th. In the main attack three British divisions had used six brigades to assault a strong enemy position with powerful artillery support, and four of those brigades had advanced to a depth of 1,200 yards and held their gains. In defence against this main attack, elements of five German divisions had been engaged, each comprised of three regiments, the regimental strength available to the Germans in defence of their position being therefore eighteen. The effective strength of some battalions was however seriously below full establishment. Plumer's theory was now working in practice.

Subsequent operations

The Germans may have been down but they were certainly not out. On the 27th September further counter-attacks attempted to throw the British back at key points along the front, but were accompanied by the now usual lack of success. South of the Menin Road three separate attempts against the 39th Division at Tower Hamlets spur were all broken by artillery fire, and on the night of 27th/28th the 39th Division was relieved by the 37th Division.
North of the Reutelbeek the 2nd Royal Welsh Fusiliers of 98th Brigade, in a period of fierce and confused fighting advanced past Cameron House which had been secured by the Australians overnight, and by 3:50 p.m. were near Cameron Covert in support of the Australian right flank. That night 23rd Division, after only two days rest relieved 33rd Division which during those two days had sustained high casualties.

The morning of the 27th saw 76th Brigade and 8th Brigade still holding the 3rd Division line in front of Zonnebeke and the foot of Hill 40. In the early hours, 8th Brigade had been ordered to push forward patrols and if possible advance across Hill 40 to the final objective, a task which proved impossible. At 2:00 p.m. orders were received from V Corps to complete the capture of the Blue Line at an early date, and orders were therefore issued to 9th Brigade for the attack to be carried out at 6:30 p.m. on the 28th. The brigade planned to use the 13th King's Liverpool and 4th Royal Fusiliers, with the 12th West Yorks and 1st Northumberland Fusiliers in support. At 6:35 p.m. an intense German barrage descended on the whole divisional front line, which was exceptionally severe on the positions of 8th Brigade at Hill 40. An attack then developed along the whole front except on the far left where 7th King's Shropshire Light Infantry held the line. Again the attack was unsuccessful, being driven off by artillery, machine gun and rifle fire. The 12th West Yorks and 1st Northumberland of 9th Brigade, which had moved up into support of 8th Brigade the previous evening, had suffered serious casualties during the shelling, and it was considered most unwise by G.O.C. 8th Brigade to move them up to the attack positions for the 28th. G.O.C. 9th Brigade who had witnessed the bombardment concurred. After

---

[469] In their influential account, Prior and Wilson claim that Hill 40 was captured after a second attempt on the 26th October. Although they cite the War Diary of the 3rd Division as their source this is clearly not the case. See *Passchendaele the Untold Story* pp129-130 and 212. Hill 40 was to be captured by the 3rd Australian Division on the 4th October.

giving the matter careful consideration Major-General Deverell felt that using a tired brigade which, although not having been directly engaged, had been subjected to severe shelling was unwise. Further he felt that the position on the reverse slope beneath Hill 40 was an acceptable position from which to jump-off for the next attack, and was not as exposed to hostile shelling as would be the Blue Line on top of the hill. On presenting his views to V Corps, he was subsequently informed that they had been approved by Gough.

On the 28th September, the 58th Division of XVIII Corps was relieved by the 48th and in XIV Corps the 20th Division was relieved by the 29th. Plumer's Chief General Staff Officer at Second Army, Major-General C. H. Harington, in a summary of the battle wrote, 'The desperate efforts made by the enemy to retain his positions between Tower Hamlets and Polygon Wood indicates the importance he attaches to denying us ground observation facilities from the heads of the valleys between Gheluvelt and Becelaere, and how much he was willing to pay to hold that area'.[470] He further commented that it was clear that the Germans recognized the serious threat to the ridge north of Becelaere, 'where our line is now within a short distance of looking over the eastern edge'. He warned that the Germans might make even stronger efforts to hold this area which shielded the assembly and dispositions of their forces. His warnings were about to be proved correct, as the Germans were now to make further attempts to disrupt the coming British attack. The weather had remained fine and dry with early morning ground mists, beneath which on the morning of the 30th September the Germans assembled to launch another counter-attack, at the vital point between the Menin Road and the Reutelbeek, to regain the Gheluvelt Plateau. At 4:30 a.m. a severe artillery and trench mortar bombardment fell upon the 70th Brigade holding the right of 23rd Division line. The 800 yard front was held by the 8th King's Own Yorkshire Light Infantry and 11th Sherwood Foresters and at around 5:00 a.m. German infantry of the *8th Division* preceded by specially trained assault groups of *Fourth Army Sturmbatallion* using flame throwers, light machine guns, smoke bombs and grenades, advanced towards the British line. The S.O.S. fired along the front went unseen owing to the mist, and it took two hours for messages to get back by runner to brigade headquarters in Sanctuary Wood. The K.O.Y.L.I. and Sherwood Foresters meanwhile stood firm and subjected the enemy to a withering fire from rifles, Lewis guns and machine guns, the Germans breaking and fleeing in confusion. At 6:00 p.m. a weaker counter-attack suffered the same fate. On the same day 5th Australian Division was relieved, part by 21st Division, and part by 7th Division of X Corps, and 3rd Division were relieved by 3rd Australian Division of II Anzac Corps.

At 5:00 a.m. on the following morning, the 1st October, to prove the German artillery still had plenty of bite, a hurricane bombardment announced another counter-attack along a 1,500 yard front from the Reutekbeek northwards, along the line east of Polygon Wood, the intense shelling engulfing the whole area back to a depth of 1,000 yards. This position was held by elements of three British divisions; on the right the 69th Brigade of 23rd Division about Cameron Covert, in the centre the 110th Brigade of 21st Division, and on the left the 22nd Brigade of 7th Division, both in front of Polygon Wood. At about 5:30 a.m. German infantry, (*210th Reserve Infantry Regiment* of the *45th Reserve Division* and *93rd Infantry Regiment* of *8th Division*) were seen advancing in strength especially towards Polygon Wood. The 1st Royal Welsh Fusiliers holding the right of 22nd Brigade line in Jetty Trench reacted quickly and stubbornly, as at around 6:15 thick waves of German infantry swarmed towards their front posts, and to a lesser extent towards those of the 20th Manchester to their left in Jubilee Trench. Despite heavy rifle fire the enemy pressed their attack right up to the Fusiliers' line, but were wiped out without achieving a lodgment in the British position. Further waves, caught squarely by the S.O.S. barrage, faltered a then withdrew, at one point being counter-attacked by the right company of the Fusiliers, which drove them deeper into the thickest of the shell-fire and succeeded in taking some prisoners. The Welsh Fusiliers had 131 casualties and the Manchester 104 in their spirited defence of the position.

---

[470] Harington *Plumer of Messines*. p119

In 110th Brigade line the 9th Leicestershire Regiment gave some ground at first, retiring from Joist Farm back towards the edge of the wood.[471] On the right the 9th Green Howards of 69th Brigade swung back its left in Cameron Covert to conform to the Leicester. Both battalions immediately counter-attacked retaking the lost ground with the exception of two pillboxes in Cameron Covert. For bravery and inspiring leadership during this counter-attack Lieutenant - Colonel Philip Eric Bent of the 9th Leicestershire was to be posthumously awarded the V.C. On seeing the Leicester and Green Howards being driven back he gathered all available reserves and succeeded in retaking the line. He was killed at the objective after giving orders for consolidation. Two more German counter-attacks over the next three hours also resulted in failure, at which point they withdrew to their original shell-hole outpost line. Their artillery continued to pound the British positions throughout the day and infantry persisted in infiltrating forward in numbers threatening another attack. Prompt and accurate artillery fire in response to S.O.S. signals, plus rifle and machine gun fire dispersed these incursions with great loss. The history of the *210th R.I.R.* states that on the right its advanced was limited to 140 yards and in the centre by 80 yards, and repeated the attack in the afternoon only after protest, suffering the loss of 6 officers and 350 other ranks.

On the 2nd October 23rd Division was relieved by 5th Division.

The German counter-attacks of the 1st October were intended as a preliminary to a much greater assault to be made on the 3rd October to the north of Polygon Wood. This major operation was intended to re-take some of the observation positions captured on the 26th September, especially Tokio spur. The counter-attacks on the 1st had been a total failure, and the attacking units had been so roughly handled that the assault was postponed from the 3rd October to the 4th which was to have disastrous repercussions on the enemy as will soon be revealed.

An appraisal of the second step

The second step by Second and Fifth Armies had successfully established the British across most of the Gheluvelt plateau and across the main ridge at Polygon Wood between the Reutelbeek and (southern) Hanebeek valleys, and had at last advanced north-east of the Zonnebeke – Langemarck road. The German reaction had been typically robust but the enemy defence in depth system had failed for the second time in 6 days and there seemed little they could do about it The concentration of enemy batteries east of the plateau which had been assembled in support of the attack of the 25th September was estimated by Second Army Intelligence to amount to the equivalent of ten divisional artilleries of an average strength of 22 batteries. The guns of both sides had fought a tremendous duel. The battle had been especially costly and tiring on the gunners, X Corps guns being in action throughout both the 25th and 26th and I Anzac Corps field artillery maintaining protective barrages from dawn until dusk on the 26th. The increase in German artillery strength prior to their spoiling attack on the 25th September, (44 field batteries and 20 heavy batteries of the Terhand (Becelaere) group alone firing on the Glencourse Wood, Inverness Copse area), had added to the British artillery casualties, as had the more exposed battery positions on the plateau. At nearly 2,300, Second Army artillery casualties had been about twice those incurred on the 20th.

In his usual but understandable fashion of understatement, Haig recorded in his diary on the 26th September, 'Our operations were entirely successful.... At 5:00 p.m. I (accompanied by Kiggell, Birch and Davidson) met Generals Plumer and Gough with their CGS at Cassel. They explained the situation on their fronts, and I decided on the extent of the next operation – and a subsequent one when it will be necessary for the French to join in to cover the left of the XIV Corps'.[472] At this time, (i.e. at 5:00 p.m.), the final German counter-attacks at around 6:00 p.m. had not taken place, and the guns were still firing until 8:00. Given the time delay in obtaining accurate information from the front to Army headquarters, Plumer and Gough appear to have

---

[471] National Archives, War Diary 110th Brigade WO95/2163
[472] Douglas Hiag. Diaries and Letters p330

already accepted that they had the Germans beaten for the day, which was indeed the case. The subsequent operation to which Haig's diary entry referred would be the fourth step, to come about a week after the third step, which should see Second Army up onto the whole of the main ridge as far north as Passchendaele. By this stage Fifth Army should be just east of Poelcappelle. How did he really see the situation developing from this point? How many more 1,500 yard steps would be required before Fifth Army could make a possible breakout to the north-east? Conjecture must have been rife amongst G.H.Q. Staff. The point would soon be reached when the French First Army would need to skirt the southern end of the inundations east of Draaibank and begin to threaten the Germans within their bastion in Houthulst Forest, to protect Fifth Army left, which would otherwise be left dangerously exposed. Between Poelcappelle and Westroosebeke, the northern end of the Flanders I Line with its associated wire entanglements and blockhouses ran 1,000 yards west of the ridge through Spriet. On top of the ridge through the western outskirts of the village of Westroosebeke, the concrete Mebus and wire entanglements were already under construction as the Flanders III position progressed. Even if things went well in the third step, it appeared that at least three further steps would be required before the position at Westroosebeke on the ridge was gained, and winter was fast approaching. Obviously this situation was not unknown to the Commander-in-Chief. A Second Army Intelligence Summary of activity both British and German, between 16th to 30th September noted, 'A considerable amount of work has been done on the Passchendaele – Terhand Line [Flanders II]; further communication trenches have been dug at short intervals north east of Gheluwe and numerous dug-outs are being constructed south of Terhand. A new line has been traced from south of the Ypres – Roulers Railway through Oostniewkerke to the Westroosebeke – Hooglede road, and new trenches are dug south and west of Hooglede'.[473] If Passchendaele fell as hoped in the fourth step, Second Army would have outflanked the Flanders I Line and be in a position to attack north from Goudberg, along the ridge towards Westroosebeke and Stadenberg, while Fifth Army attacked from the west. At this point Houthulst Forest would also be outflanked, with the British about 5,000 yards behind it. Had the Germans not always recognized Gheluvelt and Houthulst as the twin pillars on which the Flanders position stood? They had fought tooth and nail for the plateau, but now it was virtually in British hands, and if Houthulst was to be outflanked, the position would surely be as good as broken. Passchendaele, on top of the ridge, behind Flanders I, was the key to unlock the German position on the Yser. From the Passchendaele ridge to the Lichterveld railway junctions was about 8 miles of relatively open country, with no series defence line to break through, suitable at last for cavalry operations. Was it not possible therefore that Passchendaele may also be the key to evicting the Germans from the Belgian coast? But a successful attack along the ridge would demand four main elements; sufficient fresh forces, a general weakening of enemy resistance, domination of the enemy artillery, and a continuation of the dry weather, and none of these things were likely let alone guaranteed.

All these matters had undoubtedly been given careful consideration by Haig and his Staff, but what was not known was the true state of the German forces ranged against him. Their artillery strength and dispositions could be established reasonably accurately from the R.F.C's air reconnaissance. Four main groups had been identified; Tenbrielen (one large group of long range guns) firing mostly northwest towards Tower Hamlets spur; Kruiseeke (two groups) firing towards Menin Road and Polygon Wood; Becelaere / Terhand (two groups) and Keiburg (one group) firing towards Polygon Wood and Broodseinde ridge; Passchendaele (and possibly Goudberg) groups firing towards Gravenstafel ridge. The condition of the German infantry was less easy to establish. A good estimate could be made of the numbers of divisions so far engaged and the number withdrawn from the battle. Elements of four counter-attack divisions, (*17th, 236th, 4th Bavarian and 234th*) had been identified on the 26th September, the *236th* and *234th* having also been in action on the 20th and suffered grievous casualties. It was believed that of the front line divisions in action on the 20th September, the *Bavarian Ertsatz, 121st, 2nd Guard Reserve, 9th Reserve* and *36th* had all been withdrawn from the line by the 21st. Of the counter-

---

[473] National Archives, Second Army intelligence summary WO 153/490

attack divisions the *16th Bavarian* had been relieved on the 24th / 25th, the *236th* on the 22nd and the *234th* on the 23rd, but the two latter had been identified back in the line on the 26th. On the 20th, *234th Division* by German admission had lost in some battalions 60% of their officers and up to 50% of their strength.

The successful British attacks and subsequent German lack of success in counter-attacks had obviously caused great confusion in the German command and control system. It seemed that isolated parties from both front line and counter-attack divisions were still holding out in the line, and on other occasions had been carried forward in attack with other units, after the division had nominally been relieved. The capture of prisoners of the *452nd Regiment* of the *234th Division* by 3rd Division at Zonnebeke on the 26th September was one example. If the status of their own forces was confusing to the Germans, it was inevitably even more confusing to the British. What was certain was that the enemy now held the front sector in greater strength, keeping all three regiments of the front line divisions as close as possible to the front, in order to hold the position for sufficient time to allow for the arrival of the counter-attack divisions. On the 26th September they had repeated the mistake of the 20th in releasing the counter-attack divisions too quickly before the situation at the front was clear, only to have them broken by British artillery fire. Those that approached the front line were held by machine gun and rifle fire, from already well dug-in and wired British positions, and only succeeded in strengthening the line to which the front divisions had previously withdrawn.

The defence in depth system was obviously not working and the reason was simple. To work effectively von Lossberg's scheme assumed the enemy would attempt a deep penetration; but the British were not attacking to any great depth, and were always under the protection of their artillery. It was clear to the German high command that a change in tactics was required and this was soon to come. Ludendorff bitterly complained, 'the enemy managed to adapt himself to our method of employing counter-attack divisions'.[474] On the 29th September he hurried to Roulers to confer with commanders on the spot, in an effort to find a solution to the problem. Although still believing in the principle of 'defence in depth' his analysis of the problem, possibly influenced by field officers, led him to conclude that the counter-attack divisions were arriving too late, and therefore not able to confront the British during their assault when they would be most off balance. Neither could effective artillery support be provided as the exact position of the front line was usually unclear. Ludendorff struggled with the dilemma. 'Our defensive tactics had to be developed further, somehow or other. We were all agreed to that. The only thing was, it was so infinitely difficult to hit on the right remedy.'[475] The solution, which he either came to, or agreed with, would see the return of the traditional German defence arrangement of one strongly defended line. The counter-attack divisions would be held back until the day following an attack, at which time the position of the front line would be clearer and they could receive the necessary artillery support. In this case it would be essential that the front line division could hold out pending the arrival of the counter-attack divisions. To achieve this there would be a strengthening of the line divisions with an increase in the number of machine guns in the front line, these guns coming from the back areas of the divisional position, and from the support and reserve battalions. These battalions would not wait to carry out local counter-attacks but would be moved quickly towards the front as soon as an attack threatened, and each *Eingreif* division would send forward one battalion behind each front line regiment, as far as the artillery protection line. This plan seems indicative of the fact that Ludendorff had no real idea of how to confront Plumer's new tactics. He obviously knew the power of the British artillery, yet he was planning to provide that artillery with a concentrated target in a largely unprotected position, for there was no shelter for this number of infantry on the open slopes of Passchendaele ridge.

Haig was obviously unaware of Ludendorff's unhappy contemplations. He did know however that Plumer's attritional tactics were working. But was there yet the chance of a breakthrough? Of course there was the possibility that the German defence system had been so

---

[474] Ludendorff *War Memoirs ii* p480
[475] AOA p857

damaged, that the difficulty of reinforcing the Flanders position through the narrow corridor into Western Belgium with limited railway access, might result in a general withdrawal. If German divisions and artillery were being used up in the battle of attrition faster than they could be replaced, their position would become untenable. Also might it not be the case that if the British could gain a foothold upon the Westroosebeke – Stadenberg ridge, the enemy may see his Flanders position as being ruptured to the extent that necessitated withdrawal from Houthulst Forest and the Yser, uncovering the coast and the U-boat bases?

On the 24th September Crown Prince Rupprecht wrote in his diary that he hoped another attack would not happen too quickly, as he did not have sufficient reserves behind the front.[476] Since 20th September it was believed that 17 German divisions had been in action around Ypres, of which 12 had been withdrawn with heavy casualties. German records now show that there were 25 divisions in Flanders and that 9 had been withdrawn.[477] In the same period, between the Menin Road and Langemarck the British had employed 12 divisions, one, the 58th twice. By the 4th October three of the divisions used on the 20th September would be back in action again (1st and 2nd Australian and 20th), giving a net British withdrawal of 9 divisions, which had suffered heavy casualties but retained their fighting capability.

The quality of the German divisions engaged had been variable. On the 20th September some divisions had been in the line a long time, and had suffered the prolonged British bombardment and attack before being relieved. This had inevitably had a demoralizing effect and there was general dissatisfaction amongst prisoners that they had been left in the line so long. On the 26th the *3rd Reserve Division* in the front line opposite the Australians had proved a poor lot, whereas *50th Reserve* and *17th Divisions* in the counter-attacks along the Reutelbeek had fought well. Prisoners also spoke of their heavy losses especially when in reserve positions and in moving forward. They spoke of the accuracy of the British artillery fire, of the harassment of the indirect machine gun fire, and of fear of ground attack from aircraft. They were impressed by ability of the British infantry to be on top of them as soon as the barrage had passed, and were unimpressed with their own artillery which invariably fired short. It appeared that relations between officers and men were often poor, with many reports of ill discipline. Although this was all good news to their captors, there was still no indication of an imminent German collapse, and there were differing interpretations of the evidence available. The actual fighting value of German divisions withdrawn from the line, and how quickly they could be restored to full capability was very difficult to establish. There were many unknowns in the British intelligence arsenal, but the next 'bite' was about to be taken out of the German position, after which perhaps things may become a little clearer.

From the British perspective the battle had been an undoubted success, albeit a costly one. The artillery casualties had been much greater than on the 20th September, and proportionately so had the infantry. On the 20th twelve divisions had been in action and had sustained casualties of 20,305. The 15,375 casualties sustained by seven divisions on the 26th represented a proportional increase in infantry casualties of 30%. It is evident that the German spoiling attack of the 25th had a severe impact upon 33rd British and 5th Australian Division in their attacks on the 26th, and the difficulties of 3rd Division in front of Hill 40 were reflected in their losses. From their own official account German casualties for the period 11th to 30th September had amounted to 38,500 compared with about 36,000 British. To more accurately compare these figures on a like for like basis it is possible that around 30% needs to be added to the German figure to allow for lightly wounded who were not included in the enemy totals. All casualties including lightly wounded were included in the British totals.

---

[476] BOH p294
[477] The *3rd Bavarian Ersatz, 9th Reserve, 36th, 121st, 3rd Reserve, 50th Reserve, 208th, 234th* and *236th*

British casualties on 26th September

Second Army	Total	Killed
39th Division	1,577	
33rd Division	2,905	444
5th Aust. Division	3,723	
4th Aust. Division	1,529	
Fifth Army		
3rd Division	4,032	497
59th Division	1,110	176
58th Division	499	98
	15,375	

German casualties for the period 20th September to 27th September

	Total
206th Division	2,524
10th Ersatz Division	672
23rd Reserve Division	2,119
234th Division	1,850
236th Division	1,227

3rd *Reserve Division* and 4th *Bavarian Division* casualties unknown.
Total casualties for *Ypres Corps* for month of September were 25,089[478]

---

[478] National Archives, CAB45/172 p128

Building Corduroy road

Anzac Spur

Chapter Six

"We could have captured Passchendaele"

The Third Step

The Battle of Broodseinde 4th October

It was obvious to all that the battle on the 26th September had been another great success, but the nature of the success varied depending upon the perspective from which it was viewed. For many in the front line and involved in the fighting it had been the usual terrifying, bloody onslaught to which everyone had become accustomed. The shattering thunder of the barrage, the hot concussion of exploding shells, the taste of acrid smoke and dust, the crack of shrapnel shells and the incessant chattering of the machine guns, which both filled the air with zipping and whining bullets, each deadly but unseen. All were now a normal part of life, and death. The churning fears before action, the utter confusion and unfettered violence in action, the death and mutilation of both friend and foe alike, all had become commonplace. They had embraced the elation of victory and the sadness of mates lost or maimed. Training, determination and comradeship had helped overcome the great difficulties with which they had been faced and they had won through and achieved virtually all that had been required. But even the uninjured were totally exhausted, filthy, and shocked. The only thing about which they were sure was that the War was hell. This time they had beaten their enemy, but sooner or later they would have to come back and beat him again.

In the more anesthetized and insulated atmosphere at G.H.Q. the harsh emotions of the battlefield were somewhat remote, and a more clinical assessment of the situation was being made. The new lines on the map showed that another neat incision had been made into the German position in accordance with the plan. Another step had been taken in grinding down the enemy, and towards the Passchendaele ridge. The fine weather still held, and as all indications pointed towards a continuation of the run of positive results, hopes of a breakthrough did not seem unreasonable. As usual an over optimistic judgment was given as to the declining fortunes of the enemy, whose defences in Flanders were hoped by all, and believed by some, to be near breaking point, but in these heady days was it not better to be positive, rather than to pander to more cautionary councils? Compared with the disappointing results of previous campaigns in this mystifying War, things now looked rather encouraging, and given the level of commitment that the Germans were having to make to the Flanders battle, the French front remained safe. For the moment the initiative was still denied to the enemy.

Robertson wrote to Haig on the 2nd October to inform him of the conclusions of the conference held at Boulogne on the 25th September, covering the two main issues, both close to Haig's heart, the first being the 100 guns, the second being the imposition of taking over more of the French front line. The first conclusion read: 'The British and French Governments while greatly regretting the decision of General Cadorna not to pursue the offensive operations for which 100 French guns were recently sent to the Italian Front, are agreed that no action can usefully be taken in order to obtain a reversal of this decision. The whole of the British and French artillery will in consequence be withdrawn from the Italian Front.' [479] So much for the guns for Italy. The second conclusion read: 'The British Government, having accepted in principle, the extension of the line held by the British Army on the Western Front, the two Governments are agreed that the question of the amount of the extension and the time at which it should take place should be left for arrangement between the two Commanders-in-Chief.' So much for Haig's request, that no discussions would take place regarding dispositions of the British Army without him being present. He had previously written to Robertson on the 21st July. 'I am very strongly of opinion

---

[479] National Archives, Robertson to Haig 2nd October WO158/28

that questions concerning the conduct of operations – present or future, the distribution of my troops, or similar matters relating to my command, should not be discussed with the French authorities in my absence, and I shall be glad if you will inform the War Cabinet that I hold this view.' [480] Nothing however had been confirmed with the French, beyond an agreement in principle, but the final outcome was to be as Haig feared.

Taking advantage of his trip to Boulogne, the Prime Minister had met with Haig on the afternoon of the 25th, and again on the 26th, when he had visited the rear areas behind the Salient on the day of Polygon Wood, and had been shown the poor condition of enemy prisoners, which some claimed had been specially chosen for the purpose. He had, according to General Gough, also visited his headquarters at la Lovie Chateau with Brigadier-General Charteris, but had failed to give notice of his visit or meet with Gough upon his arrival. Gough was less than impressed. 'I was struck by the discourtesy of the Prime Minister in actually visiting the Headquarters of one of his Army Commanders and not coming in to him, and I therefore let him pass on. It was an amazing attitude for a man in his position and with his responsibilities.' [481] Lloyd George returned to London impressed by the poor condition of the enemy and the high morale of the British officers and men he had met and talked with. He was however impressed with little else, especially disappointed with the relative inaction of the French, adamant that Haig's predictions of further advances were worthless, and very doubtful that the Army would even reach the 'Clerken' (Passchendaele – Staden) ridge.

There is little doubt that a rift, however minor, had developed between Haig and Robertson, due primarily to the fact that although they had met on the 26th and the subject of extension of the British line had been raised, there had been no mention of any *agreement* with the French having been reached. After subsequently receiving Robertson's note, Haig recalled the content of the meeting of the 26th, and commented in his diary on the 3rd October: 'All the P.M. said was that "Painlevé was anxious that the British should take over more line". And Robertson rode the "high horse" and said it was high time for the British now to call the tune, and not play second fiddle to the French, etc. etc., and all this when shortly before he must have quietly acquiesced at the conference in Painlevé's demands! Robertson comes badly out of this, in my opinion – especially as it was definitely stated (with the War Cabinet's approval) that no discussion re. operations on the Western Front would be held with the French without my being present.'[482] An uncontested agreement in principle to the effective reduction in Haig's divisions was not the most obvious way for the C.I.G.S. to support the operation in Flanders, of which to date, in the absence of a sound alternative, he had been an advocate. Over the following weeks Robertson was to do his best to smooth the matter over.

Haig's plans for future steps

Emboldened by the conviction born out of success, Haig, at a conference with Plumer and Gough on the 28th September had made it clear that the next step planned for the 6th October, which should see British forces across the whole of the Gheluvelt plateau and along the main ridge as far north as Broodseinde, would conclude a definite phase of the offensive; the securing of a firm right flank. The following or fourth step, planned for the 10th October, although conforming to Plumer's successful bite-and-hold technique, should allow for the possibility of exploitation and not be firmly shackled to fixed limited objectives. The optimistic intelligence summaries indicating the serious degradation of German units had led Haig to believe that rapid exploitation might be possible on the 10th October, following the defeat of the inevitable counter-attacks, and provided there were also indications of a general enemy withdrawal. On the 2nd October he expressed his views to his Army Commanders thus: 'There are signs that the enemy's resistance is approaching the breaking point and, while fully recognizing that it may not have been reached even after two more defeats, we must be ready to seize the first

---

[480] National Archives, Haig to Robertson 21st July WO158/28
[481] General Sir Hubert Gough (1931) *The Fifth Army* London: Hodder and Stoughton p211
[482] Douglas Haig. Diaries and Letters p332

opportunity for a rapid advance...This opportunity may arise on the afternoon of the 10th, night of the 10th/11th, or morning of the 11th'.[483] A reserve of fresh formations was to be ready to push forward with all speed on the heels of the retreating Germans. The infantry would be supported by tanks and artillery which would move forward with them in pursuit, either eastward towards Moorselede, 3,000 yards east of Passchendaele, or northwards to outflank and roll-up the German line along the ridge, while the cavalry would move on Roulers disrupting transport and communications.

As we shall soon see, partly due to elements beyond Haig's control, this plan was not to be fulfilled, and with the benefit of hindsight appears optimistic in the extreme. But optimism was the mood of the moment, and if the conditions for a break through had in fact presented themselves on the 10th October, with his Armies not in a position to react, Haig would have appeared negligent in the extreme. Had it not always been the responsibility of the Commander-in-Chief to explore all possibilities with his Army Commanders? Plumer and Gough were requested to submit their requirements in men and material for the 10th October attack, which they did by the 30th September and 1st October respectively. Whether both commanders had conferred independently of Haig or not, they both sent covering letters expressing caution with regard to any possible break through, and that any idea of imminent exploitation was premature. They were both of the opinion that at least two more steps at three day intervals would be required to gain the line Passchendaele – Westroosebeke along the ridge top, followed by a four day break to build the roads and lay the tracks necessary to move the Armies forward before any considerable exploitation could be considered. Gough expressed doubt, that as the limited advances of 1,500 yards did not threaten the German gun line and would therefore not allow for the capture of enemy field artillery which would therefore be largely still intact, that the general situation on the 10th would provide the opportunity of exploitation. Haig's response to these letters showed understanding and indicated forethought. He argued that he did not necessarily mean that exploitation of any success on the 10th should follow immediately whatever the situation, but that all possible preparations should be made in the case that a favourable opportunity arose. In any event he required that the reserve formations should be available if not for use on this occasion, then when circumstances allowed in the future.

On the 1st October Haig visited Lieutenant-General Godley at II Anzac Corps H.Q. and explained the importance he placed on him, 'making his arrangements so as to be able to exploit any success gained without delay. Thus guns should be placed behind Gravenstafel Hill (as soon as it is captured) for dealing with Passchendaele – and the reserve brigades of attacking divisions should be used *at once* to exploit a success if the Enemy counter-attacks and fails'.[484] He made no mention of the necessity of a general enemy withdrawal being evident before getting on their heels, but just that the counter-attacks should have failed. In the last two assaults the failure of the counter-attacks had left the enemy holding their forward outpost line in greater strength, as the counter-attack divisions had gone to ground and reinforced the line divisions. From past experience therefore the failure of a counter-attack had not resulted in a collapse of the enemy line, but a strengthening. The limitations of bite and hold were obvious, but Haig still hoped for a break through.

Army Commanders Conference, Cassel 2nd October

An Army Commanders Conference was held at Haig's house in Cassel on the 2nd October at which Kiggel, Davidson, Charteris, Major-General Nash (Director General of Transport) and Plumer, Gough and their senior Staff Officers were present. Haig emphasized how favourable he considered the situation to be, his diary entry for the day stating that he had explained, '....how necessary it was to have all the necessary means for exploiting any success gained on the 10th, should the situation admit, e.g. if the Enemy counter-attacks and is defeated, then the reserve

---

[483] National Archives, notes on conference at Lovie Chateau, 6p.m. 2nd October 1917, (following C-in-C's conference at Cassel) WO95/520
[484] Douglas Haig. Diaries and Letters pp330-331

brigades must follow after the Enemy and take the Passchendaele ridge at once'. He went on to write, 'both Gough and Plumer quite acquiesced in my views, and arranged wholeheartedly to give effect to them when the time came. At first they adhered to the idea of continuing our attacks for limited objectives'.[485] Again he made no mention of the previous requirement, that an indication of a general enemy withdrawal would be a proviso of any attempted exploitation, but maybe he considered Plumer and Gough would take this as read. Haig also stated that he still intended total commitment to the Flanders campaign and for the time being had abandoned plans for the Cambrai offensive. All forces available to him were to be employed for the Ypres operation, six divisions moving from other sectors to reinforce Fifth Army, and the Canadian Corps of four divisions to move up from Lens to Second Army about the 20th October. The 1st and 5th Cavalry Divisions were to arrange to be assembled within a day's march of the battlefield by the 10th October, one division to be assigned to Second Army and one to Fifth Army.[486] He was adamant that he did not want the same mistake to befall his Armies that had so cheated the Germans of success on the 31st October 1914 during "First Ypres", when they had failed to exploit the exhausted state of the British. As a general observation upon the necessity for preparedness it was not an unreasonable comment. To add the icing to the cake, 'Charteris emphasized the deterioration of German Divisions in numbers, moral and all round efficiency'.[487] It appeared that all that remained necessary to at last make some real progress, was that the fine weather should continue to hold. But the planning, relying on slim evidence of German weakness, envisaged a complete break with the bite-and-hold tactics which had so far proved very effective at grinding down the enemy. Corps Commanders were for the first time since the 20th September questioning their objectives, the Earl of Cavan enquiring: 'In the event of full and complete success, G.O.C. XIV Corps wishes to know his ultimate objectives. He pointed out that he could not keep touch with XVIII Corps on his right, and simultaneously clear Houthulst Forest on his left'.[488] In a hardly helpful or reassuring answer which succeeded in little but avoiding the issue, Gough indicated that 'complete success' presupposed the French moving *north* of Houthulst Forest to the extent of outflanking the German garrison within the wood (implying an advance of 4,000 to 5,000 yards), a risk the enemy would not run, (and a task the French could not realistically be expected to achieve). In any case he believed that a brigade of cavalry would be usefully employed in protecting XIV Corps' flank. The fighting along the *south* face of Houthulst Forest was soon to become amongst the worst experienced throughout the whole campaign.

Further detailed instructions were given regarding the composition of the reserves to be at hand to pursue the faltering enemy. Each division was to have one reserve assault brigade, lightly equipped and at instant readiness to move forward along selected routes, accompanied by its own horse-drawn artillery train comprising of two 60-pounder batteries, two 6-inch howitzer batteries, and four batteries of field artillery. It was considered that if after about four hours following the initial attack, the forward brigades reported the situation favourable, the reserve brigades were to continue the assault in the early afternoon to a much greater depth and towards specific objectives to be reached before nightfall. But the specific objectives show a startling degree of wishful if not totally unrealistic thinking. Second Army reserve brigades were to be over the ridge to the east and north of Passchendaele, their left in touch with Fifth Army on the Passchendaele – Westroosebeke road along the ridge top. The reserve brigades of I Anzac were to reach Droogenbroodhoek on the Moorslede road, 2,750 yards east of Broodseinde, while those of II Anzac, advanced to a line with their right on Passchendaele station 1,500 yards east of the ridge top and its left north of Passchendaele and in touch with Fifth Army. This would see the reserve brigades spread across a frontage of over 3,000 yards. Droogenbroodhoek, the objective of I Anzac, lay on the Flanders II Line, and to reach the Westroosebeke road Fifth Army

---

[485] Douglas Haig. Diaries and Letters p331
[486] National Archives, Advanced GHQ order OAD 646 2nd October WO158/311
[487] Douglas Haig. Diaries and Letters p331
[488] National Archives, notes on conference at Lovie Chateau, 6p.m. 2nd October 1917, (following C-in-C's conference at Cassel) WO95/520

would have to negotiate the Flanders I Line, 2,500 yards east of Poelcappelle, and still 1,750 yards short of the ridge top road. Any chance of success would depend on the resistance of both German infantry and artillery totally collapsing, and of equal if not greater importance, the dry weather holding. The roads to the west and east of the ridge had been constantly pounded by British artillery since July, and across what was left of them the horse teams were to drag the support artillery, and its ammunition. Movement forward of medium artillery had also been planned. Even if the predictions of German weakness made by Charteris were correct, and assuming the weather held, this would still be a momentous task.

The planning went even further, with each corps having a reserve division ready to move up towards Ypres, with each brigade moving in two trains carrying 1,800 men per train. Major-General Nash, the D.G.T. stated that given three hours notice he could have the reserve divisions on the battlefield within three and a half to four hours. The cavalry were also drawn closer to the front, 1st Cavalry Division allotted to Second Army, and 5th Cavalry Division allotted to Fifth Army, whilst the remainder of the Cavalry Corps remained behind the Yser canal, (to concentrate by G.H.Q. orders on the line Vlamertinghe – Elverdinghe on the morning of the 10th), until the Passchendaele ridge was clear of the enemy. Gough's opinion was that: *'Until the infantry are on the line Passchendaele – Westroosebeke, it is improbable that the Cavalry Corps could take an active part'*.[489]

The tanks were also required to cooperate with the reserve brigades, two tank battalions being allotted to Second Army, and one tank brigade (three battalions) to Fifth Army, Haig commenting hopefully that the firmer ground and better going beyond the shell-torn area, which should shortly be reached would give the tanks a better chance, and would permit their employment in large numbers.[490] How they were to reach the firmer ground across the ravaged valleys of the Hanebeek and Steenbeek was not disclosed. The problems faced by the tanks were already well known by all. Even under the recent relatively dry conditions it had been difficult for them to get forward over the crater field, and their limited speed and range did not lend them to rapid deep penetrations. At least the cavalry were capable of this task, once the wire entanglements, blockhouses and machine gun lines, of which there were many, were cleared. Nevertheless 80 tanks would be available, 50 to 56 with XVIII Corps, and 24 to 30 with XIV Corps, a large proportion of the total to be held back in reserve. Gough commented hopefully that: *'they would be very useful in pushing on as a sort of advanced screen, and might achieve greater results even than in a normal pitched battle'*. The results of the 19th August may have continued to raise false hopes, as senior commanders struggled to understand the limited capabilities of the tanks, even in the hands of the most courageous crews. However unlikely it now seems that this plan would ever be put into action with any degree of success, Haig was undoubtedly correct and cannot be criticized in exploring all possibilities to take advantage of any opportunity which presented itself. To expand the thinking of his Army Commanders with bold plans was surely his responsibility, even if subsequently those commanders found them unworkable within the reality of weather, ground, and pressure of action. There is almost a vision of the future in these plans, which given the equipment of the time, his Armies unfortunately did not have the technical capability to carry out.

Meeting of the War Policy Committee, the 3rd October

In London, the War Policy Committee reconvened on the 3rd October, only its second sitting since the offensive opened, but again was not to consider the achievements or otherwise of its Army fighting the greatest battle of its long and illustrious history. It was to consider Lloyd George's latest obsession, to bring about the downfall of Turkey. After discussing the apparent superiority in manpower enjoyed by the Central Powers, it was pointed out that Turkey was the weakling in the enemy pack offering the Allies the likelihood of an advantage, which in the

---

[489] National Archives, notes on conference at Lovie Chateau, 6p.m. 2nd October 1917, (following C-in-C's conference at Cassel) WO95/520
[490] BOH p299

opinion of the Committee was, after the Italian disappointment, the only significant one open to them. The dislocating of Turkey from Germany, Lloyd George now argued, was the best way to proceed. As Italy had declined the offer to take the lead rôle, that option was for the moment out. But rather than attack the colossus head on, better to dispense with a weaker partner first, by means of a vigorous offensive in Palestine, followed by generous terms of peace. Lloyd George proposed that once Turkey had suffered a major military reversal, such as an advance from Gaza and the capture by the British of the Jaffa – Jerusalem line, the time would be right to negotiate a peace acceptable to Turkey, by offering that Palestine, Syria, and Mesopotamia should be created Protectorates under the suzerainty of the Sultan of Turkey. With Turkey thus pacified and hopefully appeased, the British Army could resume the offensive on the Western Front in the spring of 1918 in more favourable weather conditions. Luckily, and purely because Cadorna had suspended the Eleventh Battle of the Isonzo, there were 100 guns doing nothing in the Mediterranean, which with a couple of infantry divisions sent from the Western Front, would greatly assist General Allenby's efforts on his way to Jerusalem. General Smuts introduced another dimension to the debate by relaying to Lloyd George, in Robertson's absence, a comment the C.I.G.S. had made recently claiming that the Cabinet had changed the plans of the military in early 1917. Lloyd George rounded on the absent Robertson, vehemently denying doing any such thing, protesting that he had left the planning and arrangements up to Haig and Nivelle, and had only intervened in insisting on a joint commander, in the event Nivelle. He then went on to explain that the Nivelle offensive had been the only operation on the Western Front in 1917 which had shown signs of success, and nothing achieved since had come close to the results the French had gained. The question as to why the French had found it essential to quickly remove Nivelle, was not raised by any Committee member. It can only be assumed that Lloyd George had forgotten the reports of Spears, Maurice, Wilson and Lord Esher, which had all indicated that Nivelle's offensive had in fact brought France to the very brink of disaster, from which she had not yet fully recovered. As far as the Flanders offensive was concerned the Prime Minister claimed that it was living up to all he had expected of it, and further claimed that the Committee had been misguided by the over optimistic promises given by Haig, and if they had not been so considerably influenced, they would not have agreed to it in the first place.

With Lloyd George so stung by Smut's suggestion, and fired into condemnation of the fighting at Ypres, of which he now had no confidence whatsoever, surely this was crunch time for the Flanders operation? As we have seen on the 25th July Haig had received a telegram from the Committee (or more properly Robertson) stating, 'having approved your plans being executed, you may depend upon our whole hearted support; and that if and when we decide to reconsider the situation, we will obtain your views before arriving at any decision as to the cessation of operations'. The time for 'reconsideration' must now have arrived, for according to Lloyd George there was nothing about the campaign which either looked like succeeding or remained within the guidelines of the initial approval. The French were not fully supporting the British, and it seemed most unlikely that the 'Clerken' ridge would be taken by the winter. Haig he claimed, had grossly misled them with his over-optimistic promises of success. How much more would need to go wrong before the Committee would finally call a stop to Haig's battle? Perhaps a change in the weather, bringing back intolerable conditions, would finally prompt the Committee to act? But in the meantime all that was demanded was that the Shipping Controller should report on the availability of transport to move the divisions to Egypt, and that Robertson was to proffer his advice on inflicting such a military defeat on the Turks guaranteed to ensure that their Government would be happy to sue for peace.[491] The meeting was summed up by Hankey in two words; 'very desultory'.[492] In Flanders meanwhile, preparations towards General Plumer's next step to take place on the following day were nearing completion.

---

[491] National Archives, 18th meeting of the Cabinet Committee on War Policy, 3rd October CAB27/6
[492] Hankey Diaries, 3rd October

The plan for the 4th October

Weather conditions, rainfall Vlamertinghe, temperature Ypres[493]

	27th Sept	28th Sept	29th Sept	29th Sept	1st Oct	2nd Oct	3rd Oct	4th Oct
Rainfall	Trace	Trace	Nil	Nil	Nil	2.7mm	1.2mm	4.6mm
Temp	67F	65F	65F	67F	69F	76F	64F	60F

On the 28th September Plumer issued orders for the battle and the artillery plan, and over the next three days the necessary adjustments to corps boundaries took place. The great blow, which he intended to carry Second Army onto the Passchendaele ridge, was to be struck in the centre of the attack by both I and II Anzac Corps, and for the first time three Australian Divisions, 1st and 2nd of I Anzac, and 3rd of II Anzac, would be in action side by side, the 3rd Australian Division accompanied on its left by the New Zealand Division. Initially it had been doubted that I Anzac would be available for the third step, as higher casualties had been expected in the first two steps, a concern which thankfully had proven unfounded. On the afternoon of the 26th September Haig issued the order for II Anzac to take over the front of V Corps. A degree of urgency however hastened the movement of II Anzac from its rest area just west of St. Omer, 40 miles behind the front, for the planned date of the operation on 6th October was partly dependant on the speed with which the corps could make preparations to take up its position in the line. This it did swiftly by the 28th September, and Haig, concerned that the period of dry weather might not hold, after consultation with Plumer and Gough, brought forward the operation to the 4th October. Since the 20th September, Second Army had arranged the date for its operations solely on military considerations to ensure of success. Now for the first time preparations were to be hurried due to concerns regarding the weather.

To allow I Anzac to concentrate along a 2.000 yard front for its attack on Broodseinde, it was to move its southern corps boundary about 1,750 yards north, but its northern boundary also moved north by 750 yards to the Ypres – Roulers railway, to include the whole of Zonnebeke village, the net reduction in corps front being 1,000 yards. II Anzac, taking over the front from V Corps, would attack with its two divisions along a front of 3,000 yards, 3rd Australian front around 1,000 yards, and the New Zealand Division around 2,000 yards. The distance to the final objectives, although still limited, varied between corps. From Zonnebeke towards Broodseinde I Anzac was required to advance about 1,200 to 1,500 yards while to their left II Anzac would advance in places 2,000 yards over Gravenstafel ridge towards the Ravebeek. North of the Menin Road and south of Molenaarelsthoek, in a simultaneous advance to support the Australians right, X Corps, which would side step 1,500 yards to the north and take over the front previously held by I Anzac, would attack with the two reserve divisions of Second Army along a front just under 2,500 yards.

Fifth Army, with XVIII Corps using two divisions and XIV Corps using one division, would attack towards Poelcappelle, with a second division of XIV Corps forming a defensive flank into the Broenbeek valley. The Army would attack along a front of around 4,000 yards, and to a depth approaching 2,000 yards with their left flank astride the Ypres – Staden railway just north of Langemarck.

The German spoiling attack on the 25th September, although not holding up the major offensive on the 26th, had in one way been successful. On the 26th it had been necessary for General Plumer to limit the actions of 100th and 98th Brigades to recapturing the ground lost on the 25th. This left the enemy still desperately clinging to the eastern edge of the Gheluvelt plateau, holding the Polderhoek spur just south of the Reutelbeek and most of Cameron Covert,

---

[493] National Archives, GHQ statistics WO95/15

which had both been part of the day's final objective. Haig stressed the importance of driving the Germans off their last toehold on the plateau, both for greater observation and ease of defence. True to character Plumer was not willing to attack south of Polygon Wood with a tired division, and to achieve this new task he requested another fresh division for X Corps, a request to which Haig agreed. The 23rd Division which had seen its fair share of fighting since the 20th September with only two days rest, was relieved on the 2nd October by the 5th Division from Fifth Army, which moved into the line between Polygon Wood and the Menin Road. X Corps southern boundary was moved north to the Menin Road, the line south of the road around Tower Hamlets being taken over by IX Corps which was to form a protective right flank with the 37th Division. This was to be a big battle, and in all 12 divisions were to be engaged along a frontage of approximately 14,000 yards.

Arrangement of British divisions engaged south to north:

Second Army:
IX Corps, 37th Division: X Corps, 5th, 21st and 7th Divisions
I Anzac Corps, 1st and 2nd Australian Divisions
II Anzac Corps, 3rd Australian and New Zealand Divisions.

Fifth Army:
XVIII Corps: 48th and 11th Divisions
XIV Corps, 4th and 29th Divisions

German dispositions

The German Flanders position had taken a fearful battering and had been severely dented, but was far from broken. The first three lines of defence had been crushed, as had a small sector of the fourth (Flanders I), just east of Polygon Wood. The loss of the Gheluvelt plateau was serious and preparations were in hand to attempt its re-capture, but the central core of the Passchendaele ridge, obviously the primary British objective, still lay protected behind 10,000 yards of the Flanders I Line, with its wire entanglements, blockhouses and bunkers, from Molenaarelsthoek northwards to Stadendreef, just east of Houthulst Forest.

The method of defeating the limited penetration attacks of the British had been given careful consideration at Roulers on the 29th September. In a long instruction issued on the 30th Sixt von Armin, in line with Ludendorff's conclusions, ordered a much greater concentration of better armed infantry with a greater number of machine guns into front line positions, to check the British assault in the forward fighting zone, and to hold back the counter-attack divisions until the situation was better understood, possibly until the following day. Only then would the artillery have a clear knowledge of the British position, and could then effectively support the counter-attack in driving it back.[494]

---

[494] National Archives, CAB45/172 pp129-130

Arrangement of German divisions engaged south to north[495]

Front Line divisions:

25th Division (117th, 116th and 115th I.R's.) and *19th Reserve Division (78th, 92nd and 73rd R.I.R's.)* opposite IX and X Corps; *4th Guard Division (93rd R.I.R., 5th Foot Guard Regiment, 5th Guard Grenadier Regiment)* and *20th Division (79th, 77th and 92nd I.R's.)* opposite I and II Anzac; *10th Ersatz Division (370th, 369th and 371st I.R.'s)* and *6th Bavarian Division* opposite XVIII and XIV Corps.

Counter attack divisions:

16th Bavarian, 17th, 8th, 22nd Reserve, 4th Bavarian, 16th, and *187th Divisions*
Attack division: *45th Reserve Division* was to pass through the *4th Guard* with the *210th, 212th* and *211th R.I.R's* and attack towards Tokio spur.

British preparations for transport and communications

The now familiar tasks of moving artillery and communications closer to the front were repeated to support the third step. More timber tracks and light railways, essential for the movement of guns and ammunition were laid, new battery positions were constructed, and the guns moved up 1,000 to 1,500 yards. All along the front great difficulty was repeatedly experienced in moving supplies towards the lines. Enemy shelling continually damaged the roads and light railways and it was still necessary to move field gun ammunition and other supplies forward by pack mules and horses. Rarely could wagons make the journey to the forward dumps and back without becoming bogged, shelled, or caught in frustrating delay. The engineers and pioneers worked endlessly to keep the supply arteries open, without which there would be little success possible in the front line. The casualties amongst mule-handlers and their animals, drivers and engineers were commensurate with their enormous effort.

II Anzac found preparations on its front less advanced than those of I Anzac to its right, and made hurried efforts to improve the situation. Numerous duckboard tracks were laid forward to assist in crossing the still marshy ground around the shattered Hanebeek and Zonnebeek streams, with seven duckboard bridges being thrown across the mire by 3rd Australian Division alone. It was however impossible within the time available to bring the tracks forward as far as required. Neither was there sufficient time to timber all the roads intended for the artillery. Considering the difficulties which had been experienced moving men and equipment across the battlefield in August, it was clear that if the weather broke, with the now extended lines of supply to the forward artillery positions, both further movement of the guns and replenishment of ammunition would become near impossible. Communications were not neglected in the preparations. The telephone cable head in I Anzac sector ran forward to a position 1,500 yards beyond Frezenberg ridge to near Anzac spur, but in II Anzac sector it stopped 800 yards behind Frezenberg ridge. A trench 5 to 7 feet deep and near 2,300 yards long was rapidly dug in which to bury the cables up as far as Zevenkote, about 1,000 yards behind II Anzac front line.

The Artillery

With the movement of corps boundaries there was an inevitable transfer of guns, those of V Corps taken over by Second Army to support the long front of II Anzac. I Anzac firepower had been drastically reduced since the 20th September, having previously consisted of eight field brigades of the divisional artillery of 1st and 5th Australian Divisions, plus three Army brigades of R.F.A. In what appears on paper as a confusing deployment, the eight brigades of 1st and 5th

---

[495] National Archives, maps showing distribution of enemy forces at 5 pm on the 20th September, in WO153/601

Divisions had now been transferred to II Anzac, with I Anzac supported only by the five brigades of field artillery of 3rd Australian Division. This reduction was to be very clear to the infantry of 1st and 2nd Australian Divisions by the comparative weakness of the barrage. In the centre of the main attack I Anzac was supported by 152 heavy / medium guns and 192 field guns, and II Anzac 227 heavy / medium guns and 384 field guns. By comparison, in its attack against the plateau X Corps artillery support and barrage was on the same scale as on the previous two steps, comprising 226 heavy guns and howitzers, and field artillery of 250 18-pounders and 84 4.5-inch howitzers. Of this total 5th British Division, holding the vital sector between the Menin Road and the Reutelbeek, fielded 108 18-pounders and 36 4.5-inch howitzers, Second Army's total strength being 796 heavy / medium, and 1,548 field guns. The total figures were however nominal and were in fact much lower, some guns still on strength being out of action due to mechanical wear or damage. Replacement of worn or damaged guns was only gradual, and Second Army had lost 584 18-pounders alone since the beginning of August. Much of II Anzac Corps heavy artillery, including 60-pounder gun, 6-inch howitzer, 8-inch howitzer, and 9.2-inch howitzer batteries were now established just behind the old front line of the 31st July, between Potijze and Hellfire Corner. A 12-inch howitzer battery was sited 500 yards east of the Menin Gate with another near English Farm 500 yards north of St. Jean, and a 15-inch howitzer of the 12th Battery Royal Marine Artillery 300 yards north-east of the Menin Gate. Orders issued on the 27th September emphasized the necessity to 'push forward batteries as far as possible with a view to the next operation, in order to be able to place barrages beyond the next objective and to engage the enemy's most distant batteries'. Contrary to some accounts wire cutting remained a major objective of the artillery, both field and heavy batteries.[496]

From the 27th September the artillery fired full scale deceptive barrages including gas shell at varying times on several days. From the 1st October these barrages were fired twice daily, each corps' guns sweeping across the area of attack and into the rear areas beyond. Counter-battery fire and destruction of identified strong-points continued, but in an attempt to mystify the enemy, no long preparatory barrages were to be fired. The thousand yard deep protective barrage would be fired with massed strength at Zero hour (6:00 a.m.), laid 150 yards forward of the jumping-off tapes. The pattern used on the 20th and 26th September would be largely repeated, but at the first objective protective line, the filed guns would stand 200 yards forward of the infantry positions, while the barrage wandered 1,000 yards into the enemy position and then suddenly returned. At Zero+130 minutes it would lift towards the final objective. At the final objective, after a pause, the barrage would creep forward at intervals of an hour to a depth of 1,500 yards to break up any enemy counter-attacks by reserve regiments of the line divisions. At 11:20 a.m. the protective field gun barrage would cease, apart from on S.O.S. signals, and the heavy and medium guns would cease fire at 1:44 p.m.

The assembly

By the 3rd October the attack divisions brought up all their assault battalions east of Ypres, where many bivouacked in the unpromising shelter of shell-holes during the day. An insidious change in the weather, destined to become the second major turning point in the campaign, and therefore to be of huge significance to the future course of the War, slowly became apparent.

---

[496] See Prior and Wilson *Passchendaele the Untold Story* p 209, note 10. 'By September no such continuous belts of wire existed in the salient. From this point on the British artilleryman discounted barbed wire as an obstacle to be dealt with.' But a memorandum issued to II Anzac artillery on the 27th September throws this statement into question. It states: 'Artillery policy. Field Artillery…In addition to wire cutting and the bombardment of strong points and trenches, the ground in front of our line will be continually swept backwards and forwards by HE and shrapnel.' It continues: 'Heavy Artillery. Bombardment Groups will carry out wire cutting and the destruction of strong points and trenches as asked for by the Divisions.' Wire was obviously still an important target for the artillery. Australian War Memorial , War Diary II Anzac Corps, General Staff Headquarters, II Anzac R.A. Preliminary instructions and appendix 2. AWM4-1/32/20 part 3

The meteorological forecast reported an atmospheric depression passing, and predicted cold, squally showers. The sun had set in a stormy sky and in the late evening a south-westerly wind blew up, bringing with it sharp, chilly showers. By 12:30 a.m. as the assault battalions began the march up to the front it was raining lightly in the strong wind, and the surface of the ground became slippery, making movement difficult other than by the duckboard tracks. The clouds hid a full moon and even the well taped tracks became difficult to follow. Some of the pontoons which had been thrown across the muddy crossings of the Hanebeek and Zonnebeke had been either been wrecked by hostile shell-fire, or could not be found in the dark, and there was no choice but to plough on through the mud. There was some enemy shelling which caused a few casualties, but it was not heavy. The Germans appeared jumpy and many white flares were being fired along their line, but the ingoing infantry were used to these displays and took scant notice.

Previous experience had shown that the safest place for the infantry to assemble was close up to the jump-off tapes, to avoid the worst of the enemy defensive barrage, and this night was to be no exception. By 4:00 a.m. the battalions about to attack were close up by the front lines, some just forward, others just in rear. All were suffering the discomfort of rain in the muddy shell-holes, and took what shelter they could beneath their waterproof capes. Towards dawn, although the battlefield had fallen quiet tension levels rose, as the time for action approached and the possibility of detection increased. At about 5:20 a.m. the tension changed to apprehension, as from Broodseinde ridge in front of I Anzac, an enemy flare arced across the overcast sky to burst in a shower of yellow brilliance. Only minutes later an enemy barrage began to develop along the Hanebeek valley, in front of Zonnebeke and around Molenaarelsthoek, mainly along the front of I Anzac Corps, but also towards Polygon Wood. As the barrage intensified more flares burst, soon to be followed by a whole display, which gradually spread to right and left along the German positions. By 5:30 the hostile shelling had become intense, and many crouching anxiously in their wet shell-holes were sure the attack had been discovered.

The German counter-attack 4th October

The Australian attack had not been discovered, and the sudden German barrage had been fired for a very different reason. The inability of the previous counter-attacks to dislodge the British from their new positions had been of serious concern to German high command. Von Armin, was still convinced that although the counter-attacks were having little tactical effect, they had at least forced the British to maintain a large number of troops in the front line, which in turn exposed them to German shelling, and accordingly it had been ordered that the attacks would continue.

The staff of the *4th Guards Division* which had on the 27th September taken over the sector between Zonnebeke and Molenaarelsthoek, were concerned about their poor tactical position, lacking room to deploy other than on the exposed face of Broodseinde ridge, and urged that an attempt should be made to re-capture at least the Tokio spur. Their opinion was that any German counter-attack moving over the ridge was totally exposed to observation from Tokio spur and risked heavy shelling, whereas with the spur back in their hands it would be possible to assemble in greater safety in the upper Zonnebeke valley about Retaliation Farm, from where Anzac ridge and Polygon Wood could again be threatened. The plan codenamed 'Höhensturm' was endorsed by high command but the failure of the two counter-attacks on the 30th September and the 1st October, resulting in heavy losses, had caused a change in German timing. The attack which had at first been planned for the 3rd October, was now to take place on the 4th. The *4th Guard Division*, holding the line in greater strength since the Roulers meeting of the 29th September, was not to carry out the counter-attack, this dubious honour being bestowed upon the three battalions of the *212th Reserve Infantry Regiment* of *45th Reserve Division*. The three regiments of *4th Guard Division*, the *5th Guard Grenadier, 5th Foot Guard* and *93rd Reserve*, were to hold the front line in strength, while the three battalions of *212th* passed through them, supported by 16 heavy and 16 light *minenwerfer* on each flank, and 8 sections of *Fourth Army's*

Sturmbatallion for seizing strong-points. The attack, initially to be made on the left flank by the *III Battalion* to the south of Polygon Wood was curtailed, this battalion now to support the *I* and *II*. At 5:35 a.m. the *4th Guard* divisional artillery was joined by the *minenwerfers*, while the guns of the divisions on either flank shelled along their own fronts as a diversion. Initially the barrage in front of *212th R.I.R.* fell short, upon their own infantry, laying out in shell-holes awaiting the moment to attack. The host of flares seen by the Australians of I Anzac, were fired by the forward German infantry, urgently requesting that the range be lengthened. We shall soon return to discover the outcome of the German attack against I Anzac, coming as it did only minutes before the British barrage was to descend.

The attack of the Second Army 6:00 a.m. the 4th October
The southern defensive flank

IX Corps

South of the Menin Road, the much disputed German positions on Tower Hamlets spur were again to be attacked, this time by 37th Division of IX Corps to protect the flank of X Corps north of the road.

37th Division
Major-General H. Bruce Williams

The 37th Division had relieved the 39th Division on the 27th September, and on the 4th October was to attack with two brigades, the 63rd and 111th to once more attempt to evict the enemy from his last toe-hold on the south-eastern face of the Gheluvelt plateau, at Tower Hamlets and Gheluvelt Wood. Although the bunkers on the ridge had taken a fearful hammering from the British artillery, the defences at the Quadrilateral and east of Tower Trench were as firm as ever, seemingly unaffected by the endless barrages.

63rd Brigade [497]
At 6:00 a.m. prompt the barrage came down and the 8th Somerset Light Infantry and the 8th Lincolnshire Regiment attacked from the quagmire of the Bassevillebeek,[498] up the slope which had already seen so much endeavor and carnage. One company of the 10th York and Lancaster Regiment and two companies of the 4th Middlesex were up in support in the valley. The right of the Somerset demonstrated against the Quadrilateral whilst the centre and left advanced up the slope under heavy machine gun fire. Having virtually reached their objective at Joist and Tower Trenches, they were counter-attacked by bombers, and fell-back down the slope to their start line. In the bombing melee a bomb was dropped by a Somerset soldier who was shot down as he was about to throw it. Private Thomas Henry Sage of the 8th Somerset threw himself on the bomb, saving the lives of a number of men, a selfless and courageous act for which he was to be posthumously awarded the V.C. On the left the Lincoln also tried to advance up the slope but was caught by heavy machine gun fire from Joist Trench and Berry Cottage in the Quadrilateral defences, and also fell back to the start line. Throughout the day an enemy barrage pounded the valley of the Bassevillebeek causing many casualties, and neither the York and Lancs or Middlesex were called upon to renew the attack.

---

[497] National Archives, War Diary 63rd Brigade WO95/2528
[498] National Archives, War Diary 8th Somerset Light Infantry and 8th Lincoln WO95/2529

111th Brigade [499]

From their position higher up the valley side 111th Brigade were to attack with the 13th King's Royal Rifle Corps towards Tower Hamlets and Tower Trench,[500] and the 13th Royal Fusiliers towards the bunkers in Gheluvelt Wood. The K.R.R.C. succeeded in advancing across the ridge track and entered Tower Trench. Machine gun fire from the Lewis Farm blockhouse 150 yards east of the trench made the position untenable, the assault parties then falling back to the shelters about Tower Hamlets. On the left the Royal Fusiliers advanced towards Tower Trench and attempted a wheel to the left to attack the bunkers along the northern edge of Gheluvelt Wood near the Menin Road. While attempting to deploy they were also raked by machine gun fire Lewis Farm and took shelter in shell-holes west of the wood. (The 10th Royal Fusiliers were in support but not heavily engaged).

The attack against the last German hold on the plateau west of Gheluvelt had cost 37th Division 818 casualties of which 178 had been killed. This was to be the last major British effort south of the Menin Road and east of the Bassevillebeek until the 26th October. The Quadrilateral and Gheluvelt Wood were destined to remain in enemy hands at the end of the offensive ended.

X Corps
The right flank guard north of the Menin Road

To provide a right flank for the I Anzac Corps attack against the Broodseinde ridge, X Corps was to advance towards the eastern edge of Gheluvelt plateau with three divisions, to a depth of about 500 yards on the right flank and about 1,000 yards on the left. The Corps boundaries were, in the south, the Menin Road, and in the north, a line just short of Molenaarelsthoek. The final objective line ran through Cameron Covert, across the Polygonbeek valley near Reutel hamlet, through Noordemhoek, to a point 500 yards east of the Broodseinde road near Molenaarelsthoek. As in most divisions in Second Army this day, 5th, 21st, and 7th were to have two objectives designated the Red and Blue Lines. Four tanks were allotted to 21st Division to support their attack.

5th Division
Major-General R. B. Stephens

Attacking between the Menin Road and the Reutel track with its 13th and 95th Brigades, the division had the difficult task of advancing across ground which was still heavy with deep mud. Between the Menin Road and the hamlet of Reutel three streams drained the south-eastern slopes of the Gheluvelt plateau, the Scherriebeek, the Polygonbeek, and the Reutelbeek. The streams, which had in some places been little more than ditches, were now totally smashed by shellfire and rather than draining the ground, just collected the water in the mud about their courses. Between the Scherriebeek and the Reutelbeek was the pronounced Polderhoek spur, but even here on higher ground the surface was a deep cratered quagmire. Between the Reutelbeek and the Polygonbeek, on another small spur sat Cameron Covert, a small enclosure to the east of Polygon Wood, and here the ground was no better. Cameron Covert, which had been counter-attacked by the Germans on the 1st October, when they had re-occupied two pillboxes, was the division's objective on the left flank. Throughout the advance across the muddy waste the German protective barrage was severe causing many casualties.

---

[499] National Archives, War Diary 111th Brigade WO95/2531
[500] National Archives, War Diary 13th KRRC WO95/2533

13th Brigade [501]

The 13th Brigade attacked with the 1st Royal West Kent along the north side of the Menin Road,[502] and the 2nd King's Own Scottish Borderers across the Polderhoek spur, with their left flank on the Reutelbeek. The right company of the West Kent came under heavy machine gun fire from Lewis Farm, south of the road, this flank being exposed due to the check of the 13th Royal Fusiliers. The right company established a defence line towards the road to cover this flank. The centre and left of the West Kent maintained their advance up with the K.O.S.B. gaining their objective on the left by 12:30. With their right on the Scherriebeek and left on the Reutelbeek, the K.O.S.B. attacked with the barrage, through awful ground across Polderhoek spur. Towards the eastern end of the spur, the objective, the ruins of Polderhoek Chateau, had been reinforced with steel and concrete to provide a small fortress. The park contained a number of bunkers which protected the approaches, and had an excellent field of fire along the spur and across the shallow valleys either side. The whole area presented a churned up mass of mud and shell-holes. Under heavy fire, across the atrocious exposed ground, the K.O.S.B. advanced about 800 yards and attacked and seized several of the pillboxes in the Chateau park, a small party continuing the advance right into the Chateau defences. Being few in number and continually sniped and bombed, the party withdrew from the Chateau by nightfall, a ragged line being consolidated in shell-holes near the park.

95th Brigade [503]

The 1st Devonshire Regiment had an unfortunate start,[504] as on the way up from Sanctuary Wood to battalion headquarters, in the old *Wilhelm Stellung* just forward of Northampton Farm, both the Commanding Officer, Lieutenant -Colonel D. H. Blunt D.S.O. and the Adjutant, Captain Sir B. R. Williams Bart. were killed by shell-fire. The Devon advanced astride the Reutelbeek, under continuous enfilade fire from the German bunkers about Polderhoek Chateau, their final objective being across the Poezelhoek to Reutel track, about 1,200 yards forward. On the left No.4 Company reached the final objective as did part of No. 3 Company on the right, but the fire from Polderhoek spur, now coming from their right rear, was so intense that they fell-back about 750 yards to a line across the Reutelbeek, with the left pulled back another 250 yards, to allow some protection from the machine gun fire, in the lea of Polderhoek spur. This waterlogged line was then consolidated and touch was gained on the right with the K.O.S.B. in the chateau park. During the operation the Devon had taken about 50 prisoners.

As the 1st Duke of Cornwall's Light Infantry advanced past Cameron House,[505] they came under heavy machine gun fire from pillboxes in Cameron Covert. Due to the dreadful state of the ground, it had been decided that no tanks would work with 5th Division. Nevertheless a tank operating with 21st Division to the left, advancing along the Reutel track, supported the attack by the Cornwall, and assisted with its gunfire in the hard fighting to capture the pillboxes in Cameron Covert. The Cornwall worked northwards across the Reutel track and gained contact with the 21st Division, but a gap had opened on their right, and a company of the 1st East Surrey Regiment being brought forward to bridge it. To examine the ground over which his tanks would have to operate towards Reutel, Captain Clement Robertson of the Tank Corps had carried out a close reconnaissance of the area. Knowing that it would be impossible from inside the tanks to negotiate the muddy and cratered ground without the risk of ditching, he guided them forward on foot and under intense fire. Shortly after reaching the objective Captain Robertson was killed. He was to be posthumously awarded the V. C. for his outstanding valour. Throughout the advance and the consolidation the 5th Division had been pounded by the German barrage. The ferocity of the fighting on the Polderhoek spur and along the Reutelbeek was reflected in the total casualties of 2,557.

---

[501] National Archives, War Diary 13th Brigade WO95/1550
[502] National Archives, War Diary 1st RWK WO95/1554
[503] National Archives, War Diary 95th Brigade WO95/1576
[504] National Archives, War Diary 1st Devonshire WO95/4217
[505] National Archives, War Diary 1st DCLI WO95/1577

21st Division
Major-General D. G. M. Campbell

In the centre of X Corps line the 21st Division was to attack from the eastern edge of Polygon Wood, towards the Flanders I Line defences which ran obliquely across the division's front from north-west to south-east. Also running across the front, 200 yards south-west of Flanders I was the quagmire of the Polygonbeek depression, which both the 64th and 62nd Brigades would have to cross. From the start the German protective barrage was extremely heavy.

64th Brigade [506]
At Zero Hour as the right of the 9th King's Own Yorkshire Light Infantry advanced, it was hit by machine gun fire from Joist Farm, causing many casualties. The farm was successfully attacked and captured. The left meanwhile advanced across the mire of the Polygonbeek, and straight into machine gun fire from unsuspected dug-outs in the Flanders I Line. Concrete shelters along the Line were attacked and suppressed, Juniper Trench was outflanked and captured, and the final objective 150 yards east of the Flanders I Line was consolidated with the 10th K.O.Y.L.I., and a defensive right flank was thrown back to conform to the 1st Cornwall.

62nd Brigade [507] (See map below)
The 62nd Brigade was also confronted with the quagmire of the Polygonbeek, as it attacked out of the splintered remains of Polygon Wood, from the line established by the 5th Australian Division on the 26th September. The brigade attacked with the 3/4th Queens forward to seize the first objective, and the 12/13th Northumberland Fusiliers and the 1st Lincolnshire Regiment to secure the final. The Lincoln had replaced the 10th Green Howards at the last moment.

Having advanced slowly and with great difficulty through the mire while continually under heavy fire, the Queens attacked their section of Juniper Trench and an associated pillbox, successfully securing both, and moved on to their objective at Judge Trench by 6:40 a.m. As the Northumberland and Lincoln moved up close behind the Queens they also came under machine gun fire, and as the Lincoln crossed the old German front line they were struck by some of their own shells which fell short. A bunker on the line, although one section of it was burning, still held out firing into the Lincoln at close range. Lieutenant -Colonel Evans worked up to the bunker and opened fire through the loophole with his pistol, causing the garrison to surrender. For his gallant leadership he was to be awarded the V.C. The barrage stood in front of the Red Line at Judge Trench, and the Northumberland and Lincoln organized their lines for the next advance. After the one hour forty minute halt, the barrage thickened and lifted towards the final objective, both battalions coming under machine gun and sniper fire from Judge Copse, causing further casualties as they advanced. An outpost line was consolidated in shell-holes near the final objective, being linked up after dark, and in touch with the K.O.Y.L.I. on the right and with 91st Brigade on the left. At this point the Lincoln were reduced to four officers and 160 men in the line, casualties in the battalion having been 24 killed, 167 wounded and 36 missing. These figures were considered light, 'in the face of the fact that the German artillery fire in the battle was considered to be the heaviest and most concentrated of the whole war'.[508] By midday on the 4th the Northumberland had lost its Commanding Officer and all four company commanders. The Queens and Northumberland each lost 40% of their fighting strength. Of the 86 officers of 62nd Brigade who went into action on the 4th October, 74 had become casualties by the 8th October. There were a total of 2,616 casualties in 21st Division, of which 374 had been killed.

---

[506] National Archives, War Diary 64th Brigade WO95/2160
[507] National Archives, War Diary 62nd Brigade WO95/2152
[508] National Archives, War Diary 1st Lincoln WO95/2154

7th Division
Major-General T. H. Shoubridge

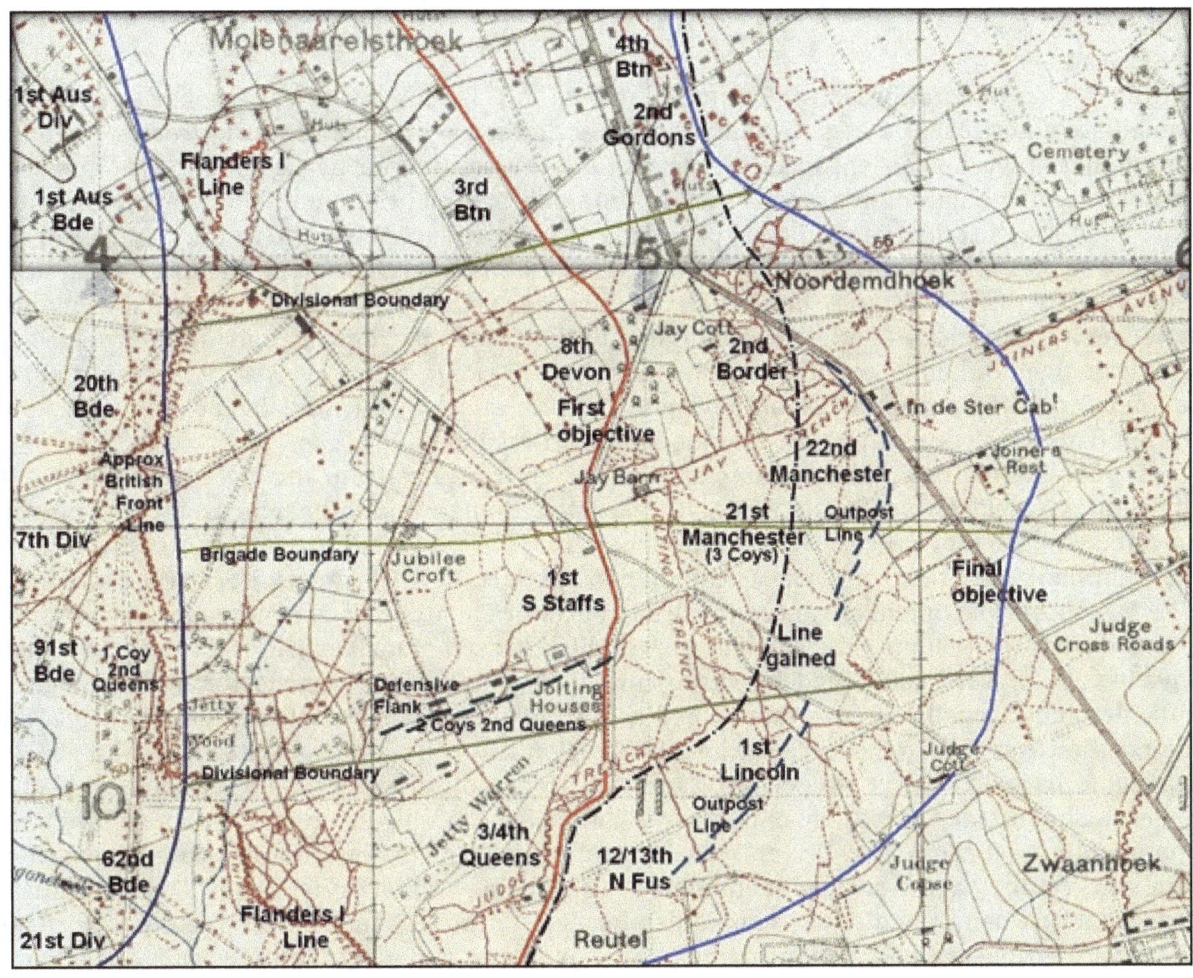

The attack of the 91st and 20th Brigades 7th Division towards in de Ster Cabaret

Without the hindrance of the muddy streams draining off the south-eastern edge of the plateau, which had hampered the 5th and 21st Divisions, the 7th Division's objectives were more straightforward, as was the ground over which they were to attack, being across the flat, but very exposed plateau top. The attack was towards the In de Ster Cabaret, a slight eminence at 58 metres on the Becelaere – Broodseinde road and overlooking the eastern edge of the plateau, with the first objective, the Red Line being about 400 yards short of the road, and the final objective, the Blue Line 200 yards beyond. The 91st and 20th Brigades would be used in the attack, each on a 500 yard front and each with one battalion forward to capture the Red Line. To capture the Blue Line 91st Brigade would use one battalion, with another in support, while the fourth remained in brigade reserve, and 20th Brigade would use two battalions to capture the Blue Line, with the fourth in brigade reserve.

The divisional forming-up line was marked by a tape positioned about 50 yards behind the forward British outposts in Jubilee Trench, the old German Flanders I Line, along the north-west corner of Polygon Wood. The assault battalions were closed up to a depth of 120 yards, with the support battalions 200 yards to the rear. The ground was now in a very bad state although before dawn the rain had stopped, and it was to take great effort to keep up with the slow barrage. German shelling on the forward waves had not been heavy as they assembled, but the 21st Manchester in support, and the 2nd Queens in reserve, both of 91st Brigade, and well behind the front lines, had suffered many casualties. Around 5:30 a.m. a German barrage hit the 7th Division, falling between the assembled forward waves and the supports. The rear companies of the forward battalions moved up closer to the front and the barrage mainly fell harmlessly behind them. This barrage was the precursor of the enemy counter-attack launched mainly against the Australians to the left of 7th Division.

91st Brigade [509]

As the 1st South Staffordshire Regiment moved off behind an excellent barrage it was immediately noticeable that the enemy was holding their front line in much greater strength. Two bunkers were soon engaged, the garrison being smothered by Lewis gun fire and rifle grenades whilst bombing parties worked around and bombed them out. Many enemy infantry were sheltering in small camouflaged pits, and many were bayoneted where they lay. Prisoners from three divisions were taken, the *4th Guard* and *19th Reserve Division* in the line, having been reinforced by the *45th Reserve Division*, all of which were close up to the front line, subsequently suffering huge casualties under the pounding of the British barrage, and giving themselves up with little fight. Unknown to the 1st South Staffs the *210th R.I.R.* of the *45th Reserve* was part of the southern edge of the main thrust of the enemy counter-attack against the line held by I Anzac, as the left flank of the German attack extended into 7th Division sector.

The South Staffordshire soon came under enfilade fire from the right, where the 21st Division was held up about the Polygonbeek, but although taking heavy casualties from the machine gun fire they succeeded in taking the Red Line. Two Vickers guns were set up to cover the right flank until the 3/4th Queens came up in support. At 8:10 a.m. as the barrage lifted, the 22nd Manchester Regiment advanced towards In de Ster Cabaret and came under heavy machine gun fire from the Joiner's Rest blockhouse,[510] which caused many casualties and checked their advance. They were reinforced by three companies of the 21st Manchester and with great difficulty and in small numbers established an outpost line just short of the final objective. But the position was far from secure as the 21st Division was still not up on the right, and the 2nd Queens in brigade reserve was ordered up from Hooge by the Divisional Commander, Major-General Shoubridge, to stiffen a defensive flank. As the Queens began to move up their Commanding Officer Major Driver was hit and killed, and a few minutes later the senior company commander was wounded. There was an inevitable delay in the Queens getting forward, but when they did, two companies formed up facing south protecting the right flank along Jolting Houses Road. The third company moved into support in Jetty Trench, 1,400 yards behind the forward outpost line and in the old German Flanders I Line, with the fourth in reserve at the Butte in Polygon Wood. The South Staffs consolidated the Red Line, and the forward outposts on the Blue Line were strengthened with Vickers guns covering the eastern slopes of the plateau. Touch was obtained with 21st Brigade north of Reutel and by evening the position was reasonably secure.

20th Brigade [511]

The 8th Devonshire Regiment captured several pillboxes in their advance to the Red Line, which they reached successfully up with the excellent barrage, taking about 200 prisoners. The 2nd Border Regiment passed through on the right with the 2nd Gordon Highlanders on the left, following the barrage through to the Blue Line between In de Ster Cabaret and Noordemdhoek with little resistance, the enemy streaming away down the eastern slopes of the plateau before them. The Gordons however veered somewhat to the left, following the Australians, leaving the Borders a longer front to hold than planned, but it mattered little as the resistance had been so light. The line had been taken five minutes before schedule and consolidation on a shell-hole line commenced. Casualties had been remarkably light, the Devon loosing around 120 and the Borders and Gordons about 70 each.

From their commanding position the 7th Division could look out over the German rear areas, which had for so long been hidden from view. The valley of the Heulebeek was at the foot

---

[509] National Archives, War Diary 91st Brigade WO95/1667
[510] National Archives, War Diary 21st Manchester WO95/1668 and 22nd Manchester WO95/1669
[511] National Archives, War Diary 20th Brigade WO95/1654

of the plateau, beyond which, 3,000 yards to the north-east was the Keiberg spur, east of Passchendaele village and still in enemy hands. It was clear that huge numbers in the densely packed enemy forward line had perished in the barrage, and in the 1,500 yard advance 600 prisoners had been taken. The only footing on the plateau remaining to the enemy was the small spur which ran 2,000 yards to the south-east and at the end of which lay the ruins of Becelaere. Total casualties in 7th Division had been 2,123 of which 351 had been killed.

The main attack on the Broodseinde ridge, the advance to the Red Line

I Anzac Corps

It is now opportune to return to the moment when the forward battalions of 1st and 2nd Australian Divisions, crouching in their wet shell-holes, believed the whole attack may have been discovered by the Germans, as an intense enemy barrage descended upon them. The barrage which fell upon the Australian lines at about 5:30 landed most heavily on 1st Division but also on 2nd Division. Those close up on the jumping-off tapes suffered least, and where room permitted the rear lines edged forward to avoid the worst of the shelling. The barrage was so intense that 20 officers were known to have been killed, and about one seventh of the striking force of I Anzac had been either killed or wounded. In front of Zonnebeke the 25th Battalion had, since about 11:00 p.m. on the 3rd, noticed German infantry passing across its front, believing this at first to be a routine relief. By the time the German barrage opened it became clear that the movements had not been a relief, but the assembly prior to a German attack. By the time the 25th had reached this conclusion it was too late to fire an S.O.S. as the artillery were forbidden to respond in the last ten minutes before Zero Hour, that is after 5:50 a.m. The German barrage was so intense that officers along the line were concerned how the men would react when Zero Hour and the moment to advance arrived. At 6:00 a.m. the British barrage thundered down, at the very moment the German barrage had planned to lift to 200 yards beyond the British line, to allow the forward movement of their infantry. It appears that the German lift never took place, their artillery being smitten at that moment by British counter-battery fire. Although the British barrage roared with great power it was noticeably less powerful than on the 20th and 26th September. At Zero Hour, the Australian infantry lifted themselves from their shell-holes, and in their inimitable fashion, lit their cigarettes and bayonets thrust advanced towards the enemy.

1st Australian Division to the Red Line
Major-General H. B. Walker

The 1st Australian Division front extended approximately 1,000 yards, from the base of Tokio spur just south of Molenaarelsthoek, to a point just east of Retaliation Farm in the upper Zonnebeke valley. On the right, in front of Molenaarelsthoek the Australian line was up very close to the enemy. At this point the Flanders I Line left the Gheluvelt plateau and ran north along the bare gentle western slope of the Passchendaele ridge. The line of wire entanglements and blockhouses was here still held by the enemy. If all went to plan, the 1st Australian Division would break through this line, which was the first objective, climb the slope, cross the ridge-top road and descend about 400 yards down the eastern slope to the final objective, the total advance being around 1,300 yards. The division was to attack with its 1st and 2nd Brigades, across the bare, churned up, and since the recent rain, very slippery ground.

1st [512] and 2nd [513] Australian Brigades

The 1st Brigade was soon into the Flanders I defences and the forward enemy outpost line was quickly overrun by the 3rd and 8th Battalions. On the left, 8th Battalion had at first to cross the slight depression of the upper Zonnebeke valley, across the head of which ran the German line. The barrage was noticeably thin, not the usual solid curtain of shells, and due to the wet ground it did not create the usual dense cloud of smoke and dust. As the Australians rushed forward and caught up with the protective shell bursts they became aware of figures rising from shell holes 30 yards beyond. A dense wave of men stretching to right and left appeared unsure of what to do, as if waiting for an order. Some were moving forward with bayonets fixed, but with rifles slung. The target was difficult to miss as the Australians fired rifle volleys and put their Lewis guns to good effect, some fired from the hip, whilst continuing the advance. The German front waves, which had missed the worst of the British barrage, were now face to face with the advancing Australians, whilst others 200 to 300 yards further back could be seen desperately running to the rear. The enemy forward wave was checked and then broken by the momentum and aggression of the Australian infantry. Many were shot down, bayoneted, or captured, to be later identified as belonging to the *212th Reserve Infantry Regiment*, the regiment ordered to carry out the main attack towards Tokio spur.

Breaking into the Flanders I defences the Australians came upon many trench mortars crews with their weapons hidden in shell-holes, undoubtedly those that had thickened the barrage at the flanks of the *212th R.I.R.* attack. Those that did not run were bayoneted or shot. But the 3rd and 8th were soon receiving severe machine gun fire from the blockhouses at Retaliation Farm, and from the concentration of bunkers about Molenaarelsthoek. In the left company of the 8th all the officers were hit, but the advance continued still under heavy hostile machine gun and shell-fire. The bunkers were quickly outflanked and taken, including Retaliation Farm where the garrison and three machine guns were captured. The prisoners taken from the trenches and bunkers were identified as belonging to the *4th Guard Division*. As the shattered stumps of Romulus and Remus Woods were cleared, the leading waves lost direction amongst the blasted trenches and entanglements of Flanders I and began to veer to the left along the face of the ridge, and as they emerged from the scrub were struck by well aimed short range fire from German field batteries. The Australians reached the first objective line a few hundred yards short of the ridge-top road by around 7:00 a.m. where the protective barrage was to hold just east of the road until 8:10. The rearward fringe of this barrage was landing near the road, and from numerous blockhouses, dug-outs and trenches along the crest the enemy could be seen hurrying towards the rear. The heavy searching barrage which continued to penetrate deeper into the enemy position was now more evident and could be clearly seen through the light protective barrage. On the right the temptation was too great for some of the 1st Brigade who chased on across the road on the heels of the fleeing Germans. The 4th Battalion coming up in support of the 3rd had become mixed with parties of the 2nd Gordons of 20th Brigade who had followed the general drift to the left. Now both Australians and Highlanders ran through the protective barrage as if it were not there, and chased the terrified enemy over the crest, nearly reaching their second objective before finally being checked and recalled by their officers.

Further to the left 2nd Brigade were not finding things so easy, for in 8th Battalion casualties began to rise as field guns on the crest opened fire over open sights. On the very crest of the ridge, 1,000 yards south of the Broodseinde crossroads, a huge crater, possibly the result of an ammunition dump explosion, had been established as a German regimental headquarters defended by a pillbox. Numerous other bunkers and lengths of trench housing battalion

---

[512] National Archives, War Diary 1st Aus Brigade WO95/3213, National Archives, War Diary 1st Battalion WO95/3217, National Archives, War Diary 3rd Battalion WO95/3221, National Archives, War Diary 4th Battalion WO95/3223

[513] National Archives, War Diary 2nd Aus Brigade WO95/3231, National Archives, War Diary 6th Battalion WO95/3235, National Archives, War Diary 7th Battalion WO95/3238, National Archives, War Diary 8th Battalion WO95/3240

headquarters and observation posts, and all well defended with machine guns opened fire on the Australians lower down the slope. The field guns that pounded 8th Battalion were situated amongst other bunkers, several hundred yards along the road north of the crater. The 8th attempted to work up the slope towards the bunkers and the guns, but were hit by enfilade fire from the machine gun at the crater. It appeared impossible to outflank the bunkers, or even get close enough to rush them, as one gave the other covering fire. A bank about 80 yards short of the road gave the forward parties of the 8th, and also some of 6th Brigade (2nd Division) moderate shelter from the fire. They were not destined to take shelter for long however, as groups organized themselves for action, bringing the enemy posts under Lewis gun and rifle fire from the bank, while rifle grenadiers further down the slope rained their bombs into the enemy position. The crater proved a stubborn obstacle, until the garrison of 30 men in an open trench, bombed out by the rifle grenades, emerged with raised hands and stumbled towards the Australians. The crater which had held out for 20 minutes was then rushed and the pillbox captured, but a number of determined German officers fell back east of the road to another trench where they continued to resist with bombs and pistols. More rifle grenades soon subdued the group sufficiently for the position to be rushed by the Victorians of the 8th and all except one surrendered. The last officer, a captain who was bayoneted rather than surrender, was believed to have been the commander of *II Battalion 211th R.I.R.*

A few hundred yards north meanwhile, parties of the 7th and 8th Battalions were working forward towards the field guns. The guns, which ceased fire as the attackers moved in were protected by numerous entrenched machine guns, one in a sunken bunker. Lewis gun fire kept enemy heads down as sections moved in close enough to charge the guns, and as they approached a white flag appeared from the bunker which had been an artillery observation post. Most of its occupants were shot. The whole position including the guns was captured, and rifle fire hastened the fleeing enemy on their way east of the ridge top.

2nd Australian Division to the Red Line
Major-General N. M. Smythe

The 2nd Division was to attack on a 1,000 yard front from Retaliation Farm to the Ypres – Roulers railway, and it was immediately confronted with the rubble heap which had once been the village of Zonnebeke. What had once been an ornamental lake in the grounds of Zonnebeke Chateau now appeared as a foul black pond about 200 yards long and 75 yards wide, which bisected the front between the 6th and 7th Brigades. The road uphill out of the ruins of Zonnebeke eastwards towards Moorslede, led in about 1,000 yards to the hamlet of Broodseinde on top of the ridge at the crossroad with the Becelaere – Passchendaele road. The Zonnebeke – Broodseinde road formed the brigade boundary, with 6th Brigade south of the road and 7th Brigade to the north.

6th [514] and 7th [515] Australian Brigades
An unsuccessful attempt was made by the 22nd and 25th Battalions, leading 6th and 7th Brigades, to link up around the sides of the lake prior to the main attack. At Zero Hour, advancing behind the barrage the 22nd immediately met with the counter-attack of *212th R.I.R.* as the enemy infantry came forward with fixed bayonets. A volley of rifle fire from the right company caused the enemy to withdraw, but in Zonnebeke the Germans pressed their attack, the Australians gradually falling back in stages 30 to 40 yards at a time, section by section, one giving the other covering fire. As the 25th advanced through the rubble enemy machine gunners in cellars in the

---

[514] National Archives, War Diary 6th Aus Brigade WO95/3323, National Archives, War Diary 21st Battalion WO95/3326, National Archives, War Diary 22nd Battalion WO95/3330, National Archives, War Diary 23rd Battalion WO95/3332, National Archives, War Diary 24th Battalion WO95/3334

[515] National Archives, War Diary 7th Aus Brigade WO95/3338, National Archives, War Diary 25th Battalion WO95/3340, National Archives, War Diary 26th Battalion WO95/3341, National Archives, War Diary 27th Battalion WO95/3342, National Archives, War Diary 28th Battalion WO95/3344

ruins behind them opened fire, but were soon flushed out by the 26th Battalion moving up in support. The advance continued towards the Flanders I defences, and 22nd Battalion attacked and bombed out a number of blockhouses. The garrison of one blockhouse at de Knoet Farm, 400 yards east of the lake and in the Flanders I Line, refused to surrender and were all killed with bombs.

By around 7:00 a.m. the barrage, which was somewhat thicker in front of 2nd Division, stood around 150 yards forward of the 22nd and 25th Battalions on the Red Line. The sight of the enemy fleeing over the crest was too great a temptation for some of the 22nd, who chased off in pursuit accompanied by some of the support waves of the 24th and 21st Battalions which should have been assembling behind the 22nd at the first objective, waiting for the attack on the final objective. Despite the efforts of their officers to restrain them, some occupied a trench on the crest while others attempted to turn round the four captured field guns and use them on the enemy, although one had already had the breach-block removed and another had been damaged. Sniping increased from the direction of Broodseinde, and up the eastern face of the ridge German reinforcements were quickly moving forward to counter-attack the Australians now on the ridge top. There was thankfully little smoke, and the atmosphere was clear enough for signalers with a Lucas lamp on the ridge to flash a warning signal back to the artillery. The guns scattered and broke the counter-attack.

The Flanders I Line along the lower slopes of the ridge, and the many bunkers along that line and up the slopes behind it had been broken and overrun and about an hour. The infantry farthest forward, who were in some cases well beyond their objective, could look across the Heulebeek valley towards the Keiberg spur, across which ran the Flanders II Line, 2,500 yards distant. From Keiberg on the southern tip, the spur ran towards the northwest, joining the main ridge 1,500 yards south of Passchendaele, near the hamlet of Keerselaarhoek, where the Ypres – Roulers railway ran across a slight saddle at the point the spur joined the ridge. To the east of the ridge the world appeared a very different place when compared to the devastated brown wasteland back to the west, towards the stark ruins of Ypres. Although the woods on the eastern slope of the Passchendaele ridge had already been smashed and splintered by shellfire and the ground was heavily cratered, the Keiberg spur looked green and fringed with trees. What smoke there was from the shells of the heavy batteries was quickly blown away on the strong wind. To the south-east the view was even more spectacular and it appeared that in that direction a normal life continued amongst the tress and hedgerows, and occasionally 'carts could be seen moving, cows grazing, smoke going up from chimneys'. At about 7:20 signal rockets were fired along the forward positions to indicate the success of the advance to the first objective.

II Anzac Corps

To the north of Zonnebeke the Flanders I Line ran due north, following the lower western slopes of the Passchendaele ridge, whereas the British Front Line, following the northern arc of the Salient veered to the north-west, the distance between the two lines therefore becoming progressively greater. The 3rd Australian Division was to attack on a frontage of about 1,000 yards, north of the Ypres – Roulers railway. On the right flank Flanders I lay 1,100 yards forward, while on the left it was 1,800 yards away, at the limit of the divisional objective. To the left of 3rd Australian, the New Zealand Division was to attack along a front of about 2,000 yards, with a final objective around 1,500 yards distant. The Flanders I Line was beyond the New Zealand objective, but the task faced by the division was complicated initially by the muddy valley of the Hanebeek, then by Gravenstafel ridge which ran obliquely across the front, and finally by the equally muddy valley of the Stroombeek – Ravebeek, to the north in which lay the final objective. To enable the New Zealand Division time to cross the wide and muddy Hanebeek valley and maintain touch with the Australians, the 3rd Australian Division had arranged for a short halt, where the barrage would stand for twelve minutes on an intermediate objective, 400 yards beyond the Langemarck road.

The Ravebeek stream, from its source 700 yards west of Passchendale village, created a valley between the main Passchendaele ridge and the Bellevue spur, a 2,000 yard projection of the main ridge, jutting towards the south-west. As the New Zealand final objective lay south of the Ravebeek the stream was not to be crossed, and the Flanders I Line which ran across the south-western end of Bellevue spur would still be 1,000 yards distant, to be tackled in the next step.

As we have seen, to cover its extra length of front, and objective depth, II Anzac had been given greater gunfire support, one and a half times as many heavy guns, and twice the number of field guns as I Anzac.

3rd Australian Division to the Red Line
Major-General Sir John Monash

The upper Zonnebeke valley, 400 yards behind the 3rd Australian jump-off tapes, still presented a muddy quagmire restricting the assembly positions of the 41st and 40th Battalions of the 11th and 10th Brigades, which were to carry forward the attack to the Blue Line. It had been proposed by Major-General Monash, commanding 3rd Division that the 41st should assemble beside 11th Brigade Headquarters 1,200 yards back on the old German third line, but due to consistent shelling of this area both the 41st and 40th were squeezed up behind the other six battalions detailed to lead the attack. On the right, 250 yards north of the railway, the low hump of Hill 40 loomed in front of 11th Brigade, while in the centre and to the left the shallow muddy depression of the Hanebeek valley, itself containing many blockhouses and fortified farm ruins, confronted 10th Brigade before they could come to grips with the Flanders I position.

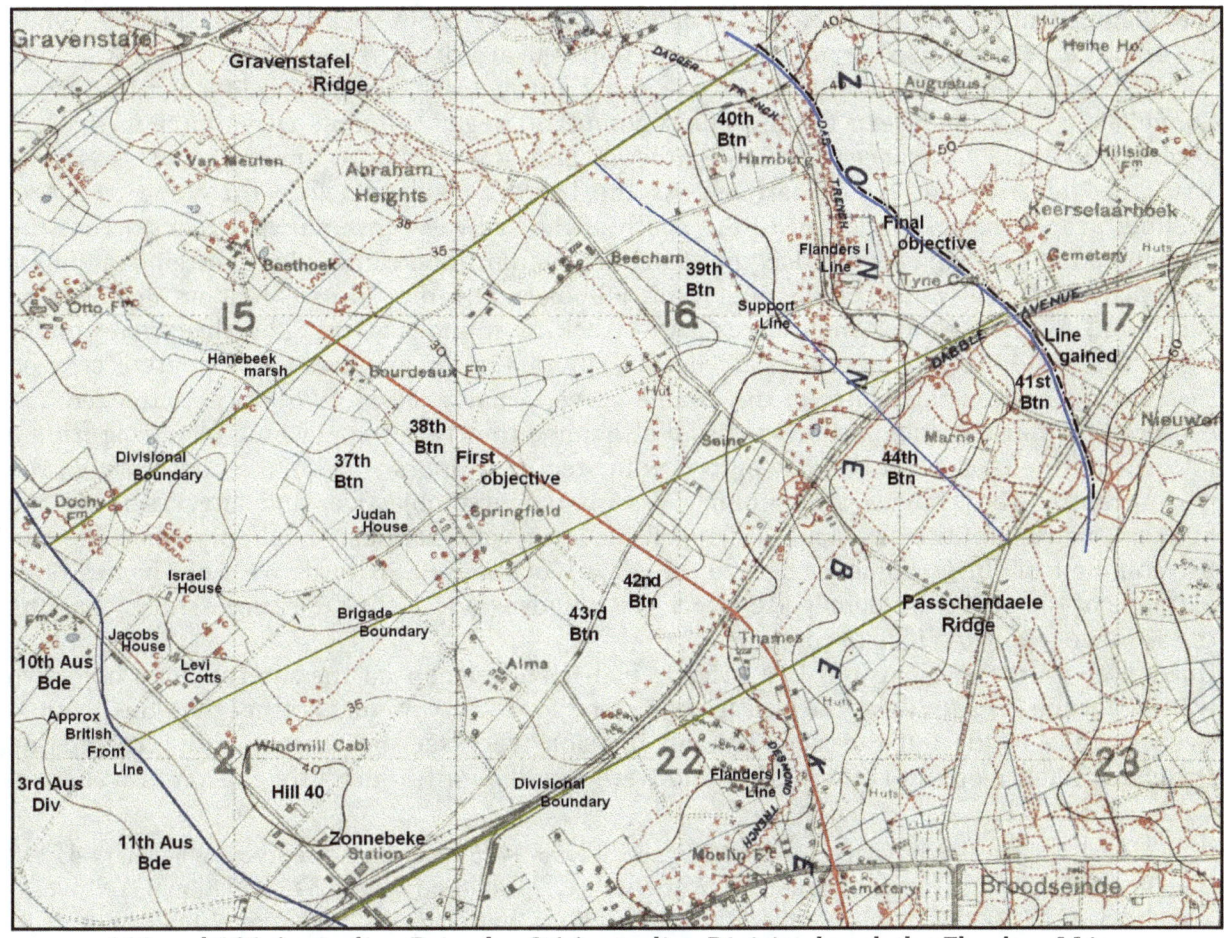

11th and 10th Australian Brigades 3rd Australian Division break the Flanders I Line

11th[516] and 10th[517] Brigades

The hostile barrage which had opened the German counter-attack had hit the 3rd Australian Division, although less severely, and as the British barrage came down all the attacking waves moved up close behind it to avoid the worst of the enemy shelling. The 43rd and 37th Battalions led off behind the barrage which was described here as, 'like a wall of flame', with the supports close behind. There was immediate resistance from the enemy, as a machine gun in a bunker near Zonnebeke station on the right opened fire on the 43rd, while stick bombs were hurled from Hill 40. Casualties began to mount, and officers in both the 43rd and the 42nd following up were killed. The resistance was soon overwhelmed as the 43rd Battalion with bayonet and bomb stormed the hill, and the enemy either fled or died in their gun pits. On the left in 10th Brigade sector, to avoid the enemy shelling the 37th had crept well forward to within 30 yards of Levi Cottages on the Langemarck road. As the battalion advanced they came face to face with the Germans. The close quarters fighting became brutal, and many of the enemy were bayoneted. Machine gun fire from the blockhouses was quickly suppressed by Lewis guns and rifle grenades and the garrisons bombed out. Lance-Corporal Walter Peeler of the 3rd Pioneer Battalion led the fight with his Lewis gun against many posts and for his gallantry was to be awarded the V.C. At Levi Cottages three machine guns were captured, and the advance proceeded beyond the Langemarck road into the depression of the Hanebeek. A fight broke out about the pillbox at Israel House 200 yards beyond the road, the garrison being smoked out with a phosphorous bomb as the advance continued. The 10th Brigade veered to the left, but were soon able to orientate their position on recognition of the blockhouse at Alma, in 11th Brigade sector, and the row of pillboxes at Judah House to their front, which were attacked and captured by the 38th. Here on the first intermediate objective there was to be a twelve minute pause in the barrage, to enable the New Zealand Division on the left time in which to negotiate the quagmire of the Hanebeek. The 43rd and 37th took shelter in shell-holes on this line, while the 42nd and 38th organized in readiness to continue the attack to the Red Line.

On the right flank of 11th Brigade the railway track, which for 500 yards beyond Zonnebeke station had been the divisional boundary, began a double curve, first to the left, across the line of advance of 42nd Battalion, and then back to the right to cross the Passchendaele ridge at Keerselaarhoek. As the barrage began its forward creep, the 42nd keeping proper direction crossed to the south of the railway. Most railway tracks across the battlefield had for long been used as convenient communication routes along the embankments of which were built numerous bunkers and pillboxes, and the Ypres – Roulers line was no exception. As the 44th Battalion crossed the track in support of the 42nd they came under machine gun fire from two bunkers at Thames, situated in the Flanders I line where it crossed the railway, right in the centre of the double curve. A party led by two officers attacked and captured the bunkers and 30 Germans, and also killed the crew of a machine gun firing from a pit beneath the tracks. Yet another pillbox with steel rear doors was bombed out through the gun aperture. The Thames strong-point was on the first objective, and after securing the bunkers the right of the 42nd paused. The left however were seriously held up by machine gun fire coming from three pillboxes behind the Alma blockhouse 550 yards west of Thames. Two platoons of the 42nd were detailed to attack the pillboxes which they did successfully, enabling the advance to the Red Line to continue.

On the left of the 3rd Division, 10th Brigade had been held up on the intermediate objective waiting for the guns to lift, as the barrage had stood for twenty minutes rather than the planned twelve, while to the left the New Zealand Division were seen to have already crossed the Hanebeek, shaken out into attack order and were heading for Abraham Heights on Gravenstafel

---

[516] National Archives, War Diary 11th Aus Brigade WO95/3425, National Archives, War Diary 41st Battalion WO95/3431, National Archives, War Diary 42nd Battalion WO95/3434, National Archives, War Diary 43rd Battalion WO95/3436, National Archives, War Diary 44th Battalion WO95/3438

[517] National Archives, War Diary 10th Aus Brigade WO95/3411, National Archives, War Diary 37th Battalion WO95/3414, National Archives, War Diary 38th Battalion WO95/3415, National Archives, War Diary 39th Battalion WO95/3417, National Archives, War Diary 40th Battalion WO95/3420

ridge. The German artillery, which had been persistently shelling the advance, now found the range with great accuracy, and began pounding the 10th Brigade in their stationary and exposed position, south of the Hanebeek. They were also under heavy machine gun fire from a fortified ruined farm at Springfield 250 yards in front. Captain Moule of the 37th accompanied by his batman attempted a frontal attack, but although both badly wounded another soldier worked around the back of the bunker and bombed it out. At last the barrage lifted, and the 38th continued the advance into the muddy depression and up the slope to their first objective 250 yards beyond the stream, where, albeit a little late, they were up in line with 11th Brigade. Along the railway mopping-up of strong-points and pillboxes continued. Localized fighting still flared up amongst the bunkers and dug-outs, and prisoners were taken in greater numbers than the Australians had ever experienced before.

New Zealand Division to the Red Line[518]
Major-General Sir A. H. Russell

The New Zealand Division had begun the relief of the 59th Division on the night of the 29th September, the 2nd New Zealand Brigade taking over the front line. On the evening of the 2nd October, the 4th and 1st Brigades which were to carry out the attack, relieved the 2nd Brigade in the forward trenches.

Each Brigade was to attack with two battalions in the line. The forward battalions were to secure the Red Line, at which point the two support battalions would pass through and attack the Blue Line. The line held by the division roughly followed the track of the Zonnebeke – Langemarck road, 200 yards north of the road on the right near Dochy Farm, and 700 yards north on the left near Wurst Farm. The first objective was around 750 yards forward, on the right across the near slope of the Gravenstafel ridge at Abraham Heights, in the centre just short of the crest near Gravenstafel hamlet, while on the left where the front line passed over the top of Gravenstafel ridge it was on the northern slope, from where it dropped into the Stroombeek valley. The division had placed its jump off tapes about 200 yards behind the forward outpost line, and the assault companies formed up on the tapes with the support companies about 40 yards behind. Shortly before Zero the outpost sentries withdrew behind the tapes. The New Zealand assault companies had witnessed the enemy signal rockets lighting up the sky to the south, soon to be followed by hostile shelling, which erupted along the Australian front and gradually spread left towards the New Zealand positions. Here however it did little damage falling generally in the unoccupied area behind the support companies.

At 6:00 a.m. the British barrage opened and in front of the New Zealand the concentrated fire of 240 18-pounders and 4.5-inch howitzers screamed into No-Mans-Land and detonated with a mighty and reassuring roar. The vivid description of this moment written by a New Zealand artilleryman serves as a tribute to all gunners in this battle: 'Those who heard it say it was tremendous, the din, but we in the pit heard it not at all, or only in a subconscious way, to be remembered afterwards, heard nothing but the vicious whanging of our own guns, nothing but the jerk of the breach as it opened and the snap as it closed again, nothing but the clang of falling "empties" and the rattle of the live shells as the No.4 jammed them on, nothing but the ticking of the watch covering the interval between the rounds and the No.1's voice, "Thirty more left! Elevate five minutes! Drop one hundred!" then the watch's ticking again till he opened his mouth once more, and before the "Fire" had hardly left it, the spiteful tonguing of the gun, her rattle and quiver as she settled down, and the hiss of the buffer coming home.

Normally our old B gun is the pick of the bunch, but the whang she got the day before had put her on edge, and she behaved not nearly as sweetly as usual. Still, we were lucky to have her going at all, for that was more than we thought possible at first. The firing lever slipped occasionally, and No.3 swore bitterly; the bubble developed tricks, and his curses became deeper, the range-drum jumped at each shot like a nervous maid, and the trail stuck like a mule in the Flanders mud. But when the buffer on the run-up stopped within a few inches of home

---

[518] Col. H. Stewart *The New Zealand Division* pp256-274

each time, I, too, felt that language was needed. As the range lengthened and her nose pointed further skyward the brute got worse, and between sticking trail and sticking buffer, the sweat came down in streams, blinding my eyes and tasting salt on my tongue; but we got there with the best, neither skipped nor lagged behind. Of the two, that last is the greater crime, for a late shot in the lifting barrage often means death to many of our fellows.'[519]

4th and 1st New Zealand Brigades [520]

In the attack to the Red Line, 4th Brigade were to use the 3rd Auckland and the 3rd Otago on an 800 yard front, while 1st Brigade used the 1st Wellington and the 1st Auckland to cover 1,200 yards.[521]

On the right the 4th Brigade moved off at Zero Hour and was soon up against stiff opposition, as, protected from the barrage in their blockhouses, the enemy opened up with vicious machine gun and rifle fire. 3rd Auckland quickly overran the Dochy Farm blockhouse, 15 German emerging with their hands raised, with four more killed and 4 machine guns captured. Closer to the Hanebeek 3rd Otago attacked Otto Farm with similar tenacity, the garrison of 35 and 4 machine guns being captured, while the 1st Wellington had captured Riverside and were nearing the stream.

Soon after the first waves moved forward an intense hostile machine gun barrage struck the left of 1st Brigade, and within four minutes the machine gun rounds were whipping and ricocheting along the length of the Langemarck road. Minutes later the German artillery also dropped a barrage along the road tearing gaps in the lines of the 2nd Wellington advancing in support.[522] The barrage remained heavy for about 30 minutes and then became more scattered, and upon answering signal flares for support from the enemy pillboxes, fell mostly behind the foremost New Zealand waves. The advance continued between the shell craters towards the blasted reedy marsh, through which the Hanebeek brook had once flowed, the assault companies pushing on across the heavy ground in sections in single file with a forward screen of skirmishers, who in around 200 yards came across the devastating effects of the British barrage. Rather than meting the enemy coming forward, they passed numerous shell holes, full of enemy dead, most for some unknown reason not wearing their steel helmets. A few survivors opened fire with their rifles, but at close quarters were no match for the New Zealand, many being dispatched with the bayonet, while others surrendered willingly. In another 200 yards the congested shell-holes revealed that the enemy second wave had been similarly smitten, 500 of their dead being counted along 1st Auckland front alone.

---

[519] Col. H. Stewart *The New Zealand Division* pp260-261
[520] National Archives, War Diary 4th NZ Brigade WO95/3712, National Archives, War Diary 1st NZ Brigade WO95/3685
[521] National Archives, War Diary 1st Wellington WO95/3689
[522] National Archives, War Diary 2nd Wellington WO95/3690

The attack across Gravenstafel Ridge 4th and 1st New Zealand Brigades
New Zealand Division

Crossing the Hanebeek was expected to cause a delay to the right and centre of the attack, although due to the stream bending west and bisecting the front line, the 1st Auckland on the left of 1st Brigade was already beyond the worst of the boggy ground. Once the protective barrage had passed beyond the stream, it stood 150 yards beyond the mire. Generally the crossing was not as bad and did not take as long as expected, and as the assault waves gathered the other side of the stream awaiting the barrage to lift, they began sustaining casualties from German shellfire. At last the barrage lifted and the advance to the Red Line continued up the slopes of the ridge, the leading wave keeping up as close as 40 yards to the impressive curtain of shells. Working forward up the slope, sections of 3rd Auckland supported by rifle grenades and Lewis guns attacked the Boethoek pillboxes capturing 3 machine guns and the garrison, and to their left 3rd Otago pushed on past the Van Meulen bunkers, leaving them to be cleared by the mopping-up parties, who subsequently took 50 prisoners and a machine gun. As the assault neared the top of the slope the left gun of each 18-pounder battery fired smoke shell into the barrage for five minutes, to indicate the one hour halt on the first objective, which both 3rd Auckland and 3rd Otago had reached up to time. The 4th Brigade began to dig-in, but with the barrage standing 150 yards forward, enemy machine gunners in the pillboxes and gun-pits between the line of bursting shells and the New Zealand posts maintained a harassing fire. Sections were quickly sent forward to silence them. The enemy positions were close up to 3rd Auckland line, and parties of the battalion worked forward and captured 8 machine guns. In front of 3rd Otago the barrage was falling beyond the ruins of the hamlet of Gravenstafel on the crest of the ridge, and sections moved forward to clear pillboxes and a blockhouse in the ruins, where 100 prisoners were captured. With the dangerous bunkers silenced, the assault parties returned to the Red Line to assist with the consolidation which was rapidly progressing, the sandy soil on the ridge aiding the work of entrenchment.

On the left meanwhile in 1st Brigade, 1st Wellington had also crossed the Hanebeek, and 1st Auckland, already beyond the stream, had advanced alongside them with the barrage. But as it did so 1st Auckland had veered to the left, across the front of 48th Division. This presented a problem for 1st Wellington, as attempting to maintain touch with the Otago on their right, and the Auckland now moving too far to their left, gave them a much greater length of front to cover than intended. The bunkers at Boetleer near the ridge-top track, which were to be attacked by the Auckland, put up a stout resistance, machine gun fire slowing the thin Wellington ranks. The bunkers were however successfully attacked and captured as were many others along the ridge, largely due to many acts of individual bravery. On reaching the Red Line, on the crest of the ridge, the Wellington with the Otago to their right began to dig-in, but came under heavy machine gun fire from two bunkers at Korek 250 yards north-east of Gravenstafel. The bunkers stood about 120 yards forward of the New Zealand line and just forward of the standing barrage. Through the fierce machine gun fire, parties of both battalions rushed forward almost into their own barrage, and threw many mills bombs into the bunker entrances. The larger of the two bunkers contained two chambers, and when the outer chamber was entered by an N.C.O. of the Wellington was found to contain around 30 dead killed by the bombs. An officer in the inner chamber attempted to burn his papers, and in so doing set fire to the bunker, incinerating himself and several wounded men. The 1st Wellington continued to dig-in, but could establish no more than a weakly held line of shell-holes as the battalion was now holding about 800 yards of front.

On the far left, 1st Auckland had attacked from north of the Hanebeek, and had immediately been faced with the south slope of the ridge and Hill 32. Along the ridge top were sited numerous bunkers and blockhouses, which commenced to bring down a hail of machine gun fire upon the Auckland, causing many casualties in the front wave. The bunkers at Dear House and Aviatik Farm near the ridge-top track were barely 200 yards beyond the New Zealand tapes. Machine gun fire checked the first wave, but the leading platoon worked forward and surrounded Dear House, capturing the machine guns and crews. Aviatik Farm fell in similar fashion with the assistance of a Stokes mortar team, and the advance soon caught up with the barrage. Enfilade machine gun fire now struck the Auckland from the bunkers at Winzig, 400 yards to their left, within the sector of 48th Division, and threatened a major hold up. Further machine gun fire from the east, in the direction of the Bellevue spur, beyond the day's objective, was coming down the Ravebeek – Stroombeek valley and hitting both the Auckland and the 48th Division in enfilade. This fire appeared to have caused a check to the 48th Division, and in consequence the Auckland veered left to knock out the guns they could threaten at Winzig. This attack was successful and the Winzig machine guns were silenced, but for reasons not entirely clear the left of the Auckland, rather than maintaining its correct line of attack to the north-east, continued to work towards the north, attacking and capturing the blockhouse at Albatross Farm, and then crossing the Stroombeek to capture Winchester Farm, around 700 yards to the left of their divisional boundary. It appeared that 48th Division still could not get forward, and the Auckland held their position, the support company of the Wellington as we have seen then filling the gap in the front line. Both battalions were now on the Red Line, with the Wellington desperately attempting to hold an 800 yard front. On the ridge the ground was good for digging, but in the valley of the Stroombeek, the Auckland soon struck mud and water.

The attack by the 3rd Australian Division and New Zealand Divisions to the Red Line had been a magnificent achievement, and a skillful and courageous feat of arms. To the first objective alone, the two divisions supported by accurate and consistent artillery had attacked and defeated no fewer than 24 major enemy strong-points, where the withering fire of multiple machine guns emanating from their concrete embraceors had failed to preserve them from a tenacious and gallant adversary. For the enemy, more terror was soon to follow.

I Anzac to the final objective

As the time approached 8:00 a.m. 3,500 yards to the south-east of Gravenstafel ridge, 1st and 2nd Australian Divisions were preparing to launch the next phase of the attack to the final objective on the eastern slopes of the main ridge at Broodseinde.

1st Australian Division to the Blue Line

1st and 2nd Australian Brigades

On the right of 1st Brigade the natural tendency to advance straight up the slope, and not slightly to the right as correct alignment required, had led to both the 3rd and 4th Battalions, and their pals in the 2nd Gordon to become intermingled and too far to the left, and a wave of enthusiasm hot on the heals of the fleeing enemy had carried them too far forward. Parties of the 2nd Brigade, imbued with the same spirit, had also crossed the ridge-top road, even after great efforts on the part of their officers to stop them. All along the division front there were gaps in the line and now officers urgently attempted to fill them by adjusting positions on the ridge and bringing up supports. Some groups were only brought back from east of the road just in time to miss the barrage as it thickened at 8:10 a.m. Captain Judge of the 4th Battalion, who had received orders from his Colonel to get the men back in line had to report that it was just not possible, and that they would lay out in shell-holes and risk the barrage.

At 8:10 as the barrage intensified once more, the 4th, 1st, 6th and 7th Battalions advanced towards the eastern side of the ridge. On the left, 6th and 7th came under sharp fire from German reinforcements which had come up during the pause, and also from field guns dug-in in the woods along the slopes. The track of a field railway marked the line of the 1st Brigade's final objective 300 yards from the road, and here the 4th Battalion dug-in to the sandy soil behind some enemy wire, while the 1st improved an old trench. To the right the 7th British Division was digging-in on the In de Ster Cabaret promontory, and their machine guns covered any possible enemy movement towards the 1st Australian front in enfilade. A few hundred yards north 2nd Brigade had advanced 500 yards down the slope to their final objective, coming under fire from machine guns on Keiberg spur, and facing some resistance from dug-outs which was soon overcome. The division then commenced to dig-in and consolidate its hard won gains.

2nd Australian Division to the Blue Line

6th and 7th Australian Brigades

The 24th and 21st Battalions advancing a few hundred yards down the eastern slope of the ridge were keen to reach a hedge in which they knew existed an active German headquarters, but before they reached it white smoke shell in the barrage indicated that they were already on the final objective of the 6th Brigade. As they began to dig-in enemy sniping from close in front became intense, unaffected by the high bursting shrapnel as the field guns fired over the ridge top.

South of the Broodseinde – Moorslede road the final advance had proceeded without serious opposition. 7th Brigade were to attack north of the road using only the 26th Brigade, the 27th having been retained in support and for consolidation. The 26th advanced through the German cemetery at the Broodseinde crossroads, and crossed the ridge top road they were struck by fire from a machine gun dug-in amongst the scrub of Daisy Wood 700 yards down the slope. Making towards the wood they came under fire from hedges and ruined houses along the Moorslede road, which caused so many casualties that part of the line fell back to the shelter of an old trench just forward of the road. Supports were called forward from the 27th and at 9:50 two companies were sent up to Broodseinde. A gap had developed between the 6th and 7th Brigades that was now filled by the supports of the 27th. It was decided by officers on the spot that nothing would be gained by moving the line forward towards the final objective near Daisy

Wood, and the battalions began to dig-in on the old trench line. As they dug-in they came across numerous remnants of tattered khaki uniforms; the sad remains of the British units which had held the ridge in the winter of 1914-1915. Touch was gained with the 6th Brigade on the right and the line on the left was far enough forward to be in touch with the 41st Battalion of the 3rd Australian Division.

Except for the slight check in front of Daisy Wood, I Anzac was now on it final objectives, in a commanding position on the east slope of the ridge, but as we have seen, German resistance had not completely broken and in places the enemy still showed great resilience.

II Anzac to the final objective

3rd Australian Division to the Blue Line

If the whole British attack on the 4th October were to be considered as an arrow head shot towards the ridge at Passchendaele, then the 3rd Australian Division was at the very tip of the arrow. The position it was to attack was at the very base of the Gravenstafel ridge where it left the main Passchendaele ridge as a spur to thrust slightly north of west. The Flanders I Line continuing its northern path along the face of the Broodseinde – Passchendaele ridge ran right across the base of the spur. The Division was now faced with the enormously difficult task of advancing out of the Hanebeek valley, up the totally exposed slopes at the junction between the two ridges, and towards the massed machine guns waiting in the serried ranks of low concrete blockhouses guarding the approaches to Passchendaele, which, scornful of the power of the British guns, morosely dared flesh and blood to approach them.

11th and 10th Brigades

Both brigades had experienced tough fighting to reach the first objective, and now before they achieved the final objective it was to become even tougher towards the Flanders I Line. The line ran diagonally across the front, was close up on the right on the railway track at the Thames blockhouse which had already fallen, while on the left it was 900 yards forward to the Hamburg blockhouses and Dagger Trench. In the attack on the Blue Line both brigades were to use one battalion up to a position 200 to 300 yards short of the final objective, where they would dig-in and a support battalion would pass through. Both brigades were to use one battalion to capture the final objective in each brigade sector, but with another battalion leading the way to within 200 to 300 yards of the final objective, where they would dig-in and give close support. At 8:10 as the barrage thickened the 11th Brigade advanced and were instantly amongst the tumbled enemy wire entanglements. The ground north of the railway was very heavy, and as the leading 44th Battalion struggled forwards followed by the 41st, the barrage was lost. In the shattered remains of Dab Trench German machine gun crews succeeded in bringing their guns into action, while fire from the Seine blockhouse impeded progress. Seine, which was found to be the headquarters of a battalion of *79th R.I.R. (20th Division)*, was outflanked and fell, one senior German officer being killed with a second and 30 men being captured. Another bunker was attacked with rifle grenades and rushed, with 10 Germans being killed and 21 men and 3 machine guns captured, allowing the advance to proceed.

On the left meanwhile, the 10th Brigade was held up by machine gun fire from posts in an old enemy switch trench. Whilst the leading 39th Battalion was engaged with these they were also checked by fire from a machine gun pit in the New Zealand sector. Moving forward in support the 40th attacked this gun and with the assistance of a Stokes mortar silenced it, while the 39th secured the switch trench. Whilst the fighting continued the barrage steadily moved on, and when the 40th once more continued the advance it was unable to catch up with the protective curtain of shells and now came under intense machine gun fire from the Flanders I Line. Back on the right in the 11th Brigade sector, the 41st, attacking each side of the railway track had swept forward to its objective at the Nieuwemolen crossroads on top of the ridge, 2,400 yards from the rubble of Passchendele village. Two Vickers machine guns of 11th Machine Gun Company were set up at the crossroads, with two more of the 7th M.G.C. to the right, and with the Lewis guns of the 41st to the left, swept the slope of the facing spur from Keiberg hill to the railway.

On the left the 40th Battalion were to attack the most significant point along the whole of the British front. The battalion's objective on the right was 500 yards beyond Flanders I, but just short of the crest of the main ridge, whilst on the left it was beyond the crest of Gravenstafel ridge at the point where it was crossed by Dab Trench, the main earthwork of the Flanders I Line. As the 40th approached this defensive amphitheatre, the cratered ground became the only possible cover available, and as the advance commenced at least ten machine guns scythed into their ranks from front and sides. Casualties quickly mounted especially in officers as the enormity of the task become apparent and the battalion for the moment was checked. Much of the machine gun fire was coming from the battered Dab Trench. The company on the left led by Captain Ruddock, who recognized the only chink in the German armour, worked in short rushes between shell-holes, behind some precariously sheltered ground in the New Zealand sector. They were soon in a position from which Dab Trench could be engaged sufficiently to suppress the enemy fire, enabling the remainder of the battalion to begin the hazardous work of clearing the blockhouses. From the top of a blockhouse in front of Hamburg a machine gun was firing from the roof causing another hold-up. Sergeant Lewis McGee of the 40th ran forward 50 yards alone, and shot the crew with his revolver and captured others. For his conspicuous bravery he was to be awarded the V.C. The Hamburg blockhouse was also rushed and taken at great cost, and 25 prisoners and 4 machine guns were captured. Casualties were mounting and the battalion right was strengthened by part of the reserve company, and a combined group of 40th and 41st proceeded to attack and knock out, with numerous acts of individual bravery, the whole line of blockhouses in front of and along Flanders I. Another blockhouse on the left continued to resist until the garrison of eight officers and N.C.O's were all killed. Two further blockhouses on the right were finally seized, and by 9:12 a.m. 44th, 41st, 39th and 40th Battalions had captured and secured the whole of their objective.

In all 15 machine guns had been captured by the 40th Battalion alone. Of these, 7 guns, which had all been in action, were captured in Dab Trench.

New Zealand Division to the Blue Line

4th and 1st New Zealand Brigades
Moving up from their assembly areas the 3rd Canterbury and 3rd Wellington of 4th Brigade and 2nd Auckland and 2nd Wellington of 1st Brigade were by just after 8:00 a.m. in position to advance. The barrage behind which the New Zealand moved off at 8:10 a.m. was considered equally as good as that fired at 6:00. The enemy barrage was fired too long to worry the forward companies, falling mainly on the south-western slopes of Gravenstafel ridge and in the Hanebeek valley. Hostile machine gun fire was however more troublesome, and as the 3rd Canterbury and 3rd Wellington crested the ridge they were lashed by fire down the Ravebeek valley, from the Passchendaele ridge and from Bellevue spur, which had earlier hampered the 1st Auckland.

On the right the Canterbury were checked by two blockhouses in Berlin Wood, 400 yards north-east of the ridge top track, where two platoons carried out a model set-piece attack with rifle grenade and Lewis gun and seized the position, capturing 17 Germans. Machine gun fire from three more unsuspected pillboxes just over the crest held up 3rd Wellington, until outflanked and bombed from the rear. Blockhouses at Berlin 300 yards beyond Gravenstafel crossroads caused a twenty minute check, until pounded by Stokes mortars and rushed by bombers of the Canterbury. Fire from blockhouses at Waterloo 50 yards north of the Mosselmarkt road, which turned out to be a battalion headquarters, held up the advance until a mixed party of 3rd Wellington and 2nd Auckland attacked and captured them. By 9:30 4th Brigade moppers-up had cleared all enemy positions and the forward companies were consolidating on the Blue Line and establishing outposts 300 yards behind on the Blue Dotted Line. In the advance the Canterbury had captured 86 prisoners and 8 machine guns, and 3rd Wellington 150 prisoners and 8 machine guns.

To the left in 1st Brigade, as 2nd Auckland crested the ridge at Korek, machine guns in bunkers within the farm ruins opened a destructive fire at close range. A Stokes mortar team immediately brought their weapon into action, smothering the ruins with bombs, and so discouraging the garrison that 80 came out and surrendered. As the Auckland worked down the lower slopes, although covered by an element of smoke in the barrage, they were hit by the intense machine gun fire coming down the Ravebeek valley, which resulted in the loss of all senior officers. The battalion, including the Stokes mortar crews who had shouldered their tubes, rushed on as quickly as their barrage would allow, clearing the enfiladed area. Near the final objective machine guns in two further pillboxes opened fire, but were again seized with the aid of the mortar. Pillboxes in the ruins of Calgary Grange were attacked and taken by a combined party of the Auckland and Wellington.

To the left in the Stroombeek valley 2nd Wellington was also hit by the enfilade machine gun fire coming down the valley, but to a lesser extent than had 1st Auckland, and 3 platoons were also to far left in 48th Division sector. The advance to the Stroombeek faced little resistance but on approaching the muddy brook the forward wave came under machine gun fire from a blockhouse carefully hidden in the well wired and entrenched ruins of Kronprinze Farm. The trench in front of the ruins also held machine gun posts, and gradually a section worked forward from shell-hole to shell-hole towards the post. Once close enough, the party led by Sergeant Foot, rose from cover, and with a yell rushed the trench at the point of the bayonet. Sergeant Foot was awarded a bar to the D.C.M. he had won at la Basse-Ville back in July, and 39 prisoners and 7 machine guns were captured. The trench was also left full of enemy dead. The 2nd Auckland had captured 200 prisoners and 9 machine guns, the 2nd Wellington 213 prisoners and 10 machine guns, and the New Zealand Division had reached the Blue Line along the whole divisional front, and part of XVIII Corps front. The 3 platoons in the 48th Division sector were brought back to their correct positions, the 48th taking up the line, while on the right the New Zealand was in touch with 3rd Australian. The division had taken a total of 1,159 prisoners and had captured 59 machine guns.

I and II Anzac had smitten the Germans a mighty blow, and their bravery and tenacity had brushed aside the best defence that enemy ingenuity could produce. The attack had been like a mighty wave beating upon a massive sea wall, and the wall had crumbled and fallen. The guns had supported them admirably, and without them they may not have succeeded. But it was not the guns that had overwhelmed and shattered the resistance of the concrete and steel blockhouses, it was flesh and blood, driven forward by courage, and backed by a fundamental belief in their own ability.

Consolidation of both the Red and Blue lines continued at a pace, especially on the northern slopes of Gravenstafel ridge where the new positions were under fire from the blockhouses on Bellevue spur. The field guns covered the digging with much smoke shell and at 11:20 the protective barrage ceased. At 1:44 p.m. after bombarding strong-points and approaches the heavy barrage also ceased. The 1st Australian Division dug-in on a series of unconnected outposts, many in improved shell-holes which were quickly camouflaged with netting and were generally not seen by enemy artillery. 2nd Australian used existing trenches which they improved and linked up into a continuous line, with a line of outposts thrown forward. 3rd Australian produced a well engineered continuous line of trenches and supports as did the New Zealand. Communication trenches were dug across the ridges to enable relief of the front line, without exposure to sniping. Machine guns were set up at vantage points, positions were wired, and 1st Australian taped out the tracks to both battalion and company headquarters. The new line was firmly secured.

Casualties in I and II Anzac were commensurate with the ferocity of the fighting, and possibly with the varying density of the protective barrage.

Total casualties in I Anzac: 1st Australian Division 2,448, 2nd Australian Division 2,174

Total casualties in II Anzac: 3rd Australian Division 1,810, New Zealand Division 1,643

Initial German response.

Initially German retaliation was limited to an intense shelling of the western side of the Broodseinde ridge, and south of Broodseinde hamlet to shelling along the crest, making movement in these areas hazardous. In front of the 7th Division and the right of the 1st Australian Division no attempt at counter-attack was made by the enemy, so well did 7th Divisions machine guns cover the eastern slope of the ridge from their position at In de Ster. On the left of the 1st Australian, and in front of the 2nd Australian, continual movement of infantry behind the woods in the Heulebeek valley about the German artillery protection line resulted in no aggressive forward movement.

Soon after the 1st Australian Division had reached its final objective, hundreds of Germans were seen to be advancing only a few hundred yard away, towards Broodseinde south of the Moorslede road, with another column further back, strung out like ants. The two Vickers guns at the Nieuwemolen crossroads enfiladed the enemy, breaking up the cohesion of the counter-attack, which however still tried to work forward using shell-holes, but got no closer than a sniping line in front of the 2nd Australian.

Twenty minutes after the 3rd Division had begun to dig-in on the final objective, a party of Germans were seen working forward in sections, by rushes, towards a hedge along Keerslaarhoek cemetery beside the railway. Rifle and Lewis gun fire drove them off, but at about 11:00 a.m. another force appeared moving down the ridge in sections from the direction of Passchendaele, crossed to the south of the railway track, and occupied an old section of trench 200 yards in front of the 41st, from where they began sniping at the Australians. Return fire did not shift them, and Lieutenant Skewes led some men forward working towards the trench using shell-hole cover. Within 50 yards of the trench the party charged forward with a yell, bayonets fixed. The Germans abandoned their position but Lieutenant Skewes had been killed in the charge.

The Attack of Fifth Army 6:00 a.m. the 4th October

The northern defensive flank

In the practice which had now become the norm, Fifth Army was to advance beside Second Army to protect the left flank of the main attack. The assault was to be along a front of about 4,500 yards between the Stroombeek valley on the right, and just north of the Ypres – Staden railway on the left. XVIII and XIV Corps were to use two divisions each to attack towards an objective at an average depth of 1,500 yards. The surface was everywhere heavy and cloying, made more so by the recent rain. But the landscape was not without contour, as from the British outpost line, at around 15 metres above sea level, it rose gently towards the north-east and the Passchendaele ridge. The western slope of the ridge was here drained by a number of small streams, the Stroombeek, Lekkerboterbeek, Laudetbeek, and the Broenbeek, all tributaries of the Steenbeek. The streams were in fact no longer streams at all, there being little sign of any flow of water, the evidence of their original course only identified by the even wetter quagmire amongst the water-filled craters. The Lekkerboterbeek had carved a pronounced depression between two spurs, the southern at Wallemolen and the northern at Poelcappelle, and had once meandered between steep banks. North of the Polecappelle spur the land was predominantly flat, towards the Ypres – Staden railway, the only relief being 19 Metre Hill between the

Laudetbeek and the Watervlietbeek, a small tributary brook of the Broenbeek. The most substantial road in the area ran north-east from St. Julian, towards the rubble mounds which had once been the village of Poelcappelle, and then on to Westroosebeke at the northern end of the Passchendaele ridge. This wasteland of low spurs, shallow valleys, and flat fields, was undoubtedly the most featureless, dismal, shell-torn landscape, along the whole of the bare muddy arc which was the battle zone of the Ypres Salient. The only shapes rising above the mire were the low concrete blockhouses, the remnants of a few shattered farms, and the short stout trunks of few willow trees, their foliage totally stripped by the guns.

Even in the drier weather of September the trenches had remained muddy, and now with just a little rain they were once more reverting to ditches. The soil here was not heavy clay, as it contained a high proportion of sand, which in dry weather would blow around like dust. But when it rained it became soft and cloying, and anything of any weight upon it simply sank. It was easy to dig, and a trench line could be quickly established, but when it rained, the trench, unless supported by strong revetments would simply collapse.

XVIII Corps

The XVIII Corps was to use the 48th Division to attack along a line between Vale House – Cemetery Trench / Stroom Trench, (close to the confluence of the Stroombeek and the Lekkerboterbeek), and towards the Wallemolen spur. To their left 11th Division was to advance up the Poelcappelle spur towards the ruins of the village. The road to Poelcappelle although cratered and strewn with fallen trees, was the only hard surface on this forlorn battlefield, as was the only route along which tanks stood any chance of operating, without the certainty of becoming bogged. A few side tracks would just support the weight of a tank, but only if negotiated with extreme care and skill. They had succeeded in this area before, and now twelve tanks of "D" Battalion I Tank Brigade were to support the 11th Division in their attack on Poelcappelle.

48th (1st South Midland) Division
Major-General N. Fanshawe

The 48th Division had relieved the 58th on the 28th September, and was to use the 143rd Brigade to make the attack with three battalions in the line.

143rd Brigade [523]
The 1/5th, 1/6th, 1/7th and 1/8th Warwickshire Regiment of 143rd Brigade began to move up from shelters on the canal bank at 6:00 p.m. on the 3rd October.[524] Soon after midnight the battalion began to assemble along the taped lines. They then spent an unpleasant night laid out in shell-holes in the wind and drizzle waiting for the 6:00 a.m. Zero Hour. The brigade was to attack with the 1/5th on the right. The Stroombeek which ran diagonally across the battalion front would immediately have to be crossed and presented an area of very bad ground. In the centre, the 1/6th Warwick were also hampered by the Stroombeek which was on their right, and the 1/7th on the left faired little better with the mire around the Lekkerboterbeek on their left.

The barrage came down at 6:00 prompt, and as the 1/5th set off, their right immediately came under fire from a number of bunkers at Vale House and Winzig, and machine gun fire from a post near the Stroombeek also hit the left company. Vale House was successfully attacked, but the machine gun fire from the Winzig bunker was also hitting the 1st Auckland in enfilade, and had caused them to veer left across the Warwick to subdue the position. Winzig was taken but as we have seen the Auckland continued to the north across the front of 1/5th taking Albatros

---

[523] National Archives, War Diary 143rd Brigade WO95/2754
[524] National Archives, War Diary 1/7th and 1/8th Warwick WO95/2756

Farm, then crossing the Stroombeek and taking Wellington and Winchester Farms, which were around 700 yards into the Warwick's sector. Machine gun fire from the Bellevue - Wallemolen spur, coming down the valley from a range of 2,000 yards also hit the 1/5th. At the same time the battalion was heavily shelled, and casualties began to increase.

The 1/6th jump-off line was on very bad ground astride the Stroombeek. They struggled forward and came under heavy machine gun fire from a bunker at York Farm, 500 yards ahead on slight rise, at the western end of Wallenmolen spur. Machine guns in the bunker near Winchester Farm, 200 yards behind York also opened fire. Under a hail of fire the 1/6th gradually worked forward. Resistance from the bunkers was stubborn, but eventually after intense and costly fighting, both were outflanked and taken. Machine guns at Burns House and Vacher Farm caused a further check. Casualties in the 1/6th were now so severe that around 1:00 p.m. "C" and "A" Companies of the 1/8th Warwick in support were brought up to Hubner Farm, and came under orders of the 1/6th. Companies of both battalions attacked Burns House and Vacher Farm, but were pinned down under heavy fire, which continued to cause severe casualties.

On the left of the brigade front "C" and "D" Companies of the 1/7th Warwick advanced towards their first objective 750 yards forward, and immediately came under machine gun fire from the bunker at Tweed House. The ground was dreadful, being a mass of water-filled craters, and a machine gun in a post on the right also opened fire upon "C" Company, checking further movement and causing many casualties. On the left "D" Company pushed on slightly and used its support platoon to form a defensive right flank to deal with the Machine gun. After half an hours fighting amongst the shell-holes they were successful, killing the crew and capturing the bunker. "C" Company was then able to continue the advance, moving forward around 700 yards and capturing 10 prisoners. With the limited view possible from a muddy shell-hole in the midst of the featureless wastes it was very difficult to be sure of correct position. But it was soon realized the company had advanced too far as they had entered a German cemetery, which was the only identifiable landmark just to the west of a small track. Here "C" Company was within the British barrage line and so withdrew around 300 yards and dug-in. "D" Company meanwhile was held up by the bunker at Tweed House, but the position was successfully attacked, the crew and the gun being captured. The company then pushed on across another 250 yards of shell-holes to its objective, where it began to dig-in, contact being made with the 9th Lancashire Fusiliers on the left and "C" Company on the right. "B" and "A" Companies, which were to attack the second objective, had kept as close to the barrage as possible, while attempting to not get involved with the initial fighting. After the pause at the first objective, and as the barrage lifted, 'B" Company pushed forward 450 yards, through the cemetery to the far side of the track. The position was found to be untenable as both flanks were exposed, and the British barrage was standing dangerously close on the cemetery. "B" Company therefore withdrew around 200 yards through the shelling, to the western side of the cemetery, making contact with the 1/6th on their right. "A" Company advanced behind the barrage across boggy ground along the southern side of the Lekkerboterbeek, and attacked and captured the bunker at Terrier Farm. Pushing on another 250 yards they came under machine gun fire from a strong-point 150 yards forward of the cross-track at Country Cross Roads. All the officers and N.C.O's of the attacking platoon had become casualties, and a party worked forward amongst the shell-holes and attacked the enemy strong-point. The party soon became pinned down, and Private Arthur Hutt ran forward alone, shooting an officer and 3 men in the pillbox, taking the position and capturing 50 other ranks. For his courage and initiative he was to be awarded the V.C. With little means of knowing where they were, "A" Company also advanced too far, coming within the barrage, and withdrew to a line just forward of Terrier Farm and through Country Cross Roads, in touch with "B" Company on the right and the Lancs Fusiliers on the left. On the left the enemy were seen to be assembling a large party about Gloster Farm 300 yards in front of the Lancs Fusiliers and Manchester of 34th Brigade, and soon counter-attacked towards their forward positions. Lewis gun and rifle fire of the Warwick in enfilade, helped drive them off. Five more counter-attacks were launched against the Warwick shell-hole outposts, three from Beek House against the left, and two from near Vacher Farm against the right, but all were broken by Lewis gun and rifle fire. The 1/7th positioned two Vickers guns at Tweed House from where they could sweep the whole of the front.

The brigade was now checked short of its objectives, all companies had been engaged, and casualties were very high. At 2:00 p.m. "D" Company of the 1/8th Warwick were also brought up to Hubner Farm, and at 3:30 the battalion received orders to gather as many of the 1/5th, 1/6th and 1/7th as possible, to make a renewed attack behind a special barrage at 5:00 p.m. in which the 5th Gloucester and 4th Ox and Bucks of 145th Brigade were to participate. The objectives included the bunkers at Burns House, Vacher Farm, Oxford House and Berks Houses, around 400 yards forward of the present position. At 5:00 p.m. the special barrage fell beyond Burns and Vacher Farms, and as the remnants of the Warwick battalions advanced without its support, they were again cut down by heavy machine gun fire. The survivors withdrew to the line which had already been consolidated 400 yards behind Vacher Farm and Country Cross Roads, a rainstorm and oncoming darkness thankfully precluding any further offensive action.

At dusk the 1/5th moved up into the positions relinquished by the New Zealand, the left companies of which moved back into their own sector.

The 48th Division was therefore around 400 yards short of its objectives. That was not through any lack of effort or courage, for in the attacks across the terrible ground, against the numerous blockhouses, and under continuous shellfire, the Warwick battalions had suffered 1,160 casualties of which 242 had been killed, a casualty rate of 300 per battalion, compared with 200 per battalion in the superb New Zealand on their right.

11th Division and Tank Corps
Major-General H. R. Davies

The 11th Division which had relieved the 51st Division on the 25th September was to use the 34th and 33rd Brigades in its attack on Poelcappelle. The twelve supporting tanks of "D" Battalion were to use the St. Julien road to approach Poelcappelle, ten tanks to attack the village, while two were to turn right at Retour Crossroads down the track, to attack Gloster and Terrier Farms. The tanks had moved up from Oosthoek Wood, across the canal at Essex Farm, and come up to St.Julien on the night of the 2nd/3rd October. Carefully hidden under special brick-rubble camouflage netting, they had not been spotted by the Germans. On the night of the 3rd / 4th they advanced along the Poelcappelle road, (which was not much wider than the tanks), to a point 800 yards beyond Vancouver Corner, close behind the British outpost line, and in front of the waiting infantry. They had been loaded up with pit props, fascines and other baulks of timber, to be used for filling the worst of any craters they may encounter.

The attack on Poelcappelle 34th Brigade / 33rd Brigade / I Brigade Tank Corps[525]

In the 34th Brigade sector the 9th Lancashire Fusiliers were to advance with their right on the Lekkerboterbeek, with the 11th Manchester Regiment to their left to attack the southern outskirts of Poelcappelle.[526] From their start line near Stroom Trench the Lancs Fusiliers, confronted by the pillbox at Malta House, attacked under cover of a Stokes mortar bombardment and captured the position. One tank of "D" Battalion had mechanical problems at the start and had to retire, while the remainder, moving slowly along the Poelcappelle road silenced a machine gun at Delta House with their 6-pounders, but then had to stop 400 yards short of the village at Retour Crossroads, to await the barrage to lift from the first objective. Movement along the road was difficult, it being badly cratered and strewn with the trunks of

---

[525] National Archives, War Diary 33rd Brigade WO95/1811, National Archives, War Diary I Tank Brigade WO95/98
[526] National Archives, War Diary 9th Lancs Fusiliers WO95/1820, National Archives, War Diary 11th Manchester WO95/1821

fallen trees, which the tanks had encountered previously. As the larger of the craters in the road were encountered, the timber and fascines carried forward were used to help bridge the holes, tunnellers of the Royal Engineers going forward under fire with the tanks to assist with this work. In some cases the tanks had become stuck, and it was necessary for up to three crew members to get out, and fix the unditching beam to the tracks. Eventually all machines successfully reached the village. At Retour Crossroads two tanks turned right, towards the south-east, along a nearly obliterated track which they followed with great difficulty. Their objective, Gloster Farm, was found to be camouflaged with a pile of discarded timber, but was quickly recognized for what it was and effectively shelled with the 6-pounders. A number of Germans fled, becoming targets for the Lewis gunners. One tank then moved off the track towards the blockhouse, at which point the whole garrison surrendered to the 11th Manchester, which, having been held up by machine gun fire, was already attacking the position with Stokes mortars. The two tanks, which were also detailed to attack Terrier Farm, crossed the Lekkerboterbeek without even noticing the stream as it contained so little water, but upon approaching the farm found it had already fallen to the Warwick. A number of bunkers and machine gun posts which held up the Lancs Fusiliers and Manchester were attacked by Sergeant Charles Harry Coverdale of the 11th Manchester. Showing an utter disregard for danger, he attacked a number of strong-points killing two machine gun detachments. He was subsequently to be awarded the V.C. for his gallantry. Both battalions then took their first objective with little further trouble, but sniping and machine gun fire from bunkers around Poelcappelle caused casualties as they began to consolidate. Advancing towards the Blue Line the Lancs came under heavy machine gun fire from Beek House, little further progress being made, and a line of shell-holes was consolidated in touch with the Warwick on the right.

On 33rd Brigade front the 7th South Staffordshire Regiment and the 9th Sherwood Foresters advanced from their jumping-off line towards Poelcappelle.[527] A German machine gun dug-in beside the road, beneath a tank disabled in a previous attack, held up the South Staffs until being knocked out. Fortified shell-holes hampered the advance but were gradually overcome, but soon machine gun fire from bunkers in the village began to cause casualties. Fire from a bunker at Ferdan House held up the Sherwood Foresters, until it was successfully attacked and knocked out. Corporal Fred Greaves, on seeing his platoon commander and sergeant were casualties, rushed forward to the bunker and bombed it through the rear entrance, killing or wounding the entire garrison, and capturing four machine guns. For his initiative and gallant leadership in this attack he was later awarded the V.C.

As the barrage lifted from the first objective, the tanks on the St. Julien road continued their advance into Poelcappelle, accompanied by parties of the Manchester and South Staffs. The road junction at the entrance to the village was a mass of craters, which the tanks successfully negotiated, and the crews detailed to turn left down Tragique and Red House roads found this unnecessary, as the South Staffs and Sherwood Foresters were already forward of these tracks. Machine gun fire from blockhouses and bunkers within the ruins continued to take its toll. As the tanks worked along the main street they engaged the well hidden bunkers with 6-pounder shells, and as the garrisons emerged and attempted to run back they were shot down with Lewis guns and case shot. The infantry followed behind, mopping-up and clearing any Germans still remaining in the bunkers, as the tanks continued their attack towards the east of the village. Each machine had carried forward five boxes of small arms ammunition, and these, plus Lewis guns and ammunition drums were handed out to the infantry. The Meunier House blockhouse, prominent on a slight rise east of the village was engaged with 6-pounders, the garrison running out and down the slope to the rear, many being shot down by the tank's Lewis guns. One tank, which had so far been successful in knocking out bunkers, became bogged east of the village while attempting to move across a field to attack another position. Machine gun fire wounded the Tank Commander and killed the Sergeant as they attempted to fix the unditching beam.

By noon, the infantry were consolidating on the final objective, and the tanks began to withdraw down the road towards St. Julien, being sniped all the way by heavy high explosive

---

[527] National Archives, War Diary 7th South Staffs and 9th Sherwood Foresters WO95/1813

shells. Most carried wounded back from Poelcappelle, and only one tank became bogged and hit by shell-fire on the return. Except for the tank abandoned beyond Poelcappelle, and the one which had become bogged on the way out, all the others which had been in action returned to the rallying-point, the only tank crew casualties being those shot down east of the village. The operation had been another excellent example of how effective the tanks could be in cooperation with the infantry, given reasonably good ground, which had not been totally destroyed by the guns. To carry out such a successful operation, was only possible with crews trained to an exceptionally high level of skill, and with tanks which were in perfect mechanical condition. On this day the men and tanks of "D" Battalion had fulfilled both criteria, and the enemy had once again shown that they could not stand up to close quarter encounters with the tanks. One German officer was reported to have said: 'There were tanks - so my company surrendered - I also'. But the fighting amongst the rubble of Poelcappelle had been severe for the infantry, 11th Division suffering 1,340 casualties of which 206 had been fatal.

XIV Corps

To secure the northern flank of the attack, XIV Corps was to us the 4th Division and the 29th Division, which would be astride the Ypres – Staden railway. The mire of the Laudetbeek ran diagonally across the Corps front, the area being generally flat, except for the gentle slopes of 19 Metre Hill, the slight crest of which was around 400 yards from the northern bank of the stream. Although of no great elevation, the hill had a 9 metre height advantage over the surrounding country. The forward slope and flanks were totally exposed to machine gun fire, and even the reverse slope was exposed to fire from the left, beyond the railway to the north in the direction of Koekuit.

4th Division
Major-General T. G. Matheson

The 4th Division was to attack along a 750 yard front, 500 yards in front of Eagle Trench, between White Mill on the lower Langemarck – Poelcappelle road and Schreiboom on the upper road. The first objective was 1,000 yards forward, and the final objective 250 yards beyond on the Poelcappelle – Houthulst road on the right, while curving back to the first objective on the left. The 11th and 10th Brigades were to be used in the attack.

11th Brigade [528] / 10th Brigade [529]   The fight for 19 Metre Hill
The 11th Brigade was to use the 1st Somerset Light Infantry and 1st Hampshire Regiment in the attack, with the 1st East Lancashire Regiment in support, while 10th Brigade was to use only the 2nd Seaforth Highlanders to capture 19 Metre Hill, with the 3/10th Middlesex in support. The 1st Rifle Brigade and 1st Royal Warwickshire Regiment were in brigade reserve.[530] The assault battalions were assembled east of Eagle Trench, in shell-holes along their jump-off tapes by around 2:00 a.m. while the East Lancs and Middlesex were assembled just west of the trench by 2:30. All spent the night in the wind and drizzle, attempting to sleep. Trench boards had been brought up by 2nd Seaforth, and were to be carried forward to assist in crossing the bad ground expected about the Laudetbeek. The first objective was along a track 150 yards beyond 19 Metre Hill.

---

[528] National Archives, War Diary 11th Brigade WO95/1492
[529] National Archives, War Diary 10th Brigade WO95/1480
[530] National Archives, War Diary 1st Somerset Light Infantry WO95/1499, National Archives, War Diary 1st Hants WO95/1495, National Archives, War Diary 1st Rifle Brigade WO95/1496, National Archives, War Diary 2nd Seaforth WO95/1483 National Archives, War Diary 1st Warwick WO95/1484

At 6:00 the Somerset and Hampshire advanced behind a barrage which was noticeably ragged, some shells falling short and causing casualties, but enemy machine gun fire and shelling was relatively light. Kangaroo Trench was quickly seized, a number of prisoners and machine guns being captured. By 6:51 the forward waves of the Hampshire were on a line about Beek Villas, around 200 yards short of the first objective. At 8:00 as the barrage lifted the Hampshire right support company passed through and quickly found themselves beneath their own shell-fire, forcing them to fall-back to a line to the left of Beek Villas, with the most advanced platoon 150 yards further forward on the south-east side of 19 Metre Hill. By midday the Hampshire line had been pushed forward around 300 yards on the right, close to the first objective and in touch with the Somerset, while on the left it was still below 19 Metre Hill, 150 yards short of the first objective. Two companies of the East Lancs meanwhile had moved up in support, "A" Company having two platoons consolidating east of Kangaroo Trench, the remaining two holding the old front line, in touch with East Lancs "D" Company on their right, but not with the 3/10th Middlesex on their left. Both companies were receiving considerable machine gun fire from the left.

Map next page

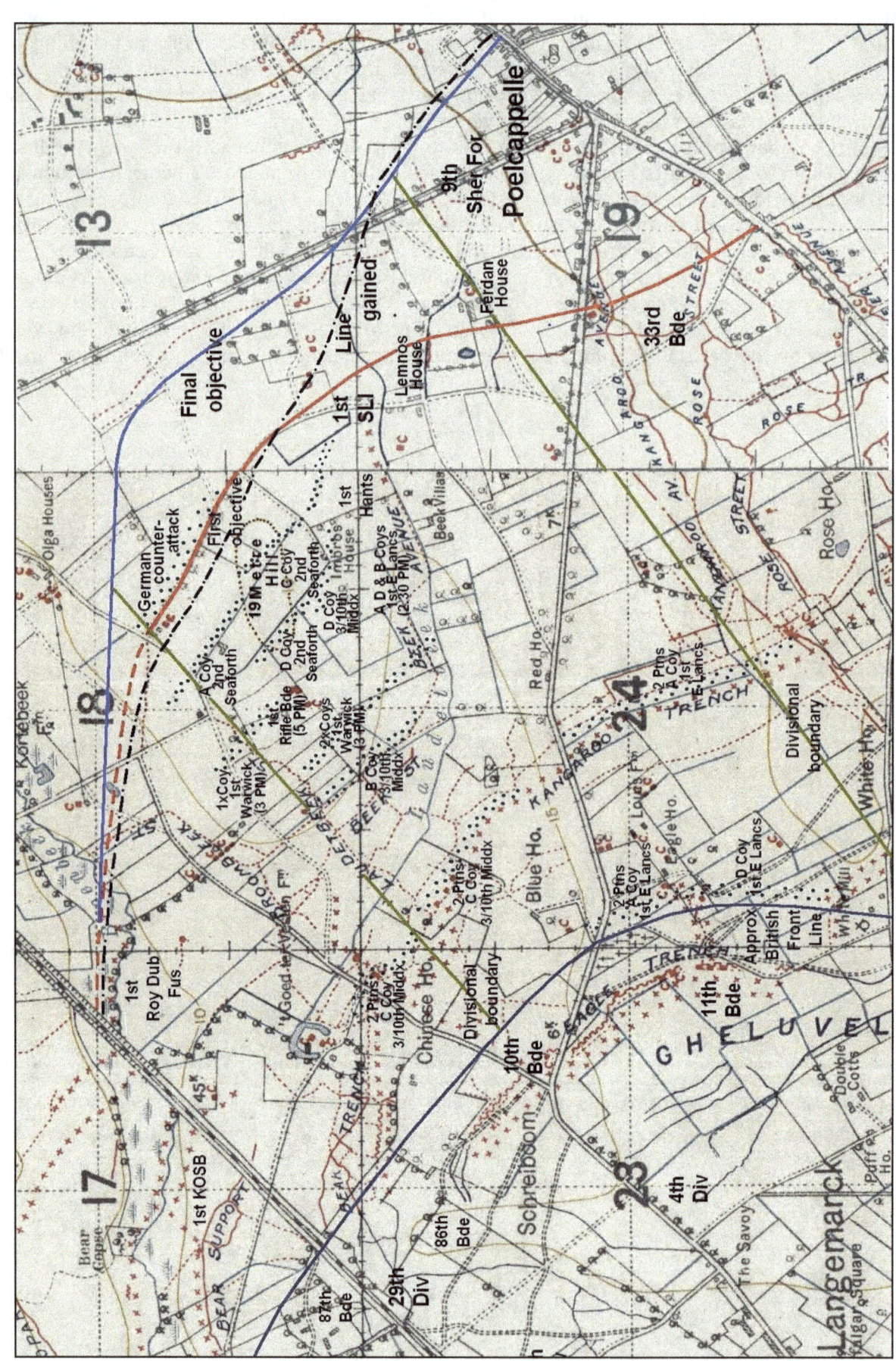

The attack of the 11th and 10th Brigades - 4th Division, and the fight at 19 Metre Hill

In 10th Brigade, and to the left of the Hampshire, the 2nd Seaforth with "C" and "A" Companies leading and "D" and "B" in support, had moved off behind the 6:00 barrage, the two leading platoons of each company carrying trench boards to help them across the marsh. The front waves immediately had difficulty keeping proper alignment, as patches of waterlogged ground caused them to attempt to find a passable route around the mire. There was great confusion, especially on the left in "A" Company, where they walked into their own barrage. The disorganization continued towards Kangaroo Trench, but any enemy who showed resistance was bayoneted. In the advance "C" Company had taken about 25 prisoners, some of whom, upon being sent to the rear, were caught by their own barrage. "A" Company became embroiled in a close-quarters fight in which few prisoners were taken, and the C.S.M. was seen to kill 15 of the enemy 'to his own bayonet'. As the advance continued it proved impossible to regain formation due to confusion and 'the excited condition of the men'. Up to Beek Street Trench, 350 yards short of 19 Metre Hill, casualties had been light, but from this point on they began to rise sharply due to machine gun fire from two bunkers just short of the hill, and from fire from the left flank coming across the Broenbeek. Both company commanders of the two left companies, "A" and "B", and six of the eight platoon commanders became casualties. The advance continued, "C" Company moving on to the reverse slope of 19 Metre Hill, while on the left "A" Company captured a fortified house 200 yards to the north. Due to heavy machine gun fire from the left flank, "A" Company could make little more progress, establishing a shell-hole line from near the top of the rise to a point 300 yards to the north-west. As "C" Company moved out of the lea of the rise and onto the crest, they immediately came under severe machine gun fire, could make no further progress, and dropped into shell-holes about 75 yards forward of "A" Company, and in touch with the Hampshire on their right. The strength of "C" Company at this time was down to one officer and 30 other ranks. Moving up in support of "C" Company, "D" Company under Captain Gjers came under heavy machine gun fire from the left, sustaining many casualties, and the advance came to a halt, around 150 yards short of the crest but on their objective.

At 6:20 the Officer Commanding the Seaforth Lieutenant -Colonel Laing, had ordered forward two companies of the 3/10th Middlesex, (then under his command), to Eagle Trench. Middlesex "B" and "C" Companies had anticipated the order and by 6:30 "B" was up at Eagle Trench, from where it was immediately sent forward to Kangaroo Trench. On the arrival of two platoons of "C" Company (the other two having been detailed to close up the left flank with 87th Brigade), they were sent up to Kangaroo Trench in support of "B" which was then to move forward 350 yards to Beek Avenue, just beyond the Laudetbeek. There they would be in a position to resist any counter-attack against 19 Metre Hill, or against the right flank of 10th Brigade. Upon arrival at Eagle Trench, "D" Company of the Middlesex was also sent forward to reinforce the right "C" Company of the Seaforth on the hill, and to attempt to work forward on the right. Using the cover of craters the Middlesex got forward to a line running through Imbros House, 100 yards south of the crest, before being checked by heavy machine gun fire from the left, then forming a defence line in shell-holes. Machine gun fire from a concrete bunker to their left was seen to be causing many casualties, and a party of the Middlesex worked across and silenced the gun, the position then being handed over to the Seaforth.

By 9:30 the battalions were considerably mixed, a party of Middlesex "D" and Seaforth holding the bunker just south of the rise, with Middlesex "B" and "C" Companies dug-in just in rear. A thin line of Seaforth "C" Company under their one remaining uninjured officer, Captain Wood, still held their shell-holes about 80 yards down the forward slope, with two platoons of Seaforth "D" under Captain Gjers dug-in 150 yards short of the crest. The whole position held by the Seaforth and Middlesex was under murderous machine gun fire, movement being virtually impossible, the only safe way to communicate between the shell-holes being to dig from one to the other.

At 9:30 Captain Wood, from his exposed position with "C" Company on the forward slope, managed to get a report back to his battalion commander: 'Have reached 18.d.7.4. [forward crest of hill] Present strength about 30. The Hants are up in line on my right. We also hold farm at 18.d.2.5. We are also held up by machine gun fire from farm at 18.d.2.8. [about 125 yards away] also by other guns which we cannot locate. 2nd Lieut. Macrae is with me (wounded). Lewis gun ammunition urgently required.'[531] At 9:40 a.m. 2nd Lieutenant Lovegrove, 6 Platoon, "B" Company, reported: 'The general line seems to be about 200 yards short of the objective. We are held up by M.G. fire from hedge in front (along the objective road) and the barrage has passed over it and remains stationary beyond.' Soon after, 2nd Lieutenant MacDonald also "B" Company reported: 'Very heavy standing barrage in front of me seems to indicate I have reached my objective. Immediately in front are a number of ruined farms, some are occupied by machine guns, which are worrying us. We are digging-in here. I have a sergeant and 16 men in shell-holes. Lewis gun in farm on right, but are not in touch with the left. Cannot identify my position on the map, but bearer will give as clear an account as possible.'

Captain Gjers then attempted to get forward beyond the crest with one platoon to stiffen "C" Company, ordering the second of his platoons to remain on the reverse slope and dig-in. On leading the platoon over the crest Gjers became a casualty, (and was later reported as missing). The men, being left in a totally exposed position and with no officers began to fall back off the hill, through the lines of the Hampshire and East Lancs. It was then reported incorrectly that the position on the hill was being evacuated, as Wood and "C" Company still held the forward slope.

At about 1:00 p.m. the Germans began shelling heavily with 8-inch guns along the old front line, and heavy machine gun and rifle fire was experienced from the left front. Soon a German counter-attack developed against 19 Metre Hill mainly from the direction of Olga Houses 400 yards to the north. This was easily repulsed on the left by Seaforth "A" Company, but on the right the Germans worked forward and crossed the track only 100 yards short of the hill top, and managed to establish a position in the road bank and in shell-holes just in rear, but were unable to advance further. In "C" Company holding the forward slope the one remaining officer, Captain Wood, had become a casualty being killed by machine gun fire whilst distributing Lewis gun drums. The 30 men remaining, who were now dangerously short of ammunition for both rifles and Lewis guns, held firm to their exposed positions, as did the second platoon of "D" Company on the rearward slope.

At 2:40 p.m. upon receiving the report that the front line was falling back, 10th Brigade sent the following message to the Commanding Officer of the Warwick in brigade reserve: 'Line reported to be falling back from 19 Metre Hill. You will move your Battalion forward to reinforce the firing line and regain possession of 19 Metre Hill counter-attacking if necessary.' The three companies of the 1st Warwick were sent up to Eagle Trench, under command of Colonel Laing of the Seaforth, who then sent one company up to fill an exposed gap to the left of the crest, with the remaining companies disposed across the brigade front, behind, but in striking distance of the hill. The Warwick was already weak in numbers before it advanced and Laing sent up two Vickers guns with them to stiffen their position.

The retirement between 1:00 and 2:00 p.m. of the platoon of Seaforth "D" Company, was believed to have exposed the left flank of the Hampshire. Captain Tinling of "A" Company 1st East Lancs, in support, now moved forward towards the hill to protect the Hampshire flank, followed by East Lancs "D" and "B" Companies, all sustaining severe casualties as they advanced, inflicted by the persistent and deadly machine gun fire from the Broenbeek valley on the left. Captain Tinling was killed in this advance.

At around 4:00 p.m. another German counter-attack developed against the hill. This time the enemy were shot up in enfilade by the machine guns of 29th Division on the left, but groups of five different regiments, without officers, began once more to retire from the hill. The line was once more, and this time finally restored, on the rearward slope by the 1st Rifle Brigade from 11th Brigade reserve. At around 6:30 p.m., on an S.O.S. call from another part of the line, the British artillery began shelling the front heavily, but between 7:00 and 8:00 calm finally descended over the battlefield.

The fighting for 19 Metre Hill had been severe and confusing, and as we shall see was of great concern right up to Army level. Losses in 2nd Seaforth Highlanders for 4th October were 341, of which 94 were killed or missing. Losses in 1st Hampshire for October, most of which had

---

[531] National Archives, War diary 2nd Seaforth WO95/1483

occurred on the 4th were, 232, of which 59 had been killed. Total losses in 4th Division had been 1,279 of which 228 had been killed.

29th Division
Major-General Sir B. de Lisle

The buttress on the far left

At the far left of the British Line, the 29th Division was to provide a left flank to protect the left of the 4th Division. Two battalions were to be used, the 1st Royal Dublin Fusiliers of 86th Brigade on the right of the railway, and the 1st King's Own Scottish Borderers of 87th Brigade to the left. The ground over which they were to attack was heavy, especially about 't Goed ter Vestern Farm, where the Laudetbeek ran into a moat about the farm, but was flat and along the southern side of the Broenbeek.

86th and 87th Brigades [532]
South of the railway the Dublin Fusiliers on a two company front of 500 yards, were to advance their right by around 1,000 yards to conform with and protect 10th Brigade, while on the left, they were to move forward around 300 yards and establish a strong-point on the embankment where the railway crossed over the Broenbeek. As the line advanced it was to drop a line of posts back to the left to face north, and form the final left defensive flank of the whole British advance. Two strong German positions guarded the approach to the Laudetbeek, a blockhouse at Chinese House, and another in the moated ruins of 't Goed ter Vastern Farm. Both places had received special attention from the divisional and corps artillery, and the farm had also been pounded by 6-inch mortars of 20th Division. North of the railway the Scottish Borderers were to capture and consolidate three strong-points, one on the railway, and two just north-west of it, the far left position being astride the Langemarck – Koekuit road, about 100 yards beyond the German cemetery. The Dublins, which were under orders to join 16th Division in two days time, had requested one last action with 29th and marched to the front in high spirits singing Irish Republican songs. It was envisaged that there would be dangers to their left, as at the end of the line, that flank would inevitably be exposed.

The Dublins advanced with the barrage in good order, but as expected difficulties were experienced with the open left flank. Two platoons, in file, had been detailed to follow up the left attacking company, two machine guns being sent forward behind the rearmost platoon with the task of defending the exposed flank. The determined Irishmen quickly took their objectives, being stopped only by the quagmire along the Broenbeek, and the two machine guns did excellent work in supporting 4th Division on 19 Metre Hill on the right. At one point an enemy machine gun held up their advance, shooting down a platoon officer. Sergeant James Ockenden rushed the gun crew single handed, killing all except one, who he chased down and killed. In the afternoon he attacked another bunker while under heavy fire, killing four more of the enemy, and taking 16 prisoners. For these courageous actions he was subsequently awarded the V.C. North of the railway the K.O.S.B. took their objectives with little resistance taking 12 prisoners, and established a line of posts.

In the fighting to secure the left flank, 29th Division had sustained 286 casualties, of which 41 had been killed and 39 were reported missing. The terrible casualty figures of 4th Division in the fighting for 19 Metre Hill were, in retrospect inevitable. The 4th was the last division in the line to have an objective along the whole divisional front, the objective of the 29th as we have seen being drawn back on the left along the Broenbeek. This left the Broenbeek valley, and all the higher ground north of the stream in enemy hands, and their machine guns, as recalled so many

---

[532] National Archives, War Diary 87th Brigade WO95/2303, National Archives, War Diary 86th Brigade WO95/2298

times in stoic terms in the battalion accounts, had smitten 4th Division in enfilade as they approached and crested the exposed 19 Metre Hill. That they had finally retained a foothold on the hill with so many officer casualties was a credit to all units involved, not the least of which was the 2nd Seaforth Highlanders.

The results of the Third Step – A most significant day

The change to the German defensive scheme, introduced in an attempt to find a solution to the gradual British successes had resulted in a disastrous day for the enemy. A large part of the disaster had been brought about by the coincidence in the timing of their major counter-attack towards Tokio spur, which, coupled with the recent decision to strengthen the front line had just served to heighten their losses beneath the barrage. They were down, but they were certainly not out. The German artillery continued its harrying and destructive fire seemingly unabated. The shellfire from the medium and heavy guns was placing even more strain on the British infantry as it was now arriving in enfilade, the Passchendaele group firing predominantly south-west towards the Gheluvelt plateau, while the Tenbrielen group fired mainly north towards Broodseinde. The British positions, exposed on the eastern face of the plateau, and along the crest and forward slopes of the Broodseinde ridge, were now prime and obvious targets for enemy field-gunners. Strong resistance had been met at Tower Hamlets, in the Reutelbeek valley, and east of Polygon Wood. To the east of the main ridge at Daisy Wood 2nd Australian had faced a still determined enemy, although at times the officers may have appeared more determined than the men. The Warwick had endured a trying time amongst the foul quagmires south of Poelcappelle, and at 19 Metre Hill there had nearly been a serious setback.

There had been checks, but it was obvious nevertheless that a great victory had been won. Virtually all objectives had been achieved, and by 10:30 a.m. the situation appeared so promising to Gough, that he had told Sir Ivor Maxse to push on with XVIII Corps along the Wallemolen and Poelcappelle spurs to the eastern outskirts of the village. On the left XIV Corps was to conform, pushing forward to the Poelcappelle – Staden road, the attack to recommence at 5:00 p.m. But the optimism was prior to the news of the difficulties at 19 Metre Hill, and upon receipt of this information the order was cancelled. After a morning meeting at Cassel with Haig, Charteris head of G.H.Q. Intelligence Branch was sent to liaise with Plumer at Second Army headquarters nearby, to discuss the possibility of exploiting what appeared to be an extremely promising situation. True to form, and probably wisely, Plumer was more cautious, pointing out that there was no sign of a general enemy withdrawal, and that the *Eingreif* divisions had not been fully engaged. This was correct, and unbeknown to Plumer was in line with latest German policy. Furthermore, at Broodseinde and at Nieuwemolen the field artillery had been firing at the extremity of its accurate range of about 5,000 yards, and there was around 3,500 yards of shell-cratered mud to negotiate to move the guns forward.

Plumer had however been impressed by the apparent magnitude of the morning's achievement, and at 11:00 a.m. consideration was given to a suggestion by Lieutenant-General Godley of II Anzac, who believed the enemy to be sufficiently demoralized for his Corps to push on across the Roulers railway, northwards along the ridge towards Passchendaele. The plan was to also involve I Anzac, 2nd Australian Division taking over the line about Nieuwemolen up to the railway from 41st Battalion of Major-General Monash's 3rd Australian Division. At 11:39 a.m. Monash informed Godley that his two leading battalions had suffered heavy casualties, but that by concentrating his right above the railway, he considered an advantageous position could be reached, farther along the ridge towards Passchendaele, to improve the jump-off line for the next attack. I Anzac was to cooperate by resuming the attack eastward towards the Keiburg spur, and preparations were commenced to put this plan into operation.

At noon Lieutenant-General Moorland commanding X Corps telegraphed Major-General Shoubridge, 7th Division, indicating that he favoured an advance northwards from the In de Ster Cabaret spur along the eastern face of the ridge, towards the Germans facing I Anzac in front of

Broodseinde. Shoubridge was aware of the difficulties 21st Division had experienced in the Polygonbeek valley and at Reutel, and was therefore anxious regarding his right flank, which was in any case thrown well back. In the early afternoon Plumer visited Lieutenant-General Birdwood, commanding I Anzac, and found him equally indisposed to attack eastward with the 1st and 2nd Australian Divisions, pointing out that his battalions would be moving beyond the range at which the field artillery could give effective support, a fact of which Plumer was undoubtedly well aware. This decided the issue in Plumer's mind, and at 2:00 p.m. any idea of exploitation was abandoned.

German counter-attacks of the afternoon

What counter-attacks there had been, and they were few, had been largely driven off. The exception was along the Reutelbeek valley at about 3:00 p.m., where the Germans, in an attempt to gain a firmer footing on the eastern edge of the Gheluvelt plateau, launched a major counter-attack using battalions from all three regiments of the *17th (Eingreif) Division* together with reserve battalions of the *19th Reserve Division* in the line. This thrust against the 5th and 21st Divisions, was successful in retaking Reutel and Cameron Covert, and in working its way across the mire and craters of Polderhoek spur to supply the garrison at Polderhoek Chateau with new machine guns and ammunition. The thrust was finally broken with heavy losses by the artillery and by the massed machine gun fire of both 5th and 21st Divisions.

Except for the counter attack in the Reutelbeek valley, no serious German movement had threatened the new British line. But against Broodseinde the enemy continued to threaten, their facility to concentrate being limited by the British machine guns to the dead ground about Daisy Wood, and in the upper Heutebeek valley near the railway. From Australian observation posts near Broodseinde and Nieuwemolen, a force was seen about 2:00 p.m. to be moving along the ridge from Passchendaele, while another worked along the western face of the Keiberg, and moved tentatively forward towards Daisy Wood. Between 3:30 and 4:00 in response to an S.O.S. the artillery placed a heavy and effective barrage on Daisy Wood, on the Moorslede road and on Dame Wood. The Germans advancing from Passchendaele were also dispersed by artillery and by Stokes mortar teams of the 41st Battalion.

The German counter-attacks against Broodseinde were in fact heavier than the British at the time realized, or the enemy intended. In line with their new defence policy the reinforcements of the German front line regiments were moving up at around 8:00 a.m., just as the British launched their second attack towards the Blue Line. The *93rd R.I.R. (4th Guard Division)*, attempting to regain its position on the In de Ster spur, was driven back even further by 7th Division. Opposite the 1st Australian Division, the reserve battalions of both the front line division, *II/5th Foot Guard (4th Guard Division)*, and counter-attack division, *III/211th R.I.R (45th Reserve Division)*, advanced across the valley from the Keiberg under heavy machine gun fire from 7th Divisions guns on the In de Ster spur, and through troops retiring from the front. They were unable to get further forward than the hedges and copses at the foot of the slopes beneath the Australians. The headquarters of the forward battalions, fearful of being overrun, retired to the rear headquarters in the artillery protection line, about 1,300 yards from the ridge crest. A few hundred yards to the north, opposite 2nd Australian, the *II Battalion, 5th Guard Grenadier Regiment, (4th Guard Division)*, with battalion headquarters in a sandpit on the Moorslede road, had concentrated some of its scattered companies in front of Daisy Wood, but now seeing a general withdrawal along the slopes to the south, became apprehensive that they may soon be cut off. At about 10:00, upon the arrival of reinforcements, (part of the reserve *II Battalion* of the *5th Foot Guard* and *II/211th R.I.R.)*, these forces were positioned to establish a defensive left flank. The Australians were next seen moving along the ridge to the north, causing further panic, and to avoid the risk of encirclement, the *II/5th Foot Guard* and the *II/211th R.I.R.* were withdrawn to Daisy Wood. Message of a possible breakthrough was passed back to the *Guard Grenadier* regimental commander, which warned (incorrectly), that the Australians were advancing towards the Keiberg. At 11:00 a.m. an urgent request for reinforcement was received by *5th*

Bavarian I.R. of the neighboring *4th Bavarian Division*, (which had been moved forward as counter-attack forces for the *20th Division* opposite 3rd Australian and the New Zealand Division). By about 1:30 p.m. the dangerous gap, which for a while had exposed the Keiberg, was filled by companies of the *5th Bavarian I.R.* At 11:25 a.m. the *5th Bavarian I.R.* had received another urgent request for reinforcement from the *5th Guard Grenadier Regiment*, and its two remaining battalions passed through the gap in the Flanders II wire near Eddy Farm, on the crest of the Keiberg, and advanced straight towards Broodseinde. Moving forward along the Moorslede road it soon came under heavy machine gun fire from the Australian guns on the ridge, and moved a few hundred yards to the north into the shelter of Daisy Wood, there joining the remnant of *5th Guard Grenadier*.

The two remaining regiments of *4th Bavarian Division* were ordered at about noon to attack astride, and north of the Staden railway, the *9th Bavarian Infantry Regiment* against Broodseinde and the *5th Bavarian R.I.R.* against the New Zealand Division. On crossing the Keiberg south of the railway, *II Battalion* of the *9th Bavarian* came under a heavy barrage, and subsequently into heavy machine gun fire, which broke up the advance, the survivors taking shelter in Daisy Wood with the remnants of the *4th Guard Division*. The same fate befell the *I Battalion* advancing north of the railway, those who could working southward and also taking shelter in the wood. *III Battalion* advancing along the crest from Passchendaele, came under such heavy machine gun fire that they veered right, down into the Ravebeek valley in front of Gravenstafel ridge, and became mixed with the *5th Bavarian R.I.R.* which had unsuccessfully attempted a counter-attack against the New Zealand.

The reports of an Australian breakthrough continued to reach *4th Bavarian Division*, and at 3:00 p.m. its one remaining battalion, *II/5th Bavarian I.R.* was ordered to attack from Eddy Farm, towards the Broodseinde crossroads. This direction of advance brought the battalion straight to Daisy Wood, where it found both the *I* and *III Battalions* of its own regiment, plus parties of the *9th Bavarian Regiment* and the remnants of the *5th Grenadier Guard*. The *II/5th Bavarian* continued its advance up the slope towards the 26th Battalion of 2nd Australian Division, and that battalion fired its S.O.S. The answering barrage broke the German advance, driving the survivors back into Daisy Wood. The chaos and confusion amongst the enemy is clearly illustrated by the fact that at this point the front of the *5th Guard Grenadier Regiment* was held by parts of the *I/9th Bavarian I.R.*, the *II/9th Bavarian I.R.*, the *I/5th Bavarian I.R.*, the *II/5th Bavarian I.R.*, parts of the *III/5th Bavarian I.R.*, the remainder of the *II/5th Guards Grenadier*, and a few men of the *II/211th R.I.R.*, most of them sheltering in or near Daisy Wood.

The general situation

During the days fighting Second Army had captured 114 officers, and 4,044 other ranks, and Fifth Army had captured 12 officers and 589 other ranks. Opposite I Anzac Corps, where the ill timed German counter-attack had been destroyed either beneath the British barrage, or at the hands of the Australian infantry, the *45th Reserve Division* had lost 83 officers and 2,800 other ranks, (not including lightly wounded), and the *4th Guards Division* 86 officers and 2,700 other ranks. Of the eight counter-attack divisions available in striking distance of the battlefront, all three regiments of the *17th Division* (*75th I.R.*, *89th Grenadier* and *90th Fusilier*) had been in action in the Reutelbeek valley, the *93rd Regiment* of the *8th Division* and the *94th R.I.R.* of the *22 Reserve Division* had attacked towards In de Ster, all three regiments of the *45th Reserve Division* had been in action against I Anzac Corps, and all three regiments of the *4th Bavarian Division* (*9th Bavarian I.R.*, *5th Bavarian R.I.R.*, and *5th Bavarian I.R.*) had been in action against I and II Anzac. Four counter-attack divisions, the *16th Bavarian Division*, *16th Division*, *187th Division* and the *6th Bavarian Division* had not been engaged.

The *5th Foot Guard Regiment* described it as the worst day yet experienced in the War. Ludendorff went even further in his description of the day. 'The battle on the 4th October was extraordinarily severe, and again we only came through it with enormous losses. It was evident that the idea of holding the front line more densely, adopted at my last visit to the front in

September, was not the remedy.' [533] The German official monograph called it 'the black day of October 4th'.[534]

At one point the Keiberg and possibly Passchendaele had been exposed, with little defences to have prevented their capture. But to have moved on Keiberg out of the accurate range of the field artillery, would have gone against all of Plumer's firmly held beliefs, which had been proved so tragically correct by previous events, and the enemy were still showing the will and ability to resist.

British casualties had also been severe, 16,189 in Second Army, and 4,283 in Fifth Army. If Second Army had ordered a continuation of the advance to commence at 4:00 p.m., (Fifth Army had been considering this for 5:00 p.m.), the battalions to perform the operation would have already been in the field and involved in severe fighting for over ten hours, after spending the previous night in wet shell-holes. Extra ammunition, additional materials for consolidation, replenishment of water and food, and great reserves of energy would be required for the further advance, and it was not part of the plan. At 3:00 p.m. Haig met with Plumer and Gough at Cassel to discuss the situation, and Plumer again reiterated his belief that only the leading troops of the enemy's front divisions had been engaged. Charteris was of the opinion that in consideration of the number of German regiments represented among the prisoners all divisions had been seriously engaged and that there were few more available reserves. The truth, as we have seen, was probably somewhere between the two opinions, but in any event there was to be no exploitation. That evening, to add to the Commander-in Chief's dilemma, Charteris informed Haig that, 'I am of opinion that, at the present moment, there is no formed division (of enemy reserves, beyond those on that morning's map) within immediate reach of the battlefront. I do not think that any formed division can reach the battlefront until early morning on the 6th October'.[535]

The Germans, in line with their new policy, had held back the main body of their counter-attack forces, only the *17th Division* and the *45th Reserve Division*, having been fully engaged. This situation had been foreseen in a Second Army intelligence summary of the 1st October, in which Lieutenant -Colonel Mitchell had suggested that after the huge setbacks of the 20th and 26th September, the enemy would deliver organized counter-attacks twelve or more hours after the assault, and make the utmost use of his artillery, especially in enfilade. This had been an astute observation, but now the Germans, after their bitter experiences, and still floundering for an answer to counter Plumer's tactics, were to make further changes. Ludendorff's solutions to the problem swung like a pendulum from one extreme to another. The order to concentrate a greater number of better armed infantry in the forward positions had resulted in a disaster on the 4th October, with huge and unsustainable losses in manpower. Nine German divisions were required to bolster the Italian front and a limited French attack was expected in the Champagne at any time. Ludendorff was doubtful if he had the necessary forces to continue to reinforce the Flanders battle and a new and less costly defensive solution had to be found, and quickly. In a complete reversal of the latest policy he insisted that Crown Prince Rupprecht should not allow his troops to be shattered by enemy fire but should give way before it.[536] The forward area was to be held by a few lightly manned posts, while the main line of resistance was to be around 800 yards farther back. On the 7th October the commander of *Fourth Army*, General Sixt von Armin ordered that the foremost line of shell craters, if no natural obstacle was available, was to be occupied by a quite thin screen of posts with light machine guns. A main line of resistance was to be constructed 500 to 600 yards behind this screen.[537] The enemy was obviously running out of tactical options. The one bright light on their horizon did not rely for its luminance upon their tactical prowess, or upon any tactical blunders the British may make. Plumer's three great

---

[533] BOH p316
[534] BOH p316
[535] AOA p880
[536] AOA p881
[537] BOH p316

attacks had required a relatively firm ground surface to allow for the forward movements of huge numbers of men, and massive quantities of weapons and materials. But now the rains had returned.

To the British, the battle had been a wonderful boost to morale, seen in the light of what had gone before in this dreary War, which had been continually punctuated with disappointment. Following close on the heels of two clear successes in the last fortnight, this latest and greatest triumph must surely signify a distinct turning point, beyond which the longed for vision of final victory appeared achievable, and for now concerns about the weather were not going to spoil the moment.

Haig had foreseen this battle, the third step, as the end of a first and distinct phase in the campaign. The right flank of the offensive was now securely anchored on the Gheluvelt plateau. Passchendaele and the ridge northwards were the objectives for the next step, and in view of the progress made in the three preceding steps this seemed realistic and achievable. Moreover when these objectives were gained in the next attack on the 10th October, given the believed deterioration in the enemy's fighting capacity, the success could then be exploited in line with Haig's views outlined to Plumer and Gough on the 2nd October, and the advance could proceed beyond Passchendaele and towards the Keiberg. This also seemed reasonable, if by the 10th October the guns would be brought forward as on previous occasions to protect the advance. It is clear that the commanders in the field who were responsible for putting the plans into action also found them reasonable, as an intelligence summary of II Anzac Corps commented subsequently regarding the situation on the 4th October, 'there can be little doubt that, if it had been in accordance with the wishes of the High Command, we could have captured Passchendaele this day with slight opposition'.[538] II Anzac obviously believed that exploitation on the 4th had been possible given the situation at that time, but would the conditions be the same on the 10th?

In fact there were to be two drastic changes. First, as forecast, the weather had begun to deteriorate and at 12:30 p.m. in the afternoon of the 4th further rain fell from a leaden sky. By the end of the day there had been 4.6 mm. Over the next four days there would be another 30.2 mm. Second, the moment of greatest German vulnerability, due to weakness in forces immediately available had past. On the 5th October opposite I and II Anzac the *195th Division* had relieved the battered *4th Guard Division*. Before the 9th October the whole battlefront was held by fresh enemy troops and an extra division had been put into the line opposite 7th Division at In de Ster, the German front line then being held by six divisions. The *1st Bavarian Reserve, 4th Guard, 5th Bavarian Reserve, 15th Division, 27th Division, 220th, 227th, 228th,* and *240th Divisions*, 5 of which had come from the French front, had all arrived in Flanders since the 4th October.

Charteris, whilst recognizing the great achievement of the 4th was beginning to feel that the offensive could make little more progress. He did however acknowledge that there were other important reasons to continue, as his diary entry on the 5th October explained. 'There was a conference late in the afternoon (4th October) – D. H. and the Army Commanders. We are far enough on now to stop for the winter, and there is much to be said for that. Unless we get fine weather for all this month, there is now no chance of clearing the coast. With fine weather we may still do it. If we could be sure that the Germans would attack us here, it would be far better to stand fast. But they would probably be now only too glad to remain quiet here and try elsewhere. Anyhow, *there are reasons far more vital than our own interests here that give us no option.* But it is a tremendous responsibility for D. H. Most of those at the conference, though willing to go on, would welcome a stop.'[539] (Authors italics) The Germans were still firmly pinned in Flanders, so whilst the tactical battle raged at least one of the two primary strategic issues remained satisfactory and as planned. There could be no hope for the moment of the coastal operation being undertaken, as insufficient progress had been made from the Salient for it to link up with. But the situation within the French Army was gradually improving. Its recovery was in large measure due to the granting of regular leave, lack of which had been

---

[538] AOA p879
[539] Brig-General John Charteris *At G.H.Q.* pp258/259

partly responsible for the initial problems. But this had inevitably created the adverse effect of reducing its fighting strength. The French front was now so thinly manned as a result of extra leave allowances, following the requests of Painlevé and Foch at the conference at Boulogne, the British had been asked to take over a sector of the French front. But it was not only in the French recovery that the operations at Ypres were assisting. Continuously German reserves were being drawn into the Flanders sector, and not being able to deploy elsewhere. The *195th Division*, mentioned above as facing I and II Anzac, had been withdrawn from the Cambrai sector, and then specially equipped to go to Italy, as part of the planned German September offensive in support of the Austrains. On the 1st October, the division handed back its special equipment and was ordered to proceed to Flanders. Ludendorff later wrote regarding the mid October period: 'The wastage in the big actions in Flanders was extraordinarily high. Two divisions which had been held in readiness in the East and were already on their way to Italy were diverted to Flanders. The Italian operation (Caporetto), could not be started before 22nd October, and the weather held it up until the 24th. These days were the culminating point of the crisis.' [540]

Word of the French mutinies from escaped German prisoners had reached the German High Command back in May. But incredibly the Germans still seemed unaware of, or unwilling to believe in the French difficulties, and the weakness of the French line. Crown Prince Rupprecht was expecting an attack by the French against the *Seventh* and *Third Armies* timed to correspond with another attack by the British. With this probability in mind, on the 9th October he wrote, 'O.H.L. will no longer be in a position to help us by bringing up fresh forces', and again on the 11th, 'our troops, on the chief fighting front in Flanders, are in a fair degree of confusion. Most troublesome is the fact that our fighting force becomes all the time of poorer quality, and that every means that we thought out is ineffective as a counter to the overpowering superiority of the enemy's artillery. As it is a matter, for us, of fighting to gain time, nothing else remains except by repeated withdrawal to force the enemy to a fresh time-consuming advance of his artillery'.[541] Kuhl, Rupprecht's Chief of Staff, later wrote regarding the manpower weakness, that on the whole front except Flanders only the most indispensable defence garrisons against partial attacks could be provided, even at the most threatened places like Lens and St. Quentin. The situation was so extreme that Rupprecht began preparations for a withdrawal from the Flanders position, to take up a shorter line, despite the disadvantages to morale and the inevitable relinquishing of the Belgian coast and the U-boat bases.

By the 4th October this is how close Haig had come to achieving his aims. Charles Bean's often quoted words resound with the possibilities following the Broodseinde attack. Let the reader looking at the prospect as it appeared at noon on October 4th ask, 'in view of the results of three step-by-step blows, what will be the result of three more in the next fortnight?' [542]

But Rupprecht's greatest ally now took to the field, and was more powerful and destructive to British aspirations than any number of field-grey clad legions. The rain had returned to the Flanders fields..

---

[540] BOH p324
[541] AOA p881
[542] AOA p881

Zonnebeke church

Zonnebeke

Corduroy road. Zonnebeke to Broodseinde

Chapter Seven

"Almost unimaginable difficulties"

The Fourth Step

The Battle of Poelcappelle 9th October

Casualty clearing

On the 4th October the rain which had set in by 4:00 p.m. not only placed the success of future operations in extreme doubt, but had the immediate consequence of making the clearance of the huge number of casualties from the battlefield an immense and heartbreaking task. It was becoming a repeat of the conditions in August, as the ground rapidly deteriorated into the same atrocious state, but the distance to carry the injured from the front was even greater.

In II Anzac sector where the duckboard tracks were totally inadequate, to get closer to the battlefield casualties the Regimental Aid Posts had by mid morning been moved forward 2,500 yards, beyond Hill 40 to Alma and Bordeaux, in the depression of the northern Hanebeek. Stretcher parties slipped and stumbled across the shell-torn slopes as they valiantly attempted to carry their comrades back to the Aid Posts. From the R.A.P's the stretcher carry led back across the foul valleys of the Hanebeek and Stroombeek and across the exposed Tokio spur, along duckboard tracks, as and where those tracks existed, towards Ypres, a distance of anything up to 5,000 yards to the ambulance loading posts. Horse drawn ambulance wagons were of limited use on the forward 'one-way' timber track circuits, as artillery limbers were making continuous two-way journeys to provide the ever hungry guns with ammunition, and with few passing points the tracks became hopelessly congested. On the I Anzac front, the wagon loading posts were driven back to the Menin Road, and on that of II Anzac to Bavaria House 1,000 yards west of Frezenberg and 5,000 yards from the front line. In the afternoon after the rain, the Model T Ford ambulances could no longer operate from the loading posts at Bavaria and Frost House, and a team of four horses was required to move each wagon along the wet slippery tracks from the most forward point accessible on the Frezenberg – Zonnebeke road at the old Bremen Redoubt.

At 8:00 p.m. the officer in control of the R.A.P. at Helles (between Anzac and Tokio spurs) reported: 'Carry from right and left R.A.P's impossible until dawn. At 7:00 p.m. about 40 stretcher cases remain beyond the (Zonnebeke) swamp at R.A.P., all under cover.' [543] The bearer parties worked until exhausted, but some of the wounded were not cleared from the battlefield before dark. The captured German blockhouses, many of which improvised as forward R.A.P's, could not begin to shelter all of the casualties awaiting evacuation, and some men spent the night lying out in the mud and rain, exposed to the continuous shelling. The slippery timber roads and poorly repaired tracks were totally inadequate for the job as hundreds of motor and horse drawn ambulances desperately struggled to transport the wounded from the loading posts to the A.D.S's around Ypres, or to the railhead for onward movement to the Main Dressing Stations, or out of the battle area to the Casualty Clearing Stations to the west of the city. Canadian engineers had completed a 60 cm railway to Anzac ridge by the 5th October. This eased the situation, as where possible, and for the first time, the light railway was used to move stretcher cases from the railhead the full distance to the C.C.S's, considerably saving on the use of road transport. The Royal Army Medical Corps, battalion bearer parties and bearers from Corps reserve, with the assistance of infantry seconded as stretcher parties, had cleared the majority of the wounded off the battlefield by 8:00 a.m. on the 5th, but many wounded remained at the R.A.P's. For the carry from the forward R.A.P's back to the A.D.S's, enemy prisoners were

---

[543] A.G.Butler. *Official History of the Australian Medical Services 1914-1918 Vol.2 The Western Front.* p236.

also employed. Captain L May of the 3rd Australian Field Ambulance gives a graphic account. 'Oct.4th. It has been a cruel day for the bearers; the enemy pounded our supports and the guns in front of us. At Helles Major Hunt killed and the M.O's cut off by shell-fire all day. Prisoners carried here [Tunnel Relay Post, Westhoek] from 'Ideal House' [R.A.P.] for 2 or 3 carries; then as we were congested I pushed them off to the rear in twos....Oct.5th. Going again – dugout crowded, almost impossible to move...Went to Ideal Post and Helles, and got the men down and sent them to Westhoek. I appreciated the awful time the bearers had on their carries, as I slipped and slopped along without any weight to bother me. Met my men from Nun's Wood Post [Nonne Bosschen] and went along the Decauville track and onto the Corduroy Road with its dead horses on the side and overturned limbers; with guns and wagons and howitzers and mules in hundreds, and carrying parties, squeezing us off the track and into muddy shell-holes. At Birr Cross-Roads on familiar ground, and on to A.D.S., the [Menin] road thick with lorries and ambulances, horsed and motor. At C.M.D.S. hot food, rum issue, cigarettes and an extra blanket.' [544] The bearers and drivers, both motor, and horse with their tragically vulnerable teams had performed magnificently.

Whilst this forlorn work to clear the results of one operation was still underway, the planning continued at a pace for the next. At a meeting with Plumer and Gough at Cassel at 3:00 p.m. on the 4th, after discussing the general situation of the battle, Haig announced that, in order to maintain the momentum against the shaken enemy and allow them no time to recover, he wished to bring forward the date of the next attack from the 10th to the 8th October. This was assuming General Anthoine, whose French First Army was to co-operate, could hasten his preparations. At 4:00 p.m. Haig met with Anthoine who seemed anxious to do everything possible to advance his plans, but felt that he would not be ready until the 9th. The date for the next step to capture Passchendaele was therefore fixed for the 9th October, with the subsequent and optimistic step to capture Westroosebeke scheduled for the 12th.

On the 5th October Haig discussed future plans with his Chief of Staff Lieutenant-General Kiggell who advocated a scheme for the Belgians to attack across the Yser at Dixmude. Haig was of the opinion that this operation would be extremely difficult due to the limited crossing points over the inundations. Most importantly, he again made clear his belief that once the Passchendaele ridge as far north as Stadenberg had been captured, the risk of encirclement would force the Germans to withdraw from their positions in Houthulst Forest and east of the Yser, without the Belgian effort.

Weather conditions, rainfall Vlamertinghe, temperature Ypres[545]					
	5th October	6th October	7th October	8th October	9th October
Rainfall	3.1mm	2.1mm	10.4mm	14.6mm	Nil
Temp	53F	47F	53F	54F	53F

The 7th October was another cold blustery day with heavy downpours bringing over 10 mm of rain. Haig had given careful consideration to the requirements for railway transport, to move forward the reserve divisions which were to carry out the deeper exploitation as outlined by him at the Cassel meeting on the 2nd October. To concentrate the necessary rolling stock to move forward the reserves on the 9th, would mean taking wagons from their daily tasks of carrying

---

[544] A.G.Butler. *Official History of the Australian Medical Services 1914-1918 Vol.2 The Western Front.* pp227/8
[545] National Archives WO95/15 GHQ statistics

ammunition, animals and road materials, and assembling them at the infantry boarding points 15 miles west of Ypres. To assemble the rolling stock on the 9th would mean the wagons being unavailable to transport normal loads for 24 hours. If the rain continued, and the ground conditions worsened, it would be inadvisable (and probably impossible), to continue the advance in the afternoon of the 9th, which would mean the wagons being dispersed and then concentrated again for the next attack on the 12th. This would result in a three day loss in freight movements causing serious shortages at the front, which in turn could bring any hoped for advance to a halt. The rain was already exerting its influence over tactical planning. Haig balanced the options and decided that exploitation on the 9th looked less likely the longer the rain continued, but postponed his decision until the following day.

It was not just the exploitation planned for the 9th which hung in the balance, but the wisdom of continuing with the offensive at all, while the present wet conditions lasted. The terrible difficulties of the August battles had not been forgotten, and it was obvious that dryer conditions had to a large part contributed to the series of successes since the 20th September. The firmer ground had enabled the guns to be moved up, allowing for careful preparation and a protective artillery barrage. Mobility had vastly improved, allowing the battalions which had attacked to then be quickly relieved and moved out of the line. These carefully planned and coordinated arrangements had been collectively essential to guarantee success. But with the return of quagmire conditions it was unlikely that the well oiled machine could work nearly as smoothly.

There is little doubt that had the decision been left to them, given the level and scope of their responsibilities, Plumer and Gough would have called off the offensive at this stage, and they told Haig as much at a G.H.Q. conference on the 7th. They were however acutely aware of the fact that Haig still regarded the Passchendaele – Westroosebeke ridge as a minimum objective as the only possible line to hold for the winter, and were ever mindful of the possibility of a general German withdrawal should this be achieved. The final decision to attack or not, was to be made by Plumer after consultation with the corps commanders, although Haig made his position clear by stating that there should be no postponement unless absolutely necessary. As may be imagined there was not a consensus of opinion, Godley of II Anzac wishing to go ahead, whilst Birdwood of I Anzac hoped for a postponement. All corps commanders were to consult with Plumer at 8:00 a.m. on the 8th October, and he was to give Haig the answer at 9:00.

Whilst undoubtedly preoccupied with the forthcoming operation, Haig had on the 8th October replied in writing to a fundamental question posed by Lloyd George during the visit the Prime Minister made to G.H.Q. at the end of September. Lloyd George had requested Haig's views regarding the rôle of the British forces in the event of Russia no longer taking an active part in the War, or making a separate peace, and also having regard to the weakened state of both France and Italy. Typically the Prime Minister had asked a virtually insolvable question, with too many imponderables to reach a firm conclusion. Haig opened his 14 page reply by admitting that, 't*he number of considerations affecting a decision on the problem is so great that it is impossible to deal with them in a short paper*'.[546] The cornerstone of his answer was that Germany and her allies relied primarily on the invincibility of the German Army to secure for them favourable peace terms and that if the power of the German Army was broken, or appeared to be on the point of breaking down, the Central Powers would gladly accept such terms of peace as the Allies might offer. The great question was (and for that matter still remains), bearing in mind the scenario suggested by the Prime Minister, was it justifiable to believe that the resistance of the enemy could be overcome by direct attack, before the endurance of the British Empire and those of her Allies which remained in the conflict broke down? Haig considered his possible answers, both positive and negative, admitting that there were conditions when indirect action was wise and offered the best chance of success in war. But he did not feel that was the case in the present situation, and came down firmly of the

---

[546] National Archives, Haig to War Cabinet 8th October WO158/24 and CAB27/8

opinion that the Western Front was the only place where the German Army could be beaten, and that no alternative course offered any prospect of defeating her. He conceded that the defeat of Russia would release forces of the Central Powers to fight on other fronts but that this would be balanced by the arrival of American forces. The Austrians would be in a position to deploy sufficient reserves against Italy to throw the Italians on to the defensive, but the price of supporting Italy would be at the cost of operations on the Western Front. He remained pessimistic regarding any imminent contribution from the French believing that neither the French Government nor the military authorities would commit their Army to offensive operations until the German strength was definitely and finally broken. Haig went on to emphasise the degradation of German divisions through the Flanders fighting and gave an estimate of the probable number of German divisions on the Western Front by 1918 as 179.[547] Ever mindful of his own vulnerability in manpower, he begged that no more frontage should be taken over by British divisions from the French, and that drafts in England, once trained should immediately be sent to France to replace wastage. Finally he also asked that the Cabinet should have, 'firm faith in the possibility of final success'.[548] The Cabinet in their usual irresolute fashion never felt able to agree to any of these three requests.

On the morning of the 8th it had stopped raining and there was a drying wind. The decision was made to go ahead with the attack, although by 4:00 p.m., and still with plenty of time to cancel, the rain again came down in torrents. Gough telephoned Kiggell at G.H.Q. questioning the wisdom of attacking, stating that Caven of XIV Corps wished to proceed, while Maxse of XVIII Corps wished to postpone. Haig ordered them to carry on. On this day, on the eve of the attack, with the weather conspiring against it and giving serious cause for concern, Major-General Harington, M.G.G.S. Second Army, gave an extraordinary address to war correspondents. He made it clear that in his opinion the series of successes so far had been attributable to the planning and methods of Second Army, and irrespective of whether or not Fifth Army agreed, Second Army was to make the attack. He went on to claim that after one or two more steps the cavalry may be pushed through, and in any case the sandy crest of the Passchendaele ridge was 'as dry as a bone'.[549] Whether this was pure bravado, painting the best possible picture to the press of an operation which was definitely going to proceed, right or wrong, or whether Harington believed his words to be true remains a mystery. There was however to be an element of truth in his predictions of the condition of the ground on the ridge top. It was certainly not to be found as dry as a bone, but as we shall see it was to be dry enough to proceed with the operation.

The 8th October was to be a day of great decisions. Haig met with Davidson and Major-General Nash, (Director General of Transportation), and requested 10 trains for Second Army, sufficient to carry five brigades, and 4 trains for Fifth Army, sufficient to carry two brigades, to be available on the 12th October. The exploitation which had been planned for the 9th was therefore postponed until the 12th.

That momentous consequence hung on the forthcoming battle, and that the whole enterprise was held in jeopardy as a result of the weather was not lost on G.H.Q. Staff. Charteris noted in his diary entry on the 8th: 'We go on again tomorrow, and yesterday and today there have been heavy downpours of rain, a last effort. Documents taken on the 4th show that the Germans are very hard pressed to hold their ground. They have given up their new plan of thinly held front lines and gone back to their old scheme, which is all to the good; but unless we have a very great success tomorrow it is the end for this year as far as Flanders is concerned, and next year the Germans will have their troops from Russia. With a great success tomorrow,

---

[547] It was to be 210.
[548] National Archives, Haig to War Cabinet 8th October WO158/24 and CAB27/8
[549] AOA p884

and good weather for a few more weeks, we may still clear the coast and win the war before Christmas. It is not impossible, but it is pouring again today.' [550]

The plan for the Fourth Step

From its conception the fourth step was to be fundamentally different to the previous three. For the first time the well proven tactics of bite and hold, would be augmented by an additional deployment of separate forces to exploit the initial success and thrust deeper into the German position. In effect Haig was about to attempt a break through. It was to be an exceedingly bold stroke. The main attack by the divisions in the line would be in two phases, the first in the morning by the leading brigades to reach a first objective, the Red Line, the second in the afternoon to a final objective, the Blue Line. If all was reported to be going well, designated brigades of the reserve divisions would, on the same day, be brought up from west of Ypres by train towards the front, two trains per brigade, to continue the pursuit of the broken enemy, beyond the Broodseinde – Passchendaele ridge, and both along the ridge, and eastward from Poelcappelle, towards Westroosebeke.

I Anzac was to use the 1st and 2nd Australian Divisions in the preliminary attack, with the 4th and 5th Australian Divisions in reserve, while II Anzac used the 66th and 49th British Divisions in the main attack towards Passchendaele, with the 3rd Australian Division and New Zealand Division in reserve.[551] On the left in Fifth Army, XVIII Corps would use the 48th and 11th Divisions to attack towards Poelcappelle, with the 18th and 9th Divisions in reserve, and XIV Corps would use the 4th, 29th, and Guards Divisions to secure the left flank. Beyond the Guards, French First Army would attack from the line of the Broenbeek – St. Jansbeek towards Houthulst Forest. On the southern flank X Corps was to hold the German reserves about Gheluvelt and Becelaere, attacking with the 5th Division across Polderhoek spur, in a further attempt to take Polderhoek Chateau. East of Polygon Wood 7th Division was to extend its right by 700 yards to just south of Jetty Wood, to renew the attack on Reutel and Noordemdhoek. Between 5th and 7th Divisions 21st Division was to stand fast. Within a day's march of the battlefield 1st and 5th Cavalry Divisions would assemble behind Second and Fifth Armies, with the remainder of the Cavalry Corps assembled and in readiness to move up if required.

The preparatory barrage would follow the pattern for the previous attacks, except this time they would be interspersed with periods of silence. The protective barrage was to commence at the same moment the infantry advanced, Zero Hour being set at 5:20 a.m. The clocks had gone back an hour on the 7th October in line with the end of British summer time. The barrage creep and lift timings would be as on the 4th October, but due to the rain, the infantry had much more difficult ground to contend with. At 10:27 a.m. the barrage would cease.

The preparations

Up until the 4th October, the condition of the roads and tracks had been tolerable, allowing for the forward movement of batteries, ammunition, stores, and men. The drier ground had helped the repair of shellfire damage to the timber tracks and light gauge railways. From that day onwards the situation worsened rapidly, as the battlefield once more reverted to a swamp. On the 5th there had been continuous drizzle, which by the 6th had become constant showers. The 7th had brought bitter drenching squalls. The Steenbeek and Zonnebeek valleys behind II Anzac front were especially bad, being described by a Divisional C.R.E. as a porridge of mud. Under such conditions the tanks could take no part.

---

[550] Brig-General John Charteris *At G.H.Q.* p259 Charteris was obviously not to know that the enemy had once again changed their tactics for holding the front line.
[551] Australian War Memorial, 2nd Anzac Instructions for the Offensive. 5th October 1917. AWM4 1/32/20 Part 2

Little progress was possible in laying the timber roads closer to the front lines of the two Anzac Corps, even with the assistance of six infantry battalions of X Corps sent by Plumer to help, the planks simply sinking into the oozing mud. The much repaired track, 'Smith's Road', from Westhoek over Anzac spur, across Albania valley and over Tokio spur to Zonnebeke, was the main supply artery for I Anzac. The rains quickly reduced the track to little better than useless, as the first echelon of guns to be moved forward over Anzac spur caused it to collapse irreparably beneath them and sink into the mud. The guns were then moved with great difficulty off to the side of the track, to be mounted as well as possible on hastily prepared platforms 1,500 yards behind where they should be. This situation led to Lieutenant-General Birdwood commanding I Anzac, informing Plumer that exploitation towards the Keiberg was not practical, as the necessary artillery support would not be available.

To enable effective and accurate support for the critical forthcoming attack by II Anzac, the field artillery was to be brought forward to the line of the Zonnebeke – Langemarck road, 4,000 yards from Passchendaele. But the lack of tracks capable of bearing the weight of the guns resulted in most of the artillery remaining west of the Steenbeek, 1,750 yards short of the desired position. The field batteries to support 66th Division in their attack on Passchendaele were having a terrible time moving up, getting little further forward than Frezenberg, then being man-handled through the mud into positions along the side of the Zonnebeke road, between Frezenberg ridge and the Steenbeek, one mile behind where they were intended to be. Most of the field guns supporting 49th Division, in their attack across the Ravebeek towards Bellevue spur, were along the Wieltje – Gravenstafel road, between Weiltje and the Steenbeek, with a few 500 yards east of the stream along the track behind Hill 35. Passchendaele village was visible from many battery positions by the still standing spire of its church, which was 750 yards short of the day's final objective. But from the most forward batteries near Hill 35 the church was still 6,000 yards distant, and the German field battery positions on the eastern slopes 1,500 yards beyond Passchendaele, were therefore out of range. Even those guns still west of the Steenbeek were on hopelessly soft ground, many sinking up to their axles, or even muzzles, before the hurriedly prepared platforms were completed. Plank tracks were essential to be laid off the remaining metalled roads towards the batteries, to enable pack animals to reach the guns with ammunition. To construct a sound gun platform took two days hard work, and much materials, requiring a foundation of fascines and road aggregate, on which was placed a double layer of beech slabs nailed together to provide a platform. With all these preparations the platforms were still beginning to sink after only a few rounds, making accurate shooting exceedingly difficult.

The carrying forward of field artillery ammunition, now almost entirely performed by pack animals, reached new levels of toil and difficulty. From the wagon lines to the batteries, a journey which had taken about an hour, now, along the treacherous tracks, was taking anything between six and sixteen hours to complete, assuming the animals had kept their footing, and not slipped off the timber to flounder and finally drown in the morass. Everything, men, animals, guns and ammunition, was saturated and caked with mud, and rest was near impossible. The journeys to the batteries, under constant fear of shelling or stumbling into the mire, were endless, and shelters on the gun lines, and dug-outs at the wagon lines were flooded out. For the first time since the 20th September, the previously smooth-running operation was quickly breaking down, and the essential support of the infantry by the field artillery looked in serious doubt.

The deteriorating conditions that were having such a retrograde effect upon the artillery, equally depressed the infantry, the continuous rain and mud making life even worse than it normally was. Understandably the engineers had placed most emphasis on constructing tracks to move the guns, but the duckboards along which the infantry were to pass had received scant attention. All that could be done was done, but was limited to improving the passage across the worst of the swamps around the streams. Three duckboard tracks, No.4, No.5, and No.6, led from Ypres, roughly following the line of the St. Jean, Wieltje, Kansas Cross road, towards the front line held by II Anzac Corps. No.4 Track, which started just north of the Menin Gate, ran approximately 750 yards to the south of, the Wieltje road and was already in poor condition and intended for mule traffic only. No.5 Track started at the Dixmude Gate as a mule track, but was joined by a double duckboard infantry track 750 yards beyond the gate, just east of Well Cross Roads. Both mule and infantry track ran parallel to, and 250 yards south of the Wieltje road. At Wieltje hamlet the infantry track reduced to single file, finally skirting to the south of Hill 35 and Hill 37, and reaching the Zonnebeke – Langemarck road near Dochy Farm. No.6 Track started on the Ypres – Yser canal bank near bridges 1, 1A and 1B, close to the junction of the Ypres – Comines canal. Again beginning as a mule track at the canal, it was joined by a double duckboard infantry track near La Brique, both tracks running around 250 yards north of the Wieltje road. Beyond Wieltje for 1,000 yards the infantry track ran across bare ground with no duckboards. The track crossed the Steenbeek 800 yards south of St. Julien, and continued, some parts boarded, some parts not, to meet the Zonnebeke – Langemarck road near Schuler Farm. The tracks, one of which was allocated to each brigade sector, ended within 1,500 yards of the front lines and from here forward the path across the awful muddy ground was indicated with tapes supported between stakes, upon which at night lamps would be fixed. These were the totally inadequate paths over which in the dark, the mud, and the rain, the many thousands of men of 66th and 49th Divisions of II Anzac Corps, would move up towards the front line. From the Menin Gate to Kansas Cross in a straight line was 7,000 yards, and Kansas Cross, where the poor tracks ended, was 2,400 yards short of the Ravebeek from where 49th Division were to jump-off. But the tracks were anything but straight, which meant the heavily laden infantry which were to carry out the most difficult and important attack of the day, must struggle forward for over six miles. Long before the battle started, the men would inevitably be exhausted by the dreadful march up to their jumping-off positions. But there was absolutely no alternative, as by the Commander-in Chief's order the battle was to proceed.

During the first few days of October, the battalions detailed to take part in the forthcoming attack, had begun to move up into camps west of Poperinghe. Those members of the battalion not to take part in the action left for their respective corps reinforcement camps. During the 6th and 7th October, with the final decisions regarding their fate still to be taken by High Command, by a combination of route marches and bussing, the divisions began to assemble in camps around Vlamertinghe, between Poperinghe and Ypres.

The 66th Division, to take up its position on the right of II Anzac Corps, was not a first line division, and had only landed in France at the end of February and beginning of March 1917. It had not previously been in action, and was now to be placed at the arrowhead of the British attack upon Passchendaele. Not only were the battalions untried but the Divisional Staff were also an unknown quantity, and there were grave misgivings in some circles as to whether they would be up to the job. On the night of the 5th October, the 199th Brigade of 66th Division had relieved 3rd Australian Division in the line. The relief was generally considered a shambles, the whole affair having been totally mismanaged. In an effort to ensure that the 197th and 198th Brigades, which were to carry out the forthcoming attack, were close enough up to the line to ensure of their timely arrival they were moved up to the east of Ypres on the evening of the 8th October, leaving a full ten hours to reach their jumping-off tapes 4,500 yards forward. Having started forward at about 5:45 p.m., by 12:30 p.m. after struggling on through the rain and mud, with intermittent enemy shelling, it became clear that the right brigade, the 197th, would not make it up to the line in time. All available staff officers were sent up with orders, 'to push forward all men who were able to move quickly and leave those who were exhausted to come on later. Men struggled up throughout the night but were unable to get right up to the tape line by Zero Hour'.[552] The commanding officer of the leading battalion of Lancashire Fusiliers, waiting at the front for the battalion to arrive, eventually believed the attack to have been postponed, and returned to his battalion headquarters, just before the weary first companies arrived. The 2/8th Lancs Fusiliers, the second battalion of the brigade following up, reported that the conditions were, 'almost indescribable. The night was inky, the track led over ground covered with innumerable shell-holes full of mud and water. This march, which would normally

---

[552] National Archives, War Diary 197th Brigade WO/95/3135

take about one to one and a half hours to complete, occupied eleven and a half hours, with the result that the battalion arrived in the front line 20 minutes late'.[553]

The approach march of the 66th Division

The approach march of the 66th Division is deserving of examination in detail. At around 7:00 a.m. on the morning of the 8th October the division began the movement up to the line, initially to an assembly area on the western side of Frezenberg ridge, which was reached by around noon. It was considered unwise to proceed beyond the ridge in daylight, but even in its shelter hostile shell-fire, mostly directed at battery positions about Frezenberg was responsible for casualties in several battalions. During the afternoon as they sheltered in the lea of the ridge, the 2/9th Manchester and the 2/4th East Lancs sustained 50 to 60 casualties before moving out of the shelled area. Forward Brigade headquarters were established, with 197th Brigade at Springfield, and 198th Brigade at Levi Cottages. At 5:45 p.m. in fading light the 198th Brigade commenced the final march up via "K" Track, while the 197th Brigade left at 6:00 p.m. and marched up via "Jack and Jill" Tracks, guided by officers of the 10th Field Company Australian Engineers . On account of the darkness, the rain, and the appalling state of the ground where the tracks were smashed, the progress of the novice division was painfully slow. Any slip or stumble off the track risked a fall into a water-filled shell-hole, and the efforts of many men were required to pull one man out. In places east of Frezenberg ridge in the valley of the Zonnebeke mud waist deep had to be avoided, and it was obvious by 3:00 a.m. that 197th Brigade would not be up on its tapes by Zero Hour. At 5:05 a.m. the 199th Brigade holding the line and awaiting relief was placed at the disposal of the G.O.C. 197th Brigade in the event of his own Brigade's late arrival. From Frezenberg ridge to the front line was around 4,500 yards, the usual time to cover the distance being about 3 hours at the most. On this night some battalions were to take around 12 hours. At 12:30 a.m. all available Staff Officers had been sent out in an effort to get the battalions forward, but by Zero Hour the head of the 197th Brigade column was just reaching the front line. The first men of the 3/5th Lancs Fusiliers were just arriving at the tapes, while the 2/8th was still 400 yards from the line, the 2/7th was just crossing Hill 40, and the 2/6th was still on the west side of Hill 40 behind Levi Cottages. The 198th Brigade began arriving a little earlier, the 2/9th Manchester being in position by 3:20 a.m. and the 2/4th East Lancs by 5:10. The more men that crossed the tracks the worse the ground conditions became, and the 2/5th East Lancs and 2/10th Manchester, despite all efforts were not finally up until 7:00 a.m. The troops were arriving at the tapes in an already exhausted state, soaked through, with uniforms and equipment coated in the clinging Flanders mud. With some battalions not in position by Zero Hour the attack was inevitably going to lack cohesion. Upon arrival at the tapes the ground from which the 198th Brigade were about to attack, especially on the left near the Ravebeek, was found to be nearly as bad as it had been in the Zonnebeke valley.

    The situation for the 49th Division, the left division of II Anzac was little better, but this was a seasoned force having been in France since April 1915. On the morning of the 8th the Yorkshire and Lancashire battalions of the 148th and 146th Brigades had moved up by bus from Vlamertinghe to resting positions about St Jean, La Brique and Potijze, where ammunition and other stores were drawn, and between 4:30 and 5:00 p.m. began the march up via Tracks 5 and 6 towards the low ridges and the front line. Most battalions were in position on their tapes by between 3:00 and 3:30, but all were in a state of exhaustion before battle commenced. Lieutenant -Colonel Tetley of the 1/7th West Yorkshire Regiment of 146th Brigade commented: 'The night was very dark and rain commenced to fall shortly before 5:00 p.m. and continued during the night, making the march up to Calgary Grange very difficult, many parts of the tracks being almost impossible to follow. Shortly after leaving the St. Julien road it was found that all the trench grids [duckboards] had been removed for a considerable distance.' [554] **The 1/8th West**

---

[553] AOA p887
[554] National Archives, War Diary 1/7th Battalion West Yorkshire Regiment WO/95/2795

Yorks reported: 'Owing to the darkness, gaps in the grids and halts, the rear company only arrived in assembly position for the attack west of Passchendaele five minutes before Zero. In spite of almost unimaginable difficulties of weather conditions and ground the battalion advanced under the barrage towards its objectives.' [555]

Since the 4th October the weather had gradually deteriorated, except for a brief spell on the 8th when until around 4:00 p.m. there had been a strong drying wind. Then the rain had once more come down in torrents which lasted until midnight. It was not a promising start. For the first time, a major attack to be made by Plumer's Second Army looked to have little chance of success from the outset.

Arrangement of German divisions engaged south to north

Front Line divisions:

233rd Division, opposite I Anzac;

195th Division (233rd R.I.R, 8th Jäger regiment, and 6th Jäger Regiment), and *16th Division (29th I.R.28th I.R. and 68th I.R.)* opposite II Anzac and XVIII Corps;

227th Division and elements of *6th Bavarian Division (477th I.R, 441st I.R, 6th Bavarian I.R. and 417th I.R.)* opposite XIV Corps.

Counter-attack divisions:

220th Division, 20th Division and *45th Reserve Division* opposite I and II Anzac;

18th Division opposite XVIII and XIV Corps.

The attack of the Second Army 5:20 a.m. the 9th October

X Corps

The Southern Flank

On the southern flank, the X Corps was to pin down German reserves by threatening Gheluvelt and Becelaere, and in so doing was again to attempt to push the enemy off the few positions they retained on the south-eastern corner of the Gheluvelt plateau. Polderhoek Chateau at the eastern tip of the spur was to be attacked by the 5th Division with their left on the Reutelbeek, while 1,250 yards north 7th Division was to attempt to retake Reutel and push a little further east along the In de Ster spur. The ground had been bad enough when both divisions had attacked on the 4th October, but now it was infinitely worse. The artillery extended the barrage to cover the X Corps attacks, but did not bombard Gheluvelt.

5th Division

15th [556] and 95th Brigades
For the attack to be made by 5th Division the preparatory barrage was described as scanty, probably due to the close proximity of the lines, and Polderhoek Chateau had received nothing

---

[555] National Archives, War Diary 1/8th Battalion West Yorkshire Regiment WO/95/2795
[556] National Archives, War Diary 15th Brigade WO95/1568

like the pounding necessary to subdue its bunkers. In a forlorn effort, across indescribable ground, the 1st Norfolk and 16th Warwick lost what barrage there was and failed in their attempt to capture Polderhoek Chateau.[557] Movement across the shell-pitted bog was near impossible, rifles and Lewis guns quickly becoming choked with mud and useless. Unaffected by the weak barrage, the Germans were soon in action, and heavy machine gun fire from the pillboxes in the park, in the chateau ruins, and from Gheluvelt in enfilade, soon brought the floundering attack to a standstill. Nothing was gained. The enemy remained in possession of their strong-point on the spur, and the British line fell back to virtually where it had started. The 1st East Surrey Regiment of 95th Brigade was to establish a line of posts for 500 yards between the Reutelbeek and Polygonbeek, to link 15th Brigade with 7th Division,[558] but due to the lack of progress on the spur the attempt did not take place. Thankfully the 12th Gloucester in support was not sent into action.

7th Division [559]

20th, 91st and 22nd Brigades [560]
On the night of the 6th - 7th October the 9th Devonshire Regiment of 20th Brigade had relieved 91st Brigade and had moved their right flank a little further south, taking over some of the front held by 21st Division. The line established on the 4th October by 91st Brigade had not been counter-attacked, but it had been constantly and accurately shelled, the brigade sustaining more casualties on the 5th and the 6th than it had in the attack. On the night of the 7th / 8th the 22nd Brigade came up, the 1st Royal Welsh Fusiliers relieving the 6th Leicester of 21st Division opposite Reutel, while the 7th Leicester (21st Division) on the right remained in the line and came under orders of 7th Division. The 20th Manchester Regiment entered the line to the left of the Welsh, with the 2/1st Honourable Artillery Company and 2nd Royal Warwickshire Regiment, (which were to carry out the attack on the 9th), in reserve. On the morning of the 9th the assembly on the tapes was hampered by the awful conditions, but before Zero Hour the H.A.C. and Warwick were in position. Their objective, the Blue Line, was the same as it had been on the 4th, with the intention of retaking Reutel.

At 5:20 a.m. the H.A.C. followed behind the barrage towards the hamlet of Reutel, and soon came up against stiff opposition, machine gun fire causing many casualties. The enemy were driven from the rubble, many being shot down as they ran, and the advance continued 500 yards east of the hamlet to the cemetery, part of which was secured. At Juniper Cottage 250 yards south of the hamlet, machine gun fire checked further advance, and casualties especially amongst officers began to mount. Attacking north of the cemetery the Warwick came under heavy machine gun fire from Judge Copse and a gap opened between the two battalions. A platoon of the reserve company of the Warwick attempted unsuccessfully to capture the copse. A company of the 9th Devon from brigade reserve was then sent forward, but only succeeded in making contact with the right of the Warwick. For the time being the copse remained in enemy hands. By 5:50 a.m. green lights along the objective gave indication that it had been taken. At dusk a second company of the 9th Devon had moved up, and attacking Judge Copse from the south-east finally secured the position and the whole of the Blue Line.

Lacking in the necessary weight of artillery support to subdue the enemy defences, the 5th Division attack had come to a predictable halt in the mud and shell-holes of Polderhoek spur. 7th Division in a costly encounter, in which the H.A.C. alone had lost 16 officers, had secured its objective, gaining Reutel which provided an excellent observation point down the Reutelbeek valley to the south-east. Since the 1st October, 20th Brigade had lost 56 officers and 1,039 men, 91st Brigade 45 officers and 1,028 men, and 22nd Brigade 57 officers and 1,256 men, a total loss to the division of 3,481, of which 51 officers and 1,032 men were either killed or missing.

---

[557] National Archives, War Diary 1st Norfolk and 16th Warwick WO/954217
[558] National Archives, War Diary 1st East Surrey WO95/1579
[559] C.T. Atkinson *The Seventh Division 1914-1918* London: John Murray pp419-422
[560] National Archives, War Diary 22nd Brigade WO95/1661

I Anzac Corps
The protective right flank to the main attack

Both the 1st and 2nd Australian Divisions were to be in action on the 9th October. In order to cause the Germans to spread their artillery fire, and prevent at least for a short time its concentration on the main attack, the 1st Australian Division was to again carry out a diversionary attack against Celtic Wood which was known to be heavily defended by a number of pillboxes. On the night of the 6th October, two officers and 60 other ranks of the 11th and 12th Battalions of the 3rd Brigade had raided the western edge of the wood, 1,000 yards south of the Broodseinde – Moorslede road, and 25 prisoners of the *448th I.R.* of the *233rd Division* had been taken. Birdwood was fully aware that I Anzac was nearing exhaustion, but as it only had a subsidiary role to play along side II Anzac, and Godley was all for going ahead, he had not felt able to protest. It was little wonder that Birdwood had been opposed to exploitation. To support the right flank of II Anzac, the 2nd Division was to attack south of the Staden railway, with two brigades. The right brigade, the 6th, was to make a shallow advance of only a few hundred yards, whilst the left brigade, the 5th, would attack north-eastwards towards the Keiberg.

Desperate efforts had been made by I Anzac to improve by all means available the access towards the front for both men and guns, but with little success. The 1st and 2nd Pioneer Battalions had worked non stop on 'Smith's Road', with the assistance of the six infantry battalions sent by Plumer, and the 5th Pioneers had worked on the tramways. Infantry fatigue parties working under engineers had attempted to improve the duckboard tracks and bury telephone cables. When the 6th Brigade came out of the line on the 6th, after only a few hours sleep in shell-holes in the rain, they were immediately put back to work for six hours cable laying, 7th Brigade being detailed for a similar task. At dusk they returned to their water-filled shell-holes to rest and next day returned to the same work of track repair and cable laying. Inevitably exhaustion and sickness quickly overcame both brigades. By the 9th October, 6th Brigade were reduced to 600 men, and 7th Brigade to 800 hundred.

On the morning of the 9th, the 24th and 21st Battalions of 6th Brigade, to carry out the attack against the woods, moved up into the line either side of Broodseinde. They were so weak in numbers that the 23rd Battalion in support was sent up with a strength of 8 officers and 220 men to stiffen the attack to the left of the 21st. The 17th and 20th Battalions of 5th Brigade, to attack between Nieuwemolen and the railway, had not been engaged on the 4th October, but also went into the line with company strengths down to around 50 to 60 men.

1st Australian Division

The attack at 5:20 a.m. was made against Celtic Wood, by a party of 85 officers and men. A barrage 800 yards wide fired by five batteries of field artillery was to cover the attack, but due to the problems moving the guns forward the fire was so weak and ragged that the infantry was unsure when it opened. Some ground was gained into the north-western end of the copse. The *448th I.R.* initially retreated, but then counter-attacked from the eastern end. Of the 85 who attacked only 14 returned. The remainder were never found subsequently, or reported as prisoners of war.

2nd Australian Division

6th [561] and 5th [562] Australian Brigades

---

[561] National Archives, War Diary 6th Aus Brigade WO95/3323, War Diary 21st Battalion WO95/3326, National Archives, War Diary 22nd Battalion WO95/3330, National Archives, War Diary 23rd Battalion WO95/3332, National Archives, War Diary 24th Battalion WO95/3334

The 6th Brigade was to use four weak battalions in the line along a 1,200 yards front. The 22nd Battalion was to attack south of the Moorslede road towards the old German battalion headquarters in the sandpit on the road. The 24th Battalion was advance about 500 yards through the scrub of Daisy Wood to the edge of Busy Wood, while the 21st Battalion moved forward about 650 yards to Knoll 38. 23rd Battalion on the left would have the deepest advance of around 800 yards towards the fortified farm ruin at Rhine. To the left of the 6th, the 5th Brigade was to form up on its tapes just south of Defy Crossing, its final objective being along a line through Rhine, Assyria, and a point 900 yards along the railway from Defy Crossing. The 20th Battalion was to lead the advance with the 17th in close support.

As the 22nd Battalion moved forward, German machine guns immediately cut into the forward ranks, so thin was the protective barrage. The survivors worked forward under constant fire and reached the sandpit by the Moorslede road. Here they dug-in close up to the enemy posts, still exchanging fire but sustaining many casualties. The 24th Battalion had 200 yards to cross to reach Daisy Wood, but half way across they came under heavy rifle fire from the copse, the defenders being little hampered by the weak barrage. Fire in enfilade from hedges near the sandpit checked the advance. German positions in the undergrowth were difficult to identify in the gloom, only recognisable by the muzzle flashes, and a bombing attack towards the hedges was unsuccessful. A dozen men then established a post at the southern corner of the wood. The left company of the 24th were just reaching the edge of the copse when machine gun fire opened upon them from the direction of Dairy Wood 150 yards to the north which almost wiped them out. The centre had managed to enter the western edge of the undergrowth, and now swung left to face this fire. The gun position was at first difficult to identify, but it was eventually found to be coming from a strong-point in a rubble pile between the two woods. The gun was engaged with rifle fire, which for a time subdued its crew. The 21st Battalion working forward between the woods came under heavy fire, many of its number being shot down before reaching the undergrowth. A few managed to pass through and establish posts 400 yards beyond the eastern edge at Rhine. To the left of the 21st, the 23rd Battalion had veered too far towards the north, and skirting the face of Dairy Wood had passed behind the supporting battalion of 5th Brigade. Machine guns in Dairy Wood opened fire on the flanks of the 23rd and into the rear of the 17th Battalion. The 23rd worked forward and established a line of posts to protect this right flank as far forward as Rhine. The German artillery, on the assumption that their forward line near the woods had fallen, had quickly started to shell both their own posts and the Australian, the infantry of both sides sending desperate messages to contact aircraft to try to indicate their position. The situation of 6th Brigade was unsatisfactory and confused. Some posts had been established forward on the objective, while others were well behind it. Enemy machine guns, which had not been attacked and cleared by the sparse number of infantry, were interspersed between them, holding some up and firing into flanks and rear of others. The 28th Battalion (7th Brigade) had already been sent up to stiffen the pitifully thin ranks, but a good many men of every battalion had already been driven back to the British front line. The 27th (7th Brigade) Battalion was also ordered up to the line in front of Daisy Wood, but finding it already crowded with retiring troops, could do little but stay there and suffer the shelling. Dairy Wood and half of Daisy Wood were still in enemy hands and continued to threaten the right of 5th Brigade. To address this situation two companies of the reserve 19th Battalion of 5th Brigade, were sent up to clear Dairy Wood, which they partly succeeded in doing, capturing a machine gun post just south of it. The Germans continued to fire on 5th Brigade from a trench in Daisy Wood, until this also fell to an attack by the 19th with the assistance of the 24th. Daisy Wood was then secured within the outpost line, and at this point 6th Brigade had captured most of its objectives.

Although the 5:20 barrage was obvious to 5th Brigade by its noise, the thin curtain of 18-pounder shells were less easy to discern. As the 20th Battalion moved off, followed by the 17th,

---

[562] National Archives, War Diary 5th Aus Brigade WO95/3308, War Diary 17th Aus Battalion WO95/3314, War Diary 19th Aus Battalion WO95/3318, War Diary 20th Aus Battalion WO95/3319, War Diary 28th Aus Battalion WO95/3343, War Diary 27th Aus Battalion WO95/3342

the barrage either did not lift or began to fall short and fell amongst them. Worryingly there was no sign of any advance north of the railway in the 66th British Division sector. Enemy fire from in front was slight, but a machine gun opened damaging enfilade fire from north of the railway, just beyond Defy Crossing near the first objective of 66th Division. Another German sandbagged post in a cement dump near the crossing fired into the left rear of the 20th until a party worked behind and knocked it out, taking 40 prisoners. An enemy post further forward held up the 20th with machine gun fire, and was attacked with a rifle grenade. The only grenade available went wide. But the post was rushed and bombed, at which point a large number of Germans and several machine guns were captured. By the time the first objective, 400 yards beyond the Nieuwemolen crossroads was reached, the 17th Battalion had caught up with the 20th. The two battalions now paused in the muddy depression between the main ridge and the Keiberg whilst the barrage played along the western face of the spur, about Assyria 800 yards forward. In places the shells were striking pillboxes but due to the wet ground and reduced fire the usual dust cloud and smoke was not created, giving the enemy a clear view of the Australian assembly. During the halt, a machine gun fired continually from Decline Copse 500 yards along the railway, while another gun firing at closer range from Decoy Copse was quickly knocked out by a section of the 20th.

The British guns lifted towards the second objective, but the thickening of the barrage was not easy to detect. As the Australians advanced towards Decoy Copse and the hedges along the slopes of the Keiberg, many Germans fled, helped on their way by Lewis gun fire. The 23rd Battalion having veered north of Dairy Wood, had not got forward as quickly as the advanced parties of 5th Brigade, and the right of the 20th now swung slightly right and took the ruins of Rhine farmhouse, in 6th Brigade's sector. On the right of 17th battalion a party of two officers and 30 men pushed on up the slope of the Keiberg towards the ruined barn at Assyria, clearing enemy posts from the hedges, capturing 17 men and 3 machine guns, and gradually establishing a right flank as they moved forward. This flank was checked by severe machine gun fire from hedges around Assyria, but several enemy posts were cleared between there and the railway cutting.

The German dug-outs along the railway cutting near Decline Copse were the scene of the heaviest fighting. As a party of the 17th bombed out the bunkers along the northern face of the cutting others of the 17th and 20th advanced along the top, either side of the track. Most of the enemy fled along the cutting to the east, many being shot down by a Vickers gun, carried up and mounted on top of the northern bank.

The 5th Brigade was now mostly upon its objectives but was hopelessly few in number, and with the 66th Division apparently not up on the left was dangerously exposed in a local salient. Australian and German posts were in close proximity, and the enemy, some of whom were still behind the Australians began to fight back, sweeping away the Vickers gun post on top of the cutting with their own machine gun fire. Greater numbers of the enemy, fighting at close quarters, gradually drove back the hard pressed Australians. Right across the 5th Brigade front the line began to fall back, from Assyria, the slopes of the Keiberg and the railway cutting. The retirement continued to the line of the first objective, but here it stopped and the line held firm. At 9:15 a.m. the 66th Division was seen to be advancing along Passchendaele ridge and the 18th Battalion, and remaining two companies of 19th Battalion were sent up. By this time the final objective had been lost, and the 18th and 19th merely helped stiffen the left flank along the railway.

The results of the morning's fighting had been much as Birdwood had predicted. Too few troops, many already exhausted, and with too little artillery support had resulted in the least efficient and least satisfactory operation carried out by Australian forces in the campaign so far. By evening the situation was to get even worse.

II Anzac Corps
The attack on Passchendaele

66th (2nd East Lancashire) Division
Major-General Hon. H. A. Lawrence

49th (1st West Riding) Division
Major-General E. M. Perceval

If all went to plan, before the morning was over the attack of 66th Division, advancing to the left of the 2nd Australian Division, would carry it to the south-western edge of the village of Passchendaele, 700 yards short of the church, and in the afternoon the perimeter would be beyond the village. But for the first time since the 20th September nothing appeared to be going to plan. The division was to attack with two brigades on a front of approximately 1,200 yards with its right on the railway and on top of the ridge, and its left on the Ravebeek stream. The valley of the stream had been described in a Second Army intelligence summary on the 7th October as, 'saturated ground. Quite impassable. Should be avoided by all troops at all times'.[563] In a typically measured tone the War diary of the 198th Brigade describes, 'the ground over which the brigade was to attack, was on the lower S.W. slopes of the Passchendaele ridge and extended down to the Ravebeek. The whole of the brigade front was very marshy, and all the shell holes, however recent, were half full of water. The going was very bad and exceptionally so on the left. A certain number of old German trenches, which had been shelled almost out of recognition, still remained in the shape of wide ditches full of water.[564] The first objective, the Red Line, was to be around 650 yards forward, and the final objective, the Blue Line 600 to 800 yards beyond. On the 4th October, the 3rd Australian Division had broken through the Flanders I Line here, so the worst of the wire entanglements and forward trenches were already cleared. The two brigades had very different ground to cover. On the right the 197th Brigade was to advance across the marginally drier ground on the top of the ridge, while, as the battlefront dipped towards the Ravebeek, 198th Brigade's left would be in the quagmire of the valley. On the other side of the valley, to the north-west, the Bellevue – Goudberg spur rose to around 50 metres. Along the top of the spur were situated a number of blockhouses, which covered the Ravebeek valley, and the slopes of the main ridge beyond with their machine guns, over ranges varying between 600 and 1,400 yards. Both the 197th Brigade and the left of the 198th Brigade were totally vulnerable to fire from these guns in enfilade, and there would be no cover on the exposed valley side. The capture of the Bellevue spur by the 49th Division was therefore imperative to the successful attack of the 66th Division.

There was however a problem, which would soon prove to be extremely serious. When the New Zealand Division had advanced over Gravenstafel ridge on the 4th October, it had quite properly stopped on its final objective on the south-west side of the Ravebeek. The 49th Division was now to attack with its 148th and 146th Brigades on a front of around 1,500 yards, from this line, reached on the 4th by the New Zealand Division. The attack of the 49th Division was therefore immediately confronted with crossing the quagmire of the Ravebeek – Stroombeek, a 30 to 50 yard expanse of mud, with water in places waist deep, under the machine guns of the Bellevue blockhouses on the spur. To make an already bad situation infinitely worse, the Flanders I Line, continuing on its northwards path, ran directly across the nose of the Bellevue spur, 600 yards beyond the Ravebeek. An extensive system of wire entanglements, 20 to 40 yards deep, guarded the nose of the spur giving excellent protection to the Bellevue blockhouses, fire trenches, and numerous organised shell-holes. The unenviable task of 49th Division was therefore, to cross the Ravebeek mire, pass through the wire entanglements, and then tackle the blockhouses and strong-points which would meanwhile be raining machine gun

---

[563] AOA p885
[564] National Archives, War Diary 198th Brigade WO/95/3138

fire down upon them. With sufficient artillery preparation before the battle the wire could have undoubtedly been thoroughly broken. But with the guns 5,000 yards back behind the Steenbeek, on their soft, flimsy platforms, there had not been sufficient preparation. An effective creeping barrage may have saved the day, shielding the advance of the 49th from view, and suppressing the machine guns long enough to allow the bombing parties to cut through the wire entanglements and close with the bunkers. Undoubtedly had the guns been further forward where they were intended to be, this would have been the case. But they were not, and if the 49th Division could not clear the bunkers on Bellevue, the 66th Division had precious little hope of taking the ridge up towards Passchendaele. The position and strength of the wire should not have come as a surprise. It was clearly shown on the September dated maps, and it could be plainly seen from Gravenstafel ridge. However there was little if any warning of the existence of extensive wire given in the intelligence summaries of II Anzac Corps. A report dated the 5th October titled 'Notes of examination of aeroplane photographs taken on II Anzac Corps front' describes an air photograph of the area. 'S.W. of Bellevue. Shows trench between Bellevue & Lamkeek [Dad Trench] with remains if wire in front of blockhouse at D.10.b.55.80, other trenches in area very weak & shallow.' [565] There is no mention of a heavy wire belt, but the erection of extra wire had been ordered by the enemy. A captured extract from the pocket book of the Adjutant of the *II Battalion, 29th Infantry Regiment* of the *16th Division* holding the line between Bellevue and Wallemolen was later found to reveal: 'In Regimental sector the *I and II Battalions* will each have two companies in the outpost line and two companies behind on the road Bray Farm – Wallemolen. Each company to have two platoons in front and one behind. Posts are to occupy foremost craters. Close behind these, wire entanglement will be erected and 20-30 paces behind the wire is the 1st line which will be held at all costs. Wire is also to be erected behind the other line.' [566] The lack of accurate intelligence regarding the new enemy wire was to cost the British dearly.

Map next page

---

[565] Australian War Memorial, Intelligence report, Headquarters II Anzac Corps. AWM4-1/33/18
[566] Australian War Memorial, Intelligence report, Headquarters II Anzac Corps. AWM4-1/33/18

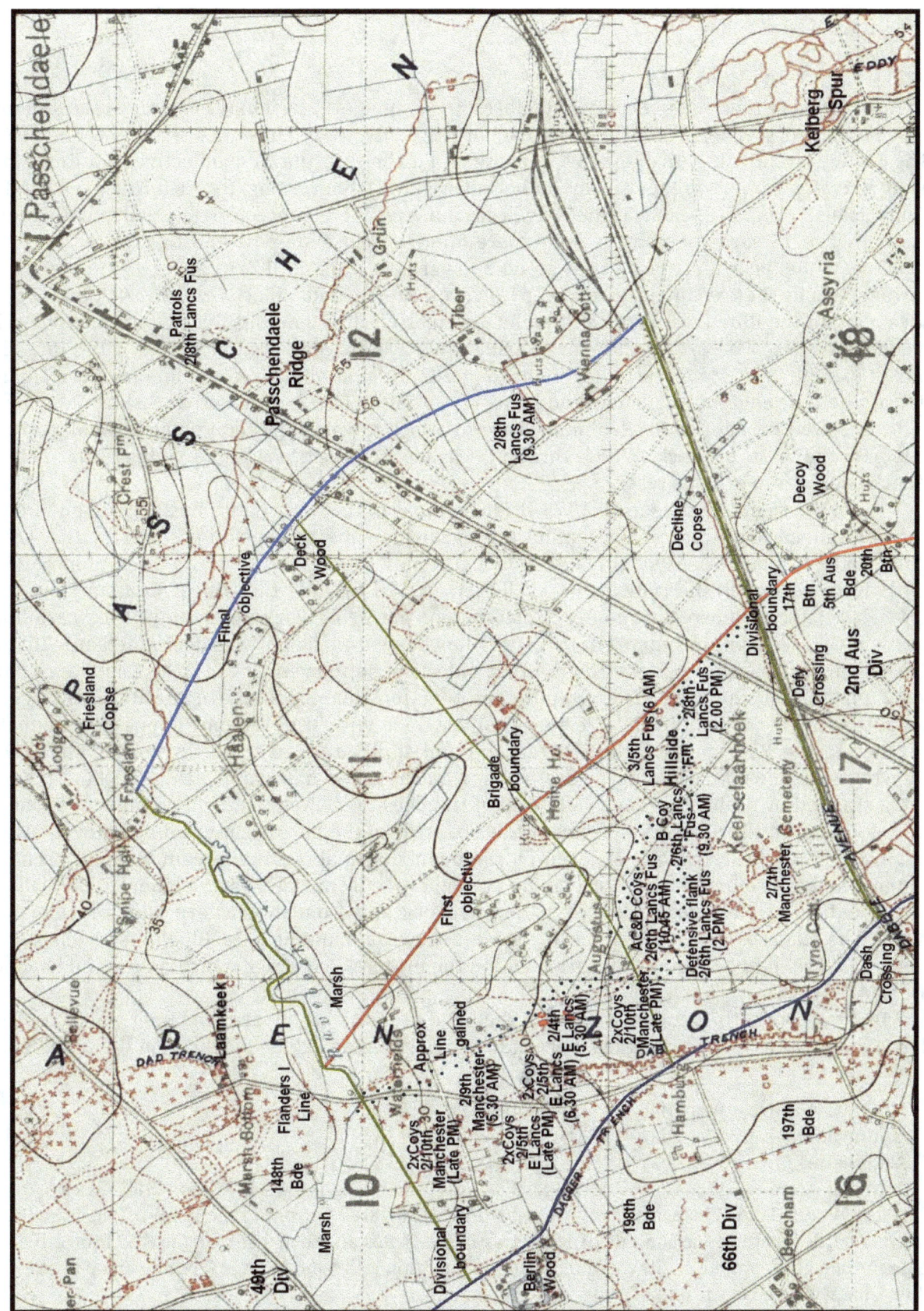

The attack of the 197th and 198th Brigades - 66th Division towards Passchendaele

66th Division [567]

197th [568] and 198th [569] Brigades

Having landed at Havre in February and March 1917, the 66th Division was about to see serious action for the first time, and the weather had already conspired to upset its first show. The 197th Brigade was to attack with the 3/5th Lancashire Fusiliers to the first objective, the Red Line being between a point on the railway 200 yards east of Defy Crossing, through Hillside Farm to Heine House. The 2/8th Lancashire Fusiliers and the 2/6th Lancashire Fusiliers, with their leading wave 15 yards behind the 3/5th were follow in close support and to wait on the first objective while the protective barrage stood 200 yards in front until Zero plus 106 minutes. The barrage would then commence to creep towards the second objective, the 2/8th and 2/6th advancing to the Blue Line, between Vienna Cottages on the right and the eastern end of Deck Wood on the left. The 2/7th Lancashire Fusiliers were in brigade reserve.[570] The 198th Brigade was to use the 2/9th Manchester Regiment to attack the first objective on a line between Heine House, the east edge of Augustus Wood and Waterfields. The 2/4th East Lancashire Regiment and the 2/5th East Lancashire Regiment were to attack towards the final objective along a line between the east of Deck Wood through Haalen Copse to Friesland, whilst the 2/10th Manchester was in brigade reserve.[571]

On the right at 5:20 a.m. in 197th Brigade, those of the 3/5th Lancs Fusiliers who were in position moved forward across dreadful ground behind the barrage, supported by the 2/7th Manchester Regiment of 199th Brigade, which was only to advance as far as the cemetery 250 yards forward beside the railway.[572] To the left in 198 Brigade the Officer Commanding the 2/4th East Lancs upon realising only 2 platoons of the 2/5th were up, deployed his battalion across the whole front in support of the 2/9th Manchester. As the barrage descended at 5:20 the 2/9th Manchester advanced towards the first objective, supported by the 2/4th East Lancs and the 2 platoons of the 2/5th. The ground conditions on the slopes above the Ravebeek were appalling. On the right the 3/5th Lancs Fusiliers met with little enemy opposition in their advance to the Red Line, which they reached and secured up to time. On the left the 2/9th Manchester followed closely up to the barrage and reached half way to the Red Line before being stopped by difficult ground. Old German trenches presented water-filled obstacles which were found difficult to cross, and even at the slow rate of the barrage, it gradually moved away leaving the Manchester totally exposed on the open slopes above the stream. Enemy machine gun and sniper fire became severe, coming at long range from Crest Farm higher up the valley, and in enfilade from Laamkeek across the Ravebeek and from the eastern edge of Augustus Wood. The Manchester took what muddy shelter they could amongst the blown in trenches and water-filled shell-holes, some 300 yards behind the protective barrage which now stood beyond the Red Line.

At 7:05 the barrage thickened with smoke shell and began to lift towards the final objective. The delayed battalions of 197th Brigade were at last arriving in an exhausted state on the battlefield,

---

[567] National Archives, War Diary 66th Division WO95/3120

[568] National Archives, War Diary 197th Brigade WO/95/3135

[569] National Archives, War Diary 198th Brigade WO/95/3138

[570] National Archives, War Diary 3/5th Lancs Fusiliers WO95/3137, 2/6th, 2/7th, and 2/8th Lancs Fusiliers WO95/3136. The barrage was to come down 150 yards in front of the jump-off tapes and creep towards the Red Line at a rate of 100 yards in 6 minutes and then stand on the Red Protective Line for one hour. Smoke shell would indicate the intention to lift the barrage, and the creep to the Blue Line would be at the rate of 100 yards in 8 minutes.

[571] National Archives, War Diary 2/9th and 2/10th Manchester, 2/4th and 2/5th East Lancs, all in WO95/3141

[572] The account of the 198th Brigade of 66th Division describes the barrage as dense and accurate. This is possibly because they had no previous experience for comparison. It can be assumed from the accounts of the Australians to the right and the 49th Division to the left that the barrage was in fact rather thin.

and as the 3/5th Lancs Fusiliers consolidated on the Red Line, the 2/8th passed through and took up the attack towards the Blue Line. By 7:30 the 2/6th had also arrived and passed the old front line, but as they moved forward could see no sign of the other battalions of 197th Brigade. They could however see the 2/4th East Lancs to their left and "A", "C", and "D" Companies of the 2/6th moved in that direction gaining touch with the East Lancs right flank. It was clear that a gap existed to the right where there appeared no sign of the 3/5th or 2/8th. Initially only the 2/6th "B" Company shifted to the right, eventually making touch with the 3/5th at around 9:30 a.m. Having subsequently also moved further to the right "A", "C" and "D" Companies of the 2/6th formed up just in rear of the Red Line at about 10:45, along a line running from Hillside Farm to the south of Augustus Wood. The 2/8th meanwhile had continued its advance towards the final objective which it had reached by 9:30 a.m. So far enemy resistance had been weak and around 250 prisoners had been sent back to the British lines.

On the left the 198th Brigade was still dreadfully exposed and pinned down by severe machine gun and sniper fire, now coming mainly from Bellevue spur across the Ravebeek, and from Crest Farm further up the valley. Any attempt to advance to the Blue Line was impossible, as other German machine guns had come into action after the barrage had passed over them. Although small groups of the 2/4th and 2/5th East Lancs had attempted to push forward, the majority had been driven to ground, as the bullets zipped overhead and smacked into the mud rims of the filthy trenches and water-filled craters in which they sprawled.

There was now a widening gap between 197th and 198th Brigades but nevertheless the 2/8th Lancs Fusiliers, with their left and right flanks exposed, were on the Blue Line, and at 9:40 had driven off a counter-attack with rifle fire.[573] By 10:10 a defence line had been established in shell-holes on the final objective between Vienna Cottages and the northern end of Deck Wood, and patrols pushed forward to the edge of Passchendaele village. On two occasions during the morning the enemy launched local counter-attacks against this line, which were successfully driven off. But it quickly became clear that due to the check of 198th Brigade this line was hopelessly exposed with no support on the left flank, and possibly due to officer casualties, at around 1:35 p.m. the 2/8th fell-back 750 yards under heavy hostile shell-fire to the Red Line. At 2:00 p.m. the 2/6th was also ordered to protect its left by throwing back a defensive flank from Hillside Farm to 20 yards in rear of the enemy bunkers at Augustus Wood which were unoccupied. By 4:00 p.m. contact between the 197th and 198th Brigades had been lost. 197th Brigade issued orders that patrols were to be sent out to attempt to gain touch, and 198th Brigade ordered 2 companies to move up to try and fill the gap. The line now held by the division ran from a point on the railway, 200 yards east of Defy Crossing to Hillside Farm, then to the south of Augustus Wood and to Waterfields. The 2/8th Lancs Fusiliers, having fallen-back from the Blue Line made desperate efforts to establish a defendable position on the Red Line north of the railway, while to their left 2/6th held Hillside Farm and were establishing a defensive left flank.

At 3:00 p.m. orders had been issued for a renewed attack to retake the Blue Line to commence at 5:15, behind a 29 minute barrage. Arrangements were made for the attack, but at around 5:10 the German artillery opened a heavy bombardment along the British positions, which fortunately fell mostly behind the new outpost line. German infantry were seen advancing along the whole divisional front, and the S.O.S. signal was fired from the thinly held British positions. On seeing the S.O.S. signals the Commanding Officer of the 2/9th Manchester gathered about 100 men from several different units, and rushed them forward to stiffen the 198th Brigade line. The British artillery responded quickly, coming down on the Blue Protective Line and disrupting the enemy advance. Those that were already forward of the Blue Line were checked by Lewis gun and rifle fire and were unable to approach the defence line.

On the far left of the divisional line on the slope above the Ravebeek, the casualties in the 2/9th Manchester and the two forward companies of the 2/5th East Lancs were increasing alarmingly, exposed as they were in their muddy scrapes to the vicious enfilade fire from the

---

[573] The 5th Australian Brigade on the right had by 9:00 already fallen-back from its exposed position at the railway cutting.

Bellevue bunkers, which 49th Division had been unable to reach. Being continuously shelled, mostly from the south-east in enfilade, and threatened by counter-attack, the position was most precarious, and the 2 support companies of the 2/5th East Lancs and 2 of the 2/10th Manchester were moved up into a support line in shell-holes between the southern edge of Augustus Wood and the road bridge over the Ravebeek at Marsh Bottom. Four Vickers machine guns from 198th Brigade Reserve were sent up to cover the position. To further strengthen the line the 2/8th Manchester and a small detachment of the 2/5th Manchester, both from 199th Brigade in Divisional Reserve were moved up to establish a second defensive line in a series of extended posts in the old British front line. By this time touch had been gained with the 49th Division on the left, but so fire swept and chaotic was the battlefield along the slopes of the Ravebeek, no contact had been possible with 198th Brigade on the right. The garrisons of the forward positions in their water-filled shell-holes, held by the 2/9th Manchester and the two forward companies of the 2/5th East Lancs were mostly either killed or wounded, and the front line eventually consolidated on the support position held by the 2/10th Manchester and 2 support companies of the 2/5th East Lancs. The 2 remaining companies of the 2/10th Manchester also moved forward to try to fill the gap between 198th and 197th Brigades.

The line remained in this position at midnight, while to the right the front line of 197th Brigade had been drawn back to Defy Crossing, then west of Hillside Farm, to west of Augustus Wood. The untried division had acquitted itself admirably in its first action under the most trying and appalling conditions. Battalions coming into action as and when they managed to reach the tapes, after an horrendous march up, had inevitably meant a very bad start. Cut down by the machine guns of the un-assailed blockhouses on Bellevue, and continually subjected to heavy shell-fire, it had achieved all that could be expected of even a seasoned division. The position handed over by the 66th Division to the 3rd Australian Division on the night of the 10th / 11th October remained the same as it was on the night of the 9th, roughly midway between the old British front line and the first objective on the Red Line. So terrible were the conditions that even by the time of relief, touch had not been gained between 197th and 198th Brigades. Evacuation of the wounded from the battlefield was considered the overwhelming difficulty of the whole operation. To assist the stretcher bearers any spare men, stragglers and enemy prisoners were all put to the task of carrying those wounded that could be reached off the field. For those that could not be reached, lying out in the cold and rain amongst the obscene sloughs of mud, death would be a blessing. Some were found still just alive when the Australians attacked again on the 12th.

Casualties in 197th Brigade had been 1,295 and in 198th Brigade 1,250. In 197th Brigade which had advanced to the Blue Line, and subsequently fallen-back to the Red Line, 408 men were reported missing.[574]

---

[574] In Denis Winter's account of the action, due to the late arrival of the 66th in the line, the barrage was brought back and proceeded to 'open fire on their own men and cut the 66th to pieces'. Winter goes on to say that Birdwood 'brought this tragedy to G.H.Q's attention, but the divisional commander involved countered by demanding the name of Birdwood's informant (he was in fact one of the Tasmanian Maxwells, a family distingushied by a vast array of military decorations won in the field) and threatened to block all promotions within the Australian Corps unless he withdrew the witness'. He then goes on to claim that the 'episode with its mixture of chance and gross ineptitude, would have been lost to us but for the eye witness of [the Australian Official Historian] Charles Bean'. *Haig's Command* pp106-107. Bean's actual account has nothing to do with a short barrage cutting the 66th Division to pieces, but is in reference to the (as we have seen) chaotic movement of the 199th Brigade towards the front line, 4 days before the battle. Bean says: 'The relief in which its 199th Brigade took over the 3rd Australian Divisions line on the night of October 5th was marked by an almost incredible degree of mismanagement.' In a footnote to this passage Bean then goes on to say: 'Birdwood was so shocked by the particulars which reached his ears that he conceived that the [II Anzac] Corps and [66th] Divisional Commanders should be frankly informed of them. The sole effect of this representation, however, was to imperil the career of a splendid officer of the division (a brother of the Maxwell's of Mouquet Farm and of Messines) who indirectly and unwittingly had been

49th Division [575]

148th [576] and 146th Brigades [577]

The last few thousand yards of the march up from Ypres, across the Hanebeek, up over Abraham heights, and past the Gravenstafel crossroads, were over appalling ground. The battalions had begun to arrive, muddy, soaked, and exhausted by around 2:30 a.m. and by 3:30 most were on their taped out lines, attempting to rest in water filled shell-holes, in the valley of the Ravebeek.

The 148th Brigade, on the right of the divisional line, was to attack with the 1/4th York and Lancaster Regiment on the right to both the first and final objectives, and on the left the 1/5th York and Lancs to the first objective, with the 1/5th King's Own Yorkshire Light Infantry to pass through to the final objective. The 1/4th K.O.Y.L.I. was in brigade reserve.

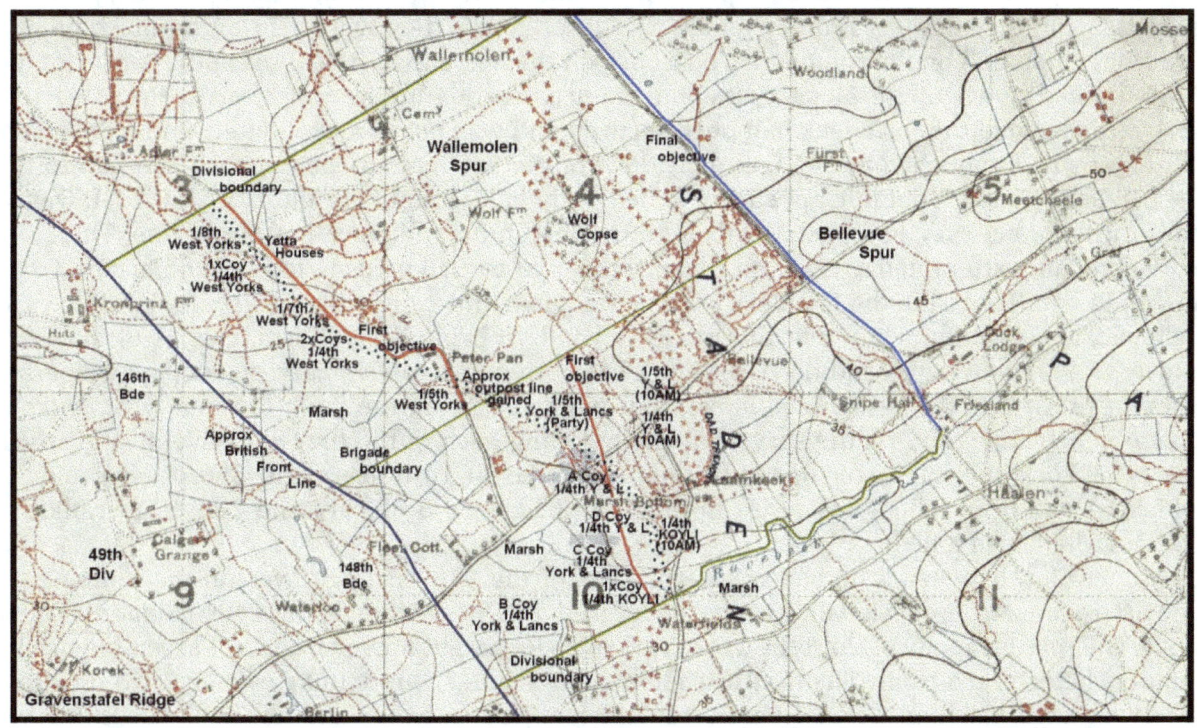

The attack of the 148th and 146th Brigades against the Flanders I Line at Bellevue

At Zero Hour the 1/4th and 1/5th York and Lancs,[578] from their jumping-off line just forward of the Waterloo blockhouses, followed the thin barrage for a short distance up to the Ravebeek. The water was in places waist deep, the stream bed totally cut up into a mass of shell-holes, with deep mud anything up to 30 yards on either side. Machine gun fire from pillboxes near the Ravebeek was quickly suppressed, one gun at Fleet Cottage being captured and turned on the enemy. But generally the initial resistance was weak, the enemy front posts seemingly lightly held.

The right "C" Company of the 1/4th floundered in the mud around the stream, as little as 50 men finally getting across. "B" Company, detailed to attack the second objective and following behind "C", came under severe machine gun fire from the Waterfields and Laamkeek bunkers, and mostly failed to reach the stream. The machine gun fire on the left was less heavy,

---

the channel through which Birdwood received the information.' AOA p886. Readers must therefore judge if they consider Winter's account (which appears to imply that Bean witnessed the 66th Division being hit by their own barrage) to be misleading.

[575] Laurie Magnus *The West Riding Territorials in the Great War* p141
[576] National Archives, War Diary 148th Brigade WO95/2804
[577] National Archives, War Diary 146th Brigade WO95/2793
[578] National Archives, War Diary 1/4th and 1/5th York and Lancs WO95/2805

"A" and "D" Companies crossing the Ravebeek by the bridge on the Gravenstafel road, and deploying on the far bank. "A" Company succeeded in reaching its first objective and dug-in about 300 yards beyond the stream. As the barrage appeared to lift, "D" Company attempted to advance, but was immediately raked by machine gun fire and at once pinned down. Their final objective was 650 yards further forward near Snipe Hall, but they were not destined to get there. Meanwhile on the right, the 50 men of "C" Company that had managed to cross the Ravebeek, had now been reduced to about 10, who had succeeded in establishing posts in shell-holes near the Nieuwemolen road, 100 yards beyond the stream, with a few men of 198th Brigade. A company of the 1/4th K.O.Y.L.I. from brigade reserve was sent up to reinforce the 1/4th York and Lancs, and parties were detailed to help stiffen this weak line of posts.

As the leading waves of the 1/5th struggled through the Ravebeek swamp and began to climb the gentle rise towards the spur, they came under long range heavy artillery fire in enfilade from the south.[579] From a somewhat closer range, they were also hit by machine gun fire from Snipe Hall on the right and Wolf Copse on the left, either side of the spur. Parties of the 1/5th worked slowly up the slope, sustaining many casualties, but by 6:00 a.m. the first objective 650 yards beyond the Ravebeek had been secured and was being consolidated, and a defensive left flank was established by "D" Company. Few of the enemy had been encountered up to the first objective, their front line appearing to be lightly held. From here the 1/5th K.O.Y.L.I. was to pass-through, but they had been delayed on the march up and were not in the line. The 1/5th York and Lancs attempted to take the advance forward by 650 yards to the final objective. To do so would entail crossing the Flanders I wire entanglements, capturing the group of pillboxes at Bellevue, and continuing another 500 yards beyond. At around 10:00 a.m. parties of the 1/5th and 1/4th York and Lancs and the 1/4th K.O.Y.L.I., with no protective barrage, made a desperate attempt to capture the Bellevue pillboxes, but were caught on the fresh German wire, and cut down by machine gun fire, the survivors finally falling-back to the first objective. In the attack the 1/5th York and Lancaster had sustained casualties of 10 officers and 358 other ranks, of which 64 had been killed. Casualties in the 1/4th had been 8 officers and 289 other ranks, of which 45 had been killed.

Earlier, between 3:00 and 3:30 a.m. most of the 146th Brigade was on the jumping-off line across the Stroombeek valley in the same tired and filthy state as the 148th Brigade to their right. The rear company of the 1/8th West Yorkshire Regiment however did not assemble until 5 minutes before Zero Hour. The first brigade objective was around 300 yards forward on a line through Peter Pan and Yetta Houses, the final objective being another 900 yards further forward along the Bellevue – Wallemolen road.

At 5:20 a.m. the 1/5th, 1/7th and 1/8th West Yorks advanced,[580] in spite of what were described as unimaginable difficulties of weather conditions and ground, behind the barrage and across the shell-torn bog towards the Ravebeek – Stroombeek valley. So bad was the ground that the barrage was quickly lost, but in any event the shellfire was so weak and indeterminate that it had little effect on suppressing the intense enemy machine gun and sniper fire. Casualties were severe, but the first objective was reached. The right company of the 1/7th consolidating near Peter Pan, and in touch with the 1/5th on its right, had only two officers uninjured, while the three remaining companies about Yetta Houses had lost all their officers and the majority of senior N.C.O's. Little information was reaching battalion headquarters which was in a shell-hole near Calgary Grange, and the Battalion Commander went forward personally to clarify the situation. The 1/8th West Yorks battalion headquarters was at the old German bunker at Kronprinz Farm. "B" and "C" Companies had been detailed to attack the first objective and "A" and "D" Companies to pass-through to the final. Machine gun and sniper fire had effectively checked the advance at the first objective, and was entirely unaffected by the weak barrage. The 1/8th dug-in just short of the first objective, around 300 yards beyond the jumping-off line. Their Commanding Officer Lieut.-Colonel R. A. Hudson D.S.O. had been killed early in the

---

[579] Probably fired by the Tenbrielen group at a range of 14,000 yards.
[580] National Archives, War Diary 1/5th West Yorks WO95/2794, 1/7th and 1/8th West Yorks WO95/2795

attack, along with eight other officers. Eight more had been wounded and one was missing, and there had been around 300 casualties amongst other ranks. During the morning two companies of the 1/4th West Yorks from brigade reserve were sent up to support the 1/7th, and around 2:00 p.m. one company was sent forward to fill a gap which existed on the left between the 1/7th and 1/8th. At 1:20 p.m. a report from an air observer wrongly informed divisional headquarters that flares had been seen along the final objective, well beyond the Bellevue blockhouses, and orders were sent forward to push on in strength to reinforce this line. The orders failed to reach those intended to carry them out.

From the German viewpoint the Flanders I defences had held firm, and the low grey pillboxes, fortified shell-holes, and trenches behind the wire belts, all seemingly unaffected by the barrage, remained to fight another day. To a great extent they had saved Passchendaele, and that in turn was to have a major influence on the outcome of the whole campaign. The high water mark of the 49th Division attack in front of Bellevue corresponded to the alignment of the wire belts, the posts of the decimated York and Lancs and K.O.Y.L.I. just over the Ravebeek, being no more than 300 yards beyond the start line on the right, while a few parties of the West Yorks were in shell-holes around 300 yards forward on the left. In the attack 49th Division had sustained around 2,500 casualties.

The attack of the Fifth Army 5:20 a.m. the 9th October

Since the 4th October, when the tanks had given excellent support to the infantry in clearing Poelcappelle, the enemy had reoccupied most of their lost positions and bunkers within the ruins. The XVIII Corp plan was to push forward another 1,200 yards from the outpost line on the western fringes and capture the village. The task of clearing the ruins would have to be repeated, without tanks support, with a much weaker barrage, and against the additional machine guns the Germans had brought up into their front line. If the 1,200 yard advance was achieved, the front would be pushed forward beyond the eastern fringe of the village, but would still be 1,700 yards short of the Flanders I Line and 3,000 yards short of Westroosebeke on the northern end of the Passchendaele ridge.

The XVIII Corps thrust through Poelcappelle was to have greater support on its left flank than had been the case on the 4th October, with XIV Corps pushing forward with the Guards Division north of the Broenbeek to a final objective depth of 2,000 yards, only 1,000 yards short of the edge of Houthulst Forest. The line was to be extended to the left, where the French First Army was to attack towards Mangelare, with its left flank thrown back on the inundations near St. Janshoek.

XVIII Corps

The push towards Westroosebeke

48th and 11th Divisions

The same terrible ground about the Lekkerboterbeek and Laudetbeek was to be attacked by the same divisions which had attempted to push forward through Poelcappelle towards Westroosebeke on the 4th October. Except this time the ground was not terrible, but in the word used so many times by those who were there, it was indescribable.

In 48th Division, the Warwick battalions of 143rd Brigade had been relieved by 145th Brigade on the 7th October. Prior to this relief the enemy had been very active in the area, with continual sniping and machine gun fire, especially from Beek House. Although little enemy movement had been detected, other strongly held posts had been located at Oxford House, and Berks Houses, and machine guns had been in action both in and near the cemetery, on the road near Vacher Farm. Subsequently the 144th Brigade, which was to carry out the attack, had relieved the 145th. The aggressive sniping activity corresponded with the arrival of a fresh German division that now held the Passchendaele – Westroosebeke high ground. To prevent the

British outflanking their positions in Houthulst Forest the enemy were intent on holding the approaches to the northern section of the ridge at all costs. In accordance with the latest defence tactics the *16th Division* had been ordered to hold the front line posts with numerous machine guns, and this revised tactic had been noticed opposite 48th Division.

At about 8:45 p.m. on the 7th October, 32nd Brigade of 11th Division had received orders to relieve 33rd Brigade in the line and the battalions began to move off from Siege Camp, just west of Ypres at 9:30. One of the tracks leading to the front line around Langemarck, crossed the Ypres – Yser canal at Bridge No.4 at Essex Farm, passed La Belle Alliance where it followed Boundary Road north towards Gournier Farm. This is the route 32nd Brigade had followed, and up to Gournier Farm, owing to the number of men on the move all at once, the march up had been delayed by a series of checks. The forward companies eventually relieved those of 33rd Brigade in the outpost line, while the support companies occupied the support line about Pheasant Farm. The relief was completed by 3:40 a.m. on the 8th. At 11:00 p.m. the orders arrived for the attack on the 9th and runners left Pheasant Farm to carry them up 1,100 yards to the forward company headquarters on the Red House road 600 yards from the centre of Poelcappelle. The night was so dark all the runners became lost, the orders not arriving until 1:00 a.m. on the 9th. Difficulties in laying out the tapes in the dark and rain prevented the attacking battalions being in position until 4:30. At 5:00 a.m. the outpost line was brought in, in anticipation of the barrage.

The attack of the 144th and 32nd Brigades along the Lekkerboterbeek and at Poelcappelle

144th Brigade [581] and 32nd Brigade [582]

Already exhausted by the march up, at Zero Hour 144th Brigade moved forward along its 1,500 yard front, amongst the water-filled craters, and behind an ineffective barrage. It soon came under severe machine gun fire from the numerous blockhouses and ruined farms, now garrisoned by the *16th Division*. In all directions the battlefield appeared as a foul muddy waste relieved only by the low enemy bunkers and ruined farms. On the right, parties of the 7th Worcestershire Regiment attacked towards the trench in front of Adler Farm, capturing the position, while others 500 yards to the north made an unsuccessful assault on Inch Houses. The 6th Gloucestershire Regiment in the centre overwhelmed the machine gun position in the cemetery and advanced across the track at the eastern end and past Vacher Farm, but under fire from Inch Houses and Berks Houses made little further progress. On the left the 4th Gloucester advanced 150 yards past Country Crossroads, but was checked by heavy machine gun fire from Oxford House and Berks Houses, on slightly higher ground further up the road. At 2:45 p.m. a company of the 8th Worcester in brigade reserve, unsuccessfully attacked Inch Houses, being partly caught by a barrage fired to protect the 6th Gloucester. An attempt by a second company of the 8th Worcester in the early evening to capture Oxford House was also unsuccessful.

The 9th West Yorkshire Regiment of 32nd Brigade, advancing to the right of the ruins of Poelcappelle came under severe machine gun fire in enfilade from Gloster House on the right, and on the left from the bunkers in the village which had been reoccupied by the Germans since the 4th October. The battalion sustained many casualties. The 6th Yorkshire Regiment advanced into the ruins behind an ill-defined barrage, with many high explosive and heavy shells landing very short. As they moved forward into the rubble they met with little opposition until reaching the fork in the road just before the Brewery. Here they came under machine gun fire in enfilade from Meunier House on the right and from String Houses on the left. Working forward, parties attacked and captured several pillboxes just north-west of the Brewery, but the machine gun and rifle fire was so destructive that the position could not be held, and around 8:00 a.m. the line fell back and dug-in across the fork junction. One bunker was attacked by Corporal William Champ, who crept forward alone and threw mills bombs through the aperture, returning under heavy sniper fire with a machine gun and about 20 prisoners. Later in the day Corporal Champ was shot and killed by a sniper, but for his most conspicuous bravery he was to be posthumously awarded the V.C. The tanks, which were to have taken the Brewery, were now greatly missed. Casualties to sniper fire increased as the Green Howards attempted to dug-in in an exposed position, their line not being in touch to right or left. A line of posts was established from near the fork junction 400 yards west of the brewery, with flanks of around 200 yards thrown back to left and right. The position was very weak, and at 11:05 "D" Company of the 8th Duke of Wellington was sent up in support, and dug-in across the road around 75 yards behind the Green Howards. Ammunition was running short, and at 12:25 a party from 32nd Brigade bravely succeeded in reaching the forward posts to replenish small arms ammunition and bombs.

In the valley of the Lekkerboterbeek little had been gained by 48th Division, the forward outposts being moved up by only a few hundred yards. The 11th Division had pushed the line forward about 400 yards. The centre of Poelcappelle was now precariously in British hands, while 100 yards forward, the machine gun infested rubble of the Brewery, and the eastern fringe, was still in the hands of the enemy. Between the Stroombeek and Poelcappelle, Fifth Army had gained little ground towards the ridge. The extra machine guns in the German line, and the stubborn resistance of the *16th Division* had caused many casualties and for the moment the advance was checked. In the attack on Peolcappelle the Green Howards had sustained casualties of 43 killed, 31 missing and 161 wounded.

---

[581] National Archives, War Diary 144th Brigade WO95/2757
[582] National Archives, War Diary 32nd Brigade WO95/1808

XIV Corps, the left flank

4th Division, 29th Division, and Guards Division

On the 9th October the left defensive flank was to be thrown well forward, across the Broenbeek, and would afford greater protection than on the 4th when enemy machine gun fire from across the Broenbeek valley had caused a near disaster at 19 Metre Hill. 4th Division was to conform to 11th Division, and advance with one brigade north of Poelcappelle, across the Poelcappelle – Houthulst road to a depth of about 1,200 yards on the right, and to 1,500 yards on the left. 29th Division was to advance with two brigades along a 1,400 yards front astride the Staden railway track, from the point where the Broenbeek past beneath the low embankment, to conform to 4th Division on the right, and to a depth of 2,000 yards on the left to conform to the Guards Division. The Guards were to attack with two brigades along a 1,500 yard front, and had a final objective on a line between Poelcappelle Station and Veldhoek, 2,000 yards forward.

The divisions of XIV Corps had a few slight advantages in the northern sector of the battlefield. The tracks up to the front lines were in better condition, and less heavily used than those further south, and as the front here had not advanced so far, the field artillery was on Pilckem ridge, and within 4,000 yards of the line. The 29th and Guards Divisions however were confronted by the considerable obstacle of the over-spilling Broenbeek, at least 3 feet deep, with a swamp along the southern bank.

4th Division

12th Brigade [583]

The 12th Brigade completed the relief of the 11th Brigade at 9:30 p.m. on the 7th October, the 2nd Essex Regiment and the 2nd Lancashire Fusiliers taking over the line from the 1st Rifle Brigade and the 1st Hampshire Regiment. The 2nd Duke of Wellington's moved up in support and the 1st King's Own Royal Lancaster was in brigade reserve.[584] The Essex and Lancs Fusiliers were to use two companies in the line with one in support and one in reserve.

At Zero Hour, a heavy barrage stood in front of the tapes for four minutes before commencing to creep forward. As the forward companies advanced across the Houthulst road they immediately came under heavy machine gun and rifle fire. Due to the check of the 11th Division on the right, the pillboxes in Poelcappelle opened machine gun fire on the Essex as did the blockhouse in front at String Houses, but the battalion succeeded in reaching its first objective around 300 yards forward. On the left the Lancs Fusiliers came under fire from blockhouses at Compromise Farm and Landing Farm on their right, and from Millers Farm on their left. Both battalions were already clear of the front line before the German barrage came down, five minutes late. Early in the advance both the commanding officer and the adjutant of the Essex became casualties, as did the commanders of "A" and "C" Companies. The Essex worked a little way beyond its first objective, finally being checked about 400 yards forward of the start line by heavy small arms fire, much of it in enfilade. A gap of 200 yards had developed on the right where the 6th Yorks were held up in Poelcappelle. The Lancs Fusiliers attacked and secured Millers Farm, finally being stopped by machine gun fire after an advance of around 600 yards. The new line was established in muddy shell-holes half filled with water, which were organised as well as possible against counter-attack. The Essex had lost 18 officers, of which 6 had been killed and 3 were missing. 42 other ranks had been killed, 144 were wounded 25 were missing and 4 had been gassed.

---

[583] National Archives, War Diary 12th Brigade WO95/1503
[584] National Archives, War Diary 2nd Essex and 2nd Duke of Wellington's WO95/1505, National Archives, War Diary 2nd Lancs Fusiliers WO95/1507

29th Division, 86th Brigade [585] and 88th Brigade [586]

The shape of the outpost line from which the 29th Division was to attack, introduced problems of its own. On the 4th October the division had established a buttress to the left flank of the attack, the final forward positions not presenting a normal line at a uniform depth of advance, but rather a series of posts swung back to the left. In simple terms the right had gone forward, dropping-off posts as it went, whilst the left had marked time.

To the south of the railway, 86th Brigade, using the 1st Lancashire Fusiliers,[587] with the 2nd Royal Fusiliers in support, was to advance to a depth of 1,650 yards to the final objective. On the left, astride the railway, 88th Brigade, using the 4th Worcestershire Regiment, with the Royal Newfoundland Regiment in support, had a full 2,500 yards to cover to reach its final objective, to keep in touch with the Guards on its left. There were to be three objectives, the first and second to be taken by the leading battalions at which point the support battalions would pass through to secure the final objective. After the attack had gone through, the 2nd Hampshire, in reserve, was to advance to and consolidate on the first objective, and the 16th Middlesex was in brigade reserve for counter-attack purposes. The two attacking brigades had moved up to the forward assembly positions on the night of 7th-8th October, the six mile march having taken four hours, which was considered slow progress, but did not compare with the difficulties farther south. Most battalions marched up the track bed of the railway, moving up through Vulcan Crossing and Langemarck Station. All attacking battalions were in position in shell-holes behind the jumping-off tapes, some around 1:00 a.m. and all before 5:20 a.m. Throughout the night the Germans shelled the assembly areas heavily especially between 2:30 and Zero Hour. In places the line was moved slightly forward to avoid the shelling and few casualties occurred.

The British barrage came down right on time, some guns concentrating on a known German strong-point in Bear Copse on the far bank of the Broenbeek, 500 yards north of the railway. On the right, the 1st Lancs Fusiliers advanced, alongside their 2nd Battalion, who were moving up with the 4th Division. Machine gun fire from Olga Houses raked the front wave of the 1st, which was checked for about 15 minutes sustaining many casualties, and the barrage was lost. Seeing his company pinned down Sergeant Joseph Lister rushed a machine gun post in a shell-hole in front of Olga Houses, shot the crew and captured the gun. He then shouted to the enemy, demanding the surrender of the garrison of Olga Houses, at which point 100 men from the blockhouse and surrounding shell-holes, laid down their arms. Sergeant Lister was to be awarded the V.C. for his act of bravery and initiative, which enabled the advance to continue and catch up behind the barrage at the first objective. Kortebeek Farm near the Broenbeek was attacked and seized, but the casualties to the Lancs Fusiliers had been so severe that their now thin ranks were soon supported by two companies of the 2nd Royal Fusiliers. Machine gun fire from another bunker, protected by a forward earth work now checked a company of the Royal Fusiliers. Sergeant John Molyneaux gathered a bombing party, attacked and took the trench, and then in hand-to-hand fighting seized the blockhouse behind it, killing a number of the enemy and capturing 20 to 30 others. Sergeant Molyneaux was to receive the V.C. for his gallant action. With the bunkers defeated the composite force of Fusilier companies moved on another 100 to 150 yards, to a point between Olga Houses and the Houthulst road, where they halted on the first objective.

As the barrage thickened, about 35 of the Lancs Fusiliers worked forward towards Conde House on the Houthulst road. As a direct result of the check in Poelcappelle, the 2nd Lancs Fusiliers of 4th Division were still held up on the right, and the right flank 1st Lancs Fusiliers was dangerously exposed. As his company moved forward, Second Lieutenant Le Mesurier ordered 30 men to establish a number of defensive posts to guard this flank. Of the depleted Lancs Fusiliers, about 20 had managed to cross the Houthulst road, and had gone to ground in shell-

---

[585] National Archives, War Diary 86th Brigade WO95/2298
[586] National Archives, War Diary 88th Brigade WO95/2307
[587] National Archives, War Diary 1st Lancs Fusiliers WO95/2300

holes under heavy rifle fire, while a small party of 10 to 15 men remained in shell-holes west of the road. Two platoons of the right leading company of the Royal Fusiliers moved across the road to give support, and under heavy fire succeeded in working forward by rushes, from shell-hole to shell-hole, 300 yards east of the road. Rifle fire from Senegal Farm caused around 20 casualties and the remaining Royal Fusiliers then also took shelter in shell-holes. A patrol was sent to the right, which reported a 300 yard gap to the nearest troops of 4th Division. As further movement was impossible, the Royal Fusiliers then consolidated a line of posts in their shell-holes about 300 yards from the road, 250 yards in front of Conde House and 100 yards north of Millers Houses.

The two left companies of the Royal Fusiliers, moving forward with the barrage from the first objective, passed through the leading wave of Lancs Fusiliers, which had taken shelter from small arms fire coming across the Houthulst road, in shell-holes short of the second objective. The Royal Fusiliers moved on to a line just short of the Houthulst road and here took shelter, short of the second objective. Here they attempted to re-organise prior to moving on to the final objective. They were in touch with the Worcester on the left, but could not obtain touch with anybody in front or on the right. As the barrage again advanced, the Royal Fusiliers tried to follow it across the road, but were thwarted by short shooting which caused them casualties. Working forward amongst their own shellfire, it soon became clear that there was nobody forward, and the second objective had not been secured. The advance was checked about 150 yards east of the road, on a line between a point 400 yards north of Conde House and Tranquille House. No further advance was made. The second objective was still not secured, there were no supports, and the machine gun and rifle fire from the enemy was too severe.

Mixed groups of the Lancs Fusiliers and Royal Fusiliers were now held up just beyond Conde House by rifle and machine gun fire from two pillboxes around 700 yards forward, and bunkers in the ruined farms. At about this time, and from the direction of the two pillboxes, eight waves of Germans were seen to be moving forward to counter-attack, but were severely swept by rifle and machine gun fire. At 8.55 a.m., with some of the enemy still approaching, the British barrage descended to indicate the advance to the final objective, fully catching the counter-attack which immediately disintegrated. Further movement forward proved impossible and the Fusiliers consolidated their final line where they were, about 500 yards short of the final objective. The 16th Middlesex was ordered up to support the Fusiliers, by which time Le Mesurier's defensive right flank was reduced to four men.

On the left front of the division, north of the railway, the 4th Worcester had advanced behind the barrage, which had been stiffened by a few Stokes mortars. The mortars proceeded to pound a strong-point in Bear Copse with 50 mortar rounds, suppressing damaging machine gun fire. To help ford the Broenbeek mats and timber bridges had been taken forward and placed across the boggy areas around the stream, resulting in a natural funnelling effect as the attacking waves attempted to cross. Some Guardsmen also became involved in the struggle to cross the marsh and the stream. Once across, the advance continued, gradually clearing the dug-outs along the railway, and a large number of the enemy in Bear Copse surrendered, abandoning two *minenwerfer* and a large quantity of ammunition.

The Newfoundland, following in support of the Worcester came under harassing machine gun fire from dug-outs along the railway. Crossing very bad ground the two battalions became mixed, the Newfoundland passing through the Worcester too soon at the first objective, rather then following them to the second objective and passing through there. A strong-point at Namur Crossing, on the railway 1,000 yards from the start line, and a bunker at Pascal Farm were engaged by a Stokes mortar from 300 yards, the enemy soon emerging to surrender. One stubborn bunker between Namur Crossing and the Broenbeek was tackled by Private Fredrick Dancox of the 4th Worcester, who worked his way around to the rear entrance and threatened the garrison with a Mills bomb. Forty of the enemy soon emerged from the bunker followed by Private Dancox carrying an enemy machine gun. He was to be awarded the V.C. for his courageous action. Sniping continued to cause the Worcester and Newfoundland casualties, but both the first and second objectives were taken up to time. The Worcester consolidated on the second objective, while the Newfoundland moved on to the final objective, where a line of shell-holes was consolidated and prepared for counter-attack. This line was established from near Tranquille House on the Houthulst road, 250 yards south of Poelcappelle Station, to a point 250 yards north of the station and just east of the Staden road. Heavy sniping was directed at the Newfoundland throughout the day, mainly from Taube Farm at a range of 500 yards, about which the enemy could also be seen collecting in large numbers. A counter-attack from the farm developed around noon against the Newfoundland outpost line, but was driven-off by rifle and Lewis gun fire. The 2nd Hampshire had moved up to the first objective at Zero plus 3 hours 35 minutes to support the Worcester.

In places the enemy had not shown their usual resilience in defence. At 4:00 a.m. on the morning of the 9th October, the *227th Division* had taken over the sector for 2,500 yards south of Houthulst Forest from the *6th Bavarian Division,* and this was given as a reason by the Germans for the only slight resistance offered at some points. On the other hand the small-arms fire across the Houthulst road had been severe, and had checked both Fusilier battalions short of the final objective, and had caused heavy casualties. On the left the Newfoundland were on the final objective, and the 29th Division had captured 7 officers, 494 other ranks, 30 machine guns, and 2 trench mortars, at a cost in casualties of 51 officers and 1,110 other ranks.

The Guards Division[588]
The attack towards Houthulst Forest

To reach its final objective on the Vijfwegen spur, close to the edge of Houthulst Forest, the Guards Division had to make the deepest penetration of the day, at around 2,500 yards. This was a full 1,000 yards deeper than Plumer's bite and hold tactics normally allowed for, but at least the field artillery back on Pilckem ridge and Hill 20 could give effective barrage support at this range, the distance from the gun line to the final objective between Veldhoek and Le 5 Chemines being around 5,500 yards.

The division was to attack on a 1,500 yards front along the Broenbeek, using two brigades, each brigade using two battalions to capture the first and second objectives, with two support battalions to pass through to the final. The 1st and 2nd Guards Brigades,[589] relieved the 3rd Guards Brigade in the line on the evening of the 7th October, the 2nd Grenadier and 2nd Coldstream of 1st Brigade, relieving the 4th Grenadier Guards on the right, and the 1st Scots and 2nd Irish of 2nd Brigade, relieving the 2nd Scots Guards on the left. In 1st Brigade, the 1st Irish and 3rd Coldstream were in support to pass through to the final objective, as were the 3rd Grenadier and 1st Coldstream in 2nd Brigade. The French First Army was to attack on the left flank.

The Broenbeek was an obvious obstacle of deep mud and water, and to assist in crossing, during the three preceding nights the Royal Engineers had brought forward 355 mats and 180 infantry bridges. In this northern sector the field artillery situation had been somewhat neglected. As the front line had remained along the line of the Broenbeek since August, it had not been necessary to continually move the guns forward, and since taking over the line, the 1st Grenadier and 1st Welsh Guards of 3rd Guards Brigade had worked hard to establish forward ammunition dumps and to man-handle the batteries into their firing positions. But the field batteries here were on firmer firing positions on the higher ground of Pilckem ridge, with a much shorter carry to bring up ammunition, as the guns were only 2,000 yards from the canal bank, a distinct advantage to those in the Steenbeek valley. All attacking formations were in their designated positions by midnight, occupying the usual water filled shell-holes, but their discomfort was eased slightly by an early morning issue of rum and hot tea, the tea brought up to the line in petrol tins wrapped in hay.

---

[588] Cuthbert Headlam *History of the Guards Division Vol I* pp271-276
[589] National Archives, War Diary 1st Guards Brigade WO95/1214 , National Archives, War Diary 2nd Guards Brigade WO95/1218

At Zero Hour the barrage came down along the Broenbeek and stood for four minutes, a much heavier curtain of fire than was experienced further south. On the right the 2nd Grenadier and 2nd Coldstream advanced from their tapes in front of Leopard and Panther Trenches and approached the stream. It was found unnecessary to use mats or bridges, some wading over, while others used fallen trees and old duckboards to cross. As the forward waves organised on the northern bank, Germans of the *417th I.R.* and *6th Bavarian Regiment* ran forward to surrender, apparently stunned into submission by the barrage. The 2nd Grenadier and 2nd Coldstream continued across the heavy cratered ground towards the first objective, the enemy either rising from their defended shell-holes to surrender or running towards the rear. By 6:00 a.m. the brigade first objective between Gruyterszale Farm and Koekuit had been reached.

Map next page

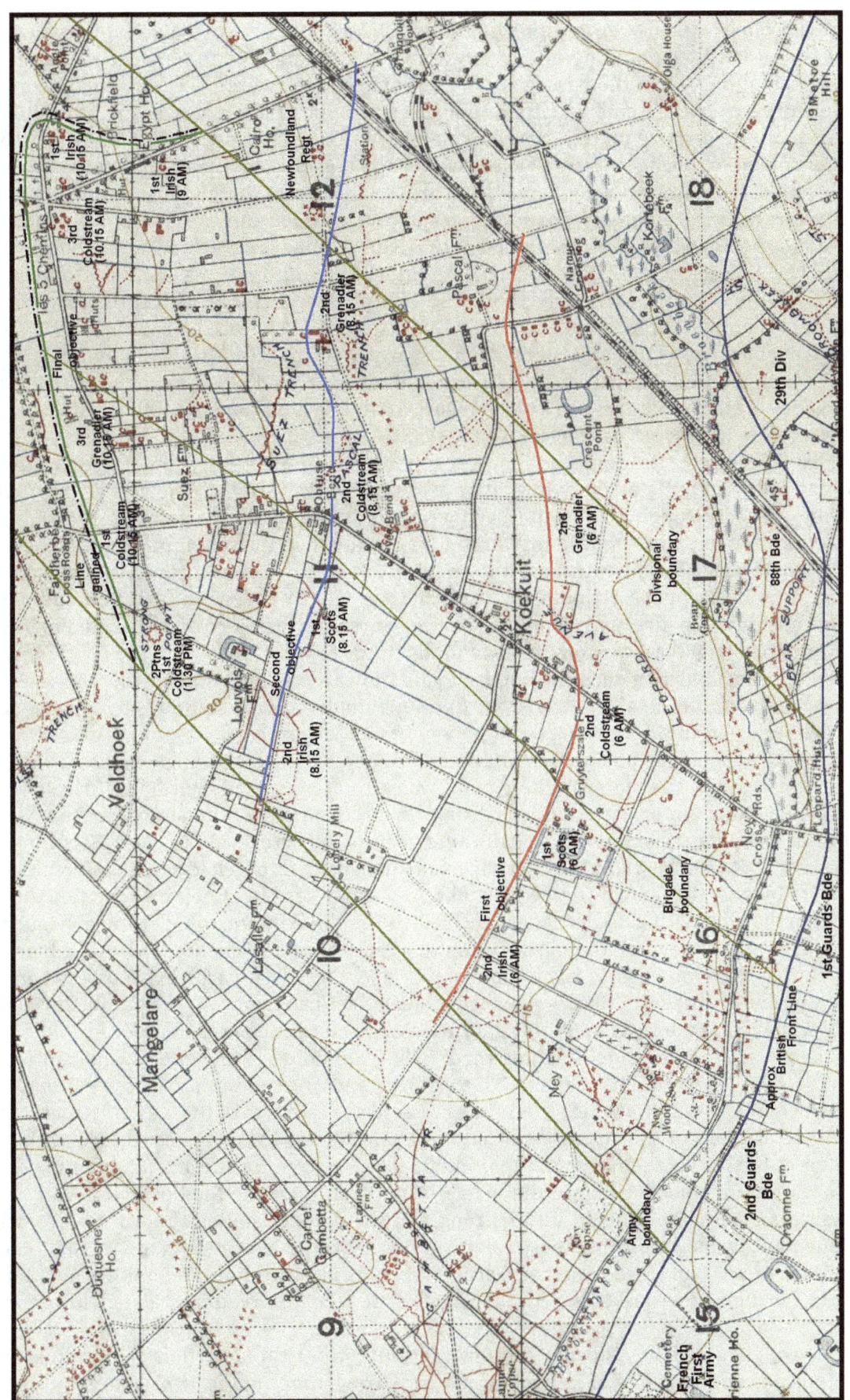

The attack of the 1st and 2nd Guards Brigades – Guards Division towards Houthulst Forest
On the left, 2nd Brigade moved off behind the barrage, and walked into very bad ground just short of the stream, where the deep water- filled shell-holes amidst the general quagmire

presented a major obstacle. A machine gun in Ney Wood just across the stream opened up on the 2nd Irish Guards, hampering an already difficult crossing, but the enemy made no other serious attempt to contest the passage of the stream. Bridges were necessary to get across the mire, but once over the Scots and Irish moved swiftly forward against slight opposition and reached the first objective on the Carrefour Gambetta road, and up with the 1st Brigade on the right. Consolidation began by the forward two companies of each attacking battalion along the first objective, and after 45 minutes as the barrage thickened the support companies passed through towards the second objective. On the right the sparse ruins of Koekuit were cleared by the 2nd Coldstream, which then came under fire from pillboxes at Vee Bend, about 400 yards beyond. The Guards worked forward and threatened to outflank the pillboxes and without further fight the enemy surrendered, about 35 being taken prisoner, and three machine guns captured. Little other opposition delayed the Guards, as by 8:15, both brigades had advanced to the second objective, which ran along a line nearly west to east through a point 500 yards beyond Koekuit, on the Langemarck – Houthulst road, that road being near the junction of the two brigades. At this point the 29th Division were up in touch on the right, 300 yards west of the railway, as were the French on the left, 300 yards east of Lasalle Farm.

By 8:30, as the leading battalions consolidated the new line, the support battalions, which had followed up in artillery formation had reached the second objective. Thirty minutes later they passed through behind the barrage towards the final objective. On the right of 1st Brigade the 1st Irish Guards moved forward more quickly than the Newfoundland, subsequently exposing their right flank, which began to receive fire in enfilade. As the Irish attacked Egypt House, on the Poelcappelle – Houthulst road, and the stoutly defended brickfield just beyond, enfilade machine gun fire was coming from the direction of Cairo House and Poelcappelle Station, in their right rear. After much stiff fighting, Egypt House and the brickfield were captured, the Irish pushing on a few hundred yards towards Angle Point on the Vijfwegen road. They were now on the final objective, but the Newfoundland was still not up, and the sniping from shell-holes on the right was causing many casualties, especially amongst officers as they attempted to organise the position. A flank was dropped back west of Angle Point, facing east in an effort to suppress the sniping. The enemy was also active on the left of 1st Brigade, the 3rd Coldstream coming under fierce rifle fire from the direction of Houthulst Forest, from the road junction at Les Cinq Chemins, and also under a hostile barrage about Suez Farm, near the Langemarck – Houthulst road. Neither rifle nor artillery fire checked the Coldstream, which pushed on towards the final objective. The pillboxes about Les Cinq Chemins road junction were heavily bombarded with rifle grenades, and fell to the Coldstream, which now consolidated a shell-hole line just beyond the road running west from the junction. In the advance the Coldstream had veered slightly right and a gap of a few hundred yards existed between it and the 3rd Grenadier of 2nd Brigade advancing near the Langemarck – Houthulst road. The Grenadier moved to the right to fill this gap, attacking and capturing the numerous blockhouses about Suez Farm and Les Cinq Chemins road, killing a number of the enemy and capturing 23 prisoners and 2 field guns. The garrison of a strong-point on the far left of the 2nd Brigade front put up an obstinate defence which for a time checked the advance of the 1st Coldstream. For the moment the capture of the strong-point was left, and the advance was continued with the 3rd Grenadier to the final objective up to time, and by 10:15, except for the strong-point the division was along its final objective across the whole front. Soon after the final objective was reached eight Vickers guns were brought up to strengthen the defences along the front of 1st Brigade, with four more guns supporting the weak right flank. On the left 2nd Brigade by 3:00 p.m. had fifteen Vickers guns and two captured German Maxims in position to defend the new line, but the task of bringing forward sufficient ammunition across the dreadful crater-field remained a problem.

Throughout the day, hostile sniping continued from the direction of Houthulst Forest which took a continual toll of officers. At 1:30 p.m., two platoons of the 1st Coldstream supported by two Vickers guns, carried out a carefully organised attack against the stubborn strong-point, 40 Germans and a machine gun being captured. During the afternoon a counter-attack looked imminent as German aircraft flew low over the Guards positions, and infantry and transport were seen moving within Houthulst Forest, but for the moment no attack developed.

The great depth of the Guards advance to the Vijfwegen spur, brought with it its own problems, as much difficulty was experienced in bringing forward sufficient quantities if wire and pickets to consolidate the new line, although by the evening of the 9th, duckboard tracks had been pushed forward across the Broenbeek. No fewer than 29 foot-crossings were thrown across the stream, one of which was carried on piles for 70 yards to cross the swamps. For all the difficulties, and given that in places the enemy had not been at their best, the attack towards Houthulst had been a fine achievement, and as the French were up on the left, this flank was also secure.

The French First Army

With their left flank resting close to the Yser inundations near Draaibaak, the French First Army attacked successfully to the left of the Guards. The ground conditions between the Broenbeek and the Corverbeek were uniformly awful and they were also confronted with a strongly fortified position within the ruins of the hamlet of Mangelare. Behind a slow and powerful barrage along a front of around 2,000 yards the French advanced steadily across the marsh, and made good progress for 1,000 yards towards their first objective near the Gambetta track. After a pause to reorganize and bring forward supports the guns lifted, and the attack went forward successfully clearing the reinforced cellars and bunkers of Mangelare. On the left equal progress was made along the Corverbeek towards Zevekoten. By 10:00 a.m. the French were on their final objective, an advance of around 2,000 yards, in touch with the Guards on the right, and with their left now resting on the fringes of Houthulst Forest.

The final actions of the 9th October

Towards dusk on the edge of the Gheluvelt plateau, to the east of Reutel, another company of the 9th Devon were sent forward to make a final attempt to capture Judge Copse. The attack from the south-east was successful and the copse was cleared. 7th Division had completed the capture of the final objective along its front. Also at dusk, the situation of the Australian 5th Brigade about Rhine, between the main ridge and the Keiberg was again threatened, as Germans were seen advancing north of the railway against the 66th Division, and over the northern end of the Keiberg against the Australians. The line on the western slopes of the Keiberg was so weakly held, that the forward outposts fired their S.O.S. signal, and began to fall back, while others who remained were either killed or captured. As the enemy descended the Keiberg slope they were caught by the barrage, and no counter-attack approached the main ridge. About 5:00 p.m. in Poelcappelle, the enemy infiltrated forward and recaptured the pillboxes north-west of the brewery, previously captured by the Green Howards. A forward post of 7 men within the fork of the road and close up to the brewery, were forced to retire to the main line. Just north of the Staden railway, a counter-attack at about 6:30 in the evening at the junction of the 29th Division and Guards Division, drove in the Newfoundland line by about 200 yards towards Cairo House, the Irish Guards dropping back their exposed right flank to the Poelcappelle road near Egypt House. The ground in 29th Division sector was soon retaken and consolidated by the 2nd Hampshire.

The day had been one of great effort and bravery but had not produced the results to which, since the 20th September all had become accustomed. The weather had undoubtedly saved the enemy from greater destruction, throwing the plans upon which the carefully contrived offensive relied into a shambles of sunken guns and muddy exhausted men. Were Second Army and G.H.Q. Staffs surprised by the lack of success, or were the facts not yet clear to them? The 7th Division had achieved its limited objectives, but in the centre the attempt by the Australians to advance towards the Keiberg, with too few men, and inadequate gunfire support, had been stopped in its tracks exactly as Birdwood had predicted. After an appallingly difficult start, 66th Division had done remarkably well, but the failure of 49th Division on the Flanders I wire had by midday caused the inevitable withdrawal of the 66th. In contrast, the operation of Fifth Army had been successful with certain reservations. The attack of the 29th Division and the Guards Division had been magnificent, but this was the defensive flank, not the main drive to the ridge. The 48th and 11th Divisions had been checked, and the road to Westroosebeke was still blocked by the enemy at the ruins of Poelcappelle, the 4th Division right being held up in consequence.

Possibly it was not just the men who were getting tired. At Second Army the belief was that the weather, which had led to the atrocious ground conditions, was mainly responsible for the failure to reach the objectives. There was some truth in this argument, but it did not recognize the core problem. Somehow the infantry had struggled to the front, and had attacked across the broken and flooded streams and marshes. The ground had slowed them but it had not stopped them. At the root of the day's failure lay a thirty yard deep wire entanglement across the nose of the Wallemolen spur, which had prevented the 49th Division from supporting the flank of the 66th Division, which by the end of the day had resulted in a withdrawal of the 66th nearly to its start line. If this fact was not quickly realized by Second Army, any further attack would have the same result, and would come to grief on the same wire. Certainly the mud was a major factor in the failure, not principally due to its effects on the infantry, but more because it had immobilised the artillery, which in turn had not been able to cut the wire.

Was it possible that the nineteen days of battle had had such a wearying effect on the once so careful and thorough Second Army Staff that their work was becoming careless and shoddy, to the point that Plumer, who back in June would not send his infantry against Gheluvelt plateau without proper artillery preparation, would now send them against uncut wire and blockhouses? As the 49th Division were aware of the wire, it would be reasonable to believe that Godley at II Anzac knew of it too. If Godley knew of it then why did Plumer not known of it? The wheels did not turn as quickly as we would now logically expect. It is unlikely that the ground conditions were to blame for a lack of information from the front, which could have been passed by telephone line from brigade headquarters to division. Had 49th Division Staff had not thought fit to mention the wire entanglements? Haig in his diary entry for the 9th October wrote: 'The results were very successful.... The 66th Division advanced without the barrage and took all objectives – 49th gained all except a small piece on the left.' [590] Either communication had completely broken down and Haig had absolutely no idea what was happening at the front, or he truly believed that the enemy was so near to breaking that the price being levied on his gradually depleting divisions would in the long term be worth paying. In any event, he seemed unaware of the total failure at Bellevue.

If the Second Army Staff had been unaware of the dangerous threat presented by the wire up to the 10th October, they were certainly made aware of it by the 11th. The 3rd Australian Division had relieved the 66th Division on the night of the 10th-11th October and on the same night the New Zealand Division had relieved the 49th Division. Patrols of both Australian and New Zealand divisions reported the existence of the wire protecting the Bellevue blockhouses. A patrol of the 2nd Otago under Sergeant Travis had carried out a close reconnaissance, which revealed that the belts, especially around the strong-points and blockhouses had been assiduously strengthened, and the entanglements remained in clear view from Gravenstafel. Revealingly the New Zealand Division account states, regarding the wire belts: 'Their formidable nature was even now insufficiently realised by the outgoing Division.' [591] It appears the reason why Godley, Plumer and Haig all seemed unaware of the obstacle, was simply that 49th Division had not told anybody. But whatever the reason, the New Zealand Division was faced with the awful prospect of attacking through this wire on the 12th October, with no likelihood of the artillery being able to break it up in the meantime.

The Germans subsequently admitted that they too had paid a high price on the 9th October stating that, 'the German losses were, however very considerable...The sufferings of the

---

[590] Douglas Haig. Diaries and Letters p335
[591] Col.H.Stewart, *The New Zealand Division* p279

troops bore no relation to the advantage obtained'.[592] On the 7th October the *Fourth Army* Staff had begun discussing the possibilities of withdrawing from the Flanders Position, and thus uncovering the U-boat bases. But the suggestion was not approved by Ludendorff, the Chief Quartermaster-General obviously believing that the price he would pay to defend them was as great as it seemed the Commander-in-Chief was willing to pay to try to disable them.

In the Second Army attack on Passchendaele on the 9th October, the casualties sustained had been:
I Anzac Corps: Total 1,253 (2nd Australian Division).
II Anzac Corps: Total around 5,700 (66th Division 3,119, and 49th Division 2,585).

Robert A. Perry
Langemark   30-8-2006

Chapter Eight

---

[592] BOH p337 footnote 3

"Every Man Steeled His Heart"

The Fifth Step

The First Battle of Passchendaele 12th October

Weather conditions, rainfall Vlamertinghe, temperature Ypres[593]			
	10th October	**11th October**	**12th October**
Rainfall	2.5mm	4.9mm	7.9mm
Temp	49F	50F	55F

Irrespective of the success or failure on the 9th October, the conditions on the battlefield remained utterly atrocious, and for those lying wounded, cold, wet, and in pain and shock, out beyond the British forward posts, their situation was unimaginable. There had been a drying wind on the 9th but the 10th was again wet and cold. After the withdrawal of the 66th Division, many wounded still lay where they had fallen amongst their dead comrades, on the foul, sodden slope above the Ravebeek, without a hope of being recovered. On the other side of the valley a high watermark of the dead and dying of the 49th Division indicated the line where the wire had presented them up as targets for the machine guns of the Bellevue pillboxes and slit trenches. Those lucky enough to have been collected by the stretcher parties were mostly laid outside the captured blockhouses, now commandeered as Regimental Aid Posts, in the mud and rain, still in view of German snipers, and awaiting attention which likely would not come in time, or evacuation across the mile of shell-torn swamp, before even a duckboard track could be reached. For men to walk this distance unencumbered was exhausting, but to struggle through with a wounded man on a stretcher, demanded the efforts of up to eight bearers. Death reached many of the wounded, long before the overwhelmed medical officers.

On the 10th October relief of the 66th Division began. As the 11th Australian Infantry Brigade of the incoming 3rd Australian Division came up towards the line it became clear that 66th Division was not holding the front line reported. Lieutenant Fisher of the 42nd Battalion, against the advice of British officers, pressed on over Abraham Heights and into the Ravebeek valley in daylight, to ascertain the true situation before the arrival of his company. The terrible sights with which he was confronted left a vivid impression. 'The slope was littered with dead, both theirs and ours. I got to one pillbox to find it just a mass of dead, and so I passed on carefully to the one ahead. Here I found about 50 men alive, of the Manchesters. Never have I seen men so broken or demoralised. They were huddled up close behind the box in the last stages of exhaustion and fear. Fritz had been fighting them off all day, and had accounted for 57 that day – the dead and dying lay in piles. The wounded were numerous – unattended and weak, they groaned and moaned all over the place….some had been there four days already.' [594]

However hopeless the situation appeared at the front, the whole process was to be repeated three days later, by order of the Commander-in-Chief and with the acquiescence of the Army Commander.

Meeting of the War Cabinet the 10th October
and the War Policy Committee the 11th October

---

[593] National Archives WO95/15 GHQ statistics
[594] AOA p907

The War Cabinet met on the 10th and discussed further the proposals which had been made by Premier Painlevé at Boulogne on the 25th September, the meeting which had so rattled Haig. Painlevé remained anxious about his Army, wishing to give more leave, but unable to do so due to the length of line they were required to hold and the need for men to be transferred to the land to assist with agriculture. The French had considered Lloyd George's proposal to land at Alexandretta behind the Turks and threaten their communications. This they were willing to consider, but only if the British *had already defeated* the Turks and drawn off all their reserves.[595] Perhaps it had slipped everyone's minds that this is what Haig was presently doing to the advantage of the French, with the main enemy in Flanders. Painlevé had required that the British take over another 60 miles of their line on the Western Front. Amidst renewed French demands, with his mind set more resolutely than ever against the policies of his chief military advisors, and desperately seeking the confidence to abandon the Flanders offensive, Lloyd George seized this moment as the opportunity he required to call a council of war. He would gain a second line of military opinion on what future War policy should be by consulting Sir John French and Sir Henry Wilson. Alarmed at the proposal Robertson met with Lloyd George in the afternoon of the 10th, but the outcome of the meeting was unsatisfactory. The drums began to thunder around the War Office and Whitehall. For Robertson, the proposal appeared as a vote of no confidence, and he offered his resignation that evening to Minister of War Lord Derby. In turn Lord Curzon made it clear to Cabinet Secretary Hankey that if Lloyd George drove out Robertson, it would undoubtedly bring about the resignations of himself, Lord Cecil, Balfour, Derby and Carson which would result in the breaking of the Government. Sensing the danger Hankey resolved to defuse the situation. Before the War Cabinet on the morning of the 11th, he warned Lloyd George of the potential trouble brewing over the introduction of French and Wilson to the circle of policy making. The Prime Minister took the warning seriously and was on best form at the Cabinet meeting, at which French, Wilson and Robertson (who according to Hankey was 'as sulky as a bear with a sore head') were present, carefully handling the situation, and largely diffusing Robertson's resentments.

Since the sitting of the War Policy Committee on the 3rd October the fortunes of the campaign in Flanders had been mixed. The outstanding success of the 4th October (although it may not have appeared such to Lloyd George as it had not been mentioned) had been negated by the failure on the 9th. The return to foul weather and atrocious battlefield conditions had provided the Committee with an unarguable reason to evoke their powers and stop the offensive, should they feel obliged to do so. If they were not going to stop it now, then when would they? The Committee met again for the twenty-first and final time on the afternoon of the 11th October. Incredibly the main topic for discussion was not to be deciding on the continuance or cessation of the campaign in Flanders, but the attack against the Turks in Palestine.

Three days earlier on the 8th at the twentieth meeting of the War Policy Committee the former Chief-of-Staff in Egypt, General Lynden-Bell had been asked by the Committee, in an attempt to gain military credence for the Palestine venture, to offer his advice, which Lloyd George hopefully believed would be positive to his cause. Much to the chagrin of the Prime Minister, Lynden-Bell had failed to oblige, warning caution and casting doubt on the winter campaign against the Turks. Lord Curzon summed up the General's advice as follows: 'That if asked the question as what would be required to achieve a great success he would reply that, in view of the limitations of water and transport, the difficulties of sea communications, the lack of harbours, and the dangers from submarines, nothing more than was now being done was possible, except for the doubling of the railway [to Gaza].' [596] **Lynden-Bell concurred that this correctly summed up his views. But having sought and received military advice, Lloyd George now explained to his Committee colleagues why that advice was unsound, claiming that military officers were afraid of saying what they believed, in fear of the affect it may have on their future**

---

[595] Hankey Diaries 10th October
[596] National Archives CAB27/6, minutes of meeting of the War Policy Committee 8th October

chances of promotion. The fact that Jellicoe, Wemyss and Robertson had given him the same advice apparently counted for nothing.

Robertson was absent from the meeting on the afternoon of the 11th, although he had compiled an 8 page memorandum advising that as the country did not possess the resources to engage in major action on more than one front at a time, the main military effort should be confined to the Western Front. Recognising the inability of the Cabinet to decide on one course of action and to stick to it Robertson urged: 'The consequences of our adopted policy, whatever that policy may be, must be clearly faced, and we must determine to carry it through although possibly at considerable cost to other operations and interests...This is my advice and I can only leave the matter in the hands of the War Cabinet. I need hardly say that success in the West, or indeed any where requires that the War Cabinet should feel able to support in practice the policy of which they approve in principle. Whatever that policy may be, once the decisive theatre has been selected it must be regarded as such, and all other theatres be ruthlessly treated as secondary and made to do the best of what is given them.' [597] Paying little attention to Robertson's advice, Lloyd George, clearly in a bullish mood and taking advantage of the absence of his military advisor, stuck his head farther above the parapet than was his usual practice, and claimed that the Committee should make a decision in favour of the Palestinian operation and the General Staff should be informed of (and not consulted on) that decision. Of the Committee, Milner, Smuts and Curzon were in accord with the Prime Minister. Only Bonar Law, after considering the testament of Lynden-Bell and the contents of Robertson's missive expressed doubt, concerned that the Palestine venture may lead to another Dardanelles fiasco. This did not however imply that Bonar Law was about to support the only operation that really mattered. Smut's was in fine fettle, and in a brave effort to add the value of his opinion to the proceedings pronounced, 'we must take the offensive somewhere; the Western Front had always produced an insoluble problem. If the Russians went out it would become a hopeless problem'.[598] In a gesture worthy of pantomime, which typified the general absence of reality from the political debate, and a continual unwillingness to address the matter of prime importance, Bonar Law suggested Italy should again be considered as a theatre of operations. The groans are almost audible across the years. Smuts suggested to Bonar Law, that as Cadorna had already proven unreliable, Italy was probably not the best place to lay British hopes. It is to be assumed Bonar Law withdrew his suggestion, and so, with only the mildest of dissention now overcome, in line with the Prime Minister's wishes, and completely at variance with the advice of the military, Palestine it would be. As, in the opinion of the Committee nothing had been, or would be achieved in Flanders, and Italy was for the moment not an option, there was no other choice open to them. Lord Curzon, practical and astute as usual, wished to take the considerations one step further and asked of Lloyd George what exactly he meant by Palestine? Did he mean stopping at the Jaffa – Jerusalem line, or did he advocate advancing into Syria? The Prime Minister's answer indicated an advance into Syria with the agreement of the French, or if their consent was not forthcoming the Jaffa – Jerusalem line. No one questioned the military benefits of advancing to the Jaffa – Jerusalem line as opposed to simply staying at Gaza.

The deterioration of the conditions in Flanders were ignored or at best avoided. Lloyd George got as close to the subject as he dare by once more eulogising over the Nivelle offensive, whilst predicting the inability of the Army to capture the Clerken ridge, a point which he promised *to bring to the Committee's attention in three weeks time*. He claimed that he had taken an overoptimistic view of Haig's predictions of success in Flanders, and that if an offensive of the type that he proposed in Palestine was not undertaken, in a year's time they would find themselves in the same position that they were in now. More difficulties than Lloyd George could begin to imagine were to engulf Haig's Army on the Western Front over the next year, and, in spite of the Prime Minister's gloomy predictions, through its own courage, tenacity, and ability it was to win through. But this was for the future, and meanwhile Lloyd George condemned Robertson's latest recommendations which urged concentration on the Western

---

[597] National Archives, Robertson to War Policy Committee 11th October CAB27/7
[598] National Archives, minutes of meeting of the War Policy Committee 11th October CAB27/7

Front as being no different to that which Joffre and all the military Commanders on the Western Front had always proposed; implying that they had always been wrong. Curzon and Smuts were in accord with the Prime Minister's summary, Curzon believing that Haig and Robertson *were* wrong.

The Committee had shown that, in theory at least, it could determine War policy independently of its official military advisors. But the ground upon which The Prime Minister was treading, he clearly considered far from firm, as to move forward in blatant disregard of the military left him dangerously isolated and therefore responsible. The solution was simple; obtain another fount of advice more in keeping with his views on which to strengthen his position. Lloyd George now unveiled his plan to circumvent the hold which Haig and Robertson allegedly held over policy making, and to generally reduce the strength of their positions. In contradiction of his earlier emphasis that the Committee should make the decisions and dictate the implementation of them upon the military, he formally proposed obtaining a second line of military opinion. His somewhat tenuous pretext was that Prime Minister Asquith had in the first days of War in August 1914 consulted military leaders other than the then C.I.G.S. (General Douglas) and Commander-in-Chief (Field-Marshal French). In an ironic twist of fate, Haig had been present with Douglas and French at a meeting of the War Council at Downing Street on the 5th August 1914. Lloyd George also proffered the totally unrelated analogy that if a patient was very sick it would be quite natural to seek a second medical opinion. We shall hear more of this proposal soon.

One important aspect of the Flanders fighting was raised by Smuts, who suggested that the relative casualty rates between the British and German Armies should be considered by the Committee, and that they should enquire into the condition of the 42 divisions with which Haig had begun the offensive. Curzon added that an examination of the reserves of manpower in consequence of the losses in Flanders should also be considered. The consensus of the rather disgruntled Committee was that they had been inadequately provided with statistics of losses through wastage and sickness, whilst they conveniently turned a blind eye to the fact that due to their preoccupation with other matters, they had never actually asked for them. In their deliberations the Committee had therefore established some important principles and conclusions. All were agreed that the fighting in Flanders had achieved and would achieve nothing. Lloyd George would confirm this conclusion to his colleagues in three weeks time (which would serve no benefit other than to prove him right). But of greatest importance the Committee were to force their decision upon the military to carry out an offensive in Palestine. Here was proof that they *were* in a position to determine and dictate military operations after all. They had taken up and accepted the mantle of responsibility, control, and power, although another opinion was to be sought which would hopefully lend support to this determined stance. So action in Palestine had been decided, but what of Flanders? According to Lloyd George, during the next three weeks he was going to be proved right; Haig would not reach the Clerken ridge, and nothing would be achieved. But by the indirect sanction of the Prime Minister and his colleagues, who were clearly in a position to stop it, *the fighting at Ypres would continue.*

The Canadians come north

The colossal operation in Flanders, with its enormous drain on manpower, continued to generate an ever growing demand for fresh divisions both German and British. In August the Canadian Corps had been involved in severe but successful fighting for Hill 70 and the town of Lens, and had sustained in excess of 7,000 casualties. On the 2nd October Haig had ordered General Horne of British First Army to withdraw two of his Canadian divisions from the line near Lens and to place them in G.H.Q. reserve. By the 5th the decision had been made to withdraw all four Canadian divisions from First Army, and to transfer the whole Canadian Corps under Lieut.-General Currie to Second Army around the 14th October.
On the 6th October G.H.Q. had requested Plumer to consider the best way to use the Canadian Corps upon its arrival; which corps it should relieve, and where it should enter the line. He proposed that the Canadians should relieve II Anzac, and strengthen the position on the ridge by

advancing the line towards Moorslede, while II Anzac moved to the right of I Anzac and took over part of X Corps and I Anzac front between the Reutelbeek and Celtic. The alternative plan under consideration prior to the 9th October was that the Canadians would relieve X Corps on the Gheluvelt plateau, north of the Menin Road, and drive the Germans from their last strongpoints at Gheluvelt and Becelaere, whilst IX Corps south of the Menin Road attacked Zandvoorde from the north and I and II Anzac strengthened the position which should have been gained by the 12th October. Corps Commanders were asked for their opinions. Godley, felt that the Canadians should go for Passchendaele, but was cool about II Anzac taking over the line between X and I Anzac Corps, suggesting that the 66th and 49th Divisions should be handed over to assist X Corps in securing Gheluvelt. He proposed II Anzac, less the 66th and 49th Divisions, should initially be withdrawn into Army Reserve, with a view to receiving two fresh divisions and preparing for a later thrust either towards Zandvoorde, assuming Gheluvelt had been secured, or to relieve the Canadians in a drive towards Roulers. He thought highly of his Australians and New Zealanders stating, 'I cannot help thinking that the New Zealand and 3rd Australian Divisions contain such fine attacking material that they can be best employed in that role, on a considerable scale. The 49th and 66th Divisions have so recently joined the Corps, that no special advantage is gained by maintaining their association with it'.[599] After the fight the 49th and 66th Divisions had put up on the 9th, perhaps Godley subsequently felt his remarks somewhat inappropriate.

By the evening of the 9th October it is clear that General Plumer was still unaware of the failure on the slopes either side of the Ravebeek, and believed the gains towards Passchendaele to be more satisfactory than in fact was the case. His misapprehension of the true situation, and his knowledge of the fact that Haig wished him to push on to Passchendaele with all speed, led him to inform G.H.Q. that II Anzac Corps had done well in the day's fighting. 'I am of opinion that the operations of the 49th and 66th Divisions, carried out today under great difficulties of assembly, will afford a sufficiently good jumping-off line for operations on October 12th, on which date I hope that II Anzac Corps will capture Passchendaele.' [600]

Preparations for the 12th October - the difficulties multiply

The general plan for the next step, which had been agreed upon before the attack on the 9th October was to stand in its entirety. If the objectives of the 9th October had been reached, this would have been reasonable. But they had not. This meant that although ground conditions had not improved, and the enemy defences were still as formidable as they had been on the 9th, the attacking divisions would have to advance to objectives of up to a depth of 2,500 yards, 1,000 yards beyond that which had already been found impossible. Due to the failure of the attack on the 9th the plans already drawn up by the attacking divisions had therefore to be changed on the 11th, with precious little time to change them, as the jumping-off lines and dispositions of the battalions would now be completely different.

Once more under Godley's II Anzac Corps was to thrust at Passchendaele, this time with the 3rd Australian Division and the New Zealand Division.[601] Gough it seems, was at this stage a little better informed than both Plumer and Godley. Gough's XVIII Corps was aware that II Anzac was not as far forward as it thought, and informed Godley of the fact. Fifth Army was now short of fresh divisions. This, coupled with the appalling ground, made Gough less than enthusiastic to continue, beyond supporting the main attack on Godley's left flank, and pushing on through Poelcappelle, while pivoting his left on Houthulst Forest. Birdwood, on Godley's right flank, was of firm opinion that his I Anzac Corps was unable to engage in any further operation beyond

---

[599] Library and Archives of Canada, Godley to H.Q. Second Army 8th October. Canadian Corps Headquarters RG9 III-D-3 Vol4957 T-10775
[600] AOA p901
[601] Australian War Memorial, 2nd Anzac Instructions for the Offensive. 10th October 1917. AWM4 1/32/20 Part 2

supporting Godley's right, as Plumer had earmarked I Anzac for future operations against the Keiberg. Australian 5th and 4th Divisions had relieved 1st and 2nd on the night of 10th / 11th October, but already on the 8th Birdwood had warned that due to the exhaustion of his troops, he could do no more than maintain the II Anzac flank with 4th Division. Godley was therefore to be out in front and very much on his own.

With the deeper penetration to be attempted by the infantry, the artillery, already weak and outranged on the 9th, would need to be brought further forward, with its ammunition, across the worsening ground, and had to be set on new gun emplacements in two days. While the backbreaking job of trying to move the guns was in hand they were not available to begin the breaking up of the wire. The Frezenberg – Zonnebeke road was jammed with ammunition wagons, ration carts and pack-horses and was in full view from Passchendaele, but there appeared to be no enemy observation, as the road was not heavily shelled. An Australian gunner described the scene on Frezenberg ridge, either side of the Zonnebeke road: 'The guns sank lower into the mud with each shot. But planks, timber and sandbags were secured from all round the district, and eventually fairly good platforms were obtained. Further forward, down the hill, about 150 yards, our other four batteries had to get in. In front of them the country [the Steenbeek valley] was an absolute quagmire and impossible to occupy. The whole eight batteries were as close to the Zonnebeke road as possible in the hope of getting ammunition up, for it was quite impossible to move across country at any time. As it was many horses, on the short stretch of road from the road to the battery, 80 yards of ground, sank down out of sight, the driver just keeping the horse's head up until assistance arrived'.[602] On the 9th October the 11th Australian Field Artillery Brigade reported: 'Our guns which were bogged yesterday we found impossible to move. Also three guns which were ordered forward were bogged 400 yards from their position.'[603]

The situation was not unknown to Army and Corps headquarters who ordered that if a battery was short of guns to support the attack, those guns in action should increase their rate of fire to compensate. The soaking conditions and water-filled shelters, had reduced through exhaustion and sickness, the number of crew operating the guns, and the system of relief had completely broken down. The ammunition, all of which needed cleaning before use, was in short supply. Fewer gunners with fewer guns and with inadequate supplies of ammunition would therefore have to fire more rounds for the infantry to succeed. On the afternoon of the 10th October, a New Zealand gun team of 15th Battery of the divisional field artillery, attempting to move two 4.5-inch howitzers along the road north of St. Julien came under heavy hostile shelling, at the same time the guns becoming firmly bogged. The road continued to be shelled during the night, and the gun teams returned before dawn to a scene of utter shambles. Dead men, dead horses and smashed wagons and limbers littered the road, but by superhuman efforts the howitzers were moved to there new positions by 7:30 a.m. accompanied by 6 18-pounders. With all the efforts of the gunners, the C.R.A. of the division reported that, owing to the difficulties of getting batteries across the Steenbeek and the instability of the gun platforms, effective artillery support for his division could not be depended upon.

By the 11th October the planned positions for the field artillery of the Australian divisions were to be concentrated in three areas close to the line of the Zonnebeke – Langemarck road; the first group 500 yards north of Zonnebeke, the second group south-west of Hill 40, the third group east of the Fokker Farm crossroads. Their actual positions were: 1st Australian Division, part behind Westhoek ridge and part on Anzac ridge, south-east of the Anzac blockhouse. 2nd Australian Division, on Anzac ridge just north-west of the Anzac blockhouse. 3rd Australian Division, mostly between Frezenberg ridge and the Steenbeek along the Frezenberg – Zonnebeke road, with part behind Hill 35. 4th Australian Division, on Tokio spur. 5th Australian Division just west of Polygon Wood. All were around one mile behind where they were supposed to be.

---

[602] AOA p904
[603] AOA p905

On the 12th October, many guns still lay temporarily abandoned, or out of action and un-replaced. The artillery was confronted with other problems. The barrage start line was still based on the outposts it was believed the 66th and 49th Divisions were holding, rather than the true position discovered by 3rd Australian and the New Zealand Divisions on the 11th. It was too late to alter the whole barrage plan, but in front of 3rd Australian it was drawn back about 350 yards, to creep forward at a quicker rate for 500 yards, where it would catch up with the general line of the Second Army barrage. This meant that 3rd Australian would have to cover 500 yards of the worst possible ground, more quickly than had been attempted on the hard dry ground of September. Everything about the forthcoming attack pointed to a disaster in the making, as all the difficulties of the 9th which had led to failure still existed, plus a few more.

It is still difficult to understand the series of errors and misunderstandings, which led Corps, Army, and G.H.Q. Commanders to agree to renew the attack against Passchendaele on the 12th October. It can only be assumed that Godley did not know what had happened on his Corps front on the 9th - the thinness of the barrage, the complete absence of a smoke screen, the ineffectiveness of the bombardment especially to smash the Bellevue wire, and the exhaustion of the troops - until it was too late to stop the action on the 12th. Haig perhaps, still clung to the hope that to maintain the momentum, one final push with two prime divisions would be sufficient to clear Passchendaele of the enemy, which may shatter their mantle of will and resolve, and at last open the portal to boundless strategic possibilities. After coming so far and being so close to success, how could it be called off while the forces were still available to carry on? The fact that he had the Germans fully engaged in Flanders was a success in itself, but more importantly he believed they were nearly beaten, and had it not been for the intervention of the weather he may well have been right. After the series of devastating blows Plumer had dealt the enemy, his thinking may have been closely aligned with Haig's. He certainly appeared to be much less cautious, and his approach had changed drastically since Messines or even Menin Road. Of late his control of the battle had lost the clinical precision, which as the result of thorough planning had previously been his hallmark. But to continue at that level may have been expecting too much of him, as the enormity of the offensive unfolded, physically and mentally exhausting everyone involved, and the adverse weather once again intervened. There is every chance that Plumer too hoped that the next blow may create an exploitable crack in the weakened enemy wall. The high command on both sides were finding the tactical situation near impossible to control, as the great battle which carried with it so many critical but imponderable issues, imposed its will on them, rather than the other way round.

The usual optimism of Brigadier-General Charteris was rapidly slipping into pessimism. On the 10th he wrote in his diary: 'I was out all day at the attack. It was the saddest day of this year. We did fairly well but only fairly well. It was not the enemy but the mud that prevented us doing better. But now there is now no chance of complete success here this year. We must still fight on for a few more weeks, (Footnote: The French were still appealing for the protection provided by out attacks) but there is no purpose in it now, so far as Flanders is concerned. I don't think I ever really had great hope of a big success yesterday, but until noon there was, at least, still a chance......Yesterday afternoon was utterly damnable. I got back very late and could not work, and could not rest. D. H. sent for me about 10:00, to discuss things. He has to bear the brunt of it all. He was still trying to find some grounds for hope that we might still win through here this year, but there is none.' [604] On the 11th October Haig told a meeting of war correspondents: 'It was simply the mud which defeated us on Tuesday. The men did splendidly to get through it as they did. But the Flanders mud, as you know, is not a new invention. It has a name in history – it has defeated other armies before this one.' [605] He went on to claim that his Army was practically through the enemy's defences: 'He has only flesh and blood against us, not blockhouses – they take a month to make.' In one way Haig was quite correct. It was the Flanders mud which had caused the disaster on the 9th. Not because it had stopped the infantry from attacking, but because it had bogged down the guns, preventing them providing a sound

---

[604] Brig-General John Charteris, *At G.H.Q.* p259
[605] AOA p908

barrage, and smashing the Bellevue wire. In another way he was to be proved disastrously wrong. The blockhouses at Bellevue stood as defiantly as ever, safe behind the wire.

On the evening of the 10th October those brigades of the 3rd Australian Division and the New Zealand Division which were to hold the line until the night of the 11th moved up across the foul desolate landscape to relieve the battered 66th and 49th Divisions. The attacking brigades of the 3rd Australian spent the night bivouacked on the wet ground near Potijze, the tents that were intended to shelter them not having arrived. At around 6:00 p.m. on the cold, bleak evening of the 11th October those brigades of both Second and Fifth Armies which were to carry out the attack began the long struggle forward beneath a leaden sky, across the inhospitable and forbidding wastes, and towards the bare dark ridges, where in the early morning their fate would once again be held in the balance. Lieutenant Fisher of the 42nd Battalion who had carried out the earlier reconnaissance near the slopes of the Ravebeek wrote: 'Finally the company came up – the men done after a fearful struggle through the mud and shell-holes not to speak of the barrage which the Hun put down and which caught numbers. The position was obscure – a dark night – no line – demoralised Tommies – and no sign of the enemy. So I pushed out my platoon ready for anything, and ran into the foe some 80 yards ahead. He put in a few bursts of rapid fire and then fled. We could not pursue as we had to establish the line, which was accomplished about an hour later. I spent the rest of the night in a shell-hole, up to my knees in mud and with rain teeming down.'[606]

During the evening Gough phoned Second Army headquarters once more to request a postponement. He later wrote: 'It poured with rain the previous afternoon, and in the evening I telephoned to Plumer to say that I thought the attack should be postponed. He said he would consult his corps commanders, and shortly after 8 o,clock he called me up to say that they considered it best for the attack to be carried out. The only course for Fifth Army was to follow suit.'[607] At around midnight the weather worsened, with a rising wind and cold drizzling rain.

The attack of the Second Army 5:25 a.m. the 12th October

The capture of Passchendaele was to be the task of Major-General John Monash's 3rd Australian Division, attacking between the Roulers railway and the Ravebeek, while the New Zealand Division of Major-General Russell attacked along the ridge north-west of the Ravebeek from Bellevue to Mosselmarkt to protect the Australian left, and if all went to plan close on Passchendaele from the north-west. The attack was to be effected in three phases, with three objectives, the first, the Red Line, being at a depth of around 900 yards, the second, the Blue Line about 600 yards further, with the final objective, the Green Line another 900 yards. Just beyond the village, there was to be an intermediate objective, the Green Dotted Line. There were to be long halts to allow for reorganization at each objective, and except for the initial sharp 500 yard barrage unfortunately imposed in front of 3rd Division, the general pace would be slow. The halt on the first objective would be from 6:37 to 8:25, the second objective from 9:21 to 10:25, and the third objective from 11:29 to 11:55.

I Anzac Corps

---

[606] AOA p907

[607] General Hubert Gough, *The Fifth Army* p213. Harington's account is different in detail. He claims that Gough rang Plumer at 2:30 on the morning of the 12th October requesting a postponement. Plumer ordered Harington to phone the Corps Commanders, (whether just Second Army, or Second and Fifth Army is not stated). All except one, who did not express a definite opinion, agreed that it was too late to postpone as the infantry were already on their way to the lines, and to communicate an order to stop would be impossible. Plumer then called Gough with a simple message, "Is that you Gough? The attack must go on. I am responsible not you. Good night and good luck". Harington, *Tim Harington Looks Back* p63

To protect the right flank of II Anzac, the 4th Australian Division was to use the 12th Brigade, which was to advance in strength across the Keiberg, to the south of the railway. The first and second objectives were to be occupied in contact with the 3rd Australian Division, but only a post would be sent forward to the final objective. As the 3rd Australian advance progressed along the main ridge towards Passchendaele, its right flank would become gradually more exposed, and this had been a concern at Second Army. On the north-eastern face of the Keiberg a small stream, the Broubeek, had washed a shallow valley across which the railway passed along an embankment, before cutting through another low spur projecting eastwards from the main ridge. This low spur, 2,000 yards beyond the start line at Defy Crossing, was to be the forward point of junction between I and II Anzac and special mention had been made of it in the Second Army orders issued to Birdwood: 'Particular attention must be given to the high ground north and south of the Broubeek, (beyond the Keiberg), which must either be seized or kept under such fire as to prevent the right flank of II Anzac being interfered with therefrom.'[608]

4th Australian Division, 12th Brigade, the morning advance[609]
The 12th Brigade was to use the 47th Battalion to seize the first objective, about 800 yards forward on the neck of the Keiberg near Decline Copse,. The 48th Battalion was to throw out a series of posts into the Broubeek valley 1,500 yards from the start line, and if the 3rd Division reached its third objective on the left, was to establish a single post beyond Passchendaele Station.

    As the 47th advanced at 5:25 a.m. there was no movement noticed north of the railway in the sector of the 3rd Australian Division. The same German post in the cement dump near Defy Crossing now shot up the 47th as it had the 20th Battalion on the 9th October. The 48th Battalion following closely, lined the embankment, and engaged the machine gun from the railway, suppressing its fire as the 47th moved on. Working forward just south of the railway cutting the 47th bombed out and seized a post in Decoy Wood. The enemy dug-outs along the railway cutting opened rifle fire upon the mixed parties of 47th and 48th, but for some reason did not use their machine guns, and were quickly overrun. Two Vickers guns were set up above the cutting to cover the infantry advance, and rifle fire in enfilade from the ruined barn at Assyria 300 yards to the south soon ceased, as at the approach of the Australians the enemy fled to the rear. In the short advance, 12th Brigade casualties had been severe, but they had reached the first objective and could see forward into the depression of the Broubeek and towards Moorslede 3,000 yards distant. From their shell-holes on the first objective the forward parties observed a company of Germans rush from Tiber Copse, 200 yards north of the railway and proceed to line the embankment from where they opened fire on the right of the 12th Brigade, but the Vickers guns further along the embankment opened fire in enfilade and scattered the enemy riflemen. At this point, about 8:25, the 3rd Division were seen to be advancing north of the railway, working forward in the face of heavy fire from right and left and still behind the left flank of the 48th. This released the party of the 48th lining the embankment, which now moved forward to reinforce the forward positions.

    The situation forward of the first objective was going to make further advance for the 48th a costly business. Fire from Vienna Cottages 150 yards north-east of the railway was severe and had virtually closed the far end of the cutting. North of the railway the 3rd Division were held up on the first objective with little hope of getting forward and had apparently decided to dig-in where they were. The left of the 48th Battalion also commenced to dig-in to conform to the 3rd Division, and the centre stayed in position awaiting any movement on the left. On the right Captain Whittington worked forward with a party of about 18 men, to a position which he believed was his objective and established an isolated post. A little later around 100 men of the 3rd Division were seen to be advancing further along the ridge in the direction of Passchendaele.

---

[608] AOA p910 footnote
[609] National Archives, War diary 12th Aus Brigade WO95/3506, National Archives, War Diary 45th Battalion WO95/3509, National Archives, War Diary 46th Battalion WO95/3510, National Archives, War Diary 47th Battalion WO95/3512, National Archives, War Diary 48th Battalion WO95/3514

II Anzac Corps
Attack towards Passchendaele

The goal towards which the whole dreadful series of battles had been striving was now limited to the capture of the high ground around the ruins of Passchendaele village. To conceive of greater hopes was agreed by all to be pointless. With the benefit of knowing what faced Godley's II Anzac Corps this day, we are compelled to view the 12th October as a hopeless dawn. However, the Australians and New Zealanders awaiting the moment to advance were under no illusions regarding the difficulty of their task. But they did not see it as hopeless, and no two finer divisions existed to make the attempt.

3rd Australian Division, 9th [610] and 10th [611] Brigades, the morning actions

The advance to the first objective.

The duckboard tracks had been taken a little closer to the front since the 9th October, but as the 3rd Division moved up the tracks they were under persistent and accurate hostile shelling with both high explosive and gas. The 9th Brigade which was to attack on the right between Defy Crossing and Augustus Wood, marched up along the Roulers railway track, an operation made more difficult as the route was also used by I Anzac going in, and other troops coming out of the line. The 10th Brigade which was to attack between Augustus Wood and Marsh Bottom, marched up over 'K Track', crossing the Zonnebeke – Langemarck road near Van Isackers Farm, across the Hanebeek, and up the gentle slope of Abraham Heights past Bordeaux and Beecham Farms. As the 10th crossed the Hanebeek gas shells were landing on the windward side of the track, but largely thanks to the strong wind there were few casualties. The gas shelling, which affected the whole front to a greater or lesser extent, was part of a German plan, *"Mondnacht"*, pre-arranged for the 2nd October, but then postponed until the evening of the 11th. By 2:30 a.m. the drizzle had turned to steady rain and by 3:30 it was raining heavily.

---

[610] National Archives, War Diary 9th Aus Brigade WO95/3397, National Archives, War Diary 33rd Battalion WO95/3402, National Archives, War Diary 34th Battalion WO95/3405, National Archives, War Diary 35th Battalion WO95/3408, National Archives, War Diary 36th Battalion WO95/3409
[611] National Archives, War Diary 10th Aus Brigade WO95/3411, National Archives, War Diary 37th Battalion WO95/3414, National Archives, War Diary 38th Battalion WO95/3415, National Archives, War Diary 39th Battalion WO95/3417, National Archives, War Diary 40th Battalion WO95/3420

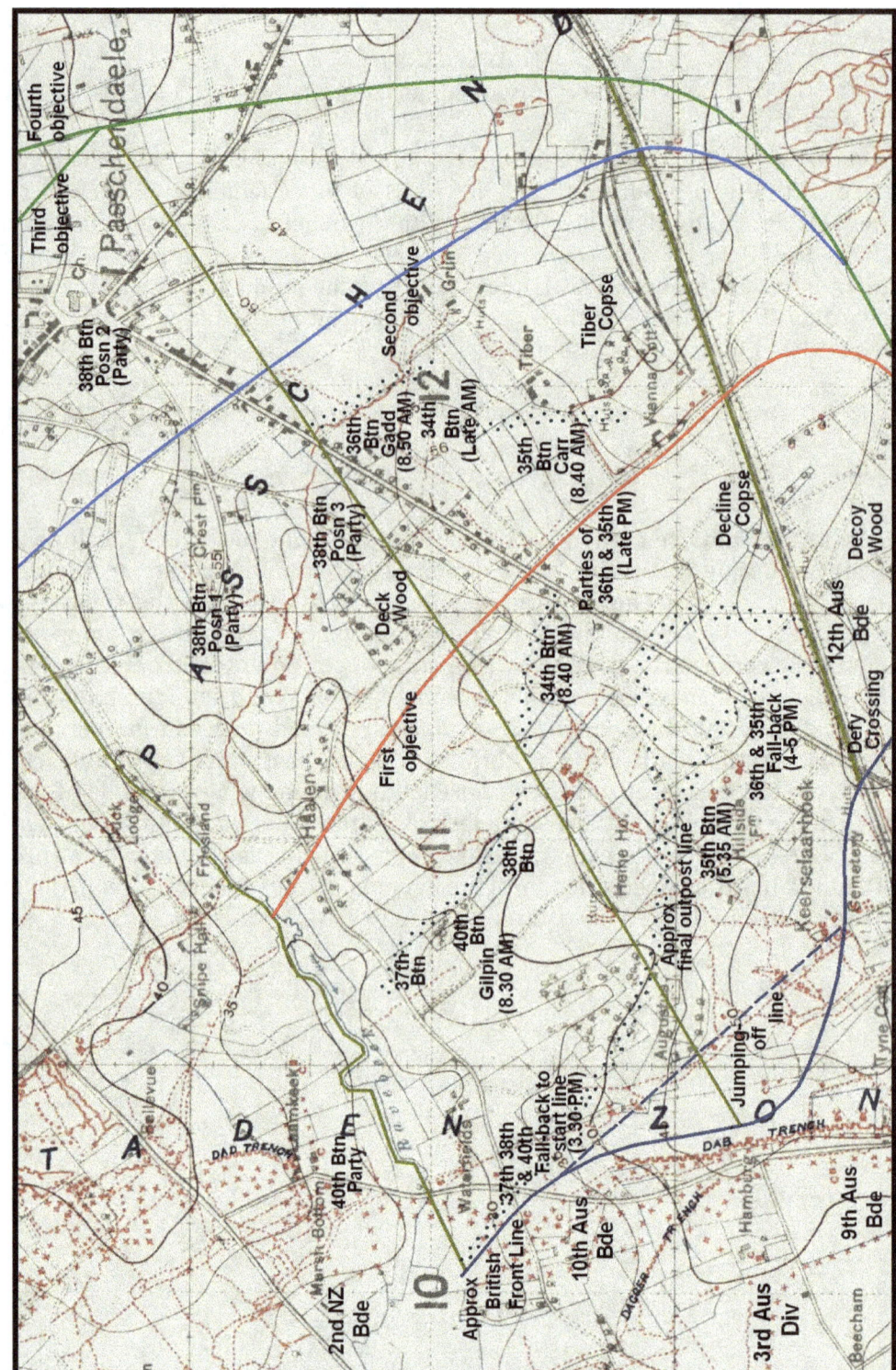

The attack of the 3rd Australian Division towards Passchendaele

As we have seen, it had soon become apparent that the line reported held by the 66th Division was not held, and rather than walk into enemy posts officers of the incoming battalions went forward to reconnoitre. The forward battalion of the 9th Brigade, the 34th, was held at Thames at the entrance to the Nieuwemolen railway cutting, until it was ascertained that the tapes were correctly laid at Keerselaarhoek cemetery, and by 3:00 a.m. the 34th was extended on its jumping-off position, with the 35th and 36th close behind, both having been shelled throughout the whole assembly. By 3:20 the 37th, 38th and 40th Battalions of 10th Brigade were laid out in shell-holes beneath their capes, but were also being shelled and suffering heavy losses.

Around 4:20 the rain had ceased but at 5:25 when the barrage opened in front of the 3rd Australian Division it bore no resemblance to that which they had so confidently followed on the 4th October. There was no solid curtain of clearly defined explosions, or dense smoke, or earth kicked up by showers of scything shrapnel. Many howitzer shells buried themselves into the soft mud, and upon detonation produced geysers of steaming mire, with little detrimental effect on the enemy. Others did not detonate at all. The Australians, so used to closing up behind a protective wall of exploding projectiles found it difficult to differentiate between the barrage and hostile shelling. The usually subdued enemy was not going to be troubled by the scattered shell-fire, and the machine guns would quickly be in action, as through the thin casual bursts, they could clearly see their targets. This was the real results of what the rain could do. The infantry were going forward but without the essential protection of the guns. Not only was the barrage weak in front of 3rd Australian Division, but it was out of phase with that of the 4th Australian and the New Zealand Division. The hostile shelling on the tapes, the 350 yard step in alignment, and the instant response from the enemy's machine guns, threw the 3rd Division advance into a state disorder, which the awful ground conspired to exacerbate. What there was of the barrage, at its increased initial rate, soon left the struggling troops behind, who were now not only disorganised but veering too far to the north. The jump-off line between Defy Crossing and Augustus Wood was nearly at right angles with the road which ran along the spine of the ridge, and along the ridge top was where the 9th Brigade now advanced, instead of crossing the road and following the railway track a good 40 degrees further east. It is little wonder 12th Brigade south of the railway could not see them.

The thin barrage enabled the German machine guns to take an early toll on the 9th Brigade, fire lashing in to the 34th from a ruined house near Defy Crossing on the right, from the blockhouse supported by a slit trench at Hillside Farm in the centre, and from the battered remains of Augustus Wood on the left. The fire from Hillside Farm caused a one hour hold-up which threatened the whole operation, until the blockhouse was rushed and the trench seized by parties of the 35th Battalion, with the capture of 35 Germans and 4 machine guns. Another blockhouse close to the Passchendaele road and near the highest point of the ridge caused a further check, in a position completely devoid of shelter. Captain Jefferies and a party of the 34th worked around to the rear and charged the position capturing 25 Germans and 2 machine guns. As the blockhouse was near the first objective, the 34th commenced to dig-in in nearby shell-holes. The capture of these positions allowed the advance to continue, but the 34th had sustained many casualties, the assault groups now very thin and with only three officers remaining. The right flank of the battalion had now veered far to the left of its correct position on the railway. On the left, the 38th Battalion of 10th Brigade was digging-in 70 yards in rear of the 34th left company, which fell back and dug-in to conform to the 38th.

The 37th Battalion, which had led the attack of 10th Brigade had also met with heavy machine gun fire from gun-pits and bunkers in Augustus Wood to their front, and sniper fire from the blockhouse at Waterfields in the bog of the Ravebeek to the left. Forward movement was limited to dashes between shell-holes, the barrage was lost, and the 38th and 40th soon caught up, parties of all three battalions becoming intermingled. A mixed party gradually worked around the rear of the shattered stumps of the wood and quickly overcame resistance from enemy posts within. In this attack Sergeant Lewis Mc Gee who had attacked the blockhouse near Hamburg on the 4th October, and was to be posthumously awarded the V.C., was shot and killed. Another group, scrambled between the craters through the quagmire, and edged their way towards Waterfields, until close enough to rush and bomb the blockhouse into submission. Casualties in the 10th had already been severe, and as the scattered parties of the brigade attempted to make their way forward along the slope above the Ravebeek they came under heavy enfilade fire from the pillboxes on Bellevue spur, as the 66th Division had done before them. The Bellevue wire belts had held up the New Zealand as they had held up the 49th Division, in a re-run of the disaster of the 9th October. The advance was reduced to a series of short rushes between water-filled craters, each rush adding to the toll of casualties, as the machine guns across the Ravebeek tore into the Australians. An old trench, battered by shell-fire and situated in a slight fold in the slope between two swamps, gave a modicum of protection.

Here, men of the 37th, 38th and 40th, still under fire, attempted to dig-in. Suddenly to better illuminate the drama unfolding on the battlefield, the clouds lifted and the sun shone in patches of blue between high cirrus clouds.

The advance to the second objective

On the ridge top, the advance to the first objective had been so held up, that as the 34th Battalion dug-in at about 8:25, the 35th, which was to attack the second objective arrived and passed straight through. The barrage was still indiscernible, and two officers standing on the ridge-top road had difficulty in deciding whether it was landing in front or behind them. The confusion created at Zero Hour still existed and mixed groups of the 34th and 35th moved forward together, the main body of around 100 moving on towards the ruins of Passchendaele village. This was the group seen by Captain Whittington's party of the 48th Battalion from the railway cutting. A German machine gun in the gap between the advancing party of the 9th Brigade and the railway opened a deadly fire, killing the senior forward officer of the brigade Major Buchanan of the 36th. Captain Jefferies again gathered a few men and worked towards the gun, which was shooting in short bursts which allowed them to creep up close. As the gun fired towards the north Jeffries and his men rushed it from the west. At that moment the gun swung back round to the west killing Jefferies and sending his men to ground. As its fire shifted from them the survivors rushed the position capturing 25 Germans and 2 machine guns. For his conspicuous bravery in the attacks on both blockhouses, Captain Clarence Smith Jefferies was to be posthumously awarded the V.C. Once more the bravery of a small group enabled the advance to continue, but as the 35th crossed to the eastern side of the ridge the dangers of the exposed right flank became clear, as enemy guns both field and medium opened fire upon them over open sights, from the direction of Moorslede. After passing a copse on its right, (probably Tiber Copse), the 35th believing it was on its second objective, stopped and dug-in, establishing three posts, although in fact its right was still short of the first objective. At 8:35 a.m. Captain Carr, the senior officer on the spot reported: 'On objective, with about 100, with Captain Dixon and three officers. Casualties 25 or 30 percent. Captain Cadell, Lieuts. Main and Day reported killed, Lieuts. Horne, Mears, Henry wounded. Prisoners sent back 400-500. Contact on flanks uncertain. Being heavily shelled.'[612] At the second objective the 36th Battalion was to pass through the 35th towards the final objective. In the confusion at the start, the 36th had in fact advanced with the 35th, and had moved forward on the left towards the second objective, establishing a line 600 yards from the church, with its left on the road. No fire came down the road from the rubble of the village, but two 5.9-inch howitzers along the Moorslede road to the east opened fire on Captain Gadd's 36th as they dug-in.

Over on the western side of the ridge, in the old German trench on the slope above the Ravebeek, the number of men that had finally struggled forward amounted to no more than 100 to 150, and there they were held by Major Giblin of the 40th battalion awaiting reinforcement or further instructions. At 8:40 Giblin sent back a message that he had insufficient men to continue the advance, but unbeknown to him a small force of around 20 men mainly of the 38th Battalion, had worked forward up the valley of the Ravebeek, until confronted with the blockhouse on the side-spur at Crest Farm. The enemy garrison of about 20 surrendered without a fight. On the other side of the valley, more Germans, who were not in a threatened position, could be seen withdrawing in numbers towards the north-east, along the Bellevue – Meetcheele spur, 1,000 yards behind the wire where the New Zealand was obviously held up. The small Australian force moved carefully forward from Crest Farm, across a slight depression, and in about 500 yards up to the remains of Passchendaele church. Within the wrecked village there were no enemy to be seen, but neither were there any more Australians, so the small group fell back out of the village by the same route they had entered. Crest Farm had to be skirted with care as it had be reoccupied by the enemy, their machine guns again active, while across the valley order had

---

[612] AOA p916

been restored in the enemy ranks, as the grey-clad figures (possibly the *II/10th Bavarian R.I.R.* counter-attack forces of the *5th Bavarian Reserve Division,* and/or the *I/55th R.I.R.* of the *220th Division*) rallied and moved forward again towards Bellevue and the New Zealand line. The small patrol of the 38th finally withdrew to the left flank of 9th Brigade.

The situation of 3rd Australian Division by midday

By midday the position of the 3rd Division was exposed and extremely precarious. On the right, the 9th Brigade was around the second objective, with Captain Carr and around 150 men of 35th Battalion on the eastern slope of the ridge near Tiber. They were being continually sniped by both enemy small arms and artillery fire, and requesting instructions of what to do. They could see small numbers of the 4th Division south of the railway, forward to their right, and by 10:55 it was discovered that 36th Battalion was established forward to their left.

But on the western slopes overlooking the Ravebeek, 10th Brigade was still held up about the first objective, with little hope of getting forward. It was clear to Giblin's mixed group from their position in the old trench line that something had gone badly wrong over in the New Zealand sector, as the fire from the Bellevue pillboxes, which should by now have been seized, was still acute, much of it ripping into the Australians left flank. In a desperate attempt to subdue this fire a small party of the 38th were detailed to move across the Ravebeek and attack the pillboxes. They were never seen again. Another attempt was made by a few of the 40th who crossed the Ravebeek by the Laamkeek road bridge, the only possible crossing place, and gradually worked along the road, silencing one bunker, and after cooperating with a small party of the New Zealand in some stiff fighting captured two more with 60 prisoners. From the bunkers the Australians opened fire on the enemy snipers up on the spur at Bellevue, but with little effect. The Germans were now recovering from their earlier timidity, as they poured in a constant stream back along the spur to reinforce the trenches and pillboxes at Bellevue, and worked their way down into the valley of the Ravebeek, in left rear of Giblin's force on the opposite slope. The New Zealand was seen to make another desperate assault on the wire, but the attack was scythed down by machine gun fire from the spur and floundered against the unbroken entanglements. Giblin's hard pressed force was coming under increasing fire from many directions; from the Crest Farm blockhouse, from Bellevue, and from enemy snipers who had now worked down into the Ravebeek mire to their left rear.

The first reports of the action to reach Monash shortly after 7:00 a.m. at his divisional headquarters in the Ramparts at Ypres, indicated that all was going well and by 8:26 it seemed the first objective was secured. The incoming reports remained optimistic, word arriving at 9:25 that the second objective was taken, and at 10:28 that the attack had gone forward towards the third, although a report at 9:55 implied that the 10th Brigade was held up by fire from Bellevue. Most of what Monash had heard pointed towards success, but worryingly nothing had been reported regarding the situation of the New Zealand Division. On the assumption that the 3rd Australian Division was still advancing Monash asked that all possible fire-power of the New Zealand artillery should be laid upon Bellevue spur, and ordered the 39th Battalion in 10th Brigade reserve to be prepared to assist in holding the ground already won, while the 33rd Battalion in 9th Brigade reserve should stand by to assist in the final capture of Passchendaele. Just after noon, news of the true situation at the front arrived in Ypres. A lamp signal station, set up in one of the captured bunkers near Waterfields flashed an accurate message back to 40th Battalion headquarters, which passed it up to 10th Brigade, which in turn forwarded it to 3rd Division at the Ramparts. Monash now knew of the precarious situation of Giblin's weakly held line, and that casualties were very high. At the same time a pigeon arrived at Poperinghe from Captain Gadd of the 36th Battalion on the east slope of the ridge with the message: 'We are on Blue Line, with composite force all three battalions, both flanks in air.'[613] Monash believed the situation remained salvageable, especially as he had been informed that the New Zealand

---

[613] AOA p916

Division had been ordered to make yet another attempt at breaking through to Bellevue at 3:00 p.m. He therefore ordered the 39th Battalion to reinforce Giblin above the Ravebeek, whilst the 9th Brigade was to use its reserve 33rd Battalion to work further along the ridge, and at 4:30 to attack the Crest Farm blockhouse from the north.

Before following the Australian story further we must first examine the fortunes of the New Zealand Division throughout the morning.

The New Zealand Division attack on Bellevue

The New Zealand Division was to attack along a 1,200 yard line which ran from Marsh Bottom, through Peter Pan to Yetta Houses, the tapes being laid about 250 yards north-east of the Stroombeek – Ravebeek. To assist in crossing the mire, five coconut mats had been laid by the 1st Field Company New Zealand Engineers. The task facing the 2nd New Zealand Brigade,[614] and the New Zealand Rifle Brigade,[615] was undoubtedly one of the toughest faced by any division in the whole campaign. In both brigades each battalion was allotted an objective line, at which point the support battalions were to leap-frog through to the next objective. 2nd Brigade was to use the 2nd Otago to the first objective (Red Line) beyond the Bellevue defences, the 1st Otago to the second objective (Blue Line) between the Ravebeek and the Paddebeek at the point where Bellevue spur abutted the main ridge, and the 1st Canterbury plus one company of the 2nd Canterbury to the final objective (Green Dotted and Green Lines) on Goudberg spur.[616] The other three 1st Canterbury companies were to be held as local reserves, two for 2nd Otago and one for 1st Otago. In the Rifle Brigade the 2nd Battalion was to capture the first objective, the 3rd Battalion the second, and the 3rd Battalion the final objective.[617] The 4th Battalion was to act as brigade reserve, and to follow up the leading assault waves. The account of the New Zealand Division throws an interesting light upon the feelings of the men on the eve of the battle: 'They were insensibly affected by their exposure to miserable weather in undrained shell-holes, the sight of unbroken wire, and the knowledge of the previous failure. None the less, every man steeled his heart and, checking dispiriting speculation, grimly determined to do his duty...As the troops waited under the rain, there were few whose thoughts in those last moments did not revert to the barbed wire and the pillboxes, and whose prayers were not fervent for an overwhelming barrage, sufficient of itself to blast a passage through the thicket of wire, or to spread such an efficient shied before them that they could cut their way through by hand with the minimum of aimed hostile fire.'[618] The enemy shelling which had struck the 3rd Australian Division also struck the New Zealand as they assembled, causing some casualties, and had unfortunately destroyed those Stokes mortars and limited quantities of mortar ammunition, which had been carried forward with huge effort along the tracks and across the mire.

As the barrage opened at 5:25, the very worst fears of the waiting infantry were realised. It was ragged and thin, and some of the guns, inadequately mounted on their spongy emplacements back near the Steenbeek were firing dangerously short. Any hopes of the barrage thickening as it climbed the slope towards the wire and blockhouses were dashed, as if anything it became even thinner. What should have been a destructive bombardment of the defences on top of the spur by the howitzers, was largely dissipated as the shells exploded almost harmlessly in the thick mud, having little or no effect on the enemy positions. The German artillery responded to the British barrage, but its fire was heaviest on the assembled lines behind the forward battalions, those in rear suffering most. But the forward battalions could not

---

[614] National Archives, War Diary 2nd NZ Brigade WO95/3695
[615] National Archives, War Diary NZ Rifle Brigade WO95/3706
[616] National Archives, War Diary 1st Otago WO95/3701, 2nd Otago WO95/3703, 1st Canterbury WO95/3697, 2nd Canterbury WO95/3699
[617] National Archives, War Diary 1st NZ Rifle Brigade WO95/3708, National Archives, War Diary 2nd NZ Rifle Brigade WO95/3709, National Archives, War Diary 3rd NZ Rifle Brigade WO95/3710, National Archives, War Diary 4th NZ Rifle Brigade WO95/3711
[618]) Colonel H.Stewart, *The New Zealand Division* p282

escape the barrage of machine gun fire which raked them from the pillboxes and trenches on the spur, and from the blockhouse and trenches at Crest Farm 1,400 yards to the east over the Ravebeek. Machine gun fire from Source Trench, a continuation of the Flanders I system to the left in XVIII Corps sector also hit the New Zealand in enfilade.

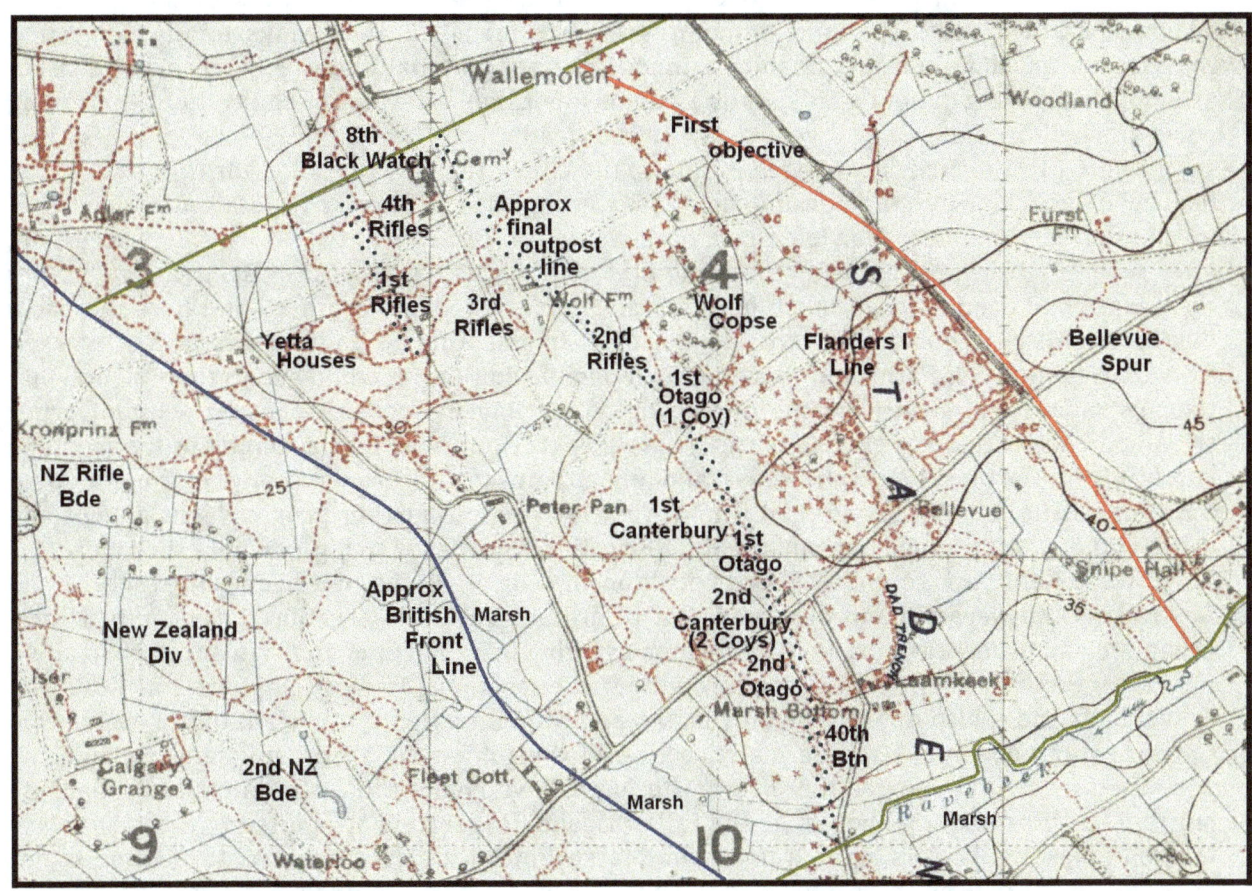

The attack of the 2nd New Zealand Brigade and New Zealand Rifle Brigade - New Zealand Division at Bellevue

On the New Zealand right, just across the Ravebeek from the Australians, in Marsh Bottom and astride the Gravenstafel road, 2nd Otago soon realised that here the Germans were holding their forward positions in strength, as they pressed forward towards the wire entanglements and came under a storm of machine gun and rifle fire. The wire belts were found to be between 25 and 50 yards wide and had been totally unaffected by the bombardment. The only possible way through was by following the line of the Gravenstafel road, but this inevitably created a defile into which many of the Otago now funnelled. They were shot down in large numbers by machine guns in two carefully positioned blockhouses either side of the road. Enemy fortified shell-holes beside the blockhouses were more vulnerable, and were effectively engaged with rifle grenades and Lewis guns, and with this covering fire some of the Otago attempted to cut their way through the wire to attack the blockhouses. Two companies of the 2nd Canterbury in brigade support were soon in action with the Otago, all desperately trying to find a way through or round the wire to come to grips with the enemy garrisons. The 1st Otago which was to attack the second objective moved up, but could do no more than fill the ever widening gaps in the ranks of the 2nd Otago. Some succeeded in cutting through the first belt of wire, to be shot down before reaching the second. Others managed to cut through the second, only to find the blockhouses protected by a new inner belt of wire. Incredibly 2nd Lieutenant J.J. Bishop, and 2nd Lieutenant N. F. Watson cut right through the entanglements, and attacked a blockhouse, there to be shot down and killed in the act of bombing it out. The left company of 1st Otago was reduced to about 28 of the original 140 that had attacked, and this small party now worked to the left in an effort to find a way around the flank of the pillboxes, eventually reaching Wolf Copse where they were finally checked along with the Rifle Brigade. Of the reserve company of the 1st Otago, all officers but one were killed or wounded.

In the Rifle Brigade sector over on the left, as the forward waves of the 2nd Rifles struggled up the lower slope some initial progress was made, but their ranks, totally exposed to the viscous machine gun fire, rapidly thinned. The support battalions moved forward in an attempt to fill the gaps but gradually the advance became a desperate choice between taking cover in shell-holes or being swept away by the hostile fire. The painfully slow progress was soon limited to short rushes between craters, the closer the New Zealand got to the wire, the heavier the machine gun fire became. Composite groups of 2nd, 3rd, and 4th Rifles all struggled to make progress, and on the far left a party assisted by some Scots of the 9th Division succeeded, after severe fighting, in capturing the cemetery 1,000 yards north-west of Bellevue. Twenty of the enemy had been killed, 3 taken prisoner and 3 machine guns captured and here the party dug-in establishing posts 150 yards to the east. In the Rifle Brigade centre, a few worked forward beyond Wolf Farm, and reaching the edge of Wolf Copse could see to their right, what the Australians had seen from the other side of the Ravebeek, as the enemy, without arms, streamed back across the spur towards Mosselmarkt. There was no slackening of the machine gun fire from the blockhouses however, and any attempt to cut through the wire brought down a hail of hostile fire. At around 8:00 a.m. it was clear that no further progress was going to be made without being wiped out, and the Rifle Brigade was ordered to dig-in where they were. 1st Rifles were held back to dig a support position in rear. Again as had been witnessed by the Australians the New Zealand observed that at around 9:00 a.m. the Germans regained their discipline and orderly groups, with some men carrying light machine guns advanced back along the ridge, the movement continuing throughout the morning. Artillery observers at Korek on Gravenstafel ridge also noticed the movement, and brought as heavy a weight of fire as possible to bear on the enemy. As the Germans recovered their offensive spirit, still safely behind the wire, they strongly reinforced the slit trenches on Bellevue mounting an additional two machine guns on the tops of the pillboxes. As the Rifle Brigade desperately attempted to establish posts in shell-holes and craters along a line from Marsh Bottom to the cemetery, they came under intense sniper fire from these guns, and the number of casualties climbed steadily.

From the start a gap had developed between the 2nd Brigade and the Rifle Brigade, where the advance had parted around an area of swamp, and to avoid the worst of the fire from the pillboxes. In an effort to reduce this fire which lashed the 2nd Brigade, two platoons of the Rifle Brigade were pushed forward into the gap and with their Lewis guns attempted to suppress the enemy fire. They were too few in number to fully bridge the gap, and the enemy fire continued to sweep the Otago, preventing further advance. The 3rd, 2nd, and 4th Battalions of the Rifle Brigade, caked in the thick mud into which they were trying to consolidate, were reduced to around 500 men along the whole front. As further movement was impossible attempts were made to clean the mud choked rifles and Lewis guns. The 1st Battalion of the Rifles moved up, and crossed the Stroombeek to carry the attack forward to the final objective, but they too came under a hail of sniper and machine gun fire and it was soon clear that the line had not advanced as planned. With the three forward battalions all pinned down on the slopes of the spur, the 1st Rifles made no further attempt to advance, but dug-in on a support line 150 yards in rear of the track between Wolf Farm and the cemetery.

On the far right of the New Zealand line, in the quagmire at Marsh Bottom, two enemy bunkers, with a communicating slit trench, which had been viciously enfilading the 2nd Brigade, appeared to offer a greater opportunity of attack, seemingly protected by less dense wire belts. A platoon led by 2nd Lieutenant A. R. Cockerell worked forward by rushes under cover of rifle grenades, and by taking cover in shell-holes. Under the hail of grenades, some of the Germans in the trench took shelter in the bunkers, while others surrendered. As we have seen an Australian party was working towards the same position from Waterfields across the Ravebeek. Some of the Otago suppressed the hostile fire from the bunker with their Lewis guns, while Cockerell led others, many of whom were shot down, in rushes towards the rear entrances, where under the threat of

Mills bombs the garrison surrendered. Out of his platoon only Cockerell and one man survived the assault, and as that man was sent back for reinforcements he too was shot down. Five of the Australians were also sent back to Otago headquarters but all became casualties, whilst Cockerell assisted the others of the 40th Battalion to garrison the bunkers. For his courageous action he was to be awarded the D.S.O.

Whilst this attack was in progress, the 1st Canterbury, detailed to attack the final objective, crossed the Ravebeek unaware of the disaster unfolding at the front. It soon became clear that the two forward battalions were pinned down on the bare slope before the wire, but the Canterbury continued in its efforts to press home the attack against the inaccessible machine guns. Their gallant efforts ended with the same result. All battalions of the 2nd Brigade and Rifle Brigade had now been engaged, and what was left of the assault force clung to their shell-holes and shallow scrapes, the dead and wounded all around, but especially thick along the wire in front. Between Marsh Bottom and the cemetery beyond Wolf Farm the New Zealand Division lay prostrate, while the Bellevue wire remained impassable and the enemy in their pillboxes remained un-assailed.

At forward battalion headquarters in the Waterloo blockhouse, 700 yards from the front, the situation on the slopes of the spur was now crystal clear. Battalion commanders had been forward to ascertain the position for themselves and concluded that there was no possible way of advancing the line. When news reached 2nd Brigade headquarters around midday, the Brigade Major, Major Richardson, went up to Waterloo to discuss the hold-up with the battalion commanders. Soon after his arrival, Richardson received a message from Corps headquarters, which to all those present appeared to seal the fate of the New Zealand Division. Godley had been made aware that Bellevue was not taken, and that 3rd Australian was pinned down around the first objective on the slopes the opposite side of the Ravebeek by machine gun fire from the spur. In places the 3rd Australian Division was believed to be somewhere near the second objective, and it seemed that the 9th Division of Fifth Army on the left had got forward to the final objective near Goudberg Copse 1,200 yards north of Bellevue. But the advance on Passchendaele village was at deadlock, unless the New Zealand Division could take Bellevue spur. Godley ordered the temporary suspension of the attack, but also that it should be renewed at 3:00 p.m. This was the news Monash had received at the Ramparts. The New Zealand Division headquarters ordered that the barrage should be brought back to the Red Line, and in line with the instructions from II Anzac headquarters ordered that two battalions of the reserve brigade should move up to the western slope of the Gravenstafel ridge, while at the front the 2nd Brigade and Rifle Brigade were to reorganise, and prepare to attack again at 3:00. The final objective was limited to the Blue Line, which had been the second objective for the day, with the advance to the final objective on Goudberg spur being postponed. It was hoped that this would at least release the 3rd Australian to advance on Crest Farm and Passchendaele. It was naively suggested that the Bellevue pillboxes should be attacked from the north-west by the Rifle Brigade, while 2 companies of 2nd Brigade feinted an attack from the south-west, the remaining force of two battalions pushing forward abreast of the Gravenstafel road. How the wire which had been impenetrable during the morning would be penetrated in the afternoon was not made clear in the orders. Just to move on the slopes below Bellevue was impossible, and the order to reorganise was unachievable. All those presently in the Waterloo blockhouse in touch with the situation in the front line knew the order to be nothing short of a death sentence for the New Zealand Division and urged its abandonment. Their protestation however fell on deaf ears, and the battalion commanders reluctantly put in place the best measures possible to reorganise their battalions, and made ready to accompany them into action from which they knew few would return.

It is now necessary to return to the plight of the Australians.

3rd Australian Division, 9th and 10th Brigades, the afternoon withdrawal

The orders issued by Monash, to engage the 33rd Battalion of 9th Brigade to attack Crest Farm, and to 39th Battalion of 10th Brigade to reinforce Gilpin on the slopes above the Ravebeek, were sent, but none of them fulfilled. Neither Gilpin's nor Carr's requests for instructions, sent several hours earlier had been received. The mixed battalions of the 9th Brigade were still holding out on the eastern side of the ridge, with Captain Carr's 35th back on the first objective near Tiber Copse just north of the railway, and Captain Gadd's 36th pushed forward near the second objective along the ridge-top road, 600 yards short of Passchendaele church. Both detachments were being pounded by German artillery at short range and casualties were mounting alarmingly. Meanwhile the battalion commander of the 36th Lieutenant-Colonel Milne had come up to Hillside Farm, and learnt of the situation, but determined that the positions must be held until dark. In Carr's three posts all officers were out of action, as were most officers of the 36th. At 3:15, although facing annihilation, Gadd was reluctant to withdraw against the orders of his colonel, and Carr agreed to remain in position on his right. The enemy artillery continued to shell both positions and Carr again urged Gadd to request of Milne at Hillside Farm permission to fall-back. Carr had already at 12:30 sent back for instructions to 35th Battalion headquarters at the Seine blockhouse, and had received no reply. The steady rain which had begun again at 3:00 added to the misery of the situation. With no further instructions coming back from any quarter, Carr with Gadd's agreement ordered the remnants of the 35th to retire. At about 4:00 p.m. the 36th and 35th commenced to fall back, with orders to rally with the 34th which was believed to be dug-in near the first objective. This however was not the case as the 34th had already gone forward in an effort to strengthen the second objective, and the first objective now lay empty. The majority of the 36th and 35th, having no idea where to take up a new position, continued to fall back past Hillside Farm to the start line. Here some were rallied by Milne and sent back up to the line of the first objective, where they stayed until after dark.

On the other side of the ridge, by shortly after noon, Giblin had come to the same conclusion as Carr as no word of instruction had come forward. With the Germans working steadily into the Ravebeek swamps to his left rear, retirement was the only option, and after thorough consultation with other officers present, and with careful instructions to the men, an orderly withdrawal in fours and fives was begun. The withdrawal was completed by 3:30 p.m. and a new line was established near the morning's jumping-off tapes and here the exhausted and soaked men dug-in.

I Anzac Corps, 4th Australian Division, the withdrawal of 12th Brigade

At around 3:00 p.m. a heavy German barrage extending deep behind the Australian front heralded a counter-attack, as the roads to the south-east were seen to be full of enemy infantry. Impressively well ordered waves advanced over the eastward slope towards the 4th Division on the Keiberg, but were swiftly broken by rifle and machine gun fire. Captain Whittington's exposed post in the northern saddle of the Keiberg at the right of 12th Brigade line was now outflanked, and commenced falling-back. One hour later as another counter-attack approached, the outposts of the 48th fired their S.O.S. but there was no response from the British artillery. Again the Australians opened accurate rifle and machine gun fire upon the enemy, but this time it was noticed that the 3rd Division was streaming back along the main ridge to their left. The position of the 12th Brigade, isolated on the Keiberg, with both flanks exposed was hopeless, and a general withdrawal was ordered. Most of the 48th and 47th fell back along the railway track, the Germans following them across the Keiberg and capturing the outpost in Decoy Wood. At around 5:15 the men trudged back across Broodseinde ridge, and past the bunker that was headquarters for both battalions, where the commanders attempted to check the withdrawal. The line finally consolidated was back near Defy crossing, from where the attack had started in the morning.

II Anzac The New Zealand Division stands fast in the afternoon

In front of the New Zealand Division the barrage planned for 3:00 p.m. came down on time and was noticeably heavier than that of the morning, but still had little effect on the enemy so firmly established on Bellevue. By chance it caught three groups of Germans concentrating for a counter-attack. The southern and centre group were heavily hit, and those that did attack were driven off with rifle and Lewis gun. The northern group with better shelter in the folded ground continued with their attack, and rushed a forward post just east of the Wallemolen cemetery. But even before the barrage had started the order for the renewed New Zealand attack had thankfully been rescinded. News of the Australian withdrawal from the other side of the Ravebeek, and knowledge that the Scots on the left were also falling-back, made any further New Zealand effort pointless.

In the wind and rain of the early October evening, in atrocious conditions of mud and misery, the exhausted troops of I and II Anzac were almost back to where they had started, about 12 hours before. As the weary survivors dug-in once more in a vain attempt to improve water-filled holes, they were still subjected to rifle and machine gun sniping, and desultory artillery fire, from an enemy who knew full well they had had the best of the fight. Dead and wounded from four British divisions lay on the bleak muddy slopes and in the filthy morass of the Ravebeek valley. Some had been there for nearly four days. Some were to be there for seven days before they were recovered. In the heart-braking fighting the 12th Brigade of the 4th Australian Division had sustained 1,018 casualties, and the 3rd Australian Division the New Zealand Division around 3,000 casualties each.

German units opposite Second Army[619]

The German front line had been held by part of the *233rd Division* opposite 4th Australian, and part of the *233rd Division (448th, 450th and 449th I. Regiments)* and the *195th Division (8th and 6th Jäger Regiments)* opposite 3rd Australian, and part of the *195th* and part of the *16th Division (29th I.R.)* opposite the New Zealand Division. The *220th (Eingrief) Division* sent two battalions, the *II/55th R.I.R.* to the *233rd Division*, and the *I/55th R.I.R.* to the *195th Division* for the counter-attacks, and to increase the defences at Bellevue. The *II/10th Bavarian R.I.R., 5th Bavarian Reserve Division* is believed to have counter-attacked around the Ravebeek at 9:30 a.m. In the fighting on the 9th and 12th October, the *195th Division* had sustained a total of 3,325 casualties.

The attack of the Fifth Army 5:35 a.m. the 12th October

The purpose of the Fifth Army attack on the 12th October is conventionally described as to provide support to the left flank of the main attack against Passchendaele. On the 9th, Second Army, from a position already on the ridge, and partly through the Flanders I defences had been checked before Passchendaele, while 7,000 yards to the north-west, on the far left, the 29th and Guards Divisions, with far stronger artillery support had advanced over 2,000 yards. As Haig's sole aim was now limited to the capture of the Passchendaele – Westroosebeke high ground, it was becoming a case of the tail wagging the dog, as the so called supporting left flank made progress along the southern edge of Houthulst Forest, while the main attack at Passchendaele and Poelcappelle was repulsed. The weakness in the German tactics to prevent Plumer's limited depth attacks were obvious to both sides, but their strategy of locking the British between the high ridge and Houthulst Forest was proving to be correct and was working. Even if Fifth Army pushed forward another 3,000 yards along the Vijfwegen spur it would be of little benefit, as any advance made north of Poelcappelle did not threaten the ridge between Passchendaele and Westroosebeke.

---

[619] National Archives, maps showing distribution of enemy forces at 5 pm on the 12th October, in WO153/601

German units opposite Fifth Army[620]

The German Front Line between Wallemolen and Poelcappelle opposite XVIII Corps was held by the centre and right regiments, *28th I.R.* and *68th I.R.* of the elite *16th Division*. Opposite XIV Corps north of Poelcappelle and up to Houthulst Forest the line was held by elements of the *227th Division* (*477th I.R.* and *441st R.I.R.*) which were at the point of relief by elements of the *240th Division* (*471st I.R.* and *470th I.R.*) and possibly elements of the *6th Bavarian Division*. Houthulst Forest was held by the *27th Division* (*124th I.R., 120th I.R.* and *123rd Grenadier Regiment*).

XVIII Corps
The second attack on Poelcappelle

After the failure of the 9th October, XVIII Corps was to attempt on the 12th, under even worse conditions, the capture of Poelcappelle. On the night of the 10th/11th October, the 9th Division relieved 48th Division in the line between Wallemolen and the Lekkerboterbeek, their task to support the left of the main attack by the New Zealand Division. On the same night the 18th Division relieved 11th Division on the Poelcappelle spur, to renew the attack against Poelcappelle.

9th (Scottish) Division [621]
Major-General H. T. Lukin

26th (Highland) Brigade [622] and 27th (Lowland) Brigade [623]
The wastes between Wallemolen and the Lekkerboterbeek, which had become more putrid with each successive attack, and each shower of rain, were to be the scene of the next fight of 9th Division, which had only been out of the line since the 22nd September. The 26th Brigade was to lead the attack, supported by the 27th Brigade which was to advance to the final objective. Across a front of 1,500 yards the 26th Brigade was to attack with four battalions, with two battalions in three waves, each on a two company front. This was a broad front for one brigade to cover and there were inevitable gaps between companies. The jumping-off line was to be between a point 200 yards south-east of Adler Farm, along the road running north-west past Vacher Farm, to Terrier Farm. In the forward wave the two forward companies of the 8th Black Watch and the 10th Argyll and Sutherland Highlanders were to capture the first intermediate objective (Green Line), with the two companies following going through to the first objective (Yellow Dotted Line). At this point the 7th Seaforth Highlanders and the 5th Cameron Highlanders would pass through and capture the second objective, (Blue Dotted Line).[624] At Zero plus 5 hours the 12th and 11th Royal Scots of 27th Brigade, with the 9th Scottish Rifles and 6th Kings Own Scottish Borderers in reserve, would pass through, and follow behind a slow barrage of 50 yards in 4 minutes. They would then advance to the final objective (Purple Dotted Line), which ran from 50 yards north of Goudberg Copse, then north-east past the western edge of Double and Middle Copse, with the left of the line thrown back to a point 100 yards north of Lind Cottages. On reaching the final objective, the Royal Scots were to push out posts to the eastern edge of Double and Middle Copse, to watch for the approach of counter-attacks. These posts would be around 2,700 yards from the start line, and every step would be across the worst ground conditions imaginable. By the time the 11th Royal Scots, on the left of the line reached the final objective, they would also have crossed the quagmire of the Lekkerboterbeek,

---

[620] National Archives, maps showing distribution of enemy forces at 5 pm on the 12th October, in WO153/601
[621] John Ewing *The History of the 9th (Scottish) Division* pp240-242
[622] National Archives, War Diary 26th Brigade WO95/1763
[623] National Archives, War Diary 27th Brigade WO95/1772
[624] National Archives, War Diary 8th Black Watch WO95/1766, National Archives, War Diary 7th Seaforth WO95/1765

as at one place the path of the stream passed obliquely across their front. Across a dry battlefield and behind a dense barrage it would have been a very tough job. Across this battlefield the plan was wishful thinking, and it just could not be done.

On the night of the 10th/11th October, the 26th Brigade had relieved 144th Brigade in the line. On the evening of the 11th, after a hot meal, the 27th Brigade left the canal bank dug-outs between 8:00 and 10:30 p.m. and made their weary way across the ugly landscape, up the duckboard tracks, in the rain towards the front line. Part way up, the enemy began shelling with mustard gas, part of the general gas barrage, which necessitated the wearing of respirators. As the brigade crossed the western end of Gravenstafel ridge, overlooking the Stroombeek, the Germans also put down a heavy 5.9-inch barrage which caused much delay and disorganisation, the 12th Royal Scots only arriving in their allotted positions 15 minutes before Zero Hour.

At 5:25 a.m. the Black Watch and Argyll set off behind a noticeably weak and patchy barrage. The German barrage which had been moderate before Zero Hour now became heavy, and machine gun fire from all quarters quickly found its target. The ground was beyond description, and many fell wounded, only to drown in the myriad of mud-filled shell-holes. Many of those who were not hit stumbled or slipped into the treacherous craters, to sink up to their waists in the mire, from which it was impossible without help to escape. The advance soon lost direction and cohesion, but the right company of the Black Watch, which had managed to keep their weapons clear of the choking mud, attacked Adler Farm. As Lewis gunners kept a suppressing fire on the embrasures bombers worked forward amongst the shell-holes and captured the blockhouse, taking several prisoners. Sustaining heavy casualties the right company carried on and made its way forward to the first intermediate objective. The left company came beneath its own barrage and completely lost direction. Under continuous machine gun fire from Germans in organised shell-holes, they veered to the left and eventually took what cover they could in craters, about 200 yards forward of the start line. The situation worsened as the left support company veered still further to the left, and came up on the left flank of the front company. The support company on the right succeeded in passing through the right forward company and advanced to Source Trench near the first objective. The 7th Seaforth had followed up closely, also sustaining many casualties from the German machine guns, but attempted to move forward and fill the gap which had developed between the Black Watch companies. Seeing that the advance of the 26th Brigade was held up the 12th Royal Scots had also followed the Seaforth, and the two battalions had become much intermingled. The blockhouse at Inch House was captured, amongst many local actions with small parties of Germans, who put up stout opposition until outflanked. Small mixed groups from all three battalions worked their way forward as far as Source Trench and the bunker at Banff House, some even as far as Source Farm, 1,300 yards forward. They were few in number, but held out until the night of the 13th/14th when they were finally relieved. A mixed party also entered the hamlet of Wallemolen, but being heavily enfiladed from both flanks fell back on the cemetery – Inch House line. It was obvious that the New Zealand were in serious trouble on the right.

On the left of the division, The Argyll had immediately floundered into ground which was in places absolutely impassable, and in desperate attempts to avoid it and get forward the barrage was lost. The right company and its support company kept direction, but were held up by machine gun fire from a blockhouse, 300 yards from the British front line, and 250 yards south of Oxford Houses, which checked the whole advance. The Camerons, 11th Royal Scots and K.O.S.B. had already moved forward behind the Argyll, and composite groups of all four battalions attacked the blockhouse, which showed a white flag whilst keeping up its machine gun fire. The garrison paid the price, 21 were killed, 4 wounded, 5 taken prisoner, and four machine guns captured.

The Argyll left company, without knowing it, and with no landmark on which to take a bearing, had dragged themselves through the shattered course of the Lekkerboterbeek, veered too far left, and strayed into 18th Division sector. Within 80 yards they were stuck in knee deep mud and under fire from the blockhouses at Beek House and Meunier House. The attack stalled, and those who could, took cover in adjacent shell-holes. Most had clogged weapons, were up to their waists in mud and water, and little more than 100 yards from the start line.

The ragged line of posts ran from the cemetery near Wallemolen, where touch was gained with the New Zealand on the right, then north-west, in front of Inch Houses to Oxford House where it curved back to the original line on the left, in touch with 18th Division. This was back on the approximate line from where it had started. The plan had been to advance to a depth of 2,500 yards. In reality, in the 100 yard trudge across the bog, 9th Division had sustained over 1,000 casualties.

In his post-battle report, Lieutenant -Colonel Campbell of the 11th Royal Scots made this poignant observation: 'In the event of future operations in similar conditions I would suggest that stretcher bearers should be issued with a length of rope for the purpose of facilitating the extrication of the wounded and unwounded men from morass and shell-holes. As many cases occurred where it was only after a long period of hard work men were got out and in some cases were left owing to the difficulty and exposed position until a more favourable opportunity offered and in two cases the prolonged exposure proved fatal.'[625]

18th (Eastern) Division [626]
Major-General R. P. Lee

55th Brigade [627] and 53rd Brigade [628]
The squalid rubble heaps which had once been the village of Poelcappelle continued to guard the road to Westroosebeek. Twice already the centre of the village had been penetrated and on the 4th October the tanks had reached the eastern fringe. On the 9th October the 11th Division, had made some progress, bunkers within the ruins being cleared, only for the line to be driven-in, back west of the Brewery. Since then the enemy had reoccupied his blockhouses in the rubble of the Brewery, and with those at Meunier House, Point 37 and Helles House, denied with their machine guns the road towards the ridge. The importance the Germans placed on Poelcappelle was emphasised by the employment of their élite *16th Division* to defend it.

On the night of the 10th/11th October, 55th Brigade had attempted to relieve 32nd Brigade in an operation which was less than straightforward, as in the pitch dark guides became lost or did not rendezvous at all, and the positions held by the 32nd were unclear. By about 3:30 a.m. the attacking battalions were in position. The 18th Division was to attack on a 1,200 yard front between Gloster Farm and a point on the Houthulst road, 500 yards to the north of the four-way junction at the western end of the village. The 55th Brigade was to lead with the 8th East Surrey Regiment and the 7th Royal West Kent,[629] with the 7th East Kent in support of the Surrey, and the 7th Queens in brigade reserve. 53rd Brigade was to be in support with the 8th Suffolk Regiment and the 6th Royal Berkshire.[630] At around dusk on the 11th modified orders arrived from Brigade headquarters with information of a revised barrage plan, necessitating verbal distribution of the order to the exposed company outposts.

At 5:25 the British barrage was seen to be weak and ragged. But within two minutes, as the forward companies waited for their barrage to lift, a hostile barrage came down 150 yards behind the tapes causing many casualties. When the British barrage did lift, it immediately moved 100 to 150 yards forward affording no protection to the infantry. The East Surrey, West Kent, and Buffs advanced in unison with platoons in files, sustaining casualties from the shell-fire and also coming under machine gun fire from the numerous German blockhouses. On the right, attacking to the south of Poelcappelle and into the centre of the village, the East Surrey and the two leading "C" and "D" Companies of the Buffs came under heavy fire from machine guns at the Brewery on their left and from Meunier House on their right. Offensive action was exceedingly difficult, and attempts at fire and movement impossible due to the atrocious state of

---

[625] National Archives, War diary 11th Royal Scots WO/95/1773
[626] Captain G.H.F. Nichols *The 18th Division in the Great War* pp234-238
[627] National Archives, War Diary 55th Brigade WO95/2047
[628] National Archives, War Diary 53rd Brigade WO95/2037
[629] National Archives, War Diary 8th East Surrey WO95/2050
[630] National Archives, War Diary 8th Suffolk WO95/2039

the ground. Weapons became quickly clogged and inoperative with mud. Two enemy machine guns near Gloster Farm, and others at Point 37, immediately brought the right companies of the Surrey and Buffs under heavy fire. As the two support "A" and "B" Companies of the Buffs came forward they were similarly struck from all sides and by 7: a.m. the whole attack was checked a few hundred yards from the start line, with the enemy still holding Gloster House in the rear. Soon after midday the enemy fire slackened. They were seen to be advancing to the south of the village carrying red cross flags and approached a post of the Buffs. Increasing numbers worked forward apparently unarmed. The ruse was not discovered until an officer and 30 of the Buffs had been taken prisoner and ordered back to Meunier House. Attempts to consolidate a shell-hole line were hampered by the depth of water and mud in the holes, but by noon a line of posts was established around 400 yards west of Meunier House.

The West Kent, advancing with "B" and "C" Companies from the Houthulst road towards the northern fringe of the village, made a little progress before "B" Company with "D" Company in support were checked by machine gun fire from the Brewery. On the left "C" Company got a few hundred yards farther until stopped by machine gun fire from Helles House and Requete Farm, 350 yards north of the Brewery. The West Kent also attempted to establish a line of posts, around 250 yards forward of the Houthulst road. The Surrey had moved up in support of the West Kent and a gap had developed between their left flank and the right of the 4th Division. The enemy attempted to work into the gap between the two divisions at noon but were driven off by Lewis gun fire. About 2:00 p.m. an attempt by the Germans to counter-attack from the Brewery through the centre of the village was driven off by rifle and Lewis gun fire of the Surrey and West Kent, and the 7th Queens moved up in support of the Buffs as a precaution. The Germans made another attempt around 5:30 p.m. to infiltrate towards the gap between the East Surrey and West Kent, but once more were driven off by Lewis gun and rifle fire.

Again the Germans had succeeded in holding Poelcappelle, and the road to the ridge remained secure. The failure was attributed to several factors. These included, the thinness of the barrage, the excessive lift which offered no protection, the number of enemy machine guns well forward, heavy officer casualties, and the deplorable condition of the ground. The ineffective attack, enacted with much bravery and resolve, but with next to no result, had cost 18th Division 1,669 casualties of which 278 were killed and 287 were missing.

XIV Corps

The XIV Corps was to develop the defensive left flank by a slight advance intended to improve its tactical position. The 4th Division and Guards Division, which had remained in the line since the 9th October, were to be used again, with the 17th Division, which had relieved the 29th Division on the 11th October, interposed between them along the Staden railway.

4th Division

12th (Composite) Brigade
The 4th Division was to use a composite brigade under Brigadier-General Carton de Wiart, V.C., D.S.O., consisting of the Household Battalion (10th Brigade), and 1st Royal Warwickshire Regiment (10th Brigade) to lead the assault,[631] 1st King's Own Royal Lancaster Regiment (12th Brigade) in support, and the 1st Rifle Brigade (11th Brigade) in reserve. The brigade was to push forwards to the north-east of Poelcappelle, from a start line 400 yards east and parallel to the Houthulst road to a depth of around 800 yards. The attack front was around 1,000 yards, from a point 200 yards south of String Houses, to a point 200 yards south of Senegal Farm. The task was to support the left of 18th Division in their attack on Poelcappelle, and to capture the final objective in touch with the right of the 17th Division.

---

[631] National Archives, War Diary Household Battalion WO95/1481, National Archives, War Diary 1st Warwick WO95/1484

As the brigade advanced, fire from the enemy machine guns around the Brewery and Helles House cut into the right flank of the Household Battalion, and caused an immediate check. On the left the Warwick and 1st King's Own made better progress, fighting their way forward past Basace Farm and Bower Farm, as far as the final objective near Memling Farm. For a time machine gun fire from a blockhouse had held up the advance causing many casualties, until Private Albert Halton of the 1st King's Own worked forward alone for about 300 yards and captured the gun and crew, an act of great courage for which he was to be awarded the V.C. The hold up of the 18th Division at Poelcappelle prevented any further advance by the Household Battalion. A 500 yard defensive right flank was established strengthened by two platoons of the King's Own and by "I" Company of the 1st Rifle Brigade, from Requete Farm back towards the start line to the south-west, facing the Brewery blockhouses.

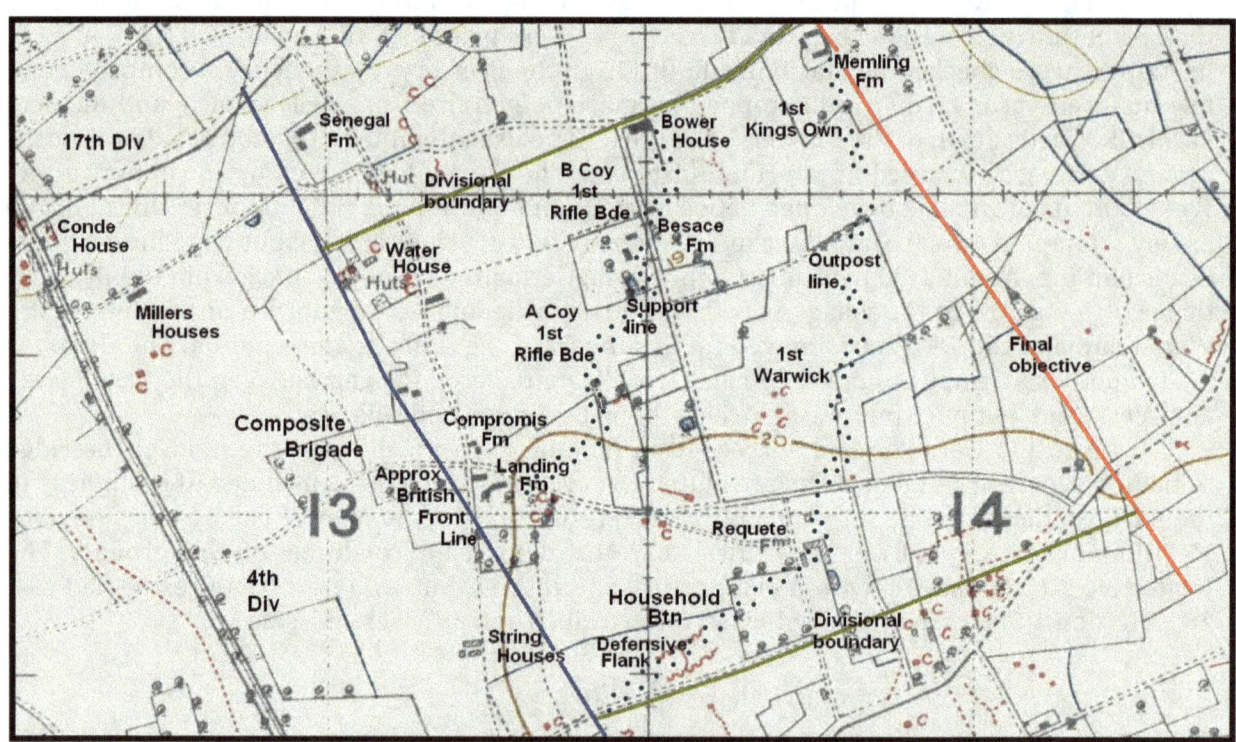

The attack of the 12th (Composite) Brigade - 4th Division from the
Poelcappelle – Houthulst Road
north of Poelcappelle

By the evening a ragged line of shell-hole posts had been established, from close to the start line on the right, in touch with 18th Division, along the defensive flank facing the Brewery to Requete Farm, then 800 yards northwards to Memling Farm, where the division was on its final objective. "A" and "B" Companies of the 1st Rifle Brigade formed a support line 200 yards to the rear, on a line from Landing Farm through Besace Farm to Bower House. The ground conditions were equally as bad north of Poelcappelle towards the Watervlietbeek as they were to the south, and the barrage had been equally as ragged. In the attack the 4th Division had suffered around 1,000 casualties.

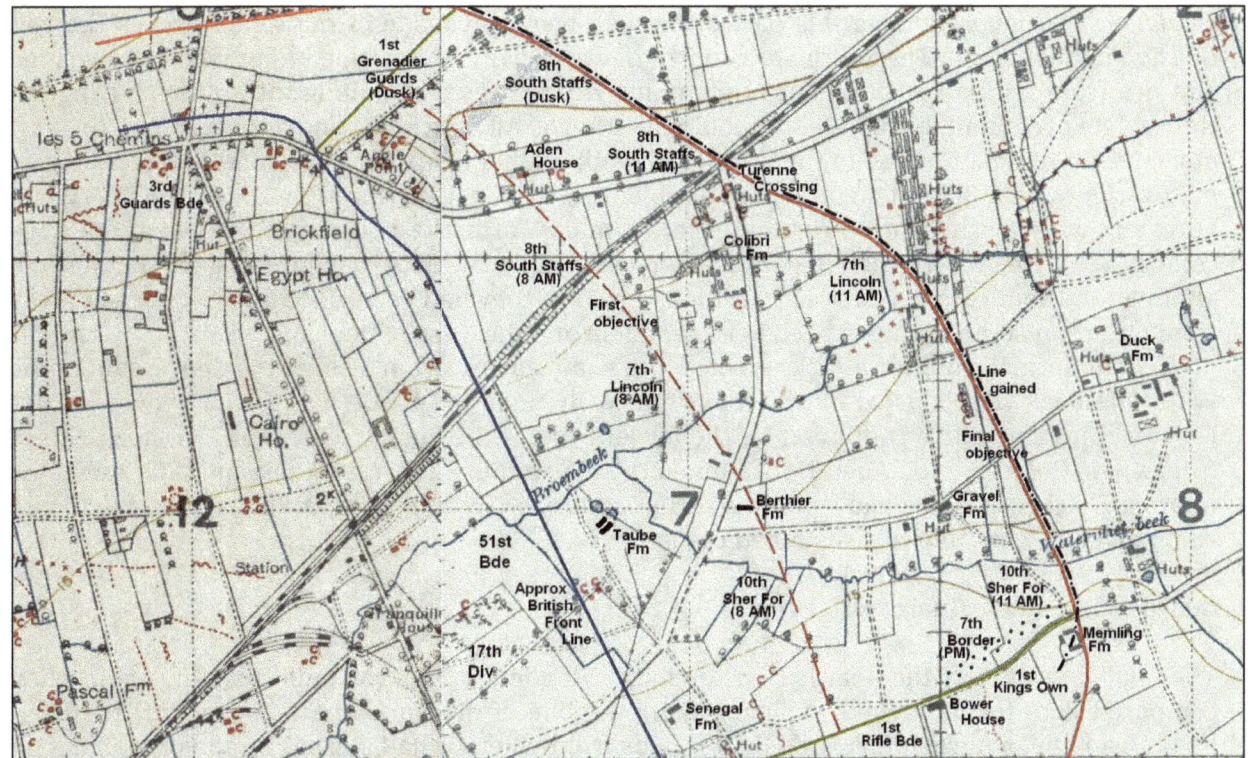

The attack of the 51st Brigade - 17th Division along the Watervlietbeek and the Broembeek

17th (Northern) Division [632]
Major-General P. R. Robertson

51st Brigade [633]

The 17th Division, although fresh to the Flanders battle, had only been withdrawn from the line at Arras in September, at which time several of its battalions were 50% below full war establishment. On the way north efforts had been made to bring the division closer to strength, with drafts from Lines of Communication, Kite Sections and other non-combatant roles. The training of these men was necessarily rudimentary given the time available. On October the 8th the division moved from Herzeele and by the morning of the 11th had one brigade in the line, two in support and one in reserve, and the 17th Divisional Artillery also covered the front. The position taken up by the division was a line of around 1,600 yards, parallel to and 400 yards east of the Poelcappelle – Houthulst road with the right 200 yards south of Senegal Farm, and the left on the road 400 yards east of les Cinq Chemins road junction near Angle Point. The marshes and craters which had linked into small pools along the Broenbeek and Watervlietbeek, would add an extra obstacle to an already awful area of ground. The division was to attack with the 51st Brigade which was to use the 10th Sherwood Foresters, the 7th Lincolnshire Regiment and the 8th South Staffordshire Regiment in the line, with the 7th Border Regiment in support.

From the outset the brigade made good headway, the Sherwood Foresters getting forward of the held-up 4th Division, overcoming resistance at Senegal Farm and arriving at the first objective about 300 yards forward by 8:00 a.m. The enemy trickled forward to reinforce their bunkers as the advance proceeded but on coming under fire showed little stomach for a fight. A signalling party of three of the Lincoln, all unarmed, accepted the surrender of 90 Germans from one bunker, which had not been cleared in the advance. The garrison emerged, 'in a pitiable condition on the verge of complete shell shock'.[634] It seems the *227th Division* and

---

[632] Hilliard Atteridge *History of the 17th (Northern) Division* pp 250-255
[633] National Archives, War Diary 51st Brigade WO95/2005
[634] Hilliard Atteridge *History of the 17th Division* p254

6th Bavarian Division holding this part of the line were not made of the same stuff as the *16th Division* further south. The South Staffs north of the railway, soon came under rifle and machine gun fire from German positions at Angle point, Aden House, and along the southern fringe of Houthulst Forest, and in enfilade from Colombo House. All attacking companies reached the first objective up to time but due to the 4th Division still not being up, the Sherwood Foresters threw back a right flank. By 11:00 a.m. the final objective had been captured, but now the Sherwood Foresters were out in a sharp right angle at Memling Farm, their right flank still exposed. Two companies of the 7th Border Regiment were sent up to fill the dangerous gap. On the left, although the South Staffs were on their final objective, they had veered slightly to the right away from Aden House, and a gap existed between them and the Guards Division.

No German counter-attacks ensued, but some enemy groups along the depression of the Watervlietbeek were shelled out by the artillery. By noon the battle was virtually over, except for some fighting which continued on the far left, where the enemy was finally evicted at dusk from Angle Point and the Aden House bunkers by a combined force of the South Staffs and the Guards. The 17th Division had captured 218 prisoners of 13 different battalions, plus a field gun and 4 machine guns, but had sustained casualties of 1, 207.

Guards Division, 3rd Guards Brigade[635]

The final operation by the Guards Division in the Flanders battle was to be a simple affair when compared with their previous exploits. Along the line of the Ypres – Staden railway the front had already been pushed forwards 8,500 yards from where it had started on the canal bank on the 31st July. The division already held most of the higher ground of the Vijfwegen spur 500 yards south of the fringe of Houthulst Forest. The final task was to push the right forward a few hundred yards to cover the whole of the spur.

In the heavy rain on the night of the 11th/12th October the 4th Grenadier and 1st Welsh Guards of 3rd Guards Brigade had moved their outpost line forward by a few hundred yards. At the same time the Germans put down a heavy gas barrage along the Wijdendrift road and in the valleys of the Steenbeek and Broenbeek, the Guards fearing this may be a prelude to a counter-attack against their advance. In fact the barrage was part of the general *Mondnacht* gas-shoot, which in any event caused a number of casualties and much disruption to communications. The only advance at Zero Hour was to be on the right of the 4th Grenadier, and before Zero the right company pulled back to the old British front line to avoid the barrage. The attack was carried out by the 1st Battalion of the Grenadier, which moved off behind a barrage which was noticeably ragged, but succeeded in advancing the few hundred yards to their objective. The 4th Battalion moved up in support to the line they had occupied the previous night. The gap which had developed between the 17th Division on the right was filled by two platoons of the 2nd Scots Guards, although initially touch was still not gained with the 17th. Sniper fire from Colombo House and the edge of the forest continued to be troublesome throughout the day, until at dusk the 1st Grenadier with troops of the 51st Brigade drove the Germans from the Angle Point and Aden House bunkers.
From the canal bank to Houthulst Forest, in every assault they had made, the Guards had been successful in reaching their final objective. The division had paid a high price, for in the battles of the 9th and 12th October it had sustained casualties of 2,375, of which 444 had been killed.

The depth of the failure on the 12th October

As the overall situation had improved not a jot since the 9th, and as the likelihood of success must have appeared negligible when the orders were issued, it is not unreasonable to argue that the battle on the 12th October should never have been fought. At the main point of the offensive, facing Passchendaele, the day had been a re-run of the 9th October and had ended once more in

---

[635] National Archives, War Diary 3rd Guards Brigade WO95/1222

painful and heartbreaking failure. Casualties had been high in all of the Flanders battles, but when they had come with victory the price had seemed more worth paying. This time there was no victory, just rain-drenched cold, and raw shell-shocked misery.

From Broodseinde to Houthulst Forest, on the blood soaked shell-blasted slopes and in the overflowing swamps, lay countless hundreds of the dead, and thousands of the wretched wounded who would take days to evacuate. At least there had been an unofficial truce to enable the exhausted stretcher bearers to try to reach the wounded. The Commanding Officer of the 7th Buffs wrote: 'It is worthy of note that during the daylight on both the 12th and the 13th, the enemy and ourselves were able to attend to the wounded by flying a white handkerchief, a piece of rag, or a red cross flag. The enemy never fired at a wounded man.'[636] Buffs casualties had been 9 officers and 375 other ranks, of which 56 were killed and 328 were wounded or missing. The War Diary of the 12th Royal Scots states: 'Our casualties were fairly heavy and the stretcher bearers and doctors worked magnificently, but in spite of these efforts many wounded died of exhaustion and exposure.'[637] Their casualties had been 8 officers and 300 other ranks; fairly heavy indeed.

In the Ravebeek valley stretcher parties struggled in the quagmire with their burdens, unmolested by the enemy snipers, who in places directed them to the wounded. Some were not wounded, but just stuck fast in the mud, and with every chance of dying of exposure. Those lucky enough to have been recovered and taken to a blockhouse dressing station mostly lay outside in the rain, now more likely to be killed by shell-fire, for although the snipers had refrained from shooting the wounded the more detached artillery had not and the blockhouses became prime targets. Little by way of rations had reached the front, and as iron rations and water had by now been consumed, hunger and thirst compounded the wretchedness. Lieutenant Fisher of the 42nd Australian Infantry Battalion described the relief of another battalion of the 3rd Australian Division. 'The next day on the 13th October we were ordered to retake the old line, and then our units sank to the lowest pitch of which I have ever been cognisant. It looked hopeless - the men were so utterly done. However the attempt had to be made, and accordingly we moved up that night – a battalion 90 strong. I had "A" Company with 23 men. We got up to our position somehow or other – and the fellows were dropping out unconscious along the road – they have guts, my word! That's the way to express it. We found the line instead of being advanced, some thirty yards behind where we had left it – and the shell stricken and trodden ground thick with dead and wounded – some of the Manchesters were there yet seven days wounded and not looked to. But men walked over them – no heed was paid to anything but the job. Our men gave all their food and water away, but that was all they could do. That night my two runners were killed as they sat beside me, and casualties were numerous again. He blew me out of my shell-hole twice, and so I shifted to an abandoned pill-box. There were twenty-four wounded men inside, two dead Huns on the floor and six outside, in various stages of decomposition. The stench was dreadful. We got the wounded away at last as well as two wounded Huns. When day broke I looked over the position. Over forty dead lay within twenty yards of where I stood, and the whole valley was full of them.'[638]

The sacrifice of the New Zealand Division had been a tragedy, made worse by the fact that their digger mates in the 3rd Australian Division had witnessed the carnage without the ability to intervene. It was the only time the Division had failed, but they had done everything that flesh and blood could do against barbed wire and concrete. The bodies of 40 officers and 600 men lay in swathes about the wire and along the Gravenstafel road. The 2nd Brigade had casualties of 1,500 men and the 3rd Brigade 1,200 men. About 20 wounded who had fallen into water-filled shell-holes beyond the first belt of wire were taken prisoner. Officers and men of the Division expressed a wish to try again at Bellevue, after the artillery had time to smash the wire, but thankfully they were not to be granted their wish. Enough New Zealand blood had saturated the ground in front of Bellevue.

---

[636] National Archives, War Diary of the 7th Buffs, WO/95/2049
[637] National Archives, War Diary 12th Battalion The Royal Scots WO93/1773
[638] AOA p927

It had been a good day for the Germans, and it was obvious to them that the series of British victories, which they had seemed so helpless to avoid, had floundered to an end, in the rain and the mud of Flanders. The same enemy divisions which had held the line on the 9th had done so again on the 12th and for the first time since the introduction of Plumer's step-by-step attacks there had been no need for relief. The new lightly held forward zone system of defence was not yet in operation for the final order for its introduction was not issued until the 12th October. Very few German reinforcements had been required. When the 1st and 3rd Australian Divisions had broken through between the Keiberg and Passchendaele the *I Battalion* of the *55th Reserve Infantry Regiment* of the *220th Division* had been brought up in support of the *195th Division* and the *II Battalion* of the *55th R.I.R.* had supported the *233rd Division*. Crown Prince Rupprecht noted in his diary: 'Sudden change of the weather. Most gratifying – rain; our most effective ally.'[639] The devout Haig must have really begun to wonder exactly whose side God was on.

Second Army casualties 12th October

II Anzac Corps
Total in excess of 6,250 (3rd Australian and New Zealand Divisions).

I Anzac Corps
Total about 1,000 (4th Australian Division, 12th Brigade)

Fifth Army casualties 9th to 14th October

XVIII Corps
Total about 5,250

XIV Corps
Total about 4,700

Probably little noticed by those on the ground, the Royal Flying Corps had been fighting above them throughout the day in very poor conditions, flying contact patrols, spotting for the guns, bombing and ground strafing, and flying offensive patrols. During the day, from the ten squadrons in the air over the Flanders battlefield, there had been either shot down or damaged: four RE8's, two SPAD 7's, three DH4's, three Sopwith Camels, five Sopwith Pups, and a Nieuwport 17. It had also been a tough day in the air.[640]

---

[639] BOH p341 footnote
[640] Trevor Henshaw (1995) *The Sky Their Battlefield* London : Grub Street p237

Corduroy road towards Broodseinde

Captured German blockhouse

Passchendaele
16th June 1917

Passchendaele
3rd September 1917

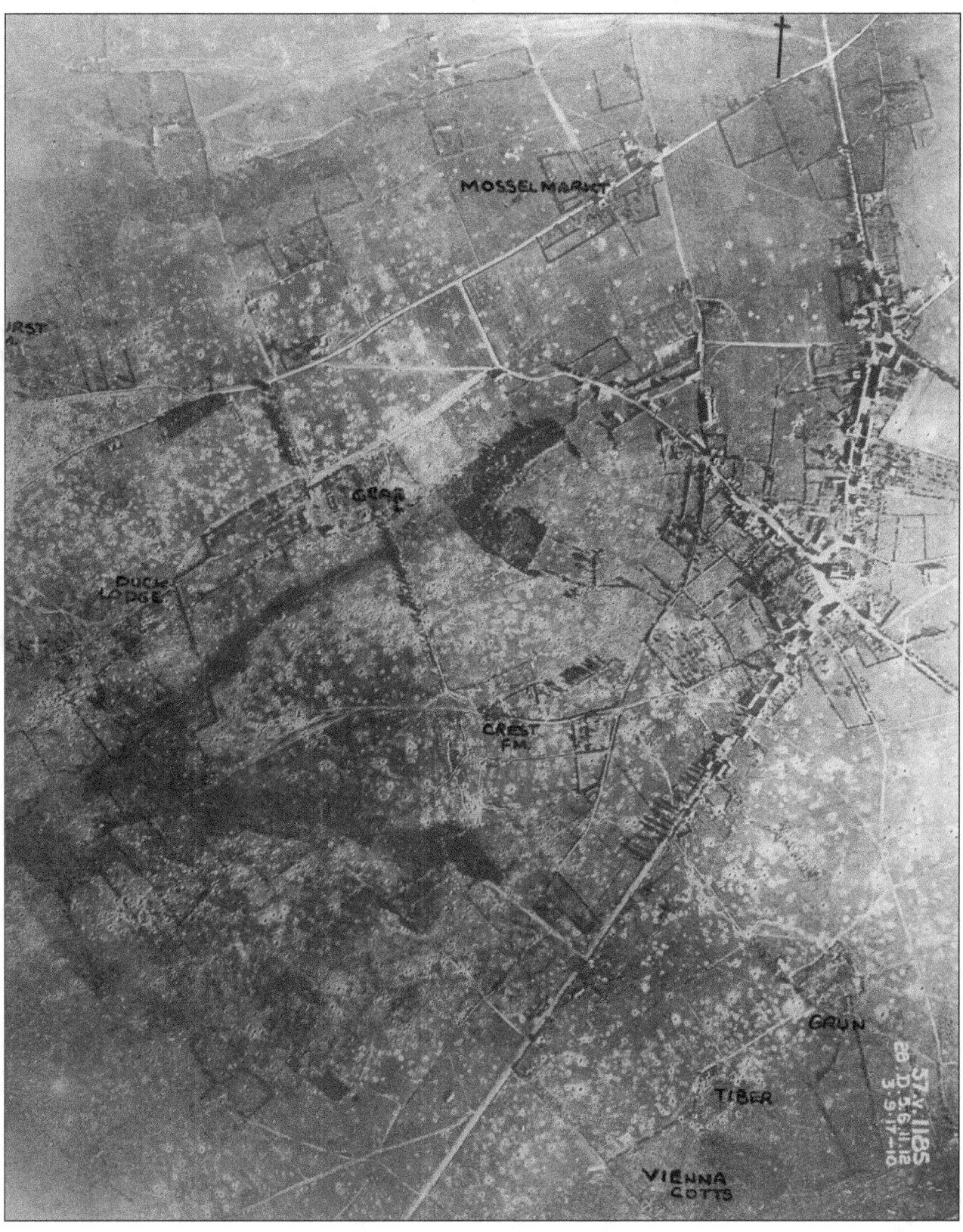

Passchendaele
27th October 1917

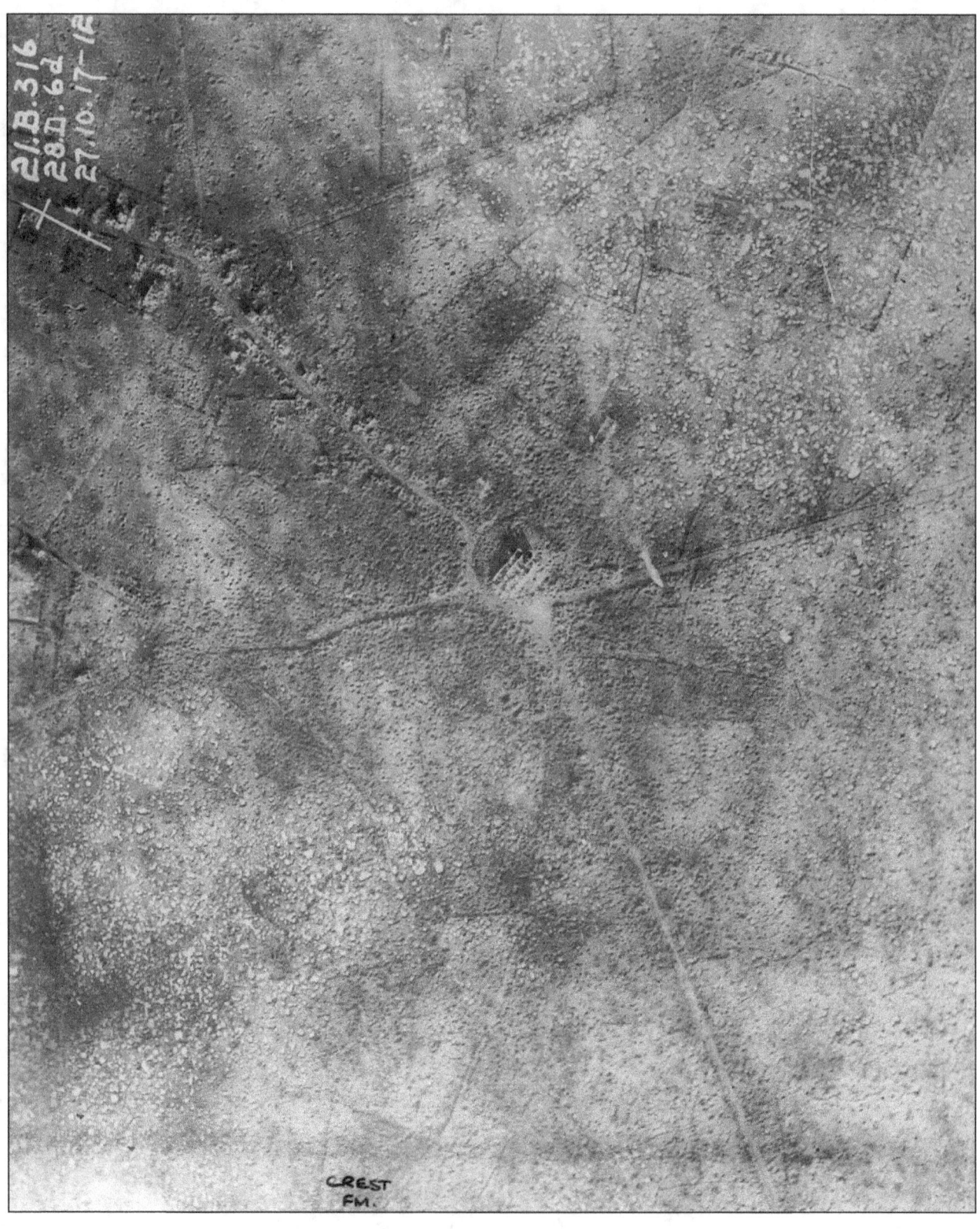

Chapter Nine

"All that was humanly possible"

The Second Battle of Passchendaele
26th October to 10th November

Part One

'It is evident from yesterday's operations that the enemy intends to resist our operations against Passchendaele to the utmost. Success will only be achieved by a thoroughly prepared attack to be carried out in good weather and with improved communications, road and railway. From now onwards wire cutting and bombardment of strong points will be carried out together with vigorous counter battery work and gassing of enemy batteries.'[641] So read the appraisal of Second Army on the 13th October. Gough's Fifth Army Conference at Lovie Chateau on the evening of the 12th was a sombre affair. The Earl of Cavan pointed out that owing to the mud it was almost impossible to distinguish friend from foe, making the job of contact patrols near impossible. Sir Ivor Maxse agreed wholeheartedly with Gough, that no further attacks should take place until there was a marked improvement in the weather.

The optimism and hopes, fostered by the successes of the 20th and 26th September and the 4th October, were now gone, as if they had never existed. The decision to hit the enemy again on the 9th October before he had time to recover from the blow of the 4th, had been a gamble that had not paid off. To attack under such dreadful conditions and with inadequate artillery support was out of keeping with Plumer's usual approach, and however much he wished to accede to Haig's desire to quickly gain the Passchendaele – Westroosebeke high ground, the issue of the atrocious state of the battlefield over which the troops had to fight could no longer be ignored. Haig bowed to the inevitable and wrote in his diary on the 12th October: 'Owing to the rain and bad state of the ground General Plumer decided that it was best not to continue the attack on the front of his Army.'[642] On the 15th October a report of an examination of an air photograph of the Bellevue area finally stated: 'Laamkeek: Blockhouse D.10.b.55.60 shows very clearly and is still intact. Dad Trench waterlogged in southern part. Wire still appears good from D.10.b.44.75 to D.10.b.56.82 and on to D.10.b.45.86. West of Bellevue: Two wire belts in front of Dad Trench have been much damaged, as is also the wire north of the road, but still probably an obstacle.'[643] The intelligence regarding the wire was sadly too late for the 49th and New Zealand Divisions.

The respite was to be short lived, only to allow enough time for an improvement in road, track and light-rail access to enable more batteries to be moved across the Steenbeek, and to give the Canadian Corps time to make its preparations. The absolute necessity of smashing the wire at Bellevue had at last been grasped, and no further attempts were to be made against it until sufficient fire-power had been dragged forward to accomplish the task. There was no apparent question in Haig's mind of whether to continue with the campaign, simply a question of when. On the morning of the 13th October, Haig met with Plumer, Gough and their Staff officers at a G.H.Q. conference at Cassel, at which Kiggell, Nash, Birch, Charteris and Davidson were present. Haig announced, as if there could be any lingering doubt in the mind of anyone present, that Passchendaele and the ridge about it was the immediate objective, and that once taken, the ridge to the north would fall more easily. It was confirmed that the Canadian Corps would go to Second Army to renew the attack on Passchendaele, and it was announced that the 1st and 63rd Divisions would go to Fifth Army to protect the Canadian left, and continue the push towards

---

[1] Library and Archives of Canada, Second Army to Canadian Corps. Canadian Corps Headquarters. RG9 III-D-3 Vol4957 T-10774
[642] Douglas Haig, Diaries and Letters p336
[643] Australian War Memorial, Intelligence, Headquarters II Anzac Corps, AWM4-1/33/18

Westroosebeke. Haig was fully aware of the atrocious conditions noting in his diary: 'Ground is so soft in places the D.G.T. (Nash) told us that he has light engines on the 60 centimetre railways sunk halfway up the boilers in the mud! Track has disappeared.'[644] The work to build new tracks and light railways across the quagmire behind the battlefront would take 10 to 12 days, and it was agreed there should be no further attack until the weather allowed some promise of success. The last proviso would prove difficult to achieve.

The situation of the Allies – Disaster at Caporetto

The situation beyond the Flanders battlefield continued to focus Haig's mind on the necessity of maintaining the offensive. The French were to make their long awaited large scale but limited attack at Malmaison on the 23rd October. Haig was anxious to do all in his power to continue to pin down German forces, recognising the prime importance of a French victory in nurturing the improvement in morale and fighting spirit of his principle and vital Ally. He had also begun to devote his attention to a proposed Third Army operation at Cambrai to commence around mid-November, using massed tanks. It had been proposed by Sir Julian Byng commanding Third Army that the Flanders campaign should be continued as long as possible to give his attack on the Hindenburg Line the best chance of success.

Since the end of August the Italians had captured the Bainsizza plateau, but after pushing back the Austro-Hungarian line over 6 miles the advance had finally been held. As we have seen, with over-extended lines of supply and communication, and upon learning that German forces were soon to be sent against him, Cadorna had ordered his Armies to stand on the defensive, and the Eleventh Battle of the Isonzo had been abandoned on the 12th September. Political pressure had already resulted in the despatch of a number of British and French heavy batteries to Italy which were still desperately required on the Western Front. There was soon to be more than guns going to Italy.

Although the situation on the Eastern Front was in turmoil, any slight hope left of keeping the Russians in the fight was seen to be dependent on reducing the German pressure upon them. Between the 1st and 21st September, a further Russian defeat at Riga at the hands of the German *Eighth Army* had led to the release of seven German divisions which were now to move south and form, with nine Austrian divisions the *Fourteenth Army*, to reinforce the Austro-Hungarian position east of the Isonzo. The direct result of this movement was to be the total rout of the Italian Second Army on the 24th October at the Battle of Caporetto, and the Italian withdrawal by the 12th November to the River Piave, only 19 miles north of Venice. This great German success, leading to an advance of around 70 miles was soon to create for the victors the inevitable problem of inadequate and impossibly over-stretched lines of supply and communication, allowing the Italians time to regroup and resist.

Meeting of the War Cabinet 17th October

At the final meeting of the War Policy Committee on the 11th October, Smuts and Curzon had asked for information to be made available regarding casualties and reserves. On the 17th the war Cabinet was not however to inquire into why Haig's earlier predictions had not come to fruition, and how the present achievements compared with the original objectives, but just to examine the casualty figures. Perhaps *this* would be the final catalyst which would prompt the Cabinet to draw the Flanders fighting to a close. But after paying scant regard to the perceived lack of achievement over the last eleven weeks, and whilst being generally of the opinion that the offensive was getting nowhere, the Cabinet on the 16th had, confusingly, sent Haig a note of congratulations, 'on his continuous, persistent, and dogged advance of 4½ miles in conditions of great difficulty'.[645] The requested casualty figures had been prepared by Sir Frederick Maurice,

---

[644] Douglas Haig. Diaries and Letters. p336
[645] National Archives, minutes of meeting of the War Cabinet 16th October CAB23/3

Director of Military Operations at the War Office, and showed that up to the 5th October the British casualties amounted to 148,470 whilst German casualties were estimated at over 255,000. Lord Derby added that from the 1st October there had been an additional 41,000 British casualties. The first time the Cabinet had troubled to ask for the figures they had received them. On the assumption that the figures were accurate British casualties were therefore approaching 190,000, but the actual number did not appear to overly concern the Cabinet. Of greater importance to them was the fact that in the country there were exaggerated rumours of even greater losses, and talk that the brunt of the fighting was being maintained by the Australian, Canadian and New Zealand forces, which were sustaining a disproportionate level of casualties. The War Cabinet decided that, 'it was not in the public interest to publish the whole of the casualties, but opportunity should be taken from time to time to dispose of the various rumours in circulation by an occasional statement by the Prime Minister'.[646] It was therefore not the *actual* number of casualties that concerned the Cabinet, but the *rumours* in the country of even greater numbers. Clearly, the actual level of casualties was not considered sufficient to call a halt. The congratulatory telegram and the apparent nonchalance regarding casualties did not in any way indicate that the Cabinet was softening its attitude towards Haig or his offensive. Sir John French and Sir Henry Wilson, now the Prime Ministers preferred choice of military opinion, had been asked to submit their views of present and future war policy, and all knew full well that neither man was likely to be a strong advocate of the policies of Haig or Robertson.[647] It was gradually becoming clear however that irrespective of the impressive accumulation of valid reasons to call off the Flanders fighting, nothing was going to induce the Cabinet to do so; in fact they were about to effectively authorize its continuation.

The question of the British front

The difficulty which had arisen over the negotiations of the Boulogne Conference of the 25th September to extend the British line, had rumbled on throughout October, the issue in Haig's mind being not that a *decision* had been made behind his back, but that *negotiations* had been undertaken and an agreement in principle had been made without him being present. Haig was to write to Robertson again on the 16th October. 'I regret that the British Government should have seen fit to decide a matter which may involve such serious consequences without giving me an opportunity of stating my views.' Robertson was obviously at pains to heal the rift, and made that clear in a minute to the War Cabinet on the 18th October.[648] 'At the recent Boulogne Conference between the Prime Minister, M. Painlevé, General Foch and myself, the question of extending our front was raised by the French representatives. The reply given was that while in principle we were of course ready to do whatever could be done, the matter was one which could not be discussed in the absence of Sir Douglas Haig or during the continuance of the present operations, and that due regard must also be had to the plan of operations for next year. It was suggested that it would be best for the Field-Marshal to come to an agreement with General Pétain, when this could be done. So far as I am aware no further formal discussion has taken place, and therefore the matter cannot be regarded as "decided". Further, I feel sure that the War Cabinet would not think of deciding such an important question without first obtaining Sir Douglas Haig's views. I am replying to him in the above sense.'

---

[646] National Archives CAB23/3, minutes of meeting of the War Cabinet 17th October. This quote from the minutes of the War Cabinet indicates that Prior and Wilson's claim that 'the publication of these figures would scotch unwelcome rumours of heavy losses, and would so put the public's mind at rest' is incorrect. In fact the opposite was decided. See *Passchendaele the Untold Story* p187.
[647] Haig had been promoted Commander-in Chief in place of French after the Battle of Loos in 1915, and Wilson had been passed over by Kitchener, who had appointed Robertson as C.I.G.S., an appointment recommended by Haig.
[648] National Archives. Minute from C.I.G.S. to cabinet Committee on War Policy OAD658 18th October CAB27-8

'I should add that on the day following the Boulogne Conference the Prime Minister verbally informed Sir Douglas Haig of what had passed, and the latter then laid stress on the necessity of settling the plan for next year and then adjusting the line accordingly. He also emphasized the great importance of having divisions out of the line for training purposes during the Winter if we were to take the offensive next Spring. He has since emphasized the necessity of giving our men, who have recently done much hard fighting, adequate leave of absence.' That he and Haig should continue to present a united front was clearly of paramount importance to Robertson. But the C.I.G.S. was in an unenviable position; doing his best to support Haig, whilst continually trying to maintain a working relationship between G.H.Q. and Downing Street, a juggling act further complicated by a steadily deteriorating, and mutually mistrustful relationship with the Prime Minister, and unfortunately dogged at times through differences of opinion between the intelligence departments of Charteris at G.H.Q. and Macdonogh at the War Office.

In a 6 page memorandum on the 17th October Haig laid out his argument against taking over more line. His first point was that whilst maintaining the offensive, which he considered vital, it would not be possible to take over more line for at least 6 to 8 weeks. He emphasised the exhaustion of his own divisions and the need for leave, the necessity for training due to the level of drafts, and the amount of work which would be required in consolidating the ground gained during the winter. The arguments repeated so often before the offensive began were driven home again. Haig recognised the necessity for a common Allied plan for 1918, but was understandably weary regarding the capacity of the French Army to engage in major offensive operations. 'If the general state of the French Armies and of the manpower available behind them will admit of a great and sustained offensive then there is a fair case for consideration as to whether the Flanders offensive or a main offensive on the French front should be given precedence. The Allied resources on the Western Front, especially in view of Russia's failure, are insufficient to enable us to prepare for and undertake two great offensives in full force : one or other must be subsiderary if both are not to be spoilt....I am decidedly of opinion that the British efforts should again be concentrated on the Flanders front as offering the best prospects of a decisive allied success with the means at our disposal.' That the Germans could not refuse to fight if attacked in Flanders had been proven, but Haig hammered home the very reasons for his present continuation of the offensive : 'In my opinion there is no other part of the Western Front where such great strategical results are obtainable by the forces available next year; and I therefore urge that in the general interests of the allies the clearing of the coast should constitute the first and ruling feature of next year's general plan of operations on the Western Front. The results attainable in Flanders should be carefully compared with those attainable on other parts of the Western Front where the enemy can retire to avoid a blow, devastating the country as he goes.' [649]

The memorandum had been used as much as an explanation of current policy as it had for protesting about taking over more line. At the time nobody knew that the deteriorating situation in Italy would change matters considerably, or that the great German offensive of the spring of 1918 would relegate most of the argument to the waste bin. That does not detract from the basic truth of much of Haig's case. Under no circumstances could the enemy refuse to fight by withdrawing in Flanders. The same principles were to deny the enemy victory in 1918, as the Allies, attacked in front of Amiens, had the room to withdraw and avoid total annihilation. If Ludendorff had risked an early attack in Flanders (where the British too had little room to manouvre) and not in Picardy, the outcome for him may have been greatly different.

Robertson replied to Haig's memorandum on the 24th after a meeting of the War Cabinet that day had considered the situation, and surprisingly acknowledged that : 'The War Cabinet are of opinion that in deciding to what extent British troops can take over line from the French regard must be had to the necessity for giving them reasonable opportunity for leave, rest, and training during the winter months and to the plan of operations for next year ; and further, that *while the*

---

[649] National Archives, GHQ memorandum 'Considerations bearing on the question of taking over more line from the French' OAD675 WO158/24

present offensive continues it would not be possible to commence taking over more line. The general military policy for next year is now under consideration and must subsequently form the subject of a Conference with the Allied Governments. In these circumstances the War Cabinet feel that until this policy is settled it would be premature to decide, finally, whether the British front can be extended by four divisions, or to a greater or less extent than this'.[650](Authors italics) The decision on British dispositions must therefore wait until considered at an Inter-Allied Conference to be held in November. So what had been the point of the agreement in principle made at Boulogne which had caused such upset and bad feelings, or did Haig have more influence than he believed with the Cabinet? The centiments of Robertson's note bore a strange resemblance to Haig's own memorandum to the War Cabinet, and it may reasonably be questioned exactly who, if anyone, was operating the merry-go-round? One thing was for certain; the note confirmed unequivocally that the Cabinet were not considering imposing a cessation of the offensive, at least until after the next Inter-Allied Conference.

The French and Wilson memorandums

The 26 page report prepared by Sir John French dated the 20th October, and the 16 page report of the same date prepared by Sir Henry Wilson, both grandly entitled 'The present state of the war, the future prospects, and future action to be taken' were, as was expected by their instigator, condemnatory of both Haig and Robertson. The recommendations presented to the Cabinet, proposed curbing the decision-making powers of the positions of both Commander-in-Chief and C.I.G.S. Lord French's report was written largely in reply to the memorandum of the 8th October prepared by Haig in response to the question posed by Lloyd George when he visited Haig's G.H.Q. on the 26th September. The Prime Minister had asked that Haig submit his views on the rôle of British forces in the event of Russia being unable to continue the War, and in consideration of the weakened state of both France and Italy.

As we have seen Haig's reply of the 8th October was founded on the belief that not only Germany but also her allies relied primarily and practically entirely on the invincibility of the German Armies to secure for them favourable terms of peace. Having identified the main enemy, and explained that peripheral attacks against Austria or Turkey would not quickly bring that enemy down, he stuck firmly to his often repeated conviction that to maintain the greatest possible force against the Germans on the Western Front, and not to disseminate forces to other theatres, was the only sound policy for the future. His mind was still focused clearly on the French difficulties. *'Though the French cannot be expected to admit it officially, we know that the state of their armies and the reserve manpower behind the armies is such that the French Government nor the military authorities will venture to call on their troops for any further sustained or offensive effort, at any rate before the enemy's strength has been definitely and finally broken. Though they are staunch in defence and will carry out useful local offensives against limited objectives the French armies would not respond to a call for more than that and the authorities are well aware of it.'*[651] As this left the British Army as the only fully operational offensive Allied force Haig pointed out that he was not in a position, without compromising his offensive capabilities, of taking over more of the French line. To continue with the offensive on the Western Front was the only possible course open. *'The alternative for us of accepting an unsatisfactory peace instead of maintaining our offensive is still more impossible of acceptance. It would mean not only the almost certain renewal of the War hereafter at a time of Germany's choosing but the entire loss of the faith and respect of our Overseas Dominions, America, and our other allies, and indeed the whole world East and West. More, it would entail a loss of self respect from which Great Britain could never recover. The effect on the 2,000,000 men in France, who have done so much and suffered so much, and are so confident in their power to win, would be calamitous and immediate…I urge unhesitatingly the continuance of the offensive*

---

[650] National Archives, Robertson to Haig 24th October WO158/24
[651] National Archives, Haig to Robertson for War Cabinet 8th October OAD 652, CAB27/8

on the Western Front, with all our strength, as the correct rôle of the British forces even under the conditions laid down by the Prime Minister.'

In his memorandum Lord French saw things very differently. He divided it into two sections; the first section an answer to Haig and Robertson's arguments, the second his own proposals. His first point was that the Germans were relying as much on U-boats and the terror threat of air raids as they were on their Army. He went on to dispute almost all of Haig's conclusions, especially and quite reasonably, those predicting an Allied superiority in men, guns and aircraft in 1918. How much Sir John knew of the French mutinies is unclear but it can be reasonably assumed that Sir Henry Wilson had informed him of at least what he had gleaned whilst at G.Q.G. Sir John was however unimpressed with any consideration of, or belief in, the debilitated state of the French, commenting on Haig's memorandum: 'It is chiefly devoted to advocating a continuation of the offensive in the west. The condition of the French Army, the political situation in France, the suggestion of lack of patriotism in that country, their supposed distrust in American help, etc. are all matters of opinion; nor in my judgement do they bear so materially on the question under review.'[652] Conversely it was clearly only Lord French's *opinion* that such a situation did not exist in France, and even though there was ample evidence to indicate that it did, it better suited his swipe at Haig to suggest that it did not. But little of great immediate material assistance to the War Policy Committee came from French's long review. In respect of offensives in other theatres, he considered there had been too great a delay to take action in Syria against the Turks and gain a decision before the spring of 1918, and felt that action against Austria could only be successful if coordinated through an Allied Supreme Command. The proposal of the creation of a Supreme Command was therefore the only constructive recommendation he made, and he considered that meanwhile the War policy should be, 'that which was termed by the Prime Minister the "Pétain scheme", namely to stand everywhere on the defensive, only resorting to such offensive action as will render the defence effective. To await the development of the forces of the United States; and in the meantime to rely on a drastic economic war to weaken the enemy.' French was obviously not possessed of any panacea with which to solve the perpetual conundrums, whilst benefiting from the enormous advantage of condemning the military decision makers from outside the circle of responsibility. His ideas were however aligned very much with those of Lloyd George who had for the moment returned him to the periphery of policy making.

Wilson's memorandum was very different. Rather than a slogging match in the fashion of Sir John, who had traded blow-for-blow with Haig, paragraph-by-paragraph disputing every aspect of his memorandum, Sir Henry's work was more his own creation, and not just an opposite reaction to the thoughts of the Commander-in-Chief. He took a more philosophical approach to the question, beginning with his views on how the War had reached the position it had, and that with the virtual elimination of Russia from the conflict, it had become a contest of three Allied powers facing four Central powers whilst awaiting the arrival of the forces of the United States. But Wilson, with a commendable honesty which was unlikely to impress the Prime Minister, made his general support of the Western Font policy quite clear. 'If I may be allowed here to interpose a remark about myself, it is to say that I shall always remain, an ardent "Westerner", for the simple reason that it is along the west front that the bulk of the forces of our principle enemy is disposed and the death-grapple must always be with these forces; but, on the other hand, I hold that this death-grapple must be engaged in at the time and place and in the manner best suited to our cause.' Wilson's main point was that *in his opinion* (and who other than Lloyd George was to say whether he was more correct than Robertson and Haig), the final decision could only be reached when decisive numbers were applied at the decisive place (i.e. on the Western Front) at the decisive time, and that 'the numbers and the place and the time are not yet, and the Germans are trying their best that they never shall be'. It was too late in his opinion to hope for a result against Turkey before the spring, and he felt the question of a separate peace with Austria was so involved, entangled, and interwoven into the fabric of Europe, that he did not believe he was qualified to state an opinion as to its possibility.

---

[652] National Archives, memorandum by Field-Marshal French for War Cabinet, CAB27/8

The main conclusion he reached was the necessity for the creation of a superior direction; a 'War Cabinet of the Allies'. The eloquent report read more like an application for a job, the author being the creator of the vacancy.

The tenor of Sir John French's report induced even Lloyd George to prompt a degree of softening in its content, especially in the remarks French had made against Robertson. He also cunningly proposed that Sir John should go so far as to praise Haig's tactical handling of the Flanders offensive. This French refused to do, admitting to Cabinet Secretary Hankey, who was assisting him with the required amendments, that in his opinion Robertson was not up to the job of C.I.G.S. and that, 'we shall do no good until we break down the Haig – Robertson ring'.[653] According to Hankey, 'there was envy, hatred and malice in the old boy's voice as he spoke'. To his credit the Cabinet Secretary took a dim view of the Prime Minister's skulduggery, clearly aimed as it was at undermining Haig and Robertson, and in view of the inside information he possessed commented darkly, 'I could, by raising my little finger, smash Lloyd George, his Government and Lord French! But this would end the War in a manner most unfavourable to us'. Hankey understood full well the Prime Ministers devious intentions, further revealing: 'Incidentally I may remark that the whole thing is a plot on L.G's part. Earlier in the year at Lindfield he sounded them both [French and Wilson] and ascertained this was their view, no doubt playing on their ambition, and known jealousy and dislike of Robertson, by letting them see that he agreed, accompanying this no doubt with a good deal of suggestion. Then he lets Haig go on, even encourages him to do so, knowing that the bad weather was preventing a big success, in order to strengthen the argument. Then he guildenly proposes the War Council, knowing perfectly well that the jury is a picked one, which will only report in one direction.' But if Lloyd George had hoped for military guidance from French and Wilson which offered him a clear course of action he had been disappointed, for they had come up with none. On the other hand he had gathered further damning advice against Haig and Robertson from his chosen men, and was now in possession of more than enough valid reasons to stop the Flanders offensive. These included the condemnation of Haig's performance by his advisory team, casualty figures, lack of progress towards defined objectives, the degradation of the offensive into a battle of attrition, deterioration in the weather, and lack of manpower resources in respect of the demands made on him by the French at Boulogne on the 25th September. Any or all could be cited as a valid political reason to stop the Flanders fighting. But the fighting was not yet to be stopped.

Preparations and plans for the next attack

In Flanders, all concerned were now in agreement that the offensive would not resume until adequate preparations had been made to allow the Canadians a reasonable chance of success. Across the waterlogged wastes the timber tracks were to be pushed further forward towards Zonnebeke and the Zonnebeke – Langemarck road. It was discovered that although cratered and covered with a deep layer of mud, the metalled surface of the Ypres – Frezenberg – Zonnebeke road still existed, and with much mud-scraping and shell-hole filling it could be put back into service. The planked 'Smith's Road' was repaired and continued beyond Anzac spur to join with it, and so create a circuit, Ypres – Hooge – Westhoek – Zonnebeke – Frezenberg – Ypres. Laying of further light railways and tramways proved less successful, as they were easily damaged by shell-fire and were difficult to repair, although work progressed to carry forward the track of the main Roulers railway line on towards Zonnebeke. The working parties, clearly visible to the enemy from the Passchendaele ridge, were continually exposed to hostile shelling, an activity to which the Germans had applied their endless ingenuity, and that now took on a novel form. Hostile shoots of 'Blue Cross' or sneezing gas, which could penetrate the filters and made the wearing of a respirator near impossible, would quickly be followed by a drenching of 'Yellow Cross' or mustard gas. Rear areas and camps were subjected to the same treatment rendering

---

[653] Hankey Diaries October 24th

sleep near impossible and bivouacs untenable due to the lingering mustard oil. On the nights of the 14th, 16th, 18th and 19th October, the Hanebeek, Zonnebeke, and Steenbeek valleys were saturated with mustard gas causing 116 casualties on one night in I Anzac alone. A party of the 43rd Battalion of II Anzac, working on the Roulers railway near Zonnebeke sent 40 men to hospital, blistered and gassed. Batteries were another key target for the enemy gas bombardments, many being temporarily put out of action with heavy casualties.

Weather conditions, rainfall Vlamertinghe, temperature Ypres[654]					
	14th Oct	**15th Oct**	**16th Oct**	**17th Oct**	**18th Oct**
Rainfall	Trace	Nil	0.1mm	7.1mm	Trace
Temp	52F	52F	54F	56F	58F
	19th Oct	**20th Oct**	**21st Oct**		
Rainfall	2.9mm	Trace	1.3mm		
Temp	59F	54F	53F		

Between the 14th and 21st October the rainfall decreased to an average of 1.4 mm per day, and conditions although awful, did not worsen. On the 17th October four Canadian Pioneer battalions joined the British and Australians at work on the forward roads.[655] Amongst the mud and the mustard gas the work continued. Haig was kept fully informed of the appalling conditions of the battlefield, the most critical area in the forthcoming Canadian attack on Passchendaele village being the Ravebeek valley. This was recognised as impassable and would inevitably split the attack down the centre by 1,500 yards, the right flank concentrating along the main ridge, the left along the Bellevue - Wallemolen spur. Haig had informed Plumer that no pressure should be applied to Currie to begin before he was satisfied with his preparations.

With the Canadian Corps thrusting at Passchendaele, the I Anzac Corps would protect the Canadian right flank, whilst the Fifth Army with the XVIII and XIV Corps would protect the Canadian left and continue the advance towards Westroosebeke. The French First Army using two divisions, would protect the left of Fifth Army and broaden the front with an attack towards Houthulst Forest. In an attempt to prevent the enemy artillery concentrating on the main front of the attack, Second Army was to also attack with the X Corps on the Gheluvelt plateau, using one division astride the Menin Road, towards Gheluvelt and the Quadrilateral on Tower Hamlets spur, and a second division towards Polderhoek Chateau. In the interval prior to the Canadian attack, Fifth Army were to continue, on the 22nd October, to maintain pressure on the enemy by a renewed attack on Poelcappelle by one division of the XVIII Corps, and to advance further along the Broenbeek and towards the southern face of Houthulst Forest with two divisions of the XIV Corps. The French First Army was to give support on the left with one regiment of its 1st Division.

Currie held a Divisional Commanders conference on the 15th October, during which the proposed plan to use two Canadian divisions to carry out both the first and second phases of the

---

[654] National Archives, GHQ statistics WO95/15
[655] The average daily labour employed then being 2 infantry battalions, 7 pioneer battalions, 10 field companies R.E., 7 tunnelling companies, 4 Army Troop companies R.E., and 2 labour companies.

attack was discussed and the objectives agreed upon. It was considered that 8 days were required to complete the necessary work on the roads, and if the planks were readily available 400 yards of corduroy road could be completed every day. The field artillery could be moved forward without too much problem, but the movement of the heavier guns was going to be more difficult for the road beyond Frezenberg ridge was badly damaged. The heavy batteries could be supplied with ammunition by road vehicle, and then by push trucks on trench tramways from the roads to the batteries, while the field batteries could be supplied by mule transport. Currie considered that if his guns and ammunition could be up to the Zonnebeke – Winnipeg road, within 2,500 yards of the front, by the 21st / 22nd October he would be ready, given reasonable weather, to carry out the first attack using two divisions on the 24th. He foresaw making his second attack on the 27th, using the same divisions as on the 24th, and then introducing two fresh divisions for a third attack four days later.

At a further conference at Canadian Corps headquarters on the morning of the 16th October with Plumer present, after a more thorough appraisal of the situation, Currie announced that he had reassessed the time necessary to make his artillery preparations, and indicated that he would not be ready until the 29th. Although Haig had instructed Plumer that Currie should be given the time he needed to prepare, the Commander-in-Chief was as ever anxious to attack at the earliest possible moment. It had been clear since the 15th October that the Germans had been moving the heavy and medium guns of their Tenbrielen Group to the north-east, and re-positioning the batteries east of Passchendaele. Moreover the French were to attack at Malmaison on the 23rd and Haig wanted to support them with action in Flanders at the earliest opportunity. After a thorough discussion Plumer expressed his hope that, given a period of reasonable weather Currie might bring the date of his attack forward to the 26th and asked that he think the possibility over and give his decision by the afternoon. The conference was reconvened at I Anzac Corps headquarters. Currie agreed that he could bring forward his attack date to the 26th, but only if the weather held and that the necessary road construction was completed by 6 p.m. on the 22nd. The date for the second phase of the operation was provisionally set for 3 days after the first, and the third phase, to allow for relief by 2 fresh divisions, 4 to 5 days after that.

Currie's artillery requirements were not going to be easy to fulfil, as he wished to get medium as well as field artillery forward to form two groups, the southern behind Windmill Hill - (Hill 40) north-east of Zonnebeke, and the northern behind Gravenstafel ridge. His plan required that by the 21st / 22nd October, six 6-inch howitzer batteries, and two 60-pounder batteries should be moved forward to the vicinity of Kansas Cross, while three R.F.A. brigades in the vicinity of Hill 40 should form a southern group, and four R.F.A. brigades behind Gravenstafel ridge should form a northern group, with 8,000 tons of ammunition dumped near at hand. On the night of 17th / 18th October the Canadian Corps Artillery Headquarters relieved II Anzac Corps Artillery. A personal reconnaissance by Currie's G.O.C. Royal Artillery, Brigadier - General E.W.B. Morrison, had confirmed the terrible difficulties under which II Anzac gunners had been fighting. The guns were handed over in position, much of the field artillery still west of the Steenbeek, and bunched, out of necessity, into two groups, one close to the Zonnebeke road near Frezenberg ridge and one just east of the stream close to the tracks behind Hill 35. Morrison discovered serious gun shortages, due to damage, wear, and weapons generally being bogged. Of 250 heavy guns to be taken over in situ he could find only 227, and of these 87 were out of action. Of a nominal strength of 306 18-pounders less than half were in action and many of these were 'dotted about in the mud wherever they happened to get bogged'. Morrison was face to face with the reason for the failures of the 9th and 12th October, and he quickly initiated a programme to move damaged guns out of the line for repair, a task for which there had neither been time or track facilities to accomplish previously.

Whilst the Canadians proceeded with their preparations, part of their artillery was instructed to support the attack of the Fifth Army on the 22nd. For four hours prior to Zero enemy batteries threatening Fifth Army front were to be subjected to a gas bombardment, and 4.5-inch howitzers were to shell with gas suspected enemy shell-hole outposts in front of XVIII Corps.

The Air Offensive

The constant air attacks by enemy aircraft which bombed the rear areas at night and ground attacked the forward areas by day were of great concern to the Army, and bitter complaints had been expressed to the Royal Flying Corps. It was recognised by the airmen that to attack the enemy on his airfields and destroy his aircraft on the ground was one of the most effective ways of lessening these intrusions, and plans were in hand to do just that. On the 20th October 45 single-seater scouts attacked Rumbeke airfield in a raid which was at that time considered unusual and ambitious. The attack was to be made at three levels, one low down to bomb and strafe aircraft and installations on the ground, one just above to catch any aircraft attempting to take off, and a higher level defence flight to prevent the intervention of enemy scouts. During the morning eleven Sopwith Camels of 70 Squadron armed with bombs, escorted by a further eight Camels, carried out the low level attack, whilst eighteen Camels from 28 Squadron dealt with any enemy attempting to get airborne. The high level offensive patrol was flown by seven SPAD 7's of 23 Squadron. The attack was a great success, much damage being inflicted to installations and aircraft on the ground, and seven enemy scouts were shot down in air combat.[656]

According to the Royal Flying Corps the enemy were in any event suffering much more from aerial bombing than were the British, and at a Corps Commanders conference on the 24th it was claimed that a comparison of results showed that eight times the number of bombs were being dropped behind their lines. Further arrangements were in hand to support the Canadian attack by G.H.Q. Wing. On the night of the 25th/26th raids were to be made on all aerodromes between the Lys valley and a line through Roulers, Sparappelhoek, and Varssenaere, and billets in Hooglede, Roulers, Berthem, Ledeghem, Moorselede, and Menin were to be attacked. On the 26th aerodromes at Coutrai, Hersaux and Sparappelhoek, and the railway stations at Courtrai, Inglemunster and Thourout were to be bombed. On the 26th/27th, railway stations, trains, and troop movements on the roads in the areas of Hooglede, Oostnieuwkerke, Rolleghem Capelle, Ingelmunster, Ardoye, Ledeghem, Halliun, Wevelghem, Oyghem, Thourout and Lichtervelde were all to receive the attention of the Royal Flying Corps. Offensive patrols of 6 scouts were to accompany the bombers on the 26th and Army Wing scouts were to patrol a southern sector from Quesnoy to Gheluve and a northern sector between Oostnieuwkerke, Dadizele and Gheluve. To protect the air space over the lines, Rovers (low flying scouts) were to operate from ½ hour after Zero to 6 hours after Zero at a height of around 500 feet behind the enemy's forward areas, and were to report any troop movements by dropping messages at the Army Report Centre at Locre. One flight of Bristol Fighters was to stand by for photography or reconnaissance duties.

Revised German tactics

Before being relieved by the Canadians, the 3rd Australian Division reoccupied part of the ground lost on the 12th October, which had subsequently been given up by the enemy. On the 11th October the *Fourth Army* had ordered yet another variation in its defence dispositions. The main line of resistance was withdrawn around 800 yards from the front, and between the two lines a fore-field zone, or *Vorfeld,* was only to be lightly held by outposts and patrols. In the event of an attack the patrols were to retire to the main line and the *Vorfeld* was to be purposely left unmanned, to enable the artillery and machine gun barrages a free field of fire to break up any advance, which was then to be stopped at the main line. This line was to be held at all costs, but if lost was to be re-taken immediately by counter-attack. This new deployment, with most of the enemy pulling back from forward positions, had been noticed by Australian observers, and subsequently on the nights of the 15th, 17th and 18th October, posts had been established within

---

[656] The RFC losses amounted to two Camels of 70 Squadron, both probably being shot down around 11:20 a.m., one over Gravenstafel and one over Passchendaele.

the fore-field zone at Hillside Farm and in Augustus Wood, half way to the first objective of the 12th.

The Canadian Corps Headquarters took over from II Anzac Corps on the 18th October, the 3rd Australian Division being relieved by the 4th Canadian Division on the 22nd and the New Zealand Division being relieved by the 3rd Canadian Division on the 24th. Since the 17th October the incoming Canadians had been studying details of the German defences, and intelligence officers, accompanied by infantry and artillery officers had made careful observations of the enemy positions. The information gathered was quickly passed back to the guns, and from the 21st October a systematic bombardment of blockhouses, strong-points and wire began in earnest, and on each day preparatory barrages in depth combed the enemy positions.[657]

The attack of the Fifth Army 5:35 a.m. 22nd October

Whilst the Canadian preparations advanced at a pace, Fifth Army was to maintain a continuous pressure and attempt once more to wrest the ruins of Poelcappelle from the stubborn enemy, while pushing its left towards Houthulst Forest. Previous attacks against the village had left a ragged outpost line through the centre of the rubble, the German line being of a similar irregular pattern a few yards to the east. So close were the opposing positions that it had been decided to carry out a partial withdrawal prior to the next attack, to enable the artillery to carry out a thorough bombardment. The dangers of attacking on a relatively narrow front were to be obvious throughout the day, as the enemy artillery concentrated its firepower along the 6,000 yards between the Lekkerboterbeek and Veldhoek, to the cost of the three attacking divisions.

On the 19th October the softening-up of the defences of Poelcappelle began with a gas bombardment of 136 Livens canisters and 285 Stokes mortar shells. To add to the general preparatory barrage, which Second Army artillery had commenced on the 21st, Fifth Army on the same day carried out a heavy bombardment to further soften the enemy defences along the front of XVIII and XIV Corps prior to the attack on the 22nd, heavy howitzers concentrating on concrete structures and strong-points. The German artillery responded in kind, shelling heavily with high explosive and shrapnel all approaches to the front, battery positions of field and forward heavy guns (especially in the Steenbeek valley), and the rear assembly and support areas with an added thorough saturation of mustard gas.

The attack to be carried out by Fifth Army was fraught with the usual difficulties. Along the whole front the duckboard tracks still ended 1,000 to 1,500 yards short of the line. From there onwards the route to the forward positions across the quagmire was marked only by tapes laid across the cratered mud, assuming the tapes had not been broken by the continuous shell-fire. The state of the ground greatly enhanced the efficiency of the enemy blockhouse defence system. Previously when the ground had been harder, rushes could be made against the concrete forts that stood a good chance of success, and with the support of Lewis guns, rifle grenades, and Stokes mortars creating dust and smoke to cover the attacks, the blockhouses had fallen one after the other. The mud now precluded any swift movement, Lewis guns and rifles quickly became clogged, and exploding shells and mortar rounds raised little more than fountains of filthy water and mire. It was virtually impossible for the Trench Mortar Battery teams to carry the Stokes guns and their heavy ammunition forward, and the advantage once more lay firmly with the defence.

---

[657] During this period the daily requirements of each Corps in the Fifth Army area were : Heavy artillery ammunition 800 tons, Field artillery ammunition 200 tons, Royal Engineers stores 25 tons, Infantry stores and small arms ammunition 5 tons, other supplies 10 tons, Average total per Corps per day 1,040 tons. National Archives, War Diary Fifth Army, Conference at Army HQ 25th October 1917, WO95/520

XVIII Corps
The third attack on Poelcappelle

Between the attacks on the 12th and 22nd October the conditions on the battlefield remained perpetually atrocious. Attempts to drag forward at least some of the field artillery in the sector of XVIII Corps were endless. The field batteries to support the next attack on Poelcappelle by the 18th Division, were mostly 4,000 yards back, near St. Julien, and many were still west of the Steenbeek. Battery C/82 of the 18th Divisional Artillery struggled to move up 2,000 yards, from Kitcheners Wood to the Winnipeg cross-roads on the Zonnebeke – Langemarck road. It was often necessary for 40 men to try to man-handle one 18-pounder field gun across the rutted tracks and shell-cratered roads. Across the deeper mud it was simply impossible. The timbered approach tracks were littered with derelict vehicles and dead horses, and in one 300 yards stretch fifteen wagons were stranded where they had slipped into the mud. None of C/82's guns got closer than within 500 yards of their intended position before getting stuck, and wherever that occurred they were swung round with great effort at the side of the track, to face the enemy with nothing but a makeshift mounting, simply to be fired from where they lay. To supply sufficient ammunition to the guns remained a nightmare, ponies being the only way of reaching most the field batteries. Usual requirements were for a supply of 1,500 rounds of 18-pounder ammunition per gun to be dumped at each battery, as on occasions 800 rounds were fired in one night. For a pony to bring forward 6 rounds in panniers could take six hours or longer across the tracks from Ypres, always assuming it and its handler got there at all.

18th Division

53rd Brigade[658]
Having remained in the line since the attack on the 12th October, 18th Division was to again use its 53rd Brigade but this time with the 8th Norfolk Regiment to capture the first objective, the Dotted Blue Line, and the 10th Essex Regiment to advance to the final objective,[659] the Blue Line. The attack was to be in three phases. In phase one three companies of the Norfolk, were to attack into the village and evict the enemy from bunkers in the ruins of the Brewery, whilst the fourth company attacked Helles Houses, 350 yards north of the Brewery, from the north. The attack was to be supported by the 53rd and 54th Trench Mortar Batteries. Phase two would see three Essex companies move up about one hour later, pass through the Norfolk, and advance behind the barrage at Zero plus two hours, towards the final objective which ran between Meunier House and Nobles Farm, 500 yards forward of the Brewery. If phases one and two went to plan, in phase three the fourth Essex company, formed up to the right of the other three near Gloster Farm, would attack towards and seize the blockhouse at Beek Houses, supported by the 55th Trench Mortar Battery. Bad visibility and heavy enemy shelling were to hamper operations throughout the day.
Reaching bivouac camp at Cane Post in the old German second line on Pilckem ridge on the 20th October, both battalions had suffered casualties due to hostile shelling of H.E. and gas, which over the last few days had become more intense. On the night of the 21st the march up across the shell-torn swamps of the Steenbeek valley had been as bad as ever, and due to the gas shelling, respirators were ordered to be worn in the 'alert' position. Losses had been inevitable and the attacking companies entered the line in already depleted numbers. The Norfolk companies were in shell-holes along their tapes by around 1:00 p.m. with the Essex in position by 2:00, contact being made between the battalions by 2:30. Since 1:00 it had been raining steadily, and the continuous enemy shell-fire, landing amongst the men whilst they lay in their filthy shell-holes, added considerably to the misery.

---

[658] National Archives, War Diary 53rd Brigade WO95/2037
[659] National Archives, War Diary 10th Norfolk and 10th Essex WO95/2038

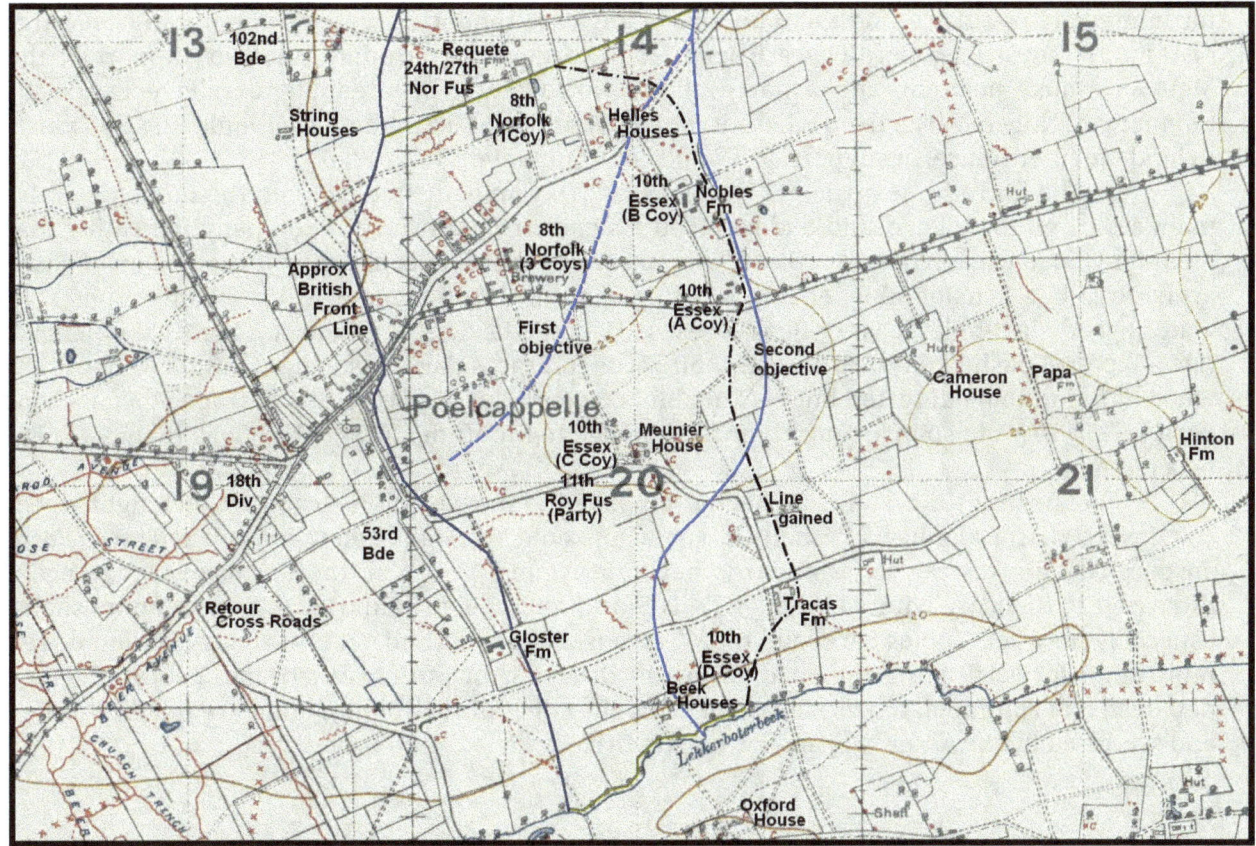

The capture of Poelcappelle 53rd Brigade - 18th Division

At 5:35 the British barrage came down and stood before the waiting infantry for 8 minutes, and then began its slow creep forward at the rate of 100 yards in eight minutes. The Norfolk got away well, and although facing some resistance moved through the village and secured the blockhouses about the Brewery. About one hour later the Essex moved forward with "C" Company on the right, "A" Company in the centre and "B" Company on the left. Machine gun fire from a strong-point which still held out 200 yards west of Helles Houses checked "B" Company and the left flank of "A", until outflanked and bombed, an enemy officer and a number of men being taken prisoner. All three companies then moved up and took cover behind the Norfolk amongst the rubble and shell-holes, awaiting the advance to the final objective. The enemy barrage had increased in intensity since the attack began, and due to the awful state of the ground it had taken time for the men to get clear of the shelling. "C" Company on the right suffered most heavily and only reached the forming up position in greatly diminished numbers and with rifles and Lewis guns already choked with mud.

At about 7:35 as the British barrage thickened, the Essex passed through the Norfolk and moved off towards the final objective. Hostile machine gun and rifle fire was slight, but enemy artillery fire remained severe. The casualties in "C" Company had been so high that the Company Commander considered it wise to concentrate his remaining force on capturing the blockhouse at Meunier House, 500 yards south-east of the village, a task successfully accomplished, the enemy withdrawing as the Essex approached. Patrols were pushed forward to establish posts to the east and south of the blockhouse and "A" Company sent a small party to help garrison the position. In the centre "A" Company had also suffered casualties from the enemy barrage, but had taken all its objectives and was consolidating its gains. Meanwhile on the left "B" Company had secured Nobles Farm, where the enemy had shown little fight, the garrisons of a few organised shell-holes being scattered by rifle fire and grenades. By 8:00 a.m. all three Essex companies were consolidating along a line between Meunier House and Nobles Farm, but were dangerously weak in number, "C" and "A" companies being reduced to around 80 men between them. Ammunition, especially for Lewis guns was running short but there was none available for immediate re-supply, and the mud was in any case rendering weapons inoperative. A party of the 11th Royal Fusiliers of 54th Brigade were ordered up around 10:00 in support of the Meunier House position, and a party of the Norfolk was ordered up to relieve Essex "B" Company at Nobels Farm, from where it moved at around 10:20 into a shell-hole line 200 yards behind Meunier House, in support of "C" and "A" Companies.

On the far right near Gloster Farm, Essex "D" Company had awaited the outcome of the main attack on the village, and had received a signal at 8:00 from "C" Company indicating that Meunier House was secure. At 8:35 "D" Company advanced, encountering little by way of small arms fire, but considerable enemy shelling, and by 9:00 a.m. was establishing posts in waterlogged shell-holes, east of Beek Houses along the Lekkerboterbeek, on the final objective. A small patrol pushed forward another 250 yards to Tracas Farm, a strong-point on a slight rise, which it found to be deserted but was unable to secure due to the British barrage. A signal sent back to 53rd Brigade soon arranged for the barrage to lift off the farm, which was then occupied by a platoon.

For the first time a line had been established to the east of Poelcappelle, in a fight which had cost the Essex alone 257 casualties. The whole objective had been taken and at Tracas Farm an outpost line was pushed 250 yards beyond. Around 4:30 p.m. the German barrage again increased in intensity with a hail of '4.2' (105mm) and '5.9' (150mm) H.E. and shrapnel shells, especially between Nobles Farm and the Westroosebeke road, and enemy infantry could be seen infiltrating forward along the road from the direction of Spriet. At around 200 yards they deployed and continued to work forward using the cover of shell-holes, but were finally checked and scattered by the Essex rifle and Lewis gun fire.

XIV Corps

The push towards Houthulst Forest

On the 13th October the 4th Division had been relieved by the 34th Division, which also took over part of the 17th Division front, and on the 17th October the 17th Division and Guards Division were relieved by the 35th Division. The intension of XIV Corps was to push the left of the British line onto the higher and more commanding ground deeper into the southern edge of Houthulst Forest, and further east along the Vijfwegen spur. The 34th Division was to use its 102nd and 101st Brigades to push the line forward up the Watervlietbeek and Broenbeek valleys, along a front of around 2,000 yards between the northern fringe of Poelcappelle and the Staden railway. On the left, the 35th Division was to use its 104th and 105th Brigades to advance to a depth of around 800 yards, threatening the German positions in Houthulst Forest, along a front of just over 2,000 yards, from the Staden railway to a point 500 yards east of Veldhoek. The ground conditions in this sector of the battlefield were uniformly dreadful, although the still intact trees within Houthulst Forest broke the grey–brown monotony of the foul, gas soaked, and sodden terrain. Machine gun attacks from low flying enemy aircraft along the Corps front, during the 21st and 22nd caused considerable casualties, seemingly operating un-accosted by the Royal Flying Corps. German reconnaissance aircraft were also active in reporting forward positions, and appeared responsible for accurate enemy barrages. Element of the *3rd Naval Division (2nd and 3rd Marine Regiments)*, the *26th Reserve Division (119th R.I.R.)*, and the *58th Division (103rd R.I.R.)*, amongst others, were to be in action on the front of XIV Corps.

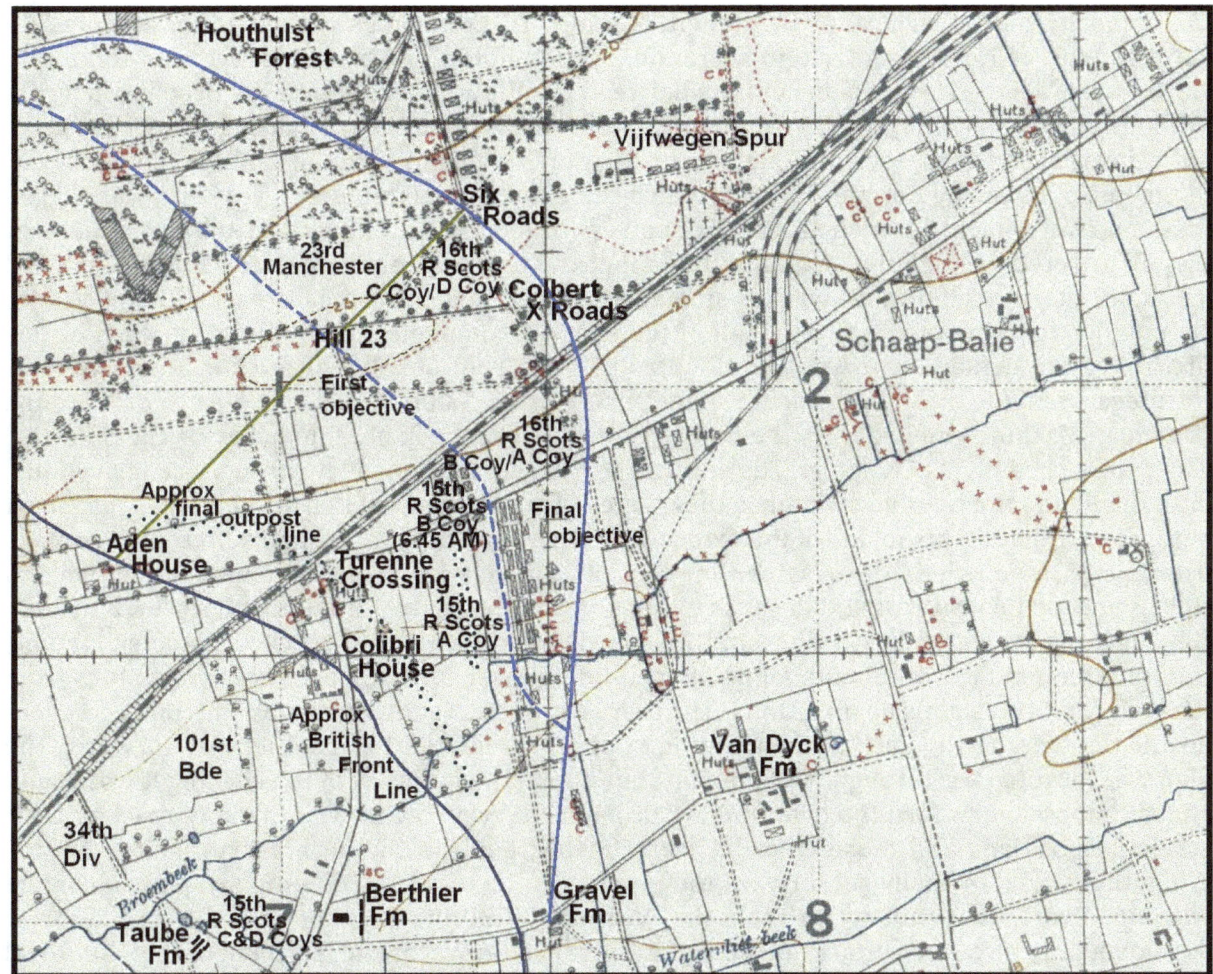

The attack at Hill 23 and along the Vijfwegen Spur 101st Brigade - 34th Division

34th Division

102nd [660] and 101st [661] Brigades

The 34th Division was to attack on a two brigade – three battalion front, using a composite battalion of the 24th and 27th Northumberland Fusiliers of 102nd Brigade on the right between Poelcappelle and the Watervlietbeek, and north of the stream the 101st Brigade with the 15th Royal Scots in the centre and the 16th Royal Scots on the left.[662] During the 21st October the 15th Royal Scots had been shelled by their own artillery causing around 80 casualties which had an understandably detrimental affect on the morale of the men. It appeared that the barrage map showed the barrage line to be behind the forward position, and the battalion was subsequently ordered to move back 200 yards, not a simple task in the appalling conditions. Throughout the day of the attack, drizzle and smoke were to make visibility poor, and to create great difficulty in maintaining direction and touch.

The British barrage came down punctually at 5:35 a.m., and was dense and landed on target. On the right flank the Northumberland seized Requete Farm 500 yards north of Poelcappelle, and reached their objectives along a line between Requete Farm and Rubens Farm, in touch with the Norfolk on their right. In the centre the 15th Royal Scots attacked with two companies in the line, between Gravel Farm and Turenne Crossing on the Staden railway,

---

[660] National Archives, War Diary 102nd Brigade WO95/2460
[661] National Archives, War Diary 101st Brigade WO95/2456
[662] National Archives, War Diary 14th Royal Scots WO95/2457, 15th Royal Scots WO95/2458

"A" Company on the right and "B" the left. "C" and "D" Companies were held in support 700 yards in rear, at Taube Farm and in surrounding shell-holes. The first objective was about 300 yards forward, just short of a line of huts between the Vijfwegen road and the Broenbeek. From the start enemy machine gun fire from numerous directions was heavy causing many casualties, but especially so from a series of bunkers on the northern bank of the Broenbeek, and adjacent to the line of huts. The German barrage, which came down at 10 minutes after Zero, was ragged on the forward lines, a few shells raising showers of muddy water amongst the Royal Scots as they floundered through the quagmire. But about the rear assembly area near Taube Farm and its associated shelters it was systematic and heavy, causing great difficulty with communications and enabling only half of the support companies to get forward. Much of this fire arrived in enfilade and was identified as coming from hostile batteries in the vicinity of Nachtegaal on the northern side of Houthulst Forest, 5,000 yards *north-west* of Turenne Crossing. Machine gun fire from the bunkers on the Broenbeek became heavy as the objective was approached by "A" Company. The survivors struggled on some way through the heavy mud, until finally the fire became so intense they were driven into the shelter of shell-holes just short of the huts. All attempts to attack the extensively wired position, which had suffered no damage from the barrage failed. At the same time German infantry were seen assembling just beyond Hill 23 and Six Roads Cross, 1,000 yards to the north in the edge of Houthulst Forest. To the left, "B" Company struggled forward around 300 yards and by 6:45 had reached its objective line. Here it attempted to consolidate a line of shell-holes, but had sustained severe casualties from the enemy machine guns near the huts. The rear area about Taube Farm was still under a severe hostile enfilade barrage as "C" Company in support attempted to make its way forward. The plan was for it to pass through "B" Company, but due to the intensity of the shelling it was found almost impossible to ford the over-spilling Broenbeek. Very few of "C" Company reached their assembly positions and those who did were further held up by machine gun and shell-fire. When the survivors finally got forward they could find no trace of "B" Company, and no contact was made with "A" Company on the right. At around 7:30 the German assembly in the forest developed into a counter-attack, as the enemy advanced towards the left flank of the 15th Royal Scots and directly towards the front of the 16th Royal Scots to the left. With mud fouled weapons defence was difficult, and the 15th began to fall-back to their original front line, and due to the poor visibility lost touch with the 16th Battalion on the left flank. The S.O.S. was fired but no apparent response came from the British artillery.

At Zero Hour the 16th Royal Scots had attacked astride the railway along a line between Colibri House and Aden House, with "A" and "D" Companies leading and "B" and "C" Companies in support. The shelling and air attacks on the 21st had already caused many casualties, and the attacking lines were subsequently thin. On the right, "A" Company leading, with "B" Company in support, advanced with the barrage but in small numbers, and immediately came under machine gun fire from the bunkers near some huts on their right flank. Reaching a point on the Vijfwegen road, 600 yards forward of Turenne Crossing, they came under further machine gun fire from blockhouses near Schaap-Balie, 750 yards to the east. On the right there was no contact with the 15th Battalion which was already pinned down, and the enemy, using local reserves, soon counter-attacked into the gap from the direction of the huts. With the risk of being outflanked and with weapons rendered useless by the mud, the remnants of "A" and "B" Companies fell-back towards Turenne Crossing. On the left "D" and "C" Companies with a party of "B" Company struggled forward behind the barrage from the Aden House – Turenne Crossing line, across atrocious ground towards Hill 23 to the north-east. They finally reached a point 900 yards forward near Six Roads on the edge of the Forest, approximately on the final objective, but with their right flank dangerously exposed due to the withdrawal of "A" and "B" Companies. Here a double apron of wire, unaffected by the barrage and running along an east to west track was guarded a number of pillboxes. The machine gun crews opened fire upon the 16th Royal Scots and the 23rd Manchester to their left. A Lewis gun team cut through a section of the wire and attacked one of the pillboxes, from where six prisoners were sent back to the British lines. While others of the Royal Scots maintained a heavy covering fire on the other pillboxes, the

Manchester attempted to work around the wire and attack the German position from the left.[663] The enemy counter-attack at around 7:30 from the direction of the huts south of the Vifjwegen road, which had driven in the right flank of "A" and "B" Companies, was partly driven-off by the right flank of "D" and "C" Companies. Soon, the main German effort which had driven back the 15th Battalion also compelled the remaining 16th to withdraw from Six Roads, with the Manchester also falling-back to their left towards Turenne Crossing. The final line was established back where it had started, between Colibri Farm and Aden House. Some stragglers drifted back along the railway as far as the Egypt House – Poelcappelle road.

The 34th Division had attacked into an apex in the British line, where it turned from south – north to east – west, and directly at the point of the apex had been the German strong-point at the huts with five concrete machine bunkers. This had the effect of splitting the attack in half, and the enemy counter-attacks from the edge of Houthulst Forest, which they had always intended to hold at all costs, had sealed the fate of the enterprise. The German infantry, of the *3rd Marine Division*, and *58th Division*, had maintained a skilful and determined defence from their strong, carefully prepared, and well camouflaged positions. The weakness of the Royal Scots battalions due to continuous enemy shelling of the rear areas, plus the intolerable state of the ground, and inoperative weapons, had added in no small measure to the failure.

35th Division [664]
104th Brigade [665] and 105th Brigade [666]

Continued page 483.

---

[663] According to the Royal Scots report.
[664] Lieut-Colonel H.M. Davson (1926) *The History of the 35th Division in the Great War* London : Sifton Praed pp159-166
[665] National Archives, War Diary 104th Brigade WO95/2482
[666] National Archives, War Diary 105th Brigade WO95/2486

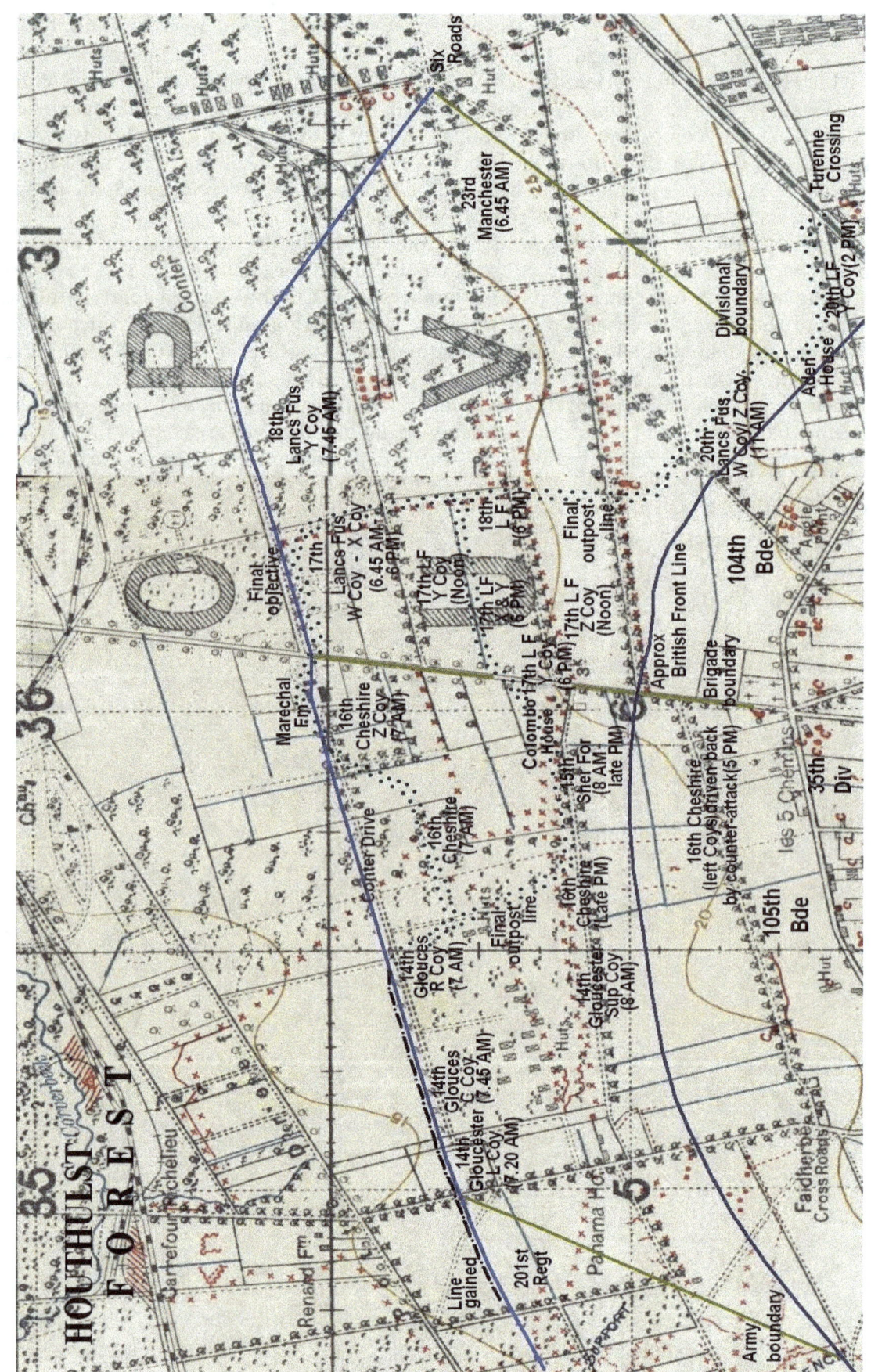

The attack towards Houthulst Forest 104th and 105th Brigades 35th Division

The problems faced by 35th Division were different, as its attack was to diverge from a front of 2,000 yards at the jumping-off line, to around 2,500 yards at the objective, which was within the southern edge of Houthulst Forest, from Six Roads through Marechal Farm to a point 400 yards north of Panama House. On the right 104th Brigade was to attack with the 23rd Manchester Regiment, and the 17th Lancashire Fusiliers, with the 20th Lancashire Fusiliers and 18th Lancashire Fusiliers in support,[667] and the 17th Royal Scots (106th Brigade) in reserve. On the left 105th Brigade was to attack with the 16th Cheshire Regiment, and the 14th Gloucestershire Regiment,[668] with the 15th Sherwood Foresters in support and the 15th Cheshire in reserve. After enormous effort, 157th Brigade R.F.A. had dragged three batteries of 18-pounders off Pilckem ridge, across the Steenbeek, and had positioned them along the Langemarck – Wijdendrift road in old gun-pits just north of Passerelle Farm, in support of the 35th Division attack.

By 2:00 a.m. the division was formed up along the tapes, slightly forward of the original line, to be clear of the German barrage which was usually timed to come down on the front line at dawn. At 5:35 a.m., as the British barrage began its slow creep forward, the 23rd Manchester struggled after it towards Six Roads. Due to the hold up of the 16th Royal Scots in front of the huts on the Vijfwegen road, the Manchester immediately lost contact with them, but continued to advance under heavy machine gun fire from front and flanks. Enemy machine guns situated near a row of huts 750 yards north of Aden House seriously hampered the advance. In greatly reduced numbers the Manchester got forward to the first objective near Six Roads, there being checked by the uncut wire along the track, (which had also checked the 16th Royal Scots), and machine gun fire from the bunkers just beyond. By this stage all officers and a large proportion of N.C.O's of the Manchester had become casualties. No further progress was possible, and with mounting losses, the surviving 50 men of the front wave began to fall-back towards the old front line. On the left, the 17th Lancashire Fusiliers, attacking in four waves made good progress along the Cinq Chemins – Marechal Farm road, initially in touch with the 16th Cheshire on their left. By 6:00 a.m. Colombo House had fallen to "W" Company, and by 6:45 "W" and "X" Companies were on the objective at Marechal Farm and along 400 yards of Conter Drive to the east of the farm. The Cheshire soon came up on their left. It became clear that all was not well on the right as stragglers of the Manchester and 16th Royal Scots were seen falling-back along the railway, being finally checked by officers of the Lancashire Fusiliers near their headquarters at Egypt House. "W" and "X" Companies of the 17th Lancs Fusiliers holding the front line, with "Y" Company in support, realised their right was dangerously exposed, and threw back a flank to cover the gap. One company of the support battalion, the 18th Lancs Fusiliers was detailed to fill the gap, a manoeuvre which was expected to occur in any event due to the diverging objective line. But the 18th had veered too far left and now found itself on the left, rather than the right of the 17th Battalion. After some delay the company of the 18th was brought round behind the 17th, and advanced into the edge of the forest. It here sustained serious casualties from machine gun fire from the right flank, which was also totally exposed. After loosing the company commander and other officers, the remainder of the company fell-back to the edge of the forest. Meanwhile, "Y" Company of the 18th Battalion had come up on the right of the 17th and had taken up positions in shell-holes along Conter Drive, and in turn their right flank was not covered, as the Manchester had already withdrawn to Turenne Crossing. At around 8:00 a.m. word was received by the 20th Lancs Fusiliers in brigade reserve 1,000 yards back near Pascal Farm that the right of the division had fallen back. An order from 104th Brigade was received by the 20th Battalion at 8:35, to move two companies up to the line Aden House – les Cinq Chemin. At 9:20 "W" and "Z" Companies of the 20th moved off with orders to take up the defensive line, and gain touch with 101st Brigade on the right and the 18th Lancs Fusiliers on the left, the two companies subsequently reporting to the officer commanding 23rd Manchester at Egypt House at 10:15. Under heavy hostile fire, mostly from the direction of the forest, both companies proceeded to organise in shell-holes 100 yards north of Aden House and 250 yards north of Angle Point. The enemy could be seen moving 600 to 800 yards away to the north-east, and fired on officer

---

[667] National Archives, War Diary 17th and 20th Lancs Fusiliers WO95/2484
[668] National Archives, War Diary 14th Gloucester WO95/2488

patrols sent out to make touch with the battalions on either flank. The 18th Battalion could not be found, but at 12:15 p.m. touch was at last gained with the 17th Battalion, 600 yards north of the Angle Point line. Amongst the mud and shell-holes on the right all that could be found of the 16th Royal Scots by 1:00 p.m. were 5 wounded men. At 10:30 a.m., with the situation on the right still unclear, the two remaining support companies "X" and "Y" of the 20th Lancs Fusiliers were also sent up to strengthen the line, and at 2:00 p.m. an order was received from brigade for "Y" Company to take up defensive positions along the Aden House – Turenne Crossing road, with "X" Company in reserve near Angle Point.

At noon the position held by 104th Brigade ran from Aden House, to a point 500 yards north-east of Angle Point, this line held in depth by "W", "Y" and "Z" Companies of the 20th Lancs Fusiliers, then north to Conter Drive, this line held weakly by "Y" Company of the 18th Lancs Fusiliers, and west to Marechal Farm, held in depth by "W", "X", "Y" and "Z" Companies of the 17th Lancs Fusiliers. All movement, difficult enough in the atrocious mud, was made more trying in the face of heavy machine gun fire and sniping mainly from the direction of the forest. At around midday hostile shelling became heavy, as the new British shell-hole positions became known to the enemy.

On the left in 105th Brigade sector, the 16th Cheshire and 14th Gloucester had got away well behind the 5:35 barrage, but the going was very heavy and keeping up with the slowly creeping shell-fire proved exhausting. The right "Z" Company of the Cheshire, advancing to the west of the Cinq Chemin – Marechal Farm road arrived at Colombo House shortly after the Lancs Fusiliers, and then moved on to Marechal Farm which they reached at around 7:00 a.m. and began to secure the position. Around 500 yards north-west of Colombo House, the centre and left companies were held up by machine gun fire from a blockhouse, and Lieutenant - Colonel Dent went forward personally to organise the attack. The blockhouse was seized, but heavy fire soon caused another check short of the objective. No further advance appeared possible and a line of posts was then consolidated, in touch with "Z" Company at Marechal Farm, and with the Gloucester on the left. A company of the 15th Sherwood Foresters was sent up to support the Cheshire and occupied a position about Colombo House. The 14th Gloucester had also made good progress, the right company advancing 600 yards to its objective along the track to the west of Marechal Farm with little opposition. This company had however veered too far to the right, loosing touch with the centre company. The Gloucester centre company seized a pillbox 150 yards east of Panama House, taking 5 prisoners with 9 more collected from adjacent organised shell-holes, and then moved on to its final objective. On the left the enemy machine guns at Panama House checked the advance, until a small party, all except one of which became casualties, outflanked the blockhouse and bombed the rear entrance. Two German officers and 3 men were killed, and as others attempted to escape they were shot down by a Lewis gunner, another officer and 5 men being captured inside the blockhouse and 5 more from adjacent trenches. By 6:15 Panama House was secured and the Gloucester pushed on towards the final objective, but soon came under heavy machine gun fire from another blockhouse 200 yards to the north. A small party led by Captain Russell worked forward by shell-holes until close enough to rush the position, at which point the garrison fled. By 7:20 the whole left company of the Gloucester was up and consolidating on the final objective, which was by 7:45 held along the battalion front, but in places by only very small numbers. Captain Russell gathered as many moppers-up and stragglers as possible and sent them forward to strengthen the line. Meanwhile the fourth support company of the Gloucester established a rear defence line between Colombo House and Panama House, and was at about 8:00, reinforced by a company of the 15th Sherwood Foresters. Russell then attempted to gain touch with the Cheshire to the right, which he finally located 200 yards to the right and 200 yards in rear of the Gloucester position. A platoon of the Sherwood Foresters were sent up to fill the gap, but found great difficulty in doing so due to heavy sniping from the forest, some of which was coming from the tree tops. Notwithstanding the difficulties, by 1:00 p.m. the mixed groups of Gloucester and Sherwood Foresters had secured the objective and were in touch with the Cheshire on the right and the French 201st Regiment, which had reached all its objectives, on the left. Close touch and cooperation had been maintained with the French throughout the morning, a platoon of the Gloucester being detailed for the purpose by the brigade commander.

Between 2:00 and 4:30 p.m. it fell comparatively quiet along the whole line from Aden House to Panama House. Urgent digging-in and wiring under dreadful conditions was attempted by the British battalions to consolidate their new positions. The lull was not to last and at just after 4:30 the enemy counter-attacked in force against the left of the Cheshire outpost line to the west of Marechal Farm, and broke through threatening to surround the three left companies, which fell-back around 100 yards, and then stopped and attempted to make a stand. The Germans pressed their attack, driving many of the Cheshire, and some of the company of the Sherwood Foresters which had formed a support line at Colombo House, back to the old front line near the Vijfwegen road. At Marechal Farm "Z" Company of the 16th Cheshire desperately clung to their forward positions, some of which were just in front of the farm, but with their left flank now totally exposed an attempt was made to throw back a long defence line of posts towards Colombo House. To the right, the 17th Lancs Fusiliers had at 4:15 p.m. observed the enemy massing in the forest, and had warned the artillery of the impending counter-attack. At 4:31 the S.O.S. rockets had been fired in the front line and from battalion headquarters at Egypt House. The answering barrage, plus the rifle and Lewis gun fire from the Fusiliers broke up the German counter-attack on their front, the enemy falling-back into the edge of the forest. But it did not break the attack on the left in front of the Cheshire. To support the Cheshire, the Lancashire Fusiliers had also been enfilading the left flank of the German counter-attack with rifle and Lewis gun fire, but upon observing parties of the Cheshire "Z" Company falling back from Marechal Farm to form their defensive flank, mistook the movement for a general withdrawal. It was now believed by Captain Kitchen, the senior Lancashire Fusilier officer on the spot that his "W" and "X" Companies were alone in a salient 1,000 yards deep by 300 yards wide with both flanks totally exposed, and he deemed it wise to withdraw at around 6:00 p.m. to the "Y" Company support line at Colombo House. "Y" Company of the 17th Lancashire Fusiliers were instructed to swing back their left to gain touch with those of the Cheshire and Sherwood Foresters which were still at Colombo House, while to their right, "Y" Company of the 18th were also to swing back to the right to conform to the 20th Battalion in the Angle Point – Aden House line. Upon realising the 17th Lancashire Fusiliers had fallen back Captain Millington of the 16th Cheshire, still holding on but now completely isolated, had no alternative but to order his "Z" Company to withdraw from Marechal Farm to the Colombo House line. On the left the enemy counter-attack against the Gloucester had been largely broken by the artillery, and it was the only battalion still holding its objective. The right flank had been turned back to conform to the Cheshire, and here a platoon of the 15th Sherwood Foresters had moved up to strengthen the line.

The line finally consolidated ran from Aden House, where it was held by remnants of the 23rd Manchester and by 2 companies of the 20th Lancs Fusiliers, roughly north-west where it was held by part of the 20th, part of the 18th and part of the 17th Lancs Fusiliers, to Colombo House, then west for 300 yards, along the track towards Panama House, this section held by the 15th Sherwood Foresters and the 16th Cheshire, where it turned towards the north, meeting Conter Drive, then turning west along that track, there held by the 14th Gloucester.

The day had been exhausting and trying for all concerned. The weather had been miserable and the ground was as bad as everyone fighting at Ypres had now come to expect. Every soldier on the battlefield had been lying chilled to the bone in water-filled holes for hours. Hostile shelling had been severe, especially in the rear assembly areas and along the lines of approach. Battalion headquarters located mainly in old blockhouses and fortified farms had received a systematic bombardment of H.E. and gas, and communication with the line had become very difficult. Sniping and machine gun fire from well camouflaged enemy positions amongst the still intact trees within the forest had taken a steady toll of casualties, and the Germans, by the tenacity of their counter-attacks, had made it clear that they were not about to give up Houthulst Forest without a serious fight. The British infantry were now utterly exhausted.

Although quiet for a few hours the fighting was not yet over. The machine gun bunkers near the row of huts 750 yards north of Aden House were identified as being mainly responsible for the failure of the Manchester, which with the withdrawal of 104th Brigade had led to the collapse on the right, and at 7:00 p.m. the 20th Lancashire Fusiliers was detailed to carry out a local attack in an effort to seize or destroy the position. At 2:00 a.m. on the morning of the 23rd October, two officers and 20 other ranks set off on a forlorn mission, across the foul dark morass towards the enemy position that lay 350 yards beyond the wire belts which had held up the 16th Royal Scots and the Manchester on the 22nd. The party surprised a German machine gun post, bayoneting the crew, and capturing the gun and 4 prisoners. The Germans, now aware of the attack, sent up their S.O.S., and the Fusiliers were hit by artillery and small arms fire, suffering considerable casualties including both officers before withdrawing to the British line. At 5:30 the Germans made another thrust at the 105th Brigade line, at the point where it met with the French. The Gloucester had been relieved by the 15th Cheshire and a company of the 15th Sherwood Foresters, and their rapid fire, combined with an accurate protective barrage broke the enemy attack, many taking cover in adjacent shell-holes. A subsequent field artillery shrapnel barrage, requested by the infantry, decimated those Germans which had taken cover, 40 dead being counted in front of the position.

On the 24th October, relief of the 105th Brigade by the 106th was under way, when at 5:15 p.m. the enemy made yet another counter-attack. The 19th Durham Light Infantry was in direct line of the attack, but the 15th Cheshire, at that moment being relieved by the 18th Highland Light Infantry was also involved. The attack was preceded by red rocket signals, soon followed by a hostile barrage, which crept forward over the British outposts. Around 300 to 400 of the enemy approached but were dispersed by small arms and artillery fire, 60 or 70 being killed and a few prisoners taken.

For the moment the fighting along the southern edge of Houthulst Forest subsided, to be renewed in earnest on the 26th October. Over the period 22nd / 23rd October the 35th Divisional Artillery and attached brigades had fired around 66,500 rounds in support of the infantry. On the 22nd October the 17th Lancashire Fusiliers had sustained casualties of 36 killed, 150 wounded and 12 missing, and 20th Lancashire Fusiliers 28 killed, 173 wounded and 12 missing, these figures being typical for all battalions engaged .

The attacks by XVIII and XIV Corps had achieved little beyond occupying the ruins of Poelcappelle, but they had produced the desired affect of pinning down German forces and not enabling them to deploy elsewhere. German artillery fire had, of necessity, been dispersed over a wider area, and not been allowed to concentrate on the Canadian build-up. Enemy response had been variable, relying mainly on artillery at Poelcappelle with scant infantry intervention; whereas in Houthulst Forest a hornets nest had been disturbed, and the German reaction had shown the importance which they attached to their leafy bastion.

The Sixth Step

The attack of the Second Army 5:40 a.m. 26th October

Weather conditions, rainfall Vlamertinghe, temperature Ypres [669]				
	22nd Oct	**23rd Oct**	**24th Oct**	**25th Oct**
Rainfall	3.2mm	4.0mm	7.7mm	4.5mm
Temp	56F	50F	49F	50F
	26th Oct	**27th Oct**	**28th Oct**	**29th Oct**
Rainfall	7.8mm	Nil	1.3mm	Trace
Temp	48F	49F	45F	47F

In keeping with what had become the pattern for the whole campaign, the weather between the 22nd and 24th October had worsened, there being an average of around 5.5 mm of rain per day over the period, with the inevitable adverse affect on the battlefield. The night of the 25th / 26th however had been fine, and up until about 3:00 a.m. it had been dry. But it was not to last and just after 3:00 a.m. a driving rain once more set in, topping up the shell-holes and saturating the already wet surface.

The attack was to be split into two separate geographical parts. The southern sector on the Menin Road, was to be attacked by X Corps of Second Army. The northern sector was to be attacked by the Canadian Corps of Second Army towards Passchendaele and Goudberg, by XVIII Corps of Fifth Army towards Westroosebeke, and by XIV Corps of Fifth Army towards Vijfwegen. The attacks of X, XVIII, and XIV Corps were intended to give width to the front, preventing a concentration of hostile shelling on the main Canadian attack, and to confuse the enemy as to the main objective, although it is unlikely if at this stage there was any doubt in German minds as to what that objective was. The gap between the left of the X Corps attack on the Reutelbeek in the southern sector, and the right of the Canadian Corps attack at Defy Crossing on the Roulers railway in the northern sector, was around 5,500 yards, although a general barrage was to be fired along the whole front.

X Corps

Another attempt at Gheluvelt

Since the 4th October and the unsuccessful attempt by 37th Division to seize Tower Hamlets and the Quadrilateral, no further major attacks had been made south of the Menin Road. On the 4th the ground conditions, although bad in the Bassevillebeek valley, had been manageable on the higher ground, and the artillery had been near the peak of its efficiency. On the 9th October the

---

[669] National Archives, GHQ statistics WO95/15

5th Division, in appalling conditions, had tried to attack along Polderhoek spur towards the Chateau. Neither on the 4th or on the 9th had the attacks been successful. Further rain and further shelling had now rendered both the Kroomebeek valley (which ran across the front of 7th Division) and the Polderhoek spur impassable to infantry. Those areas which were just passable were denied by the sweep of numerous machine guns. Across this ground the 7th and 5th Divisions were about to attack, towards the concrete bunkers still unbroken after over two months of bombardment by the artillery. It could reasonably be said that the outcome was predictable. There can have been few armies in history, in which the discipline was so sure, and the officers and men so steady, that an attack under these conditions could have even been contemplated let alone attempted.

7th Division [670]
Major-General T. H. Shoubridge

91st Brigade [671] and 20th Brigade [672]
The 7th Division, after ten days out of the line, had relieved elements of the 14th Division north of, and 39th Division south of the Menin Road on the 24th October. The prime tactical objective of the forthcoming attack was the capture of the Gheluvelt spur and the ruins of Gheluvelt village. In support of the division XXII Brigade Royal Field Artillery was in positions around Glencorse Wood, 2,000 yards back, with extra artillery brigades attached under command of the Divisional C.R.A., with 144 18-pounders and 48 4.5-inch howitzers. Heavy gunfire support was provided by 32 medium and 20 heavy howitzers, and 94 Vickers guns would fire a machine gun barrage. The 5:40 a.m. creeping barrage was to land 150 yards forward of the jumping-off tapes and stand on this line for four minutes. It was then to do two lifts of 100 yards in six minutes, followed by two more at eight minute intervals, the final 100 yard lifts taking twelve minutes to the Red Line. Here the protective barrage would stand 150 yards in front of the line. After a halt of 30 minutes the barrage would creep towards the Blue Line at a rate of 100 yards in twelve minutes, to stand 200 yards forward of the Blue Line. A secondary barrage would then search backwards and forwards across the German position throughout the day.

The division was to attack with five battalions in the line along a 1,500 yard front, between the southern sector of the German Quadrilateral position on the right, to near Jackson Trench, 300 yards north of the Menin Road on the left. The first objective, the Red Line about 500 yards forward, ran from Joist Trench (part of the Quadrilateral), roughly north-west towards Gheluvelt church, where it swung slightly to the north in the direction of Polderhoek Chateau. At Zero plus 45 minutes it was hoped the infantry would have fought their way forward to the first objective, across the 500 yards of churned, clinging mud. The final objective, the Blue Line, formed an arc 450 yards deep in the centre which included most of the ruins of Gheluvelt village, and the remains of Gheluvelt Chateau, 500 yards north of the Menin Road.
On the southern flank, 91st Brigade was to use the 1st South Staffordshire Regiment on the right,[673] with the 21st Manchester Regiment in the centre, and the 2nd Queens on the left, with one company of the 22nd Manchester in support of the South Staffs, and one company in support of the 21st Manchester and the Queens. Upon the capture of the first objective, the 21st Manchester and the Queens were to push their support companies through to seize the final objective. To the left, astride the Menin Road, the 20th Brigade was to use the 2nd Border Regiment south of the road and the 9th Devonshire Regiment to the north to seize the first objective,[674] with the 2nd Gordon Highlanders in support of the Border Regiment and the 8th Devon in support of the 9th, both to push through to take the final objective. The 22nd Brigade

---

[670] C.T. Atkinson The Seventh Division 1914-1918 pp426-423
[671] National Archives, War Diary 91st Brigade WO95/1667
[672] National Archives, War Diary 20th Brigade WO95/1654
[673] National Archives, War Diary 1st South Staffs WO95/1670, National Archives, War Diary 2nd Queens WO95/1670
[674] National Archives, War Diary 9th Devon WO95/1656

provided the divisional reserves, with the 20th Manchester supporting 91st Brigade and the 1st Royal Welsh Fusiliers supporting the 20th Brigade.

At daybreak on the 25th October the weather situation seemed a little better, as with a clear sky and a strong wind, the higher and sandier parts of the battlefield began to improve. Throughout the day hostile shelling was light, the enemy keeping relatively quiet. By 9:00 p.m. the sky remained clear and moonlit. The laying of tapes was hampered by sniping which caused some officer casualties. But about 2:00 a.m. the battlefield darkened as clouds covered the moon and by 4:30 as the assembly along the tapes was completed, and the men lay out in their shell-holes, the rain began to fall.

At 5:40 a.m. with the first hint of dull light appearing in the overcast sky, the division moved off behind the barrage. The Germans retaliated almost immediately, but their shells fell mostly behind the support battalions which had intentionally closed up on the front line to avoid them. On the right of 91st Brigade the South Staffs started well, with "B" Company on the right, "D" Company in the centre and "C" Company on the left, with two platoons of "A" in support of "C" and the remainder of "A" in support of "B" and "D". Attacking towards a significant knoll on the side of the Bassevillebeek valley, known as "The Mound", "B" Company advanced with relatively light casualties, being protected by the shape of the ground from the machine guns in the blockhouses behind the Quadrilateral. They approached the position successfully, but it proved to be strongly held by the enemy, and a savage and costly fight ensued. After a prolonged struggle, in which all officers and most N.C.O's. were killed or wounded the position fell to "B" Company, now commanded by a corporal. The remaining Germans withdrew leaving behind many of their dead and a machine gun. "B" Company began to consolidate the position against counter-attack, and sent back for reinforcements. All the runners were killed and no reinforcements were to arrive. In the centre of the South Staffs, "D" Company, attacking towards Hamp Farm, did not have the benefit of the ground, and was cut down by machine gun crossfire from the farm and Berry Cottage, the survivors taking cover in shell-holes 50 yards from their start line. On the left "C" Company, although sustaining heavy casualties, made some progress, until finally checked by machine gun fire from Berry Cottage just forward of their objective, and from the group of blockhouses at Lewis House 500 yards to the north-east. Now, 50 yards from Berry Cottage, they too took cover in shell-holes under a shower of stick grenades hurled by the enemy. Most weapons were by this time choked with mud, and the company was reduced to an officer and about 20 men. There was nothing to be done but to wait for a suitable opportunity to withdraw.

If it were possible, the situation of the centre and left battalions of 91st Brigade was even worse. On the right flank the South Staffs had attacked across a spur of higher and slightly drier ground jutting south-east from Tower Hamlets ridge, whereas the 21st Manchester and Queens were to descend the eastern slope towards the Kroomebeek and into a quagmire. The line held by the 21st Manchester was dominated by the guns of the Lewis House blockhouses, and its advance was immediately checked by severe machine gun fire and fell-back to the assembly position. The Queens had formed up with three companies in the line, "D" on the right, "B" in the centre, and "C" on the left, with "A" Company in support of "C". The barrage crept forward at its slow rate, but the Queens, floundering forward through the morass were unable to keep pace with it, and soon came under severe fire from the Lewis House machine guns. By about 6:20 the Queens were also checked and parties of the Manchester and Borders which had converged on the same position, prevented the planned Stokes mortar attack on the blockhouses, and provided the enemy with a dense target. Of the officers of the four Queens companies, all except 2nd Lieutenant Howells M.C. commanding "A" Company, and Captain Streeter commanding "D" Company had become casualties. These officers organised several attempts to outflank the Lewis House position but without success, finally establishing a composite line of Queens, Manchester, and Borders in shell-holes 200 yards short of Lewis House. There were now many gaps in the front line, and the two reserve companies of the 22nd Manchester were brought up to fill the gap between the Queens and 21st Manchester and two Vickers guns sections were brought forward to cover the front.

The failure of the centre and left of 91st Brigade was to have a knock-on effect on 20th Brigade. The 2nd Border Regiment, attacking with its "C" Company on the right and "D" Company on the left between Tower Trench and the Menin Road, advanced across terrible ground over which movement was only just possible. "C" Company began descending the slope into the Kroomebeek valley and became stuck in thigh deep mud, and were raked by the machine guns at Lewis House and by fire from bunkers along the Menin Road. On the left "C" Company found the ground to their immediate front totally impassable, and moved left towards the only way forward, which was along the Menin Road. Parties worked along what remained of the cobbled surface towards a group of German bunkers situated 250 yards from the start line, but came under heavy machine gun fire. The state of the ground on either side prevented the company from deploying off the road. The group provided a concentrated target for the enemy guns and were badly shot up, the remnants taking shelter in a large crater near the 7th kilometre marker post, just short of the bunkers. "B" Company, detailed to mop-up behind the forward companies, also found the ground impossible and struggled onto the Menin Road. Suffering the same fate as "C" Company, the survivors also took shelter in the crater. Another attack against the bunkers was organised from the crater by Captain Moore and 2nd Lieutenant Inkpen, but both were killed in the attempt, and the attack failed. Coming forward in support, "A" Company worked along the road coming under fire from the shelters and from Lewis House 350 yards to the left, sustaining many casualties, but succeeding in capturing one pillbox and a machine gun. All further attempts to seize the remaining bunkers proved hopeless. Leaving "A" Company to suppress the enemy machine gun fire, Captain Little, who had gathered the remnants of "B" and "D" Companies and a few stragglers of the Devon, worked forward by shell-holes another 250 yards to within 150 yards of the rubble of Gheluvelt where at around 7:00 a.m. the small party established a line of shell-hole posts, and awaited reinforcements. That reinforcement should have come from the 2nd Gordon Highlanders but as they advanced across the position of the old front line, without the support of the barrage, they were cut down by machine gun fire from Lewis House and Swagger Farm, which lay 650 yards to the south-east. Survivors of the Gordons right company veered right and joined the Queens pinned down before Lewis House. Another party moved along the Menin Road to the crater, where they were cut down attempting to attack one of the troublesome pillboxes. Others moved north of the road finally entering Gheluvelt with the Devon. All five battalions of the 7th Division were now completely pinned down and only on the extreme right at The Mound had the objective been secured. Worse was soon to come.

North of the Menin Road the 9th Devon were to attack along a 200 yard front just forward of Jackson Trench, their right being on the road, with "1" and "2" Companies in the line, "3" Company mopping-up, and "4" Company in reserve. All four companies were formed up to a depth of 140 yards, and the 8th Devon was in support 50 yards in the rear. Both battalions moved forward and kept up reasonably with the barrage, but were soon hit in enfilade from the machine guns at Lewis House and Swagger Farm firing across the Menin Road, and from other machine guns and snipers in the ruins of Gheluvelt. By around 7:30 parties of "1" and "2" Companies of the 9th Devon had got forward into the village ruins, as had groups of the 8th. Some of the 9th under Captain Pridham had proceeded beyond a light railway cutting, while the 8th had attacked and cleared a line of pillboxes along Johnson Trench. Some had even approached close enough to the church to attempt to rush the position, but all were hampered by rifles and Lewis guns choked with mud. At around 8:00 a.m. the enemy appeared to be infiltrating forward covered by machine gun fire, and the companies of the 9th in their exposed position fell-back to the light railway cutting. At 10:00 a.m. around 100 Germans were seen to emerge from the ruins of the church, and with few serviceable weapons available to resist them, a general withdrawal from the village began. Some of the Devon fell-back to their left rear into the sector of 13th Brigade, where some were rallied by the commanding officer of the 1st Royal West Kent. Others fell-back to the crater held by the Borders, while a few joined Captain Pridham who intended to make a stand at the railway cutting. At the crater near the 7 kilometre marker, Major Kerr of the Borders rallied a mixed group of 40 of his battalion, plus men of the Gordons and Queens, and established a defensive flank in shell-holes along the southern side of the Menin Road, back towards Tower Hamlets. But there was a large gap between this group and the main body of the Queens in front of Lewis House.

The whole division, with battalions scattered and well out of position, was now back around the start line, but of greatest danger, there were few serviceable weapons to fight off the expected counter-attack. At 2:00 p.m. two companies of the Royal Welsh Fusiliers were sent up in support of the Devon, one company forming a defence line in shell-holes behind the forward Devon position, the second held back in reserve to counter-attack. As the runners had not got through with their reports from The Mound, the fact that "B" Company of the 1st South Staffs was in possession of the position was still not known, and as the artillery put down a barrage to dissuade any enemy counter-attack, their position was heavily shelled. It had subsequently to be abandoned, and the only success of the day was therefore lost.

The General Officer Commanding the 7th Division, Major-General Shoubridge, C.M.G., D.S.O. wrote later to his battalion commanders: 'I have just seen the army commander. Though he regrets we did not get our objectives, he fully realises that officers and men did all that was humanly possible in the face of great difficulties. He also told me that the enemy had a railway reserve between Menin and Passchendaele intending to employ it at the most threatened point. Our attack showed such determination that he retained all reserves against us. This helped the Canadians materially to gain and hold their objectives. Therefore we did not fight in vain. The 7th Division has taken hard knocks before – but it never losses its splendid spirit, and yesterday's battle will only be an incentive to get our own back on the next opportunity. Will you convey the contents of this letter to all officers N.C.O's. and men, and also tell them how proud I am of the way in which they went forward under the worst conditions of mud and fire and would not give in until they died or stuck in the mud. No soldiers can do more. Yours Sincerely, Herbert Shoubridge.' [675]

The doubts and fears before the action had been well founded, for in the attack on Gheluvelt the 91st and 20th Brigades had been shattered. Total losses sustained by the division were 110 officers and 2,614 other ranks, of which 179 had been killed and 730 were missing. The opportunity for the 7th Division to get its own back on this enemy was not to come about. On the 8th November the order was received to embark for Italy, and it arrived there on the 23rd. The division which had landed at Zeebrugge on the 6th October 1914, and had been in the thickest of the fighting at First Ypres was to finish the War far away from Flanders, at Pozzo, on the River Tagliamento, east of Pordenone.

5th Division
Major-General R. B. Stephens

13th Brigade [676]

The German blockhouses in the ruins of Polderhoek Chateau had been located in a position of great tactical strength. Situated on the eastern edge of the Gheluvelt plateau, on a small spur between the Scherriabeek and the Reutelbeek, the Chateau commanded the slopes of the plateau to north and south, and the bunkers in the park a few yards to the west of the ruin covered the approach from that direction.

The 13th Brigade was to use the 1st Royal West Kent Regiment along the valley of the Scherriabeek, the 15th Royal Warwickshire Regiment towards the Chateau, and the 14th Royal Warwickshire along the Reutelbeek. As there was to be no attack across the ground to the left of the brigade the objective was limited to keeping touch on the right with the 20th Brigade, and seizing the Chateau. From the start the West Kent was presented with a hopeless task along the impassable Scherriabeek, becoming physically stuck in the mud, with mud-choked weapons and under fire from the ruins of Gheluvelt. The going along the spur was a little better, and against all odds the 15th Warwick successfully seized the bunkers in the park and took the Chateau,

---

[675] National Archives War Diary 1st South Staffs WO/95/1670
[676] National Archives, War Diary 13th Brigade WO95/1550

capturing a battalion commander, a liaison officer and 100 men in the cellars beneath the ruins. The left of the 14th Warwick was stuck in the bogs of the Reutelbeek, but the right got forward sufficiently to keep touch with the 15th at the Chateau. Believing himself to be in an extremely exposed position, and with few serviceable weapons, the company commander at the Chateau made the unfortunate decision to withdraw to straighten the brigade line. The Germans quickly reoccupied the bunkers and again swept the ground to the west with machine gun fire, under cover of which they mounted a successful counter-attack. By nightfall, the 13th Brigade had been driven back to its start line.

Under the prevailing conditions the advantage was firmly with the defenders, who generally fought from their fixed positions with weapons free of the filthy mud. The carefully practised routine of fire and movement, which had been the downfall of so many of the Flanders blockhouses, was just not possible over ground which clung to, and sucked down the attackers. The inability of the enemy to launch any concerted counter-attacks, other than to recover their lost positions was evidence that they realised the hopelessness of the endeavour. It was not a question of why X Corps had not done better, but rather how they had mounted an attack at all. As General Shoubridge had written, it was to be hoped that the sacrifice was to significantly help the Canadians at the vital point of attack. Total casualties in X Corps had amounted to 119 officers and 3,202 other ranks.

The capture of Passchendaele – The First Phase

Canadian Corps

Lieutenant-General Sir Arthur Currie

4th Canadian Division
Major-General D. Watson

10th Canadian Brigade [677]

3rd Canadian Division
Major-General L. J. Lipsett

9th [678] and 8th [679] Canadian Brigades

I Anzac Corps

Lieutenant-General Sir William Birdwood

1st Australian Division
Major-General H. B. Walker

2nd Australian Brigade [680]

---

[677] National Archives, War Diary 10th Can Brigade WO95/3896
[678] National Archives, War Diary 9th Can Brigade WO95/3875
[679] National Archives, War Diary 8th Can Brigade WO95/3868
[680] National Archives, War Diary 2nd Aus Brigade WO95/3231

The proposed step by step stages of the Canadian Corps operation to capture Passchendaele

Since the 21st October Lieutenant -General Currie's artillery had been constantly pounding the German defences around Passchendaele. At the beginning of October, what had still been recognisable from the air as roads and settlements of the village of Passchendaele, now appeared as a featureless extension of the massive, waterlogged crater-field, which stretched back 6,000 yards to the old July front line. The only structures tall enough to cast even a short shadow, were the rubble remains of the church, and the skeletal frames of a few houses near the five cross way at the northern fringe of the village. A Canadian Corps Summary of Intelligence 19th October had at last spelt out the danger. 'Reports from patrols and from observers show that the enemy's wire very thick across Bellevue Spur, varying from 25 to 40 yards in depth, and is of the low picket pattern.'[681] This wire was now to be systematically smashed.

The artillery strength available to Currie was considerable, comprising a total of 15 Field Brigades of field artillery, of which 4 were Canadian and 2 were New Zealand, with around 210 18-pounders and 70 4.5-inch howitzers. There were 52 heavy or siege batteries of which 5 were Canadian, with approximately 20 60-pounders, 80 6-inch howitzers, 25 8-inch howitzers, 15 9.2-inch howitzers, and 1 15-inch howitzer. During the 21st and 22nd October, 62nd Heavy Artillery Group fired in excess of 750 rounds of 6-inch shells against various targets on and around the German lines, 200 being fired at Vocation Farm alone. From 6:00 a.m. on the 22nd

---

[681] Library and Archives of Canada. RG9 III-D-3 Vol4816 T-7177 File-13

October to 6:00 p.m. on the 23rd the Northern Double Bombardment Group concentrated in earnest on the 500 yard by 500 yard square on Bellevue spur, in which were situated some of the blockhouses and wire that had previously caused so much trouble. Into this area of less than a tenth of one square mile, were fired 20 15-inch, 80 8-inch and 400 6-inch projectiles. The 15-inch shells were seen to do considerable damage to the concrete structures, in places causing the garrisons to evacuate, and due to the ferocity of the bombardment some of the defenders were observed to cross to the British lines. On the 24th Decline Copse, Crest Farm, Graf, Meetcheele and several prominent Mebus were engaged with good results, and lanes were cut through the wire belts on and north of the Bellevue spur. On the next day an intelligence report stated that at last the wire on Bellevue spur, and to the north and south of it was passable to infantry.

The Ravebeek valley between the main ridge and the Bellevue – Wallemolen high ground remained a major obstacle, presenting an impassable muddy corridor right down the centre of the 2,600 yard front, which would inevitably split the attack in two. It had wisely been decided, possibly upon reflection of the disasters of the 9th and 12th October but more likely due to Currie's tactical common sense, that the final objective for the first attack, the Red Line, would once more be strictly limited to an advance of about 800 yards along the railway on the right, and 1,200 yards to around Vapour Farm on the left. The final objective of the 4th Canadian Division, which was to attack south of the Ravebeek, would be along an approximately 1,400 yard line between a point just forward of Decline Copse beside the Roulers railway 700 yards east of Defy Crossing, to Friesland in the marsh of the Ravebeek. For the 3rd Canadian Division attacking north of the stream, the final objective would be along a 1,400 yard line running towards the north-west from Friesland to Vapour Farm in the valley of the Paddebeek, a small marshy depression on the northern slope of Wallemolen spur.

The 4th Canadian Division was to attack with a single brigade, the 10th, and that brigade with a single battalion, the 46th (South Saskatchewan) Battalion.[682] The 47th (British Columbia) Battalion was in close support near Levi Cottage and the 44th in reserve at Potijze. Before the main attack, outposts were to be pushed forward on the 23rd October by the 50th (Calgary) Battalion holding the line, from where the 46th would jump-off, reducing the distance to the first objective to 500 yards.
North of the Ravebeek, the 3rd Division was to attack with the 9th Brigade, using two battalions, the 58th (Central Ontario) Battalion towards Laamkeek, and the 43rd (Cameron Highlanders of Canada) towards Bellevue,[683] and the 8th Brigade using the 4th Canadian Mounted Rifles towards Wallemolen.[684] As the division had a deeper final objective than the 4th, there was to be an intermediate objective, the Dotted Red Line, upon which there was to be a one hour halt. The 9th Brigade had the 52nd Battalion in support with the 116th Battalion in reserve, while the 8th Brigade had the 1st C.M.R. in close support, the 2nd C.M.R. in support and the 5th C.M.R. in reserve. To cover the right flank of the 4th Canadian Division, the 1st Australian Division was to use three platoons, (around 80 men in total), of the 6th Battalion, 2nd Australian Brigade, to be supported by the 2nd Field Company of Australian Engineers, to seize the Keiberg railway cutting near Decline Copse.
As the infantry crouched in their shell-holes awaiting the moment for action, the rain which had fallen throughout the early hours gradually worsened the already appalling state of the ground below the ridges. Due to the weather, poor visibility was going to hamper precise observation throughout the day. South of the Ravebeek, two hours before Zero, the 46th Battalion worked forward to their assembly positions just behind the 50th Battalion outposts. At 5:40 the barrage

---

[682] National Archives, War Diary 46th Can Battalion WO95/3898, National Archives, War Diary 47th Can Battalion WO95/3899

[683] National Archives, War Diary 52nd Can Battalion WO95/3877, National Archives, War Diary 43rd and 58th Can Battalion WO95/3878

[684] National Archives, War Diary 1st CMR WO95/3870, National Archives, War Diary 2nd CMR WO95/3871, National Archives, War Diary 4th CMR WO95/3872, National Archives, War Diary 5th CMR WO95/3873

crashed down 100 yards in front, and commenced its slow forward creep of 100 yards in eight minutes, followed as closely as possible by the Canadians. South of the Roulers railway, from their assembly position 250 yards forward of Defy Crossing, the right flank guard party of three Australian platoons also started forward. But they were immediately stopped as the barrage collapsed back upon the front platoon. The survivors quickly fell-back out of the barrage, reformed, and again moved forward accompanied by the support platoon. To gain some protection from the errant shell-fire they crossed the railway and worked forward under the dubious shelter of the northern side of the low embankment. The Canadians of the 46th, after initially experiencing the same problem with the barrage, made good progress astride the Passchendaele road, and reached the Red Line, one company pushing out posts 350 yards along the road beyond its objective. As the Australians entered the Keiberg cutting the garrison of an enemy dug-out attempted to get one of their machine guns into action, but were quickly shot up. Thirty subsequently surrendered and 3 machine guns were captured. On the other side of the railway, 30 more prisoners and a machine gun were captured at a dug-out south-east of Decline Copse. With the 46th Canadians up on the left, the small Australian party began to establish posts on the crest of the Keiberg, and at 7:30 a.m. were assisted with the consolidation by the arrival of the engineers and the reserve platoon.

It had appeared before the attack that the Flanders I wire entanglements across the Bellevue – Wallemolen spurs in front of the 3rd Canadian Division had at last been well broken by the artillery, and as the 43rd advanced up the slope this proved to be the case. By 6:21 they were seen to be north of the pillboxes at Bellevue which had so decimated the 49th Division and the New Zealand Division, and by 6:25 a stream of enemy prisoners was being sent to the rear. Down by the Ravebeek however the 58th Battalion were held up by the blockhouses and wire at Laamkeek, and by machine gun fire from the Crest Farm blockhouse 1,200 yards up the valley. On the far left meanwhile, on the other side of Bellevue spur, the 4th C.M.R. had by 7:45 attained its intermediate objective, and after bitter fighting had overwhelmed the strong-points and pillboxes of Flanders I and taken Wolf Copse. In the attack Private Thomas William Holmes on his own initiative and single-handed, ran forward and threw two bombs at a machine gun post which was holding up the advance, killing the crew. Later he again went forward alone under heavy fire and threw a bomb into a bunker, causing the garrison of 19 to surrender. He was to be awarded the V.C. for his conspicuous bravery and resource. Over at Laamkeek by the Ravebeek there had been no progress, and at 8:15 it was reported by the 9th Brigade that the 58th Battalion and elements of the 43rd were back on their jumping-off lines, but were being reinforced by the 52nd Battalion and a renewed attack was to be made.

At 8:20 a.m. a severe enemy artillery and machine gun barrage, which caused many casualties, heralded a counter-attack. On the left in the 8th Brigade a company of the 1st C.M.R. were ordered up to support the 4th C.M.R., and by 9:05 the brigade was on its final objective. But at 8:50 the 58th Battalion was confirmed as being back on its start line, and most worryingly was under machine gun fire from blockhouses up on Bellevue spur where the 43rd Battalion was supposed to be. Up on Bellevue spur the advance of the 43rd had been stopped 450 yards short of the objective, both by hostile artillery fire, and machine gun fire from pillboxes along the Wallemolen track, 250 yards east of Bellevue. The rain was now pouring down, and by 9:00 parties of the 43rd were falling-back down the slope. South of the Ravebeek the 46th Battalion, seeing the withdrawal of the 43rd, and itself under machine gun fire from Laamkeek, from Meetchele along the spur, and under shelling from the hostile barrage, threw back a defensive flank along the Ravebeek facing north-west. On the left near Wolf Copse, the 4th C.M.R. also fell-back around 300 yards, to keep touch with the 43rd to their right and to conform to the 63rd Division of Fifth Army, which was not up on the left.

It was beginning to look like a re-run of the 9th and the 12th. By 11:00 a.m. the artillery had been ordered to bring the barrage back to the protection line forward of the first intermediate objective and slacken its fire, as it was known that groups were still holding out on the spur. Two companies of the 52nd Battalion were ordered forward in support. Two acts of great leadership and courage now saved the day. Up on Bellevue spur Lieutenant Robert Shankland D.C.M. of the 43rd Battalion, had in the general confusion of withdrawal, reinforced his platoon with men of other companies and two detachments of the 9th Machine Gun Company. With this force of around 50 men, he had managed to establish and hold on to a strong-point, in pillboxes and shell-holes behind the Flanders I Line, and just north of the Gravenstafel – Mosselmarkt road. Enemy counter-attacks failed to dislodge the group and just before noon Captain Christopher Patrick John O'Kelly led the two companies of the support 52nd Battalion over 1,000 yards of open ground under heavy fire, without barrage support, and organised an attack against the obdurate Bellevue pillboxes. The stubborn position had at last been outflanked, and working gradually towards the south, with the support of Shankland's party, O'Kelly's companies brought their Lewis guns and rifle grenades to bear, while others crept up close and bombed out 6 pillboxes, capturing 100 prisoners and 10 machine guns. Continuing down the slope towards the Ravebeek they attacked the Laamkeek blockhouses from the rear, inflicting the same punishment. The Flanders I defences at Bellevue which had wrought such havoc, and had been culpable in stalling the whole offensive had at last collapsed, lanced like a great abscess, opening the way to Passchendaele. Both Lieutenant Shankland and Captain O'Kelly were to receive the V.C. for their actions, the importance of which of which at the time they may not have fully realised.

The near disaster north of the Ravebeek had a knock on affect on the 46th Battalion south of the stream, on the main ridge and along the Passchendaele road. At about 11:30 the Germans were seen to be concentrating on the southern fringes of Passchendaele, culminating in a counter-attack at about 1:30 p.m. which was driven off by rifle and Lewis gun fire, resulting in heavy enemy losses. But around 2:00 p.m. with enemy pressure increasing from the front, and the withdrawal underway on the left, (and enfiladed by the same German guns firing from Moorslede which had previously decimated the 66th Division and 3rd Australian Division), the 46th Battalion posts which had been pushed forward 350 yards along the Passchendaele road, gradually began to fall-back to the Decline Copse line. Two companies of the 50th Battalion were rushed up in support of the 46th. At 4:15 p.m. in the face of another counter-attack against the Australians holding the Decline Copse cutting, Company-Sergeant-Major Palmer of the 6th Battalion, was sent across to the Canadians in the copse to advise that so long as they were supported, the Australians would not retire from the cutting and would hold on at all costs to protect the Canadian right. Canadian artillery and Australian machine guns scattered the German counter-attack, but the Australians had observed the Canadian forward outposts falling-back along the crest, and taking this for a general withdrawal, which would expose their small group on the Keiberg, abandoned the Decline Copse line and fell-back towards Defy Crossing.

At around 4:00 p.m. on Bellevue spur, two enemy groups of around 500 each were observed to be advancing from Meetcheele, towards the line held by the 43rd and 52nd Battalions, but the counter-attack was broken by artillery and small arms fire. By 4:15 the 52nd Battalion had secured a line between Bellevue and the Wallemolen track in touch with the 43rd Battalion on the right and the 4th C.M.R. on the left.

Casualties sustained by the 46th Canadian Battalion had been extremely heavy, amounting to over 290 out of 420 engaged, and on the evening 26th/27th the 47th Battalion relieved the 46th in the line. The C.O. of the 47th, believing his position to be too exposed and beyond the S.O.S. barrage line, carried out a poorly arranged withdrawal at 3:00 a.m. on the morning of the 27th which, falling back farther than necessary, finally abandoned Decline Copse. Great confusion arose as to who had withdrawn first, the Canadians initially believing that they were still in possession of the copse, and that 6th Australian Battalion had exposed their right flank. Lieutenant Lay of the 8th Australian Battalion spent the afternoon of the 26th and the morning of the 27th reconnoitring Decline Copse, and liaising between the Canadian and Australian headquarters. The Australians tactfully agreed to recapture Decline Copse if it could be shown the Canadians were still forward, but managed to put off doing so until Lieutenant Lay's information proved to all concerned that they were not. This was to be the last major infantry action by Australian forces in the Flanders offensive, although they still continued to hold their section of the line. The magnificent contribution that all five Australian Divisions had made in the Third Battle of Ypres was now coming to an end, the torch being safely passed on to the Canadians.

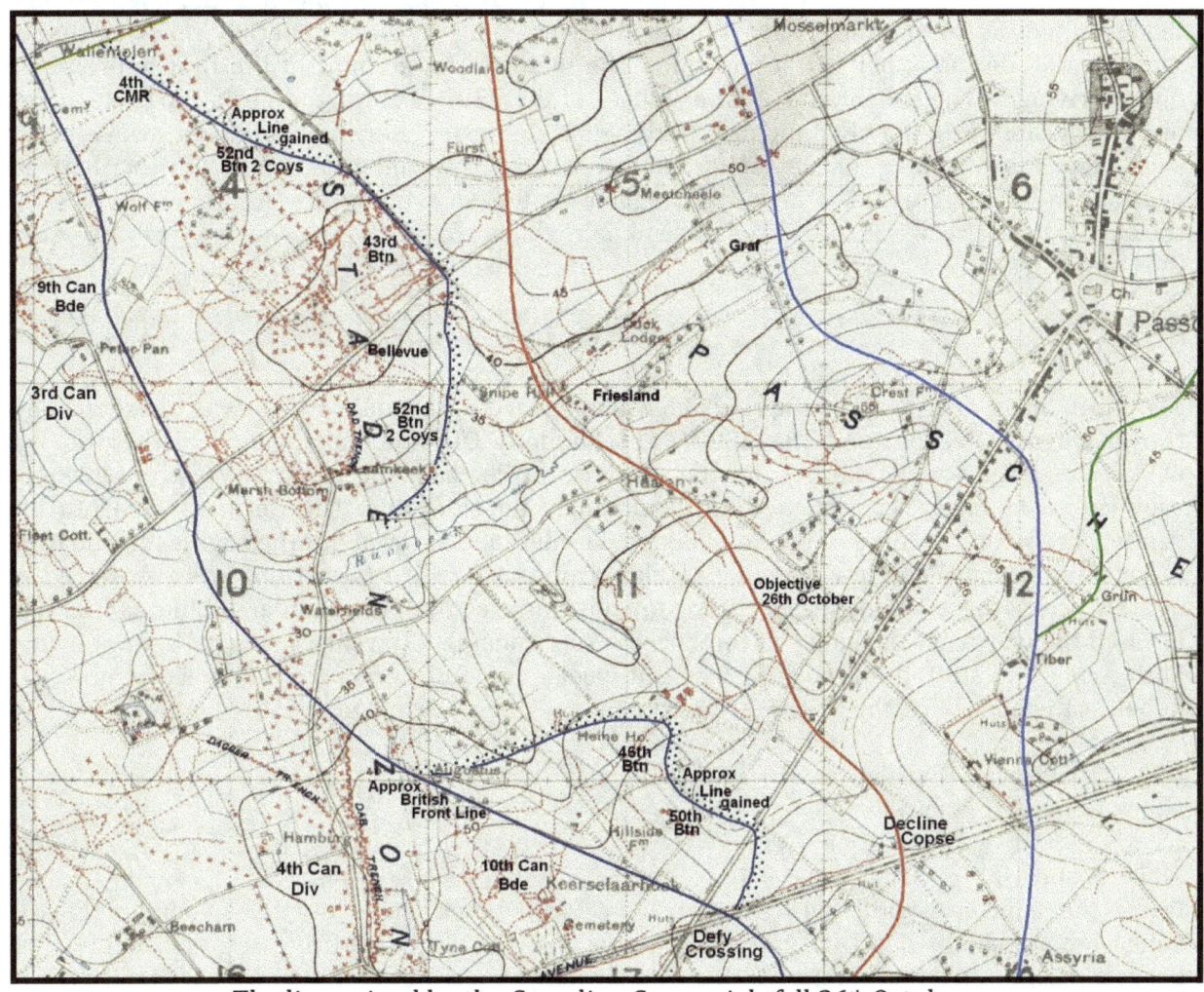

The line gained by the Canadian Corps nightfall 26th October
10th Canadian Brigade - 4th Canadian Division   9th Canadian Brigade - 3rd Canadian Division

The days objectives had not all been achieved, and in places the forward outposts were more than 500 yards short of the Red Line. At times it had looked as though the attack on Passchendaele might fail once more. But it had not failed, due largely to the resilience and fortitude of a few Canadians at Bellevue, and the vital section of the Flanders I Line across the Bellevue – Wallemolen spur had fallen. These actions had made it certain that Passchendaele would be taken, however much the enemy insisted that it was to be defended at all costs. The sandy high ground held by the Canadians on either side of the Ravebeek provided to be excellent for digging and slightly better under foot, and at last the ruins of the village were threatened with attack from the south-west and the west. Over 500 enemy prisoners of the *3rd, 13th,* and *22nd Bavarian R.I.R's* of the *11th Bavarian Division* had been taken.[685]

---

[685] The *11th Bavarian* had transferred to Flanders from the Champagne on the 14th October, and had entered the line on the 21st. The *238th Division*, which had been transferred from Artois on the 7th October, was in support of the *11th*.

The attack of the Fifth Army 5:40 a.m. 26th October

The XVIII and XIV Corps had between them brought four fresh divisions into the line to renew the attack on the 26th October, the artillery of the incoming divisions generally relieving that of the outgoing divisions before the arrival of the infantry. An account of the first impressions upon arriving in The Salient, of a gunner officer of the 250th (1st) Northumbrian Brigade, R.F.A. of 50th Division, paints a vivid picture: "Fifty square miles of slime and filth from which every shell that burst threw up ghastly relics, and raised stenches too abominable to describe; and over all, and dominating all, a never-ceasing ear-shattering artillery fire and the sickly reek of the deadly mustard gas. Such was the inferno into which, after a long journey by train and road, the Colonel led the four Battery Commanders in the early morning of the 23rd October 1917".[686]

XVIII Corps

The XVIII Corps, once again in the role of left flank guard to the main attack, was to use the 63rd (Royal Naval) Division, and the 58th (2/1st London) Division, to advance further up the Lekkerboterbeek valley, and beyond the outskirts of Poelcappelle towards Westroosebeke. It sounded so familiar, yet remained so dispiritingly unachievable. The Germans clung to the gentle, bare western slopes of the Passchendaele ridge, and showed not the slightest inclination to give any ground. The low concrete blockhouses and fortified farm ruins were scattered as densely across these muddy wastes, along the northern sector of the Flanders I Line, as they had been all the way from the banks of the Ypres – Yser canal 8,000 weary yards back, from where Fifth Army had started forward 12 frightful weeks ago. But it remained a fact that however hopeless the objectives, the British Army still had the enemy firmly pinned in Flanders.

63rd (Royal Naval) Division [687]
Major-General C. E. Lawrie

188th [688] and 189th [689] Brigades
From the junction with the Canadians on Wallemolen spur to the quagmire of the Lekkerboterbeek, the 63rd Division was to attack along a 1,500 yard front, across ground which got gradually worse towards the north, being virtually impassable near the course of the stream. The first objective was along a line roughly between Varlet Farm and Banff House around 300 yards forward, while the final objective, about 500 yards beyond the first, lay across another brook, the Paddebeek, around which the ground was also a shell-holed quagmire. The Flanders I defences lay around 700 yards forward on the right flank, and 1,200yards forward on the left. Having relieved the 9th Division on the 24th October, the 63rd Division was to use the 188th Brigade to attack with its Anson Battalion on the right on a 600 yard front, with the 1st Royal Marine Battalion on the left on a front of 900 yards. The Howe Battalion was to support the Anson and the 2nd Royal Marine Battalion to support the 1st Royal Marine.[690] Two battalions of the 189th Brigade were attached, Hood as a counter-attack battalion and Hawke as reserve.[691]

By 2:00 a.m. all attacking battalions were laid out in shell-holes along the tapes, in the drenching rain that had started soon after midnight. The dreary landscape was suddenly illuminated by the flashes of gunfire, as at 4:40 the artillery began the preparatory barrage. At

---

[686] Everard Wyrall, History of the Fiftieth Division, p239
[687] Douglas Jerrold *The Royal Naval Division* London : Hutchinson pp252-257
[688] National Archives, War Diary 188th Brigade WO95/3108
[689] National Archives, War Diary 189th Brigade WO95/3112
[690] National Archives, War Diary Anson Battalion ADM137/3063, National Archives, War Diary Howe Battalion WO95/3111, National Archives, War Diary 1st and 2nd RM Battalion WO95/3110
[691] National Archives, War Diary Hawke Battalion ADM137/3063, National Archives, War Diary Hood Battalion WO95/3064

5:40, behind the barrage, two thin lines of skirmishers of the Anson and 1st R.M. trudged forward around the lips of the water-filled craters, followed by small columns of platoons by sections, each detailed with an objective. Machine gun fire from across the Paddebeek was severe and losses mounted rapidly, most company commanders becoming casualties. Progress across the dreadful ground was painfully slow and it took over an hour and a half for a platoon of the Anson to advance around 500 yards and report the capture of the ruins of Varlet Farm. This report proved subsequently to be wrong, as the party under Lieutenant Stevenson had in fact advanced past the practically invisible Varlet Farm, (which was not occupied by the enemy), and was in possession of other ruins 200 yards farther to the east close up to Source Trench in the Flanders I defences. On the left, groups of 1st R.M. had followed the barrage forward across the morass and by 7:20 had reported the capture of their objective, the blockhouse at Banff House. In the centre the attack was held up by machine guns in dug-outs and organised shell-holes 200 yards east of the Bray Farm – Wallemolen track. At about 8:00 parties of the Howe passed through the Anson beyond Varlet Farm but due to heavy machine gun fire could make no more progress towards the Paddebeek. To the left the 2nd R.M. passed through the 1st and continued the slow advance east of Banff House. In the centre however east of the Wallemolen track no further progress was possible, and as the barrage crept on towards the Paddebeek, parties of 1st and 2nd R.M. remained pinned down in shell-holes 150 yards east of the track by the fierce enemy machine gun fire. At just after 8:00, two companies of the Hood were sent forward to attempt to push the centre on, and as no movement had been achieved by 8:30 a third company was sent up. There seemed a real possibility of the enemy cutting off the battalions which were now close to the Paddebeek on the right flank, and those already across the stream on the left. On the far left "A" Company of the 2nd Royal Marine Battalion had got across the brook, and were on their final objective which they continued to hold throughout most of the day, but from where they could not influence the situation in the centre. The position at 9:00 was unclear as there was no further news from the front and it was understood that there was no contact with the Canadians on the right. An officer's patrol led by Commander Asquith, went forward to clarify the situation. By scrambling for over two hours amongst the foul shell-holes, he finally established touch between the Canadian Mounted Rifles and the Anson and Howe Battalions on the Flanders I position at Wallemolen. Knowledge of the location of the division's outposts was now known sufficiently to allow the artillery to protect the new front line. Lieutenant Stevenson's party of the Anson were also discovered beyond Varlet Farm and promised relief.

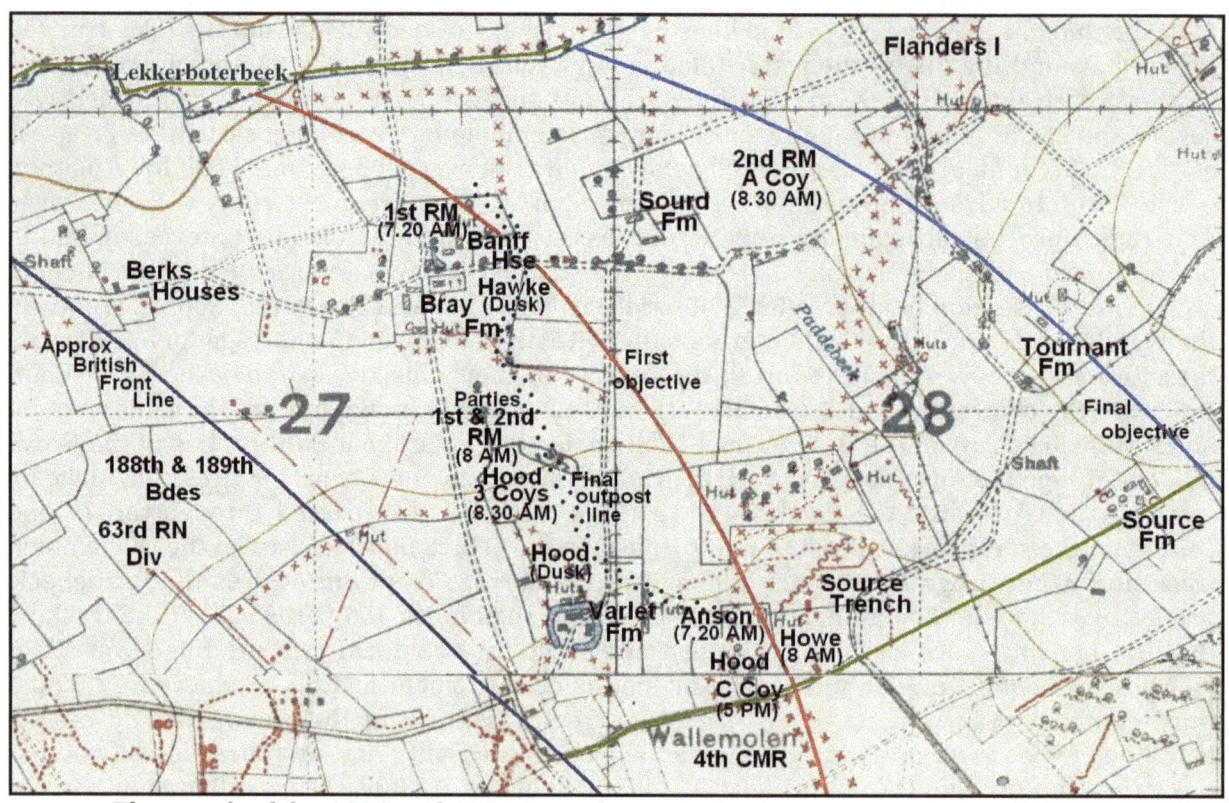

The attack of the 188th and 189th Brigades - 63rd (RN) Division on the Paddebeek

By mid-morning the division was at a standstill driven into a shell-hole line, forward on both flanks but back near the start line in the centre. With many weapons clogged with mud no further advance was considered either practical or possible. Four German officers and 111 other ranks had been captured during the morning's fighting. At around 5:00 p.m. the enemy counter-attacked in force on the right towards the outposts of the Howe, and only swift support from "C" Company of the Hood prevented a withdrawal. At dusk both the exhausted Anson and Howe Battalions were relieved, Hood taking over their outposts, and Hawke Battalion from reserve relieved the 1st and 2nd R.M. On the left "A" Company of the 2nd R.M., out of ammunition, without water, and nearly surrounded, had fallen-back across the Paddebeek and continued to retire past Banff House and Bray Farm, to the old front line near Berks Houses, and the garrisons holding these blockhouses had followed them back. Prompt action by "C" Company of the Hawke under Lieutenant Bartholomew, R.N.V.R. recaptured all the abandoned blockhouses and regained touch with the Hood. Further confusion arose on the right. As a scouting party of the Hood had as promised gone forward to locate Lieutenant Stevenson's party of the Anson beyond Varlet Farm, they reported coming under fire from the position, seeming to indicate that it had fallen. Commander Asquith again went forward personally and discovered Stevenson still holding out, his party reduced to seven men. Asquith returned to his lines and led forward a platoon of the Hawke to finally relieve Stevenson. Asquith was awarded a bar to his D.S.O. for his actions this day. Fourteen officers of the division had been killed and many more wounded. In the four battalions of 188th Brigade, the total casualties amongst N.C.O's and men had been around 800.

58th 2/1st (London) Division
Major-General H. D. Fanshaw

173rd Brigade [692]
The 58th Division had relieved the 18th Division in the line on the 25th October. There must have been a degree of apprehension as to the outcome of the forthcoming attack, as the ground conditions were near impossible, especially on the right near the Lekkerboterbeek where the mud was knee deep. The 173rd Brigade was to attack with the 2/2nd and 2/3rd London Regiment, with the 2/4th in close support,[693] on a 1,500 yard front between the Lekkerboterbeek just south of Tracas Farm, and Helles House 500 yards north-east of Poelcappelle. The 2/1st London was in support and the 2/7th in reserve. It had taken the 2/2nd 9 hours to march up the 8,000 yards from the canal bank to Poelcappelle, but all assembly was complete by 2:00 a.m.

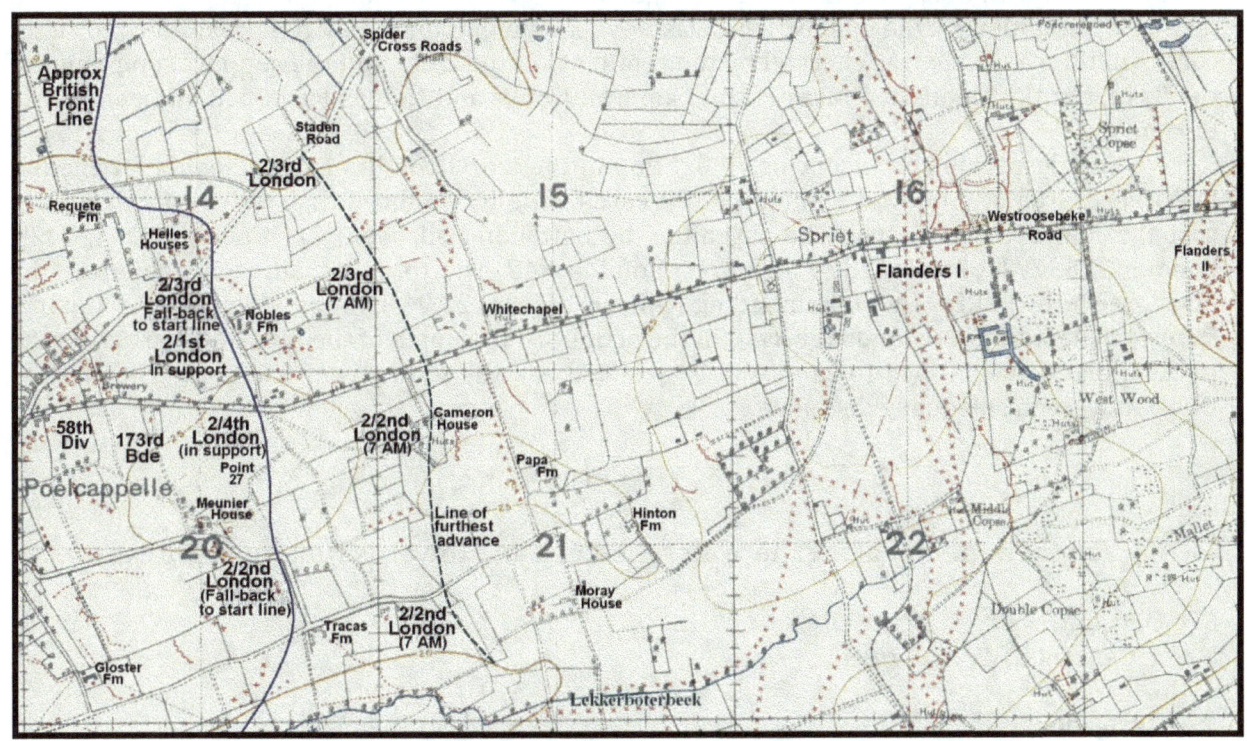

The attack of the 173rd Brigade - 58th Division east of Poelcappelle

Across the appalling ground, worsened by the rain which had again set in around 3:00 a.m., the 2/2nd attacking on a 4 company front, made initially good progress, but the thin barrage even at its slow pace was soon lost. It had landed about 150 yards in front of the forward wave, and from the start the London had never managed to reach it. Fire from the Mebus 250 yards east of Tracas Farm was suppressed with a Lewis gun and rifle grenades until bombing parties worked across the shell-holed quagmire, when at risk of being surrounded, the enemy fled to the rear. A little to the north, after moving forward a few hundred yards another party of the 2/2nd captured 3 of the 4 pillboxes at Cameron House. To their left parties of the 2/3rd just north of the Westroosebeke road tackled the Mebus at Nobles Farm, while another group worked forward along the Staden road, towards Spider Crossroads. In a state of exhaustion and with largely mud choked weapons they were checked by heavy machine gun fire at what was believed to be the objective at Spider Crossroads. They were in fact at the junction 350 yards south-west of the crossroads, but it mattered little. Further movement across the quagmire under the relentless machine gun fire was just not possible and the survivors took what cover was available in

---
[692] National Archives, War Diary 173rd Brigade WO95/3000
[693] National Archives, War Diary 2/2nd, 2/3rd, 2/4th London Regiment WO95/3001

water-filled craters. With the 57th Division held up to the left, that flank was dangerously exposed and at about 7:20 a.m. the enemy counter-attacked towards Spider Crossroads, and also 1,000 yards to the south along the Spriet road towards Poelcappelle. On the right the enemy appeared to emerge from a camouflaged trench near the sunken lane between Papa Farm and Whitechapel, and advance towards Cameron House. The initial counter-attack was by a skirmishing line of sharpshooters, soon followed by an attacking wave which passed through while the riflemen kept the British under fire. By this stage the rifles and Lewis guns of the London battalions were mostly choked with mud, while the enemy who had just emerged from their trench had all the advantages of relatively clean weapons. The small party of the 2/3rd near Spider Crossroads were soon overwhelmed, the survivors falling-back towards Poelcappelle. In front of Cameron Farm, the Germans pressed their attack, the 2/2nd also falling-back towards the start line. With the situation deteriorating at the front the 2/4th had moved up in support of the 2/2nd, and with the added fire of Vickers guns of the 206th Machine Gun Company, prevented further exploitation by the enemy, who was now equally hampered by the dreadful conditions. On the left the advance was checked by the remnants of the 2/3rd and the support companies of the 2/1st, but the Mebus at Tracas Farm, Cameron House and Nobles Farm had all been lost to the enemy.

The desperate and inconclusive fighting in the worst conditions imaginable for the flat featureless area of muddy shell-holes 1,500 yards wide by no more than 800 yards deep, had cost the 58th Division dearly. The casualties by battalion had been: 2/1st London 103, 2/2nd London 326, 2/3rd London, 378 and 2/4th London 348. The total casualties sustained by the division were 1,208. The Commanding Officer of the 2/3rd London, Lieutenant -Colonel Beresford had died of wounds received in the action. To the north of the 58th Division across the pocked, blood soaked bog towards the Watervlietbeek their pals from Lancashire in the 57th Division were in an equally dire state.

XIV Corps

Another attempt along the Watervlietbeek and towards Houthulst Forest

57th Division
Major-General R. W. R. Barnes

170th Brigade [694]
The 57th Division had come into the line on the 23rd October and had relieved the 34th Division, subsequent to the costly attack of the 22nd. The 170th Brigade was to attack along a 1,400 yard front between Requete Farm and the Broenbeek, just north of Gravel Farm, with the 2/5th Loyal North Lancashire Regiment on the right between Requete Farm and Belace Farm, the 2/4th Loyal North Lancs in the centre astride the Watervlietbeek between Belace Farm and Gravel Farm, and the 4/5th Loyal North Lancs on the left between Gravel Farm and the Broenbeek.[695] The 2/5th King's Own Royal Lancaster Regiment was in support and the 2/8th King's Liverpool Regiment, (attached from 171st Brigade for use in an emergency), was held in brigade reserve at Eagle Trench. The 57th Division was faced by the *239th Division* with the *3rd Marine Division* in support. The *239th Division* had arrived in Flanders from Reims on the 12th October.

The ground across which the brigade was to attack was as near impassable to infantry as it could possibly be, and from the outset the prospects appeared hopeless. This did not however lessen the planning and preparation which was to go into the attempt. Considering the great difficulties involved and the probable lack of success, the instructions issued were very precise, showing no preconception of failure. The objective, which was an average of 1,000 yards from

---

[694] National Archives, War Diary 170th Brigade WO95/2977
[695] National Archives, War Diary 2/4th Loyal North Lancs WO95/2978, National Archives, War Diary 2/5th and 4/5th Loyal North Lancs WO95/2979

the start line, and ran from Spider Crossroads in the south to the Broenbeek near Shaap–Balie in the north, displayed optimism, or naivety, in the extreme, the brigade being confronted by the quagmires around the Watervlietbeek and Broenbeek, which spread across most of the front. Each battalion was to attack on a three company front, with one in reserve. The three stated aims of the attack were, first to reach the objective, second to mop-up all the pillboxes in the area, and third 'to hold on to the last man the ground won'. Three distinct lines of defence were to be established on achieving the objective, the first line in shell-hole posts on the objective, the second 50 to 100 yards in rear of the first at intervals between the front line posts, and the third manned by the counter-attack companies 300 to 400 yards behind the front line. The dreadful state of the ground about the Watervlietbeek and the Broenbeek was recognised, and the 2/4th Loyal North Lancs was instructed to attack with two companies either side of the swamps. The 2/5th King's Own was to carefully watch the left flank along the Broenbeek, where the 50th Division was to attempt to advance north of the stream and deal with pillboxes on that bank. The reality was very different to the hopes apparent in the planning.

In the darkness, in pouring rain and driving wind, the slow and difficult forming-up on the taped lines, set about 150 yards behind the barrage line, was completed by the forward companies 2 hours before Zero. The 2/5th King's Own in support formed up 500 yards to the rear between Compromise Farm and Water House. As the attack began great efforts were made to catch up to the barrage, but the right company of the 2/5th Loyal North Lancs, the right battalion of the brigade, immediately came under heavy machine gun and rifle fire from the Mebus at Helles House and Nobles Farm in 173rd Brigade sector. It also became clear that the enemy were holding their front line with a strong force situated in prepared shell-holes right in front of them between the British Front Line and the barrage line. Machine gun fire smashed into the front ranks knocking out all the company officers and most of the N.C.O's. Showing great courage the men rushed the shell-holes bayoneting 40 Germans and continued to advance across the quagmire. After slogging forward for around 600 yards up to their knees in mud, the remnants could go no further, stopped by exhaustion, the ground, and the severe machine gun fire which had decimated their number. They were now reduced to 40 men out of 112. Two sergeants who had survived gathered together what men they could, amounting to about 5 each, and with great difficulty fell-back to the original line.[696] The Germans had obviously strongly reinforced their front line, for as the centre and left companies attempted to gain the protection of the barrage, they too were struck by machine gun fire from organised shell-hole position in No-Mans-Land. Again all the officers and most N.C.O's became casualties, but as the survivors pressed their attack the enemy paid dearly for their actions, for around 100 were bayoneted before they were able to retire. The centre company pushed on another 500 yards, under constant fire from both flanks, before being checked by another organised line of defence. The reserve company had moved up at Zero Hour, and soon getting into the firing line had already lost all its officers. The remnants now endeavoured to support the survivors of the left company, but within 500 yards were forced to take cover by machine gun fire from a bunker directly ahead of them. With rifles and Lewis guns inoperative and rapid movement impossible in the mud, no attack could be made against the bunker. The exhausted and shattered remains of three companies laid out in the poor protection of shell-holes, in the rain and under continuous sniper fire. Throughout the dreadful day at the slightest sign of movement bullets zipped overhead or smacked and spattered into the mud about them, until a little after dusk just 10 men crawled back to the British lines. The 2/5th Loyal North Lancs had ceased to exist as a fighting force.

The brigade centre battalion, the 2/4th Loyal North Lancs, initially had better luck. Attacking astride the Watervlietbeek, the forward waves succeeded with great effort in closing with the barrage and reached the first objective. Only on the left company front, north of the Watervlietbeek was stiff resistance met, once more from prepared shell-hole positions which were soon overrun, all the defenders being killed. The blockhouse at Memling Farm was quickly seized. The garrison of 17 surrendered with little fight, and the King's Own established a

---

[696] In the right company sector between Requete Farm and Besace Farm, 10 enemy machine gun positions were identified which had not been shown on the maps.

support position north-west of the farm. The fortified remains and pillboxes of Rubens Farm were also easily mopped-up. While the barrage was halted beyond the first objective the enemy attempted a counter-attack across the Spider Crossroads – Devoust Farm road, which was successfully driven-off with rifle and Lewis gun fire. Two officers and about 30 men of the left company worked forward to some huts just south of Van Dyck Farm, but came under severe machine gun fire from pillboxes at the farm and were driven to take cover in shell-holes. Here they remained until dark, when only two wounded men returned to the British lines. As the barrage lifted towards the final objective the first two waves of the centre and right companies, now very weak in numbers, moved off and were seen to reach a bunker 500 yards east of Rubens Farm. None of them were seen again. Enemy bunkers 350 yards beyond the Memling Farm – Rubens Farm line continued to hold out, as the leading waves were not of sufficient strength to mop them up, and fire from these bunkers now held up the support waves around Rubens Farm and a hedge east of Memling Farm. This became the line finally consolidated by the 2/4th Loyal North Lancs, 25 men holding Memling Farm and 30 men holding Rubens Farm, supported by 2 platoons of the 2/5th King's Own.

On the brigade left the 4/5th Loyal North Lancs also started well gaining the protection of the 5:40 barrage and following it forward until about 6:00 a.m. At this point their luck ran out as they were swept by machine gun fire in enfilade from the huts 400 yards east of Turenne Crossing and from emplacements to the left front along the Broenbeek. Struggling forward under fire for another 20 minutes, the forward waves were finally checked 100 yards short of Van Dyck Farm, by machine gun fire from bunkers amongst the farm ruins, from across the Broenbeek in the direction of Schaap-Balie, and from Davoust Farm 400 yards forward. The problem which had bedevilled British infantry since the 31st July was now again evident. Although the ground had been utterly devastated by shell-fire, the reinforced concrete structures in which sheltered the enemy machine guns remained unscathed. The right company of the 4/5th, with support from a platoon of the King's Own which had waded the flooding Watervlietbeek to assist in the attack on the farm, made desperate attempts to work forward amongst the craters, their movements slowed to a literal crawl through the mud. Van Dyck Farm consisted of a number of bunkers each giving the other covering fire, the whole area also covered by the guns in the huts and further concrete structures north of the Broenbeek. Under intense close range fire and sustaining severe casualties, a party of the right company succeeded in approaching one of the Van Dyck Farm bunkers and knocking it out killing about 30 of the enemy. Fire from the other bunkers at between 50 and 100 yards prevented any further frontal attacks. At around 6:20 a.m. an attempt at envelopment of the farm from the north resulted in the attack party being wiped out by the fire from across the stream. The platoon of the King's Own which had waded the Watervlietbeek had also lost heavily from the fire across the Broenbeek, and the survivors had fallen-back and established a defence line south-east of Gravel Farm. At 7:20 about 100 of the enemy attempted a counter-attack from the direction of Davoust Farm, but were driven off with the few Lewis guns and rifles still operative, with casualties of about 40. The weak position at Van Dyck Farm, in close contact with the enemy was held by the remnants of the 4/5th until dusk. Then at 9:00 p.m. with no touch gained with troops of 50th Division to the left, and with weapons useless, in a state of total exhaustion, soaked through and caked from head to foot in the clinging all pervading mud, what remained of the 4/5th withdrew painfully to the original front line.

The 2/5th King's Own meanwhile, with the troops it had available and any stragglers that could be gathered, established a defence line between Belace and Requete Farm, supporting the shattered 2/5th Loyal North Lancs. Except for the two forward posts at Memling and Rubens Farm the 170th Brigade line was back where it had started from.

The 170 Brigade had entered the action with a total of 2,504 men in the line. It had sustained casualties of 1,229. The total casualties by battalion were: The 2/4th Loyal North Lancs 11 officers and 348 other ranks, the 2/5th Loyal North Lancs 15 officers and 283 other ranks, the 4/5th Loyal North Lancs 7 officers and 272 other ranks, and the 4/5th King's Own 6 officers and 235 other ranks. Out of the total personnel that attacked with the companies, 62%

of the officers and 59% of the men were casualties. To the left of 57th Division the dreadful story was the same.

50th (Northumbrian) Division [697]
Major-General P. S. Wilkinson

149th Brigade [698]
The 50th Division were to continue where the 34th Division had left off threatening the southern edge of Houthulst Forest in inconclusive fighting of the 22nd October. The 34th Division had been relieved on the night of the 24th/25th October. Three battalions of the Northumberland Fusiliers of 149th Brigade had taken over the outpost line, after a trying march up over the desolate cratered ground, which was new and unknown to them. The 35th Division still held the line to the left as it had on the 22nd October, and although its divisional artillery was to support the attack of the 50th Division and the French, its infantry were not to be directly involved on the 26th October. The part of the line between Aden House and Colombo House which had been held by 104th Brigade of 35th Division on the 22nd was also taken over by the left and centre battalions of the 149th Brigade.

The 50th Division plan called for an attack by three battalions in the line, the 1/4th Northumberland Fusiliers on the right, the 1/5th in the centre and the 1/7th on the left,[699] with the 1/6th held in brigade reserve. The 1/4th Green Howards of 150th Brigade was at the disposal of 149th in case of emergency. Each battalion was to attack on a three company frontage, with the fourth company in reserve, and each company was to attack with one platoon in the line, the others to leap frog through. This tactic of passing one platoon through another, so commonplace in the Flanders fighting, was new to the incoming division and although they had trained for it, they were about to use it in action for the first time. Each battalion was to be supported when consolidating by two Vickers guns of 149th Machine Gun Company, and two Stokes mortars of the 149th Trench Mortar Battery, always assuming these heavy weapons could be brought forward across the quagmire.

The line from which the 1/4th was to attack was approximately that of the start line on the 22nd October, from a point 500 yards south-east of Turenne Crossing on the right, across the Staden railway just west of the crossing. The 1/5th in the centre and 1/7th on the left, were to attack along the line of around 1,000 yards which had been gained on the 22nd, from slightly east of Aden House, and then north-west towards a point 400 yards east of Colombo House. The objective was limited to an advance of around 700 yards towards the north-east, to include the area of hutments 700 yards along the Schaap-Balie road from Turenne Crossing, Colbert Crossroads, and Hill 23. The divisional boundary was the Broenbeek on the right, and a line east of Colombo House on the left. Before the final assembly it was found by the Commanding Officer of the 1/4th that it was not possible, due mainly to the dreadful state of the ground south of Turenne Crossing, to form up on any more than a one company front and this arrangement was agreed to. His reasoning is well worthy of note. 'From reports received from the 11th Suffolk,' (104th Brigade, 34th Division), 'the right of my Battalion front is a swamp. Even if it is possible to assemble the right company, I do not consider they would be able to advance, but would have to be dug out. I propose with your permission to attack with two companies,' [subsequently changed to one company], 'only in the front line, one in support, and to keep the fourth company in reserve in the Tranquille House area. Conditions on rest of front are such that if a man steps of a firm piece of ground into the slightest hollow he has to be dug out. There are very few firm pieces of ground away from the railway and roads.' [700]

---

[697] Everard Wyrall *The History of the Fiftieth Division 1914-1919* London : Percy Lund, Humphries pp238-249
[698] National Archives, War Diary 149th Brigade WO95/2827
[699] National Archives, War Diary 1/4th, 1/5th and 1/7th Northumberland Fusiliers WO95/2828
[700] Everard Wyrall, *History of the Fiftieth Division*, p243

Between 7:00 and 9:00 p.m. on the 25th the attacking companies began the arduous task of marching up to their jump-off lines, which lay in shell-holes facing the dark forest, 800 to 1,000 yards to the north. The 1/5th had been first up, being assembled by 11:00 p.m., and by 5:00 a.m. all battalions were reported to be in position. Hot food had been brought up by pack animals in containers tightly packed with hay in an effort to keep it warm, but other comforts were few. The rain which had come on heavily at 3:00 a.m. gradually filled the craters in which the infantry huddled. Out in front across the bleak, inhospitable No-Mans-Land, the water filled shell-holes could be seen forming pools which gradually spread into small lakes, the reflection of a gun-flash or flare shimmering off the sheets of water defining the swamp over which they must soon attack. The vision became even more vivid, when at 4:40 it was illuminated more clearly by the countless flashes of the preparatory barrage.

A few minutes after 5:40 a.m., the protective barrage lifted. The Northumberland Fusiliers numbed by the wet and cold, raised themselves from their watery holes and trudged heavily forward, avoiding the worst of the pools where possible, but still knee deep in mud. By the time the German barrage came down on the brigade line, most of the 1/4th on the right was forward of the start line. Much of the hostile shell-fire landed at around Zero plus 3 minutes well behind the 1/5th, along the Poelcappelle road between Tranquille house and Egypt House, but "A" Company just behind Colibri Farm on the 1/5th right was heavily shelled before getting clear. On the left the 1/7th was only just away when at Zero plus 1 minute the enemy shelled the line between Aden house, Angle Point, and towards the 5 Chemin road junction.

The British barrage although only moving at a rate of 100 yards in 8 minutes proved impossible to follow, many men becoming fixed firmly in the mud. It appeared that the barrage consisted of mostly shrapnel, which had no effect in subduing the hostile machine gun and rifle fire from the concrete pillboxes. A hail of fire, from the bunkers amongst the row of huts 350 yards east of Turenne Crossing, now lashed into the forward platoon of the floundering 1/4th, the survivors of which finally splashed to ground 80 yards short of the huts, taking what miserable cover they could in shell-holes. In the centre the 1/5th had more luck as by 7:10 their left "B" Company had worked painfully forward and reached Hill 23. But here their luck ran out. Between the trees, along the track which ran along the Vijfwegen spur, was an uncut entanglement of wire beyond which was the heavily manned enemy position near Six Roads Cross which had checked the advance on the 22nd. As the first two waves reached the wire at about 7:40 and attempted to cut their way through, they were struck in enfilade by machine gun fire from a bunker beside the railway 300 yards to the south-east, which practically wiped them out. By 9:00 a.m. "C" Company of the 1/5th which had advanced to the left of the 1/4th was also pinned down by machine gun fire from the huts east of Turenne Crossing. The survivors of 1/5th "A" Company, which had been heavily shelled at the start made little progress north of the Vijfwegen road, and by 11:30 a platoon of the 1/6th from brigade reserve had come up in support and both had established a line in shell-holes between Turenne Crossing and Aden House.

On the left, the hostile barrage which had come down at the start mostly behind the 1/7th gradually shortened its range to catch the advancing waves, as the enemy were seen to retire. "A" Company on the right and "D" Company on the left made remarkably good progress, "D" getting forward up to 1,000 yards and securing and holding its objective, all the while under intense and accurate sniper fire from the forest. But in the centre "B" Company was checked within 150 yards of the start by machine gun and rifle fire from pillboxes to their front. After severe fighting in the most appalling conditions, these shelters were eventually cleared, but at great cost. By now "A" Company were also pinned down by fire from their right front, and two platoons of "C" Company in reserve were sent up, one to support "B" Company and one to support "A". With the assistance of the support platoon, "A" Company pressed on to a position 300 yards west of Hill 23 where they were once more checked by machine gun fire from a wired German trench, probably the same system which was holding up "B" Company of the 1/5th to their right. A third platoon of "C" Company was sent forward to the beleaguered "A", only to loose its commander and many men before getting up.

Officer casualties along the entire brigade front had become extreme, as the attack, now virtually leaderless stalled in the mire, under fire of the enemy strong-points from front and flanks. In "A" Company of the 1/7th, all three Platoon Commanders and the Company Commander had been killed as had most of the N.C.O's. With the enemy reinforcing in front of them, the remainder, with the survivors of "C" Company were compelled to fall-back to the line of "B" Company, which in turn had also sustained grave casualties, two platoon officers and many other ranks having been killed. In a hopelessly tired, weary, and filthy condition, the survivors of the right and centre companies, under ceaseless machine gun and sniper fire continued to fall-back until a defensive line could be established about 150 yards forward of the tape line, this position being consolidated as well as possible in shell-holes by the utterly exhausted men. On the far left of the 1/7th, "D" Company was now dangerously exposed with its right flank unprotected due to the retirement of "B" and "A" Companies. A right defensive flank was hastily thrown back to cover the lost ground, which the enemy was now quickly re-occupying.

It had been a tragedy for the 50th Division. On the right the 1/4th Northumberland Fusiliers, having fallen-back from the huts was consolidating upon its start line, having lost nearly half its number. In the 1/5th, "C" Company on the right had fallen-back with the 1/4th and by 2:15 was on its start line, in touch with "A" Company, which had hardly got forward. By 4:15 what was left of "B" Company which had succeeded in reaching Hill 23 was back at Aden House, near where it had started. Only on the extreme left did "D" Company of the 1/7th precariously hold on to its slender gains.

The French attack to the left of 50th Division had advanced slightly, across ground in the same condition. After a three day bombardment the 1st and 133rd Divisions of the First Army had established bridgeheads across the inundated St. Jansbeek, strengthened their position east of the inundations, and had advanced the line towards Zevekoten.[701]

The 1/4th Northumberland Fusiliers had gone into action with 20 officers and 578 other ranks. At roll call it had lost 10 officers and 256 other ranks, killed, wounded, or missing. The 1/5th Northumberland Fusiliers had lost 12 officers and 439 other ranks. The 1/7th Northumberland Fusiliers had lost 11 officers and 246 other ranks. Total casualties in 149th Brigade over the 26th/27th October 1917 were 38 officers and 1,080 other ranks. The commanding officer of one of the attacking battalions upon learning of his casualties is reported to have said 'This has fairly done me,' as tears trickled down his weather beaten face. Five days later on the 31st October, 50th Division was destined to attack the Turenne Crossing – Colombo House line again.

In his diary entry for the 26th October Haig recognised the importance of the Canadian achievement at Bellevue, remarking that, 'the positions won by the Canadians and 63rd Division today are of the greatest importance'.[702] He made no mention of the total failure of the five other divisions which had attacked over the worst ground conditions imaginable. Neither however did he make any mention of the fact that although the flank attacks had resulted in failures, they were continuing to limit Ludendorff's capacity to develop his own strategy, by continuing to dictate the movement of his reinforcements to Flanders, while his interests may well have been better served sending them elsewhere. Was it Haig's iron will, absolute clarity of purpose, and total determination that prompted him to continue? Or had he totally lost sight of what he was trying to achieve, and lost touch with the reality of what was, and what was not achievable with the forces at his disposal, and in the conditions in which they were having to fight? The cost of continuation was surely becoming dangerously high, the scales tipping precariously towards the unjustifiable. At this moment lofty sermons relating their sacrifice to the salvation of the French Army, would have struck few chords with the Tommies stuck in the mud on Polderhoek spur, in

---

[701] On the 27th the French continued their advance, with the Belgians supporting their left by crossing the Yser opposite Knockehoek, capturing Merckem, Kippe and Aschhoop, and working northwards, to the east of the inundations as far as the southern tip of Blankaart Lake. On the 28th the French and Belgians completed the capture of the whole Merckem peninsula.
[702] Douglas Haig. Diaries and Letters. p337

the Lekkerboterbeek valley, or along the face of Houthulst Forest. But they had no say in the matter, and although they might grumble and grouse bitterly about the apparent futility, they continued to obey orders. There is no doubt that both Haig and Gough were fully aware of the terrible conditions in which their soldiers were fighting. It can be argued that possession of that knowledge makes Haig's decision to continue appear even worse. He sent the following message to Fifth Army on the 27th October: 'Please ensure all troops engaged that I thoroughly appreciate their fine effort yesterday (26.10.17) under the terrible conditions of ground and weather. The ground gained by the 63rd Division is of great importance and the determined fighting of the other divisions contributes in no small degree to the important success achieved on the main ridge.' [703] In a similar vein Gough wrote to his Corps Commanders: 'Please convey to all ranks engaged in today's (26.10.17) operations my very great appreciation of their gallant efforts. They have all my sincere sympathy as no troops could have had to face worse weather conditions of mud than they had to face owing to the sudden downfall of rain this morning. No troops could have done more than our men did today; and given a fair chance I have every confidence in their complete success every time.' [704] But Gough now had serious doubts about going on given the present condition of the ground, considering it, in the words of the Earl of Cavan, more advisable to await the hardening of the winter frosts before proceeding further. At the Fifth Army Conference on the evening of the 26th the Cavan also pointed out that: 'the enemy's position on his front was very much stronger than had been anticipated; Schaap Bailie was practically a concrete village. Very careful and particular artillery preparation would be required before the next attack was launched'. Brigadier-General Hollond the B.G.G.S. of XVIII Corps added that Maxse concurred with Cavan. Gough communicated his thoughts and those of his Corps Commanders to Kiggell. But with his Fifth Army Commander wavering Haig would not be moved. Kiggell suggested a conference with Plumer to discuss the matter. Haig rejected this, preferring that Plumer and Gough consult with their corps and divisions and report their findings in two days time, adding in his diary: 'In my opinion today's operations at the decisive point (Passchendaele) had been so successful that I was entirely opposed to any idea of abandoning the operations till frost set in. If wet continues, a day or two's delay may be advisable before we launch the next attack.' [705]

It was at the time, and it still remains, unwise to generalise about the state of the battlefield. As we have seen, many areas were considered impassable, but on the higher sandy ground of the Passchendaele ridge and Bellevue spur the going was much better. On the 24th October the 4th Canadian Division had reported that they were under fire from enemy positions on the western slope of the Passchendaele ridge, between the ridge-top road and the Ravebeek, about 750 yards north of Defy Crossing. In the report they describe the ground thus: 'The ground from our forward posts to the enemy positions is a gentle slope, on the whole quite dry and hard, sloping gently off to the left [towards the Ravebeek] where it becomes wetter.' It was also reported: 'The Hamburg – Laamkeek road is passable and the crossing of the Ravebeek stream is fairly good. The ridge from Heine House to D.11.a.2.0. [250 yards north of Augustus Wood and 200 yards from the Ravebeek] is sandy and free from water.' [706] It was quite understandable for Gough to be concerned about his sector of the battlefield, but Haig's view of the ability of the Canadians to carry on towards Passchendaele, judging by their own reports, appears also to have been correct.

---

[703] National Archives, War diary 170th Infantry Brigade. Special order by Brigadier General Goggisberg C.M.G. 30th October 1917 WO/95/2977
[704] National Archives, War diary 170th Infantry Brigade. Special order by Brigadier General Goggisberg C.M.G. 30th October 1917 WO/95/2977
[705] Douglas Haig. Diaries and Letters. p337
[706] Library and Archives of Canada, War diary 4th Canadian Division RG9 Srs III-D-3 Vol 4860.

The re-capture of Decline Copse 27th/28th October

By 7:45 a.m. on the morning of the 27th October, upon receipt of a report from 10th Canadian Brigade, it was finally established by 4th Canadian Division that they were not in possession of Decline Copse. As far as could be ascertained the front line ran from a point on the railway 125 yards forward of Defy Crossing, to a point 400 yards along the Passchendaele road from the crossing, thence north-west for 500 yards down the western slope of the ridge, to where the left flank was drawn back facing the Ravebeek as far as Augustus Wood. At 8:15 a.m. an order was issued to 10th Brigade for the re-capture of the copse at the earliest possible moment. Arrangements were made, including for the support of an artillery and machine gun barrage, to both assault the copse and capture the remaining portion of the Red Line still in enemy hands, Zero Hour at 10:00 p.m. that evening. Throughout the day the enemy had been shelling the newly won ground with guns of all calibres, causing disruption and casualties, but at 10:00 p.m. under the protection of their own barrage the 44th Battalion attacked along the railway towards the copse, while the 47th Battalion advanced along the line of the road and the western slope of the ridge. The 44th soon came under considerable machine gun fire from Assyria, Vienna Cottages and Tiber, and as the 47th moved along the western slope of the main ridge they were also hit by fire from Crest Farm and Haalen Wood in the Ravebeek valley. The attack was pressed home through the darkness and by 3:45 a.m. the 10th Brigade reported that in spite of heavy shelling the new line was being consolidated, forward of Decline Copse, and touch had been gained with the 1st Australian Division 100 yards south of the railway near the copse. From then until daylight the artillery of both sides remained active, and at times the enemy shelling of the new front becoming intense. By 9:00 a.m. the line was reported as being firmly consolidated, but the hostile shelling remained heavy until around 2:00 p.m. when there was a one hour lull. At 3:00 p.m. however the Germans again opened severe shell fire on the Canadian front line and forward positions, and intense neutralising fire with both high explosive and mustard gas upon the British batteries, greatly hampering their ability to retaliate. During this period the 44th Battalion pushed patrols forward to secure some pillboxes 300 yards north of Assyria, and there captured two prisoners of the *463rd Regiment*, indicating that the *238th Division* were supporting the *11th Bavarian* in the front line.

The effects of the counter-battery gas bombardments are well illustrated by an account by Colonel Shiel of the British 50th Division artillery: 'The enemy's artillery was very active, especially at night when he deluged us with mustard gas. So intense was this gas that everything one touched was infected with it. Nobody had a voice left after the first few days. We did not at first realise the full danger of this, and just laughed because no one had a voice; but when people began to blister and swell, and two men of my old Battery died horribly from eating bread which had been splashed with the stuff, we got wind up thoroughly. The whole area was tainted: one could touch nothing with safety; even our own doctor who came to see us, slipped in the mud and was so badly blistered by it that we never saw him again. The gas casualties were bad enough but oh! the shell casualties were pathetic. I lost many of my great friends in the Battery, horribly mutilated in the mud, and towards the end was near a raving lunatic as possible. Our guns were in the open; the only protection for the gunners the piles of high explosive; and the mud was over everything tainted with mustard gas.' [707]

British divisions for Italy and the aftershocks of the Italian disaster

Events far from Flanders and beyond Haig's control, now conspired, with the direct intervention of the War Cabinet, to deprive him of essential forces, which, even had they not been used again in the Passchendaele fighting were still desperately needed on the Western Front.

---

[707] Everard Wyrall, *History of the Fiftieth Division* p248

In the wake of the Italian disaster on the 24th October at Caporetto, an order sent directly from Lloyd George arrived at Haig's G.H.Q. on the 26th, requiring as a preliminary measure the immediate dispatch of two divisions to Italy. Although the huge Flanders battle was drawing to a closure, another was planned to commence in a few weeks at Cambrai and divisions that could not be spared from the theatre of greatest importance were within two days on their way to Italy, to fight at the end of lines of communication and supply which, compared with the Western Front, would be a logistical nightmare. On the 28th October the advance parties of 23rd and 41st Divisions of X Corps were on there way, with the able Lieutenant -General Lord Cavan and XIV Corps Staff soon sent to command them, the northern sector of the British front being handed to Lieutenant-General Watts' XIX Corps by the 30th. By the 8th November 7th and 48th Divisions were also ordered to Italy under Lieutenant -General Haking's XI Corps, as was the 5th Division on the 14th November. Corps artillery was sent in support of the divisions, and by the 29th November VII Brigade of the Royal Flying Corps was for the first time in action over the Montello front with Camels of 28 Squadron escorting RE8's of 34 Squadron upon a mission of photographic reconnaissance, by which time the Italian front had already stabilised on the Piave, with the Italians already on their way to recovery. However, the Camels of 45 and 66 Squadron and the RE8's of 42 Squadron were soon to follow. Haig, with the possibility of placing his hands around the enemy's throat was being ordered to send forces to a theatre where at best they might tread on the enemy's toe.

Premiere Painlevé in an obvious state of alarm wrote to Lloyd George on the 27th demanding that the British send divisions to Italy, and pronouncing that the French Government attached the greatest importance for the common cause of the Allies in reinforcing the Italians. Lloyd George replied that he had already taken action and that two divisions were on their way. Robertson he told Painlevé, was also on his way to Italy to establish the true situation, and further action would not be taken until he had reported. The French position was virtually the same as it had been in September. Painlevé, in obvious and considerable agitation over a possible Italian collapse which may allow the enemy to descend upon him, was demanding that the British send divisions to Italy whilst they were still engaging the main body of the enemy in Flanders, in an operation which was already preventing them attacking the French.[708]

Robertson found it difficult to obtain any information about the situation at the Italian front, assuming this was due to Cadorna moving his headquarters, but began making railway arrangements to get the two British divisions, each with a 60-pounder battery to Italy. He also wrote to Haig on the 28th telling him of the situation as best he knew it, but warned: 'What effort will be demanded from us to restore the situation it is quite impossible to say as the Italian troops are so unreliable,'[709] and adding that four more of Haig's divisions and a quantity of heavy artillery would probably be required.

At the meeting of the War Cabinet on the 29th October, Lloyd George, using the Italian disaster as incontrovertible evidence to prove his argument, set out to show that he had been right all along, and that if the heavy artillery which he had always entreated should be sent to Italy had in fact been sent, the Allies would not be in the serious peril in which they now found themselves. He requested that the paper he had issued at the Rome Conference in January 1917 outlining his proposals at that time should be added as an appendix to the minutes of the meeting. The paper had advocated sending heavy guns with British and French gunners to Italy, to resist any German attack on the Italian front, and had proclaimed encouragingly, 'by adopting this plan we might well convert a repulse into a rout just as the Germans, by massing artillery on the Rumanian front, converted the Rumanian invasion of Transylvania into an utter defeat'.[710] For the moment the Prime Minister held the high ground. But his elevated position was only maintained through the ill-considered acceptance by his colleagues of his illogical and baseless assumptions. Nobody felt compelled to question whether it was reasonable to compare the efficiency of the German storm-troops, now so purposefully and efficiently demolishing the

---

[708] Parliamentary Archives, Lloyd George Papers. LG/F/50/1/19 and 20
[709] Parliamentary Archives, Lloyd George Papers, Robertson to Haig LG/F/44/3/30
[710] National Archives, minutes of War Cabinet No.259 CAB23/3

Italians, with that of the Rumanian infantry that had attacked Transylvania. Nobody questioned if the extra Allied artillery he had continuously urged sending to Italy would have been an ounce of benefit in stemming the enemy thrust, when 25 divisions of the Italian Second Army had been routed, the Third Army much knocked about, and the Fourth Army pressed into a desperate retreat through most difficult mountainous country, when confronted with an attack by a spearhead of 7 crack German divisions backed by 9 mediocre Austrian divisions. Nobody asked how likely it was that the Allied guns would have chanced to be in the right place at the right time, or how easily they and their ammunition could have been moved to counter the swift tactical strikes of the German storm-troop groups amongst the peaks and gorges. The 120 miles of threatened Italian front ran through the Dolomites, the Ampezzo Alps, the Carnic Alps, the Venetian Alps, the precipitous upper valley of the Tagliamento, the Julian Alps, the Bainsizza plateau and the Carso plateau, but nobody felt it appropriate to enquire where the guns, along all this great front, would have been best deployed to make any material difference to the outcome. And nobody questioned the removal, at the instruction of the Cabinet, of the 100 guns which, taken from the Western Front, had already been on their way to or with the Italians, prior to the cessation of Cadorna's offensive, and were now on their way to Allenby. That it was unlikely the disaster could have been prevented even by an additional 500 heavy guns, was a thought which may have lurked silently at the back of many minds, but as nobody felt in a position to say so and oppose the Prime Minister's thesis, it remained Lloyd George's hour, and, 'the members of the War Cabinet expressed their appreciation and approval of the prompt decisions taken by the Prime Minister on their behalf during the past 48 hours'.[711] After a brief meting with Lloyd George in the afternoon Hankey noted: 'He told me he would not go on unless he obtained control of the War. He meant to take advantage of the present position to obtain this.'[712] At the Cabinet meeting at 11:30 a.m. on the 30th October the principle of the Supreme War Council was accepted, and Lloyd George was well on his way to achieving his goal. It was not considered important in London, but seven hours earlier, in Flanders, the British artillery had roared out again, and the Canadians had begun working ever closer to the beleaguered, devastated ruins on top of the muddy, low ridge.

---

[711] National Archives, minutes of War Cabinet No.259 CAB23/3
[712] Hankey Diaries

The Second Battle of Passchendaele
26th October to 10th November

Part Two
The Seventh Step

The attack of Second Army 5:50 a.m. the 30th October

	30th Oct	31st Oct	1st Nov	2nd Nov	3rd Nov	4th Nov	5th Nov
Rainfall	2.3mm	Trace	0.2mm	0.7mm	Nil	Nil	Nil
Temp	44F	54F	51F	56F	52F	47F	49F

Weather conditions, rainfall Ypres, temperature Vlamertinghe [713]

Since the 26th October the weather had improved, there being only just over 1 mm of rain during the three day period 27th to the 29th October. The requirements for ammunition, trench stores and supplies of all kinds for the divisions about to continue the attack on the 30th were still huge, and the endless efforts of the engineers, pioneers, and tunnelling companies proceeded at a pace to improve and extend the tracks towards the forward lines. Work on communications and the movement of stores and rations, was made difficult during the day, due to constant enemy shelling, and sniping nearer the lines. At night hostile aircraft continued to bomb camps and dumps west of Ypres, from where the vital ammunition and equipment began its treacherous and arduous journey towards the front. Ammunition for the bigger guns could only be moved forward by light gauge railway, or by horse drawn limbers or motor lorries across the corduroy tracks, shells for some of the medium guns having to be brought to the battery positions as far up as the Zonnebeke – Langemarck road, whilst ponies struggled on to the field batteries with six 18-pounder shells at a time in panniers. Two double-plank roads now led towards the front, the southern (South Road) extending the Frezenberg road as far as the crossing of the Roulers railway south-west of Zonnebeke, and the northern (Panet Road) finish 200 yards east of the Zonnebeke – Langemarck road at Kansas Cross. In each Canadian brigade sector a track, hastily constructed from planks, supported by fascines across the hollows, led from the forward dumps up towards the fighting lines, and 250 pack ponies per brigade were provided to ensure the arrival of adequate supplies.

On the 27th October the improvement in the weather enabled an increase in air activity on both sides, the RE8's of the Corps Squadrons spotting for the guns which concentrated on counter-battery fire, targeting 116 enemy batteries. Enemy aircraft bombed the British rear areas from the early hours and throughout the morning of the 28th, and their artillery disrupted the Canadian support areas with intermittent gas shelling. The day, although fine, was misty over the lines but this did not prevent the enemy taking revenge for the previous days bombardments, shelling heavily all approaches and tracks around Bellevue and Wallemolen with 4.2's and 5.9's from the direction of Moorslede, and once more drenching the British battery positions with mustard gas. But however hard the German airmen, and the gunners who were now concentrated east of the ridge, may have tried to disrupt the preparations, all was as ready as it could be for the next drive on Passchendaele.

---

[713] National Archives, GHQ statistics WO95/15

The capture of Passchendaele – The Second Phase

Canadian Corps

The task of the Canadian Corps on the 30th October was entrusted to the 4th Canadian Division; to push the line forward along the main ridge and capture a strong jumping-off position for the final assault on Passchendaele, whilst the 3rd Canadian Division completed the capture of the Red Line objective of the 26th along the Bellevue – Meetecheele spur. On the right, contact was to be maintained with I Anzac Corps near Vienna Cottages, and on the left with XVIII Corps of Fifth Army near Vapour Farm.

The Canadians were opposed by the *463rd, 464th*, and *465th Regiments* of the *238th Division*, with the *126th, 132nd*, and *172nd Regiments* of the *39th Division*, which had arrived in Flanders from Artois on the 13th October, in support.

4th Canadian Division – 12th Canadian Brigade [714]
3rd Canadian Division – 7th [715] and 8th Canadian Brigades [716]

On the night of the 28th/29th October the 12th Canadian Brigade relieved the 10th Brigade in the line, along the 4th Canadian Division sector between the Roulers railway and the Ravebeek, the 85th (Nova Scotia Highlanders) Battalion on the right, the 78th (Winnipeg Grenadiers) in the centre, and the 72nd (Seaforth Highlanders of Canada) on the left,[717] with one company of each attacking battalion holding the line that night. The Germans showed their determination to hold the Passchendaele position, for as the relief was beginning on the right, the *463rd Regiment* attacked Decline Copse, driving the 44th Battalion from their posts either side of the Roulers railway before the 85th could effectively intervene. A determined counter-attack by the 85th drove the enemy out once more and secured the front line on both sides of the railway, but did not recover the forward outposts which remained in the hands of the Germans. The position of the 85th was carefully reconnoitred under a bright moon by Staff Officers, who found the Germans in possession of the outpost line and in dangerously close proximity to the 85th. This situation necessitated altering the barrage plan for the right of the attack, bringing the initial protection zone back towards the 85th to cover the enemy posts, the final arrangements only completed a little before Zero Hour. The 78th Battalion was to attack along the line of the Passchendaele road, with the 72nd Battalion attacking north-west of the road towards Crest Farm.

North of the Ravebeek in the sector of 3rd Canadian Division, the 7th Brigade relieved the 9th on the night of the 28th/29th at Bellevue, while to the left the 8th Brigade remained in the line just forward of Wallemolen. It was known that the Germans were still holding the strong-points at Snipe Hall, Friesland and Duck Lodge in the Ravebeek valley, and at Furst Farm 200 yards north of the Mosselmarkt road, which were all very close to the Canadian line, as patrols of the 116th Battalion had come under fire from these positions on the night of the 27th/28th. On the 30th, the Princess Patricia's Canadian Light Infantry was to attack the strong-points along the north of the Ravebeek, while the 49th (Edmonton) Battalion attacked from Bellevue towards Furst Farm.[718] Each attacking battalion was to be close-supported by two platoons of the Royal Canadian Regiment, the remainder of the R.C.R. being in support on Gravenstafel ridge, and the 42nd Battalion in reserve 4,500 yards back at Pommern Castle. The 7th Brigade was to use the 5th Canadian Mounted Rifles on a one battalion front in the attack towards Vapour Farm, with the

---

[714] National Archives, War Diary 12th Can Brigade WO95/3906
[715] National Archives, War Diary 7th Can Brigade WO95/3864
[716] National Archives, War Diary 8th Can Brigade WO95/3868
[717] National Archives, War Diary 85th and 78th Can Battalion WO95/3909, National Archives, War Diary 72nd Can Battalion WO95/3908
[718] National Archives, War Diary 49th Can Battalion WO95/3876

2nd C.M.R. in support,[719] one company of which was to occupy the old front line as the attack began. The 9th Brigade was held in reserve at Wieltje.

The assembly, carried out under a full moon, was completed successfully by 5:43 a.m. The assault companies lay out in their shell-holes, chilled by a blustery cold wind, but although the sky had clouded over, for the moment at least it was not raining. A short time before Zero, the forward posts of the 78th and 76th Battalions were pulled back to the front line, unseen by the enemy whose artillery remained remarkably quiet, sending over no more than twenty shells.

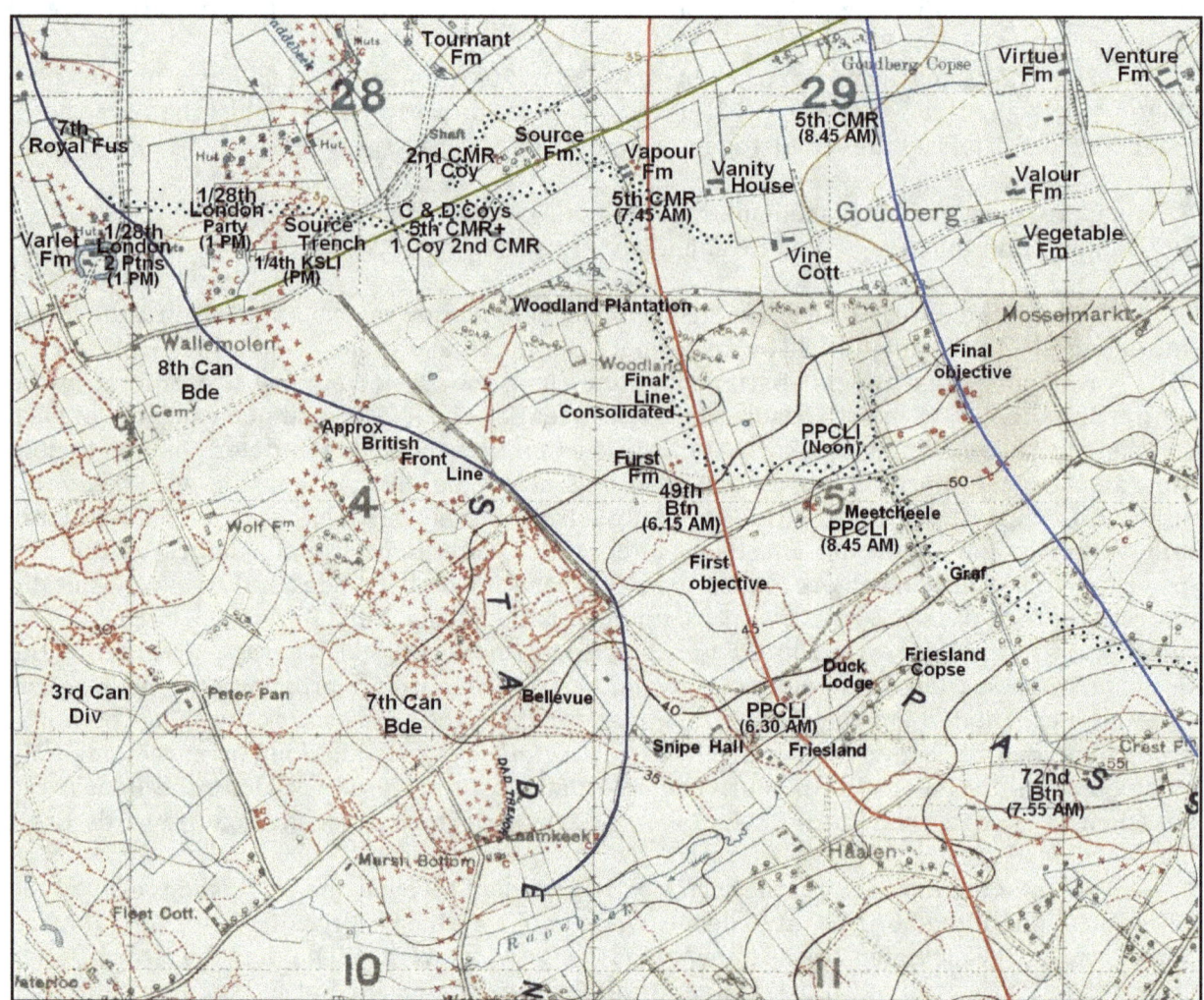

Attacks at Meetcheele and the Paddebeek 7th and 8th Canadian Brigades - 3rd Canadian Division and 190th Brigade - 63rd (Royal Naval) Division

At 5:50 the Canadian barrage, fired as on the 26th by some 420 guns and howitzers crashed down, and the three attacking battalions of 4th Division followed it closely, quickly overrunning all in their path. It was at least eight minutes before the enemy artillery responded, by which time the Canadians were well away. As the 85th crossed to the eastern edge of the Keiberg saddle they came under heavy machine gun fire, but continued to their final objective, clearing the blockhouses in their path and turning captured machine guns on the retreating enemy, but sustaining around 50% casualties in the operation. Along the Passchendaele road the 78th reached its objective around 250 yards short of the church, and began to consolidate. On the left, by 7:55, the defences at Crest Farm were overwhelmed by the 72nd before the Germans could

---

[719] National Archives, War Diary 5th CMR WO95/3873, National Archives, War Diary 2nd CMR WO95/3871

man their machine guns. As the barrage past beyond the objective line some groups pushed on another few hundred yards to the ruins of Passchendaele church, and found that the enemy had evacuated the southern end of the village. With a counter-attack expected the small Canadian parties were soon brought back to the objective, to work on the consolidation of new the position. Digging-in to the drier sandy soil on the ridge was found to be easy. By 8:30 a.m. the divisional objective was taken and digging and wiring was making it secure. Only in the Ravebeek valley, north-west of Crest Farm was the ground found to be too flooded to dig-in on the objective, and as the 3rd Division north of the quagmire were not yet up on their objectives, a flank was dropped back to the left facing the stream. Canadian snipers were quickly active along the new line. The enemy infiltrated out of the village in small parties in an effort by the *464th Regiment* to form an outpost shell-hole line close to the Canadians, many being shot down by the snipers. But 78th and 72nd had also lost around 40% of their number in the attack.

The P.P.C.L.I. had amongst the worst ground of any Canadian battalion to cross that day, their right being in the swamp of the Ravebeek. The blockhouse at Snipe Hall 150 yards north of the stream, and just forward of the front line had been captured before Zero Hour. At 5:50 as the barrage came down along the 3rd Division front the P.P.C.L.I. floundered forward, keeping as well up as they could to the line of bursting shells towards Duck Lodge which was on the intermediate objective. Enemy machine gun fire from pillboxes and organised shell-holes further up the valley was intense, causing many casualties, and by 6:50 most junior officers were lost. On the spur at Bellevue the advance of the 49th had been even harder hit, being heavily shelled and swept by machine guns from the main ridge and from the direction of Meetcheele. One machine gun which held up the advance appeared particularly difficult to assault. Private Cecil John Kinross stripped off his equipment and carrying only his ammunition bandolier and rifle worked forward alone, finally rushing the position, killing the crew of six and destroying the gun. For his most conspicuous bravery in action Private Kinross was later to be awarded the V.C. The survivors of the 49th continued the advance and had succeeded in capturing Furst Farm 600 yards from the Bellevue start line by 6:15. The German artillery was noticeably more aggressive north of the Ravebeek, a heavy barrage being put down 100 yards west of Bellevue three minutes after Zero, and again at 6:31 along the old support line. The enemy were obviously intent on isolating the forward Canadian units, firing a smoke barrage into Marsh Bottom, Waterloo and Peter Pan at 6:50. Communication with the front line was to remain difficult throughout the day.

North-west of Bellevue spur, in the 8th Brigade sector, the 5th C.M.R. were confronted by the marshy ground of the Woodland Plantation in the upper Paddebeek depression, but advanced steadily and by 7:00 a.m. one company was on the first objective. Here parties of the *465th Regiment* had little stomach to stop and fight and soon after 7:00 many were seen leaving the battlefield without weapons, over the top of the main ridge between Venture Farm and Wallis Copse about 1,200 yards to the north-east. At about 7:45 the 5th C.M.R. had succeeded in pushing forward across the Paddebeek marsh and capturing the blockhouses at Vanity House, and Vapour Farm and was close to Source Farm, the attack on the blockhouses being led personally by Major Pearkes. By 8:45 flares indicated that the 5th C.M.R. had achieved its objectives, but was not in contact with the 63rd Division to the left near Source Farm, or with the 49th Battalion across the Paddebeek bogs in the Woodland Plantation to its right.

Around 1,000 yards to the south, as the left company of the P.P.C.L.I. climbed the southern side of the Bellevue spur from the direction of Snipe Hall, they were checked by machine gun fire from blockhouses at the fortified position 150 yards east of the Meetcheele crossroads, which guarded the road to Mosselmarkt. The company had already lost all its officers, and Lieutenant Hugh Mackenzie D.C.M. of the 7th Machine Gun Company, with Sergeant George Harry Mullin M.M. a regimental sniper, rallied the men and took control of an attack on the blockhouses nearest the crossroads. Working towards the position Mackenzie drew the fire of the machine guns upon himself and was killed in doing so. Mullin continued the attack alone and climbed on top of one blockhouse, shooting the two machine gunners and taking ten of the garrison prisoner. Meetcheele crossroads soon fell to the P.P.C.L.I. Lieutenant Mackenzie and Sergeant Mullin were subsequently to be awarded the V.C. for their heroic actions. Machine gun fire remained heavy and destructive from the group of blockhouses towards Mosselmarkt. Along the Ravebeek the P.P.C.L.I. was continuing to face stiff opposition and difficult fighting, where the enemy still held out in shell-holes in the bogs of Friesland Copse, supported by heavy machine gun fire from the strong-point at Graf House 350 yards up the valley which caused many casualties.

On the Bellevue spur the Germans appeared to rally at around 8:00, and there were signs of a counter-attack developing from Mosselmarkt. But although the concentration was supported by artillery, which shelled the 49th positions around Furst Farm at about 8:50, the attack was not pressed, dissuaded by bursts of suppressing fire from the 3rd Division machine gun batteries. The hasty withdrawal over the main ridge south of Wallis Copse had also been checked, and at 9:15 small bodies of the enemy were reported regrouping in the area. Half an hour later a much larger number began to assemble on the ridge top around Vindictive Crossroads, 900 yards north of the church, and the Canadian artillery and machine guns were quickly turned upon them. This group was not easily scattered, for although a great weight of artillery was also directed upon them they continued to advance on a line between Vindictive Crossroads and Venture Farm, in open order, and in a south-westerly direction towards Mosselmarkt.

On the Canadian left about the Paddebeek meanwhile the situation was becoming serious. The 5th C.M.R. still clung to their objective but in small numbers and with both flanks dangerously exposed. To their left 63rd Division had been seriously checked, but at 8:45 "A" Company of the 1/28th London Regiment, (Artists Rifles) reported that they were consolidating a line 200 yards east of Source Trench, near the Paddebeek, but had suffered appalling casualties having lost 90% of their strength. It appeared to the Canadians that the 1/28th had advanced little more than 100 yards, and was not as far forward as it thought, leaving the left of the 5th C.M.R. in a precarious position. Major George Randolphe Pearkes M.C. of the 5th, who had been wounded earlier in the day, was still holding Vapour Farm and was close up to the blockhouse at Vanity House, which still held out. He had pushed out small parties of his "C" and "B" Companies to his left, 20 men to the east of the Paddebeek bogs and 20 men to the west. With counter-attacks threatening he was in urgent need of reinforcement, and sent a message by carrier pigeon to the Poperinghe communication centre. The message was telephoned to Divisional H.Q. on the canal bank requesting rapid assistance, the 3rd Division relaying the message to 8th Brigade. But due to heavy machine gun fire from the direction of Source Trench on his left flank, his position was considered by 8th Brigade H.Q. to be cut off, and the best that could be done was to request that 63rd Division should reinforce their right flank and continue to push forward in support of the 5th C.M.R. The request was not easily met by 63rd Division which replied that it would do what it could, but that it was extremely short of men, and would attempt to send up two companies of the counter-attack battalion. Within a quarter of an hour the danger of the situation was fully appreciated, as the reserve company of the 5th C.M.R. and two companies of the 2nd C.M.R. from brigade reserve were ordered up by Brigadier-General Elmsley and were on their way to reinforce Pearkes. The 63rd Division had also confirmed that they were sending two companies to attack Source Trench. A degree of confusion arose over who should carry out the attack on Source Farm, which was of ultimate importance, for if the line was not connected and strengthened at this point it threatened the success of the whole Canadian attack on Passchendaele. Elmsley considered that the 63rd Division stood a greater chance of attacking before him, 'even if they took one and a half hours'. Corps, divisional, and brigade staffs all became involved in the arrangements, and meetings were suggested between representatives of 8th Canadian Brigade and 63rd Division. Meanwhile, as the debate continued, Pearkes held on at Vapour Farm. Towards late morning, to add to the difficulties of the operation, the rain which had held off for a few days again began to fall.

At Meecheele the P.P.C.L.I. had by midday extended their front across the spur, and dug-in 300 yards forward of Furst Farm, where they were in touch with the 49th a little to their rear. From here a line of posts ran over the spur, towards the south-east, to the quagmire of Graf Wood on the Ravebeek, where there was still a gap between them and the 72nd Battalion south of the stream. At Graf Wood they were 300 to 400 yards short of their objective, 400 to 500 yards short in the centre at Meetcheele, and up-close to their objective on the left beyond Furst Farm. The Patricias had suffered grievous casualties in the attack mainly from machine gun and sniper fire, and the German barrage was continuing to fall along the crest of Bellevue spur and around Marsh Bottom, hampering reinforcement and communication, although supports were now moving forward. Pearkes was also beginning to receive reinforcements at Vapour Farm, where the 5th C.M.R. had dug-in along a 300 yard line either side of the strong-point. The enemy still held out in Vanity House, with the 5th C.M.R. established in shell-holes just south of it. Around 60 men had got up in support, and parties of the two left Companies, "C" and "D" were still attempting to secure the gap amongst the bogs of the Paddebeek on the left. Of the two right 5th C.M.R. Companies, "A" and "B", nothing had been heard. Soon after 1:00 p.m. a small party of around 14 of the left company had succeeded in entering Source Trench 200 yards west of the Paddebeek, with around 40 of the Artists Rifles apparently holding a blockhouse nearby, with two more platoons of the Artists in Varlet Farm 350 yards to the east. But the Germans were still in possession of another blockhouse 100 yards north of Source Trench, and soon more were seen to be massing 500 yards to the north of Pearkes line at Vapour Farm. One Company of the 2nd C.M.R. had now got up and was establishing a defensive flank in shell-holes around the north and west of Source Farm, with a second company supporting "C" and "D" of the 5th at Vapour Farm, whilst a third company was moving up under Pearkes orders. The fourth company of the 2nd was in reserve in the old jumping-off trench. The 1st C.M.R. had also been ordered to move towards the front, and at around 2:30 the 42nd Battalion was ordered up in support to Gravenstafel ridge. Elmsley had realised the extreme danger of the situation and was doing all in his power to address the problem, the dilemma regarding whether he or the 63rd Division should attack first now being academic. Both Canadian and Imperial support was now converging on the danger spot as at 2:00 p.m. a company of the 1/4th King's Shropshire Light Infantry of 190th Brigade, 63rd Division, passed Kronprinz Farm 2,000 yards back, with orders to pass through the Canadian rear and attack Source Trench from the east.

Soon after 3:00, the enemy counter-attack gathering north of Vapour Farm began to threaten the Canadian line and the S.O.S. was fired requesting a barrage, the enemy subsequently making little further progress. Around 5:00 p.m. the S.O.S. was again fired on both the right and left of the Canadian front, and all guns came into action firing a general barrage on the S.O.S. lines. The gunfire gradually slackened first on the right, and by 5:40 on the left. Although a few more S.O.S. calls were made, for the Canadians the fighting was virtually over for the day, and most of the jump-off position required for the next assault on Passchendaele had been gained. For his tireless, skilful leadership and bravery throughout the day, which had gone a long way to saving a precarious situation, Major Pearkes of the 5th Canadian Mounted Rifles was to be awarded the V.C.

The artillery had been kept very busy and the counter-battery group especially had experienced a gruelling day. They had started with 41 hostile batteries engaged against them, of which the enemy had pulled 18 into rear positions. Two silent batteries just east of Passchendaele had come into action, and during the day the British guns had expended 15,000 rounds in neutralising fire. The enemy infantry had been kept at bay by the field artillery, machine guns and sniper fire, and no counter-attack had seriously threatened the Canadian line, although during the afternoon no less than five counter-attacks had been launched from north of Passchendaele.

The advisability of holding on to the precarious position at Vapour Farm was questioned, but it was felt that giving it up would only mean fighting for it again. The line finally consolidated by 3rd Canadian Division on a line of shell-hole posts, ran from Graf Wood, to just west of the Meetcheele Crossroads, to a point 150 yards west on the Gravenstafel – Mosselmarkt road, thence to Furst Farm, then along a line east of the Paddebeek, to a point 200 yards north-west of Vapour Farm, to Source Farm and then to Source Trench. Posts were pushed forward of this line where possible, and the area of bog around the upper Paddebeek between the 7th and 8th Brigades was patrolled. The 7th Brigade was also charged with capturing the group of blockhouses just north-east of the Meetcheele Crossroads as soon as possible.

The attack of Fifth Army 5:50 a.m. the 30th October

The protection of the Canadian left flank.

XVIII Corps

The 63rd Division on the Paddebeek and the 58th Division east of Poelcappelle.

63rd Division [720]

190th Brigade [721]

The objectives confronting 190th Brigade were the same as those faced by 188th Brigade on the 26th, and the battlefield had not improved underfoot in any way. German observation from the Passchendaele - Westroosebeke ridge straight down the Lekkerboterbeek depression remained undiminished, enabling accurate sniping by rifle, machine gun and field artillery upon the slightest movement. But the protective flank to be established by the 190th Brigade was of vital importance to the main Canadian attack as any weakness in the line on the Paddebeek, left exposed to exploitation by the enemy, would threaten the attack along the Bellevue spur, and thus the main attack on Passchendaele.

From the outset things went badly, as the enemy drew back the line of their protective barrage, catching the assembly of the attacking battalions before they began to advance. On the right the 1/28th London Regiment (Artists' Rifles),[722] sustained severe casualties before re-organising sufficiently to proceed, by which time the barrage, doing little more than raising fountains of mud and filthy water, had passed on beyond their reach. The survivors wallowed forward towards Source Trench, harassed by heavy machine gun fire, and were soon checked by an uncut wire entanglement protecting it. As we have seen, by 8:45 "A" Company of the Artists' Rifles reported that they were attempting to consolidate 200 yards east of Source Trench and that they had suffered 90% casualties. It is most probable that they were still west of Source Trench, and this was the Canadian opinion, with the benefit of the view from another position on the battlefield. It is likely that they were pinned down by heavy fire from machine gun posts near the trench, which were also enfilading the Canadians east of the Paddebeek about Source Farm and Vapour Farm. At this point the Canadians had requested that 63rd Division should address the situation by sending up supports to Source Trench.

To the left of the Artists Rifles, the 7th Royal Fusiliers and the 4th Bedfordshire Regiment could make no progress in the face of the appalling ground and heavy machine gun fire,[723] which conspired to make movement impossible. To continue to hold the line on which they stood was all that could be achieved. By 1:30 a weak party of the Artists Rifles had entered Source Trench accompanied by 14 Canadians. The Rifles also held a blockhouse just east of the trench, and two platoons were in or about Varlet Farm. The enemy held on close at hand, a garrison remaining in a blockhouse 100 yards north of the trench, and touch between the 3rd Canadian and 63rd Divisions across the Paddebeek was at best tenuous, possession of Source Farm still being bitterly disputed. The two companies of the 1/4th King's Shropshire Light Infantry from brigade reserve, which had moved up past Kronprinz Farm at 2:00 attacked northwards through the Canadian rear towards Source Trench. This was the first action the battalion had fought on the Western Front, and initially it was reported that they had reached Source Trench. The report was later proved incorrect, but touch was gained with a third company of the 1/4th which had been sent up to support the Canadians at Source Farm, and by dusk the three companies had

---

[720] Douglas Jerrold *The Royal Naval Division* London : Hutchinson pp252-257
[721] National Archives, War Diary 190th Brigade WO95/3117
[722] National Archives, War Diary 1/28th London (Artists Rifles) WO95/3119
[723] National Archives, War Diary 7th Royal Fusliers WO95/3119, National Archives, War Diary 4th Bedford WO95/3118

established a line in contact with the Canadians near Source Farm and the Artists Rifles at Varlet Farm, from where the line ran to the northwards 600 yards to Bray Farm, and thence westwards 500 yards to Berks Houses and the Lekkerboterbeek.

In the two attacks made on the 26th and 30th October, the division had sustained casualties of 32 officers and 954 other ranks killed or missing and 83 officers and 2,057 other ranks wounded. The sacrifice across the 1,500 yards of battlefront had been huge, but although threatened, the Canadian left had remained secure.

58th Division, 174th Brigade [724]

North of the Lekkerboterbeek the 174th Brigade was to cover the left flank of the 63rd Division by capturing specific blockhouses up to 700 yards forward of the British outpost line, advancing over the same ground attacked by the 173rd Brigade four days earlier. The 2/8th London Regiment was to advance on Moray House, Hinton Farm, Papa Farm and Cameron House, while to their left the 2/6th was to seize Nobles Farm and the group of pillboxes 200 yards to the south-east of the farm.[725] The 57th Division, although not to take part in the attack, was in possession of Requete Farm on the left flank.

As an indication of the state of the ground it was accepted that the 58th Division was not in touch on the right flank with the 63rd Division along the Lekkerboterbeek, and that under the conditions prevailing contact between the two divisions was not possible. The 2/8th London, floundering in the quagmire soon lost the weak barrage, and succeeded in only pushing forward to a line of shell-holes around 100 yards from their start line. The 2/6th was to attack with only its "A" Company, which assembled across the Staden road about 250 yards north-east of the Poelcappelle Brewery. The company moved off behind the barrage towards the south-east, two platoons seizing what little remained of Nobles Farm, whilst the third captured the group of pillboxes, and there stopped and attempted to dig-in.

To the north of 58th Division, the 57th Division of Watts' XIX (late XIV) Corps, although not part of the main attack had been shelled out of Rubens and Memling Farms in the Watervlietbeek valley, but was ordered to re-occupy them that night.

The results of the 30th October

The operations on the 30th October had not been an unparalleled success, but neither had they been the failure many had expected given the conditions. The Canadians had done extremely well, advancing up to 1,000 yards along their 2,800 yard front, and had mostly secured the final jumping-off line which would enable them to capture Passchendaele in the next attack, and that had been the requirement of their operation. On the left flank, in ground so bad that it was at the very limit in which men could operate, 63rd and 58th Divisions had done all they could do; in fact they had done enough to prevent the Germans wheeling into the Canadian flank.

Along the southern edge of Houthulst Forest, the 50th Division, after the terrible day of the 26th, had not been involved in the fighting on the 30th, but the 150th Brigade was required in the early hours of the 31st to make another attempt to push towards Hill 23 across the Vijfwegen – Veldhoek spur, between Turenne Crossing and Colombo House. In the centre, two companies of the 1/4th East Yorkshire Regiment were to advance around 400 yards and establish a line along the Colbert Crossroads track with posts out in front, while the third and fourth companies protected the flanks. Two companies of the 5th Green Howards were in support. At 2:00 a.m. and behind a very heavy barrage, the two companies of the East Yorks moved off and were immediately checked under a hail of enemy machine gun fire. The flanking companies

---

[724] National Archives, War Diary 174th Brigade WO95/3003
[725] National Archives, War Diary 2/8th London WO95/3006, National Archives, War Diary 2/6th London WO95/3005

succeeded in continuing the advance, and eventually a line around 100 yards short of the objective was established.

Throughout the day of the 31st the Germans continued, without success, to probe the new Canadian positions about Passchendaele. At around 4:00 a.m. S.O.S. signals were fired by the 4th Canadian Division, as the enemy were believed to be massing. A heavy barrage was put down and no attack materialised. German shelling was intermittent on both forward and battery areas, and at times it became severe, but at no time was the new line seriously threatened.

The six day preparation period between the end of the second and beginning of the third phase of the attack on Passchendaele, had been foreseen by Currie as allowing for movement of the guns, divisional reliefs, and to enable Fifth Army to fully participate on the 6th November. This participation now became academic as on the 31st October G.H.Q. ordered General Plumer to take over from Fifth Army the XVIII Corps sector, replacing the corps staff with that of Lieutenant -General Sir Claud Jacob's II Corps, enabling unity of command for the forthcoming operation. Plumer instructed Currie and Jacob to make all efforts possible to work their batteries forward, and to proceed apace with counter-battery fire against the increasingly powerful German artillery concentrations east of Passchendaele. The now commonplace procedure of road and track improvement and repair continued, a seemingly endless stream of ammunition and supplies being trundled towards the front, as the build up for the Eighth Step commenced. The gunners, drivers, and pioneers toiled ceaselessly, and suffered the same pervading awfulness of the Salient in equal measure with the infantry in the line. A Canadian gunner described the period: 'Sometimes the sun shone, pale and wintry in that November air; but most of the time rain came and the shells landed, now blowing up black spouts of mud, now white columns of water like ghosts that drifted and danced and vanished over the gloomy landscape. And every night there were one on two more casualties amongst the drivers; and few indeed, were the days when some gunner did not fall. Yet there was nothing to do but 'stick it out'; and day after day, the men set their teeth, wondered, "Who's next?" and went about the business of war.'[726]

In an attempt to secure the important jumping-off sections of the Blue Dotted Line objective about Vapour Farm, which had not been achieved on the 30th October, the 8th Canadian Brigade was to use the 1st Canadian Mounted Rifles to carry out an attack at 1:15 a.m. on the 2nd November. The 14th Battalion of the 3rd Brigade, of the incoming 1st Canadian Division was placed at the disposal of the 8th Brigade to support the operation. The attack was to be made by two parties, each consisting of 1 officer and 20 men, to be given covering fire by two Vickers guns brought up for the purpose, while the enemy approaches were covered by the artillery. The right party seized and mopped-up Vine Cottage with ease, but were then counter-attacked by a strong force of Germans from a trench behind the blockhouse, and came under heavy machine gun fire from the right. The party subsequently moved to their left towards Vanity House to assist the situation there. The left party captured Vanity House, taking one prisoner and killing the remainder of the garrison. The prisoner taken was from the *76th Fusilier Regiment* of the *111th Division* that had come to Flanders from Verdun and into the line on the 17th October and which he claimed when questioned had suffered severe casualties on the 26th October, but was obviously still in the line. In accordance with Haig's planning the Flanders fighting was still drawing in enemy reserves, the *238th Division* being relieved at this time by the *39th Division* which had been moved north from the Lens sector on the 13th October. The harassing British artillery fire was causing great difficulty and confusion to the relieving parties, a mix up of units in the various regimental sectors being the inevitable result.

A major movement of Canadian divisions was also under way. In order to reduce the length of the Canadian attack front, on the night of the 1st / 2nd November the right boundary of the 4th Canadian Division was moved 350 yards north of the Roulers railway to Tiber Copse, the

---

[726] W.B. Kerr, Shreiks and crashes bring memories of Canada's Corps, 1917, Hunter Rose Company Ltd. 1929 Toronto P189.

section of line being subsequently occupied by the 1st Australian Division. Over the same period the 1st and 2nd Canadian Divisions began to move by rail from their reserve area near Caestre east of Cassel. During the night of the 2nd / 3rd November the 2nd Canadian Division relieved the 4th Division in the line, 2nd Division advanced headquarters being established at the Ramparts in Ypres on the 3rd November. Also on the 3rd, a dull, overcast and misty day, the 1st Canadian Division relieved the 3rd Division, the advanced headquarters of the 1st Division moving to the Yser canal bank. It was not long before the 2nd Division was in action on the Passchendaele ridge.

German counter-attack of the 3rd November

At 4:40 a.m. on the morning of the 3rd November the enemy artillery opened very heavy shelling of the forward areas and at 4:55 a heavy shrapnel barrage along the whole Canadian and the left of the Australian front between the Roulers railway and the Meetcheele – Mosselmarkt road, which ominously stood just forward of the outposts for 5 minutes. From the forward positions the Germans were seen to be massing behind their barrage, and as it lifted towards the Canadian line the S.O.S. was sent up, and heavy machine gun and rifle fire lashed the advancing groups. The enemy shelling effectively cut communication between the line companies and battalion headquarters and it was not until 6:30 that the strength of the attack became clear. The S.O.S. rockets were repeated and the artillery soon responded, the protective barrage and the small arms fire generally breaking the attack. The Germans succeeded in gaining a foothold near Crest Farm, and struck at Tiber Copse, at the junction between the 1st Australian Division and the 4th / 2nd Canadian Divisions, (the relief was still under way), but were quickly evicted from both positions by counter-attacks. Hostile artillery was active for the remainder of the day on front and rear areas, the British guns replying with an effective counter-barrage.

The 3rd November was also a busy day north of the Ravebeek, where the 7th Brigade in line with the orders issued after the attack on the 30th was, in the early hours of the morning, to attempt to capture the pillboxes just east of the Meetcheele crossroads. The 42nd (Highlanders of Canada) Battalion was detailed to seize the Graf House pillbox on the track 50 yards north of the crossroads, and a machine gun emplacement 200 yards to the east. The Germans were in close proximity to the Canadian forward posts, and there were indications that they had dug a short section of trench in front of the pillboxes, about 150 yards west of the junction. The 42nd was to make a stealth attack, without the assistance of artillery, but supported by rifle grenadiers, bombers, Lewis gunners, and if possible Stokes mortars. At 2:00 a.m. the small groups of the 42nd attacked, and after heavy fighting the right party, having sustained severe casualties seized the objective at Graf House. Around 4:30 the enemy responded in strength against the pillbox, the fighting so severe that the Canadians were soon out of ammunition, and the three or four men that remained of the attack party fell-back to their own line. As a precaution against further incursions the German artillery opened a heavy barrage along the Canadian front at 5:00 a.m., the British guns countering in response to the S.O.S. rockets, until at around 7:00 the firing subsided. The attempt at securing the ideal jump-off line had failed, but in the evening, after dark, posts were pushed a little further forward.

Operations of the 63rd Division,[727] from the 31st October to the 4th November

It was not only the Canadians who attempted to improve the position of their line prior to the attack on the 6th November. The weakness of the front about the Paddebeek was of concern to 63rd Division who determined to push the Varlet Farm – Banff House line forward and get across the mire closer to their original objectives. Commander Asquith had recognised the weakness of conventional morning attacks behind the usual protective barrage, and planned a series of surprise night raids to seize the troublesome blockhouses and pillboxes along the Paddebeek.

---

[727] Douglas Jerrold *The Royal Naval Division* London : Hutchinson pp259-262

He considered that mobility, prior reconnaissance, surprise and the personal leadership of senior officers were essential ingredients in overcoming the German system of defence.

On the night of the 30th / 31st October, the 189th Brigade relieved 190th in the line, the Nelson Battalion taking up position on the right and the Hawke Battalion on the left.[728] By this time the sector had passed to the control of Second Army, which gave instructions that the crossing of the Paddebeek was to be secured under divisional arrangements before the 6th November, and XVIII Corps gave approval to the night attacks. Upon reconnoitring the line, officers from Hawke Battalion found the divisional advanced post at Banff House to have been abandoned, while patrols of the Nelson located the enemy defences near Source Trench. Plans were made to secure Banff House and seize Source Trench on the following night. At 6:10 p.m. on the 1st November a party of the Nelson comprising Sub-Lieutenant Brearly and 11 men crept forward across the muddy crater-field towards Source Trench, and the concrete bunker which defended it. About 80 yards from the position they came across the uncut wire belt which had checked the Artists Rifles on the 30th, and here the party split into three groups, an N.C.O. and 3 men working around each flank, while Brearly and 2 men found a way through the wire. Within 20 yards the group on the left were discovered and the enemy in the pillbox opened fire. The Germans had not seen Brearly or the right group however and he now decided to draw the whole party to the right flank and attack the bunker from there. The attack worked perfectly, an N.C.O. eleven men and a machine being captured at no cost to Brearly's party, and the pillbox which had defied capture by frontal assault on the 30th had fallen. Brearly was to be awarded the Military Cross for his daring attack.

The Hawke operation to secure Banff House was equally successful. An enemy pillbox, which had checked the advance on the 26th October and commanded the battalion left front, had also been responsible for the evacuation of Banff House, having kept the post under fire. An officer and one and a half platoons of "D" Company worked stealthily forward, and in similar fashion to the Nelson seized the pillbox, killing 2 of the enemy and capturing 9 men and a machine gun. With the pillbox secure posts were pushed out on either flank and to the north of Banff House, which was now safely in the hands of the Hawke. Four hours later a German ration party arrived at their pillbox, and were also captured.

On the night of the 2nd / 3rd November the Nelson was relieved by the Hood Battalion and the Hawke by the Drake Battalion.[729] The two fresh battalions continued with reconnaissance with a view to further operations on the night of the 3rd / 4th. The Drake planned to seize the one remaining bunker on their battalion front west of the Paddebeek at Sourd Farm. At 9:00 p.m. two and a half platoons of "C" Company worked forward from Banff House, between the craters, towards Sourd Farm 250 yards in front, while one and a half platoons moved round to the left of the objective to give covering fire to the attack. The enemy were obviously more vigilant this night as the two groups were soon discovered, the garrison opening machine gun fire, which owing to the darkness was practically un-aimed and failed to hit anybody. The pillbox was however very clear, the gun-flashes making it an excellent target for the Lewis gunners and rifle grenadiers who temporarily silenced the fire, as others closed on the position and rushed it. Only one prisoner was taken as the remainder of the garrison of Sourd Farm had fled. On the right front of the Division on the same evening the Hood Battalion pushed the line forward to the Paddebeek, in touch with the Drake at Sourd Farm, and the ground west of the Paddebeek marsh was now clear of the enemy.

For the next attack Tournant Farm, 150 yards east of the stream was the target, which Commander Asquith proceeded to reconnoitre that night. This was however going to be a much harder task, as the blockhouse within the ruins appeared strongly held, was supported by a pillbox on either flank, and was protected by wire and trench-works which would have to be overcome first. With the difficulties of the attack outlined to Corps Staff, 63rd Division was instructed, as the line of the Paddebeek was now secure, not to proceed with the attack against Tournant Farm as part of the preliminary operations. An attack was however made on the night

---

[728] National Archives, War Diary Nelson Battalion WO95/3114
[729] National Archives, War Diary Drake Battalion WO95/3114

of the 4th / 5th, which, against stiff opposition, succeeded in securing the trench outposts and capturing a few machine guns, the attack then being called off. On the 5th November the 63rd Division was relieved by the 1st Division.

The operations carried out in the dark had resulted in greater gains than had been achieved on the 26th and 30th October and at negligible cost, and were a tribute to the resourcefulness and abilities of the Royal Naval Division. The divisional objectives that had been so elusive under conventional attack had been virtually achieved. The division had shown that with proper training it was possible to carry out complex night operations and that even against an alert enemy, the cover of darkness could be worth more than a barrage.

Political moves to curb the power of Robertson and Haig

During the next two days, as the preparations for the assault on the 6th November continued, infantry action along the front quietened, although on the 4th, in 63rd Division sector, the 189th Brigade used the Drake Battalion to push its outpost line a little further forward, and Hood Battalion, in order to shorten the Canadian left flank, took over Vapour and Source Farms from the 3rd Canadian Brigade. Activity by German artillery had become intermittent, with some shelling of the forward areas by long range guns, and occasional vigorous bombardments of field battery positions. The weather was generally fine with little rain, the mornings being dull and misty, but improving in the afternoons.

But away from the front the clouds of a future storm were gathering. The War Cabinet were well aware that Passchendaele was about to be seized by the Canadians, but could not decide whether the situation in Italy was the more critical. Two meetings at Downing Street on the 2nd November, one in the morning and one in the evening, left them still undecided. The French were understandably in a state of great alarm regarding the situation in Italy. Pétain, in London with Premier Painlevé had gone so far as to propose that as a fighting force the Italian Army, (after being attacked primarily by 6 German divisions) had ceased to exist and the only way Italy was going to stay in the War was by the direct intervention of the British and French, the French taking control of the Italian forces. He suggested a dividing of the whole allied front from the Channel to the Adriatic, Haig to Command as far south as near Verdun, and himself the line to the south and east, including the Italian front, and to cover the Swiss border in case of a German adventure through that country. Someone present had the sense to venture that the Italians may not agree to such a scheme. On the other hand it was reported that General Cadorna had complained that the British and French forces promised so far in his support were totally inadequate, there being the possibility of a military débâcle if more were not forthcoming. The military débâcle had already occurred on Cadorna's watch. Almost as an aside the D.M.O. gave the casualty figures for the Flanders fighting for October, which amounted to 4,956 officers, and 106,409 other ranks. It was pointed out however that normal wastage amounted to around 35,000 per month so, 'the actual casualties, therefore, for the month of October, due to the Third Battle of Ypres, were about 76,000'.[730] The Prime Minister agreed with a proposal of Premier Painlevé that they should both repair to Italy for urgent talks, Lloyd George to be accompanied by Smuts, Wilson, Maurice, and Hankey. Haig, equally concerned over the Italian disaster, but for different reasons, had sent Kiggell to London with a memorandum contending that the only way to effectively support Italy was to continue fighting on the Western Front, which did not impress the Prime Minister. Concerned as ever that he might be deprived of the forces enabling him to maintain the initiative on the Western Front, or that if more divisions were sent to Italy even the *defence* of the Western Front might be compromised, Haig summarised in his 7 page note by way of a warning. 'It is not possible to determine now whether direct or indirect assistance to Italy would prove most effective in saving her from collapse. But either method may fail and it is beyond doubt that failure in one case would be far more dangerous than in the other and that it would be wiser to risk the loss of Italy from the

---

[730] National Archives, minutes of meeting of War Cabinet No.263, morning 2nd November. CAB23/3

alliance than to risk the loss of the War.'[731] Lloyd George had in any event arranged to meet Haig in Paris on his way to Italy.

In Paris on the 4th November, Lloyd George had a brief meeting with the American Commander-in Chief General Pershing, immediately introducing Pershing to his idea of increased unity of Allied command, and urging him to come to Italy, if only as a spectator with a watching brief. Later Haig was apprised by the Prime Minister of his deliberations regarding the establishment of an Inter-Allied Supreme War Council and associated Staff, in line with the proposals of French and Wilson. Being fully aware of the difficulties of fighting a coalition war, directed by a committee, Haig made his position clear, that for the three years during which period the matter had been on the political agenda he had been wholeheartedly against it. Lloyd George announced that in any event the two Governments had decided to form it, making his seeking of Haig's opinion somewhat superfluous. The manoeuvring continued with Haig raising the question of whether the Prime Minister intended to further strip his forces on the Western Front and send more of his desperately needed divisions to fight in Italy. Lloyd George agreed to send no more divisions to Italy until he had a clearer view of the situation. On the same day in response to Pétain's suggestion to divide command of the Allied front between himself and Haig, the latter sent a telegram to Robertson in Rome. Haig wisely saw no reason for Pétain to take command of the Italian Army, but rather that he should coordinate their operations with his own, and that as the greatest need of the Italians was training, Pétain should arrange and oversee this. Resisting the pressure which was becoming overwhelming for a Supreme Allied Command he added, 'I suggest that Pétain and I should agree regarding general plan of allied operations on Western and Italian fronts which should be considered as one. Our joint proposals will then be submitted to our respective Governments through usual channels. This proposal seems preferable to new allied staff sitting in Paris which in my opinion is quite unworkable'.[732] The Commander-in Chief was swimming desperately, and ultimately unsuccessfully, against an increasingly powerful current.

On the 5th the entourage continued on its journey from Paris to the Levant, and the Anglo-French-Italian Conference at Rapallo, where the scheme for the organization of a Supreme War Council was finally adopted. The decision had been made, but the Russians, and more importantly the Americans had not been present. Lloyd George was to telegram London on the 8th for the information of the King and the War Cabinet. 'Decision to make a beginning on Western Front was precipitated by recent events on Italian Front which rendered absolutely indispensable adoption of immediate steps to secure united direction amongst Allied Armies operating on Western Front.'[733] The actions of the few German central reserve divisions in Italy had therefore, at last, enabled the Prime Minister's will to prevail, for better or worse; the first major step had been taken in curtailing Haig's and Robertson's future control over military policy and operations on the Western Front.

---

[731] National Archives Haig to CIGS, 31st October WO158/24
[732] National Archives Haig to CIGS 4th November WO158/24
[733] National Archives Lloyd George to War Cabinet 4th November WO158/24

The Eighth Step

The attack of the Second Army 6:00 a.m. the 6th November

Weather conditions, rainfall Ypres, temperature Vlamertinghe[734]						
	6th Nov	**7th Nov**	**8th Nov**	**9th Nov**	**10th Nov**	**11th Nov**
Rainfall	1.0mm	1.4mm	2.6mm	1.6mm	13.4mm	1.8mm
Temp	52F	48F	44F	50F	45F	48F

The Canadian perimeter alone was now the attack front, limited to around 2,500 yards along the irregular jumping-off line, widening to 3,000 yards at the days objective, the Green Line, which formed an approximate semi circle with a 1,000 yard radius centred on Graf Wood. Within this arc were included the village of Passchendaele, and the hamlet of Mosselmarkt, and the Goudberg spur. The assault front had become so short that it offered a target upon which the hostile artillery could concentrate, at great danger to the Canadians, unless heavily countered by the British batteries. Although the divisions of XVIII Corps on the Canadian left were now under command of II Corps and Second Army, they were to play no part in the fighting on the 6th November, but were only to give artillery support. On the southern flank the VIII, IX, and I Anzac Corps were also to give artillery support and to simulate attacks against Zandvoorde, Gheluvelt, Becelaere, and Droogenbroodhoek on the Keiberg spur. It had also been decided that in X Corps sector just north of the Menin Road not only would the artillery demonstrate, but the 5th Division would make another attempt to seize the bunkers of Polderhoek Chateau.

All guns that could be moved forward, given the time available and the state of the ground, were in position to support the Canadians, with sufficient levels of ammunition. The rear-most field batteries had been brought forward to stay within range and the new plank road to Kansas Cross had allowed a few 60-pounders and 6-inch howitzers to be brought up, to better deal with the enemy batteries further east of the ridge. The 2nd Canadian Division, south of the Ravebeek was to be supported by the Southern Double Group of 8 siege batteries, and the 2nd and 4th Divisional Artillery with 7 Brigades of field artillery. The 1st Canadian Division north of the Ravebeek was supported by the Northern Double Group of 9 siege batteries, and the 1st Divisional artillery right and left main groups with 8 brigades of field artillery. In addition the Canadian Corps commanded 5 groups of heavy artillery, totalling 21 siege and 5 heavy batteries to support its two divisions. The guns had commenced to soften-up the enemy defences on the evenings of the 1st, 2nd and 3rd with preliminary barrages and bursts of fire in depth. Casualties in the Canadian Corps artillery had reached 1,200 in October, but in contradiction of many accounts which report enormous gas casualties during the period, only 6 were due to gas.[735]

During the early hours of the 5th November, the Canadian battalions to carry out the attack on the 6th relieved the battalions holding the line. The day dawned cloudy with light winds that brought some showers. The enemy artillery was in an aggressive mood, shelling battery positions, the area around Augustus Wood and Hamburg, and the more forward outposts. Roads and tracks towards the front received intermittent bursts of shrapnel, whilst a high velocity gun pounded Ypres, as the Germans did their best to disrupt the forthcoming attack. On the evening of the 5th the British artillery retaliated in strength as destructive shoots were fired by all guns and howitzers on the Canadian Corps front against enemy battery

---

[734] National Archives, GHQ statistics WO95/15
[735] Library and Archives of Canada, War diary Royal Artillery Canadian Corps. Appendix 'B' sheet 3. RG9 III-D-3 Vol4957 T-10774 P66

positions, wire entanglements, forward positions and known assembly areas. What remained of the buildings in Passchendaele were further reduced to drive out the defenders.

Facing the 2nd Canadian Division was the *11th Division* which had arrived from the Champagne on the 31st October, and relieved the *39th Division* on the nights of the 4th / 5th and 5th / 6th November. The line was held from south to north by the *51st Infantry Regiment*, the *10th Grenadier Regiment*, and the *38th Fusilier Regiment*, each with one battalion in the line, one in support, and one in reserve. From information provided by prisoners, company strengths in these regiments averaged around 150 men. The 1st Canadian Division faced the left sector of the *4th Division*, which had arrived in Flanders from Reims on the 1st November, with the *49th Infantry Regiment* in the line. The *44th Reserve Division* which had arrived in Flanders on the 25th October from Verdun was in close support of the *11th Division,* and was destined to relieve the *11th* after the fighting of the 6th November. *The 3rd Guard Division* which had returned to Flanders on the 9th October, having left on the 5th August, was behind the Passchendaele sector as counter-attack division.

The capture of Passchendaele – The Third Phase

X Corps

5th Division, 95th Brigade [736]

The bunkers at the bitterly contested Polderhoek Chateau represented one of only a few remaining German footholds on the eastern edge of the Gheluvelt plateau. The 5th Division was to make a final attempt to seize the position, the 95th Brigade using the 1st Devonshire Regiment and the 1st Duke of Cornwall's Light Infantry in the attack.[737] Although the 5th Division action would attract enemy artillery fire away from the Canadian front, the reason for the isolated attack, 7,000 yards south of the main battlefront remains obscure. The medium and heavy guns had pounded the ruin and the bunkers in the Chateau park on numerous occasions, but with little result, the enemy machine guns being unmolested by the shelling. The D.C.L.I. was to attack the Chateau, while one platoon of "2" Company of the Devon attacked a small defended mound just south of the ruin, and "3" Company supported the D.C.L.I. At 6:00 a.m. behind a dense 18-pounder barrage of shrapnel and high explosive the D.C.L.I. and Devon advanced across the foul tortured spur. The Cornwall were immediately struck by machine gun fire from the bunkers in the Chateau grounds, and made little progress. Checked by the fire, they subsequently fell-back through the Devon "C" Company, which had established a support line in shell-holes 70 yards west of the Chateau. The mound meanwhile had been taken successfully by the Devon platoon which had quickly established a defendable position. A German counter-attack was launched at around 10:00 a.m. as small parties worked up the Scherriabeek valley intent on recapturing the mound, but the S.O.S. was fired by the Devon at 10:05 and the enemy were dispersed by the artillery. The Devon positions were exposed, and subjected to sniper and machine gun fire throughout the day, the outposts finally being withdrawn to the original front line at dusk, when the line was also reinforced by 2 companies of the East Surrey Regiment. Of the 2 Devon companies engaged 15 were killed, 11 missing and 79 were wounded, and the enemy still held on tenaciously to Polderhoek Chateau.

Canadian Corps

In the main attack, 7,000 yards north of Polderhoek, the Ravebeek marsh would again split the assault of the Canadian Corps. The 2nd Canadian Division was to attack Passchendaele towards the north-east along the main ridge whilst the 1st Canadian Division attacked along the Bellevue

---

[736] National Archives, War Diary 95th Brigade WO95/3868
[737] National Archives, War Diary 1st Devonshire WO95/4217, National Archives, War Diary 1st DCLI WO95/1577

spur from Meetcheele also in a north-easterly direction towards Mosselmarkt, to push the northern perimeter towards Goudberg. The jumping-off line was well positioned and on firm ground on the main ridge, and reasonably positioned on the Bellevue spur, but the area in the Ravebeek valley about Graf Wood and that north of Meetcheele in the upper Paddebeek depression, (where a line was only held securely between Vanity House and Vapour Farm), was still in places impassable.

2nd Canadian Division
Major-General H. E. Burstall

5th and 6th Canadian Brigades [738]

1st Canadian Division
Major-General A. C. Macdonell

1st Canadian Brigade [739]

South of the Ravebeek, the 6th Canadian Brigade of the 2nd Division was to attack on a front of nearly 1,000 yards between Tiber Copse and Graf Wood, with the 27th (City of Winnipeg) Battalion on the right, 31st (Alberta) Battalion in the centre, and 28th (North West) Battalion on the left, whilst the 26th (New Brunswick) Battalion of the 5th Brigade protected the right flank of the attack.[740] The 6th Brigade had an intermediate objective on the left divisional front, the Green Dotted Line, (700 yards from the jump-off line), which ran from 250 yards north-east of the church, to a point 150 yards east of the Mosselmarkt road junction, the final objective at the Green Line being around 250 yards beyond. Three Vickers guns of the 1st Australian Division were to give support on the right divisional boundary, to subdue enemy sniping from the Keiberg, whilst three more of 6th Canadian Brigade, positioned at Crest Farm and firing over Graf Wood were to support the left.

North of the Ravebeek the 1st Canadian Brigade of the 1st Division was to attack with the 1st (Western Ontario) and 2nd (Eastern Ontario) Battalions, from a jump-off line 170 yards east of the Meetcheele road junction, on a 300 yard front across Bellevue spur. Seven hundred yards to the north, from the Vanity House – Vapour Farm position, the 3rd (Toronto) Battalion had the special task of attacking south-eastwards,[741] towards the stubborn Vine Cottage blockhouse on the left flank of the main attack. In the 1,100 yard advance to the Green Line 1st Brigade had two intermediate objectives. The first, the Red Line, was about 250 yards north-east of the Meetcheele crossroads and the second, the Brown Line about 600 yards further on. The final objective, the Green Line formed an arc between Valour Farm and a point on the road 250 yards east of Mosselmarkt crossroads.[742]

---

[738] National Archives, War Diary 6th Can Brigade WO95/3828
[739] National Archives, War Diary 1st Can Brigade WO95/3759
[740] National Archives, War Diary 27th Can Battalion WO95/3831, National Archives, War Diary 31st Can Battalion WO95/3835, National Archives, War Diary 28th Can Battalion WO95/3832, National Archives, War Diary 26th Can Battalion WO95/3825
[741] National Archives, War Diary 1st Can Battalion WO95/3860, National Archives, War Diary 2nd Can Battalion WO95/3861, National Archives, War Diary 3rd Can Battalion WO95/3862
[742] The 1st Battalion was to attack on a two company frontage to the first objective, each company with two platoons in the forward wave. At the first objective the two following companies would take up the attack to the second objective, from where one company from the first objective would pass through to the final objective. As soon as the second objective was secure one company would advance to the final objective to support the position. The 2nd Battalion was to attack on a one company frontage to the first objective, where the two following companies would continue the attack to the second objective. From here the fourth company would continue the attack to the third objective. As soon as the second objective was secure one company would advance to the final

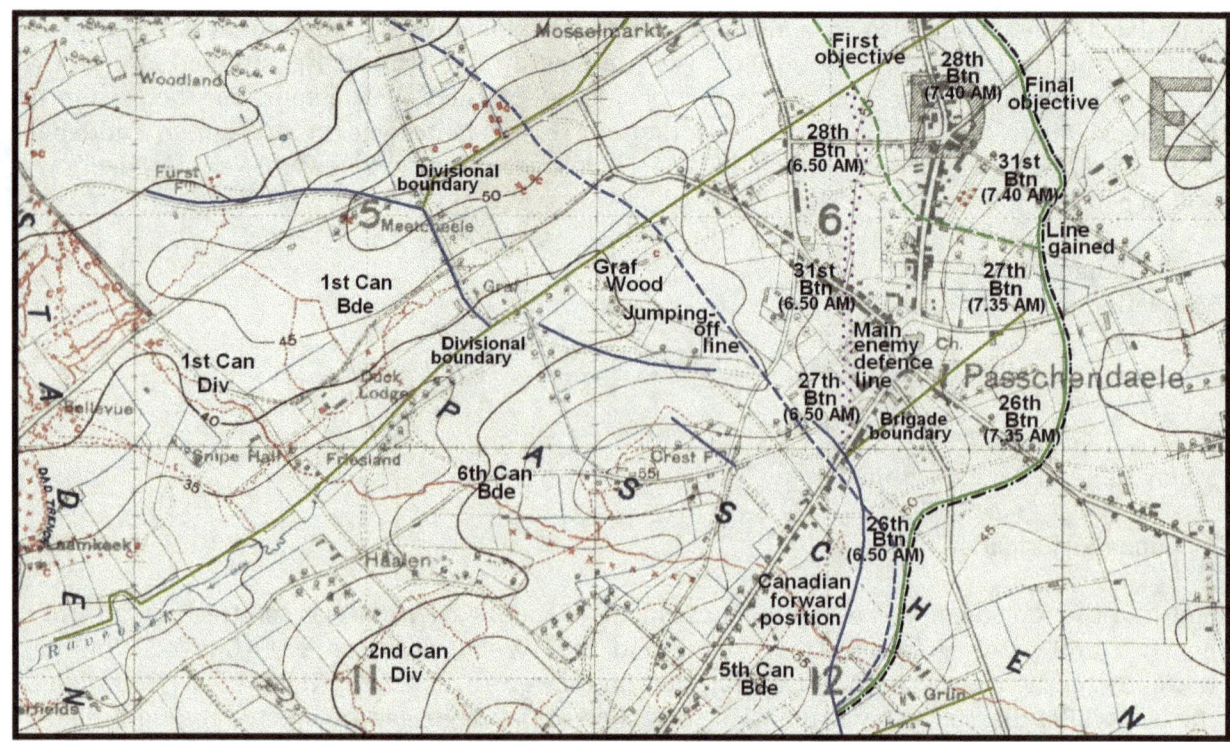
The capture of Passchendaele 6th Canadian Brigade - 2nd Canadian Division

Three Vickers guns of 1st Brigade, positioned just south of the Meetcheele crossroads near the jump-off line were to cover the upper Ravebeek valley from north of the stream. In addition to the specially positioned Vickers, each brigade was to fire a machine gun barrage from 32 guns, which in 6th Brigade were ordered to pay special attention to the area about Vindictive crossroads, where it was felt counter-attack troops might assemble. Eight further mobile guns and 4 sniping guns per brigade were to be taken forward when the final objective was gained to cover the new support and reserve line, and 2 Stokes mortar teams were to be under the direction of the Commanding Officers.[743] Infantry Contact Patrols were to be flown by 21 Squadron, Royal Flying Corps, and a counter-attack patrol was also to be flown to locate and inform the artillery of any threatening counter-attack.

For once the weather for the attack was good, being initially fine and cold, later to become overcast with occasional showers. By 4:00 a.m. on the 6th November the assembly of all troops to carry out the attack was complete, and most were laid out forward of the front line. Careful observation of the timing and position of the German morning barrage line had determined the forward assembly positions, and when a considerable hostile defensive barrage of 5.9's came down just after 4:00 a.m. there were few casualties. The barrage became heavy on Bellevue however between 4:30 and 5:15 and some casualties were caused in the 1st Battalion including the Commanding Officers of "A" and "C" Companies who were both wounded. At 6:00 a.m. the waiting was over as a great ripple of brilliant flashes lit the sky heralding the British barrage. Within seconds the first salvos came down with a reassuring thunder more reminiscent of the September battles, the first burst standing before the jump-off lines for two minutes

---

objective to support the position. The 3rd Battalion would attack with one company from Vanity House with another company in support at Yetta Houses 1,700 yards back.

[743] At Zero to Zero plus 4 minutes the barrage depths for the various guns were to be: 18-pounder barrage, 100 yards deep fired 100 yards forward of the jump-off line. 18-pounder and 4.5-inch howitzer barrage 200 yards deep up to 400 yards from the jump-off line. Machine gun barrage 200 yards deep and up to 600 yards from the jump-off line. 6" howitzer barrage, 200 yards deep up to 800 yards from the jump-off line. 60-pounder, 8" and 9.2" howitzer, 200 yards deep and up to 1,000 yards from the jump-off line.

before lifting. Two minutes after the artillery, the machine gun barrage joined in the general cacophony. Along the whole front the Canadians were away instantly, close up to the barrage. When the enemy artillery retaliated a few minutes later, heavy but erratic and mainly upon Bellevue, it was too late as their targets had already moved forward.

The suddenness and ferocity of the shelling stunned the Germans, and the Canadians, keeping frighteningly close to the rolling barrage, were upon them with their bayonets before they had time to react. Ferocity was not the reserve of the guns alone, as along the enemy front line few prisoners were taken. The bodies of the German dead clearly marked their line. In the usual practice 6th Brigade had ordered its leading waves not to fire from the hip as they advanced, and most of the enemy had been despatched with the bayonet. In the 6th Brigade sector 4 machine guns were captured in the front line before they had time to fire a shot. But the enemy were not about to abandon Passchendaele without a fight and as the 27th and 31st Battalions passed over the forward outposts and moved astride the ridge-top road the resistance stiffened considerably. As the 27th worked towards the village, still 200 yards from the church, every machine gun and rifle which could be brought to bear, opened fire from strong-points in the rubble, whilst the 31st to their left were lashed by fire from pillboxes which had survived the barrage. The 28th Battalion in the swamps along the Ravebeek wallowed through mud knee deep, and in places waist deep, and came under heavy machine gun and rifle fire as they desperately struggled to come to grips with the enemy. Even under this damaging fire the Canadian advance remained relentless, overwhelming the opposition before it. The main German defence position ran roughly parallel to the Westroosebeke road 150 yards west of the church, and as this line was approached many of the enemy dropped their weapons and fled. Some however continued to resist, a hail of fire from pillboxes, machine gun emplacements, and fortified shell-holes amongst the rubble causing many casualties. The thorough training in suppressing the defences with Lewis gun and rifle grenade, while bombing parties outflanked the strong-points was put into practice once more and soon brought the resistance to an end, most enemy garrisons surrendering as the bombers approached. Many acts of personal bravery aided the momentum of the attack. With his platoon pinned down by machine gun fire Private James Peter Robertson of the 27th worked towards a heavily wired position, as the platoon kept the gun under rifle and Lewis gun fire. He gradually outflanked the strong-point and when close enough rushed the gun and bayoneted four of the enemy, then turning the gun on the remainder as they fled. Robertson then led his platoon to their objective and as they dug-in he kept down snipers with the enemy machine gun. Later in the day he was twice to rescue wounded men from in front of the Canadian line while under fire, but on the second occasion was tragically killed by a shell. Private Robertson was to be posthumously awarded the V.C. for his gallantry.

By 6:50 a.m. the main defence line west of the village had been broken, and the Canadians fought their way through the rubble with free use of their bayonets, mopping-up any enemy resistance remaining in bunkers or cellars amongst the ruins. The attack soon moved on to the Green Dotted, (intermediate objective) line 200 yards north-east of the church. In the southern end of the village resistance had now virtually ceased, but in the sectors of 31st and 28th Battalions the enemy remained active from pillboxes and strong-points. There was much bitter fighting before they were finally silenced. But even then machine gun fire remained intense from positions further along the Westroosebeke road and from guns on the eastern side of the ridge. The attack to the Green Line, (the final objective) past the five ways cross 400 yards north of the church placed the whole of Passchendaele village in Canadian hands. By 7:35 a.m. the 27th Battalion were on the Green Line and by 7:40 the 28th Battalion had also reached the objective. Once clear of the Ravebeek marsh the 28th had swung its left flank to the north and opened fire upon the enemy positions at Mosselmarkt, in front of the 1st Canadian Battalion fighting along Bellevue spur. In the centre there was more fighting for the 31st Battalion before pillboxes to the north-east of the village and just within the final objective were eventually taken. Whilst the fighting for the village proceeded, on the right of the 27th Battalion, the 26th Battalion of 5th Brigade had established a flank guard from Tiber Copse towards the north-east. The attack was entirely successful and by 6:58 a.m. the 26th was upon its objective along the eastern slope of the ridge towards the Moorslede road. Messages relating the success of the operation and the position of the new line had already been sent back to the 6th Brigade headquarters, but at 10:00 a.m. a 21 Squadron RE8 observed the Canadian flares all along the line, confirming the initial reports.

North of the Ravebeek the attack had also proceeded well. The forward assembly positions had been as close to the enemy outpost line as possible, and the prompt advance of the 1st Brigade, had saved its 1st and 2nd Battalions from the German barrage which came down two minutes after Zero. "A" Company on the right of 1st Battalion immediately came under sniper and machine gun fire from the Graf House blockhouse 200 yards south of Meetcheele, but the position was quickly brought under fire by a Stokes mortar team, which scored several hits, suppressing the fire and driving the garrison out. None of them escaped, and two machine guns were captured. The other three companies met with little opposition towards the first objective, a few of the enemy in organised shell-holes being knocked out. The swampy ground north of the Ravebeek hampered the progress of "A" Company which veered towards the left to avoid it and crowded upon "D" Company. By 6:30 a.m. both leading companies were digging-in on the first objective, and "B" and "C" Companies passed through and advanced towards the second objective near the Mosselmarkt crossroad junction which was reached up to time at 7:40. Near the crossroads a 77 mm field gun in good order with 200 rounds of ammunition was captured. About Mosselmarkt many of the enemy had taken cover in shallow shelters or cellars and had been killed by the barrage. Those that remained with their machine guns in shell-hole gun pits were attacked from the front by 1st Battalion, and hit by enfilade fire from rifles and Lewis guns of the 28th Battalion, which had advanced up the other side of the valley. The enemy soon raised their hands in surrender. From a blockhouse near the road junction the garrison of 4 officers and 50 men emerged and surrendered without a fight. After a 20 minute pause at the first objective, "D" Company moved forward, passed through "B" and "C" now digging-in on the second, and with a support platoon from "B" Company, attacked towards the final objective 150 yards short of Vindictive Crossroads which by 7:45 had been taken. The three other platoons of "B" Company now moved up from the second objective and "B" and "D" began to dig-in and consolidate the new line, in touch with the 28th Battalion on the right and 2nd Battalion on the left.

The left wing of the Canadian Corps attack 1st and 3rd Canadian Brigades - 1st Canadian Division

To the north of the Meetcheele – Mosselmarkt road 2nd Battalion had advanced successfully and pushed the line 800 yards to the north-east across the Goudberg spur. By 6:15 the first objective (the Red Line) was reached, and by 7:30 the battalion was on the second objective (the Brown Line) between Vegetable Farm and the Mosselmarkt road junction. Confirmation of the successful attack on the final objective was received by 9:30 a.m., the Green Line then extending from near Vindictive Crossroads to Valour Farm. The enemy remained active from strong-points just beyond the final objective, sniping with rifle and machine gun as the Canadians dug-in. In the sunken road 100 yards south of Virtue Farm 12 men with a machine gun put up a stiff resistance until a party worked up close enough to dissuade them, and snipers in a hedge on the east side of Venture Farm kept up a harassing fire until routed by rifle grenades. A local counter-attack was attempted by about 25 men with two machine guns who advanced from the west of Virtue Farm, but they were driven off by the Canadian rifles and Lewis guns.

Although by the 5th November, the Royal Naval Division had pushed posts forward to the Paddebeek, the dreadful muddy area east of the stream continued to be bitterly disputed. In front of the Division the enemy as we have seen had clung to Tournant Farm, on slightly higher ground 150 yards east of the stream. Hood Battalion had also taken up position east of the Paddebeek, taking over the posts 250 yards south-east of Tournant Farm, at Source Farm and Vapour Farm where they were in touch with the Canadian left. To the east of Vapour Farm the Canadian 3rd Battalion held the outpost line to Vanity House, but the Germans still clung firmly to the blockhouse at Vine Cottage 200 yards to the south-east, the strong-point sticking into the Canadian left flank, and endangering the main assault on Passchendaele. The 3rd Battalion was now to eradicate this danger by seizing the Vine Cottage blockhouse, thus nipping out the local salient, and linking the Vapour Farm – Vanity House line with Valour Farm, the objective of 2nd Battalion. Behind the 3rd Battalion lay the bogs of the upper Paddebeek at its source in the Woodland Plantation, which lay due west of Vine Cottage and virtually cut-off the 3rd Battalion from the 2nd Battalion.

The attacking force consisted of 10 platoons; "C" Company, "D" Company and 2 platoons of "A" Company, three platoons to carry out the attack, three to be in local support, with the remaining four in reserve. The attack was a very difficult and complicated operation to perform given the obstruction of the impassable Paddebeek bog. The obvious direction to approach Vine House was from the west but the ground conditions made this impossible. The only possibility was to attack with one platoon from Vanity House towards the south-east, while the remainder of the force wheeled to the north to secure the Vanity House – Valour Farm line. The assault force formed up on a line about Vanity House facing east. At Zero hour the northern group advanced a few yards, to shelter beneath the barrage, which was not to lift off the objective until Zero plus 10 minutes. As the barrage at last crept to the east they moved off, the left almost marking time as the right flank wheeled towards the north. The southern group headed south-east towards Vine Cottages. The difficulties of the awful ground and the severity of enemy shelling and machine gun fire made communications near impossible, 3rd Battalion headquarters knowing more of the progress of 1st and 2nd Battalions than they did of their own groups. It was not until later in the day that a message was received confirming that the Vanity House – Valour Farm line was held in touch with 2nd Battalion on the right and the Hood on the left. From the moment the attack began, enemy machine gun fire had been extremely heavy, pinning down the advance, three guns opening fire from Vine Cottage and two from a track just north of the blockhouse. The garrison at Vine Cottage stubbornly resisted the attack but was eventually overwhelmed. As the Canadians worked forward to within 20 yards of the blockhouse the enemy machine gunners attempted to surrender, but the men from Toronto already decimated by the fire were in no mood to take prisoners, and at least 12 of the enemy were killed with the bayonet. During the operation Corporal Colin Fraser Barron of the 3rd Canadian Battalion rushed and knocked out three machine guns, and turned one of the guns on the enemy as they ran off, an act of bravery and determination for which he was to be awarded the V.C. With the difficult manoeuvre on Goudberg spur, carried out in dreadful conditions of mud, the 3rd Battalion had secured the northern flank of the main attack on Passchendaele and in doing so had captured forty prisoners and two heavy and three light machine guns.

Throughout the early morning the enemy shelling had been sporadic, but heavy at times on Bellevue and Goudberg spurs. It had been at its heaviest in support areas and on approaches, where communications especially in 1st Brigade had been seriously disrupted. The German artillery had also engaged in considerable counter-battery fire. At about 11:30 a.m. it shortened its range and began a severe bombardment of the newly won positions, but by this time it was too late. At around 9:00 a.m. it had begun to rain, but the Canadians were already well dug-in to the sandy ridge-top soil which was found to be fairly dry and most suitable for rapid entrenchment. German aircraft, sometimes in flights of up to 9 harassed the consolidating infantry, machine-gunning the new trenches and improved shell-holes, but little damage was done. At 2:50 p.m. it seemed that the enemy had realised the futility of further shelling the positions which they were to have held at all costs, and the bombardment ceased. In front of 1st Battalion three advanced posts were thrown out by "D" Company to a depth of around 30 yards, where Lewis guns were set up, and around 2:00 p.m. a small patrol worked forward to Vindictive Crossroads where they found no trace of the enemy. In their sector just north of the village 31st Battalion were still checking captured bunkers at 3:00 p.m. A low sunken concrete dug-out, which as it had been silent had not been discovered in the morning attack, was found to contain 6 officers and 6 other ranks. Amongst the 6 officers was a Battalion Commander of the *10th Grenadier Guards* and a Bavarian battalion commander, together with their Adjutants. The Bavarian battalion had been under orders to immediately counter-attack Passchendaele, and the disappearance of its C.O. who had gone forward to confer may have accounted for no counter-attack being launched. During the day 8 German officers and 315 other ranks were to pass through the 2nd Division cage, while 1st Division captured 11 officers and 199 other ranks. Information from prisoners indicated that orders had been issued that Passchendaele was to be held at all costs, and that if any ground was lost it was to be retaken immediately by counter-attack. But this had not happened. No serous counter-attacks had developed, although there had been some half-hearted attempts by small local groups during the morning which had been quickly broken by artillery, Lewis gun and rifle fire. A report at about 5:15 p.m. that the enemy had be seen concentrating near Wrath Farm 1,000 yards north-east of Passchendaele resulted in a 45 minute bombardment of the area, and no attack materialised. Around 6:30 p.m. an enemy counter-attack appeared imminent and the S.O.S. went up on the 1st Brigade front, gradually spreading across the Corps front. The artillery opened fire on the S.O.S. lines, heavily for the first five minutes, then slackening and finally ceasing fire at 7:25. There was no counter-attack and from that point on the night quietened.

It had taken a long time, much longer than anyone had initially believed possible, to capture the ruins on the ridge which had been Passchendaele. The suffering experienced since the 31st July in doing so had been unimaginable. This latest action had cost 1st Canadian Division 8 officers killed, 34 officers wounded, and approximately 1.068 other ranks either killed, wounded or missing, and 2nd Canadian Division 14 officers killed, 49 officers wounded, 313 other ranks killed or missing, and 1,154 other ranks wounded. But even these losses could not detract from the sense of pride and achievement felt by the Canadians. In his report of the action written on the 20th November 1917, the Commander of 6th Canadian Brigade, Brigadier -General Ketchen wrote the following: 'I may say knowing all the particulars from start to finish, of what very strenuous efforts had to be made by all ranks to attain the complete success met with, words entirely fail me to do justice to the determination, initiative and gallantry displayed by all ranks, who were well aware of the difficulties of the situation, but met their many hardships and trials with the utmost cheerfulness, outstanding spirit and high courage, which carried them through a memorable day, and once again decisively proved their fighting superiority over the enemy.'[744]
Another interesting summary of the operation of the 6th November was written on the 16th November 1917, not by a Field-Marshal, or a General, or even a Lieutenant -General, but by the

---

[744] Library and Archives of Canada, War diary 6th Canadian Infantry Brigade RG9 Series II-D-3 Vol.4890

Brigade Major of the 5th Canadian Brigade, Major W. Clark Kennedy: 'Passchendaele remains in our hands without any serious attempt of the Germans, so far, to retake it and this victory means that every piece of elevated ground in this war area is now commanded by our guns. Passchendaele also commands Houthulst Forest, which is in the process of being encircled. The capture of Passchendaele and other Ridges is symbolical of much larger strategic conception, for the development whereof their recovery from the enemy is an essential prelude. Their capture is the first and probably the far most difficult step. The worst work is over and the enemy must either recover ground – which he is unlikely to be able to do – or submit to domination which no troops could endure for any length of time. But the measure of our success in Flanders, is not only to be estimated by the value of important positions taken. It is to be found also in the declining strength of the enemy's defences and diminished vigour of his counter attacks. He no longer meets an attack with an immediate counter offensive, and operations since 20th September bear evidence of the gradual decline of German morale and general exhaustion. This is not surprising, considering his long succession of reverses and gigantic efforts to avert defeat by piling division on division. During the last three months, 68 German Divisions have been through the mill in Flanders. Of these, 14 were put in during September. In October, 19 fresh divisions were added. Such was the state of the German reserves that 20 divisions had to be subjected to a second grinding, while two underwent that for a third time. Thus, counting those which re-appeared after having been renovated, our troops in Flanders met and defeated during the last 3 months, 90 German Divisions among the best the German Army can provide.'[745] If this passage had been written by Haig, or the optimistic Charteris, the sentiments expressed would have contained a very similar message. The accuracy or otherwise of the claims of the enemy forces engaged will be examined shortly. More to the point the passage gives an indication that the views of the Commander-in-Chief were also held by others of a much lower rank, who still maintained a positive outlook, whilst at the time having no idea that their sacrifice had further helped the recovery of their hard pressed Ally. It is clear that not all of Haig's Army considered themselves 'tipped into the slough of despond'.[746] The work of the Canadian Corps was far from over, but for the moment the Canadian flag flew over Passchendaele.

The Ninth and Final Step

The shattered, desolate prize had been seized, and the Canadians set about securing what they had won. The 6th Brigade did not sit on its laurels, and by the next day the defences around the village were becoming well established. A forward outpost line of isolated sections of trench, with 4 to 10 men in each provided the first screen. An almost continuous trench formed the front line, situated in a good position, in touch on both flanks, and giving an excellent field of fire. A support line had been started but was not yet a continuous trench, and a main line trench was being dug just in rear. A reserve position was also being established in dry ground, consisting of short sections of trench, echeloned in depth and protected from enemy fire by the reverse slope of the ridge. From the front line good observation was possible over the German rear areas to the east, and along the ridge top towards Westroosebeke. The state of the ground varied greatly, some areas being good for consolidation while others were near impassable. The remaining priorities were to wire the whole position, and make the front and support trench lines continuous.

Evacuation of the wounded from the battlefield was the usual deplorable struggle. The Regimental Aid Posts, mostly situated in old blockhouses had themselves inevitably been targets for the enemy artillery, but had done the very best they could before passing casualties down the line. Many casualties survived the initial trauma of injury, only to be blown to pieces along with their carrying party on the way out. The same fate befell many enemy prisoners, some being pressed into service as bearers, to be subsequently annihilated by their own

---

[745] Library and Archives of Canada, War diary 5th Canadian Infantry Brigade RG9 Series III-D-3 Vol.4885
[746] John Keegan (1998) *The First World War* London: Hutchinson p395

artillery as they streamed down off the ridges. Once off the higher ground there was no other route for the stretcher bearers but to cross the hundreds of yards of mud before reaching the flimsy and often broken duckboard tracks, which eventually led to the muddy shattered roads, on the long, exhausting journey back towards Ypres.[747]

Haig was extremely pleased with the operation, but his initial information of there being only a small loss of "under 700 men" proved woefully short of the mark. At this moment of muted triumph the Italian situation intervened to spoil his reverie. Before his great Flanders operation was completed, General Plumer, the chief architect of the plans which had brought about the downfall of the vaunted German in-depth defence system, was ordered to Italy. Haig mused ruefully in his diary on the 7th November: 'Was ever an Army Commander and his Staff sent off to another theatre of war in the middle of a battle?'[748] Perhaps 'middle' was stretching the point, but the battle was certainly still in progress. Haig immediately replaced Second Army H.Q. with Fourth Army Staff under General Sir Henry Rawlinson, and after a final meeting with Haig on the 10th, Plumer duly left for Italy.

On the 7th November Currie gave the order for the Canadian Corps to attack again on the 10th November, with the object of pushing the front line further forward to the north of the village, to a point 600 yards north of Vindictive Crossroads, and along the line of the 45 metre contour on the eastern slope of the ridge. The left of the objective would encompass the high point at Hill 52. The 1st Canadian Division would carry out the attack, with its 2nd Brigade using the 7th (1st British Columbia), and 8th (90th Rifles) Battalions. The 5th (Western Cavalry) Battalion would be in support, with the 10th (Alberta) Battalion in reserve, and the 3rd Canadian Brigade would be in Divisional reserve. The right flank was to be protected by the 2nd Canadian Division, with the 4th Brigade using the 20th (Central Ontario) Battalion.

To the left of 1st Canadian Division in the II Corps sector, the 1st British Division would attack with its 3rd British Brigade, using the 1st South Wales Borderers and the 2nd Royal Munster Fusiliers, with the 1st Gloucestershire Regiment in support. The 3rd British Brigade was to attack in a north-north-easterly direction from the much disputed Valour Farm – Source Farm line, to a depth of about 800 yards, on to a small spur projecting west from the main ridge on which sat the blockhouses of Void Farm and Veal Cottage. The II Corps protective barrage would of necessity be fired in enfilade from the west, the guns, many of which were still back near the Langemarck – Zonnebeke road, having to traverse towards the north in front of the 3rd Brigade advance rather than lengthening their range. From the Canadian Corps boundary on the right to the II Corps boundary on the left presented a dangerously short length of attack front of around 2,000 yards, against which the enemy could concentrate the whole of his extensive artillery.

The Canadian and British artillery continued with its nightly harassing shoots by guns of all calibres. The heavy guns were active shelling blockhouses, ruined farms, and searching woods and rear areas for enemy troop concentrations. Army barrages were fired each morning at 5:00 a.m. which brought a prompt retaliation from the enemy, usually starting on the Canadian forward areas then lifting towards approaches, rear areas and batteries. Between 10:00 and 11:00 a.m. on the 9th, under the directing eye of an enemy reconnaissance aircraft, their batteries pounded the vicinities of Gallipoli and Kansas cross in an attempt to disrupt

---

[747] On the right flank of 1st Canadian Division the wounded recovered from the battlefield were carried to the Regimental Aid Post at Waterloo 2,500 yards from Mosselmarkt. After first aid they were transferred, by another 3,000 yard carry to the Somme Advanced Dressing Station, and from there by motor ambulance to Bridge House on the Steenbeek. From Bridge House they were transferred by light gauge railway to Culloden sidings at Vlamertinghe, and then to the Main Dressing Station at Vlamertinghe Mill. If trains were not available, the transfer from Bridge House was completed by motor ambulance direct to Vlamertinghe. From the left flank of 1st Canadian Division the route was initially via Kronprinze Farm, 2,000 yards back from Vanity House, and across some of the worst ground imaginable through the upper Paddebeek bogs, and thence to Bridge House.
[748] Douglas Haig. Diaries and Letters p339

movement and communication with the front lines. Hostile shellfire on and around Passchendaele was practically continuous, the rubble mound of the church being an excellent registration point. German aircraft were also very active, bombing forward and rear positions and batteries, and on occasions machine-gunning the Canadian trenches. On the 9th the weather became squally, south-west winds and occasional showers punctuating fair, bright intervals.

The forces with the dubious honour of carrying out what was to become the last major attack of the whole offensive began to move into position about Passchendaele, and although the rain was not heavy, there was an intermittent drizzle. On the night of the 8th/9th November 4th Canadian Brigade relieved 5th Canadian Brigade in the 2nd Canadian Division sector. By 4:50 a.m. on the 9th the relief was complete with the 18th and 19th Battalions holding the front line exclusive of the attack front. The 20th Battalion, to carry out the attack, moved into position by midnight with 2 companies in the outpost line 250 yards north of the five ways cross at the northern end of the village, and two companies in support. The 21st Battalion were held in reserve at Seine.

In the 1st Canadian Division sector, the attack battalions of the 2nd Brigade began to assemble in the line in front of Vindictive Crossroads and just east of Valour Farm. The 7th Battalion Battle Headquarters was established in a pillbox at Mosselmarkt 400 yards behind the front line by 9:00 a.m. on the 9th. The enemy artillery were obviously well aware by the level of troop movements and the number of practice barrages fired, that the attack was about to be renewed, and swept the forward Canadian positions throughout the afternoon, eventually relenting just after dark. At around 7:00 p.m. the 7th Battalion began moving to its assembly positions for the attack, and by 11:30 p.m. the movement was complete. The 8th Battalion had also moved its Battle Headquarters to Mosselmarkt by 8:00 a.m. on the 9th. During the afternoon the battalion was heavily shelled in its support and reserve trenches and before nightfall at least 25% of the men had been buried in the soft sandy soil and had to be dug out, sustaining casualties of 5 officers and 60 other ranks. After dark the 5th and 10th Battalions also moved up into their support and reserve positions and by 10:30 p.m. were well dug-in.

The 1st British Division prepared to take its place in the line to the left of the Canadians. At 5:50 p.m. on the 9th, the 1st South Wales Borderers left Irish Farm and began its 10,000 yard march up along No.6 Track, past Spriet Farm, Kansas Cross and over Bellevue, towards the line at Valour Farm on Goudberg spur. There were few casualties on the march up, but once in position accurate hostile shelling knocked out all but 5 men of one platoon of "A" Company, and "B" Company also sustained 17 casualties. Forward Battle Headquarters were established at Valour Farm.[749] The 2nd Royal Munster Fusiliers left Irish Farm around 7:20 p.m., arriving at its position in the line close to Source Farm, where battalion headquarters were established at 2:00 a.m. Enemy shell-fire had accounted for 5 casualties en route. By 4:15 the battalion was formed up on its tapes facing north-northeast.

The attack of Second Army 6:05 a.m. the 10th November

All possible preparations for the forthcoming attack had now been made and the long wait for the 6:05 Zero Hour began. The enemy had been making his own arrangements and more guns had been moved into position east of the ridge, batteries from eleven groups being in position to unleash a storm of fire into the small Passchendaele salient. But the continuous and sometimes intense German barrages had failed to prevent the assembly, although the night was still punctuated with sporadic shellfire. The 20th Canadian Battalion sent out patrols to a depth of 300 yards to check the flanks of the attack, but found no trace of the enemy and withdrew before Zero Hour. At around 3:00 a.m. the tension was heightened as the nervous German artillery dropped a heavy barrage of '4.2's' and '5.9's' which fell about 50 yards behind the assembled waves, causing few casualties but succeeding in cutting off the front lines from

---

[749] Disputed by 8th Canadian Battalion account which states that as no suitable accommodation was available in 1st South Wales Borderers sector, and agreement was reached with the Canadians for the battalion to use a pillbox just forward of the Meetcheele road junction.

battalion headquarters. The hostile shelling finally quietened at around 5:00 a.m., picking up again at 5:30 with sporadic shelling just in rear of the Vapour Farm - Source Farm assembly line but causing little damage. At 6:05 prompt the British barrage came down 150 yards in front of the jump-off tapes, where it stood for 3 minutes. As the barrage fell the tension was released, as Canadians and British climbed stiffly from trench or shell-hole, and when it finally lifted advanced towards the enemy.

Facing the Canadians and British from south to north were the *208th R.I.R.* of *44th Division*, which had relieved the *11th Division* on the night of the 8th / 9th November, the *140th Infantry Regiment*, the *14th Infantry Regiment* and the *49th Infantry Regiment*, all of *4th Division*.

The extension of the Passchendaele perimeter

The Canadian Corps and the British II Corps

The 2nd Canadian Division   4th Canadian Brigade[750]
The 1st Canadian Division   2nd Canadian Brigade[751]
The 1st British Division   3rd Infantry Brigade[752]

Shortly after Zero the rain began to fall heavily to add its misery to the proceedings. At 6:08 in the 2nd Canadian Division sector, the three leading companies of the 20th Battalion,[753] "1" on the right, "3" in the centre and "2" on the left moved forward and followed up closely behind the excellent barrage, while "4" Company in support took over the jumping-off line. Above the German lines flares arced into the dark rainy sky to burst into points of red and white brilliance. Within 3 minutes the enemy artillery opened fire in retaliation, but on the ground their infantry were nowhere to be seen. By 7:10 a.m. all objectives had been seized and consolidation began in good ground which was relatively dry beneath the surface, while an outpost line was established 150 yards forward. On the battalion left flank, the southern end of Venison Trench, 500 yards east of Vindictive Crossroads had been entered with no opposition. From the air the Germans were more aggressive their aircraft machine-gunning the new line, but the nearest enemy infantry that could be seen to the east of Venison Trench were at least 1,000 yards away. Either the 20th Battalion had gone too far forward or their artillery was falling short, as the barrage seemed dangerously close. A message was sent back to increase the range by 300 yards.

---

[750] National Archives, War Diary 4th Can Brigade WO95/3812
[751] National Archives, War Diary 2nd Can Brigade WO95/3765
[752] National Archives, War Diary 3rd Infantry Brigade WO95/1276
[753] National Archives, War Diary 20th Can Battalion WO95/3817

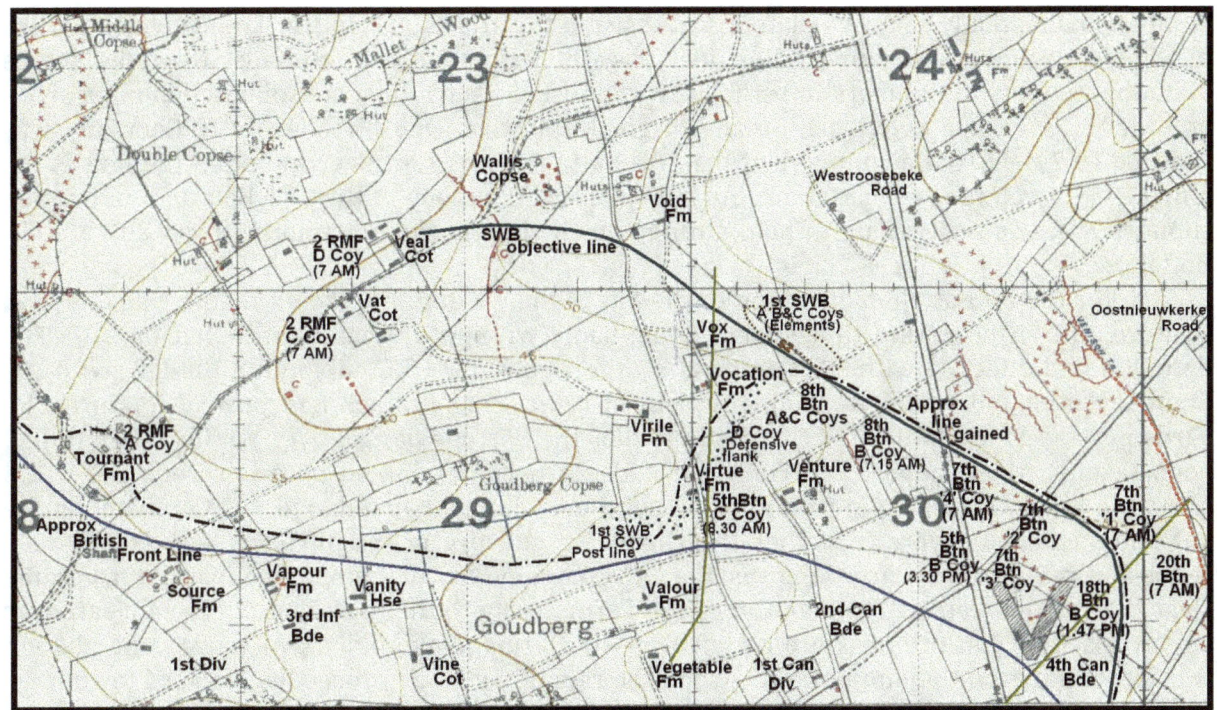

The northern extension of the Passchendaele perimeter (until 4.00 PM)

To the left of 20th Battalion, in 1st Canadian Division sector, the 7th Battalion attacked with "1" Company on the right, "4" on the left, with "3" following in support, while "2" remained in the assembly position.[754] Light opposition was encountered in taking Vindictive Crossroads, but on advancing further towards the objective enemy resistance stiffened, and heavy rifle and machine gun fire (mainly from Venison Trench) for the final 200 yards caused many casualties. The enemy retaliatory barrage at first landed mainly behind the assembly areas causing little damage, but it shortened its range and was now landing amongst the attack waves and inflicting further casualties. Indirect machine gun fire from German barrage guns also swept the advance. Due to the fire from Venison Trench it was found very difficult to consolidate and some on the right of "1" Company entered the southern end of the trench with the 20th Battalion, but sniping and machine gun fire from the centre and left sections of the trench still raked the left of "1" Company and "4" Company as they advanced towards their objectives, drastically thinning their ranks. A successful attack was made by the remainder of "1" Company on the central section of the trench, where 20 prisoners were taken, and touch was made with the 20th Battalion moving up the trench from the south. Two machine guns firing from outside a pillbox situated in the trench where it crossed the Oostnieuwkerke road, opened fire. One gun fired down the trench while the other raked "4" Company as it attempted to reach its objective. The enemy position was brought under Lewis gun fire, suppressing the hostile fire sufficiently for the pillbox to be rushed and seized. Two more machine guns were captured inside the bunker and another 18 prisoners taken. "1" Company also found themselves in front of the barrage, and the artillery was requested to lift the range to east of Venison Trench. Heavy machine gun fire in enfilade then raked the party at the pillbox, coming from an enemy strong-point in the northern end of the trench, 150 yards north of the Oostnieuwkerke road. Too short of men to attack the strong-point, the remnants of "1" Company fell-back down the trench to the south to the original objective, after first destroying the enemy machine guns which could not be taken back. It was necessary to crawl along the muddy trench to avoid being hit as the machine gun fire whistled close overhead. "4" Company meanwhile had reached its objective, but in doing so had lost all its officers and most N.C.O's to the machine gun fire. It now attempted to dig-in. Two platoons from "2" Company were sent up to fill the gap between the decimated "1" and "4" Companies. "3"

---

[754] National Archives, War Diary 7th Can Battalion WO95/3768

Company had already sent two platoons to assist in the attack on Venison Trench whilst a third platoon consolidated a support line just easy of Vindictive Cross Roads. Now the whole battalion, too few in numbers to establish a connected trench line, consolidated along a shell-hole line, 2 men per hole, back on the original objective. One platoon of "1" Company was reduced to 7 men, and a company of the 20th Battalion was sent over to stiffen the line at the junction between the two battalions. At 1:47 p.m. "B" Company of the 18th Battalion in brigade support was also ordered up to help strengthen the line at the junction between 20th and 7th Battalions.[755]

For the 8th Battalion attacking to the left of the 7th Battalion, towards the ridge beyond Venture and Virtue Farms, things were going badly wrong, especially on the left flank.[756] The battalion had attacked with "B" Company on the right and "C" Company on the left, with "D" Company in support and "A" Company held in reserve. The attack had pushed forward 250 yards north-east of Vindictive Crossroads, and as the barrage passed over Venture Farm it had been taken without opposition. The farm had not been reinforced with concrete, but it did contain 4 serviceable 77 mm field guns which the enemy had abandoned. "C" Company on the left had sustained severe casualties from machine gun fire in the advance, and at 7:00 a.m. requested reinforcement from the reserve "A" Company. As "A" Company advanced it became clear that the bunkers at Virile and Vocation Farms away to their left had not been cleared, as enemy machine gun fire tore into its left flank. With this flank obviously exposed one platoon was left to garrison the jump-off line, while the remaining three proceeded forward to support "C" Company. "B" Company was by 7:15 on its objectives at all points and was in touch with 7th Battalion on the right and "C" Company on the left, but had sustained serious casualties from machine gun and shellfire in the advance. The attack of "C" Company meanwhile had been turned into a shambles through no fault of its own, as both it and the 3 platoons of "A" which had come up in support, were mown down by machine gun fire from their left flank and rear. The reason for the enfilade fire soon became clear.

The 1st British Division was in the line for the first time in the Passchendaele fighting, and had been out of a front line situation for some time. The 1st South Wales Borderers and the 2nd Royal Munster Fusiliers were to carry out a difficult attack in a north-north-easterly direction, across unfamiliar and featureless ground, with their artillery supporting them in enfilade.[757] They were responsible for protecting the left flank of the Canadian Corps. The 1st South Wales Borderers had formed up about Valour Farm, with "A" Company and one platoon of "C" Company on the right, "B" Company on the left. "C" Company were in support and "D" Company in reserve. It is probable that they assembled about 60 yards forward of their jump-off line, or it is possible that their barrage fell short. Whatever the reason, at 6:05 the front wave advanced and within 30 yards walked into their own barrage sustaining severe casualties including 4 officers. To the right the Canadian barrage rolled forward in a dense wave, and the leading Welsh companies veered right towards the Canadians, and the safety of the regular advancing curtain of exploding shells. This manoeuvre had the effect of crowding the left "C" Company of the Canadian 8th Battalion forcing them to the right and off their objective. Some of the Borderers got as far as 600 yards forward to the 52 metre ring contour on top of the ridge, which was part of the 8th Battalion objective. Two platoons of "D" support Company of the 8th had correctly followed "C" Company forward and had reached a line 150 yards east of Vocation Farm, and were in touch with "B" Company on the right, but found its flank completely exposed, as there were no troops to the left where the South Wales Borderers should have been. The

---

[755] National Archives, War Diary 18th Can Battalion WO95/3814
[756] National Archives, War Diary 8th Can Battalion WO95/3769
[757] National Archives, War Diary 1st South Wales Borderers WO95/1280, The 1st Division had undergone considerable training at the high security Clipon Camp near Dunkirk in preparation to undertake the seaborne landings east of Nieuport, which had been finally called off on the 15th October. Regarding the night of the 8th of November, an officer of the 1st South Wales Borderers of 3rd Brigade wrote: 'Rather a disturbing night at Irish Farm after being behind the line for so long. Heavy guns are apt to keep one awake'…

situation became serious as "D" Company were soon struck by the same punishing machine gun fire from Vocation and Vox Farms, which had already smitten "C" and "A" Companies. At 7:00 a.m. the remnants of the left platoons of "C" Company of the 8th Battalion, began falling-back from the ridge, crowded off their objective and with their left flank totally exposed. Realising the situation, with troops streaming back through his position, Lieutenant Smith commanding "D" Company dug-in under fire, on a line east of Vocation Farm and threw back a flank to cover the 500 yard gap back to the South Wales Borderers jump-off line on his left.

The forward elements of the South Wales Borderers had meanwhile continued to advance beyond the 52 metre ring contour, a few hundred yards beyond the final Canadian objective, well beyond the top of the main ridge. They were still moving at Zero plus 59 minutes when the creeping barrage stopped on the defence line, and they again walked into friendly shell-fire. Daylight had made it clear that they were not on their objective, and being under the fire of their own guns, some of the Borderers fell-back through the 8th Canadian Battalion, and some even through the 7th Canadian Battalion about Vindictive Crossroads. The objective line, Hill 52 – Void Farm – Veal Cottage was therefore left unoccupied.

The three platoons of the 8th Battalion reserve "A" Company had already been sent forward to reinforce "C" Company, but the line was still precariously weak. At 8:30 a.m. the Officer Commanding 8th Battalion ordered forward "C" Company of the 5th Battalion from brigade support to establish a defensive flank on the left.[758] The situation of the 8th Battalion line then was: "B" Company on the right, which had reached its objectives and had established a consolidated position. "C" Company on the left had been decimated by the machine guns at Vocation and Vox Farms, had lost all its officers and was reduced to 40 men, but the survivors were dug-in on the left of "B" Company, about 50 yards in rear of the right section of its objective. "D" Company in support had a line of posts from the left of "C" Company, to a point about 150 yards east of Vocation Farm. One platoon of "A" Company from reserve was garrisoning the Venture Farm locality, with the remainder of the company reinforcing the front line and the left flank. "C" Company of the 5th Canadian Battalion was moving up to establish a left flank between Venture, Vocation and Virtue Farms, on the junction at the left of the Canadian Corps and the right of II British Corps. This situation remained largely the same until about 2:00 p.m.

The account of the action from the perspective of the 1st South Wales Borderers is different in detail. But for certain the battalion had veered right and followed the Canadian barrage. The Borderers barrage had come down only 30 yards in front of the assembly positions and on moving forward they had soon been amongst it, suffering casualties, and confusion which the few officers remaining found impossible to correct. The attack, rather than advancing north-northeast towards Void Farm swung drastically to the right towards Venture Farm and the Canadians, leaving only a few men west of the Venture Farm – Vocation Farm road. The left battalion boundary between the Borderers and the Munster should have been along a line from Goudberg Copse to a point 100 yards west of Mallet Copse, and there was now a gap of at least 600 yards between the two British battalions. At around 7:00 as parties of the Borderers approached within 100 yards of Vocation Farm the enemy artillery had shortened its range and came down very heavily amongst the Welshmen. There was also heavy enemy machine gun and sniper fire from Virile and Vox Farms and apparently from a trench running between them, but a few men succeeded in establishing a Lewis gun post just south of Vocation Farm. The reserve "D" Company moved up and established a defence line with Lewis gun posts just south of Virtue Farm. In the advance the ground between Vocation and Virile Farms had not been cleared, but Venture and Virtue Farms were reported as not occupied by the enemy.[759] Three hundred yards to the north-east elements of "A", "B", and "C" Companies had continued to the 52 metre ring contour on top of the main ridge where they had dug-in, (600 yards to the right of where they should have been), in touch with Canadians on their right. At 7:15 a.m. an enemy counter-attack

---

[758] National Archives, War Diary 5th Can Battalion WO95/3767
[759] Venture Farm had by this time been occupied by the 8th Canadian Battalion and 4 77 mm field guns captured.

developed from the direction of Mallet Copse, heading south towards Goudberg Copse and Vox Farm and also upon the Canadian front.[760] The counter-attack was disrupted by the Lewis guns of "D" Company, and by the Lewis gun team at the post near Vocation Farm, although some of the enemy worked forward into the trench near Virile Farm and into Goudberg Copse, (250 yards from the start line). The Germans were also reported to have forced back the Canadian left. Hostile artillery remained constant throughout the morning, directed onto the Borderers positions by enemy aircraft which at times also machine-gunned their posts.

To the left of the South Wales Borderers the 2nd Royal Munster Fusiliers had got away well at 6:05 behind a good barrage, with "A" Company on the left opposite the ruin of Tournant Farm, "D" Company on the right, and "B" and "C" Companies in support.[761] Although it was raining, short range visibility was reasonable and no difficulty was experienced either in keeping direction, or moving across the wet slippery ground. Around 15 minutes after Zero the enemy artillery shortened its range by 300 to 400 yards and a heavy barrage fell about Tournant Farm, and remained constant throughout the morning. Notwithstanding the barrage, and a hail of sniper fire which appeared to come from many directions, "A" Company succeeded in capturing Tournant Farm, and 2 bunkers 150 yards to the north-west, but machine gun fire from another bunker 150 yards to the north of the farm checked the advance. On the right "D" and "C" Companies had followed the barrage forward to the objective line which they took up to schedule, and after stiff fighting captured the blockhouses at Vat and Veal Cottages. Many enemy prisoners were sent to the rear, but the hostile sniping, which proved impossible to suppress continued, and casualties steadily rose as rifles and Lewis guns became inoperative, their actions clogged with mud. At around 7:15 the same German counter-attack seen by the Borderers was also observed by the Munsters, estimated at battalion strength, approaching over the ridge from the direction of Valuation Houses, and directed towards the largely unoccupied 600 yard gap in the line between Void Farm and Veal Cottages where the Borderers should have been. Being armed with largely inoperative weapons, an urgent S.O.S. was fired by the Munsters at Vat Cottages, soon repeated by the Battalion Commander from Tournant Farm. The enemy counter-attack was supported by a barrage, and 3 enemy observation aircraft were seen to be operating over the lines, after which shell-fire was directed at the Munsters positions. The S.O.S. appeared to have gone unnoticed as no protective barrage was fired, and as no British contact aircraft were operating at the time no assistance came from the air. The positions held at Veal and Vat Cottages were now most precarious. Having few operative weapons with which to fight, threatened with encirclement by the counter-attack, and with casualties especially of officers and N.C.O's increasing alarmingly, the Munsters fell-back towards the Vapour Farm – Source Farm start line. On the left a small party rallied and succeeded in retaking Tournant Farm.

Between noon and 1:00 p.m. the enemy again infiltrated into the trench between Vox and Virile Farms, in front of the South Wales Borderers, and at 1:30 with the Germans working round to the left rear, the post at Vocation Farm was withdrawn. This infiltration was also observed by the Officer Commanding "C" Company of the 5th Canadian Battalion, who reported to the 8th Battalion that about 100 of the enemy were assembling about Virtue Farm and appeared intent on launching a counter-attack. At the same time in 7th Battalion sector the enemy were seen to be assembling on both sides of the Oostnieuwkerke road north of Vindictive Crossroads and in Venison Trench. At 2:30 a general counter-attack commenced and considerable numbers of the enemy were seen coming over the crest of the ridge at 52 Metre Hill. The S.O.S. was fired but there was no immediate response from the artillery. A brigade observation post at Korek spotted the flare signals and informed the artillery by telephone. The subsequent barrage broke the enemy counter-attack. Both at noon and at 2:30 the artillery had fired protective barrages along the whole front in response to S.O.S. calls which effectively broke up enemy counter-attacks, and forced them to retire in apparent disorder.

---

[760] There is no mention of this counter attack in the accounts of either the 8th, 7th, or 5th Canadian Battalions, but it is mentioned by both battalions of 1st British Division.
[761] National Archives, War Diary 2nd Royal Munster Fusiliers WO95/1279

Being very anxious about his exposed left flank the O.C. 8th Battalion ordered 5th Battalion to send up its "B" Company to occupy the Canadian jump-off line but not to be used unless the Germans threatened the jump-off line of the South Wales Borderers to the left, which still appeared not to be garrisoned. Before moving up "B" Company had already been reduced to 1 officer and 20 other ranks. As the situation in 7th Battalion sector at Vindictive Crossroads was considered even more precarious, at 3:30 p.m. the remnants of "B" Company were moved 400 yards east and dug-in 80 yards in rear of the 7th Battalion front line.

So far the day had been enormously costly and exhausting for all battalions involved. At 4:00 p.m. the survivors of the South Wales Borderers established a defence line between Venture and Valour Farms. When the S.O.S. was fired at 2:00 p.m. the Officer Commanding 10th Canadian Battalion in 2nd Brigade reserve had ordered the battalion to be at readiness to move.[762] It was soon realised that the 5th Battalion from support was already fully engaged, and "A" Company of the 10th was ordered forward to take up the support position. They were soon moved up to the left of 8th Battalion near Venture Farm to reinforce the weak left flank. A major misunderstanding now occurred as the 8th Battalion, believing "A" Company to be their relief, began to move out of the line. The front line from a point 250 yards north of Vindictive Crossroads to just south of Vocation Farm was now thinly held only by "A" Company of 10th Battalion. This was not the intention but little could be done as the 8th Battalion were in a state of total exhaustion, and three support companies of 5th Battalion were already holding the line about Venture Farm, with one company supporting 7th Battalion at Vindictive Crossroads. At around 6:30 p.m. it was agreed between the battalion commanders that, although it was not in the orders, 10th Battalion would take over the whole front from 7th and 8th Battalions, "B", "C" and "D" Companies relieving 7th Battalion, which would for the moment remain in support of the right flank. The 5th Battalion would hold the left flank and support the centre. "B", "C", and "D" Companies of the 10th then took over the front line about 150 yards east of the Passchendaele – Westroosebeke road, 250 yards either side of Vindictive Crossroads. The Officer Commanding "C" Company reported that he was unhappy with the position of the line, believing it short of the objective. The Battalion Commander agreed with this view and the line was pushed out to 300 yards beyond the road. The 10th Battalion now held 1,250 yards of the front line.

At about 7:00 p.m. in 1st British Division sector, a company of the 1st Gloucestershire Regiment moved up to the Valour Farm Source Farm line,[763] "C" and "D" Companies to support the Munster on the left and "A" and "B" Companies occupying the line Vine Cottage, Vanity Farm, Vapour Farm in support of the Borderers on the right. Touch was at last gained with the Canadians on the right at Valour Farm, and the line was back virtually where it had been after the fighting on the 6th November. At 10 p.m. the 1st Loyal North Lancs of 2nd Brigade relieved the decimated Munster, which by 4:00 a.m. on the 11th November was back at Irish Farm its ranks emptied by casualties of 13 officers and about 400 men. The Loyals also relieved the South Wales Borderers on the night of the 11th / 12th, the Welsh battalion having sustained casualties of 10 officers and 372 other ranks. They were not to have the opportunity to put the hard learnt lessons of this unforgiving battlefield into practice.

Between 7:00 a.m. and 6:00 p.m. there had been 6.3mm of rain. There had been not a sign of the sun all day and a chill wind had been blowing from the west-north-west at about 13 miles an hour. By the time the 8th Canadian Battalion came out of the line, it was reduced to 150 totally exhausted, shocked and mud-caked men, with no serviceable Lewis guns and with mud-choked rifles. At the forward Regimental Aid Post, which had been moved up to Meetcheele, three men died of exhaustion and on the march out two men drowned in the Ravebeek, too tired to get across the swollen stream. On marching out on the 11th November the 8th (90th Rifles) Battalion strength was; "A" Company 63, "B" Company 56, "C" Company 59, "D" Company 35, and "F" Company 30. The total casualties for the battalion were 19 officers and 393 other ranks. The 7th (British Columbia) Battalion had found it impossible to clear the wounded from the Regimental Aid Post during the 10th due to the exceptionally heavy shell-fire, with the result that

---

[762] National Archives, War Diary 10th Can Battalion WO95/3770
[763] National Archives, War Diary 1st Gloucester WO95/1279

the post remained crowded with stretcher cases during the night. A special brigade party of 200 men worked through the 11th and by 8:00 p.m. all the wounded had been carried out. Many of the dead remained unburied, the shell-fire and exhaustion preventing the burial parties providing even this last act of dignity, and for those few who were buried there was no way of marking their hastily dug graves. The 7th Battalion was eventually relieved after dark on the 11th, the operation being complete by 9:00 p.m. In the days fighting the battalion had suffered total casualties of 14 officers and 362 other ranks. On the evening of the 11th the 5th (Western Cavalry) Battalion was relieved and marched out having sustained casualties of 28 officers and 313 other ranks. Also on the evening of the 11th, the 10th Battalion was relieved in the front line and marched out having sustained total casualties of 4 officers and 150 other ranks. In 2nd Canadian Division the 20th (Central Ontario) Battalion was relieved on the 11th November and marched back to Seine, having sustained casualties of 9 officers and 176 other ranks.

What the enemy losses were on the 10th November was not known. It was known however that 506 prisoners had been taken, and 6 field guns, 2 heavy trench mortars, 1 light trench mortar and 20 machine guns had been captured.

So ended the last major engagement of the Northern Offensive, which was soon to become known to the world as the Battle of Passchendaele. The professionalism, discipline, and fighting capabilities of the Canadian Corps had been proven once more. In the final stages of the great Flanders campaign they had been in the vanguard of the attacks to seize the high ground, part of which had been the naïve target of the first day back on the 31st July. They had overcome hardships and achieved success in conditions in which many would have just sat and wept. The cost had been extraordinarily high. Between the 26th October and the 11th November the Canadian Corps had sustained total casualties of 12,403, of which 4,047 had been killed. Only 2 officers and 20 other ranks had been taken prisoner.

Total Canadian Casualties 26th October to 11th November

	Officers	Other Ranks
1st Canadian Division	116	2870
2nd Canadian Division	113	2849
3rd Canadian Division	162	3369
4th Canadian Division	114	2836
Canadian Corps Troops	16	479

The Offensive comes to an end

Haig expressed himself pleased with the day's operation, recognising the failure of 1st Division but satisfied with the improvement in the tactical position, which the Canadian Corps in reaching its objectives had achieved. But the position on the ridge formed a dangerously exposed salient 4,000 yards wide across the neck between Broodseinde and the Paddebeek, and 2,500 yards deep to the furthest point of the advance just east of Vindictive Crossroads. This had not been in the plan even in its much revised and curtailed form. It had been hoped that the ridge as far north as Westroosebeke would be captured, threatening Houthulst Forest, but that was not to be. The supply arteries across the devastated wasteland between Ypres and the Passchendaele ridge remained choked with mud, derelict vehicles, and the carcases of dead horses and mules, and were continuously shattered by shell-fire. There was no reason why this would soon change. The German artillery had not been dominated as Haig had always hoped but was stronger than ever, and a perpetual threat to both communications and the troops holding the precarious narrow salient on the ridge.

Events rather than planning now conspired to bring the offensive to a close, something that to this point Haig had considered undesirable, and the War Cabinet had never felt quite sure enough of themselves to do. Winter was close, and although the ground on top of the ridge was reasonable, the approaches towards Westroosebeke up the shallow valleys east of Poelcappelle were near impassable. The Battle of Cambrai was only 10 days away, creating a natural pressure on the limited resources of artillery and infantry. Five Divisions with guns and aircraft were on their way to Italy. The four divisions of Fourth Army, held on the coast for the stillborn landings operation, were, on agreement between the British Government and the French soon to take up positions along 40 miles of the French front line south of the Somme. On the 10th November, while the bitter fighting was in progress around Passchendaele, Haig met with Robertson at Cassel, with Kiggell, Butler, Davidson, Plumer and Harington also present. Haig remained of the opinion that a renewal of the Flanders offensive in the spring was the best policy, and once more emphasised the importance of the Belgian coast to Great Britain. Robertson briefed the assembly on the Italian situation, and stated that the Government had decided that saving Italy, subsequent to the disaster at Caporetto, was to be the priority and another 3 or 4 British divisions may yet have to be sent, with an equal number of French, bringing the total to nearly 20. Robertson asked for Haig's views on the subject in writing. Haig questioned quite reasonably whether sending even 20 divisions would save the Italians from disaster, pointing out that the loss of 20 divisions to the Western Front might lead to the loss of the War. With the German lines of communication overstretched, and unable to press their pursuit, actions taken meanwhile by the Italians had already saved them from disaster.

In a few weeks Haig's optimistic hopes of a renewed offensive were to look very different, as the Germans moved further divisions from east to west, while some his own divisions were shifted to other theatres, and an inadequate number of drafts were sent to France to restore those that remained. On the 14th December G.H.Q. was to issue a 7 page: 'Memorandum on defensive measures. The general situation on the Russian and Italian fronts may enable the enemy to release a considerable number of effectives both as formed units and as reinforcements to the Western Front. At the same time the condition of our own man power and the paucity of reinforcements which we are likely to receive during the next few months will make it impossible for our units to be brought up to establishment. In consequence the British Army in France will probably have to adopt a defensive attitude for some time to come and be prepared to meet a strong and sustained hostile offensive, adequately supported by artillery. At the same time we must consider the possibility of having to assume the offensive at some point, as the surest means of assisting either the French, should the weight of the enemies blow fall on them, or some other portion of our line.' [764]

But for the present no direction had yet been given by Haig to Corps or Army Staffs to indicate the end of the offensive, and planning for further attacks continued. On the 9th November II Corps artillery headquarters, recognising the inadequacies of many of their battery positions which were still west of the Langemarck – Zonnebeke road, had asked for a 10 day pause before resuming the attack. Sir Henry Rawlinson had taken over command of Second Army from Plumer on the 9th November, and on the 14th November the Fifth Army front also passed to Rawlinson's command, Fifth Army headquarters being withdrawn into G.H.Q. Reserve.[765] On the 19th November Haig met with Rawlinson to discuss the future of operations around Passchendaele. Rawlinson advocated extending the front northwards from Passchendaele, but did not wish to take Westroosebeke, undoubtedly recognising the difficulties of attempting another attack from the west across the terrible ground. Haig suggested night

---

[764] National Archives, G.H.Q. memorandum 14th December issued with OAD291/29 WO158/311. OAD 291/29 was specifically issued as a guide to the defensive organisation for the Passchendaele salient, which it was recognised was impossible to hold if attacked in force.

[765] Rawlinson commanded Second Army from the 9th November to the 19th December. Second Army was designated Fourth Army on the 20th December.

attacks by small units, as nothing of that nature had been attempted at the Ypres battle front, seemingly unaware of the activities of the Royal Naval Division. Rawlinson was directed to work out his plans but not to give effect to them until the results of the next day's attack at Cambrai were known, when Haig would decide on future operations. The next day, the 20th November, Haig took the decision to finally close down the Flanders Operation.

Robert Alan Perry
Essex Villa
Langemark
15-12-2006

Chapter Ten

The Ragged Sword

In the Shadow of Passchendaele

On the 20th November 1917 the Third Army under General Byng attacked at Cambrai. The show had moved on, and instantly the limelight turned away from Ypres and its wretched, tortured Salient. At the time there was neither the opportunity nor the necessity to attempt a post-mortem to establish the success or otherwise of the Flanders Offensive. The Battle was over but the War went on. The great inquisition was to come later.

When the appropriate time came to reflect upon what had happened, and what if anything had been achieved in Flanders between the end of July and the middle of November 1917, the consensus of opinion was generally negative towards the campaign itself, its outcome, and the senior commanders who had controlled its progress, with the possible exception of General Plumer. Over the years, as many critics became increasingly less well informed, their opinion became increasingly more vociferous and obdurate. In the arena of informed debate, the 'anti' and 'pro' lobbyists firmly entrenched their polarised positions, each trying to prove the validity of their own case, and in consequence the fallacy of the opposing argument. Some wise and learned historians have produced volumes, expounding their own theories, often leaving out or trivialising important issues which would weigh against their argument, whilst emphasising and discussing in great detail matters which to the 'other camp' would be considered equally trivial or irrelevant. Precise and detailed analysis, however sincerely it may be undertaken will never reconcile the arguments over Passchendaele to the satisfaction of all, and to ever believe that it will, deludes nobody but those attempting the analysis. Better to tell what happened as precisely as possible and allow the reader to make up her or his own mind.

As we have seen, to attempt to describe all aspects of the Battle meaningfully is a lengthy process. Some accounts, while spending little time describing the fighting, have gone to great lengths to explain in minute detail how misguided was Haig's command, and how in their opinion the Flanders campaign, and to an extent the whole War should have been conducted. To make such bold assertions 90 years after the event enjoys the benefit of 20:20 hindsight. But it is of vital importance to examine evidence from all sides of the debate, irrespective of how well that evidence supports the projected point of view. It is a worthwhile exercise therefore to examine whether some of these so earnestly made assertions stand up to close scrutiny. Of course it is understandable that after discussion of certain issues they are subsequently disregarded by some as irrelevant; but this should only be *after* discussion not before. It is worth identifying a few important, often contentious, but sometimes trivialised areas, and then looking at them in more detail.

The big picture

To better consider the value of the Flanders campaign it is first essential to establish that it did not stand alone as an independent operation, but was a part of a much larger whole; a move upon an enormous chess board, but only a move, not the game itself. This point had certainly been grasped by Lloyd George and Henry Wilson, although the reasonings behind their contentions were different. It is also of fundamental necessity to review what were the original aims of the offensive, and how well did the results, taking into consideration the costs, compare with those aims.

As the aims were stated so many times by Sir Douglas Haig they are straightforward enough to establish. There were three. First and foremost was the capture of the Channel ports. Second, from June onwards when the situation was made clear, the necessity to maintain the offensive independently to allow for the recovery of the French. Third, the wearing down of the German Army. From there on little is straightforward. The order of importance and the validity of the degree of concern over the U-boat threat, or the French situation, can be argued ad-infinitum, but nevertheless these were the objectives that Haig recognised at the time.

How can the cost of the campaign be quantified from the British perspective? The cost is largely to be measured by the number of casualties and any loss of morale. But can the number of casualties be accurately established, as there is a marked variation in figures, even between different official sources? Further research continues to lead to differing conclusions. Which of the figures quoted are correct, or have they been arranged to suit the varying arguments? One thing is certain; there are so many different figures, they cannot all be correct.

How can the results, or positive achievements of the Battle be gauged, assuming any exist? Are they to be measured in square miles of ground captured from the enemy? The very nature of the Western Front being two fixed opposing lines, suggests that for an offensive to have been successful, it must have resulted in a break through, or at least to have pushed the enemy back, and taken ground. Of Haig's three objectives, only reaching the Channel ports required a forward movement of any distance. The other two objectives could be achieved, with less effort, and with very little if any movement. With bite-and-hold tactics, under the fire of the British guns the German counter-attack methods could be used against them. But if the enemy was concentrated and held in this (for him), critical sector, whilst other forces who would eventually help strike the enemy a mortal blow recovered and assembled, would this not also constitute a positive result? It may well, but without the immediate clear-cut victory or large gain in ground the argument is as difficult to make now with any conviction, as it was to the War Cabinet in 1917. There were to be few clear-cut victories in the Great War, but while the British held the ring and drew the Germans to Flanders, the French recovered and the Americans gathered their strength.

For certain it is impossible to always measure success or failure by conquest of territory, as is clearly shown by the German experience in the spring of 1918, where huge gains in territory led ultimately to their downfall. To produce a map which shows that in an attack very little or no ground was taken, as in the case of Third Ypres, although visually provocative in supporting the 'futile' argument, really proves little, other than the attempted break through did not work, for as we have seen there was much more to Passchendaele than a failed break through. It can be equally justifiable to claim damage inflicted on the enemy force in a battle of attrition, as evidence of a positive result, even if the argument is more difficult to establish. The attrition argument is more difficult still if the casualty levels are no better than equal, and trying to prove that Haig wore down the enemy strength to a greater extent than he reduced his own is also problematic. To establish German casualty figures is just as controversial as establishing those of the British. It is also necessary to consider the level of casualties each side could sustain long term. To find an answer to the enormous question 'was it all worth it?' it is necessary to review the aims, and also to examine the contentious area of casualties and tangible results.

The aims

To remove the threat on the Flemish coast

From the moment in August 1914 that the Germans occupied the ports along the Flemish coast, that which the British had dreaded for centuries had become reality. A powerful enemy was in possession of harbours from which it could operate small naval craft against the east coast, the Thames estuary and the Straights of Dover. It is only 60 nautical miles from Ostend to the North Foreland. Britain's cross-channel communications with Dunkirk, Calais and Boulogne, the life-line of her Army in France, were threatened with attack within a few hours sailing time. The military use of aircraft was in 1914 at the point of conception, but it did not escape the notice of strategists on both sides that from the Belgian bases, not just the French ports and sea routes, but the coast of England, and the ports on the Thames and at Harwich were in range of even the earliest aircraft. The development of the submarine had introduced a new and alarming threat, which coupled with the sea mine, asked questions of the Royal Navy for which at first there were few answers. Enemy torpedo boats, soon to be joined by larger more powerful destroyers, were far too close to the movements of troop-ships for comfort. As technology improved both the capability and the range of submarines and aircraft, so the importance of maintaining the Belgian coastal bases grew to the Germans, and the importance of their elimination grew to the British. The British perceived even greater dangers, in that the Germans, although wreaking havoc had not recognized the full potential of their position. The dagger was truly 'held at the throat of England'.

The Battle of the Somme had precluded the 1916 Flanders offensive. But the insistence of the War Cabinet on the 26th October, reiterated on the 23rd of November, of the importance of the expulsion of the enemy from the Belgian coast, and that the occupation of Ostend and Zeebrugge should form one of the objectives of the campaign of 1917, left Haig with no misunderstanding of the Governments requirements. Jellicoe's deep concerns regarding shipping losses due to U-boat operations, and the activities of the destroyers in the Channel, reiterated at the War Committee meeting in late June, at the very least saw that Haig's plans for the Northern Operation were not summarily rejected. The expulsion of the enemy from the Belgian coast was to be, at least initially, the first aim. Were the British correct in their fear of the enemy bases on the Belgian coast? Did they really pose such a threat to British communication and supply? If they did not, as some claim, then the first aim of the Northern Offensive was flawed from the outset. But on the other hand if they did pose a major and virtually irreplaceable (to the enemy) threat, then the Germans would pay a high price to retain their sally-ports, a price which in the long run and for varied reasons, may eventually prove too high.

No account of the Passchendaele offensive can be considered complete without consideration of the threat posed by the Flanders U-boat bases, and how *or more especially if* that threat influenced policy making. It can reasonably be argued that the impossibility of reaching the Belgian coast became clear to Haig by mid August, but that does not alter the fact that the U-boat operations were a key element in British strategic planning prior to the offensive. Not once during the offensive did the War Cabinet indicate to Haig that the submarine threat had declined, or the bases were no longer to be considered a legitimate objective. There has always been a question mark over whether Jellicoe's statements to the War Policy Committee, both written and verbal, had any influence over the deliberations of the Committee when considering sanctioning the Flanders offensive. It has been strongly alleged by some that there is no evidence that Jellicoe's words carried conviction either way with the politicians or the military, and that even Haig was not convinced by them. As we have seen Haig considered the announcement a 'bombshell' and the minutes of the War Committee for the 20th June noted the Prime Minister to have said in response to Jellicoe's assertions, 'this statement made in such a quarter must be tested'.[766] It has been claimed that the records of the War Policy Committee provide no confirmation that either the political or the military leaders came down in favour of Third Ypres on account of Jellicoe's fears. But this omission in the Committee records is irrelevant, as neither do the records tell us why they *did* come down in favour of Third Ypres. In any event the Committee did not all say yes to Third Ypres; they simply did not all say no. That they did not comment on whether they were or were not moved by Jellicoe's statement cannot be used as proof that his word carried no weight at the time. The fact is we do not know whether they influenced the proceedings or not, but it is most likely that the Committee felt it unwise to totally disregard them. The dangers to maritime operations in the English Channel, which threatened the maintenance of every material requirement of the Army, were clear to all long before June 1917, and that knowledge was not dependent on anything Jellicoe had said. Haig had been warned of the seriousness of German destroyer operations from the Flemish coast by Admiral Bacon in November 1916. We shall examine the operations of the *MarineKorps Flandern*, and once more it will be up to the reader to decide whether the fear of their activities was genuine and justified, or simply an added excuse adopted by Haig to enhance the reasons for his chosen path.

---

[766] National Archives, minutes of ninth meeting of the Committee on War Policy CAB27/6

The target of the break through – *MarineKorps Flandern* [767]

On the 23rd August 1914 Admiral Alfred von Tirpitz requested of General Headquarters the creation of a naval division which would garrison the Flemish coastline, as and when it was captured. During the 1890's Germany had recognised the importance of the Belgian coast ports of Zeebrugge and Ostend, and Bruges linked by canals, in any war with Great Britain. To reach the British cross-Channel supply arteries from the Heligoland Bight required over 350 nautical miles of sailing; the Flanders ports cut this by 300 nautical miles, enabling U-boats to stay on station much longer. The numerical superiority of the British Battle Fleet was to be addressed partly with the strategy of *Kleinkrieg*. This foresaw the steady attrition of British warships by attack from small torpedo craft and U-boats, and the Flemish ports offered excellent opportunities for attacking both British commercial and naval assets. The principle role of the new *MarineDivision* would be to build and defend the bases from which the German boats would operate. On the 24th August Admiral Ludwig von Schröder, was called out of retirement to command the 20,000 men of the new division forming at Keil, and on the 29th August the new unit was officially designated *MarineDivision Flandern*. An aggressive admiral who favoured an active naval policy, von Schröder's views were very much in line with those of von Tirpitz.

By the end of the First Battle of Ypres in November 1914, the war had reached a stalemate of fixed position on the Western Front. The decision was taken to enlarge the *MarineDivision* with the addition of a second infantry division. The *1st MarineDivision* which to date had been employed in front line duties on the Yser, was to take over its main role of coastal defence and to prepare the port facilities for naval warfare. The *2nd MarineDivision* was to take up position in the line on the 4th December, the two divisions then becoming officially designated *MarineKorps Flandern*. A third division of infantry was to be added on the 3rd June 1917.

The ports had been captured virtually intact on the 15th October 1914. On the 9th November the *U-12* of the *High Seas Fleet* sailed into Zeebrugge, to be soon followed by the *U-11*, the first U-boats to enter the Flemish ports. During the first months of 1915 work proceeded at a pace to develop the necessary facilities, with around 5,000 Belgian civilians pressed into labour, and a further 5,000 German workers, all involved in the construction of docks and coastal defences. By the beginning of March, Ostend and Zeebrugge were ready to begin receiving the first naval forces from Germany, and by the 31st March the initial coastal fortifications were complete. These consisted of 6 batteries of guns from 105 mm to 280 mm at Ostend, and 7 batteries from 105 mm to 280 mm at Zeebrugge, a total of 55 heavy guns. There were also a number of 88 mm anti-aircraft batteries. This fire-power was to grow enormously over the next few years. The guns were augmented by 3 defensive minefields laid off the Flemish coast.

Stark warnings regarding the commencement of a U-boat campaign against shipping in British coastal waters had been given by the Chief of the German Admiralty Staff von Pohl on the 4th February 1915, when in the Imperial Gazette it was announced: 'The waters around Great Britain and Ireland, including the whole of the English Channel, are herewith declared to be in the War Zone. From February 18, 1915, onward, every merchant ship met with in this War Zone will be destroyed, nor will it always be possible to obviate the danger with which the crews and passengers are thereby threatened'.[768] The Flanders bases were now in the front line.

The first of the small UB-I type U-boats arrived on the 27th March. Only one craft, the *UB-2* arrived by sea. The remainder were shipped by train to Antwerp in around 15 pieces, where they were assembled at Hoboken by Cockeril and tested in the Scheldt. They were then moved via canals to Ghent, where they were loaded on a floating dry-dock for onward shipment to

---

[767] See, Johan Ryheul (1997) *MarineKorps Flandern 1914-1918* Hamburg: E.S. Mittler and Mark D. Karau *Wielding the Dagger, TheMarineKorps Flandern and the German War Effort* Westport: Praeger

[768] Reinhard Scheer (1919) *Germany's High Seas Fleet in the War* London: Cassell

Bruges. The UB-I boats displaced 120 tons and were armed with 2 x 45cm torpedo tubes, and with 1 deck mounted machine gun. Their radius of action was 800 nautical miles on the surface and 80 nautical miles submerged with a speed of 6 knots on the surface, and 5 knots submerged. The first flotilla was formed on the 28th March with the arrival of the second boat. Their patrol area included the English Channel and the British east coast as far north as Flamborough Head. This was soon to be expanded to include the French west coast, the Bay of Biscay, and the southernmost parts of the Irish Sea. On the 9th April active patrols commenced on the route between the Netherlands and Britain, the *UB-4* sinking 4 steamers on its first patrol. A newer and larger UC class boat was soon under production, the design completed in November 1914. These boats displaced 150 tons with a similar range and speed as the UB boats, but of greatest importance carried 12 mines. On the 31st May the first minefield *Sperre I* was laid near the Goodwins.

The sinking of the Lusitania on the 7th May 1915 placed a temporary restriction on U-boat activities, as the German Chancellor Theobald von Bethman Hollweg, fearful of further antagonising the United States, lobbied for an end to the unrestricted submarine campaign. On the 1st June the *MarineKorps* received official notification to cease attacking neutral ships. This had an immediate and serious affect on the operations from the Flanders bases. The U-boats had already been restricted by order from entering the main British sea route across the straights of Dover, for fear of encountering British naval patrols, minefields, or net barriers. In an attempt to recover the initiative, *UB-6* was ordered to sail west to Boulogne on the 21st June to test the theory that the British Channel defences could be breached. This it did successfully, the patrol area of the Flanders' boats then being extended westwards to a line Portland – Cap de la Hague. It was still however a quiet time for the U-boats.

Operations of the UB and UC boats increased in July, 26 missions being undertaken, resulting in 41 vessels being sunk. Over 100 mines were laid in the areas of Calais and the Downs and these were credited with severely disrupting commercial traffic. In August and September a further 36 British vessels were sunk, and by the end of the period the Flanders boats had sunk 142 allied ships for the loss of one UB and one UC submarine. Throughout the last 3 months of 1915 the patrol and mine-laying activities continued. By February 1916 the UB boats had sunk a further 17 British steamers in the Channel, and the UC-I boats had laid 119 minefields around the Thames, Flamborough Head, the Isle of Wight and le Havre, which had accounted for 112 vessels totalling 167,702 tons, at the cost of two UC boats sunk and one interned in the Netherlands. A new submarine class the UB-II with a displacement of 270 tons was introduced in early 1916, with greater endurance and speed than the UB-I, and with improved sea keeping. In September 1916 the new UC-II class boat was introduced, which was to become the most successful of the Flanders U-boat types. Displacing over 400 tons and with a radius of action of 7,000 to 9,000 nautical miles they were a powerful and flexible weapon. Armament consisted of 18 mines, three torpedo tubes and an 88 mm deck gun. By April 1917, 17 of these boats operated from Flanders ports.

At the beginning of December 1914 von Schröder had recommended that in addition to the submarine forces, a half-flotilla of torpedo-boats and a light cruiser should also be sent to Flanders. After protracted arguments, during which undoubted possibilities to strike harder at the British in the Channel were missed (a situation not lost upon the British Admitalty), the Flanders Torpedo Boat Flotilla was officially formed on the 28th April 1915. In some ways the new vessels were disappointing. The boats were specifically designed for Flanders operations, and were transported, in the same way as the UB-Is, in pre-fabricated subassemblies to Hoboken. Designated "A" Class they displaced a mere 100 tons, and mounted 2 torpedo tubes, a 50 mm deck gun, and carried 4 mines. The flotilla was fully operational by the 16th June 1915 with 15 "A" Class boats available. On the 1st May the *A-2* and *A-6* were both sunk in an inauspicious first encounter with British destroyers, against which, with their extremely limited armament they were no match. It was clear that a vessel with more punch was required and after much wrangling over where the new crews were to come from, a half flotilla of three V-25 Class boats, the *V-47, V-67* and *V-68* finally left Heligoland to arrive at Zeebrugge on the 3rd

March 1916. These boats were in a very different class, displacing 1,200 tons, with a range of 2,050 miles, carrying 24 mines and equipped for minesweeping. They were also equipped with 6 torpedo tubes, three 105 mm guns and four machine guns.

Von Schröder had not neglected the potential of the Flanders coast for air operations, and one of the *MarineDivision's* original missions had been to create a naval air station in Flanders. From simple beginnings of training, escort and reconnaissance, offensive operations gradually increased. On the 21st December 1914 the first raid by a Flanders based aircraft was made on Dover. Targets increased and were soon to include Dunkirk, Calais, Boulogne, le Harve, the Thames estuary and Harwich, and torpedo carrying float planes made attacks on shipping and boom patrol vessels. As a portent of things to come, on the 28th November 1916 an LVG biplane with a crew of two flew from Gistel to London, where it took pictures and dropped six 10-kilo bombs from 13,000 feet aimed at the Admiralty building and Whitehall. The bombs missed, falling between Brompton Road and Victoria station; but the point had been made. The only enemy airfields close enough from which to attack London were those in Flanders. Although the *MarineKorps* was not involved in mounting the Gotha raids on London, (to combat which the British Government in 1917 diverted two squadrons of fighter aircraft from the Western Front), it was from the Flanders airfields that the Gothas flew.

The year 1916 was to see three distinct phases of development for the *MarineKorps*. Between late March and the 1st June it remained an auxiliary service. From June to October the Flanders theatre took on greater importance as major decisions were taken regarding the evolution of submarine warfare. Between October 1916 and continuing into May 1917 the Germans launched serious destroyer raids into the Channel. In October it was decided to send 2 full destroyer flotillas, 20 boats in total, to Flanders on a temporary basis. Given the fact that their operations were still restricted, the Flanders submarines continued to be successful. In August 39 Allied vessels were sunk totalling 21,769 tons. In September the figure rose to 53 vessels of 74,695 tons. Between June and October the UC-Is laid a total of 67 minefields between the Thames, Yarmouth, and the French harbours on the Channel which accounted for 41 vessels of 62,347 tons.

From October 1916 to January 1917 the pace of *MarineKorps* activity rose drastically. On the 26th October a major raid into the Channel was planned by the two full destroyer flotillas and the Flanders half flotilla. The raid was a near total success, and claimed to have sunk 11 drifters, 2 destroyers and a steamer, without loss.[769] But the main benefit of having the large destroyers in Flanders was to enable the "A" Class boats to proceed with their mine sweeping operations without molestation by British destroyers, keeping the exit routes from the ports clear for the submarines. It also became necessary for the British to move extra destroyers from the north into the Channel, this limiting to an extent the actions of the Home Fleet. Between October and January the UC-Is laid an additional 48 minefields which accounted for 24 ships of 35,052 tons, while the UB-IIs renewed their attack against Allied commerce between Britain and the Netherlands sinking 149 ships of 151,990 tons. During the same period, the UC-IIs laid their own minefields, claiming 34 ships of 77,190 tons by mine, while sinking another 146 vessels of 141,805 tons by surface action.

A major point of escalation came on the 1st February 1917 when Germany again declared unrestricted U-boat warfare. After the Battle of Jutland German Naval policy, with the agreement of the Army, swung towards a demand to continue with the unrestricted U-boat campaign to defeat Britain, and as the submarines again took centre stage in naval planning and overall German strategy the importance of the Flanders bases increased. The prediction of Chief of the German Naval Staff, Admiral von Holtzendorff, was that if the U-boat flotillas could sink 600,000 tons of Allied shipping per month over the next six months the British would be compelled through shortage of shipping to carry vital raw materials and foodstuffs to stop fighting. This is a policy that von Holtzendorff had been advocating since January 1916. The tonnage sunk in the first six weeks of the new campaign was to equal the total tonnage sunk throughout the whole of 1915.

---

[769] This is the raid mentioned to Haig by Admiral Bacon.

At the re-opening of the unrestricted U-boat campaign on the 1st February, the *MarineKorps* submarine flotilla numbered 23 U-boats of all types for immediate use. This number soon rose to 32 and was to stay at around this level for the next three months.[770] In February the Flanders flotilla sunk 115 ships of 164,455 tons, slightly more than 25% of the total of 520,412 tons for the German Fleet as a whole. Over the next few months the figures for the Flanders boats soared. In March they reported sinking 195 ships totalling 234,871 tons, approaching half the fleet total of 564,497 tons. April saw the fleet total rise to a staggering 860,334 tons, of which 545,282 tons had been British, the flotilla's share being 117 vessels of 253,840 tons. On April the 27th a reluctant but desperate Jellicoe ordered the implementation of a number of trial convoys which sailed from Gibraltar and North America, in an attempt to do something to staunch the maritime haemorrhage. May witnessed a slight improvement for the Allies, the tonnage of allied and neutral shipping lost dropping slightly to 616,316 of which the Flanders boat total was 146 ships of 217,743 tons.[771] June saw an improvement from the German perspective, with 696,725 tons of Allied and neutral shipping sunk of which 417,925 tons was British. Jellicoe's outburst at the June meeting of the War Cabinet was therefore understandable and was hardly an overreaction. The losses were horrendous and at that time there appeared little that he could do to appreciably reduce them. In the month leading up to the beginning of the Flanders offensive the allied losses improved slightly, but still amounted to 555,514 tons, 85 ships of 203,066 tons being claimed by the Flanders boats.

It was not that the Royal Navy or the Royal Flying Corps had not attempted to curb the activities of the *MarineKorps,* because they had certainly tried. Monitors had attacked the bases with gunfire, but had been reduced to duals with the shore defences, and even with their 15-inch guns had to stand so far off to avoid the fire from the German batteries that the raids had caused little damage. The *MarineKorps* had vastly increased the coastal defence batteries to a total of 41 including anti-aircraft units, most batteries mounting four guns. The *Deutschland* battery near Bredene alone mounted four 380 mm guns in defence of Ostend. Throughout 1917 the Royal Flying Corps had carried out numerous bombing raids against the port installations. Around 6,000 bombs had been dropped on the installations at Bruges, but most had caused more damage to the civilian population than they had to the base, 123 people being killed, 243 injured and some 700 homes destroyed. There had been some success however. On the 7th February some stored munitions had been destroyed at Bruges. The raids had concerned the Germans to the extent that in the event of an air-raid they had begun to move the warships out of the inner harbour at Zeebrugge, mooring then alongside the outer mole. This behaviour had been noticed by the British airmen and on the morning of the 8th April an air-raid was launched in conjunction with an attack by coastal motor-torpedo boats. The attack was a spectacular success and the 1,100 ton destroyer *G-88* was hit and sunk by a torpedo. But the success was not to be repeated. The air weapon was not yet sufficiently powerful to threaten the *MarineKorps*, and the coastal defences were more than adequate to see off bombardment from the sea. During 1917 construction had begun at Bruges of a massive eight dock concrete U-boat pen to protect the boats from air attack.

---

[770] In a desperate effort to prove the irrelevance of the U-boat campaign, Denis Winter says the Germans could keep no more than 20 U-boats at sea at any one moment during this period. *Haig's Command* p100. In fact there were 32 U-boats in the Flanders flotilla alone in May 1917. Later in the year the Flanders flotilla number was to rise to 46. See Mark Karau's *Wielding the Dagger* p128 and p146.

[771] Denis Winter claims that 'by May, it appeared that a U-boat threat, which seemed critical at the end of 1916, had become equally insignificant'. *Haig's Command* p100 Figures from the Official History of the Great War 'Merchant Navy', Vol III Appendix C, p379 tells us that British Merchant shipping lost in January 1917 amounted to 49 ships of 153,666 tons. By May the figure had risen to 122 ships of 352,289 tons. Hardly an insignificant number. (BOH p103) In June the Flanders boats alone sank 117 Allied ships for the loss of 1 U-boat, *UC-66*. See Mark Karau's *Wielding the Dagger* p146. Of all Winter's extraordinary claims this must rank amongst the most extraordinary. By examining the actual figures, it is clear that Winter's statement is totally inaccurate.

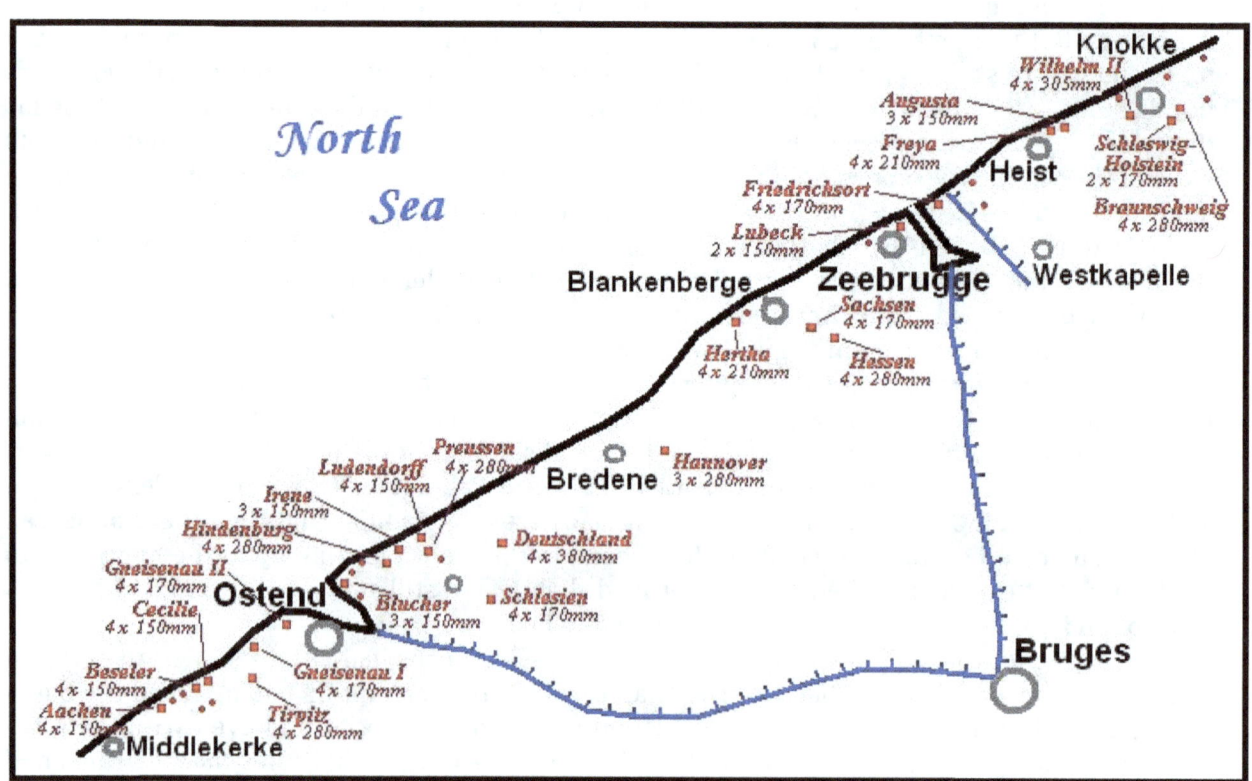

The artillery defences of the Flemish coast – with details of batteries 150mm and over

There is no doubt whatsoever that the threat imposed by the enemy possession of the Flanders bases was enormously real and had a fundamental strategic influence upon British War policy. It can be argued that both von Holtzendorff's prediction of a British collapse after six months unrestricted U-boat warfare, and Jellicoe's deep pessimism regarding the future were both to be proved unfounded, but that was not at all clear to either side at the time. The first aim of the Northern Offensive to capture the coastal bases was therefore perfectly valid.

To keep the French in the fight

Any account of Passchendaele which disregards the dangerous repercussions upon British policy of mutiny in the French Army must also be considered seriously incomplete. Some historians may fail to discuss the problems within the French Army, as in their own minds they have already dismissed them as unimportant and of no relevance to Haig's strategy and conduct of the campaign. As we have seen on so many occasions, the mutinies were of enormous concern to Haig, but it has proved much more convenient to build a case against the Commander-in-Chief's handling of the offensive by not mentioning them at all. To imply that the mutinies were unimportant enables the development of a stronger case against Haig, as it conveniently sidesteps possible explanations for his actions and reasoning behind his motives. This can hardly be acceptable in any account intended to provide all available facts and information, and not to be considered selective by omission.

The rationale for dismissing the impact of the mutinies upon Haig's conduct of the campaign is founded primarily, but not solely, on three main expositions. The first is that the mutinies are now seen to have been of no great danger to the Allied cause, and therefore Haig was not, or should not, have been concerned about them. The second is that although the mutinies may have presented some danger, Haig deliberately over exaggerated the peril, to provide a further reason to persevere with his offensive. The third is that the French had quickly recovered their composure, were not overly concerned for their safety, and in any event were unimpressed with Haig's strategy to draw off German reserves to Flanders. The latter argument has been further expanded by some to the point where it is claimed that French confidence was based on the belief that the Germans were not in a position to mount an offensive against them.[772] But this argument makes little sense. First, there is little to indicate that the French felt their position to be safe from attack; in fact there are more reasons to believe the contrary.[773] Second, if the unlikely scenario of French confidence is accepted, that confidence could only be founded on Haig's operations in Flanders drawing off German reserves. It is strange therefore to suggest that the French were not wholly supportive of Haig's offensive which virtually ensured them time for recovery.[774]

If the Germans had become aware of the French predicament, (and how was Haig or Pétain to know they would not?), whilst the British had stood on the defensive or mounted a limited attack, there would have been nothing to prevent the enemy offensively deploying some of the divisions and guns against the French that they were to use in defending their Flanders position against the British? The German Official History says of the period: 'No one could have been more eager to give the order to attack [the French] than the High Command, if this had been considered possible; but it was unable to do so.' [775] The reason it was unable to do so was that 30 divisions were required to mount an offensive on the Aisne, but only 23 were available as, '8 were already (in early June) on their way to strengthen the Northern Group of Armies in order to meet the British offensive in Flanders which appeared imminent'. That the Germans had withdrawn to the Hindenburg Line in February, did not in any way guarantee that they would not attack the French if they detected a hint of weakness, or 'mutiny'. In his book on the French mutinies *Dare Call it Treason,* Richard Watt describes the period at the end of June 1917 on the Chemin des Dames thus: 'And over the battlefront there had descended an unaccountable quiet. The German attacks had ceased, and to G.Q.G. this could mean only one thing – the Germans were preparing their long dreaded assault.'[776] This implies the French were in fact expecting an attack. We also know from the German Official Account that the Crown Prince was lobbying to make an attack across the Aisne in May and June, but could not be assigned sufficient forces to do so as divisions were already on their way to the expected battle in Flanders. It is enlightening to review the German records which show the following distribution of forces in the summer and autumn of 1917 on the Western Front:

---

[772] See Prior and Wilson *Passchendaele the Untold Story* p33: 'the French command were not impressed by Haig's strategic nostrums. And whatever their problems, they were aware that the enemy was in no position to mount an offensive against them in the foreseeable future'. The second sentence can be considered correct if it is underscored by the fact that Haig's actions in Flanders were the reason why the Germans did not have the strength to attack the French.

[773] On the other hand Denis Winter claims that 'the Germans sent 105 of their 157 Western Front against the French and by the end of July (so the War Office told the Cabinet) the Germans had used forty more divisions and made seventy attacks on the Chemin des Dame, east of Soissons'. Obviously both assertions cannot be right.

[774] There is a fourth scenario offered by Denis Winter, shrouded within his theories of 'smoke screens of lies and fiction', 'clouds of poison gas' and 'dastardly plots' allegedly cast abroad by the British military faction in the 1920's. His claim is that the mutinies did not contribute much to the French defensive policy, but that policy was adopted as a direct result of instructions from the French Government to await the arrival of the Americans. *Haig's Command* p87

[775] BOH p-xvi

[776] Richard Watts (1964) *Dare Call it Treason* London: Chatto & Windus p180

Third Armee:

From 28th May to the 30th June, *Stellungskampfe in der Champagne*: 6 divisions. *Stellungskampfe in den Argonnen*: 6 divisions. *Stellungskampfe bei Reims*: 6 divisions.

Second Armee:

From the 21st June [1917] to 31st January [1918], *Kampfe in der Siegfried Stellung:* 44 divisions [of which 7 were transferred to Ypres during the period of the offensive].

Seventh Armee:

From the 9th July to 23rd October, *Stellungskampfe am Chemin des Dames*: 23 divisions.

Fourth Armee:

From the 27th May to 3rd December *Schlacht in Flandern:* 86 divisions.

It was not the case that the French *knew* they would not be attacked, but that the Germans *could not* attack them, as they did not possess the strength.[777] Their reserves were continuously heading north against the British. But if the British had not attacked in Flanders, the forces necessary to attack towards Paris would have been available to the Crown Prince. It must be considered a strong possibility, if not a probability, that if the Germans had used even half (43) of the divisions against the weakened French, that they eventually used to defend their Flanders Position, the result would have been an Allied disaster. The enemy certainly believed this was the case. It is reasonable to argue that the principle reason that the French were not seriously attacked by the Germans during their critical period of recovery, was because of Haig's operations at Ypres drawing the enemy's reserves away to Flanders, and saving a possibly disastrous situation.

The French attacks on the 20th August (in beautiful weather) at Verdun, and on the Chemin des Dames on the 23rd October (the Battle of Malmaison) were both a great success. This success has often been attributed to the adoption of 'Pétain tactics' with limited objectives, with attacks made after an overwhelming artillery bombardment, over three days in the case of Verdun (where 60% of the French forces engaged were artillerymen), and over six days and six nights in the case of Malmaison. At Verdun the attack began at 4:40 a.m. and by 7:30 a.m. the objectives had been reached all along the line, capturing the summits of Mort-Homme and Hill 344. On the 24th August Hill 304 was stormed, the fighting continuing with further success until the 26th. French losses were relatively light. On the 23rd October at 5:15 a.m. the French Sixth Army attacked the German *Seventh Army* on the Chemin des Dames along a seven mile front, this time in dense fog and heavy drizzle. Within four days the French had advanced to a depth of four miles and had captured 11,500 prisoners and 180 guns.

How had the French turned the tables on their enemy so dramatically in seven months? Admittedly their attacks had been long delayed, but their recovery was nevertheless extraordinary. We have been led to believe that the French Army was a spent force and in disarray. There had obviously been an enormous recovery of spirit. It also appears that the 'limited objective-broad front' attack, or 'Pétain tactics' had after all provided the miracle ingredient, lacking in all other offensives mounted to this time. What had happened to the Germans, usually so effective and efficient in defence as well as attack? Maybe Pétain had found

---

[777] John Mosier puts a different slant on the subject. He claims that the French infantry 'mostly stayed in their positions and defended them – not that much defence was necessary, as the Germans saw little need to mount attacks on an adversary who could be counted on to destroy himself'. If the French appeared a walkover was that not an even better reason for the Germans to attack them? See *The Myth of the Great War* p277

the answer to the conundrum which had faced the high commands since late 1914. It has been claimed that the French had achieved in four days the equivalent to that which the British had achieved in ninety-nine.[778] But *'what if'* the British Army had not been drawing such large numbers of German reserves into Flanders, and the French had faced an enemy defensive force sufficient in artillery and counter-attack reserves, as the British were facing at Ypres? As we have seen from the distribution of division figures, even the German Army did not have the resources to be in the same strength at Ypres, where over the period it fielded 86 divisions, and on the Chemin des Dames where it fielded 23 divisions. To have achieved the success they had, with *relatively* light casualties, the French must have come very near to dominating the German artillery, the position which Haig had always wanted to achieve at Ypres, but due to insufficient guns never had. Did this indicate superior equipment, capability, and tactics on the part of the French artillery, or was it that they were facing a weaker opponent? All the available facts point to the latter. If Pétain had been faced with the relays of German divisions, and unsuppressed enemy artillery which had faced Haig's Armies at Ypres, he would not have dared risk threatening the newly restored, and possibly still fragile morale of his Army. On the other hand if Haig had been faced with the same level of enemy resistance at Ypres as Pétain had faced at Verdun and on the Chemin des Dames, the story of Passchendaele would have been very different. The British offensive in Flanders had allowed for the recovery and the new found successes of the French Army, which Pétain and Haig knew were so imperative to the Allied cause. The French could throw their weight at the Chemin des Dames in the full knowledge that the Germans were still engaged in a life and death struggle with the British in Flanders. That Pétain was not willing to risk failure and further problems with morale is borne out by the letter presented to Haig on the 30th June by Anthoine, in which he impressed on the British Commander-in-Chief the necessity, from the French point of view, of a sure victory; l'offensive des Flandres doit etre assure d'un success absolu, *'imperieusement exige par les facteurs moraux du moment'*.[779] There was no doubting Pétain's priorities, and the French Armies in Flanders, at Verdun, and on the Chemin des Dames, thanks to the Passchendaele offensive, had acquired their 'success absolu'. Some have argued that to have engaged over 80 enemy divisions at Passchendaele was of no great significance as this was only one third of the German Army, whilst Haig had used 'more than half' of his.[780] But this is to completely miss the key point. The question is, what havoc would the Germans have created against the French with those eighty-odd divisions if they had not been engaged in Flanders?

It is clear therefore that for a whole host of reasons, it is impossible to disregard the added complexities and influences brought about by the weakening of the French Army due to the mutinies, the consequences of which were inevitably imposed upon Haig and the British Army. We shall now look briefly at what actually happened within the French Army in consequence of the Nivelle offensive.

The threat of disaster – the French mutinies[781]

If, in line with Haig's plan, the first aim of the Northern Offensive, (that is the capturing of the ports) was successful, then undoubtedly the German Army in Belgium would suffer a major defeat, and the repercussions of that defeat may well lead to a general collapse, at least at the northern end of the Western Front. If however the campaign was less successful and the British failed to break-out beyond the ridge east of Ypres, there remained the major aim of wearing down the German Army in a battle of attrition. Following the failure of the Nivelle offensive, the subsequent upheavals in the ranks of the French Army had been foremost in Haig's mind

---

[778] John Keegan (1998) *The First World War* London: Hutchinson p394
[779] 'The offensive in Flanders must be an absolute success, *as strictly required by the moral factors of the moment'*.
[780] John Keegan (1998) *The First World War* London: Hutchinson p394
[781] See John Williams, *Mutiny 1917* London: Heinemann, and Richard M. Watt *Dare Call it Treason* London: Chatto and Windus

throughout the long weeks of battle. To keep the bulk of the German Army on the Western Front focused on Flanders had become his main aim, once a break-out beyond the Passchendaele ridge looked unlikely. But how weakened had the French really been? Had Haig been hoodwinked by Pétain into believing the situation was worse than it truly was, for Pétain was well known for his pessimism. Or had Haig deliberately and grossly over-emphasised the French problem for some other devious reason of his own? Were some of the often mentioned 'pleas' for Haig to continue the battle never actually made by Pétain? An understandable cloak of military secrecy had shrouded the whole affair. We know for certain that the mutinies occurred, but what more do we know, and were they as significant as Haig obviously believed them to be?

Under Nivelle's plan and Command, on the 16th April 1917, 19 divisions of the French Fifth and Sixth Armies under General Mazel and General Mangin had attacked on the Aisne along a 50 mile front between Soissons and Reims. On the 17th the Fourth Army under General Anthoine had attacked east of Reims. Although some small gains were made, generally the attacks were unsuccessful when measured against their objectives, and the French had incurred extremely heavy losses. To the French troops it was not so much the magnitude of the failure that so infuriated them, but rather the depth of disappointment, which came in sharp contrast to the promises they had been given of rapid success. This disappointment came upon the heels of the massive losses the Army had incurred since early 1916 at Verdun. For the rank and file, the conditions, never to be considered good in times of war, had got steadily worse. Sporadic leave arrangements, lack of acceptable food and unsatisfactory medical attention all added to an ever increasing ground-swell of dissatisfaction. The problem was not confined to the military. Political agitation against the war in the large cities was rife. The dreadful military situation, brought to a head by the Nivelle disaster, encouraged and emboldened the political subversion, and the political subversion helped to fuel the military dissatisfaction and disgruntlement.

In the Army the trouble had started soon after the first attacks, but began in only a minor way. On the 16th and 17th April in the Sixth Army, the II Colonial Corps attacking on the Craonne plateau had sustained casualties of around one third of its effective strength, and by the 19th it had been withdrawn from the line. The I Corps in a similar plight had been withdrawn soon after. As the shattered troops were transported out through Epernay and Chateau-Thierry, dissension and unruly behaviour was plainly rife, the men cursing their own artillery and showing disrespect to officers. The fighting had died down by the 22nd April, and those men that had witnessed the disaster began to write home in huge numbers in a markedly defeatist tone. The general consensus of dissatisfaction and hostility towards their commanders was quickly picked up by field censors, amazed at the swing from optimism prior to the offensive, to the depths of pessimism over the short two week period. But for the moment the troops still obeyed orders.

Dissatisfaction was not limited to the ranks. On the 22nd April deputations by officers at Corps level were made to President Poincaré in an effort to stop further attacks. Poincaré immediately intervened, sending a message to Nivelle at G.Q.G. stating that he thought the proposed attacks at Craonne and Vauclerc inadvisable. Upon informing the French War Cabinet that morning of his unofficial intervention, he received their unanimous approval. Political pressure was already mounting against Nivelle, and a deep rift was also developing between the Commander-in Chief and his senior commanders. General Mangin became a scapegoat and was dismissed. His Sixth Army, in which most of the unrest had centred, was placed under command of General Maistre and transferred from General Micheler's Reserve Army Group, (Nivelle also having fallen out with General Micheler), to the Northern Army Group under General Franchet d'Espèray. News of the unrest in the Sixth Army, which was now preparing for an attack on the river Ailette, soon reached the ears of Franchet d'Espèray, who was sufficiently concerned to report the matter on the 26th April to Nivelle. He received a swift rebuke from Nivelle who basically told him to concentrate on military matters and not involve himself with the morale of the Nation. Discontent in the ranks continued to simmer.

On the 1st May, International Labour Day, at Montmort and Baye 25 miles south-west of Epernay, discontent did not just simmer but flared-up to an open state of anarchy. But this was not in French ranks. The 1st and 3rd Russian Brigades had been fighting alongside the French and their casualties had been enormous, 1st Brigade alone losing 3,000 men in an attack on Fort Brimont. Revolutionary ferment had been rife and the attack had been the final spark to send the tinder into flame. Out of the 16,000 men, 10,000, mostly in 1st Brigade, had downed their arms and were refusing to parade. The agitation spread as Soviets and Soldiers Councils took over, with delegates elected from the ranks. Insubordinate demonstrations spilled onto the streets, the unruly rabble passing a camp of bewildered French troops recently returned from the front.

On the 4th May the general offensive resumed. During the middle fortnight in May protest from all levels of command poured into War Minister Painlevé's office in Paris, and on the 10th May the French War Cabinet decided to relieve Nivelle of his command. Initially Nivelle refused to go but bowed to the inevitable on the 15th. On the same day Pétain was appointed in his place and on the morning of the 17th he began the long and painful task of restoring the French Army to a reliable fighting force. His main aim was to call off the offensive as soon as possible, and pull the battered and dejected Army back from the Aisne for rest and reorganisation. His intention was then to soon resume limited local attacks, and launch a further assault by the Sixth Army against the Chemin des Dames to support the British attack at Messines on the 7th June. Pétain did not realise it at the time, but he was to be completely unable to fulfil any of these intentions. By the monitoring of mail and observation of the behaviour of the men, G.Q.G. had by the 15th May become sufficiently alarmed to compile a report concerning the lack of discipline in the ranks along the 40 mile front. The report was sent to War Minister Painlevé, the first official notification of just how bad matters had become.

The Tenth Army of General Duchêne had been in reserve of the initial attacks on the Chemin des Dames, held back to exploit the hoped for breakthrough. It had later been moved up in support of the weakening front of the Fifth Army, when some regiments had remained in the line for 9 days, before relief. One regiment, the 128th, having been pulled out of the line on the 15th May, rather than receiving the news expected that they were to be moved back for rest, were ordered on the 20th back into the line. At first, most of the regiment emboldened by their wine ration refused the order. By evening all except 55 had obeyed the order to march, with the remainder locked in a barn guarded by military police until the following morning. On reflection of the hopelessness of their situation, and having sobered from the effects of the wine of the previous afternoon, they too marched for the front the next morning. The ringleaders were soon to face court-martial.

On the 18th May, Haig had met with Pétain at Amiens, not due to concerns over the French Army, but rather to discuss the wording of the written commitments made by the French after the Paris conference. The British Official History tells of Pétain being outspoken on the unrest within the French Army. In his diary Haig makes no mention of it, but he did ask for Pétain's assurance of co-operation in the forthcoming British offensives, which at that point Pétain gave. At the same time, indiscipline, and a general refusal to obey orders was occurring at random along the Fifth and Tenth Army fronts. On the 19th May a battalion in the IX Corps of the Fifth Army refused to march for the front. On the same day in the 69th Division, the 162nd Regiment refused to leave their base as reinforcements for the line. But on the 22nd May matters were to quickly escalate, and take on a more serious tenor. In the 18th Division, for 3 weeks in the line without relief, men of the 66th Regiment in the trenches refused to carry out orders. This was very different from refusing to march to the front, as serious as that may be; this was mutiny in the face of the enemy. The Army Group Commander, General Duchêne acted immediately, and with the utmost severity. The men of the 66th were paraded, and a number of men chosen seemingly at random. They were disarmed, marched away to the roll of drums and summarily shot. The zone behind Soissons and Reims simmered with unrest, and further isolated outbreaks of disobedience occurred. Worse still on the 26th May, 100 miles to the east in the Vosges sector, a unit refused to march for the line and two days later disorder broke out in Lorraine. Trouble was flaring up at many places along the French sector of the Western Front. On the 26th it was in the 18th and 158th Regiments; on the 28th the 111th, the 258th and the 109th. The 29th May saw trouble spread to another ten regiments along the Aisne, and at G.Q.G. at Compiegne, Pétain and his staff faced a situation unprecedented in the War. But so far except in the 66th the front line units had held firm, and news of the crisis had not yet leaked beyond the military zone. Even the President was not formally told until the 29th.

The unrest began to spread more widely, and most importantly, away from the front, as those disenchanted soldiers lucky enough to be given leave gathered at railway stations and joined together in general protest. In Paris the platforms of the Gare de l'Est and the Gare du Nord swarmed with troops arriving on, or returning from leave. The subversive elements of Paris society merged with the crowd, distributing pacifistic and defeatist literature amongst the soldiers, the bad news from the front serving to enhance the power and meaning of their message, and better ensuring it of a welcome reception. For the enormity of the web of political agitators the French Government had to a point only themselves to blame. Before the War their security services had listed some 2,500 people, suspected spies, revolutionaries, and pacifists, who it was considered would be dangerous in time of war. But it had been decided for political reasons not to act fully on the information, and 2,000 of those on the 'Carnet B' list had retained their freedom. The results were now being felt. The intrigues and complicity in acts of subversion and propaganda spread even within Government circles, specifically within the Ministry of the Interior. Continual requests from the Army to the security services to suppress the publication of subversive literature, which was spread widely amongst the troops on leave, were not acted upon due to political pressures. One such disreputable Paris news sheet was the 'Bonnet Rouge'. The paper was financed directly by the German security services, and although caught on his way back from Switzerland by French security, with a German backed cheque for 150,000 francs, the editor Duval, with the complicity of Minister of the Interior Malvy, was able to continue with his publication and even had his cheque returned. The colourful headlines of Bonnet Rouge recognised few boundaries of truth or integrity: 'Why go on fighting when Germany is ready with a generous peace and will make Britain pay all the war-costs? Why do all the fighting while Britain shrinks in the rear? Britain not Germany was responsible for the war!'[782] Duval was to be shot at dawn for treason at Vincennes on the 17th July 1918, and Malvy was to vanish into disgrace, but in the meantime serious damage was being done to morale both in the Army and on the home front.

The cancer which ate away at the very heart of the French war effort was difficult to eradicate. As had been pointed out to the British Cabinet by Spears, it had no central co-ordination, and was led by no single personality. It fed upon the strife and misery caused at the front and in the cities by the hardships and privations of the War. On the 15th May a procession of protesting midinettes saw the beginning of industrial unrest, and before June was out there were over 170 stoppages in war factories in Paris and the provinces, involving 70,000 workers. The trouble soon spread to Bordeaux, Toulouse, Limoges, Saint-Etienne, Marseilles, Grenoble, and other centres. Provocateurs were infiltrating the factories, lecturing and calling for the establishment of Communist cells. One man had given the same violent and treasonous speech in 30 different factories without apprehension by the police.

On the 29th and 30th May at the front, the unrest had spread to the 36th and 129th Regiments at Coeuvres. There had been a plan to seize a train and bring their grievances to Paris; in fact to send a delegation to the Chamber to demand immediate peace. The plan had been thwarted. Although it was still being kept a closely guarded military secret, on the 31st May the French War Cabinet was at last made aware of the full magnitude of the military threat hanging over France. Pétain was called to Paris on this day to give an account of the revolt in the 36th and 129th. The burning political question of the moment concerned a proposed Socialist peace conference to be held in Stockholm. Poincaré demanded Pétain's views regarding the effect on the Army if the conference should take place: 'General, if there is an International Socialist Conference at Stockholm and the French and Germans meet there to discuss peace-terms, could you keep your armies under control? Would you be able to ensure that they continued fighting?'[783] Pétain replied with an emphatic "No". War Minister Painlevé then said gravely, 'gentlemen, after the General's declaration, it's impossible to grant the passports. But, all the

---

[782] John Williams, *Mutiny 1917* London: Heinemann p108
[783] John Williams, *Mutiny 1917* London: Heinemann p128

same, there are dangers on both sides. If the Congress takes place, our Army stops fighting. If the Russian invitation to attend is refused, then the Russian Army stops fighting – and 75 German divisions will be forced to move to our front!' Pétain turned to the War Minister. 'Quite true Minister, but the danger of 75 German divisions attacking us is much less than that of the demoralisation of our Armies!' If Haig had been present he would have agreed wholeheartedly, as his awareness of the true situation two days later led to the foundation of another of his prime aims; to allow time for the rebuilding of morale in the French Army. This was to form the bedrock of his policy during his British fought battle in Flanders. It was however a matter that for reasons of great military security, he was able to say little about, even to the War Cabinet.

On the 1st of June trouble spread to the 97th and 159th regiments, and to the 57th, 60th and 61st Chasseurs. On the 3rd General Maistre informed Pétain that the 6th Army was no longer capable of attacking and must be rested. Protests by striking workers on the streets of Paris on the same day were larger than ever. In Soissons on the 2nd June a wine train standing in a siding was the catalyst for a drunken riot, which led to a 700 strong armed body of the 298th Regiment marching 5 miles outside the town and making camp in woodland, where they commenced to set up soldier's councils. They were soon to be surrounded by cavalry. That evening, again at Coeuvres a few hundred mutineers of the 310th Regiment, the remnants of a band of 1,500 who had not already been rounded up by the Republican Guard, also lay low in woodland a few miles south of the town. At the time of the bedlam in Coeuvres that had led to the march out of the town, General Debeney had been on his way to see Haig with Pétain's message regarding the extent of the unrest, and explaining that the attack at Malmaison on the 10th June could not take place. In the morning at Coeuvres plans were afoot amongst the 310th to march south and join forces with the mutineers of the 17th Regiment from Mercin, and from there march on Paris.

At Compiegne, on the 4th June Pétain held a conference at which Foch, Franchet d'Espèrey, Castelnau, Fayolle, Maistre, Duchêne and Gouraud were present. Pétain opened by saying: 'Gentlemen, I have called you here to hear your reports of the state of the various Army commands. The High Command regards the situation as grave in the extreme. Like an infection the revolts are spreading with disastrous speed. We must face the facts. Now it is not a question of indiscipline in several regiments, as it was at Verdun in 1916, but the whole French Army is filled with the spirit of revolt!'[784] Whilst the meeting considered the reasons and remedies, news arrived of a major German attack on the Sixth Army front at Craonne on the Chemin des Dames. The 70th Division were in reserve and were ordered to counter-attack immediately, which they did successfully, driving the Germans from a significant lodgement area. As Pétain received the report from Maistre of the excellent performance of the 70th Division he also received news that the XXII Corps would take over the front line but refused to attack, and the VII Corps would not go into the trenches at all.

On the 5th June the 310th gave up their revolt at Coeuvres, and on the 8th the 298th finally came out of the woods at Soissons. Two days later the British Second Army attacked at Messines. From the 13th June onwards, with the threat of stiffer repressions coupled with the promise of better leave periods and conditions, the storm of mutiny began to blow itself out. Over the next few weeks Pétain was to ensure he was seen by his Army, making morale-boosting visits to 90 divisions. He was very careful not to overestimate the improvement in the situation. On the 20th he cautioned the Government that there was no certainty that order had been fully restored, and that trouble could flare up again with little provocation. He warned that the future morale of the Army was dependant on the Governments action against the defeatists.[785]

---

[784] John Williams, *Mutiny 1917* London: Heinemann p162
[785] The troublesome Russian Brigades had been moved on the 25th May to a camp at Neufchateau in the Vosges. With the danger of them causing further unrest amongst French troops it was considered necessary to move them once more this time to La Courtine Camp, high on an isolated plateau in Limoges in central France. Friction between the 1st and 3rd Brigades led to 6,000 the 3rd Brigade leaving camp to pitch camp 5 miles away. By the end of July the 10,000 of the 1st Brigade were in open revolt. The siege of the camp was finally broken by the shells of French 75's on the 17th

Hiag understood as clearly as Pétain that to restore the French Army to full fighting efficiency would take many months, always assuming that given its shortages of manpower, and general war-weariness in the country, that could ever be achieved. Pétain was doing his best to encourage and re-establish the fighting spirit in his Army, but he could not do that unless any possible enemy pressure upon him was relieved. Of the one hundred and nineteen "collective acts of indiscipline" that had taken place between the 29th April and the end of September one hundred and ten had been serious, In addition to the one hundred and nineteen there had also been fifty-one of a lesser nature. The one hundred and ten worst cases had been spread throughout fifty-four divisions of the French Army, a force approximating to the size of the whole B.E.F. It is clear therefore that Haig was totally correct to consider the trouble in the French Army as an absolute danger to the security of the Allies, although at the time his knowledge of what was really happening was limited to what Pétain had told him by letter on the 2nd June, and at their meeting at Cassel on the 7th.

Of the period around the end of May and the beginning of June, Richard Watt describes the situation in the French camp thus: 'Pétain's staff combed and recombed every unit on the Western Front in an effort to find enough loyal troops to man the defences. Somehow it was done; with dismounted cavalry, a good battalion here, a sturdy regiment there, the front was held closed. But this was a stop-gap measure of the most desperate nature. These loyal units could not hold the trenches forever, and they could not hold the front at all in the face of a large scale German attack which seemed every day more imminent. Time would soon run out, and before it did the pressure had to be removed from the French front and the mass of the Army returned to health. Thus the crucial question bearing on Pétain's strategy was whether the British could be persuaded to launch an offensive to draw German pressure off the tiny group of desperate Frenchmen who were now defending the trench lines.'[786] Richard Watt's understanding of Haig's willingness to raise the sword (he needed little persuading) may be slightly naïve, but he makes the point well regarding the main theme of his book, the terrible situation of the French.

The wearing-down battle

That the fighting was appalling and traumatic for those directly involved has been thoroughly and painstakingly exposed in these chapters. But this is no measure of the relative success or failure of the Battle, for the fighting would not have been pleasurable even had it been an obvious and outstanding success. However much we may empathise with the sufferings of those who fought, we cannot judge the outcome by emotional considerations alone. It is essential to try to establish not just what affect it had on the British Army, or what immediate affect it had on the enemy, but moreover to establish what affect it had on the final outcome of the War. Neither is it sufficient to simply examine the casualty figures of the protagonists in direct comparison, as there are other key factors to consider. Any attempt to establish a view of the overall effectiveness or otherwise of the offensive must of necessity take into account consequences beyond casualty figures or gains in ground, for Passchendaele was one offensive, not the whole War.

In order to strengthen the case against Haig, it has been questioned why he should risk the morale of the British Army by continuing with the Flanders offensive?[787] It is argued that with the French, Russian, and at some points the Italian Armies in either a state of indiscipline or

---

September, the rebellious Russians gradually being dispersed to voluntary labour, the final hardcore of 3,000 being shipped to Africa.

[786] Richard M. Watt *Dare Call it Treason* London: Chatto and Windus p184

[787] Prior and Wilson *Passchendaele the Untold Story* p196 'Nevertheless, the clear weakening of resolve of the French army in the first half of 1917, and the utter collapse of the Russian army in the second half, renders it bewildering that the British military command should have risked their own troops' fighting spirit by persisting in the Third Ypres battle.'

collapse, why risk the British Army with a similar fate?[788] Was there ever a clearer case of the wood not being seen for the trees? It was for the precise fact that the other Allied Armies *were* in a state of collapse or turmoil that Haig found it essential to continue with the offensive, sure (and justifiably so) in the solidarity of his own Army. His confidence was clearly justified, for the Army fought its heart out through the worst imaginable conditions without a hint of loss of fighting spirit even during the dark days of August in the Steenbeek valley. This is not to claim that it did not grumble, complain, suffer miserably, and undoubtedly at times despair at what was being asked of it, but that is a good British mile short of indiscipline, mutiny, or lack of 'fighting spirit'. As John Tolland says, 'the British troops groused and made up more caustic poems, but they did not mutiny'.[789] One measure of the morale of an army must be the attitude of prisoners under interrogation. Documents taken from a German officer captured by II Anzac Corps in October revealed the morale of some captured British soldiers. 'Extracts from report on examination of an officer and men of "B" Company the 8th East Yorkshire Regiment, and a man of 1st Gordon Highlanders. Attack: Regarding dispositions and objectives of the attack the men knew nothing and the officer refuses to say anything. Further prospect of an offensive: Prisoners cannot, or will not, give any information in this matter. Battle Dispositions: Of their own brigade are unknown to both men in like manner the higher formations to which they belong. The officer refuses absolutely to answer any questions on military matters.' [790] Not a bad result for an Army with questionable fighting spirit. But should Haig have curbed the offensive operations of the British Army, and limit the scope of actions he believed essential, after giving consideration to the poor morale and levels of indiscipline in the Russian and French Armies? The conditions, problems, and political-social stresses in each Army were totally different. For Haig to have cited lack of morale in the Armies of France or Russia, as a reason not to fight with the British Army in which he had every confidence is plainly absurd, unless there was a major gain to be made by standing on the defensive, which there certainly was not. Furthermore with Russia out of the fight after the 1st September, France temporarily limited in offensive capability and with severely shaken morale after the Nivelle offensive, Italy temporarily limited to defensive action after the 12th September, and the Americans not yet in the fight at all, for the British Army to have also stopped offensive action would have placed the Germans in a position to prepare for their offensive of 1918 which from their point of view could not have been bettered. If Germany had been allowed to run the build up race unimpeded there would have been only one outcome in the spring of 1918.

Flanders had long been Haig's preferred point of attack and that preference was now to be of great significance. The Germans had attacked the French at Verdun for the very reason that they knew full well the French could not refuse to fight. They would hold Verdun come what may, and at all costs. The great battles of attrition in 1916 at Verdun and on the Somme had caused Ludendorff to be less than enthusiastic at the prospects of fighting another such wearing-out battle, which German manpower shortages were making him unwilling to contemplate. At a meeting at Pless on the 1st January 1917 at which the German Chancellor, Hindenburg and Ludendorff were present, the latter had stated: 'The U-boat war will improve the situation even of our armies…We must spare the troops another Somme battle.'[791] The withdrawal to the

---

[788] Prior and Wilson *Passchendaele the Untold Story* p196 'In the year when the command structure of the Russian army disintegrated utterly and large numbers of French soldiers mutinied, the question poses itself: how close did Haig's forces come to acts of 'collective indiscipline?' But they go on to explain that at no point during the offensive did discipline in the British Army brake down. So whilst virtually ignoring and failing to discuss the French mutinies, which *did* happen and therefore arguably had an impact on the overall conduct of the campaign, we are thrown a red herring, and asked to consider how close the British Army came to mutiny in the field, a hypothetical scenario which *did not*.
[789] John Tolland (1980) *No Man's Land* New York: Konecky & Konecky p xvi
[790] Australian War Memorial, Intelligence report, Headquarters II Anzac Corps, AWM4-1/33/18
[791] Ludendorff, The General Staff and its Problems, Dutton, New York, p305

Hindenburg Line in the spring of 1917, to shorten the line and so save manpower had also saved the enemy from greater losses during the Nivelle offensive, which they would undoubtedly have suffered if they had maintained their old line. The 'give-not-an-inch' policy that von Falkenhayn had adopted on the Somme, was very different to that now displayed by Ludendorff, who was obviously willing to give up ground if he considered it to be in his long-term strategic interest. So what was the German policy to be in Flanders, where it was clear by late spring the British were going to mount a serious attack? To hold the great defensive position in Flanders would inevitably lead to another costly battle of attrition. A lot may depend on how persistently the British pressed their attack. But there were other considerations, for to withdraw in Flanders meant more than just giving up ground. Admiral Reinhardt Scheer, Commander of the High Seas Fleet later wrote: 'At the beginning of the year of 1916 the Chief of the General Staff of the Army, von Falkenhayn, had also strongly advocated our embarking on an unrestricted U-boat campaign, because he had realised that our only hope of future salvation lay in overcoming English resistance. In the autumn of 1916 Field-Marshal von Hindenburg took over Supreme Command of the Army, to save the serious situation which had arisen in the land war. At that time there was under discussion a new demand on the part of the Chief of the Naval Staff to resume the U-boat campaign with full intensity. At the meeting of September 3rd at General Headquarters in Pless, at which the matter was considered, the following were present: the Imperial Chancellor, the Field-Marshal, General Ludendorff, Admiral von Holtzendorff, Admiral von Capelle, as Secretary of State of the Imperial Ministry of Marine, the Secretary of State of Foreign Affairs, von Jagow, the Secretary of State, Helfferich, and the War Minister, Wild von Hohenborn. The outcome of the proceedings was that, after consulting all who were concerned in the question of the U-boat campaign, they unanimously declared that the decision must for the time being be postponed, because the general situation, and especially the military situation, was by no means clear, and they resolved that the final decision should lie with the General Field-Marshal Hindenburg

I took occasion after that to send the Chief of Staff of the High Seas Fleet to General Headquarters, to consult with General Ludendorff, and they agreed upon the following: 1/ There is no possibility of bringing the war to a satisfactory end without ruthless U-boat warfare. 2/ On no account must a half-and-half campaign be started, which could not achieve anything of importance, but involve the same military dangers, and would probably result in a new limitation for the nation.....The Chief of Staff returned from this conference under the impression that the question of the U-boat campaign could not be in better hands than in those of the Chief of the General Staff of the Army. I was able to confirm this view later, when on November the 22nd I had occasion myself to discuss the question at General Headquarters with the Field-Marshal and with General Ludendorff. The refusal of our peace proposal of December brought about a new situation in the U-boat war. Our enemies had given us clearly to understand that they would accept no peace of understanding. This led to the decision to open the unrestricted U-boat campaign on February 1st 1917. The Chief of the Naval Staff, with the approval of the General Field-Marshal, succeeded in bringing about this decision, in which the Imperial Chancellor acquiesced. So on that date the most effective period of our war against England actually began. On December 2nd 1916, the Chief of the Naval Staff had again, in a detailed memorandum, given explicit reasons for adopting this form of campaign. He summed up his arguments as follows: '1/ A decision must be reached in the war before the autumn of 1917, if it is not to end in the exhaustion of all parties, and consequently disastrously for us. Of our enemies, Italy and France are economically so hard hit that they are only held up by England's energy and activity. If we can break England's back the war will at once be decided in our favour. Now England's mainstay is her shipping, which brings to the British Isles the necessary supplies of food and materials for war industries, and ensures their solvency abroad......6/ I am most emphatically of opinion that war with the United States of America is such a serious matter that everything must be done to avoid it. But in my opinion, fear of a break must not hinder us from using this weapon which promises success'......With the unrestricted U-boat campaign we had probably embarked on the most tremendous undertaking that the world-war brought in its long train. Our aim was to break the power of mighty England vested in her sea trade in spite of the protection which her powerful fleet could afford her. Two and a half years of the world-war had passed before we addressed ourselves to this task, and they had taxed the strength of the Central Powers to the uttermost.'[792]

Here lay a dilemma for the Germans of unimaginable proportions. Scheer had received agreement in the necessity of the U-boat campaign from Ludendorff, as the only method to bring England down, even if it risked war with the United States. The Flemish bases as we have seen, were of immense value in pursuance of the U-boat offensive. To relinquish them would risk condemning the whole enterprise to failure, on which Germany by admission had based her future hopes. But to protect them may cost Germany more than she could possibly afford to pay. Continued possession of the U-boat bases threatened to place the Germans in the same position as they had placed the French at Verdun. Whether they wanted to fight a battle of attrition in Flanders or not, if the British attacked there they would have to. The magnitude of the problem would undoubtedly depend on how persistently the British pressed their attack, and the question would have to be revisited when that was known.

The necessity to keep the attention of the enemy away from the French had occurred mainly in consequence of the Nivelle disaster. The Allied objective prior to the adoption of Nivelle's ideas had been to degrade the enemy defences in terms of manpower, equipment and morale, by a series of wearing down battles in furtherance of the agreements of the Chantilly Conference of the 15th November 1916. After the disastrous Nivelle offensive it had been agreed to return to wearing down attacks with limited objectives, within the protection of the field artillery, and this had been settled at the Paris Conference in May. The fact was that by the 2nd June, at least two of Haig's objectives, wearing down the German Army, and keeping the Germans off the French, went hand in glove. To do one would achieve the other. So how had Haig's Northern Offensive performed in this respect?

If the Germans had thought themselves capable of winning the War on land at the beginning of 1917, it is reasonable to assume that they would not have resorted to a form of warfare which was most likely to bring the United States into the conflict and thus guarantee, if the Allies were given the vital time, Germany's own long-term defeat. It has been argued that the true reason for the United States entering the War was not the resumption of the U-boat campaign, but this does not alter the fact that German diplomats were convinced at the time that this would be the result. The German ambassador in Washington had made this very clear in a telegram to the Foreign Office in Berlin on the 27th January 1917 in which he stated: 'If the U-boat campaign is opened now without any further ado, the President will regard this as a smack in the face, and war with the United States will be inevitable. The war party here will gain the upper hand and the end of the war will be quite out of sight, as whatever people say to the contrary the resources of the United States are enormous.'[793] The re-opening of unrestricted U-boat warfare appears as an act of folly by desperate men. At the beginning of 1917 the German Field Army numbered a staggering 5,253,000 men (238 divisions), 680,000 more than at the beginning of 1916. But the year had started badly, and in the spring battles at Arras, on the Aisne, and at Messines, it was believed to have sustained casualties of over 384,000, of which 121,000 had been killed or were missing. So widespread were the demands on this huge Army that it was insufficient for the task, and by July the general reserve amounted to no more than 6 divisions.[794] It was still an enormous force but it was stretched beyond its means, and sufficient wearing down, or attrition, applied at a strategically vulnerable point, such as Flanders, may well, by further reducing its strength, stretch it beyond its limits with disastrous results. This was not an unreasonable argument, and in fact came within a whisker of fruition.

---

[792] Reinhard Scheer (1919) *Germany's High Seas Fleet in the War* London: Cassell
[793] Ludendorff *The General Staff and its Problems* Dutton: New York p333
[794] This reserve had been used first in Russia to defeat the Kerenski offensive between the 8th and 28th July, then at Riga on the 1st September, and most spectacularly in Italy at Caporetto on the 24th October.

German records show that from the 31st July 1917 to the end of November, within General von Armin's *Fourth Army*, 86 German divisions were at varying times present in Flanders, not including the 3 divisions of the *MarineKorps*. Of these 86 divisions, (which amounted to about half the total strength of 156 divisions on the Western Front), 37 were transferred from the French sector of the Western Front to Flanders. The number of German divisions in Flanders fluctuated throughout the period. During the battles of Pilckem Ridge, Langemarck, Menin Road, Polygon Wood and Broodseinde, the figure remained fairly constant at around 22 divisions. After Broodseinde, around the time of Poelcappelle, it leapt to 31, reducing to 28 for the period of First Passchendaele. For the period of Second Passchendaele it again reached an extraordinary 40 divisions. During the final phase of the offensive, that is after the 26th October, a further 9 German divisions were transferred to Flanders from sectors of the French front including St.Mihiel, Champagne, and Verdun. Even after the fighting at Passchendaele finished on the 10th November another 5 German divisions were transferred to the sector. The attack on the 4th October prompted the Germans to move 9 fresh divisions into the battle sector. No fewer than 22 fresh divisions were moved into Flanders during the final period after the First Battle of Passchendaele, and 9 of these subsequent to the Canadian attack that threatened Passchendaele (which was to be held by the enemy at all costs), on the 26th October. Rupprecht's Chief of Staff, General von Kuhl expressed his personal viewpoint. 'About the middle of October, the greater part of the divisions on the rest of the front of the Group of Armies (which extended from la Fere 15 miles south of St. Quentin to the sea) had already been engaged in Flanders. On the whole front outside Flanders, even at the most threatened places like Lens and St. Quentin, we had no more than the very minimum of defenders to meet any diversion attacks which might be attempted. The Supreme Command, which hitherto had helped as far as its reserves permitted, was now, in view of the general situation, hardly in a position to provide reinforcements from other Groups of Armies on the Western Front. It was, amongst other things, reckoned that the French would proceed to partial attacks to fix German forces on other parts of the front. This actually happened on the 23rd October at Malmaison. Crown Prince Rupprecht found himself compelled to consider whether in the case of his forces proving inadequate, in spite of the many disadvantages involved thereby [including the abandonment of the Flanders coast], he should not withdraw the front in Flanders so far back that the Allies would be forced to carry out an entirely new deployment of their artillery. The time gained thereby could be used for the building of a new defence front, with a shortening of its length and consequent economy of troops. The loss of ground and moral disadvantage of retirement would have to be accepted. Preparations were duly made for this operation.'[795] Knowing the importance the Germans had placed on the U-boat bases, and the hope they still held that the U-boat campaign was the only way they were going to win, that they were seriously considering a withdrawal to relinquish them indicates the level of desperation and anxiety within Rupprecht's Army Group at this time. Crown Prince Rupprecht summed up what the cost to the German Army of continuing to hold on in Flanders had been in his Order of the Day on the 5th December 1917: 'Divisions disappeared by dozens into the turmoil of the battle, only to emerge from the witches' cauldron after a short period, thinned and exhausted, often reduced to a miserable remnant, and the gaping spaces left by them were filled by fresh divisions.'[796]

From the British perspective (and we now know the same view was also held by the Germans), the wearing-down battle had been entirely successful, but at the time there was little by way of evidence to show that a great deal had been achieved. There were a few (like the Canadian Major) who recognised the temporary tactical advantage of the captured ridge, and the decline in the spirit of the enemy, but to the majority the cost in life, limb and misery had been too high. They had no way at the time of knowing the enormity of their achievement.

The Germans had missed a major opportunity to finish the War at the height of the French mutiny, an event about which they had at least some knowledge. A thrust across the Aisne from Soissons towards Paris in late May could well have sealed the fate of France. But by

---

[795] BOH p-xii
[796] BOH p-xiv

early June it was too late. Between the 1st May and the 7th June, with a general movement to the north, the strength of the *Fourth Army* in Flanders increased by 13 divisions and by 106 batteries, 85 of which were heavy, with a consequential reduction in the forces in the south. The German Official Account says that as early as the 12th of May that reports of a British attack in Flanders began to increase, and O.H.L. saw that it must be reckoned with. The Armies of the Crown Prince were being reduced and he was ordered to fall-back if attacked. As 8 German divisions began to head north to face an imminent British attack the resources were just not available to mount an offensive, but in any event the German High Command had placed its faith in the unrestricted U-boat campaign to finish the War. The six month period in which Admiral von Holtzendorff had claimed the U-boats could bring the British to their knees was up on the 1st August. The time period had not been kept a military secret but had been announced to the German public, which by the time of the opening of the Flanders offensive, was expecting positive results from their navy. Instead they got a major attack by the British. But the *Fourth Army* had withstood Gough's first two hammer blows well, and the British had become bogged down in August, both by the enemy and the mud. In September and the beginning of October the pendulum had swung the other way as in better weather Plumer's three steps had clinically cut into, and then broken the German defences. The golden challis on the coast once more appeared to Haig to be within his grasp, even though the weather had then turned sour.

On the 4th October, progress towards two of Haig's three objectives was going very well, and even the third looked hopeful. Was this the right time to call-off the offensive as many have subsequently claimed? The rain which returned on the 3rd October, Rupprecht's 'best ally', had improved the German hand once more; certainly improved it to the extent that the challis again slipped away. But the rain was not going to stop the grinding down of further German divisions still being moved to Flanders, and it was not going to stop the gradual recovery of the French. Kuhl's opinion written later regarding the Battle was that, 't*he supply of reinforcements was bound to become even more difficult in the ensuing years, so that in the end the conduct of the War was definitely influenced by it. On this point Field-Marshal Haig has been quite right: if he did not actually break through the German front, the Flanders battle consumed the German strength to such a degree that the harm done could no longer be repaired. The sharp edge of the German sword had become ragged'.*[797]

So throughout October and into November Haig continued to grind away at the enemy, fully aware of the conditions on the battlefield under which his soldiers were fighting, but also fully aware of the dangerous consequences of stopping. A further 33 German divisions were to be transferred to Flanders from the period starting 9th October until the end of the offensive, this at a time when the British effort was largely limited to attacks on Passchendaele, Poelcappelle and along the southern edge Houthulst Forest. Until the very end of the campaign the Germans continued to be anxious of a British breakthrough to the coast. After the fall of Passchendaele to the Canadians in November, the *Fourth Army* Commander General von Armin met with Admiral von Schröder of the *MarineKorps* to determine what the effect on the submarine war would be if the German Army was forced to abandon the Belgian coast. This alarmed von Schröder to the extent that he immediately wrote to the Naval Staff to find out whether or not this was seriously being considered.

It is quite clear therefore, and made even more so by the opinions of the enemy who new their situation better than anyone, that the Passchendaele Offensive had been entirely successful in focusing the German Army's strength, much against its own will, to a battle of attrition in Flanders, and in so doing had also been successful in wearing down that Army, causing it significant and long-term irreparable damage. Whilst the British had battled on for over 14 weeks through horrendous hardships, the French had been given the time to recover, and Pétain had used it well. The fledgling American Army also slowly gathered its strength. To have stood on the defensive for the second half of 1917 would have been a totally unjustifiable gamble. To have gained the advantage for the Allied cause in so doing, it would have been necessary to build up forces at a greater rate than the Germans throughout the period, and there

---

[797] BOH p-xv

was no guarantee that this could be done. Given the production capacity of German industry, backed by the output of the captured facilities in Belgium, Luxembourg and Northern France, the German build-up, without the drain Passchendaele had placed on their resources, may well have been greater than the Allies. Throughout 1917 Germany produced around 14 million metric tons of coal per month from its own mines.[798] France managed to produce around 1.7 million metric tons per month,[799] whilst Great Britain produced just over 21 million metric tons per month, much of which was destined not for industry and armaments production, but for fuel for most of its merchant, and part of its Royal Naval fleets.[800] An examination of steel production reveals a large German superiority in the output of this vital strategic material. In 1917 France produced 1.8 million metric tons of steel ingots and castings.[801] In the same year Germany produced 16.2 million metric tons.[802] Britain produced about 9.5 million long tons (9.7 metric tons) of steel,[803] but much of the British steel production was going to the shipbuilding industry to make up losses due to the U-boat campaign, which between January to June 1917 had amounted to 694 ships totalling 2,136,126 gross tons.[804] For use in its armaments industry Germany was producing as much coal, and over 50% more steel than Britain and France. Passchendaele, whilst being a gamble in itself, had without question removed the risk of a far greater gamble, and had denied the enemy time in which to accumulate an unstoppable offensive energy. This was to be proven in 1918, when at the beginning of the great spring offensive, on the main front of attack against the British Fifth and Third Armies, Germany had accumulated 6,473 guns and 3,532 trench mortars,[805] an enormous assembly which still proved insufficient to force a final decision. But the essential time, of which the Germans had successfully been deprived, had been won by the British Army at a fearful cost.

The Casualties – the cost of the achievement

By the end of the offensive the U-boat bases remained for the time being in the hands of the enemy, and the damage they continued to inflict was grievous; but not terminal. For the men who had fought at Passchendaele there was for the moment little tangible sense of achievement. But the memories of the awful conditions, the suffering, and the casualties were all too vivid and would remain so. The casualty figures have always been at the centre of the ongoing

---

[798] National Bureau of Economic Research, Inc. Cambridge, Massachusetts. NBER macrohistory I. Production of commodities. Ref: m01119b Source: Data for 1914-1918: Institut fur Weltwirtschaft und Seeverkehr of Kiel University. The figure of 167 million metric tons accounted for the production of the Rhur, Upper Silesia, the Saar, Lower Silesia, Saxony and Aachen. See also *Annals of the American Academy of Political and Social Science*, Vol. 92, Social and Industrial Conditions in the Germany of Today (Nov., 1920), pp. 66-75

[799] National Bureau of Economic Research, Inc. Cambridge, Massachusetts. NBER macrohistory I. Production of commodities. Ref: a01214 Source: Direction des Mines, Statistique de l'Industrie. Minerale, 1870-1872 and later issues.

[800] National Bureau of Economic Research, Inc. Cambridge, Massachusetts. NBER macrohistory I. Production of commodities. Ref: m01133c Source: Computed by NBER from data found in Board of Trade Journal, 27th February 1919, p269; 12th June 1919, p744 and later issues.

[801] National Bureau of Economic Research, Inc. Cambridge, Massachusetts. Ref: a01213 Source: Annuarie Statistique 1935 p81

[802] National Bureau of Economic Research, Inc. Cambridge, Massachusetts. Ref: a01261 Source: Verein Deutscher und Stahl Industrieller, Deutschlande Gerwinnung an Roheisen, Rohstahl, und Walzwerkserzengnissen, 1933, pp 28-29

[803] National Bureau of Economic Research, Inc. Cambridge, Massachusetts. NBER macrohistory I. Production of commodities. Ref: a01183ba Source: National Federation of Iron and Steel Manufacturers, Statistics for the Iron and Steel industries, 1934, p9

[804] BOH p-viii and footnote p103. See also Mark D. Karau *Wielding the Dagger, TheMarineKorps Flandern and the German War Effort* Westport: Praeger pp128-130, 146-147, 163-164.

[805] John Terraine (1978) *To Win a War* Sidgwick & Jackson p60

controversy surrounding Passchendaele. From the outset it is essential to state that to attempt to be precise regarding the number of casualties sustained throughout the Third Battle of Ypres is an impossible exercise. There have been numerous assessments, both official and unofficial, all purporting to be correct, but resulting in very different figures. But it is not a simple matter to even specify what constituted a casualty, the extent of the geographical area included as a catchment for statistics, or from what start date to what finish date the figures apply. For example, do (or should) the quoted figures include the large number of casualties sustained by Fifth Army in the Salient during the build-up period before the 31st July? There are other complications for the British Official History tells us that some official figures were based on the number of wound casualties, not the wounded men, causing inflation in the British wounded total.[806] It also states that the German wounded figures did not include wounded whose recovery was to be expected in a reasonable time.[807] There was therefore no consistent and directly comparable calculation for the number of casualties of each side, and few date or geographical parameters given to explain how the figures were arrived at.

British losses approaching 400,000 have been quoted in some accounts, the figure used as primary evidence in condemning the whole concept and management of the Battle, and the abilities and characters of the commanders who directed it. The origin of this figure of 400,000 is obscure but may be the Bavarian Official Account, undoubtedly not the best point of reference for British casualty figures, which stated that the British had lost about 400,000 men on the battlefields of Flanders.[808] After the War, Lloyd George began using the 400,000 figure, and others followed, either in full knowledge that it was incorrect, or in total ignorance of what the numbers really were but happy to accept a figure which best reinforced their argument. The enormous figure provided Lloyd George with the proof that at the time he had been quite correct in his reticence to support the Flanders offensive. The consequence of the repetition of the 400,000 figure, with no proof offered as to its provenance, was to ensure an ongoing assault on Haig's reputation. Since then many disparaging written or spoken commentaries on Passchendaele, come with the inevitable 400,000 figure, or something very near it. It certainly has the effect of sensationalising the story, but is the figure in any way accurate? As time passes, rather than becoming better researched, or at least more realistic, the reports of Passchendaele casualties become more lurid, as a modern media demands even greater sensationalism to add spice to a subject that they would otherwise consider dull and un-newsworthy. The 90 year anniversary ceremonies held at Ypres on the 12th July 2007 in remembrance of Passchendaele are a notable recent example. On that day various British national television news programmes, whilst briefly acknowledging the occasion, gave in the early evening broadcast the casualty figures for the Battle of Passchendaele as 350,000 dead (a quite ridiculous figure), increasing to 500,000 casualties mid-evening, and then later to 550,000 casualties, the carnage increasing as the evening progressed. On the 29th July 2007 a BBC news broadcast, giving an account of the visit of a Passchendaele veteran to Ypres on that day, gave the casualty figure as 250,000 dead.

One thing is for certain; totally verifiable figures are not available to accurately establish what the total casualties in the Third Battle of Ypres were. In the British Official History Edmonds gives a total of 238,313 casualties, calculated from returns made weekly by Fifth and Second Armies to G.H.Q.[809] So whose figure is nearer correct, Edmonds or Lloyd George? The Fifth Army totals, obtained by the author from the Fifth Army headquarters War Diary, give an approximate figure of 142,307 total casualties, with 18,697 killed, from week ending 6th July to week ending 28th October.[810] From week ending 27th July to week ending 28th October the figure is approximately 124,163 with 16,443 killed. The figure given to the Supreme War Council at Versailles on the 25th February 1919, when according to the British Official Historian an

---

[806] BOH p-vi
[807] BOH p362
[808] BOH p-vi
[809] BOH pp364-365
[810] National Archives, War Diary Fifth Army headquarters, weekly casualty reports WO95/520. Some entries, for instance that of the 3rd August, acknowledge that the figures given are approximate.

endeavour was made to make them as large as possible, was 244,897.[811] The figure quoted in the Australian Official Account based on the official compilations of the "Statistics of Military Effort of the British Empire in the Great War" is 448,416, but this figure also includes casualties for the Battle of Cambrai.[812] The figure quoted by Edmonds in the British Official History, from the same source, (Statistics of Military Effort of the British Empire in the Great War), is 380,002, from the 31st July to the 31st December.[813] If the Cambrai figures are accepted as around 45,000, then a figure of 400,000 British and Empire casualties is claimed in the Australian account, but 335,000 in the British. Edmonds claims that the figure of 335,000 has been inflated by incorporating the total number of wounds (284,684) rather than the number of wounded men (172,994), that is by 111,690, bringing the figure back to 223,310. The Australian Medical Services Official Account gives a figure of 720,000 as a combined British and German total for the whole Battle,[814] but it seems this is a rough addition of the British (448,614) and German (270,710) figures quoted in the Australian Official Account. It also gives a figure of 109,000 British casualties for the period 5th August to 9th September, when Fifth Army fought at Westhoek and the Battle of Langemarck,[815] whilst Fifth Army records for the same period give approximately 60,000. To try to make sense of the figures is like walking into an endless maze; but try we must.

A review of the casualty figures given in unofficial accounts becomes even more confusing, and rarely if ever is an explanation given as to how the figures were arrived at. In *The Myth of the Great War* John Mosier says his best estimate is that the B.E.F. lost 399,821 officers and men in casualties of all kinds (killed, wounded, and missing).[816] Nigel Steel and Peter Hart in *Passchendaele the Sacrificial Ground*, although admitting that analysis of the casualty figures is an unrewarding minefield claim that the British Empire suffered some 275,000 casualties and the French in the region of 8,500.[817] Lyn Macdonald in *They Called it Passchendaele* tells us there were quarter of a million casualties and that official estimates of the number of dead made after the War ranged from as few as 36,000 to as many as 150,000.[818] Richard Holmes in *Western Front* believes a figure of 260,000 to be a fair estimate.[819] Prior and Wilson put the figure at 275,000 including the Battle of Messines.[820]

The author has attempted to examine the figures using a different approach. Between the 31st July and the 10th November, a total of 54 British divisions had been engaged, which during the offensive made divisional scale attacks on just short of 100 occasions. These divisional attacks had resulted in around 165 brigade engagements, which had in turn resulted in approximately 550 battalion engagements. On the 9th October in the fighting at Passchendaele, the 8 battalions of the 197th and 198th Brigades of the 66th Division, in one of the bloodiest fights of the campaign, had sustained casualties of 2,545, and the division as a whole 3,119, an average of around 390 casualties per infantry battalion engaged. At the extreme end of the casualty scale, the 1/5th Northumberland Fusiliers, 149th Brigade, 50th Division, on the 26th October at Houthulst Forest had sustained 451 casualties, and had been virtually wiped out. An average

---

[811] BOH p361
[812] AOA p943
[813] BOH p-vii
[814] See A.G.Butler. *Official History of the Australian Medical Services 1914-1918 Vol.2 The Western Front.* P183
[815] See A.G.Butler. *Official History of the Australian Medical Services 1914-1918 Vol.2 The Western Front.* P184
[816] Mosier (2002) *The Myth of the Great War* Perennial p284
[817] Steel and Hart (2002) *Passchendaele the Sacrificial Ground* London: Cassell p303
[818] Lyn Macdonald (1993) *They Called it Passchendaele* Penguin Chapter 19. With regard to the ratio of dead to wounded a rule of thumb figure from the Australian Medical Services account gives 1:3.7 as an average rate. See A.G.Butler. *Official History of the Australian Medical Services 1914-1918 Vol.2 The Western Front.* p249
[819] Richard Holmes (1999) *Western Front* London: BBC p174
[820] Prior and Wilson *Passchendaele the Untold Story* p195

(but still horrendous) casualty figure for a battalion action in the Flanders fighting is about 300. To make a rule of thumb calculation, if extended over 550 battalions, this gives a figure of 165,000 combat casualties. To this "combat" casualty figure must be added a whole host of others, which may have occurred out of the line, or other than on days of major attacks, and must include engineers, artillery, transport and medical personnel, and these figures are difficult to estimate. Casualty figures for battalions just holding the line, or even providing labour out of the line could be extraordinarily high, as in the case of the 16th and 36th Divisions, which sustained 2,000 and 1,500 casualties respectively prior to going into action on the 16th August; but these figures seem to be an exception rather than the rule. The estimated figure of 165,000 combat casualties is all that the author can reasonably establish by applying the known figure of the number of battalions engaged multiplied by an estimated number of average battalion casualties. But encouragingly (from the point of view of corroboration) this number does correspond fairly well with the number obtained by adding together the individual divisional combat casualty figures per battle from the British Official History, which gives a total of 168,846. To this figure must then be added the difficult to estimate non-combat casualties mentioned above. If we accept for a moment the figure of around 165,000 infantry combat casualties, to bring this up to the consensus figure of 260,000 to 270,000 means adding another 95,000 to 105,000 casualties. For 94 days of fighting this would mean adding 1,000 casualties per day to the "combat" casualty figure, which does not seem unreasonable. If the total casualty figure *was* as high as 400,000 it would mean a daily loss of 2,500 to add to the combat casualties, which seems most unlikely. The author therefore tentatively places his head on the block and would concur that between 250,000 and 270,000 casualties is a believable figure. To attempt to be more precise without further evidence is pointless.

As if that were not enough dreadful arithmetic, bearing in mind that an average of approaching one in four of these huge numbers resulted in a fatality, we must now examine the possible German casualty figures. From the outset it is important to note that the establishment of a German division in 1917 was about 12,000, whereas a British division at War strength at this time was nominally over 20,000. The total strength of 86 German divisions therefore amounts to around 1,032,000 men and 54 British divisions 1,080,000 men. In reality they were well below these figures. Considering the numbers of men and not the numbers of divisions gives a different perspective of relative strengths.

The British Official History by applying certain calculations tells us that there is every possibility that the German Army sustained about 400,000 casualties. This figure is obtained by a calculation which is based on the assumption that before relief, a German division sustained casualties of around one third of its strength, which is not unreasonable accepting the superiority (not supremacy) of firepower of the British artillery, and is comparable with a worse case British division experience of casualties amounting to a quarter of rifle strength. But the calculation is also based on the assumption that all German divisions were engaged sufficiently to loose one third of their strength. In the introduction to Chris McCarthy's *Passchendaele, The Day-by-Day Account*, John Lee claims that 88 divisions – over half of the total serving in France and Flanders – were drawn into the battle and thoroughly pulverised.[821] But were all of the German divisions present in the Ypres sector during the period of the Battle 'thoroughly pulverised'? If they were, then Edmonds' figure of 400,000 enemy casualties is about right. But not all British divisions present were engaged to the same extent, one to another, and did not therefore sustain casualties of the same severity before relief, so why is it assumed that all 86/88 German divisions did? Edmunds also quotes Kuhl, in explaining that:

'During the period 15th June to 15th December 1917, 77 divisions were transported to the *Fourth Army* front [from the Lille – Armentiers road to the Belgian coast], and 63 transferred from it....From the beginning of the battle on the 31st July to the 20th August, that is in the first three

---

[821] Chris McCarthy (1995) *The Third Ypres Passchendaele, The Day-by-Day Account* London: Arms and Armour, introduction

weeks, 17 divisions were used up.'[822] Kuhl's figures, as would be expected, correspond with the official German *Divisiongefechtskalender*. But what is omitted from Kuhl's statement is that out of the 63 divisions moved out of Flanders, 14 divisions had already left before the 31st July. Between the 31st July and the 6th November, the actual period of the Battle, 49 German divisions were moved out. Of the total of 86 divisions, (or 88 including the *MarineKorps*), 24 formed the garrison on the 31st July and a further 62 were added to the *Fourth Army* strength during the Battle. But of these 62 divisions, 22 were moved into Flanders after the battle on the 26th October. It is just not possible that these 22 divisions sustained thirty percent casualties at the hands of 1 British and 2 Canadian divisions on the 6th November and 1 Canadian and 1 British division on the 10th of November, plus casualties caused by British artillery or other means. The German casualty calculations in the British Official History are based it would seem on the false premise that all 86 divisions were fully engaged and badly damaged to the same extent. It is more likely that about 68 German divisions, (the initial garrison of 24, plus 40 moved in before the 26th October, and probably 4 others seriously engaged on the 6th and 10th November), were badly mauled to a greater or lesser extent during the offensive. In this case, if Edmonds figure of 4,000 casualties per division is applied, it gives a total of around 272,000 German casualties. This figure closely corresponds with the Australian Official History which gives a German casualty figure of 270,710, with which, although probably arrived at by completely different methods of calculation, the author would largely concur. But as the German divisional strength was probably less than 12,000, a figure of 3,500 casualties per division is probably more appropriate, which would give a German casualty figure of about 238,000. A figure of between 238,000 and 270,000 German casualties would therefore appear to be about right. Again to try and establish greater precision is pointless.

It seems likely therefore that both sides lost about the same number. But as the Germans had fewer men engaged, 68 divisions with (nominally) 12,000 men per division = 816,000 men, against 54 British divisions with (nominally) 20,000 men per division = 1,080,000 men, enemy casualties would have to be at a rate of around 33% to give 272,000 casualties, while those of the British would be around 25% to giving a figure of 270,000. Clearly there is not a great deal of science or precision applied in estimating these figures, but if they are *about* right then the conclusion must be that the battle of attrition was at least as costly for the British as it was for the Germans, although the Germans may have sustained a higher casualty rate per division engaged.

One final word is necessary on casualties. To place in perspective the sometimes over emphasised effect of the German use of Mustard Gas throughout the period of the Third Battle of Ypres it is important to examine actual figures. In the Australian Imperial Force the number of casualties from gassing as a percentage of the total casualties per month was 4.42%, compared with a figure of 32.18% wounded through other causes. The rate of deaths through poison gas was 0.09% of the total monthly casualty figure, less in fact than the rate for self inflicted wounds which was 0.11%.[823]

The tangible achievements

A little more science can be applied to establishing the tangible achievements of the battle measured by way of ground gained. During the whole period of the offensive, around 33.50 square miles of ground was captured, this including about 1.75 square miles captured by the Second Army south of the Klein Zillebeke road during the Battle of Pilckem Ridge on the 31st July. The approximate figures for each Battle were; Pilckem Ridge 11.25 square miles; Langemarck (including the attack at Westhoek) 2.75 square miles; Menin Road 4.5 square miles; Polygon Wood 2.00 square miles; Broodseinde 7.00 square miles; Poelcappelle 2.5 square miles; 1st Passchendaele 1.5 square miles; and 2nd Passchendaele 2.0 square miles. These figures

---

[822] BOH p362
[823] See A.G.Butler. *Official History of the Australian Medical Services 1914-1918 Vol.2 The Western Front.* p243

represent ground captured and held on the day of the Battle, or over three days of battle in the case of 2nd Passchendaele, and do not include ground captured and subsequently lost, as occurred on the 31st July when Fifth Army withdrew from 2.75 square miles of ground east of the Steenbeek.[824]

In themselves these figures tell us little as far as the achievements of the Battle are concerned, although they do constitute a measurable result. At face value, they give an insight into how efficiently each battle was fought, but even this comparison is fraught with complexity. On the 31st July Gough's Fifth Army captured 9.5 square miles of ground at a cost of around 27,000 casualties; approaching 2,850 casualties per square mile. The Battle of the Menin Road Ridge saw Second and Fifth Armies capture only 4.5 square miles at a cost of 20,255 casualties; around 4,500 casualties per square mile. The figures appear to indicate that the Pilckem battle was less costly in casualties per square mile than Menin Road. But the greatest gain in ground in the Pilckem battle was north of the Ypres – Roulers railway where around 7 square miles was captured at a cost of approaching 2,000 casualties per square mile. The remaining 2.5 square miles south of the railway and on the Gheluvelt plateau cost nearer 5,250 casualties per square mile, and of more importance did not achieve its objectives. Also as the German Second Line was not threatened on the plateau, in this area the German counter-attack divisions were not engaged. On the 20th September, in this key area between the Klein Zillebeke road and 700 yards south of the Roulers railway, 2.1 square miles were captured by Second Army at a cost of 4,928 casualties per square mile, more in line with the figures of the 31st July. But all objectives were captured and the German Second and Third Lines were broken, except at Tower Hamlets and the Quadrilateral. Of greatest importance, the German counter-attack divisions were engaged and sustained heavy casualties. Nobody had doubted that the casualties would be high on the 20th September, and this had certainly been the case. But there was no disputing the relative efficiency in the two methods of attack. On the 20th September there was no doubting which side had won and which had lost; and both sides knew it.

The Battle of Broodseinde was another demonstration of the greater efficiency of Plumer's bite-and-hold methods, the last time that the weather, upon which the whole operation relied, was to be with the British. The capture of 7 square miles cost Second and Fifth Armies 2,925 casualties per square mile. Again the greatest number of casualties for the least achievement in ground captured was on the Gheluvelt plateau, where in the fighting along Polderhoek spur and in the Reutelbeek valley, 5th Division had sustained 2,557 casualties for the capture of a quarter of a square mile of ground. However the New Zealand Division across Gravenstafel ridge had captured 1.3 square miles at a cost of 1,643 casualties, 1,263 casualties per square mile. As with the casualties, the permutations are endless, and their meaning, as with all statistics, can be interpreted to suit almost any argument.

Was Haig negligent in not considering Weather and Ground Conditions?

Haig had wanted to launch the British offensive in Flanders in the spring, and had been prevented from doing so by Nivelle's insistence that the British supported his offensive by attacking at Arras. Lloyd George had supported the Nivelle offensive as it offered the chance of a spectacular success, without the risk of huge British casualties, and with Haig in a subordinate role. The timing of the Flanders offensive was therefore not entirely of the Commander-in-Chief's choosing, and neither were all the subsequent delays.
There is nothing odd or unusual about the unpredictability of rainfall in Flanders to anybody used to the weather conditions of most of the British Isles, Belgium or north-west France. On the

---

[824] An explanation of the calculation of the figures for ground captured on the 31st July north of the Klein Zillebeke road (i.e. by Fifth Army), are based on analysis of positions projected on the 1/10,000 map sheets as follows. Map sheet Bixschoote, 20SW4 3.5 million square yards. Map sheet St. Julien, 28NW2 17 million square yards. Map sheet Zillebeke, 28NW4 and NE3 (parts of), 8 million square yards. Map sheet Zonnebeke, 28NE1 1 million square yards. This gives and approximate total of ground captured *and held* on the 31st July as 29.5 million square yards, or 9.5 square miles.

night of the 5th July in the summer of 2004 there was very heavy rain at Langemark. By the morning the Steenbeek had risen by around 12 feet from its normal July level and had covered the Boesinghe road, (at the bridge near the site where the Au Bon Gite blockhouse once stood, known to the British as Piccadilly Bridge), to a depth of one foot of water. The stream had burst across the meadows to flood an area about 200 yards wide, and this with the drainage and water control systems in good order. In a few hours the stream had returned between its banks, and within days the ground was again hard and dry. Flanders weather, like that in Britain, is fickle.

Remarking on Haig's choice of Flanders to launch an offensive, Lloyd George in a further effort to besmirch the Commander-in-Chief's reputation, wrote in his War Memoirs: 'Flanders was the wettest area on the front...in Flanders the weather broke early each August with the regularity of the Indian monsoon.'[825] He claimed that Haig had sufficient information to be forewarned of the inevitable August weather: 'The August failures were put down to the wet weather. As if it had never rained before in that dripping climate!....Figures show what a reckless gamble it was to risk the life of the British Army on the chance of a rainless autumn on the Flemish coast.' Allowing for a limited understanding of geography it seems odd that the ex-Prime Minister should consider the weather in Flanders to be so different from the weather in south-east England, given that the Flemish coast is only 70 miles in a straight line from Kent.[826] The monthly weather summary of the Meteorological Office reporting on the depression which had brought bad weather to south east England and Flanders for August 1917 says: 'The excessive wetness of this particular disturbance will be realised from the fact that for the week ending the 4th [August] a number of stations had totals aggregating from ten to sixteen times the normal, Margate's 144mm being 1,600 per cent of the weeks usual total.'[827] Lloyd George had therefore experienced the conditions for himself in England, and knew full well they were not simply confined to Flanders. His reference to tropical weather conditions had been taken out of context from a somewhat inaccurate off-hand remark by Brigadier-General Charteris who had stated in his book *Field Marshal Earl Haig*: 'Careful investigations of the records of more than eighty years showed that in Flanders the weather broke early each August with the regularity of the Indian monsoon'.[828] Lloyd George had taken little else Charteris had said at face value, but this colourful description of the Flemish weather appeared to suit his purpose. Charteris was to provide a different account three years later in another book which presumably Lloyd George did not see. In his 1931 book *At G.H.Q.*, quoting from his diary on the 30th July 1917 Charteris had written: 'We have carefully prepared statistics of previous years – there are records of eighty years to refer to – and I do not think that we can hope for more than a fortnight, or at the best, three weeks of really fine weather.'[829] He had dropped the word 'monsoon' but Lloyd George was to maintain the myth. Charteris had also written prophetically on the same day regarding the unfortunate delays required by Gough and Anthoine: 'With reasonable luck it will make little difference, but we have so often been let in by the weather that I am very anxious.'

That there would be wet weather in the summer and autumn of 1917 was quite predictable. It was the extent, the persistency, and the lack of drying periods between that was totally unpredictable. Haig could not be found guilty of recklessness in the face of wayward nature, however much Lloyd George may have later wished he could. The recorded historic weather patterns showed August rainfall as normal, September as increasing and October as generally giving most rain, but that the ground was generally dry enough to absorb most of the rain quickly.[830]

---

[825] Lloyd George (1938) *War Memoirs Vol 2* Odhams: London p2207
[826] Denis Winter talks of the 'foul climate of Flanders'. The author has lived in Flanders for four years and has not found it such. Perhaps Winter was referring specifically to 1917. *Haig's Command* p91
[827] National Archives, monthly weather summary of the Meteorological Office August 1917, WO106/407
[828] John Charteris (1929) *Field Marshal Earl Haig* London: Cassell p272
[829] John Charteris (1931) *At G.H.Q.* London: Cassell p237
[830] BOH p211

The actual rainfall figures for the area for the years 1915, 1916, 1917, were: [831]

	July	Aug	Sept	Oct	
1915	2.12"	1.5"	5.11"	N/K	Weather station St. Omer
1916	1.02"	2.91"	2.20"	2.72"	Weather station unknown (Second Army)
1917	3.14"	5.00"	1.58"	4.21"	Weather station Vlamertinghe

Lloyd Georges Memoirs gave the following rainfall statistics (with no reference to where they were recorded):

	July	Aug	Sept	Oct
1915	2.91"	4.21"	2.56"	Not given
1916	3.86"	2.79"	3.07"	Not given
1917	4.095"	4.17"	0.692"	Not given

It is very difficult to see what Lloyd George was trying to prove with these figures, as for 1916 they do not show 'monsoon' conditions for August, which leaves only the 1915 figure of 4.21 inches as the evidence to prove his case. The Army figure for August 1915 however was 1.5 inches.

Historic average monthly figures for Lille,[832] in years which saw heavy rainfall in August, September or October show:

	August	September	October
1893	38mm	117mm	83mm
1894	126mm	138mm	216mm
1895	132mm	1mm	130mm
1896	45mm	103mm	141mm
1897	102mm	69mm	16mm
1907	69mm	122mm	64mm
1908	80mm	81mm	23mm
1909	69mm	122mm	20mm
Average	82mm	94mm	86mm

These figures disprove Lloyd George's claim. The post War attempts by the ex-Prime Minister to condemn Haig for blatantly disregarding weather predictions for a 'monsoon' August were finally shown up for what they were by Lieutenant-Colonel Ernest Gold head of the

---

[831] BOH p212. To add further confusion to the argument the wartime statistics were kept in millimetres, whereas all the post-war quotations were given in inches.
[832] National Archives, Meteorological Section R.E. General note on the weather of August, September and October 1917 in the British Army Area, table IV, WO106/407

meteorology section of the B.E.F. who in 1958 wrote an article on the subject for the Spectator. He made it very clear that the August 1917 rainfall was unprecedented, at 57mm above average for the month at Vlamertinghe. Others were still claiming it was foreseeable, which prompted him to write: 'It is quite contrary to the evidence of the actual records which show that the weather in August 1917, in and around the battle area, was exceptionally bad. The rainfall directly affecting the first month of the offensive was more than double the average; it was over five times the amount for the same period in 1915 and 1916. The period is July 29 to August 28. The rainfall at Vlamertinghe was 157mm (6.18") in 1917 and 28mm in 1916. At St. Omer it was 30mm in 1915 (there was no rain gauge then at Vlamertinghe). The quite exceptionally heavy rain from July 29 to August 4, 1917, was followed by muggy, stagnant weather which prevented the drying by evaporation, normal in the intervals of fair weather at that time of year.'[833]

The figures are also at variance with the findings of Denis Winter who claims that figures from the previous thirty years showed July and August were the most unpredictable months, that September was the best month (dry one year in four) and October was dry only one year in ten and had historically been the wettest month of the year.[834] But a report compiled by Gold, dated 20th October 1917 titled 'General note on the weather of August, September and October 1917 in the British Army Area' says: 'The beginning of August is not usually a wet time as the attached diagram based at Lille shows.' Gold summarized his report thus: 'The tables indicate roughly that August [1917] was bad and nearly as bad as August has ever been: that September was good though not as good as some previous Septembers notably 1888, 1898, 1907: that so far October has been bad with conditions in the first half of the month similar to those which prevail in the latter half of a wet October.' [835]

Lloyd George was fully aware at the time that the weather conditions could not have been predicted, as the Cabinet had been kept informed that not only had the August rainfall been heavy, but it had also been abnormal. Haig had produced a report on the 22nd October for Robertson, who sent it on to Hankey on the 23rd, for the attention of the War Cabinet. It read: 'The weather at the beginning of August was exceptionally and unexpectedly bad; heavy rain began to fall late on July 31st and continued almost without ceasing till August 4th. During this time the average rainfall of three places in the battle zone was 76mm, whereas records of thirty years show that the average rainfall at Lille during the first five days of August amounts to 8mm only. After four dull and foggy days which gave the ground little chance to dry up, a period of changeable weather with some showers, drizzle and thunderstorms lasted for a fortnight, but heavy rain set in again on the night of the 26th and the last days of the month were wet and stormy. The abnormal wetness of this month in Flanders may be seen from the fact that whereas the August rainfall at places in the battle zone where records are available is normally 70mm, it amounted this year to no less than 162mm. During September the rainfall in Flanders was below normal, but the weather broke again on October the 3rd and rain fell on every day except two up to the 19th, by which date the normal rainfall for the whole month of October had been surpassed.'[836]

That the rainfall had brought with it atrocious conditions was agreed by all, but the subsequent attempts which continue to pin the responsibility on Haig for not foreseeing the possibility of extremely bad August weather were nonsense, and have been proved to be wrong. For certain the rain had quickly softened the surface of the battlefield, and beneath the feet of tens of thousands of men and animals, and countless narrow, iron-rimmed wheels that surface had rapidly turned to soft creamy mud. But the ground conditions in Flanders when it rained were no worse than they would have been at Loos, Arras, or on the Somme under the constant load of marching feet and shifting guns. There is no doubt that the mud at Ypres is different to

---

[833] Lieut.-Col Ernest Gold, Meteorological Section, Royal Engineers, G.H.Q. in The Spectator, 17th January 1958.
[834] Denis Winter *Haig's Command* p 92
[835] National Archives, Meteorological Section R.E. General memorandum by Major E. Gold WO106/407
[836] National Archives Haig to CIGS 22nd October 1917, WO106/407

that found on other Western Front battlefields. The soil is very light with a high proportion of fine sand, which in dry weather blows off the fields and across the tracks, like the sand at the fringes of a beach. In the wet it soon turns to a very soft quicksand, which will support very little weight. A high water table means the surface does not drain well, and after a short period of rain the surface becomes saturated and pools quickly form. The mud is however nowhere near as clinging as that of Loos or the Somme. The author made the mistake of leaving a heavy plastering of mud on his car overnight, from the tracks around Hulloch on the Loos battlefield. By the next morning it had set to an almost concrete like hardness. From recent experience, for impeding movement the mud of the Loos battlefield takes some beating. The wet August 1917 at Loos, where there had been a total of 110mm of rain, 60mm above average, or on the Somme, where there had been 98mm of rain, 55mm above average, would have produced equally dire conditions as those experienced in Flanders. The mud at Ypres made movement slow and exhausting, but only on rare occasions did it actually stop the movement of the infantry. In October when it became necessary to move the artillery forward in pace with Plumers attacks, the mud did temporarily stop the movement of guns and ammunition. When it rained, the utter devastation of the whole area by shellfire and the enormous damage done to the man made drainage systems, on which the control of surface drainage relied, added greatly to the problems of movement. But the Australians reported that for them the Somme in late 1916 had been worse.[837] The conditions of mud were never sufficient to call off the offensive, given the overwhelmingly serious reasons for maintaining the initiative at that time. Even under the worst conditions in late October, the Canadians, with superhuman efforts, repaired roads, laid tracks, and moved forward sufficient guns to support their attack on Passchendaele. As John Buchan so aptly put it: 'The British movements became an accurate barometer; whenever it was more than usually tempestuous it was safe to assume that some zero hour was near.'[838] It was not foresight that Haig had lacked, it was luck; and it was not a disregard of possible bad weather which had helped damned his reputation, it was the knowingly false claims of Lloyd George. The clamour of erroneous claims has hardly subsided over the years.[839]

Conclusions and the long-term achievements

At the time, the amount of ground taken in relation to the cost appeared but little, and 1917 was to close without the conclusive result expected, or at least hoped for by either side. The hugely costly defence of the Flanders position by the *Fourth Army* had allowed the German Navy twice the length of time its leaders had required to bring down Britain, and with her the Allied cause. It had not happened, and as defences against submarines were refined and Allied shipbuilding

---

[837] AOA p890/1 and p930

[838] Sir John Hammerton *World War 1914-1918* London: Amalgamated Press p1151

[839] Denis Winter claims that no commander could have been better informed about the enemy defences, the terrain or the weather he was likely to encounter, and that Haig had acknowledged that fact, warning on the 5th July that 'the progress of events may demand modifications, especially in view of the comparatively short period of fine weather we can count on'. *Haig's Command* p92 But Winter only partially quotes Haig. As we saw in Chapter 1 the full passage reads 'the Commander of the Second Army will also be prepared with plans to develop an advance towards the line Warneton – Menin, or push forward on the right of the Fifth Army to the line Courtrai – Roulers (throwing out a flank guard along the line of the Lys), if circumstances should render such movements desirable as the situation develops - the above outline of possibilities is issued to enable Army Commanders to foresee and prepare for what may be required of them. The progress of events may demand modifications or alterations of plan from time to time and, - especially in view of the comparatively short period of fine weather we can count on, - our progress before winter sets in may fall short of what would otherwise have been within our power for this year' This was a perfectly reasonable warning and would have made sense for any long term offensive being considered in any part of northwest Europe, and in no way implied that Haig expected the appalling weather he was to actually experience. National Archives, Haig to Army Commanders 5th July, WO158/311

at last began to outstrip losses, it never would. The U-boat and destroyer bases had not been closely threatened, although at times, the enemy had quivered at the possibility. But the threat to Britain of the U-boats and destroyers on the Flemish coast, for long recognised, and so dramatically reiterated by Jellicoe, had set the Army upon a course for which it had long planned. From the German viewpoint the outcome was somewhat ironic. They had defended at great cost, an asset which at the time was erroneously believed to be their only hope of victory, and like the French at Verdun they could do nothing but defend it. What they had been defending turned out eventually not to have been worth the effort. But they had been defending more than just the U-boat bases. They had been defending the most strategically vulnerable part of their great defence system in the west, the northern end of the Western Front. Here they were sensitive to any British threat, and as they had shown, they would defend the position at all costs.

In addition to the task of eliminating the threat on the coast, Haig was also burdened in June with the alarming news of the troubles within the French Army, and the Northern Offensive had taken on a new and added urgency. Haig's choice of Gough to command the offensive rather than Plumer, was undoubtedly a mistake. But the vision of a break through to the coast mesmerised the Commander-in Chief. Detrimental to the clarity of thinking required to fight either a break through battle, or a wearing down battle, his objectives confusingly now called for both. The plans of General Gough, did in his opinion constitute a step-by-step approach. But to most others they looked like an attempt at a break through, and this conspired to cloud Haig's judgement. This was a major error. A firmer hand at this point would have reined in Gough's proposed advance and kept it within the range of the field artillery, although ironically Gough was probably doing no more than he believed Haig had ordered him to do, and Plumer's vehement support of Gough's plan (according to Davidson), adds further to the confusion from an unexpected quarter.

The delay between the end of Messines and the beginning of Passchendaele cost six weeks of good campaigning weather. But as the resources in manpower or guns were not available sooner to begin making the massive arrangements necessary for the offensive little could be done, and subsequently both Gough and Anthoine had asked for longer to make their artillery preparations. The delay was down to logistics, and certainly had nothing whatsoever to do with Gough's appointment, Mustard gas, or Belgian reticence.

The withdrawal on the 31st July of in some places 2,500 yards, back to the Steenbeek, proved that the warnings of Davidson and others had been valid. The deep penetration attack had fallen into the trap of von Lossberg's counter-attack divisions. North of St. Julien, where the advance had stopped on the Steenbeek, it had held firm. The failure to break the German Second Line at Gheluvelt had also been predicted, but here Gough was less culpable. To achieve a broad front attack by Fifth Army with the forces available, virtually eliminated the possibility of sufficient preparation and concentration of strength at the Gheluvelt plateau. As we have seen there were totally insufficient guns for the purpose. The break in the weather before the 31st would not have been such a problem had it not continued for so long, and had there been sufficient warmth in the air to dry the battlefield quickly when the rain stopped. It had been hoped that by the 8th August the advance would have reached the Roulers – Thourout railway.

With the front line stuck in the mud along the Steenbeek the artillery had continued to pound the ground east of the stream, creating a waterlogged, cratered wilderness, near impassable to men and hopeless for the operation of supporting tanks. The attack on the 16th August, with weaker forces, an unsuppressed enemy artillery, and in worse ground conditions, was guaranteed to fail, especially at the Gheluvelt plateau. The subsequent piecemeal local attacks in an attempt to batter through the *Albrecht Stellung* on the plateau, and reach the *Wilhelm Stellung* beyond the Steenbeek, had unfortunately sealed the image of muddy futility upon the whole campaign, and throughout the period it had proved impossible to dominate the enemy artillery.

Since becoming aware in May that the French would not be taking a major rôle in the summer offensive the War Cabinet, although fully aware of the U-boat menace, had been unhappy at the prospect at the British Army fighting alone. They had eventually but reluctantly agreed to the initial phase of the offensive, allowing Robertson to write, in his words not theirs, 'having approved your plans being executed, you may depend upon our whole hearted support; and that if and when we decide to reconsider the situation, we will obtain your views before arriving at any decision as to the cessation of operations'. But the situation, which undoubtedly was not to the satisfaction of the War Cabinet, was never reviewed to the point that any intervention had been made, although Robertson had regularly kept the Cabinet updated. As early in the campaign as the 6th August Lloyd George had mentioned his desire to send men and guns to Italy, irrespective of the requirements of the Italians, and irrespective of the requirements of the Western Front. By the 4th September, the Prime Minister and most members of the War Cabinet would have much preferred that the main pressure point of British war making strength should be shifted to quite another front, either Italy or Salonica. But even a *major* Italian expedition was not likely to have provided an offensive of such magnitude as to ware down and incapacitate sufficient numbers of the German Army and sufficient quantities of their war-making equipment to have made any material difference to the final outcome of the conflict. At best it would be a holding tactic awaiting the arrival of American forces to tip the balance of strength on the Western Front, and as we have seen this was a very dangerous race to run. The Australian Official Historian summed it up clearly: 'In both of these theatres [Italy or Salonica] not only were the natural difficulties at least equal to those of Flanders, but anything less than overwhelming success of the Entente could be watched by the German command almost with indifference. But in Flanders there could be no question of indifference – there the Germans were vitally sensitive to every advance of even a thousand yards. The exertion of all available strength there would definitely keep the main enemy engaged.'[840]

Lloyd George, consistently maintaining his dislike and distrust of the Flanders campaign did little but talk of support for Italy, and subsequently operations against Turkey. In the view of the War Cabinet, the August battles appeared to have achieved little. Neither had they achieved what Haig had hoped, but they had certainly made a major impact on the Germans. Ludendorff wrote: 'From the 31st July 1917 till well into September was a period of tremendous anxiety. The fighting on the Western Front became more serious than any the German Army had yet experienced, while in the east we had to keep on hammering at Russia in order to bring about the fall of the Colossus. On the 31st July the fighting caused us very heavy losses in prisoners and stores, and a large expenditure of reserves; and the costly August battles imposed a great strain on the western troops. I was myself being placed in a difficult predicament. The state of affairs in the west appeared to prevent the execution of our plans elsewhere. Our wastage had been so high as to cause grave misgivings, and exceeded all our expectations.'[841] As feared by many, Gough's battles had not created a break through, but they *had* stretched the hard pressed enemy still farther. Nevertheless Gough's tactics had been costly and wrong, and so had Haig's leadership been wrong in not rejecting them. Gough had been allowed to proceed on the incorrect assumption that he had sufficient fire-power to dominate the enemy guns east of the high ground, and that he had the strength to capture the Gheluvelt plateau. In the event he had neither.

Haig's replacement of Gough with Plumer heralded a most significant and fundamental change in planning, which corresponded with an equally significant change in the weather. Another serious consequence of the mistaken initial appointment of Gough, was the loss of three weeks good campaigning weather during the beginning of September whilst Plumer made his intricate preparations, but he was however ready on time. There had been two major tactical changes. The first change was at the Gheluvelt plateau. An overwhelming and unprecedented

---

[840] AOA p939
[841] BOH p210. It must be noted that Prior and Wilson warn us to be wary about Ludendorff's statements claiming: 'His memoirs are by no means a disinterested or impartial document.' Prior and Wilson, *Passchendaele, the Untold Story* Introduction xxi. They do not tell us however if we should be equally sceptical concerning the writings of Rupprecht, Kuhl, and the German Official Account, which all say very much the same thing, and concur with Ludendorff's conclusions.

weight of artillery was to engage the enemy batteries east of the plateau, and the length of a divisional front was to be reduced to 1,000 yards. The punch to be packed by Second Army at Gheluvelt was to be enormous. The second change was to limit the depth of attack along the whole line to 1,000 to 1,500 yards, and then stop. This principle was to hold good over the next three battles. Menin Road Ridge, Polygon Wood and Broodseinde, fought in better weather and on harder ground were to prove the validity of the tactics. The enemy proved incapable of devising a defensive scheme to halt the gradual but unstoppable steamroller, which by precise advances, and protected by a vigilant air force and superior artillery, edged ever closer to the Broodseinde – Passchendaele ridge. For the enemy to deploy their counter-attack divisions, so capable on the 31st July and throughout August, meant subjecting them to a crushing volume of British artillery fire, which prevented them ever challenging the newly won positions. But as with August, never during September and October had the British artillery achieved complete dominance over the enemy as had been required by Haig at every step, and given the shape and cramped nature of the Ypres Salient, the number of guns available, and the skilful handling of the German batteries east of Gheluvelt, it was not surprising. The Germans had however suffered three crushing defeats in a fortnight, and a certain momentum had developed in the succession of British attacks, which it was hoped would be maintained. From Broodseinde, on top of the Passchendaele ridge, to Roulers was the same distance as from Ypres to Broodseinde. The capture of Passchendaele village looked like a foregone conclusion in the next step. East of the ridge the ground had not suffered anything like the same devastation, and there was comparatively little by way of German defence lines and blockhouses to overcome. The British stood on the brink of a break through. But then the weather broke down and the rain again tipped the scales heavily in favour of the defence.

It did not take much rain in early October to return the bare, churned, ill-drained surface of the Salient back into the atrocious mud of August. In places the mud had never dried and where the tracks towards the front crossed the valleys of the two Hanebeeks, the Steenbeek and the Zonnebeke it had always remained a quagmire. That quagmire now spread quickly. The movement forward of the guns and ammunition, a prerequisite of the three previous successes, slithered and sunk hopelessly into the mire. A degree of exhaustion, the results of the exertions of the last two weeks undoubtedly took its toll, as the gunners, sappers, and engineers struggled desperately to get the weighty pieces on their skinny artillery wheels up into position to support the next advance. Frantic work continued on the corduroy roads to assist the movement of the guns, hampered by continuous hostile shellfire. Urgent efforts were made to carry forward the duckboard tracks to enable the infantry to move up to the lines. Under the worsening conditions the five days to prepare were totally insufficient. The guns could not be brought forward in sufficient numbers. But the mud did not prevent the infantry getting forward. In one of the most gruelling marches of the whole campaign the 66th and 49th Divisions succeeded in getting forward on the 9th October, although some were late arriving. Neither did the mud stop the attack of the 66th Division. The uncut wire which prevented the 49th Division getting onto Bellevue spur was the reason for the failure, and the wire was not cut because the guns could not get forward. The Battle of Poelcappelle was a failure due to uncut wire stopping the infantry, not the mud. The mud had stopped the guns. But Poelcappelle was from the outset to be fundamentally different from Plumer's three previous attacks. Haig had considered Broodseinde a pivotal point of the campaign, and had conceived the 9th October as the time for a possible break through and drive towards Roulers. If the weather had not intervened the battle may have developed into a hybrid; first phase bite-and-hold, second phase break through. The theory was attractive, but unless the enemy had shown serious signs of breaking, the successful execution even in dry conditions appeared extremely doubtful.

Three days later there was another attempt to capture Passchendaele, this time with the 3rd Australian and New Zealand Divisions. The lack of control and clear thinking, and either unwillingness or inability of Corps and Army Staffs to alter plans at short notice and call of the attack was tragically displayed. With no foreseeable improvement in artillery support, even deeper objectives, 1,000 yards beyond those of the 9th October, remained the day's target. The result was the same as on the 9th and for the same reasons. It now seems inexcusable that

Second Army Staff knew nothing of the impassable wire entanglement obstacle, guarded by the Bellevue machine guns. If intelligence had been available to Second Army that identified the uncut wire, then the attack should have been stopped. But as we have seen there is nothing to indicate that such intelligence existed. By the time the New Zealand Division knew of it, it was too late. For the lack of battlefield intelligence the buck must stop with Second Army. The attack should not have taken place. But this is not the same as to argue that the weather or the mud were sufficient reasons to call off the offensive, for the efforts of II Anzac had proved they were not.

The Battle of Poelcappelle and the First Battle of Passchendaele were both failures at the key point of attack. For the first time the Second Army planning and attention to detail was poor and well below their previous standards. The casualties of the four divisions of II Anzac, approaching 12,000, were unnecessary and even by the standards of the time were unacceptable. To continue with the attacks had been a costly error of judgement. To have lost momentum would have been a far lesser handicap than to suffer the near destruction of the magnificent II Anzac Corps. But the weather and ground conditions had not render fighting impossible, and could not be considered a valid reason to have called off the offensive. Conversely, to have delayed the next attack due to uncut wire would have been a perfectly valid reason, and after the failure on the 12th October this became obvious and was acted upon. The Ravebeek valley was certainly the worst ground in the Passchendaele area. But on two occasions the enemy had found it possible to work down into the valley, behind the left rear of 66th Division and subsequently the 3rd Australian Divisions. The state of the higher ground above the valley was bad, but mention of it did not feature highly in the accounts of the battalions fighting there. The conditions at Polderhoek, and in the Lekkerboterbeek and Watervlietbeek – Broenbeek depressions was certainly a lot worse.

The pause between the First Battle of Passchendaele on the 12th October and the opening of the final phase of the campaign, the Second Battle of Passchendaele on the 26th October, indicated that tactically, and largely thanks to Lieutenant-General Currie, clear logical thinking had been re-established. The Canadians would not attack until sound artillery preparations were completed to Currie's satisfaction. The attacks were finally made under ground conditions which remained atrocious, but which did not prevent the Canadian infantry, once more supported by effective artillery being completely successful, albeit at a terrible price. The return to the old bite-and-hold tactics, backed by careful preparation had worked. The cost of over 16,000 Canadian casualties to achieve all their objectives was easier to accept than 12,000 II Anzac casualties to achieve nothing. Of course in reality it is incorrect to say that the II Anzac Corps had 'achieved nothing'. They had engaged the enemy at his most sensitive point, and this was part of the object of the exercise. That the divisions of the Corps had not been used carefully and effectively is the contentious issue. The cost of 16,000 Canadian casualties to capture a wrecked village on the top of a shattered muddy ridge also appears questionable. But this is only one side of the story, and it must be set against the eventual price levied on the enemy in defending the muddy ridge.

What had been gained by continuing with the offensive after the success of the 4th October? Several things had been gained, not the least of which was time, which had however been bought at a high price. Throughout this period the enemy were denied the initiative, and the ability to make their own strategic decisions. Between the 8th October and the middle of November, another 31 German divisions had been moved into Flanders. The capture of Passchendaele may not have been a great strategic prize, but denying the enemy the initiative at this dangerous moment of the War was. This was the way the Germans viewed it, as they confirm in their official monograph: 'There remained to the Allies as their one positive gain from the Flanders Battle the certainty that, by tying down the Germans under intensely severe strain, they survived the crisis which arose in the interval between the breakdown of Russia, the onset of the unlimited submarine campaign, and the reverse of the French in April, on the one side, and, on the other, the hoped for time when American help would begin to be effective. In the year 1918 it turned out that this success definitely contributed to the result that the war ended in the favour of the Allies, but when the Flanders Battle broke off they had no inducement to look upon it as decisive.'[842] Given the tempo that Plumer's three attacks had achieved, it is inconceivable that Haig would have called of the offensive after the 4th October. He was right not to do so, and as we now know, on the 11th October Rupprecht was suggesting to O.H.L. the possibility of a major withdrawal. By this time the coastal plan was long dead, but the attritional battle before the ridge at Passchendaele had come very close to achieving a decision in its own right.

That the Battle had multi objectives may have in some ways clouded the precision of thought required to efficiently attain any one of them. The separate aims of the break through and wearing-down battles had become intermingled and confused. On the other hand, as one aim had become less likely to be achieved, the other aim had quickly taken its place, ensuring the battle a continuation of justifiable goals. After Langemarck the coastal operation looked unlikely, although Gough's attacks *had* done significant damage to the enemy. Plumer's next three attritional attacks did even more damage, and reopened the possibilities of a break through. Poelcappelle had been planned on the assumption that the Germans had sustained substantial damage, and with the hope of break through in mind, but had been thwarted by conditions. The First Battle of Passchendaele had been a gravely miscalculated re-run. But from the 26th October the return to the tactics of attrition had served a valuable and long term purpose. The Germans had been able to reinforce their front to the point that a further break through by the tired British divisions was impossible, but only at the cost of relinquishing the strategic initiative and their own freedom of action. Whilst the 40 German divisions remained with the *Fourth Army* in Flanders throughout November, they were not in the most favourable position to re-organise, re-equip, and re-train for a new offensive to be unleashed in just over three short months. The habits of 3 years of defensive warfare had to be eradicated, and indoctrination in the new Storm Troop offensive tactics could not be achieved quickly. That the Germans urgently wished to regain the initiative and mastery of independent decision is shown by the fact that all 40 divisions present in Flanders in late November had been moved out by the end of the year. The delay and loss of over two months training and preparation time, imposed by Haig's continuation after Broodseinde undoubtedly cost them dearly.

The importance of keeping the French in the fight had been the beacon guiding Haig's policy throughout the Flanders campaign. In the spring of 1940, Churchill, recognising the same desperate importance, went so far as to propose a merger of the two nations as a last ditch effort to keep the French in the fight. In 1917 the British could not continue without the French and vice versa. The conclusions of the Australian Official Historian are important, and the passing of time since they were written has not in any way changed the concise correctness of their meaning: 'The condition of the French Army after the Aisne was the determining factor of the campaign on the Western Front in 1917. The long-drawn-out effort of the British at Ypres, planned and authorised with other intentions, came to be, first and foremost, a diversion to keep the Germans engaged while the French recovered. As long as military history has its students, they will probably differ over the question whether that effort was justified. But those who maintain that the British Army could have played a more or less passive role are out of touch with the realities of that situation. It is not sufficient to show that French resentment at British inaction *might* not have had fatal consequences, or that the Germans *might* not have attacked the French Army, or that, if relieved by the British on part of its front, that army *might* have shattered a German offensive. The situation was such that Great Britain could not afford to take a risk. The crisis in France and Russia forced the British Army to play a giant's part, carrying the main weight of the war for the time being on its shoulders, and suffering whatever exhaustion might be involved in the process.'[843] From the other side of the line Kuhl adds: 'There can be no doubt today, that in point of fact, the English stubbornness bridged over the

---

[842] AOA p940
[843] BOH p-xviii

crisis in France. The help which England brought to the cause of the Entente was compensated by the result.'[844]

The aim of greatest and overriding importance had therefore been achieved. Haig had remained resolutely committed to the offensive, in the face of opposition and interference from Lloyd George and his War Cabinet, which would have reduced a man of lesser character to despair. The forces of the British Empire had alone engaged the mighty enemy, and done him enormous damage, whilst France had regained her composure and the United States had gathered her strength. There had been times when even his Army Commanders had wavered, mainly in consequence of the bad weather and atrocious ground conditions. Haig's soldiers had proved that it was possible to fight on in conditions which to any rational judgement looked impossible. To their great credit so had the Germans. The severity of the campaign had been the result of the tenacity and obstinacy of the men of both sides. If either side had weakened it would soon have been over. But neither side had.

The Prime Minister and the War Cabinet, had been in full knowledge of the progress of the battle, Robertson had made sure of that, and eventually after bothering to enquire, had been informed of casualty figures. Whilst paying scant attention to Flanders they had considered every possible alternative theatre of operations open to them. They had numerous valid reasons, and the political power to stop the fighting, but they had neither the will to do so nor a rational alternative, and they had failed to act. Why did Lloyd George and his Cabinet protest so much but in reality do so little? It cannot be argued that they were in ignorance of the situation, or they lacked the power to intervene, because as has been shown neither was the case. Was simple incompetence or lack of will to blame? Perhaps: but maybe there is another reason, to be found in the welter of post-war denials of responsibility, and artful shifting of blame towards Haig. As Lloyd George persisted with his protests of futility, and pointed plaintively towards what he saw as less painful alternatives, whilst allowing Haig to (in his view) mindlessly hammer away in Flanders, the Prime Minister distanced himself from the centre of the only operation that really mattered, and removed himself from culpability in and responsibility for its outcome. How could Passchendaele possibly have been Lloyd George's *fault* when he had so condemned the whole affair? Had he not repeatedly wished to shift the centre of gravity elsewhere? The Prime Minister was no strategist, this much he had admitted, so if the military who were running the show believed their plans to be right, who was he to stop them from getting on with it, whilst avoiding agreeing with or condoning their actions. Better to privately and publicly condemn Hiag, whilst not militarily stopping, or even curtailing him. To order a curtailment or even down-scaling of the operation from Downing Street would indicate direct involvement, or even control, and therefore imply joint responsibility. If Haig was successful then there was nothing to stop the Cabinet receiving at least part of the credit. But if the military were unsuccessful, which was believed most likely, then the Prime Minister could claim he had been right all along and therefore not responsible, and as he had no alternative plan which stood a chance of ultimate success, there was really little to loose and everything to gain from the non-intervention policy. The scheming towards a Supreme Command would eventually solve the Haig – Robertson problem, and this he had well in hand. In the meantime Lloyd George hoped he could benefit from both sides of the deal. He had wanted the goods, but had not been willing to pay the price. But the political lesson was obvious then, and still holds good now. To declare war is like writing a blank cheque. Once committed, the price, however excessive it may be, has to be paid.

Whilst describing all aspects of the Flanders campaign, this account has not attempted to portray the performance of Haig, Gough or Plumer in any other than a balanced light. It has however attempted to point out that they were dealing with real problems in real time, not theoretical games, with little pressure and infinite time to draw conclusions. The performance of the Commander-in-Chief and his Army Commanders left each of them vulnerable to criticism

---

[844] BOH p-xviii

to a greater or lesser extent, which has already been levelled throughout these chapters. Haig must stand primarily responsible for the lack of control and direction, leading to confusion over the precise aims of the offensive. Gough thought he knew what Haig required of him and set about doing it with over ambitious plans and inadequate tools at his disposal. If he had misunderstood the Commander-in-Chief's requirements it was up to Haig, for whom verbal communication was never easy, to correct him. Gough was warned to be cautious but the warnings were insufficient, Gough's overall plan was not changed, and was for too long left to run its course. Plumer's performance is somewhat of an enigma. If we are to believe Brigadier-General Davidson, Plumer did not disagree with Gough's initial plan, which seems out of character. But this is not to say that he would have proposed a similar plan. By September it was very clear what Haig required of him, and up until the 4th October his planning worked very well. The lack of control over the attacks of the 9th and 12th October, the lowest point of Plumer's career, is still difficult to explain, a situation made infinitely worse by lack of battlefield intelligence, and Haig's insistence to quickly gain the high ground, with the added urgency and complication of a back-up break through plan. The arrival of Lieutenant-General Currie led to a return to the only tactics with a hope of working under the conditions imposed both by the state of the battlefield and the strength of the enemy. Control of the battle at this point was largely the responsibility of a Corps Commander.

From the British viewpoint the Third Battle of Ypres must be recognised as a catalogue of tactical command and control errors, on numerous occasions, but made under the enormous stresses and strains of every conceivable problem and difficulty, and against a backdrop of massive strategic considerations beyond the Flanders theatre. The performance of the War Cabinet was weak, probably misguided, but largely irrelevant to the offensive. So where does this leave the outcome of the battle and the long bestowed stigma of futility? We began by asking 'was it all worth it'? All evidence points to the fact that as a stand alone operation the answer must be, 'no it was not'. But it was not a stand alone operation; it was simply a move in a much larger game. The battle had serious and profound repercussions, not just on the British Army which without doubt had taken a fearful hammering, but also on the German Army and upon the forward planning and preparations of the German High Command. From July to November Haig had done what he said he would do from the very start. On the 25th July he had written to the Cabinet, 'even if my attacks do not gain ground, as I hope and expect, we ought still to persevere in attacking the Germans in France. Only by this means can we win; and we must encourage the French to continue fighting'. He had not gained a lot of ground, but he had successfully 'ground' away at the main enemy, and the French were still in the fight. He had therefore achieved two of his three aims.

There undoubtedly came a defining moment when the ultimate outcome, not of the battle, but of the War itself, pivoted upon the cusp of a final delicate balance. From the moment that balance tipped, however imperceptible was its movement, the advantage had turned, and although great setbacks were still to befall the final victor, the ultimate loser was locked into an inevitable downward spiral towards defeat. When the German Army returned to the offensive four months later, it did so not only lacking the men and equipment it had lost at Ypres, but also having lost the vital window of opportunity to build up its store-house of war materials unmolested. If left unmolested the Germans certainly had the industrial capacity to do this more quickly than the Allies. On the 21st March 1918 the German Army, reinforced from the Eastern Front numbered 192 divisions. From the 21st March and throughout April and May the enemy made great advances and did much damage, although eventually stopped and finally driven back. But the mighty Army, at the moment of its greatest power and success, was not of uniform capability, already having fragmented into a two tier force of attack divisions – the much vaunted Storm Troops providing the vanguard, and trench divisions of far less fighting quality. This was not from choice, but rather from expediency, brought about by the losses sustained in the fighting of

1917.[845] If the men and material lost in the Ypres fighting had been available to the Germans in the spring of 1918, what had been a very close run thing, and the gravest Allied crisis of the War, would have ended in Allied defeat. Some turn the argument around and suggest that the British losses at Ypres pushed them closer to defeat in the spring of 1918. This approach turns a blind eye to an obvious counter argument. There were in Britain at the beginning of 1918 a total of 74,403 officers and 1,486,459 other ranks of whom 607,403 were trained "Category A" men, and nearly 450,000 of them were available for drafts.[846] The Army in France received 100,000 of them. There were therefore 350,000 men, (the equivalent of about 25 divisions) immediately available in Britain, but which the War Cabinet felt should not be sent to France. The Germans on the other hand threw everything they had into their last great offensive, except for the folly of retaining one million men to support the increasingly paranoid Ludendorff's fantasies of a 'Greater Germany' in the east. The British Army in France fought with the forces it had at its disposal and eventually checked the full might of the enemy, whilst a host of reinforcements were held back in Britain. It was not the Ypres fighting that nearly led to Allied defeat in the spring of 1918, but the Cabinet's retention of available and vitally needed drafts, and (as will be seen) the refusal of Foch to release French reserves. The situation for the enemy at the beginning of 1918 was very different. The only reinforcements left to them were the 1899 class of 'just called up' 18 year olds, and recovered sick and wounded. Due to the mauling received at Passchendaele, the balance had tipped imperceptibly against the Germans, and even with the addition of the eastern reserves and new assault techniques, they still possessed insufficient men, material, and ability, to achieve the great victory. As Kuhl had so poignantly put it: 'The sharp edge of the German sword had become ragged.'[847]

The British Army had truly 'played a giant's part', and more by chance than by design, the terrible fighting at Passchendaele was to lead to the ultimate undoing of the greatest Army that until that time the world had ever seen. This had not been achieved by any sound and consistent captaincy on the part of Lloyd George. Neither had it necessarily been achieved by the effective leadership or tactical prowess of the High Command, although Haig had repeated on so many occasions that the War would only be won by wearing-down the German Army on the Western Front. It had however been achieved by the fighting spirit of the officers and men of the British Army, tens of thousands of whom still lie at Ypres.

The input of British and Dominion effort had been extraordinary. Out of a total of 60 British infantry divisions on the Western Front in 1917, 54 had been in the Ypres sector at some time between the 31st July and the 10th November. Of the 54 that had been at Ypres, 5 divisions had been in action 4 times, 8 divisions had been in action 3 times, 15 divisions had been in action twice, and 25 divisions had been in action once. One division had been present but not engaged.

To those that had fought during the 103 days of conflict, it would have been unimaginable at the time to believe that their massive endeavours would in the long term seal the fate of the enemy. The Battle had been without equal in the misery it had imposed upon the fighting soldiers, and the lasting impression it left with them was not one of victory. But that cannot alter the fact that their enormous sacrifices, which in all truth only they understood, were in no way pointless or futile. To discard their Battle as futile casts a long dark shadow. To dwell on the horrors is understandable, but only encompasses one aspect of the momentous struggle. Far better to remember the Battle as a forge from which was lit a beacon of freedom and liberty – handed down to us, by those who fought – a flame that shines brightly across the years, to chase away the long dark shadow of Passchendaele.

---

[845] The Germans were acutely aware that as a matter of policy dictated by necessity, two distinct capability levels existed amongst infantry divisions, requiring separate training regimes and differing equipment levels. Ludendorff commented: 'General Headquarters regretted that the distinction became established in the Army. We tried to eradicate it, without being able to alter the situation which gave rise to it'. See John Terraine (1978) *To Win a War* Sidgwick & Jackson p38
[846] See BOH p-xvi and John Terraine (1978) *To Win a War* Sidgwick & Jackson p50
[847] BOH p-xv

Postscript

"The Army that died in the mud"

Part 1

For a while Haig's attention was taken up with the Battle of Cambrai. The attack at first showed much promise having breached the Hindenburg Line, only to be driven back virtually to its starting point. Plumer and Harington had gone to Italy, Gough's Fifth Army Staff into G.H.Q. Reserve, and Rawlinson had taken up the reins in the now relatively quiet Salient.

France was in a much improved state, both militarily and in terms of national morale. Georges Clemenceau, 'The Tiger', who had succeeded Paul Painlevé as premier, had on the 20th November told the nation: 'No more pacifist campaigns, no treachery, no semi-treachery – only war. Nothing but war!...The country shall know it is being defended.'[848] The situation in the French Army was better, but could not be considered fully restored. Captain Cyril Falls, serving as a liaison officer with the French at the beginning of 1918 when asked, 'was the French Army's recovery complete?', had replied: 'I should answer in the best formations and units it was, but on the whole not. Even the best did not come up to scratch, as when, in the assault on Kemmel Hill in 1918, the Germans were surprised to see men of a division wearing the fourragere of the Crois-de-Guere running down the slope to surrender.'[849]

    Italy was still in a parlous state following the debacle at Caporetto, but *before* the arrival of 11 French and British divisions, had already rallied and was holding the Austro-German offensive on the Piave. The only realistic hope of Italian action however was that the line could be held; there would be no new Allied offensive here soon. Plumer wrote to Robertson on the 21st November informing him of the improvement in the Italian situation, and requesting two British Corps be sent with additional heavy artillery.

    On the 28th November the firing had ceased on the Eastern Front. By the 20th December full-scale peace negotiations with the Bolshevik Government had opened at German headquarters at Brest-Litovsk. The harshness of the terms offered resulted in failure of the negotiations, which led in turn to another German thrust into Russia. Meeting with little opposition, in five days the Germans advanced 150 miles, occupying the Ukraine, Livonia and Estonia. With the enemy only 120 miles from the gates of Petrograd, Russia finally surrendered. Germany had ended its nightmare period of war on two fronts, and through the Russian example the Allies now knew exactly what peace negotiations with the Germans really meant. On the 3rd March the Treaty of Brest-Litovsk was signed and the full attention of the enemy could be turned to the West.

    As ever Haig was short of manpower, his Armies starved of the replacements they needed by the intervention which the War Cabinet had considered necessary. To resolve the question of the Army's long term requirements a Cabinet Committee on Manpower was set up in December 1917, with Lloyd George in the chair. It did not include one soldier amongst its number. The Army asked for 650,000 men to prepare to face the forthcoming German spring offensive, evidence of which gradually mounted throughout December. As we have seen they received 100,000 Category "A" men. At the end of 1917 there were 1,560,862 officers and men in Britain, compared with a total of 1,097,906 officers and men comprising the B.E.F. in France and Flanders. To disguise the dangerous manpower shortage at the front whilst nominally maintaining the same number of divisions, the Cabinet Committee decided, despite the formal opposition of the Army Council and the explicit protest of the Commander-in-Chief to reduce the brigade strength from 12 battalions to 9, and the divisional strength from 4 brigades to 3. On the 3rd January the War Office was compelled to order a total reorganisation of forces along these

---

[848] Quoted in John Terraine (1978) *To Win a War* Sidgwick & Jackson p15
[849] Quoted in Richard Watt (1963) *Dare Call it Treason* London: Chatto and Windus forward by Cyril Falls p10

lines. In the midst of the Passchendaele battle Lloyd George had ordered Haig to send men and guns to Italy. Now as the Army braced itself to meet the greatest enemy attack to fall upon the Allies since 1914, he forced Haig to disband 2 out of the 5 existing cavalry divisions, and 141 infantry battalions, the equivalent of 9 full infantry divisions. With great foresight, and to their credit, especially as their manpower situation was far more serious than that of British, the Governments of Australia, Canada and New Zealand, declined to adopt similar measures. It was not to be long before the blow, of unparalleled might, was to fall on the reduced British Army. On the 7th December Haig mused in his diary: 'It is just 6 months today since I held the last Conference with Army Commanders at Doullens (7th May) and issued orders for the offensive against Messines etc. We expected at that time help from Russia, Italy and France!! In reality the British Army has had to bear the brunt of it all. I added that we [Commanders] might well be proud of the achievements of the Armies this year and I thanked them one and all for their help and support.'[850] Haig had every right to feel proud. It was not a question of why the Northern Offensive had not achieved greater success, but rather how, in the face of every conceivable obstacle and hardship, it had possibly achieved what it had.

Part 2

At about 4:40 am on the morning of the 21st March 1918 the long expected blow fell along a 42 mile front, between the Somme valley in the south and Cherisy in the north, summoned by the roar of 6,473 enemy guns and 3,532 trench mortars. Germany was making its final major move in the enormous game of which Passchendaele had been but a part. There were now 192 German divisions on the Western Front, and the race for victory had begun in earnest. Would the American Army, slowly building its strength, arrive in sufficient numbers and in time, or would the war-weary British and French collapse beneath the onslaught? To the British the fortitude of the French was still an unknown quantity. The British had suffered grievous casualties at Passchendaele, which had not been made up due to the policy of the Cabinet. Some claim that in early 1918 the British Army was a spent force. John Mosier says that whatever was left of the B.E.F. after the Somme and Arras, had died in the mud at Passchendaele.[851] This allegedly broken Army which had 'died in the mud at Passchendaele' and was constantly starved of reserves, was, over the next 16 days to check the German onslaught. Both the damage inflicted on the enemy, and the precious time which had been gained at Passchendaele, would play their vital parts in the forthcoming struggle.

The German plan was to separate the bulk of the British Army from the French by thrusting, mainly at the British Fifth and Third Armies, between the river Somme and Cherisy, towards the old Somme battlefield, and thence towards Amiens. The British Army would then be isolated and rolled up northwards towards the sea. The attack was to be delivered by the *Eighteenth, Second* and *Seventeenth Armies*, with a total of 71 divisions, 32 of which would be in the first line of assault.

On the morning of the 21st March, holding a 5,000 yard sector of the Third Army front line astride the Bapaume to Cambrai road, six miles east of Bapaume, was the 51st Highland Division, which had been in the thick of the fighting at Passchendaele. The divisional front north of the road, was held by the 153rd Brigade which had fought alongside the Welsh in the Battle of Pilckem Ridge in the previous July. The initial bombardment upon 153rd Brigade was of exceptional severity. Most of the troops in the Forward Zone were killed, buried by the bombardment, or taken prisoner. The few who survived were not capable of much resistance, and none returned to tell the tale. To the left of the 51st Division was the 6th Division, which had been spared the Passchendaele fighting. The right of the 6th Division sector, beside the 153rd Brigade, was held by the 18th Brigade, with the 1st West Yorkshire Regiment holding the right

---

[850] Douglas Haig, Diaries and Letters, p358 It had in fact been seven months.
[851] Mosier (2002) *The Myth of the Great* War Perennial p284

brigade sector of the Front Line, and the 2nd Durham Light Infantry holding the left. The 11th Essex Regiment was in support 4,000 yards to the rear near Morchies. For five hours the two forward battalions and the Essex were subjected to a tornado of high explosive and gas shelling. Around 10:00 am the enemy infantry advanced, concealed by a thick fog which blanketed most of the 42 mile attack front. On the Cambrai road Lieutenant -Colonel Dumbell of the Essex was ordered to take charge of all troops in the Brigade sector of the corps line between Beaumetz and Morchies. Upon the front of the 153rd and 18th Brigades now fell the *119th, 3rd Guard*, and *20th Divisions*, with the *4th* and *39th Divisions* in reserve. Communications were soon virtually non existent, but it was evident that the Front Line was under severe attack. "C" and "D" Companies of the Essex moved up in support of the West Yorks and at 12:30 p.m. "A" Company was ordered forward to support the Durham. A mixed force, 267 strong, of Essex "B" Company, 12th Field Company Royal Engineers, and a Pioneer company of the 11th Leicester, remained holding the corps line. Having held the enemy onslaught throughout the afternoon, under an ever increasing weight of hostile artillery and machine gun fire, the remnants of the West Yorks, the Durham, and the three Essex companies attempted to fall-back on the corps line. At midnight Colonel Dumbell again reorganized his force, which by this time was reduced to 210 men of the Essex on the right, 98 of the West Yorks in the centre and 128 of the Durham on the left, in touch with the remnants of the 7th Gordons of 153rd Brigade on the right, and the 3rd Worcester of 7th Brigade (25th Division) on the left. The morning of the 22nd was again misty, and the enemy took every advantage to establish machine guns and mortars close up to the 18th Brigade line. Having been in action since early on the 21st the remnants of the three battalions were practically exhausted and had lost most of their officers. Under constant enemy pressure, Dumbell's force remained in position throughout the 22nd, until at 4:30 p.m. the Germans broke through the corps line north of Morchies, and began to move south-west against the brigade left flank. By 6:30 after a short but intense bombardment the flank to the right was also penetrated, although two platoons of the 8th Royal Scots gave great material support before being overwhelmed. The battered remnants of the 18th Brigade were left isolated in an advanced position with both flanks open. The position was now untenable and at midnight Brigade headquarters ordered Colonel Dumbell: 'You will withdraw at once without being relieved. Buses will be found at the Monument, Favreuil – Sapignies road whence you will proceed to Buchanan Camp, Achiet area.'[852] The troops handed what little ammunition they had left to the machine gunners, who were to remain in position. The enemy were shelling the neighbourhood of the Monument and no buses could be seen. It is about 10 miles from Morchies to Achiet-le-Grand. The exhausted remnants of the 11th Essex marched to their destination. In the words of Colonel Dumbell: 'All ranks fell asleep on the road at each ten minutes halt. There was however no straggling and at about 6:30 a.m. on the 23rd instant 7 officers and 77 other ranks marched steadily into Buchanan Camp.' In holding the German advance on the road to Bapaume for 43 precious hours the 11th Essex had sustained casualties of 17 officers and 411 other ranks. The author's grandfather had been one of the few survivors who escaped without injury.

Two weeks later on the 5th April the great German gamble was finally stopped just nine miles short of Amiens. After 16 days of ferocious fighting the *Kaiserschlacht*, the 'Emperor's Battle', was suspended. Ludendorff recognised that further effort was pointless. British casualties had amounted to 178,000, of whom over 70,000 were prisoners. The French had sustained 77,000 casualties. Hindenburg wrote with commendable honesty: 'Our advance became slower and slower. The hopes and wishes which had soared beyond Amiens had to be recalled. Facts must be treated as facts…. We ought to have shouted in the ear of every single man: 'Press on to Amiens. Put in your last ounce. Perhaps Amiens means decisive victory. Capture Villers-Bretonneaux whatever happens, so that from it heights we can command Amiens with masses of our heavy artillery!' It was in vain, our strength was exhausted.'[853] It was not the distance that they had marched which had exhausted the Germans and prompted their failure. The Australians had been in Villers-Bretonneaux. Ludendorff concluded: 'The enemy's

---

[852] National Archives, War diary 11th Battalion the Essex Regiment WO/95/1616
[853] Hindenburg (1920) *Out of My Life London*: Cassell, p350

resistance was beyond our powers….O.H.L. was forced to take the extremely hard decision to abandon the attack on Amiens for good.'[854] The under-strength Army which had 'died in the mud at Passchendaele' was obviously resurrected and had given a good account of itself. The Cabinet Committee on Manpower had based its judgement on reinforcement levels on the premise that as the British Army would be standing on the defensive for the foreseeable future, the draft requirement would in their estimation be much lower than the Army had suggested. Once more Lloyd George had been proved hopelessly wrong. British casualties at Passchendaele had been about 2,600 per day. In the March Offensive they had been over 6,800 per day. Even taking out the prisoner of war figures they had been nearly 3,900 per day.

After the terrible mauling at Morchies, the 6th Division, and the 11th Essex, was moved to Ypres, now a quiet sector of the Western Front, to rest and reorganize.

The aim of Ludendorff's offensive had been to crush the British Army by rapidly splitting them from the French and then rolling up the British line towards the coast. The Somme had not been Haig's first choice of area to attack in 1916 and neither had it been Ludendorff's in 1918. Flanders had been the first choice of both, not possible for Haig due to French considerations in 1916, and not risked by Ludendorff due to concerns over the ground conditions in March 1918. But a Flanders attack code named '*Georgette*' had already been planned, and retained as a possible second stage. With the failure before Amiens, the German weight was now to be shifted to the alternative front. The new attack opened on the misty morning of the 9th April.

Two Portuguese divisions, seconded to the British First Army and recognised as being of dubious value, held the line between Neuve Cappelle and Laventie. In the same way that electricity follows the line of least resistance the Germans threw their weight against the unfortunate Portuguese. The attack was carried out by four corps of the *Sixth Army*, between the line of the La Bassee Canal and Armentières. The main attack was intended to smash through the Portuguese, which it did with ease, and then to 'at all costs' cross the Rivers Lys and Lawe, which it did not, mainly due to a very fine defensive action by the 55th Division. A small bridgehead across the Lys was however secured by the enemy at Bac St. Mar. British divisions moved south from the Ploegsteert - Messines ridge front to stem the German tide but were unable to dislodge the bridgehead. German penetration continued at this point, determining the future course of the offensive. But the attack was to be in two parts, and in the early hours of the morning on the 10th after a heavy bombardment two corps of the *Fourth Army* attacked north of Armentières. By the end of the day Armentières, Ploegsteert and Messines had fallen and the Bac St. Mar bridgehead had been extended to a depth of around 6,000 yards, the forward German units being within 3,000 yards of Bailleul. Haig was virtually out of reserves, but in a complete reversal of fortunes, due largely to the relative levels of combat over the past eight months, the French now had ample. On the 26th March at Doulens an agreement had been drafted, entrusting to General Foch (soon to become French Commander-in-Chief and Marshal of France), 'the co-ordination of the action of the British and French Armies in front of Amiens'. It had appeared that to place Foch in a position to co-ordinate the action of all the Allied Armies on the Western Front was the best way to ensure the French Army maintaining touch with the British, as at the time Pétain had seen his main responsibility as falling-back on Paris, a movement destined to create a gap between the two Armies. So it was Foch who at this critical juncture on the 11th April controlled the reserves, and he flatly refused to release them. Haig's Armies had no alternative but to fight on with the resources they already possessed. To the Commander-in-Chief the situation was so grave that he made his famous appeal to all troops of the B.E.F.: 'To all ranks of the British Forces in France. Three weeks ago to-day the enemy began his terrific attacks against us on a 50 mile front. His objects are to separate us from the French, to take the Channel ports and destroy the British Army. In spite of throwing already 106 Divisions into battle and enduring the most reckless sacrifice of human life, he has as yet made little progress towards his goals. We owe this to the determined fighting and self- sacrifice of our troops. Words fail me to express the admiration which I feel for the splendid resistance

---

[854] Ludendorff (1919) *War Memoirs* London: Hutchinson, p600

offered by all ranks of our Army under the most trying circumstances. Many amongst us are now tired. To those I would say that victory will belong to the side which holds out the longest. The French Army is moving rapidly and in great force to our support. There is no other course open to us but to fight it out! Every position must be held to the last man: there must be no retirement. With our backs to the wall, and believing in the justice of our cause each one of us must fight on to the end. The safety of our Homes and the Freedom of mankind alike depend upon the conduct of each one of us at this critical moment. D. Haig F.M. Thursday 11 April 1918.'[855]

By the 14th April the enemy were over six miles beyond the Lys and threatening the strategically vital railway junction at Hazebrouck, lines from which carried by far the greatest amount of stores and supplies into the Ypres Salient. The German thrust now seriously compromised the British position in Flanders, as the Ypres – Yser line was becoming increasingly outflanked and the Channel ports were threatened, Calais being only 40 miles north-northwest of Hazebrouck. At its deepest point the German penetration was now 12 miles *south-west* of Ypres. On the 15th April Foch informed Haig that in his opinion the German offensive in Flanders was *'finie'*, but that night, Plumer, (who had returned from Italy in mid March to the command of Second Army), reluctantly and with great personal distress, pulled his Army out of the now hopelessly exposed Passchendaele salient. Harington described the scene: 'We had lost our Messines Ridge. Was our immortal Ypres to go? Think of the effect on the Germans with their eyes on the Channel Ports if they got Ypres. I think now of a conference in my room. I think of the stout and gallant troops holding on to Passchendaele at the risk of being cut off. The Army Commander was with me standing at my desk examining the map. We both knew that the limit had been reached. We should have to come out. The risk was too great. No more help could come from anywhere. Meteren was in flames. Hazebrouck was threatened. At last I summoned up courage to say what I had feared for days. 'I think, Sir, you will have to come out of Passchendaele.' The effect was magic. My old chief, always like a father to me, made one last bid. He turned on me and showed the most wonderful example of his bulldog tenacity that I have ever seen. I can hear it now – 'I won't!' It was indeed a plucky effort. The next moment I felt, and I have often felt it since, his hand on my shoulder – 'You are right, issue the orders.' He knew it all the time. He knew it was coming. We both did. We did not talk about it. He went of to his room'.[856]

All the ground which had been gained in the great battle of 1917 had of necessity been given-up. The new defence line established around Ypres ran along the eastern slope of Pilckem ridge, through Wieltje, and crossed the Menin Road near Hellfire Corner. From there it ran south to Zillebeke Lake where it passed along the bund on the western end of the lake, and then continued to Lock 8 on the Ypres – Comines canal.

---

[855] Quoted in AOA p437
[856] Sir Charles Harington *'The Ypres Salient in 1918' The Ypres Times, Vol 2 No.2*, 4-1924 p36

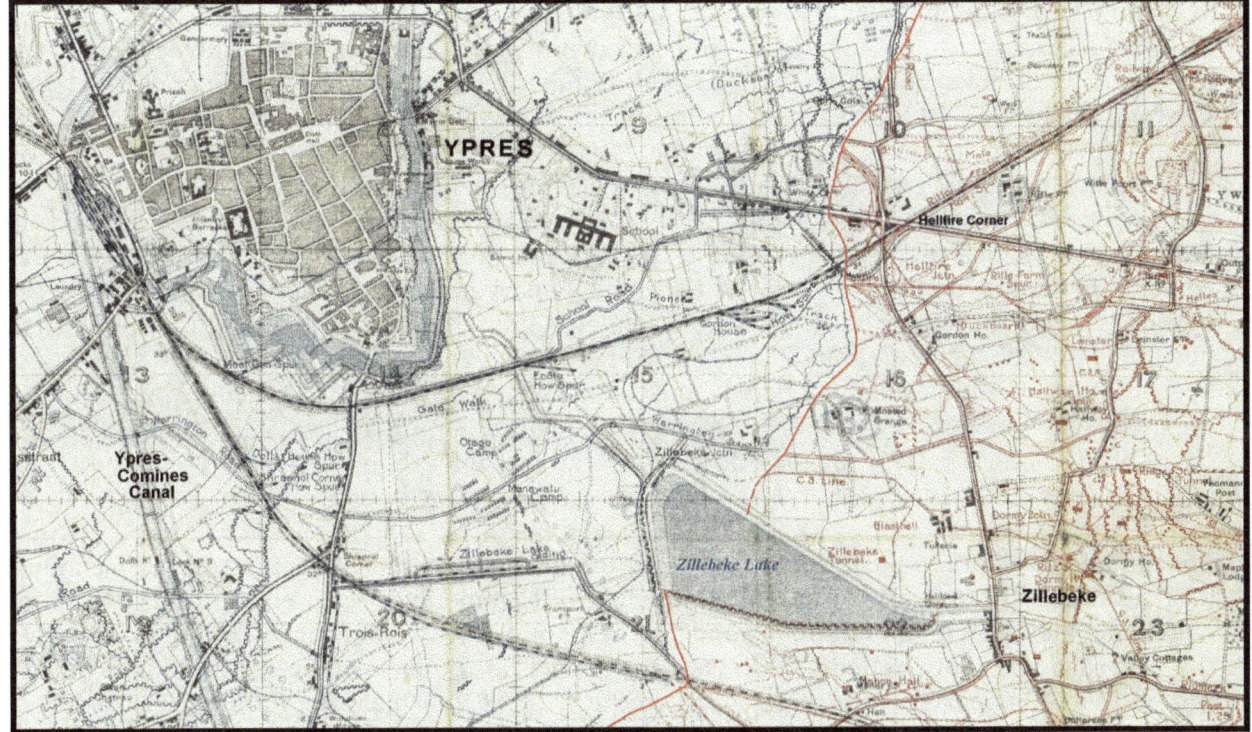
The German outpost line in front of Ypres - May 1918

The 6th Division, having moved north to recover from the mauling on the Somme, was on the 13th April holding a quiet sector of the line east of Ypres between Broodseinde and Polygon Wood, 17 miles north of the main German break-in. With the new deployment of forces after the withdrawal on the 15th April the Division took up the line south of Hellfire Corner, with the 11th Essex holding the new Front Line along the bund with outpost positions to the south of Zillebeke lake.

By the 18th April the enemy thrust towards Hazebrouck had slackened, and Mount Kemmel, the eastern-most of five hills forming the Monts des Flandre became their prime objective. At a height of 159 metres, and little more than 9,000 yards *south-west* of Ypres, the hill commanded observation over the flat plain to the north towards Ypres and the main supply artery into the Salient from Poperinghe. Second Army daily expected the offensive to be renewed and was now holding the line with exhausted, worn-out forces. Haig and General Sir Henry Wilson, (recently appointed C.I.G.S. in place of Robertson), made the British situation very clear to Foch. Either French reinforcements would be forthcoming or the British would have no alternative but to abandon the Ypres-Yser defence line and fall-back on St. Omer and the Channel ports, and plans were already in hand to flood extensive low-lying areas to cover their left flank. At last Foch grasped how serious the situation had become and promised four French divisions, to be organised as the Army Detachment of the North, under General de Mitry. Plumer immediately ordered three of the fresh French divisions to relieve his exhausted IX Corps around and south-west of Kemmel.

Kemmel village, at base of the hill on the north-east side, was near the point of junction of the *X Reserve Corps*, and the *XVIII Corps* of the *Fourth Army*, and the German plan called for both to be engaged in the attack on Mount Kemmel, the objective being the line St, Eloi, Vierstraat, Kemmel, Dranoutre. At 6:45 a.m. on the 25th April, following a severe gas and high explosive bombardment, and supported by low flying aircraft, the German attack began. On the right the *XVIII Corps* took Kemmel village and later St. Eloi. The *Alpine Corps*, of the *X Reserve Corps,* (which had failed against the British at Bailleul on the 14th), stormed over Mount Kemmel, driving the newly arrived French division from the hill, but being finally checked near Locre in the valley between Kemmel and the next mounts, the Scherpenberg and Mont Rouge. Haig was far from impressed with the French performance, as his diary entry for the 26th indicated: The

> French 28th Division did not fight well. We all thought Kemmel impregnable. Yet the place was abandoned after two hours fighting.'[857] He foresaw the loss of Kemmel as possibly leading to the imminent withdrawal from the Ypres Salient: 'Plumer reported to me that Enemy had taken Voormezeele and were north of Kemmel. In view of this, he had decided to withdraw to the Ypres Canal line, leaving outposts on the Pilckem Ridge line. I told him that my Army Commander on the spot could decide when the moment had come to retire. Looking at the points already reached by the Enemy south of Ypres, I considered that the time had come to retire from the salient and I concurred in the dispositions that he had ordered.' It was not to come to that; quite. On the 29th April the German offensive, to become known as the Battle of the Lys, or the Fourth Battle of Ypres, was suspended. General von Kuhl summed up the German position: 'The storming of Kemmel was a great feat, but, on the whole, the objective set had not been attained. The attack had not penetrated to the decisive heights of Cassel and Mont des Cats, the possession of which would have compelled the evacuation of the Ypres Salient and the Yser position. No great strategic movement had become possible; the Channel ports had not been reached....The second great offensive had not brought about the hoped for decision.'[858]

But the enemy effort to push the British from the Salient was not altogether dead. Spasmodic local attacks were to continue into May. The loss of Kemmel had resulted in the British Front Line being withdrawn tighter still around Ypres. By mid May, south of the City, the line crossed the Lille road just south of Bedford House, little more than 2,000 yards south of the Lille Gate in the southern Ramparts. From there it ran to the west of Voormezeele, the British Front Line being just east of the Kemmel road at Elzenwalle. To this area, near Dickebusch Lake, the 6th Division had moved in May to relieve the 19th Division, and now held the line beside the French 14th Division.

On the 27th May the *18th Reserve Infantry Regiment* carried out a local attack from the direction of Voormezeele, which succeeded in capturing a section of the Front Line held by the French between Elzenwalle and Kruistraathoek, and threatened to further encircle Ypres by working around the south-west flank of the city. At this point the enemy were 3,000 yards *south west* of the Lille Gate, the closest they would ever get to completely outflanking the city. On the morning of the 28th May the 11th Essex were instructed to move from billets at Cat Farm at Vlamertinghe, to the neighbourhood of Belgian Chateau, about one mile behind the line, to await orders, a sure indication that they would soon be in action. Battalion headquarters was established at the ruined chateau. In the afternoon company commanders were informed of the loss of the Front Line on the previous day, and instructed that the 11th Essex, with the 13th French Chasseurs to their left and another French battalion to their right were to recapture the line on the morning of the 29th.

The Essex was to form up in three waves, "B" and "A" Company in the first wave, 1,000 yards from the objective, "C" Company in the second wave 400 yards behind "A", and "D" Company in the third wave 200 yards behind "C". At 3:00 a.m. on the 29th the battalion deployed 600 yards east of Dickebusch lake, with the forward wave through the low scrub of English Wood. About 300 yards forward the enemy had established an outpost line close up to the edge of the scrub. The attack was to be preceded by a heavy bombardment and a standing barrage which was to open 10 minutes before Zero Hour, which was set for 4:00 a.m. By 3:50 as neither French battalion had arrived, it was obvious that the Essex would have to attack alone. The enemy were wide awake and busy firing flares along their front, as were the French further to the right. Heavy hostile shells began falling behind the Essex formations, and although '4.2's' were also landing intermittently in front, the battalion avoided the worst of the shelling. At 3:50 the planned British bombardment failed to materialise, but at 4:00 the Essex advanced to the assault behind a punctual creeping barrage. The enemy quickly fired their S.O.S., but with little immediate response. The Essex soon walked into trouble as a friendly field battery failed to lengthen its range, the shells falling amongst the forward wave. In the confusion the support

---

[857] Douglas Haig, Diaries and Letters, p407
[858] Quoted in BOH 1918 Vol2 p454

companies were quickly amongst the barrage, and it was not long before the enemy artillery answered the calls of its infantry. Little more is known about the attack, except that by 5:30 a.m. all objectives were reported as captured. Casualties, especially in officers were high. One message sent by a young Lieutenant typifies the terrifying experience: 'The men in my post have all become casualties. May I return to H.Q. I am sick with shock.'[859] It is not known which company the author's grandfather was with at the time. What is known is that all officers of his company had become casualties and acting Company Sergeant Major Leonard William Perry took command of the company. He was to be awarded the D.C.M. and Croix-de-Guerre for his actions this day, 3,000 yards south-west of Ypres. The 11th Essex held the line until relieved by the 13th Chasseurs at 12:55 a.m. on the 30th May.

The British did not withdraw from Ypres. General Plumer's Second Army, which had died in the mud of Passchendaele, was to advance victoriously from the old Salient in September 1918. But that story is for another book.

Robert A. Perry
Essex Villa
Langemark   1-1-2007

---

[859] National Archives, War diary 11th Battalion the Essex Regiment WO/95/1616

To Play a Giants Part

Non published sources of information

Battle of Pilckem Ridge 31st July

II Anzac Corps

1st New Zealand Infantry Brigade WO95/3687. 2nd Wellington WO95/3690
11th Australian Infantry Brigade WO95/3425. 42nd Battalion WO95/3434. 43rd Battalion WO95/3436

IX Corps

56the Infantry Brigade WO95/2075-76. 7th Loyal North Lancs WO95/2080.
X Corps
122nd Infantry Brigade, 18th KRRC, 11th RWK, 12th East Surrey all in WO95/4243
123rd Infantry Brigade WO95/4243

II Corps

72nd Infantry Brigade, WO95/2211. 8th Queens, WO95/2214. 1st North Staffs WO95/2213. 9th East Surrey WO95/2215.
73rd Infantry Brigade, WO95/2217. 2nd Leinster & 7th Northants, both in WO95/2218. 13th Middlesex, WO95/2219.
17th Infantry Brigade, WO95/2204. 1st Royal Fusiliers, WO95/2207. 12th Royal Fusiliers, WO95/2208
21st Infantry Brigade, WO95/2327-28. 2nd Green Howards, 2nd Wilts & 19th Manchester all in WO95/2329.
90th Infantry Brigade, WO95/2337. 16th,17th & 18th Manchester WO95/2339
89th Infantry Brigade, WO95/2332. 20th King's WO95/2335
53rd Infantry Brigade, WO95/2037. 6th Berkshire WO95/2037. 8th Suffolk WO95/2039
24th Infantry Brigade, WO95/1717. 2nd East Lancs WO95/1720. 1st Sherwood Foresters WO95/1721
2nd Northants WO95/1722
23rd Infantry Brigade, WO95/1710. 2nd Devon WO95/1712. 2nd West Yorks WO95/1714.
25th Infantry Brigade, WO95/1727.

XIX Corps

44th Infantry Brigade, WO95/1935. 8/10th Gordons WO95/1938. 8th Seaforth WO95/1940.
46th Infantry Brigade, WO95/1950. 10/11th Highland Light Infantry WO95/1952.
45th Infantry Brigade, WO95/1943. 6th Cameron WO95/1945. 13th Royal Scots WO95/1946.
165th Infantry Brigade, WO95/2925.
166th Infantry Brigade, WO95/2928.
164th Infantry Brigade, WO95/2920-21. 1/4th King's Own WO95/2922
XVIII Corps

116th Infantry Brigade, WO95/2581.
117th Infantry Brigade, WO95/2928.
118th Infantry Brigade, WO95/2588-89, 1/1st Cambridge WO95/2590
152nd Infantry Brigade, WO95/2862. 1/5th Seaforth WO95/2866. 1/6th Seaforth WO95/2867
153rd Infantry Brigade, WO95/2872-73. 1/7th Black Watch WO95/2879. 1/5th Gordons WO95/2881

XIV Corps

114th Infantry Brigade, WO95/2558.
113th Infantry Brigade, WO95/2553
115th Infantry Brigade, WO95/2560
2nd Guards Brigade, WO95/1218
3rd Guards Brigade, WO95/1218
1st Guards Brigade, WO95/1214

The Attack at Westhoek 10th August

II Corps
55th Infantry Brigade, WO95/2047
54th Infantry Brigade, WO95/2041. 7th Bedford WO95/2043
74th Infantry Brigade, WO95/2245

Battle of Langemarck 16th August

II Corps
53rd Infantry Brigade, WO95/2043
169th Infantry Brigade, WO95/2958. 1/2nd London WO95/2960. 1/5th London WO95/2961-62
167th Infantry Brigade, WO95/2947. 1/1st London WO95/2949
25th Infantry Brigade, WO95/1727
23rd Infantry Brigade, WO95/1710. 2nd West Yorks WO95/1714

XIX Corps

48th Infantry Brigade, WO95/1973
49th Infantry Brigade, WO95/1976
108th Infantry Brigade, WO95/2504
109th Infantry Brigade, WO95/2508-09

XVIII Corps

145th Infantry Brigade, WO95/2761
34th Infantry Brigade, 8th Northumberland Fusiliers, 11th Manchester, all in WO95/1821. 5th Dorset WO95/1820

XIV Corps

60th Infantry Brigade, WO95/2118-19
61st Infantry Brigade, WO95/2124
88th Infantry Brigade, WO95/2307. 1st Newfoundland & 2nd Hampshire WO95/2308, 1st Essex WO95/2309
87th Infantry Brigade, WO95/2303. 2nd South Wales Borderers WO95/2304. 1st Border WO95/2305.

Battle of the Menin Road Ridge 20th September

IX Corps

58th Infantry Brigade, WO95/2088. 9th Cheshire WO95/2091
57th Infantry Brigade, WO95/2084. 8th Gloucesterm & 10th Warwick WO95/2085.
X Corps
117th Infantry Brigade, WO95/2585. 17th KRRC & 16th Rifle Brigade WO95/2586
122nd Infantry Brigade, 15th Hampshire WO95/2634
124th Infantry Brigade, WO95/2641. 10th Queens & 21st KRRC both in WO95/2643
123rd Infantry Brigade, WO95/2636. 11th Queens & 10th RWK both in WO95/2638
68th Infantry Brigade, WO95/2181
69th Infantry Brigade, WO95/2183

I Anzac

2nd Australian Infantry Brigade, WO95/3231. 5th Battalion WO95/3233. 6th Battalion WO95/3235
7th Battalion WO95/3237. 8th Battalion WO95/3240
3rd Australian Infantry Brigade, WO95/3243. 9th Battalion WO95/3247. 10th Battalion WO95/3248
11th Battalion WO95/3251. 12th Battalion WO95/3252
7th Australian Infantry Brigade, WO95/3338. 25th Battalion WO95/3340. 27th Battalion WO95/3342
5th Australian Infantry Brigade, WO95/3308. 18th Battalion WO95/3316. 20th Battalion WO95/3319

V Corps

27th Infantry Brigade, 11th Royal Scots & 12th Royal Scots all in WO95/1773. South African Infantry Brigade WO95/5345
165th Infantry Brigade, WO95/2925.
164th Infantry Brigade, WO95/2921. 4th King's Own WO95/2922

XVIII Corps

173rd Infantry Brigade, WO95/3000.
174th Infantry Brigade, WO95/3000. 2/5th & 2/6th London both in WO95/3005
154th Infantry Brigade, WO95/2844

XIV Corps

60th Infantry Brigade, WO95/2119. 12th Rifle Brigade WO95/2121
59th Infantry Brigade, WO95/2113. 11th Rifle Brigade WO95/2116

Battle of Polygon Wood 26th September

X Corps

118 Infantry Brigade, WO95/2589. 1/1st Cambridge WO95/2590
116th Infantry Brigade, WO95/2581
100th Brigade, WO95/2429. 100th Machine Gun Company WO95/2431
98th Infantry Brigade, WO95/2425. 1st Middlesex WO95/2426. 1/4th Suffolk WO95/2427
1/5th Scottish Rifles (19th Infantry Brigade attached 98th Infantry Brigade) WO95/2422

I Anzac

15th Australian Infantry Brigade, WO95/3638. 59th Battalion WO95/3651
8th Australian Infantry Brigade, 29th Battalion WO95/3614, 31st Battalion WO95/3619
14th Australian Infantry Brigade, WO95/3625. 53rd Battalion WO95/3631. 56th Battalion WO95/3633
55th Battalion WO95/3631
4th Australian Infantry Briade, WO95/3488. 16th Battalion WO95/3499. 15th Battalion WO95/3498
14th Battalion WO95/3495
13th Australian Infantry Brigade, WO95/3518. 50th Battalion WO95/3522. 49th Battalion WO95/3521
51st Battalion WO95/3523

V Corps

3rd Division-General Staff, WO95/1379. 76th Infantry Brigade, WO95/1433. 1st Gordons WO95/1435
8th Infantry Brigade, WO95/1418. 2nd Royal Scots WO95/1423
177th Brigade, 2/4th & 2/5th Leicester WO95/3022. 2/4th & 2/5th Lincoln WO95/3023
178th Infantry Brigade, 2/5th & 2/6th Sherwood Foresters WO95/3025

XVIII Corps

175th Infantry Brigade, WO95/3008. 2/9th (Q.V.R.) & 2/12th (Rangers) London WO95/3009

Battle of Broodseinde 4th October

IX Corps

63rd Infantry Brigade, 8th Somerset WO95/2429, 8th Lincoln WO95/2529
111th Infantry Brigade, WO95/2531. 13th KRRC WO95/2533
X Corps

13th Infantry Brigade, WO95/1550. 1st RWK WO95/1554
95th Infantry Brigade, 1st Devon WO95/4217. 1st D.L.I. WO95/1577. 1st East Surrey WO95/1579
64th Infantry Brigade, WO95/2160.
62nd Infantry Brigade, WO95/2152. 1st Lincoln WO95/2154
91st Infantry Brigade, WO95/1667. 1st South Staffs WO95/1670. 21st Manchester WO95/1668.
22nd Manchester WO95/1669. 2nd Queens WO95/1670
20th Infantry Brigade, WO95/1654. 2nd Borders WO95/1655

I Anzac

1st Australian Infantry Brigade, WO95/3213. 1st Battalion WO95/3217. 3rd Battalion WO95/3221
4th Battalion WO95/3223
2nd Australian Infantry Brigade, WO95/3231. 6th Battalion WO95/3235. 7th Battalion WO95/3238
8th Battalion WO95/3240
6th Australian Infantry Brigade, WO95/3223. 21st Battalion WO95/3326. 22nd Battalion WO95/3330
24th Battalion WO95/3334
7th Australian Infantry Brigade, WO95/3338. 25th Battalion WO95/3340. 26th Battalion WO95/3341
27th Battalion WO95/3342

II Anzac

Headquarters II Anzac Corps General Staff, AWM4-1/32/20 Parts 1-3
Headquarters II Anzac Corps Intelligence, AWM4-1/33/18
11th Australian Infantry Brigade, WO95/3425. 41st Battalion WO95/3431. 42nd Battalion WO95/3434
43rd Battalion WO95/3436. 44th Battalion WO95/3438
10th Australian Infantry Brigade, WO95/3411. 37th Battalion WO95/3414. 38th Battalion WO95/3415
39th Battalion WO95/3417. 40th Battalion WO95/3420
4th New Zealand Brigade, WO95/3712
1st New Zealand Brigade, WO95/3685. 1st Wellington WO95/3689. 2nd Wellington WO95/3690

XVIII Corps

143rd Infantry Brigade, WO95/2754. 1/7th & 1/8th Warwick WO95/2756
33rd Infantry Brigade, WO95/1811. 9th Sherwood Foresters WO95/1813

XIV Corps

11th Infantry Brigade, WO95/1492. 1st S.L.I. WO95/1499. 1st Hants WO95/1494.
1st Rifle Brigade WO95/1496
10th Infantry Brigade, WO95/1480. 2nd Seaforth WO95/1483. 1st Warwick WO95/1484
87th Infantry Brigade WO95/2303
86th Infantry Brigade, WO95/2298.

Battle of Poelcappelle 9th October

X Corps

15th Infantry Brigade, WO95/1568. 1st Norfolk & 16th Warwick both in WO95/4217
22nd Infantry Brigade, WO95/1661

I Anzac

6th Australian Infantry Brigade, WO95/3323. 23rd Battalion WO95/3332
21st, 22nd & 24th Battalions see Broodseinde
5th Australian Infantry Brigade, WO95/3308. 17th Battalion WO95/3314
28th Battalion (7th Brigade) WO95/3343.
20th Battalion & 27th Battalion (7th Brigade) see Menin Road.

II Anzac

197th Infantry Brigade, WO95/3135. 3/5th Lancs Fusiliers WO95/3137.
2/6th 2/7th & 2/8th Lancs Fusiliers WO95/3136.
198th Brigade, WO95/3138. 2/9th & 2/10th Manchester, 2/4th & 2/5th East Lancs, all in WO95/3141
148th Infantry Brigade, WO95/2804. 1/4th & 1/5th York & Lancs WO95/2805
146th Infantry Brigade WO95/2793. 1/5th, 1/7th & 1/8th West Yorks all in WO95/2795

XVIII Corps

144th Infantry Brigade, WO95/2757.
32nd Infantry Brigade, WO95/1808. 6th Yorks WO95/1809

XIV Corps

12th Infantry Brigade, WO95/1503. 2nd Lancs Fusiliers WO95/1507. 2nd Essex WO95/1505
86th Infantry Brigade, WO95/2298. 1st Lancs Fusiliers WO95/2300. 2nd Royal Fusiliers WO95/2301
88th Infantry Brigade, WO95/2307. 1st Newfoundland WO95/2308
1st Guards Brigade, WO95/1214
2nd Guards Brigade, WO95/1218

1st Battle of Passchendaele 12th October

I Anzac

12th Australian Infantry Brigade, WO95/3506. 47th Battalion WO95/3512. 48th Battalion WO95/3514
II Anzac

9th Australian Infantry Brigade, WO95/3397. 34th Battalion WO95/3405. 35th Battalion WO95/3408
36th Battalion WO95/3409
10th Australian Infantry Brigade, WO95/3411. 37th Battalion WO95/3414. 38th Battalion WO95/3415
40th Battalion WO95/3420
2nd New Zealand Brigade, WO95/3695. 2nd Otago WO95/3703. 1st Otago WO95/3701
1st Canterbury WO95/3697
3rd New Zealand Rifle Brigade, WO95/3706. 4th Rifles WO95/3711. 2nd Rifles WO95/3709
3rd Rifles WO95/3710. 1st Rifles WO95/3708

XVIII Corps

26th Infantry Brigade, WO95/1763. 8th Black Watch WO95/1766. 7th Seaforth WO95/1765
27th Infantry Brigade. 11th & 12th Royal Scots WO95/1773. 9th Scottish Rifles WO951772
55th Infantry Brigade, WO95/2047. 8th East Surrey WO95/2050. 7th East Kent WO95/2049
53rd Infantry Brigade. 10th Essex WO95/2038. 8th Suffolk WO95/2039

XIV Corps

Composite Brigade. Household Battalion WO95/1481. 1st Warwick WO95/1484
51st Infantry Brigade, WO95/2005
3rd Guards Brigade, WO95/1222

Attack at Poelcappelle and Houthulst Forest 22nd October

53rd Infantry Brigade, 8th Norfolk WO95/2040
102nd Infantry Brigade, WO95/2460. 15th Royal Scots WO95/2457. 16th Royal Scots WO95/2458
104th Infantry Brigade, WO95/2482. 17th & 20th Lancs Fusiliers WO95/2484.
105th Infantry Brigade, WO95/2486. 14th Gloucester WO95/2488.

2nd Battle of Passchendaele 26th October to 10th November

26th October

X Corps

91st Infantry Brigade, WO95/1667. 2nd Queens WO95/1670.
1st South Staffs, 21st & 22nd Manchester see Broodseinde
20th Infantry Brigade, WO95/1654. 9th Devon WO95/1656
13th Infantry Brigade, WO95/1550

Canadian Corps

4th Canadian Division General Staff, RG9 Srs.III, D-3 Vol 4860 Reel T-1938-39 File 161
10th Canadian Infantry Brigade, WO95/3896. 46th Battalion WO95/3898. 47th Battalion WO95/3899
3rd Canadian Division General Staff, RG9 Srs.III, D-3 Vol 4854 Reel T-1935 File 141
9th Canadian Infantry Brigade, WO95/3875. 43rd & 58th Battalions WO95/3878.
8th Canadian Infantry Brigade, WO95/3868. 1st C.M.R. WO95/3970. 2nd C.M.R. WO95/3871
4th C.M.R. WO95/3872. 5th C.M.R. WO95/3873

XVIII Corps

188th Infantry Brigade, WO95/3108. Anson & Hawke ADM137/3063. Howe WO95/3111
1st Royal Marine & 2nd Royal Marine WO95/3110
173rd Infantry Brigade, WO95/3000. 2/2nd, 2/3rd, & 2/4th London WO95/3001

XIV Corps

170th Infantry Brigade, WO95/2977. 2/4th Loyal North Lancs WO95/2978.
2/5th & 4/5th L.N.L. WO95/ 2929

149th Infantry Brigade, WO95/2827. 1/4th & 1/5th Northumberland Fusiliers WO95/2828
1/7th N.F. WO95/2830

30th October

Canadian Corps

12th Canadian Infantry Brigade, WO95/3906. 85th & 78th Battalions WO95/3909.
72nd Battalion WO95/3908
7th Canadian Infantry Brigade, WO95/3864. 49th Battalion WO95/3876
8th Canadian Infantry Brigade, WO95/3868. 5th C.M.R. & 2nd C.M.R. see above.

XVIII Corps

190th Infantry Brigade, WO95/3117. 1/28th London (Artists Rifles) & 7th Royal Fusiliers WO95/3119.
4th Bedford WO95/3118
174th Infantry Brigade, WO95/3003. 2/8th London WO95/3006. 2/6th London WO95/3005

6th November

X Corps

95th Infantry Brigade, see Broodseinde
Canadian Corps
2nd Canadian Division General Staff, RG9 Srs.III, D-3 Vol 4846 Reel T-1928 File 111
6th Canadian Infantry Brigade, WO95/3822. 27th Battalion O95/3831. 31st Battalion WO95/3835
28th Battalion WO95/3832. 26th Battalion (5th Infantry Brigade) WO95/3825
1st Canadian Division General Staff, RG9 Srs.III, D-3 Vol 4834 Reel T-1917 File 72
1st Canadian Infantry Brigade, WO95/3759. !st Battalion WO95/3760. 2nd Battalion WO95/3761
3rd Battalion WO95/3762

10th November

Canadian Corps

4th Canadian Infantry Brigade, WO95/3812. 20th Battalion WO95/3812. 18th Battalion WO95/3814
2nd Canadian Infantry Brigade, WO95/3765. 5th Battalion WO95/3767. 7th Battalion WO95/3768
8th Battalion WO95/3769. 10th Battalion WO95/3770

II Corps

3rd Infantry Brigade, WO95/1276. 1st South Wales Borderers WO95/1280. 2nd Munster WO95/1279
1st Gloucester WO95/1278

Published accounts, see bibliography

H. Stewart, The New Zealand Division.
C.E.W. Bean, Official History of Australia in the War
Everard Wyrall, The Die Hards in the Great War
J. Aston & T.B. Lawford, The History of the 12th East Surrey Regiment
R.O. Russell, The History of the 11th RWK
Chronicle of the KRRC
Everard Wyrall, The History of the King's Liverpool Regiment
G.H.F. Nichols, The 18th Division
C.E.O. Bax, The 8th Division
J.H. Borarston, the Eighth Division in War 1914-1918
W. Seymour, The History of the Rifle Brigade
J. Stewart & J. Buchan, The Fifteenth (Scottish) Division
J.O. Coop, The 55th (West Lancs) Division
C.T. Atkinson, The Royal Hampshire Regiment
F.W. Bewsher, The History of the 51st (Highland) Division
Cyril Falls, The Gordon Highlanders
J. Sym, Seaforth Highlanders
J.E. Munby, The 38th (Welsh) Division
C. Headlam, The History of the Guards Division
T. Denman, Ireland's Unknown Soldiers, the 16th (Irish) Division
H.C. Wylly, The Historical Records of the 2nd Battalion Royal Dublin Fusliiers
V.E. Inglefield, The History of the 20th (Light) Division

S. Gillon, The Story of the 29th Division
J.W. Burrows, Essex Units in the War
H.R. Sandilands, The 23rd Division
F.P. Gibbon, 42nd (East Lancashire) Division
L. Magnus, The West Riding Territorials (49th Division) in the Great War
J. Ewing, The History of the 9th (Scottish) Division
A.H. Hussey & D.S. Inman, The Fifth Division in the Great War
A. Hilliard Atteridge, History of the 17th (Northern) Division
H.M. Davson, The History of the 35th Division
C.T. Atkinson, The Seventh Division 1914-1918
G.W.L. Nicholson, Canadian Expeditionary Force 1914-1918
D. Jerrold, The Royal Naval Division
Everard Wyrall, The History of the Fiftieth Division